2018
U.S. Master™ Bank Tax Guide

Ronald W. Blasi

Wolters Kluwer

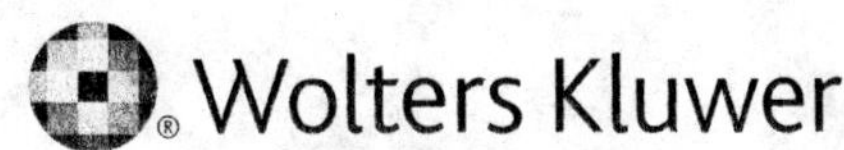

Editorial Staff

Editor .... Barbara L. Post, Esq.
Production .... Christopher Zwirek, Manjula Mahalingam, Prabhu Meenakshisundaram

ISBN: 978-0-8080-4739-1

2700 Lake Cook Road
Riverwoods, IL 60015
800 344 3734
CCHGroup.com

Printed in the United States of America

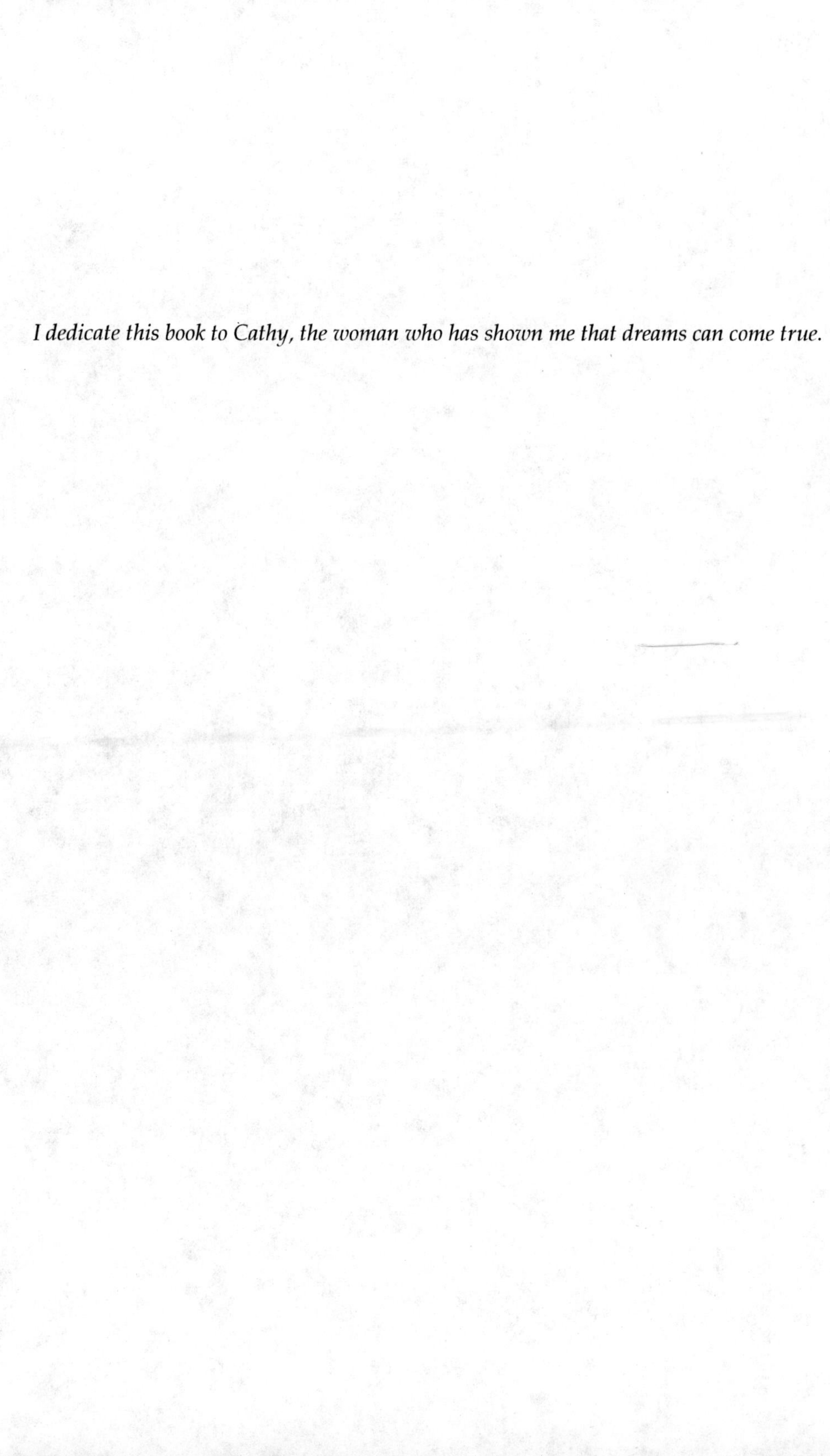

I dedicate this book to Cathy, the woman who has shown me that dreams can come true.

Preface

This book is written for tax practitioners who advise financial institutions on federal income tax matters. It has been designed to be an up-to-date desk-top reference that contains a comprehensive discussion of federal income tax rules applicable to banks and bank holding company groups. It requires no annual filing of updates and no checking of appendices to see if developments have occurred. The reader does not have to, on his or her own, integrate any developments into the discussion in the text. Instead, the book is annually revised from cover-to-cover and all important developments occurring during the preceding year are integrated into the text. If the reader needs a more exhaustive analysis of any topic addressed in the book, numerous references are provided to sections of the Internal Revenue Code, Treasury Regulations, Revenue Rulings, other IRS pronouncements, judicial opinions, and legislative history.

The book begins with an examination of the issues associated with selecting the most appropriate entity within a consolidated group to earn an item of income or incur an item of expense. It is assumed that there is some degree of flexibility as to which entity is properly treated as accruing an item. Because a "bank" is taxed differently than an entity that does not meet the technical tax definition of a "bank," both opportunities and pitfalls are present when booking an item of income and expense. The choice of entity that a tax advisor makes with respect to securities gains and losses, interest on tax-exempt income, and loan losses, just to name a few, could affect the overall tax liability of the consolidated group.

Following this important threshold discussion, all of the items of income and expense that are likely to be incurred by most financial institutions are analyzed. With respect to income items, the treatment of interest income, original issue discount, and the various categories of fee income is carefully examined. Throughout the book, those areas where controversy exists between the IRS and taxpayers are identified. The positions taken by both parties are set forth as are the authorities on which each relies.

Readers of the *2018 U.S. Master Bank Tax Guide* are encouraged to submit their suggestions on how to improve the book to the author at *RonBlasi@gmail.com*. Any suggestions will be taken into account in preparing next year's edition.

Acknowledgments

The author wishes to acknowledge, with gratitude, the tireless support provided by Karen Butler, Georgia State University Administrative Coordinator, and Pamela Brannon, Faculty Services Librarian, without whose efforts the organization and preparation of this volume would not have been possible. The author also wishes to thank research assistants Laura Devoe, Spencer Johnson, Susan Goldfarb, Sean Dunn, Bruce Clements, Jennifer L. Judkins, Robert Kiser, Elizabeth C. Millwood, Jennifer Wilson, Kara Williamson, L. Alyson Graham, Laura Reinhold, Greg Swartzberg, Patrick Wheaton, Reed White, Viraj Deshmukh, Michael Kennerty and, in connection with the preparation of the 2015 and 2016 editions of this book, Jeffrey Hawkins.

The author is indebted to the many practitioners from whom he has learned bank tax law, including members of the American Bar Association's Tax Section Committee on Banking and Savings Institutions, the tax accountants and attorneys in the Tax Departments at Citibank, N.A. and at Chemical Bank (currently J.P. Morgan-Chase) during his employment in those institutions, his co-speakers at the Executive Enterprise's Annual Bank Tax Institute, the individuals in the firms with whom he consults on bank tax matters, and his good friends at the IRS.

About the Author

Ronald W. Blasi was the Mark and Evelyn Trammell Professor of Tax Law at the College of Law at Georgia State University in Atlanta, Georgia, where he specialized in federal income taxation. He retired from that position in June 2016. Professor Blasi has over forty years of experience in bank tax matters. He managed the tax planning and audits groups in the tax department at Chemical Bank (currently J.P. Morgan-Chase), and he was earlier employed as a tax attorney at Citibank, N.A. He also practiced law at a New York City tax litigation firm. Professor Blasi served as chairman of the American Bar Association Tax Section's Banking Committee, and he has testified as an expert witness and served as a consulting expert for accounting firms, banks, the IRS, and the New York State Legislative Tax Study Commission. Professor Blasi has an LL.M. (Taxation) from New York University Graduate School of Law, a J.D. from St. John's University, School of Law, and an APC (Accounting) from New York University Graduate School of Business.

The author welcomes suggestions for improving this book. Professor Blasi can be reached at (404) 314-6183 or *RonBlasi@gmail.com*.

Summary Contents

		Page
Chapter 1	Entities Subject to Bank Tax Rules	1
Chapter 2	Interest, Fee, and Other Income	67
Chapter 3	Discount and Premium	155
Chapter 4	Securities Dealers and Investors	199
Chapter 5	Nonperforming Loans	257
Chapter 6	Modified Debt	285
Chapter 7	Foreclosures	311
Chapter 8	Business Expenses	335
Chapter 9	Interest Expense	437
Chapter 10	Bad-Debt Deductions	485
Chapter 11	Acquisitions	593
Chapter 12	Business Tax Credits	709
Appendix A	IRS Banking Industry Issue Papers	783
Appendix B	Audit Technique Guide for Commercial Banking	899
	Finding Lists	1065
	Index	1123

Detailed Table of Contents

Section

Chapter 1: Entities Subject to Bank Tax Rules

Tax Planning Suggestions 1.1
Financial Modernization Act 1.2
Financial Holding Company 1.2.1
Electing FHC Status 1.2.2
Financial Subsidiaries 1.2.3
Insurance Activities 1.2.4
Securities Activities 1.2.5
State Bank Provisions 1.2.6
Commercial Banks and Thrifts Treated Alike 1.3
Taxation of Banks 1.4
Overview 1.4.1
Accumulated Earnings Tax 1.4.2
Banks as Limited Liability Companies 1.4.3
Definition of a "Bank" 1.5
Classical Definition 1.5.1
Judicial Definition 1.5.2
Regulatory Definition 1.5.3
Tax Definition 1.5.4
Scope of Code Section 581 . . . . . 1.5.5
Chartering Requirement 1.5.6
Deposit Requirement 1.5.7
Supervisory Requirement 1.5.8
Fiduciary Institutions 1.5.9
Cooperative Banks 1.5.10
Banks as S Corporations 1.6
Qualifications for S Corporation Treatment 1.6.1
Trusts, Estates, and ESOPs as Shareholders 1.6.2
QSub and Corporate Structure 1.6.3
Electing S and QSub Treatment 1.6.4
Advantages 1.6.5
Disadvantages 1.6.6
Passive Investment Income 1.6.7
Built-in Gains Tax 1.6.8
Estimated Tax Payments 1.6.9
Domestic Building and Loan Associations 1.7

Section

Tax Definition ... 1.7.1
Evolution of Thrift Taxation ... 1.7.2
Special Bank Tax Rules ... 1.7.3
Eligible Entities ... 1.7.4
Supervisory Test ... 1.7.5
Business Operations Test ... 1.7.6
Asset Test ... 1.7.7
Regulatory Definition Contrasted ... 1.7.8
Quick Reference Table ... 1.7.9

Chapter 2: Interest, Fee, and Other Income

Tax Planning Suggestions ... 2.1
General Accounting Rules ... 2.2
Overall Methods of Accounting ... 2.2.1
Requirements for Acceptable Accounting Methods ... 2.2.2
Change in Accounting Method ... 2.2.3
Accounting for Different Businesses ... 2.2.4
Allocation of Receipts ... 2.3
Interest Income ... 2.4
Tax-Exempt Interest ... 2.5
Private Activity Bonds ... 2.5.1
Fire Department Loans ... 2.5.2
ESOP Loans ... 2.5.3
Accruing Interest Income ... 2.6
Rule of 78s Method ... 2.6.1
Liquidation, Actuarial, Composite Methods ... 2.6.2
Service Fee Income ... 2.7
Service Fee Income v. Interest Income ... 2.7.1
When to Include Service Fee Income ... 2.7.2
Credit Card Annual Fees ... 2.7.3
Mortgage Servicing Fees ... 2.7.4
Affinity Cards ... 2.7.5
Gift Cards ... 2.7.6
Other Income ... 2.8
Commitment Fees ... 2.8.1
Commissions on Loans ... 2.8.2
Commissions on Purchase or Sale of Securities ... 2.8.3
Repurchase Agreements ... 2.9
Overview of Tax Treatment ... 2.9.1
Sale vs. Loan ... 2.9.2
Mortgage Backed Securities ... 2.10
Types of Mortgage Backed Securities ... 2.10.1

Section

Tax Treatment of CMO and Other Pass-Through Transactions . . . 2.10.2
REMICs . . . 2.10.3
REITs . . . 2.10.4
Asset Backed Securities . . . 2.11
FASITs . . . 2.11.1
Hedging Transactions . . . 2.12
The Volcker Rule . . . 2.12.1
Definition of Notional Principal Contracts . . . 2.12.2
Accounting for Notional Principal Contracts . . . 2.12.3
Periodic Payments, Termination Payments and Nonperiodic Payments . . . 2.12.4
Swaps . . . 2.12.5
Caps and Floors . . . 2.12.6
Currency Gains or Losses . . . 2.12.7
Premature Withdrawal Penalties . . . 2.13
FHLB Distributions . . . 2.14
The FHLB System . . . 2.14.1
FHLB Stock Dividends . . . 2.14.2
FHLB of Redemptions . . . 2.14.3
Tax Basis . . . 2.14.4

Chapter 3: Discount and Premium

Tax Planning Suggestions . . . 3.1
Discount Income . . . 3.2
General Rules . . . 3.2.1
Original Issue Discount . . . 3.3
Accruing O.I.D.–General Rules . . . 3.3.1
O.I.D. on Worthless Debts . . . 3.3.2
O.I.D. for Prepaid Interest . . . 3.3.3
Debt Obligations Subject to O.I.D. Rules . . . 3.3.4
O.I.D. on Short-Term Loans . . . 3.3.5
Accruing O.I.D. Computation . . . 3.3.6
Basis Adjustments for O.I.D. . . . 3.3.7
Recordkeeping Requirements for O.I.D. . . . 3.3.8
De Minimis O.I.D. . . . 3.4
Determining the *De Minimis* O.I.D. . . . 3.4.1
Accruing *De Minimis* O.I.D. . . . 3.4.2
Points as *De Minimis* O.I.D. . . . 3.4.3
Pre-Regulation Treatment of Points . . . 3.4.4
Points under O.I.D. Regulations . . . 3.4.5
Accruing Points . . . 3.4.6

Section

Grace Period Interest . . . 3.4.7
Mortgage Buy-Down Fees . . . 3.4.8
Odd Days Interest . . . 3.4.9
Credit Card Fees . . . 3.5
Credit Card Fees as O.I.D. . . . 3.5.1
Over-the-limit Fees as O.I.D. . . . 3.5.2
Late Charge Fees as O.I.D. . . . 3.5.3
Cash Advance Fees as O.I.D. . . . 3.5.4
Intercharge Fees as O.I.D. . . . 3.5.5
ATM Fees as O.I.D. . . . 3.5.6
Merchant Fees . . . 3.5.7
Non-sufficient Funds Fees . . . 3.5.8
Market Discount . . . 3.6
Ordinary Income Treatment . . . 3.6.1
Special Rule for Short-Term Obligations . . . 3.6.2
Deferral of Interest Deduction . . . 3.6.3
Current Inclusion Election . . . 3.6.4
Bond Premium . . . 3.7
Premium Amortization Election . . . 3.7.1
Basis Adjustment . . . 3.7.2
Bonds Defined . . . 3.7.3
Amortization Methods . . . 3.7.4
Computing Premium . . . 3.7.5
Chapter 4: Securities Dealers and Investors
Tax Planning Suggestions . . . 4.1
Permissible Securities Activities . . . 4.2
Determining Amount and Character of Gains or Losses . . . 4.3
Wash Sale Rule . . . 4.3.1
Stripped Bonds . . . 4.3.2
Character of Gain or Losses—Debt Securities . . . 4.3.3
Character of Gain or Losses—Certain Preferred Stock . . . 4.3.4
Character of Gain or Loss—Mutual Fund Investments . . . 4.3.5
Securities Dealer Transactions . . . 4.4
Recognition Rules: Pre-Code Section 475 . . . 4.4.1
Recognition Rules: Code Section 475 . . . 4.4.2
Exceptions to Section 475 Recognition Rules . . . 4.4.3
Identification of Securities . . . 4.4.4
Who Is a Dealer? . . . 4.4.5
Traders, Investors and Speculators . . . 4.4.6
What Is a "Security"? . . . 4.4.7
Measuring Mark-to Market Gain or Loss . . . 4.4.8

Section

Characterizing Mark-to Market Gains or Losses 4.4.9
Tax-Free Acquisitions 4.4.10
Other Mark-to-Market Rules 4.4.11
Change of Accounting Method 4.4.12
Security Investment Transactions 4.5
Statement of Financial Accounting Standards No. 115 . . . . 4.5.1
Loans of Securites 4.6

Chapter 5: Nonperforming Loans

Tax Planning Suggestions 5.1
Book Treatment of Delinquent Interest 5.2
Treatment 5.2.1
Statement of Financial Accounting Standards No. 114 . . . . 5.2.2
Tax Treatment of Delinquent Interest 5.3
General Rule 5.3.1
"All Events" Test for Nonperforming Loans 5.3.2
Reasonable Expectancy Standard 5.3.3
Banks Not Using Conformity Bad Debt Method 5.3.4
Loans Not Completely Charged-Off 5.3.5
Safe Harbor Method 5.3.6
Charge-Off of Accrued Interest 5.3.7
Banks Using Conformity Bad Debt Method 5.3.8
Mark-to-Market Loss 5.3.9
Resumption of Accrual 5.3.10
Payments After Non Accrual 5.3.11
O.I.D. on Nonperforming Loans 5.3.12
Open and Speculative Transactions 5.3.13
Coordinated Issues Papers 5.3.14
Code Sections 166 and 451 Contrasted 5.3.15
Appeals Guidelines 5.3.16
IRS Historical Practice 5.3.17
Audit Protection 5.3.18

Chapter 6: Modified Debt

Tax Planning Suggestions 6.1
Elements of Exchange Treatment 6.2
Cottage Savings Association 6.2.1
Foundation for Regulations 6.2.2
Cottage Savings Regulations 6.2.3
Measuring Gain or Loss 6.3
Statutory Rules 6.3.1
IRS Positions 6.3.2
O.I.D. Rules 6.3.3

Section

Chapter 7: Foreclosures

Tax Planning Suggestions 7.1
Legal Aspects of Foreclosure 7.2
Treatment of Gain or Loss 7.3
General Rules 7.3.1
Foreclosures by Thrifts: Pre-1996 Acquisitions 7.3.2
Interest Income on Foreclosure 7.4
Holding Security Property 7.5
Post-Acquisition Expense 7.5.1
Post-Acquisition Income 7.5.2
Disposing of Security Property 7.6
Capital Asset Treatment 7.6.1
Stock Acquired at Foreclosure 7.6.2
Interest Income at Sale 7.6.3
Nominee Corporations 7.6.4

Chapter 8: Business Expenses

Tax Planning Suggestions 8.1
General Rules for Taxable Year of Deduction 8.2
Economic Performance Requirement 8.2.1
Deducting Refunded Interest 8.2.2
Capitalization of Expenditures 8.3
General Rules 8.3.1
Separate and Distinct Asset Test 8.3.2
Future Benefits Test 8.3.3
Loan Origination Costs 8.3.4
Capitalization of Acquisition or Creation of Intangibles 8.4
Overview of Capitalization Regulations 8.4.1
Acquired Intangibles 8.4.2
Created Intangibles 8.4.3
Capitalized Transaction Costs 8.4.4
Special Rules for Pooling Methods 8.4.5
Accounting Method Changes 8.4.6
Acquisition Costs 8.5
Capitalization Regulations 8.5.1
Judicial Background to Regulation Section 1.263(a)-5 . . . . 8.5.2
Debt Issuance Costs 8.6
Amortization of Capitalized Costs 8.7
Pre-Regulation IRS Pronouncements 8.8
Home Equity Lines of Credit 8.8.1
Origination of Mortgage Loans 8.8.2
Advertising and Other Expenditures 8.8.3

Section

Start-Up and Expansion Expenditures 8.9
Overview 8.9.1
Start-Up Expenditures—Code Section 195 . . . . . 8.9.2
Organizational Expenditures—Code Section 248 . . . . . 8.9.3
Comparison of Code Sections 195 and 248 . . . . . 8.9.4
Electing Code Section 248 . . . . . 8.9.5
Business Expansion and New Product Expenditures 8.10
Branch Pre-Opening Costs 8.10.1
Geographic Branch Expansion Costs 8.10.2
Training Costs 8.10.3
Promotional and Selling Costs 8.10.4
Advertising Costs 8.10.5
Mutual Fund Costs 8.10.6
Credit Card Costs 8.10.7
Bailout Costs 8.10.8
Expenditures Reducing Future Costs 8.10.9
Year 2000 Costs 8.11
FDIC Deposit Insurance Assessment 8.12
FDIC Exit and Entrance Fees 8.13
Regulatory Examination Assessment 8.14
Farm Credit System Assessment 8.15
Directors' and Officers' Insurance 8.16
Premiums on Debtor's Life Insurance 8.17
Discount for Early Mortgage Pay-off 8.18
Supervisory Goodwill 8.19
Net Operating Losses 8.20
Pre-1987 Net Operating Losses 8.20.1
1987-1993 Net Operating Losses 8.20.2
Election to Forego Carryback 8.20.3
2008-2009 Net Operating Losses 8.20.4
Abandonment Losses—Customer Lists and Goodwill 8.21
Abandonment Loss for Customer Lists 8.21.1
Abandonment Loss for Supervisory Goodwill 8.21.2
Covered Asset Losses 8.22

Chapter 9: Interest Expense

Tax Planning Suggestions 9.1
Allowance of Deduction 9.2
Deducting Dividend Payments on TARP–Preferred Stock . . . 9.2.1
Timing of Deduction 9.3
General Rule 9.3.1
Special Rule for Thrifts 9.3.2

Section

When Crediting Takes Place 9.3.3
Savings Certificates and O.I.D. 9.3.4
Deferred Interest Expense 9.4
Prepaid Interest by a Thrift 9.4.1
Market Discount Bonds 9.4.2
UNICAP Rule 9.4.3
Disallowed Interest Expense 9.5
Overview of Automatic Disallowance Rules 9.5.1
Overview of General Disallowance Rule 9.5.2
The TEFRA Disallowance 9.5.3
The TRA '86 Disallowance Rule 9.5.4
Qualified Tax-Exempt Obligations 9.5.5
Interest Expense 9.5.6
Acquisition Date 9.5.7
Consolidated Disallowance 9.5.8
Tax Basis of Assets and Tax-Exempts 9.5.9
S Corporations Banks 9.6
Registration-Required Obligations 9.7

Chapter 10: Bad-Debt Deductions

Tax Planning Suggestions 10.1

Basic Rules

Deduction for Worthless Debt 10.2
Available Methods 10.2.1
Amount of Deduction 10.2.2
What Constitutes a "Bad Debt"? 10.2.3
Direct Charge-Off Method 10.3
Establishing Worthlessness 10.3.1
The Meaning of "Charge-Off" 10.3.2
Presumptions of Worthlessness 10.4
Industry Directive 10.4.1
Bank Specific Rules 10.4.2
Historical Presumption 10.4.3
The Conformity Election 10.4.4
Rebutting Conclusive Presumption 10.4.5
Involuntary Charge-Off 10.5
Recoveries 10.6

Reserve Methods

Allowable Reserve Methods 10.7
Electing a Reserve Method 10.7.1
Legislative History of Code Section 585 .... 10.7.2
Pre-1987 Rules 10.7.3

Section

Post-1986 Rules—Overview ... 10.7.4
Commissioner's Discretion Revoked ... 10.7.5
Eligible Taxpayers ... 10.7.6
Minimum Reserve Addition ... 10.7.7
Alternative Formula Within Code Section 593 ... 10.7.8
Recoveries ... 10.7.9
Establishing and Maintaining Reserves ... 10.7.10
Acceptable Bookkeeping for Reserves ... 10.7.11
The Experience Method ... 10.8
Moving-Average Formula ... 10.8.1
Reserve Restoration—General Rule ... 10.8.2
Reserve Restoration—Decline in Loan Balance ... 10.8.3
Shorter Experience Period ... 10.8.4
"Loans" Defined ... 10.8.5
Extraordinary Loan Losses ... 10.8.6
Percentage of Taxable Income Method ... 10.9
Loans That Are Qualifying ... 10.9.1
Loans That Are Nonqualifying ... 10.9.2
Specially Computed Taxable Income ... 10.9.3
Applicable Percentages ... 10.9.4
Limitations on Reserve Additions ... 10.9.5
Limitations on Reserve Additions (Pre-1987 Law) ... 10.9.6
Commercial Bank Bad-Debt Reserve Recapture ... 10.10
"Large Bank" Defined ... 10.10.1
Code Section 481(a) Adjustments ... 10.10.2
Advantages/Disadvantages of Recapture Methods ... 10.10.3
Financially Troubled Banks ... 10.10.4
Thrift Bad-Debt Reserve Recapture ... 10.11
Applicable Excess Reserves—Large Bank ... 10.11.1
Applicable Excess Reserves—Small Bank ... 10.11.2
Acquisitions and Dispositions ... 10.11.3
Residential Loan Requirement ... 10.11.4
Tax Preference Issues ... 10.12
Alternative Minimum Tax ... 10.12.1
Corporate Preference Item ... 10.12.2

Chapter 11: Acquisitions

Tax Planning Suggestions ... 11.1
Interstate Opportunities for Banks and BHCs ... 11.2
Permissible Interstate Bank Activities ... 11.2.1
Permissible Interstate BHC Activities ... 11.2.2
Taxable Acquisitions ... 11.3

Section

Taxation of Selling Corporation 11.3.1
Cost Recovery Rules to Acquiring Corporation 11.3.2
Cost Recovery: Code Section 197 Intangibles 11.3.3
Code Section 197 Intangible Assets 11.3.4
Code Section 197 Intangibles: Exceptions 11.3.5
Code Section 197 Intangibles: Dispositions 11.3.6
Loan Premium 11.3.7
Qualified Stock Purchase 11.3.8
Limitation on Loss Carryovers 11.4
Code Section 382 Limitation 11.4.1
Loss Corporations 11.4.2
Pre-change Loss and Post-change Year 11.4.3
Entity 11.4.4
Short Tax Year 11.4.5
Net Operating Loss Carryovers: Built-in Gain and Loss 11.4.6
Net Unrealized Built-in Gain and Loss 11.4.7
Taxable Year of Net Unrealized Built-in Loss 11.4.8
Recognized Built-in Gain or Loss 11.4.9
Threshold Requirement 11.4.10
Calculating RBIL and RBIG 11.4.11
Ownership Changes 11.4.12
Owner Shift Involving Five-percent Shareholders 11.4.13
Equity Structure Shift 11.4.14
Multiple Transactions 11.4.15
Testing Periods 11.4.16
Stock Ownership Rules 11.4.17
Disregarded Stock 11.4.18
Options 11.4.19
Worthless Stock 11.4.20
Mutual Funds 11.4.21
Separate Accounting 11.4.22
Seized Financial Corporations 11.4.23
Capital Contributions 11.4.24
Recapitalized Financial Institutions 11.4.25
Tax-Free Acquisitions 11.5
Overview 11.5.1
Type A Reorganizations 11.5.2
Acquisitions with Solely Voting Stock—Type B and Type C Reorganizations 11.5.3
Type D Reorganizations 11.5.4
Charter Stripping of Type C and D Reorganizations 11.5.5

Section

Type E Reorganizations 11.5.6
Type F Reorganizations 11.5.7
Type G Reorganizations 11.5.8
Federal Financial Assistance 11.6
Federal Financial Assistance, Defined 11.6.1
Principles Used in Prescribing Regulations 11.6.2
Income Inclusion of FFA 11.6.3
Transfers of Property by Institution 11.6.4
Bridge Banks and Residual Entities 11.6.5
Taxable Transfers 11.6.6
Limitation on Collection of Income Tax 11.6.7
Miscellaneous Rules 11.6.8
Phantom Income from Loan Modifications 11.6.9

Chapter 12: Business Tax Credits

Research and Development Credit 12.1
Expenditures Eligible for Credit 12.1.1
Expenditures Ineligible for Credit 12.1.2
Internal Use Software 12.1.3
Norwest Corp. 12.1.4
Calculating the R&D Credit 12.1.5
Research and Experimental Expenditures as Tax Preference Items 12.1.6
Election to Claim Accelerated Research Credit in Lieu of Bonus Depreciation 12.1.7
Low-Income Housing Credit 12.2
Applicable Percentage 12.2.1
Low-Income Housing Credit: Qualified Basis 12.2.2
Low-Income Unit 12.2.3
Low-Income Housing Project 12.2.4
Credit Period 12.2.5
Additional Credit 12.2.6
Disposition of Building 12.2.7
Tenant's Right to Acquisition 12.2.8
Agency Authorization 12.2.9
Housing Use Agreement 12.2.10
Maximum Allocable Credits 12.2.11
Allocation Authority 12.2.12
Acquisition of Existing Buildings 12.2.13
Recapture of Credit 12.2.14
New Markets Tax Credit 12.3
Overview 12.3.1

Section
Qualified Equity Investment 12.3.2
Qualified Community Development Entity 12.3.3
Low-Income Community 12.3.4
Low-Income Community Investment 12.3.5
Qualified Active Low-Income Community Business 12.3.6
Allowance Date 12.3.7
Recapture of Credit 12.3.8
Appendix A: IRS Banking Industry Issue Papers
Interest on Cap Loans (Discussed at § 2.6.3) A.1
Premature Withdrawal Penalties (Discussed at § 2.14) A.2
Deferred Loan Fees—Composite Method (Discussed at § 2.6.2) A.3
Deferred Loan Fees—Loan Liquidation Method (Discussed at § 2.6.2) A.4
Mortgage Buy-Down Fees (Discussed at § 2.7.2) A.5
Nonperforming Loans—Accrued Interest (Commercial Bank) (Discussed at § 5.3.14) A.6
Nonperforming Loans—Accrued Interest (Thrift) (Discussed at § 5.3.14) A.7
Nonperforming Loans—Accrued Interest (Commercial Bank)—Appeals (Discussed at § 5.3.14) A.8
Nonperforming Loans, LMSB Industry Directive with IDR (Discussed at § 5.3.2) A.9
Foreclosures: Gain or Loss on Foreclosures (Discussed at § 7.6.1) A.10
Foreclosures: Interest Income on the Sale of Foreclosed Debt (Discussed at § 7.6.3) A.11
Foreclosures: Interest Income on the Sale of Foreclosed Debt—Appeals (Discussed at § 7.6.3) A.12
Validity of Treasury Regulations Section 1.593-6A(b)(5)(vi) A.13
Core Deposit Intangibles (Commercial Bank) (Discussed at § 11.3.4(g)) A.14
Core Deposit Intangibles (Thrift) (Discussed at § 11.3.4(g)) A.15
Debt-Equity Swaps A.16
Gross Up of Net Foreign Loans A.17
Supervisory Goodwill—Settlement Guideline (Discussed at § 11.6.1) A.18
Supervisory Goodwill—LMSB Coordinated Issue (Discussed at § 11.6.1) A.19
Bad Debts: Industry Director Guidelines on Auditing Bank Bad Debt Conformity Election (Discussed at § 10.4.2(f)) A.20

Section

Bad Debts: Attachment to Industry Director Guidelines on Auditing Bank Bad Debt Conformity Election (Discussed at § 10.4.2(f)) A.21
Bad Debts: Uniform Agreement on Classification of Securities (Discussed at § 10.4.2(e)) A.22
LB&I Directive Related to § 166 Deductions for Eligible Debt and Eligible Securities A.23
Mark-to-Market: I.R.C. § 475 Field Directive on Valuation A.24

Page

Appendix B: Audit Technique Guide for Commercial Banking 899
Finding Lists:
Table of Cases 1065
Table of I.R.C. Sections 1077
Table of Other Statutory Provisions and Statements of Financial Accounting Standards 1093
Table of Treasury Regulations 1097
Table of Revenue Rulings and Procedures 1111
Table of IRS Private Letter Rulings and Other Releases 1117
Index 1123

Chapter 1
Entities Subject to Bank Tax Rules

Contents

§1.1 Tax Planning Suggestions
§1.2 Financial Modernization Act
  §1.2.1 Financial Holding Company
  §1.2.2 Electing FHC Status
  §1.2.3 Financial Subsidiaries
  §1.2.4 Insurance Activities
  §1.2.5 Securities Activities
  §1.2.6 State Bank Provisions
§1.3 Commercial Banks and Thrifts Treated Alike
§1.4 Taxation of Banks
  §1.4.1 Overview
  §1.4.2 Accumulated Earnings Tax
  §1.4.3 Banks as Limited Liability Companies
§1.5 Definition of a "Bank"
  §1.5.1 Classical Definition
  §1.5.2 Judicial Definition
  §1.5.3 Regulatory Definition
  §1.5.4 Tax Definition
  §1.5.5 Scope of Code Section 581
  §1.5.6 Chartering Requirement
  §1.5.7 Deposit Requirement
  §1.5.8 Supervisory Requirement
  §1.5.9 Fiduciary Institutions
  §1.5.10 Cooperative Banks
§1.6 Banks as S Corporations
  §1.6.1 Qualifications for S Corporation Treatment
  §1.6.2 Trusts, Estates, and ESOPs as Shareholders
  §1.6.3 QSub and Corporate Structure
  §1.6.4 Electing S and QSub Treatment
  §1.6.5 Advantages
  §1.6.6 Disadvantages
  §1.6.7 Passive Investment Income
  §1.6.8 Built-in Gains Tax
  §1.6.9 Estimated Tax Payments
§1.7 Domestic Building and Loan Associations
  §1.7.1 Tax Definition
  §1.7.2 Evolution of Thrift Taxation
  §1.7.3 Special Bank Tax Rules
  §1.7.4 Eligible Entities
  §1.7.5 Supervisory Test
  §1.7.6 Business Operations Test

§1.7.7 Asset Test
§1.7.8 Regulatory Definition Contrasted
§1.7.9 Quick Reference Table

§1.1 Tax Planning Suggestions

Whether an entity is classified as either a bank or as some other institution that does not meet the tax definition of a bank will affect the tax treatment of items of income and expense.[1] Within a bank or thrift group there will be a commercial bank or thrift, the parent holding company and, depending upon the size of the institution, often a variety of other nonbank or nonthrift entities that may include a mortgage company, credit card bank, brokerage firm, investment advisory company, and other special purpose subsidiaries.

The different tax treatment of members of a bank or thrift group presents potential traps for the unwary, but also opportunities for tax planning. Income or assets properly recorded on the books of one type of entity may be subject to more or less favorable tax rules depending upon the classification of the entity. Thus, selecting the proper entity to earn the income or incur the expense could increase after tax income.

Tax planning usually has at least three objectives: to reduce exposure to tax, to reduce the rate of tax, and to defer tax. Exposure to tax can be reduced by shifting the tax burden to another taxpayer. The rate of tax can be reduced by converting ordinary income into capital gain. Tax deferral can be achieved by qualifying a transaction under one of the tax-deferral provisions of the Code. With careful tax planning, all three of these objectives can be attained when stock representing an ownership interest in an S Corporation is sold.

Banks are eligible to elect S corporation status, a change from pre-1997 law. Within a bank holding company group that has an S corporation as its parent there can be both corporations taxed as S corporations and corporations taxed as C corporations. This flexibility offers opportunities for tax minimization never before available to banks. It also places increased significance on the choice of a corporate structure. For example, a C corporation holding company as a subsidiary of an S corporation can be used to isolate earnings from shareholder taxation of some subsidiaries. If S corporation status is elected, care must be taken to properly value all assets for purposes of determining exposure to the tax on built-in gains. The assets that must be valued at the effective date of election include intangible assets, such as goodwill.

The American Jobs Creation Act of 2004 made a number of changes to the S corporation rules that allow more corporations to qualify as "Small Business Corporations."[2] Effective for tax years beginning after December 31, 2004, the maximum number of eligible shareholders is increased from 75 to 100. For purposes of counting the number of shareholders, all family members can elect

[1] *See The Art of Tax Efficiency in Community Banks*, by M. Gula, J. Brew, and R. Blasi, 2007, Red Room Publishing, *http://www.mraeresources.com/bookstore/*.

[2] Pub. L. No. 108-375 (2004).

to be treated as one shareholder. Effective on October 22, 2004, banks (but not bank holding companies) with stock held in IRAs can elect S corporation status without first having to redeem those shares. Effective for transfers made after December 31, 2004, the beneficiary of a qualified subchapter S trust ("QSST") is generally allowed to deduct suspended losses under the at-risk rules of Code section 465 and the passive loss rules of Code section 469(g) when the trust disposes of S corporation stock. The Act also clarifies the definition of a potential current beneficiary for purposes of electing a small business trust. For tax years beginning after December 31, 2004, current potential beneficiaries no longer include those who might benefit from an unexercised power of appointment. Also effective for tax years beginning after December 31, 2004, the IRS is authorized to provide guidance regarding information returns of qualified subchapter S subsidiaries.

The tax rules for determining the proper classification of an entity are partially dependent on the bank regulatory rules. Accordingly, whenever the provisions governing the definition of an entity for regulatory purposes are altered, the tax definition also may be automatically altered. However, the regulatory definitions of a commercial bank and a thrift are not the same as the tax definitions. Accordingly, an entity can be qualified as a commercial bank or as a thrift for regulatory purposes but fail to meet the corresponding tax tests. Bank tax specialists should carefully monitor the tax qualifications to ensure that expected tax treatment is obtained. This is particularly a problem for credit card banks, which usually qualify as a bank for regulatory purposes but may not meet the tax definition of a bank.

A bank or thrift holding company group that files a consolidated income tax return is in a position to achieve unique planning advantages. Opportunities arise from an interplay of provisions contained in the consolidated return regulations that require consolidated computations and those statutory provisions that require separate entity computations. In a bank holding company group, the separate entity computations can be quite significant because of the many special rules contained in the Code[3] that apply only to banks or thrifts.[4] For example, if a bank disposes of property and recognizes a capital loss, and in the same tax year it recognizes a gain by disposing of a debt security that it held for investment, the capital loss may not be offset against the gain.[5] If instead the debt security were owned by a nonbank affiliate, the gain would most likely be capital gain.[6] Pursuant to the consolidated return regulations, a consolidated capital gain net income computation must be made.[7] Thus, the separate entity computation of a bank's gain or loss on debt instruments coupled with the consolidated taxable income computation of capital gain net income may result in the capital loss being allowed to offset the capital gain. This is only one illustration of the potential opportunities for tax reductions from a planned interplay of the consol-

[3] Unless indicated to the contrary, all references to the "Code" or to "I.R.C." are to the Internal Revenue Code of 1986, as amended.

[4] In fact, there are over 100 provisions contained in the Code that contain special bank tax rules.

[5] I.R.C. §§582 and 1202.

[6] I.R.C. §1221.

[7] Reg. §1.1502-11(a)(3) and -22.

idated return and separate entity rules. Others include the interest expense disallowance rules of Code sections 265(b) and 291(e) and the bad debt rules of Regulation section 1.166-2(d).

This chapter describes the characteristics that distinguish commercial banks and thrifts from other C corporations. Subsequent chapters discuss the implications of an entity being a commercial bank or a thrift. The more significant differences relate to: the application of special mark-to-market rules for securities dealers; the characterization of gains or losses from disposing of debt instruments; the recognition of income from acquiring security property; and the deductibility of bad debts. This chapter also outlines the bank specific S corporation rules and describes the advantages and disadvantages of making an election for the parent of a bank to be treated as an S corporation.

§1.2 Financial Modernization Act

The Financial Modernization Act (the "Act")[8] of 1999 contained sweeping changes in the statutes governing the regulation of financial services providers. The centerpiece of the Act is a provision that permits the formation of Financial Holding Companies ("FHC"). These are entities that are authorized, directly and through affiliates, to engage in commercial and merchant banking, full service broker-dealer activities, life, title, and other insurance businesses, as well as other activities "financial in nature."

The Act dismantled long-standing statutory proscriptions designed to fragment the financial services industry. It did so by amending the Banking Act of 1933, commonly referred to as the Glass-Steagall Act,[9] the Bank Holding Company Act of 1956,[10] the Securities Exchange Act of 1934,[11] the Federal Reserve Act,[12] the Federal Deposit Insurance Corporation Act,[13] and the National Banking Act.[14] The removal of the restrictions on affiliation among banking, securities, and insurance firms permits a single affiliated groups of corporations to offer a complete range of financial products and services. Proponents assert that, by removing these restrictions, the resulting diversification will enhance the institution's financial strength. On the other hand, critics claim that the resulting concentration of financial resources may lead to entities the failure of which could seriously disrupt the entire financial structure of the nation.

Taxpayers that elect the FHC structure participate in a more complex federal income tax regime. The affiliated group will have entities that are taxed quite differently. Some entities may not be permitted to join in a consolidated federal income tax return. For example, insurance companies are subject to taxation under special provisions largely contained within Subchapter L of the Internal

---

[8] Often referred to as the Gramm-Leach-Bliley Act, Pub. L. No. 106-102 (1999).

[9] Banking Act of 1933, Pub. L. No. 73-66 (1933), codified as amended in scattered sections of 12 U.S.C.

[10] Bank Holding Company Act of 1956, Pub. L. No. 84-511 (1956) & 12 U.S.C. §§1841 *et seq.* (2006).

[11] Securities Exchange Act of 1934, 48 Stat. 881, 15 U.S.C. §§77b *et seq.* (2000).

[12] Federal Reserve Act: 63 Stat. 906, 12 U.S.C. §§371 *et seq.* (1991).

[13] Federal Deposit Insurance Corporation Act, 48 Stat. 162, 12 U.S.C. §§462a-1, 1811 to 1831 (1993).

[14] National Banking Act, 13 Stat. 99 (codified as amended in scattered sections of 12 U.S.C).

Revenue Code, and they are not "includible corporations" for purposes being allowed to offset the capital gain. This is only one illustration of the potential opportunities for tax reductions from a planned interplay of the consolidated return and separate entity rules. Others include the interest expense disallowance rules of Code sections 265(b) and 291(e) and the bad debt rules of Regulation section 1.166-2(d) of the consolidated return rules.[15] Special bank tax provisions are contained in Subchapter H and in numerous subsections sprinkled throughout the Code. Some of these provisions are applicable only to banks that do not meet the definition of a "large bank,"[16] while others apply to all entities that meet the definition of a "bank."[17] Although securities firms are not singled out for any unique treatment, there are provisions in the Code that are particularly applicable to the activities in which they engage, including rules that deal with inventory accounting, the character of gains and losses, and the accrual of discount and premium.[18] Furthermore, the formation or acquisition of entities that will be members of the FHC group may raise issues relating to the deductibility of "start-up" expenses,[19] the deductibility of acquisition expenses,[20] and the treatment of Code section 197 intangibles that may be acquired.

§ 1.2.1 Financial Holding Company

The creation of the FHC is made possible by amendments to the Bank Holding Company Act of 1956 (the "BHCA"). The amendments authorize and set forth the requirements for the creation of FHCs.[21] In most situations, the entity will be a reincarnation of the bank holding company ("BHC"), within which the bank conducted its historical banking businesses. There will be no tax consequences associated with conversion to FHC status; however, if the entity engages in a new trade or business, it is likely to incur expenses that are required to be deferred under Code section 195.

In general, a FHC may engage in any activity that is (1) "financial in nature," (2) "incidental to such financial activity" or (3) "complementary to a financial activity and does not pose a substantial risk to the safety or soundness of depository institutions or the financial system generally."[22] Previously, a BHC was limited to engaging directly and through its subsidiaries in activities that were "so closely related to banking as to be a proper incident thereto."[23] FHCs are permitted to engage in a broader range of activities either directly or through subsidiaries.[24] They may own entities that engage in banking, insurance, securities, and other financial activities, assuming they are financial in nature.[25]

---

[15] I.R.C. § 1504(b)(2). However, I.R.C. § 1504(c)(1) permits two or more insurance companies to affiliate. An affiliated group comprising of life and nonlife companies may file a consolidated return after a five-year affiliation period. I.R.C. § 1504(c)(2), Reg. § 1.1502-47.

[16] I.R.C. § 585(c).

[17] I.R.C. § 581. *See, e.g.*, § 582 that classifies all gains and losses on the disposition of debt obligations as ordinary gains or losses for all banks.

[18] *See e.g.*, I.R.C. §§ 475, 165, 171, 1256, 1271, *et seq.*

[19] I.R.C. § 195.

[20] I.R.C. §§ 162 and 263.

[21] *Id.* at 1342.

[22] *Id.*

[23] Bank Holding Company Act of 1956, 12 U.S.C. § 184(c)(8) (2006).

[24] 113 Stat. 1338, 1342.

[25] *Id.* at 1344.

§1.2.2 Electing FHC Status

A BHC that wishes to become a FHC must declare its intent to do so and certify that it has met all of the statutory and regulatory requirements.[26] No special tax election is required. Among the bank regulatory requirements that must be met is the condition that all BHC depository institution subsidiaries must be well capitalized and well managed. If at any time a FHC fails to remain well capitalized and well managed, the FHC may be required to either divest itself of control of any depository institution subsidiary or, at the election of the FHC, it must limit its activities or its subsidiaries' activities to those permissible for BHCs under section 4(c)(8) of the BHCA.[27] Of course, any divestiture or sale of business assets will have tax implications that will depend upon whether the transaction is structured as a taxable sale or a nonrecognition transaction.[28]

In order to engage in the newly permissible insurance or securities activities, each of the bank's depository subsidiaries must have received at least a rating of "satisfactory" in its most recent examination under the Community Reinvestment Act ("CRA"). The CRA requires banks to extend their services to low and moderate income areas of the community where a bank is operating. However, failure to meet CRA requirements will not require divestiture.[29] If a national bank or any of its subsidiaries does not satisfy its CRA requirement of a "satisfactory" rating in its last examination, then the FHC may be required to confine its activities to those permissible for BHCs. Once the rating has been restored to "satisfactory," all financial activities may resume.

A BHC that does not elect to become a FHC or does not qualify as a FHC will continue to engage in the same activities permissible for BHCs under the BHCA prior to its amendment. As such, the BHC will be subject to the narrower limitations of section 4(c)(8) of the BHCA that limit permissible nonbank subsidiary activities to those that are "closely related" to banking.[30]

§1.2.3 Financial Subsidiaries

The Act contains provisions that amend the National Bank Act to permit national banks to engage in a broad range of financial activities through a new entity called a "financial subsidiary." A financial subsidiary may engage in several activities that are impermissible for a bank to engage in directly.[31] Thus, banks themselves are not authorized to offer significantly different financial products under the Act. Rather, banks will engage in the new activities through affiliations with other financial services companies, including its financial subsidiary. The financial subsidiary may be either an existing corporation or a newly formed corporation. In the event that a new entity is formed and the new

[26] The Federal Reserve Board issued interim guidance for BHCs to convert to FHCs in 65 Fed. Reg. 3785 (January 25, 2000); 12 C.F.R. Pt. 225.

[27] 113 Stat. 1338, 1347.

[28] *See* discussion in Ch. 12 of taxable and tax-free transactions. In particular, *see* discussion of §355 transactions.

[29] 113 Stat. at 1346-47.

[30] *Id.* at 1346.

[31] The Office of the Comptroller of the Currency issued guidance for National banks that wished to create financial subsidiaries. 65 Fed. Reg. 12905-01; 65 Fed. Reg. 15526-01 & 65 Fed. Reg. 14810-01 (March 20, 2000).

business activities are either acquired or created by the financial subsidiary, the treatment of expenditures will implicate Code sections 162, 195, 197, 248 and 263.[32]

A national bank may control, or hold an interest in, a financial subsidiary if the financial subsidiary engages in activities that are financial in nature, incidental to activities financial in nature, or activities that the national bank may engage in directly.[33] Financial activities are those authorized for FHCs with a few exceptions. Among the most significant new activities is a full service broker-dealer business. However, there are certain activities that financial subsidiaries may not engage in as a principal, but they may be engaged in by other affiliates of the FHC. These include insurance underwriting, real estate development or investment, and merchant banking. Nevertheless, the financial subsidiary may sell financial products as an agent without any geographic restriction.

Because the financial subsidiary is permitted to engage in several activities that are not permitted to be engaged in by the bank, and these activities comprise most of the activities authorized to the FHC, a national bank is now in a position to operate without a holding company. If it chooses this operating mode, it would avoid Federal Reserve Board regulation. The elimination of the holding company can be accomplished tax-free because the transaction will probably meet the definition of a Code section 368(a)(1)(D) "reorganization."[34]

To engage in financial activities through a financial subsidiary, a national bank and all of its affiliated depository institutions must be well capitalized, well managed, and the bank must have received a rating of "satisfactory" on its most recent CRA examination.[35] A bank that fails to meet these requirements must cure the default, or it may be required to divest control of the financial subsidiary.[36] A bank would then be prohibited from acquiring additional financial subsidiaries directly or through another subsidiary until all requirements are met. Bank financial subsidiaries are required to be separately capitalized and funded and comply with additional requirements that are not required of directly owned FHC subsidiaries.[37]

Restrictions are imposed by amendments to sections 23A and 23B of the Federal Reserve Act on activities that may be conducted between a bank and its financial subsidiary. The effect of these "firewall" restrictions is to treat a financial subsidiary as though it is dealing at arm's length with a brother/sister corporation. The tax allocations of expense should be consistent with the required regulatory allocations to substantiate that the entity has adhered to the firewall restrictions.

---

[32] *See* discussion in Ch. 8 of start-up expenditures, organization expenditures, and business expansion expenditures. *See also* discussion in Ch. 11 of acquisitions in general, and § 197 in particular.

[33] 113 Stat. 1338, 1373.

[34] *See* discussion in Ch. 11 of Type D Reorganizations.

[35] 113 Stat. 1374.

[36] *Id.* at 1377. A bank that fails to comply with these requirements may be subject to limitations imposed on its conduct or activities of its subsidiaries.

[37] *Id.*

§1.2.4 Insurance Activities

The Act permits FHCs to engage in insurance activities such as "insuring, guaranteeing or indemnifying against loss, harm, damage, illness, disability, or death or providing and issuing annuities and acting as principal, agent, or broker" for those purposes.[38] Thus, the FHC or any of its affiliates (except for the bank) are authorized to sell insurance as agent or broker and to engage in life insurance, casualty insurance, and title insurance and to sell annuities.[39]

Because the FHC group must file separate federal income tax returns for the life insurance business and determine life insurance taxable income under the special rules prescribed by Subchapter L of the Internal Revenue Code, intercompany transactions and the proper booking of income and deductions may have a significant effect on the aggregate tax liability of the FHC group. Furthermore, dividend distributions will not qualify for the intercompany elimination that applies to members of a group filing a consolidated return; however, the 100 percent dividends received deduction will be available. Although the effect on federal taxation may be limited to the effect on the tax basis that the FHC has in the stock of the life insurance company, there may be significant state tax implications. If the insurance company is located in one state and the holding company is located in another state, the dividend may be subject to tax in the FHC's home state, without any offsetting deduction for dividends paid.

Although the Act authorizes banks to affiliate with insurance companies, national banks themselves are prohibited from underwriting almost all types of insurance,[40] including title insurance,[41] with the following exceptions. First, a national bank and its subsidiaries may provide insurance in a state as principal where the national bank was already providing a product as principal prior to the passage of the Act.[42] Second, a national bank is authorized to sell title insurance as agent, but only in the same manner and to the same extent as permitted to state banks.[43] Third, there is a grandfathering provision that permits a national bank and a subsidiary of a national bank to conduct title insurance activities that the bank or its subsidiary were lawfully conducting before the date of the Act. However, if a national bank has either an affiliate or a subsidiary that provides insurance as principal, then the national bank may not directly engage in any activity involving the underwriting of title insurance.

§1.2.5 Securities Activities

The Act repeals section 20 of the Glass-Steagall Act, which contained the historical restriction on banks affiliating with securities firms. Banks are now permitted to affiliate with companies, and to own subsidiaries, that are principally engaged in securities underwriting and other securities activities com-

---

[38] 12 U.S.C. §1843(k) (2006).

[39] There is no change to the provision allowing national banks to sell insurance in towns with populations of no more than 5000. Furthermore, national banks have been permitted to sell annuities. *Nationsbank v. VALIC*, 513 U.S. 251 (1995).

[40] 113 Stat. at 1409.

[41] *Id.* at 1408.

[42] 113 Stat. 1338, 1407.

[43] *Id.* at 1409.

monly referred to as investment banking.[44] The Act also repeals section 32 of the Glass-Steagall Act,[45] which restricted banks from having any person serve on the board or from employing anyone who was affiliated with a securities firm. The effect of these amendments is to formally approve the affiliation of banks and bank holding companies with securities firms.[46]

In an action that constituted a *de facto* limited repeal of section 20 of the Glass Steagall Act, the Federal Reserve Board has permitted the formation, during the several years prior to the enactment of the securities provisions of the act, by bank holding companies of so called Section 20 subsidiaries. These entities were allowed to engage in limited securities underwriting activities. The extent of securities underwriting depended, in part, on the volume of income from bank qualified investments. This limitation provided a motivation for some banks to conduct their government security investment business in the Section 20 subsidiary. An unintended consequence of this action was to possibly relieve the bank of the interest expense disallowance associated with holding tax-exempt obligations.[47] It appears that it is no longer necessary to comply with these Federal Reserve Board rules. Consequently, banks may be inclined to shift their tax-exempt portfolios back to the bank. This could have significant adverse tax consequences because of the application of Code section 265(b).[48]

Accompanying the implementation of these changes is a provision in the Act that amends the Securities Exchange Act of 1934 to eliminate the registration exemptions that banks were once afforded.[49] Although the Act replaces the exemptions with specific exemptions for banking products and activities, if a bank engages in non-exempt securities activity it will have to register with the Securities and Exchange Commission ("SEC") as a broker-dealer. A bank can conduct securities activities without SEC regulations by taking advantage of the incentives under the Act for banks to "push out" their securities and investment advising activities into registered broker-dealer affiliates.

§ 1.2.6 State Bank Provisions

The Act amends the Federal Deposit Insurance Act to allow state banks to engage in the new activities that may be engaged in by national banks, assuming that the bank is permitted to engage in the activities under state banking law.[50] Furthermore, a state bank may control or have an interest in a subsidiary that engages as principal in activities permissible for national banks to conduct

[44] 12 U.S.C. § 377, repealed by Pub. L. No. 106-102, Title I, Sec. 101(a), 113 Stat. 1341 (Nov. 12, 1999).

[45] 12 U.S.C. § 1843(k)(4)(E) (2006). Subsidiaries are given broader authority in the area of securities than subsidiaries conducting insurance activities.

[46] 12 U.S.C. § 78, repealed by Pub. L. No. 106-102, Title I, Sec. 101(b), 113 Stat. 1341 (Nov. 12, 1999).

[47] Many bank holding companies were allowed to circumvent the Glass-Steagall restrictions by forming so called Section 20 subsidiaries. These entities were authorized by the Federal Reserve to engage in limited securities underwriting activities. 61 Fed. Reg. 68650 (December 30, 1996). *See also, Securities Ind. Assoc. v. Board of Governors,* 468 U.S. 207 (1984).

[48] I.R.C. § 265(b) contains a special bank tax interest expense disallowance rule. It does not apply to nonbank members of the BHC group, including the Section 20 subsidiary. However, § 7701(f) could cause a reconsolidation of the tax-exempt obligations of the Section 20 subsidiary with the bank if tax avoidance is found.

[49] *See* discussion in Ch. 9 of disallowed interest expense.

[50] 113 Stat. 1338, 1384, 1390.

through a financial subsidiary.[51] State banks must also comply with the strictures applicable to national banks relating to capitalization, CRA ratings, safety and soundness, firewalls, and financial disclosure. However, state banks apparently do not have to meet the "well managed" criteria.

The Act prohibits any state from preventing or restricting a depository institution or any of its affiliates from being affiliated with an insurance company.[52] The Act also prohibits states from preventing or restricting a depository institution or its affiliates from engaging in any insurance activities permissible under the Act. However, current law remains unchanged with respect to state insurance regulators; that is, anyone engaging in insurance as principal or agent must follow state licensing requirements.[53]

§1.3 Commercial Banks and Thrifts Treated Alike

Throughout this volume, the term *bank* or *banking institutions* will be used to describe both commercial banks and thrifts, except where expressly noted to the contrary.[54] Included within the definition of a *thrift* is any domestic building and loan association,[55] any mutual or stock savings bank,[56] or any cooperative bank without capital stock that is organized and operated for mutual purposes and without profit.[57] Organizations included within these definitions are, among others, any domestic savings and loan association, any federal savings and loan association, and any other savings institution chartered and supervised as a savings and loan or similar association under federal or state law.[58] The term "thrift" is not herein as broadly defined as it is for regulatory purposes. Regulators customarily include within the definition credit unions, which continue to be completely exempt from federal income taxation.[59]

Including both thrifts and commercial banks in the definition of a *bank* for purposes of this book may, by historical standards, be overly broad. As will be explained in detail below, the Internal Revenue Code has contained provisions that were applicable to just commercial banks or just to thrifts. However, at this

[51] Several state banking laws contain a "wild card" provision that has the effect of authorizing state banks to engage in any activity that may be engaged by national banks operating within the state.

[52] 113 Stat. 1338, 1353.

[53] 113 Stat. 1338, 1352. Prior to the Act, the U.S. Supreme Court held that a state could not prevent a national bank from selling insurance. *Barnett Bank of Marion County, N.A. v. Nelson*, 517 U.S. 25 (1996).

[54] In a case involving a foreign tax credit issue, the Sixth Circuit concluded that an entity that met the definition of the term "bank" used in I.R.C. §581 was not necessarily an entity that conducted a "banking business" for purposes of I.R.C. §956. It arrived at the different meaning of those two terms by applying statutory construction principles. It noted that although neither the Internal Revenue Code nor the United States Code defines the phrase "banking business," it could apply two canons of statutory construction to assist it in interpreting that term: (1) undefined terms are construed in accordance with their ordinary and natural meanings, and (2) the meaning of an undefined term may be deduced from nearby words under *noscitur a sociis*. *The Limited, Inc. v. Commissioner*, 286 F.3d 324 (6th Cir. 2002).

[55] I.R.C. §7701(a)(19).

[56] I.R.C. §591(b).

[57] I.R.C. §7701(a)(32).

[58] I.R.C. §581.

[59] I.R.C. §501(c)(14). The "Unlimited Savings Allowance Act of 1995," S 722, introduced in the Senate on April 25, 1995, but never enacted, would have, in effect, repealed the long-standing exemption from federal income taxation accorded credit unions.

point in the evolution of financial institution taxation and activities, it is appropriate because the different tax provisions have been repealed.[60]

The elimination of many differences between the activities historically conducted by commercial banks and by thrifts was accelerated by the Garn-St. Germain Depository Institutions Act of 1982.[61] Although vestiges of the historical differences in business activities remain, they are insufficient to justify a disparity in taxation. Notable among the historical variances in taxation that were eliminated by the Small Business Job Protection Act of 1996[62] are the differences in the treatment of foreclosure transactions and bad-debt deductions.[63]

Although, historically, thrift institutions enjoyed more favorable tax treatment than other financial institutions, Congress demonstrated in the Tax Reform Act of 1986 that changes in regulatory policies had expanded the activities of thrift institutions and encouraged other institutions, namely commercial banks and mortgage companies, to expand their activities in areas that were traditionally serviced by the thrift industry.[64] Acknowledging this new competitive framework, Congress substantially reduced the bad debt deduction available to thrift institutions.

§ 1.4 Taxation of Banks

§ 1.4.1 Overview

Banks that have not elected to be treated as S corporations are C corporations subject to the imposition of federal income tax by Code section 11.[65] At one time, the Code expressly stated that banks were taxable as C corporations. Section 104(b) of the Revenue Act of 1936 provided, "Banks shall be taxable in the same manner as other corporations. . . ."[66] No such express language is currently contained in the Code.[67] Regulations state that "[a] bank, as defined in Code section 581, is subject to the tax on corporations imposed by Code section 11."[68] This reference to a bank includes both commercial banks and thrifts.[69] Regulation section 1.581-2(a) states further that "[m]utual savings banks, building and loan associations, and cooperative banks not having capital stock repre-

[60] Small Business Job Protection Act of 1996, Pub. L. No. 104-188 (1996).

[61] Garn-St. Germain Depository Institutions Act of 1982, Pub. L. No. 97-320 (1982).

[62] Small Business Job Protection Act of 1996, Pub. L. No. 104-188 (1996).

[63] *See* discussions of I.R.C. § 595 in Ch. 7 and Code §§ 585 and 593 in Ch. 10.

[64] Pub. L. No. 99-514.

[65] A C Corporation is defined in I.R.C. § 1361. *See also*, Reg. § 301.7701-2(b). I.R.C. § 542(c)(2) expressly exempts banks from the personal holding company tax, and I.R.C. § 7507 exempts insolvent banks from federal income taxation. PLR 9044046 (Nov. 1990). For purposes of I.R.C. § 7507, no substantial difference exists between deposits in a savings and loan or building and loan association and deposits in a bank or trust company. Generally, the holder of a share account in a savings and loan or building and loan association is no more an investor than is a holder of a deposit account in a bank or trust company. Thus, depositors in a savings and loan association or building and loan association are entitled to the protection provided by Code section 7507. Rev. Rul. 88-18, 1998-1 C.B. 402.

[66] Revenue Act of 1936, Pub. L. No. 74-740 (1936).

[67] For tax years beginning after December 31, 1997, a bank that qualifies as a "small corporation" under the provisions of I.R.C. 55(e) will be exempt from the Alternative Minimum Tax. The Taxpayer Relief Act of 1997, Pub. L. No. 105-34, 111 Stat. 788 (1997) amended the Alternative Minimum Tax provisions of the Code to clarify the application of the small business exemption, which generally applies to a corporation that has gross receipts of $5 million or less.

[68] Reg. § 1.581-1.

[69] I.R.C. § 581.

sented by shares are subject to tax as in the case of other corporations." Code section 591(b) provides that a "mutual savings bank," for purposes of Code sections 591-596, includes any bank that had capital stock represented by shares and that is subject to and operated under federal or state laws relating to mutual savings banks.[70]

Regulation section 301.7701-13A provides that "[i]n general. For taxable years beginning after July 11, 1969, the term 'domestic building and loan association' means a domestic building and loan association, a domestic savings and loan association, a federal savings and loan association, and any other savings institution chartered and supervised as a savings and loan or similar association under federal or state law which meets the supervisory test (described in paragraph (b) of this section), the business operations test (described in paragraph (c) of this section), and the assets test (described in paragraph (d) of this section)."[71]

§ 1.4.2 Accumulated Earnings Tax

Banks are not exempt from the accumulated earnings tax, although the tax is seldom imposed on banks.[72] For the accumulated earnings tax to be imposed on a bank, one federal government agency (the IRS) may be taking a position that is contrary to another federal agency (the FDIC or OCC).

(a) *Bank Regulatory Rules*

Federal banking regulators police bank capital levels. Federal banking regulations provide that a bank shall be deemed to be "adequately capitalized," in general, only if the bank: (i) has a total risk-based capital ratio of 8 percent or greater; (ii) has a Tier 1 risk-based capital ratio of 4 percent or greater; (iii) has (A) a leverage ratio of 4 percent or greater, or (B) a leverage ratio of 3 percent or greater if the bank is rated composite 1 under the CAMEL rating system in the most recent examination of the bank and is not experiencing or anticipating

[70] This provision was added to the Code by the Economic Recovery Tax Act of 1981, Pub. L. No. 97-34 (1981). I.R.C. § 591(b) was enacted in response to changing regulations in the banking industry that allowed mutual savings banks to convert to stock savings banks. H. Conf. Rept. 97-215, at 284-285 (1981). In order to facilitate the conversions and not frustrate regulatory policy, I.R.C. § 591(b) provided that "for purposes of this part, the term 'mutual savings bank' includes any bank . . . which has capital stock represented by shares, and . . . which is subject to, and operates under, Federal or State laws relating to mutual savings banks." Accordingly, mutual savings banks that converted to stock savings banks continued to qualify as mutual savings banks for purposes of the reserve method of accounting for thrift institutions under § 593. The amendments were intended to "apply to both mutual savings banks which convert into stock associations and to newly formed stock associations so long as the institution is operated as a savings institution and is subject to the same Federal or State regulatory scheme as a mutual savings bank chartered under Federal or State law." H. Conf. Rept. 97-215, at 284-285 (1981).

[71] The definition of a "building and loan association" under section 101(4), I.R.C. 1939, was expanded to include "a domestic building and loan association, a domestic savings and loan association, and a Federal savings and loan association, substantially all the business of which is confined to making loans to members" by the Revenue Act of 1951, ch. 521, sec. 313, 65 Stat. 490. In that Act, Congress eliminated the exemption from Federal income tax for domestic building and loan associations and instead enacted generous rules for calculating deductions for additions to bad debt reserves. Revenue Act of 1951, ch. 521, sec. 313(e), 65 Stat. 490-491. The legislative history for the 1951 Act indicates: "This amendment is of a clarifying nature and is not intended to change the existing meaning of a domestic building and loan association." S. Rept. 781, 82d Cong., 1st Sess. (1951), 1951-2 C.B. 563-564.

[72] I.R.C. § 532.

significant growth; and (iv) does not meet the definition of a "well capitalized" bank. A state member bank is deemed to be "well capitalized" if the bank: (i) has a total risk-based capital ratio of 10 percent or greater; (ii) has a Tier 1 risk-based capital ratio of 6 percent or greater; (iii) has a leverage ratio of 5 percent or greater; and (iv) is not subject to any written agreement, order, capital directive, or prompt corrective action directive issued by the Federal Reserve Board to meet and maintain a specific capital level for any capital measure.[73]

(b) *Tax Rules*

The accumulated earnings tax is imposed on a bank in addition to the other taxes to which a bank is subject.[74] The tax is imposed on the accumulated taxable income of a bank that is formed or availed of, for the purpose of avoiding the income tax with respect to its shareholders or the shareholders of any other corporation, by permitting earnings and profits to accumulate beyond its reasonable business needs instead of being divided or distributed.[75] Currently, accumulated taxable income is taxed at a rate of 15 percent. According to prospective sunset amendments made by the Economic Growth and Tax Relief Reconciliation Act of 2001, for tax years beginning after December 31, 2010, accumulated taxable income will be taxed at the highest rate of tax under Code section 1(c).[76] Code section 7701(a)(23) provides that the term taxable year means, "[I]n the case of a return made for a fractional part of a year under the provisions of subtitle A or under regulations prescribed by the Secretary, the period for which such return is made."

The reasonable business needs of a bank will include the reasonable anticipated needs of the business. In order for a corporation to justify an accumulation of earnings and profits for reasonable anticipated future needs, there must be an indication that the future needs of the business require such accumulation and the bank must have specific, definite, and feasible plans for the use of such accumulation.[77]

The accumulation need not be used immediately, nor must the plans for its use be consummated within a short period after the close of the taxable year. However, such accumulation must be used within a reasonable time depending upon all the facts and circumstances relating to the future needs of the business.[78] Where the future needs of the business are uncertain or vague, where the plans for the future use of the accumulation are not specific, definite, and feasible, or where the execution of such plan is postponed indefinitely, an accumulation cannot be justified on the grounds of reasonable anticipated needs of the business.

In a situation in which the bank had a total risk-based capital ratio and Tier 1 risk-based capital ratio over 3.6 times its peer group, a leverage ratio 2.6 times its

[73] 12 C.F.R. § 208.33(b)(2); Section 208.33(b) defines three additional categories or levels of capitalization: "undercapitalized," "significantly undercapitalized," and "critically undercapitalized."

[74] I.R.C. § 531.

[75] I.R.C. § 532(a).

[76] I.R.C. § 531.

[77] Reg. § 1.537-1(a)-2(b).

[78] Reg. § 1.537-1(b).

peer group, and a dividend to net income ratio approximately 1.5 times its peer group, the IRS concluded that the bank was subject to the accumulated earnings tax.[79] The bank was not able to demonstrate that the accumulation of its earning was entirely justified on the grounds of reasonable anticipated needs of the business. However, the IRS found that to the extent that the accumulation was for the purpose of constructing a new building for its home office and to maintain adequate financial strength, it was reasonable. The taxpayer was unable to persuade the IRS that it had definite plans for buying the minority stock of one of its affiliated banks. Thus, to that extent, the accumulation was unreasonable.[80]

§ 1.4.3 Banks as Limited Liability Companies

One of the statutory requirements for a state-chartered bank to be eligible for federal deposit insurance is that it be "incorporated under the laws of any state."[81] To satisfy this rule, and recognizing the potential attractiveness of the limited liability company ("LLC") form of organization, the FDIC adopted a regulation that permits a bank that is chartered as an LLC under state law to be treated as "incorporated" under state law if it meets certain criteria.[82]

In the regulation the FDIC states, "We note that one of the entities specifically classified as a corporation in the [income tax] regulation is a '[s]tate-chartered business entity conducting banking activities, if any of its deposits are insured under the Federal Deposit Insurance Act.' As a result, an FDIC-insured, state bank that is chartered as an LLC would not qualify for partnership tax treatment for federal income tax purposes."

The Internal Revenue Service rules that determine whether an entity is to be taxed as a corporation or as a partnership were substantially amended in 1996. Prior to their amendment, Treasury regulation § 301.7701-2 classified an association of two or more persons who had the purpose of carrying on a business and dividing the profits as either a partnership or a corporation depending upon whether the association possessed more corporate characteristics than noncorporate characteristics. The four corporate characteristics that the IRS utilized were: continuity of life (perpetual succession), centralized management, limited liability, and free transferability of interests. Under the old IRS regulations, if an association possessed at least three of the four corporate characteristics, then it would be treated as a corporation for federal income tax purposes.

After 1996 the IRS no longer utilized the corporate characteristics test and now permits business entities that are not specifically classified as corporations in the regulation to elect partnership tax treatment.[83] One of the entities specifically classified as a corporation in the regulation is a "[s]tate-chartered business entity conducting banking activities, if any of its deposits are insured under the Federal Deposit Insurance Act."[84] Apparently, for this reason, the FDIC volun-

[79] TAM 9822009, May 29, 1998. *Cf.* PLR 8821002, January 27, 1988.

[80] If a bank allocated retained earnings to stock distributions, it does not thereby reduce accumulated earnings and profits ("E & P") for tax purposes.

[81] 12 U.S.C. § 1813(c)(1) (2007).

[82] 67 FR 48054-01, July 23, 2002. 12 C.F.R. Part 303.

[83] Reg. § § 301.7701-2, 7701-3 (1997).

[84] Reg. § 301.7701-2(b)(5) (1997).

teered that an FDIC-insured state bank that is chartered as an LLC would not qualify for partnership tax treatment for federal income tax purposes.[85]

In 1995, the IRS examined whether the Texas legislature created limited banking associations ("LBA") with the same essential characteristics as Texas limited liability companies and, therefore, LBAs should be considered a special type of limited liability company. The taxpayer argued that a Texas LBA is not a corporation *per se*. However, the IRS concluded that a Texas LBA is "better viewed" as a special form of state bank, which is a corporation under state law. Accordingly, it must be treated as a corporation under federal income tax law.[86] The reasoning of the IRS seems to turn on the conclusion that under Texas state law the LBA was regarded by both the taxpayer and Texas bank regulators as incorporated for certain (although not all) purposes.

The IRS has been urged to reconsider the apparent prohibition contained in the regulations on banks electing to be taxed as partnerships.[87]

§ 1.5 Definition of a "Bank"

The tax definition of a bank derives its key components from the historical legal definition of a bank.

§ 1.5.1 Classical Definition

In *Bouvier's Law Dictionary*, a bank is defined for commercial law purposes as "[a] place for the deposit of money . . . ."[88] *Ballentine's Law Dictionary* describes a bank as "[a]n institution, usually incorporated, the business of which is primarily receiving deposits of money, the collection of commercial paper, discounting commercial paper, lending money . . . ."[89] In *Black's Law Dictionary*, a bank is described as "an institution . . . whose business it is to receive money on deposit, cash checks or drafts, discount commercial paper, make loans, and issue promissory notes payable to bearer . . . ."[90]

§ 1.5.2 Judicial Definition

The classic judicial definition of a bank was enunciated by Justice Clifford for the U.S. Supreme Court in *Stoulton v. Savings Institution*.[91] It was expressed at a time when the nation's commercial banking system reached a form resembling its current structure. The opinion reads, in part:

> Strictly speaking, the term "bank" implies a place for the deposit of money, as that is the most obvious purpose of such an institution. Originally the business of banking consisted only in receiving deposits, such as bullion, plate and the like, for safekeeping until the depositor should see fit to draw it out for use, but the business, in the progress of events, was extended, and bankers

[85] Certainly, the FDIC's interpretation of a federal income tax regulation is not authoritative. However, the existence of the Treasury regulation appears to prevent LLC banks from electing, under the "check-the-box" regulations, partnership tax treatment.

[86] PLR 9551032, September 27, 1995.

[87] *See* letter from Senators Orin Hatch (R-Utah), John Breaux (D-La.), and Gordon Smith (R-Ore.) dated July 9, 2004 to Gregory F. Jenner, Acting Assistant Secretary for Tax Policy.

[88] *Bouvier's Law Dictionary and Concise Encyclopedia* 318 (3d rev. 1914).

[89] *Ballentine's Law Dictionary* 121 (3d ed. 1969).

[90] *Black's Law Dictionary* 98 (6th ed. 1990).

[91] *Stoulton v. Savings Institution*, 84 U.S. 109, 118-119 (17 Wall.) (1872).

> assumed to discount bills and notes and to loan money upon mortgage, pawn or other security, and at a still later period to issue notes of their own intended as a circulating currency and a medium of exchange instead of gold and silver.[92]

§ 1.5.3 Regulatory Definition

For federal bank regulatory purposes, a commercial bank is defined in terms of the type of business in which it is engage or the "powers" it exercises.

(a) *National Bank Act*

Federal banking law sets forth those powers today in substantially the same form as set forth in the National Bank Act of 1864. A national banking association is permitted under current law:

> To exercise subject to law, all such incidental powers as shall be necessary to carry on the business of banking; by discounting and negotiating promissory notes, drafts, bills of exchange, and other evidences of debt; by receiving deposits; by buying and selling exchange, coin, and bullion; by loaning money on personal security; and by obtaining, issuing, and circulating notes according to the provisions of this chapter.[93]

The scope of this clause has been, and continues to be, the subject of judicial examination and bank regulatory pronouncements, which are uniform in holding that, to be a "bank" for federal banking law purposes, the institution need only accept deposits *or* make loans.[94]

(b) *Bank Holding Company Act*

The tax definition of Code section 581 adheres, in part, more closely to the definition of a bank contained in the Bank Holding Company Act of 1956. The latter adopts a conjunctive approach to the definition; that is, the institution must accept deposits *and* make loans.[95]

The Bank Holding Company Act definition of a bank has been changed several times since 1956. At first, a "chartering" definition was provided: a bank was originally defined as "any national banking association or any state bank, savings bank, or trust company."[96] The definition was substantially modified in 1966 to include "any institution that accepts deposits that the depositor has a legal right to withdraw on demand."[97] In 1970, the definition was further amended to read: "[b]ank means any institution . . . which (1) accepts deposits that the depositor has a legal right to withdraw on demand, and (2) engages in the business of making commercial loans."[98] This conjunctive definition had the effect of promoting the formation of so-called nonbank banks—institutions that accept deposits but do not make commercial loans. Finally, the Competitive

---

[92] *Id.*

[93] 12 U.S.C. § 27 (1994), R.S. 5136, July 1, 1922, ch. 257, § 1, 42 Stat. 767. R.S. 5136 was derived from Act of June 3, 1864, ch. 106, § 8, 13 Stat. 101, which was the National Bank Act. The Act was actually passed in 1863 but amended in 1864.

[94] *See, e.g., First National Bank in Plant City, Fla. v. Dickinson*, 396 U.S. 122 (1969).

[95] 12 U.S.C. § 1841(c) (2006).

[96] Bank Holding Company Act of 1956, Pub. L. No. 511, § 2(c) (1956).

[97] An Act to amend the Bank Holding Company Act of 1956, Pub. L. No. 89-485 (1966).

[98] Bank Holding Company Act Amendments of 1970, Pub. L. No. 91-607 (1970).

Equality Banking Act of 1987 provided that a bank is an "insured bank" if it meets the definition in Section 3(h) of the Federal Deposit Insurance Act and is a domestic institution that *both* accepts demand deposits or deposits that the depositor may withdraw by check or similar means (NOW accounts) *and* is engaged in the business of making commercial loans.[99]

(c) ***Farm Credit Act***

The Farm Credit Act of 1933[100] created various lending institutions within the Farm Credit System to meet the specific credit needs of farmers. Among these institutions were banks for cooperatives, one in each of 12 farm credit districts, and a Central Bank for Cooperatives. These banks were designed to make loans to cooperative associations engaged in marketing farm products, purchasing farm supplies, or furnishing farm services. Today, the Farm Credit System includes banks for cooperatives, production credit associations, farm credit banks, and federal land bank associations.[101] By statute, each of these institutions is designated as a "federally chartered instrumentalit[y] of the United States."[102]

§ 1.5.4 Tax Definition

The Code adopts the central component of the classical and the regulatory definitions of a bank; that is, that the entity accept deposits. The definition of "bank" for tax purposes is contained in Code section 581, where it provides:

> For purposes of section 582 and 584, the term "bank" means a bank or trust company incorporated and doing business under the laws of the United States (including laws relating to the District of Columbia) or of any State, a substantial part of the business of which consists of receiving deposits and making loans and discounts, or of exercising fiduciary powers similar to those permitted to national banks under authority of the Comptroller of the Currency, and which is subject by law to supervision and examination by State, or Federal authority having supervision over banking institutions. Such term also means a domestic building and loan association.

The definition requires the institution to be one of two types of entities:

1. A bank or trust company
    a. Incorporated
    b. Doing business under the laws of the United States (including laws relating to the District of Columbia) or of any state
    c. A substantial part[103] of the business of which consists of receiving deposits and making loans and discounts, or of exercising fiduciary

99 12 U.S.C. § 1841(c), as amended by the Competitive Equality Banking Act of 1987, Pub. L. No. 100-86 (1987). Similar definitions have been contained in earlier Revenue Acts. *See, e.g.*, Internal Revenue Code of 1939, Code § 104(a).

100 48 Stat. 257, as amended, 12 U.S.C. §§ 2001 *et seq.* (1986)

101 12 U.S.C. § 2002(a) (1988).

102 12 U.S.C. § 2121 (1998) (banks for cooperatives and Central Bank for Cooperatives); § 2141 (National Bank for Cooperatives); §§ 2071(a) and (b)(7) (production credit associations); § 2011(a) (farm credit banks); §§ 2091(a) and (b)(4) (federal land bank associations). The Farm Credit Act also addresses the taxation of these institutions. For a discussion of the state taxation of banks for cooperatives, *see Director of Revenue of Missouri v. CoBank ACB*, 531 U.S. 316 (2001).

103 For a discussion of what constitutes "substantial," *see Austin State Bank v. Commissioner*, 57 T.C. 180 (1974), *acq.*, 1974-1 C.B. 1.

powers similar to those permitted to national banks under authority of the Comptroller of the Currency

d. Subject by law to supervision and examination by state, or federal authority having supervision over banking institutions, or

2. A domestic building and loan association.

Although the introductory clause in the first sentence expressly limits the scope of Code Section 581 to Code sections 582 and 584, there is no other definition of a "bank" elsewhere in the Code. Moreover, whenever the term "bank" is used, the Code section 581 definition is made applicable. Accordingly, the introductory clause should be read "For all purposes . . . ."

The definition prescribes a rule that allows only two types of entities to qualify as a "bank" for federal income tax purposes, one is a "bank," referred to in the first sentence of the section, and the second is a "domestic building and loan association," referred to in the second sentence. These are the only two types of depository institutions that are subject to federal income tax. For an entity referred to in the first sentence of Code section 581 as a "bank," it also must meet the four listed requirements. If an entity is a domestic building and loan association, it must meet the requirements prescribed in Code section 7701(a)(19).

Long before the enactment of the nation's first constitutionally valid income tax in 1913, the term "bank" was commonly used to describe only a commercial bank.[104] When the initial version of Code section 581 was enacted, federal income tax was imposed only on commercial banks, not domestic building and loan associations or any other depository institution. The latter entities were exempt from federal income taxation. Much later, when Congress withdrew the tax-exempt status from domestic building and loan associations and subjected them to federal income tax, the second sentence was added. It was needed because it was understood that the reference to a "bank" in the first sentence referred to a commercial bank. The presence of the second sentence also indicates that the term "bank" used in the first sentence refers to a commercial bank.

In *MoneyGram International*, the Firth Circuit Federal Court of Appeals stated that " . . . § 581 is not a model of statutory clarity. Its construction and circular use of the term "bank" are inherently ambiguous."[105] Undeniably, when a term is defined using a term that has the same meaning as the term being defined, the definition is circular. However, if the term has a commonly understood meaning independent of the term being defined and that term is being imported into the definition, the definition is not circular.[106] Because the Court did not interpret the

---

[104] *See* discussion of regulatory definition of a commercial bank at §1.5.3. In 1913, the same year that Congress enacted federal income tax law, Congress enacted legislation that permitted deposit insurance.

[105] *MoneyGram International and Subsidiaries v. Commissioner*, 664 Fed. Appx. 386 (5th Cir. 2016). The Court admitted that " . . . being a 'bank' within the commonly understood meaning of that term is an independent requirement." It appears that the Court did not consider what the "commonly understood meaning of that term" was.

[106] I.R.C. §61 defines "gross income" as "all income from whatever source derived . . . ." In this definition, containing language found in the Sixteenth Amendment, Congress used the word "income" in the definition to base federal income tax law on the accountant's concept of income that predated the Sixteenth Amendment. That definition requires realization to take place before income is

reference in the first sentence to a "bank" to mean a commercial bank, it assumed the definition to be circular.

The federal income tax definition of a "bank" for tax purposes begins with the entity that is a commercial bank, but it doesn't end there. The tax definition is more limited and for an important reason. To ensure uniformity and consistency in the application of federal income tax law, Congress specified additional requirements for the commercial bank to meet to qualify for the then very favorable bank tax rules. Had it not done so, bank regulators with their chartering authority would be able to qualify entities for the favorable tax rules for which they were not intended to qualify. The existence of a dual banking system, one where both federal and state governments determine which entities will qualify as banks, would compound this distortion by permitting 51 chartering agencies to determine which entities qualified for the favorable federal income tax rules.

§ 1.5.5 Scope of Code Section 581

Code section 581 expressly defines a bank only for purposes of Code section 582 ("Bad Debts, Losses, and Gains with respect to Securities Held by Financial Institutions")[107] and Code section 584 ("Common Trust Funds"). However, the Code section 581 definition is linked to the operative provisions of several other Code sections, including Code section 585, which specifies the allowable bad-debt reserve addition available to certain commercial banks;[108] Code section 265,[109] which disallows interest expense allocable to tax-exempt obligations; Code section 291, which specifies the cutback in deductions for certain corporate preference items, including interest expense,[110] and Code section 1277, which defers the deduction of interest expense allocable to accrued market discount.[111]

(a) *Thrifts*

By including a "domestic building and loan association" within the Code section 581 definition of a bank, the term "bank" is expanded to include a variety of institutions commonly referred to as "thrifts."[112] Prior to the enactment of the Small Business Job Protection Act of 1996, these entities were subject to some special Code provisions not applicable to commercial banks or other taxpayers, including: the deduction for dividends paid on deposits;[113] more generous loan

(Footnote Continued)

earned. This type of income is to be distinguished from the historical definition of income employed by economists, which measures income by reference to appreciation in the value of property plus consumption.

[107] I.R.C. § 582(c)(5). In that section, the term "financial institution" is defined more broadly than a "bank" and includes any small business investment company operating under the Small Business Investment Act of 1958 and any business development corporation.

[108] I.R.C. § 585(a)(2). Other sections that refer to I.R.C. § are I.R.C. § 165(l)(3)(A); I.R.C. § 246A(c)(3)(B)(i); I.R.C. § 271(a); I.R.C. § 279(c)(5)(A); I.R.C. § 465(c)(7)(D)(iv); I.R.C. § 542(c)(2); I.R.C. § 585(a)(2)(A); I.R.C. § 593(d)(1)(B)(ii); I.R.C. § 1281(b)(1)(C); I.R.C. § 6032; I.R.C. § 6695(f); I.R.C. § 7512(b).

[109] I.R.C. § 265(b).

[110] I.R.C. § 291(a)(3).

[111] I.R.C. § 1277(c).

[112] For regulatory purposes, credit unions are usually embraced within the definitions of a thrift.

[113] I.R.C. § 591.

loss deduction rules;[114] provisions for deferring foreclosure gains and losses;[115] and limitations on the dividends-received deduction.[116] A financial institution chartered as a bank cannot meet the threshold requirements of Code section 7701(a)(19).[117] Thus, if a taxpayer converts its thrift charter to a bank charter it may no longer use the reserve method of accounting for bad debts under Code section 593.

(b) ***Foreign Banks***

Under several provisions, certain foreign financial institutions are treated "as banks" for tax purposes, despite the fact that they do not technically fit within the Code section 581 definition of a bank. For example, Code section 585(a)(2)(B) extends the commercial bank loan loss reserve methods to any corporation that would otherwise meet the Code section 581 definition of a bank except that it is a foreign corporation. However, in the case of any foreign bank, the loan loss rule applies only with respect to outstanding loans on which interest is effectively connected with the conduct of a banking business within the United States.[118]

§ 1.5.6 Chartering Requirement

The Code section 581 definition of a bank appears on its face to require the institution to be "incorporated and doing business under the laws of the United States (including laws relating to the District of Columbia) or any state . . . ." The "laws" referred to are, presumably, the banking laws of the jurisdiction that charters institutions because banking powers are normally not conferred simply by complying with general laws of incorporation, and certainly not under tax law. However, the weight of authority establishes that the state and federal banking law definitions of a bank do not control for federal income tax purposes. There is a lack of uniformity among jurisdictions as to what constitutes a bank. Definitions of banks are found in federal (nontax) statutes and the laws of each of the 50 states.[119]

Banking law definitions of a bank are usually expressed in terms of the powers that the entity may exercise.[120] Thus, the Fourth Circuit Court of Appeals held that the laws of Virginia, which classified an entity as an "industrial loan association," and not a bank, would not disqualify the institution from being treated as a bank for federal income tax purposes.[121] The opinion reads, in part:

> We cannot accept the proposition that a special classification given by state law can so act as to withdraw an institution, which possesses the essential characteristics of a bank, from the protection afforded by the wording of, and

[114] I.R.C. § 593.

[115] I.R.C. § 595.

[116] I.R.C. § 596.

[117] *Barnett Banks, Inc. & Subsidiaries v. Commissioner*, T.C. Memo. 2002-168 (2002), *aff'd*, slip op. No. 03-15055, 2005 WL 1864724 (11th Cir. Aug. 8, 2005).

[118] I.R.C. § 864(c). *Cf.* Rev. Rul. 70-385, 1970-2 C.B. 156. Most foreign banks that are subject to U.S. income tax would be barred from using the reserve method for computing bad-debt deductions because they would be "large banks." *See* I.R.C. § 585(c). *See* also PLR 200027021, April 6, 2000.

[119] *Morris Plan Bank of New Haven v. Smith*, 42-1 U.S.T.C. ¶ 9239, 125 F.2d 440 (2d Cir. 1942).

[120] *See, e.g.*, New York Banking Law, art. 1, § 2(1), and art. 3, § 96. *See also* federal banking laws at 12 U.S.C. § 24, in which the powers permitted to be exercised by national banks are enumerated.

[121] *Staunton Industrial Loan v. Commissioner*, 41-2 U.S.T.C. ¶ 9544, 120 F.2d 930 (4th Cir. 1941).

the policy underlying [the predecessor to Code section 581]. Furthermore, we are mindful that, wherever possible, federal taxing statutes are to be uniformly interpreted.[122]

§ 1.5.7 Deposit Requirement

The deposit requirement traditionally has been recognized as critical to the definition of a bank for general legal purposes. Similarly, unless the institution meets the fiduciary exception (as a trust company), it must receive deposits to be classified as a bank for federal income tax purposes.[123] However, standing alone, the authorization to accept deposits will not qualify an institution as a bank for tax purposes.[124] If an entity is not a "fiduciary," the fact that it actually receives deposits, and is not just authorized to do so, is critical.[125] Moreover, it must also make loans.

Prior to 2005, the FDIC managed the insurance for both commercial banks and thrifts in different funds. Thrift deposits were insured by the Savings Association Insurance Fund ("SAIF") and commercial bank deposits were insured by the Bank Insurance Fund ("BIF").[126] BIF and SAIF served in largely identical roles as deposit insurance funds for separate sectors of the depository industry.[127] The funds were established in 1989 in the wake of the savings and loan crisis upon the abolition of the Federal Savings and Loan Insurance Corporations (FSLIC).[128] Originally, the two separate funds were ostensibly intended to regulate different types of financial institutions.[129]

Soon after the creation of these two funds, however, commercial banks began to acquire SAIF insured deposits through the purchase of thrift institutions.[130] Over the past three decades, the popularity of state chartered thrifts has waned and the state chartered thrift industry has undergone a period of prolonged decline.[131] Thus, the necessity of a separate insurance fund devoted solely to state chartered thrifts became questionable. At the same time, banks began to engage in tactics designed to shift deposits from one insurance fund to the other to avoid higher premiums.[132] As a result, the parallel approach to deposit

---

[122] *Id.* (citations omitted). *See also Mutual Savings and Loan Co., Inc. of Norfolk v. Commissioner*, 44 B.T.A. 1204, Dec. 12,034 (1941).

[123] PLR 200027021, April 6, 2000; PLR 8113004, November 28, 1980 and PLR 8001006, September 26, 1979. Traditionally, savings and loan associations and domestic building and loan associations were nonstock corporations that secured their funds through "shares" and not deposits. The distinction is largely irrelevant. *See* I.R.C. § 591, which allows a deduction for dividends paid on deposits as a substitute for the interest expense deduction allowed under I.R.C. § 163. *See also* Reg. § 301.7701-2(b).

[124] *La Caisse Popularire Ste. Marie (St. Mary's Bank) v. United States*, 77-2 U.S.T.C. ¶9698, 563 F.2d 505 (1st Cir. 1977).

[125] *United States v. Seattle First International Corp.*, 79-2 U.S.T.C. ¶9495, 1979 WL 1414 (W.D. 1979).

[126] In some situations involving acquisitions and charter conversions, an entity chartered as a commercial bank could have deposits included in SAIF.

[127] David B. Sicilia & Jeffrey L. Cruikshank, The Greenspan Effect: Words That Move the World's Markets 96 (New York McGraw-Hill Professional 2000).

[128] Arthur E. Wilmarth, Jr., *Wal-Mart and the Separation of Banking and Commerce*, 39 CONN. L. REV. 1539, 1584 n. 264 (2007).

[129] *See id.*

[130] *Id.*

[131] Arthur J. Wilmarth Jr., *The OCC's Preemption Rules Exceed the Agency's Authority and Present a Serious Threat to the Dual Banking System and Consumer Protection*, 23 Ann.. Rev. Banking & FIN. L. 225, 281 (2004).

[132] Sicilia & Cruikshank, *supra* note 129 at 97 ("If there is no substantial difference between BIF and SAIF insurance, and if there is no substantial differ-

insurance funding that was adopted in the wake of the savings and loan crisis of the 1980's fell into disfavor.

The existence of two separate, but largely coextensive, depository insurance funds came to an end with passage of the Federal Deposit Insurance Reform Act of 2005 ("FDIRA").[133] The FDIRA did away with the two-fund approach entirely and established a single Deposit Insurance Fund ("DIF").[134] All assets and liabilities held by the former insurance funds transferred to DIF upon the merger and dissolution of BIF and SAIF.[135]

DIF, like its predecessors, is managed by the FDIC.[136] The fund originally set the initial standard maximum deposit amount at $100,000.[137] The maximum deposit amount is indexed to inflation and will be subject to review every five years, starting on April 1, 2010.[138] However, in July 2010, Congress passed the Dodd-Frank Wall Street Reform and Consumer Protection Act, which permanently increased the maximum deposit amount to $250,000.[139] This modification applied retroactively to deposits held by institutions "for which the [FDIC] was appointed as receiver or conservator on or after January 1, 2008, and before October 3, 2008."[140] For the purpose of calculating the net amount due to depositors, all of the deposits made by a single depositor into an insured depository institution must generally be aggregated.[141] The term "deposit," as currently defined in the Federal Deposit Act, was not modified by the FDIRA.[142] DIF does not insure against all bank liabilities that could be termed deposits under the Federal Insurance Corporation Act.[143]

(Footnote Continued)

ence between the advantages granted to BIF institutions or SAIF institutions, then anytime one deposit insurance fund has difficulties that result in substantially higher premiums, members will try to shift to the other deposit insurance fund. In the process, the disadvantaged fund becomes increasingly vulnerable to insolvency as its premium base declines.") (quoting Alan Greenspan).

[133] Federal Deposit Insurance Reform Act of 2005, Pub. L. No. 109-171, 120 Stat. 4 (codified as amended in scattered sections of 12 U.S.C.). *See id.* at 97 ("Deposit insurance (at least the SAIF version) was starting to look like HMOs in their worst days: the departure of the healthiest insurees led to higher premiums for those less-healthy insurees who remained behind."); § 2102, 120 Stat. at 9–21.

[134] 12 U.S.C. § 1821(a)(4)(A) (2006).

[135] Federal Deposit Insurance Reform Act of 2005, Pub. L. No. 109-171, § 2102, 120 Stat. 4 (codified as amended in scattered sections of the U.S.C.).

[136] 12 U.S.C. § 1821(a)(4)(A) (2006).

[137] 12 U.S.C. § 1821(a)(1)(E) (2006). *See also* 12 U.S.C. § 1821(a)(1)(C) (2000) (requiring that the FDIC aggregate the amount held in multiple accounts by a single depositor in a single deposit institution to reach the net amount due to the depositor).

[138] *Id.*

[139] Dodd-Frank Wall Street Reform and Consumer Protection Act, Pub. L. No. 111-203, § 355, 124 Stat. 1376 (codified as amended in scattered sections of the U.S.C.).

[140] *Id.*

[141] *But see* 12 U.S.C. § 1821(a)(1)(C) (2006) (specifically excluding from aggregation trust funds as described in 12 U.S.C. § 1817(i)(1-2) that have a separate insurance requirement, and funds separately insured under 12 U.S.C. § 1817(i)(3)).

[142] 12 U.S.C. § 1813(l) (2006). *See also* § 2102, 120 Stat. at 9–21 (containing no mention of the definition of deposit). *See also* 12 C.F.R. § 327.8(a) (specifying that for the purposes of assessments under Part 327, the term deposit has the meaning provided by 12 U.S.C. § 1813(l)).

[143] 12 U.S.C. §§ § 1813 and § 1832(a)(5) (2006). For example, liabilities arising under an investment contract between an insured depository institution and an employee benefit plan may not be considered insured deposits if it is determined that the benefit plan "expressly permits benefit-responsive withdrawals or transfers." The United States Code defines benefit responsive withdrawals or transfers as " . . . any withdrawal or transfer of funds (consisting of any portion of the principal and any interest credited at a rate guaranteed by the insured depository institution investment contract) during the period in which any guaranteed rate is in effect, without substantial penalty or adjustment, to pay

A deposit, in its broadest sense, is a borrowing by a bank; however, not all borrowings are deposits. According to *Black's Law Dictionary*, a deposit is:

> The act of placing money in the custody of a bank or banker, for safety or convenience, to be withdrawn at the will of the depositor or under rules and regulations agreed on. Deposit, according to its commonly accepted and generally understood meaning among bankers and by the public, includes not only deposits payable on demand and subject to check, but deposits not subject to check, for which certificates, whether interest bearing or not, may be issued, payable on demand, or on certain notice, or at a fixed future time.[144]

Regulatory definitions of deposits are contained in Title 12 of the United States Code for purposes of defining insured deposits, and in the Code of Federal Regulations for purposes of determining reserve requirements at depository institutions.[145] The distinction between deposits received from governmental instrumentalities and those received from other unrelated sources is not material to the definition of a bank.[146] Further, a production credit association organized and operated pursuant to the Farm Credit Act of 1933[147] that did not receive deposits properly avoided the Code section 56 corporate minimum tax imposed on the bank bad debt preference item described in Code section 57(a)(4) because it was not a "bank."[148] Certificates of deposit that an industrial bank issued to customers have been regarded as "deposits,"[149] and labeling funds received as "investments" did not alter their character as deposits for purposes of qualifying the entity as a bank.[150]

In *The Limited, Inc. v. Commissioner*, the Sixth Circuit addressed the issue of whether a credit card bank is a "person carrying on a banking business" for purposes of Code section 956.[151] Code section 956 describes what constitutes

(Footnote Continued)

benefits provided by the employee benefit plan or to permit a plan participant or beneficiary to redirect the investment of his or her account balance." 12 U.S.C. § 1832(a)(5)(B)(i). The term employee benefit plan encompasses two types of employee benefits described specifically outlined elsewhere in Titles 29 and 26 of the United States Code. *See* generally 29 U.S.C. § 1002(3) (defining employee welfare benefit and employee pension plans), 26 U.S.C. § 401(d) (limiting contributions of owner employees to trusts "forming part of a pension or profit-sharing plan which provides contributions or benefits for employees some or all of whom are owner-employees . . ."). Such plans may be excluded from coverage by DIF due to statutory requirements that such deposits be separately insured by the depository institution. 12 U.S.C. § 1832(a)(5) (2006).

[144] *Black's Law Dictionary* 302# (6th ed. 1990).

[145] 12 U.S.C. § 1813 (2007); 12 C.F.R. § 204.2.

[146] *Austin State Bank v. Commissioner*, 57 T.C. 180, Dec. 31,056 (1974), *acq.*, 1974-1 C.B.

[147] 12 U.S.C. § 2091 (1988).

[148] This minimum tax provision has been repealed. Rev. Rul. 81-172, 1981-1 C.B. 39. 12 U.S.C. § 2093 enumerates the corporate powers conferred on production credit associations. A production credit association may not exercise the trust powers permitted to national banks. *See also* TAM 8001006, September 26, 1979, and PLR 8113004, November 28, 1980. *But cf.* Rev. Rul. 81-37, 1981-1 C.B. 368, in which an industrial loan association that met the I.R.C. § 581 definition of a bank was precluded from availing itself of the bank exemption from the personal holding company tax. The IRS ruled that because I.R.C. § 542(c)(6) is a specific provision with respect to lending or finance companies, including industrial loan companies, it takes precedence over the more general banking exemption found in I.R.C. § 542(c)(2).

[149] *Morris Plan Bank of New Haven v. Smith*, 42-1, U.S.T.C. ¶ 9239, 125 F.2d 440 (2d Cir. 1942). *See also*, Rev. Rul. 88-18, 1988-1 C.B. 402, where the IRS ruled that there was no substantial difference between deposits in a commercial bank and a thrift.

[150] *Staunton Industrial Loan Corp., v. Commissioner*, 41-2 U.S.T.C. ¶ 9544, 120 F.2d 930 (4th Cir. 1941). An interdivisional task force under the FDIC's Division of Finance has begun to examine assessment of premiums for "deposit" insurance. In that connection, what constitutes a "deposit" may be formulated with more precision. *See* BNA's "Banking Report," Vol. 62 (April 11, 1994).

[151] *The Limited, Inc. v. Commissioner*, 113 T.C. 169 (1999). An institution qualifies as a credit card bank

"investment of earnings in United States property." For purposes of this section, United States property does not include "obligations of the United States, money, or deposits with persons carrying on the banking business . . . ." The IRS argued that the Code section 956 test was not passed because the entity was not a "bank" as that term is used in Code section 581. The IRS reasoned that to be a Code section 581 "bank" a substantial part of the business of the taxpayer must consist of accepting deposits from unrelated parties. The Limited's nationally chartered credit card bank accepted deposits, but they were all jumbo CDs and many were from related parties.[152]

The Sixth Circuit reasoned that, while the Commissioner's arguments all support the conclusion that it is improbable that the transfer would have occurred between unrelated parties, that argument is tangential to the question of whether the CDs that were purchased were "deposits" under Code section 956(b)(2)(A). Thus, according to the Sixth Circuit, the question of whether independent parties would have engaged in the transfer was not the issue. Rather, the question is whether the certificates of deposit constituted "deposits." Because the term "deposit" is not defined for purposes of Code section 956(b)(2)(A), the court looked to its ordinary meaning. It concluded: "Rather than belabor this point with dictionary definitions, we think that it is sufficiently clear that a certificate of *deposit* constitutes a deposit absent a specialized definition of 'deposit.' For that reason, we reject the Commissioner's final argument on the 956 issue as well."[153]

§ 1.5.8 Supervisory Requirement

The supervisory requirement is independent from the general requirement that the entity be a bank, yet it is intertwined with it. The statutory requirement that the entity be "subject by law to supervision and examination by state or federal authority having supervision over banking institutions" is loosely construed whenever the entity possesses all of the other characteristics of a bank.[154] Thus, the Ninth Circuit Court of Appeals has held that an industrial loan company having all the attributes of a bank was a "bank" for federal tax

(Footnote Continued)

if it (1) engages only in credit card operations, (2) does not accept demand deposits or deposits that the depositor may withdraw by check or similar means for payment to third parties or others, (3) does not accept any savings or time deposits of less than $100,000 (except for certain deposits held as collateral), (4) maintains only one office that accepts deposits, and (5) does not engage in the business of making commercial loans. 12 U.S.C. § 1841(c)(2)(F) (1994).

[152] For a discussion of banking income and activities, *see* preamble to Prop. Reg. § 1.1296 at 60 F.R. No. 82 (April 28, 1995). For a discussion of related person factoring income, *see* preamble to temporary and final regulations issues under I.R.C. § 864 at 53 F.R. No. 114 (June 14, 1988).

[153] *The Limited, Inc. v. Commissioner*, 286 F.3d 324, 340 (6th Cir. 2002).

[154] The power of the Office of the Comptroller of the Currency to regulate national banks is derived in large part from 12 U.S.C. § 1 (1994), which provides: There shall be in the Department of the Treasury a bureau charged with the execution of all laws passed by Congress relating to the issue and regulation of a national currency secured by United States bonds and, under the general supervision of the Board of Governors of the Federal Reserve System, of all Federal reserve notes, the chief officer of which bureau shall be called the Comptroller of the Currency and shall perform his duties under the general directions of the Secretary of the Treasury.

purposes, although it was supervised by the California Corporations Commissioner and not the state's bank regulatory authority.[155]

Conversely, an institution subject by law to state banking regulatory supervision, but not accepting deposits or performing trust services for the public, did not qualify as a bank for federal income tax purposes.[156] Furthermore, an entity that was in the business of providing payment services, including issuing money orders and transferring funds from one customer to another, was found not to be a bank.[157]

Moreover, the IRS has ruled that the Federal National Mortgage Association (FNMA) does not "carry on a banking business for purposes of determining income from sources within the United States, since FNMA is subject by law to supervision and examination by the Department of Housing and Urban Development rather than by federal (or state) bank regulatory agencies."[158]

§ 1.5.9 Fiduciary Institutions

If an entity exercises fiduciary powers similar to those permitted to national banks under authority of the Office of the Comptroller of the Currency, and if it satisfies the chartering and the supervisory requirements, it need not accept deposits to qualify as a bank. Trust powers granted to national banks under the authority of the Comptroller of the Currency include the right to act as trustee, executor, administrator, registrar of stocks and bonds, guardian of estates, assignee, receiver, committee of estates of lunatics, or in any other fiduciary capacity in which state banks, trust companies, or other corporations which come into competition with national banks are permitted to act under the laws of the state in which the national bank is located.[159]

Whether an entity is a "fiduciary" will depend upon the activities it conducts and not its legal characterization. Thus, it has been held that an entity that merely met a state's banking law definition by qualifying as a "fiduciary" under state law did not qualify as a bank for tax purposes.[160] The Tax Court determined that it was insufficient for the entity's fiduciary operations to consist solely of acting as trustee under certificates of beneficial interest covering mortgages held by it for the benefit of its stockholders and their children and grandchildren, and of collecting and transmitting payments of principal and interest thereunder.[161]

However, the IRS has ruled that a state chartered trust company, organized under the banking laws of a state to serve as corporate trustee or co-trustee of trusts initially on behalf of its parent company, qualified as a "bank" for tax purposes.[162] The IRS has ruled that an entity classified as an insurance company

---

[155] *Commissioner v. Valley Morris Plan*, 62-2, U.S.T.C. ¶9596, 305 F.2d 610 (9th Cir. 1962).

[156] *Palm Beach Trust Co. v. Commissioner*, 49-1 U.S.T.C. ¶9246, 174 F.2d 527 (DC Cir. 1949), *cert. denied*, 338 U.S. 825 (1949).

[157] *Moneygram International, Inc. v. Commissioner*, 144 T.C. 1 (2015).

[158] Rev. Rul. 83-176, 1983-2 C.B. 111, issued under I.R.C. § 861(c)(1).

[159] 12 U.S.C. § 92a(a) (1986). *See also* PLR 8903016, September 30, 1988.

[160] *Palm Beach Trust Co. v. Commissioner*, 491-1 U.S.T.C. ¶9246, 174 F.2d 527 (DC Cir. 1949), *cert. denied*, 338 U.S. 825 (1949).

[161] *Id.*

[162] PLR 8814053, January 13, 1988.

under state law and not subject to bank regulatory supervision would not be treated as a bank for federal income tax purposes despite the fact that the entity was permitted to exercise fiduciary powers similar to those permitted to national banks under the Federal Reserve Act.[163]

§1.5.10 Cooperative Banks

In general, a cooperative bank is an institution similar to a building and loan association but, by definition, it may not have capital stock and must be organized and operated for mutual purposes and without profit.[164] Although not expressly encompassed within the Code section 7701(a)(19) definition of a domestic building and loan association, a cooperative bank is treated in Regulations as a domestic building and loan association.[165] Under the laws of some states, cooperative banks are permitted to issue stock, just as mutual savings and loan associations have been permitted. A state stock cooperative bank is treated as a domestic savings and loan association.[166]

The Code has expressly made several "thrift" sections applicable to cooperative banks, including: the Code section 591 allowance for a deduction for dividends paid on deposits; the Code section 593 loan loss rules; the Code section 595 foreclosure rules; and the Code section 596 limitation on the dividends-received deduction.[167] An institution that fails to qualify as a cooperative bank under this definition, but meets the broader and less precise general definition of a bank contained in Code section 581, will be treated as a bank for federal income tax purposes.[168]

§1.6 Banks as S Corporations

Under current law, banks are eligible to qualify as S corporations.[169] The Small Business Job Protection Act of 1996 provides that for tax years beginning after December 31, 1996, a bank that does not utilize the reserve method for computing its bad debt deduction may elect S corporation status.[170] The historical prohibition imposed on a bank from electing S corporation status was justified, in part, because of the inappropriateness of permitting a S corporation shareholder to realize the tax benefits associated with a bank's reserve method of accounting. That "benefit" was the subsidy accorded banks from deductible reserve addition that exceeded actual experiences. In the four years immediately following the S corporation election, a bank must include its loan loss reserve in income. Special rules apply to a thrift, which limit the amount of reserve recapture.[171] The limitations will not apply if the thrift fails to meet the tax definition of a bank.

---

[163] Rev. Rul. 58-605, 1958-2 C.B. 358.

[164] I.R.C. §7701(a)(32). *See* above discussion of Farm Credit Act and banks for cooperatives. 12 U.S.C. §§2000 *et seq.*

[165] Reg. §301.7701-14.

[166] PLR 9836030, September 4, 1998.

[167] Small Business Job Protection Act of 1996, Pub. L. No. 104-188, 110 Stat. 1755 (1996). The special treatment afforded these sections has been repealed.

[168] Rev. Proc. 65-332, 1965-2 C.B. 175.

[169] I.R.C. §1361(b)(2). *See* discussion of advantages, disadvantages, and potential taxes below.

[170] Small Business Job Protection Act of 1996, Pub. L. No. 104-188 (1996).

[171] *See* discussion of a thrift bad debt reserve recapture in Chapter 10.

For banking corporations that qualify as small business corporations, this change in the law, which became effective for taxable years beginning on or after January 1997, provides an opportunity for the bank-shareholder unit to significantly reduce federal tax liability and to experience other advantages. However, except as expressly provided to the contrary in Subchapter S, or as would be inconsistent with the S Corporation rules, a bank that elects S Corporation treatment will continue to be subject to general rules contained in Subchapter C of the Code and all other tax provisions to which C Corporations are subject.[172] Thus, rules dealing with redemptions and the recognition of gain on the distribution of appreciated property by the corporation will continue to apply.

§ 1.6.1 Qualifications for S Corporation Treatment

To qualify for S corporation status, a corporation must be a "small business corporation," as defined in Code section 1361(b)(1), and it may not be an "ineligible corporation" as defined in Code section 1361(b)(2). To be a "small business corporation," a corporation may not have more than 100-shareholders (75 shareholders for tax years beginning before January 1, 2005); it may not have as a shareholder a person other than an individual and certain trusts and estates; it may not have a nonresident as a shareholder;[173] and, it may not have more than one class of stock. Family members may elect to be treated as one shareholder, effective for tax years beginning after December 31, 2004.[174] A family is defined as a common ancestor, the lineal descendants of the common ancestor, and the spouse (or former spouse) of the ancestor and the descendants. The common ancestor can be no more than six generations removed from the youngest shareholder who is treated as a member of the family. Any family member can make the election to treat family members as one shareholder. The election can be terminated only as prescribed in regulations.[175]

(a) *Ineligible Corporation*

An ineligible corporation includes a bank that uses the reserve method of accounting to determine its bad debt deduction. A bank that does not use the reserve method of accounting for bad debts and is therefore an eligible corporation, is not disqualified from meeting the definition of a small business corporation merely because it also meets the definition of a bank regardless of its asset size.[176]

[172] I.R.C. § 1371.

[173] A nonresident alien is not an eligible S corporation shareholder. In addition, if a U.S. shareholder's nonresident alien spouse has a current ownership interest in the shareholder's stock under applicable local law, such as a state community property law or a foreign country's law, the S corporation does not qualify as a small business corporation from the time that the nonresident alien spouse acquires the interest in the stock. Reg. § 1.1361-1(g)(1)(i). Relief from an inadvertent termination of an S corporation election that is caused by a nonresident alien spouse's ownership interest in the stock may be available.

[174] I.R.C. § 1361(c)(1), as amended by the American Jobs Creation Act of 2004 (Pub. L. No. 108-357).

[175] The Treasury Department has not yet promulgated regulations.

[176] Small Job Protection Act of 1996, Pub. L. No. 104-188, § 1315, amending I.R.C. § 1361(b)(2).

(b) *Directors' Shares as Second Class of Stock*

The IRS ruled that under Code section 1361(b)(1)(D) a bank holding company that elected S corporation treatment had inadvertently terminated its election when the BHC parent of a Qsub bank entered into a special shareholder agreement with its directors.[177] However, subsequent amendments made to the agreement that created the second class of stock were found to eliminate the second class. Consequently, the parent company was permitted to be treated as an S corporation effective with the date of its initial election.

The agreement with its directors restricted the transfer of directors' shares to anyone other than the parent company. The agreement also provided for the repurchase of each director's shares to the parent company in consideration for a fixed dollar amount upon the director ceasing to hold the office of director. Finally, the agreement provided that each director assigned to the parent company any and all dividends or distributions of whatsoever kind or nature.

Under federal banking law, a national bank director generally must own a qualifying equity interest of $1000 in the stock of a national bank or its holding company.[178] In an interpretive ruling, the OCC has stated that the qualifying equity interest may include common or preferred stock having an aggregate par value of $1000 or an aggregate fair market value of $1000. The value of the qualifying interest is determined as of the date purchased or the date on which a person became a director, whichever value is greater.[179]

After the election to be an S corporation became effective, the parent company determined that due to the agreement, the company may have inadvertently created a second class of stock. As a result, the company possibly was not in compliance with Code section 1361(b)(1)(D). Consequently, the agreement with the directors was amended and restated to remove the limitation on dividends and distributions, and to provide for the payment of fair market value to the directors upon their sale of the stock back to the parent company.

(c) *Retirement Plans as Shareholders*

In general, an organization described in Code section 401(a) and exempt from taxation under Code section 501(a) is an eligible S corporation shareholder and will count as one shareholder for purposes of the 100-shareholder limit. An organization described in Code section 401(a) includes most qualified retirement plans, but it does not include individual retirement accounts.[180] An IRA or a Roth IRA may hold stock in a bank S corporation if the IRA held the stock on or after

---

[177] PLR 200217048, January 24, 2002.

[178] 12 U.S.C. §72 (2006). The OCC has discussed PLR 200217048 in an Advisory Letter dated January 2, 2003, and directed to the chief executive officers of all national banks, department divisions heads, and all examining personnel.

[179] 12 C.F.R. §72 (2006). The OCC has also endorsed legislation that would amend 12 U.S.C. §72 to enable the OCC to allow a national bank director to satisfy the qualifying share requirement by holding a subordinated debt instrument that would not be treated as a separate class of stock for Subchapter S purposes. *See* Financial Services Regulatory Relief Act of 2002, H.R. 3951, 107th Cong. 101.

[180] The author understands that the Labor Department has permitted a beneficiary of an IRA to purchase the IRA shares and the transaction would not be classified as a prohibited transaction. This is a possible method for ameliorating the prohibition on IRAs being S corporation shareholders.

October 22, 2004.[181] If the IRA decides to sell the stock, it can sell the stock to the IRA beneficiary within 120 days after the corporation made the S corporation election without violating the prohibited transaction rules in Code section 4975. Other limitations apply that prevent certain persons who are not individuals from owning S corporation stock and that prevent stock from being owned by a person who is not a citizen or a resident.

(d) *Purchasing S Corporation Stock*

The purchasers of S corporation stock are permitted to continue the status of the S corporation if each purchaser is an eligible S corporation shareholder and if the corporation continues to qualify as a small business corporation eligible to be an S corporation.[182] No new election need be filed. The purchasers, however, may elect to terminate the election.[183]

An acquired S corporation ceases to be an S corporation if the purchaser:

- Causes the S corporation to exceed the 100-shareholder limit;[184] or
- Is not an individual, other than a qualified Subchapter S estate or trust, a specified tax-exempt organization[185] or an electing small business trust;[186] or
- Is a nonresident alien.[187]

The IRS has issued guidelines that allow for an S corporation to keep its status when an employee stock ownership plan ("ESOP") distributes the entity's stock to a participant's individual retirement account (IRA) in a direct rollover. First, the terms of the ESOP must require that the S corporation repurchase its stock immediately upon the ESOP's distribution to the IRA. Second, the S corporation must (1) actually repurchase its stock contemporaneously with, and effective the same day as, the distribution, or (2) the ESOP is permitted to assume the rights and obligations of the S corporation to repurchase the stock immediately upon the distribution to an IRA and the ESOP actually repurchases the stock contemporaneously with, and effective on the same day as, the distribution. Third, no income, loss, deduction, or credit attributable to the distributed S corporations stock under Code section 1366 can be allocated to the participant's IRA.[188]

An S corporation also ceases to be an S corporation if it has more than one class of stock,[189] or if it is one of the following types of ineligible corporation:

- Any financial institution[190] using the reserve method to account for bad loans,[191] thus excluding large banks, and small banks using the specific charge-off method;[192]

---

181 I.R.C § 1361(c)(2), as amended by the American Jobs Creation Act of 2004 (Pub. L. No. 108-357).

182 I.R.C. § 1361(b).

183 I.R.C. § 1362(d)(1).

184 I.R.C. § 1361(b)(1)(A).

185 I.R.C. § 1361(b)(1)(B), (c)(6).

186 I.R.C. § 1361(e).

187 I.R.C. § 1361(b)(1)(C).

188 Rev. Proc. 2004-14, 2004-7 I.R.B. 489, modifying and superseding Rev. Proc. 2003-23, 2003-1 C.B. 599.

189 I.R.C. § 1361(b)(1)(D).

190 I.R.C. § 581.

191 I.R.C. § 585.

192 I.R.C. § 1361(b)(2)(A).

- An insurance company;
- A corporation to which an election applies under the pre-1996 Puerto Rico and possession tax credit;[193]
- A foreign corporation; or
- A corporation that is or was a domestic international sales corporation.[194]

The purchaser or purchasers take a tax basis in the stock equal to the amount paid for the stock.[195] A corporate purchaser of an S corporation can elect to adjust the basis of its assets by making the qualified stock purchase election.[196] Because an S corporation cannot be a subsidiary of another corporation the purchase, however, ends the corporation's status as an S corporation, and no election to treat the target corporation as a member of the selling group can be made on the stock purchase to shift liability for any tax resulting from the basis adjustment from the S corporation to its former owners.[197]

§ 1.6.2 Trusts, Estates, and ESOPs as Shareholders

(a) *General Rules*

In general, a trust or an estate may not be an S corporation shareholder. Code section 1361(b)(1)(B) provides the following exceptions to this general rule:

1. A qualified Subchapter S trust ("QSST") or other trust that is treated as owned by an individual who is a U.S. citizen or resident (subpart E trust).[198]
2. A trust that qualified as a QSST before the owner's death and continues in existence after the owner's death. This rule is applicable for the two-year period beginning on the day of the deemed owner's death.[199]
3. A trust to which stock is transferred according to the terms of a will. This rule is applicable for a two-year period after the stock is transferred.[200]
4. A voting trust that is a subpart E trust and that is created primarily to exercise the voting power of stock transferred to it.[201]
5. An Electing Small Business Trust.[202]

---

[193] I.R.C. § 936(j).

[194] I.R.C. § 1361(b)(1), (2)(A) through (D).

[195] I.R.C. § 1012.

[196] I.R.C. § 338.

[197] I.R.C. § 1361(b)(1)(B).

[198] I.R.C. § 1361(c)(2)(A)(i) and I.R.C. § 1361(d).

[199] I.R.C. § 1361(c)(2)(A)(ii).

[200] I.R.C. § 1361(c)(2)(A)(iii). An estate of a decedent may be a shareholder of an S corporation. Even if title to the stock technically passes under state law to a beneficiary, the estate is considered to be the shareholder as long as the executor or administrator has power to administer the estate. A beneficiary of an estate that does not qualify as an S corporation shareholder, such as a corporation or nonresident alien, will thus not cause the corporation to fail to qualify as a small business corporation. If the estate is unreasonably prolonged, however, the IRS may disregard the estate and treat the beneficiaries as shareholders (*Old Virginia Brick Co., Inc.*, 66-2 USTC ¶9708).

[201] I.R.C. § 1361(c)(2)(A)(iv); Reg. § 1.1361-1(h)(1)(v). A voting trust agreement does not invalidate an S corporation election (I.R.C. § 1361(c)(2)(A)(iv)). Each beneficiary of the voting trust is treated as a separate shareholder (I.R.C. § 1361(c)(2)(B)(iv)). As is the case with other trusts in which the beneficiaries are treated as the shareholders in the corporation, the fact that the trustee or nominal owner of the shares is a nonqualifying shareholder will not terminate an S corporation election.

[202] I.R.C. § 1361(c)(2)(A)(v).

6. A beneficiary of an IRA holding bank S corporation stock, effective October 22, 2004.[203] An IRA or a Roth IRA may hold stock in a bank S corporation if the IRA held the stock on or after October 22, 2004.[204] If the IRA decides to sell the stock, it can sell the stock to the IRA beneficiary within 120 days after the corporation made the S corporation election without violating the prohibited transaction rules in Code section 4975.
7. A qualified retirement trusts (as described in Code section 401(a)) and certain charitable organizations (as described in Code section 501(c)(3)).[205]

(b) *Qualified Subchapter S Trust*

A qualified subchapter S trust ("QSST") is an eligible S corporation shareholder if the individual beneficiary of the trust, or his legal representative (or parent of a minor beneficiary if there is no legal representative), elects to be treated as the owner of the trust for purposes of Code section 678.[206] Under the rules for counting shareholders, the deemed owner of a subpart E trust or QSST is considered to be the shareholder in the S corporation.[207] Thus, a corporation will not cease to qualify as a small business corporation because its shares are held by an ineligible bank or other nonqualifying shareholder as part of such a trust arrangement. Similarly, shares held by a custodian that is a nonresident alien, ineligible bank or corporation will not cause the S corporation election to terminate, provided that the beneficial owner of the shares is a qualifying shareholder. The election is irrevocable (except with IRS consent) and applies from the date of the trust's election until the trust ceases to be a QSST. The election by a QSST may apply retroactively for up to two months and 15 days,[208] a grace period that conforms to the time provided for making an S corporation election.

A QSST is a trust with respect to which an election is made and which:

1. Owns stock in one or more electing S corporations;
2. Distributes or is required to distribute all of its income to a citizen or resident of the United States;
3. Has certain trust terms, including the requirement that there be only one income beneficiary;
4. Does not distribute any portion of the trust corpus to anyone other than the current income beneficiary during the income beneficiary's lifetime, including the time at which the trust terminates; and
5. The income interest of the current income beneficiary ceases on the earlier of such beneficiary's death or the termination of the trust.[209]

---

[203] I.R.C. § 1361(c)(2)(A)(vi), as added by the American Jobs Creation Act of 2004 (Pub. L. No. 108-357).

[204] I.R.C. § 1361(c)(2), as amended by the American Jobs Creation Act of 2004 (Pub. L. No. 108-357).

[205] I.R.C. § 1361(c)(6).

[206] I.R.C. § 1361(d)(1).

[207] I.R.C. § 1361(c)(2)(B)(i).

[208] I.R.C. § 1361(d)(2).

[209] I.R.C. § 1361(d)(3); Reg. § 1.1361-1(j)(1).

The determination of whether a trust satisfies each of the aforementioned requirements is dependent upon the applicable state law and the specific terms of the trust instrument.[210] For example, even though a trust instrument provides for a single income beneficiary, if there is a possibility that the corpus of the trust will be distributed during the lifetime of the current income beneficiary to someone other than the beneficiary, the trust is not a QSST.[211]

If a husband and wife file a joint return, are both U.S. citizens or residents, and are both designated income beneficiaries of a trust, they are treated as one beneficiary for purposes of meeting the QSST requirements.[212] However, if any distribution from the trust satisfies the grantor's legal obligation to support the income beneficiary, the trust ceases to be a QSST as of the date of the distribution.[213]

While it is possible to reform trust provisions that do not conform to the requirements of a QSST by obtaining an appropriate court order, the IRS will not recognize retroactive reform orders for purposes of curing a defective S corporation election.[214]

To be treated as a QSST, the current income beneficiary must make an election by signing and filing a statement with the IRS service center where the S corporation files its income tax return. With respect to minors, if a legal representative has not been appointed, the natural or adopted parents may make this election.[215] The statement must:

1. Give the name, address, and taxpayer identification number of the current income beneficiary, the trust, and the S corporation;
2. Identify the election as being made under Code section 1361(d)(2);
3. Specify the date on which the election is to become effective (not earlier than 15 days and two months before the date on which the election is filed);
4. Specify the date (or dates) on which the stock is to be transferred to the trust; and
5. Provide any other information necessary to establish that trust requirements have been met.

A QSST that holds stock in more than one S corporation must make a separate election for each corporation in which the trust holds stock. If S corporation stock is transferred to a trust, or if a C corporation that has made an S corporation election transfers stock to a trust before that election goes into effect, the QSST election must be made within the 16-day-and-two-month period beginning on the day that the stock is transferred to the trust.[216] If a trust holds C corporation stock and the C corporation makes an S election effective for the first day of the tax year in which the S election is made, the QSST must be made

[210] Reg. § 1.1361-1(j)(2)(ii).
[211] Reg. § 1.1361-1(j)(1)(iii).
[212] Reg. § 1.1361-1(j)(2)(i).
[213] Reg. § 1.1361-1(j)(2)(ii)(B).
[214] Rev. Rul. 93-79, 1932-2 C.B. 269.
[215] Reg. § 1.1361-1(j)(6).
[216] Reg. § 1.1361-1(j)(6)(iii)(A).

within the 16-day-and-two-month period beginning on the day that the S election is effective. If the corporation makes an S election effective for the first day of the tax year following the tax year in which the election is made, the QSST election must be made within the 16-day-and-two-month period beginning on the day that the S election is made.[217]

Upon the death of a beneficiary, the QSST election remains in effect following the succession of a new current income beneficiary, unless the current income beneficiary terminates the election.[218] In order to terminate the election, the new current income beneficiary must affirmatively refuse to consent to the election by signing and filing a statement within 15 days and two months after the date on which he became the income beneficiary with the IRS service center where the S corporation files its income tax return. The termination is effective as of the date on which the successive income beneficiary became the income beneficiary.[219]

A QSST election may be revoked only with IRS consent. A revocation will not be granted if one of its purposes is the avoidance of federal income taxes or if the tax year is closed. The application for consent to revoke the election must be submitted to the IRS in the form of a letter ruling request. It must be signed by the current income beneficiary and must:

1. Contain the name, address and taxpayer identification number of the current income beneficiary, the trust, and the corporation with respect to which the QSST election was made;
2. Identify the election being revoked as an election made under Code section 1361(d)(2); and
3. Explain why the current income beneficiary seeks to revoke the QSST election and indicate that the beneficiary understands the consequences of the election.[220]

(c) *Electing Small Business Trust*

An Electing Small Business Trust ("ESBT") may be a shareholder of an S corporation for tax years beginning on or after January 1, 1997.[221] In order for a trust to qualify as an ESBT and as a shareholder in a subchapter S corporation, only certain types of persons are permitted to be beneficiaries. Once a trust makes the ESBT election, each potential current beneficiary ("PCB") of the trust is treated as a shareholder of the S corporation. Thus, the identity of the beneficiaries affects whether a trust can be an ESBT, while the identity and number of PCBs affect whether the corporation can be an S corporation.[222]

---

217 Reg. § 1.1361-1(j)(6)(iii)(B).

218 Reg. § 1.1361-1(j)(9).

219 Reg. § 1.1361-1(j)(10).

220 Reg. § 1.1361-1(j)(11).

221 I.R.C. § 1361(c)(2).

222 The IRS has released final regulations governing the qualification and treatment of ESBTs. T.D. 8994, 2002-1 C.B. 742. The final regulations are effective May 14, 2002. The regulations interpret the rules added to the Code by section 1302 of the Small Business Job Protection Act of 1996, section 1601 of the Taxpayer Relief Act of 1997, and section 316 of the Community Renewal Tax Relief Act of 2000. In addition, the regulations provide that an ESBT, or a trust described in I.R.C. § 401(a) or I.R.C. § 501(c)(3) and exempt from taxation under I.R.C. § 501(a), is not treated as a deferral entity for purposes of Regulation § 1.444-2T.

An ESBT is defined as any trust if:

1. Such trust does not have as a beneficiary any person other than an
   (a) individual,
   (b) estate, or
   (c) organization described in paragraph (2), (3), (4), or (5) of Code section 170(c);
2. No interest in such trust was acquired by purchase; and
3. A proper election is made for the trust to be treated as an electing small business trust.

Each potential current beneficiary of the ESBT is counted as a shareholder for purposes of the 100-shareholder limit. However, in order to qualify, all beneficiaries of the ESBT generally must be individuals or estates eligible to be S corporation shareholders. A technical amendment to Code section 1361(c)(1)(B) enacted in 1997 provides that a charitable remainder annuity trust, a charitable remainder unitrust, as well as other exempt trusts may not qualify as ESBTs. A potential current income beneficiary is any person, with respect to the applicable period, who is entitled to, or at the discretion of any person may receive, a distribution from the principal or income of the trust.

Each potential current beneficiary of the trust is treated as a shareholder, except that, for any period if there is no potential current beneficiary of the trust, the trust itself is treated as the shareholder during this period.[223] A potential current beneficiary is a person who is entitled to, or at the discretion of any person may receive, a distribution from the principal or interest of the trust.[224] For tax years beginning after December 31, 2004, the American Jobs Creation Act of 2004 provides that any person who may benefit from a power of appointment is not a potential beneficiary if the power has not been exercised.[225] If the potential current beneficiaries of an ESBT would disqualify an S corporation, the ESBT has a grace period to dispose of its stock in the S corporation, thereby avoiding disqualification. For tax years beginning before January 1, 2005, the grace period is 60 days. For tax years beginning after December 31, 2004, the grace period is extended to one year.[226]

This provision permits a nonresident alien to enjoy the benefits of S corporation status, which was previously reserved only for residents or citizens of the United States. Thus, as beneficiaries of an ESBT, nonresident aliens may have an interest in the S corporation without violating the rule that nonresident aliens may not be shareholders of an S corporation.

---

[223] I.R.C. § 1361(c)(6).

[224] Reg. § 1.1361-1(m).

[225] I.R.C. § 1361(e)(2), as amended by the American Jobs Creation Act of 2004 (Pub. L. No. 108-357)).

[226] I.R.C. § 1361(e)(2), as amended by the American Jobs Creation Act of 2004 (Pub. L. No. 108-357)).

(i) Taxation of ESBT. The portion of the ESBT that consists of stock in one or more S corporations is treated as a separate trust for purposes of computing the income tax attributable to the S corporation stock held by the trust. This portion of the trust's income is taxed at the highest rate imposed on estates and trusts. The taxable income attributable to this portion includes: (1) the items of income, loss or deduction allocated to the trust as an S corporation shareholder under the rules of subchapter S; (2) gain or loss from the sale of the S corporation stock; and (3) any state or local income taxes and administrative expenses of the trust properly allocable to the S corporation stock. Capital losses are allowed only to the extent of capital gains.

In computing the trust's income tax on this portion of the trust, no deduction is allowed for amounts distributed to beneficiaries and, except as described above, no additional deductions or credits are allowed. Because this income is not included in the distributable net income of the trust, it is not included in the beneficiaries' income. No item relating to the S corporation stock is apportioned to any beneficiary. Furthermore, when computing the tax imposed on an ESBT, the available alternative minimum tax exemption amount under Code section 55(d) is zero.

In determining the tax liability of the remaining portion of the trust, items taken into account by the S corporation portion of the trust are disregarded. Also, although distributions from the trust are deductible in computing the taxable income of this portion of the trust, the trust's distributable net income does not include any income attributable to the S corporation stock.

(ii) Electing ESBT Treatment. The IRS has provided guidance for making an election to treat a trust as an ESBT, which applies rules similar to those that apply to a Qualified Subchapter S Trust ("QSST").[227] Pursuant to these rules, the trustee of the ESBT must file an election and the election must be filed within the time requirements prescribed for filing QSST elections.[228]

Under the general rule, a QSST must file an election within the 16-day-and-2-month period beginning on the day that the stock is transferred to the trust. When a trust already holds the stock of a C corporation and the C corporation makes an S election, the regulations set forth three situations that illustrate when the election must be made:

1. If the S corporation election is to be effective for the first day of the taxable year in which the S election is made, the QSST election must be made within the 16-day-and-2-month period beginning on the day that the S election is effective;
2. If the S corporation election is to be effective for the first day of the taxable year following the taxable year in which the S election is made, the QSST election must be made within the 16-day-and-2-month period beginning on the day that the S election is made;

[227] Notice 97-12, 1997-1 C.B. 385. (*See* Notice 97-49, 1997-2 C.B. 304, for guidance on how distributions of a ESBT are treated.)

[228] Reg. § 1.1361-1(j)(6)(iii).

3. If the S corporation election is to be effective for the first day of the taxable year in which the election is made, but such S election is subsequently treated as effective for the first day of the taxable year following the taxable year in which the S election is made, an otherwise valid QSST election will, in general, be treated as effective for the first year in which the corporation's S election is effective.

§1.6.3 QSub and Corporate Structure

(a) *Consolidated Returns*

For taxable years beginning on or after January 1, 1997, an S corporation is permitted to own any percentage of stock in a C corporation. Prior to the 1996 amendments to the S corporation rules, an S corporation was not permitted to be a member of an affiliated group of corporations.[229] Thus, an S corporation was not permitted to own 80 percent or more of the stock of another corporation, nor could it have as a shareholder another corporation. The purpose of the rule was, presumably, to prevent a controlled group from isolating some income in a C Corporation and allowing only some other income (or loss) to flow through to the shareholders. A C corporation subsidiary of an S corporation is now permitted to elect to join in the filing of a consolidated return with its affiliated C corporations if stock ownership equals or exceeds 80 percent. However, neither any S corporation nor a QSub is permitted to join in the consolidated return.

(b) *Qualifying a QSub*

Under the post-1996 rules, a corporation treated as an S corporation may be permitted to be owned by another S corporation if its parent corporation owns 100 percent of its outstanding stock and if the parent corporation elects to treat its subsidiary as a Qualified Subchapter S Subsidiary ("QSub").[230] To qualify as a QSub, the corporation must be eligible to be an S corporation if it were not owned by another corporation. Thus, it may not be an "ineligible corporation" as that term is defined in Code section 1361(b)(2). Furthermore, the QSub must be a domestic corporation and its stock must be held by a corporation that has elected S corporation status. Subsidiaries of a QSub may, but need not, also be QSubs. Thus, the election is available for both chains and brother-sister affiliates of eligible corporations.

(c) *Deemed Liquidation or Disposition of Stock*

In general, a QSub is not treated as a separate corporation.[231] Its assets, liabilities, items of income, deductions, losses, and credits are treated as if they appeared on the books and records of its parent S corporation.[232] Thus, a QSub is treated as disregarded as a separate entity for federal tax purposes and its items of income, deduction, loss, and credit are treated as items of its parent S corporation. If the subsidiary corporation ceases to be a QSub (e.g., fails to meet

[229] Exceptions were made for ownership in inactive corporations.

[230] §1361(b)(3). On April 22, 1998, the Treasury Department issued proposed regulations relating to the treatment of corporate subsidiaries of S corporations. 26 U.S.C. §1361(b)(3) (2007).

[231] I.R.C. §1361(b)(3)(A)(i).

[232] I.R.C. §1361(b)(3)(A)(ii).

the wholly-owned requirement) the subsidiary is treated as a new corporation acquiring all its assets (and assuming all of its liabilities) immediately before such cessation from the parent S corporation in exchange for its stock. Under Treasury regulations, the tax treatment of the termination of the QSub election is determined under general principals of tax law, including the step transaction doctrine.[233] The regulations set forth an example in which an S corporation sells 21 percent of the stock of a QSub to an unrelated party.[234] In the example, the deemed transfer of all the assets to the QSub is treated as a taxable sale because the S corporation was not in control of the QSub immediately after the transfer by reason of the sale, and thus the transfer did not qualify for nonrecognition treatment under Code section 351.

For taxable years beginning after December 31, 2006, where the sale of stock of a QSub results in the termination of the QSub election, the sale is treated as a sale of an undivided interest in the assets of the QSub (based on the percentage of the stock sold) followed by a deemed transfer to the QSub in a transaction to which Code section 351 applies.[235]

In the above example, the S corporation will be treated as selling a 21-percent interest in all the assets of the QSub to the unrelated party, followed by a transfer of all the assets to a new corporation in a transaction to which section 351 applies. Thus, the S corporation will recognize 21 percent of the gain or loss in the assets of the QSub.

The provision does not change the treatment of the disposition of stock of a QSub by an S corporation in connection with an otherwise non-taxable transaction. Thus, the transfer of stock of a QSub by an S corporation pro rata to its shareholders can qualify as a distribution to which Code sections 368(a)(1)(D) and 355 apply if the transaction otherwise satisfies the requirements of those sections.[236]

When the parent corporation makes the election to treat its subsidiary as a QSub, the subsidiary will be deemed to have liquidated under Code sections 332 and 337 immediately before the election is effective.[237] The deemed liquidation will not trigger the recognition of any built-in gain.[238] However, the de-consolidation will introduce the specter of Code section 482 reallocations, which were of little or no concern when a consolidated return was filed. Moreover, it is unclear whether transactions with members of the controlled group will be treated as

---

[233] Reg. § 1.1361-5(b).

[234] Reg. 1.1361-5(b)(3), Ex. 1.

[235] Small Business and Work Opportunity Tax Act of 2007, Pub. L. No. 110-28. *See* explanation by Joint Committee on Taxation at JCX-29-07, May 25, 2007.

[236] Reg. § 1.1361-5(b)(3), Ex. 4.

[237] S. Rep. No. 281, 104th Cong., 2d Sess. 53 (1996); H.R. Rep. No. 586, 104th Cong., 2d Sess. 89 (1996). Congress has authorized Treasury regulations to provide exceptions to the general rule that a QSub election is treated as a deemed Code section 332 liquidation of the subsidiary in appropriate cases. In addition, Congress has provided that if the effect of a QSub election is to invalidate an election to join in the filing of a consolidated return for a group of subsidiaries that formerly joined in such filing, Treasury regulations may provide guidance as to the consolidated return effects of the S election. Joint Committee on Taxation Staff's General Explanation of Taxpayer Relief Act of 1997 (H.R. 2014), Title XVI, p. 459. *See also* H.R. Rep. No. 105-220. The Final Treasury regulations were released January 25, 2000, and were effective as of January 20, 2000.

[238] PLR 9801015, January 5, 1998.

transactions with a party who is not a "customer" for purposes of the Code section 475 rules applicable to dealers in securities.[239]

The IRS has ruled that a recognition event does not occur, for purposes of the built-in gains tax, when a subsidiary is merged into its parent in a transaction intended to qualify as a complete liquidation under Code section 332. Thus, a parent's unrealized built-in gain on the subsidiary stock is not recognized. However, the parent corporation will be subject to the built-in gains tax on any net recognized built-in gain attributable to the assets it acquired from its subsidiary in the merger for any taxable year beginning in the ten-year recognition period.[240]

(d) ***Separate Treatment of Bank***

As a general rule, those provisions that are unique to banks will continue to apply to the bank items after the QSub election. This general rule may be subject to an exception for certain interest expense disallowance rules.[241]

In a 1997 technical correction to the QSub statutory provisions, Congress authorized the Treasury Department to promulgate regulations that would require a bank that is a QSub to be subject to bank tax rules and regulations.[242] The legislative history of this technical correction provides that:

> if a S corporation owns 100 percent of the stock of a bank (as defined in sec. 581) and elects to treat the bank as a qualified subchapter S subsidiary, it is expected that Treasury regulations would treat the bank as a separate legal entity for purposes of those Code provisions that apply specifically to banks (*e.g.* sec. 582).[243]

The IRS has specifically applied this treatment with respect to interest expense that is disallowed under Code section 265(b).[244] Other sections of the Code that have specific application to banks are the following: Code section 291 (the TEFRA interest expense disallowance), Code section 582 (the characterization of gains and losses on the disposition of debt instruments), and Code section 1281 (the treatment of interest on short-term obligations).

Code section 291 disallows a deduction for 20 percent of a bank's interest expense that is allocable to tax-exempt obligations held by a bank that were acquired after 1982 and before August 9, 1986. Code section 265(b) applies the Code section 291 interest expense disallowance percentage to "qualified tax exempt obligations." However, Code section 1363(b)(4) indicates that the Code

---

[239] Reg. § 1.475(c)-1(a)(3)(ii); Reg. § 1.1502-13(c)(7)(ii), Ex. 11.

[240] PLR 9801056, January 2, 1998.

[241] I.R.C. § 1363(b)(4).

[242] Taxpayer Relief Act of 1997, Pub. L. No. 105-34, § 1601(c)(3), 111 Stat. 788 (1997). I.R.C. § 1361(b)(3) was amended by this provision. Language added provides: "Except as provided in regulations prescribed by the Secretary . . . ."

[243] Joint Committee on Taxation Staff's General Explanation of Taxpayer Relief Act of 1997 (H.R. 2014), Title XVI, p. 459. *See also* H.R. Rep. No. 105-220. The Report Prepared by The Joint Committee on Taxation, often referred to as the Blue Book, states: "Thus, if an S corporation owns 100 percent of the stock of a bank (as defined in § 581) it is expected that Treasury regulations would treat the bank as a separate legal entity for purposes of those Code provisions that apply specifically to banks (e.g., sec 582)." General Explanation of Tax Legislation Enacted in 1997, Prepared by the Staff of the Joint Committee on Taxation, December 17, 1997, pages 459-460.

[244] Notice 97-5, 1997-1 C.B 352.

section 291 "TEFRA" interest expense disallowance will not apply to a bank after the expiration of the three-year period following the S election. The IRS first promulgated then withdrew a proposed regulation that provides for continued application of Code section 291 after the three-year period expires.[245]

There are other provisions of the Code that may have specific application to the collection of assets and liabilities and income and expense of the separate corporations that are treated as one entity after the QSub election. For example, if the QSub is a bank that is a dealer in securities for purposes of Code section 475, it is unclear whether the parent will thereby become a dealer. Because of the required segregation of certain items of income, deduction, etc., a continuation of the separate accounting for the two corporations will be necessary; however, there will be no further "intercompany transactions" for purposes of the consolidated return rules, except with C corporation affiliates. Guidance from Congress may be needed with respect to this provision as well as others, including the interest expense disallowance rule.

A provision that treats the parent bank as an entity separate from a subsidiary when the subsidiary is treated as a disregarded entity is contained in Reg. § 301.7701-2(c)(2)(ii). Thus, if a bank owns an LLC that is treated as a disregarded entity, the assets of the LLC may not be combined with the assets of the bank for purposes of determining the banks interest expense disallowance under Code sections 291 or 165.

(e) *C Corporation Holding Company in S Corporation Group*

When a bank holding company group is considering making an S corporation election and also a QSub election, the group should consider whether all members of the group should elect S corporation status or only some members, and if only some members, whether the group should be reorganized. Among the possible corporate structures that could maximize the tax advantages of both S corporations and C corporations within a controlled group is one that has the effect of isolating some portion of the group's income from shareholder taxation. This corporate structure would thereby take advantage of the graduated corporate tax rates and avoid the immediate and higher rate of tax imposed on individual income. Furthermore, by interposing a C corporation holding company between the parent S corporation and the subsidiary C corporations, the profits of the C corporations can be transferred among the lower tier group without being subject to the pass-through shareholder taxation.

(f) *Sale of S Corporation Stock*

There is a unique interplay of the tax rules that apply to S corporations and to reorganizations when the ownership interest of a bank is sold. In order to understand how these rules affect the opportunity to save tax on the sale of an S bank, it is first necessary to review the tax rules that prescribed the taxation of the transaction when the S election was made.

---

[245] ANPR Reg-158677-05, FR 50007, Aug. 24, 2006. Announcement 2011-75, Nov. 28, 2011. *See* discussion in Chapter 9 of S corporation banks.

The statutory provisions enacted in 1996 that permitted a bank holding company group to elect S corporation status treat the bank as having been liquidated into its bank holding company parent in a tax free transaction when the election took effect. After the election, the bank and the bank holding company are treated as a single entity for most purposes of the Code.

When a sale of the bank or bank holding company stock takes place, Treasury regulations indicate that the deemed liquidation is, in effect, reversed when the acquiring corporation is a C corporation.[246] The bank holding company is then treated as having transferred the bank's assets and related liabilities to a newly formed bank in exchange for newly issued stock of the bank. This fictitious reincorporation transaction has the effect of then separating the bank and the bank holding company for tax purposes, and any sale of the bank may be a taxable transaction. With proper planning, however, this tax liability may be avoided.

When a bank is the target of an acquisition, the shareholders of the bank holding company may be in a position of either transferring the stock of the bank or the stock of the bank holding company to the acquirer. Depending on whether the stock of the bank or the stock of the bank holding company is disposed of, the tax treatment of the deemed reincorporation may vary significantly.

As the following examples illustrate, the preferred way to structure the transaction is as a disposition of the stock of the bank holding company. If the shareholders of the bank holding company dispose of their stock, the deemed reincorporation of the bank should be tax-free to the shareholders. In effect, the tax liability inherent in the bank's assets (including goodwill with a zero tax basis) is shifted to the acquirer. Conversely, if the bank holding company disposes of its stock in the bank, it is likely that all of the gain inherent in the assets of the bank (including the goodwill) will be immediately taxed to the shareholders, and that portion of the tax attributable to the ordinary assets of the bank will probably be computed using ordinary income tax rates.

Example 1: Holding Company Disposes of Bank Stock. Holding Company exchanges 100 percent of the stock of Bank for stock of Acquirer. Holding Company then distributes Acquirer's stock to the shareholders of Holding Company in liquidation. Holding Company will probably recognize gain on the deemed reincorporation of Bank, a portion of which will likely be characterized as ordinary income. All income will flow through to, and be reported on, the personal income tax returns of Holding Company shareholders, while retaining its character as either ordinary income or capital gain. Holding Company shareholders may have additional gain to report when Holding Company liquidates. Any such gain will be taxed at capital gains rates. Thus, there could be taxes on two transactions and one of the transactions may generate some ordinary income.

Example 2: Shareholders Dispose of Holding Company Stock. Shareholders of Holding Company exchange 100 percent of the stock

[246] Reg. § 1.1361-4(a)(3).

of Holding Company for stock of Acquirer. Holding Company recognizes no gain on the deemed reincorporation of Bank. The shareholders will have gain to report when they transfer their stock to Acquirer. This gain will be taxed at capital gains rates. Thus, there will be a tax on only one transaction, and it will be at favorable capital gains rates.

If the exchange of Holding Company stock for stock of Acquirer meets the definition of one of the Code's tax-deferred reorganization provisions, the shareholders would be able to defer the tax liability they would otherwise pay on the stock exchange. Under one of the commonly utilized reorganizations, tax-deferred treatment will be permitted whenever the shareholders who transfer their stock receive stock of the Acquirer. This form of reorganization, referred to as a Type B Reorganization because it is defined in Code section 368(a)(1)(B), permits only stock in the Acquirer to be received by the exchanging shareholders. If in Example 2 above, the transaction qualified as a Type B Reorganization, there would be no tax paid by either Holding Company or the shareholders on the reincorporation or on the exchange of Holding Company stock for Acquirer stock.

However, there is one significant disadvantage of the Type B Reorganization, from the standpoint of the selling shareholders. In the Type B Reorganization, the exchanging shareholders are prohibited from receiving even the smallest amount of cash or other non-stock consideration. If they do, the exchange of stock will not qualify as a Type B Reorganization, with the likely consequence that the transaction will be entirely taxable to the shareholders.

The S corporation rules contain a special provision that may allow the shareholders to secure the advantages of tax-deferred treatment, while receiving cash at the time of the exchange of stock. This unique phenomenon can occur if the cash that the shareholders receive is properly treated as a distribution from the bank holding company's Accumulated Adjustment Account ("AAA"). The AAA is the account that keeps track of the income of the S corporation that has previously been taxed to its shareholders. A distribution from the AAA account will be tax-free to the extent of the shareholder's tax basis in the stock of the bank holding company. Example 3 illustrates the favorable consequences of a distribution from AAA followed by a Type B Reorganization.

Example 3: AAA Distribution Followed by Shareholders Disposing of Holding Company Stock. In anticipation of the disposition of the stock of Holding Company, the shareholders cause Holding Company to distribute to themselves cash from Holding Company's AAA in an amount not to exceed their tax basis. Shareholders then exchange 100 percent of the stock of Holding Company for stock of Acquirer in a transaction that conforms to the definition of the Type B Reorganization. Neither the reincorporation, nor the exchange of stock, nor the receipt of the cash will be taxable events.

Of course, any distribution of cash of Holding Company will affect the value of Holding Company stock. An adjustment in the number of shares of

Acquirer given in the exchange would probably be required. Nevertheless, an exchange of Holding Company stock for stock of Acquirer in a Type B Reorganization, which is preceded by a distribution of AAA, will usually accomplish all three of the tax planning goals.

§1.6.4 Electing S and QSub Treatment

An entity that is a small business corporation and that is not an ineligible corporation must make an election in order to be treated as an S Corporation. If any member of an affiliated group wishes to be treated as a QSub, the parent corporation of the group must elect to be an S corporation. With respect to an election to treat a subsidiary as a QSub, the parent also makes the election. A requirement that must be met before a subsidiary may be treated as a QSub is that the QSub parent own 100 percent of the stock of the QSub. Not all subsidiaries are required to be treated as a QSub if one elects. Thus, an S Corporation may have some subsidiaries which are C Corporations and some of which are QSubs. The C Corporations need not be 100 percent owned by the S Corporation parent.

The parent corporation makes the election to be classified as an S corporation by filing a Form 2553, "Election by a Small Business Corporation," with its local IRS Service Center no later than the 16th day of the 3rd month of the taxable year for which the election is to be effective.[247] The form should be accompanied with the requisite consents from all shareholders. That would include both spouses if there are any married shareholders, even though they are considered to be one shareholder for purposes of the 100 shareholder limit. A trustee will consent on behalf of the beneficiaries of an Electing Small Business Trust, but the income beneficiaries of a Qualified Subchapter S Trust file the consent.[248]

If one or more of the subsidiaries of the S corporation parent wish to be classified as a QSub, the parent corporation must file a Form 8869, "Qualified Subchapter S Subsidiary Election," with the Service Center.[249] Although Form 8869 does not have to be filed with the Form 2553, it is advisable that it be filed at that time. It may be filed at any time within the 16-day-and-2-month period beginning on the first day of the taxable year that the S election is first effective, if it is intended that it will be effective coincident with the S election.

In addition to these forms, a bank that is treated as a QSub or an S corporation must elect to change its method of accounting for loan losses from the reserve method to the specific charge-off method of Code section 166 to avoid being classified an "ineligible corporation." The election is made on Form 3115,

---

[247] The Internal Revenue Service has issued procedures that provide relief for late S corporation, QSST, and ESBT elections. Pursuant to this procedure, if a taxpayer files one of those three elections after the statutory due date but within 12 months of the due date, the taxpayer may obtain relief under I.R.C. §1362(b)(5) in the case of the late S election, and under I.R.C. §1362(f) in the case of the QSST and the ESBT, without applying for a private letter ruling.

[248] It is strongly recommended that the trustee execute a stock transfer restriction at the time that the consent is given. Furthermore, it is advisable to file the election to treat any trust as an Electing Small Business Trust at the same time.

[249] Announcement 2000-83 requires Form 8869. Earlier, Form 966 was required. Notice 97-4, 1997-2 I.R.B. 24. Proposed regulations issued April 22, 1998, indicated that a revised form will be developed by the IRS prior to the time that the regulations become final. The final Treasury regulations were issued January 25, 2000, effective as of January 20, 2000.

"Application for Change in Accounting Method," which is filed with the National Office of the IRS, and a copy must be attached to the income tax return of the parent corporation for the first year in which the S election is effective. The IRS has provided automatic change procedures, granting the taxpayer permission to change its method of accounting for loan losses.[250] Of course, as with any accounting method change, Code section 481(a) adjustments must be taken into account, and the period specified for recapturing the reserve is four years, using a straight line rate.

Following the elections, the QSub and the parent will file one Form 1120S, and not a consolidated return. However, there is uncertainty associated with whether the separate corporate status is ignored for purposes of employment tax returns. The IRS has not been clear on how to handle this issue. Moreover, it would seem proper to continue filing Form 1099s and other information returns using the bank's name.

§ 1.6.5 Advantages

By far the most significant advantage associated with S corporation status is the elimination of the corporate level income tax, which for most banks is at the highest marginal rate of 35 percent.[251] However, the attractiveness of S corporation status can fluctuate along with comparable individual and corporate tax rates. S corporation earnings passed through to shareholders are not considered dividends taxed at the lower tax rate for dividends. Furthermore, for tax years beginning after December 31, 1997, an Employee Stock Ownership Plan ("ESOP") is permitted to be a shareholder of an S Corporation. To the extent that income is attributable to the stock held by the ESOP, it escapes all (individual and corporate) current income taxation.[252] However, there are other important advantages.

A bank that elects S corporation status eliminates the specter of corporate alternative minimum tax,[253] accumulated earnings tax,[254] and personal holding company tax.[255] Furthermore, the 20 percent interest expense disallowance of Code section 291 may not apply to the S corporation bank (or Qsub bank) after it has been subject to S corporation treatment for three years.[256] Although it may not file a consolidated return with C corporations, it may be a member of an affiliated group of corporations that includes C corporations.[257]

---

[250] Rev. Proc. 2002-9, 2002-3 I.R.B. 327. *See also* Rev. Proc. 2008-18, which provides additional guidance with respect to I.R.C. § 1361(g).

[251] I.R.C. § 1362(a); I.R.C. § 11. Not all states have adopted the federal tax treatment of S corporations.

[252] If a shareholder holds stock in his name directly, it may be possible to engage in a nonrecognition transaction by which the stock is sold to the ESOP. This may be a technique that could be used to reduce the number of shareholders of the corporation for the purpose of complying with the 75-shareholder limitation. *See* I.R.C. § 1042. A survey conducted by the ESOP Association indicates that over 50 percent of those S corporations that are owned almost entirely by ESOPs converted from C to S corporation status in 1988. The expectation is that practically all of the ESOP owned C corporations will convert to S corporation status in subsequent years. Certain issues relating to the treatment of distributions may be discouraging some ESOP owned corporations from converting.

[253] I.R.C. § 55.

[254] I.R.C. § 531.

[255] I.R.C. § 542(c)(2).

[256] I.R.C. § 1363(b)(4). *See* discussion in Chapter 9 of S corporation banks and *Vainisi v. Commissioner*, 599 F.3d 567 (7th Cir. 2010).

[257] In general, an S corporation may own the stock of C corporations, but its stock may be owned

The shareholders of an S corporation will have their tax basis adjusted annually for income and distributions of the S corporation, with the likely consequence that tax basis of shareholder stock will increase over time.[258] Tax basis is increased for both separately and nonseparately stated items, including tax-exempt income. The net positive adjustment will reduce any capital gains tax liability if the stock of the bank is sold by the shareholder.[259] This is generally advantageous. However, if the shareholder is elderly, it may be preferable to avoid current inclusion of the S corporation's earnings in the shareholder's taxable income and receive the step-up in tax basis that occurs at the date of death.

An S corporation, unlike most C corporations, may employ the cash receipts and disbursements method of accounting.[260] However, any accrued interest receivable on the books of an accrual method C corporation on the date the election takes effect will have to be recognized as built-in gain.

The flow-through treatment of specially taxed items of income and expense will permit bank and shareholder capital gains and losses to be netted, and, to the extent that there are net capital gains, the favorable individual tax rate of 15 percent would apply.[261] The opportunity for reducing the tax rate on capital gains by nearly one-half will probably result in a renewed focus by the taxpayer on the possibility of capital gains treatment when real estate that is acquired by a bank at foreclosure is subsequently sold.

The limitation on charitable contributions made by the bank is significantly increased[262] from the ten percent limit applicable to corporations to the 50 percent limit applicable to individuals, and an S corporation and its shareholders are not subject to the consequences of a denial of the deductibility of unreasonable compensation.[263] To the extent that a bank has passive income or loss it would be eligible to be netted against the passive loss or income of the shareholder.[264] Finally, the after-tax yield on tax-exempt obligations is increased because of the higher tax rate to which individuals are subject.

§ 1.6.6 Disadvantages

A bank that is considering whether to elect S corporation status should also recognize and evaluate the potential disadvantages.[265] Among the more signifi-

(Footnote Continued)

only by individuals and certain trusts. *See* the discussion of Qualified Subchapter S Subsidiaries below.

[258] I.R.C. § 1367. The Treasury Department issued proposed regulations relating to the pass through of items, adjustments to basis, and the treatment of distributions. 63 FR 44181 (August 18, 1998).

[259] However, a lower rate of tax on capital gains reduces the cost of retaining C corporation status.

[260] I.R.C. §§ 446(c) and 448(a). Certain C corporations are permitted to use the cash method of accounting. I.R.C. § 448(c); Notice 2001-76.

[261] I.R.C. §§ 1(h) and 1366(b).

[262] I.R.C. § 170.

[263] I.R.C. § 162.

[264] I.R.C. § 469.

[265] One possible disadvantage to S corporation status was related to certain distributions by thrifts. However, the Taxpayer Relief Act of 1997 amended I.R.C. § 593(e) to clarify that the I.R.C. § 1368 accumulated adjustments account of an S corporation would be treated the same as post-1951 earnings and profits for the purpose of determining whether the thrift will be required to recapture any portion of the thrift's pre-1988 bad debt reserve. Furthermore, the clarification of I.R.C. § 593(e) will have the effect of imposing the I.R.C. § 1374 tax on built-in gains on distributions that trigger I.R.C. § 593(e) even if such distributions occur after the expiration

cant disadvantages is associated with the prohibition imposed on the use of the reserve method of accounting for loan losses.[266] An electing bank is required to employ the specific charge-off method for determining loan loss deductions. Consequently, an electing bank must recapture its loan loss reserve on a straight-line basis over four tax years.[267] A thrift that was eligible for the Code section 593 loan loss rules recaptures only "applicable excess reserves," and such reserves are recaptured on a straight-line basis over six years.[268] In general, "applicable excess reserves" are reserve balances in excess of the thrift's base year reserve balance; that is, the balance at the end of the last taxable year ending in 1988.[269] The special rule that permits a portion of a thrift's reserve to avoid recapture is available only if the thrift remains a "bank," as defined in Code section 581. Thus, among other requirements, it must both accept deposits and make loans.[270]

To qualify and maintain its status as a small business corporation, the bank will have to comply with several strict Code provisions that define a small business corporation, including the 100-shareholder limit on the number of shareholders and the single class of stock limitation.[271] Detailed rules contained in Treasury Regulation § 1.1361-1(l) address the one-class of stock requirement. Among the instruments and agreements that may constitute a second class of stock are special shareholder arrangements with directors.

An S corporation is not entitled to the dividends received deduction,[272] and distributions from C corporation subsidiaries will not be eliminated as they are when a consolidated return is filed. An S corporation is not entitled to deduct the cost of certain tax-free fringe benefit plans for 2 percent shareholders.[273] However, a shareholder may deduct up to 40 percent of the amount paid for medical insurance for the shareholder, the shareholder's spouse, and the shareholder's dependents. The deductible percentage of this cost is scheduled to be increased to 80 percent by the year 2006. Because of the loss of the deduction, if the corporation provides disability insurance for the shareholder/employees, it would be highly beneficial for the policy to be transferred to, and owned and paid for by, the employee. In the event that proceeds are paid on such a policy, the recipient would be permitted to exclude the proceeds from gross income.

An S corporation must account for its income on a calendar year basis,[274] and its income will be subject to individual tax rates that are as high as 35 percent.[275]

(Footnote Continued)

of the normal ten-year period of I.R.C. § 1374. Pub. L. No. 105-34, § 1601(f)(5)(A).

266 I.R.C. § 1361(b)(2)(A).

267 I.R.C. § 1361(b)(2); Rev. Proc. 97-27, 1997-1 C.B. 680.

268 I.R.C. § 593(a).

269 I.R.C. § 593(g)(2). *See also* discussion of thrift reserve recapture rules in Ch. 10.

270 *See* definition of a bank in Section 1.5.

271 I.R.C. § 1361(b). These restrictions could inhibit the acquisition of capital that may be necessary for business expansion. However, the S corporation may be terminated, at the election of the shareholders, if it becomes necessary to raise capital through stock offerings that would be prohibited to an S corporation.

272 I.R.C. § 243.

273 I.R.C. § 1372.

274 I.R.C. § 1378. The IRS has published procedures by which a taxpayer may automatically change its annual accounting period in order to elect to be an S corporation effective for the taxable year beginning January 1, 1997. Notice 97-20, 1997-1 C.B. 406.

275 I.R.C. § 1.

In the first year of S Corporation status, the corporation should be careful not to make a distribution in excess of the corporation's Accumulated Adjustments Account ("AAA"). Such a distribution by a corporation with C Corporation earnings and profits would be taxable to the shareholders as dividend income. Because tax-exempt income is not included in AAA, it would be an oversight to assume that all of the income of the S Corporation could be distributed on a tax-free basis.

Adjustments will have to be made to deferred income tax accounts, and any deferred tax asset must be written off on the books. Furthermore, a deferred tax liability will have to be provided for all built-in gains tax, including gain triggered by the recapture of the bank's loan loss reserve.

An S corporation is not entitled to utilize any predecessor C corporation net operating losses and capital loss carryovers, as well as any alternative minimum tax credits.[276] However, net operating losses and capital loss carryovers from C Corporation years are available to offset any built-in gains tax.[277] Furthermore, if an S corporation has any C corporation earnings and profits, as an electing bank normally would, it could incur a special tax on passive investment income depending upon its future business activities, and this may cause its S corporation status to be terminated.[278] The specter of a tax on passive investment income is more likely for an investment affiliate of the book than it is for the bank itself.

An S corporation will have to value all of its assets as of the beginning of its first taxable year for which an S election is in effect, and it will incur a special tax imposed on certain built-in gains.[279] The built-in gains tax will cause all built-in gains, including the recaptured loan loss reserve, to be taxed at both the corporate and individual shareholder levels. Significant built-in gains tax may also be triggered if the bank, or a large portion of its assets, are acquired in a taxable asset acquisition.

§ 1.6.7 Passive Investment Income

An S corporation, with C corporation earnings and profits, and gross receipts more than 25 percent of which are passive investment income that generates excess net passive income, is subject to the Code section 1375 tax on "excess net passive income."[280] The tax is imposed at the highest marginal corporate income tax rate of 35 percent. Moreover, if passive investment income constitutes more than 25 percent of the corporation's gross receipts for each of three consecutive years, and during that period the corporation has accumulated earnings and profits, the S corporation election automatically terminates.[281]

---

[276] I.R.C. § 1371(b).

[277] I.R.C. § 1374(b)(2).

[278] I.R.C. § 1375. A corporation contemplating S corporation status should consider eliminating C corporation earnings and profits by declaring a pre-election dividend.

[279] I.R.C. § 1374.

[280] I.R.C. § 1375(a). The IRS may waive the tax on excess net passive income if the S corporation establishes that it made a good-faith determination at the close of the tax year that it had no C corporation earnings and profits and that it distributed such earnings and profits within a reasonable time after determining that they existed. I.R.C. § 1375(d); Reg. § 1.1375-1(d).

[281] I.R.C. § 1362(d).

Passive investment income is defined as gross receipts derived from royalties, rents, dividends, interest, annuities, and sales or exchanges of securities.[282] It does not include gross receipts directly derived from the active and regular conduct of a lending or finance business, which include gains and interest income from loans originated in a lending business.[283] Expressly excepted from the definition, in the case of a bank or a bank holding company, is (a) interest income, and (b) dividend income on assets required to be held by the bank or holding company, including stock in the Federal Reserve Bank, the Federal Home Loan Bank, or the Federal Agricultural Mortgage Bank, or participation certificates issued by a Federal Intermediate Credit Bank.[284] However, as a general rule, interest income earned from the investment of idle funds in short-term securities is not treated as gross receipts directly derived in the ordinary course of a lending or finance business.[285] Furthermore, passive investment income does not include any recognized built-in gains or losses.[286]

The IRS has ruled that income and gains earned by an S corporation on certain banking assets will not be considered subject to the passive investment income limitation regardless of whether the assets are short-term securities that are purchased with idle funds.[287] The assets that qualify for this exception are:

- All loans and REMIC regular interests owned, or considered to be owned, by the bank regardless of whether the loan originated in the bank's business. For this purpose, securities described in section 165(g)(2)(C) are not considered loans. The latter comprise any bond, debenture, note, or certificate, or other evidence of indebtedness, issued by a corporation or by a government or political subdivision thereof, with interest coupons or in registered form. Thus, when a bank contributes a portion of its loans to a partnership in which it holds an interest, the interest income derived from the loans owned by the partnership will be treated as gross receipts directly derived in the ordinary course of a banking business and will not be considered passive investment income.[288]
- Assets required to be held to conduct a banking business (such as Federal Reserve Bank, Federal Home Loan Bank, or Federal Agricultural Mortgage Bank stock or participation certificates issued by a Federal Intermediate Credit Bank, which represent nonvoting stock in the bank).
- Assets pledged to a third party to secure deposits or business for the bank (such as assets pledged to qualify as a depository for federal taxes or state funds).
- Investment assets (other than assets specified in the preceding paragraphs) that are held by the bank to satisfy reasonable liquidity needs

[282] I.R.C. §§1375(b)(3) and 1362(d)(3).

[283] Reg. §§1.1362-2(c)(5)(iii)(B)(1)(i) and 1.1362-2(c)(6), Ex. 8. The S corporation must meet the requirements of I.R.C. §542(c)(6) that exclude a lending or finance company from the personal holding company tax.

[284] I.R.C. §1362(d)(3)(C)(v).

[285] Reg. §1.1362-2(c)(5)(iii)(B)(2).

[286] I.R.C. §1375(b)(4). This exclusion appears to be available regardless of whether the recognized built-in gain results in a built-in gains tax.

[287] Notice 97-5, 1997-1 C.B. 352. This exception may not apply to a C corporation subsidiary that is not a bank.

[288] PLR 199938035, September 24, 1999.

(including funds needed to meet anticipated loan demands). Of the four categories of banking exceptions, this will prove to be the most controversial. The IRS has not indicated what test should be applied to determine whether a liquidity need is reasonable.

For this purpose, an entity is a "bank" if is meets the definition contained in Code section 581. This exception to the tax on passive income also applies to a bank holding company (within the meaning of section 2(a) of the Bank Holding Company Act of 1956)[289] and a financial holding company (within the meaning of section 2(p) of the Bank Holding Company Act). The exception for assets applies to stock in the Federal Reserve Bank, Federal Home Loan Bank, or Federal Agriculture Mortgage Bank, and participation certificates issued by a Federal Intermediate Credit Bank. This provision applies to tax years beginning after December 31, 2004.[290]

There appears to be no exception for rental income derived by a QSub bank from renting property, including property acquired as foreclosure, a portion of the bank's headquarters building, or other property. Even if such income does not result in the Code section 1375 tax on excessive net passive income, it is likely to be treated as passive income reportable to the shareholders of the S Corporation as such.[291]

In the event that a tax is imposed on excess net passive income, the amount of passive investment income that is passed through to the S corporation shareholders is reduced.[292] The reduction for each item of passive investment income is equal to the amount of the passive income tax multiplied by a fraction, the numerator of which is the amount of the item, and the denominator of which is total passive investment income for the year.[293]

As discussed above, an S corporation is not required to make the QSub election for any of its subsidiaries. Moreover, if a QSub election is made for one subsidiary, the S corporation is not required to make the election for all of its subsidiaries. Thus, an S corporation is not prohibited from having C corporation subsidiaries. Any distributions from a C corporation subsidiary to its S corporation parent will not necessarily be treated as passive income.[294] Treasury Regulations section 1.1362-8 provides that a dividend from a C corporation subsidiary will not be treated as passive income to the extent that those dividends are attributable to "active earnings and profits." The term "active earnings and profits" means the earnings and profits of the C corporation derived from activities that would not produce passive investment income (as defined in Code section 1362(d)(3)) if the C corporation were an S corporation. If any portion of the dividend is attributable to a dividend from a subsidiary of the C corporation, the distribution from the lower tier subsidiary will be considered attributable to

[289] 12 U.S.C. § 1841(a) (2006).

[290] I.R.C. § 1362(d)(3)(F), as amended by the American Jobs Creation Act of 2004 (Pub. L. No. 108-357).

[291] I.R.C. § 469; Reg. § 1.469-1T(e).

[292] I.R.C. § 1366(f)(3).

[293] I.R.C. § 1366(f)(3)(A) and (B).

[294] Reg. § 1.1362-8(a).

active earnings and profits according to the same rules that apply to the C corporation subsidiary.[295]

Any reasonable method may be used to determine to what extent the earnings and profits of a C corporation subsidiary are active earnings and profits.[296] The Treasury Regulations contain a safe harbor method by which active earnings and profits are determined by reference to the ratio of active gross receipts to total gross receipts.[297] Furthermore, a *de minimis* exception is provided, which allows a taxpayer to treat all earnings and profits of a C corporation subsidiary as active earnings and profits if less than ten percent of the subsidiaries earnings and profits for a taxable year are derived from activities that would produce passive investment income if the C corporation were an S corporation.[298] Finally, a special rule applies for earnings and profits accumulated by a C corporation prior to an acquisition that satisfies the 80 percent test of Code section 1504(a)(2). In this situation, a corporation may treat earnings and profits accumulated by the corporation in all taxable years ending before the S corporation held stock meeting the 80 percent test as active earnings and profits. This treatment must be in the same proportion as the C corporation's active earnings and profits for the three taxable years ending prior to the time when the S corporation acquired 80 percent of the C corporation bears to the C corporation's total earnings and profits for those three years.[299]

§1.6.8 Built-in Gains Tax

(a) *General Rules*

A bank that has been operating as a C corporation is required to value its assets as of the beginning of the first taxable year for which the S corporation election is in effect for the purpose of determining its exposure to the special tax imposed on S corporation net recognized built-in gains.[300] The tax on built-in gains is imposed at the highest marginal corporate rate of tax (currently 35 percent) on net recognized built-in gains. A built-in gain will be recognized upon disposal of any asset that had built-in gains at the election date. However, no tax is payable if an asset that had built-in gain is held for 10 years from the election date. For tax years beginning in 2009 and 2010, the recognition period is reduced to seven years.[301] The net unrecognized built-in gain at the date when the S election becomes effective will establish the ceiling on the S corporation's exposure to the built-in gains tax.[302]

(b) *Amount of Built-in Gains and Losses*

To the extent that the fair market value of an asset exceeds the corporation's tax basis in the asset at the election date, the excess is treated as a built-in gain. An excess of basis over fair market value is a built-in loss. All assets of the

---

[295] Reg. §1.1362-8(b)(2).

[296] Reg. §1.1362-8(b)(1).

[297] Reg. §1.1362-8(b)(5).

[298] Reg. §1.1362-8(b)(3).

[299] Reg. §1.1362-8(b)(4).

[300] I.R.C. §§1374 and 1374(d)(3).

[301] I.R.C. §1374(d)(7). I.R.C. §1374(d)(7)(B) and (C) provides special rules that reduce the recognition period for taxable years beginning in 2009 through 2014.

[302] I.R.C. §1374(d)(1).

corporation enter into this computation, including tangible and intangible assets and assets that are not recorded on the books of the corporation. Thus, if a bank has an unbooked core deposit intangible, customer list, or goodwill asset, it would have to be valued for purposes of determining exposure to the tax on built-in gains. Unless these assets were purchased in earlier acquisitions, it is unlikely that the corporation will have a tax basis in them. For example, if a bank has accrued on its books interest income that has not been included in taxable income, for a cash method taxpayer the accrued interest receivable may be an asset with built-in gain. The collection of the interest would be treated as recognized built-in gain.

Any gain recognized at the time of disposition of a built-in gain asset, which is in excess of the built-in gain, is not subject to the built-in gains tax. Furthermore, if a corporation disposes of an asset with built-in losses, also determined as of the election date, the built-in loss may be applied to offset any built-in gains that would otherwise be subject to the tax on built-in gains.[303] However, all gains recognized during the recognition period are presumed to be recognized built-in gains; all losses recognized during the recognition period are presumed not to be recognized built-in losses.[304] Any built-in gains tax is treated as a loss sustained by the S corporation during the taxable year. The character of the loss is determined by allocating the loss proportionately among the recognized built-in gains that gave rise to the tax.[305]

(c) *Loan Loss Reserve Recapture*

The entire amount of a bank's loan loss reserve, at the effective date of the S corporation election, is treated as a built-in gain. Thus, a bank that elects S corporation treatment will incur a tax imposed on built-in gains from the income from the recapture of the bank's loan loss reserve. For a thrift, only the "applicable excess reserves" will be treated as built-in gain assets.[306]

Any loans charged-off in the first year of the recognition period are built-in losses, which are permitted to offset the recognized built-in gain from reserve recapture.[307] After the first recapture year, taxpayers are permitted to offset the reserve recapture if they can establish that a loan loss is attributable to a built-in loss that existed at the date the S election became effective. For this reason, a taxpayer should analyze its book reserve for loan losses and attribute the reserve to loans that are recorded on the books of the taxpayer at the date that the S election took effect.

A bank expecting to make an S election or that will be treated as a QSub should evaluate the potential benefit of electing to begin to recapture its reserve in a tax year prior to the year in which the S election becomes effective.[308] To the extent that any reserve is recaptured prior to an S corporation year, there would be no built-in gains tax payable on the recaptured amount. Thus, double taxation

[303] I.R.C. § 1374(d)(4).

[304] I.R.C. §§ 1374(d)(3) and (4).

[305] I.R.C. § 1366(f)(2).

[306] I.R.C. § 593(g).

[307] Reg. § 1.1374-4(f).

[308] *See* Rev. Proc. 2002-9, 2002-3 I.R.B. 327, for automatic accounting method change procedures.

would be avoided. A bank also should explore the implications of maximizing its bad debt deductions in the tax year prior to the first recapture year. By doing so, the taxpayer would receive an immediate benefit from the deduction while the increased reserve balance would be recaptured over four subsequent tax years. The reserve recapture rules contained in Code sections 585 and 593 do not apply when a commercial bank or a thrift changes its reserve method of accounting by reason of electing S corporation or QSub status. Thus, the optional cut-off method provided in Code section 585(c) and the six-year recapture period provided in Code section 593 are unavailable.

When a bank recovers on loans that were on the bank's books at the effective date of the QSub election, the bank should consider whether to refrain from reducing charge-offs by these recoveries on or after the effective date of the election. In general, it could be argued that the bank never benefited from the deduction because it is required, as a condition to making the QSub election, to recapture its loan loss reserve. Code section 111(a) provides that "[g]ross income does not include income attributable to the recovery during the taxable year of any amount deducted in any prior taxable year to the extent such amount did not reduce the amount of tax imposed by this chapter." This provision embodies the tax benefit rule. The tax benefit rule generally applies when an amount deducted from the taxpayer's gross income in one tax year is recovered in a later year. The purpose of the tax benefit rule is to permit a balancing entry when a seemingly proper expense turns out to be improper—that is, when a transaction has been reported on the basis of assumptions that in a subsequent year prove to have been erroneous. However, Treasury Regulation section 1.111-1(a)(1) provides, "If a bad debt was previously charged against a reserve by a taxpayer on the reserve method of treating bad debts, it was not deducted, and it is, therefore, not considered a section 111 item."[309]

The tax benefit rule has two parts. The first part provides that an amount deducted from gross income in one year is included in income in a subsequent year if an event occurs in the subsequent year that is fundamentally inconsistent with the premise on which the deduction was previously based (sometimes referred to as the "inclusionary component" of the rule). The second part of the tax benefit rule limits the income that must be recognized under the inclusionary component to the amount of the tax benefit that resulted from the deduction (sometimes referred to as the "exclusionary component" of the rule).

Under the tax benefit rule, an amount must be included in gross income in the current year if, and to the extent that the amount was deducted in a prior year, the deduction resulted in a tax benefit, an event occurs in the current year that is fundamentally inconsistent with the premises on which the deduction was originally based, and the inclusion of the recovery in gross income is not precluded by a nonrecognition provision of the Code.

---

[309] This regulation may be designed to prevent the exclusion when the earlier bad debt reserve addition was not based on actual experience. Most banks use actual experience to determine their reserve addition.

(d) *Valuation of Assets*

Each asset held at the beginning of the first taxable year in which a corporation is an S corporation must be valued not only for purposes of determining any built-in gain or loss with respect to the asset itself, but also because it could affect the computation of built-in gains tax when another asset is disposed of. The unrealized built-in gain on all assets, not only those disposed of, as of the first day of the S Corporation's tax year, becomes the ceiling for the computation of potential net recognized built-in gain. In other words, if an asset with built-in gains is undervalued, or not valued at all, the ceiling on potential net recognized built-in gain is reduced accordingly.

Exposure to built-in gains tax liability should be a concern not only for those shareholders of the S corporation at the time that the election is made, but also for anyone who becomes a shareholder after the election is made and during the recognition period. If the liability is not properly taken into account, the bank's book value may be overstated in a purchase and sale agreement. Although bankers are generally aware that built-in gains tax liability will be incurred as the bank's loan loss reserve is recaptured, exposure to the built-in gains tax may be significantly greater if the assets are undervalued.

Regardless of whether goodwill, the core deposit intangible, or any other asset with built-in gain is disposed of during the recognition period, the very existence of one of these built-in gain assets is taken into account when determining the bank's exposure to the built-in gains tax. This aspect of the built-in gains tax provision is sometimes overlooked. The rudimentary example that follows will illustrate how built-in gains tax liability may be increased when goodwill is not properly valued.

Example: Bank X elected to be taxed as an S corporation effective January 1, 1977, after being taxed as a C corporation for all of its prior tax years. On the date the election took effect, the bank had numerous assets, but only three assets had a tax basis different from fair market value: a loan, a bank building, and goodwill. Those assets had a fair market value and an adjusted basis at January 1, 1997 as follows:

Asset	*Adjusted Basis*	*Fair Market Value*
Loan	$100,000	$95,000
Building	$35,000	$50,000
Goodwill	$-0-	$20,000

Assume that in 1999, Bank X disposes of the building for $55,000. Also, assume that when the bank converted to an S corporation it did not value the goodwill. Because the built-in gains tax ("BIG Tax") provision limits total exposure to the BIG Tax to the amount of the net built-in gain at the conversion date, the bank would incorrectly determine that its maximum exposure to BIG Tax is $3,500 (*i.e.*, 0.35 ($15,000 – $5,000)).

In fact, Bank's maximum exposure to BIG Tax is $10,500 (*i.e.*, 0.35 ($20,000 + $15,000 – $5,000)). Because the ceiling on tax liability is increased, the sale of the building in 1999 will generate $5,250 of BIG Tax (*i.e.*, 0.35 × $15,000), which is a 50 percent increase in tax. Furthermore, the underestimation of the BIG Tax will also result in an underestimation of personal income tax liability to the shareholders of the S corporation when the gain is reported to them.

Given the sensitivity of the IRS to this issue, a bank would be operating at its peril if it did not properly value all of its assets at the date that the election to be taxed as an S corporation takes effect. Buyers and sellers of bank stock also should take into account the exposure to BIG Tax, which may not be disclosed on financial statements.

§1.6.9 Estimated Tax Payments

S corporations are required to make estimated tax payments for tax liability attributable to the Code section 1374(a) built-in gains tax, the Code section 1375(a) excessive passive investment income tax, and any tax due by reason of investment credit recapture[310] if the total of these taxes for the year is $500 or more.[311] The required annual estimated tax payment is the lesser of: (1) 100 percent of the tax shown on the return for the tax year or (2) 100 percent of the tax liability incurred by virtue of the built-in gains tax and tax due because of investment credit recapture, plus 100 percent of the tax due on the passive investment income reported by the S corporation in the preceding year.

An S corporation cannot utilize the exceptions prescribed in Code sections 6655(d)(1)(B)(ii) and 6655(d)(2)(B) that allow estimated tax payments to be based on the corporation's prior tax year when it is computing estimated tax payments attributable to built-in gains and to investment tax credit recapture. The prior year's tax exception is available to all S corporations with respect to the portion of required estimated tax payments attributable to excess passive income, even if there was no tax attributable to excess passive income in the prior year. In all cases, an S corporation can use the annualization exception.[312] The term "taxable income" as used in Code section 6655(e) includes built-in gain and excess passive income for the purpose of computing lower required installment payments of estimated tax.[313]

§1.7 Domestic Building and Loan Associations

§1.7.1 Tax Definition

The first detailed definition of a building and loan association was incorporated into the Code by the Revenue Act of 1962, ten years after thrifts were first subject to federal income tax.[314] It was modified by the Tax Reform Act of 1969 to liberalize the asset and income tests discussed below.[315] The Economic Recovery Tax Act of 1981 did not disturb the Code section 7701(a)(19) definition of a

---

[310] I.R.C. § 1371(d)(2).

[311] I.R.C. § 6655(g)(4).

[312] I.R.C. § 6655(e).

[313] I.R.C. § 6655(g)(4)(E).

[314] Revenue Act of 1962, Pub. L. No. 87-834, 76 Stat. 960 (1962).

[315] Tax Reform Act of 1969, Pub. L. No. 91-172, §432(c), 83 Stat. 742 (1969). The Tax Reform Act of 1969 also modified the definition of a building and loan association in certain respects to embrace mutual savings banks and other mutual institutions.

domestic building and loan association, but it did amend the now repealed Code section 591. This amendment provided that the definition of a mutual savings bank could include a savings bank that has capital stock represented by shares and that is subject to and operates under federal or state laws relating to mutual savings banks.[316] The Tax Reform Act of 1986 also did not change the Code section 7701(a)(19) definition of a building and loan association, except to add subdivision (19)(C)(xi), which deals with Real Estate Mortgage Investment Conduits ("REMICs").[317]

Because a detailed definition of a domestic building and loan association is contained in the Code and in regulations, it is inappropriate to rely on the bank regulatory classification of a thrift for purposes of determining whether the entity is a thrift for purposes of the Code. However, an entity that fails to qualify as a thrift for regulatory purposes is likely also to be disqualified as a thrift for tax purposes.[318] For example, an entity that fails the regulatory "qualified thrift lender test" ("QTL test") would probably not meet the tax definition of a domestic building and loan association, as one which passes the QTL test is not assured of thrift tax status.[319]

The current significance of an entity qualifying as a thrift for tax purposes is practically meaningless, except for transitional issues associated with loan loss reserve recaptures and as it may affect the taxation of the entity for pre-1997 tax years. With the repeal of all favorable thrift tax provisions, an entity that is a thrift for regulatory purposes will be taxed as a commercial bank.

§ 1.7.2 Evolution of Thrift Taxation

(a) *Thrift Exemption*

Until 1952, thrifts were exempt from federal income tax.[320] Exemption was granted on the theory that the money belonging to members of these institutions, nearly all of which were organized in mutual form, was being used for loans to the members, and there was no profit since the earnings belonged to the members.[321]

---

[316] Economic Recovery Tax Act of 1981, Pub. L. No. 97-34 & 12 U.S.C. § 1813(f) (2007), § 245(a)(2), 95 Stat. 172 (1981). For bank regulatory purposes, a mutual savings bank is defined as "a bank without capital stock transacting a savings bank business, the net earnings of which inure wholly to the benefit of its depositors after payment of obligations for any advances by its organizers." 12 U.S.C. § 1813(f).

[317] Tax Reform Act of 1986, Pub. L. No. 99-514 § 671, 100 Stat. 2085 (1986).

[318] A savings bank chartered under state law may not meet the regulatory definition of a thrift, but it still may qualify as one for tax purposes. I.R.C. § 591(b).

[319] The QTL test was added to the law by the Financial Institutions Reform, Recovery and Enforcement Act of 1989, Pub. L. No. 101-73, 103 Stat. 183 (1989). Title III, § 301 (60% test) and § 303 (70% test) 12 U.S.C. § 1467a(m)(1) (2006). Temporary and limited exceptions are granted.

[320] *See* Revenue Act of 1913, Pub. L. No. 63-16, § II(G)(a), 38 Stat. 114 (1913). Prior to the enactment of the Revenue Act of 1951, a thrift was exempt from federal income tax under the provisions of § 101(4) of the 1939 I.R.C. This exemption was repealed by § 313(b) of the Revenue Act of 1951, effective for all taxable years beginning after December 31, 1951.

[321] Tax Reform Act of 1969, Pub. L. No. 91-172, 83 Stat. 487, H.R. Rep. No. 413, at p. 123, 91st Cong., 1st Sess. 123 (1969), reprinted in 1969 U.S.C.C.A.N. 1645. By the early 1960's there were approximately 500 stock savings and loans. "Treasury Dept. Report of July 1961 on The Taxation of Mutual Savings Banks and Savings and Loan Associations," p. 3.

(b) *Repeal of Exemption*

The Revenue Act of 1951 repealed section 101(2) of the Internal Revenue Code of 1939, which was the final blanket exemption granted thrifts from federal income tax.[322] The change was justified, in part, by the fact that these mutual institutions were no longer dealing with themselves. Instead, a significant portion of their lending business was with nonmembers.[323] There also was a realization that these institutions were actively competing with commercial banks for public savings and in the security and real estate lending markets.[324]

As a practical matter, the exemption continued until generous loan loss deduction rules, enacted simultaneously with the elimination of the exemption, were modified. The Revenue Act of 1951 permitted thrifts to deduct, as a reasonable addition to their reserve for loan losses, an amount not greater than the lesser of: (a) the amount of its net income for the taxable year, computed without regard to the bad-debt deduction, or (b) the amount by which 12 percent of the total deposits or withdrawable accounts of its depositors at the close of the taxable year exceeded the sum of its surplus, undivided profits, and reserves at the beginning of the taxable year.[325] The limitation based on deposits provided no practical constraint on a thrift's loan loss deduction, since most thrifts were below the limitation for several years following the enactment of the Revenue Act of 1951. It also bore no relationship to economic reality since deposit liabilities can never result in a bad debt. Thus, for nearly every thrift an exemption from federal income taxation continued after the enactment of the Revenue Act of 1951. The loan loss deduction rules eliminated taxable income. These generous rules were justified, in part, by the policy objectives to encourage thrift formation and encourage appropriate housing expansion and overcome the constraints on mutual organizations that resulted in lack of access to capital markets. They were able to secure additional reserves only from retained earnings whereas stock institutions could secure capital cushions by the sale of additional stock.

(c) *Elimination of Practical Exemption*

The Revenue Act of 1962 eliminated this virtual exemption by reducing the percentage of taxable income that could be claimed as a bad-debt deduction to 60 percent; however, it continued to provide significantly more generous methods for computing bad-debt deductions for thrifts than were allowed commercial banks and other taxpayers.[326] Subsequent revenue acts reduced the allowable percentage. Between 1969 and 1979, the percentage was phased down to 40 percent of taxable income, and the Tax Reform Act of 1986 dropped the percent-

---

[322] Federal banking law contained an exemption from federal and state taxation for "[a]ll notes, bonds, debentures, or other obligations issued by the (FSLIC) . . . ." This exemption also has been repealed. Section 802(b), ch. 649, Tit. VIII, 68 Stat. 642, *repealing* 12 U.S.C. § 1725(e).

[323] *Id.*

[324] S. Rep. 71, 82d Cong., 1st Sess., 25-28 (1951). Banks and thrifts have been making a similar argument with respect to credit unions.

[325] Revenue Act of 1951, Pub. L. No. 82-183, § 313(e), 65 Stat. 452 (1951).

[326] Revenue Act of 1962, Pub. L. No. 87-834, 76 Stat. 960 (1962).

age to 8 percent.[327] Finally, the Small Business Job Protection Act of 1996 completely repealed all special thrift loan loss deduction rules.[328]

§ 1.7.3 Special Bank Tax Rules

There are several Code sections contained in Subchapter H that expressly modify the general C corporation rules for purposes of arriving at a bank's federal income tax liability. Other provisions contained in subsections, divisions, and paragraphs of sections sprinkled throughout the Code are expressly applicable to banks. Moreover, Code section 7507 provides a special exemption from federal income tax for "any bank or trust company" that has ceased to do business by reason of insolvency or bankruptcy. A savings and loan association and a building and loan association come within the term "bank and trust company" as those terms are used in Code section 7507. Since, for purposes of Code section 7507, there is no substantial tax difference between deposits in a savings and loan or building and loan association and deposits in a bank or trust company, depositors in savings and loan or building and loan associations were granted entitlement to that section's protection.[329]

§ 1.7.4 Eligible Entities

For federal income tax purposes, a domestic building and loan association is defined in Code section 7701(a)(19) to include:

1. A domestic building and loan association;
2. A domestic savings and loan association;
3. A federal savings and loan association; and
4. Any other savings institution chartered and supervised as a savings and loan or similar association under federal or state law.

To qualify as a domestic building and loan association, each of these institutions must meet a supervisory test, a business operations test, and an asset test.[330] Failure to satisfy all three of the tax tests disqualifies the institution from thrift status, but not necessarily from bank status. The IRS has ruled that a federally chartered savings and loan association subject to regulation by the Federal Home Loan Bank Board is a bank, even though it failed to meet the more restrictive Code section 7701(a)(19) definition of a domestic savings and loan association.[331] The IRS reasoned that an institution that fails to meet the Code section 7701(a)(19) criteria can nevertheless qualify as a bank under Code section 581 so long as a substantial part of the institution's business consists of receiving deposits and making loans or of exercising fiduciary powers similar to those granted national banks. Retaining "bank" status for an institution that fails to

---

[327] I.R.C. § 593. Chapter 10 contains a complete discussion of this provision.

[328] Small Business Job Protection Act of 1996, Pub. L. No. 104-188, 110 Stat. 1755 (1996).

[329] Rev. Rul. 88-18, 1988-1 C.B. 402.

[330] I.R.C. § 7701(a)(19)(A)-(C); Reg. § 301.7701-13A(b)-(d).

[331] PLR 8701041, October 8, 1986. The Federal Home Loan Bank Board has been replaced by the Office of Thrift Supervision as the regulator of thrifts. Financial Institutions Reform, Recovery & Enforcement Act of 1989, Pub. L. No. 101-73, Title IV, 103 Stat. 183 (1989) (hereinafter "FIRREA").

qualify as a thrift will permit the institution to avoid recapture of its base year loan loss reserve.[332]

Although a savings bank, whether operated in mutual or stock form, is not expressly included among the institutions that meet the definition of a domestic building and loan association, such an institution will qualify as a thrift for tax purposes. According to the Home Owners Loan Act ("HOLA"), "[A]ny reference in any other law to a federal savings and loan association shall be deemed to be also a reference to . . . a federal savings bank, unless the context indicates otherwise."[333]

§ 1.7.5 Supervisory Test

To pass the supervisory test, a domestic building and loan association must be either:

1. Subject by law to supervision and examination by the state or federal authority given supervision over such associations; or
2. Insured by a federal insurance agency.[334]

The "federal authority given supervision" had been the Office of Thrift Supervision ("OTS"). All OTS duties and functions have been transferred to the Federal Reserve, the Office of the Comptroller of Currency, and the FDIC.[335] The Federal Reserve now supervises thrift holding companies, the Comptroller supervises federal thrifts, and the FDIC supervises state-chartered thrifts.[336] Earlier amendments to federal banking laws abolished the supervisory authority of the Federal Home Loan Bank Board and established the OTS as the primary federal regulator of thrifts.[337] Treasury regulations provide that the insurance aspect of the supervisory test is met if the association is an insured institution within the meaning of Section 401(a) of the National Housing Act.[338] Treasury regulations further provide that an *insured institution* is one whose accounts are insured by the Federal Savings and Loan Insurance Corporation ("FSLIC").[339] Section 401(a) of the National Housing Act has been repealed, and the FSLIC was abolished by the Financial Institution Reform, Recovery, and Enforcement Act of 1989 ("FIRREA").[340] FIRREA transferred the insurance of thrifts from FSLIC to the Federal Deposit Insurance Corporation ("FDIC").[341] As a result of the modifications made

---

[332] *See* discussion of a thrift's loan loss reserve recapture rule in Ch. 10.

[333] 12 U.S.C. § 1462(d) (1989). HOLA authorizes the organization, incorporation, examination, operation and regulation of federal savings banks and other savings associations. 12 U.S.C. § 1464 (2006). *See also*, the FDIC Act which treats the term federal savings association as synonymous with a federal savings bank as chartered under HOLA. 12 U.S.C. § 1813(b)(2) (2007); 12 C.F.R. §§ 561.43, 546.1, 574.2. *See also*, the Home Mortgage Disclosure Act which includes in the definition of a depository institution "any savings institution." 12 U.S.C. § 1813(b) (2007); 12 U.S.C. § 2802(2)(A)(ii) (1989).

[334] Reg. § 301.7701-13A(b). The "subject by law" language is repeated in I.R.C. § 581.

[335] Section 312 of the Dodd-Frank Wall Street Reform and Consumer Protection Act (Pub. L. No. 111-203, 124 Stat. 1376-2223).

[336] H. Rep. No. 111-517, 111th Cong., 2d Sess. 866 (2010).

[337] Financial Institutions Reform, Recovery and Enforcement Act of 1989, Pub. L. No. 101-73, 103 Stat. 183 (1989).

[338] Reg. § 301.7701-13A; 12 U.S.C. § 1724(a).

[339] Reg. § 301.7701-13A(b).

[340] Financial Institutions Reform, Recovery and Enforcement Act of 1989, Pub. L. No. 101-73, 103 Stat. 183 (1989) at §§ 401 and 407.

[341] *Id.* at §§ 205 and 211. Sections 4 and 11(a) of the Federal Deposit Insurance Act (12 U.S.C. § 1821(a)) was amended by FIRREA.

to the federal deposit insurance laws, the tax supervisory test should be read to substitute a reference to the FDIC for the reference to the FSLIC, and a reference to the Federal Deposit Insurance Act for the reference to the National Housing Act.

The FDIC now handles the insurance for both commercial banks and thrifts, albeit in different funds. Generally, thrift deposits are insured by the Savings Association Insurance Fund ("SAIF") and commercial bank deposits are insured by the Bank Insurance Fund ("BIF").[342] In some situations involving acquisitions and charter conversions, an entity chartered as a commercial bank can have deposits included in SAIF.[343]

In *Barnett Banks, Inc. & Subsidiaries v. Commissioner*, the Tax Court concluded that two financial institutions chartered as banks under Florida law, but earlier chartered as savings and loan associations, were not entitled to use the reserve method of accounting for bad debts prescribed in Code section 593.[344] During the taxable years in question the Florida Code provided the Florida Department of Banking and Finance with the authority to supervise and examine all financial institutions chartered under state law, including savings and loan associations, banks, industrial savings banks, trust companies, international bank agencies or representative offices, and credit unions. However, banks and trust companies were subject to the statutory provisions set forth in chapter 658 of title XXXVIII of the Florida Code. Savings, savings and loan, and building and loan associations were subject to the statutory provisions set forth in chapter 665 of title XXXVIII of the Florida Code.

The IRS took the position that the taxpayers lost qualification to use the Code section 593 reserve method of accounting for bad debts when they obtained bank charters and relinquished their savings and loan charters in order to be acquired. The IRS interpreted the language of Code section 7701(a)(19) and of Regulation section 301.7701-13A(a) to preclude use of Code section 593 by any entity chartered as a bank. The IRS relied on legislative history emphasizing the historically different tax treatment afforded to banks, on the one hand, and to savings and loan associations, on the other.

The taxpayer contended that the language of the applicable statutes allows for use of the reserve method of accounting under former Code section 593 by any association actually functioning as a savings and loan. Taxpayer also asserted that banks functioned the same before and after the change in their charters from savings and loan associations to commercial banks. The taxpayer argued that precedents in the subject areas repeatedly apply substance over form analysis, even when a taxpayer is attempting to repudiate the form that the taxpayer has chosen.

---

342 *Id.*

343 For a discussion of charter conversions *see* Ch. 11.

344 T.C. Memo. 2002-168, July 10, 2002.

§1.7.6 Business Operations Test

To pass the business operations test, an association must employ its assets so that its business consists "principally of acquiring the savings of the public and investing in loans."[345] Included within these activities are ancillary or incidental activities which are, nonetheless, directly and primarily related to acquiring savings and investing in loans. Such activities include: advertising for savings, appraising property on which loans are to be made by the institution, and inspecting the progress of construction in connection with construction loans.

Regulations contain two standards for determining when the business operations test is met: (a) if the institution's business consists principally of acquiring the savings of the public, *and* (b) if the institution's income is derived from an approved list of investments.[346]

(a) *Acquiring Savings*

The requirement that an association's business must consist primarily of acquiring the savings of the public will be considered met if the association's business operations meet either a subjective "conformity" test with regard to the percentage of its deposits placed by the general public or acquired in conformity with federal and state regulatory requirements, or an objective 75 percent test.

(i) Conformity Test. An association's business operations will pass the subjective test if its operations consist principally of "acquiring savings of the public." The savings must be acquired in conformity with the rules and regulations of the Federal Home Loan Bank Board ("FHLBB") or substantially equivalent rules of state law or supervisory authority.[347] The reference to the FHLBB in the Regulations is no longer valid. As discussed above, FIRREA abolished the FHLBB,[348] and the regulatory functions of the FHLBB have been transferred to the OTS. The OTS was created as an Office of the Department of Treasury under the general oversight of the Secretary of the Treasury.[349]

The IRS has ruled that a federal savings bank chartered and supervised by the OTS is essentially the same as a savings and loan association, and it will satisfy the savings prong of the business operations test, even though it did not meet the 75 percent objective test. As a result of the transfer to a savings bank by its parent multi-bank holding company of a nationwide consumer finance business operated by nonbank subsidiaries of the parent, the savings bank turned to the parent for intercompany advances, both as to loans and deposits, to partially fund the finance business.[350] These loans or deposits were disqualified under the 75 percent test (and 25 percent sub-tests) because they were amounts deposited

[345] I.R.C. §7701(a)(19)(B); Reg. §301.7701-13A (c)(1).

[346] Reg. §301.7701-13A(c).

[347] Reg. §301.7701-13A(c)(2). The regulation has not been updated to reflect Congressional action to remove supervisory authority from the FHLBB. The power of a Federal Home Loan Bank to accept deposits is described in 12 U.S.C. §1431(e) (2006).

[348] Financial Institutions Reform, Recovery and Enforcement Act of 1989, Pub. L. No. 101-73, 103 Stat. 183 (1989) at §703.

[349] Financial Institutions Reform, Recovery and Enforcement Act of 1989, Pub. L. No. 101-73, 103 Stat. 183 (1989) at §301. Thus all reference to rules and regulations of the FHLBB should be construed as similar rules and regulations of the OTS.

[350] PLR 9312017, December 23, 1992.

or held by members of a related business group. Nevertheless, the ruling concluded that the savings prong of the business operations test was satisfied because the deposits were acquired, in all material respects, in conformity with the rules and regulations of the FHLBB or substantially equivalent rules of a state law or supervisory authority.

(ii) The 75 Percent Test. Alternatively, an association's business operations will consist principally of acquiring the savings of the public if more than 75 percent of the dollar amount of total deposits, withdrawable shares, and other obligations of the association are held by the general public during the taxable year.[351] The *general public* excludes family or related business groups or persons who are officers or directors of the association.[352] The term *other obligations* means notes, bonds, debentures, or other obligations and debt securities issued by the association in conformity with the rules and regulations of the OTS or substantially equivalent rules of a state law or supervisory authority. *Other obligations* does not include certain secured advances made by a Federal Home Loan Bank.[353]

A further limitation applies: other obligations outstanding during the taxable year may not exceed 25 percent of the total of deposits, withdrawable shares and other obligations.[354]

> **Example:** Association B has $1,500,000 total deposits and withdrawable shares of which greater than 75 percent are held by the general public. Additionally, the association has "other obligations" in the amount of $400,000 of which greater than 75 percent are held by the general public. Association B's operations consist principally of acquiring the savings of the public. "Other obligations" are only 21 percent ($400,000 ÷ [$1,500,000 + $400,000]) of the total of deposits, withdrawable shares and other obligations. If the association has other obligations of $600,000, then the association does not have operations that consist principally of acquiring the savings of the public because the 25 percent rule is not met:
>
> [$600,000 ÷ ($1,500,000 + $600,000)]= 29 percent.

Both the percentage of total deposits, withdrawable shares, and other obligations of the association and the percentage of "other obligations" may be determined either at year-end or on the basis of a yearly average. The yearly average may be computed by reference to either monthly, quarterly, or semiannual balances. The averaging method employed may be changed from year to year without requesting permission from the IRS It is not treated as a method of

---

351 Reg. § 301.7701-13A(c)(2).

352 *Id.*

353 Sections 10 and 106 of the Federal Home Loan Bank Act, 12 U.S.C. §§ 1430, 1430b (1992). Each Federal Home Loan Bank is authorized to make secured advances to its members upon such security as the Board may prescribe. The FHLBB's authority to make secured loans was modified by FIRREA. Under the amendment, secured loans are permitted to be made if, in the judgment of the FHLBB, the collateral is sufficient to secure advances obtained from the FHLBB under Sec. 10 and Sec. 11(g) of the Federal Home Loan Bank Act. Other modifications have been made concerning advances by Federal Home Loan Banks.

354 Reg. § 301.7701-13A(c)(2).

accounting. However, the method selected must be applied uniformly to all deposits and obligations during any single taxable year.[355]

(b) *Investing in Loans*

A thrift's business will consist principally of "investing" in loans if, and only if, for a taxable year, more than 75 percent of the gross income of the thrift is derived from one or more specified sources.[356] Unlike the savings prong of the business operations test, there is no alternative to meeting this 75 percent test. However, there is an exception, discussed below, which deals with "exceptional circumstances."[357]

(i) The 75 Percent Test. For all purposes of this calculation, gross income does not include:

1. Gains or losses on the portion of "property used in the association's business," as described below;[358]
2. Gains or losses on the sale or exchange of that portion of "property used in the association's business" which is rented to others;[359] or
3. Gains or losses on sales of loan participations, other than participations of taxable state and federal government (including instrumentality) obligations.[360]

To meet this test, 75 percent of the institution's gross income must be derived from:

1. Interest or dividends on:
   (a) Cash on hand;
   (b) Time or demand deposits with, or withdrawable accounts in, other financial institutions; or
   (c) Deposit insurance company securities;[361]
2. Interest, discounts, premiums, commissions or fees (including late charges and penalties) and other income (but not gains or losses) on loans, including passbook loans, residential real property loans, church loans, urban renewal loans, institutional loans, and educational loans. However, to the extent that the amount of these items of income, other than interest, exceeds 20 percent of gross income, they shall not count toward satisfying the 75 percent test;[362]
3. Interest and net gain from sales and exchanges of taxable state and federal government obligations, including government agency obligations;[363]

---

355 *Id.*

356 Regulations require the thrift to include a statement on its return that shows the amount of gross income broken down into the several categories, as set forth in Reg. § 301.7701-13A(c)(3)(iii).

357 Reg. § 301.7701-13A(c)(3)(ii).

358 Reg. § 301.7701-13A(c)(3)(ii)(a).

359 Reg. § 301.7701-13A(c)(3)(ii)(b).

360 Reg. § 301.7701-13A(c)(3)(ii)(c).

361 Reg. § 301.7701-13A(c)(c)(i)(a).

362 Reg. § § 301.7701-13A(c)(3)(i)(b) and (d).

363 Reg. § 301.7701-13A(c)(3)(i)(e).

4. Gross income and recognized gain or loss attributable to property acquired at foreclosure or pursuant to a deed-in-lieu-of-foreclosure.[364] Income or loss deferred by reason of Code section 595 is not taken into account;[365] and

5. Income attributable to property (real or personal, tangible or intangible) used by the association in the conduct of its business of acquiring savings and investing in loans.[366] Real property which is held for the purpose of being used primarily as the principal or branch office of the thrift will be considered property used in the thrift's business so long as it is reasonably anticipated that such property will be occupied as the principal or branch office of the thrift, or construction work preparatory to such occupancy will commence thereon, within two years after the acquisition of the property.[367] Stock of a wholly-owned subsidiary corporation will be considered for this purpose as "property used in the thrift's business" if the subsidiary has as its exclusive activity the ownership and management of property, more than 50 percent of the fair market value of which is used as the principal or branch office of the thrift.

A thrift may not include within the category of property used in its business any real property held for investment or sale, even if it is held for the purpose of obtaining mortgage loans thereon. Moreover, if real property is rented to others and is not held for the purpose of being used primarily as the principal or branch office of the thrift, it will generally not constitute property used in the association's business.[368] However, if the rental value of the rented portion of a parcel of real property used as the principal or branch location constitutes less than 50 percent of the fair rental value of the property, or if the property has an adjusted basis of not more than $150,000, the entire property shall be considered used in the thrift's business and all income therefrom shall be counted toward the 75 percent test. If the rented portion constitutes 50 percent or more of the fair rental value of the property, and the property has an adjusted basis of more than $150,000, an allocation based on relative fair rental values must be made. The portion of total adjusted basis of such property that is deemed to be used in the thrift's business shall be equal to the total adjusted basis of the property multiplied by a fraction, the numerator of which is the fair rental value of the portion used as the principal or branch office, and the denominator of which is the total fair rental value of the property.

If the property that is rented to others is not real property used or to be used as the principal or branch office of the thrift, the entire property shall be considered used in the thrift's business if the fair rental value of the rented portion constitutes less than 15 percent of the total rental value of the property. If the rented portion constitutes 15 percent or more of the fair rental value, an

---

[364] Reg. §§301.7701-13A(c)(3)(i)(a), (c)(3)(i)(e), (e)(1), and (e)(11).

[365] Reg. §301.7701-13A(c)(3)(i)(f).

[366] Reg. §301.7701-13A(c)(3)(i)(c).

[367] Reg. §301.7701-13A(e)(11)(i).

[368] Reg. §301.7701-13A(e)(11)(ii).

allocation based on fair rental values is required to determine to what extent the property is used in the thrift's business.

Example: Bank H has $1,000,000 gross income consisting of the following items:

1. $150,000 interest and dividends on cash;
2. $180,000 income from loans;
3. $150,000 gain from exchange of a government obligation;
4. $150,000 income attributable to business property;
5. $150,000 income attributable to property acquired at foreclosure; and
6. $220,000 other income.

Because 78 percent ($780,000 ÷ $1,000,000) of gross income is attributable to Items 1 through 5 above, the association's business is considered to consist principally of "investing."

(ii) Exceptional Circumstances Exception. Excluded from the computation of total gross income and from the five categories of gross income listed above is any gross income that arises out of transactions "necessitated by exceptional circumstances and which are not undertaken as recurring business activities for profit."[369]

The IRS has ruled that "exceptional circumstances" were present when a savings and loan association triggered $7 million in deferred fee income, due to the mechanical operation of the loan liquidation method of accounting, by contributing the loans to the capital of a subsidiary.[370] Because the contribution to its subsidiary was made during a short taxable period, the loan fee income of the savings and loan association constituted 90 percent of the association's gross income for the period. This exceeded the 20 percent limitation contained in Regulation section 301.7701-13A(c)(3)(i)(d). Under that Regulation, income from "other loan transactions" will be taken into account for purpose of the 75 percent test so long as that income is not in excess of 20 percent of the association's gross income. Because an "exceptional circumstance" was found to exist, the association's gross income was computed without regard to the deferred fee income that was triggered by the contribution to capital. The IRS noted that if a short-period return had not been required, 97 percent of the association's gross income would have been qualifying income.

It also has been held that a savings and loan association that acted as a conduit for a mortgage lender, deriving more than 50 percent of its gross income from fees for making "brokered" mortgage loans, did not qualify as a bank for tax purposes.[371] Similarly, because an association's real estate investments be-

---

369 Reg. § 301.7701-13A(c)(3)(ii).

370 The loan liquidation method is described in Rev. Rul. 64-278, 1964-2 C.B. 120. It has been modified by Treasury regulations under the O.I.D. sections of the I.R.C. *See* Rev. Procs. 94-28, 29 and 30 discussed in Ch. 3.

371 *Permanent Savings & Loan Association v. United States*, 77-2 U.S.T.C. ¶ 9625, 439 F. Supp. 917 (S.D. Ohio 1977).

came so extensive that its method of operation was comparable to that of a real estate corporation, it did not meet the definition of a bank for tax purposes.[372]

§ 1.7.7 Asset Test

To pass the asset test at least 60 percent of a thrift's assets must consist of Code section 7701(a)(19)(C) assets. These are often referred to as *qualifying assets.*[373]

The percentage of total assets is computed as of the close of the taxable year or it may be computed on the basis of a monthly, quarterly, or semi-annual average of the assets outstanding during the taxable year. The choice of averaging is not a method of accounting, but it must be applied uniformly for the taxable year to all categories of assets. It may be changed from year to year.

Code section 7701(a)(19)(C) assets consist of:

1. Cash on hand, time and demand deposits with other financial institutions, and withdrawable accounts in other financial institutions;[374]
2. Federal and state taxable government obligations but not municipal obligations exempt under Code section 103;[375]
3. Deposit in and other securities of state deposit insurance funds;[376]
4. Five types of loans:
   (a) Loans secured by deposit, withdrawable share savings account, or shares of a member, for which a deduction is allowable under Code section 591 for a distribution;[377]

   (b) Loans secured by interest in church or residential real property, including multiple family dwellings and facilities in residential developments dedicated to public use, but not including mobile homes used on a transient basis. If the structure securing the loan is partially used for nonresidential purposes, the entire loan will be deemed a residential real property loan if the planned residential use exceeds 80 percent of the property's planned use. Moreover, if the loan is made to finance the acquisition or development of land, it shall be a loan secured by an interest in residential real property if there is a reasonable assurance that the property will be residential real property within a three-year period from the date of acquisition of the land, but only if within the three-year period the land becomes residential real property;[378]

   (c) Loans secured by real property located within an urban renewal area to be developed for predominately residential use;[379]

---

[372] *Guaranty Employees Association, Inc. v. United States*, 57-1 U.S.T.C. ¶9336, 241 F.2d 565 (5th Cir. 1957).

[373] Reg. § 301.7701-13A(d). With few exceptions these are the same assets the income from which will qualify in the 75 percent "investing in loans" test, discussed below.

[374] Reg. § 301.7701-13A(e)(1).

[375] Reg. § 301.7701-13A(e)(2).

[376] Reg. § 301.7701-13A(e)(3).

[377] Reg. § 301.7701-13A(e).

[378] Reg. §§ 301.7701-13A(e)(5) and (6).

[379] Reg. §§ 301.7701-13A(e)(5) and (7).

(d) Loans secured by an interest in educational, health or welfare institutions or facilities including structures used for students, residents and persons under care, employee or staff housing;[380] and

(e) Loans made for the payment of college or vocational training;[381]

5. Two types of "property:"

(a) Property acquired through liquidation of defaulted loans other than loans secured by deposits or loans for the payment of college or vocational training;[382] and

(b) Property used by the association in the conduct of its business of acquiring savings and investing in loans;[383] and

6. Any regular or residential interest in a REMIC, but only in the proportion which the assets of the REMIC consist of loans and property described above; except that if 95 percent or more of the assets of the REMIC are assets described above, the entire interest in the REMIC shall qualify.[384]

§ 1.7.8 Regulatory Definition Contrasted

There are sufficient differences between the regulatory and the tax definitions of a thrift, which could result in an entity meeting the regulatory definition but not the tax definition. For instance, a savings association passes the QTL Test if: (a) "Qualified Thrift Investments" equal or exceed 65 percent of the savings association's portfolio assets, and (b) the association's qualified thrift investments continue to equal or exceed that percentage on a monthly average basis in nine out of every 12 months. As mentioned above, the tax test is multi-pronged: there is a supervisory, a business operations, and an asset component. The asset test requires that at least 60 percent of the total assets of the entity consist of assets listed in the Code and in Regulations.[385]

Both the percentage and the types of assets or investments vary for regulatory and tax purposes. For example, QTL investments include loans to small businesses, qualified Federal Home Loan Bank stock, certain service corporation

[380] Reg. § § 301.7701-13A(e)(5) and (8).

[381] Reg. § § 301.7701-13A(e)(5) and (10).

[382] Reg. § 301.7701-13A(e)(9).

[383] Reg. § 301.7701-13A(e)(11). *See* discussion of property used in the conduct of the association's business, above, under "Investing in Loans" for additional detail on this property.

[384] Reference to I.R.C. § 7701(a)(19) assets is made in I.R.C. § 593 and is used for purposes of qualifying an entity for the favorable loan loss deduction rules of that section. I.R.C. § 593(a)(2). In PLR 8715011, January 5, 1987, the ownership of stock in a cooperative housing corporation entitled the stockholder to occupy the cooperative apartment for dwelling purposes pursuant to a proprietary lease. As a result, loans secured by stock in a cooperative housing corporation constituted loans secured by an interest in residential real property for purposes of I.R.C. § 7701(a)(19)(C)(v). Furthermore, because the aforementioned section is construed as specifically including single as well as multi-family dwellings in its definition of residential real property, a cooperative apartment, as well as a single-family dwelling, falls within the category of residential real property as that term is used in the section. Thus, loans made by the taxpayer for the purpose of cooperative apartments and secured by the apartment owner's stock in the cooperative housing corporation constitute loans secured by an interest in residential real property. A collateralized mortgage obligation is not a qualified asset but an investment in a REMIC is a qualified asset.

[385] I.R.C. § 7701(a)(19)(C); Reg. § 301.7701-13A (d).

stock, and so on, but such investments are not included among qualified assets for purposes of the tax test.[386]

Further, an institution may temporarily violate the QTL Test but remain a thrift for regulatory purposes because of a forgiveness provision in banking law.[387] No such flexibility appears to be present in the Code or Regulations.

§1.7.9 Quick Reference Table

The following table summarizes the types of assets that meet the Code section 7701(a)(19) asset test and compares them to the assets that meet the QTL test and that constitute qualifying assets for purposes of the Code section 593 loan loss computation. Qualifying assets are discussed in detail in Chapter 11.

Type of Asset	*§7701*	*§1467*	*§593*
Cash	Y	N	N
Federal and state government taxable obligations	Y	N	N
Deposits in, and obligations of, state deposit insurance funds	Y	N	N
Obligations of deposit in federal insurance agencies	N	Y	N
Loans secured by deposit	Y	N	N
Loans secured by an interest in improved residential real property or residential property to be improved out of the proceeds	Y	L	Y
Mortgage-backed securities	N	Y	N
Home Equity Loans	L	Y	Y
Loans made, purchased, refinanced to construct, improve, etc., residential housing	Y	Y	Y
Loans secured by interest in residential or church real property including some portion of property with non-residential use	Y	L	Y
Loans secured by real property located within urban renewal areas for predominately residential use	Y	L	Y
Loans secured by an interest in educational, health or welfare institutions, including structures used for housing	Y	L	Y
Loans for personal, family, household or educational purposes	N	Y	N
Loans for college or vocational training	Y	L	N
Property acquired through liquidation of defaulted loans not including loans for college or vocational training or loans secured by deposits	Y	N	N
Property used by the association in the conduct of its business	Y	N	N
Any regular or residential interest in REMIC	Y	N	L
Federal Home Loan Bank stock	N	Y	N
Certain service corporation capital stock or obligations	N	L	N

L = This type of asset may be included to satisfy the test subject to various conditions and limitations as set forth in the statute.

N = This type of asset is not included to satisfy the test.

Y = This type of asset is included to satisfy the test.

[386] Moreover, a collateralized mortgage obligation is not a qualified asset for tax purposes, but it is for purposes of the QTL Test.

[387] 12 U.S.C. §1467(a)(m) (1989).

Chapter 2
Interest, Fee, and Other Income

Contents

§ 2.1 Tax Planning Suggestions
§ 2.2 General Accounting Rules
  § 2.2.1 Overall Methods of Accounting
  § 2.2.2 Requirements for Acceptable Accounting Methods
  § 2.2.3 Change in Accounting Method
  § 2.2.4 Accounting for Different Businesses
§ 2.3 Allocation of Receipts
§ 2.4 Interest Income
§ 2.5 Tax-Exempt Interest
  § 2.5.1 Private Activity Bonds
  § 2.5.2 Fire Department Loans
  § 2.5.3 ESOP Loans
§ 2.6 Accruing Interest Income
  § 2.6.1 Rule of 78s Method
  § 2.6.2 Liquidation, Actuarial, Composite Methods
§ 2.7 Service Fee Income
  § 2.7.1 Service Fee Income v. Interest Income
  § 2.7.2 When to Include Service Fee Income
  § 2.7.3 Credit Card Annual Fees
  § 2.7.4 Mortgage Servicing Fees
  § 2.7.5 Affinity Cards
  § 2.7.6 Gift Cards
§ 2.8 Other Income
  § 2.8.1 Commitment Fees
  § 2.8.2 Commissions on Loans
  § 2.8.3 Commissions on Purchase or Sale of Securities
§ 2.9 Repurchase Agreements
  § 2.9.1 Overview of Tax Treatment
  § 2.9.2 Sale vs. Loan
§ 2.10 Mortgage Backed Securities
  § 2.10.1 Types of Mortgage Backed Securities
  § 2.10.2 Tax Treatment of CMO and Other Pass-Through Transactions
  § 2.10.3 REMICs
  § 2.10.4 REITs
§ 2.11 Asset Backed Securities
  § 2.11.1 FASITs
§ 2.12 Hedging Transactions
  § 2.12.1 The Volcker Rule
  § 2.12.2 Definition of Notional Principal Contracts
  § 2.12.3 Accounting for Notional Principal Contracts
  § 2.12.4 Periodic Payments, Termination Payments and Nonperiodic Payments

§2.12.5 Swaps
§2.12.6 Caps and Floors
§2.12.7 Currency Gains or Losses
§2.13 Premature Withdrawal Penalties
§2.14 FHLB Distributions
§2.14.1 The FHLB System
§2.14.2 FHLB Stock Dividends
§2.14.3 FHLB of Redemptions
§2.14.4 Tax Basis

§2.1 Tax Planning Suggestions

The timing of income recognition from financial transactions may vary depending upon whether an item is properly characterized as interest income, as fee income, or as some other type of income.[1] Neither the label that is placed on an item nor the book accounting treatment will be controlling for tax purposes. Instead, it will be the substance of the transaction that will be controlling.

Special accounting methods may be mandated by the Code or by the IRS for certain financial products or services. For example, the IRS has issued pronouncements that constrain or mandate the choice of accounting method for certain installment loans, including loans that have been accounted for under the Rule of 78s method, certain credit card fees, and points.

Mortgage service fee income will be treated as fee income or possibly as gain from the sale of property depending upon several factors, including the reasonableness of the amount charged for services and whether the loans sold had an above market interest rate. Various loan origination fees, late payment fees, overdraft fees, and other payments incident to a lending transaction may properly be characterized as prepaid interest income, thereby creating O.I.D. that must be deferred.[2]

Taxpayers who pool credit card receivables are required, in accordance with statutory original issue discount rules, to accelerate into income grace period interest based on a reasonable assumption regarding the timing of the payments by the obligors of the receivables.

In general, the tax accounting for an item, once established, may not be changed without the Commissioner's permission. Thus, general ledger accounts must be monitored to ensure that the tax accounting for an item is not inadvertently changed because of a change in book accounting without first receiving consent from the Commissioner. Furthermore, if a bank expects to have an adjustment to an accounting method made when the bank comes under audit, it is critical to determine whether it is advisable to request an accounting method change under Revenue Procedure 2011-14, which contains incentives to en-

[1] *See The Art of Tax Efficiency in Community Banks*, by M. Gula, J. Brew, and R. Blasi, 2007, Red Room Publishing, *http://www.mraeresources.com/bookstore/*.

[2] *See* Chapter 3 for a discussion of the O.I.D. rules.

courage voluntary compliance with proper tax accounting principles. If this is done, audit protection is received for years preceding the method change year.[3]

§2.2 General Accounting Rules

§2.2.1 Overall Methods of Accounting

Code section 446(c) generally allows a taxpayer to select the method of accounting it will use to compute its taxable income. The IRS has issued pronouncements that permit advantageous accounting methods for various financial products and services. As a general rule, the method of accounting used by the taxpayer to compute income for financial accounting purposes shall be used to compute income for tax purposes.[4] A taxpayer's accounting methods will be its overall method of accounting and its accounting treatment of any item.[5]

The Tax Court has held that late fees are a separate and distinct item of income because they are earned for reasons independent of the reasons other types of income from credit cards are earned, such as finance charges, over-the-limit fees, interchange fees, and cash advance fees. Thus, late-fee income, and other credit card receivable income, are "items" themselves and not components of the "item" of interest. Consequently, a taxpayer may not change its method of accounting for any of these "components" of interest without first receiving consent from the Commissioner.[6]

A taxpayer is entitled to adopt any one of the permissible methods for each separate trade or business, including the cash method and an accrual method, subject to certain restrictions. Code section 446(b) provides that the selected method must clearly reflect income. In addition, Regulation section 1.446-1(c)(2)(i) requires that a taxpayer use an accrual method with regard to purchases and sales of merchandise whenever Code section 471 requires the taxpayer to account for inventories, unless otherwise authorized by the Commissioner under Regulation section 1.446-1(c)(2)(ii). Under Regulation section 1.446-1(c)(2)(ii), the Commissioner has the authority to permit a taxpayer to use a method of accounting that clearly reflects income even though the method is not specifically authorized by the regulations.

Code section 446(c) provides that any one of the following may be adopted as an overall accounting method:

1. The cash receipts and disbursements method;
2. An accrual method;
3. Any other method permitted by the Code; or
4. Any combination of the foregoing methods (a hybrid method) permitted under the regulations.[7]

---

[3] Rev. Proc. 2011-14, 2011-4 I.R.B 330. This revenue procedure amplifies, clarifies, modifies, and supersedes Rev. Proc. 2008-52, 2008-2 C.B. 587, as amplified, clarified, and modified by Rev. Proc. 2009-39, 2009-38 I.R.B. 371, and provides additional changes in methods of accounting for which a taxpayer may obtain automatic consent.

[4] I.R.C. §446(a); Reg. §1.446-1(a).

[5] Reg. §1.446-1(a).

[6] *Capital One Financial Corporation and Subsidiaries v. Commissioner*, 130 TC 147, May 22, 2008.

[7] Early in the development of the U.S. income tax system, only two methods were acceptable. In *Ap-*

Most banks are prohibited, by amendments to tax accounting rules made by the Tax Reform Act of 1986,[8] from employing the cash receipts and disbursements method of accounting.[9] Moreover, with respect to purchases and sales of items in a bank's securities inventory, the accrual method must be used even though the bank may be permitted to account for interest income on the cash basis.[10] S corporations, or subsidiaries of S corporations for which an election is in effect to treat the subsidiary as a qualified subchapter S subsidiary, are not required to use the accrual method.

(a) *Cash Method*

The Tax Reform Act of 1986 added section 448 to the Code, which provides for taxable years beginning after December 31, 1986, that for C corporations, as well as for certain partnerships and tax shelters, taxable income may not, with limited exceptions, be computed under the cash receipts and disbursements method of accounting. Exceptions are provided in two situations:

1. If for any prior taxable year beginning after December 31, 1985, the average annual gross receipts for the three-year period ending with such prior taxable year are equal to or less than $5,000,000;[11] and
2. If a loan, a lease, or any transaction with a related party was entered into on or before September 25, 1985, and an election was made to employ the cash receipts and disbursements method of accounting.[12]

Any change from the cash method mandated by Code section 448 will be treated as a change in a method of accounting that is initiated by the taxpayer with the consent of the Secretary of the Treasury.[13] Code section 481 adjustments that may be necessitated by the change must be taken into account over a period not to exceed four years.[14]

The cash receipts and disbursements method of accounting requires all items that constitute gross income, whether in the form of cash, property or services, to be included in income for the taxable year in which they are actually or constructively received. Similarly, expenses are deductible when paid.[15] Congress occa-

(Footnote Continued)

peal of Chatham & Phoenix National Bank, 1 B.T.A. 460, Dec. 174 (1925), it was stated: In income taxation there are two recognized methods of accounting employed to reflect income: one called the cash receipts and disbursement basis in which income is reported when either actually or constructively received and the other known as the accrual basis, in which income is reported when due, in the sense of owing, although it may be payable in the future. Early cases discussing accounting methods should be read in light of this judicial perception.

[8] I.R.C. § 448; Tax Reform Act of 1986, Pub. L No. 99-514, 100 Stat. 2085 (1986). *See* exception for taxpayers with average gross receipts not in excess of $10,000,000. Notice 2001-76, 2001-2 C.B. 613, December 10, 2001.

[9] *See* discussion of exception for S corporations in Ch. 1.

[10] Reg. § 1.446-1(c)(1)(iv)(b)(2); *see also* Rev. Rul. 74-280, 1974-1 C.B. 121.

[11] I.R.C. § 448(c)(1).

[12] Tax Reform Act of 1986, Pub. L. No. 99-514; § 801(d)(2)-(4), as amended by Pub. L. No. 100-647, § 1008(a)(5)-(6). This election may be made on a loan-by-loan or lease-by-lease basis.

[13] Reg. § 1.448-1(g); Rev. Proc. 99-49, 1999-52 I.R.B. 725, *modifying and superseding,* Rev. Proc. 98-60, 1998-2 C.B. 761.

[14] I.R.C. § 448(d)(7).

[15] Reg. § 1.446-1(c)(1)(I). *See also* Rev. Rul. 63-57, 1963-1 C.B. 103 which permits a cash method taxpayer to defer interest recognition when the parties to the lending agreement designate that all payments are first applied to principal.

sionally overrides this general rule and requires cash method taxpayers to include items in income under the accrual method. This has been done for cash method banks with respect to short-term obligations,[16] original issue discount generally,[17] and to gain or loss on a securities dealer's portfolio.[18] Other provisions of the Code or regulations applicable to cash method taxpayers may change these general rules; for example, Code section 263 (requiring the capitalization of expenses paid out for a new building or for permanent improvements or betterments made to increase the value of any property or estate, or for restoring property or making good the exhaustion of property for which an allowance is or has been made); Code section 263A (requiring capitalization of direct and allocable indirect costs of real or tangible personal property produced by a taxpayer or real or personal property that is acquired by a taxpayer for resale); and Code section 460 (requiring the use of the percentage-of-completion method for certain long-term contracts).

In Notice 2001-76, the IRS expanded the availability of the cash method of accounting.[19] The Notice applies to a "qualifying small business taxpayer," which is defined as any taxpayer with "average annual gross receipts" of more than $1,000,000, but less than or equal to $10,000,000, that is not prohibited from using the cash method under Code section 448.[20] For taxable years ending on or after December 31, 2001, a qualifying small business taxpayer that reasonably determines that its principal business activity (*i.e.*, the activity from which the taxpayer derived the largest percentage of its gross receipts) for its prior taxable year is described in a North American Industry Classification System ("NAICS") code, other than one of the ineligible codes listed in the Notice, may use the cash method for all of its trades or business.[21] None of the ineligible codes would appear to exclude a bank from use of the cash method of accounting.

---

[16] *See, e.g.*, I.R.C. § 1281.

[17] I.R.C. § 1272 *et seq.*; Reg. § 1.446-2(a)(2). *See* discussion in Ch. 3.

[18] I.R.C. § 475.

[19] 2001-2 C.B. 613. In Notice 2002-14, 2002-1 C.B. 548 & 2002-1 C.B. 327, the IRS stated that any qualifying small business taxpayer within the scope of the proposed revenue procedure may change to the cash method of accounting with respect to its eligible trades or businesses for any taxable year ending on or after December 31, 2001. Pending publication of a final revenue procedure in the Internal Revenue Bulletin, a small business taxpayer may obtain automatic consent to change to the cash method and the materials and supplies method by complying with the procedures provided in the proposed revenue procedure. These procedures state that a small business taxpayer may change to the cash method and the materials and supplies method for any taxable year ending on or after December 31, 2001, by attaching the original Form 3115, Application for Change in Accounting Method, to its timely filed (including extensions) federal income tax return for that year (or on an amended return filed within six months of the original due date of the return), filing a duplicate of the Form 3115 with the Internal Revenue Service's National Office, and complying with the provisions of Rev. Proc. 2002-9, 2002-3 I.R.B. 327, as modified by the proposed revenue procedure. Both changes may be made on a single Form 3115. A taxpayer that has fully complied with these procedures has obtained the consent of the Commissioner under I.R.C. § 446(e) to change its method of accounting to these methods. Rev. Proc. 2002-9 has been modified and superseded. *See* Rev. Proc. 2011-14, 2011-4 I.R.B. 330.

[20] Although this Notice does not apply to a taxpayer with average annual gross receipts of $1,000,000 or less, such taxpayer generally is allowed to use the cash method pursuant to Rev. Proc. 2001-10, 2001-1 C.B. 272.

[21] However, the Notice states that the IRS will not challenge a taxpayer's use of the cash method under § 446, or a taxpayer's failure to account for inventories under I.R.C. 471, for a trade or business in an earlier year if the taxpayer, for that year, was a qualifying small business taxpayer as described in section 3 of the Notice and the taxpayer was eligible to use the cash method for such trade or business under section 4.01 of the Notice.

A taxpayer has average annual gross receipts of $10,000,000 or less if, for each prior taxable year ending on or after December 31, 2000, the taxpayer's average annual gross receipts for the three-taxable-year period ending with the applicable prior taxable year does not exceed $10,000,000. Gross receipts is defined consistent with Temporary regulation section 1.448-1T(f)(2)(iv). Thus, gross receipts for a taxable year equal all receipts derived from all of a taxpayer's trades or businesses that must be recognized under the method of accounting actually used by the taxpayer for that taxable year for federal income tax purposes. For example, gross receipts include total sales (net of returns and allowances) and all amounts received from services, interest, dividends, and rents. However, gross receipts do not include amounts received by the taxpayer with respect to sales tax or other similar state and local taxes if, under the applicable state or local law, the tax is legally imposed on the purchaser of the good or service and the taxpayer merely collects and remits the tax to the taxing authority.[22]

A qualifying small business taxpayer that wants to use the cash method as described in Notice 2001-76 for an eligible trade or business must follow the automatic change in accounting method provisions of Revenue Procedure 2002-9 with the certain modifications.[23] The net amount of the Code section 481(a) adjustment must take into account both increases and decreases in the applicable account balances such as accounts receivable, accounts payable, and inventory.

(b) *Accrual Method*

Under the accrual method, the "all-events" test controls income inclusion.[24] Accordingly, interest is taxable when all the events have occurred that establish the right to receive the income and the amount thereof can be determined with reasonable accuracy.

The "all-events" test is a judicially crafted test.[25] Congress has set it aside in a variety of situations, including the inventory mark-to-market rules and original issue discount rules, as well as other statutory provisions dealing with income recognition predicated on the time value of money. All events that fix the right to receive income occur when: (1) the required performance occurs; (2) payment is due; or (3) payment is made, whichever happens earliest.[26] Thus, a taxpayer was not permitted to recognize income on loans that was neither received nor earned.[27]

Although expenses generally are deductible when incurred, taxpayers using the accrual method of accounting may not deduct items of expense prior to the time of economic performance.[28] Economic performance occurs when the goods,

---

[22] *See also* I.R.C. § 448(c)(3)(C).

[23] Rev. Proc. 2002-9, 2002-1 C.B. 272, January 22, 2002.

[24] Reg. § 1.446-1(c)(1)(ii); Reg. § 1.451-1(a).

[25] *Spring City Foundry Co. v. Commissioner*, 292 U.S. 182 (1934).

[26] Rev. Rul. 77-135, 1977-1 C.B. 133.

[27] *National Bank of Fort Benning v. United States*, 79-2 U.S.T.C. ¶ 9627; 1979 WL 1466 (M.D. Ga. 1979).

[28] I.R.C. § 461(h). Proposed regulations under I.R.C. § 446 explicitly include reference to the requirement that economic performance occur before an item may be deducted. Reg. § 1.446-1(c)(1)(ii)(A) provides: "[A] liability is incurred, and generally is taken into account for federal income tax purposes, in the taxable year in which all the events have

services, or payments due under the taxpayer's liability are provided. For example, a calendar-year, accrual method bank could not accrue on December 31 the semiannual assessment that the bank was required to pay to the Comptroller of the Currency on or before January 31 for the six-month period beginning January 1 because all the events that determine the fact of the liability had not occurred as of December 31.[29] A taxpayer, using the accrual method of accounting, must accrue an item in the year in which the taxpayer acquires a fixed and unconditional right to receive the amount, even though actual payment is deferred. Therefore, when there is an "unreasonable uncertainty" as to whether the taxpayer will receive an amount, accrual of such income is not required.[30]

The economic performance rule is waived for any item in those very few situations "for which a deduction is allowable under a provision which specifically provides for a deduction for a reserve for estimated expenses."[31] Thus, those banks permitted to use the reserve method of accounting for bad debts do not run afoul of the economic performance rule when they deduct a reasonable reserve addition.[32]

(c) *Hybrid Method*

A combination of the cash and accrual methods is referred to as a "hybrid method." Where, pursuant to the regulations of a bank regulatory agency, the accrual method is employed for discount income and interest expense, but the cash method is required for rents and collection fee income as well as for other items, the bank is using an acceptable hybrid method.[33] The repeal of the cash receipts and disbursements method by the Tax Reform Act of 1986 for most banks, effective for tax years beginning after 1986, all but eliminates the availability of the hybrid method as an overall method.

A hybrid method will not be acceptable if it fails to clearly reflect income.[34] Thus, the Sixth Circuit Court of Appeals disallowed a claim for refund computed using the cash method where the taxpayer failed to establish that the hybrid method of accounting historically used by the taxpayer clearly reflected income.[35] Similarly, the IRS ruled that a bank used an impermissible accounting method when it employed the accrual method for all items of income and expense, except that the cash method was used to account for interest income from commercial and mortgage loans.[36] A taxpayer who uses the accrual method in computing

(Footnote Continued)

occurred that establish the fact of the liability, the amount of the liability can be determined with reasonable accuracy, and economic performance has occurred with respect to the liability." Prior to the proposed amendment, there was no requirement in the regulations that economic performance occur in order for an amount to be incurred by a taxpayer using an accrual method of accounting. *See also Helvering v. Enright's Estate*, 41-1 U.S.T.C. ¶9356, 312 U.S. 636 (1941); Reg. § 1.446-1(c)(1)(ii). *See* discussion of economic performance rule in Ch. 8.

[29] Rev. Rul. 80-230, 1980-2 C.B. 169.

[30] *San Francisco Stevedoring Co. v. Commissioner*, 8 T.C. 222 (1947).

[31] I.R.C. § 461(h)(5).

[32] An exception also is provided for "recurring items." I.R.C. § 461(h)(3). Reg. § 1.461-5 provides that the exception does not apply to the accrual of liabilities to pay interest.

[33] *Appeal of Bank of Hartsville*, 1 B.T.A. 920, Dec. 336 (1925); *Appeal of Madison & Kedzie State Bank*, 1 B.T.A. 922, Dec. 337 (1925).

[34] Reg. § 1.446-1(c)(1)(iv).

[35] *Schram v. United States*, 41-1 U.S.T.C. ¶9290, 118 F.2d 541 (6th Cir. 1941).

[36] Rev. Rul. 86-35, 1986-1 C.B. 218.

business expenses must use the accrual method in computing items affecting gross income in the same business. Similarly, a taxpayer who uses the cash method in computing gross income must use the same method in computing the expenses of such business.

(d) ***Other Methods***

The Code permits or mandates methods of accounting for individual items of income and expense. For example, original issue discount is generally accrued into income using the constant yield method "regardless of the holder's regular method of accounting."[37] Recoveries of bad debts realized by a bank using the reserve method of accounting must be credited to a reserve account,[38] and interest income on certain installment loans may be accounted for using the Rule of 78s Method.[39] Each of the special accounting methods applicable to banks is hereinafter discussed.

(e) ***CAP Loans***

The IRS succeeded in requiring current inclusion of income where payments to a bank were refundable regardless of whether the period of proration (accrual) was definite or indefinite. In an IRS Coordinated Issue Paper, IRS examining agents were advised that amounts received on so-called CAP loans were immediately includible in income on the theory that the amounts were either prepaid income or interest income (considered current income), which was subject to a risk of forfeiture.[40]

A CAP loan is one in which the borrower is required to make payments to the lending bank based on a floating rate. However, the borrower's liability for interest is based on a fixed rate negotiated when the funds are advanced. When payments exceed the borrower's liability the bank refunds to the borrower the excess amount at the maturity of the loan.

The IRS's position appears to be founded, at least in part, on the claim of right doctrine. This doctrine was first described by the U.S. Supreme Count, as follows:[41]

> If a taxpayer receives earnings under a claim of right and without restriction as to its disposition, he has received income which he is required to return (report on a tax return), even though it may still be claimed that he is not

[37] Reg. § 1.446-2; Reg. § 1.1272-1(a); I.R.C. § 1272. Exceptions are provided for *de minimis* amounts.

[38] I.R.C. §§ 585 and 593. This provision may be qualified by the tax benefit rule contained in I.R.C. 111. *See* discussion of the reserve method of accounting in Ch. 10.

[39] Rev. Rul. 83-84, 1983-1 C.B. 97.

[40] *See* IRS Industry Specialization Program Coordinated Issues Paper on Cap Loans at A.1 and on Deferred Loan Fees at A.3 and A.4; *Schlude v. Commissioner*, 62-1 U.S.T.C. ¶ 9137, 296 F.2d 721 (8th Cir. 1962), *aff'g*, 32 T.C. 1271 (1959). *See also* Rev. Rul. 60-85, 1960-1 C.B. 181, *as modified by* Rev. Rul. 71-299, 1971-2 C.B. 218. Rev. Rul. 66-347, 1966-2 C.B. 196; *Corliss v. Bowers*, 2 U.S.T.C. ¶ 525, 281 U.S. 376 (1930); *Brown v. Helvering*, 4 U.S.T.C. ¶ 1223, 291 U.S. 193 (1934).

[41] *North American Oil Consolidated v. Burnet*, 3 U.S.T.C. ¶ 943, 286 U.S. 417 (1932). *Cf.* I.R.C. § 83's reluctance to include an item in income that is subject to "a substantial risk of forfeiture." *See also* Rev. Rul. 66-49, 1966-1 C.B. 36, in which the IRS ruled that an accrual basis bank's earnings on Federal Savings and Loan Insurance Corporation (FSLIC) premiums are not includible in income until the earnings are not available for losses of the FSLIC. A cash basis bank would be required to include such earnings in income when they are applied to satisfy its obligations or when they become available to the institution without substantial restriction or limitation.

> entitled to retain the money, and even though he may still be adjudged liable to restore its equivalent.[42]

The scope of this doctrine and whether it properly applies in the CAP loan situation is unclear. The IRS has recently taken the position that it does not apply to prepaid interest.[43] Moreover, if, as some have argued, it is a rule concerned only with the timing of income inclusion, its application is doubtful.[44] But, if the rule can be employed to determine *whether* an item is income, it would constitute judicial support for the IRS's position.[45]

The Seventh Circuit Court of Appeals has decided the issue in favor of the IRS.[46] The Court found that a bank's method of accounting for such floating rate loans did not clearly reflect income. Although borrowers were entitled to repayment of a portion of the payment, the "all-events" test was found to have been met with respect to the entire amount paid since all of the events necessary for the accrual of interest income had occurred. Any obligation to refund an excess payment was considered a contingent liability that had no bearing on the bank's right to accrue the income.

In *Morgan Guaranty Trust Co. of New York*,[47] another prepaid interest case, the Claims Court held that deferring income inclusion of prepaid interest did not constitute a distortion of income. In *Morgan*, the court reached the "inescapable" conclusion that no material distortion of income occurred when a bank accrues (defers) prepaid income. The court's holding rested primarily on three observations: (1) the amount of prepaid income was *de minimis;* (2) the accrual method was consistently used and was the taxpayer's overall method of accounting; and (3) the Federal Reserve Board required use of the accrual method. In addition, the court noted that a series of insurance company cases cited by the government in support of its position contained a "critical difference"—the loan agreements in the insurance company cases all required prepayment of the interest as a condition of the loan. In *Morgan*, the prepayments were voluntarily made.[48]

§2.2.2 Requirements for Acceptable Accounting Methods

The choice of a method of accounting is subject to two requirements: the method must clearly reflect income, and it must conform to the method of accounting on the basis of which the taxpayer regularly computes his income in keeping his books.[49] However, the IRS recognizes that no uniform method of

---

[42] *Id.* at 423.

[43] CCA 200019041, March 3, 2000.

[44] *James v. United States*, 61-1 U.S.T.C. ¶9449, 366 U.S. 213 (1961). *See also* Lister, *The Use and Abuse of Pragmatism: The Judicial Doctrine of Claim of Right*, 121 Tax L. Rev. 263 (1966).

[45] *Commissioner v. Wilcox*, 46-1 U.S.T.C. ¶9188, 327 U.S. 404 (1946); *James v. United States id.; see also* Mullock, *The Claim of Right Rule: A Postscript to a Footnote*, 47 Taxes 54 (1969); Dubroff, *The Claim of Right Doctrine*, 40 Tax L. Rev. 729, 732 (1985).

[46] *Continental Illinois v. Commissioner*, 998 F.2d 513 (7th Cir. 1993), *cert. denied* 510 U.S. 1041 (1994).

[47] *Morgan Guaranty Trust Company of New York v. United States*, 78-2 U.S.T.C. ¶9753, 585 F.2d 988 (Ct.Cl. 1978).

[48] *See also* Notice 89-21, 1989-1 C.B. 651, in which the IRS took the position that lump-sum payments with respect to notional principal contracts that require future payments must be taken into income over the life of the contract. *See also*, Reg. §1.446-3.

[49] I.R.C. §446(a); Reg. §1.446-1(a).

accounting can be prescribed for all taxpayers and that "[e]ach taxpayer shall adopt such forms and systems as are, in his judgment, best suited to his needs."[50]

(a) *Clear Reflection of Income*

Although the phrase "clearly reflect income" is not defined in the Code, attempts at defining it have been made by the courts and the IRS. The Second Circuit Court of Appeals has stated that to clearly reflect income means "that income should be reflected with as much accuracy as standard methods of accounting practice permit."[51] In determining whether income is clearly reflected under a taxpayer's accounting method, the IRS is given broad discretion. The IRS's determination as to whether income is clearly reflected is unreasonable only if the taxpayer proves an abuse of discretion.[52] If a taxpayer contends that the IRS has abused its discretion, the taxpayer carries the very heavy burden of proving that there is not an adequate basis in law for the IRS's position.[53]

In *Barnett Banks of Florida, Inc.*[54] and in *Bank of Kirksville,*[55] two banks were found to have carried this burden. In the former, the taxpayer argued successfully before the Tax Court that it was entitled to defer credit card service fee income, and in the latter, the taxpayer was permitted by a federal district court to discontinue accrual of interest and to deduct certain debts charged off on its books.[56]

(b) *Conformity With Accounting Rules*

Proof that a taxpayer's method of accounting is in accordance with generally accepted accounting principles does not establish that the method clearly reflects income under the income tax laws.[57] For example, Statement of Financial Accounting Standards No. 91 requires deferral of loan origination fee income. It does not distinguish between such fees that are interest and fees that are amounts actually received for services. The tax rule, as discussed below, does distinguish between these items. Thus, book/tax conformity, while a starting point for calculating taxable income, is frequently modified.

(c) *Conformity With Regulatory Rules*

Compulsory accounting practices imposed by regulatory or supervisory agencies do not necessarily dictate federal tax consequences, as these rules are not binding on the IRS. Accounting methods and practices prescribed by regula-

---

[50] Reg. §1.446-1(a)(2).

[51] *Caldwell v. Commissioner*, 53-1 U.S.T.C. ¶9218, 202 F.2d 112 (2d Cir. 1953). *See* IRS Coordinated Issue Paper: "Accrual vs. Cash/ Hybrid Accounting Method" published in *MSSP - Health-care Industry Audit Technique Guide*, in which the IRS prohibits the cash method for health care providers. The Coordinated Issue Paper contains a discussion of the standards it applies when examining the acceptability of a method of accounting.

[52] *Bank of Kirksville v. United States*, 943 F. Supp. 1191 (W.D. Md. 1996).

[53] *J.T. Bennett v. Commissioner*, 9 T.C.M. 72, Dec. 17,476(M) (1950); *Bradstreet Co. of Maine v. Commissioner*, 3 U.S.T.C. ¶1138, 65 F.2d 943 (1st Cir. 1933); *RCA Corp. v. United States*, 664 F.2d 881, 886 (2d Cir. 1981).

[54] *Barnett Banks of Florida, Inc. v. Commissioner*, 106 T.C. 103 (1996). *Cf, Signet Banking Corp. v. Commissioner*, 118 F.3d 239 (4th Cir. 1997) *aff'g*, 106 T.C. 117 (1996).

[55] *Bank of Kirksville v. United States*, 943 F. Supp. 1191 (W.D. Mo. 1996).

[56] These cases are discussed in detail in subsequent sections relating to the issues in question.

[57] *Thor Power Tool Company v. Commissioner*, 79-1 U.S.T.C. ¶9139, 439 U.S. 522 (1979).

tory agencies, like all other accounting practices, will not be accepted for federal tax purposes unless the method clearly reflects income.[58] This does not mean that the method prescribed by the agency is irrelevant and will be accorded no significance. The U.S. Supreme Court has commented that, where a taxpayer's generally accepted method of accounting is made compulsory by a regulatory agency *and* that method clearly reflects income, the method "is almost presumptively controlling of federal income tax consequences."[59] The Claims Court has stated, "[T]he Supreme Court has indicated that, when reviewing tax accounting questions, deference should be paid to accounting methods that a regulatory body or agency imposes upon a business enterprise."[60]

Thus, accounting strictures imposed by bank regulators are not necessarily adhered to for tax purposes, yet they are considered when determining whether a bank's accounting method clearly reflects income. Where the books of a bank are required by bank regulators to be kept on the accrual basis, the bank must continue the cash method for tax purposes unless and until permission to change is received from the IRS.[61] Similarly, where the primary federal regulator of thrifts required a cash basis savings and loan association to take loan fees into income over a period of years, for tax purposes the income was includible in income in the year received.[62] Additionally, where commercial bank regulators mandate the writedown of fixed assets and additional depreciation for book accounting purposes, the taxpayer was not permitted an automatic tax deduction.[63]

When accrual of an item of income differs for state law purposes from federal treatment, federal law prevails.[64] Whenever the book and the tax methods differ, permanent records must be maintained that reconcile the two.[65]

§2.2.3 Change in Accounting Method

Once a method of accounting is adopted for tax purposes, it may not be changed without actual or deemed consent having been received from the Commissioner.[66] Code section 446(e) and Regulation section 1.446-1(e) state that,

---

[58] *Commissioner v. Idaho Power Co.,* 418 U.S. 1 (1974).

[59] *Id.* at 15.

[60] *See Commissioner v. Idaho Power Co.,* 74-2 U.S.T.C. ¶9521, 418 U.S. 1 (1974); *Commissioner v. Standard Life & Accident Ins. Co.,* 77-2 U.S.T.C. ¶9480, 433 U.S. 148 (1977); *Morgan Guaranty Trust Co. of N.Y. v. United States,* 78-2 U.S.T.C. ¶9753, 585 F.2d 988 (Ct.Cl. 1978). In *NCNB Corp. v. United States,* 82-2 U.S.T.C. ¶9469, 684 F.2d 285 (4th Cir. 1982), the Fourth Circuit found that the required regulatory accounting policy was "presumptively controlling" for federal income tax purposes. 684 F.2d 285, 292.

[61] Rev. Rul. 68-83, 1968-1 C.B. 190. *Appeal of First National Bank of Kulm,* 4 B.T.A. 317, Dec. 1526 (1926). Note that national bank regulatory requirements mandate the accrual method for banks with assets in excess of $25 million. The rules of the Federal Home Loan Bank Board provide that insured institutions shall use the accrual basis of accounting to prepare and maintain their accounting records and/or to prepare their financial statements and reports to the corporation, except that this requirement shall not apply to insured institutions whose total assets do not exceed $10,000,000. 12 C.F.R. §563(c)(10)(b). *See also Merchants National Bank v. Commissioner,* 6 B.T.A. 1167, Dec. 2423 (1927).

[62] Rev. Rul. 68-220, 1968-1 C.B. 194.

[63] *Barretville Bank & Trust Company v. Commissioner,* 17 T.C.M. 749, Dec. 23,122(M) (1958), T.C.M. 1958-148; *Schuylkill Haven Trust Company v. United States,* 66-1 U.S.T.C. ¶9344, 252 F. Supp. 557 (E.D. Pa. 1966).

[64] *Roy Moody Bell v. Commissioner,* 12 T.C.M. 1321, Dec. 19,999(M) (1953).

[65] Reg. §1.446-1(a)(4); Rev. Rul. 68-83, 1968-1 C.B. 190; Rev. Rul. 74-383, 1974-2 C.B. 146.

[66] I.R.C. §446(e), Reg. §1.446-1(e), Rev. Proc. 97-27, 1997-1 C.B. 327, contains rules for inclusion of net negative or net positive I.R.C. §481 adjustments.

except as otherwise provided, a taxpayer must secure the consent of the Commissioner before changing a method of accounting for federal income tax purposes. Unless specifically authorized by the Commissioner, a taxpayer may not request, or otherwise make, a retroactive change in method of accounting, regardless of whether the change is from a permissible or an impermissible method.[67] Consent is normally requested by filing Form 3115 ("Application for Change in Accounting Method") during the year of change.[68]

When a Code section or its legislative history provides that a change is treated as made with consent, the taxpayer must still comply with I.R.S. procedures in order to effect the change. Thus, if the taxpayer does not file a timely Form 3115, automatic consent will not be granted. Similarly, at least one court has held that if the taxpayer files an incomplete or otherwise deficient Form 3115, automatic consent is not deemed to be granted.[69] The Form 3115 must specifically refer to the item of income for which a change is requested. Thus, by failing to mention late fees or to account for late fees as O.I.D. on its originally filed returns, the fact that permission was properly requested for other credit card fees did not allow the taxpayer to change its method of accounting for late fees.[70] Even if permission to change is granted, the taxpayer usually is required to make Code section 481 adjustments to avoid omission or duplication of income or expense.[71]

The Code section 446(e) consent requirement is intended to prevent distortions of income that usually accompany a change of accounting method and that could have an adverse effect upon revenue.[72] By doing so, consistency will lessen the Commissioner's burden of administering the Code[73] and secure uniformity in collection of revenue.[74] The Fourth Circuit stated that "[t]o allow such changes without the prior consent of the Commissioner would roil the administration of the tax laws, sending revenue projection and collection into a churning and unpredictable state. Belated attempts to change accounting methods 'would

(Footnote Continued)

Recognition of such items affect taxable income in the year of change and up to the fifth succeeding year, depending upon the type of adjustment. Rev. Proc. 2002-9, 2002-3 I.R.B. 327, contains procedures by which a taxpayer may obtain automatic consent to change accounting methods.

67 Rev. Rul. 90-38., 1990-1 C.B. 57.

68 *See* Reg. § 1.446-1T(e)(3)(i) for the year of change.

69 Reg. § 1.448-1(h)(4).

70 *Capital One Financial Corporation and Subsidiaries v. Commissioner*, 130 TC 147 (2009).

71 These adjustments are computed in accordance with I.R.C. § 481 and the regulations thereunder. Further, numerous judicial opinions have dealt with a bank's treatment of income and expense when a method of accounting is changed. *See Appeal of National Bank of New Jersey*, 1 B.T.A. 1238, Dec. 480 (1925) (loss of interest deduction); *Appeal of Chatham & Phenix National Bank*, 1 B.T.A. 460, Dec. 174 (1925) (Acq.) and *Chemung Canal Trust Company v. Commissioner*, 30 B.T.A. 230, Dec. 8489 (1934), *aff'd per curiam*, 74 F.2d 1009 (2d Cir. 1935), *cert. denied*, 295 U.S. 751 (double inclusion of interest); and *National Bank of South Carolina v. Lucas*, 1930 CCH ¶ 9031, 36 F.2d 1013 (App. D.C. 1929).

72 *See Commissioner v. O. Liquidating Corp.* 61-2 U.S.T.C. ¶ 9508, 292 F.2d 225, 231 (3d Cir. 1961), *rev'g* T.C. Memo. 1960-29; *Casey v. Commissioner*, 38 T.C. 357, 386-387 (1962); *Wright Contracting Co. v. Commissioner*, 36 T.C. 620, 634 (1961), *aff'd*, 63-1 U.S.T.C. ¶ 9416, 316 F.2d 249 (5th Cir. 1963); *Advertisers Exch., Inc. v. Commissioner*, 25 T.C. 1086, 1092-1093 (1956), *aff'd per curiam* 57-1 U.S.T.C. ¶ 9414, 240 F.2d 958 (2d Cir. 1957).

73 *See Lord v. United States*, 61-2 U.S.T.C. ¶ 9767, 296 F.2d 333, 335 (9th Cir. 1961); *Casey v. Commissioner, supra* at 386.

74 *FPL Group, Inc. & Subs. v. Commissioner*, 115 T.C. 554, 574 (2000) (quoting *Barber v. Commissioner*, 64 T.C. 314, 319-320 (1975)).

require recomputation and readjustment of tax liability for subsequent years and impose burdensome uncertainties upon the administration of the revenue laws.'"[75] The Supreme Court also has held that once a taxpayer has reported income according to a particular method the taxpayer has "made an election that is binding upon it and the commissioner."[76]

The Commissioner has discretion to accept or reject a request for a retroactive change in a taxpayer's choice between two permissible methods of computing taxable income. If the Commissioner, acting within his discretion, does not consent to the taxpayer's request to make a change in the taxpayer's method of computing taxable income, the taxpayer is required to continue computing taxable income under the taxpayer's old method of accounting. In deciding whether to consent to a change of accounting method, the Commissioner is invested with wide discretion.[77]

(a) *Code Section 481(a) Adjustments*

Code section 481(a) provides that in computing a taxpayer's taxable income for the tax year for which there has been a change in method of accounting, there shall be taken into account those adjustments that are determined to be necessary solely by reason of the change in order to prevent amounts from being duplicated or omitted. Regulation section 1.481-1(c)(1) provides that the term "adjustments," as used in Code section 481, has reference to the net amount of the adjustments required by Code section 481(a). In the case of a change in over-all method of accounting, such as from the cash receipts and disbursements method to an accrual method, the term "net amount of the adjustments" means the consolidation of adjustments (whether the amounts thereof represent increases or decreases in items of income or deductions) arising with respect to balances in various accounts, such as inventory, accounts receivable, and accounts payable, at the beginning of the taxable year of the change in method of accounting.

In effect, a Code section 481(a) adjustment represents the aggregate amount of net income or expense that would have been reported in years prior to the year of change if the taxpayer had been on the new method in such prior years. Accordingly, the amount of a taxpayer's Code section 481(a) adjustment is generally computed at the beginning of the year of change by comparing the amounts of income and/or expense the taxpayer reported under its prior method and the amounts that the taxpayer would have reported if the taxpayer had used the new method in prior years.[78]

(b) *What Constitutes a Change*

A change in the accounting treatment that results from a change in the facts underlying a transaction is not a change in a method of accounting.[79] "[A] change

---

[75] *Capital One Financial Corporation and Subsidiaries v. Commissioner*, 659 F.3d 316, 322 (4th Cir. 2011), *Pac. Nat'l Co. v. Welch*, 304 U.S. 191, 194, 58 S.Ct. 857, 82 L.Ed. 1282 (1938).

[76] *Id.* at 195, 58 S.Ct. 857.

[77] *See, e.g., Commissioner v. O. Liquidating Corp., supra* note 72, at 231; *Capitol Fed. Sav. & Loan Association & Sub. v. Commissioner*, 96 T.C. 204, 213 (1991); *Drazen v. Commissioner*, 34 T.C. 1070, 1075-1076 (1960), at 1076.

[78] Reg. § 1.481-1(c)(1).

[79] Reg. § 1.446-1(e)(2)(ii)(b).

in [a] method of accounting includes a change in the overall plan of accounting for gross income or deductions, or a change in the treatment of any material item."[80] If a taxpayer has been engaging in an activity and, later, the required method of accounting for that activity is altered for whatever reason, the taxpayer has experienced a change in a method of accounting.[81] Thus, if a taxpayer had been computing and recording interest earned on installment loans on a monthly basis, but later changes to a daily basis, a change in an accounting method requiring IRS consent has occurred.[82]

A change in the billing policy and practice is not a change in an accounting method requiring consent if the change was produced by the taxpayer's change in the terms of the sale of its product and not from any change in its accounting system. Thus, taxpayers may argue that a change in a credit card cardholder agreement to conform it to the terms approved by the Tax Court is not an accounting method change.[83] A method of accounting[84] is not established for an item unless there is a pattern of consistent treatment. Thus, there would be no change in a method of accounting unless there has been a pattern of consistent treatment of the item. The IRS defines consistent treatment as "[t]he treatment of a material item in the same way...for two or more consecutively filed federal income tax returns,..."[85] The focus of the Code and regulations appears to be on the item and not the status of the taxpayer.

(c) *Automatic Change Procedure*

The IRS has provided various procedures by which a taxpayer may obtain automatic consent to change the methods of accounting for certain items.[86] A taxpayer complying with all the applicable provisions of the procedure will be deemed to have obtained the consent of the Commissioner to change its method of accounting under Code section 446(e) and the regulations thereunder. The taxpayer will also secure audit protection for taxable years prior to the year of change.

(d) *Involuntary Change Procedures*

The IRS has provided guidance with respect to final involuntary change-of-accounting-method procedures under Code section 446 and Regulation section 1.446-1(b).[87] Taxpayers under examination, who otherwise could not request a voluntary change in method of accounting under the advance consent revenue procedure or the automatic consent revenue procedure, are permitted to do so prospectively, but without audit protection. Also, the IRS has reduced the Code section. 481(a) adjustment period for changes that result in a negative adjustment

[80] Rev. Proc. 2011-14, 2011-14 I.R.B. 330.

[81] Rev. Rul. 90-38, 1990-1 C.B. 57.

[82] Rev. Rul. 79-378, 1979-2 C.B. 201.

[83] *Barnett Banks of Florida, Inc. v. Commissioner*, 106 T.C. 103 (1996). *Cf*, *Signet Banking Corp. v. Commissioner*, 118 F.3d 239 (4th Cir. 1997) *aff'g*, 106 T.C. 117 (1996).

[84] Rev. Proc. 2011-14, 2011-4 I.R.B. 330.

[85] *Id.*

[86] Rev. Proc. 2011-14, 2011-4 I.R.B. 330 and Rev. Proc. 2016-29, 2016-21 I.R.B. 880. These revenue procedures also consolidate automatic consent procedures for changes in several methods of accounting that were published subsequent to the publication of Rev. Proc. 99-49 and provide automatic consent procedures for changes in several other methods of accounting.

[87] Rev. Proc. 2002-18 and Announcement 2002-37, 2002-13 I.R.B. 703, March 14, 2002.

from four years to one year, effective for tax years ending on or after December 31, 2001. The IRS also prescribed the latitude that revenue agents and appeals offices have to adjust or compromise the application of an IRS imposed accounting method change.[88]

(e) *Voluntary Change Procedures*

The IRS has provided procedures under which taxpayers may obtain the advance consent of the Commissioner to change a method of accounting.[89] The revenue procedure prescribes rules to follow by taxpayers under examination, who otherwise could not request a voluntary change in method of accounting under the advance consent procedure or the automatic consent revenue procedure. These taxpayers may receive advance consent to prospectively change their method of accounting without audit protection.

§2.2.4 Accounting for Different Businesses

A taxpayer engaged in more than one trade or business may use a different method of accounting for each separate and distinct trade or business.[90] To be a separate and distinct trade or business, each business must have a complete and separable set of books and records.[91] A taxpayer will not be treated as having separate and distinct trades or businesses if the use of different methods of accounting shifts the profits or losses between the trades or businesses, thereby resulting in the taxpayer's income not being clearly reflected.[92] Such proscribed shifting may result from inventory adjustments, sales, purchases, or expenses.

Thus, a bank's method of accounting for its lending business may differ from its method of accounting for its other business segments.[93] Not infrequently, a bank's trust business is accounted for under the cash method and its lending transactions under the accrual method.[94] Also, a bank may utilize a variety of accounting methods for different types of lending transactions. Each taxpayer can adopt a system that best reflects its needs.[95]

A business is considered separate only if a separate set of books are kept reflecting each line of business.[96] The IRS has approved the use of the accrual method to account for dealer securities activities and the cash method for all

---

[88] Rev. Proc. 97-27, 1997-1 C.B. 680, as modified by Rev. Proc. 2002-19, 2002-1 C.B. 696, and Rev. Proc. 2002-9, 2002-1 C.B. 327, as modified by Ann. 2002-17, 2002-1 C.B. 561, and Rev. Proc. 2002-19, 2002-1 C.B. 696, which provide the procedures for voluntary requests to change an accounting method.

[89] Rev. Proc. 2002-19, 2002-1 C.B. 696, March 14, 2002. In addition, this revenue procedure modifies Rev. Proc. 2002-9, which provides procedures for taxpayers within the scope of that revenue procedure to obtain automatic consent to change a method of accounting. The changes to Rev. Proc. 97-27 and Rev. Proc. 2002-9 include: (a) allowing a taxpayer to change its method of accounting prospectively, without audit protection, if the method to be changed is an issue pending for a taxable year under examination or an issue under consideration by either an appeals office or a federal court; (b) providing that, in the case of changes in method of accounting that result in a negative (*i.e.*, taxpayer-favorable) Code section 481(a) adjustment, the entire amount of the adjustment will be taken into account in the year of change; and (c) certain other conforming and clarifying changes.

[90] I.R.C. §446(d); Reg. §1.446-1(d)(1).

[91] Reg. §1.446-1(d)(2).

[92] Reg. §1.446-1(d)(3).

[93] I.R.C. §446(d); Reg. §1.446-1(d)(1).

[94] Rev. Rul. 74-270, 1974-1 C.B. 109.

[95] Reg. §1.446-1(a)(2). *See, e.g.*, Rev. Rul. 77-135, 1977-1 C.B. 133, for the proper method for reporting interest income under Graduated Payment Mortgage Plans implemented by the Department of Housing and Urban Development.

[96] Reg. §1.446-1(d)(2).

other business activities.[97] A taxpayer may be a dealer or merchant as to one class of securities and at the same time it may be holding other securities as to which it is not a dealer in securities.[98] Withdrawn Regulation 94, article 41-2, provided a method for withdrawal from the inventory system of securities. One that is seeking to withdraw from the inventory system must obtain approval from the Commissioner and adjust its inventory so that the new accounting method will clearly reflect income. In *Stokes*, the Court stated that the plaintiff was not permitted to disregard this regulation and arbitrarily withdraw from inventory to avoid the effect of a rising stock market on the income reflected in inventory.[99]

§2.3 Allocation of Receipts

As a general rule, amounts received prior to a loan's maturity and in partial repayment of the loan are treated first as interest and then as repayments of principal.[100] This payment ordering rule applies to O.I.D. as provided in final regulations issued under Code section 1275, where it is stated, with certain exceptions, that "each payment under a debt instrument is treated first as a payment of O.I.D. to the extent of the O.I.D. that has accrued as of the date the payment is due and that has not been allocated to prior payments, and second as a payment of principal."[101] There is, however, some authority for arguing that amounts received at maturity are applied proportionally to interest and principal.[102]

The IRS has stated that this general rule does not apply when it can be inferred from the circumstances that the parties understood that a different allocation of the payments would be made.[103] Thus, the IRS has ruled that if the parties have entered into a bona fide and arm's-length agreement to apply installment loan payments first to reduce principal, no interest is realized by a cash method lender until after the principal is repaid.[104] This ruling conforms with an earlier Board of Tax Appeals decision in which a nonbank, cash-method taxpayer was permitted to reallocate a payment to principal pursuant to an arm's-length agreement with a debtor.[105]

---

97 Rev. Rul. 74-280, 1974-1 C.B. 121.

98 *Stokes v. Rothensies*, 61 F. Supp. 444 (1944), 45-2 U.S.T.C. ¶9360, *aff'd per curiam*, 54 F.2d 1019 (3d Cir. 1946), 46-1 U.S.T.C. ¶9251. *See also Harriman National Bank v. Commissioner*, 43 F.2d 950 (2d Cir. 1930); *Hammitt v. Commissioner*, 79 F.2d 494 (3d Cir. 1935). These cases were decided under the law in effect prior to the enactment of Code section 475. Under current law, a taxpayer may be a dealer yet may be treated as an investor or trader with respect to identical securities.

99 *See* I.R.C. §475 (d)(2) for a subsequently enacted statutory rule that penalizes a taxpayer for improper identification. *See also* discussions of mark-to-market rules at section 4.3 *infra*.

100 Reg. §1.446-2(e); *European American Bank and Trust Company v. United States*, 940 F.2d 677 (Fed. Cir. 1991). *See also Motel Corp. v. Commissioner*, 54 T.C. 1433, Dec. 30,214 (1970); *E.P. Wright, Executors v. Commissioner*, 2 T.C. 1, Dec. 13,230 (1943) (Acq.); *Theodore R. Plunkett v. Commissioner*, 1 U.S.T.C. ¶9373, 118 F.2d 664 (1st Cir. 1941).

101 Reg. §1.1275-2(a). Chapter 5 contains a discussion of the allocation of receipts when a loan is in default.

102 *Warner Co. v. Commissioner*, 50-1 U.S.T.C. ¶9291, 181 F.2d 599 (3d Cir. 1950), *aff'g* 11 T.C. 919 (1948); *William Justin Petit, et al. v. Commissioner*, 8 T.C. 228, Dec. 15,576 (1947) (Acq.).

103 *European American Bank and Trust Co. v. United States*, 940 F.2d 677 (Fed. Cir. 1991); Rev. Rul. 70-647, 1970-2 C.B. 38.

104 Rev. Rul. 63-57, 1963-1 C.B. 103.

105 *Huntington-Redondo Company v. Commissioner*, 36 B.T.A. 116, Dec. 9679 (1937). Similarly, the payor is not entitled to a deduction under Code §163 for interest until the amount borrowed has been repaid.

Under unusual circumstances, the IRS may take the position that a taxpayer is required to take the entire amount distributed to it from a defaulted bond into income as a return of principal in computing gain or loss on the bonds.[106] This may occur, for example, when the total sum received was sufficient only to restore the capital value that existed at the commencement of the period under consideration. The IRS argued that since there was no profit, there was no income. "To hold otherwise would be to 'enter into the refinements of lexicographers or economists'—to substitute form for substance—and to lose sight of the commonly understood meaning of the words."[107]

§2.4 Interest Income

Interest is defined as any amount received or accrued for the use, forbearance, or detention of money.[108] Whether a particular payment constitutes interest is determined by the facts, not by the terminology used.[109] This is also true with respect to regulatory labels. For example, federally chartered banks are required to comply with the National Banking Act, pursuant to which a national bank may charge the same fees as any state bank chartered in the same state although the national bank is not bound by the labels used in the state. Thus, even if the state bank is required under state law to call a charge a "service fee," the proper classification of the fee charged by the national bank for regulatory purposes is made under the National Bank Act.[110] For tax purposes, "[L]abels are unimportant."[111] Thus, loan origination fees that are additional amounts substituting for stated interest paid to obtain a loan are interest income.[112] However, origination fees that are not a substitute for interest are not properly accounted for as interest income. Furthermore, if a commitment fee is in fact an amount received by a bank for granting the right to draw on a sum of money, it is neither interest income nor service fee income.[113] Instead, it is an amount received for selling an intangible property right.[114]

§2.5 Tax-Exempt Interest

In general, gross income does not include interest on any state or local bond.[115] A state or local bond is any obligation of a state or political subdivi-

---

[106] PLR 8650035, September 12, 1986.

[107] *Id.* Why would the IRS take the position that the payment was principal and not interest? Answer. The obligation produced interest excludable as municipal bond income under I.R.C. §103.

[108] *Deputy v. DuPont*, 40-1 U.S.T.C. ¶9161, 308 U.S. 488 (U.S. Del. 1940); and *Old Colony Railroad Co. v. Commissioner*, 3 U.S.T.C. ¶880, 284 U.S. 552 (1932). *See also The Theory of Interest*, Irving Fisher, New York, Macmillan, 1930, in which he states that the nominal interest rate is equal to the rate of return on real assets together with the expected rate of inflation on those assets and a risk premium.

[109] *Goodwin v. Commissioner*, 75 T.C. 424, Dec. 37,502 (1980), *aff'd without published opinion*, (3d Cir. 1982).

[110] CCA 200145013, August 3, 2001. *See* 12 U.S.C. §85 (interest includes any kind of charge imposed by a national bank for the use or forbearance of money).

[111] *Metropolitan Mortgage Fund, Inc. v. Commissioner*, 62 T.C. 110, Dec. 32,562 (1974). Rev. Rul. 69-188, 1969-1 C.B. 54. *Helvering v. Lazarus & Co.*, 308 U.S. 252, 255 (1939); 1939-2 L.B. 208; *Mapco Inc. v. United States*, 556 F.2d 1107, 1110 (Ct. Cl. 1977); PLR 9839001, September 25, 1998.

[112] Reg. §1.61-7(c). *Vancoh Realty Company v. Commissioner*, 33 B.T.A. 918, Dec. 9204 (1936).

[113] Rev. Rul. 81-160, 1981-1 C.B. 312; Temp. Reg. §1.1273-2(f); Rev. Rul. 74-395, 1974-2 C.B. 45.

[114] *See* discussion of "Committment fees" below.

[115] I.R.C. §103.

sion.[116] This definition is sufficiently broad to encompass loans and other financing arrangements that are in fact loans but which may be labeled as leases. However, if the state or local bond is an arbitrage bond, or a bond not in registered form, the interest is included in gross income.[117]

§ 2.5.1 Private Activity Bonds

A private activity bond that is not a "qualified bond" will not generate tax-exempt interest.[118] A private activity bond is any bond issued, or part of an issue, which meets a "private business use test" and a "private security or payment test."[119] The private business use test is met if more than ten percent of the proceeds of the issue are to be used for any private business use. In general, the private security or payment test is met if the payment of the principal of, or the interest on, more than ten percent of the proceeds of such issue is directly or indirectly secured by: (a) any interest in property used or to be used for a private business use, (b) payments in respect of such property, or (c) to be derived from payments or respect of property, or borrowed money, used or to be used for a private business use.[120]

A "qualified bond" is any private activity bond that also qualifies as any one of the following types of bonds:

1. An exempt facility bond,
2. A qualified mortgage bond,
3. A qualified veterans' mortgage bond,
4. A qualified small issue bond,
5. A qualified student loan bond,
6. A qualified redevelopment bond, or
7. A qualified 501(c)(3) bond.

However, only if a "qualified bond" is also a state or local bond will the interest thereon be tax-exempt for federal income tax purposes. Thus, the interest on loans made to a university was not tax-exempt. A university may qualify as a Code section 501(c)(3) organization; however, the university is not a state or political subdivision.[121] Moreover, obligations issued by a university are not treated as issued "on behalf of" a state or local governmental unit "by constituted authorities empowered to issue such obligations."[122]

---

[116] I.R.C. § 103(c).

[117] I.R.C. § 103(b). An arbitrage bond is defined in I.R.C. § 148. If a bond not in registered form meets the requirements of I.R.C. § 149, the interest on the bond may be eligible for exclusion.

[118] I.R.C. § 103(b)(1).

[119] I.R.C. § 141(a).

[120] I.R.C. § 141(b)(2).

[121] *Philadelphia National Bank v. United States*, 666 F.2d 834 (3d Cir. 1981).

[122] Reg. § 1.103-1(b).

§2.5.2 Fire Department Loans

An obligation of a volunteer fire department issued after December 31, 1980, is treated as an obligation of a political subdivision of a state if two conditions are met:[123]

1. The volunteer fire department is a "qualified volunteer fire department," and
2. Substantially all of the proceeds of the issue of which the obligation is a part are to be used for the acquisition, construction, reconstruction, or improvement of a fire house or fire truck used or to be used by the qualified volunteer fire department. The "substantially all" requirement is satisfied if 90 percent or more of the proceeds are so used.

If an obligation is issued by an ambulance and rescue squad that is a "qualified volunteer fire department," but substantially all of the proceeds of the issue of which the obligation is a part are to be used for the furnishing of emergency medical services, the obligation will not be treated as an obligation of a political subdivision of a state.[124] For this purpose, the term "qualified volunteer fire department" means an organization that meets three requirements:

1. It is organized and operated to provide firefighting services or emergency medical services in an area within the jurisdiction of a political subdivision;
2. It is required to furnish firefighting services by written agreement with the political subdivision; and
3. It serves persons in an area with the jurisdiction of the political subdivision that is not provided with any other firefighting services.

§2.5.3 ESOP Loans

If a loan was made to an employee stock ownership plan pursuant to a written binding contract in effect prior to June 10, 1996, it was eligible for a partial exclusion.[125] This partial exclusion allowed a bank, or any other entity that was engaged in the business of lending money, to exclude from gross income 50 percent of the interest received on loans to an employee stock ownership plan or to an employer corporation, the proceeds of which are used by the plan to acquire employer securities.

The exclusion will continue to apply to refinancing loans made on or after June 10, 1996, if: (1) the refinancing loan meets the requirements of Code section 133, prior to the repeal by the Small Business Job Protection Act of 1996; (2) immediately after the refinancing, the outstanding principal amount of the loan is not increased; and (3) the term of the refinancing loan does not extend beyond the term of the original employee stock ownership loan.

---

[123] Reg. §1.103-16. In a case that pre-dated this change in the law, a volunteer fire department was not treated as a political subdivision of a state. *The Seagrave Corp. v. Commissioner*, 38 T.C. 247 (1962). *See also* Rev. Rul. 77-232, 1977-2 C.B. 71.

[124] A piece of legislation that was never enacted, The Emergency Medical Services Enhancement Act of 1993, would have allowed medical groups providing emergency medical services to issue tax-exempt obligations.

[125] Section 1602(a) of The Small Business Job Protection Act of 1986, Pub. L. No. 104-188, repealed I.R.C. §133, which allowed the partial exclusion.

§2.6 Accruing Interest Income

Taxpayers must use a method of accounting for interest that accurately reflects the economic accrual of interest. As a general rule, interest is included in taxable gross income in accordance with a bank's overall method of accounting,[126] and if the bank employs the accrual method, it is usually accrued using the constant yield method.[127] This is true even if a loan agreement provides that interest shall be earned in accordance with some other method, such as the Rule of 78s method or a method required under state law for purposes of computing finance charges and rebates on installment loans.[128]

The amount of interest that properly accrues for a period between payment dates is determined by applying the effective rate of interest on the loan to the unpaid balance for that period.[129] Under this method, a constant rate is applied to a declining balance. The constant yield method is similar to that used for accruing original issue discount under Code section 1272.

Example: Assuming the following facts, under the constant yield method interest income for the three months in 19X1 would amount to $46.01 and for the nine months in 19X2 would amount to $63.99, computed as follows:

Loan Amount	$2,000
Loan Term	12 months
Annual Percentage rate	10%
Interest compounded monthly.	
Loan begins	10/01/X1

Payments are due last day of each month and are paid when due.

Date	*No.*	*Payment*	*Interest*	*Principal*	*Balance*
10/01/X1	0	—	—	—	$2,000.00
10/31/X1	1	$175.83	$16.67	$159.16	1,840.84
11/30/X1	2	175.83	15.34	160.49	1,680.35
12/31/X1	3	175.83	14.00	161.83	1,518.52
01/31/X2	4	175.83	12.65	163.18	1,355.34
02/28/X2	5	175.83	11.29	164.54	1,190.80
03/31/X2	6	175.83	9.92	165.91	1,024.89
04/30/X2	7	175.83	8.54	167.29	857.60
05/31/X2	8	175.83	7.15	168.68	688.92
06/30/X2	9	175.83	5.74	170.09	518.83
07/31/X2	10	175.83	4.32	171.51	347.32
08/31/X2	11	175.83	2.89	172.94	174.38
09/30/X2	12	175.87	1.49	174.38	-0-
		$2,110.00	$110.00	$2,000.00	

[126] I.R.C. §446; Reg. §1.446-1(a).

[127] Reg. §1.446-2; Rev. Rul. 69-188, 1969-1 C.B. 54.

[128] Rev. Rul. 83-84, 1983-1 C.B. 97. Case law has supported allocations of interest and principal for tax purposes based on arm's-length agreements between the borrower and lender. *European American Bank and Trust Co. v. United States*, 940 F.2d 677 (Fed. Cir. 1991). *See also* Rev. Rul. 70-647, 1970-2 C.B. 38.

[129] Conf. Rep. No. 760, 97th Cong., 2d Sess. 553 (1982), 1982-39 I.R.B. 4, 41; S. Rep. No. 494 (Vol. 1), 97th Cong., 2d Sess. 209 (1982); Supplement I to Regulation Z, 12 C.F.R. §§226.6 and 226.40 (1979).

§2.6.1 Rule of 78s Method

In addition to a bank's overall method of accounting for interest, a bank may employ special methods of accounting for individual items of income. A method of accounting occasionally used for interest (or discount) income on installment loans for both cash and accrual basis taxpayers is the Rule of 78s method.[130] It is the IRS's position that the Rule of 78s method is no longer an acceptable method of accounting. An exception to this position applies to stated interest on short-term consumer loans that were issued prior to the first day of the taxpayer's first taxable year that begins on or after January 1, 1999 and that have certain characteristics described in Revenue Ruling 83-84.[131] For all other loans, the Rule of 78s method is not permitted to be used. The IRS has issued automatic accounting method change procedures pursuant to which permission to change to an acceptable method will be automatically granted.[132]

Under the Rule of 78s method a cash basis bank includes in income the annual interest thus determined when actually or constructively received.[133] An accrual basis bank will recognize income at the earlier date of receipt or when the installment is due.[134]

Under the Rule of 78s method, interest income for the taxable year is equal to an amount determined by multiplying total interest income by a fraction, the numerator of which is the number of payment periods (usually months) remaining on the term of the loan at the time of calculation (including the period for which the calculation is made), and the denominator of which is the sum of the number of payments during the term of the loan.

Example: Assuming the facts of the preceding example for 19X1, interest income would amount to $45.12, as follows:

Date	*No.*	*Payment*	*Fraction*	*Interest*	*Principal*	*Balance*
10/01/X1	0		—	—	—	$2,000.00
10/31/X1	1	$175.83	12/78	$16.92	$158.91	1,841.09
11/30/X1	2	175.83	11/78	15.51	160.32	1,680.77
12/31/X1	3	175.83	9/78	12.69	163.14	1,355.90
01/31/X2	4	175.83	9/78	12.69	163.14	1,355.90
02/28/X2	5	175.83	8/78	11.28	164.55	1,191.35
03/31/X2	6	175.83	7/78	9.87	165.96	1,025.39
04/30/X2	7	175.83	6/78	8.46	167.37	858.02
05/31/X2	8	175.83	5/78	7.05	168.78	689.24
06/30/X2	9	175.83	4/78	5.64	170.19	519.05
07/31/X2	10	175.83	3/78	4.23	171.60	347.45
08/31/X2	11	175.83	2/78	2.82	173.01	174.44
09/30/X2	12	175.87	1/78	1.43	174.44	-0-
		$2,110.00		$110.00	$2,000.00	

[130] It is sometimes referred to as the sum-of-the-months-digits method, so named because the sum-of-the-months-digits for a 12-month period is 78.

[131] Rev. Rul. 83-84, 1983-1 C.B. 97.

[132] Rev. Proc. 2011-14, 2011-14 I.R.B. 330.

[133] *Appeal of Chatham & Phenix National Bank*, 1 B.T.A. 460, Dec. 174 (1925); *Appeal of Bank of Hartsville*, 1 B.T.A. 920, Dec. 336 (1925); *Appeal of Madison & Kedzie State Bank*, 1 B.T.A. 922, Dec. 337 (1925).

[134] Reg. § 1.451-1.

In 1983, the IRS ruled that the Rule of 78s method was an acceptable method of accounting but only for consumer loans that have the following six characteristics:

1. Self-amortizing;
2. Level payments;
3. Payments made at regular intervals;
4. Payments made at least annually;
5. Payments made over a period not in excess of five years (with no balloon payments at the end of the loan term); and
6. The loan agreement that interest is earned, or upon the prepayment of the loan interest is treated as earned, in accordance with the Rule of 78s.[135]

The IRS's disallowance of the Rule of 78s method of accounting for a partner's distributive share of partnership interest expense deductions for 1981 and 1982 has been upheld, even though these years pre-date the IRS's 1983 revenue ruling. Although use of the method was allowed for short-term consumer loans, the partner's interest expense resulted from a long-term mortgage of the partnership and, thus, did not qualify for such treatment.[136]

If any one of the above six conditions is not met, the lender's installment loan interest income (and the borrower's interest expense) may not be computed using the Rule of 78s method. The IRS has reasoned that the Rule of 78s is not a method of accounting that reflects the economic accrual of interest because the method "fails to reflect the true cost of borrowing."[137] It is an acceptable method, as a matter of administrative convenience, only in the limited circumstances described above.[138]

§2.6.2 Liquidation, Actuarial, Composite Methods

Among other methods of accounting for interest income that were acceptable prior to the issuance of Revenue Ruling 83-84 were the liquidation and actuarial methods described in Regulation Z of the Truth-in-Lending Act.[139] Although the actuarial method was approved by the IRS, it is not widely employed.

---

[135] Rev. Rul. 83-84, 1983-1 C.B. 97; Rev. Proc. 83-40, 1983-1 C.B. 774.

[136] *K.L. Mulholland v. United States*, 89-1 U.S.T.C. ¶9161, 16 Cl. Ct. 252 (1989). *See also Prabel v. Commissioner*, 89-2 U.S.T.C. ¶9488, 882 F.2d 820 (3d Cir. 1989).

[137] Rev. Rul. 83-84, 1983-1 C.B. 97; Rev. Proc. 83-40, 1983-1 C.B. 774.

[138] For guidelines to follow when changing from the Rule of 78s to an acceptable method, *see* Rev. Proc. 84-27, 1984-1 C.B. 469; Rev. Proc. 84-28, 1984-1 C.B. 475; Rev. Proc. 84-29, 1984-1 C.B. 480; Rev. Proc. 84-30, 1984-1 C.B. 482. Rev. Proc. 2002-9 provides automatic accounting method change procedures from the Rule of 78's method. 2002-1 C.B. 327.

[139] Rev. Rul. 79-228, 1979-2 C.B. 200, *as modified by* Rev. Rul. 83-84, 1983-1 C.B. 97. Regulation Z is found in 12 C.F.R. §226 (1969) of the Consumer Credit Protection Act, Pub. L. No. 90-321, 82 Stat. 146 (1968).

The liquidation method is a composite method that has the effect of apportioning interest income on a loan over the term of that loan. Purchase discount accounted for under the composite method is not included in the tax basis of mortgages sold.[140] The loan liquidation method may not be used where a specific agreement, established practice of the lender, applicable law, or directive of an appropriate bank regulatory agency apportions the interest to be paid on the loan by a method other than the straight-line method.[141] Presumably, because the liquidation and the actuarial methods use arbitrary formulas for allocating interest income, the IRS may determine that they do not "reflect the true cost of borrowing."[142]

Loan origination fees that are interest income must be recognized as income in accordance with original issue discount rules.[143] Those rules permit limited use of the liquidation method.[144]

When a pool of installment obligations is purchased at a discount, the IRS has ruled that the discount may be accounted for on a composite basis if: (1) the taxpayer regularly employs the composite method; (2) the annual discount income is clearly reflected; and (3) the total of the discount from such obligations is eventually included in income.[145]

§ 2.7 Service Fee Income

Whether an item is a fee for services, a payment for the use or forbearance of money, or some other type of income, such as the payment for the sale of property, is a question of fact that is not resolved by the terminology used.[146] The burden of proof on this issue is on the taxpayer.[147] After a loan has been made, including credit card loans, it is likely that any "fees" charged will be properly classified as interest income;[148] however, the inquiry is whether the charge compensates the lender for the use of money or for specifically stated services it provided to or for the benefit of the borrower beyond the lending of money.[149]

---

[140] PLR 8519011, February 6, 1985. For discussion of the composite method of accounting, *see* Rev. Rul. 53-216, 1953-2 C.B. 38; Rev. Rul. 54-367, 1954-2 C.B. 109; S.M. 3820, C.B. IV-2, 32 (1925).

[141] Rev. Rul. 64-278, 1964-2 C.B. 120, *as modified by* Rev. Rul. 72-100, 1972-1 C.B. 122.

[142] Private letter rulings authorizing the use of the actuarial and liquidation methods have not been revoked by the IRS.

[143] I.R.C. § 1272; Reg. § 1.1273-2. *See* Ch. 3 for detailed discussion of original issue discount rules and the loan liquidation method. *See also* Rev. Proc. 94-28, 1994-1 C.B. 614; Rev. Proc. 94-29, 1994-1 C.B. 616; Rev. Proc. 94-30, 1994-1 C.B. 621.

[144] Although Rev. Proc. 94-29 declares obsolete certain revenue rulings that allowed the composite and the loan liquidation methods, Rev. Rul. 53-216, 1953-2 C.B. 38; Rev. Rul. 54-367, 1954-2 C.B. 109, Rev. Rul. 64-278, 1964-2 C.B. 120, it authorized modified composite or aggregate and loan liquidation methods.

[145] Rev. Rul. 77-349, 1977-2 C.B. 20.

[146] *Goodwin v. Commissioner*, 75 T.C. 424, Dec. 37,502 (1980); *Signet Banking Corp. v. Commissioner*, 118 F.3d 239 (4th Cir. 1997), *aff'g* 106 T.C. 117.

[147] Rule 142(a), Tax Court Rules of Practice and Procedure.

[148] CCA 200145013, August 3, 2001.

[149] *W. Credit Co. v. Commissioner*, 38 T.C. 979, 980, (1962), *aff'd*, 325 F.2d 1022 (9th Cir. 1963); *Noteman v. Welch*, 108 F.2d 206, 213 (1st Cir. 1939); *Seaboard Loan & Sav. Association v. Commissioner*, 45 B.T.A. 510, 516 (1941).

§2.7.1 Service Fee Income v. Interest Income

Factors that have been found to indicate that an amount is not a fee for services but rather interest income include:

1. A dependency of the amount charged upon the same factors relied on in determining the stated rate of interest to be charged. Such factors include the degree of risk involved and the current money market.[150]
2. An inverse relationship between the stated interest rate and the fee rate; that is, the higher the one the lower the other should be.
3. No relationship between the cost incurred by the petitioner in underwriting the loan and the fee charged thereon. Such a relationship would be evident if the fee were computed as a percentage of the amount borrowed.[151]
4. No liability for the fee if the loan did not close, even though the bank performed a substantial amount of services in connection with the loan.
5. No liability for the fee if other services were performed for which the borrower was charged.
6. The fees were treated by the lender as interest for purposes of complying with federal truth-in-lending requirements and state usury and tax laws.[152]
7. An agreement to refund the payment if all services are not performed.[153]

Thus, amounts received for specific services such as appraisals, credit investigations, maintaining escrow amounts, and servicing mortgages are properly classified as service fee income.

§2.7.2 When to Include Service Fee Income

As a general rule, a cash method bank must include service fees in income when received.[154] However, the Claims Court has held that unearned payments received for services are not includible in income in the year received if the taxpayer's contractual obligation to provide the future services is "fixed and definite."[155] The IRS does not embrace this fixed and definite theory. It has taken

[150] *Goodwin v. Commissioner*, 75 T.C. 424, Dec. 37,502 (1980) in which the amount of each loan fee was computed as a percentage of the loan amount and bore no direct relation to the actual cost of the specific services performed, yet was found to be a payment for services. *Pacific First Federal Savings & Loan v. Commissioner*, 79 T.C. 512, Dec. 39,365 (1982); Rev. Rul. 70-540, 1970-2 C.B. 101; *Metropolitan Mortgage Fund, Inc. v. Commissioner*, 62 T.C. 110, Dec. 32,562 (1974).

[151] *Blitzer v. United States*, 82-2 U.S.T.C. ¶9465, 684 F.2d 874 (Ct.Cl. 1982); *Western Credit Co. v. Commissioner*, 64-1 U.S.T.C. ¶9207, 325 F.2d 1022 (9th Cir. 1964).

[152] *Pacific First Federal Savings & Loan v. Commissioner*, 79 T.C. 512, Dec. 39,365 (1982)

[153] *Barnett Banks of Florida, Inc. v. Commissioner*, 106 T.C. 103 (1996).

[154] *Schlude v. Commissioner*, 62-1 U.S.T.C. ¶9137, 296 F.2d 721 (8th Cir. 1962) *aff'g*, 32 T.C. 1271 (1959).

[155] *Boise Cascade Corp. v. United States*, 76-1 U.S.T.C. ¶9203, 530 F.2d 1367 (Ct.Cl. 1976). The Solicitor General did not authorize certiorari in *Boise Cascade*. However, he has stated that "[a]dvance payments for services to be rendered in future years and received without restriction as to use are income in the year received by an accrual basis taxpayer." Action on Decision No. 1986-014.

the position that an accrual basis bank has income when a fee is earned, or received, whichever occurs earlier.[156]

Under limited circumstances, the IRS concedes that there will not be a material distortion of income if service fee income is deferred. In Revenue Procedure 2004-34, the IRS allowed taxpayers using an accrual method of accounting to defer the inclusion in gross income of "advance payments" in certain limited situations.[157] The revenue procedure is intended to reduce the administrative and tax compliance burdens on taxpayers and to minimize disputes between the IRS and taxpayers regarding advance payments. The procedure modifies and supersedes Revenue Procedure 71-21, discussed below. Advance payments for non-services (and often, for combinations of services and non-services) do not qualify for deferral under Revenue Procedure 71-21, and taxpayers and the IRS frequently disagreed about whether advance payments were for "services." In addition to the issue of defining "services" for purposes of Revenue Procedure 71-21, questions also arose about whether advance payments received under a series of agreements, or under a renewable agreement, were within the scope of Revenue Procedure 71-21.

Inclusion in gross income of these "advance payments" may generally be deferred to the next taxable year, to the extent the advanced payments are not recognized in book income in the taxable year of receipt. A taxpayer that wishes to defer advance payments must use the advance consent procedures for a change of accounting method set forth in Revenue Procedure 97-27. However, Revenue Procedure 2004-34 includes a safe harbor allocation for which the taxpayer may use the automatic change of accounting method procedures in Revenue Procedure 2002-9.

Revenue Procedure 2004-34 provides that a payment is eligible for deferral in part or in whole into the next tax year as an "advance payment" only if:

1. The payment is received by the taxpayer in one taxable year;
2. Including the payment in gross income for the taxable year of receipt is a permissible method of accounting for federal income tax purposes (without regard to this revenue procedure);
3. The payment is included by the taxpayer (in whole or in part) in gross receipts for financial reporting purposes for a subsequent taxable year, whether or not the inclusion is contingent upon a future act by the taxpayer or any other party; and

---

[156] Rev. Rul. 70-540, 1970-2 C.B. 101.

[157] Notice 2002-79, 2002-2 C.B. 964, December 2, 2002. In conjunction with this proposed revenue procedure, the Treasury Department and the Service plan to propose regulations that will modify Reg. §1.61-8(b) to conform to the proposed revenue procedure. The current regulation states that "advance rentals" are includible in gross income for the year of receipt (except as provided by I.R.C. §467 and the regulations thereunder); the proposed regulation will allow the Commissioner to provide rules allowing for inclusion in gross income for a taxable year other than the taxable year of receipt. Revenue Procedure 2006-12 superseded Revenue Procedure 2004-23 for taxable years ending on or after December 31, 2005, and for certain earlier taxable years.

4. The payment is solely for:
   a. Services;
   b. The sale of goods (other than for sales of goods for which the taxpayer uses a deferral method provided in § 1.451-5(b)(1)(ii));
   c. The use (including by license or lease) of certain intellectual property;
   d. The occupancy of space or the use of property if the occupancy or use is ancillary to the provision of services;
   e. The sale, lease, or license of computer software;
   f. Guaranty or warranty contracts ancillary to the items described in (a), (b), (c), (d), and (e), above;
   g. Subscriptions (other than for subscriptions for which an election under Code section 455 is in effect), whether or not provided in a tangible or intangible format;
   h. Membership in an organization (other than for memberships for which an election under Code section 456 is in effect); or
   i. Any combination of subsections (a) through (h).

The Notice excludes from the term "advance payment" most forms of rent, insurance premiums, and payments with respect to financial instruments.

For this purpose, financial instruments include: debt instruments, deposits, letters of credit, notional principal contracts, options, forwards, futures, foreign currency contracts, credit card agreements, financial derivatives, *etc.*, including purported prepayments of interest.

Prior to the effective date of Revenue Procedure 2004-34, the IRS allowed a more limited deferral of fee income. Revenue Procedure 71-21 allows prepayments for services to be performed before the end of the taxable year following the taxable year of receipt to be deferred until the year following the year of receipt.[158] The amount of deferral is proportionate to the portion of services remaining unperformed at the end of the year of receipt. The application of this pronouncement has been the subject of considerable recent controversy, which surrounds the proper tax accounting for credit card fees. Revenue Procedure 71-21 was designed to reconcile the tax and financial accounting treatment of payments received for services to be performed by the end of the next succeeding taxable year without permitting extended deferral of the inclusion of those payments in gross income for federal income tax purposes.

§ 2.7.3 Credit Card Annual Fees

According to Revenue Ruling 2004-52, the annual fee that a cardholder pays an issuer of credit cards for the privilege of accessing a revolving line of credit and for various benefits and services is not interest income to the issuer, and it is includible in gross income when the fee becomes due and payable by the cardholder under the terms of the credit card agreement.[159] This treatment is

[158] Rev. Proc. 71-21, 1971-2 C.B. 549.

[159] Rev. Rul. 2004-52, 2004-1 C.B. 973. *See* also TAM 2005533023, May 10, 2005. *See* discussion of credit card fees in Ch. 3.

appropriate regardless of whether the annual fee is nonrefundable or refundable. Normally, the annual fee becomes due and payable when the fee is posted to the cardholder's account.

The IRS reasoned that because the annual fee is not for any specific benefit provided by the credit card issuer, but instead covers all benefits and services that are available to the cardholder, the annual fee is not compensation for the use or forbearance of money. Thus, it is not interest income. Oddly, the IRS failed to specifically comment on the possibility that the annual fee was paid for the right to draw on credit, in which case it would be received for the sale of an intangible property right. Only the oblique reference to the fee being paid for "benefits" may possibly embrace the fee being paid for the right to draw on credit. Earlier, as discussed below, it was the position of the IRS that the annual credit card fee was in the nature of a commitment fee.

Notwithstanding the characterization of the fee as an amount received for "benefits and services," for taxable years ending on or after December 31, 2003, the IRS in a companion pronouncement granted taxpayers permission to recognize the annual fee ratably over the period covered by the fee.[160] Entitlement to this income deferral is conditioned on the taxpayer: (a) recognizing any unrecognized fee income at the time that a credit card account is cancelled, and (b) if a credit card annual fee is due and payable in installments, each installment must be recognized ratably over the period to which the installment relates.

For those taxpayers who wish to change their method of account for annual credit card fees, the IRS granted permission to automatically change their accounting method in accordance with the general rules of Revenue Procedure 2002-9, as modified.[161] Any taxpayer that currently uses the ratable inclusion method for annual credit card fees will receive audit protection for all open years.[162]

In an earlier pronouncement the IRS took the position that the annual fee charged credit card holders is neither a payment for services nor an interest charge.[163] Rather, it was determined to be in the nature of a commitment fee and should be treated as a payment for the transfer of a property right, thereby requiring immediate inclusion in income. According to the pronouncement, although services are rendered by the bank as partial consideration for the credit card fee, the services are insufficient to overcome the appearance of the fee being "similar to a loan commitment fee." The IRS's pronouncement did not appear to take into account the compensation that the bank receives from the merchant, which may indirectly pay the bank for a portion of the cardholder's credit advanced by the bank.[164]

---

[160] Rev. Rul. 2004-32, 2004-1 C.B. 621.

[161] *Id.* Sec. 5.

[162] *Id.* Sec. 6.

[163] TAM 8537002, May 22, 1985. General Counsel Memorandum 39434, May 31, 1985, underlies the Technical Advice Memorandum. *See also* TAM 8543004, July 18, 1985.

[164] The IRS has issued a Coordinated Issue Paper on the treatment of mortgage buy down fees paid on behalf of a borrower. *See* Appendix A 1.105. These fees constituted interest income paid to the bank.

The historical position of the IRS is consistent with the treatment of credit card fees prescribed by the Financial Accounting Standards Board. Statement 91 provides, in part:

> A credit card fee represents a payment by the cardholder to obtain the ability to borrow from the lender under predefined conditions. Such borrowings take place at the option of the borrower. The Board noted that such arrangements provide opportunities to lend and concluded that the related fees represent commitment fees.[165]

Of course, the FASB does not appear to be concerned with the important distinction between those "fees" that are, in fact, interest income (such as points), those "fees" that are, in fact, amounts received for the sale of a property right (such as commitment fees), and those "fees" that are, in fact, received for services. All of these items of income are pooled and treated as "fees" for purposes of Statement 91.

In *Barnett Banks*, the Tax Court determined that the taxpayer was permitted to defer credit card fee income in accordance with the provisions of Revenue Procedure 71-21,[166] while in *Signet Banking Corp.*, decided on the same day by the Tax Court, the credit card fee income earned by the bank could not be deferred.[167] Under Revenue Procedure 71-21,[168] the portion of fee that may be deferred is the amount which represents the services to be performed during the next taxable year. This treatment, of course, is a method of accounting. Thus, a taxpayer may either adopt it on the return for the first tax year when the income is earned,[169] or the taxpayer must request permission to change its method of accounting to the deferral method.[170] Among the distinctions in the facts that had an apparently significant influence on the court in these two cases were these: in *Barnett Banks*, the taxpayer's credit card agreement did not state that the fee was received for the issuance of the card and for the extension of credit; in *Signet Banking Corp.*, it did so provide. Also, in *Barnett Banks*, the fee was refundable, while in *Signet Banking Corp.* it was nonrefundable. Furthermore, in *Signet Banking Corp.*, the court found that all services were performed when the card was issued, but in *Barnett Banks* the services were found to have been performed over the life of the card.

In light of the significance of the factual distinctions that the Tax Court noted existed in the agreement that *Barnett Banks* and that *Signet Banking Corp.* had with their cardholders, banks may want to consider amending cardholder agreements. If the nontax disadvantages can be overcome, the *Barnett Banks* type agreement would appear to ensure tax deferral of fee income. If a change in the cardholder agreement is treated as a change in the facts associated with this business activity, an accounting method change would not occur when the credit card fee income is deferred.

---

[165] Financial Accounting Standards Board, Statement of Financial Accounting Standards No. 91, Acct. Series, Dec. 1986, at 24, para. 51.

[166] *Barnett Banks of Florida v. Commissioner*, 106 T.C. 103 (1996).

[167] *Signet Banking Corporation v. Commissioner*, 118 F.3d 239 (4th Cir. 1997), *aff'g* 106 T.C. 117.

[168] Rev. Proc. 71-21, 1971-2 C.B. 549.

[169] Reg. § 1.446-1(d)(1).

[170] Rev. Proc. 97-27, 1997-1 C.B. 680.

The holdings in *Barnett Banks* and *Signet Banking Corp.* are to be compared with the more recent decision of the Court of Federal Claims in *American Express.*[171] Unlike the approach to resolving the cases taken in the former two Tax Court decisions, the Court of Federal Claims was asked to rule on cross motions for summary judgment made by the parties in connection with the taxpayer's claim for refund filed when its application for an accounting method change was denied The denial precluded the taxpayer from including annual card fees in gross income ratably over the 12 month period for which a card was valid in accordance with Revenue Procedure 71-21. Oddly, the court and the parties found that there were no factual disputes in the case. Yet, there appeared to be considerable disagreement over whether the fee paid was for services or for making a commitment to lend money. This is clearly a question of fact.

The IRS argued that the taxpayer was not permitted to account for its credit card fee income in accordance with that procedure because the fees were not for services and also because the taxpayer's methodology for determining the amount of fees used for services did not produce the level accuracy required by Revenue Procedure 71-21. The taxpayer claimed that the IRS had abused its discretion in denying the taxpayer's request for a change in accounting method under Revenue Procedure 71-21 because the card fees met all the criteria for deferral under Revenue Procedure 71-21. Prior to the year in issue, the taxpayer included card fees in income when the fees were billed. Beginning in late 1987, the taxpayer changed its method of financial accounting to conform with FASB Statement No. 91.

The IRS denied the application because, as it announced in General Counsel Memorandum 39,434, it did not view card fees as payments for contingent services, but rather as payments for credit. The taxpayer acknowledged that a portion of the fees may have been paid to acquire credit but insisted that the credit aspect of its cards was *de minimis*. The government countered that the primary reason for paying the fee was to acquire credit, and therefore the fee was not a payment for services.

The court noted that the Commissioner enjoys broad discretion to determine whether a taxpayer's accounting method clearly reflects income. The task of the reviewing court is not to determine whether, in its own opinion, a taxpayer's method of accounting clearly reflects income, but to determine whether there is an adequate basis in law for the Commissioner's conclusion that it did not because of its longstanding position on this issues first expressed in General Counsel Memorandum 39,434. The court relied heavily on this Memorandum as a clear expression of the IRS's position that credit card fees are not received for services but, rather, for promising to extend credit.

Surprisingly, the court acknowledged that the memorandum was based on different facts than the present case, but it concluded, nevertheless, that the existence of the Memorandum satisfied the requirement that the IRS not abuse its

[171] *American Express Co. and Affiliated Subsidiaries v. United States,* 47 Fed. Cl. 127 (Cl. Ct. 2000).

discretion when denying an application for an accounting method change. This determination appears to be a serious logical inconsistency in the courts reasoning.

As in *Barnett Banks,* the taxpayer in the case at issue provided considerable services to its cardholders.[172] A study performed by the taxpayer indicated that these benefits were one of the most important reasons why cardholders carried its cards despite higher fees than for cards of competitors. Moreover, as with *Barnett Bank's* card fee, the taxpayer's fee was refundable to the cardholder on a pro rata basis if the card was canceled. The arrangement between the taxpayer and its cardholder provided that if the cardholder or the taxpayer canceled the card without cause, the cardholder was refunded a portion of the fee reflecting the amount of time that was left on the 12-month period. These facts distinguished the holding in *Barnett Banks* with the holding in *Signet Banking Corp.*[173] The court noted that neither *Barnett Banks* nor *Signet Banking Corp.* fully addressed the question of whether there was an adequate basis for the Commissioner's exercise of discretion under Revenue Procedure 71-21. The court also noted that in both cases, the Tax Court "appears to decide anew the facts of those cases." However, the Tax Court decisions in those cases helped to define when a credit card fee is in fact a fee for services and therefore eligible for amortization pursuant to Reserve Procedure 71-21.

§ 2.7.4 Mortgage Servicing Fees

A servicer of mortgages receives a fee for collecting and remitting monthly payments and providing various documentation and other services. The servicer also is entitled to the use of the funds collected until the funds are required to be remitted to the owner of the mortgage, tax authorities, or insurance companies. A servicer of mortgages can be the originator, who may sell mortgages but retain the servicing rights, the purchaser of mortgages, who may also purchase the servicing right, or simply an entity that purchases the servicing rights.[174]

(a) *General Tax Accounting Rules*

Reasonable compensation for the services to be performed by a bank that services mortgages for third parties are included in taxable income in accordance with a taxpayer's overall method of accounting. Thus, an accrual basis taxpayer would recognize income when the fee is earned or when it is received, whichever occurs earlier. The fee may not be averaged over the life of the mortgage.[175] If all services are to be performed in the future and payments have not been received (including the receipt of notes constituting payment), income may be deferred.[176]

---

[172] *Barnett Banks of Florida v. Commissioner,* 106 T.C. 103 (1996).

[173] *Signet Banking Corp. v. Commissioner,* 106 T.C. 117 (1996), *aff'd,* 118 Fed. 3d 239 (4th Cir. 1997).

[174] For special rules pertaining to the treatment of a purchaser of mortgage servicing rights, *see* Ch. 11, at Section 11.3.2. Generally, mortgage servicing rights retained in a sale of mortgages are not subject to the I.R.C. § 197(e)(7) rules for amortization of intangibles, because they do not constitute the acquisition of a trade or business. If mortgage servicing rights are purchased apart from a trade or business, the rights are eligible for amortization. *See* I.R.C. § 167(f)(3).

[175] Rev. Rul. 70-142, 1970-1 C.B. 115.

[176] *Schuster v. Helvering,* 41-2 U.S.T.C. ¶ 9601, 121 F.2d 643 (2d Cir. 1941), *aff'g* 42 B.T.A. 255, Dec. 11,239 (1940).

Furthermore, the Tax Court has held that an accrual-basis taxpayer must include mortgage servicing fees in income as mortgage payments are received even though the underlying agreement the taxpayer had with the mortgagee provided that the fee would be equal to a fixed percentage of the principal amount of the mortgage.[177] A cash-basis taxpayer has fee income when the fee is actually or constructively received.

(b) *Coupon Stripping Bond Rules*

For purposes of determining whether and to what extent compensation received on the sale of originated mortgages represents payment equal to the amount loaned, and also what portion may represent income on sale of the mortgages, the IRS has issued a series of pronouncements.[178] These rules establish certain safe harbors for reasonable service fees and treat the excess of any amount retained over reasonable compensation for servicing the mortgages as a stripped coupon to which the Code section 1286 coupon stripping bond rules apply.[179] The IRS's "Audit Technique Guide for Commercial Banking" sets forth examination treatment of this issue in considerable detail.[180]

Code section 1286 defines a "bond" for purposes of the coupon stripping bond rules as including certificates or other evidences of indebtedness.[181] A "coupon" is defined to include "any right to receive interest on a bond (whether or not evidenced by a coupon)."[182] A "stripped bond" is "a bond issued at any time with interest coupons where there is a separation in ownership between the bond and any coupon which has not yet become payable."[183]

The coupon stripping bond rules have the effect of treating the obligation as having O.I.D. equal to the difference between all amounts to be received (the "stated redemption price at maturity") and the basis allocated to the coupon (the "issue price"). This O.I.D. may be included in income for accrual method taxpayers using an alternative to the constant rate yield-to-maturity method.[184]

---

[177] *Guarantee Title & Trust Co. v. Commissioner*, 63-1 U.S.T.C. ¶9292, 313 F.2d 225 (6th Cir. 1963); *Etheridge and Vanneman, Inc. v. Commissioner*, 40 T.C. 461, Dec. 26,157 (1963).

[178] Rev. Rul. 91-46, 1991-2 C.B. 358; Rev. Proc 91-49, 1991-2 C.B. 777; Rev. Proc. 91-50, 1991-2 C.B. 778; Rev. Proc. 91-51, 1991-2 C.B. 779; Temp. Reg. §1.1286-1T; T.D. 8358, 1991-2 C.B. 360. Rev. Proc. 91-51 contains guidelines for obtaining consent to change from an impermissible method of accounting for mortgage servicing fees to a method that complies with I.R.C. §1286. A taxpayer under audit was permitted to effect a change in its method of accounting under the terms and conditions of Rev. Proc. 91-51 because it was found that the issue had not yet been raised on audit. TAM 9522005, June 5, 1995. IRS Information Document Requests relating to sales of mortgages that asked for information on how loan servicing fees were determined and details on sales prices, interest rates, names of purchasers, loan numbers, etc., were found to be insufficient to raise issues relating to taxpayer's method of accounting. However, a taxpayer was not permitted to retroactively change its method and obtain tax refunds. TAM 9439002, June 23, 1994. *See also* Rev. Rul. 90-38, 1990-1 C.B. 57.

[179] *See* I.R.C. §197(e)(7) for rules that apply to mortgage servicing rights acquired in a transaction (or series of related transactions).

[180] Audit Technique Guide for Commercial Banking, Ch. 8, Mortgage Servicing Rights, located at Appendix D.

[181] I.R.C. §1286(e)(1).

[182] I.R.C. §1286(e)(5).

[183] I.R.C. §1286(e)(2).

[184] FSA 199913023, April 2, 1999. The alternate became available with the addition of I.R.C. §1272(a)(6)(C)(iii) through the Taxpayer Relief Act of 1997, Pub. L. No. 105-34, §1004, 111 Stat. 787.

The alternative method allows for the deferment of income until a prepayment is actually received.[185]

If tax basis is allocated to the right to receive future income (the stripped coupon) and a portion of proceeds on the sale of the mortgages is treated as gain, the character will be determined based on the character of the mortgage in the hands of the transferor. Code section 582 would characterize any gain or loss by a bank as ordinary in nature. If only the right to sell mortgage servicing is sold, taxpayers have argued that the gain or loss is with respect to a Code section 1231 asset, thereby entitling them to capital gains and ordinary loss treatment.

(c) *Allocation of Basis*

Pursuant to the coupon stripping bond rules, a mortgagee's tax basis in the mortgage immediately before the sale is allocated between the item retained, the interest in excess of reasonable compensation for the services to be performed, and the item sold, which equals the principal of the mortgage. The allocation is made in accordance with the respective fair market values of those components.[186] The IRS has provided limited guidance to taxpayers in determining the fair market value of the stripped interest coupon. Revenue Ruling 91-46 takes the position that mortgages are "stripped bonds" if the contract entitles the taxpayer to receive amounts that exceed reasonable compensation for the services to be performed under the contract. It provides further that "the fair market value of the stripped coupons is determined on the basis of all of the relevant facts and circumstances."[187] "[F]acts to be considered in determining this amount include, but are not necessarily limited to, recent sale prices of comparable rights."[188] In any event, the fair market value of the stripped coupons will represent the value of the mortgagee's right to receive interest other than as compensation for services. Although not controlling for tax purposes, the taxpayer's accounting treatment of interest coupons may also be relevant in determining fair market value, at least from a reasonableness perspective.

(d) *Safe Harbors*

Because the period of time that a loan remains outstanding is uncertain, it is often difficult to determine the actual servicing fee portion of the amount received from the sale of originated mortgages.[189] However, to provide some certainty in the tax treatment, the IRS has provided safe harbors. An elective safe

---

[185] For a discussion of this deferment of income as applied to credit cards, *see* Section 3.5.1.

[186] I.R.C. § 1286(b). Statement of Financial Accounting Standards No. 112 (Statement No. 112) issued in May 1995 requires mortgage servicers who sell or securitize mortgage loans, but who retain the right to service the mortgages, to allocate the cost of the loans to the loan and to the retained rights based on relative fair market values. If such value cannot be determined, the cost of acquiring the loans must be allocated entirely to the loans. Statement No. 112 modifies Statement No. 65 as issued in 1982. *See also* Statement No. 125, which deals with the accounting for mortgage servicing rights in excess of "adequate compensation." Statement of Financial Accounting Standards No. 140 supersedes Statement Nos. 112 and 125. It applies to transferors of securities and the servicing of financial assets and extinguishment of liabilities occurring after April 1, 2001.

[187] Rev. Rul. 91-46, 1991-2 C.B. 359.

[188] *Id.*

[189] *See Buy, Sell, or Hold? Valuing Cash Flows from Mortgage Lending*, Economic Review, Vol 79, No. 6, Nov./Dec. 1994, published by the Federal Reserve Bank of Atlanta, for a discussion of how mortgage loans can be valued.

harbor rule set forth in Revenue Procedure 91-50 designates the amount of "reasonable compensation" for servicing mortgages to be between 25 and 44 basis points, depending upon the type of mortgage.[190] This rule is elective and the election is made by attaching a statement to the taxpayer's timely filed federal income tax return for the first taxable year for which the safe harbor is elected.[191]

Depending on several variables, the use of the safe harbors may be either advantageous or disadvantageous. For example, although many taxpayers who service mortgages benefit from the safe harbors, those taxpayers who service relatively small amounts of mortgages will have a higher cost per mortgage to service than a taxpayer who services a large quantity of mortgages. For them the use of the safe harbors will be disadvantageous.

A taxpayer operating outside of the safe harbor rules is likely to have the treatment of retained mortgage servicing rights challenged. The IRS may scrutinize the discount rate used by the taxpayer to determine the value of the rights, the prepayment and default assumptions, and the estimated costs of servicing.

For the following four categories of loans, the safe harbor rates that may be elected are:

1. 25 Basis Points for conventional fixed-rate loans with an original balance greater than $50,000;
2. 44 Basis Points for one-to-four unit residential loans with an original principal balance of $50,000 or less;
3. Federal Housing Administration, the Department of Veterans Affair, and Farmers Home Administration loans originated within one year of sale with an original balance greater than $50,000; and
4. 37.5 Basis Points for all other one-to-four unit residential loans, including conventional, variable rate loans, with an original balance greater than $50,000.

The safe harbor rates are a percentage of the principal balance of the loans. The servicer is also entitled to any customary late payment fees, prepayment fees, and assumption fees. In addition, the servicer will not violate the safe harbor rates by retaining the use of any funds in the escrow accounts.

A mortgage originator/servicer is likely to have mortgages that fall into two or more of the four safe harbor classifications. In such cases, the IRS provides that the safe harbor rates are to be blended by computing the weighted average of the rates for each of the classes. The weighted average is determined by reference to principal balances of the mortgages at the time of sale.[192]

---

[190] Rev. Proc. 91-50, 1991-2 C.B. 778.

[191] PLR 201701017, September 16, 2016, contains a discussion of the circumstances that should be present when a taxpayer requests relief under Reg. §301.9100-3 for filing a delinquent election.

[192] The method of accounting for income recognition on mortgage servicing set forth in Rev. Rul. 91-50 is mandatory, and the procedure for adopting the ruling's method of accounting is also mandated. Rev. Proc. 91-51, and not Rev. Proc. 84-74, 1984-2 C.B. 736, contains the rules for changing to the accounting method set forth in Rev. Rul. 91-50.

Example: Assume that Bank sells a $9 million conventional, fixed-rate mortgage pool to Agency for $9 million. Agency is in the business of purchasing residential mortgages and selling interests in these mortgages to investors. At the time of the transfer, Bank and Agency enter into a contract for Bank to service the mortgages transferred. The contract provides that Bank is entitled to receive 1.25 percent of the outstanding principal balance of the mortgages. In addition, Bank is entitled to retain income earned on the mortgage collections between the time they are collected and the time they are remitted to Agency, as well as on the income earned on escrow accounts and late fees, bad check charges, and so on. Bank elects to use the safe harbor provided in Revenue Procedure 91-50 for determining the extent to which amounts received under the mortgage servicing contract represent reasonable compensation.

Under Revenue Procedure 91-50, the appropriate safe harbor rate for this category of loan is 0.25 percent and thus the excess servicing component of the contract is 1 percent. The fair market value of the stripped coupon, which is the value of Bank's rights to receive interest other than as compensation for services, is determined by discounting the 1 percent payments over the estimated life of the servicing contract. The normal servicing component, consisting of the 0.25 percent payments plus other income earned on the contract, such as bad check fees, is taken into income as amounts are received or accrued over time.

Assume that Bank estimates the fair market value of the stripped coupon, using similar sales, to be $1 million. The total fair market value of the principal and stripped coupon equals $10 million ($9 million + $1 million). The relative fair market value of the interest component is ten percent ($1 million/$10 million). This percentage is then used to allocate basis of the original mortgage pool between the principal and the stripped coupon, and also for determining gain or loss on the sale and for interest amortization purposes. No basis is allocated to the normal servicing component. Assuming an original basis equal to the principal amount of the mortgage pool, basis allocations to the principal and interest components are $8.1 million and $900,000, respectively. Therefore, Bank recognizes gain on the sale of the mortgage pool of $900,000 ($9 million sales price less $8.1 million of allocated basis). The original issue discount equals the excess of the total amounts to be received by Bank for the excess servicing over the allocated basis amount ($900,000). This discount is amortized to income using the constant rate, yield-to-maturity method.

(e) *Sale of Mortgage Servicing-Character of Gain or Loss*

Normally when property is sold the character of gain or loss is determined under the general rule of Code section 1221. Occasionally, the Code provides special rules that override this general characterization rule. In the case of mortgage servicing rights, determining the character of gain or loss is complicated by the nature of the transaction. Characterization of gains or losses is particularly important for those banks that are taxed under Subchapter S of the Code.

In general, the sale of mortgage servicing involves the outright assignment, for a fair and adequate consideration, of the mortgagor's obligation to remit interest, principal, tax, and insurance amounts to the mortgagee. Thus, the seller transfers to the buyer the right to receive all payments on the mortgages. The purchaser derives from the property purchased a servicing fee, the interest free use of the funds that it collects from the mortgagor, and various other amounts, including any fees that it may charge the mortgagors for late payment of amounts due.

Code section 1221 characterizes all property as a capital asset except for the items that it expressly lists as not being capital assets. Among the exceptions are:

1. "stock in trade . . . or other property of a kind which would properly be included in the inventory of the taxpayer or on hand at the close of the taxable year, or property held by the taxpayer primarily for sale to customers in the ordinary course of his trade or business . . . ."[193]

2. "property, used in his trade or business, of a character which is subject to the allowance for depreciation provided in section 167 . . . ."[194]

3. "Accounts or notes receivable acquired in the ordinary course or trade or business for services rendered or from the sale or property described in paragraph (1)"[195]

The applicability of the first exception is questionable, especially for most banks. Banks are not in the business of selling mortgage servicing rights, even though they do so as an adjunct of their financial intermediation business. Moreover, the mere fact that such property is sold by a bank does not cause the bank to own property "held . . . primarily for sale to customers." The purpose of owning the property is not for it to be "held" for sale.

The applicability of the third exception is also questionable, as it is dependent upon the applicability of the first exception. What is sold is not an account or note receivable that was acquired by selling the property that was held as inventory or property otherwise described in the first exception. Some may argue that the property sold is a debt instrument, but even assuming it is, it is probably not with respect to property "held" as inventory, etc.

The applicability of the second exception also appears to be questionable, especially if the seller had not previously purchased the mortgage servicing. A seller of mortgage servicing that was the originator of the mortgages is not entitled to depreciate the mortgage servicing before it is sold. It is not properly classified as "property used in the trade or business" or "property held for the production of income."[196] However, a purchaser of mortgage servicing who later sells the property, would probably be entitled to amortization deductions under Code section 167 with respect to the property acquired. Moreover, if the acquired

193 I.R.C. § 1221(a)(1).
194 I.R.C. § 1221(a)(2).
195 I.R.C. § 1221(a)(4).
196 I.R.C. § 167(a)((1) and (2).

mortgage servicing constituted "a trade or business or substantial portion thereon" an amortization deduction would expressly be permitted under Code section 197.[197]

Thus, of the three possible exceptions to what constitutes a capital assets contained in Code section 1221, none appears to be clearly applicable. If no other provision were applicable, then the gain or loss on the sale or mortgage servicing would be capital gain or loss.

Code section 582 overrides Code Section 1221 and recharacterizes capital gains or losses as ordinary. The former section is, however, applicable only to certain financial institutions and to the sale of certain property.

For Code section 582 to apply, the selling entity must either meet the Code section 581 definition of a "bank" (including any corporation which would meet the definition of a bank except for the fact that it is a foreign corporation) or the Code section 591 definition of a "mutual savings bank."[198] Mortgage companies usually do not meet these definitions.

Moreover, Code section 582 is applicable only to gains or losses derived from the sale or exchange of "a bond, note, or certificate or other evidence of indebtedness . . . ."[199] The applicability of this limitation to mortgage servicing rights is unclear. Undoubtedly, what is sold is a property right, and, so too is a bond, note, etc. Of course, not all property rights are debt instruments described in Code section 582.

The IRS pronouncements (discussed above) on the tax treatment of "excess" mortgage servicing rights cast some light on this analysis and suggest that when mortgage servicing is sold, a debt instrument may have been sold. Whether these pronouncements should be read to apply only to basis allocation and not to income characterization is unclear. Moreover, it appears that they are designed to deal with "excess" servicing, not with the fee with respect to services.

(f) *Purchase of Servicing Rights-Cost Recovery*

When a servicer of loans purchases servicing rights (either with or without the underlying mortgages and whether from another servicer or from an originator of loans), the purchaser must determine the extent to which the cost of the items purchased may be recovered in any tax year. To the extent that there is cost recovery, there will be an offset to the income derived from the serviced mortgages.

To properly arrive at the cost recovery amount, the amortization method and recovery period must be determined. Resolution of these questions will depend on when the servicing was acquired, whether it was acquired as part of a transaction involving the acquisition of a trade or business, and what type of loans are being serviced.

---

[197] *See* I.R.C. § 197(e)(7). *See* discussion below.

[198] I.R.C. § 582(c)(2)(A)(i) and (ii). The definition also includes a small business investment company operating under the Small Business Investment Act of 1958 and a business development company.

[199] I.R.C. § 582(c)(1).

Mortgage servicing acquired after August 10, 1993, as part of the acquisition of a trade or business is subject to the general cost recovery rules prescribed in Code section 197(a).[200] Prior to the effective date of Code section 197, the general cost recovery rules of Code section 167 would apply.

Under Code section 197 the cost is recovered over a 15-year term using the straight line method. However, if the servicing does relate to loans secured by residential real estate, Code section 197(e)(6) excepts the servicing rights from the usual 15-year amortization period provided by Code section 197(a). It appears that such servicing is subject to the general cost recovery rules of Code section 167(a), discussed below.

Regulations provide that, for purposes of Code section 197, a group of assets constitutes a trade or business if their use would constitute a trade or business under Code section 1060 (that is, if goodwill or going concern value could, under any circumstances, attach to the assets).[201] For this purpose, all the facts and circumstances, including any employee relationships that continue (or covenants not to compete that are entered into) as part of the transfer of the assets, are taken into account in determining whether goodwill or going concern value could attach to the assets.

If the acquisition of the mortgage servicing occurs after August 10, 1993, and it is not part of the acquisition of a trade or business, cost recovery will be determined under a special rule contained in Code section 167(f).[202] That rule prescribes that the depreciation is computed using the straight-line method and a 108-month useful life, with salvage value equal to zero.[203]

Servicing rights that are not amortizable under either the general rule of Code section 197(a) (15 years, straight-line) or the special rule of 167(f) (108 months, straight-line) are subject to general cost recovery rules of Code section 167(a). Because pools of servicing rights are intangible assets,[204] the Modified Accelerated Cost Recovery System prescribed in Code section 168 for tangible property is not available. Intangible property, such as servicing rights, is eligible for cost recovery under the general depreciation rules of Code section 167.

An intangible asset known from experience or other factors to be of use in the business or in the production of income for only a limited period whose length can be estimated with reasonable accuracy may be the subject of a depreciation allowance.[205] The estimated useful life of an asset is not necessarily the useful life inherent in the asset, but is the period over which the asset may be expected to be useful in the trade or business or in the production of income.[206] The taxpayer will have the burden of proving the appropriate life of the servicing that is acquired.

---

[200] I.R.C. § 197(f)(7). The provisions of Code section 197 became effective on August 10, 1993.

[201] Reg. § 1.197-2(c)(11).

[202] Reg. § 1.197-14(d); Reg. § 1.167(b)-1.

[203] Reg. § 1.197-2(e)(1). *See also* Reg. § 1.1060-1T(b)(2).

[204] *Western Mortgage Corp. v. United States*, 308 F. Supp. 333 (C.D. Cal. 1969); *Securities-Intermountain, Inc. v. United States*, 460 F.2d 261 (9th Cir. 1972); *First Pennsylvania Banking & Trust Co. v. Commissioner*, 56 T.C. 677 (1971).

[205] Reg. § 1.167(a)-1(a).

[206] Reg. § 1.167(a)-1(b).

Treasury regulations provide that the straight line method is always deemed to be a reasonable depreciation method.[207] Furthermore, it is the position of the IRS that the income forecast method is not an acceptable method of depreciation for pools of mortgage servicing rights. It is acceptable only for specified types of property which have an erratic stream of income and a usefulness dependent upon consumer appeal.[208] Thus, the straight-line method is the method that will most likely apply to purchased pools of servicing rights, regardless of when they are acquired (prior to or after August 10, 1993) and regardless of whether the servicing that is acquired is mortgage servicing or servicing of other loans.

Mortgage servicing rights relating to a pool of mortgages are treated as a single asset under section 167(f) (relating to mortgage servicing rights not acquired as part of a purchase of a trade or business).[209] Thus, if some but not all mortgages in a pool prepay, no loss is recognized. Similarly, any amount realized from the sale or exchange of some (but not all) of the mortgage servicing rights is included in income and the adjusted basis of the pool is not affected by the realization. The Treasury Department rejected requests by taxpayers at the time that the regulations were being finalized to treat each right in the pool is a discrete asset. This would have permitted taxpayers to recognize a loss upon the prepayment of an individual mortgage within the pool.[210] The Treasury Department stated that this is generally inappropriate in cases where depreciation is based on the average useful life of the assets.[211] The Regulations also provide, however, that if a taxpayer establishes multiple accounts within a pool at the time of its acquisition, gain or loss is recognized on the sale or exchange of all mortgage servicing rights within any such account. If the taxpayer establishes multiple accounts within a pool at the time of its acquisition, gain or loss is recognized on the sale or exchange of all mortgage servicing rights within any such account.[212]

§2.7.5 Affinity Cards

A bank may enter into an arrangement with a tax-exempt or other organization pursuant to which the bank solicits members of the organization to acquire the bank's credit card. This arrangement may generate royalty or service fee income. Whether the amount that the bank pays to the organization is a royalty or a service fee will depend upon the terms of the arrangement.[213] If the payment is for the right to use intangible property rights and it is not for services, it will be a royalty payment. However, the organization need not be passive in earning the income for the income to be treated as royalty income. Thus, an organization which actively manages the mailing lists that it licenses to the bank may receive royalty income if the amount it receives is for the right of the bank to use the mailing list.[214]

---

[207] Reg. §1.167(b)-1. FSA 199941009, October 15, 1999.

[208] Rev. Rul. 89-62, 1989-1 C.B. 78.

[209] Reg. §1.197-14(d)(2)(i).

[210] *See* preamble to final regulations under §197, T.D. 8865, February 14, 2000, 2000-1 C.B. 589.

[211] *See* Reg. §1.167(a)-8.

[212] Reg. §1.197-14(d)(2)(ii).

[213] *Sierra Club, Inc. v. Commissioner*, 96-2 U.S.T.C. §50 326, 86 F.3d 1526 (9th Cir. 1996).

[214] *Oregon State University Alumni Assoc. v. Commissioner*, 71 T.C.M. 1935, T.C. Memo 1996-34.

§2.7.6 Gift Cards

Taxpayers may defer recognition of advance payments received from the sale of gift cards under a special rule promulgated in 2013 that permits gift card income to be included in taxable income when it is recognized for book accounting purposes.[215] An advance payment on a gift card sale is one where the taxpayer is primarily liable to the customer or holder of the card for the value of the card and the customer may redeem the gift card with the taxpayer or with any other entity that is legally obligated to the taxpayer to accept the gift card as payment.[216]

If a bank sells a gift card that is redeemable by an unrelated entity, the gift card income is normally recognized by the bank for accounting purposes to the extent the gift card is redeemed during the taxable year.[217] To be eligible for tax deferral, an advance payment must be recognized by the taxpayer on its "applicable financial statement" in a taxable year subsequent to the year of sale.[218] An "applicable financial statement" is one that is required to be filed with the Securities and Exchange Commission, a certified audited financial statement accompanied by the report of a certified public accountant that is used for credit purposes, reporting to shareholders, or any other substantial nontax purpose, or a financial statement required to be provided to any federal or state government or agency.[219] This would include a financial statement that is provided to a bank regulator.

(a) *The Deferral Method*

Under the deferral method of accounting that predated the 2013 rule, taxpayers were required to include in gross income all or a portion of advance payments, but only to the extent that the payment was recognized in revenues in the taxpayer's own financial statement. If the revenue were not included in the taxpayer's financial statement, it was not eligible for the deferral rule.[220] If a gift card was redeemed by an unrelated entity whose financial statement revenues were not consolidated with the taxpayer's revenues, the taxpayer would never recognize any portion of the gift card sale in revenues because that revenue was

---

215 Rev. Proc. 2013-29, 2013-33 I.R.B. 141; Rev. Proc. 2011-18, 2011-5 I.R.B. 44. "[P]rovided the other requirements of Rev. Proc. 2004-34 are met, a taxpayer that sells gift cards redeemable through other entities should be treated the same as a taxpayer that sells gift cards redeemable only by that taxpayer." Rev. Proc. 2013-29, at § 2.08. Notably, Revenue Procedure 2013-29 does not alter Treasury Regulation section 1.451-5 because the Regulation allows deferral of advance payments on agreements for the future sale of goods held by the taxpayer; goods provided by entities other than the gift card issuing taxpayer are not "held by the taxpayer" as is required by the Regulation. *Id.*

216 Rev. Proc. 2013-29, at §3. *See* Rev. Proc. 2004-34, §4.01(3)(a)-(j) for a list of acceptable items that a gift card may pay for in order to be treated as an eligible gift card sale.

217 Retailers treat gift card payments as a liability on their balance sheet and do not recognize revenue on their balance sheet from the sale of the gift card until the gift card is redeemed. Charles O. Kile, Jr., *Accounting for Gift Cards, An Emerging Issue for Retailers and Auditors,* JOURNAL OF ACCOUNTANCY, Nov. 2007, *available at* http://www.journalofaccountancy.com/NR/exeres/19C8DBEE-AD5C-4497-A487-519F4CC29CBF.htm.

218 For taxpayers without an "applicable financial statement," the payment must be earned in a subsequent taxable year to be eligible for deferral. Rev. Proc. 2013-29, at §2.03.

219 Rev. Proc. 2004-34, 2004-22 I.R.B. 991, §4.06.

220 Rev. Proc. 2004-34, at §1; *see also* Rev. Proc. 2013-29. The idea of deferring payments until subsequent taxable years is fairly common. *See, e.g.,* Rev. Proc. 71-21, 1971-2 C.B. 549, and Reg. §1.263(a)-5.

only accounted for by the unrelated entity.[221] Accordingly, because the taxpayer would not recognize the revenue on the taxpayer's financial statement, the sale of the gift card would not qualify as an advance payment and the taxpayer would be unable to use the deferral method. Under the current rule when the income is redeemed by the unrelated entity, it will be treated as recognized in the financial statements of the taxpayer. Under both the current and the rule that predated it, the taxpayer may not defer including an advance payment in gross income later than the succeeding taxable year.[222]

(b) *Effective Date*

The changes to accounting methods made by Revenue Procedure 2013-29 are effective for taxable years ending on or after December 31, 2010.[223] Accordingly, the Service will not raise the issue of whether the deferral method can apply to eligible gift card sales that occurred in taxable years ending before December 31, 2010.[224]

(c) *Example*

An example of the deferral method applied to gift card sales is provided in Revenue Procedure 2011-18, as follows:

> R corporation operates department stores. *U* corporation, *V* corporation, and *W* corporation are wholly owned domestic subsidiaries of *R* that file a consolidated federal income tax return with *R*. *X* corporation is a controlled foreign subsidiary of *R* that is prohibited from filing a consolidated return with *R*. *U* sells Brand A goods, V sells Brand B goods, *X* sells Brand C goods, and Z is an unrelated entity that sells Brand D goods. *W* administers a gift card program for the *R* consolidated group, *X*, and Z. Pursuant to the underlying agreements, *W* issues gift cards that are redeemable for goods or services offered by *U*, *V*, *X*, and Z. In addition, *U*. *V*. *X*. and Z sell gift cards to customers on behalf of W and remit amounts received to *W*. The agreements provide that *W* is primarily liable to the customer for the value of the gift card until redemption, and *U*, *V*, *X*, and Z are obligated to accept the gift card as payment for goods or services. When a customer purchases goods or services with a gift card at *U*, *V*, *X*, or Z, *W* reimburses that entity for the sales price of the goods or services purchased with the gift card, up to the total gift card value. In Year 1, W sells gift cards with a total value of $900,000, and, at the end of Year 1, the unredeemed balance of the gift cards is $100,000. In the consolidated group's applicable financial statement, the group recognizes revenue from the sale of a gift card when the gift card is redeemed. *W* tracks sales and redemptions of gift cards electronically, is able to determine the extent to which advance payments are recognized in revenues in its consolidated applicable financial statement for the taxable year of receipt, and meets the requirements of section 5.02(1)(b)(i) of this revenue procedure. The payments *W* receives from the sale of gift cards are advance payments because they are payments for eligible gift card sales under section 4.01(3) of this revenue procedure and meet the requirements of sections 4.01(1) and (2). Thus, W is eligible to use the Deferral Method. At the end of Year 1, *W*

[221] Rev. Proc. 2013-29, at § 2.04.

[222] Rev. Proc. 2013-29, at § 2.01; Rev. Proc. 2004-34, at § 1. If the taxpayer does not have an applicable financial statement, the taxpayer must include the advance payment to the extent earned in the taxable year of receipt. *See* Rev. Proc. 2004-34, § 4.06 for a detailed explanation of financial statements.

[223] Rev. Proc. 2013-29, at § 4.

[224] *See id*. at § 5; Rev. Proc. 2011-18, § 5.

recognizes $800,000 in income in its consolidated applicable financial statement. Under the Deferral Method, *W* must include $800,000 of the payments from gift card sales in gross income in Year 1 and the remaining $100,000 of the payments in gross income in Year 2.

§ 2.8 Other Income

§ 2.8.1 Commitment Fees

Commitment fees are earned for agreeing to make funds available in the future pursuant to agreed-upon terms. Thus, a commitment fee is an expenditure that results in the sale and acquisition of the intangible property right paid for the use of money. It is similar to the cost of an option, which becomes part of the cost of the property acquired upon exercise of the option.[225]

Commitment, or standby, fees are includible in the income of a cash basis bank when received and in the income of an accrual basis bank when the "all-events" test is met or when received, whichever occurs earlier.[226] Normally, the all-events test will be satisfied at the time the commitment is made because that is when the income is earned; however, deferral over the commitment period has been required for the payor of the fee.

The purchaser of the right must capitalize the cost and deduct it ratably over the term of the loan if the right is exercised. If the right is not exercised, the taxpayer may be entitled to a loss deduction under Code section 165 when the right expires.[227]

Deferring recognition of commitment fee income until a date subsequent to the date of receipt, for a cash method lender, or subsequent to the earlier of the date of receipt or when earned, in the case of an accrual method lender, is to use a method of accounting that fails to "clearly reflect income."[228] Regulation section 1.1273-2(g)(2)(i) expressly excludes commitment fees from the required deferral of loan origination income (points).

Statement of Financial Accounting Standards No. 91 provides for deferral of commitment fees. The deferred fees are recognized over the life of the related loan if the commitment is exercised, or if the commitment expires unexercised, the fees are recognized in income upon expiration of the commitment. Thus, a Schedule M adjustment should be made for commitment fees.[229]

---

[225] CCA 201136022 (2011); Rev. Rul. 81-160, 1981-1 C.B. 312; Rev. Rul. 70-540, 1970-2 C.B. 101.

[226] *See* Rev. Rul. 81-160, 1981-1 C.B. 312, *rev'g* Rev. Rul. 56-136, 1956-1 C.B. 92; Rev. Rul. 70-142, 1970-1 C.B. 115; Rev. Rul. 70-540, 1970-2 C.B. 101; Rev. Rul. 74-607, 1974-2 C.B. 149; Rev. Rul. 74-395, 1974-2 C.B. 45, for a discussion of the treatment of commitment fees earned for FNMA assumption of construction loans. *See also* IRS "Audit Technique Guide for Commercial Banking," Chapter 16, Fee Income, located at Appendix D.

[227] Rev. Rul. 75-172, 1975-1 C.B. 145; *Francis v. Commissioner* TC memo. 1977-170, 36 T.C.M. 704; Rev. Rul. 71-191, 1971-1 C.B. 77.

[228] *Chesapeake Financial Corp. v. Commissioner*, 78 T.C. 869, Dec. 39,059 (1982); Rev. Rul. 70-540, 1970-2 C.B. 101.

[229] Statement of Financial Accounting Standards No. 91, para. 8.

§2.8.2 Commissions on Loans

Commissions that are received by a bank for originating a loan are includible in the income of an accrual basis taxpayer at the time the loan is made, regardless of whether the fee is actually or constructively received or whether the fee may be refunded.[230] Loan commissions are to be distinguished from prepaid interest, or points, also paid on the origination of some loans. A commission fee is usually received by a bank to compensate it for the administrative costs, often referred to as pipeline costs, associated with originating the loan.[231] A portion of such costs may be associated with the risk that interest rates will rise during the commitment period.

If loan commissions are subtracted from the face amount of a loan at the time that the loan is made, a cash basis taxpayer takes the commissions into income when and to the extent that payments are actually received (or the loan is sold or otherwise disposed of).[232] However, the IRS has ruled that commissions that are not refundable in the event that a loan is repaid are income at the time the loan is made.[233] The Tax Court has held that refundable commissions are not immediately recognized in income.[234] An accrual method taxpayer is not entitled to defer loan commissions that are subtracted from the face of a loan under the O.I.D. deferral rules. The latter apply only to interest income. It has been held that when an accrual basis taxpayer received a time certificate in payment of its loan commission, endorsed it, and used it as additional security for endorsing loans of its clients, the commission was income in the taxable year in which the endorsement was made.[235]

§2.8.3 Commissions on Purchase or Sale of Securities

When a taxpayer purchases or sells securities on behalf of a customer, the taxpayer is essentially performing a service, the income from which is commonly referred to as a commission.

It has long been the position of the IRS that a stock brokerage business using the accrual method of accounting must accrue commission income on the trade date, rather than on the settlement date.[236] The "trade date" is the day a trade occurs. On this day, a customer's order is executed by locating a seller or

---

[230] Rev. Rul. 75-541, 1975-1 C.B. 195; *Columbia State Savings Bank v. Commissioner*, 2 U.S.T.C. ¶547, 41 F.2d 923 (7th Cir. 1930); *Bonded Mortgage Co. of Baltimore v. Commissioner*, 4 U.S.T.C. ¶1265, 70 F.2d 341 (CCA 1934); *Title Insurance Co. of Hampden County v. United States*, DC Mass., 39-2 U.S.T.C. ¶9782; *Columbia State Savings Bank v. Commissioner*, 31 B.T.A. 685, Dec. 8797 (1934).

[231] Loan commission fees are sometimes referred to as syndication fees. *See* Statement of Financial Accounting Standards No. 91, para. 11.

[232] *Blair v. First Trust & Savings Bank of Miami, Fla.*, 2 U.S.T.C. ¶501, 39 F.2d 462 (5th Cir. 1930); *Cf.* S.M. 3820, IV-2 C.B. 32 (1925). Reserves established to cover a bank's liability that may arise upon the borrower's default in paying a loan commission may not be currently deducted. *Kistler Co. v. Commissioner*, B.T.A. Memo., Dec. 12,020-G (1941).

[233] S.M. 3820, IV-2 C.B. 32 (1925); *Columbia State Savings Bank v. Commissioner*, 2 U.S.T.C. ¶547, 41 F.2d 923 (7th Cir. 1930); *Columbia State Savings Bank v. Commissioner*, 31 B.T.A. 685, Dec. 8797 (1934).

[234] *Motor Securities Co., Inc. v. Commissioner*, 11 T.C.M. 1074, Dec. 19,275(M) (1952). Compare this with the treatment of refunded interest at §2.3.5.

[235] *Vancoh Realty Company v. Commissioner*, 33 B.T.A. 918, Dec. 9204 (1936). Note that if the time certificate were received not "in payment" but as evidence of a debt, it would not give rise to current income inclusion.

[236] Rev. Rul. 74-372, 1974-2 C.B. 147.

purchaser for securities on terms acceptable to the customer. The date on which petitioner settles the accounts of a customer whose order to buy or sell securities has been executed is termed the "settlement date." Settlement is the process of transferring payment from buyer to seller and certificates from seller to buyer. When customers buy securities, the taxpayer earning the commission must receive the full confirmed amount due no later than the settlement date. When customers sell securities, the taxpayer earning the commission must receive the stock certificates, properly endorsed, by the settlement date.

Recently, the Tax Court acquiesced in this treatment.[237] The Tax Court reasoned that the taxpayer's execution of a trade for a customer is a condition precedent that fixes the taxpayer's right to receive the commission income. The functions that remain to be performed by the taxpayer after the trade date are of a ministerial nature to effectuate the mechanics of the transfer and confirm the trade executed. Although failure to perform these functions may ultimately divest the taxpayer of its right to the commission income, the court concluded that these functions are conditions subsequent and, therefore, do not preclude accrual of commission income on the trade date. Furthermore, the possibility that an executed trade may not settle due to cancellation of an entire public offering does not make the taxpayer's right to the commission income too indefinite or contingent for accrual.[238] According to the Tax Court, the possibility that a trade might not finally be settled is, if anything, a condition subsequent to the execution of the trade, which is the event that fixes the taxpayer's right to the commission.[239]

§2.9 Repurchase Agreements

Repurchase agreements consist in their most basic form of an agreement between two parties pursuant to which securities are exchanged for cash, and then, at a later date, the transaction is reversed, with cash returned in exchange for the securities. The tax consequences of the transaction can vary depending upon the substance of the transaction. The two tax issues to resolve when a repurchase agreement is entered into are: (1) whether the initial and subsequent transfers of the securities themselves are taxable events, and (2) whether the interest income yielded by the securities is reportable by the initial transferee of the securities or by the initial transferor.[240]

---

[237] *The Charles Schwab Corp. v. Commissioner*, 107 T.C. 282 (November 14, 1996).

[238] *See Brown v. Helvering* [4 U.S.T.C. ¶1223], 291 U.S. 193, 199-200 (1934) holding that overriding commissions received by a general agent for policies written must be accrued even though there was a contingent liability to return a portion of the commission in the event the policy was canceled; *Georgia School-Book Depository, Inc. v. Commissioner* [Dec. 12,934], 1 T.C. 463, 468-470 (1943) holding that a book broker that represented publishers in sales of school books to the State of Georgia must accrue commission income, despite the fact that the State was obligated to pay for the books only out of a particular fund, and, during the years in issue, the fund was insufficient to pay for the books in full.

[239] *See Central Cuba Sugar Co. v. Commissioner*, 198 F.2d 214, 217-218 (2d Cir. 1952) holding that sales commission expenses were deductible in the year the taxpayer entered the contract for sale even though they were not payable until delivery, and even though the commission expenses were subject to adjustment in accordance with final weighing before shipment and forfeiture if the contract were not carried out.

[240] Federal income tax withholding could be imposed on transactions involving securities lending for stock of U.S. corporations. Notice 97-66, 1997-2 C.B. 328.

§2.9.1 Overview of Tax Treatment

A typical repurchase agreement involves Bank A transferring securities to Broker B, for cash. Depending on the circumstances, this transaction can be described alternatively as Bank A "selling" the securities to Broker B for cash, as Bank A "loaning" the securities to Broker B for a fee, or it may be considered as Broker B "loaning" money to Bank A and receiving the securities as collateral for the loan. Regardless of the terminology used or how the parties characterize the transaction, its substance will determine the tax treatment.[241] The period between the initial transfer and when the security is returned can last for various lengths of time, depending on the needs and desires of the parties involved. The underlying securities used in the transaction are typically federal government securities, municipal bonds, or mortgage-backed securities.

If Bank A actually sells the securities to Broker B, a taxable event occurs, resulting in any gain or loss being recognized by the transferor and the transferee taking a Code section 1012 cost basis.[242] Furthermore, Broker B reports the interest earned on the securities, and if the interest is paid or accrued on a municipal obligation, Broker B is entitled to exclude the interest from gross income.[243] If the securities are simply collateral for a loan from Broker B to Bank A, then Broker B is not entitled to all incidents of ownership interest received, any interest received cannot be excluded from gross income, and no gain or loss is recognized by the transfer or special statutory rules prescribed in Code section 1058 for certain loans of securities. These rules are discussed below.

§2.9.2 Sale vs. Loan

Although certain factors are commonly regarded in judicial opinions and revenue rulings as determinative of the tax treatment of repurchase agreements, no single criterion is controlling, and the factors are seldom equally weighted. Whether a sale or a loan has occurred turns on all of the facts and circumstances in each particular situation. The term "sale" is given its ordinary meaning and is generally defined as a transfer of the ownership of property for money or for a promise to pay money.[244]

The Supreme Court of the United States issued a decision regarding a state's ability to tax interest income derived from a repurchase agreement of federal government securities.[245] Ordinarily, the interest income earned on federal government securities is exempt from state income taxation; however, in the situation before the Court, it found that the interest income earned by the repurchase agreement buyer was not exempt from state taxation.

The taxpayer involved in the case owned shares in two mutual fund trusts that invested in short-term U.S. government securities. Both trusts participated in and earned a portion of their income from repurchase agreements of such securities. The trusts purchased and agreed to resell the same, or identical,

[241] PLR 9839001, September 25, 1998.

[242] I.R.C. §1001. Consider the possible application of the wash sale rule of I.R.C. §1091.

[243] I.R.C. §103.

[244] *Commissioner v. Brown*, 380 U.S. 563, 570-71 (1965); PLR 9839001, September 29, 1998.

[245] *Nebraska Department of Revenue v. Loewenstein*, 513 U.S. 123 (1994).

securities to the initial seller. The transaction was accomplished by the trust transferring cash to the bank account of the seller-borrower and the seller-borrower transferring specified federal securities to the trust's account maintained on the Federal Reserve System's commercial book-entry system. At a later date, either specified by the parties in the original agreement or upon demand of one of the parties, the trusts would deliver the securities to the seller-borrower's account maintained on the Federal Reserve's system and the seller-borrowers would credit the trusts' bank account in an amount equal to the sum of the original cash transfer plus interest at an agreed-upon rate.

The Court determined that the taxpayer, through his participation in the trusts, did not earn interest income from the federal securities, but instead earned interest on loans with respect to which the securities were held as collateral.[246] Two crucial factors noted by the Court in reaching its decision appeared to be the absence of risk assumption by the transferee and the fact that the interest earned by the transferee was determined independently of the amount payable on the securities.[247] The Court observed that the interest that the taxpayer earned was neither "coupon interest" nor "discount interest," the only types of interest that can be earned on a federal security.

Four factors in all were cited by the Court as determinative. First, the amount of interest payable on the repurchase agreement bore no relation to either the coupon interest paid or the discount interest accrued on the securities during the term of the repurchase agreement. Second, if the seller-borrower defaulted on its obligation to pay its debt, the trust could liquidate the securities, but only retain the proceeds of the liquidation up to the amount of the debt plus expenses. If the proceeds were insufficient to satisfy the debt, the trust could recover from the seller-borrowers. An owner of the securities would be entitled to the full amount of the liquidation and would have to absorb the loss if it was insufficient. Further, the Court noted that the parties were required to maintain the value of the securities at 102 percent of the original amount of cash transferred to the seller-borrower, either by depositing more securities when the market value declined, or returning securities when the market value rose. Finally, it observed that the seller-borrower was permitted to substitute federal securities of equal market value for the federal securities initially transferred, indicating that the trusts were indifferent to the particular collateral pledged so long as it had sufficient value and liquidity.

In light of this Supreme Court opinion and prior judicial and administrative pronouncements, whether a repurchase agreement will be treated as a loan or as a sale will depend upon the answers to the following questions:

---

[246] *Id.* at 562. The Court stated that even if the taxpayer held legal title to the securities, the interest that the trusts received was, in economic reality, interest on cash lent to the seller-borrower, and not interest earned on federal obligations. *Id.* at 564.

[247] IRS revenue rulings have analyzed the issue in a similar fashion. In Rev. Rul. 74-27, 1974-1 C.B. 24, the IRS listed five factors relevant in making a determination as to whether a transaction is a sale or a loan. All five factors relate to the transfer or assumption of risk by the parties.

1. *Who has control over the securities?* The party that controls the securities will most likely be deemed the owner and will be entitled to any tax benefits including interest exclusion.[248] Control will be found to be present if the buyer-lender can dispose of the securities and exercise, without restraint, other incidents of ownership.[249]
2. *Who bears the risk of loss?* If the buyer assumes the risk of loss when the market value of the securities decreases, or if the buyer retains any profit if the market value rises, then he is treated as the owner of the securities.[250] However, if the seller is required to buy the securities back at the selling price, regardless of market fluctuations, then the risk has remained with the seller and he is likely to be treated as the owner of the securities. Similarly, if the buyer is permitted to liquidate the securities and hold the seller accountable for any deficiency, or has to return any amount over that owed to him to the seller, then the transaction more closely resembles a loan with the securities being merely collateral.
3. *Does the seller have the right to repurchase?* If the seller has the right to repurchase the securities upon repayment of the cash, then it appears that the buyer does not control the securities. The buyer lacks the right to dispose of them, and he does not have the opportunity for gain by selling to a third party.[251]

---

[248] In Rev. Rul. 82-144, 1982-2 C.B. 34, the IRS concluded that an actual sale had occurred because the taxpayer was holding the securities for its own benefit, was free to dispose of them at any time, and was entitled to the full benefit of any appreciation in the value of securities.

[249] *American National Bank of Austin v. United States,* 421 F.2d 442 (5th Cir. 1970), *cert. denied,* 400 U.S. 819 (1970) (bond dealer had complete dominion over the bonds even after they were in the bank's possession through dealer's ability to sell them at his pleasure at prices he determined); *Union Planters National Bank of Memphis v. United States,* 426 F.2d 115 (6th Cir. 1970) (dealers exercised control over the bonds while they were in possession of the bank by advertising them for sale in trade magazines in complete disregard of the fact they had been transferred to the bank); *but see Citizens National Bank of Waco v. United States,* 551 F.2d 832 (Ct.Cl. 1977) (bank not required to resell the bonds to the original seller, thus indicating that the bank was the owner of the bonds).

[250] *Higland Farms, Inc. v. Commissioner,* 106 T.C. 237, 253 (1996).

[251] The Fifth and Sixth Circuit Courts of Appeals placed significant weight on this factor. In *Union Planters National Bank of Memphis v. United States,* 426 F.2d 115 (6th Cir. 1970); *cert. denied,* 400 U.S. 827 (1970), the court held that where a bank bought municipal obligations from a bond dealer with the right to require the dealer to repurchase the obligations at the price paid by the bank, the transaction more closely resembles a loan than a sale. The court noted that "in a transaction that would be characterized as a sale for tax purposes, [the court] would expect the Bank, rather than the dealer, to assume the risk of fluctuations in the market value of the banks. *Id.* at 118. *But, cf.* in *Citizens National Bank of Waco v. United States,* 551 F.2d 832 (Ct.Cl. 1977) where a bank purchased municipal bonds from an insurance company at par value, with the agreement that the insurance company would repurchase them at par on the request of the bank. The court held that the transaction was in fact a sale, and that the bank, being the owner of the securities, was entitled to exclude the interest from those securities from taxation. In reaching its decision, the court analyzed *Union Planters* and *American National,* but distinguished their facts from the facts at hand. The court emphasized the fact that the bank was not required to sell the securities back to the insurance company, but could instead sell to a third party and keep the profit, if any, thus indicating that it had control over the securities. The court dismissed the fact that the bank could require the insurance company to repurchase the securities for the original amount, thus insulating itself from loss, as a prudent business decision made in line with good banking practices to keep itself liquid. In *American National Bank of Austin v. United States,* 573 F.2d 1201 (Ct.Cl. 1978), the seller of bonds was not required to repurchase them, but simply had the option to do so. When the seller did not exercise this option, and the market had fallen, the bank sustained a loss. The court found that, in these circumstances, the bank had borne the basic risk of ownership of the bonds, and was thus entitled to the favorable tax treatment of the interest as the owners of such securities.

4. *How is the interest determined?* If the interest payable to the seller is determined independently from the stated interest on the securities, and if the seller is obligated to pay the interest based solely on the duration of the repurchase agreement, then the transaction will appear to be a collateralized loan. However, if the buyer has a right to the interest income from the securities purchased, then it appears that he purchased them outright.
5. *Does a margin have to be maintained?* If the parties are required to keep the value of the securities constant or equal to a fixed percentage of the original selling price, then the transaction will resemble a loan, where the prudent lender required the value of the collateral to be maintained.

§ 2.10 Mortgage Backed Securities

Mortgage Backed Securities ("MBSs") are various types of debt obligations that are backed by a pool of residential or commercial mortgage loans whose monthly payments are the sole source of cash flow of the securities.[252] Many MBSs are held in securitization vehicles such as investment trusts and real estate mortgage conduits ("REMICs"). MBSs pass through to the owners' cash flows representing the principal and interest payments and any unscheduled prepayments on the pool of mortgages. Because they are much more common in practice, this section will focus on MBSs backed by residential mortgage loans. The party that makes the mortgage loans that underlie a MBS is called the "originator;" the party that issues a MBS is referred to as the "issuer;" and the party that purchases a MBS is referred to as the "purchaser." A servicing entity is responsible for collecting payments on the mortgages and distributing those payments to MBS owners. Banks may play any of these roles in a MBS transaction.

§ 2.10.1 Types of Mortgage Backed Securities

MBSs include the following types of securities: (1) mortgage participation certificates, (2) mortgage pass-through securities, (3) stripped MBSs, (4) mortgage backed bonds, and (5) collateralized mortgage obligations.

(a) *Mortgage Participation Certificates*

A mortgage participation certificate is issued with respect to a pool of mortgage loans placed with a third party custodian who reviews the loans on behalf of the purchaser to ensure that they conform to representations and warranties made by the transferor of mortgages. The seller of the loans makes representations and warranties to the effect that it will repurchase any loan that does not conform to the representations and warranties. The purchaser, as sole owner, is fully liable for all losses on loans within the pool that conform to the

[252] For a more exhaustive discussion of the various forms of MBSs, *see* Joesph Huy, Basics of Mortgage Backed Securities (1997); Paul W. Feeney, Securitization: Redefining the Bank 97-98 (1995); Tamar Frankel, Securitization Structured Financing, Financial Assets Pools, and Asset Backed Securities, Vol I, 309 (1991); K. Jeanne Person, *Introduction to Mortgages and Mortgage-Backed Securities*, in The Handbook of Asset-Backed Securities 363-64 (Jess Lederman ed., 1990); Frank J. Fabozzi, *Mortgage-Backed Securities*, in Handbook of Structured Financial Products (Frank J. Fabozzi ed., 1988).

representations and warranties made by the seller. The structure of a mortgage participation certificate makes it difficult for the seller to spread credit risk out among various purchasers because each purchaser is effectively buying a pool of whole mortgage loans and is the sole owner of those loans. The desire for credit enhancement and homogeneity, often lacking in mortgage participation certificates, led to the development of the mortgage pass-through security, discussed below.[253]

(b) *Mortgage Pass-Through Securities*

Mortgage pass-through securities ("pass-through securities" or simply "pass-throughs") are the most common type of MBS. Pass-throughs are created when mortgage loans are pooled, transferred to a grantor trust, and ownership interests in the trust are sold as securities. The pass-through investor is treated as indirectly owning a *pro rata* interest in the various cash flows generated by the underlying mortgages. A servicing agent is responsible for collecting the borrowers' monthly payments and, after deducting a fee, remitting the monthly payments to the security holders. The cash flow from the underlying mortgages, the monthly payments of scheduled interest, principal and prepayments, is thus "passed through" to the certificate holders.

The securitization process differentiates the pass-through from the mortgage participation certificate. The purchaser of a mortgage participation certificate purchases a pool of mortgage loans outright and is the sole owner of those loans. The purchaser of a pass-through security buys a *pro rata* ownership share in a pool of mortgage loans held in trust. The representations and warranties made by the seller of a mortgage participation certificate do not exist in the case of a pass-through. Unlike the holder of a mortgage participation certificate, the holder of a pass-through does not bear the entire risk of loss on any single loan within the pool. Instead, that risk is distributed among the pass-through holders according to their *pro rata* ownership shares in the pool. Thus, the pass-through allows for shifting of credit risk not possible in the case of a mortgage participation certificate.

Three government agencies issue and/or guarantee pass-throughs: (1) the Government National Mortgage Association ("GNMA" or "Ginnie Mae"); (2) the Federal Home Loan Mortgage Corporation ("FHLMC" or "Freddie Mac"); and (3) the Federal National Mortgage Association ("FNMA" or "Fannie Mae"). As discussed below, Freddie Mac and Fannie Mae issue pass-throughs directly to investors. Ginnie Mae pass-throughs are issued by private mortgage lenders and guaranteed by Ginnie Mae at the agency level. Collectively, pass-throughs that are issued and/or insured by Ginnie Mae, Freddie Mac, and Fannie Mae are referred to as "agency" pass-throughs. Pass-throughs issued by private issuers are referred to as "nonagency" pass-throughs. Nonagency pass-throughs are not guaranteed by any government agency, but are credit enhanced by the private issuers using a variety of techniques.

---

[253] Paul W. Feeney, Securitization: Redefining the Bank 97-98 (1995).

(i) Agency Pass-Throughs

(A) Ginnie Mae Pass-Throughs. Ginnie Mae is a federal corporation within the Department of Housing and Urban Development ("HUD"). Ginnie Mae pass-throughs are issued by a large number of Ginnie Mae-approved mortgage originators. Originators of Ginnie Mae pass-throughs pool mortgages are insured by the Federal Housing Administration ("FHA"), the Department of Veterans Affairs ("VA"), and the Rural Housing Service ("RHS"). The pool of mortgages is then transferred by the originator to a trust. Once the trustee of the trust notifies Ginnie Mae that all appropriate documentation has been received, Ginnie Mae provides the trustee with a pool number identifying the pass-through security to be issued. The mortgage originator then issues pass-through securities in the form of share certificates, which are sold to investment bankers for distribution to private investors. Thus, unlike Freddie Mac and Fannie Mae pass-throughs, which are both issued directly by a government agency, Ginnie Mae pass-throughs are issued privately by Ginnie Mae approved mortgage originators. Because Ginnie Mae pass-throughs are guaranteed by an agency of the federal government, however, they are still classified as "agency" pass-throughs.

Ginnie Mae guarantees full and timely payment of both principal and interest on all loans in the pool in addition to the mortgage loans pooled to create Ginnie Mae pass-throughs being guaranteed by the FHA, the VA, and/or the RHS. Because Ginnie Mae is a wholly-owned corporation of the U.S. government, that guarantee is backed by the full faith and credit of the U.S. government. The credit risk associated with Ginnie Mae pass-throughs is thus identical to that of U.S. Treasury securities.

(B) Freddie Mac Pass-Throughs. Freddie Mac is a government-sponsored private, stockholder-owned corporation that is subject to extensive government regulation by agencies including HUD and the Treasury Department. Unlike Ginnie Mae pass-throughs, which are issued by private mortgage originators, Freddie Mac pass-throughs are issued directly by Freddie Mac. Freddie Mac pass-throughs are referred to as participation certificates. Freddie Mac assembles pools of conventional mortgage loans[254] from two sources: (1) direct purchases from private mortgage lenders under its Cash Program, and (2) the Guarantor Program, which includes both conventional mortgage loans and FHA/VA insured loans. Under the Cash Program, Freddie Mac purchases pools of loans from mortgage lenders and securitizes them by issuing participation certificates, which are then sold to investment bankers through auctions. Under the Guarantor Program, loans in a mortgage lender's portfolio are exchanged directly with Freddie Mac for participation certificates backed by precisely the same mortgages.

Freddie Mac guarantees the timely payment of interest and the ultimate payment of principal on all participation certificates.[255] Freddie Mac passes

[254] In this context, a conventional mortgage loan is a standard, single-family, residential mortgage that is not insured by the U.S. government.

[255] Under Freddie Mac rules, if a borrower is delinquent or in default, part of the scheduled principal payment to the Freddie Mac pass-through holder could be delayed. Such delays are not present in the cases of Ginnie Mae pass-throughs and Fannie Mae pass-throughs because timely payment of interest and principal is guaranteed.

through all collected principal amounts to participation certificate holders and guarantees payment of the remainder within one year. Because Freddie Mac is neither an agency of the federal government nor a wholly owned government corporation, the cash flow guarantees made by Freddie Mac are not backed by the full faith and credit of the U.S. government. To reflect the marginally increased credit risk that results from cash flows not guarantees not backed by full faith and credit, the yield on Freddie Mac participation certificates is slightly higher than that of Ginnie Mae pass-throughs.

(C) Fannie Mae Pass-Throughs. Similar to Freddie Mac pass-throughs, Fannie Mae pass-throughs are comprised of conventional mortgage loans, as well as FHA and VA insured loans. Fannie Mae assembles pools of mortgage loans, the majority of which are obtained through a swap program with private lenders similar to Freddie Mac's Guarantor Program. Under Fannie Mae's swap program, the mortgage lender transfers a pool of mortgage loans to Fannie Mae and Fannie Mae issues pass-through securities to the lender backed by the same pool of loans. Though the large majority of Fannie Mae pass-throughs are issued under this swap program, Fannie Mae also issues pass-throughs under a program very similar to Freddie Mac's Cash Program.

Like Ginnie Mae pass-throughs, Fannie Mae pass-throughs carry a guarantee of full and timely payment of both principal and interest. Similar to Freddie Mac, Fannie Mae is a shareholder-owned government sponsored enterprise that is neither an agency of the federal government nor a wholly owned government corporation. Thus, the cash flows from Fannie Mae pass-throughs are not guaranteed by the full faith and credit of the U.S. government. However, because timely payment of interest and principal are guaranteed, the yield on a Fannie Mae pass-through is slightly lower than that of Freddie Mac pass-through to reflect marginally decreased credit risk. Because the cash flow guarantees of Fannie Mae pass-throughs are not backed by the full faith and credit of the U.S. government, the yield on Fannie Mae pass-throughs is slightly higher than that of Ginnie Mae pass-throughs.

The following chart summarizes the principal characteristics of the three types of agency pass-throughs.

Basic Characteristics of Agency Pass-Throughs

	Ginnie Mae	Freddie Mac	Fannie Mae
Issuer	FHA-approved lenders	Freddie Mac	Fannie Mae
Underlying Mortgages	FHA/VA	Conventional or FHA/VA	Conventional or FHA/VA
Payment Guaranteed	Full and timely payment of principal and interest	Full and timely payment of interest and ultimate payment of principal	Full and timely payment of principal and interest
Guarantor	GNMA (backed by full faith and credit of U.S. government)	FHLMC (slightly better yield than Ginnie Mae pass-throughs to reflect increased credit risk)	FNMA (yields lower than Freddie Mac pass-throughs and higher than Ginnie Mae pass-throughs)

(ii) Nonagency Pass-Throughs

Private entities also issue MBSs, which are referred to as "nonagency" MBSs or "private pass-throughs." Nonagency MBSs can take the form of either pass-through securities or collateralized mortgage obligations. In the case of a nonagency pass-through, a private entity pools mortgage loans and transfers them to a trust. The trust then issues share certificates representing *pro rata* ownership interests in the trust. The same interests are then purchased by private investors. Nonagency pass-throughs are generally composed of conventional mortgages that fail to meet the size limits or other requirements of Freddie Mac or Fannie Mae.[256] Since none of the cash flows from a nonagency pass-through are guaranteed by a government agency, the pool of loans underlying the securities will be credit enhanced to obtain the desired rating of the issuer.[257]

External credit enhancements come in the form of third-party guarantees that provide for loss protection up to a certain level. The most common types of external credit enhancements are: (1) a corporate guarantee; (2) a letter of credit; (3) pool insurance; and (4) bond insurance. The most common internal credit enhancements are reserve funds and senior/subordinated structures.[258] The senior/subordinated structure essentially employs over-collateralization to cover credit losses. The cash flows of the junior securities are subordinated to the senior class in order to provide the senior class with credit protection similar to pool insurance.[259]

(c) *Mortgage Backed Bonds*

The mortgage backed bond was developed in response to the market's demand for a securitized mortgage with greater cashflow predictability. These bonds are term debt offerings collateralized by a pool of mortgages. Unlike pass-throughs where the assets are sold, the mortgage backed bonds are debt obligations of the mortgage lending institution which retains ownership of the assets.[260] The bonds are over-collateralized with mortgages that are guaranteed by one of the federal agencies, corporate bonds, and/or Government Treasuries to ensure full payment of principal and interest in the event of default. While this structure ensured greater predictability of cashflows, it resulted in an inefficient use of collateral.

---

[256] For 2012, loans with principal amounts greater than $417,000 will not be eligible for inclusion in mortgage pools underlying Freddie Mac participation certificates or Fannie Mae pass-throughs.

[257] For a complete discussion of the external and internal credit enhancement of nonagency pass-throughs, *see* Basics of Mortgage Backed Securities (1997) by Joseph Huy, at 88-91.

[258] Frank J. Fabozzi, *Mortgage-Backed Securities*, in Handbook of Structured Financial Products 305 (Frank J. Fabozzi ed., 1998).

[259] *See* Securitization: Refining the Bank 97-98 (1995) by Paul W. Feeney, at 101-02.

[260] *Id.* at 101.

(d) *Stripped MBSs*

A "stripped" MBS is created by altering the distribution of the cash flows of the underlying pool of mortgages from a *pro rata* distribution to an unequal distribution of principal and interest. In the case of a pass-through security, the cash flows from the underlying pool of mortgages are divided on a *pro rata* basis among security holders. By altering the ratio of the interest and the principal received by investors, stripped MBS issuers can create multiple classes of coupon rates known as "strips." For example, an 8 percent Freddie Mac pass-through can be "stripped" to create two classes of securities, one with a 7 percent coupon and the other with an 11 percent coupon. The higher coupon rate is accomplished by allocating more of the interest from the underlying collateral to that strip. The ratio of interest to principal received by the 7 percent coupon holder is lower than that received by the 11 percent coupon holder, resulting in the lower coupon rate. The most common type of stripped MBS allocates all interest to one strip and all principal to another strip. Because they are extremely sensitive to changes in interest rates, stripped MBSs are more volatile than the other varieties of MBSs. Stripped MBSs are used primarily as a hedge against mortgage prepayment risk and interest rate risk.[261]

(e) *Collateralized Mortgage Obligations*

The market's response to the inefficient use of collateral by mortgage backed bonds was the cashflow bond, the most common variety of which is the collateralized mortgage obligation ("CMO"). CMOs are multi-tranche cashflow securities that are collateralized with pass-throughs or whole mortgage loans. CMOs are issued by private entities ("nonagency CMOs"), as well as Ginnie Mae, Freddie Mac, and Fannie Mae ("agency CMOs"). Agency CMOs are created from pools of agency pass-through securities. Nonagency CMOs are created from either a pool of pass-through securities or a pool of conventional mortgage loans that have not been securitized. The issuer of a CMO typically transfers the loans to a trust in a non-sale transaction as collateral for the "loan" it receives from CMO investors.[262]

The cashflows of the mortgage-related products (principal and interest) are redistributed on a *pro rata* basis to different CMO classes, or tranches, creating securities with different maturity dates. The cashflows are used to retire the bonds, one at a time. Once the fastest pay tranche of bonds is retired, all payments are applied to the next fastest paying tranche until all are retired and the CMO is repaid. The collateral levels for CMOs are substantially lower than that required of mortgage backed bonds because the CMO is valued on the

[261] *See* K. Jeanne Person, *Introduction to Mortgages and Mortgage-Backed Securities*, in The Handbook of Asset-Backed Securities 374 (Jess Lederman ed., 1990).

[262] For a discussion of the characteristics of a non-sale transaction in the case of a CMO, *see* FSA 200130009, April 20, 2001. It is the author's understanding that the Field Service Advice does not reflect the position of the IRS Thus, the typical transfer of mortgages to a trust will not be a sale for tax purposes.

present value of the cashflows from the mortgages and not their market value. Therefore, the issuer of a CMO does not need to be concerned with the marketability of the underlying collateral or periodic reevaluations as occurs with regular mortgage backed bonds.[263]

Generally, the mortgages used to collateralize a mortgage backed bond are valued at their present market value; however, the mortgages used to collateralize a CMO are valued at the present value of the cash flows from those mortgages. Because the present value method of valuation yields higher valuations than the market value method, CMOs enjoy lower collateralization levels than mortgage backed bonds. CMOs thus allow for more efficient use of collateral by the issuer than mortgage backed bonds. Additionally, the issuer of a CMO need not concern itself with the marketability of the mortgages used for collateral or periodic reevaluation of their market values.[264]

There are several other advantages to CMOs. First, CMOs are able to unbundle a product into different risk categories and diversify that risk among various classes of investors who can choose the maturity of the bonds they purchase. Second, CMO bonds have a high level of safety and high credit ratings, usually AAA, because most of the CMOs are backed by GNMA, FNMA or FHLMC pass-through securities. Third, the issuers, thrifts, mortgage banks, homebuilders, FHLMC and insurance companies receive several benefits. Because of investor segmentation and certainty of cash flows, issuers are able to raise capital more cheaply, achieve a wider diversification of investor base, and offer a more efficient use of collateral while achieving high credit ratings.[265]

Unlike a pass-through security, the issuer of a CMO retains ownership of the mortgage loans pooled to create the security and issues debt obligations backed by the same loans. In contrast, the issuer of a pass-through sells investors *pro rata* ownership interests in the mortgage loans underlying the security. CMO cash flows are not passed through to the security holders, as is the case of a pass-through, but are secured debt obligations of the issuer. Thus, the cash flow uncertainties that can exist when borrowers fail to make scheduled payments are absent in the case of a CMO. Because stripped MBSs are a variety of pass-through security, the differences between stripped MBSs and CMOs are the same as the differences between pass-throughs and CMOs.

§2.10.2 Tax Treatment of CMO and Other Pass-Through Transactions

(a) *Characterization of the Trust for Tax Purposes*

The multi-tranche structure of the typical CMO raises questions concerning the classification of the CMO as a debt instrument for tax purposes. The mortgages underlying a CMO are generally transferred to a grantor trust, which issues CMOs to investors. Because a trust that issues more than one class of

---

[263] Paul W. Feeney, Securitization: Redefining the Bank 97-98 (1995) at 103-104.

[264] *Id.* at 101-102.

[265] *Id.* at 104-107.

securities is ordinarily taxed as a business association,[266] there is the risk that the owner trust in a CMO transaction would be treated as a business entity, subjecting CMO holders to double taxation. To avoid unfavorable characterization as a business association, grantor trusts in a CMO transaction should be structured so that: (i) the issuer retains significant control or discretion over the pool's assets; (ii) the issuer meets minimum capitalization levels apart from the pledged collateral—1$^{1}/_{2}$ to 2 percent of its total assets (this requirement is usually met through over-collateralization, leaving a "residual" value of the collateral pledged to secure the CMOs); (iii) the issuer has an option to call the bonds, usually when 20 to 30 percent of the original principal amount of the CMO is outstanding; and (iv) generally no more than quarterly payments should be made on the CMOs.[267]

With the passage of the Tax Reform Act of 1986 and the creation of Real Estate Mortgage Investment Conduits ("REMICs"), CMO issuers can choose to be taxed as a REMIC and qualify for pass-through tax treatment, thereby avoiding entity taxation. Under the REMIC rules, a "taxable mortgage pool" is taxed as a corporation and thus subject to entity level tax.[268] A "taxable mortgage pool" is an entity other than a REMIC in which (i) substantially all the assets consist of debt obligations or interest in debt obligations and more than 50 percent of the obligations or interests are real estate mortgages; (ii) the entity is the obligor under debt obligations with two or more maturities; and (iii) payments on the obligations bear a relationship to payments on the obligations which are its assets.[269] Under this definition CMO issuers would be taxed at the entity level. If they wish to avoid double taxation on both trust income and distributions to noteholders, CMO issuers should elect REMIC status.[270] REMICs are discussed more fully below.

(b) *Tax Treatment of the Transfer of Mortgages into the Trust*

Historically, the transfer of the pool of mortgages underlying the CMO into a trust has been treated as a loan or financing transaction, with the issuer of the CMO retaining ownership of the mortgages for tax purposes.[271] Under this analysis, the issuer (typically a bank) does not recognize gain or loss on the transfer of the mortgages because the incidents of ownership have not passed and no sale occurs. In a 2001 Field Service Advice, however, the IRS concluded that the transfer of mortgages to a trust was a sale of mortgages to the trust.[272] In that case, a bank transferred a bundle of mortgages to a trust and the trust issued four classes of debt obligations plus two additional interests in the trust. Drawing on prior judicial decisions, the IRS employed an eight-factor analysis in determining that the transfer constituted a sale. The eight factors are:

---

[266] Reg. § 301.7701-4(c); Reg. § 301.7701-2.

[267] Tamar Frankel, Securitization Structured Financing, Financial Assets Pools, and Asset-Backed Securities, Vol. I, 309 (1991); Reg. § 301.7701(4)(c).

[268] I.R.C. § 7701(i)(1); Reg. § 301.7701(i)-1(a).

[269] Tamar Frankel, Securitization Structured Financing, Financial Assets Pools, and Asset-Backed Securities, Vol. I, 309 (1991) at 329; I.R.C. § 7701(i)(2).

[270] For a complete discussion of the REMIC election requirements, *see* discussion of the "Tax Treatment of Pass-Through Securities," below.

[271] *See* Brant Goldwyn, *IRS Taxation of Mortgage Transfers as Sales Causes Concerns for Securitization Attorneys*, Daily Tax Report, August 10, 2001, at G-1.

[272] FSA 200130009, April 20, 2001.

1. Whether the transaction was treated by the parties as a sale
2. Whether the obligors on the debt instruments were notified of the transfer
3. Which party serviced the debt interests
4. Whether payments to the transferee corresponded to collections on the debt instruments
5. Whether the transferee imposed restrictions on the operations of the transfer that are consistent with a lender-borrower relationship
6. Which party had the power of disposition
7. Which party bore the risk of loss
8. Which party had the potential for gain.[273]

In reaching its conclusion, the IRS stressed that no single factor was dispositive and that the facts and circumstances of each case determine the importance of each factor.[274] If the IRS treats transfers of mortgage loans to a trust as a sale in the case of a CMO financing, then banks will be forced to recognize any gain or loss on the loans at the time of the transfer.[275]

(c) *Tax Treatment of Transfer of Mortgages to Form Pass-Throughs*

Pass-through securities are still the most common form of MBS. The IRS has issued numerous revenue rulings addressing the income tax consequences to the various parties associated with pass-throughs.[276] The tax consequences of the various entities associated with the creation and operation of pass-throughs are illustrated as follows:

> **Example:** X and Y are unrelated commercial banks. Pursuant to a pooling and servicing agreement (the "Agreement") between them, X creates a pool of mortgage loans by assigning the loans in trust to Y. The loans assigned to the trust are all originated by X. The assignment of the loans includes all principal and interest to be received by X on all of the loans after the date of the assignment. X's assignment is without recourse, and X's obligations with respect to the loans are limited to the representations and warranties made by X in the Agreement. Pursuant to the Agreement, X will service the loans and Y will act as trustee for the pool. X agrees to service the loans by collecting principal and interest payments on the loans and passing any amounts received on to Y, as trustee, after deducting a reasonable servicing fee. Y issues share certificates (the "Certificate") in the trust to X in exchange for the mortgage loans. The Certificates, issued in registered form, represent fractional undivided interests in the pool of loans. X then sells the Certificates to capital market underwriters, who subsequently sell the Certif-

[273] *Id.* at 14-15.

[274] *Id.* at 15.

[275] The author understands that it is unlikely that the IRS will follow this Field Service Advice in the future. In any event, a Field Service Advice is not precedent under the I.R.C. and is not binding on any other taxpayer.

[276] *See* Rev. Rul. 84-10, 1984-1 C.B. 155; Rev. Rul. 81-203, 1981-2 C.B. 137; Rev. Rul. 80-96, 1980-1 C.B. 317; Rev. Rul. 77-349, 1977-2 C.B. 20; Rev. Rul. 74-300, 1974-1 C.B. 169; Rev. Rul. 74-169, 1974-1 C.B. 147; Rev. Rul. 72-376, 1972-2 C.B. 647; Rev. Rul. 71-399, 1971-2 C.B. 433; Rev. Rul. 70-545, 1970-2 C.B. 8; Rev. Rul. 70-544, 1970-2 C.B. 6.

icates to investors. Holders of the Certificates are entitled to their proportional share of the principal and interest amounts collected by X on the loans.

(i) Tax Treatment of Pass-Through Trust. In the above example, the trust is not considered an association taxable as a corporation, but is classified as a trust, and the certificate holders are the owners of the trust under Subpart E of Subchapter J of the Code.[277] The trust is not taxed on the income that is distributed to the holders of the certificates. In order for the trust to receive pass through tax treatment, the trust must hold a fixed portfolio of mortgages and should not have the power to vary the investment of the certificate holders. In addition, the trust can only issue a single class of securities representing undivided transferable interests in the trust's assets.[278]

(ii) Tax Treatment of Transfers of Mortgage Loans into the Pass-Through Trust. Concurrent with the assignment of the mortgages to the trust, the transferor receives certificates in exchange, which it then sells to investors. Ordinary income or loss will be recognized upon the sale of the certificates measured by the differences between the proportionate amount of the proceeds realized with respect to the sale of each of the mortgages and the transferor's adjusted basis in each mortgage.[279]

(iii) Tax Treatment of the Certificate Holders. Each certificate holder is treated as the owner of an undivided interest in the entire trust (corpus as well as ordinary income) and is taxed on the income it receives. The sale of a certificate transfers to the certificate holder its proportionate share of equitable ownership in each mortgage in the pool. Certificate holders are required to take into account their proportionate share of the mortgage interest and other items of income, including prepayment penalties, assumption fees, and late payment charges, consistent with their method of accounting. The certificate holders must also report their proportionate share of the discount income realized on the purchase of each of the mortgages as ordinary income, consistent with their accounting method. Certificate holders may amortize their proportionate share of any premium paid to acquire mortgages to the extent permitted by Code section 171. The certificate holders may deduct their proportionate share of the trustee's servicing fees including the monthly service charge, late payments charges, assumption fees, and prepayment penalties under Code sections 162 or 212, consistent with their method of accounting.[280]

In addition, the special rules of Code section 1272, which address the inclusion of income from debt instruments having original issue discount, may be applicable to the certificate holders' proportionate share of discount on any mortgages that are the obligations of corporations or governments or their political subdivisions, if the other conditions of that section are met.

---

[277] *See* Rev. Rul. 61-175. The trustee will file Form 1041 notifying the IRS of the entity's tax status.

[278] Rev. Rul. 77-349, 1977-2 C.B. 20.

[279] Rev. Rul. 77-349, 1977-2 C.B. 20; Rev. Rul. 84-10, 1984-1 C.B. 155.

[280] *Id.*

A certificate owned by a REIT is considered as representing "real estate assets" within the meaning of Code section 856(c)(5)(A), and the interest income is considered an "interest on obligations secured by mortgages on real property" within the meaning of Code section 856(c)(3)(B).[281]

(d) ***Reserves for Losses on Loans***

Banks that are not "large banks" are permitted to include MBSs representing interests in pools of mortgages insured by FNMA, GNMA, or FHLMC in their total loans outstanding for purposes of computing its additions to reserve for losses under Code section 585(b)(3) (the experience method).[282] However, if a bank had used the percentage of eligible loans method under Code section 585(b)(2) in computing its addition to the reserve for loan loses, it would not have been permitted to treat the pass through mortgage-backed certificates as eligible loans for loss reserves because they were insured by the United States.[283]

§2.10.3 REMICs

The Tax Reform Act of 1986 created a new form of entity known as a "real estate mortgage investment company" ("REMIC").[284] A REMIC is a securitization vehicle that issues multiple classes of investor interests (securities) in itself that are backed by a pool of mortgages. Code Sections 860A through 860G govern the tax treatments of REMICs. The securities are referred to as either "regular interests" or "residual interests." There may be only one class of regular interests. The regular interest has terms that are fixed when the REMIC is formed, and it unconditionally entitles the investor to receive a specified principal amount. This interest can be issued in the form of debt or stock.

REMICs are designed primarily for three purposes: (1) to assist the private sector in competing against the government agencies in the MBS market; (2) to provide MBS issuers with greater flexibility to create new types of mortgage securities; and (3) to eliminate the need for the structural complexities of CMOs.[285] A REMIC is not taxed on its income. Instead, its income is taxable to the holders of the interests. A bank can be a creditor of a REMIC or an owner of REMIC interests. The legislative history of the REMIC provisions indicates that Congress intended the provisions to apply only to an entity that holds a substantially fixed pool of real estate mortgages and related assets and that "has no powers to vary the composition of its mortgage assets."[286]

---

[281] Rev. Rul. 80-96, 1980-1 C.B. 317; Rev. Rul. 74-300, 1974-1 C.B. 169; Rev. Rul. 70-545, 1970-2 C.B. 8; Rev. Rul. 70-544, 1970-2 C.B. 6.

[282] I.R.C. §585(c); TAM 8928002, July 14, 1989.

[283] *Id.* The percentage of eligible loans method has long been repealed.

[284] Pub. L. No. 99-514 Sec. 671(a). The statutory provisions governing REMICs have been modified on several occasions since 1986 including significant amendments made by The American Jobs Creation Act of 2004. Pub. L. No. 108-357, Sec. 835(a). The latter liberalized the definitions of regular interests, reverse mortgages, qualified mortgages, and permitted investments so that certain types of real estate loans and loan pools can be transferred to or purchased by a REMIC.

[285] *See* K. Jeanne Person, *Introduction to Mortgages and Mortgage-Backed Securities*, in Handbook of Structured Financial Products 376 (Frank J. Fabozzi ed., 1988).

[286] S. Rep. No. 99–313, 99th Cong., 2d Sess. 791–92, 1986–3 (Vol. 3) C.B. 791–92.

(a) *Electing to be a REMIC*

A REMIC offers an issuer substantial flexibility in choosing the legal form of the pool of mortgages. A REMIC must have one or more classes of "regular interests" and a single class of "residual interests."[287] A regular interest is any interest that is issued on the start-up day for the REMIC, has fixed terms, and is designated as a regular interest but only if the interest (1) unconditionally entitles the holder to receive a specified principal amount and (2) provides that any interest payments at or before maturity must be based on a fixed rate or consist of a specified portion of the interest payments on qualified mortgages, and such portion does not vary during the period that the interest is outstanding.[288] A residual interest is defined as any interest issued on the start-up day that is not a regular interest and is designated as a residual interest.[289] All distributions with respect to residual interests must be made *pro rata*.[290] All regular interests are treated as debt instruments for federal income tax purposes and residual interests, conversely, are treated as equity interests for federal income tax purposes.[291]

An entity that would be taxed as a corporation, trust, partnership or association can elect REMIC status, provided it meets the specific requirements and makes an election for the first taxable year of its existence.[292] The election shall apply to the taxable year for which it was made and all subsequent taxable years.[293]

REMICs are permitted to invest only in "qualified mortgages" and "permitted investments."[294] A "qualified mortgage" is any obligation that is principally secured by real property that was transferred to the REMIC on the startup day in exchange for interests in the REMIC, or was purchased within three months of the start up day.[295] A qualified mortgage includes regular interests in other REMICs and regular interests in Financial Assets Securitization Investment Trusts (FASITs) if 95 percent of its assets are attributable to obligations secured primarily by interests in real property. "Permitted investments" are of three types: (1) cash flow investments, (2) qualified reserve assets, and (3) foreclosure property. However, a REMIC may hold a de minimis amount of other assets if they are less than 1 percent of the aggregate adjusted bases of all the REMIC's assets.[296]

---

[287] I.R.C. § 860D(a)(2).

[288] I.R.C. § 860G(a)(7)(C). Interest payments at or before maturity may be based on a floating rate to the extent permitted by Reg. § 1.860G-1(a)(3).

[289] I.R.C. § 860G(a)(2). *See generally* Van Brunt, *Tax Aspects of REMIC Residual Interests*, 2 Fla. Tax. Rev. 149 (1994).

[290] I.R.C. § § 860D(a)(2) and (3).

[291] I.R.C. § 860B(a).

[292] The election is made on Form 1066.

[293] I.R.C. § 860D(b). A REMIC must use the calendar year for its taxable year. I.R.C. § 860D(a)(5).

[294] I.R.C. § 860D(a)(4).

[295] I.R.C. § 860G(a)(3). Rev. Proc. 2008-47, 2008-31 I.R.B. 272, describes the conditions under which modifications to certain subprime mortgage loans will not cause the I.R.S. to challenge the tax status of REMICs or to assert that those modifications create a liability for tax on a prohibited transaction. Rev. Proc. 2007-72, 2007-52 I.R.B. 1257, provided similar guidance regarding fast-track loan modifications that were effected in a manner consistent with certain principles, recommendations, and guidelines, which the American Securitization Forum ("ASF") released on December 6, 2007. In July 2008, the ASF released an updated Framework, which covers additional fast-track loan modifications. *See* discussion of modified debt in Ch. 6.

[296] The IRS and the Treasury Department issued final regulations relating to permitted modifications of commercial mortgage loans held by REMICs. TD 9463, 74 FR (No. 178, Sept. 16, 2009). The IRS also

The REMIC must make reasonable arrangements designed to ensure that residual interests are not held by a disqualified organization.[297] This requirement is met if the residual interests are in registered form, the REMIC's organizational documents expressly prohibit a disqualified organization from acquiring beneficial ownership of a residual interest, and notice of the prohibition is provided by a legend on the instrument evidencing ownership. If, however, a residual interest is acquired by a disqualified organization, the REMIC must provide the IRS and the transferor of the interest with the information necessary to compute the tax imposed by Code section 360E(e). A disqualified organization is: (1) the United States, any state or political subdivision thereof, any foreign government, international organization, or any agency or instrumentality of the foregoing; (2) any organization which is exempt from tax under Chapter 1 of the Code, unless such organization is subject to tax imposed by Code section 511; and (3) any organization described in Code section 1381(a)(2)(c) (any organization which is engaged in furnishing electric energy, or providing telephone service to persons in rural areas).[298]

(b) *Tax Treatment of Regular Interests*

The tax consequences of REMIC transactions are governed exclusively by Code sections 860A through 860G.[299] Because all regular interests, whether they are in the form of debt or equity interests, are treated as debt instruments for federal income tax purposes, the payments that flow through to the investor are treated as interest income or principal repayments. The debt instruments are treated as market discount bonds, where the revised issue price will exceed the holder's basis in the interest. Any market premium is amortized currently under Code section 171.

Sec. 1272(a)(6)(C)(i) and (ii) prescribe rules for determining the amount of O.I.D. allocated to a period for any regular interest in a REMIC, a qualified mortgage held by a REMIC, or any other debt instrument if payments under the instrument may be accelerated by reason of prepayments of other obligations securing the instrument. The daily portions of the O.I.D. on such debt instruments are determined by taking into account a reasonable assumption regarding the prepayment of principal for such instruments.

(Footnote Continued)

has provided a procedure that sets forth conditions under which modifications of certain mortgage loans will not cause the Service to either challenge the tax status of REMICs that hold the loans or to assert that those modifications constitute prohibited transactions. Rev. Proc. 2009-45, 2009-40 I.R.B. 471; Rev. Proc. 2008-28, 2008-23 I.R.B. 1054, May 16, 2008. The IRS has also issued guidance allowing certain asset securitization vehicles to avoid a challenge to their tax status in the event disqualifying modifications are made to subprime mortgage loans held by the vehicle. Rev. Proc. 2008-47, 2008-31 I.R.B. 272, July 8, 2008.

[297] I.R.C. § 860D(a)(6)(A).

[298] I.R.C. § 860E(e)(5).

[299] The Conference Report on the Tax Reform Act of 1986 states: "The conferees intend that where the requirements for REMIC status are met, that the exclusive set of rules for the treatment of all transactions relating to the REMIC and to holders of interests therein are to be those set forth in the provisions of the conference agreement." H.R. Rep. No. 99-841, 99th Cong., 2d Sess., at II-230. The IRS has argued that if a taxpayer did not actually transfer securities to a trust in exchange for REMIC regular and residual interests, the transaction should be recast as a secured loan in the form of the notes issued by taxpayer that are collateralized by the securities. TAM 201517007 (November 21, 2014).

In addition, regular interests are treated by a bank as evidences of indebtedness under Code section 582(c)(1) so that any gain or loss from their sale or exchange by a bank would not be treated as the sale or exchange of a capital asset. Gain on the disposition of a regular interest is treated as ordinary income to the extent of unaccrued O.I.D. computed at 110 percent of the applicable federal rate at the time the interest was acquired.[300] A REMIC is subject to the reporting requirements of Code section 1275(c)(2) with respect to these interests. If the entity holding the interest is not a bank, capital gain or loss will result.

(c) *Tax Treatment of Residual Interests*

The residual interest is similar in structure to common stock. The residual interest has a variable rate of interest similar to a dividend on common stock and the payments that flow through to the investor are treated as ordinary income or loss. A holder of a residual interest must take into account their daily portion of the taxable income or net loss of the REMIC for each day during the taxable year on which the holder owned the residual interest.[301] The daily portion is determined on the basis of quarterly computations of the REMIC's taxable income or net loss and is allocated among all residual interests in proportion to their respective holdings on such day.[302] Distributions to holders of residual interests are tax free to the extent they do not exceed the holder's adjusted basis. Any excess is treated as gain from the sale or exchange of an interest.[303] A holder's basis is increased by the amount of the REMIC's taxable income that the holder takes into account and is decreased by the amount of distributions he receives and the amount of the REMIC's net loss that he takes into account.[304]

(d) *Tax Treatment of Transfers of Property into a REMIC*

No gain or loss is recognized to a transferor when he transfers property into a REMIC in exchange for a regular or residual interest.[305] The aggregate adjusted basis of the interests received in exchange for property will equal the aggregate adjusted basis of the property transferred to the REMIC. If the transferor receives a regular interest and a residual interest, his basis must be allocated among the interests in the REMIC according to their respective fair market values.[306]

If the issue price of any regular or residual interest exceeds its adjusted basis as described above: (1) in the case of a regular interest, the excess is included in gross income as if it were market discount that the sponsor elected to include currently in income under Code section 1278(b); and (2) in the case of a residual interest, the excess is included in gross income ratably over the period during which the mortgage pool is expected to be in existence.[307]

If the adjusted basis of any regular or residual interest received in a transfer exceeds its issue price: (1) in the case of a regular interest, such excess is allowed

---

[300] I.R.C. § 860B(c).

[301] I.R.C. § 860C(a)(1).

[302] I.R.C. § 860C(a)(2). REMICs must issue quarterly reports on Schedule Q of Form 1066 to all holders of residual interests reporting their share of income or loss.

[303] I.R.C. § 860C(c).

[304] I.R.C. § 860C(d).

[305] I.R.C. § 860F(b)(1)(A).

[306] I.R.C. § 860F(b)(1)(B).

[307] Reg. § 1.860F-2(b)(4).

as a deduction as if it were bond premium that the sponsor elected to amortize under Code section 171(c); and (2) in the case of a residual interest, the excess shall be a deduction over the anticipated period during which the REMIC's mortgage pool will be in existence.

(e) *Character of Sponsor's Gains or Losses*

The REMIC rules specifically envision that a REMIC sponsor has a choice of either retaining its interests in the REMIC or transferring them. If and when a sponsor sells REMIC interest to a third party, the sponsor may recognize gain or loss equal to the difference between its adjusted tax basis in the interest sold and the amount received.[308] If the issue price of a retained interest is more or less than the sponsor's basis in that interest, then the sponsor has unrecognized gain or loss in the interest, and the sponsor recognizes gain or loss with respect to the retained regular or residual interest in accordance with the applicable rules.[309] The sponsor is entitled to a capital gain or loss upon the sale of its regular interests, and is also permitted to recognize ordinary gain or loss on its residual interest ratably over the anticipated life of the trust.[310]

§2.10.4 REITs

A real estate investment trust ("REIT") is a private company that buys, develops, manages and sells real estate assets, or, in some cases, finances real estate. Thus, REITs are investment conduits specializing in real estate and real estate mortgages that allows its participants to invest in a professionally managed portfolio of real estate properties. A bank can contribute property or mortgages into a REIT, or it can be an investor in a REIT. REITs were created by Congress in 1960 and special tax provisions apply to REITs under Code sections 856 through 858. These tax rules apply only if the REIT meets income and asset tests. There are two income tests and three asset tests.

To qualify as a REIT under the Code, an entity must:

- Be structured as a corporation, business trust or similar association;
- Be managed by a board of directors or trustees who generally hold legal title to the organizations' property;[311]
- Be taxable as a domestic corporation, but for its qualification as a REIT;
- Issue shares that are fully transferable;[312]
- Have a minimum of 100 shareholders;[313]
- Have no more than 50 percent of its shares held by five or fewer individuals during the last half of each taxable year;[314]
- Pay dividends of at least 95 percent of the REIT's taxable income;

---

[308] Reg. §1.860F-2(b)(2).

[309] I.R.C. §860F(b)(1)(C) and (D) and §1.860F-2(b)(4)(i) through (iv).

[310] I.R.C. §860F(b)(1)(D)(ii); TAM 201517007 (November 21, 2014).

[311] I.R.C. §856(a)(1).

[312] I.R.C. §856(a)(2).

[313] I.R.C. §§856(a)(5) and 856(b).

[314] I.R.C. §§856(a)(6) and 856(h).

- Ensure at least 95 percent of its gross income comes from qualifying passive sources; and
- Ensure at least 75 percent of its gross income is derived from investments in real property.

(a) ***Income Tests***

Under the 95 percent gross income test, 95 percent or more of the REIT's gross income, other than gross income from prohibited transactions, must be derived from qualifying passive sources of income. Qualifying types of income include: (1) dividends; (2) interest; (3) rents from real property; (4) gains from the sale of stock, securities and real property; (5) abatements and refunds on taxes from real property; (6) income and gain from foreclosure property; (7) amounts received or accrued as consideration for agreeing to make loans secured by real estate mortgages, real estate interests, or to purchase or lease real estate; and (8) gain from the sale or disposition of a real estate asset that is not a prohibited transaction.[315] A prohibited transaction is a sale or disposition of property held for sale in the ordinary course of a trade or business other than foreclosure property.[316] A REIT is taxed 100 percent on the net income derived from a prohibited transaction[317] unless it meets the safe harbor rule.[318]

Under the 75 percent gross income test, at least 75 percent of the REIT's gross income must come from investments in real property. Qualifying types of income include: (1) rents from real property; (2) interest on obligations secured by real estate mortgages or real estate interests; (3) gain from the sale of real property; (4) dividends and other distributions from qualified REITs; (5) abatements and refunds of taxes on real property; (6) income and gain from foreclosure property; (7) amounts received or accrued as consideration for agreeing to make loans secured by real estate mortgages or real estate interests or to purchase or lease real estate; (8) gain from the sale or disposition of a real estate asset that is not a prohibited transaction; and (9) qualified temporary investment income.[319]

The interaction of the two tests means that 75 percent of the REIT's income must be derived from real property and another 20 percent must be derived from either real property or from passive source income. REITs are permitted to take advantage of any type of hedge that reduces the risks associated with fluctuating interest rates and be assured that the payments under the hedging agreement will be treated as qualifying passive income. In addition, the gain on the sale of a hedge is treated as qualifying passive income.[320]

If a REIT was formed prior to August 6, 1997, no more than 30 percent of the REITs gross income was permitted to be generated from the sale or disposition of: (1) stock or securities held for less than one year; (2) certain real property held

[315] I.R.C. § 856(c)(2).

[316] I.R.C. § 857(b)(6)(B)(iii).

[317] I.R.C. § 857(b)(6)(A).

[318] I.R.C. § 857(b)(6)(C).

[319] I.R.C. § 856(c)(3).

[320] I.R.C. § 856(c)(5)(G), as amended by Pub. L. No. 105-34.

for less than four years; and (3) property in a prohibited transaction. This test was repealed by the Taxpayer Relief Act of 1997.

(b) ***Asset Tests***

In addition to the two income tests, REITs also must meet three asset tests on a quarterly basis. Under the first test, at least 75 percent of the value of the REIT's assets must be in real estate assets, cash and cash items, and government securities.[321] Receivables arising in the ordinary course of a REIT's business, but not those purchased, can be included in cash items.[322] The second test (really a restatement of the first test) requires that no more than 25 percent of a REIT's assets may consist of assets that do not qualify under the 75 percent test. Under the third test, no more than 25 percent of the REIT's assets can be represented by securities (excluding government securities). For purposes of this calculation, the securities of any one issuer may not be in an amount greater than 5 percent of the REIT's total assets and may not be more than ten percent of the voting securities of the issuer.[323] If a REIT fails one of the asset tests at the close of any quarter, and the failure is caused in whole or in part by the REIT's acquisition of a security or other property, the REIT will lose its REIT status unless it eliminates the discrepancy within 30 days of the close of the quarter.[324]

For purposes of the asset test (and also the income test), real estate assets include real estate interests, interests in real estate mortgages, and shares or beneficial interests in other REITs. Also, both regular and residual interests in REMICs are treated as real estate assets. However, if less than 95 percent of the REMIC's assets are real estate assets, the REIT is treated as holding directly its proportionate share of the assets and income of the REMIC.[325] The fair market value of the residual interests, and not the fair market value of all the REMIC's assets, is then used in applying the REIT tests. Regular interests in Financial Asset Securitization Investment Trusts that are comprised of real estate assets are also treated as real estate assets for purposes of determining REIT status, in the same manner as REMIC interests.

(c) ***Tax Treatment of Distributions and Retained Earnings***

REITs are required to distribute 95 percent or more of their ordinary income. Any amount over the 95 percent that the REIT retains is taxed at the regular corporate income tax rate. The distributed earnings are taxed to the shareholders/beneficiaries of the REIT as ordinary income. However, only "passive" income from real estate investments, as contrasted to income from the active operation of a business involving real estate, qualifies for this treatment.

Capital gains can be retained by the REIT or distributed to the shareholders. Capital gains that are distributed to the shareholders are treated as capital gains from the sale or exchange of a capital asset held for more than one year.[326] The REIT must designate amounts as a capital gains dividend in a written notice to

---

[321] I.R.C §856(c)(4)(A).

[322] Reg. §1.856-2.

[323] I.R.C §856(c)(4)(B).

[324] *Id.*

[325] I.R.C §856(c)(5)(E).

[326] I.R.C §857(b)(3)(B).

shareholders with the REIT's annual report or within 30 days of the end of the tax year.[327] If the REIT decides to retain net long-term capital gains in order to preserve working capital, the REIT will pay tax on the gain. The shareholders include their proportionate share of the undistributed long-term capital gains in income and receive a credit for their share of the tax paid by the REIT.[328] The shareholders must be notified in writing that the REIT has designated amounts as undistributed capital gains.

(d) *Tax Treatment of Transfer of Property into a REIT*

In general, the transfer of property directly to a REIT is a taxable transaction, despite the fact that a REIT is a corporation. Pursuant to Code section 351(e), gain or loss is recognized if a person contributes property to an "investment company."[329] A transfer of property is considered a transfer to an investment company if: (1) the transfer results, directly or indirectly, in diversification of the transferor's interest; and (2) the transferee is (a) a regulated investment company, (b) a REIT, or (c) a corporation where more than 80 percent of the value of the assets (excluding cash and nonconvertible debt obligations) are held for investment and are readily marketable stocks or securities, or interests in regulated investment companies or REITs.[330] In most circumstances the contribution of property to a REIT will result in diversification of the transferor's interest, and therefore will be considered a transfer to an investment company.

In a 1977 Private Letter Ruling, the IRS held, without discussing the investment company issue, that the transfer of stock and partnership interests to a REIT was tax-free under Code section 351(a).[331] The IRS, in informal discussions, has indicated a willingness to issue rulings applying a "diversified portfolio" exception to transfers of real property to a REIT.[332] However, in the absence of such a ruling, the taxpayer should assume the contribution of appreciated property to a REIT will be treated as a transfer to an investment company and will be a taxable transaction. The contributor will recognize gain or loss to the extent of the difference between the fair market value of the REIT shares and the adjusted basis of the property contributed.[333] Alternatively, a REIT can be structured as an UPREIT described below.

(e) *Tax Treatment of Transfer of Property into an UPREIT*

An umbrella partnership real estate investment trust ("UPREIT") is a REIT in which substantially all of the assets of the REIT are owned through an "Operating Partnership" ("OP") composed of the REIT as the general partner and the contributing partners as limited partners. Partnership interests in the OP are referred to as "OP Units" and may or may not be certified. In general, the REIT will own a number of OP Units equal to the number of REIT shares outstanding. The limited partners may exchange their OP units for common

[327] I.R.C § 857(b)(3)(C).

[328] I.R.C § 857(b)(3)(D).

[329] I.R.C § 351(e).

[330] Reg. § 1.351-1(c)(1).

[331] PLR 9744003, October 31, 1977.

[332] Blake D. Rubin, Andrea R. Macintosh and Jonathan I. Forrest, *Doing a Deal with a REIT: The Property Owner's Perspective*, 443 PLI/Tax 133, 149-150 (June 1999).

[333] *Id.* at 150.

stock of the REIT on a one-for-one basis, except that the REIT may elect to pay cash equal to the value of the REIT stock.[334]

The UPREIT has a significant advantage over the traditional REIT because the contribution of property to the OP generally will be tax free.[335] The UPREIT structure was first used in 1992 and currently nearly half of all publicly traded REITs utilize the UPREIT structure.[336] Pursuant to Code section 721(a), the contribution of property to the OP in exchange for OP units will not result in the recognition of gain or loss. Code section 721(b) provides that gain may be realized on a transfer of property to a partnership that would be treated as an investment company (within the meaning of Code section 351) if the partnership was incorporated. But, the OP will not be considered an investment company if it were incorporated because 80 percent of its assets will not be "stock and securities" as defined in Code section 351(e)(1), but will be real property assets. Therefore, pursuant to Code section 722, a contributing partner's initial basis in the OP is equal to the amount of any money contributed and the adjusted basis of the contributed property. Code section 704(c) rules will have an impact on the timing and character of taxable income recognized by contributing partners in an UPREIT transaction and will also impact the timing and amount of depreciation deductions allowable to other partners in the OP, including the REIT.[337]

§2.11 Asset Backed Securities

§2.11.1 FASITs

The Small Job Protection Act of 1996 created a new type of statutory entity called a "financial asset securitization investment trust" ("FASIT"). A FASIT was designed for the purpose of facilitating the securitization of debt obligations such as credit card receivables, home equity loans, and auto loans.[338] The American Jobs Creation Act of 2004 repealed the rules that permit FASITs. However, the repeal did not apply to any FASIT in existence on the date of enactment, to the extent that regular interests already issued by the FASIT remain outstanding in accordance with their original terms.[339]

A FASIT is a pass-through entity equitably owned by a single taxable C corporation (the "Owner") that is not treated as a trust, partnership, corporation, or taxable mortgage pool. The income of the FASIT, which is roughly equal to the difference between the income earned from its loan portfolio and the interest paid to its investors, is passed through to its Owner and is not taxed at the FASIT level.[340] A FASIT issues asset backed securities that are treated as debt for federal income tax purposes. A bank may possess the ownership interest or the regular interests described below. The tax provisions that apply to FASITs can be found under Code sections 860H through 860L.

---

334 *Id.* at 144-45.

335 *Id.* at 152.

336 *Id.* at 145; Philip S. Payne, *REIT Conversions – Issues and Opportunities,* The REIT Report (Autumn 1998).

337 Rubin, Macintosh and Forrest, Doing a Deal with a REIT: The Property Owner's Perspective, 443 PLI/Tax 133, 157 (June 1999).

338 Pub. L. No. 104-188, § 1621.

339 Pub. L. No. 108-357, § 835(a).

340 I.R.C. §860H(a).

An entity can qualify as a FASIT if:

- An election of FASIT treatment applies to the tax year;
- There is a single ownership interest held directly by an eligible C corporation;
- The only non-ownership security interests in it qualify as regular interests;
- Substantially all of its interests are permitted assets no later than three months after formation; and
- It is not a regulated investment company (such as a mutual fund).[341]

An "eligible corporation" is any domestic C corporation other than exempt corporations, regulated investment companies (such as a mutual funds), REITs, REMICs, and cooperatives.[342] "Permitted assets" include: (1) cash and cash equivalents; (2) certain debt instruments; (3) foreclosure property; (4) instruments or contracts that represent a hedge or guarantee of debt held or issued by the FASIT; (5) contract rights to acquire permitted debt instruments or hedges; (6) a regular interest in another FASIT; and (7) a regular interest in a REMIC.[343]

(a) ***Tax Treatment of Regular and High-Yield Interests***

There are two types of interests in a FASIT. Regular interests held by investors, which includes high-yield interests that may be held only by eligible corporations and other FASITs, and the ownership interest held by the eligible owner.

A regular interest is an asset-backed security issued on or after the startup date that has a fixed term and meets the five requirements of Code section 860L(b)(1). Regular interests cannot have a yield that is more than five percentage points above the applicable federal rate at the time of issue. High-yield interests do not meet the five requirements of Code section 860L(b)(1) and may be held only by domestic C corporations subject to corporate level tax and dealers that acquire the interests for resale to customers (eligible corporations or other FASITs) in the ordinary course of business. Qualifying regular interests are treated as debt for federal income tax purposes and avoid double taxation because the income is not taxed at the corporate level but is taxed only to the investors.[344] Interest paid to the holders of regular interests is deductible by the FASIT in computing its net income passed through to its owner.

(b) ***Tax Treatment of the Holder of the Ownership Interest***

The owner of the FASIT is taxed on income earned by the FASIT and is liable for any penalty taxes incurred by the FASIT. All FASIT assets, liabilities, items of income, gain, deduction, loss and credit are attributable to the owner of the FASIT.[345] Any securities held by the FASIT are treated as held for investment by the owner. The character of the income received by the owner is the same as its

---

341 I.R.C. § 860L(a)(1).

342 I.R.C. § 860L(a)(2).

343 I.R.C. § 860L(c).

344 I.R.C. § 860H(c)(1).

345 I.R.C. § 860H(b)(1).

character to the FASIT, except that tax-exempt interest is treated as ordinary income.[346] Taxable income of a FASIT, passed through to the owner, is calculated on the accrual method of accounting. The constant yield method and principles that apply to determining original issue discount accrual on debt obligations apply to all debt obligations held by a FASIT in determining its interest and discount income and premium deductions or adjustments.[347]

FASIT items of income, gain, or deduction allocable to prohibited transactions are excluded from general taxable income. Instead of paying ordinary income taxes on these items, the owner is liable for a 100 percent excise tax on FASIT net income derived from the specified prohibited transactions.[348] Prohibited transactions include the receipt of income from: (1) an asset that is not a permitted asset; (2) a loan issued by a FASIT; and (3) a fee or other compensation for services (excluding certain fees for waivers and amendments, or consents under permitted assets other than foreclosure property).[349] In addition, income from the disposition of permitted assets is also a prohibited transaction. However, exceptions exist for the dispositions in the following circumstances: (1) a complete liquidation of a class of regular interests; (2) foreclosure, default, or imminent default of a FASIT asset; (3) liquidation, bankruptcy or insolvency of the FASIT; (4) dispositions that avoid a default on a debt of the FASIT attributable to a default on a loan held by the FASIT; (5) dispositions that facilitate a clean-up call; (6) dispositions that (a) substitute a permitted debt instrument for another debt instrument, or (b) return a debt instrument contributed by the owner to such owner in order to avoid over-collateralization, provided the purpose is not to avoid recognition of gain due to an increase in the asset's market value; and (7) dispositions of former hedge assets.[350]

(c) *Tax Treatment of the Transfer of Property into a FASIT*

The transfer of property by sale or contribution into a FASIT by the holder of the ownership interest (or a person related to the owner) will generally trigger gain.[351] The amount of gain recognized is the excess of the value of the property determined under FASIT valuation rules on the date of transfer over the transferor's adjusted basis in the property. For purposes of calculating gain, the valuation rules provide that the value of property transferred to a FASIT is its fair market value.[352] The value of debt instruments that are not traded on an established securities exchange is the sum of the present values of the cash flows reasonably expected from the obligations, discounted over the weighted average life of the contributed loans.[353] The discount rate shall equal 120 percent of the applicable federal rate, or such other discount rate specified in regulations, compounded semiannually.[354] Losses on assets contributed to the FASIT can not be recognized upon their contribution. However, the losses may be allowed to the owner of the FASIT upon the disposition of the assets by the FASIT.

---

[346] I.R.C. § 860H(b)(4).
[347] I.R.C. § 860H(b)(2).
[348] I.R.C. § 860L(e)(1).
[349] I.R.C. § 860L(e)(2).
[350] I.R.C. § 860L(e)(3).
[351] I.R.C. § 860I.
[352] I.R.C. § 860I(d)(1)(B).
[353] I.R.C. § 860I(d)(1)(A).
[354] I.R.C. § 860I(d)(1)(A)(ii).

Property acquired by the FASIT from someone other than the holder of the ownership interest is treated as if it were first acquired by the owner and then sold to the FASIT.[355] In determining the gain recognized, the acquisition cost to the owner of the FASIT is equal to the FASIT's acquisition cost, and the sales price is the value of the property determined under FASIT valuation rules. In addition, any assets of the owner that are contributed to the FASIT that are used to support the FASIT's obligations to holders of regular interests are treated as contributions to the FASIT. Therefore, gain is recognized to the owner as if the property was sold at its value under the FASIT valuation rules on the earliest date the property was used to support any regular interest.[356]

The provisions requiring gain recognition upon the transfer of property to the FASIT will override any other non-recognition provision that are otherwise available.[357] The basis of the property on which gain is recognized shall be increased by the amount of the gain recognized.[358]

(d) *Special Rules Regarding Losses*

The owner and the holders of high yield interests in a FASIT are not permitted to offset income or gain from their FASIT interests with any other non-FASIT losses.[359] Therefore, any increase in income of the holder of the ownership interest or the high yield interest from disallowed non-FASIT losses will be disregarded in determining the amount of the holder's net operating loss, as well as the amount of any allowable carryback or carryover.[360]

The following chart summarizes the tax treatment of FASITs, straight pass-through mortgage backed securities, REMICs and REITs.

---

[355] I.R.C. § 860I(a)(2).

[356] I.R.C. § 860I(b).

[357] I.R.C. § 860I(e)(1).

[358] I.R.C. § 860I(e)(2).

[359] I.R.C. § 860J(a).

[360] I.R.C. § 860J(b).

	Straight Pass Through Mortgage Backed Securities	*REMIC*	*REIT*	*FASIT*
Types of Ownership Interests and How Treated for Tax Purposes	Certificates - debt instrument	Regular Interests - debt instrument Residual Interests - equity instrument	Share Certificates- equity instrument	Regular Interest - debt instrument High Yield Interest - debt instrument
How Entity is Treated for Tax Purposes	Trust is not taxed on its income.	REMIC is not taxed on its income.	REIT taxed at regular corporate tax rates for income not distributed to the shareholders.	FASIT is not taxed on its income.
Taxation of Transfer to Entity	The originator of the mortgages will recognize income or loss upon the sale of its interest in each of the mortgages in the "pool."	No gain or loss is recognized upon contribution of property in exchange for either regular or residual interests. Gain or loss is deferred until sale of the regular or residual interest.	Gain will be recognized upon contribution of property (unless an "UPREIT" is formed).	Gain, but not loss, will be recognized upon contribution of property to FASIT by the holder of the Ownership Interest.
Taxation of Ownership Interest of Entity	NA	NA	NA	Taxed on FASIT's income.
Taxation of Investors	Holders of certificates will be taxed on the interest and other items of income received.	Holders of regular and residual interest are taxed on the income of the REMIC.	Holders of share certificates are taxed on the income received from the REIT. Distributed earnings are taxed as ordinary income. Capital gains distributed are treated as capital gains from the sale or exchange of a capital asset held for more than one year.	Holders of regular and high yield interests are taxed on the interest income received.

§2.12 Hedging Transactions

In 1999, Code section 1221 was amended to provide ordinary gain or loss treatment on the sale or exchange of instruments involved in hedging transactions (and consumable supplies).[361] Code section 1221(a)(7) now provides ordinary treatment for hedging transactions that are clearly identified as such before

[361] Ticket to Work and Work Incentives Improvement Act of 1999, §532; 113 Stat 1860, December 17, 1999.

the close of the day on which they were acquired, originated, or entered into. The characterization of gain or loss from hedging transactions is further governed by Treasury regulation § 1.1221-2.[362]

The statute defines a hedging transaction as a transaction entered into by the taxpayer in the normal course of business primarily to manage risk of interest rate, price changes, or currency fluctuations with respect to ordinary property, ordinary obligations, or borrowings of the taxpayer.[363] The statutory definition of hedging transaction also includes transactions to manage such other risks as the Secretary may prescribe in regulations.[364] Further, the statute grants the Secretary the authority to provide regulations to address the treatment of nonidentified or improperly identified hedging transactions, and hedging transactions involving related parties (Code sections 1221(b)(2)(B) and (b)(3), respectively). The statutory hedging provisions are effective for transactions entered into on or after December 17, 1999. Congress intended that the hedging rules be the exclusive means through which the gains and losses from hedging transactions are treated as ordinary.[365] The purchase or sale of an asset that was not acquired primarily to reduce risk, such as an investment, will not be treated as a hedging transaction even if the asset limits or reduces the taxpayer's risk with respect to other assets or liabilities.[366]

Hedging transactions entered into on or after October 1, 1994, are subject to the accounting and recordkeeping requirements of Treasury regulation § 1.446-4.[367] To the extent that other regulations governing the timing of income, deductions, gain, or loss are inconsistent with the rules of this regulation, the rules of Treasury regulation § 1.446-4 control, except as noted below.[368]

Taxpayers who use the cash method of accounting are not subject to Treasury regulation § 1.446-4 if, for all prior tax years ending on or after September 30, 1993, the $5 million annual gross receipts test provided in Code section 448(c) is satisfied (or would be satisfied if the taxpayer were a corporation or partnership).[369] Additional exceptions are provided for: (1) positions held by dealers with respect to securities marked to market under Code section 475; and (2) any Code section 988 foreign currency exchange hedging transaction if the transaction is integrated under Treasury regulation § 1.988-5 or if other regulations

---

[362] In 1994, the IRS published final regulations under Code § 1221 providing for ordinary character treatment for certain business hedges (59 FR 36360). In 1996, the IRS published final regulations on the character and timing of gain or loss from hedging transactions entered into by members of a consolidated group (61 FR 517). In 2002, the IRS published final regulations to determine the character of gain or loss from transactions that are also subject to various international provisions of the Code. T.D. 8985, T.D. 8985, 2002-14 I.R.B. 707, April 8, 2002.

[363] I.R.C. §§ 1221(b)(2)(A)(i) and (ii).

[364] I.R.C. § 1221(b)(2)(A)(iii).

[365] S. Rep. No. 201, 106th Cong., 1st Sess. 25 (1999).

[366] Reg. § 1.1221-2(c)(3).

[367] Reg. § 1.446-4(g). Book and tax accounting methods diverge with respect to hedged transactions. Under GAAP, gain or loss on a non-hedged transaction appears in current income while hedging transactions are matched to the hedged item, with gain or loss appearing in the same period. FAS 133 at ¶¶ 17 and 22. For tax, a non-hedged transaction is subject to the mark-to-market rules of Code section 1256, with gain or loss taken into account on the last business day of the taxable year. Hedging transactions are excluded from mark-to-market by Code section 1256(e) and are timed to match the hedged item. Reg. § 1.1221-2(f)(2)(ii).

[368] Reg. § 1.446-4(a) and (f).

[369] Reg. § 1.446-4(a)(1).

issued under Code section 988(d) (or an advance ruling described in Treasury regulation § 1.988-5(e)) govern when gain or loss from the transaction is taken into account.[370] Treasury regulation § 1.446-4 also does not apply to determine the issuer's yield on an issue of tax-exempt bonds for purposes of the arbitrage restrictions to which Treasury regulation § 1.148-4(h) applies.[371]

§ 2.12.1 The Volcker Rule

The rules governing banking transactions have undergone considerable changes in the wake of the most recent financial crisis. Under a new rule, named after former Federal Reserve Chairman Paul Volcker, banking entities are restricted from engaging in certain types of trading, such as proprietary trading, that do not benefit their customers. The "Volcker Rule" was passed in section 619 of the Dodd-Frank Wall Street Reform and Consumer Protection Act.[372] Congress promulgated new regulations on January 1, 2014, to clarify certain aspects of the Rule.[373] These final rules implementing section 619 of the Dodd-Frank Act were effective April 1, 2014.

(a) *Purpose of Volker Rule*

The Volcker Rule prohibits, with certain exceptions, banking entities from "engaging in proprietary trading or from acquiring or retaining an ownership interest in, sponsoring, or having relationships with a hedge fund or private equity fund ('covered fund')."[374] Exceptions include trading in U.S. government obligations, underwriting and market making-related activities, risk-mitigating hedging activities, trading for insurance companies, and foreign trading by non-U.S. banking entities.[375] For example, banks may still engage in risk-generating activities associated with "client-oriented financial services."[376] Additionally, banking entities still may engage in aggregate hedging, as the statute allows risk-mitigating trading for both individual and aggregate hedges.[377]

The Rule's allowance of certain hedging was designed to limit potential abuse while not constraining a banking entity's risk-management capabilities in certain activities.[378] With these limits, regulators sought to "prevent the type of

---

[370] Reg. § 1.446-4(a)(2)(i) and (ii).

[371] Reg. § 1.446-4(a)(2)(iii).

[372] Pub. L. No. 111-203, 124 Stat. 1376 (2010), 12 U.S.C. § 1851.

[373] *See* Prohibitions and Restrictions on Proprietary Trading and Certain Interests in, and Relationships With, Hedge Funds and Private Equity Funds [Hereinafter "Prohibitions on Proprietary Trading"], 79 Fed. Reg. 5,808 (Jan. 31, 2014) (to be codified at 17 C.F.R. pt. 75).

[374] *Id.* at 5,810.

[375] *Id.* at 5,810.

[376] *Id.* at 5,814. Such services include underwriting, market making, and asset management services. *Id.*

[377] 12 U.S.C. § 1851(d)(1)(C) (2012) ("[Permissible activities include] [r]isk-mitigating hedging activities in connection with and related to individual or aggregated positions, contracts, or other holdings of a banking entity that are designed to reduce the specific risks to the banking entity in connection with and related to such positions, contracts, or other holdings."). The regulations are clear in their allowance of aggregate hedging. "[T]he statutory language is clear on its face that a banking entity may engage in risk-mitigating hedging in connection with aggregated positions[, 'portfolio hedging,']of the banking entity." Prohibitions on Proprietary Trading at 79 Fed. Reg. 5,907.

[378] Prohibitions on Proprietary Trading, 79 Fed. Reg. at 5,901 ("[T]he Agencies believe the scope of the final hedging exemption is appropriate because it permits risk-mitigating hedging activities . . . while requiring a robust compliance program and other internal controls to help ensure that only genuine risk-mitigating hedges can be used in reliance on the exemption.").

activity conducted by banking entities in the past that involved taking large positions using novel strategies to attempt to profit from potential effects of general economic or market developments and thereby potentially offset the general effects of those events on the revenues or profits."[379]

Acceptable hedging activities must be designed to reduce *specific* risks. The hedging activity, at its inception, must "be designed to reduce or otherwise significantly mitigate and demonstrably reduce[]or otherwise significantly mitigate[] one or more specific, identifiable risks."[380] These requirements placed on hedging activity also apply to any adjustments to the activity. The Rule does not require banking entities to adopt the "best hedge," as was requested by many commenters, because positions may be complex, the market may be unpredictable, and certain hedging options may not be available, making a requirement of a "'best hedge' impractical, unworkable, and subjective."[381]

The Rule is designed to limit the risks banks undertake when engaging in certain trading activities and to ensure that banking entities engaging in permitted trading activities are doing so "in a manner designed to identify, monitor, and limit the risks posed by these activities."[382] In order to mitigate risk, the Rule requires banking entities engaging in certain activities to establish a compliance program that can monitor risk and ensure compliance with the statute, and do so in a way that "reflects the banking entity's activities, size, scope, and complexity."[383] In order for banking entities to satisfy the compliance program requirements, they must have written polices, internal controls, analysis and independent testing covering, for example, products or instruments that may be purchased or sold, and limits for a trading desk's underwriting activities.[384]

(b) *Definitions*

A "banking entity" that is covered by this rule is "any insured depository institution . . . any company that controls an insured depository institution or that is treated as a bank holding company for purposes of section 8 of the International Banking Act of 1978, and any affiliate or subsidiary of any such entity."[385] The term "proprietary trading" encompasses banking entities

> engaging as a principal for the trading account of the banking entity or nonbank financial company supervised by the Board [of Governors of the Federal Reserve System] in any transaction to purchase or sell, or otherwise acquire or dispose of, any security, any derivative, any contract of sale of a commodity for future delivery, any option on any such security, derivative, or

[379] *Id.* at 5,902.

[380] *Id.* at 5,904. "Specific risks" includes "market risk, counterparty or other credit risk, currency or foreign exchange risk, interest rate risk, commodity price risk, basis risk, or similar risks, arising in connection with and related to identified individual or aggregated positions." *Id.*

[381] *Id.* at 5,904-05.

[382] *Id.* at 5,813. The Rule also requires certain nonbank financial companies to be subject to additional capital requirements and quantitative limits if they engage in proprietary trading or certain "covered fund" activities. *Id.* at 5,810.

[383] *Id.* at 5,814.

[384] *Id.* at 5,844. *See id.* for more requirements banking entities must satisfy in order to have a satisfactory compliance program. The proposed rule did not contain the specific requirements mentioned above in order to comply with the program. *Id.* at 5,844-45.

[385] 12 U.S.C. § 1851(h)(1); *see also* 12 C.F.R. § 225.180 (2013).

contract, or any other security or financial instrument that the appropriate Federal... [agencies]determine.[386]

(c) *Effect on Hedging*

The Rule allows entities to engage in risk-mitigating hedging for aggregate positions held by the bank.[387] When the permitted hedging activity involves more than one position held by the bank, it "must be in connection with or related to aggregated positions of the banking entity."[388] The hedging activity must be designed to mitigate specific risks related to an identified position. The risk may not be a merely generalized risk that the bank believes may exist based on "non-position-specific modeling or other considerations."[389]

In determining whether a bank may properly undertake a hedge, the bank must specifically identify risk factors in the positions the bank holds.[390] The hedging must be "demonstrably risk reducing or mitigating rather than simply correlated to risk."[391] However, when banks are conducting their compliance programs to make sure their positions are allowed by law, banks must conduct "correlation analysis" in order to allow for better consideration of the facts and circumstances regarding the risks of a hedge, which is designed to reduce the administrative burden placed on the banks.[392] Additionally, banks must make a risk determination at the beginning of the hedging activity.[393] However, "[a] trade that is not risk-reducing at its inception is not viewed as a hedge for purposes of the exemption."[394] Aside from making a risk determination at the inception of the hedge, banking entities must continually review, monitor, and manage their positions to reduce or mitigate risks involved with the hedge.[395]

§2.12.2 Definition of Notional Principal Contracts

Notional principal contracts, one type of hedging transaction, are financial instruments providing for payments between the contracting parties at specified intervals. The payments are calculated according to a specified index upon a notional principal amount in exchange for specified consideration or a promise to pay similar amounts. Treasury regulation §1.446-3(c)(1)(i) defines a notional principal contract as a financial instrument that provides for the payment of amounts by one party to another at specified intervals calculated by reference to

[386] 12 U.S.C. § 1851(h)(4). However, the term does not include a bank acting solely as an agent, broker, or custodian for an unaffiliated third party because the bank is not trading as a principal when acting in these capacities. Prohibitions on Proprietary Trading at 79 Fed. Reg. 5,817.

[387] Prohibitions on Proprietary Trading at 79 Fed. Reg. 5,907.

[388] *Id.*

[389] *Id.* Examples of prohibited activity include hedging designed to "[r]educe risks associated with the banking entity's assets and/or liabilities generally, general market movements or broad economic conditions; profit in the case of a general economic downturn; counterbalance revenue declines generally; or otherwise arbitrage market imbalances unrelated to the risks resulting from the positions lawfully held by the banking entity." *Id.*

[390] *Id.* In addition, the bank must sufficiently identify aggregate hedged positions so that the specific components of the hedge may be clearly determined. *Id.*

[391] *Id.* at 5,908.

[392] *Id.* ("The type of analysis and factors considered in the analysis should take account of the facts and circumstances, including type of position being hedged, market conditions, depth and liquidity of the market for the underlying and hedging position, and type of risk being hedged.").

[393] *Id.*

[394] *Id.*

[395] *Id.*

a specified index upon a notional principal amount in exchange for specified consideration or a promise to pay similar amounts.[396]

A contract may be a notional principal contract even though its term is subject to termination or extension.[397] The notional principal amount is not actually borrowed or loaned between the parties as part of the contract.[398] It is any specified amount of money or property that, when multiplied by a specified index, measures a party's right or obligation under the contract.[399]

Notional principal contracts are customarily used by financial institutions to reduce the risk of adverse changes in interest rates, commodity prices, and currency exchange rates. Examples of notional principal contracts include interest rate swaps, currency swaps, basis swaps, interest rate caps, interest rate floors, commodity swaps, equity swaps, and equity index swaps.

In a typical interest rate swap agreement, one party agrees to make periodic payments based on a fixed rate while the other party agrees to make periodic payments based on a floating rate. The payments are calculated on the basis of a hypothetical or a notional principal amount. When payments are due on common dates, they are usually netted.

A commodity swap is similar to an interest rate swap, except that a commodity price index is used in lieu of an interest rate index and the notional principal amount is measured in units of a commodity rather than in dollars.

A collar is not itself a notional principal contract, but a taxpayer may treat certain caps and floors that comprise a collar as a single notional principal contract under Treasury regulation § 1.446-3(f)(2)(v)(C).[400] Interest rate cap agreements may take a variety of forms. Most typically, a purchaser makes an initial cash payment in exchange for a seller's (usually a financial institution's) agreement to make cash payments to the purchaser at specified future times if interest rates increase. Under an interest rate floor agreement, the seller of the floor agrees to pay the purchaser if interest rates fall. The parties to an interest rate cap or floor agreement designate an interest rate index to determine the amount by which interest rates rise or fall.

§ 2.12.3 Accounting for Notional Principal Contracts

Accounting methods for taxpayers receiving income from or making payments under notional principal contracts entered into on or after December 13, 1993, are prescribed by Treasury regulation section 1.446-3. The IRS will generally

---

[396] Proposed regulations have been issued that alter the definition of a national principal contract. REG-111283-11, Sept. 16, 2011. These regulations also describe swaps and similar arrangements that fall within the meaning of I.R.C. § 1256(b)(2)(B).

[397] Reg. § 1.446-3(c)(1)(i).

[398] Reg. § 1.446-3(c)(3).

[399] A specified index is defined as:

(1) a fixed rate, price or amount;

(2) a fixed rate, price or amount applicable in some specified period(s) followed by one or more fixed rates, prices or amounts applicable in other periods;

(3) an index based on objective financial information, that is, information not within the control of a party to the notional principal contract and not unique to any party's circumstances; and

(4) an interest rate index that is regularly used in lending transactions between a contracting party and unrelated persons.

[400] Reg. § 1.446-3(c)(1)(i).

treat a method of accounting for contracts entered into before December 13, 1993, as clearly reflecting income if it takes payments into account over the life of the contract under a reasonable amortization method, whether or not the method satisfies the rules in the previously proposed or final regulations.

The IRS may partially or totally recharacterize a notional principal contract transaction if its effect is to avoid the application of Treasury regulation section 1.446-3.[401] Moreover, if necessary to establish the appropriate timing of income and deductions derived from notional principal contract transactions, the IRS may depart from the accounting rules contained in Treasury regulation section 1.446-3 when taxpayers enter into such transactions with a principal purpose of applying the rules to produce a material distortion of income.[402]

To the extent that the regulations under Code section 446 are inconsistent with Code section 988 and the regulations thereunder (dealing with the treatment of gains or losses from certain foreign currency transactions), Code section 988 is to prevail.[403]

§2.12.4 Periodic Payments, Termination Payments and Nonperiodic Payments

Notional principal contracts will typically generate periodic payments, termination payments, and nonperiodic payments. As a general rule, the net income or net deduction from a notional principal contract within a tax year is included in or deducted from that year's gross income. The net income or net deduction is equal to the sum of all payments recognized under the contract for the year.[404]

Periodic payments are contractual payments made or received at intervals of up to one year during the entire contract term. These payments are based on a specified index and on a single notional principal amount or a notional principal amount which varies over the term of the contract in the same proportion as the notional principal amount that measures the other party's payments. The term of the contract includes any contractually fixed extension periods.[405] A nonperiodic payment commonly arises when a party to a notional principal contract makes below-market periodic payments or receives above-market periodic payments under the terms of the contract. A party making below-market periodic payments or receiving above-market periodic payments would also typically be required to make an upfront payment to the counterparty to compensate for the off-market coupon payments specified in the contract.[406]

---

401 Reg. §1.446-3(g)(1).

402 Reg. §1.446-3(i).

403 Reg. §1.446-3(c)(1)(iv).

404 Reg. §1.446-3(d).

405 Reg. §1.446-3(e)(1).

406 The IRS and Treasury issued final and temporary regulations amending the treatment of nonperiodic payments made or received pursuant to certain notional principal contracts. T.D. 9719, 80 FR 26437-01.

These regulations provide that, subject to certain exceptions, a notional principal contract with a nonperiodic payment, regardless of whether it is significant, must be treated as two separate transactions consisting of one or more loans and an on-market, level payment swap. This document also contains temporary regulations regarding an exception from the definition of United States property. These regulations affect parties making and receiving payments under notional principal contracts, including United States shareholders of controlled foreign corporations and tax-exempt organizations.

In general, regardless of a taxpayer's method of accounting, a taxpayer must recognize the ratable daily portion of a periodic payment for the tax year to which that portion relates.[407] A periodic payment is not treated as interest. Although a periodic payment made pursuant to an interest rate swap is made as a direct result of an increase or decrease in interest rates, this type of payment is not an interest expense because it is not "compensation for the use or forbearance of money."[408] This is because under a typical on-market interest rate swap there is no loan of money. The principal or notional amount upon which the payments are calculated is not normally exchanged between the parties.

With respect to contingent non-periodic payments under notional principal contracts, taxpayers have accounted for income using a wait-and-see approach before the issuance of Regulations under Section 446. Under the wait-and-see approach, taxpayers were permitted to defer recognition of income until the contingency was removed. The preamble to proposed regulations under Code section 446 noted that the wait-and-see approach has a great potential for abuse and is inconsistent with the timing regime under Regulation § 1.1275-4(b).[409] Some taxpayers intentionally designed notional principal contracts at formation to fall under the wait-and-see approach.

For contingent non-periodic payments under the notional principal contracts, a projected amount is to be included each year for contingent payments.[410] Additionally, taxpayers are required to re-project the contingent amounts each year and make adjustments. Taxpayers are also required to keep records describing their projection method, payment schedule and adjustments. Alternatively, the taxpayer may elect a mark-to-market method to reduce the administrative burden.[411]

Under the 1993 Regulations, when a notional principal contract includes a "significant" nonperiodic payment, the contract is generally treated as two separate transactions consisting of an on-market, level payment swap and a loan (the embedded loan rule).[412] The loan must be accounted for by the parties to the contract separately from the swap. The time-value component associated with the loan is recognized as interest for all purposes of the Code.

Termination payments are payments made or received to extinguish or to assign all or a proportionate part of the remaining rights and obligations of any

(Footnote Continued)

On October 13, 2015, the applicability date of the embedded loan rule for the treatment of nonperiodic payments was changed from November 4, 2015, to the later of January 1, 2017, or six months after the date of publication of the Treasury decision adopting the rules as final regulations in the Federal Register. The October 13th amendments to the temporary regulations provide guidance to taxpayers who are parties making and receiving nonperiodic payments under notional principal contracts. 80 FR 61308-01.

[407] Reg. § 1.446-3(e)(2).

[408] *Deputy v. du Pont*, 308 U.S. 488, 498 (1940).

[409] Preamble to Proposed Reg. § 1.446 issued February 26, 2004.

[410] Proposed Reg. § 1.446-3(g).

[411] Proposed Reg. § 1.446-3(i).

[412] The 1993 Regulations do not define what constitutes a "significant" nonperiodic payment. Instead, examples in those regulations illustrate contracts with and without significant nonperiodic payments and explain how to determine significance by comparing the nonperiodic payment to the present value of the total amount of payments due under the contract.

party under a notional principal contract. A payment between the original parties to the contract is an extinguishment. A payment between a party to the contract and a third party is an assignment. A payment is considered a termination both as to the person making the payment and the person receiving it. In determining whether a particular payment is a termination payment, substance governs form. Thus, any economic benefit that is given or received in lieu of a termination payment is also treated as a termination payment.[413] Gain or loss realized on the exchange of a notional principal contract for another notional principal contract is also treated as a termination payment.[414]

A payment made or received by a party in exchange for assigning all or a portion of one leg of a notional principal contract is not a termination payment if it is made or received at a time when a substantially proportionate amount of the other leg remains unperformed and unassigned. The payment, however, may be considered a nonperiodic payment or an amount loaned or borrowed, depending on the economic substance of the transaction to each party.[415]

An original party to a notional principal contract generally recognizes a termination payment in the year in which the contract is extinguished, assigned, or exchanged. If only a proportionate part of an original party's rights and obligations is extinguished, assigned, or exchanged, then only that portion of the unrecognized payments is recognized.[416] A termination payment made or received by an assignee pursuant to an assignment of a notional principal contract is generally recognized by the assignee under the rules applicable to nonperiodic payments.[417]

Payments under a notional principal contract that are not periodic payments or termination payments are nonperiodic payments. Nonperiodic payments include the premium for a cap or floor agreement (even when paid in installments), the payment for an off-market swap agreement, the prepayment of part or all of one leg of a swap and the premium for an option to enter into a swap if and when the option is recognized.[418]

As in the case of a periodic payment, a taxpayer must recognize the ratable daily portion of a nonperiodic payment for the tax year to which that portion relates regardless of the taxpayer's method of accounting. A nonperiodic payment must be recognized over the term of the contract in a manner that reflects the economic substance of the contract.[419]

A nonperiodic payment does not constitute interest expense because the payments do not serve as compensation for the use or forbearance of money. Any upfront amounts paid to purchase a cap and a collar are similar to premiums paid to purchase options.

---

[413] Reg. § 1.446-3(h)(4)(ii).

[414] Reg. § 1.446-3(h)(1).

[415] Reg. § 1.446-3(h)(4)(i).

[416] Reg. § 1.446-3(h)(2).

[417] Reg. § 1.446-3(h)(3).

[418] Reg. § 1.446-3(f)(1).

[419] Reg. § 1.446-3(f)(2)(i).

§2.12.5 Swaps

Under a general rule for swaps, a nonperiodic payment is recognized over the term of the contract by allocating it in accordance with the forward rates (forward prices in the case of a commodity) of a series of cash-settled forward contracts that reflect the specified index and the notional principal amount. The IRS will respect reasonable forward rates and prices used to determine the amount of the nonperiodic payment.[420]

A prepayment (*i.e.*, upfront payment) on a swap may be amortized, for purposes of determining the timing of income and deductions, using the level payment method and adjusted to take into account increases or decreases in the notional principal amount.[421] Nonperiodic payments on a swap, other than an upfront payment, may be amortized by treating the contract as if it provided for a single upfront payment and a loan between the parties.[422]

§2.12.6 Caps and Floors

A payment to purchase or sell a cap or floor is recognized over the term of the agreement by allocating it in accordance with the prices of a series of cash-settled option contracts that reflect the specified index and the notional principal amount. Only the portion of the purchase price that is allocable to the option contract or contracts that expire during a particular period is recognized for that period. Consequently, straight-line or accelerated amortization of a cap premium is generally not permitted.[423]

A payment to purchase or sell a cap or floor that hedges a debt instrument held or issued by a taxpayer may be amortized, with the payment adjusted to take the notional principal amount into account.[424] Amortization may be computed using the level payment method in the case of a premium paid upfront for a cap or a floor. Nonperiodic payments, other than upfront premium payments, may be amortized by treating the contract as if it provided for a single upfront payment (equal to the present value of the nonperiodic payments) and a loan between the parties.[425] A taxpayer may treat a cap and floor that comprise a collar as a single notional principal contract and amortize the net nonperiodic payment to enter into the cap and floor over the term of the collar in accordance with the rules applicable to caps and floors that hedge debt instruments.[426]

§2.12.7 Currency Gains or Losses

Special rules contained in Code section 988 prescribe the character of exchange gains or losses from transactions that are denominated in a currency other than the taxpayer's functional currency or that are determined by reference to the value of one or more nonfunctional currencies. The rules also apply to the gains or losses from the disposition of nonfunctional currency. The timing of income, deductions and loss on a Code section 988 transaction is determined in

[420] Reg. §1.446-3(f)(2)(ii).

[421] Reg. §1.446-3(f)(2)(iii)(A).

[422] Reg. §1.446-3(f)(2)(iii)(B).

[423] Reg. §1.446-3(f)(2)(iv).

[424] Reg. §1.446-3(f)(2)(v).

[425] Reg. §1.446-3(f)(2)(v)(A) and (B).

[426] Reg. §1.446-3(f)(2)(v)(C).

accordance with a taxpayer's overall method of accounting.[427] Foreign-currency denominated items comprising income or deduction are to be translated into U.S. dollars using the exchange rate that most properly reflects income; generally, the appropriate exchange rate will be the free market rate.

(a) *Definition of Section 988 Transaction*

The term "section 988 transaction" means a transaction in which the amount required to be paid or entitled to be received is denominated in a nonfunctional currency, or is determined by reference to the value of one or more nonfunctional currencies.[428] Section 988 transactions are: (1) the acquisition of (or becoming the obligor under) a debt instrument, (2) accruing (or otherwise taking into account) any item of expense or gross income or receipt that is to be paid or received on a later date, (3) entering into or acquiring an interest in any forward contract, option, or similar investment position (such as a currency swap), if such position is not marked to market under section 1256, and (4) the disposition of nonfunctional currency. The positions included in a mixed straddle that is identified under section 1256(d) are not treated as section 988 transactions. For purposes of the rule for dispositions of nonfunctional currency, the term nonfunctional currency includes not only coin and currency, but also nonfunctional currency denominated demand or time deposits and similar instruments issued by a bank or other financial institution.

(b) *Taxation of Section 988 Transaction*

Generally, gain or loss on a Code section 988 transaction is taxable as ordinary income or loss, but is not treated as interest income or expense.[429] The recognition of exchange gain or loss requires a closed and completed transaction (e.g., the actual payment of a liability). The use of a nonfunctional currency to simply establish a demand or time deposit denominated in the same currency (or the conversion of such a deposit to another deposit in the same currency) is not a recognition event.

Foreign currency gain or loss attributable to a Code section 988 transaction is calculated separately from any gain or loss on the underlying transaction. However, if any Code section 988 transaction is part of a hedging transaction all positions in the hedging transaction are integrated and treated as a single transaction, or otherwise treated consistently (*e.g.*, for purposes of characterizing the nature of income or the sourcing rules).

(c) *Forward and Future Contracts*

Capital gain or loss treatment is accorded to forward contracts, futures contracts, and options that constitute capital assets in the hands of the taxpayer, are not marked-to-market under Code section 1256, and that meet certain identification requirements. For this purpose, foreign currency gain or loss is defined as gain or loss realized by reason of a change in the exchange rate between the

---

[427] I.R.C. § 446.

[428] I.R.C. § 988(c)(1).

[429] I.R.C. § 988(a)(1); Reg. §§ 1.988-1(a)(1) and 1.988-3(a) and (c). An exception is provided for certain hedging transactions discussed in succeeding text.

date an asset or liability is taken into account for tax purposes (referred to as the "booking date") and the date it is paid or otherwise disposed of.

Code section 988 does not alter the treatment of bank forward contracts or regulated futures contracts that are marked to market under Code section 1256 or to the treatment of mixed straddles that are identified under Code section 1256(d).[430]

(d) *Hedging Transactions*

In connection with certain hedging transactions, foreign currency gain or loss will be treated as interest income or expense.[431] A hedging position may include any contract (1) to sell or exchange nonfunctional currency at a future date under terms fixed in the contract, (2) to purchase nonfunctional currency with functional currency at a future date under terms fixed in the contract, (3) to exchange functional currency for a nonfunctional currency at a future date under terms fixed in the contract (which would include parallel loans and currency swaps), or (4) to receive or pay a nonfunctional currency (*e.g.*, interest rate swaps denominated in a nonfunctional currency). Treasury regulations provide that if a taxpayer has identified multiple hedges as being part of a qualified hedging transaction, and the taxpayer has terminated at least one but less than all of the hedges (including a portion of one or more of the hedges), the taxpayer must treat the remaining hedges as having been sold for fair market value on the date of disposition of the terminated hedge.[432]

(e) *Sourcing Rules*

In general, foreign currency gain is sourced, and foreign currency losses are allocated, by reference to the residence of the taxpayer or qualified business unit on whose books the underlying financial asset or liability is properly reflected. In the case of any U.S. person (as defined in Code section 7701(a)(30)) other than an individual, the residence is the United States.[433] In the case of a foreign corporation, partnership, trust, or estate, the residence is treated as a foreign country. Where appropriate, foreign currency gain or loss that is treated under the Code section 988 hedging rules is to be sourced or allocated in a manner that is consistent with that of the hedged item. The residence of a taxpayer's qualified business unit (including the qualified business unit of an individual) is the country in which the unit's principal place of business is located.

For purposes of determining the source or allocation of exchange gain or loss from certain related party loans, loans are marked-to-market on an annual basis, and interest income earned on the loan during the taxable year is treated as domestic source income to the extent of any loss on the loan.[434] This rule is prescribed because of a concern that the general rule that looks to residence could be manipulated to artificially increase foreign source income for purposes of computing allowable foreign tax credits.

---

[430] I.R.C. § 988(c)(1)(E)(iv). A "mixed straddle" is defined for this purpose in I.R.C. § 1092(c).

[431] I.R.C. §988(d).

[432] T.D. 9736, 80 FR 53732-01.

[433] I.R.C. § 988(a)(3).

[434] I.R.C. § 988(a)(3)(C).

The special rule applies to a loan by a U.S. person or a related person (*e.g.*, a foreign subsidiary) to a 10-percent owned foreign corporation, which loan is (1) denominated in a currency other than the dollar, and (2) bears interest at a rate at least ten percentage points higher than the AFR for mid-term federal obligations at the time the loan is made. A 10-percent owned foreign corporation means any foreign corporation in which the taxpayer owns directly or indirectly at least ten percent of the voting stock. This rule applies only for purposes of subpart J and Code section 904.

(f) ***Straddles***

Neither the loss deferral rule of Code section 1092 applicable to straddles (discussed below) nor the mark-to-market regime under Code section 1256 will apply to a Code section 988 transaction that is part of a hedging transaction. Further, the general rule that treats foreign currency gain or loss as ordinary gain or loss is inapplicable to a Code section 1256 contract that is marked to market. Such gain or loss is to be treated as short-term capital gain or loss. In connection with the exception for Code section 1256 contracts, bank forward contracts with maturities longer than the maturities ordinarily available for regulated futures contracts are within the definition of a foreign currency contract in Code section 1256(g), if the requirements of that subsection are satisfied otherwise.

(g) ***Loss Deferral Rule***

An obligor's interest in a foreign currency denominated obligation is a "position" for purposes of the loss deferral rules applicable, for example, to losses sustained by a corporate lender on repayment of a foreign currency denominated loan by an affiliated corporation where the principal is determined by reference to the value of a nonfunctional currency. The rationale for this treatment is that a foreign currency borrowing is economically equivalent to a short position in the foreign currency. In addition, foreign currency for which there is an interbank market is presumed to be "actively traded" property for purposes of the loss deferral rules.

For transactions entered into after February 14, 2000, the rules under Code section 988 are coordinated with the rules of Treasury regulation § 1.446-3(e)(4)(iii) regarding currency swaps with significant non-periodic payments,[435] and exchange gain or loss on a hyperinflationary currency swap contract is realized annually under a mark-to-market methodology.[436]

Code section 988 may be applied to recharacterize transactions that do not properly reflect the economic substance of the transaction, because the IRS is concerned about the use of hyperinflationary currencies in tax-motivated transactions.[437] Accordingly, the rules covering hyperinflationary instruments in Treasury regulation § 1.988-2(b)(15), Treasury regulation § 1.988-2(d)(5) and Treasury regulation § 1.988-2(e)(7) are applied in accordance with the general economic substance principles.

[435] Reg. § 1.988-2(e)(3)(iv).

[436] Reg. § 1.988-2(e)(7).

[437] Reg. § 1.988-1(a)(11); Reg. § 1.988-2(f).

§2.13 Premature Withdrawal Penalties

Historically, when a depositor withdrew funds from certain time deposit accounts prior to the account's maturity, a penalty was incurred. Beginning in 1980, the amount of this "premature withdrawal penalty" was prescribed by the Depository Institutions Deregulation Committee ("DIDC"), which was established by the Depository Institutions Deregulation Act of 1980.[438] Although the DIDC has been terminated effective March 31, 1986, federal bank regulators have issued similar regulations.[439] The penalty reduces the originally stated rate of interest on the deposit, and it is subtracted from the principal and interest due the depositor at the time of the withdrawal.

Banks have taken the position that the forfeited interest is cancellation of indebtedness income eligible for exclusion under Code section 108(c)(1).[440] However, the Tax Reform Act of 1986 repealed this exclusion, effective for debt discharges after 1986. In the absence of this exclusion, income recognition will have the effect of simply offsetting the interest deducted in earlier years under Code sections 163 and 591.[441] The IRS has ruled that the forfeited interest does not fit the definition of cancellation of indebtedness income.[442] It has reasoned that an interest forfeiture caused by premature withdrawal is merely the "medium" for payment of the penalty.

The U.S. Supreme Court has resolved a split between the Fifth and Seventh Circuit Courts of Appeals in favor of the Seventh Circuit's view that early withdrawal penalties imposed upon certificate of deposit ("CD") account depositors constitute ordinary income to financial institutions. The Fifth Circuit held that the penalties collected from early withdrawal of CDs were excludable from gross income as discharge of indebtedness income. In framing its analysis, the Fifth Circuit focused on the spread between the amount of debt that the financial institution assumed when the depositor opened a CD account and the lesser amount that it actually paid when the depositor closed the account prematurely. The Fifth Circuit determined that the early settlement of the account for less than the amount that would have been paid at maturity was sufficient to trigger application of the discharge of indebtedness rules.

The Supreme Court dismissed the concept that premature withdrawal penalties represented discharge of indebtedness income to financial institutions and noted that, for the purposes of Code section 108, the term *discharge of indebtedness* conveys the forgiveness of, or release from, an obligation to repay. In the Supreme Court's analysis, a depositor who prematurely closes an account and pays the early withdrawal penalty does not forgive or release any repayment obligation on the part of the financial institution. Under the CD agreement, the

---

[438] Depository Institutions Deregulation Act of 1980, Pub. L. No. 96-221, §203, 94 Stat. 132 (1980), codified at 12 U.S.C. §3502 (2007). 12 C.F.R. §1204.103 (1980).

[439] *See, e.g.*, Federal Reserve Reg. §204.2(c)(1)(i).

[440] I.R.C. §1017 contains provisions for making a basis reduction whenever an election to exclude the income under I.R.C. §108 is made.

[441] I.R.C. §591 was repealed by the Small Business Job Protection Act of 1996, Pub. L. No. 104-188, 110 Stat. 1755 (1996).

[442] Rev. Rul. 83-60, 1983-1 C.B. 39. *See also* IRS Industry Specialization Program Coordinated Issue Paper on Premature Withdrawal Penalties at A.102.

depositor and the bank predetermine how much the depositor will be entitled to receive should the depositor close the account before the maturity date. Accordingly, a depositor does not discharge the bank from an obligation when the depositor accepts the exact amount that the bank was obligated to pay under terms of the parties' agreement. As a result, the Supreme Court ruled that the penalties could not be excluded from the bank's income.[443]

§2.14 FHLB Distributions

§2.14.1 The FHLB System

The Federal Home Loan Bank ("FHLB") system consists of 12 banks that are instrumentalities of the federal government and that function as a source of liquidity for its members. The FHLB was created in 1932 for the purpose of providing long-term funding to thrifts and other institutions that were mortgage lenders. In 1989, however, significant changes were made to the powers of an FHLB, which permitted all depository institutions (banks, as well as thrifts) that had residential mortgage-related assets which exceeded ten percent of their portfolios to become members.[444] Federal banking law provides that a thrift or a commercial bank that wishes to become a member and retain membership in one of the FHLBs is required to purchase capital stock in an amount equal to the greater of one percent of mortgage-related assets, 0.3 percent of total assets (the minimum subscription requirements), or five percent of outstanding FHLB advances (the advances-to-stock requirement).[445] Also, each non-thrift member whose mortgage-related assets are less than 65 percent of total assets may be required to purchase additional stock in order to borrow from its FHLB.[446]

Capital stock held by members in excess of their statutory requirements may, at the discretion of its FHLB, be redeemed at par value ($100) by the FHLB.[447] It is also permissible for one FHLB member to assign its FHLB stock to another FHLB member in the same FHLB District in the case of a merger or other acquisition between institutions, but a shareholder is otherwise prohibited from transferring or hypothecating any of its FHLB stock.[448] Dividends on FHLB stock may be paid in the form of cash or capital stock.

FHLB stock has a fixed $100 par value, and a shareholder does not share in the appreciation of the FHLB. Furthermore, shareholders do not own the excess value of the FHLB at liquidation. As stated by the Ninth Circuit in the seminal case involving the equity interest in the FHLB, the court stated:

> [I]n view of the fact that the Federal Home Loan Bank is a federal instrumentality organized to carry out public policy and having functions wholly governmental in character, neither the bank nor its association members, although the latter are nominally stockholders, acquire, under provisions of

[443] *United States v. Centennial Savings Bank FSB*, 91-1 U.S.T.C. ¶50,188, 499 U.S. 573 (1991), *aff'g in part, rev'g in part*, 89-2 U.S.T.C. ¶9612, 887 F.2d 595 (5th Cir. 1989). *See also Colonial Savings Association v. Commissioner*, 88-2 U.S.T.C. ¶9458, 854 F.2d 1001 (7th Cir. 1988).

[444] Financial Institutions Recovery and Reform Act of 1989, Pub. L. No. 101-73, 103 Stat. 183.

[445] 12 U.S.C. §1426(b) (2000).

[446] 12 U.S.C. §§1430(e)(1) (1999) and 1467(m) (1991).

[447] 12 U.S.C. §1426(a) and (b) (2000).

[448] 12 U.S.C. §1426(c) (2000).

Federal Home Loan Bank Act, any vested interest in continued existence of bank or any legally protected private rights which would enable them to invoke the due process clause upon dissolution or liquidation of bank by bank board.[449]

An FHLB issues only one class of stock and that one class has no preference with respect to any other ownership interest. The members holding capital stock are eligible to participate in the annual election of directors of the FHLB of which they are a member, but there is a cap on their right to elect directors that is designed to prevent any one institution from having controlling influence over the Board. Furthermore, shareholders do not elect all the members of the Board, and the voting rights grant the shareholder no other control over the operation of the FHLB, such as right to approve mergers or to liquidate. The Ninth Circuit stated further, "The regulatory provisions of the Federal Home Loan Bank Act disclose an intention on the part of Congress to retain the broadest kind of federal control over the number, powers and existence of the banks authorized to be created . . . ."[450] There is very little other statutory or judicial authority that describes the nature of the capital stock of the FHLB.

§2.14.2 FHLB Stock Dividends

Code section 305(a) provides that gross income does not include the amount of any distribution of the stock of a corporation made by the corporation to its shareholders with respect to its stock. Pursuant to Code section 305(b), this exclusion does not apply, and the distribution is treated as a Code section 301 distribution if, among other situations, the distribution is, at the election of any shareholder, payable either in stock of the distributing corporation or in cash or other property.

The IRS has ruled that when a bank that is a member of the FHLB system receives a stock dividend from an FHLB, it will not be treated as having an election to receive stock or property within the meaning of Code section 305(b).[451] This ruling reverses the IRS's position expressed in an earlier ruling in which it found the same type of stock dividend to be includible in gross income.[452]

The change was prompted by a ruling favorable to the taxpayer in *Western Federal Savings and Loan Association v. Commissioner*.[453] In *Western*, the taxpayer was required to maintain stock holdings in an FHLB district bank equal to one percent of outstanding loans. When the district bank issued shares to its members, the taxpayer retained the shares in order to meet its holding requirement while other shareholders requested that the district bank redeem their new shares. The district bank complied, and the IRS issued a notice of deficiency to the taxpayer when it failed to report the distributed shares as income under Code sections 305(b)(1) and 301. The Tax Court did not accept the IRS's argument that

[449] *Fahey v. O. Melveny & Meyers*, 200 F.2d 420, 446 (9th Cir. 1952).

[450] *Id.* at 443.

[451] Rev. Rul. 90-98, 1990-2 C.B. 56.

[452] Rev. Rul. 83-68, 1983-1 C.B. 75, *modified by* Rev. Rul. 90-98, *supra*.

[453] 880 F.2d 1005 (8th Cir. 1989), *aff'g* 55 TCM 372 (1988) (holding that shares issued by a district bank to a shareholder was not taxable income when the district bank had the only authority to redeem the shares). *See also Frontier Savings Ass'n v. Commissioner*, 87 T.C. 665 (1986), *aff'd* 854 F.2d 1001 (7th Cir. 1988), *acq.* 1990-1 C.B. 1.

the request to redeem the shares was an election by some of the shareholders to receive the distribution as property rather than stock. The court reasoned that since only the FHLB Board and the district bank had the authority to redeem the distributed shares from the shareholders, there could never be such an election by the shareholders. Thus the distribution of stock from an FHLB-supervised district bank does not meet the section 305(b)(1) exception to the general rule of section 305(a) that distribution of stock to shareholders is excluded from gross income. The Eighth Circuit affirmed the decision.

§2.14.3 FHLB of Redemptions

Code section 302(a) provides that if a corporation redeems its stock and if the redemption is one described in Code section 302(b), the redemption is treated as a distribution in part or in full payment in exchange for the stock. If the distribution does not fit within one of the paragraphs contained in Code section 302(b), then Code section 302(d) provides that it will be treated as a distribution of property to which Code section 301 applies. Code section 301(c) provides that a distribution to which Code section 302 applies is treated as a dividend to the extent of the distributing corporation's accumulated and current earnings and profits. Any excess is first applied against and reduces the adjusted basis of the stock and any excess is treated as gain from the sale or exchange of property.

Code section 302(b)(1), which prescribes exchange treatment if the distribution is "not essentially equivalent to a dividend," requires the application of a highly subjective test that often is difficult to pass. In *U.S. v. Davis*,[454] the Supreme Court held that in order to qualify under Code section 302(b)(1), a redemption must result in a "meaningful reduction" of the shareholder's proportionate interest in the corporation. In determining whether a reduction in interest is "meaningful," the rights inherent in a shareholder's equity interest in the corporation must be examined. The three rights inherent in a shareholder's equity interest that are generally considered most significant are: the right to vote and thereby exercise control; the right to participate in current earnings and accumulated surplus; and the right to share in net assets in liquidation.

Regulation section 1.302-2(b) provides that whether a redemption is not essentially equivalent to a dividend depends upon the facts and circumstances of each case; however, a *pro rata* redemption generally will be treated as a distribution under Code section 301. The only example in the regulations of a redemption that qualifies for exchange treatment under Code section 302(b)(1) is one where more than one-half of the nonvoting preferred stock of a shareholder who owns no shares of any other class of stock is redeemed. However, in Revenue Ruling 77-426, the IRS ruled that the redemption of any stock that is nonvoting, nonconvertible, and limited and preferred as to dividends and in liquidation represents a meaningful reduction of the shareholder's proportionate interest in the corporation if the shareholder does not own any other class of stock.[455] In this ruling, the shareholder did not own any of the corporation's common stock.

[454] *U.S. v. Davis*, 397 U.S. 301 (1970).

[455] 77-2 C.B. 87.

To qualify as a Code section 302(b)(2) redemption, three objective, mathematical tests must be passed. First, the shareholder must own less than 50 percent of the total combined voting power of all classes of stock entitled to vote immediately after the redemption. Second, the ratio which the voting stock of the corporation owned by the shareholder immediately after the redemption bears to all of the voting stock of the corporation at such time must be less than 80 percent of the ratio which the voting stock of the corporation owned by the shareholder immediately before the redemption bears to all of the voting stock of the corporation at such time. Third, the shareholder's ownership of the common stock of the corporation (whether voting or nonvoting) after and before the redemption also must meet the 80 percent requirement.

Complete termination rules are contained in Code section 302(b)(3). Under these rules, a redemption that results in the complete redemption of all of the stock of the corporation owned by the shareholder will qualify for Code section 302(a) exchange treatment.

If there were a redemption of the same percentage of all holders of FHLB stock, under Treasury regulations it will probably result in a Code section 301 distribution, as with any cash distribution. In such case, any tax basis previously allocated to the redeemed stock will be reallocated to the remaining stock held by each shareholder. In this situation, the redemption distribution will be a dividend but only to the extent of the FHLB's accumulated and current earnings and profits that have been generated from dividends from the Federal Home Loan Mortgage Corporation. To this extent, the dividends received deduction ("DRD") would be available.

In the event that a distribution is treated as a dividend, Code section 243 allows a deduction equal to a certain percentage of the amount received. Generally, the DRD is an amount equal to 70 percent of dividends received. However, Code section 246(a)(2) provides that the DRD is unavailable with respect to dividends from FHLBs unless and to the extent that a dividend from the FHLB is out of earnings and profits generated from dividends received from the Federal Home Loan Mortgage Corporation.

Code section 1211(a) provides that losses incurred by a corporation from the sales or exchanges of a capital asset are allowed to be deducted only to the extent of gains from such sales or exchanges, and Code section 1212 provides that net capital losses are permitted to be carried back three taxable years and carried over to each of the five taxable years succeeding the loss year.

§2.14.4 Tax Basis

Tax basis is used to determine the amount of gain when FHLB stock is sold or treated as exchanged under the provisions of Code section 302(a). It is also used to determine the extent to which a distribution under Code section 301 will be a return of capital. When a distribution of stock is excluded from gross income under Code section 305(a), Code section 307 provides that the basis of the distributed stock and the stock with respect to which it is distributed is determined by allocating between the new stock and the old stock the adjusted basis of the old stock in proportion to their relative fair market values on the date of distribution.[456] Applying the basis allocation rule of Code section 307, a bank must allocate basis between any basis it may have in FHLB stock that it purchased to satisfy the minimum subscription requirements or the advances-to-stock requirement, stock previously received as a stock dividend, and the stock received as a new nontaxable stock dividend.

Tax basis is different from book basis if stock dividends are included in book income when received, as they often are. Unless basis is properly allocated under the specific identification method, it has been the IRS's position that the shares sold or redeemed will be the shares that were first acquired. If this approach favors the taxpayer, it is unlikely that it will be applied. If the shares disposed of were acquired in a taxable acquisition of another member of the FHLB system, then the basis that should be allocated to those shares is their fair market value on the date of acquisition. Fair market value would be the stock's par value, $100. If the acquisition were tax-free, then the shares would have a carryover basis.

---

[456] Reg. § 1.307-1.

Chapter 3
Discount and Premium

Contents

§3.1 Tax Planning Suggestions
§3.2 Discount Income
§3.2.1 General Rules
§3.3 Original Issue Discount
§3.3.1 Accruing O.I.D.—General Rules
§3.3.2 O.I.D. on Worthless Debts
§3.3.3 O.I.D. from Prepaid Interest
§3.3.4 Debt Obligation Subject to O.I.D. Rules
§3.3.5 O.I.D. on Short-Term Loans
§3.3.6 Accruing O.I.D. Computation
§3.3.7 Basis Adjustments for O.I.D.
§3.3.8 Recordkeeping Requirements for O.I.D.
§3.4 *De Minimis* O.I.D.
§3.4.1 Determining *De Minimis* O.I.D.
§3.4.2 Accruing *De Minimis* O.I.D.
§3.4.3 Points as *De Minimis* O.I.D.
§3.4.4 Pre-Regulation Treatment of Points
§3.4.5 Points under O.I.D. Regulations
§3.4.6 Accruing Points
§3.4.7 Grace Period Interest
§3.4.8 Mortgage Buy-Down Fees
§3.4.9 Odd Days Interest
§3.5 Credit Card Fees
§3.5.1 Credit Card Fees as O.I.D.
§3.5.2 Over-the-limit Fees as O.I.D.
§3.5.3 Late Charge Fees as O.I.D.
§3.5.4 Cash Advance Fees as O.I.D.
§3.5.5 Intercharge Fees as O.I.D.
§3.5.6 ATM Fees as O.I.D.
§3.5.7 Merchant Fees as O.I.D.
§3.5.8 Non-sufficient Funds Fees
§3.6 Market Discount
§3.6.1 Ordinary Income Treatment
§3.6.2 Special Rule for Short-Term Obligations
§3.6.3 Deferral of Interest Deduction
§3.6.4 Current Inclusion Election
§3.7 Bond Premium
§3.7.1 Premium Amortization Election
§3.7.2 Basis Adjustment
§3.7.3 Bonds Defined
§3.7.4 Amortization Methods
§3.7.5 Computing Premium

§3.1 Tax Planning Suggestions

A great deal of controversy between the IRS and banks surrounds the proper treatment of prepaid interest.[1] In an attempt to resolve this controversy and implement reasonable rules, the Treasury Department promulgated final regulations in 1994 under the original issue discount ("O.I.D.") sections of the code that are broad in scope and that afford taxpayers income deferral.[2] In addition, the IRS's "Audit Technique Guide for Commercial Banking" contains a lengthy discussion of the audit procedures that an agent may follow when examining this issue.[3] Taxpayers should ensure that all forms of prepaid interest are accounted for in accordance with these rules, which allow favorable deferral treatment.

Among the types of prepaid interest that qualifies for deferral under these regulations is points. However, not all receipts labeled points will be subject to these regulations. It is the IRS's position that banks must disaggregate receipts that are labeled "points" or loan origination fees if a portion of the receipt is interest and some portion is consideration for services.[4] Only the former is subject to the O.I.D. deferral rules. However, the timing of income inclusion may vary with the type of discount; that is, whether the discount is O.I.D., acquisition discount, or market discount.[5]

As a general rule, discount is taxed as interest income. Thus, it is required to be included as income when earned. However, market discount generally is not subject to the accrual rules. Nevertheless, a taxpayer may inadvertently elect to accrue market discount if the taxpayer takes the item into account for accounting purposes and makes no adjustment for tax purposes.

The method available (constant yield, straight-line, or principal reduction) for calculating the annual amount of accrued discount may also depend on the type of discount, and different rules are provided for discount on taxable and on tax-exempt obligations. Finally, discount on certain short-term obligations may be subject to special rules depending on whether the holder is a bank or some other corporation. Recently, the IRS has issued automatic accounting change procedures for discount on short-term obligations.

This chapter will set forth the rules for determining whether O.I.D. or other forms of discount exist and how the amount of discount will be determined and taxed. The various elections available to taxpayers will be described and the advantages and disadvantages of each will be discussed. This chapter also will provide an analysis of the treatment of bond premium that banks may encounter in connection with purchased securities.

---

[1] *See The Art of Tax Efficiency in Community Banks*, by M. Gula, J. Brew, and R. Blasi, 2007, Red Room Publishing, *http://www.mraeresources.com/bookstore/*.

[2] I.R.C. §§1271-1275. 59 F.R. 4799 (Feb. 2, 1994).

[3] Audit Technique Guide for Commercial Banking, Ch. 16, located in Appendix D.

[4] Some institutions refer to these two types of points as discount points (interest) and origination points (service fees).

[5] *U.S. v. Midland Ross Corporation*, 65-1 U.S.T.C. ¶9387, 381 U.S. 54 (1965).

§ 3.2 Discount Income

§ 3.2.1 General Rules

When a debt instrument is acquired at a discount, the discount may be classified for federal income tax purposes as O.I.D., market discount, or acquisition discount.[6] O.I.D. may only arise upon the initial issuance of a debt instrument. It is defined as the excess of a debt instrument's stated redemption price at maturity over its issue price.[7] Since O.I.D. is viewed as a substitute for interest, the character of the income is ordinary.[8] Market discount and acquisition discount are defined as the excess of a debt instrument's stated redemption price at maturity over the debt instrument's tax basis at the time of acquisition, after initial issuance.[9]

§ 3.3 Original Issue Discount

§ 3.3.1 Accruing O.I.D.—General Rules

For most O.I.D. obligations issued after July 1, 1982, the amount of discount includible annually in gross income is determined by using the constant yield method—a method that attempts to approximate the actual accrual of interest.[10] For purposes of determining the accrued discount on short-term, taxable governmental obligations acquired after July 18, 1984, and for certain obligations issued before July 2, 1982, the straight-line method is normally used.[11] However, with respect to the former, the constant yield method is also permitted.[12] The straight-line method results in less taxable income in early years relative to the constant yield method.[13]

However, O.I.D. may be subject to alternative accounting methods.[14] Though these alternatives are commonly used for credit card fee income,[15] the Code language does not limit these methods to credit cards.[16]

§ 3.3.2 O.I.D. on Worthless Debts

Accrual of O.I.D. is required regardless of whether it is doubtful that the O.I.D. or the principal of the obligation is likely to be collected.[17] The general rule that permits discontinuance of accrual of interest in situations when the interest is uncollectible as the right to receive the interest accrues will not apply to O.I.D.

[6] Market discount is defined in I.R.C. § 1278(a)(2); original issue discount is defined in I.R.C. § 1273(a); acquisition discount is defined in I.R.C. § 1283(a).

[7] I.R.C. § 1273(a); Reg. § 1.1273-1(a). An instrument's stated redemption price at maturity is the sum of all payments due under the instrument, other than qualified stated interest including certain capitalized interest and other amounts payable at such time, regardless of how they are labeled in the bond indenture or other purchase agreement. The definition of an obligation's issue price depends on the circumstances under which the obligation was issued.

[8] Reg. § 1.61-7(c).

[9] I.R.C. § § 1278(a)(2) and 1271(a)(3)(C); and § 1283(a)(2).

[10] I.R.C. § 1272(a)(3); Reg. § 1.1272-1(b)(1)(iv). This method also is used by the issuer for purposes of calculating deductible interest expense.

[11] I.R.C. § § 1271(b), 1281(b)(1)(C), and 1283(b)(1).

[12] I.R.C. § 1283(b)(2).

[13] *See* discussion in Ch. 2.

[14] I.R.C. § 1272(a)(6)(C).

[15] *See* § 3.5.

[16] Cf. FSA 199913023, April 2, 1999 (applying I.R.C. § 1272(a)(6)(C)(iii) to mortgage servicing rights). For a discussion of mortgage servicing rights, *see* § 2.7.4.

[17] TAM 9538007, September 22, 1995.

obligations.[18] Whatever similarities exist between the general accrual method of accounting rules and the O.I.D. rules will not justify an exception of the doubtful collectibility rule to O.I.D. obligations.[19] The IRS reasons that the discount on O.I.D. obligations is deemed paid as it accrues and it is, thus, included in income in lieu of receipt, not in advance of receipt. This inclusion permits an upward adjustment to tax basis in an amount treated as relevant to the issuer. Of course, this position taken by the IRS does not appear to prevent a bad debt deduction for the discount that is of doubtful collectibility.[20]

§ 3.3.3 O.I.D. from Prepaid Interest

It was the IRS's longstanding position that an accrual method lender must include interest in income at the earlier of the date of receipt or when earned, as if the taxpayer were on a method that defers the recognition of interest income. This position has been reversed by regulations promulgated in 1992 under the O.I.D. sections of the Code that apply a method that defers the recognition of interest income.[21] Although the 1992 O.I.D. regulations apply to a limited type of debt instrument, they declare that deferring recognition of interest income until earned is a method of accounting that clearly reflects income for most bank loans. If the interest income is earned and payments are made then Treasury regulations provide that "each payment under a loan (other than payments of additional interest or similar charges provided with respect to amounts that are not paid when due) is treated as a payment of interest to the extent of the accrued and unpaid interest...."[22]

Under the O.I.D. regulations, a payment from the borrower to a lender at the inception of a loan, regardless of how it is labeled (a fee or as "prepaid interest,") is likely to represent an adjustment to the loan's issue price. It does not constitute interest income includible at the time the loan is made.[23]

§ 3.3.4 Debt Obligations Subject to O.I.D. Rules

In general, the O.I.D. rules apply to any debt instrument.[24] The term "debt instrument" is defined as a bond, debenture, note, or certificate or other evidence of indebtedness.[25] The Eight Circuit Court of Appeals ruled that loans made by a bank are not short-term obligations, as that term is defined in Code section 1283.[26] The latter defines a short-term obligation as a debt instrument with a fixed maturity date not more than one year from the date of issue.[27] By excluding bank loans from the definition of short-term obligation, the court appears to have excluded bank loans from the definition of debt obligations. The Office of Chief

[18] Rev. Rul. 80-361, 1980-2 C.B. 164.

[19] H.R. Rep. No. 432, Part 2, 98th Cong., 2d Sess. 1241, Footnote 2 (1984). *See also* S.Rep. 494, 97th Cong., 2d Sess. 212 (1982).

[20] I.R.C. § § 166 and 585.

[21] Reg. § 1.1273-2(g).

[22] Reg. § 1.446-2(e). *See also*, Reg. § 1.1275-2(a) that requires each payment under a debt instrument to be treated first as a payment of O.I.D. to the extent of the O.I.D. that has accrued as of the date the payment is due and has not been allocated to prior payments."

[23] CCA 200019041, March 3, 2000.

[24] I.R.C. § 1272(a).

[25] I.R.C. § 1275(a)(1)(A). An exception is provided for certain annuity contracts.

[26] *Security Bank Minnesota v. Commissioner*, 994 F.2d 432 (8th Cir. 1993), *aff'g* 98 T.C. 33 (1992).

[27] I.R.C. § 1283(a)(1).

Counsel of the IRS has issued an Action on Decision recommending that the IRS nonacquiesce in the Eight Circuit's opinion.[28] It continues to be the position of the IRS that Code section 1281, and the O.I.D. rules in general, apply to loans made by a bank in the ordinary course of business.

O.I.D. on taxable corporate and governmental bonds issued after May 27, 1969, with a fixed maturity date of more than one year is required to be accrued into income by both cash and accrual basis taxpayers.[29] For taxable governmental obligations with a maturity date of one year or less (mostly T-Bills) acquired after July 18, 1984, discount accrual also is required.[30] A *de minimis* rule permits O.I.D. not to be accrued if it amounts to less than one-fourth of 1 percent of the stated redemption price at maturity multiplied by the number of full years from the date of issue to maturity.[31] Accrual of discount income is not required for tax-exempt obligations and for corporate bonds or certain government bonds issued at a discount before May 27, 1969, and after December 31, 1954, but gain realized on a taxable sale or exchange may be characterized as ordinary income to the extent of the original issue discount.

§3.3.5 O.I.D. on Short-Term Loans

The IRS has conceded that a cash method bank that makes short-term loans with a stated interest rate to customers in the ordinary course of its business is not subject to accrual of the interest on those loans under Code section 1281(a)(2).[32] Earlier, in an Action on Decision ("AOD"), the IRS disagreed with the Eighth Circuit opinion in *Security Bank Minnesota v. Commissioner*.[33] The Service concluded, as had the Eight Circuit, the Tax Court and later, the Tenth Circuit, that Code section 1281 is not ambiguous.[34] Revenue Procedure 2002-9, as modified, permits a bank to automatically change its method of accounting for stated interest on short-term loans made in the ordinary course of business from an accrual method under Code section 1281 to the cash method.[35] A taxpayer is permitted to make the change in accounting for any taxable year ending before December 31, 2000, provided that the year is not barred by the statute of limitations, there is no closed taxable year after the year of change, and the taxpayer complies with several requirements. Among the requirements set forth in Revenue Procedure 2001-25 is one that imposes on the taxpayer the obligation to file a Form 3115 on or before December 31, 2001, along with amended returns for all prior years.

---

[28] Action on Decision 1995-014, December 16, 1995, *Security Bank Minnesota v. Commissioner*. An Action on Decision is a memorandum issued by the Office of Chief Counsel of the IRS in which it recommends acquiescence or nonacquiescence in a judicial decision.

[29] I.R.C. § 1272; Reg. § 1.1272-1(a)(1).

[30] I.R.C. § 1281. *Cf* I.R.C. § 454. If the taxpayer holding the obligation is not a bank, accrual is usually, but not always, required. *See* I.R.C. § 1281(b) for short-term obligations which are subject to the accrual rule.

[31] I.R.C. § 1273(a)(3); Reg. § 1.1273-1(d).

[32] Rev. Proc. 2001-25, 2001-12 I.R.B. 913, March 19, 2001.

[33] *Security Bank Minnesota v. Commissioner*, 98 T.C. 33 (1992), *aff'd*, 994 F.2d 432 (8th Cir. 1993).

[34] Action on Decision 1995-014 (December 26, 1995). *Security State Bank v. Commissioner*, 214 F.3d 1254 (10th Cir. 2000).

[35] Rev. Proc. 2002-9, 2002-3 I.R.B. 327.

The earlier AOD concluded that there is a strong indication that Congress intended to include loans made by a bank in the ordinary course of business within the definition of "short-term obligations."[36] According to the IRS, Congress intended to exclude from Code section 1281 only ordinary investors making unleveraged purchases of Treasury bills or other short-term discount obligations.[37] Banks are not ordinary investors and they necessarily leverage. Accordingly, Code section 1281 should apply to short-term obligations with stated interest made by a bank in the ordinary course of business. The AOD concluded that the IRS will continue to litigate this issue outside the venue of the Eighth Circuit.

In *Security Bank Minnesota,* the Eighth Circuit began its analysis with an exhaustive look at the text and background of Code section 1281. After holding the language of the statute was ambiguous, the Court turned to the legislative history and determined "the primary scope and purpose of the legislation was to apply the discount accrual rules to cash basis taxpayers that purchased short-term discount obligations pursuant to a leveraged purchase arrangement."[38] The court concluded Code section 1281(a)(2) did not apply to banks making loans in the ordinary course of business.[39]

Following the Eight Circuit's opinion, the Tenth Circuit held that Code section 1281(a)(1) also has no application to loans made by a bank in the ordinary course of its business.[40] The Tenth Circuit stated that "[i]n order to adopt the Commissioner's argument, we must ignore the common language used throughout the Code in describing loan transactions, and we must examine the text of §§1281 and 1283 in a vacuum. We will not take this approach."[41] Elsewhere the Court stated that "the phrase used to define 'short-term obligation' for purposes of §1281—'any bond, debenture, note, certificate, or other evidence of indebtedness'—appears throughout the Code to describe investment activity. In stark contrast, 'when Congress wants to refer to lending transactions, it uses the terms 'loan' and 'made.'"[42] Thus, according to the Court neither accrual of stated interest nor of discount is required on short-term loans made by a bank.

§3.3.6 Accruing O.I.D. Computation

Computing the annual amount of O.I.D. includible in income involves three steps:

1. Determining the total amount of O.I.D.;
2. Determining the accrual period; and
3. Determining the "daily portions."

---

[36] *See* S. Rep. No. 313, 99th Cong., 2d Sess. 903.

[37] H.R. Rep. 432 (Part 2), 98th Cong., 2d Sess. 1174 (1994).

[38] *Security Bank Minnesota,* 994 F.2d 432, 439.

[39] *Id.* at 441.

[40] *Security State Bank v. Commissioner,* 214 F.3d 1254 (10th Cir. 2000).

[41] *Id.* at 1257.

[42] *Id.* at 1258 (internal quotations omitted).

(a) ***Total O.I.D.***

The amount of O.I.D. is equal to the excess of an obligation's stated redemption price at maturity over its issue price.[43]

(i) Stated Redemption Price at Maturity. The stated redemption price at maturity of an O.I.D. obligation is the amount fixed by the last modification of the purchase agreement.[44] It includes any interest and all other payments provided by the debt instrument, except for qualified stated interest.[45] Qualified stated interest is stated interest that is unconditionally payable in cash or property, at a single fixed rate at fixed periodic intervals of one year or less, during the entire term of the debt instrument.[46] A "single fixed rate" is one that appropriately takes into account the length of the interval between payments.[47]

In general, interest is unconditionally payable only in arm's-length dealings and only if late payment (other than late payment that occurs within a reasonable grace period) or nonpayment is expected to be penalized, or other reasonable remedies exist to compel payment.[48] The IRS has ruled that qualified stated interest is not unconditionally payable merely because, under the terms of the debt instrument, the failure to make interest payments when due requires that a corporate issuer forgo paying dividends, or that interest accrues on past due payments at a rate that is not high enough to ensure that, absent insolvency, the corporation will make interest payments when due with reasonable certainty.[49]

O.I.D. can arise when a debt obligation is issued with a stepped interest rate, an interest holiday, another property right, or where the interest payable accrues and is not payable until the obligation matures. In these and similar cases, interest payments under the loan would not constitute qualified stated interest and, therefore, would represent part of the obligation's stated redemption price.[50]

(ii) Issue Price. The rules for determining issue price vary depending upon whether the instrument is issued for property (other than cash), whether the property is publicly traded, and whether the instrument has adequate stated interest. In the case of publicly offered debt (i.e., securities registered with the Securities and Exchange Commission) not issued for property, the issue price is the initial public offering price at which a substantial amount of the obligations are sold by underwriters, brokers or other intermediaries.[51] If the publicly offered debt is issued for property, the issue price is the fair market value of the debt instrument, determined as of the issue date.[52]

In general, in the case of privately placed debt, the amount paid by the first buyer will be the "issue price."[53] Thus, in the case of a debt instrument evidencing a loan to a natural person, the issue price is the amount loaned.[54] If privately

---

[43] I.R.C. § 1273(a)(1).

[44] I.R.C. § 1273(a)(2); Reg. § 1.1273-1(b).

[45] I.R.C. § 1273(a)(12); Reg. § 1.1273-1(b).

[46] Reg. § 1.1273-1(c)(i)(i).

[47] Reg. § 1.1273-1(c)(iii). Special rules are provided for certain first and final payment intervals.

[48] Reg. § 1.1273-1(c)(ii).

[49] Rev. Rul. 95-70, 1995-1 C.B. 124.

[50] Reg. § 1.1273-1(c)(1).

[51] I.R.C. § 1273(c); Reg. § 1.1273-2(a).

[52] I.R.C. § 1273(b)(3); Reg. § 1.1273-2(b).

[53] I.R.C. § 1273(b)(2); Reg. § 1.1273-2(a)(2).

[54] I.R.C. § 1273(b)(2); Reg. § 1.1273-2(a)(1).

placed debt is issued for property other than cash, the issue price will be equal to fair market value at the date of issuance if a part of the issue is either traded on an established securities market, or it is issued for stock, securities, or other property traded on an established securities market.[55] In the case of a debt-for-debt exchange, where neither the old nor the new instrument is publicly traded, the issue price will normally be determined under the rules contained in Code section 1274. As such, the issue price is equal to either the "stated principal amount," where there is adequate stated interest, or if interest is not "adequate," the "imputed principal amount."[56] Code section 1274 contains detailed rules for determining whether the rate of interest is adequate and for computing the imputed principal amount. Debt issued for property that is not subject to the above rules will be deemed to have an issue price equal to the stated redemption price at maturity.[57] Thus, if there is a "mere assumption" of a debt instrument that is caused by an alteration in the nature of the issuer, Code section 1274(c)(4) provides that the general rule for determining issue price contained in Code section 1274 will not apply. Consequently, the issue price will be equal to the instrument's stated redemption price at maturity, under Code section 1273(b)(4), if the instrument is not publicly traded.[58]

Prior to the effective date of the Tax Equity and Fiscal Responsibility Act of 1982 (TEFRA),[59] privately placed debt issued at a discount for property did not give rise to O.I.D. Instead, the transaction was treated as an installment sale subject to the imputed interest rules of Code section 483. Under the latter, a portion of what would otherwise be taxable as capital gain could be recharacterized as ordinary (interest) income. Code section 1274 now requires accrual into income of the imputed discount and, thus, it reduces the role of Code section 483 in preventing the conversion of ordinary income into capital gains.

Table 3.1 summarizes the rules contained in the Code and Regulations for determining "issue price."

---

[55] I.R.C. § 1273(b)(3); Reg. § 1.1273-2(c)(1). "Property" is defined to include a debt instrument. Reg. § 1.1273-2(c).

[56] I.R.C. §§ 1273(b)(4)(B) and 1274; Reg. § 1.1273-2(d).

[57] I.R.C. § 1273(b)(4); Reg. § 1.1273-2(d)(1).

[58] PLR 9615007, April 12, 1996.

[59] Tax Equity and Fiscal Responsibility Act of 1982, Pub. L. No. 97-248, 96 Stat. 324 (1982).

Table 3.1 Determining the Issue Price of Debt Instruments

Debt Category	Internal Revenue Code Definition	Treasury Regulations Definition
Publicly offered debt issued for money.	Initial offering price to public (excluding bond houses and brokers) at which price a substantial amount of such debt instruments was sold.[a]	First price at which substantial amount of the debt instruments is sold for money.[b]
Privately placed debt issued for money.	Price paid by first buyer of such debt instrument.[c]	
Publicly offered debt[d] issued for property.[e]	Fair market value of such property.[f]	Fair market value of the debt instrument, determined as of the issue date, if a substantial amount of the debt instruments are traded on an established market.[g]
Debt issued for stock or securities which are traded on an established securities market, or Debt issued for other property of a kind regularly traded on an established market.	Fair market value of such property.[f]	Fair market value of the property received in exchange for the debt instrument, reduced by the fair market value of any consideration other than the debt issued in consideration for the sale or exchange.[h]
Other debt instruments issued for property, except where Code section 1274 applies.[i]	Stated redemption price at maturity.[j]	Determined as if debt instrument were separate issue. If Regulation section 1274 doesn't apply, issue price equals stated redemption price at maturity under Regulation section 1273(b)(4).[k]
Debt instruments issued where Code section 1274 applies and no potentially abusive situation exists.[l]	Where there is adequate stated interest, the issue price is the stated principal amount.[m]	Stated principal amount.[n]
	In any other case, the issue price is the imputed principal amount.[o]	Imputed principal amount.[p]
Debt instruments issued where Code section 1274 applies and a potentially abusive situation exists.	Imputed principal amount shall be the fair market value of the property adjusted to take into account other consideration received in the transaction.[q]	Fair market value of the property.[r]

a I.R.C. § 1273(b)(1).

b Reg. § 1.1273-2(a)(1). For this paragraph, money includes functional currency and in certain circumstances, nonfunctional currency. The issue date of an issue described in (a)(1) of this section is the first settlement date or closing date, whichever is applicable, on which a substantial amount of the debt instruments is sold for money.

c I.R.C. § 1273(b)(2).

d Securities are publicly traded where a substantial amount of the debt instruments in an issue is traded on an established market. Reg. § 1.1273-2(b)(1).

e For purposes of this subsection, property includes services and the right to use property, but does not include money. Code § 1273(b)(5).

f I.R.C. § 1273(b)(3).

g Reg. § 1.1273-2(b)(1). Property is traded on an established market for purposes of this section, if, at any time during the 60-day period ending 30 days after the issue date, (1) the property is listed on (a) a national securities exchange registered under section 6 of the Securities Exchange Act of 1934, (b) an interdealer quotation system sponsored by a national securities association registered under section 15A of the Securities Exchange Act of 1934 (c) The International Stock Exchange of certain foreign countries designated by the IRS Commissioner in the Internal Revenue Bulletin, (2) the property is traded on a board of trade or an interbank market, or (3) the property appears on a system of general circulation that provides a reasonable basis to determine fair market value through dissemination of price quotations, or price quotations are readily available from dealers, brokers, or traders. Reg. § 1.1273-2(f).

h Reg. § 1.1273-2(c)(1).

i I.R.C. § 1274 generally applies to debt instruments given in consideration for the sale or exchange of property if the stated redemption price at maturity for the debt instrument (1) exceeds the stated principal amount, where there is adequate stated interest, or (2) in any other case, the imputed principal amount of the debt instrument determined under I.R.C. § 1274(b). I.R.C. § 1274(c)(1).

j I.R.C. § 1273(b)(4).

k Reg. § 1.1273-2(d)(1).

l A potentially abusive situation is defined as a tax shelter, use of certain nonrecourse financing, issuance of debt instruments with excessive interest, etc. Reg. § 1.1274-3

m I.R.C. § 1274(a)(1).

n Reg. § 1.1274-2(b)(1).

o I.R.C. § 1274(a)(2).

p Reg. § 1,1274-2(b)(2).

q Reg. § 1.1273-2(c).

r I.R.C. § 1274(b)(3).

(b) *Accrual Period and Daily Portions*

The term "accrual period" means a six-month period (or shorter period from the date of original issue) that ends on a day in the calendar year corresponding to the obligation's maturity date or the date six months before such maturity date.[60] Except for purposes of determining O.I.D. on short-term obligations, the "daily portions" are the ratable portions of the increase in the adjusted issue price of the instrument allocated to each day in the accrual period.[61] An obligation's "adjusted issue price" equals the sum of the issue price plus all preceding accrual period adjustments. For purposes of determining O.I.D. on short-term obligations, the "daily portion" is an amount determined under either a ratable accrual basis or a constant yield basis.[62] The increase in adjusted issue price is determined by multiplying the adjusted issue price at the beginning of an accrual period by the yield to maturity (determined by compounding at the close of each accrual period and adjusted for the length of the period) and then subtracting from this amount the total of the interest payable on the debt instrument during the accrual period.[63]

---

[60] I.R.C. § 1272(a)(5); Reg. § 1.1272-1(b)(1)(ii).

[61] I.R.C. § 1272(a)(3); Reg. § 1.1272-1(b)(1)(iv).

[62] I.R.C. §§ 1282(b)(1) and (2).

[63] I.R.C. §§ 1272(a)(3) and (4).

Example: Bank H acquired a wholly taxable two-year debt obligation upon issue on 1/1/X5 for $96,000. The stated redemption price at maturity is $100,000 and the nominal (coupon) rate of interest is 6 percent payable semiannually on 6/30 and 12/31, generating a yield to maturity of 8.2 percent. Under these assumptions, the O.I.D. required to be accrued into income is calculated as follows:

Step 1: Determine Total O.I.D.

Stated redemption price at maturity	$100,000
Issue price	96,000
Total O.I.D.	$4,000

Step 2: Determine the "Accrual Periods"

There are four "accrual periods" as follows: 1/1-6/30/X5; 7/1-12/31/X5; 1/1-6/30/X6; 7/1-12/31/X6

Step 3: Determine the "Daily Portions" of O.I.D.

	1/1-6/30/X5	*7/1-12/31/X5*	*1/1-6/30/X6*	*7/1-12/31/X6*
Adjusted issue price	96,000	96,936[b]	97,910	98,924
Multiplied by yield to maturity[a]	x.041	x.041	x.041	x.041
	$3,936	$3,974	$4,014	$4,056
Minus amount of interest payable	-3,000	-3,000	-3,000	-3,000
Equals increase in adjusted issue price	$936	$974	$1,014	$1,076[c]
Ratable daily portion (÷ 180 days)	5.20	5.41	5.63	5.98
Sum of daily portions for each month in period equals amount to be included in income	$156.00	$162.33	$169.00	$179.33

[a] 8.2% divided by 2

[b] 96,000 + 936

[c] Calculated amount = $1,056; $1,076 reflects rounding; Total amortized = $4,000 = (936 + 974 + 1014 + 1076)

§ 3.3.7 Basis Adjustments for O.I.D.

The unadjusted basis of a debt obligation usually is equal to the purchase price of a bond or, for a loan, the amount of funds that are loaned. As a general rule, for both taxable and tax-exempt obligations, the constant-yield method used to calculate O.I.D. determines the basis adjustment.[64] If a taxpayer uses the principal reduction method to determine income inclusion, the tax basis, as of the date each loan in a category is acquired, is deemed to be the loan's stated principal amount.[65] The principal reduction method requires the taxpayer to include O.I.D. in income as principal payments are received. Tax basis is increased by the amount of O.I.D. included in gross income, and it is decreased by the amount of any payment from the issuer to the holder other than a payment of qualified stated interest.[66] Tax basis in tax-exempt obligations also must be increased for amortized but excluded discount income. If there is a pro rata prepayment, then tax basis immediately before the prepayment is allocated

[64] I.R.C. §§ 1272(a)(1) and (d)(2); Reg. § 1.1272-1(b)(1). Prior to TEFRA, the straight-line method was available.

[65] Rev. Proc. 94-29, Sec. 5.01, 1994-1 C.B. 616. For a discussion of the principal reduction method *see* § 3.4.2(a).

[66] I.R.C. § 1272(d)(2); Reg. § 1.1272-1(g).

between the portion of the debt that is treated as retired and the portion of the debt that remains outstanding.[67] A pro rata prepayment is defined as payments made prior to maturity that are not made pursuant to the instrument's payment schedule and that result in a substantially pro rata reduction of each payment remaining on the instrument.[68] Special rules are provided for determining tax basis when a holder has elected to treat all interest on a debt instrument as O.I.D.[69] and when a debt instrument is acquired at a premium in exchange for other property.[70]

§ 3.3.8 Recordkeeping Requirements for O.I.D.

Notification and recordkeeping requirements are imposed on the issuer, the first party to sell, and the holder of O.I.D. obligations.[71] Within 30 days of issuance of publicly offered O.I.D. obligations, the issuer must file form 8281 with the IRS. The issuer of any O.I.D. obligation is required to notify the holder annually of the amount of taxable O.I.D. that accrued during the year.[72] An underwriter, broker or other "first party to sell" an O.I.D. obligation must mark the issue price and issue date on the obligation.[73] The holder of an O.I.D. obligation must record the issue price on the bond or on an attachment to the bond.[74]

§ 3.4 *De Minimis* O.I.D.

§ 3.4.1 Determining *De Minimis* O.I.D.

According to statutory law, if the amount of O.I.D. is less than the "*de minimis* amount," the amount of O.I.D. is treated as zero.[75] Presumably, this should result in no income accrual of O.I.D. over the term of the debt obligation to which the O.I.D. relates. The Code defines the *de minimis* amount as an amount equal to one-quarter of 1 percent (.0025) multiplied by the product of the stated redemption price at maturity ("SRP") and the number of complete years to maturity from the issue date.[76] If the O.I.D. is equal to or exceeds the "*de minimis* amount," it is not *de minimis*.

Thus, the calculation of the *de minimis* amount is as follows:

De minimis amount = .0025 × Complete years to maturity from issue date × SRP

Example 1: If the principal amount of a loan is $100,000, the interest rate is 8 percent, and the loan has a ten-year maturity, points less than $2,500 (i.e., 2 1/2%) will be *de minimis*, as follows:

.0025 × 10 yrs. × $100,000 = $2,500

In the case of an installment obligation, the regulations require the *de minimis* amount to be calculated under either a Weighted Average Method ("WAM") or,

---

67 Reg. § 1.1275-2(f).

68 Reg. § 1.1275-2(f)(2).

69 Reg. § 1.1272-3(c)(2).

70 Reg. § 1.1272-2(b)(6).

71 I.R.C. § 1275(c); Reg. § 1.1275-3; I.R.C. § 6049(d)(6).

72 I.R.C. § 6049(c).

73 I.R.C. § 1275(c)(1); Reg. § 1.1275-3(b).

74 *Id.*

75 I.R.C. § 1273(a)(3); Reg. § 1.1273-1(d)(1).

76 I.R.C. § 1273(a)(3). Reg. § 1.1273-1(d)(2).

in the case of a debt instrument that provides for the payment of principal no more frequently than a self-amortizing installment obligation, under a Self-Amortizing Method ("SAM").[77] An installment obligation is a debt instrument that provides for the payment before maturity of any amount other than qualified stated interest.[78] A self-amortizing installment obligation provides for equal payments, which consist of principal and qualified stated interest, that are unconditionally payable at least annually during the entire term of the debt instrument with no significant additional payments required at maturity.[79]

The weighted average maturity of a debt instrument is the sum, for each payment over the life of the loan, of the number of complete years from the issue date until the payment is made multiplied by a fraction, the numerator of which is the amount of the payment, other than qualified stated interest, and the denominator of which is the debt instrument's stated redemption price at maturity.[80]

Thus, the weighted average calculation for WAM is as follows:

WA = ΣComplete years from issue × *(Principal portion of payment/SRP)*

Using WAM, the weighted average would be substituted into the years to maturity formula for the complete years to maturity factor. Thus,

De minimis amount = .0025 × WA × SRP

Example 2: Under WAM, if, in the previous example, the loan were self-amortizing, points less than $1309 (i.e., 1.309%) will be *de minimis,* as follows:

.0025 × 5.236 × $100,000 = $1309

Alternatively, in the case of a self-amortizing installment loan under SAM, the taxpayer may substitute the factor of .00167 for .0025 in the original years to maturity formula to determine the *de minimis* amount, as follows:[81]

Example 2, *continued*

Under the SAM alternative, points less than $1670 (i.e., 1.67%) will be *de minimis,* as follows:

.00167 × 10 yrs × $100,000 = $1670

As the chart that follows indicates, for long-term obligations, the *de minimis* amounts calculated under WAM and under SAM using the reduced factor are very similar. For example, for a 30-year $100,000 mortgage loan with stated interest at 8.5 percent, the *de minimis* amount under SAM and WAM would be $5,010 and $5,085, respectively. However, for short-term obligations, the *de minimis* amount calculated under SAM is significantly higher than under WAM. For example, for a $100,000 loan with a five-year maturity and having an 8.5

---

[77] Reg. § 1.1273-1(d)(3). Neither the I.R.C. nor the regulations refer to these calculations as WAM or SAM. These acronyms were merely assigned by the author as a simple means of reference.

[78] Reg. § 1.1273-1(e)(1).

[79] Reg. § 1.1273-1(e)(2).

[80] Reg. § 1.1273-1(e)(3).

[81] Reg. § 1.1273-1(d)(3). Although Reg. § 1.1273-1(d)(3) states that the *de minimis* amount "may be calculated" using .00167, it appears, in fact, to require the use of this factor unless the debt instrument provides for payments "more rapidly than a self-amortizing installment obligation." This may mean that for non-self-amortizing installment obligations, the factor .0025 should be used.

percent stated rate of interest, the *de minimis* amount under SAM is $835, while under WAM it is $564.

Maximum De Minimis Amount Chart[82]

(Per $1,000 of Principal)

Loan Duration	*Calculation Method*	*6.00%*	*6.50%*	*7.00%*	*7.50%*	*8.00%*	*8.50%*	*9.00%*	*9.50%*	*10.00%*
1	WAM	0.21	0.21	0.22	0.22	0.22	0.22	0.22	0.22	0.22
1	SAM	1.67	1.67	1.67	1.67	1.67	1.67	1.67	1.67	1.67
5	WAM	5.51	5.54	5.56	5.59	5.61	5.64	5.66	5.69	5.71
5	SAM	8.35	8.35	8.35	8.35	8.35	8.35	8.35	8.35	8.35
10	WAM	12.69	12.79	12.89	12.99	13.09	13.19	13.29	13.39	13.49
10	SAM	16.70	16.70	16.70	16.70	16.70	16.70	16.70	16.70	16.70
15	WAM	20.47	20.69	20.91	21.13	21.35	21.57	21.78	21.99	22.20
15	SAM	25.05	25.05	25.05	25.05	25.05	25.05	25.05	25.05	25.05
20	WAM	28.82	29.21	29.59	29.96	30.33	30.69	31.05	31.40	31.74
20	SAM	33.40	33.40	33.40	33.40	33.40	33.40	33.40	33.40	33.40
25	WAM	37.72	38.29	38.86	39.41	39.95	40.48	41.00	41.50	42.00
25	SAM	41.75	41.75	41.75	41.75	41.75	41.75	41.75	41.75	41.75
30	WAM	47.11	47.90	48.67	49.42	50.14	50.85	51.53	52.19	52.82
30	SAM	50.10	50.10	50.10	50.10	50.10	50.10	50.10	50.10	50.10

§3.4.2 Accruing *De Minimis* O.I.D.

Although Treasury regulations recite the statutory rule that O.I.D. less than the *de minimis* amount shall be treated as zero,[83] they provide what appears to be mandatory income accrual rules for *de minimis* amounts.[84] Either of two permitted methods must be employed for including *de minimis* O.I.D. in income: the Principal Reduction Method ("PRM") or the Constant Yield Method ("CYM").

(a) *The Principal Reduction Method*

Under the PRM, a holder of the debt instrument is required to include *de minimis* O.I.D. (other than *de minimis* O.I.D. treated as qualified stated interest under Regulation §1.1273-1(d)(1)) in income as stated principal amounts are received. The amount to include in income with respect to each principal payment shall equal the total amount of *de minimis* O.I.D. on the debt instrument multiplied by a fraction, the numerator of which is the amount of the principal payment made, and the denominator of which is the stated principal amount of

---

[82] This chart illustrates for both the SAM and the WAM the maximum "*de minimis*" amount per $1,000 of SRP (not including points) for a range of interest rates from 6 percent to ten percent based on loan durations from 1 to 30 years.

Example: $100,000 30-yr installment obligation; 8.5 percent stated interest rate with 4 points ($4,000). To determine if the O.I.D. ($4,000) is "*de minimis*", simply compare this amount to the amount listed on the grid for the given interest rate and loan duration.

For 30 years at 8.5 percent:

WAM = $50.85 per $1000 of loan amount or $5085;

SAM = $50.10 per $1000 of loan amount or $5010.

Since $4000 < WAM and/or SAM, then $4,000 is "*de minimis*".

[83] Reg. §1.1273-1(d)(1) provides that in general "if the amount of O.I.D. with respect to a debt instrument is less than the *de minimis* amount, the amount of O.I.D. is treated as zero, and all stated interest (including stated interest that would otherwise be characterized as O.I.D.) is treated as qualified stated interest."

[84] Reg. §1.1273-1(d)(5).

the instrument.[85] The PRM may be used only for certain "categories" of loans specified in Revenue Procedure 94-29.[86] To compute loan discount, all loans in each category must be aggregated. The PRM is illustrated in the following example.

Example 3: In the case of a self-amortizing installment loan requiring repayment of $98,000 of principal and $2000 of points, an 8 percent rate of interest, with a 15-year maturity, the accrual of stated interest and *de minimis* O.I.D. under the PRM would be as follows:

$$\text{De minimis O.I.D. from each payment} = \frac{\text{Principal paid}}{\text{SPA}} = \text{De minimis O.I.D.}^{87}$$

Principal Reduction Method:

SPA	*Points*	*De Minimis WAM*[88]	*De Minimis SAM*[89]
$98,000	$2,000	$2,135	$2,505

Since $2,000 of points is less than the *de minimis* amount, the PRM can be used to spread the $2,000 over the life of the loan as principal payments on the loan are received.

Date	*Payment Number*	*Monthly Payment*	*Principal Portion*	*Amount Included in Income*[90]
1/1/X1	1	$936.54	$283.21	$5.78[91]
1/1/X2	13	936.54	306.71	6.26
1/1/X3	25	936.54	332.17	6.78
1/1/X10	121	936.54	628.61	12.83
12/31/X15	180	936.54	930.34	18.99

Thus, under the PRM, the amount included in income will increase over the life of the loan, as will principal payments.

The term *stated principal amount* is not defined in either the Code or the Regulations.[92] Regulation section 1.1273-2(g)(2)(ii) states that the stated principal amount of a debt instrument is reduced by any payment from the buyer-borrower to the seller-lender that is designated as interest or points. Moreover, Regulation section 1.1274-2(b)(1) provides that the issue price of a debt instrument that provides for adequate stated interest is the stated principal amount of the debt instrument.

---

[85] Reg. § 1.1273-1(d)(5)(i).

[86] Rev. Proc. 94-29, §§ 4.02 and 4.03, 1994-1 C.B. 616.

[87] This formula is expanded under Rev. Proc. 94-29, § 5.05, for aggregating loans as follows:

Amount to include from each payment =

(Starting principal + Current Principal – Ending principal)/(Starting principal + Ending principal) × (Starting discount + Current discount)

[88] Reg. § 1.1273-1(d)(3)

[89] *Id.*

[90] There will be amounts to include in income for each of the 12 payments during each of the 15 years of the loan totaling $2,000 over the life of the loan. Selected payments are shown and amounts are rounded for illustration purposes.

[91] Amount computed as follows: ($283.21/$98,000) × $2000 = $5.78

[92] Reg. § 1.1273-1(f) contains examples that illustrate what the "stated principal amount" of a debt instrument is equal to.

The PRM is authorized only for loans made by the taxpayer which have no O.I.D. or *de minimis* O.I.D., but are not subject to the election to use the Constant Yield Method ("CYM") for *de minimis* O.I.D.[93] Although Regulations allow a bank to elect to use the CYM to account for all interest, including *de minimis* O.I.D., the election is available only for loans made on or after April 4, 1994.[94]

The PRM is a permissible method of accounting for *de minimis* O.I.D. only for one or more categories of loans specified by the taxpayer that are acquired on or after an elected cut-off date.[95] The possible cut-off dates are:

1. December 22, 1992;
2. The first day of any taxable year beginning after December 22, 1992, and before April 4, 1994;
3. April 4, 1994; and
4. If a taxpayer is changing its method of accounting for *de minimis* O.I.D., including *de minimis* O.I.D. attributable to points, the first day of the taxpayer's first taxable year beginning after April 4, 1994.

Thus, for calendar year taxpayers, the potential cut-off dates are:

1. December 22, 1992;
2. January 1, 1993 or 1994;
3. April 4, 1994; and
4. January 1, 1995, in respect of *de minimis* O.I.D., including *de minimis* O.I.D. attributable to points.[96]

If the PRM is used for any of the loans within a category, it must be used for all loans within that category, but it need not be used for loans in other categories. If the method is used for more than one category, however, the taxpayer is required to maintain separate books and records for each category and computations must be made separately for each category. According to the IRS, there are four standard categories of loans:

Category 1: Loans secured by 1 to 4 family residential real property that are not home equity lines of credit or construction loans;

Category 2: Loans that are construction loans with terms not greater than three years;

Category 3: Loans that are secured by real property, and are not contained in Category 1 or Category 2, and are not home equity lines of credit; and

Category 4: Loans that are consumer loans with original terms not greater than seven years, are not secured by real property, and are not revolving credit loans.[97]

---

[93] Rev. Proc. 94-29, §§3.01 and 4.01, 1994-1 C.B. 616; Reg. §1.1272-3. Rev. Proc. 94-29 also contains two other limitations on the use of the PRM that will probably always apply to loans made by banks. They are: the loan may not be issued at a premium and the loan would produce ordinary gain or loss when sold or exchanged by the taxpayer.

[94] Reg. §1.1272-3.

[95] Rev. Proc. 94-29, §4.02, 1994-1 C.B. 616.

[96] Rev. Proc. 94-28, §7, 1994-1 C.B. 614.

[97] Rev. Proc. 94-29, §4.02, 1994-1 C.B. 616.

The PRM also may be used for other loans made by the taxpayer after the cut-off date that can be placed into additional categories and that have no O.I.D. or only *de minimis* O.I.D.; however, loans in the additional category or categories must be "homogeneous."[98] To be homogeneous, the category must consist solely of loans having a comparable duration; that is, a comparable weighted average time to expected payments of principal (including expected prepayments of principal). The weighted average is computed using the present value at the date of issue of the expected payments and prepayments.[99]

Duration is a critical piece of information for someone who is buying loans because it is the measure of how interest-sensitive the loans are. The exact calculations are not defined in Revenue Procedure 94-29; however, the investment definition of duration is that for a given change in the interest rate, the price will change by some related amount. For example, a duration of ten means that if the interest rate should change by 1 percent, then the price will change by ten percent. (The price is being differentiated with respect to the interest rate.) Therefore, the longer the duration, the more volatile the price. The formula for this calculation is as follows:

$$Duration = \frac{\sum_{t=0}^{n} t \times v^t \times P_t}{\sum_{t=0}^{n} v^t \times P_t}$$

where:

Pt = the principal repayment at the end of time t;

v = (1)/(1 + I) where I = the interest rate for period t;

t = the number of years from issue;

n = the time of the last principal repayment.

Without *v*, (i.e., without taking into account the time value of money), this formula is the same as the weighted average method. Even though the weighted average method is less accurate than duration, it is often used because it is simpler. (For the weighted average calculation of *de minimis* O.I.D., Regulation section 1.1273-1(e)(3) does not require that the present value of the payments be considered.)

To aggregate under this method, loans that have the same duration are combined. For example, a loan aggregation with a duration of ten might include the following: new ten-year loans, 30-year loans that originated ten years before, and 15-year loans that originated five years before.

---

[98] Rev. Proc. 94-29, §4.03, 1994-1 C.B. 616. Loans that are home equity lines of credit could be placed into a homogenous category.

[99] *Id.*

An important requirement of this section is the inclusion of any "expected prepayments." Loans are often repaid either in full or in part before the set life of the loan ends. A standard prepayment may be a necessary factor to be considered in calculating the duration of the loan. Unfortunately, Revenue Procedure 94-29 offers no guidance to the taxpayer on how to implement this requirement.

For each category of loans for which the taxpayer is using the PRM, the taxpayer must record and retain at certain dates the following information:[100]

At the Start of Each Computation Period:

1. The "Starting Principal"—The unpaid stated principal amount as of the end of the prior period of all loans in the category that were held at the end of the prior period; and
2. The "Starting Discount"—The unrecognized discount as of the end of the prior period.

During Each Computation Period:

1. The "Current Principal"—The stated principal amount at the time of acquisition of all loans in the category that were acquired at origination by the taxpayer at any time during the period, whether or not held at the end of the period. A loan will be treated as acquired at origination by the taxpayer if it refinances a loan previously held by the taxpayer or if it is a new loan received in exchange for a loan previously held by the taxpayer. In determining whether a loan is received in exchange for a previous loan, the proposed regulations issued under Code section 1001-3(g) should be taken into account. Thus, deemed debt exchanges resulting from modifications of the term of loans would probably be treated as received in exchange.
2. The "Current Discount"—The aggregate discount, including original issue discount attributable to points, at the time of acquisition on all loans acquired at origination by the taxpayer at any time during the period.
3. The "Ending Principal"—The unpaid stated principal amount of all loans in the category that are still held by the taxpayer at the end of the period. A loan will not be treated as held by the taxpayer at the end of the period if it has been refinanced or exchanged during the period. Further, to the extent that the loan has been charged off during the period, the charged off portion of the loan is excluded from the ending principal. If the taxpayer is a savings and loan association or other taxpayer permitted to account for foreclosures on security property under the provisions of Code section 595, the unpaid principal of the loan immediately before the transaction that resulted in the acquisition of the security property, less any charge off made prior to acquisition, shall be included in the Ending Principal. However, if the security

[100] Rev. Proc. 94-29, §§5.03 and 5.04, 1994-1 C.B. 616.

property has been disposed of prior to the end of the period, it appears that the Ending Principal would exclude such loan. Finally, the Ending Principal does not include the amount of any retained mortgage servicing rights. However, to the extent that the value of the retained right represents a retained participation interest in the loan it shall be included in the Ending Principal.

(b) *The Constant Yield Method*

The holder of a debt instrument may elect to include in gross income all interest, including *de minimis* O.I.D., that accrues on the instrument by using the CYM.[101] The election is made by attaching to the holder's timely-filed federal income tax return a statement that the holder is making an election under Treasury Regulation § 1.1272-3(d) and that identifies the debt instruments subject to the election.[102] Regulation § 1.1272-1(b) requires income accrual of O.I.D. to be determined under the constant yield method. The election under Regulation § 1.1273-3(a) allows this same method to be used for all forms of interest, including "stated interest, acquisition discount, O.I.D., *de minimis* O.I.D., market discount, *de minimis* market discount, and unstated interest, as adjusted by any amortizable bond premium." Therefore, O.I.D. has to be accounted for under the constant yield method regardless of this election. However, this election is available only with respect to a debt instrument acquired on or after April 4, 1994.[103] The CYM is calculated in four steps as follows:[104]

Amount to include in income for the period (month) = E

Step 1: Find *A* and *B*.

A = Present value of all future (remaining) stated monthly payments at the effective interest rate. (End of the month principal balance.)

B = Present value of all future (remaining) stated monthly payments at the stated interest rate. (End of the month principal balance under CYM.)

Step 2: *A* – *B* = C.

C = The remaining amount of O.I.D. (*Note*: Before a payment is ever made, C = the full amount of O.I.D.)

Step 3: Locate *D*.

D = The previous month's calculation of remaining O.I.D. (Balance in O.I.D. less any prior allocations.)

Step 4: *D* – C = *E*.

Example 4: Continuing the facts of the previous example, the interest accrual using the CYM over the term of the loan would be as follows:

---

[101] Reg. § 1.1272-3(a).

[102] Reg. § 301.9100-1(c) provides that the Commissioner has discretion to grant a reasonable extension of time to make a regulatory election or a statutory election (but no more than six months unless the taxpayer is abroad) under certain subtitles of the Code. For this purpose, a regulatory election is one defined in Reg. § 301.9100-1(b) as an election whose deadline is prescribed by regulations or by a revenue ruling, a revenue procedure, a notice, or certain announcements. PLR 201720004, May 5, 2017.

[103] Rev. Proc. 94-29, § 2, 1994-1 C.B. 616.

[104] Reg. § 1.1272-1.

Date	Pmt No.	PV at Effective Rate (A)	PV at Stated Rate (B)	Previous Balance in O.I.D. (D)	O.I.D. Incl. in Income (E)[105]
1-1-X1	1	$97,725.13	$99,711.01	$2000.00	$14.12
1-1-X2	13	94,273.88	96,089.18	1829.59	14.29
1-1-X3	25	90,523.67	92,166.74	1657.46	14.39
1-1-X10	121	46,128.63	46,489.82	371.81	10.62
12-31-X15	180	00	.00	.26	.26

Generally, under the CYM, the amount included in income decreases over the life of the loan. The payment of points, however, creates a difference between the stated interest rate and the effective interest rate that may result in the amount included in income initially rising to some point before declining to the end of the loan. This occurrence can be seen most readily on the amortization schedule of a loan with a relatively long life (*i.e.*, 15 years or more) or a relatively high interest rate. The increase is due to the fact that the principal repayments under the effective rate initially include more interest and less principal than the principal repayments under the stated rate. The principal repayments under the effective rate eventually catch up with those under the stated rate where the amount included in income is at its highest. After this point, the amount included in income begins to decline to the end of the loan.

§ 3.4.3 Points as *De Minimis* O.I.D.

Points often give rise to O.I.D. In general, points are often, although not always, a substitute for stated interest charged by a lender. Although other amounts may be labeled points, only points that are determined upon consideration of the factors that usually dictate the rate of interest will be treated as prepaid interest.[106] The standard practice in the industry is for points to be paid out of the borrower's funds. Congress recognized this when stating "[p]oints are additional interest charges which are usually paid when a loan is closed."[107] Whether points are paid out of the borrower's funds or financed is a question of fact.[108] Critical to the determination is the agreement between the parties, but a net disbursement by the lender creates ambiguity.[109] Historically, this was an important distinction. However, in 1994 Treasury regulations were amended to

---

[105] There will be amounts to include in income for each of the 12 payments during each of the 15 years of the loan totaling $2,000 over the life of the loan. Selected payments are shown and amounts are rounded for illustration purposes.

[106] Rev. Rul. 70-540, 1970-2 C.B. 101, *as amplified by* Rev. Rul. 74-607, 1974-2 C.B. 149, *as clarified by* Rev. Rul. 83-84, 1983-1 C.B. 97; *see also* TAM 8516003, December 28, 1984; 8516006, December 28, 1984 (accrual basis taxpayer); 8516009, December 28, 1984 (cash basis taxpayer); and 8901001, August 28, 1988 (hybrid method taxpayer). I.R.C. § 461(g)(2).

[107] H.R. Rept. No. 94-658, 94th Cong., 1st Sess. 101, 1976-3 C.B. (Vol. 2) 793. *See also R.C. Goodwin v. Commissioner*, 75 T.C. 424, CCH Dec. 37,502, *aff'd* (unpublished opinion) (9th Cir. 1980); *D.L. Wilkerson v. Commissioner*, 70 T.C. 240, CCH Dec. 35,156 (Acq.), *rev'd on other issues*, 81-2 U.S.T.C. ¶ 9657 (9th Cir. 1981); *W.B. Dozier v. Commissioner*, 44 T.C.M. 1274, CCH Dec. 39,389(M), T.C. 1982-569. IRS Pub. 530 (for 1993 returns), p. 4; IRS Pub. 936 (for 1993 returns), p. 6. The IRS, however, will treat loan origination fees on HA and VA loans as prepaid interest provided the requirements of Rev. Proc. 94-27, 1994-1 C.B. 613 are met.

[108] TAM 8516003, December 28, 1984.

[109] TAM 8516009, December 28, 1984 (cash basis bank); TAM 8516003, *id.* (accrual basis bank).

require accrual of O.I.D. regardless of whether the points were paid with fresh funds or on the net disbursement method.[110]

Points can be indirectly paid to the lender. For example, if a builder enters into an arrangement with a bank to buy down the interest rate of any borrower who purchases a home from the builder, the bank will be treated as having received a payment of points from the borrower, not a payment in the nature of a fee from the builder.[111]

§3.4.4 Pre-Regulation Treatment of Points

Prior to the O.I.D. Regulations adopted in 1994, the IRS held that if a loan application required the borrower to name the source of funds to be used for payment of settlement charges, then this identification indicated that the borrower paid the charges with "fresh" funds; that is, amounts brought to the closing by the borrower.[112] If points were paid out of the borrower's funds (not financed by the bank), a cash basis taxpayer included the points in taxable income in the year of receipt; an accrual basis taxpayer included the item in taxable income at the earlier time of receipt or when the right to receive the points arose.[113]

This treatment applied in situations where a cash method savings and loan association used the net disbursement technique; that is, where the lender issued a check for the face amount of the loan less the points and other settlement charges. The IRS noted that it was of some significance that the Housing and Urban Development settlement statement also specifically stated that the points were to be paid from borrower funds at settlement.[114] However, the IRS has ruled that points representing interest on construction loans received by an accrual method taxpayer in a single payment, along with other interest and principal paid upon completion of the construction project, were includible in gross income on a straight-line basis over the life of the loan.[115]

---

[110] Reg. §1.273-2(g).

[111] *See* IRS Coordinated Issue Paper on Mortgage Buy-Down Fees at Appendix § A.5.

[112] PLR 8901001, August 28, 1988; TAM 8710001, June 30, 1986. Since a change in accounting method occurred, the IRS applied the ruling prospectively to taxable years beginning after its issuance, pursuant to I.R.C. §7805(b). *See also* Coordinated Issue Papers on Deferred Loan Fees at Appendix A3 and A4.

[113] Rev. Rul. 70-540, 1970-2 C.B. 101; General Counsel Memorandum 14839, XIV-I C.B. 73 (1935), *modified by* Rev. Rul. 54-367, 1954-2 C.B. 109; TAM 8134013, April 30, 1981. In TAM 8724004, February 17,1987, an accrual basis federally chartered savings and loan association was required to include points in gross income at the time of the loan closing to the extent of the fresh funds provided by the borrower. In an earlier private letter ruling, the taxpayer was authorized to change its method of accounting for points from full inclusion in the taxable year of closing to a ratable inclusion as payments were due or received, if earlier, using the straight-line method. The change was based on the premise that the taxpayer's transactions were discounted loans and, therefore, the points were not paid or required to be paid by the borrower at closing. The earlier ruling was revoked prospectively. Moreover, application of the ruling resulted in a change in the taxpayer's method of accounting within the meaning of I.R.C. §446(e). The IRS found that most borrowers considered a portion of the fresh funds brought to closing to be allocable to and currently applied against so much of the points charged as constituted interest. *See also* TAM 8706001-004, 8707001, 8710001, June 30, 1986; TAM 8723005 and 8723006, February 17, 1987.

[114] *Id. See also Bell Federal Savings & Loan v. Commissioner*, 62 T.C.M. 376, Dec. 47,527(M)(1991), T.C. 1991-368.

[115] Rev. Rul. 74-607, 1974-2 C.B. 149, *as clarified by* Rev. Rul. 83-84, 1983-1 C.B. 97. If this "discount income" meets the I.R.C. §1273 definition of original issue discount, income inclusion will be calculated under the constant yield method and not the straight-line method. I.R.C. §§1273(a)(1) and 1272(d)(2); Reg. §1.1272-1(b)(1).

If points were financed, a cash basis bank was required to increase interest income ratably (straight-line basis) over the term of a loan. Points were found to be financed when they were included in the face amount of the loan and withheld by the bank.[116] An accrual basis bank would include the financed points in income as payments on a mortgage note were due, or as actually received, if earlier.[117] This was consistent with the characterization of financed points as discount income in the nature of interest.[118]

§ 3.4.5 Points under O.I.D. Regulations

In accordance with the Regulations adopted in 1994, points, as a form of prepaid interest, paid to a bank incident to a lending transaction are not included in the bank's income when received but are spread over the life of the related loan as O.I.D.[119] This treatment assumes that the lending transaction is the issuance of a debt obligation for cash, with the bank becoming the holder. A payment from the borrower to the lender incident to a lending transaction reduces the issue price of the debt instrument evidencing the loan.[120] Accordingly, the loan is subject to the O.I.D. rules that are applicable to a debt instrument not issued for property;[121] the amount loaned is treated as the stated redemption price at maturity of the instrument;[122] the points are treated as reducing the stated redemption price of the debt instrument to arrive at the issue price;[123] and the excess of the stated redemption price of the debt instrument over its issue price is O.I.D.[124]

An example contained in Regulations[125] indicates that if a bank "lends $100,000" and the points received at closing by the bank are $4,000, the stated redemption price of the debt instrument is $100,000; its issue price is $96,000; and the amount of O.I.D. is $4,000. This illustration may create some confusion. If the principal that the borrower will repay is $100,000 and the bank receives from the borrower $4,000 of points, then the stated redemption price at maturity would appear to be $104,000, not $96,000, and the issue price would be $100,000. In general, an instrument's stated redemption price at maturity is the "sum of all

[116] *Id. See also* IRS Industry Specialization Program Coordinated Issue Paper in Appendix A1.103.

[117] *Id.* In TAM 8712001, December 3, 1986, a 1 percent processing fee charged by the taxpayer in connection with loans to other lending institutions was considered in the nature of interest and thus constituted points. Accordingly, the fee was required to be ratably included in the income of the taxpayer over the life of the loan as payments on the note were due or actually received, if earlier. With respect to the accrual basis taxpayer's receipt of points, all the events that fix the right to receive income occur (1) when the required performance occurs, (2) when payment is due, or (3) when payment is made, whichever is earliest.

[118] Reg. § 1.61-7(c).

[119] Reg. § 1.1273-2(g).

[120] Reg. § 1.1273-2(g)(2).

[121] The term "debt instrument" is defined broadly to include any bond, debenture, note, or certificate or other evidence of indebtedness. I.R.C. § 1275(a)(1)(A). If a debt instrument is publicly offered and not issued for property, the issue price is the initial offering price to the public (excluding bond houses and brokers) at which a substantial amount of such debt instrument would be sold. I.R.C. § 1273(b)(1). Reg. § 1.1273-2(c) provides that the term "property" includes a debt instrument.

[122] I.R.C. § 1273(a)(2); Reg. § 1.1273-1(b).

[123] The issue price of a debt instrument is the price paid by the first buyer of the debt instrument. If a debt instrument is publicly offered and not issued for property, the issue price is the initial offering price to the public (excluding bond houses and brokers) at which a substantial amount of such debt instrument would be sold. I.R.C. § 1273(b)(1); Reg. § 1.1273-2(a)(1).

[124] I.R.C. § 1273(a)(1); Reg. § 1.1273-1(b).

[125] Reg. § 1.1273-2(g)(5), Ex. 1.

payments provided by the debt instrument," other than qualified stated interest.[126] Only if the $100,000 loan includes points would the example in the regulations appear to be accurate, since the example excludes points from the "sum of all payments under the instrument." This would be the case if the points were financed; that is, if the borrower received $96,000 cash at closing but the amount of the loan were $100,000.[127] If the points were included in the stated redemption price, the points would, inappropriately, be considered both principal and interest. Further, the payment of points would result in a higher effective interest rate. Thus, by using $96,000 as the stated redemption price when the payments are "present valued," a higher effective interest rate is achieved.

§3.4.6 Accruing Points

Generally, the amount of O.I.D., including O.I.D. in respect of points, is included in income in accordance with the statutory O.I.D. accrual rules.[128] Thus, a bank includes in gross income on a loan with O.I.D. an amount equal to the sum of the daily portions of the O.I.D. for each day during the taxable year on which the bank held the loan.[129] The daily portion of O.I.D. is determined by allocating to each day in any accrual period its ratable portion of the increase during such accrual period in the adjusted issue price of the loan.[130] The adjusted issue price at the beginning of an accrual period is equal to the original issue price of the loan increased by adjustments for daily portions taken into account for all periods before the first day of the accrual period.[131] The increase in the adjusted issue price for any accrual period is an amount equal to the excess, if any, of:

1. The product of—
   (a) The adjusted issue price of a loan at the beginning of the accrual period, and
   (b) The yield to maturity determined on the basis of compounding at the close of each accrual period and properly adjusted for the length of the accrual period, over
2. The sum of the amounts payable as qualified stated interest on the loan during the accrual period.[132]

§3.4.7 Grace Period Interest

Section 1272(a)(6)(C)(iii), which was added to the Code in 1997, has the effect of requiring taxpayers to treat credit card receivables as creating or increasing O.I.D. on the pool of credit card loans to which the receivables relate.[133]

---

[126] Reg. §1.1273-1(b); I.R.C. §1273(a)(2). The definition of an instrument's stated principal amount for purposes of I.R.C. §1274 is identical to the definition of an instrument's stated redemption price at maturity for purposes of I.R.C. §1273. Reg. §1.1274-2(b)(1).

[127] The IRS did not intend the amortization of points to be limited to those points that are financed. The O.I.D. treatment is also meant to apply to points paid at closing with fresh funds.

[128] I.R.C. §1272. For a discussion of O.I.D. from credit card fees, mortgage buy-down fees and odd days interest, *see* Chapter 3.

[129] I.R.C. §1272(a)(1); Reg. §1.1272-1(b)(1).

[130] I.R.C. §1272(a)(3); Reg. §1.1272-1(b)(1)(iv).

[131] I.R.C. §1272(a)(4); Reg. §1.1275-1(b)(1).

[132] I.R.C. §1272(a)(3); Reg. §1.1272-1(b).

[133] Taxpayer Relief Act of 1997, Pub. L. No. 105-34, sec. 1004, 111 Stat. 911. It is clear that section

As a general rule, Code section 1272(a)(6)(C)(iii) requires a taxpayer that holds a pool of credit card receivables to accrue interest and O.I.D. on the receivables during the "grace period" based on a reasonable assumption regarding the timing of the payments by the obligors of the receivables in the pool.[134]

Grace periods are generally defined in the relevant cardholder agreements although they may also appear on the billing statement. Typically, a grace period with respect to new purchase transactions may run from the date the holder of a credit card uses the card to make a purchase to the due date shown on the billing statement from the card issuer in which that purchase is reflected, provided that the card holder pays the charge in full by that due date. However, another form of grace period can occur with respect to interest if, under its cardholder agreement, the issuer does not charge the holder interest on the outstanding account balance for the period between a statement's billing date and the due date for payment, provided that the outstanding balance shown on that billing statement is paid in full by the specified due date.

Under Code section 1272, a holder of a debt instrument with O.I.D. is required to include the sum of the daily portions of O.I.D. in income for each day during the taxable year on which the holder held that instrument.[135] Section 1272(a)(6) provides rules to determine the daily portions of O.I.D. for certain debt instruments subject to prepayments. Under these rules, the daily portions of O.I.D. are determined, in part, by taking into account an assumption regarding the prepayment of principal on the debt instruments. Under certain circumstances, the fees received by an issuer of credit cards must be included with the grace period interest;[136] however, the application of section 1272(a)(6)(C)(iii) to other credit card receivables, such as late-fees, over-the-limit, and cash advance fees, generally has the effect of deferring income to later years which otherwise would be recognized in the year the fee was charged to the cardholder.[137]

The debt holder is prohibited from assuming that all credit card holders will pay their balances by the date specified in the grace period provision of the credit card agreement and, based on this assumption, defer the inclusion of grace period interest. In cases where the payments in the pool occur soon after year end and before the taxpayer files its tax return for the taxable year that includes such year end, the taxpayer may accrue interest based on its actual experience rather than based upon reasonable assumptions. To the extent that accrual in one year is different from the actual amount that should have been accrued into

(Footnote Continued)

1272(a)(6)(C)(iii) was intended to apply to credit card loans and the related receivables. *See* H. Conf. Rept. 105-220, at 522 (1997), 1997-4 C.B. (Vol. 2) 1457, 1992; however, it has not been fully resolved which credit card receivables increase O.I.D. under section 1272(a)(6)(C). For example, it is unclear whether interchange income is properly treated as O.I.D. *See* TAM 2005-33023 (Aug. 19, 2005). *Capital One Financial Corporation and Subsidiaries v. Commissioner*, 130 TC 147, May 22, 2008.

[134] Section 1004 of the Taxpayer Relief Act of 1997 added I.R.C. § 1272(a)(6).

[135] I.R.C. § 1272(a)(1).

[136] CCA 200145013, August 3, 2001.

[137] Rev. Proc. 2004-33, 2004-1 C.B. 989; Rev. Proc. 2005-47, 2005 -2 C.B. 269; TAM 2005-33023 (Aug. 19, 2005).

income, an adjustment is made in the immediately succeeding year to reflect the actual payments received during the earlier year.

Notice 2011-99 proposes a revenue procedure that would allow a taxpayer to use as safe harbor method of accounting for O.I.D. on a pool of credit card receivables a "proportional method." The proportional method generally allocates to an accrual period an amount of unaccrued O.I.D. that is proportional to the amount of the stated redemption price at maturity ("principal") of the pool that is paid by cardholders during the period. Under certain assumptions, the proportional method generally produces the same results as an implementation of the method described in Code Section 1272(a)(6).[138] If the proportional method is used, the method must be used for every pool of credit card receivables held by that taxpayer. If the proportional method is used for more than one pool, separate data for each pool must be kept, and the computations must be made separately based on the data for each pool.

§ 3.4.8 Mortgage Buy-Down Fees

In certain situations, a third party to a lending transaction may make a payment to a bank for the purpose of reducing the interest rate, which a purchaser of real property would otherwise agree to pay. These payments, commonly referred to as *mortgage buy-downs*, are intended to facilitate the sale of real property. Frequently, they are made by a home builder to a bank in order to entice a prospective purchaser to acquire a newly constructed home. The IRS Savings and Loan Association Specialist issued a Coordinated Issue Paper that addresses the issue whether such payments are required to be included in income when received.[139] The conclusion reached in the paper is that the receipt of such funds by the lending institution is required to be recognized as income when received, since the lender has unrestricted use of the funds.

Regulations now overrule this treatment by recharacterizing a payment from a party other than the borrower to the lender as a payment first from the third party to the borrower, followed by a payment, in the same amount, from the borrower to the lender.[140] In accordance with this recharacterization, the payment will then be treated as a payment from the borrower reducing the issue price of the debt instrument evidencing the loan. Consequently, it will create O.I.D. in accordance with the rules discussed previously.

§ 3.4.9 Odd Days Interest

It is customary for a bank that is in the business of making mortgage loans to charge what is referred to as odd days interest. Odd days interest is the interest that a bank will charge for the period of time between the date the loan proceeds are disbursed and the beginning of the period covered by the first mortgage

---

[138] 2011-50 I.R.B. 847 (Dec. 12, 2011). The Notice also describes the exclusive procedures by which a taxpayer may obtain the Commissioner's consent to change to the proportional method. The proposed revenue procedure would amend Rev. Proc. 2011-14 to add new section 31.02 to the APPENDIX dealing with the change procedure. It does not contain an effective date for the proposed revenue procedure.

[139] *See* IRS Industry Specialization Program Coordinated Issue Paper on mortgage buy-downs at A1.105.

[140] Reg. § 1.1273-2(g)(4).

payment. This interest is sometimes referred to as escrow interest, interim interest or simply odd days interest.

Odd days interest is probably properly accounted for in accordance with the rules prescribed for de minimus O.I.D.[141] Thus, odd days interest should, in general, be deferred as prepaid interest and spread over the life of the underlying loan in accordance with the effective interest method of accounting. However, because its accounting treatment will affect the timing of a taxpayer's income, the treatment of odd days interest is a material item for purposes of the Treasury Regulations that provide rules for accounting method changes.[142] If a taxpayer wishes to change its method of accounting for odd days interest, it must comply with the general procedures governing accounting method changes.[143]

§ 3.5 Credit Card Fees

§ 3.5.1 Credit Card Fees as O.I.D.

In appropriate circumstances certain credit card fee income may be susceptible to treatment as O.I.D. As stated in Revenue Ruling. 72-315, "It is not necessary for the parties to a transaction to label a payment made for the use of money as interest for it to be so treated."[144] Rather, the facts of the transaction (and not the label ascribed) control the character of the income received. If a fee is in fact interest income, the issuer may defer income recognition.

Relevant facts may include: (a) who is paying the fee; (b) what is the nature of the fee; (c) when (or how) is the amount of the fee determined; (d) how does the fee appear in the taxpayer's books and records; and (e) why is the fee accounted for in this manner. In addition, the capacity in which such fee income is earned, as well as the purpose for which it is earned, are also relevant. The taxpayer must establish what portion, if any, of the fees are interest where the fees are imposed for more than one purpose.[145]

Fee income that is treated as O.I.D. may receive special treatment under Code section 1272(a)(6)(C)(iii) which defers inclusion of the O.I.D. for accrual method taxpayers. While the general rule of section 1272(a) requires that the O.I.D. of a debt instrument be taken into account through the constant rate, yield-to-maturity method, an exception is provided for three categories of debt instruments in which the principal is subject to acceleration, thus making the date of maturity unknown:

(i) any regular interest in a REMIC or qualified mortgage held by a REMIC,

(ii)) any other debt instrument if payments under such debt instrument may be accelerated by reason of prepayments of other obligations

---

[141] Reg. § 1.1273-2(g).

[142] Reg. § 1.446-1(e)(2)(ii)(a); PLR 9729004, April 8, 1997.

[143] Rev. Proc. 2002-9, 2002-3 I.R.B. 327.

[144] 1972-1 C.B. 49 at 50. So, too, an item labeled interest will not be accorded interest treatment for federal income tax purposes if, on the facts, that charge is attributable to specific services performed in connection with a borrower's account. *See* Rev. Rul. 69-189, 1969-1 C.B. 55. *See* discussion of credit card annual fee in Chapter 2.

[145] *See, e.g., West v. Commissioner*, T.C. Memo. 1991-18, Dec. 47,120(M), *aff'd*, 967 F.2d 596 (9th Cir. 1992) (unpublished opinion).

securing such debt instrument (or, to the extent provided in regulations, by reason of other events), or

(iii) any pool of debt instruments the yield on which may be affected by reason of prepayments (or to the extent provided in regulations, by reason of other events).[146]

For qualifying debt instruments, the constant rate method is modified to reflect actual prepayments.[147] For an accrual method taxpayer, the result of the change is a deferral of income from the time when the payment is received to the time when the interest (O.I.D.) is earned.

Categories (i) and (ii) were added by the Tax Reform Act of 1986[148] to clarify the treatment of O.I.D. for mortgage-backed securities.[149] Category (iii) was added through the Taxpayer Relief Act of 1997.[150] This exception was intended to apply to credit card loans and the related receivables.[151] However, the I.R.S. has ruled that excess mortgage servicing rights also qualify under category (iii).[152]

While Code section 446(e) generally requires the consent of the Secretary for a change in accounting method, the I.R.S. provided procedures by which a taxpayer can receive automatic consent to a change in their method of accounting to the method described in Code section 1272(a)(6) for pools of credit card receivables and other pools of debt instruments.[153] Automatic consent is achieved by attaching Form 3115 to the taxpayer's return and filing Form 3115 with the I.R.S.[154]

(a) *Proportional Accounting Method*

Taxpayers may use a proportional accounting method to account for original issue discount ("O.I.D.") and certain other items of income on pools of credit card receivables. This method has been determined to be an acceptable method to determine the "daily portions" of O.I.D. in accordance with Code section 1272(a)(6).[155] The Taxpayer Relief Act of 1997[156] extended Code section 1272(a)(6) to cover any pool of debt instruments that are subject to prepayment.[157]

---

[146] I.R.C. § 1272(a)(6)(C).

[147] I.R.C. § 1272(a)(6).

[148] Pub. L. No. 99-514, § 672, 100 Stat. 285 (1986).

[149] H.R. Conf. Rep. 99-841, pt. II at 222-23 (1986). As stated in the Report, "The application of the O.I.D. rules is uncertain for debt instruments the maturity of which may be accelerated on account of prepayments on obligations that collateralize the debt instrument."

[150] Pub. L. No. 105-34, § 1004, 111 Stat. 787.

[151] *See* H.R. Conf. Rep. 105-220, at 522 (1997), 1997-4 C.B. (Vol.2) 1457, 1992. "If a taxpayer holds a pool of credit card receivables that require interest to be paid if the borrowers do not pay their accounts by a specified date, the taxpayer would be required to accrue interest or O.I.D. on such a pool based on a reasonable assumption regarding the timing of the payments of the accounts in the pool . . . .".

[152] FSA 199913023, April 2, 1999. For a discussion of mortgage servicing rights, *see* § 2.7.4.

[153] Rev. Proc. 2004-33, 2004-1 C.B. 989; Rev. Proc. 98-60, app. sec. 12, 1998-2 C.B. 759, 786.

[154] *Id.* sec. 6.02, app. sec. 12, 1998-2 C.B. at 765, 786. In *Capital One Financial Corporation and Subsidiaries v. Commissioner*, the Tax Court held, in relevant part, that the taxpayer must unambiguously state the types of receivables on Form 3115 so as to give effective notice to the Secretary. 130 T.C. 147, 163 (2008); *aff'd*, 659 F.3d 316 (4th Cir. 2011).

[155] *See* Rev. Proc. 2013-26, 2013-22 I.R.B. 1160. Notably, Revenue Procedure 2013-26 differs from the proposed revenue procedure predating it. *Compare* Rev. Proc. 2013-26, *with* 2011-50 I.R.B. 847 (Dec. 12, 2011). The later Revenue Procedure applies to any taxpayer that holds a pool of credit card receivables and, unlike its predecessor, is not limited to credit card issuers.

[156] Pub. L. No. 105-34, § 1004, 111 Stat. 788 (1997).

[157] H.R. Conf. Rep. 105-220, at 222-23 (1997).

The proportional method allocates to an accrual period an amount of income that is proportional to the amount of the stated redemption price at maturity ("SRPM") of the pool that is paid by the cardholders during the period.[158] The difference between the aggregate balance owed on the receivables, other than amounts representing charges or fees that are not treated as O.I.D. (such as finance charges that are qualified stated interest), and the taxpayer's basis is permitted to be treated as O.I.D. under the proportional method.[159] As a result, a taxpayer may use the proportional method for certain amounts that would not otherwise be treated as O.I.D., for example, market discount or bond premium.[160] The proportional method is available to both taxpayers who purchase a pool (or interest in a pool) of credit card receivables and taxpayers who originate the receivables.[161]

Although there is no express authority for applying the proportional method to O.I.D. on debt instruments other than a pool of credit card debt, the legislative history to Code section 1272 suggests no such limitation.[162]

(b) *Automatic Change Procedures*

A taxpayer desiring to change to the proportional method must comply with Revenue Procedure 2011-14 when making the change.[163] Revenue Procedure 2011-14 provides the procedures for a taxpayer to follow in order to obtain automatic consent for a change in the taxpayer's method of accounting. A taxpayer may not retroactively recalculate his previous years' O.I.D. using the proportional method.[164] The change to the proportional method is allowable only for taxable years ending after December 31, 2012,[165] and because the change to the proportional method is made on a cut-off basis, a Code section 481(a) adjustment to taxable income is neither permitted nor necessary.[166]

The restriction that a taxpayer may not change his accounting method if the taxpayer has changed accounting methods within the previous five years is

---

[158] Rev. Proc. 2013-26, at § 1. A "debt instrument" is defined as "a bond, debenture, note, or certificate or other evidence of indebtedness." I.R.C. § 1275(a)(1)(A). A "pool" of debt instruments can generally be thought of as an aggregated collection of a certain type of instrument, for example, credit card receivables. *See Capital One Fin. Corp. v. Comm'r*, 130 T.C. 147, 162 (2008).

[159] Rev. Proc. 2013-26, at § 4.02.

[160] *Id.*

[161] *See* Reg. § 1.1272-2(b) ("For purposes of section 1272 . . . purchase means any acquisition of a debt instrument, including the acquisition of a newly issued debt instrument in a debt-for-debt exchange or the acquisition of a debt instrument from a donor."). Additionally, see the examples in Reg. § 1.1272-1 for support of the proposition that a taxpayer may accrue O.I.D. on debt instruments purchased at original issue.

[162] *See* H.R. Conf. Rep. 105-220 at 223 ("The conference agreement applies to *any pool* of debt instruments the yield on which may be affected by reason of prepayments.") (emphasis added); H.R. Rep. 105-148, 451 (1997) ("The bill applies the special OID rule applicable to any regular interest in a REMIC, qualified mortgages held by a REMIC, or certain other debt instruments to *any pool* of debt instruments the payments on which may be accelerated by reason of prepayments.") (emphasis added); Reg. § 1.1272-1(b)(2)(i) (stating that § 1272(a)(6) applies to "certain interests in mortgages held by a REMIC, and certain other debt instruments with payment subject to acceleration).

[163] It is important to note that Rev. Proc. 2013-26 modifies Rev. Proc. 2011-14 by adding § 31.02, governing the use of the proportional method on pools of credit card receivables.

[164] *See* Rev. Proc. 2011-14, 2011-4 I.R.B. 330, § 2.04 ("Unless specifically authorized by the Commissioner, a taxpayer may not request, or otherwise make, a retroactive change in method of accounting, regardless of whether the change is from a permissible or an impermissible method.")..

[165] *See* Rev. Proc. 2013-26, at § 4.02.

[166] *Id.* at § 8.

waived.[167] This waiver applies if the taxpayer seeks to change to the proportional method in the first or second taxable year ending on or after December 31, 2012.[168] The waiver does not apply if the taxpayer attempts to change to the proportional method later than the second taxable year after 2012.

In order to change to the proportional method, the taxpayer must comply with Code section 446(e) and its regulations by filing an Application for Change in Accounting Method (Form 3115) during the taxable year the taxpayer wants to make the change.[169] If the taxpayer does not yet have an accounting method for O.I.D. on a pool of credit card receivables, then the taxpayer may adopt the proportional method by using it on a timely filed original federal income tax return for the first taxable year the taxpayer must account for the O.I.D. on an acquired pool of credit card receivables.[170]

(c) *Calculating O.I.D. under the Proportional Method*

A taxpayer using the proportional method must make the required computations on a monthly basis.[171] At the beginning of each computation period, the taxpayer must determine the SRPM as of the beginning of the period ("Beginning SRPM") and the unaccrued O.I.D. as of the beginning of the period ("Beginning O.I.D.").[172] A taxpayer's Beginning SRPM is equal to the aggregate balance owed on all credit card receivables at the beginning of the period, other than amounts that are not properly treated as O.I.D.[173] Beginning O.I.D. is equal to the O.I.D. for the pool at the beginning of the period that has not previously been taken into income.[174] During each computation period, the taxpayer must determine for each pool of credit card receivables the sum of the payments during the period that reduce the Beginning SRPM ("SRPM Payments").[175] Additionally, the taxpayer must compute the O.I.D. allocated to the period ("Monthly O.I.D.") and include the amount in income.[176] Monthly O.I.D. is the product of the Beginning O.I.D. multiplied by the quotient of the SRPM Payments divided by the Beginning SRPM.[177]

An example of the proportional method is provided in Revenue Procedure 2013-26, as follows:

> On December 1, for the taxpayer's single pool of credit card receivables, the Beginning SRPM is $100,000,000, and the Beginning OID is $1,000,000. During December, the taxpayer receives SRPM payments of $11,000,000 with respect to the pool. For December, the taxpayer computes Monthly OID for the pool in the amount of $110,000 ($1,000,000 * ($11,000,000 / $100,000,000)).

§3.5.2 Over-the-limit Fees as O.I.D.

Over-the-limit fees are charged by an issuer of a credit card when a cardholder's credit limit is exceeded. In general, an over-the-limit fee is billed directly

---

[167] *Id.* at §8.
[168] *Id.*
[169] Rev. Proc. 2011-14, at §2.03.
[170] Rev. Proc. 2013-26, at §4.03.
[171] *Id.* at §5.01.
[172] *Id.* at §5.02.
[173] *Id.*
[174] *Id.*
[175] *Id.* at §5.03.
[176] *Id.* at §5.04.
[177] *Id.*

against a cardholder's account and, once posted, is included in the outstanding account balance to which interest is charged at the stated rate. An over-the-limit fee is often a fixed amount of money (as opposed to a variable percentage). This charge appears on the cardholder's next monthly account billing statement. If an over-the-limit fee is imposed by an issuer on a cardholder with respect to the cardholder's credit card account, and that fee is not imposed for services rendered by the issuer for the cardholder's benefit, the IRS believes that an over-the-limit fee like an overdraft advance fee may be susceptible to characterization as interest.[178]

§ 3.5.3 Late Charge Fees as O.I.D.

Late charge fees are charged by an issuer of a credit card when a cardholder fails to make a payment otherwise due. In general, a late charge fee is billed directly against a cardholder's account and, once posted, is included in the outstanding account balance to which interest is charged at the stated rate. It is often a fixed amount of money (as opposed to a percentage of the delinquency). This charge appears on the cardholder's next account billing statement. Where a late charge fee is imposed by an issuer on a cardholder with respect to the cardholder's credit card account, and it is not imposed for a specific service rendered by the issuer for the cardholder's benefit, Revenue Procedure 2004-33 holds that late fees may be treated as interest income on a pool of credit card loans. The additional interest may be treated as either stated interest or as interest that creates or increases the amount of original issue discount on the pool of credit card loans to which the fees relate.[179] It is irrelevant whether the late fee is a one-time charge or a flat sum in addition to the stated periodic interest rate.

To qualify for this treatment, the fee charged to each cardholder by the taxpayer must be separately stated on the cardholder's account when the late fee is imposed.[180] Furthermore, under the applicable credit card agreement governing each cardholder's use of the credit card, no amount identified as a credit card late fee is charged for specific services performed by the taxpayer for the benefit of the cardholder.

Revenue Procedure 2004-33 is effective for tax years ending on or after December 31, 2003. However, if the issuer of the credit card treated credit card late fees as interest that creates or increases the amount of original issue discount ("O.I.D.") on the pool of credit card before the effective date of the procedure, the issue of whether the taxpayer is properly treating its credit card late fees as O.I.D. will not be raised as an audit issue for tax years ending before December 31, 2003. If the issuer treats late fees as interest that creates or increases the amount of O.I.D. on the pool of credit card loans, the issuer may obtain automatic consent to change its accounting method by filing a Form 3115, "Application for Change in Accounting Method."

---

[178] TAM 200533023, May 10, 2005; CCA 200145013, August 3, 2001.

[179] Rev. Proc. 2004-33, 2004-1 C.B. 989; TAM 200533022, May 10, 2005.

[180] *Id.* Sec. 5.

§3.5.4 Cash Advance Fees as O.I.D.

Cash advance fees are charged by an issuer of a credit card when a cardholder uses that card to obtain cash drawn (or deemed to be drawn) against the line of credit on the card. A minimum or maximum fee may be imposed in some situations. In general, a cash advance fee is billed directly against the cardholder's account and, once posted, is included in the outstanding account balance to which interest is charged at the stated rate. A transaction fee (ranging in percentages that depend on applicable state law and upon the amount advanced) is often imposed on cardholders whenever a cardholder uses its credit card to obtain cash. This charge appears on the cardholder's next account billing statement following the cash advance. If the cash advance is obtained against a credit card, this charge is in addition to any stated interest charge and any separately stated ATM charge billed to the cardholder.

Provided that the cash advance fee is not attributable to services performed by the issuer, Revenue Ruling 77-417 permitted such fees to be deducted as interest by the cardholder.[181] Revenue Ruling 77-417 holds that a cardholder may take a deduction for interest (as permitted at that time) for such fees provided they were not made to compensate the issuer for services directly chargeable to, or incurred for the benefit of, the cardholder. However, the result reached in the revenue ruling is indicative that, from an issuer's perspective, cash advance fees may be imposed to reflect the additional cost of funds in this type of credit card transaction.

§3.5.5 Interchange Fees as O.I.D.

The Tax Court has held in *Capital One* that interchange fees received by the issuer of a credit card may be treated as interest income.[182] Following the decision, the IRS announced that it will no longer challenge or litigate the issue of whether interchange fee income earned in connection with a credit card transaction by an issuer of credit cards creates or increases O.I.D. on a pool of credit card loans.[183] The notice did not address any of the other issues litigated and decided by the Tax Court, including the proper calculation of the accruals of O.I.D. on a pool of credit card loans for purposes of Code section 1272(a)(6).

In general, a merchant bank, commonly referred to as an "acquiring bank," is charged an interchange fee by the credit card issuer with respect to a purchase transaction. The issuing bank receives the majority of the interchange fee, but a small portion is paid to the applicable association clearinghouse (VISA or Master Card) to cover operating expenses. Interchange fee rates are set by, and are adjusted regularly by, the associations. The associations generally take into account costs to the parties involved in the interchange function when setting and revising their applicable interchange fee rates.

---

[181] 1977-2 C.B. 60; *see also* TAM 200533023, May 10, 2005.

[182] *Capital One Financial Corp. v. Commissioner*, 130 T.C. 147, 150 (2008); TAM 200533023, May 10, 2005.

[183] CC-2010-018, September 27, 2010.

§3.5.6 ATM Fees as O.I.D.

If a credit card issuer pays the owner or operator of an ATM the fee that a holder of a credit card incurs to obtain a cash advance from an ATM, the credit card issuer must treat the amount paid as an additional amount load to the card holder.[184] The payment by the issuer to the owner or operator of the ATM is treated as being made on behalf of the card holder. Therefore, the ATM fee is treated under Regulation section 1.1273-2(g)(4) as an additional amount loaned by the issuer to the holder of the card and as creating O.I.D.

Regulation section 1.1273-2(g) provides general rules for determining the treatment of certain cash payments made incident to lending transactions. Regulation section 1.1273-2(g)(4) provides more specific rules for determining the treatment of these payments when made between the lender and a person other than the borrower. If, as part of a lending transaction, the lender makes a payment to a third party, that payment is treated as an additional amount loaned to the borrower and then paid by the borrower to the third party. Thus, when an issuer of a credit card pays the ATM fee of the holder to the owner or operator of an ATM, the payment will be treated as made incident to a lending transaction on behalf of the borrower. This is so regardless of whether the bank reflects the ATM fee on the cardholder's account as part of the amount of the holder's cash advance or as a separately stated amount.

An issuer of credit cards is permitted to change its method of accounting for credit card cash advance fees to treat these fees as creating or increasing O.I.D. on a pool of credit card loans that includes the cash advances that give rise to these fees.[185] This treatment is available only if the amount of any credit card cash advance fee charged to a cardholder by the taxpayer is separately stated on the cardholder's account when that fee is imposed and under the credit card agreement; no amount identified as a credit card cash advance fee is charged for property or for specific services performed by the taxpayer for the benefit of the cardholder.[186]

§3.5.7 Merchant Fees as O.I.D.

The difference between the total price of the goods or services sold to cardholders and the amount remitted to the merchant by the acquiring bank[187] is known as the merchant discount or gross merchant discount. The merchant discount is typically a fixed percentage of the total price of the goods or services

---

[184] Rev. Rul. 2005-47, 2005-2 C.B. 261.

[185] Rev. Proc. 2005-47, 2005-2 C.B. 269. Rev. Proc. 2005-47 provides the exclusive procedure by which a taxpayer may obtain the Commissioner's consent to change its method of accounting for credit card cash advance fees to a method that treats these fees as creating or increasing O.I.D. on a pool of credit card loans that includes the cash advances that give rise to the fees.

[186] If a taxpayer uses a method of accounting that treats credit card cash advance fees as creating or increasing the amount of O.I.D. on a pool of credit card loans that includes the cash advances that give rise to those fees, the issue of whether that treatment is proper will not be raised by the Commissioner for a taxable year that ends before December 31, 2004. Rev. Proc. 2005-47, 2005-2 C.B. 269, Sec. 7.01.

[187] An acquiring bank recruits, screens, and accepts merchants into the associations' credit card systems. An acquiring bank enters into agreements with merchants regarding the merchants' acceptance of credit cards (merchant agreement). The acquiring bank's contractual relationship with the merchant is separate and distinct from the acquiring bank's relationship with the association.

sold and compensates the acquiring bank for the services it provides the merchant. Unlike interchange fees, the merchant discount is not determined by the association. Rather, merchant discounts are negotiated between acquiring banks and their respective merchants. The difference between the amount the acquiring bank receives from the issuing bank and the amount the acquiring bank sends to the merchant is generally known as the net merchant discount; i.e., the difference between the gross merchant discount and the interchange fee.

It is the I.R.S.'s position that merchant fees paid to an issuer of credit cards are for services and may not be treated as O.I.D. because merchant fees are paid in connection with services rendered by the issuer in authorizing and settling credit card transactions of customers that use the issuer's credit cards to purchase goods and services.[188]

The fees that a cash method bank operating a credit card plan charges for its services by deducting the fees from amounts it periodically remits for credit sales to merchants enrolled in the plan are includible in the bank's income as payments are received from the cardholders on their accounts.[189] There is no constructive receipt of the service fee when the taxpayer makes remittance to the enrolled merchants. For example, if the service fee (discount) for a particular enrolled merchant is 4 percent, then 4 percent of the payment (other than any finance charge) received from a cardholder with respect to an account created as a result of a transaction with that particular enrolled merchant would be attributable to the service fee (discount) and would be included in the taxpayer's income in the taxable year the payment was received.

With respect to when such fees are includible in the income by a taxpayer that uses an accrual method of accounting, the fee charged the enrolled merchants must be accrued by the taxpayer using the O.I.D. rules in the year in which the taxpayer makes remittances to the merchants, since all events have occurred at that time that fix the taxpayer's right to receive such amounts and the amount thereof is determinable.[190] The fee is not included in income when the cardholder pays his account.

§3.5.8 Nonsufficient Funds Fees

The IRS has reversed its position on NSF fees. In Technical Advice Memorandum 20053023, it concluded that an NSF fee is charged by the issuer of a credit card to its cardholders for the use or forbearance of money and, thus, is interest.[191] This was found to be true even though the NSF fee was not denominated as a finance charge and was imposed as a flat sum in addition to the stated periodic rate finance charge. NSF fees are usually imposed in addition to the stated finance charges and are typically added to the cardholder's outstanding principal balance, along with the amount of any prior finance charges, new purchases, and cash advances for the billing cycle. The minimum monthly

---

[188] TAM 200533022, May 10, 2005. *See also* Rev. Rul. 71-365, 1971-2 C.B. 218.

[189] Rev. Rul. 78-40, 1978-1 C.B. 136.

[190] Rev. Rul. 71-365, 1971-2 C.B. 218.

[191] *See* Rev. Ruls. 72-315, 1972-1 C.B. 49; Rev. Rul. 74-187, 1974-1 C.B. 48; Rev. Rul. 77-417, 1977-2 C.B. 60. *See also* TAM 200533023, May 10, 2005.

payment amount that a cardholder is required to pay is customarily determined based on the amount outstanding after taking into account any new items, including NSF and other fees incurred during the billing period. The amount of an NSF fee is determined, in part, based on what the cardholder's competitors charged their customers. An NSF fee is generally not charged to cardholders to compensate the issuer for services or property provided by the issuer.

More recently, in Revenue Ruling 2007-1, the IRS reached the opposite conclusion on what appeared to be identical facts. It held that a credit card NSF fee was not a payment of interest. Accordingly, it was required to be included in income by the issuer of the credit card when the event that triggers the fee occurs.[192] When the bank determined that it was not going to honor a customer's account check that a third party presented for payment because the taxpayer's line of credit would be overdrawn, the bank was found to be denying the customer the use of the bank's funds. A loan on which interest income could accrue was not being made.

The ruling also found that the NSF event fixed the bank's right to receive the income, and at that time the amount could be determined with reasonable accuracy. Thus, the all events test of Regulation section 1.451-1(a) was satisfied when the NSF event occurred.[193]

§ 3.6 Market Discount

Market discount arises when a bond, other than a tax-exempt bond, is purchased after initial issuance and there is an excess of the bond's stated redemption price at maturity over the taxpayer's basis in the bond immediately after acquisition.[194] In general, neither a cash nor an accrual basis taxpayer is required to include in gross income any (the accrued amortized portion of) market discount.[195] However, a special accrual rule is prescribed for banks that hold certain obligations.[196]

A financial institution may acquire a market discount bond in a variety of ways. For example, market discount may arise from a purchase by a mortgage company of mortgages for a price below the unpaid balance of the mortgages.[197] Market discount also may arise when a bank purchases the assets of another bank or purchases selected loans.

For accounting purposes it is customary to accrete market discount, but unless an election under Code section 1278(b) is made by a taxpayer, current inclusion of the market discount is not generally required for tax purposes. However, if market discount is accreted on the accounting books, failure to make a Schedule M adjustment to arrive at federal taxable income may cause the

---

192 *Capital One Financial Corp. v. Commissioner*, 130 TC 147, *aff'd*, 659 F.3d 316 (4th Cir. 2011).

193 A change in the treatment of NSF fees to comply with this revenue ruling is a change in method of accounting. A taxpayer wishing to change its treatment of NSF fees to comply with the revenue ruling must obtain the consent of the Commissioner under § 446(e) and § 1.446-1(e)(2)(i) by following the procedures in Rev. Proc. 97-27, 1997-1 C.B. 680 (or its successor).

194 I.R.C. § § 1271(a)(3)(c) and 1278(a)(2).

195 I.R.C. § § 1278(a)(2) and 1283(a)(2).

196 I.R.C. § 1281(a).

197 *See* exception for FHA insured loans. Rev. Rul. 53-258, 1953-2 C.B. 143; Reg. § 1016-9(c).

taxpayer to have inadvertently elected to include the discount in income for tax purposes. Because the election applies to all market discount bonds acquired by the taxpayer on or after the first day of the first taxable year to which the election applies, and the election may not be revoked without the permission of the IRS, a taxpayer may find itself in a position of having to accrue market discount on all obligations, even those not accreted for accounting purposes.[198]

Whenever the market discount bond rules apply, a taxpayer should consider the application of the Code section 475 mark-to-market rules. The mark-to-market rules require adjustment to taxable income at year-end of unrealized gain or loss on securities held by a dealer. Under the broad definitions of "securities" and "dealers" contained in Code section 475, market discount obligations acquired by a bank will likely be subject to the mark-to-market rules unless identified as held for investment, not held for sale, or a hedge of security that is not subject to mark-to-market rules.[199]

§3.6.1 Ordinary Income Treatment

Historically, the amount of gain representing market discount was granted preferential capital gains treatment. Capital gains treatment was accorded most taxpayers for the appreciation in value attributable to market discount on an obligation issued by a corporation or government unit and held for more than one year. The Deficit Reduction Act of 1984 provided for recharacterization of gain on the disposition of "market discount bonds" issued after July 18, 1984.[200] For most taxpayers, what may have been capital gain will be recharacterized as ordinary income to the extent of accrued market discount.[201] Code section 1276(a)(1) now provides that gain on redemption or sale of a debt security is characterized as ordinary income to the extent of "accrued market discount."[202]

The amount of recognized gain it treated as interest income.[203] Rules are also now prescribed for partial principal payments.[204] In general, an amount received as a partial payment of principal is treated as an amount received on disposition of part of the bond. Thus, the bond's market discount is recognized as ordinary income to the extent such payment does not exceed accrued market discount on the bond. Before the enactment of Code section 1276, an amount received as a partial payment was typically pro-rated between the principal and the discount portion of the instrument. Current law, however, is silent as to whether unscheduled partial payments are to be treated differently from scheduled partial payments.

Treasury regulations do provide payment ordering rules applicable to O.I.D. obligations. As a general rule, each payment on an O.I.D. obligation is treated first as a payment of O.I.D. to the extent of the O.I.D. that has accrued as of the date the payment is due and that has not been allocated to prior payments, and

---

198 I.R.C. §§1278(b)(2) and (3).

199 *See* discussion of mark-to-market rules in Ch. 4.

200 Deficit Reduction Act of 1984, Pub. L. No. 98-369, §41(a), 98 Stat. 494 (1984).

201 I.R.C. §1276.

202 For a bank, all gain on the disposition of debt securities is ordinary in character. I.R.C. §582(c).

203 I.R.C. §1276(a)(4).

204 I.R.C. §1276(a)(3).

second as a payment of principal. To this extent the O.I.D. and market discount rules appear to be the same.[205]

If there is a pro rata prepayment of an O.I.D. obligation, Treasury regulations provide that the amount received shall be treated as a payment in retirement of a portion of the instrument. Any gain or loss to the holder on the retirement is determined by assuming that the original debt instrument consists of two instruments, one that is retired and one that remains outstanding. Thus, there appears to be an allocation of part of the pre-payment to the O.I.D. and the principal of the portion of the debt instrument that is not treated as retired.[206] For purposes of this rule, a pro rata prepayment is one that is not made pursuant to the instrument's payment schedule and that results in a substantially pro rata reduction of each payment remaining to be paid.[207] Thus, it includes only unscheduled pre payments. This approach appears to differ from the treatment of partial principal payments prescribed for market discount obligations under Code section 1276(a)(3).

The market discount bond rules are not timing sections. They do not require acceleration of the recognition of income. For a bank, this may be the most significant difference between the O.I.D. rules and the market discount bond rules. For purposes of the market discount bond rules, the reference in Code section 1276(b) to "accrued market discount" describes the amount of gain that will be taxed as ordinary income at the time of the bond's disposal. However, at the election of the taxpayer, accrued market discount may be currently included in income.[208] The election, if made, will apply to all market discount bonds acquired on or after the first day of the first taxable year to which the election applies, including all subsequent taxable years.

§ 3.6.2 Special Rule for Short-Term Obligations

An exception to the rule allowing market discount to be deferred applies to short-term obligations held by banks and acquired after July 18, 1984.[209] With respect to such obligations, "acquisition discount" must be accrued into income on a ratable (straight-line) basis or, if the bank elects, using the constant yield method usually employed for obligations subject to the O.I.D. rules.[210] The election to use the constant-interest rate method in lieu of the ratable method may be made on a bond-by-bond basis.[211] A *short-term obligation* is defined as any bond, debenture, note, certificate, or other evidence of indebtedness that has a fixed maturity date not more than one year from the date of issue.[212] Whether a loan made by a bank in the ordinary course of its trade or business is a short-term obligation for this purpose is a matter of controversy.[213]

---

[205] Reg. § 1.1275-2(a). Congress expressly authorized the promulgation of regulations under I.R.C. § 1276 that would be similar to the rules of I.R.C. § 1245(b). I.R.C. § 1276(d). No regulations under I.R.C. § 1276 have been issued.

[206] Reg. § 1.1275-2(f)(1).

[207] Reg. § 1.1275-2(f)(2).

[208] I.R.C. § 1276(b)(2).

[209] I.R.C. §§ 1281 and 1283(a).

[210] I.R.C. §§ 1283(b) and 1276(b)(1) and (2).

[211] I.R.C. § 1276(b)(2).

[212] I.R.C. § 1283(a)(1)(A).

[213] In *Security Bank Minnesota v. Commissioner*, 93-1 U.S.T.C. ¶50,301, 994 F.2d 432 (8th Cir. 1993) the court held that a commercial bank's short-term loans are not obligations subject to I.R.C. § 1281

§3.6.3 Deferral of Interest Deduction

Whenever a taxpayer holds a market discount bond, a portion of the taxpayer's interest expense deduction is susceptible to being deferred under the rules of Code section 1277.[214] The "net direct interest expense" paid or accrued on debt that was incurred or continued to purchase or carry a market discount bond is limited for bonds acquired after July 18, 1984. The net direct interest expense is the excess of interest paid or accrued to purchase or carry the market discount bond over the interest (including original issue discount (O.I.D.)) includible in the purchaser's gross income.[215] Net direct interest expense is deductible only to the extent that it exceeds the market discount allocable to the number of days that the bond is held by the taxpayer.[216]

Any net direct interest expense that is not deductible under the above rule is deferred and deducted in the year of disposition or, if a special election is made, in a year prior to the disposition year.[217] If market discount bonds are disposed of in nonrecognition transactions, the disallowed interest expense is treated as interest paid or accrued in the year of disposition to the extent of gain recognized. Any excess interest expense is a disallowed interest expense in the case of transferred basis property or exchanged basis property.[218]

In the case of market discount bonds held by a bank, special rules apply to determine the amount of interest expense that will be deemed applicable to accrued market discount.[219] A bank (as defined in Code section 582(c)) determines whether interest is deferred under principles similar to the principles of Code section 291(e)(1)(B)(ii) used to identify interest expense attributable to tax-exempt obligations. Under these rules the portion of total interest expense that is allocable to the market discount bond is determined by using a formula based on total assets instead of any tracing method. Moreover, under rules similar to the rules of Code section 265(a)(5), short sale expenses shall be treated as interest for purposes of determining net direct interest expense.

An election may be made to deduct deferred interest expense in a tax year prior to the year in which a market discount bond is disposed.[220] If there is net interest income for a tax year with respect to a market discount bond and the taxpayer makes a proper election on a bond-by-bond basis, any disallowed interest expense, as determined at the close of the prior tax year, shall be treated as interest paid or incurred. However, the deduction will be allowed only to the extent of net interest income on the bond. Net interest income equals the excess

(Footnote Continued)

(a)(2), which requires accrual of stated interest on short-term obligations. Similarly, in *Security State Bank v. Commissioner*, 111 T.C. 210 (1998) the Tax Court held that I.R.C. §1281(a)(1), which requires accrual of acquisition discount on short-term obligations, was inapplicable to short-term loans made by a bank in the ordinary course of its trade or business. The IRS has issued automatic change procedures that are to be followed by taxpayers changing their accounting method for short-term obligations. Rev. Proc. 99-49, §13, 1999-52 I.R.B. 725, *modifying and superseding* Rev. Proc. 98-60, §13, 1998-51 I.R.B. 16. *See* discussion at §3.2.2.

[214] For a more detailed discussion of the interest expense deferral rules, *see* discussion in Chapter 9.

[215] I.R.C. §1277(c).

[216] I.R.C. §1277(a).

[217] I.R.C. § 1277(b)(2).

[218] I.R.C. § 1277(b)(2)(B).

[219] I.R.C. § 1277(c).

[220] I.R.C. § 1277(b)(1).

of interest paid on the bond over the aggregate amount of interest includible in gross income with respect to the bond.[221]

A taxpayer may elect under Code section 1278(b) to include market discount in income for the tax years to which it relates. If such an election is made, the rules provided in Code section 1276 and Code section 1277 do not apply.

Although not expressly provided for in the Code, the computation of deductible interest expense may be made on an aggregate basis.[222]

§ 3.6.4 Current Inclusion Election

Making the election to currently include market discount in gross income will avoid the deferral of interest expense deductions, but it may have the net effect of accelerating income recognition.[223]

Example 8: Assume the same facts as Example 7, except that the discount referred to is market discount and not O.I.D. Assume also that the bank elects under Code section 1278(b) to annually include the market discount in income. The amount to be accrued depends upon whether the taxpayer uses the ratable method or the constant interest rate method. Under each alternative, the calculation would be as follows:

Ratable Method:		
(a)	Stated redemption price at maturity	$100,000
	Tax basis immediately after acquisition (cost)	$96,000
	Market discount	$4,000
(b)	The amount to be amortized equals total market discount times the ratio of the number of days in which the taxpayer held the bond to the number of days after the date the taxpayer acquired the bond and up to and including the date of maturity ($4,000 × 730/730)	$4,000
(c)	Monthly amortizable amount $4,000 ÷ 24 mo.	$166.67
Constant Rate Method:		
(a)	Same as in Ratable Method	$4,000
(b)	Same as in Ratable Method	$4,000
(c)	Monthly Amounts (obtained from the previous example)	
	1/X5-6/X5	$156.00
	7/X5-12/X5	$162.33
	1/X6-6/X6	$169.00
	7/X6-12/X6	$179.33

§ 3.7 Bond Premium

Depending on the issuer and certain characteristics of the bond, as well as upon the holder's trade or business, amortization of bond premium over the holding period of an obligation is either optional or mandatory.[224] Amortization of bond premium is optional with respect to taxable bonds, but it is mandatory with respect to tax-exempt bonds.[225] If an election is made to amortize bond premium on a taxable bond, the amortized amount is deductible.[226] No deduction is allowed for amortized bond premium on tax-exempt bonds.[227]

---

221 I.R.C. § 1277(b)(1)(C).

222 H.R. Rep. No. 861, 98th Cong., 2d Sess. 806 (1984).

223 I.R.C. § 1278(b).

224 I.R.C. § 171.

225 I.R.C. § 171(c); Reg. § 1.171-1.

226 I.R.C. § 171(a)(1); Reg. § 1.171-1(a)(2).

227 I.R.C. § 171(a)(2).

The Federal Reserve Board requires deductible bond premium to be treated as an offset to interest or discount income.[228] Thus, a separate deduction is not allowed for bond premium where interest income exist on that same bond but only to the extent that the amortized bond premium exceeds interest income on the bond. The interest income is first reduced by amortized bond premium.[229]

The Claims Court has held that securities dealers are not required to amortize bond premium.[230] Moreover, dealers in tax-exempt securities are expressly excepted from the provisions of Code section 171.[231] However, the Code section 475 rules will require a dealer in securities to mark its securities to market. Further, Code section 75 requires adjustments to the "cost of securities sold" during the year if securities are inventoried other than at cost. If they are not inventoried, adjustments must be made to the adjusted tax basis of the individual bonds sold.[232] An exception to the mandatory amortization rule applies (1) when tax-exempt obligations are held by a dealer for less than 30 days, or (2) when the maturity or call date of the security is more than five years from the time the dealer acquired the bond, and the dealer realizes a gain on the sale or exchange.[233] In these two situations, the adjustment to tax basis is made at the time of sale.

§3.7.1 Premium Amortization Election

The election to amortize bond premium on taxable bonds is made by claiming the deduction on the return for the first taxable year to which the election is to apply.[234] The Tax Court has held that an election may not be made on an amended return or on a claim for refund.[235] If the election is made, it applies to all bonds held by the taxpayer at the beginning of the first taxable year to which the election applies, and it is binding for all subsequent taxable years with respect to all bonds properly fitting within the "fully-taxable" class.[236]

§3.7.2 Basis Adjustment

Any amortized premium (deductible or nondeductible) reduces tax basis.[237] A dealer in tax-exempt bonds that neither inventories its bonds nor values its inventories at cost must reduce the adjusted basis of bonds by "amortizable bond premium" for purposes of computing gain or loss on the sale of the bonds.[238] For

---

[228] *See* instructions for preparation of Form F-9A, Balance Sheet, issued by Federal Reserve Board. I.R.C. §171 (e). This provision was added by the Tax Reform Act of 1986, Pub. L. No. 99-514, 100 Stat. 2085. It applies to obligations acquired after October 22, 1986, in tax years ending after that date. The Senate Finance Committee's Report under the 1986 Tax Reform Act provides that this rule may be modified by Regulations. *See* Senate Finance Committee Report, No. 99-313, 99th Cong., 2d sess., at 802 (1986). The Conference agreement followed the Senate Report. *See* Conference Committee Report, No. 841, 99th Cong., 2d Sess.II-211 (1986).

[229] I.R.C. §171(e).

[230] *Brown v. United States*, 70-1 U.S.T.C. ¶9407, 426 F.2d 355 (Cl. Ct. 1970).

[231] I.R.C. §171(f).

[232] I.R.C. §§75(a)(1) and (2).

[233] I.R.C. §75(b)(1).

[234] I.R.C. §171(c)(2); Reg. §1.171-3(a).

[235] *Bessie A. Woodward Estate v. Commissioner*, 57-1 U.S.T.C. ¶9436, 241 F.2d 496 (5th Cir. 1957).

[236] Reg. §1.171-3(a).

[237] I.R.C. §1016(a)(5); Reg. §1.1016-5(b).

[238] I.R.C. §§75(a) and 1016(a)(6). Under a provision that is becoming largely out of date because of the passage of time, thrifts are required to adjust basis in tax-exempt bonds for amortizable premium from the date the bond was acquired, even though the thrift may have been exempt from federal income tax during a portion of the years in which bonds were held. Reg. §1.1016-9(a). Furthermore,

dealers in tax-exempt obligations who maintain inventories or value their inventories on any basis other than cost, the cost of obligations sold must be reduced by the amortizable bond premium that would be disallowed as a deduction by Code section 171(a).[239] The basis of taxable bonds is adjusted for amortizable bond premium from the effective date of the election to amortize.[240]

If a bank does not elect to deduct amortizable bond premium, the absence of a downward adjustment to basis will increase any loss or decrease any gain on a subsequent sale, exchange or redemption of the obligation. Thus, the election should be made whenever the acceleration of deductions is desired. For banks, unlike other taxpayers, gain or loss at subsequent disposition does not receive capital asset treatment even though the bond may be held for investment.[241]

§ 3.7.3 Bonds Defined

The definition of a bond qualifying for the election to deduct amortizable bond premium includes:

> [A]ny bond, debenture, note, or certificate or other evidence of indebtedness, but does not include any such obligation which constitutes stock in trade of the taxpayer or any such obligation of a kind which would properly be included in the inventory of the taxpayer if on hand at the close of the taxable year, or any such obligation held by the taxpayer primarily for sale to customers in the ordinary course of his trade or business.[242]

Thus, the definition of a *bond* for this purpose includes short-term debt or other obligations regardless of whether the obligation is in registered form or whether it has coupons attached.[243] Although mortgage loans insured by the Federal Housing Administration are not "bonds," the IRS has ruled that banks may amortize premiums on such obligations over the life of these loans.[244]

§ 3.7.4 Amortization Methods

For obligations issued before September 28, 1985, a bank may elect the straight-line or the constant yield (economic accrual, yield-to-maturity) method of amortization.[245] In addition, for such obligations, Regulations permit the use of any other reasonable method "regularly employed."[246]

If the straight-line method is used, the amortized and deducted premium is greater in the early years of the bond relative to amortization under the constant yield method. Accordingly, tax basis would be lower and gain would be larger if a disposition occurs in the early years of a bond that had premium amortization

(Footnote Continued)

with the enactment of I.R.C. § 475, a dealer in securities no longer has the flexibility to use inventory valuation methods other than the mark-to-market rules contained in that section.

[239] I.R.C. § 75(a)(1).

[240] Reg. § 1.1016-9(b).

[241] I.R.C. § 582.

[242] I.R.C. § 171(d).

[243] Reg. § 1.171-4(a). *See* discussion of loans as short-term obligations at § 3.2.2.

[244] Rev. Rul. 53-258, 1953-2 C.B. 143; *see also* Reg. § 1.1016-9(c).

[245] Rev. Rul. 82-10, 1982-1 C.B. 46.

[246] According to Reg. § 1.171-2(f):

> A taxpayer who regularly employs a method of amortization may be one, for example, who is subject to the jurisdiction of a State or Federal regulatory agency and who, for the purposes of such agency, amortizes the bond premium on his bonds in accordance with a method prescribed or approved by such agency.

calculated under the straight-line method. Conversely, if the premium is amortized under the constant yield method, the holder would realize a smaller gain from a disposition of the bond in the early years (and smaller deductions for amortized bond premium) relative to that which would result from amortization of premium under the straight-line method.[247]

For obligations issued after September 27, 1985, the amount of amortizable bond premium calculated under Code section 171 must be determined using the constant yield method.[248] However, if an election to amortize bond premium was in effect on October 22, 1986 (the date of enactment of the Tax Reform Act of 1986), the taxpayer may choose not to apply the election to obligations issued after September 27, 1985.[249]

§ 3.7.5 Computing Premium

Bond premium is equal to the excess of the taxpayer's basis in a bond over the amount payable at maturity or, in the case of a callable bond, the earlier call date.[250] However, for taxable bonds acquired after December 31, 1957, bond premium is measured by comparing tax basis to either the amount payable at maturity or the amount payable on an earlier call date, but only if comparison to the earlier call date results in a smaller amortizable premium.[251] Tax basis includes paying commissions, attorneys' fees, and other capitalized expenses incurred in reducing the asset to possession. In those cases where the purchase price of a bond, excluding commissions, does not exceed the amount payable at maturity or, if applicable, the call price, amortization of capitalized acquisition expenses is still permitted.[252]

Example 1: Basic Illustration. Bank L purchases, for investment, a tax-exempt bond on 01/03/X3 for $12,000. It has a face value of $10,000, and it matures on 01/02/X8. Under the straight-line or ratable method of amortization, Bank L's adjusted basis in the bond on 12/31/X3 would be $11,600, computed as follows:

Bond premium ($12,000 – $10,000):	$2,000
Premium amortized from 1/3/X3 to 12/31/X3 ($2,000 × 12/60):	$400
Adjusted basis on 12/31/X3 ($12,000 – $400):	$11,600 [253]

Example 2: Callable Bond with Acquisition Costs. Assume the same facts as in Example 1, except that the bond is callable on 01/02/X6 for $10,600 and that Bank L has paid commissions and attorneys' fees in acquiring the bond of $300 and $100, respectively. Bank L's tax basis in the bond on 01/03/X3 would be $12,400 ($12,000 + $300 + $100). Its tax basis on 01/02/X6 would be $10,600, computed as follows:

---

[247] *Id.*; I.R.C.; § 171(b)(3)(A).

[248] I.R.C. § 171(b)(3). The Tax Reform Act of 1986, § 1803(a)(11)(A), contains this "technical" correction to the Tax Reform Act of 1984, Pub. L. No. 98-369, 98 Stat. 494.

[249] *See* transitional rule at Pub.L. No. 99-514, § 1803(a)(11)(A).

[250] I.R.C. §§ 171(b)(1)(A) and (B)(i); Reg. § 1.171-2(a)(1).

[251] I.R.C. § 171(b)(1)(B)(ii).

[252] Reg. § 1.171-2(d).

[253] A fractional part of a month is disregarded unless it amounts to more than one-half of a month, in which case it is treated as a full month.

Premium computed with reference to the maturity date ($12,400 – $10,000):	$2,400
Premium computed with reference to the earlier call date ($12,400 – $10,600):	$1,800
Amortizable bond premium for each month, using the ratable method (1/3/X3 to 01/02/X6) ($1,800 ÷ 36 months):	$50
Tax basis on 01/02/X6 ($12,400 – [$50 × 36]):	$10,600

Under the ratable method, if the bond is not called, the amortizable bond premium for the remainder of the bond's life is $25 per month ($600 divided by 24 months). Bank L's tax basis on 01/02/X7 will be $10,300 ($10,600 – [12 × $25]) and on 01/02/X8 will be $10,000 ($10,300 – [12 × $25]).

Example 3: Straight-Line v. Accelerated Amortization. Bank E invested in a taxable bond costing $10,803 on June 5, 19X4. The bond has a face value of $10,000, is due on June 4, 19X9, and has a coupon rate of 10 percent payable each June 4. The current market rate is 8 percent. Premium amortized during the first three months during which the bond was held would be $40.14 under the straight-line method and $34.15 under the constant yield method, computed as follows:

Option 1: Straight-Line Method

Bond premium ($10,803 – $10,000): = 803

Monthly amortization ($803 ÷ 60 months [rounded]): = $13.38

Option 2: Yield Method

Step 1: Calculate the annual yield rate, as follows:

$AI = I \times [(P)/(N)]$

where AI = Average income

I = Interest (as stated)

P = Premium

N = Number of years to maturity

$AC = (C + M)/2$

where AC = Average cost

C = Cost of bond

M = Maturity value

Y = (AI)/(AC)

where Y = yield (annual rate)

Assuming the same facts, the yield method is exemplified:

AI = $1,000 – ($803/5) = $839.40

AC = $10,803 + ($10,000/2) = $10,401.50

Y = ($839.40)/($10,401.50) = 8%

Step 2: The premium to be amortized for a particular period is calculated by: (1) first applying the annual stated interest rate to the face value of the bond; (2) applying the annual yield rate to the adjusted basis in the bond; and (3) subtracting (1) from (2). Thus, the first three months' amortization would be calculated as follows:

First month:

(a) ($10,000 × 10%)/12 = $83.33

(b) ($10,803 × 8%)/12 = $72.02

(c) Amortization = $11.31 ($83.33 – $72.02)

Second month:

(a) ($10,000 × 10%)/12 = $83.33

(b) [($10,803 – $11.31)/12]× 8% = $71.95

(c) Amortization = $11.38 ($83.33 – $71.95)

Third month:

(a) ($10,000 × 10%)/12 = $83.33

(b) [($10,791.69 – $11.38)/12]× 8% = $71.87

(c) Amortization = $11.46 ($83.33 – $71.87)

APB 21 Preferred Method

Accounting Principles Board Opinion No. 21 specifies a preference for the effective interest method but permits other methods if the results obtained are not significantly different from those obtained by using the effective interest method. This method obtains somewhat different amounts than under the yield method. Assuming the same facts, the following table is created:

Year[a]	Basis	(= Mkt. Rate = 8%)	of Face	Amortization	(Year - End)	Basis	Amount
1	$10,803	$864	$1,000	$136	$667	$10,667	$11.33
2	10,667	853	1,000	147	520	10,520	12.25
3	10,520	842	1,000	158	362	10,362	13.17
4	10,362	829	1,000	171	191	10,191	14.25
5	10,191	809 [b]	1,000	191	-0-	10,000	15.92

[a] Year 1 in this example is the period 6/X4 to 5/X5 and so on.

[b] Adjusted to compensate for accumulated rounding. Note the primary difference between the yield method and the APB 21 method as illustrated is that the APB 21 method computes the yield annually and then computes monthly amortization on a straight-line where the annual yield is divided by 12. The yield method illustrated above assumed a one-month yield period. Compare this approach to the O.I.D. rules contained in Code sections 1272(a)(3) and 1283(b)(2), which use a semi-annual yield period and a straight-line method on a daily basis within the yield period. Conceptually, they are identical, but different yield periods are used.

Example 4: Gain or Loss on Sale. Bank A acquires for investment a ten-year, 8 percent bond (interest payable annually) with a face value of $1,000 on January 1, 19X0 for $1,100, plus $100 in commissions and attorneys' fees. The bond is due to mature on December 31, 19X9. Bank D sells the bond on 4/4/X1 for $1,200:

Scenario 1: Fully Taxable Bond

Option 1: Code section 171 Election Not Made

Basis on 1/1/X1	$1,200
Selling price	1,200
Gain on sale	-0-

Option 2: Code section 171 Election Made, Straight-Line Amortization

Basis on 1/1/X1	$1,200
Deductible adjustments to Basis:	
($1200 – $1000) × 3/120	-5
Adjusted basis 4/4/X1	1,195
Selling price 4/4/X1	1,200
Gain on sale	5

Option 3: Code section 171 Election Made, Yield Method Amortization

If the yield method is used, the adjusted basis on 4/4/X1 would be $1,196.32 and the gain on sale would be $3.68.

Scenario 2: Tax-Exempt Bond

For a tax-exempt bond, Bank A must adjust its basis in the bond by the amount of the nondeductible amortized bond premium in the same manner as if the Code section 171 election to deduct the amortized bond premium on taxable obligations had been made. Thus, under the straight-line method of amortization, gain would be $5.00; and under the yield method, it would be $3.68. If the yield method were used and the security were disposed of prior to maturity, a *permanent* tax savings would be realized relative to premium amortization under the straight-line method.[254]

[254] The difference in premium amortization on taxable bonds yields a timing difference, not a permanent tax savings.

Chapter 4
Securities Dealers and Investors

Contents

§4.1 Tax Planning Suggestions
§4.2 Permissible Securities Activities
§4.3 Determining Amount and Character of Gains or Losses
§4.3.1 Wash Sale Rule
§4.3.2 Stripped Bonds
§4.3.3 Character of Gains or Losses—Debt Securities
§4.3.4 Character of Gains or Losses—Certain Preferred Stock
§4.3.5 Character of Gains or Losses—Mutual Fund Investments
§4.4 Securities Dealer Transactions
§4.4.1 Recognition Rules: Pre-Code Section 475
§4.4.2 Recognition Rules: Code Section 475
§4.4.3 Exceptions to Section 475 Recognition Rules
§4.4.4 Identification of Securities
§4.4.5 Who Is a Dealer?
§4.4.6 Traders, Investors and Speculators
§4.4.7 What Is a "Security"?
§4.4.8 Measuring Mark-to-Market Gain or Loss
§4.4.9 Characterizing Mark-to-Market Gains or Losses
§4.4.10 Tax-Free Acquisitions
§4.4.11 Other Mark-to-Market Rules
§4.4.12 Change of Accounting Method
§4.5 Security Investment Transactions
§4.5.1 Statement of Financial Accounting Standards No. 115
§4.6 Loans of Securities

§4.1 Tax Planning Suggestions

Every bank should assume that it is a dealer in securities and, even if the institution may not be a dealer, to be prudent, it should make a protective identification to exempt its holdings from the mark-to-market rules.[1] The broad scope of the Code section 475 mark-to-market rules will ensnare most banks in a burdensome system of compliance. However, it also provides significant opportunities to accelerate losses when debt is renegotiated and to defer income with respect to nonperforming loans.

Gain or loss can be accelerated and its character can be affected depending on whether a security is held by the taxpayer in its capacity as a dealer, an investor, or a trader. Because of the existence of several entities within a bank

[1] *See The Art of Tax Efficiency in Community Banks,* by M. Gula, J. Brew, and R. Blasi, 2007, Red Room Publishing, *http://www.mraeresources.com/bookstore/*.

holding company group, tax planning opportunities exist with respect to substantially identical securities when one member of a group may be a dealer and another may be an investor or trader.

Characterization rules can maximize tax planning opportunities. A bank's gains and losses from debt securities transactions will be ordinary, and under 2008 legislation, gain or loss on certain Fannie Mae or Freddie Mac preferred stock also will be ordinary. A nonbank member of a bank holding company group has the opportunity to recognize capital gains, but also risks losses being characterized as capital. Mutual fund investments are likely to yield capital gains or losses.

The securities dealer rules also raise a variety of other issues. Intercompany transaction regulations may present traps for the unwary bank that is a member of a controlled group that files a consolidated return. A member of a consolidated group that is not a dealer may be treated as a dealer with respect to securities that it receives from an affiliated dealer. This problem is acute if there are sales between or among affiliated banks of mortgage and other loans. However, if a bank engages in transactions with its branches, even if those branches are located in foreign countries, the transaction is not intercompany and it is not with a "customer."

Furthermore, the interplay of the securities dealer and investor rules with the bad-debt deduction rules introduces planning potential. Bad debt deductions may be taken for tax purposes before a charge is made to book earnings. Yet, the mark-to-market rules may present a difficult problem for those banks that have made the conformity election. Finally, the mark-to-market rules will provide an opportunity for loss recognition when debt is renegotiated and the measurement of loss will be pursuant to more favorable rules than apply generally to debt renegotiation.

Instruments that meet the Code section 475 definition of a "security" include nonpublicly traded debt for which a fair market value is not readily available. To alleviate the administrative burden associated with auditing the values that taxpayers place on their securities that are marked-to-market, the IRS and the Treasury Department have promulgated regulations that permit taxpayers to elect to conform their tax valuations to their book valuations.[2] Taxpayers that have made this election and that come under audit will be requested to execute the "Industry Directive on I.R.C. § 475 Valuation Certification Statement," which states the taxpayer will provide all relevant data and records to establish that the tax and book values are in conformity.[3]

§ 4.2 Permissible Securities Activities

As a general rule, national banks are prohibited from investing in equity instruments of commercial enterprises.[4] This prohibition is implied from the

[2] Reg. § 1.475(a)-4.

[3] *See* Appendix for the Directive and the Statement that the taxpayer must sign that elects book/tax conformity on valuations at Appendix § A.23.

[4] 12 U.S.C. 24 (7th) (2006).

failure of the National Bank Act to grant the power,[5] and it is designed to avoid distortions in the allocation of credit. However, pursuant to the grant of "incidental powers" necessary to carry on a banking business, national banks are permitted to accept equity instruments in settlement of debts. The Supreme Court held, "[I]t can hardly be doubted that stocks may be accepted in payment and satisfaction, with a view to their subsequent sale or conversion into money so as to make good or reduce an anticipated loss. Such a transaction would not amount to dealing in stocks."[6] Moreover, banks are authorized to own stock in certain operating subsidiaries, which may perform "any business function which the parent bank is permitted to perform."[7] Furthermore, the Supreme Court has held that the Comptroller of the Currency has the power to interpret the National Bank Act to determine whether an activity is encompassed within the statutory term "the business of banking."[8] This ruling may signal to the Comptroller that an expansion of securities powers may be acceptable.

Federal banking law has restricted a bank holding company's underwriting activities. Historically, underwriting activities were limited to making a market in federal or municipal debt obligations.[9] The Federal Reserve Board gradually relaxed these constraints permitting bank holding companies and their nonbank subsidiaries to perform a wider range of securities dealer activities, including a limited corporate bond underwriting business and a discount brokerage business.[10] Recently, Congress stepped in and in historic legislation empowered a bank or financial services holding company group to engage in a wide range of securities underwriting activities.[11]

§ 4.3 Determining Amount and Character of Gains or Losses

A bank that invests in securities must compute its security gains and losses in accordance with the general rule of Code section 1001.[12] Under that section, if there is a "sale or other disposition of property" the resulting gain or loss must be determined.[13] A sale or other disposition will include the retirement of any debt instrument[14] and significant modifications of debt instruments.[15] The amount of gain or loss is measured by comparing the amount realized with the security's adjusted basis.[16] The amount realized is the amount of money received plus the fair market value of property other than money.[17] It is reduced by sales commissions.[18] Adjusted basis is equal to a security's cost plus any commission or other

---

[5] *First National Bank of Charlotte v. National Exchange Bank of Baltimore*, 92 U.S. 122 (1875).

[6] *Id.* at 128.

[7] 12 CFR § 5.34; 12 CFR § 7.7376(b) (1981).

[8] *NationsBank of North Carolina, N.A. v. Variable Annuity Life Insurance Co.*, 513 U.S. 251 (1995).

[9] 12 U.S.C. 24 (7th) (2006).

[10] 12 U.S.C. 1843(c)(8) (2006). A bank holding company may engage in activities that are "so closely related to banking as to be a proper incident thereto." The Federal Reserve Board has published a list of such activities under Regulation Y. 12 CFR § 225.4(a) (1981). *See also* 12 CFR § 225.126.

[11] The Financial Modernization Act, Pub. L. No. 106-102, 113 Stat. 1338 (1999). See discussion in Ch. 1.

[12] In this discussion, the term "securities" mean all debt instruments, not only those narrowly defined as meeting the I.R.C. § 165(g)(2)(C) definition.

[13] I.R.C. § 1001(a).

[14] I.R.C. § 1271(a).

[15] Reg. § 1.1001-3.

[16] I.R.C. §§ 1001(a) and 165(b).

[17] I.R.C. § 1001(b).

[18] *Spreckles v. Helvering*, 42-1 U.S.T.C. ¶9345, 315 U.S. 626 (1942).

costs incurred to purchase the security.[19] Unless otherwise provided in the Code, realized gain or loss is recognized.[20]

§4.3.1 Wash Sale Rule

One of the exceptions to recognition is contained in Code section 1091, the wash sale rule, which denies a loss deduction when a wash sale takes place. These rules do not apply to the securities accounted for under the mark-to-market rules. If a realized loss results from the sale or other taxable disposition of most debt or equity instruments held for investment and, within a period beginning 30 days before the date of such sale or disposition and ending 30 days after such date, the taxpayer purchases or enters into a contract or option to purchase "substantially identical" debt or equity instruments, the wash sale rule provides that the loss deduction is disallowed.[21] This is an exception to the general recognition rule of Code section 1001(c). Realized but unrecognized losses are deferred and are added to tax bases.

Debt or equity securities subject to the wash sale rule include stock, notes, bonds, debentures or other evidences of indebtedness, or an interest in or right to subscribe to or purchase any of these instruments.[22] Commodity futures and foreign currency transactions are not "securities" for this purpose.[23] Moreover, the wash sale rule is inapplicable to sales and repurchases of mortgage loans, unless they are found to be "securities."[24] With respect to mortgage "swaps,"[25] the IRS has attempted to apply the wash sale rule to disallow otherwise deductible losses.[26] In this situation, the IRS based its ruling on the fact that the taxpayer's true economic position did not differ after the transaction.

While the wash sale rule does not apply to dealer activities, a bank that is a dealer is subject to the wash sale rule restrictions if the security sold is held in the bank's investment portfolio. Thus, for Code section 1091 not to apply, the taxpayer must be both a dealer *and* "the loss must be sustained in a transaction made in the ordinary course of such business."[27] The wash sale limitation applies to a bank despite the disallowance of capital gains treatment under Code section 582.[28]

The inability to classify securities as capital assets renders the determination of the security's holding period moot. As a general rule, the holding period of

---

[19] I.R.C. §1011; *Helvering v. Winmill*, 38-2 U.S.T.C. ¶9550, 305 U.S. 79 (1938); *Woodward v. Commissioner*, 70-1 U.S.T.C. ¶9348, 397 U.S. 572 (1970).

[20] I.R.C. §1001(c).

[21] I.R.C. §1091; Reg. §1.1091-1(a).

[22] Rev. Rul. 74-218, 1974-1 C.B. 202.

[23] Rev. Rul. 71-568, 1971-2 C.B. 312; Rev. Rul. 74-218, 1974-1 C.B. 202.

[24] *Burbank Liquidating Corp. v. Commissioner*, 64-2 U.S.T.C. ¶9676, 335 F.2d 125 (9th Cir. 1964).

[25] Mortgage swaps involve exchanges of mortgage pools. Early mortgage swap transactions involved a simultaneous exchange of mortgage pools in which the interest rates and most other key terms were identical. More recently, mortgage swaps have involved the purchase and sale of mortgages in which cash is passed between the parties.

[26] General Counsel Memorandum 39551, June 30, 1986; 39149, March 14, 1983; and 38838, October 1, 1981. *See also* Rev. Rul. 81-204, 1981-2 C.B. 157; Federal Home Loan Bank Board Pronouncement, FHLBB-R-Memo. 49, and the more recent Pronouncement found at 12 CFR §563c.14. *See also* Rev. Rul. 85-125, 1985-2 C.B. 180; TAM 8641004, June 30, 1986 (GNMA certificates); and the discussion of *Cottage Savings v. Commissioner* in Ch. 6.

[27] I.R.C. §1091(a).

[28] *Merchants National Bank v. Commissioner*, 9 T.C. 68, Dec. 15,900 (1947).

acquired securities begins on the day after the date of acquisition and includes the date of disposition.[29]

Example: Bank X purchased a government bond for $500 in 19X4 that it sold in January of 19X7 for $400. Less than one month later, Bank X purchased a substantially identical bond for $450. Under Code section 1091, no loss is recognized, and the basis in the new bond is $550 ($500 original cost plus $50 unrecognized loss).[30]

Although the wash sale rules could be avoided if a security were identified as one in which the bank deals, a transfer to the dealer portfolio for purposes of avoiding the limitation would be without effect even though such a transfer would be a nontaxable transaction.[31]

§ 4.3.2 Stripped Bonds

For purposes of determining gain or loss on the sale or other taxable disposition of debt securities with detached interest coupons, Code section 1286(b)(3) provides that the tax basis of the bond and coupons immediately before the disposition is to be allocated between principal and interest retained and disposed of on the basis of relative fair market values. The IRS ruled that, for sales of debt securities with detached interest coupons occurring prior to the effective date of Code section 1286 (July 2, 1982), a security's tax basis was equal to its cost. Basis was not apportioned between detached interest coupons and the underlying security.[32] Thus, prior to the enactment of Code section 1286 by the Tax Reform Act of 1984,[33] a tax deductible loss often arose from the sale of such securities when coupons were detached. Of course, the interest accrued was fully includible in taxable income.

§ 4.3.3 Character of Gains or Losses—Debt Securities

As a general rule, the character of gain or loss on the disposition of debt securities (and equity securities) is determined by the character of the asset that is sold or otherwise disposed. Usually, the character of an asset is determined, in the first instance, under the rules of Code section 1221. That section provides that the term "capital asset" means any property (real, personal, tangible, or intangible) held by the taxpayer (whether or not connected with his trade or business), but not including eight listed types of property described in Code section 1221(a)(1)-(8).[34] Several Code sections alter the general rule of Code section 1221 for securities that are sold or otherwise disposed.[35]

(a) *Special Bank Rule*

Code section 582(c) provides that the gain or loss from the sale or exchange of a bond, debenture, note, or certificate or other evidence of indebtedness by a

[29] Rev. Rul. 70-598, 1970-2 C.B. 168.

[30] Reg. § 1.1091-2, Ex. 1.

[31] Rev. Rul. 73-403, 1973-2 C.B. 308.

[32] TAM 8602006, undated.

[33] Deficit Reduction Act of 1984, Pub. L. No. 98-369, 98 Stat. 494 (1984).

[34] Reg. § 1.1502-13(c)(7)(ii), Ex. 2 illustrates how the character of gain or loss can change by transferring an asset from one member of a consolidated group to another member. The general rule for determining the consolidate capital gains or loss of a consolidated group is found in Reg. § 1.1502-22.

[35] *See, e.g.*, §§ 582(c) and 1256.

financial institution shall not be considered a sale or exchange of a capital asset.[36] For this purpose, a "financial institution" is defined as a commercial bank, mutual savings bank, domestic building and loan association, cooperative bank, business development corporation and small business investment company.[37] Net losses from sales or exchanges that are covered by Code section 582(c) are treated as ordinary losses.[38]

The ordinary characterization rule of Code section 582(c) applies to debt securities regardless of whether they are held by the bank in connection with dealer activities or as investments. Although a bank is permitted to deduct net losses in full on debt securities without regard to capital loss limitations, a bank is not permitted to deduct a loss otherwise disallowed under the Code section 1091 wash sales provisions.[39] Code section 582 does not characterize the instrument itself as either a capital asset or as an ordinary asset, it does not apply to instruments that are not debt instruments, and it does not apply to any member of a bank group that is not a "financial institution."

(b) *Legislative History*

Code section 582 was enacted as part of the 1954 codification of the Internal Revenue Code. In its original form, the section provided:

> (a) SECURITIES. Notwithstanding sections 165 (g) (1) and 166 (e), subsections (a), (b), and (c) of section 166 (relating to allowance of deduction for bad debts) shall apply in the case of a bank to a debt which is evidenced by a security as defined in section 165 (g) (2) (C).
>
> (b) WORTHLESS STOCK IN AFFILIATED BANK. For purposes of section 165 (g) (1), where the taxpayer is a bank and owns directly at least 80 percent of each class of stock of another bank, stock in such other bank shall not be treated as a capital asset.
>
> (c) BOND, ETC., LOSSES OF BANKS. For purposes of this subtitle, in the case of a bank, if the losses of the taxable year from sales or exchanges of bonds, debentures, notes, or certificates, or other evidences of indebtedness, issued by any corporation (including one issued by a government or political subdivision thereof), with interest coupons or in registered form, exceed the gains of the taxable year from such sales or exchanges, no such sale or exchange shall be considered a sale or exchange of a capital asset.[40]

On September 2, 1958, the phrase "with interest coupons or in registered form" was deleted from subsection (c).[41] The section then remained unchanged until 11 years later when subsection (c) was replaced with the following language:

---

[36] See discussion below of character of gain or loss resulting from a mark-to-market under I.R.C. § 475.

[37] With respect to foreign banks, only sales or exchanges of securities that are effectively connected with the conduct of banking business in the United States will not be considered sales or exchanges of capital assets (I.R.C. § 582(c)(2)(C)).

[38] Reg. § 1.582-1(d).

[39] *Merchants National Bank*, 9 TC 68, Dec. 15,900.

[40] Available at Hein Online, Legislative session 68A Stat. 202.

[41] Pub. L. No. 85-866.

(c) BOND, ETC., LOSSES AND GAINS OF FINANCIAL INSTITUTIONS.

(1) GENERAL RULE–For purposes of this subtitle, in the case of a financial institution to which section 585, 586, or 593 applies, the sale or exchange of a bond, debenture, note, or certificate or other evidence of indebtedness shall not be considered a sale or exchange of a capital asset."[42]

In 1986, a sentence was appended to paragraph (1) that provided: "For purposes of the preceding sentence, any regular or residual interest in a REMIC shall be treated as an evidence of indebtedness."[43] Congress also added a fifth paragraph to section (c), which served to replace the original definition of the term "financial institution" found in paragraph one. It provided a Code specific definition of what entities qualify as financial institutions, and it limited the use by foreign corporations to those gains and losses connected to their banking business in the United States.[44]

In 1988, Code section 582 was again revised to delete mention of Code section 166(c) in paragraph (1) due to its repeal.[45] Subsequently in 1990, Congress repealed sections (c)(2) through (c)(4), which related to transitional rules.[46] In 1996, Congress added language to paragraph 582(c)(1) that included "any regular interest in a FASIT" with REMICs as evidence of indebtedness.[47] The inclusion of FASITs was subsequently repealed in 2004 when the FASIT vehicle was repealed.[48]

(c) *Dealers in Securities*

For dealers in securities that mark securities to market under Code section 475, there will be a deemed sale that takes place on the last business day of the taxable year. Gain or loss will be measured as if the securities were sold for their fair market value. Any gain will be included in taxable income and any loss is generally deducted under Code section 165.[49]

As a general rule, the character of the gain or loss is determined by the character of the underlying asset. For banks, any gain or loss on debt securities will be treated as an ordinary gain or loss under Code section 582. However, special rules are provided for bifurcating any loss between the Code section 165 loss deduction and a deduction for partially or wholly worthless debts allowed under Code section 166.[50] Special rules are also provided for gains and losses on notional principal contracts and derivatives.[51]

---

[42] 83 Stat. 624. In addition to this language, a transitional rule was added for banks that permitted certain gains and losses to be treated as capital in nature. In 1976 the transitional rule for banks was further amended.

[43] 100 Stat. 2318.

[44] *Id.*

[45] Pub. L. No. 100-647.

[46] Pub. L. No. 101-508.

[47] 110 Stat. 1867.

[48] 118 Stat. 1593.

[49] To the extent that any portion of a mark down is attributable to worthlessness, the deduction is taken under I.R.C. § 166.

[50] Prop. Reg. § 1.475(a)-1(f). *See also* discussion later in this chapter of the character of gains and losses on securities marked-to-market under I.R.C. § 475.

[51] Reg. § 1.475(d)-1. A proposal has been made by Senator Ron Wyden (D-Ore), The Modernization of Derivatives Act, in May 2016, to subject derivatives to a single timing, character and sourcing rule for purposes of I.R.C. § 475. The Joint Committee on Taxation has opined that if this were done, it should not trigger valuation or cash- flow problems.

Nonbank dealers in securities are subject to the characterization rules in Code section 1236. That section contains special rules for gains and losses.[52] Gains from the sale or exchange of any security may not be treated as a capital gain unless the security was clearly identified before the close of the day on which it was acquired in the dealer's records as a security held for investment.[53] Losses may not be treated as ordinary losses if the security was identified as held for investment.[54] For this purpose, the term "security" means any share of stock in any corporation, certificate of stock or interest in any corporation, note, bond, debenture, or evidence of indebtedness, or any evidence of an interest in or right to subscribe to or purchase any of the foregoing.[55]

(d) *Notes Receivable*

A nonbank member of a bank holding company group does not determine the character of gain or loss on the sale or other disposition of debt securities under Code section 582(c). Instead the general rules of Code section 1221 apply. Regulations were proposed to clarify the circumstances in which accounts or notes receivable would be treated as capital assets.[56] Under the proposed regulations, notes acquired by a creditor in a lending transaction or notes purchased in the secondary market are not to be treated as "acquired in the ordinary course of a trade or business for services rendered or from the sale of" inventory or property held by the taxpayer primarily for sale to customers in the ordinary course of his trade or business.[57] Thus, capital characterization would result. This could result in capital losses being recognized when a mortgage company sells mortgages in which it invested. These proposed regulations were withdrawn and the I.R.S. announced that it would follow the interpretation of Code section 1221(a)(4) that preceded the proposed regulations.[58]

Depending upon whether the debt security is originated or acquired, the characterization of any gain or loss may vary. It appears now that Code section 1221(a)(4) permits originated debt to be excepted from capital asset classification. However, whether the I.R.S. believes that that provision extends to acquired debt is unclear. In either case, however, it appears that Code section 166 permits partial worthlessness to be deducted before the instrument is disposed.

(e) *Worthless Stock in Subsidiary*

As a general rule, if any security that is a capital asset becomes worthless during a taxable year, the loss resulting therefrom is treated as a loss from the

---

[52] *See* discussion of gains and losses below for securities marked-to-market.

[53] I.R.C. § 1236(a). Special rules are provided for floor specialists and options. I.R.C. § 1236(d) and (e).

[54] I.R.C. § 1236(b).

[55] I.R.C. § 1236(c).

[56] REG-109367-06 Aug. 6, 2006.

[57] I.R.C. § 1221(a)(1) and (4).

[58] Announcement 2008-41, 2008-19 I.R.B. 943. The IRS stated in the Announcement that it will not challenge return reporting positions of taxpayers under I.R.C. § 1221(a)(4) that apply existing law, including Burbank Liquidating; Federal National Mortgage Association; and *Bieldfeldt v. Commissioner*, 231 F.3d 1035 (7th Cir. 2000), *cert. denied*, 534 U.S. 813 (2001). See also TAM 200839033 (June 2008), Rev. Rul. 80-56, 1980-1 C.B. 154, and Rev. Rul. 80-57, 1980-1 C.B. 157. The IRS and the Treasury Department will continue to study this area and may issue guidance in the future.

sale or exchange, on the last day of the taxable year, of a capital asset.[59] A special rule contained in Code section 582(b) permits the loss that a bank may recognize from the worthlessness of a stock investment it holds in a subsidiary bank to be treated as an ordinary loss. According to this special rule, the bank experiencing the worthless stock loss must own directly at least 80 percent of each class of the stock in the other bank.

(f) *REMIC and FASIT*

Any regular or residual interest in a real estate mortgage investment conduit ("REMIC") is treated as an evidence of indebtedness, as is any regular interest in a financial asset securitization investment trust ("FASIT").[60]

§ 4.3.4 Character of Gain or Loss—Certain Preferred Stock

In general, gain or loss on equity securities, including preferred stocks, is characterized as capital gain or loss.[61] An exception has been provided in the Emergency Economic Stabilization Act of 2008 for gain or loss recognized by an "applicable financial institution" from the sale or exchange of "applicable preferred stock." Such gain or loss may be treated as ordinary income or loss.[62]

An "applicable financial institution" is a financial institution referred to in Code section 582(c)(2) or a depository institution holding company (as defined in section 3(w)(1) of the Federal Deposit Insurance Act).[63] "Applicable preferred stock" is preferred stock of the Federal National Mortgage Corporation ("Fannie Mae") or the Federal Home Loan Mortgage Corporation ("Freddie Mac") that was (i) held by the applicable financial institution on September 6, 2008, or (ii) was sold or exchanged by the applicable financial institution on or after January 1, 2008, and before September 7, 2008. In the absence of this special rule, Fannie Mae and Freddie Mac preferred stock is not treated as indebtedness for federal income tax purposes, and therefore is not treated as an asset to which section 582(c)(1) applies. In general, the provision applies to sales or exchanges occurring after December 31, 2007, in taxable years ending after such date.

In the case of a sale or exchange of applicable preferred stock on or after January 1, 2008, but before September 7, 2008, the provision applies only to taxpayers that were applicable financial institutions at the time of such sale or exchange. In the case of a sale or exchange of applicable preferred stock after September 6, 2008, by a taxpayer that held such preferred stock on September 6, 2008, the provision applies only where the taxpayer was an applicable financial institution at all times during the period beginning on September 6, 2008, and ending on the date of the sale or exchange of the applicable preferred stock. Thus, the provision is generally inapplicable to any Fannie Mae or Freddie Mac

---

[59] I.R.C. § 165(g)(1).

[60] I.R.C. § 582(c)(1). The provisions creating FASITs were repealed by the American Jobs Creation Act of 2004 (Pub. L. No. 108-357), but a regular interest in a FASIT in existence on October 22, 2004, issued before that date, and still outstanding in accordance with its original terms of issuance, will still be treated as an evidence of indebtedness (Act Sec. 835(c)(2) of the American Jobs Creation Act of 2004 (Pub. L. No. 108-357)).

[61] I.R.C. § 1221. "Nonqualified preferred stock" is not an equity instrument. I.R.C. § 351(g).

[62] 12 U.S.C. § 5261. Sec. 301, Emergency Economic Stabilization Act of 2008, Pub. L. No. 110-903.

[63] 12 U.S.C. 1813(w)(1).

preferred stock held by a taxpayer that was not an applicable financial institution on September 6, 2008 (even if such taxpayer subsequently became an applicable financial institution).

The Treasury Department is granted the authority to extend the provision to cases in which gain or loss is recognized on the sale or exchange of applicable preferred stock acquired in a carryover basis transaction by an applicable financial institution after September 6, 2008. For example, if after September 6, 2008, Bank A, an entity that was an applicable financial institution at all times during the period beginning on September 6, 2008, acquired assets of Bank T, an entity that also was an applicable financial institution at all times during the period beginning on September 6, 2008, in a transaction in which no gain or loss was recognized under section 368(a)(1), regulations could provide that Fannie Mae and Freddie Mac stock that was applicable preferred stock in the hands of Bank T will continue to be applicable preferred stock in the hands of Bank A.[64]

In addition, the guidance, rules, or regulations may extend the provision to cases in which the applicable financial institution is a partner in a partnership that (i) held preferred stock of Fannie Mae or Freddie Mac on September 8, 2008, and later sold or exchanged such stock, or (ii) sold or exchanged such preferred stock on or after January 1, 2008, but before September 7, 2008.[65] The Secretary took such action and released Revenue Procedure 2008-64 on October 29, 2008, less than a month after the bill's enactment.[66] The "procedure primarily addresses transactions in which the applicable financial institution is a partner in a partnership which held the applicable preferred stock."[67] Moreover, the procedure extends ordinary income and loss tax treatment to five scenarios concerning these transactions.[68]

The first scenario involves sales or exchanges of "qualified preferred stock" (QPS) by a partnership in which an applicable financial institution is a partner. Specifically, for sales or exchanges on or after January 1, 2008, but before September 7, 2008, the section allowing ordinary income for gains and losses applies where (1) a partnership sold or exchanged QPS on or after January 1, 2008, and before September 7, 2008; (2) the taxpayer was a partner in the partnership on the date of the Transaction; and (3) the taxpayer was an applicable financial institution (or a Subsidiary[69]) on the date of the Transaction and at all times thereafter through the earlier of—(a) the closing of the partnership's tax year in which the Transaction occurred; or (b) the date on which the partnership's tax year in which the Transaction occurred closed with respect to the taxpayer.[70] Alternatively, for sales after September 6, 2008, the section applies

[64] JCT Rept. No. JCX-79-08.

[65] 12 U.S.C. § 5261(d)–(e).

[66] Rev. Proc. 2008-64, 2008-47 I.R.B. 1195.

[67] *Id.*

[68] *Id.* Notably, the "definition of a 'Financial Institution' . . . under Revenue Procedure 2008-64 is more restrictive than the definition of an 'applicable financial institution'" listed in the bill's text. "Therefore, not all subsidiaries of an applicable financial institution will be permitted to apply the revenue procedure to otherwise qualifying transactions involving the Preferred Stock." Denise Schwieger & Jill Gehling, *What's News in Tax: Ordinary Treatment for Fannie Mae and Freddie Mac Preferred Stock*, KPMG 1, 2-3 (February 27, 2009).

[69] Subsidiary is described in Sec. 6.01(1)(b)—(d) of Rev. Proc 2008-64.

[70] Rev. Proc. 2008-64, Sec. 3.01(1).

where (1) a partnership sold or exchanged QPS after September 6, 2008 (the Transaction); (2) the partnership held the QPS on September 6, 2008, and at all times thereafter until the Transaction; (3) the taxpayer was a partner in the partnership on September 6, 2008, and at all times thereafter through the date of the Transaction; and (4) the taxpayer was an applicable financial institution (or a Subsidiary[71]) on September 6, 2008, and at all times thereafter through the earlier of—(a) the closing of the partnership's tax year in which the Transaction occurred; or (b) the date on which the partnership's tax year in which the Transaction occurred closed with respect to the taxpayer.[72]

The second scenario involves sales or exchanges by an applicable financial institution of an interest in certain partnerships. For sales or exchanges on or after January 1, 2008, but before September 7, 2008, the section allowing ordinary income for gains and losses applies where (1) a partner sells or exchanges a partnership interest on or after January 1, 2008, and before September 7, 2008; (2) the taxpayer was an applicable financial institution (or a Subsidiary[73]) on the date of the Transaction; and (3) at the time of the Transaction, at least 95 percent in value of the partnership's assets consisted of QPS and cash or cash equivalents.[74] Alternatively, for sales after September 6, 2008, the section applies where (1) a partner sold or exchanged a partnership interest after September 6, 2008; (2) on September 6, 2008, and at all times thereafter through the date of the Transaction, the taxpayer was an applicable financial institution (or a Subsidiary[75]) and a partner in the partnership; and finally, (3) on September 6, 2008, and at all times thereafter through the date of the Transaction, at least 95 percent in value of the partnership's assets consisted of QPS and cash or cash equivalents.[76]

In the third scenario, the section applies to distributions of QPS by certain partnerships to a partner that is an applicable financial institution. Specifically, the section applies where four criteria are met: (1) after September 6, 2008, a partner (the taxpayer) acquired QPS as a result of a distribution from a partnership (the Acquisition); (2) the partnership held the QPS on September 6, 2008, and at all times thereafter until the distribution to the taxpayer; (3) on September 6, 2008, and at all times thereafter until the partnership made the distribution to the taxpayer, at least 95 percent in value of the partnership's assets consisted of QPS and cash or cash equivalents; and (4) on September 6, 2008, and at all times thereafter until the Acquisition, the taxpayer was an applicable financial institution (or a Subsidiary[77]) and was a partner of the partnership.[78]

In the fourth scenario, sales or exchanges of QPS by certain subsidiaries of applicable financial institutions are covered. For sales or exchanges on or after January 1, 2008, but before September 7, 2008, the section applies where (1) a corporation for state law or federal tax law purposes (the Subsidiary) sold or

---

[71] Subsidiary is described in Sec. 6.01(2)(b)—(e) of Rev. Proc 2008-64.

[72] Rev. Proc. 2008-64, Sec. 3.01(2).

[73] Subsidiary is described in Sec. 6.01(1)(b)—(d) of Rev. Proc 2008-64.

[74] Rev. Proc. 2008-64, Sec. 4.01(1).

[75] Subsidiary is described in Section 6.01(2)(b)–(e) of Rev. Proc 2008-64.

[76] Rev. Proc. 2008-64, Sec. 4.01(2).

[77] Subsidiary is described in Section 6.01(2)(b)—(e) of Rev. Proc 2008-64.

[78] Rev. Proc. 2008-64, Sec. 5.01.

exchanged QPS on or after January 1, 2008, and before September 7, 2008 (the Transaction); (2) at the time of the Transaction, the Subsidiary was owned (in whole or in part, directly or indirectly) by another corporation that was a financial institution referred to in section 582(c)(2)(A)(i) or (ii) (Financial Institution); (3) in the calendar quarter in which the Transaction occurred, the assets of the Subsidiary were consolidated with the assets of the Financial Institution on a line-by-line basis on the Consolidated Reports of Condition and Income and their supporting schedules (the call report) that the Financial Institution filed with its federal bank supervisory authorities; and (4) the Subsidiary and the Financial Institution joined in the filing of a federal income tax return on which gain or loss from the Transaction was reported.[79] Alternatively, for sales after September 6, 2008, the section applies where (1) A corporation for state law or federal tax law purposes (the Subsidiary) sold or exchanged QPS after September 6, 2008 (the Transaction); (2) on September 6, 2008, and at all times thereafter until the Transaction, the Subsidiary held the QPS that was the subject of the Transaction; (3) on September 6, 2008, and at all times thereafter until immediately after the Transaction, the Subsidiary was owned (in whole or in part, directly or indirectly) by another corporation that was a financial institution referred to in section 582(c)(2)(A)(i) or (ii) (Financial Institution); (4) in every calendar quarter that both ends after September 6, 2008, and begins on or before the date of the Transaction, the assets of the Subsidiary were consolidated with the assets of the Financial Institution on a line-by-line basis on the Consolidated Reports of Condition and Income and their supporting schedules (the call report) that the Financial Institution filed with its federal bank supervisory authorities; and (5) the Subsidiary and the Financial Institution joined in filing the same federal income tax return(s) for each taxable year of the Subsidiary and the Financial Institution that included all, or any portion, of the period beginning on September 7, 2008, and extending through and including the date of the Transaction.[80]

The final scenario involves sales or exchanges by a taxpayer of QPS, the basis of which in the taxpayer's hands is determined by reference to the basis of that stock in the hands of the person that had transferred it to the taxpayer. The provision applies where (1) the taxpayer acquired QPS after September 6, 2008 (the Acquisition); (2) the Acquisition was a transaction in which the taxpayer's basis in the QPS was determined by reference to the basis of the QPS in the hands of the person (the Transferor) that transferred the QPS to the taxpayer (that is, the QPS is "transferred basis property" within the meaning of section 7701(a)(43) of the Code); (3) the Transferor held the QPS on September 6, 2008; and (4) on September 6, 2008, and at all times thereafter until the QPS was transferred to the taxpayer, if the Transferor had sold the QPS, the character of gain or loss on the sale would have been governed by EESA § 301, either because the Transferor was an applicable financial institution for that entire time period or because the sale would have been described in Section 6.01(2) of the revenue procedure.[81]

[79] Rev. Proc. 2008-64, Sec. 6.01(1).

[80] Rev. Proc. 2008-64, Sec. 6.01(2).

[81] Rev. Proc. 2008-64, Sec. 7.01.

§4.3.5 Character of Gains or Losses—Mutual Fund Investments

Beginning in 1987 and continuing to the present, banks have been permitted to purchase interests in mutual funds. In 1987, the Comptroller of the Currency specifically authorized national banks to hold such assets subject to certain conditions, including:

1. The securities held in the mutual fund are securities that the bank would otherwise be authorized to own directly, and
2. The shares in the mutual fund are highly liquid.[82]

The income that a bank derives from a mutual fund investment usually takes two forms: the annual income earned by the fund, and the appreciation or depreciation in the value of the investment when the bank sells its interest in the fund.

In general, the character of the annual income that the fund earns is determined at the fund level. Thus, ordinary income and capital gains or losses will retain their character when reported to the bank. However, the character of any gain or loss when the bank sells its interest in the fund has been the subject of some controversy. The controversy relates to the absence of any capital gains preferential treatment coupled with exposure to nondeductible capital losses.

Code section 1211 allows losses recognized by a corporation from the sale or exchange of capital assets to be deductible only to the extent of gains from the sale or exchange of such assets. Code section 1221 contains the definition of a capital asset. It provides that a capital asset is any property held by the taxpayer except for five items:

1. Inventory or property held for the sale to customers in the ordinary course of a trade or business;
2. Depreciable property or land used in the taxpayer's business;
3. Certain copyrights and similar assets;
4. Receivables; and
5. Certain government documents.

For a bank, Code section 582(c) provides that capital gains or losses arising from the sale or exchange of a bond, debenture, note, or certificate or other evidence of indebtedness are recharacterized as ordinary gains or losses. Furthermore, for purposes of this rule, a regular or residual interest in a REMIC is treated as an evidence of indebtedness, thus entitling gains or losses on the sale or the exchange of such interest to ordinary treatment.

Banks may argue that ordinary treatment of losses recognized on the sale of mutual fund shares is appropriate because the fund invests in assets that if held directly by the taxpayer would be entitled to ordinary treatment. Thus, because the securities contained within the fund are debt instruments and it is with

[82] *See e.g.*, OCC unpublished interpretive letter, April 11, 1991, "Re: National Bank Investment in Investment Companies-Banking Circular 220."

respect to these assets that the value of the fund declined, the loss was incurred with respect to assets—the gain or loss on which would be ordinary under Code section 582(c). This argument was rejected by a U.S. District Court in *Community Trust Bancorp, Inc. v. United States*.[83] There the court summarized its conclusion by saying: "In order for an instrument to fall within the 'evidence of indebtedness' category, it must have the essential characteristics of debt instruments, such as the repayment of principal. Although the mutual funds at issue in this case were invested in guaranteed United States debt securities, the funds themselves gave no assurances that the investor would ever receive a return of principal." [Footnotes omitted.][84] Legislation also has been proposed, but never enacted, which would have expressly treated shares in mutual funds as bonds and not as capital assets.[85]

An alternative argument that the court in *Community Trust* did not appear to address is that the fund investment itself is an ordinary asset. Although the statutory provision that defines a capital asset appears, on its face, to be unambiguous in limiting the exceptions to capital asset characterization to eight items, considerable judicial controversy has surrounded its application. During the period 1955-1988, commentators and courts crafted what became known as the *Corn Products* doctrine, named after the 1955 Supreme Court opinion in *Corn Products Refining Co. v. Commissioner*.[86] In *Corn Products*, the Court allowed ordinary asset treatment of corn futures acquired to assure the taxpayer of an adequate supply of corn and to avoid the effect of increases in the price of corn.

In 1988, the Supreme Court again reexamined the scope of Code section 1221 and the *Corn Products* doctrine in *Arkansas Best Corp. v. Commissioner*.[87] In that case, the court held that the disposition of bank stock by the taxpayer, which had been acquired with the purpose of preventing damage to its business reputation, resulted in capital loss. The opinion appeared to cut back on the extent that there existed a sixth "judicial exception" to the definition of a capital asset.

The Tax Court, in *FNMA v. Commissioner*,[88] was called upon to decide whether certain losses incurred by the taxpayer on the sale or disposition of regulated futures contracts on debt securities, options on such regulated futures contracts, and Treasury securities were capital in nature. In what some may say was a clarification of the *Arkansas Best* opinion, the Tax Court allowed ordinary loss treatment.

In each of these cases the court ruling addressed an asset or transaction that did not squarely fit within any one of the exceptions to what constituted a capital asset. The courts refrained in all cases from propounding an absolute rule that would strictly construe Code section 1221. In fact, when ruling in favor of the taxpayer, the Tax Court in *FMNA* stated, "FNMA's hedges do not fit under any literal application of the statutory exceptions to capital asset treatment found in

---

[83] 99-2 U.S.T.C. ¶50,698, 1999 WL 594129 (E.D. Ky.).

[84] *Id.*

[85] S. 2223 introduced by Sen. Shelby, February 18, 1992.

[86] *Corn Products Refining Co. v. Commissioner*, 350 U.S. 56 (1955).

[87] *Arkansas Best Corp. v. Commissioner*, 485 U.S. 212 (1988).

[88] *FNMA v. Commissioner*, 100 T.C. 541 (1993).

section 1221 nor does petitioner appear to hold assets to which these same exceptions would apply." Yet, the court concluded that "petitioner's hedging transactions bear a close enough connection to its section 1221(4) mortgages to be excluded from the definition of capital asset." In reaching its conclusion, the court reasoned, "A business connection, although irrelevant to the initial determination whether an item is a capital asset, is relevant in determining the applicability of certain of the statutory exceptions . . . ."

Thus, if a "business connection" could be established between the asset disposed of and one of the assets excepted from the definition of a capital asset, the loss or gain on the disposition of the asset could be characterized as ordinary. How close the "business connection" must be is uncertain; however, the facts should indicate that the two assets are "integrally related" for the requisite nexus to be present.

While the facts of each situation will be controlling, it is significant that the Comptroller of the Currency requires a bank's mutual fund investment to be highly liquid and to be in a fund in which the bank may otherwise invest for liquidity purpose. If it can be established that the liquidity is for the purpose of ensuring adequate funds to meet customer loan demand (loans being an asset excepted from the definition of a capital asset by Code Section 1221(4)), the relationship between the asset disposed of and the asset excepted from the definition of a capital asset may be "close enough" to meet the test set forth in *FNMA*.

Of course, banks do acquire government securities for investment. While the Supreme Court has stated that "a taxpayer's motivation in purchasing an asset is irrelevant to the question whether the asset is 'property held by a taxpayer (whether or not connected with his business)',"[89] this proposition is applicable to an asset that does not otherwise fit within the list of exceptions, as the bank stock in *Arkansas Best*. For this reason, the business connection must be established between the asset and one of the listed exceptions in Code section 1221.

To support the argument that mutual fund shares held by a bank are ordinary assets, evidence should be gathered to establish the connection between the mutual fund asset and one of the listed exceptions to capital asset treatment.

§4.4 Securities Dealer Transactions

§4.4.1 Recognition Rules: Pre-Code Section 475

In general, a dealer in securities includes in gross income securities gains or losses regardless of whether these gains or losses are realized,[90] while investors and traders take into account gains or loss when securities are sold or otherwise disposed of in a taxable transaction.[91]

---

[89] *Arkansas Best Corp. v. Commissioner*, 485 U.S. 212, 222 (1988).

[90] I.R.C. §475. Also, dealers in tax-exempt securities must apply special rules to account for bond premium. I.R.C. §75.

[91] The Taxpayer Relief Act of 1997, Pub. L. No. 105-34 amended I.R.C. §475 to add subsection (f), which permits traders to elect the dealer in securities rules.

For taxable years ending prior to December 31, 1993, a securities dealer was permitted to value securities using one of three authorized methods:

1. Cost;
2. Cost or market, whichever is lower; or
3. Market.[92]

Under the cost method, unrealized gain or loss is not recognized. Instead, gain or loss is recognized when a taxable event that closes the transaction occurs.[93] Thus, gain or loss is recognized when a security is sold or exchanged,[94] or, in the case of a corporate or governmental debt obligations, when it is retired.[95] A bank will be deemed to have elected to inventory securities at cost if its books of account contain separate computations of the gain or loss from the sale of various lots of securities sold, made on the basis of the cost of each lot.[96]

The ability of the taxpayer to control the timing of income or deductions is a distinct advantage of the cost method over the other valuation methods. This is not unlike the relatively greater control over taxable income that can be exercised by a cash method taxpayer as compared with an accrual method taxpayer. Moreover, since the wash sale rules of Code section 1091 do not apply to security dealers, losses can be recognized without any change in position. The cost method, however, is cumbersome in that it requires specific identification of the cost of each security or lot of securities.

The lower of the cost or market method has the same disadvantage as the cost method—specific identification of securities is required. However, unlike the cost method, unrealized losses at year-end are recognized. Since only securities that have declined in value are revalued at year-end to their market values, unrealized gains are not taxed.

Under the market method, both unrealized gains and unrealized losses are recognized. The fair market value of a portfolio at year-end is compared to the fair market value at the beginning of the year, or if purchased during the year, at the purchase date, and any increase or decrease in value is a taxable gain or loss. Thus, this method adheres to an economist's accretion concept of income: unrealized gains or losses are taken into account in determining tax base. Since there is no need to specifically identify the tax bases and fair market value of each security held, this method has the advantage of administrative simplicity.

A taxpayer valuating its inventory on the basis of cost must comply with uniform rules for capitalizing costs and expenditures attributable to inventory property.[97] The uniform capitalization rules also apply to inventories valued at cost by a taxpayer using the lower of cost or market method, but these rules will not affect the valuation of inventories at market by a taxpayer who uses the

---

[92] Reg. § 1.471-5.

[93] *Eisner v. Macomber*, 1 U.S.T.C. ¶32,252 U.S. 189 (1920); Reg. § 1.165-1(b).

[94] I.R.C. § 1001(c).

[95] I.R.C. § 1271.

[96] Reg. § 1.471-5.

[97] I.R.C. § 263A; Reg. § 1.263A-3. The statutory provisions were added to the I.R.C. by the Tax Reform Act of 1986, Pub. L. No. 99-514, § 803, 100 Stat. 2085 (1986). Expenses allocated to tax-exempt income are nondeductible. Reg. § 1.265-1(a).

lower of cost or market method. The effect of the uniform capitalization rules will be to defer deductions for costs that are required to be included in inventory and capitalized.

§4.4.2 Recognition Rules: Code Section 475

Effective for taxable years ending on or after December 31, 1993, Congress amended the general inventory rules contained in Code section 471 by adding Code section 475. Code section 475 contains rules preempting the general inventory rules in respect of dealers in securities.[98] These rules require securities dealers to mark their securities inventories to market for federal income tax purposes, and for securities not held in inventory by a dealer, to treat them as if they were sold for their fair market value on the last day of the taxable year. Thus, a dealer in securities will recognize unrealized gains and losses.[99]

According to the legislative history of Code section 475, the dealer inventory methods authorized by regulations under Code section 471 generally had the effect of understating the income of securities dealers.[100] Moreover, Congress believed that the new Code section 475 method would more clearly reflect the income of securities dealers.

Final regulations under Code section 475 were issued December 24, 1996.[101] These regulations generally adopted previously proposed regulations.[102] The IRS has also issued several revenue rulings designed to provide guidance to taxpayers.[103] Temporary and proposed regulations have also been issued. The final regulations furnish guidance on several issues, including the scope of the exemptions from the Code section 475 rules, the meaning of the terms *security, dealer in security, held for investment*, and *not held for sale*, and certain transitional issues.

A securities dealer is not permitted to apply the uniform capitalization rules of Code section 263A for allocating direct and indirect costs to inventory property and property acquired for resale to the securities to which it applies the mark-to-market rules. A dealer also will not be able to capitalize under Code section 263(g) the interest and carrying charges properly allocable to a security that is part of a straddle. All those costs, interest and carrying charges will be reflected in the fair market value of the security.

---

[98] I.R.C. §475 was added to the I.R.C. by §13223 of the Omnibus Budget Reconciliation Act of 1993, Pub. L. No. 101-508, 104 Stat. 1388 (1990).

[99] There are many other implications of a taxpayer being subject to the mark-to-market rules. For example, an intercompany transaction can be a hedging transaction only if it is entered into with a member of the taxpayer's consolidated group that accounts for its position in the intercompany transaction by marking the position to market. Reg. §1.1221-2(d)(ii)(B). *See also* Notice 96-12, 1996-1 C.B. 366.

[100] Senate Finance Committee Report on Revenue Provisions (Title VIII) as Reported June 18, 1993, to the Senate Budget Committee for Inclusion in the Omnibus Budget Reconciliation Act of 1993. The I.R.C. §471 methods which resulted in this "understatement" were the cost method or the lower of cost or market method.

[101] 61 Fed. Reg. 67715 (December 24, 1996), Codified at 26 CFR pt. 1 & 602.

[102] On December 29, 1993, temporary regulations were issued (T.D. 8505, 58 Fed. Reg. 68747) cross referencing proposed regulations (F.I.-72-93, 58 Fed. Reg. 68798). Additional proposed regulations were issued on January 4, 1995 (60 Fed. Reg. 397), on June 20, 1996 (62 Fed. Reg. 31474), and on May 24, 2005 (70 FR 29663). The IRS informally announced in 2016 that it was engaged in a "clean-up" project that will update and clarify some of its earlier I.R.C. §475 pronouncements.

[103] Rev. Rul. 93-76, 1993-2 C.B. 235; Rev. Rul. 94-7, 1994-1 C.B. 151; Rev. Rul. 97-39, 1997-2 C.B. 62.

A dealer is not permitted to apply the mark-to-market rules to a security that is part of a foreign currency transaction under Code Sec. 988(d). A dealer will not apply the wash sales provision of Code section 1091, but will have to apply the straddle rules of Code Sec. 1092 to any loss it recognizes under the mark-to-market accounting rule. A special set of mark-to-market rules apply to Code section 1256 contracts.[104]

§ 4.4.3 Exceptions to Section 475 Recognition Rules

Exceptions to the general application of the Code section 475 rules are provided for:

1. Any security, whether debt or equity, held for investment;[105]
2. Any debt security acquired or originated by the taxpayer in the ordinary course of its trade or business, but is not held for sale, and any obligation to acquire such security if it is entered into in the ordinary course of the taxpayer's trade or business and not held for sale;[106] and
3. Any security that is a hedge with respect to either a security not subject to the mark-to-market rules or to any position, right to income, or liability that is not a security in the hands of the taxpayer.[107]

Failure to properly identify a security as fitting into one of these exceptions will cause the security to be subject to mark-to-market, even if the taxpayer actually invests in the security.

(a) *Held for Investment*

The term *held for investment*, as used in this exception, and the term *not held for sale* have the same meanings.[108] Both terms refer to a security that is not held by the taxpayer primarily for sale to customers in the ordinary course of the taxpayer's trade or business.[109] Thus, the concept of held for investment in Code section 1236(a) is adopted for use in Code section 475. Consequently, a dealer may identify as held for investment a security that it holds primarily for sale to non-customers, such as a trading security.[110] However, a taxpayer is generally required to treat as held for sale any securities that it expects to contribute to a REMIC.[111]

---

[104] *See* discussion below.

[105] I.R.C. § 475(b)(1)(A).

[106] I.R.C. § 475(b)(1)(B).

[107] I.R.C. § 475(b)(1)(C). Congress has given the Treasury Department express authority to promulgate regulations which may override the exception for hedges held by a taxpayer in its capacity as a dealer in securities. I.R.C. § 475(b).

[108] Reg. § 1.475(b)-1(a).

[109] *Id.* Rev. Rul. 97-39, 1997-2 C.B. 62, Holding 6.

[110] "Explanation of Provisions" accompanying final regulations under I.R.C. § 475, 61 FR 67715, 67718. The identification rules also treat these terms as synonymous. Reg. § 1.475(b)-2(a).

[111] Reg. § 1.475(b)-3(a) explains that a taxpayer is only required to treat as held for sale those securities that it expects to contribute to a REMIC. If a taxpayer and its subsidiaries securitize only a portion of their loan portfolio during the year, they will be treated as having expected that only a portion of the loans originated would ever be securitized. Consequently, a taxpayer and its subsidiaries would not be required to mark-to-market their entire loan portfolio. FSA 200047012, July 31, 2000.

(b) *Not Held for Sale*

Regulation § 1.475(b)-1 provides that a security is not held for sale if it is not held by the taxpayer *primarily* for sale to customers in the ordinary course of the taxpayer's trade or business. In determining whether a taxpayer holds property primarily for sale to customers, the Supreme Court has explained that the term "primarily" means "of first importance" or "principally."[112] A taxpayer's purpose for holding property is based on a number of factors, including: (1) the frequency and regularity of sales; (2) the substantiality of the sales and the amounts of income derived by the taxpayer from its regular business relative to the sales at issue; (3) the length of time the assets are held; (4) the nature and extent of the taxpayer's business and the relationship of the assets to that business; (5) the purpose for which the assets were acquired and held prior to sale; (6) the extent of the taxpayer's efforts to sell the property by advertising or otherwise; and (7) any improvements made by the taxpayer to the assets.[113] This determination is highly fact specific.

In Revenue Ruling 60-346 the IRS addressed whether a bank that originated mortgage loans, half of which it sold to financial institutions within three months after the loan origination, held the loans primarily for sale to customers within the meaning of Code section 1221.[114] Although this ruling pre-dates Code section 475, its holding should continue to be applicable. With respect to the loans that it sold, the bank agreed to service and collect the outstanding loan balance in return for a fee. The IRS concluded that the taxpayer held the loans primarily for sale to customers in the ordinary course of its trade or business, reasoning that: (1) the taxpayer consistently engaged in the practice converting mortgages into liquid funds for the purpose of making additional loans; (2) the loans were made with the intention of selling the mortgages; and (3) selling mortgages in this fashion is a customary function of the taxpayer's banking business. The IRS also noted that the bank sold the loans at or near par value. Thus, a taxpayer who consistently engaged in the practice of converting a portion of its mortgage portfolio into liquid funds by transferring them to a REIT would satisfy one of the three prongs of the test contained in Revenue Ruling 60-346.

§ 4.4.4 Identification of Securities

The exceptions to the mark-to-market rules can be availed of only if securities have been "clearly identified" for purposes of Code section 475.[115] In addition to the security identification rules contained in Code section 475, other Code sections contain security identification rules.[116] Complying with any of these others will not satisfy the Code section 475 identification requirements. Although the identification rules contained in regulations relating to hedging transactions contain a provision that excuses the taxpayer from the consequences of an

---

[112] *Malat v. Riddell*, 383 U.S. 569, 572 (1966).

[113] *Guardian Industries v. Commissioner*, 97 T.C. 308, 316-317 (1991).

[114] 1960-2 C.B. 217.

[115] I.R.C. § 475(b)(2); Reg. § 475(b)-2. *See* discussion following of intercompany transactions.

[116] *See, e.g.*, I.R.C. §§ 988, 1221(a)(7), 1236, 1256, and Reg. § 1.1221-2(f).

incorrect identification in the case of an inadvertent error, no such rule appears in regulations contained under Code section 475.[117]

Certain securities held by a dealer will be deemed to be properly identified as per se held for investment and, consequently, exempt from the mark-to-market requirements.[118] These securities are:

1. Stock in a corporation, or a partnership or beneficial interest in a widely traded partnership or trust, to which the taxpayer is considered a related person under provisions contained in Code section 267 or Code section 707;[119] and
2. A contract that is treated for federal income tax purposes as an annuity, endowment, or life insurance contract.[120]

Notwithstanding these exclusionary rules, stock will not be deemed to be exempt from the mark-to-market rules if it is actively traded on a national securities exchange or through an interdealer quotation system, the taxpayer (and related persons) hold less than 15 percent of all of the outstanding shares or interests in the same class of stock, and, if the stock was acquired from a related person, significant trading involving unrelated persons has taken place.[121]

(a) *When to Identify*

Generally, identification of a security must take place no later than the close of business on the day on which it was acquired, originated, or entered into, or at such other time as regulations provide.[122] The legislative history of Code section 475, however, authorizes the Treasury Department to promulgate regulations that permit a dealer that originates evidences of indebtedness in the ordinary course of its trade or business, or that enters into commitments to acquire mortgages, to identify such instruments as not held for sale based on the accounting practices of the dealer no later than the date that is 30 days after the date that such instruments are originated or commitments made.[123]

The IRS has ruled that for financial institutions defined in Code section 265(b)(5), an identification of an evidence of indebtedness originated or acquired (including mortgage loans) in the ordinary course of the taxpayer's trade or business is timely, if it is made in accordance with the taxpayer's accounting practices, but in no event later than 30 calendar days after the date of the origination or acquisition.[124] It appears that the 30-day rule applies to a non-bank

[117] Reg. § 1.1221-2(f)(2)(ii). Reg. § 1.475(b)-2(a).

[118] Reg. § 1.475 (b)-1(b).

[119] Reg. § 1.475(b)-1(b)(i). The relationships that will cause the deemed identification to apply are described in I.R.C. §§ 267(b)(2), (3), (10), (11), or (12) or I.R.C. § 707(b)(1)(A) or (B).

[120] Reg. § 1.475(b)-1(b)(ii). Such contracts are described in I.R.C. §§ 72, 817, and 7702.

[121] Reg. § 1.475(b)-1(b)(3).

[122] I.R.C. § 1236(a)(1).

[123] Omnibus Budget Reconciliation Act of 1993, Pub. L. No. 103-66, 107 Stat. 312 (1993). In IRS News Rel. IR-93-78, issued Sept. 2, 1993, the IRS extended from Sept. 9, 1993, to Oct. 31, 1993, the date when taxpayers were required to first identify securities as being excepted from the provisions of I.R.C. § 475. H.R. Rep. No. 103-111, 103rd Cong., 1st Sess. 1993, *reprinted* in 1993 U.S.C.C.A.N. 894.

[124] Rev. Rul. 93-76, 1993-2 C.B. 235, Holding 8. A financial institution defined in § 265(b)(5) is a domestic bank or a foreign bank with respect to its income effectively connected with a U.S. trade or business.

member of a bank holding company group that is a dealer in securities that are mortgages.[125] Furthermore, the IRS has ruled that a dealer in securities that enters into commitments to acquire mortgages may apply the 30 day rule to those commitments as being held for investment if the dealer acquires the mortgage loans and holds the mortgage as investments.[126]

If a loan is purchased outside the ordinary course of the taxpayer's business, it is subject to the one-day rule, not the 30-day rule. Thus, if loans are purchased as part of the acquisition of an unrelated taxpayer, the loans must be properly identified by the close of business on the day of acquisition.[127] Failure to properly identify a debt as eligible for one of the exceptions to the mark-to-market rules will require it to be marked to fair market value.[128]

The date that the dealer acquires a security is not affected by whether the dealer's basis in the security is determined, in whole or in part, by either the reference to the basis of the security in the hands of the person from whom the security was acquired or to other property held at any time by the dealer.[129] This rule is effective for securities acquired, originated or entered into on or after January 1, 1995.[130] If a taxpayer is treated as the holder of a synthetic debt instrument as the result of legging into an integrated transaction (as defined in Regulation section 1.1275-6) then, for purposes of the timeliness of an identification, the synthetic debt instrument is treated as having the same acquisition date as the qualifying debt instrument.[131] If a taxpayer legs out of an integrated transaction, the qualifying debt instrument that remains in the taxpayer's hands is treated as having been acquired, originated, or entered into immediately after the leg-out.[132] These rules regarding identification in the context of an integrated transaction apply on or after August 13, 1996.[133]

(b) *How to Identify*

As a general rule, a dealer in securities is not required to use any special procedure to comply with the identification requirements contained in Code section 475.[134] Any reasonable method may be used to satisfy the identification requirement, including the use of identification rules contained in Code sections 988(a)(1)(B), 1221, 1236(a)(1), 1256(e)(2)(C), and regulations thereunder.[135] However, the identification must clearly indicate that it was made for purposes of Code section 475, and it is made on, and retained as part of, the securities dealer's books and records. Classification of a security under financial Accounting Standards Statement No. 115 (Accounting for Certain Investments in Debt and Equity Securities) will not determine whether any security qualifies for one

---

[125] Rev. Rul. 97-39, 1997-2 C.B. 62, Holding 8.

[126] *Id.*

[127] Loan participations acquired from an affiliate would probably be subject to the identification by the seller of the participation. Because the participation is sold it may not be eligible for investment treatment.

[128] This is likely to result in a larger loss (or smaller gain) than would be permitted under Reg. § 1.1001-1(g). *See* discussion of Renegotiated Debt in Ch. 6.

[129] Reg. § 1.475(b)-2(b).

[130] Reg. § 1.475(e)-1(e)(2).

[131] Reg. § 1.475(b)-2(c)(2).

[132] Reg. § 1.475(b)-2(c)(3).

[133] Reg. § 1.475(e)-1(e)(3).

[134] Rev. Rul. 93-76, 1993-2 C.B. 235, Holding 6.

[135] Rev. Rul. 97-39, 1997-2 C.B. 62, Holding 6.

of the exceptions to the mark-to-market rules of Code section 475.[136] If a taxpayer is not otherwise a dealer for purposes of Code section 475, it will not become a dealer by making a protective identification of securities as exempt from the mark-to-market rule.[137]

The dealer's records must clearly indicate the specific security or hedge being identified, and the identification must clearly indicate that it is being made for purposes of Code section 475.[138] A "specific reference to Code section 475" may be affected by any reasonable method including booking the security in an account that identifies the security or hedge for purposes of both Code section 1236(a)(1) and Code section 475(b)(1).[139] As an alternative to indicating on a dealer's books and records the specific security or hedge, the dealer may identify specific accounts as containing only securities or hedges that are covered by a particular exception. Placing a security or hedge in the account will identify the security or hedge as being covered by that exception. Identification by account may be perilous if the dealer customarily deals in securities booked into the identified account. The IRS may take the position that all securities in the account are misidentified.

Proposed regulations had required that the identification must specify the subparagraph of Code section 475(b)(1) under which an exemption is claimed. This identification rule was a reversal from prior proposed regulations,[140] which appeared to rely on Committee Reports under Code section 475 that indicate that there is no material difference between "held for investment" and "not held for sale."[141] Although the presence in the Code of these provisions suggests that they pertain to different activities, final regulations permit an identification as a security that is exempt either by stating on the taxpayer's books and records that the security, on the one hand, is exempt as held for investment or not held for sale or, on the other hand, exempt because it is a hedge of an item not subject to mark-to-market rules.[142] Furthermore, the IRS has stated that taxpayers are permitted to make a reverse, or negative, identification; that is, a statement that all of its securities are exempt from the mark-to-market rules, except those specifically identified as subject to the rules.[143] A reverse, or negative, identification seems to be inconsistent with identification of the exemption by subparagraph.

(c) *Approved Methods to Identify*

Identification rules are contained in regulations under Code sections 988, 1221, 1236 and 1256.[144] Complying with these rules is acceptable for purposes of Code Section 475, but only if the identification makes specific reference to Code

[136] *Id* at Holding 4.

[137] *Id* at Holding 1.

[138] *Id.*

[139] Rev. Rul. 94-7, 1994-1 C.B. 151, Issue 5; Rev. Rul. 97-39, 1997-2 C.B. 62, Holding 6.

[140] Reg. § 1.475(b)-1, 60 F.R. 397, January 4, 1995.

[141] H.R. Rep. No. 103-111, at 664.

[142] Reg. § 1.475(b)-2(a). Unfortunately, the effective date of this regulation is for identifications made on or after July 1, 1997. *See also* Rev. Rul. 97-39, 1997-2 C.B. 62, Holding 6.

[143] Rev. Rul. 93-76, 1993-2 C.B. 235, Holding 6; Rev. Rul. 94-7, 1994-1 C.B. 151, Issue 6; Rev. Rul. 97-39, 1997-2 C.B. 62, Holding 6.

[144] Reg. § 1.1236-1(d)(1).

Section 475.[145] According to those regulations, a security is clearly identified when there is an accounting separation through entries on the dealer's books. Such entries should indicate, when feasible, "the individual serial number of, or other characteristic symbol imprinted upon, the individual security . . . ."[146] The Tax Court has held that adequate segregation is present where endorsements are typed on securities together with ledger entries showing the transfer of securities to an investment account.[147] When formal segregation does not occur, a taxpayer may be precluded from treating the security as includible in its dealer account even though other factors indicate that the securities are held for investment.[148] However, the IRS has ruled that dealers participating in common depository account arrangements need not indicate individual certificate numbers when identifying their dealer and investment securities.[149] Just as taxpayers need not individually value securities, they are not required to individually identify securities.[150]

Dealers have been authorized by the IRS to identify specific accounts as containing only securities held for investment for purposes of Code section 1236(a)(1).[151] Thus, a securities dealer can satisfy the identification requirements of Code section 475(b)(2) by unambiguously indicating that all of the securities or hedges in an account identified as a security held for investment for purposes of Code section 1236(a)(1) are also described in one of the exceptions contained in Code section 475(b)(1)(A),(B), or (C).[152]

Moreover a parent corporation's Code section 475 identification statement on behalf of all members of its consolidated group in combination with its ledgers and software systems was found to be sufficient for purposes of meeting the identification requirements of Code section 475(b)(2).[153] The taxpayer attached a blanket statement to its consolidated tax return designed to be applicable to all members of the group that provided that, in accordance with section 475(b)(2), all loans and securities were exempt from the mark-to-market rules except for mortgage loans identified in its books as held for sale. In its general ledger account, loans held for sale and loans not held for sale were combined in the same account. However, the taxpayer's software system produced a report used to identify the loans that it held for sale. The use of the software system was found to fall within dealer's books and records. The fact that the securities not held for sale could not be distinguished from the loans held for sale by looking only at the general ledger was not fatal.

An identification of a security as "held for investment" under Code section 1236 will no longer serve to identify that security as "held for investment" for

[145] See preamble to regulations in T.D. 8700. These rules are consistent with rules promulgated under I.R.C. § 1221(a)(1).

[146] *Id.*

[147] *Ellis, Holyoke & Company v. Commissioner*, 29 T.C.M. 18, Dec. 29,913(M) (1970), T.C. Memo. 1970-10.

[148] *Stephens, Inc. v. Commissioner*, 72-2 U.S.T.C. ¶9547, 464 F.2d 53 (8th Cir. 1972), *cert. denied*, 409 U.S. 1118 (1973).

[149] Rev. Rul. 64-160, 1964-1 C.B. 306, modified by Rev. Rul. 76-489, 1976-2 C.B. 250.

[150] FSA 199909007, March 5, 1999.

[151] *Id.*

[152] Rev. Rul. 94-7, 1994-1 C.B. 151, Issue 6.

[153] CCA 200731029 (April 26, 2007).

purposes of Code section 475.[154] A transitional rule provides, "[I]f, as of the close of the last taxable year ending before December 31, 1993, a security was identified under section 1236 as a security held for investment, the security is treated as being identified as held for investment for purposes of section 475(b)."[155] Merely identifying a security for purposes of Code section 1236 will not satisfy the identification requirements of Code section 475 for taxable years beginning on or after January 1, 1994.[156] While the same method of identification may still be used for purposes of those two sections, the identification must be specific to Code section 475.

(d) *Improper Identification*

If a taxpayer misidentifies any security or fails to identify certain hedging transactions with respect to securities at the time the identification is required, the mark-to-market rules will continue to apply to the security, except that any loss from marking-to-market prior to the disposition of the security or hedge is permitted to be recognized only to the extent of gain previously recognized under Code section 475 with respect to such security or hedge.

A security is improperly identified if the taxpayer identifies the security as eligible for one of the three exceptions contained in Code section 475(b), but the security does not properly meet any one of those exceptions. Further, improper identification will result if a taxpayer fails to identify any "hedge," described in Code section 475(c)(2)(F), at the time such identification is required. Failure to properly identify a security could result in disallowance of losses resulting from the mark-down of a security to market.[157]

The limitation on the deductibility of any loss that results from application of the Code section 475 mark-to-market rules applies throughout the period when the security is held by the taxpayer. Loss resulting from a market write down prior to the disposition of the security or position may be recognized only to the extent of the gain previously recognized under the Code section 475 rules, but not previously taken into account as a result of the improper identification provision with respect to the security or position. The loss restriction will apply whenever the taxpayer misidentifies a security as falling into one of the three exceptions from the mark-to-market rules contained in Code section 475(b)(1) or if the taxpayer fails to identify any "position" described in Code section 475(c)(2)(F) at the time identification is required.[158]

(e) *Deemed Identification*

The following items held by a dealer in securities are deemed to be properly identified as held for investment: stock in a corporation, a partnership, or a beneficial interest in a widely held or publicly traded partnership or trust to

---

[154] Rev. Rul. 97-39, 1997-2 C.B. 62, Holding 5.

[155] Reg. § 1.475(b)-4(a).

[156] Reg. § 1.475(b)-2(a)(1).

[157] I.R.C. § 475(d)(2). Rev. Rul. 93-76, 1993-2 C.B. 235, Holding 6; Rev. Rul. 94-7, 1994-1 C.B. 151, Issue 6.

[158] This appears to be the case only if the security was improperly identified as exempt from the mark-to-market rules. If the security was subject to mark-to-market, the misidentification rules do not apply.

which a taxpayer has a relationship described in Code sections 267(b)(2), 267(b)(3), 267(b)(10), 267(b)(11), or 267(b)(12) (generally, corporations considered related for purposes of the loss disallowance rules); or a relationship described in Code sections 707(b)(1)(A) or 707(b)(1)(B) (rules describing loss disallowance for controlled partnerships). In determining the existence of any of these relationships, the constructive stock ownership rules of Code section 267(c) and constructive capital or profits ownership rules of Code section 707(b)(3) are taken into account where appropriate.[159] In addition, a contract treated for tax purposes as an annuity, endowment or life insurance contract is considered held for investment.[160]

(f) *Notional Principal Contracts and Derivative Accounts*

Notional principal contracts and derivative securities (described in Code section 475(c)(2)(D) and Code section 475(c)(2)(E)) that are held by a dealer in securities may not qualify for the exemption from the mark-to-market rules for investment property unless the IRS determines otherwise in a revenue ruling, revenue procedure, or letter ruling.[161] In the case of notional principal contracts and derivatives acquired before January 23, 1997, the exemption applies if the taxpayer establishes unambiguously that the acquisition of such securities was not made in the taxpayer's capacity as a dealer. A dealer will recognize ordinary income on notional principal contracts and derivative securities that do not qualify for exemption from the mark-to-market rules as securities held for investment.[162] A taxpayer may also treat as exempt from mark-to-market treatment a security that hedges a position of another member of a taxpayer's consolidated group and meets the following requirements: (1) the security is a hedging transaction under Regulation section 1.1221-2(b); (2) the security is timely identified as a hedging transaction; and (3) the security hedges a position that is not marked to market.[163]

§ 4.4.5 Who Is a Dealer?

(a) *Historical Definition of Dealer*

Although not expressly stated in Code section 475, the legislative history indicates that dealer status is determined on an entity-by-entity basis.[164] Case law and Treasury pronouncements that pre-dated the enactment of Code section 475 have provided guidance as to what activities will constitute dealer activities. The principles these authorities establish should apply for purposes of Code section 475, except as expressly modified by statutory provisions or subsequent regulations issued under Code section 475.

According to pre-Code section 475 regulations, a dealer in securities is "a merchant of securities" who has an established place of business in which the

[159] Reg. § 1.475(b)-1(b)(2).

[160] Reg. § 1.475(b)-1(b)(1).

[161] I.R.C. § 475(b)(4); Reg. § 1.475(b)-1(c).

[162] Reg. § 1.475(d)-1(b).

[163] Reg. § 1.475(b)-1(d).

[164] *See* H.R. Rep. No. 11, 103d Cong., 1st Sess. 224, n.37 (explaining that contracts between dealers and related parties are treated as contracts between unrelated parties). *See also* CCA 200731029, April 26, 2007.

purchase of securities and their resale to customers is regularly transacted for the purpose of deriving gains and profits.[165] Courts have held that a dealer's profit is derived from the mark-up charged customers above cost basis, not from any anticipated rise in market value of the security.[166] Taxpayers are not dealers if their "status as to the source of supply is not significantly different from that of those to whom they sell."[167] A taxpayer can be a dealer despite not advertising as a dealer, not being considered a specialist, not issuing daily quotations, and not having wire connections throughout the country.[168]

Thus, a bank that maintained a regularly established bond department for the purchase of securities and their resale to customers is a dealer in securities.[169] In addition, the IRS has ruled that a mortgage corporation that originates mortgage loans for the purpose of generating profit from sales, and not from future servicing, may inventory the mortgages as a dealer despite the fact that the mortgages were technically not "purchased" within the meaning of Regulation section 1.471-5.[170] The debt obligation that evidences the mortgagor's obligation, however, could reasonably be viewed as a purchased security when that obligation was issued by the mortgagor. Similarly, the Supreme Court has held that a floor specialist was a dealer since he possessed dealer attributes.[171]

Infrequent and isolated transactions with its depositors have not been sufficient to classify a bank or trust company as a dealer in securities.[172] Similarly, a taxpayer who, as agent, buys and sells securities on customer's orders, deriving income from commissions, is not a dealer.[173] Moreover, the Supreme Court has held that an individual who purchased securities for his own account with the expectation of reselling them to others at a profit was not a dealer.[174] A dealer for purposes of registration with the Securities and Exchange Commission (SEC) is not necessarily a dealer for tax purposes.[175] However, the IRS has ruled that an options market maker by definition is a dealer.[176]

---

[165] Reg. § § 1.471-5 and 1.543-1(b)(5)(ii).

[166] *Stephens, Inc. v. Commissioner*, 72-2 U.S.T.C. ¶9547, 464 F.2d 53 (8th Cir. 1972), *cert. denied*, 409 U.S. 1118 (1973); *see also Brown v. U.S.*, 70-1 U.S.T.C. ¶9407, 426 F.2d 355 (Ct. Cl. 1970).

[167] *George R. Kemon v. Commissioner*, 16 T.C. 1026, Dec. 18,271 (1951).

[168] *Stokes v. Rothensies*, 45-2 U.S.T.C. ¶9360, 61 F. Supp. 444 (D.C.E.D. Penn. 1945). Judgement *aff'd* by *Stokes v. Rothensies*, 154 F.2d 1022, 46-1 U.S.T.C. ¶9251 (C.C.A.3Pa) (May 1, 1946).

[169] *Harriman National Bank v. Commissioner*, 20-2 U.S.T.C. ¶565, 43 F.2d 950 (2d Cir. 1920); *Union Trust Co. of Indianapolis v. United States*, 49-2 U.S.T.C. ¶9188, 173 F.2d 54 (7th. Cir. 1949), *cert. denied*, 337 U.S. 940 (1949).

[170] Rev. Rul. 72-523, 1972-2 C.B. 242, *modifying* Rev. Rul. 65-95, 1965-1 C.B. 208; *see also* Rev. Rul. 60-346, 1960 C.B. 217. *But cf. Burbank Liquidating Corporation v. Commissioner*, 64-2 U.S.T.C. ¶9676, 335 F.2d 125 (9th Cir. 1964), in which the sale and repurchase of mortgage loans were held not to be securities for purposes of the wash sale rule of I.R.C. § 1091.

[171] *Helvering v. Fried*, 37-1 U.S.T.C. ¶9004, 299 U.S. 175 (1936).

[172] *Pan-American Bank & Trust Co. v. Commissioner*, 5 B.T.A. 839, Dec. 2000 (1926).

[173] *Stokes v. Rothensies*, 45-2 U.S.T.C. ¶9360, 61 F. Supp. 444 (D.C.E.D. Penn. 1945).

[174] *Schafer v. Helvering*, 36-2 U.S.T.C. ¶9537, 299 U.S. 171 (1936); *see also Northeastern Surety Co. v. Commissioner*, 29 B.T.A. 297, Dec. 8282 (1933), for a list of "dealer" characteristics.

[175] *Van Suetendael v. Commissioner*, 46-1 U.S.T.C. ¶9124, 152 F.2d 654 (2d Cir. 1946).

[176] TAM 8141035, June 30, 1981; *see also* Committee Reports under the Deficit Reduction Act of 1984, Staff of Joint Committee on Taxation, 98th Cong., 2d Sess., General Explanation of The Revenue Provisions (1984). *But cf.* I.R.C. § 1256, which classifies option market makers as "traders" with respect to contracts governed by I.R.C. § 1256 and entered into after July 18, 1984.

If a taxpayer that was a dealer discontinues dealer activities its status as a dealer could also terminate; however, a temporary discontinuance will not result is the taxpayer no longer being a dealer for purposes of Code section 475.[177] When determining whether a taxpayer is "regularly" purchasing or selling securities, there should be an examination of the frequency of purchases and sales and the type of dealer business in which the taxpayer is engaged. Frequency of dealer activity is likely to be less if the taxpayer's dealer activities are only securitizations.

For a taxpayer to be a Code section 475 "dealer in securities," the taxpayer must acquire and hold securities "primarily for sale to customers" as that term is used in Code section 1221.[178] The "held for sale to customers" standard employed in Code section 475 is identical to that earlier adopted in Code sections 1221(a)(1) and 1236.[179] Thus, a taxpayer cannot be a dealer unless the taxpayer has "customers," and if the taxpayer merely engages in regular sales of securities, it will not, on that basis alone, qualify as a dealer. The essence of the customer standard is found in the status of the taxpayer, not in the type of buyer. Thus, traders and many investors engage in regular sales of securities, but these sales are not "primarily . . . to customers" even if the customer is a dealer in securities.[180]

For the securities to be held "primarily" for sale to customers, the security must be held "principally" or "of first importance" for the purpose of sale to customers.[181] To establish the purpose for holding the securities, it is insufficient for a taxpayer to testify that securities were purchased or held primarily for resale to customers.[182] Objective evidence is controlling. Thus, if securities are held for their income yields, they will not be treated as held for sale to customers.[183] Similarly, if the purpose of the sale was to meet business needs, the securities may not be treated as held for sale "to customers."[184]

---

[177] CCA 201238025 (September 2012).

[178] CCA 200817035 (January 17, 2008).

[179] See preamble to Reg. § 1.475(b)-1), T.D, 8700, where it provides: "By providing that a security is held for investment (or not held for sale) if it is not held primarily for sale to customers in the ordinary course of a trade or business, the regulations adopt the concept of held for investment in section 1236(a). Thus, under these regulations, a dealer in securities may identify as held for investment a security that it holds primarily for sale to non-customers (for example, a trading security). The IRS and the Treasury believe that providing a single standard for purposes of sections 475 and 1236 is consistent with the purpose of section 475."

[180] *Van Suetendael*, 3 T.C.M. (CCH) 987 [CCH Dec. 14,147(M); *Marrin v. Commissioner*, 147 F.3rd 147, 151 (2d Cir. 1998) [98-2 U.S.T.C. ¶ 50,490], *aff'g* 73 T.C.M. (CCH) 1748 [CCH Dec. 51,826(M)]; *United States v. Wood*, 943 F.2d at 1051-1052; *Bielfeldt v. Commissioner*, 76 T.C.M. (CCH) 776 (1998) [CCH Dec. 52,943(M)].

[181] *Malat v. Riddell*, 383 U.S. 569 (1966) [66-1 U.S.T.C. ¶ 9317].

[182] *Vaughan v. Commissioner*, 85 F.2d 497, 500 (2d Cir. 1936) [36-2 U.S.T.C. ¶ 9446]. *Guardian Industries Corp. v. Commissioner*, 97 T.C. 308, 316 (1991) [CCH Dec. 47,610]; *Stern Brothers v. Commissioner*, 16 T.C. 295, 313 (1951) [CCH Dec. 18,103]; *Pacific Securities v. Commissioner*, 63 T.C.M. (CCH) 2060 (1992) [CCH Dec. 48,003(M)]. *Goldberg v. Commissioner*, 223 F.2d 709, 712 (5th Cir. 1955) [55-1 U.S.T.C. ¶ 9519].

[183] *United States v. Chinook Inv. Co.*, 136 F.2d 984 (9th Cir. 1943) [43-2 U.S.T.C. ¶ 9538]; *Brown v. United States*, 426 F.2d 355 (Ct. Cl. 1970) [70-1 U.S.T.C. ¶ 9407]; *United States v. Wood*, 943 F.2d 1048 (9th Cir. 1991) [91-2 U.S.T.C. ¶ 50,432]. As stated in *Stephens, Inc. v. United States*, 464 F.2d 53, 57 (8th Cir. 1972) [72-2 U.S.T.C. ¶ 9547], "It is well established that 'investor' status attaches to anyone, including a recognized 'dealer,' who acquires securities with the primary intent to profit from their income yield." This is true even though the taxpayer has the status of "dealer" with respect to other similar securities that it properly holds in its inventory. Id. at 58.

[184] *Erfurth v. Commissioner*, 53 T.C.M. (CCH) 767 (1987) [CCH Dec. 43,897(M)].

(b) *Code Section 475 Definition of Dealer*

All relevant facts and circumstances are taken into account when determining whether a taxpayer is a dealer in securities.[185] Pursuant to Code section 475 and the regulations thereunder, a dealer is a taxpayer that, in the ordinary course of the taxpayer's trade or business, regularly holds itself out as being willing and able to enter into either side of certain acquisitions and sales of securities with customers.[186] It includes any taxpayer who either:

1. Regularly purchases securities from or sells securities to customers in the ordinary course of a trade or business;[187] or
2. Regularly offers to enter, assume, offset, assign or otherwise terminate positions in securities with customers in the ordinary course of a trade or business.[188]

Usually, the every-day business of a bank will result in a bank being classified as a dealer for purposes of the mark-to-market rules. In fact, as discussed below, it is perilous for a bank to assume that it is not a dealer in securities. Many banks will be dealers under the tax definition even though they do not consider themselves dealers for business purposes. This is because whenever a bank makes a loan it is treated as having acquired a security. The legislative history of Code section 475 contains the following example:

> For example, assume that, in the ordinary course of its trade or business, a bank originates loans that are sold if the loans satisfy certain conditions. In addition, assume that (1) the bank determines whether a loan satisfies the conditions within 30 days after the loan is made, and (2) if a loan satisfies the condition for sale, the bank records the loan in a separate account on the date that the determination is made. For purposes of the bill, the bank is a dealer in securities with respect to the loans that it holds for sale.[189]

In addition to revealing Congressional intent to subject banks to the mark-to-market rules, this statement also appears to limit its application. The quoted statement indicates that if the bank is found to be a dealer because it originates and sells certain loans that are identified as held for sale, then it is a dealer only ". . . with respect to the loans that it holds for sale." This statement may not be technically correct. If a bank originates (acquires) and sells loans, it is a "dealer in securities" for purposes of Code section 475. It may then identify particular securities as exempt, but the bank remains a dealer generally. A bank will not be a dealer only with respect to a portion of its portfolio.

No inference that a bank must engage in both sides of a lending transaction should be drawn from the statement in the legislative history that may appear to suggest that the bank is a dealer because it engages in both the origination *and* the sale of loans. The statute is clear that either purchasing *or* selling securities

---

185 Reg. § 1.475(c)-1(a).

186 Reg. § 1.475(c)-1(a)(2).

187 I.R.C. § 475(c)(1)(A).

188 I.R.C. § 475(c)(1)(B). Reg. § 1.475(c)-1(a)(2) defines a dealer in securities only for purposes of I.R.C. § 475(c)(1)(B), and even then the regulation provides that its definition is not all inclusive. It states, "For purposes of section 475(c)(1)(B), the term *dealer in securities* includes, but is not limited to . . ."

189 H. Rep. 103-111, page 664, n. 41, *reprinted in*, 7 U.S.C.C.A.N. 895; *See also* H. Conf. Rep. 103-213, page 611, *reprinted in* 7A U.S.C.C.A.N. 1300.

will qualify a taxpayer as a dealer. Chief Counsel Advise 200731029 confirmed this conclusion when it opined with respect to the members of a bank holding company consolidated group: "Members of Group A originate loans with customers. One of the affiliates, X, also sells mortgage loans into the secondary market. Therefore, based upon section 475(c)(1)(A), all members of Group A qualify as dealers in securities, unless excepted under the negligible sales rules."[190]

Under the Code section 475 identification rules, the mark-to-market rules will not apply to those securities which are properly identified as excepted from the rules. Thus, even if a bank acts as a securities dealer, not all debt instruments it holds are subject to the dealer rules. To be subject to these rules, the instrument must be a "security," and it must be one with respect to which the bank is actually "dealing."[191] However, in order to avoid mark-to-market treatment with respect to any security, including securities in which the dealer invests, the security must be "clearly identified" in the dealer's records as being not held for sale.[192] Thus, at the option of the dealer, investment securities could be subject to mark-to-market.

Following its enactment, Code section 475 was interpreted in several Treasury Department pronouncements; a news release[193] and accompanying notice;[194] revenue rulings;[195] and temporary, proposed and final regulations.[196] Certain of these pronouncements also appear to set forth nonstatutory exceptions for banks from the mark-to-market rules.

According to a Treasury Department news release:

> . . . the mark-to-market provisions apply to many financial institutions that have not traditionally thought of themselves as securities dealers. For instance, any bank, thrift, or other taxpayer that makes and then regularly sells loans is affected and must mark to market at year-end all of its loans and other securities that are not covered by an exception.[197]

Following that news release, the IRS sought to elaborate on the applicability of Code section 475 to banks in a Revenue Ruling that presented a series of "issues" and "holdings," where it was first asked:

---

[190] CCA 200731029, August 26, 2007; *See also* FSA 200047012, July 31, 2000.

[191] Reg. § 1.475(c)-1(a). *Connelly v. Commissioner*, 45 T.C.M. 49, Dec. 39,475(M) (1982), T.C. 1982-644 (1982). *See also R.E. Purvis v. Commissioner*, 76-1 U.S.T.C. ¶ 9270, 530 F.2d 1332 (9th Cir. 1976).

[192] I.R.C. § 475(b)(2). A discussion of the identification rules appears above.

[193] IRS News Rel. IR-93-78, September 2, 1993, I.R.B. 1993-29.

[194] Notice 93-45, 1993-2 C.B. 334.

[195] Rev. Rul. 93-76, 1993-2 C.B. 235; Rev. Rul. 94-7, 1994-1 C.B. 151, Rev. Rul. 97-39, 1997-2 C.B. 62. Several of the statements contained in Rev. Rul. 93-76 were clarified in the temporary regulations issued Dec. 29, 1993, including the meaning of the statutory term "dealer in securities." 58 Fed. Reg. 68798 (December 29, 1993). The 1993 temporary regulations, as revised by 1995 and 1996 proposed regulations, 60 FR 397 and 61 FR 31474, respectively, were generally adopted in final regulations promulgated in 1996, effective December 24, 1996. 61 FR 67715-01.

[196] 58 Fed. Reg. 68747 (December 29, 1993); 60 FR 397 (January 4, 1995); 61 FR 67715 (December 24, 1996); 70 FR 29663 (May 24, 2005).

[197] IRS News Rel. IR-93-78, September 2, 1993, I.R.B. 1993-29. *See also* Prop. Regulations on Intercompany Transactions § 1.1502-13(c)(4)(ii), Ex. 13.

> Is a bank or an insurance company excepted from the mark-to-market rules on the grounds that it is, per se, not a dealer in securities within the meaning of section 475(c)(1) of the Code?

The holding not only answered the question, but appears to be the first expression of a modification of the statute which may have the effect of limiting its application. The holding states:

> No. A bank or an insurance company is subject to the mark-to-market rules if its activities bring it within the definition of a dealer in securities in section 475(c)(1) of the Code. For example, many banks are dealers because they regularly originate and sell loans . . . .[198]

(c) *Related Parties as Customers*

For a taxpayer to be a dealer, it must not only enter into certain transactions in the ordinary course of its trade or business, but those transactions must be with its customers. The term *customer* is not defined in the Code or regulations. Code section 475(c)(1), however, suggests that the party with whom the taxpayer is entering into the transaction must be one with whom the taxpayer is dealing in the ordinary course of the taxpayer's business. Thus, not all parties from whom a bank purchases securities or to whom a bank sells securities are customers.

Whether a taxpayer is transacting business with customers is determined on the basis of all relevant facts and circumstances.[199] Typically, a dealer's performance of services in creating a unique source of supply enables the dealer to mark-up the price of securities. In contrast, a taxpayer that does not have customers, such as traders or investors, depends upon circumstances such as an increase in value or an advantageous purchase in order to sell at a price in excess of cost.[200]

If a bank sells securities to or purchases securities from its own branches, it is not considered to be entering into a transaction with a customer because the taxpayer and its branches are a single taxpayer. Thus, for purposes of determining the source of a notional principal contract under Code section 863, notional principal contracts between separate branches of the same corporation are disregarded.[201] However, if a taxpayer enters into those transactions on behalf of its branches, even if those branches are located in foreign countries, it could be engaged in dealer activities.[202]

If a taxpayer creates a source of supply by originating loans and then selling them to a REMIC, and it generates profits from sales of the loans from both a mortgage servicing fee and from the spread between the interest rate paid on the loans and the interest rate paid to the purchasers of the REMIC interests, it would probably be treated as a dealer. Conversely, if the taxpayer generated profits from REMIC transactions by selling appreciated loans in which it invested, the taxpayer probably will not be engaging in dealer activities.[203]

---

[198] Rev. Rul. 93-76, 1993-2 C.B. 235, Issue 2; Rev. Rul. 97-39, 1997-2 C.B. 62, Holding 2.

[199] Reg. § 1.475(c)-1(a).

[200] *See United States v. Wood,* 943 F.2d 1048, 1051-1052 (9th Cir. 1991).

[201] Reg. § 1.863-7(a)(1).

[202] PLR 9743013, July 23, 1997.

[203] FSA 200047012, July 31, 2000. See discussion of "Intercompany Transactions" below.

As a general rule, for purposes of qualifying the taxpayer as a dealer, a transaction with a related person with whom the taxpayer did not join in the filing of a consolidated return will be a transaction with a customer even if the taxpayer engages in no transactions with third-party customers.[204] If the transactions were between members of a consolidated group, the related person would not be a customer unless special election were made. Thus, the sale of loan participations among members of a group is not a sale to customers. The sale of loan participations by a dealer that invested in the loans did not take them out of the held for investment/not held for sale exception of Code section 475(b)(1).[205]

At the election of the common parent of a consolidated group, a member of a group may be a dealer even if its only customer transactions are with other members of its consolidated group.[206] This election, referred to as the *intragroup-customer election*, is made by filing a statement, signed by the common parent and attached to the return for the first taxable year to which it is intended to apply, that says:

> [Insert name and employer ID number of common parent] hereby makes the Intragroup-Customer Election (as described in § 1.475(c)-(1)(a)(3)(iii) of the income tax regulations) for the taxable year ending [describe the last day of the year] and for subsequent taxable years.

The election will continue in effect for all subsequent taxable years until revoked with the consent of the Commissioner.

(d) *Nonfinancial Goods and Services*

In general, a taxpayer will not be classified as a dealer in securities merely because the taxpayer purchases or sells debt instruments that, at the time of purchase or sale, are customer paper with respect to either the taxpayer or a member of the taxpayer's consolidated group.[207] For debt instruments to qualify as customer paper under this exception, the debt instruments, among other requirements, must arise out of the sale of nonfinancial goods or services.[208] Because of this requirement, a bank, or member of a bank holding company group, will usually not be entitled to this exemption.

---

[204] Reg. § 1.475(c)-1(a)(3)(i) and Reg. § 1.1502-13(c)(7)(ii), Ex. 11.

[205] CCA 200731029 (April 26, 2007); Reg. § 1.475(c)-1(a)(3)(ii). A consolidated group is defined in Reg. § 1.1502-1(h).

[206] Reg. § 1.475(c)-1(a)(3)(iii).

[207] Reg. § 1.475(c)-1(b)(1); Reg. § 1.1502-1(h).

[208] Reg. § 1.475(c)-1(b)(2)(i). Customer paper also must be (a) a debt instrument issued by a purchase of the goods or services at the time of the purchase of those goods or services in order to finance the purchase, and (b) at all times since the debt instrument was issued, it has been held either by the person selling those goods or services or by a corporation that is a member of the same consolidated group as that person. Reg. § 1.475(c)-1(b)(2)(ii) and (iii). Exceptions to this rule are provided for a taxpayer (a) who inventories securities, (b) who elects for the purchases and sales to cause the taxpayer to be treated as a dealer in securities, or (c) who is not a person whose principal activity is selling nonfinancial goods or providing nonfinancial services but who accounts for the customer paper in a manner that allows deductions for additions to a bad debt reserve or recognition of unrealized gains or losses.

(e) *Negligible Sales Exception*

Code section 475(c)(1) provides that a taxpayer is a dealer in securities only if the taxpayer *regularly* engages in purchase or *sale* transactions or if the taxpayer *regularly* takes positions with respect to securities.[209]

The term *sale* in this context contemplates exchanges, particularly in a case where the taxpayer immediately sells for cash the property received in the exchange. Otherwise, taxpayers could qualify for the negligible sales exception by entering into non-cash transactions with their customers. Under the Uniform Commercial Code, exchanges are treated as sales.[210] Furthermore, there is a *sale* even though the transfer is not a taxable transaction. In a situation involving the transfer of Home Equity Loans to a REMICs in exchange for a regular or residual interest, Code section 860F(b)(1)(A) treats the transfer as nontaxable transfer of property. However, the IRS has ruled that this transfer should be treated as a *sale* for purposes of Code section 475.[211] It reasoned that Code Section 1001(c) provides that a taxpayer must recognize the entire amount of gain or loss resulting from the sale or exchange of property, except as otherwise provided. Therefore, a transaction may constitute a sale or exchange for tax purposes, although it is not a taxable transaction. A Code section 351 transaction may also constitute a nonrecognition transaction that is a sale or exchange.

The IRS's position with respect to transfers to REMICs, as set forth in the proposed regulations, is consistent with this principle. Proposed regulation § 1.475(b)-3(a) provides that a taxpayer that expects to contribute mortgages to a REMIC must treat such assets as held for sale unless the taxpayer expects that each of the interests it will receive from the REMIC in return for the mortgages will be either held for investment or not held for sale to customers in the ordinary course of the taxpayer's trade or business.[212]

(f) *Negligible Sales Election*

A taxpayer who engages in negligible sales of securities will be treated as a taxpayer who does not regularly engage in sale or purchase transactions, unless the taxpayer elects to be treated as a dealer.[213] The regulations under Code section 475 contain a limited exception to dealer status for a taxpayer who purchases securities from customers in the ordinary course of its trade or business but engages in no more than negligible sales of the securities that it purchases.[214] The focus of this exception is on the securities sold, not on those that are acquired or purchased. However, the exception does not apply if the

209 I.R.C. § 475(c)(1).

210 Reg. § 1.475(c)-1(c)(1); Reg. § 1.475(c)-1(c)(1)(ii).

211 See U.C.C. § 2-304 (providing that "price" paid pursuant to a sale under U.C.C. § 2-106(1) may be in money or otherwise). The Tax Court has cited the Uniform Commercial Code's definition of "sale" for the purpose of determining whether a taxpayer has held property primarily for sale to customers. *Guardian Industries Corp. v. Commissioner*, 97 T.C. 308, 318, 319 n.5 (1991).

212 FSA 200047012, July 31, 2000.

213 The Tax Court has explained that although proposed regulations constitute a "body of informed judgment," they are accorded no more weight than a litigation position. *KTA-Tator, Inc. v. Commissioner*, 108 T.C. 100, 102-103 (1997) (quoting *Bolton v. Commissioner*, 694 F.2d 556, 560 n.10 (9th Cir. 1982)).

214 Reg. § 1.475(c)-1(c)(1)(i).

taxpayer claims to be a dealer in those securities for purposes of the general Code section 471 inventory rules.

The safe harbors for what constitutes "negligible sales" is prescribed in two rules.[215] In the first rule, the sale of fewer than 60 debt instruments, regardless of how acquired, is regarded as negligible.[216] In the second rule, the sale of debt instruments will be negligible if all debt instruments sold during the taxable year have a total adjusted basis of less than 5 percent of the total basis, immediately after acquisition, of all debt instruments that it acquires in that year.[217] In the first safe harbor rule, the comparison is between all debt instruments on the taxpayer's books and the debt instruments sold. In the second safe harbor rule, the comparison is between the debt instruments acquired in the year in which the debt instruments are disposed.

In the case of a consolidated group that does not have an intra-group customer election in effect (discussed below), the IRS applies a two-part test to determine whether the negligible sales exception excludes the entire group or any of the affiliates from dealer status. A taxpayer will satisfy the negligible sales test if either of these two tests is met.[218]

Initially, the consolidated group is tested as a whole, treating members of the group as if they were divisions of a single corporation, and taking into account all of the taxpayer's sales of debt instruments.[219] If the group fails to pass the group wide test, each member of the group is separately tested to determine whether it could qualify for the negligible sales exception.[220] In this test, all sales of debt instruments to other group members are taken into account.

A taxpayer that is not classified as a dealer in securities because of the negligible sales exception may, nevertheless, elect to be treated as a dealer in securities if an intragroup customer election is made.[221] The election is made merely by filing a return reflecting the application of the mark-to-market rules.

If a taxpayer has made the intragroup-customer election, the negligible sales rules (both the 60 loan and the 5 percent rules) are applied by taking into account all of the taxpayer's sales of debt instruments to other group members.[222] If the intragroup-customer election has not been made, the negligible sales test is met by a taxpayer that is a member of a consolidated group if either:

1. The taxpayer satisfies the test, taking into account all of the taxpayer's sales of debt instruments, including sales to other group members, or
2. The consolidated group would satisfy the test if the members of the group were treated as divisions of a single corporation.[223]

For purposes of determining whether the taxpayer sells more than a negligible portion of securities, three types of transactions are ignored:

---

[215] Reg. § 1.475(c)-1(c)(2).

[216] Reg. § 1.475(c)-1(c)(2)(i).

[217] Reg. § 1.475(c)-1(c)(2)(ii).

[218] CCA 200731029 (April 26, 2007).

[219] Reg. § 1.475(c)-1(c)(3)(ii)(B).

[220] Reg. § 1.475(c)-1(c)(3)(ii)(A).

[221] Reg. § 1.475(c)-1(c)(1)(ii).

[222] Reg. § 1.475(c)-1(c)(3)(i).

[223] Reg. § 1.475(c)-1(c)(3)(ii). This group-wide approach is consistent with the single-entity approach of Reg. §§ 1.1221-2(d)(1) and 1.1502-13.

1. Sales of securities necessitated by exceptional circumstances, and not undertaken as a recurring business activity.[224]
2. Any securities that are debt instruments, whose quality has declined while held by the taxpayer, and are sold pursuant to an established policy of the taxpayer to dispose of such debt obligations that are below a certain quality.[225]
3. Both acquisitions and sales of debt instruments that are qualitatively different from all debt instruments that the taxpayer purchases from customers in the ordinary course of its business.[226]

Frequently where debt is renegotiated, a deemed exchange of the debt occurs. This may be a taxable event that may be treated as a "recurring business activity." Thus, all loans that are renegotiated may be taken into account in determining whether the negligible sales exception applies. In addition, banks purchase and regularly sell participations in loans. Each such transaction should be counted when determining whether the negligible sales exception should apply. For these reasons alone, it is unlikely that the negligible sales exception can be relied upon for excluding any banks from dealer status.

(g) *Intercompany Transactions*

Even though a taxpayer is not a dealer in securities, it may be treated as holding securities that are subject to the mark-to-market rules. In regulations dealing with the rules relating to consolidated return intercompany transactions, the potential of dealer taint carrying over with respect to a security sold by a dealer to a nondealer affiliate is addressed.[227] However, a nondealer will not lose its status as such merely because it holds a security subject to mark-to-market that it has acquired from a dealer affiliate.[228]

In a transaction described in the consolidated return regulations, a dealer in securities sells a security to a non-dealer affiliate for its fair market value on the day of sale. The security was purchased by the dealer during the preceding tax year, and a mark-down was taken at the end of that tax year. The selling price exceeded the dealer's tax basis, which was adjusted to reflect that mark-down.[229] The regulation provides that the selling entity's "intercompany gain is taken into account by treating section 475 as applying to [the seller and buyer] as a single corporation that is a dealer . . . ."[230]

Regulations require the seller to include the deferred intercompany gain in income at year-end. The buying corporation determines its corresponding item, its mark-to-market gain or loss on the security at year-end, by reference to its cost

---

[224] Reg. § 1.475(c)-1(c)(4)(i).

[225] Reg. § 1.475 (c)-1(c)(4)(ii). *See also* discussion of "exceptional circumstances" rule in Ch. 1, § 1.5.4(b) discussion of "Investing in Loans."

[226] Reg. § 1.475(c)-1(c)(4)(iii).

[227] I.R.C. § 1504(a). Reg. § 1.1502-13(c)(4)(ii), Ex. 11.

[228] The regular purchase of securities, such as loan participations, from an affiliate would not cause the purchaser to be a dealer, unless the intra-group customer election is made.

[229] It should be noted that there is no express rule requiring or permitting an adjustment to tax basis when a security is written down.

[230] Reg. 1.1502-13(c)(4)(ii).

basis.[231] The affiliates will be treated as separate corporations for purpose of determining the character of any gain or loss. Thus, the selling corporation's gain will be ordinary, but the buying corporation's gain or loss on a subsequent disposition of the security may be capital, depending upon the character of the asset in the hands of the buyer.

Although a security once subject to the mark-to-market rules appears to remain subject to those rules after an intercompany transaction, when a security is transferred from a nondealer to a dealer, the investment status of the security does not carryover. Nevertheless, the buyer-dealer is permitted to identify the security as held for investment or not held for sale and, thus, exempt it from the mark-to-market rules.[232] Any built-in gain or loss on the security on the day that it is sold to the affiliated dealer is deferred until the security is sold outside the group. If the acquiring affiliate treats the security as subject to the mark-to-market rules, it will measure gain or loss by reference to its cost basis.

Example 1: Assume that on 7/01/X1 a dealer in securities, S, sells a security to B, an affiliated company that is a nondealer. The sales price is $100 and S had an adjusted basis in the security of $70. The security was held by B at 12/31/X1, but sold to X, an unrelated company on 7/01/X2.

S will have a deferred intercompany gain of $30, and B takes a cost basis in the securities of $100.[233] The timing of the recognition of any gain or loss and its character is illustrated under three scenarios, as follows:[234]

Tax Year X1
Dealer "S" Sells to New Dealer "B"

	Alt. 1	*Alt. 2*	*Alt. 3*
FMV (12/31/X1)	100	84	115
B's basis (12/31/X1)	100	100	100
B's G(L) (12/31/X1)	0	(16)[235]	15[236]

[231] *Id.* These regulations retain the deferred sale approach of the current intercompany transaction regulations, but the manner in which deferral is achieved is comprehensively revised. In general, the amount, location, character, and source of items from an intercompany transaction are determined as if separate returns were filed. This is referred to as separate entity treatment. However, the timing of items is determined more like the timing that would apply if the participants were divisions of a single corporation. This is single entity treatment. For a complete discussion of the operation of the regulations *see* the preamble to them at 59 Fed. Reg. 18011 (April 15, 1994).

[232] Reg. § 1.1502-13(c)(4)(ii), Ex. 13(d).

[233] Reg. § 1.1502-13(a)(2).

[234] Reg. § 1.1502-13(a)(2). The selling member and buying member are treated as separate entities for determining the amount of gain or loss and basis. The timing of gain or loss recognition is based on a single entity theory.

[235] Reg. § 1.1502-13(c)(7)(ii), Ex. 11(b). Under the matching rule of the intercompany regulations, attributes are redetermined by treating S and B as divisions of a single corporation. Since S is a dealer, the single corporation is treated as a dealer with respect to securities. Thus, B must continue to mark-to-market the security acquired from S.

[236] Id.

Tax Year X1
Dealer "S" Sells to New Dealer "B"

	Alt. 1	*Alt. 2*	*Alt. 3*
S's G(L) (12/31/X1)	30[237]	30[238]	30[239]
Character of B's G(L)[240]	N/A	Ordinary	Ordinary
Character of S's G(L)[241]	Ordinary	Ordinary	Ordinary
B's Basis (12/31/X1)	100	84	115

Tax Year X2

	Alt. 1	*Alt. 2*	*Alt. 3*
FMV (07/01/X2)	110	120	112
A/B	100	84	115
B's basis	10	36	(3)
Character of B's G(L)[242]	Capital	Capital	Capital

Example 2: Assume that on 7/01/X1 a nondealer, S, sells a security to B, an affiliated company that is a dealer in securities. The sales price is $100 and S had an adjusted basis in the security of $70. The security was held by B at 12/31/X1, but sold to X, an unrelated company, on 7/01/X2.

S will have a deferred intercompany gain of $30, and B takes a cost basis in the securities.

The timing of the recognition of any gain or loss and its character is illustrated under three scenarios, as follows:

Tax Year X1
Nondealer "S" Sells to Dealer "B"

	Alt. 1	*Alt. 2*	*Alt. 3*
FMV (12/31/X1)	100	84	115
B's basis	100	100	100
Character of B's G(L)[243]	N/A	Ordinary	Ordinary
Character of S's G(L)	N/A	N/A	N/A
B's Basis (12/31/X1)	100	84	115

[237] Reg. § 1.1502-13(c)(7)(ii), Ex. 11(c). S's $30 recognized gain is determined as follows: B's recognized gain from the security to market equals $0; Recomputed gain that would be taken into account if S and B were divisions of a single corporation equals $30, the difference equals $30. Overall, the consolidated group recognizes a $30 gain for the year, reflecting the difference between the security's initial basis of $70 and its fair market value at 1N/3N/X1 of $100.

[238] Reg. § 1.1502-13(c)(7)(ii), Ex. 11(c). S's $30 recognized gain is determined as follows: B's recognized loss from marking the security to market equals $(16); Recomputed gain that would be taken into account if S and B were divisions of a single corporation equals $14; the difference equals $30. Overall, the consolidated group recognizes a $14 gain for the year, reflecting the difference between the security's initial basis of $70 and its fair market value at 1N/3N/X1 of $84.

[239] Reg. § 1.1502-13(c)(7)(ii), Ex. 11(c). S's $30 recognized gain is determined as follows: B's recognized gain from marking the security to market equals $15; Recomputed gain that would be taken into account if S and B were divisions of a single corporation equals $45; the difference equals $30. Overall the consolidated group recognizes a $45 gain for the year, reflecting the difference between the security's initial basis of $70 and its fair market value at 1N/3N/X1 of $115.

[240] I.R.C. § 475(d)(3)(A)(i). Reg. § 1.1502-13(c)(7)(ii), Ex. 11(c). The character of S's gain and B's gain are redetermined as if the security were transferred between divisions. Thus, S's gain and B's gain are both characterized as ordinary.

[241] Id.

[242] I.R.C. § 475(d)(3)(B)(ii); Reg. § 1.1502-13(c)(7)(ii), Ex.11(c).

[243] I.R.C. § 475(d)(3)(A)(i).

Tax Year X2

	Alt. 1	*Alt. 2*	*Alt. 3*
FMV (07/01/X2)	110	120	112
B's basis	100	84	115
B's G(L)	10	36	(3)
S's G(L)	30[244]	30[245]	30[246]
Character of B's G(L)[247]	Ordinary	Ordinary	Ordinary
Character of S's G(L)[248]	Capital	Capital	Capital

§ 4.4.6 Traders, Investors and Speculators

A dealer is to be contrasted with an investor, trader, or speculator; however, a dealer may also be an investor, trader, or speculator. According to the Eighth Circuit, "Investor status attaches to anyone, including a recognized dealer, who acquires securities with primary intent to profit from their income yield, even though the taxpayer has the status of a dealer with respect to other similar securities."[249] An investor is anyone who holds securities with the expectation of deriving profits from their appreciation in value.[250] A taxpayer who only buys and sells securities for investment is not treated as a dealer even when such buying and selling constitutes a trade or business.[251]

A trader is one engaged in the trade or business of buying and selling securities for his own account.[252] A speculator, like an investor, acquires securities for the purpose of deriving profits from appreciation, not from the trading activity itself.[253]

---

[244] Reg. § 1.1502-13(c)(7)(ii), Ex. 11(d). S takes its $30 gain into account in year X2 under the matching rule, determined as follows: B's recognized gain from sale of the security to a third party equals $10; Recomputed gain (loss) that would be taken into account if S and B were divisions of a single corporations ($110 - $70) equals $40; the difference is $30. Overall, the consolidated group recognizes a $40 gain for X2, reflecting the difference between the security's $70 initial basis and the amount realized of $110 upon sale by B.

[245] Reg. § 1.1502-13(c)(7)(ii), Ex. 11(d). S takes its $30 gain into account in year X2 under the matching rule, determined as follows: B's recognized gain from the sale of the security to a third party equals $36; Recomputed gain (loss) that would be taken into account if S and B were divisions of a single corporation ($120 - $54) equals $66; the difference equals $30. Overall, the consolidated group recognizes a $66 gain in X2 and a combined $50 gain for years X1 and X2 ($66 X2 gain - $16 X1 loss), reflecting the difference between the security's $70 initial basis and the amount realized upon sale of $120 upon sale by B.

[246] Reg. § 1.1502-13(c)(7)(ii), Ex. 11(d). S takes its $30 gain into account in year X2 under the matching rule, determined as follows: B's recognized loss from sale of the security to a third party equals $(3); Recomputed gain (loss) that would be taken into account if S and B were divisions of a single corporation ($112 -$85) equals $27; the difference equals $30. Overall the consolidated group recognizes a $27 gain in X2 ($30 gain less $3 loss) and a combined $42 gain for years X1 and X2 ($27 X2 gain + $15 X1 gain), reflecting the difference between the security's $70 initial basis and the amount realized upon sale of $112 upon sale by B.

[247] I.R.C. § 475(d)(3)(A)(i).

[248] I.R.C. § 475(d)(3).

[249] *Stephens, Inc. v. Commissioner*, 72-2 U.S.T.C. ¶9547, 464 F.2d 53, 57 (8th Cir. 1972), *cert. denied*, 409 U.S. 1118 (1973).

[250] *Leach Corp. v. Blacklidge*, 38-2 U.S.T.C. ¶9401, 23 F. Supp. 622 (N.D. Ill. 1938).

[251] Reg. § 1.471-5.

[252] Rev. Rul. 97-39, 1997-2 C.B. 62, Holding 3. *C.E. Wilson v. Commissioner*, 35 U.S.T.C. ¶9245, 76 F.2d 476 (10th Cir. 1935). According to Rev. Rul. 93-76, "A taxpayer whose sole business consists of trading in securities is not a dealer in securities within the meaning of section 475(c) of the I.R.C. because that taxpayer does not purchase from, sell to, or enter into transactions with customers in the ordinary course of a trade or business." 1993-2 C.B. 235.

[253] *Lowell v. Commissioner*, 30 B.T.A. 1297, Dec. 8652 (1934).

The Taxpayer Relief Act of 1997 amended Code section 475 to permit traders in securities or commodities (as well as commodities dealers) to elect the mark-to-market rules that are imposed on dealers in securities, even though they do not deal in securities.[254] If a securities trader elects application of Code section 475(f), all securities or commodities held in connection with its trade or business as a trader in securities or commodities will be subject to the mark-to-market accounting rules.[255]

Congress was concerned with taxpayer selectivity in making identifications. It did not want a taxpayer to selectively mark-to-market some securities, and then to selectively identify other securities as exempt from the mark-to-market treatment. Congress especially did not want a taxpayer to be able to do that using hindsight. To address this concern, Congress placed a higher burden of proof for electing securities traders to identify securities as not subject to Code section 475 than is applicable to securities dealers.[256]

Securities or commodities that an electing taxpayer can demonstrate, by clear and convincing evidence, have no connection with its activities as a trader and that are properly identified are excepted from the mark-to-market rules.[257] Proposed regulation also provides a special rule for the situation where a taxpayer may identify securities as not held in connection with its trading business when the electing trader also trades the same or substantially similar securities that it uses in its trade or business. In this situation, a taxpayer can only meet the requirements of Code section 475(f)(1)(B)(i) if the security is held in a separate, non-trading account maintained by a third party.[258] The identification must occur on the day that the securities or commodities are acquired using the general identification rules contained in Code section 475(b) and the regulations thereunder.[259] If an electing trader holds a security that is not held in connection with its trading business and fails to identify the security in a manner that satisfies the requirements of Code section 475(f)(1)(B)(ii), then Code section 475(d)(2) applies. Under the latter, the security is marked to market and any losses realized with respect to the security prior to its disposition are recognized only to the extent of gain previously recognized (with respect to that security) and the character of the gain or loss is ordinary.[260]

The legislative history of the subsection provides that it is not intended that an electing taxpayer can mark-to-market loans made to customers or receivables or debt instruments acquired from customers that are not received or acquired in

[254] Pub. L. No. 105-34, § 1001(b).

[255] I.R.C. §§ 475(f)(1) and (2). Separate elections appear to be available for commodities and for securities.

[256] *See* Conf. Report 105-220, 105th Cong., 1st Sess., July 30, 1997, 1997-4 C.B. 1457, 1985; General Explanation of Tax Legislation Enacted in 1997 (Blue Book), JCS 23-97, Dec. 17, 1997, p. 182, 1997-3 C.B. 89, 292. The IRS also expressed concern with selective identification because it believes that it is more difficult to distinguish trading securities from investment securities than it is to distinguish dealer securities from investment securities. *See* Preamble to REG-104924-98, 1999-10 IRB 47, 49.

[257] I.R.C. § 475(f)(1)(B).

[258] Prop. Reg. § 1.475(f)-2(a)(3).

[259] I.R.C. § 475(f)(1)(D). The legislative history provides that the I.R.C. § 475(b)(4) rules will apply only to contracts and instruments referenced to commodities that are held by a commodities trader or dealer. Conference Report for Taxpayer Relief Act of 1997, H.R. 2014, Title X, Subtitle A, Sec. 1001(b).

[260] Prop. Reg. § 1.475(f)-2(a)(4).

connection with a trade or business as a securities trader.[261] The legislative history also expands the definition of a commodity to include: any commodity that is actively traded (within the meaning of Code section 1092(d)(1)), any option, forward contract, futures contract, short position, notional principal contract or derivative instrument that references such a commodity, and any other evidence of an interest in such a commodity.[262] Furthermore, the term commodity encompasses any position that hedges any of these items and that are identified by the taxpayer as such, using the general identification rules applicable to dealers in securities.

The election for a trader to apply the mark-to-market rules to securities may not be made separately for each trade or business but is made on an entity-by-entity basis. Only in the case of separate commodities business may the taxpayer make separate elections. Code Section 475(f)(3) expressly provides that separate elections must be made for a trader in securities election under Code Section 475(f)(1) and a trader in commodities election under Code Section 475(f)(2). Furthermore, a trader is apparently permitted to make the election for commodities or for securities, even though both activities may be engaged in by the trader. Once made, the election shall apply to the taxable year for which made and to all subsequent taxable years. It may be made without the consent of the IRS, but it may be revoked only with consent.[263]

The Conference Committee Report accompanying the enactment of Code section 475(f) describes the House Bill as providing that a "[g]ain or loss recognized by an electing taxpayer . . . is ordinary gain or loss."[264] However, it appears that this is merely an inexact reference to the general ordinary income rule of Code section 475(d)(3), which provides an exception for any security "held by a person other than in connection with its activities as a dealer in securities.[265]

The IRS has issued guidance that prescribes the exclusive procedure for traders in securities to make an election to use the mark-to-market method.[266] It applies both to existing taxpayers who change to the mark-to-market method and to new taxpayers who are adopting that method. A new taxpayer (for which no federal income tax return was required to be filed for the taxable year immediately preceding the election year) may make an election under Code section 475(f) for a tax year beginning on or after January 1, 1999, by placing in its books and records no later than two months and 15 days from the first day of the election year a statement that describes the election being made, the first taxable year for which the election is effective, and the trade or business for which the

---

261 *Id.*

262 *Id.*

263 I.R.C. § 475(f)(3).

264 H.R. Rep. No. 105-220, at 515. The section, as enacted, does not contain any characterization rule. If the character of gain or loss were determined in accordance with the House Bill, a trader would be subject to different characterization rules than a dealer. This could present a conundrum because many dealers are also traders. Legislative action may be needed to clarify this confusion.

265 I.R.C. § 475(d)(3)(B).

266 Rev. Proc. 99-17, 1999-1 C.B. 503 (section 6 superseded by Rev. Proc. 99-49, 1999-2 C.B. 725, which was clarified, modified, amplified, and superseded by Rev. Proc. 2002-9, 2002-1 C.B. 327, which was clarified, modified, amplified, and superseded by Rev. Proc. 2008-52, 2008-36 I.R.B. 587).

election is made.[267] The new taxpayer also must attach a copy of the statement to its original federal income tax return for the election year.

The election under Code section 475(f) determines the method of accounting an electing trader is required to use for federal income tax purposes for securities subject to the election.[268] A method of accounting for securities subject to the election is impermissible unless the method is in accordance with Code section 475 and the regulations thereunder. If an electing trader's method of accounting for its taxable year immediately preceding the election year is inconsistent with Code section 475, the taxpayer is required to change its method of accounting to comply with its election. A taxpayer that makes a Code section 475(f) election but fails to change its method of accounting to comply with that election is using an impermissible method. Because the election is integrally related to the change in accounting method to mark-to-market, it is an accounting method regulatory election subject to Regulation section 301.9100-3(c)(2). Any net Code section 481(a) adjustment must be taken into account for any taxpayer that changes its method of accounting.[269]

In a subsequent revenue procedure, the IRS prescribed procedures by which a trader may obtain automatic consent to change to the mark-to-market accounting method.[270] Advance written consent of the Commissioner is not required to make an election under 475(f) assuming all requirements are met.[271]

§4.4.7 What Is a "Security"?

For purposes of Code section 475, a "security" is defined as any:

1. Share of stock in a corporation. It appears that the stock that a parent bank holding company owns in its subsidiaries would be a "security";[272]
2. Partnership or beneficial ownership interest in a widely held or publicly traded partnership or trust;[273]
3. Note, bond, debenture, or other evidence of indebtedness except any debt instruments issued by the taxpayer.[274] This category includes loans and financial leases;[275]
4. Interest rate, currency, or equity notional principal contract. Any other notional principal contract, such as a notional principal contract that is

[267] Section 5.03(2) of Rev. Proc. 99-17.

[268] Section 4 of Rev. Proc. 99-17.

[269] Section 6.03 of Rev. Proc. 99-17.

[270] Section 23(2)(a) of the Appendix to Rev. Proc. 2008-52. Rev. Procs. 99-17 and 2008-52.

[271] The automatic change applies to a taxpayer only if the taxpayer has made a valid election under I.R.C. § 475(f) by complying with the requirements of Rev. Proc. 99-17 and is required to change its method of accounting to comply with the election.

[272] Stock will not be a security if I.R.C. §1032 prevents the taxpayer from recognizing gain or loss with respect to the stock. Reg. §1.475(c)-2(a)(1).

[273] A REMIC residual interest will not be treated as a security. Reg. §1.475(c)-2(a)(3).

[274] This is to be contrasted with the narrower provision contained in I.R.C. §165(g)(2)(C).

[275] Reg. §1.475(c)-2(a)(2). However, the Eighth Circuit and the Tenth Circuit have held to the contrary. In *Security State Bank v. Commissioner*, 214 F.3d 1254 (10th Cir. 2000), *aff'g* 111 T.C. 210, the court said that the phrase used to define "short term obligation" for purposes of §1281—"any bond, debenture, note, certificate, or other evidence of indebtedness"—appears throughout the Code to describe investment activity. In stark contrast, "When Congress wants to refer to lending transactions, it uses the terms 'loan' and 'made.'" *See also* *Security Bank Minnesota v. Commissioner*, 994 F.2d 432 (8th Cir. 1993).

based on the price of oil, wheat, or other commodity, is not an "equity notional principal contract;"[276]

5. Evidence of an interest in, or a derivative financial instrument in, any security described in 1, 2, 3, or 4 above, or any currency, including any option, forward contract, short position, and any similar financial instrument in such a security or currency.[277] This category of securities does not include any contract that meets the definition of a "section 1256 contract" or any regulated futures contract, foreign currency contract, nonequity option, or dealer equity option.[278] However, it does include an agreement with a prospective seller of loans to acquire a specified principal amount of loans for future delivery by a specified future date.[279]

6. Position which:
   (a) is not a security described in 1, 2, 3, 4, or 5 above,
   (b) is a hedge with respect to such a security,[280] and
   (c) is clearly identified in the dealer's records as being described as a position before the close of the day on which it was acquired or entered into (or such other time as the IRS may by regulations prescribe).[281]

Unlike under prior law, not only securities in which a bank "deals" will be subject to the dealer rules, but also any security not properly identified by a dealer as meeting one of the exceptions to the mark-to-market rules will be subject to mark-to-market.[282] Although a dealer in one type of security (*e.g.*, government securities) is not permitted to inventory other securities (*e.g.*, non-governmental securities) that it purchases for speculation or investment, it may elect to subject them to the Code section 475 mark-to-market rules.[283] A dealer can do this by simply failing to identify the security as subject to one of the exemptions. However, a dealer is prohibited from including in its securities for purposes of Code section 475 the stock of corporations it organizes and owns[284] because this type of investment is excluded from the definition of a Code section 475 security. Any other security with respect to which gain or loss will not be

---

[276] Explanation of Senate Finance Committee revenue provisions as submitted to the Budget Committee on June 23, 1993 (S.1134), § 8223, page 277.

[277] I.R.C. § 475(c)(3); Reg. § 1.475(c)-2.

[278] I.R.C. § 1256(b). These types of instruments are subject to mark-to-market rules contained in § 1256.

[279] PLR 199935017, May 28, 1999.

[280] For purposes of this provision, a "hedge" is any position which reduces the dealers risk of interest rate or price changes or currency fluctuations, including any position which is reasonably expected to become a hedge within 60 days after the acquisition of the position. I.R.C. § 475(c)(3). The special character rule of Code section 475, rather than the special character rule contained in Code section 1256(a), will apply to any Code section 1256 contract that is a hedge of a security to which Code section 475 applies.

[281] I.R.C. § 475(c)(2)(F).

[282] *Factor v. Commissioner*, 60-2 U.S.T.C. ¶ 9551, 281 F.2d 100 (9th. Cir. 1960), *cert. denied*, 364 U.S. 933 (1961). For this reason, the I.R.C. § 475 rules are referred to as being over inclusive and they can result, if elected, in nearly all assets held by a bank being subject to the mark-to-market rules.

[283] *R.O. Holton & Co. v. Commissioner*, 44 B.T.A. 202, Dec. 11,774 (1941).

[284] *Appeals of Franklin Brown and Otto Thomen*, 9 B.T.A. 965, Dec. 3258 (1927).

recognized because of the nonrecognition rule of Code section 1032 also is excluded from the Code section 475 definition of a security.[285]

(a) ***Securitization Transactions***

In recent years, sales of mortgage loans by banks have increased dramatically. Additionally, banks are becoming active in pooling other loans, such as credit card loans, lease receivables and automobile loans. The process of pooling loans and either selling the pool outright, selling interests in the pool, or borrowing and pledging the pool of receivables as collateral is commonly referred to as "securitization." Securitization is viewed by banks as a means of generating fee income, removing assets with credit or interest rate risk from the balance sheet, or obtaining funds to finance additional loans. In the situation of mortgage-backed securities, the purchaser and packager is often the Government National Mortgage Association ("Ginnie Mae") or Federal Home Loan Mortgage Corporation ("Freddie Mac") and the federal government or a private corporation acts as guarantor.[286] For other types of securitization transactions, trust are employed, including grantor trusts.

If the transaction is actually a sale and not merely a collateralized borrowing, the loans that are securitized will be treated as securities sold to customers by a dealer in securities. Regulations provide that the exceptions for securities held for investment or securities not held for sale will apply to interests that the taxpayer expects to contribute to a trust or other entity, including a REMIC, only if each of the interests received in the exchange, regardless of whether the interest is a security for purpose of the mark-to-market rules, is expected to be held for sale or held for investment.[287] The securities that are contributed to the trust are often mortgage loans, and the interests that are received in the exchange may be an owner's interest or a creditor's interest.

If the securitization transaction is a taxable transaction, the identification of the securities transferred does not control the identification of the interest received.[288] Thus, if the ownership interest of the security received is not treated as the ownership of the securities transferred to a trust in a taxable transaction, the security received may be identified as qualifying for one of the Code section 475(b) exceptions to the mark-to-market rules. However, if the transaction is not a recognition event, the identification of the security received will be the same as the securities transferred.

---

[285] Reg. § 1.475(c)-2(a)(1).

[286] *See* "Going Off the Balance Sheet," by Sylvester Johnson and Amelia A. Murphy, *Economic Review*, Federal Reserve Bank of Atlanta, September/October 1987; *See also* "Understanding Loan Sales," by Sean Becketti, *Financial Letter*, Federal Reserve Bank of Kansas City, April 1987; "Some Issues in Asset Securitizations by National Banks," *Issues in Bank Regulation*, Winter 1987, pp. 5-14; "Loan Sales: Another Step in the Evolution of the Short-Term Credit Market," by Sean Becketti and Charles S. Morris, *Economic Review*, Federal Reserve Bank of Kansas City, November 1987.

[287] Reg. § 1.475(b)-3. On December 24, 1996, the Treasury Department issued final regulations under I.R.C. § 475 (61 Fed. Reg. 67715). The final regulations generally adopt temporary regulations issued in 1993 (TD 8505, 58 Fed. Reg. 68747) as revised by proposed regulations issued in 1995 (60 Fed. Reg. 397) and 1996 (61 Fed. Reg. 31474). Certain sections of the 1995 proposed regulations that were not adopted remain proposed.

[288] Prop. Reg. § 1.475(b)-3(b).

If a taxpayer sells mortgages and establishes a book reserve for losses with respect to its repurchase and indemnity obligations that may arise from a breach of the mortgage sale contract's warranty and representations, the obligations may not be treated as "securities" for purposes of the Code section 475 mark-to-market rules.[289] The warranty and representations are standard provisions in mortgage sales contracts and not severable instruments that may qualify as securities. They are material and integral to the sales contracts, not independent financial instruments, investments, positions or bets on the value of those mortgages. Thus, unlike the value of options or similar derivative financial instruments, the value of the obligation is generally driven by non-market forces including things like discovery of a breach, failure to cure, negotiations and the quality of appeal arguments.[290] More generally, executory sales contracts that embody a provision that triggers an obligation by the taxpayer, is not treated as a severable instrument that would qualify as a "security."[291]

(b) *Other Definitions of Securities*

The Code contains several other definitions of the term "security" that could be contrasted with the Code section 475 definition.[292] For example, Code section 1236 provides that a "security" is:

> [A]ny share of stock in any corporation, certificate of stock or interest in any corporation, note, bond, debenture, or evidence of indebtedness, or any evidence of an interest in or right to subscribe to or purchase any of the foregoing.[293]

This definition is among the broader definitions of "security" found in the Code.

For purposes of identifying "worthless securities" deductible under Code section 165, instruments qualifying as debt securities are limited to ones issued by a corporation, or by a government or political subdivision thereof, *with interest coupons or in registered form*.[294] Code section 582(a) defines a "security" as a "debt which is evidenced by a security as defined in Code section 165(g)(2)(C)."[295] Further, the Code section 361 definition of securities generally encompasses only debt instruments that have a term in excess of five years.[296] Under Code section 368, a short (less than five-year) maturity date may disqualify an instrument

---

[289] CCA 201529006, April 8, 2015.

[290] *W.A. Drake v. Commissioner*, 145 F.2d 365 (10th Cir. 1944).

[291] *United States Freight Co. v. U.S.*, 422 F.2d 887 (Ct. Cl. 1970).

[292] The term *securities* also is defined in 15 U.S.C. §78a-78kk for purposes of the Securities Exchange Act of 1934. Some commentators believe that loan participations are *securities* for the purpose of the Act. *Loan Participations: Are They Securities?* Scholl and Weaver, Florida State Univ. L. Rev., Vol. 10:197, p. 215.

[293] I.R.C. §1236(c).

[294] I.R.C. §165(g)(2)(C).

[295] Note that for purposes of determining a bank's loan loss deduction under I.R.C. §585, all securities defined under I.R.C. §165(g) are excluded from the definition of "loans." Reg. §1.585-2(e)(2). Note also that in certain instances mortgages acquired or even originated may fit the definition of a "security" for purposes of I.R.C. §1236.

[296] *Lloyd-Smith v. Commissioner*, CA-2, U.S.T.C. ¶9167, 116 F.2d 642, 644 (1st Cir. 1941), *cert. denied*, 313 U.S. 588 (1941). A similar meaning of the term securities is used for purposes of I.R.C. §354. *See also, Pinellas Ice & Cold Storage Co. v. Commissioner*, 33 U.S.T.C. ¶1023, 287 U.S. 462 (1933).

from being treated as a security.[297] These definitions of the term "security" will not be controlling for purposes of Code section 475.

§ 4.4.8 Measuring Mark-to-Market Gain or Loss

Code section 475(a) requires a security that is subject to the mark-to-market rules be either "included in inventory at its fair market value," or if it is not inventory, then it shall be treated as "sold for its fair market value on the last business day of . . . [the] taxable year." The Treasury Department has stated that ease of valuation is not relevant in determining whether a security should be marked to market.[298]

Adjustments to any gain or loss resulting from a mark-to-market in a prior taxable year must take into account the current year's recognized mark-to-market gain or loss.[299] The IRS conceded that securities do not have to be valued on an individual basis.[300] Thus, it would be likely that pools of homogeneous securities that are subject to the mark-to-market valuation rules can be valued in the aggregate.

Code section 7701(g) applies to determine the year-end mark-to-market gain or loss on securities. As such, the fair market value of securities shall not be less than the amount of any nonrecourse indebtedness to which the securities may be subject.[301]

(a) *Bad Debt Deductions*

Proposed regulations have been issued that provide rules for marking a partially or wholly worthless debt to market.[302] These rules coordinate the mark-to-market rules with the bad debt rules under the Code.

In general, the amount of gain or loss recognized under Code section 475(a)(2) when a debt instrument is marked to market generally is the difference between the adjusted basis and the fair market value of the debt adjusted for prior marks. Under the proposed regulations, if a debt becomes partially or wholly worthless during a taxable year, the amount of any gain or loss required to be taken into account under Code section 475(a) is determined using a basis that is adjusted for the worthless portion of the debt.

The basis of the mark-to-market debt is treated as having been reduced by the amount of any book or regulatory charge-off (including the establishment of

[297] *Cf.* the definitions in I.R.C. §§ 165(g)(2) and 1236(c). *See also Cortland Specialty Co. v. Commissioner*, 32 U.S.T.C. ¶ 980, 60 F.2d 937 (2d Cir. 1932), *cert. denied*, 288 U.S. 599, (1932); *Pinellas Ice & Cold Storage Co. v. Commissioner*, 33 U.S.T.C. ¶ 1023, 287 U.S. 462, (1933); and the discussion at ¶ 203.01, 501, *et seq.* I.R.C. § 351 was amended by the Omnibus Budget Reconciliation Act of 1989, Pub. L. No. 101-239, § 7203(a), 103 Stat. 2106 (1989) to delete the reference to "securities."

[298] "Explanation of Provisions" accompanying final regulations under I.R.C. § 475, 61 Fed. Reg. 67715, 67719 (December 24, 1996).

[299] I.R.C. § 475(a).

[300] FSA 199909007, March 5, 1999.

[301] CCA 201507019, June 30, 2014. In that pronouncement, the IRS also stated that even if I.R.C. § 7701(g) does not apply to I.R.C § 475, the principles expressed by the Supreme Court in *Commissioner v. Tufts*, 461 U.S. 300 (1983) and in *Crane v. Commissioner*, 331 U.S. 1 (1947) require a dealer in securities to determine year-end mark-to-market gain or loss on securities to include in the amount realized the amount of nonrecourse indebtedness to which the securities are subject.

[302] Prop. Reg. § 1.475(a)-1(f). 60 FR 397-01.

a specific allowance for a loan loss) for which a deduction could have been taken, without regard to whether any portion of the charge-off is, in fact, deducted or charged to a tax reserve for bad debts. The difference between this adjusted basis and the fair market value of the debt is the amount of gain or loss to be taken into account under Code section 475(a)(2). Thus, if the debt is wholly worthless, its basis would be reduced to zero and no gain or loss would be taken into account under Code section 475(a)(2).

Computing the mark-to-market adjustment as if the debt's basis had been adjusted to reflect worthlessness preserves a taxpayer's ability to postpone claiming a deduction for partial worthlessness until the debt becomes wholly worthless.[303] To the extent that a debt has been previously charged off, mark-to-market gain is treated as a recovery.

The rules that are provided for bad debts in the proposed regulations do not apply to debts accounted for by a dealer as inventory under Code section 475(a)(1). Although it is possible for a debt that is in inventory to become partially worthless prior to sale, the likelihood or frequency of such an occurrence is difficult to ascertain given the speed with which inventory is sold.

When dealing with illiquid securities, or securities for which there is not an established securities market, fair market value is often difficult to determine. Perhaps, for this reason, the legislative history of Code section 475 provides that "the conferees expect that the Treasury Department will authorize the use of valuation methods that will alleviate unnecessary compliance burdens for taxpayers and clearly reflect income for Federal income tax purposes."[304]

Trying to determine fair market value can be a frustratingly elusive goal, as the taxpayer in *JPMorgan Chase & Co.* discovered.[305] In that case, the Seventh Circuit determined that the Tax Court properly concluded that the taxpayer's method of valuing its interest swaps did not produce a fair market value. However, once the Tax Court rejected the taxpayer's valuation method, the Seventh Circuit found that the Tax Court was required, under Code section 446, to defer to the IRS's valuation method unless it was clearly unlawful or plainly arbitrary. According to the Seventh Circuit, the Tax Court erred when it examined whether the IRS's method produced a fair market value of the interest swaps. The Tax Court's determination that the IRS's method did not clearly reflect income was vacated and remanded for the Tax Court to conduct the proper analysis under the arbitrary and unlawful standard.

(b) *Safe Harbor Rule*

For financial accounting purposes, valuation criteria for securities is provided in several pronouncements. However, the "fair value" of a security for financial accounting purposes may not always be accepted for federal income tax purposes. For example, it has been held that interest rate swaps must be valued

---

[303] *See* discussion of Involuntary Charge-off Rule in Chapter 10 that permits deferral of certain bad debt deductions.

[304] H. Conf. Rep. No. 103-213 at 616 (1993).

[305] *JPMorgan Chase & Co. v. Commissioner*, 458 F3d 564 (7th Cir. 2007), *aff'g in part, vac'g in part and reman'g* 120 TC 174.

at their fair market value and not at fair value under generally accepted accounting principles.[306] Nonetheless, to reduce the administrative burden the Treasury Department has issued regulations and a revenue procedure under Code section 475 that set forth a safe harbor for valuing securities and commodities that permit the use of financial accounting values.[307] It is unclear whether financial institutions headquartered abroad may use the safe harbor valuation regulations.[308]

The safe harbor regulations generally permit eligible taxpayers to elect to have the values that are reported for eligible positions on certain financial statements treated as the fair market values reported for those eligible positions for purposes of Code section 475, but only if certain conditions are met.[309] To qualify for the safe harbor, the regulations provide that a financial accounting method must satisfy four "basic" requirements[310] and three "limitations."[311] The I.R.S. has issued a Field Directive instructing examining agents not to challenge mark-to-market values reported on qualified financial statements that are used to satisfy valuation requirements of Code section 475. Taxpayers that have used qualified financial statement values for tax valuation are required to sign and complete an "Industry Directive on I.R.C. § 475 Valuation Certification Statement."[312]

The first of the four basic requirements is for the taxpayer to mark eligible positions to market through valuations made as of the last business day of each taxable year. Second, the taxpayer must recognize into income on the income statement any gain or loss from marking eligible positions to market. Third, the taxpayer must recognize into income on the income statement any gain or loss on disposition of an eligible position as if a year-end mark occurred immediately before the disposition. Fourth, the taxpayer must arrive at fair value in accordance with U.S. GAAP. Under GAAP, valuation criteria is provided in several pronouncements dealing with securities.[313]

The three limitations are designed to ensure minimal divergence from fair market value. Under the first limitation, the financial accounting method must

---

[306] *J.P. Morgan Chase & Co. v. Commissioner*, 458 F.3d 564 (7th Cir. 2006).

[307] Reg. § 475(a)-4; Rev. Proc. 2007-41, 2007-26 I.R.B. 1492, June 12, 2007. The legislative history of IRC § 475 indicates that the Secretary may issue regulations to permit the use of valuation methodologies that reduce the administrative burden of compliance on taxpayers but that nevertheless clearly reflect income for federal income tax purposes. H.R. Rep. No. 213, 103d Cong., 1st Sess. 616 (1993), 1993-3 C.B. 494.

[308] The IRS has requested comments regarding the possible expansion of the safe harbor valuation regulations so that financial institutions headquartered outside the United States can qualify to make the safe-harbor election. Notice 2008-71, 2008-35 I.R.B. 462, August 12, 2008.

[309] Reg. § 1.475(a)-4.

[310] Reg. § 1.475(a)-4(d)(2).

[311] Reg. § 1.475(a)-4(d)(3). The regulations apply to the valuation of securities on or after July 6, 2011. 76 FR 39281.

[312] See the Certification Statement attached to the I.R.C. § 475 Field Directive in Appendix § A.23.

[313] For, example, Statement of Financial Accounting Standards No. 65, "Accounting for Certain Mortgage Banking Activities," four criteria for valuing the securities. *See also*, The Investment Company Act of 1940, 35 Fed. Reg. 19986, § 2(a)(4) provision that regulated investment company portfolios should be stated, generally, at fair value on a daily basis, and Accounting Series Release 118 which sets forth several valuation guidelines for arriving at value for purposes of the Investment Company Act, Ch. 686, vol. 54, stat. 789, Aug. 22, 1940. Release 118 was issued Dec. 1970, but rescinded on May 17, 1982. *See also*, Statements 12 and 115.

not result in values at or near the bid or ask values, even if the use of bid or ask values is permissible in accordance with U.S. GAAP. Under the second limitation, if the method of valuation consists of determining the present value of projected cash flows from an eligible position or positions, then the method must not take into account any cash flows of income or expense that are attributable to a period or time before the valuation date. Under the third limitation, no cost or risk may be accounted for more than once, either directly or indirectly. To illustrate this limitation, the preamble to the regulations provide the following illustration:

> "For example, a financial accounting method that allows a special adjustment for credit risk generally satisfies this limitation. It would not satisfy this limitation, however, if it computed the present value of projected cash flows using a discount rate that takes into account any amount of credit risk that is also taken into account by the special adjustment. Thus, if a dealer in securities enters into an interest rate swap contract with a counterparty with a AA/aa rating, taking credit enhancement and netting agreements into account, then the dealer cannot take a special adjustment to the value of the contract for all of the risk between a counterparty with a risk-free rating and the actual counterparty if the dealer determines the present value of projected cash flows from the contract using a mid-market swap curve based upon the LIBOR AA rate. The Treasury Department and the IRS understand, however, that there may be degrees of credit quality within an established rating level, such as AA/aa, and that valuation methodologies used currently may reflect these nuances in credit quality. Accordingly, a credit adjustment reflecting these nuances may satisfy this limitation."

Only three categories of financial statements qualify under the regulations for the safe harbor.[314] In their order of priority, from highest to lowest, they are: those financial statements that must be filed with the Securities and Exchange Commission (SEC), such as the 10-K and the Annual Statement to Shareholders; those financial statements that must be provided to the federal government or any of its agencies other than the IRS, such as the Federal Reserve or the Office of the Comptroller of the Currency; and certified audited financial statements that are provided to creditors to make lending decisions, that are provided to equity holders to evaluate their investment, or that are provided for other substantial non-tax purposes and are reasonably anticipated to be directly relied on for the purposes for which the statements were created.

To elect the safe harbor rules, financial statement values must be adjusted to reflect the appropriate arm's length pricing of inter-branch transactions as of their origination date that may be called for by Code section 482.[315] The safe harbor is available to any taxpayer subject to Code section 475, and it must apply to every security position and every commodity position subject to mark-to-market under Code section 475.

Revenue Procedure 2007-41 designates eligible positions under Regulation §1.475(a)-4(g) for those taxpayers who have made the safe harbor election.[316] With respect to a dealer in securities, as defined in section 475(c)(1), which is an

314 Reg. §1.475(a)-4(h).

315 Reg. §1.475(a)-4(e).

316 Rev. Proc. 2007-41, 2007-1 C.B. 1492.

eligible taxpayer described in Regulation § 1.475(a)-4(c)(1), such eligible position includes any "security" as defined in Code § 475(c)(2) and the regulations thereunder. With respect to a dealer in commodities, as defined in Code section 475(e), that is subject to an election under Code section 475(e), which is an eligible taxpayer described in § 1.475(a)-4(c)(2), such eligible position includes any commodity within the meaning of Code § 475(e)(2) and any regulations thereunder.

(c) *Fair Market Value*

Fair market value ("FMV") has been historically defined in regulations as "the price at which the property would change hands between a willing buyer and a willing seller, neither being under any compulsion to buy or to sell and both having reasonable knowledge of relevant facts."[317] The Courts have elaborated on this general definition by adding that FMV "must be determined with respect to the particular property at the [valuation date] subject to any conditions or restrictions on marketability."[318] The identities of the buyer and seller, or donor and donee, should not be considered in determining FMV,[319] and the hypothetical "willing buyer" should be a member of the general public and not a particularly motivated buyer. Property is to be valued at the price it would have sold for if offered for sale in a prudent manner for a reasonable period of time.[320] Because fair market value is fact specific, Courts emphasize that the entire record must be considered.[321] Valuation is an approximation that should be derived from all the evidence.[322] Courts exercise broad discretion in determining what factors are most important to the valuation calculation.[323]

Regulation section 20.2031-2 outlines a fairly specific method for determining the FMV of stocks and bonds. If a market for the security exists, then FMV should be the "mean between the highest and lowest selling price on the valuation date of actual sales of identical securities."[324] The market will be deemed to take into account all relevant factors,[325] even if the market price is based on misrepresentations. If there are no sales on the valuation date, then a weighted average should be taken of sales within a reasonable time before and after the valuation date.[326] If there are no actual sales available then the bona fide bid and asking prices within a reasonable time of the valuation date may be used,[327] and if these do not accurately reflect the FMV then reasonable modifica-

---

317 Reg. § 20.2031(b) (as amended in 1965); Reg. § 25.2512-1(as amended in 1992).

318 *Cooley v. Commissioner*, 33 T.C. 223, 225 (1959), *aff'd per curiam*, 283 F.2d 945 (2d Cir. 1960).

319 *Estate of Bright v. United States*, 658 F.2d 999 (5th Cir. 1981); *Propstra v. United States*, 680 F.2d 1248 (9th Cir. 1982); *Andrews v. Commissioner*, 79 T.C. 938, 955-56 (1982); Rev. Rul. 93-12, 1993-1 C.B. 202.

320 *Bull v. Smith*, 119 F.2d 490, 492 (2d Cir. 1941).

321 Reg. § 20.2031-1(b). "All relevant facts and elements of value . . . shall be considered." *Lio v. Commissioner*, 85 T.C. 56 (1985), *aff'd sub nom, Orth v. Commissioner*, 813 F.2d 837 (7th Cir. 1987).

322 *Helvering v. Safe Deposit Co.*, 316 U.S. 56 (1942); *Silverman v. Commissioner*, 538 F.2d 927, 933 (2d Cir. 1976), *aff'g* T.C. Memo 1974-285.

323 *Colonial Fabrics, Inc. v. Commissioner*, 202 F.2d 105, 107 (2d Cir. 1953) ("Finding market value is, after all, something for judgement, experience and reason.").

324 Reg. § 20.2031-2(b).

325 *Estate of Gilford v. Commissioner*, 88 T.C. 38, 55 (1987).

326 Reg. § 20.2031-2(b).

327 Reg. § 20.2031(c).

tion will be allowed.[328] However, in *United States v. Cartwright*,[329] the Supreme Court held that the FMV of a mutual fund should be the redemption price and not the asking price at which the item could be purchased from the fund as is required by the regulations.[330] Generally, discount for a lack of marketability and for minority shareholder interest is considered as well in determining whether the number of shares being valued represents a controlling interest in the corporation.[331] However, the legislative history of Code section 475 indicates that blockage discount should not affect valuation.[332]

In the absence of comparable sales or bona fide asked prices, the following factors are often considered when valuing securities:[333]

- For debt obligations:
  1. The soundness of the security,
  2. The interest yield,
  3. The date of maturity,
  4. The sufficiency of the collateral.[334]
- For stocks:
  1. The corporation's net worth,
  2. The corporation's prospective earning power,
  3. The corporation's dividend paying capacity.
- For both stocks and debt obligations:
  1. Goodwill,
  2. Economic outlook of the industry,
  3. Management of the corporation,
  4. The size of the block and degree of control it represents,
  5. Similar corporation's stock value,[335]
  6. Cash flow and earnings record,[336]
  7. Recent sales, growth and earnings history, and dividends,[337]
  8. Total equity in its assets divided by the number of shares outstanding,[338]

---

[328] Reg. § 20.2031-2(e). For example, the size of the block and whether the block is a controlling interest.

[329] *United States v. Cartwright*, 411 U.S. 546 (1973).

[330] Reg. § 20.2031-8(b).

[331] *White v. Commissioner*, TC Memo 1976-382, 35 T.C.M. 1726 (1976).

[332] H. Conf. Rep. 103-213, 103rd Cong., 1st Sess. (1993) reprinted in 7A U.S.C.C.A.N. 1302, page 613.

[333] Reg. § 20.2031-2(f).

[334] Reg. § 20.2031-4.

[335] Reg. § 20.2031-2(h).

[336] *Lippmann v. Commissioner*, TC Memo 1965-73, 24 T.C.M. 399 (1965).

[337] *Makoff v. Commissioner*, TC Memo 1967-13, 26 T.C.M. 83 (1967).

[338] *Stratton v. Commissioner*, 70-1 USTC ¶ 9316, 422 F.2d 872 (2d Cir. 1969). *But see, Estate of Bennet v. Commissioner*, TC Memo 1993-34, 65 T.C.M. 1816 (1993) (Court was reluctant to consider the asset accumulation method without adjusting or discounting for the nature of the business, the earning and dividend history, management, and prospects for growth.).

9. Past sales of stock, net asset value, earnings per share, potential future earnings,[339]
10. Speculative nature and growth potential.[340]

There is no set weight given to each of the factors as they must be evaluated on a case by case basis,[341] and the factors set forth above are not always consistently followed by courts.

For complex instruments, such as unusual derivatives, certain dealers in financial products have installed specially designed computer software packages. On audit, the IRS has had to rely on the valuations these systems produced because the IRS lacks similar sophisticated programs. The IRS had an arrangement with the Los Alamos National Laboratory to develop valuation models for such derivative instruments. However, the IRS announced in late 1997 that it decided to temporarily suspend the project. It had been expected that the IRS would present a limited version of computer software that could be used to value sophisticated financial instruments.

The legislative history of Code section 475 provides that the Uniform Capitalization Rules contained in Code section 263(A) and the more specific rules contained in Code section 263(g) relating to "straddles" will not apply to any security subject to the Code section 475 mark-to-market rules.[342]

§ 4.4.9 Characterizing Mark-to-Market Gains or Losses

(a) *General Rule*

Code section 475(d)(3) provides that, as a general rule, mark-to-market gain or loss shall be treated as ordinary gain or loss. However, as a practical matter, the exceptions contained in that paragraph result in any gain or loss being characterized as ordinary or capital in accordance with general characterization rules prescribed in Code section 1221.[343] Thus, ordinary income or loss characterization will occur if the security is inventory in the hands of the dealer.[344] Moreover, ordinary income or loss characterization will occur if the security is not inventory in the hands of the dealer, but the security is property held by the taxpayer primarily for sale to customers in the ordinary course of the taxpayer's trade or business.[345] Ordinary income characterization cannot be avoided by disposing of a security before the close of any taxable year.[346] Conversely, if a

---

[339] *White v. Commissioner*, TC Memo 1976-382, 35 T.C.M. 1726 (1976).

[340] *Gatlin v. Commissioner*, 85-1 USTC ¶9237, 754 F.2d 921 (11th Cir. 1985).

[341] *Messing v. Commissioner*, 48 T.C. 502, 512 (1967).

[342] H. Conf. Rep. 103-213, 103rd Cong., 1st Sess. (1993) *reprinted in* 7A U.S.C.C.A.N. 1302, page 613. Costs to which the uniform rules apply include direct costs of producing or acquiring property and an allocable portion of indirect costs. Indirect costs are expenditures for general administration, pensions, stock bonuses, profit sharing, annuities or other deferred compensation, etc. (The Senate Finance Committee Report states that "[t]he uniform capitalization rules will be patterned after the rules applicable to extended period long-term contracts, set forth in the final regulations issued under § 451." S. Rep. No. 313, 99th Cong., 2d Sess. 141 (1986). Since the securities inventories of bank taxpayers typically turn over many times within the taxable year, the impact of capitalization requirements should be minimal.

[343] I.R.C. §§ 475(d)(3) and 1221(1). *See* discussion of intercompany transactions at § 4.2.

[344] I.R.C. § 1221(1). *See also* I.R.C. § 1236.

[345] *Id.*

[346] I.R.C. § 475(d)(3)(ii).

security is held by a dealer for investment and has never been held in connection with the taxpayer's activities as a dealer in securities, then the security is likely to be treated as a capital asset if properly identified as such.[347]

If a security is subject to the mark-to-market rules because it was not identified as excepted under Code section 475(b)(1)(A), (B), or (C), and not because it is one in which the dealer inventories or holds for sale to customers in the ordinary course of its trade or business, the character of mark-to-market gain or loss will probably be capital. However, for a bank, capital asset treatment may be unavailable for debt securities that are held for investment by reason of Code section 582, which provides that gains or losses on sales of debt securities held by a bank "shall not be considered as gain from the sale or exchange of a capital asset."[348] Equity instruments sold or exchanged by a bank acting as an investor could produce gains or losses that may be characterized as gain or loss from the sale or exchange of a capital asset.[349] The application of Code section 582 is likely, although not certain. On its face the section applies when there is a "sale or exchange" of a debt instrument. Code section 475 provides its rules will apply "as if such security were sold." Thus, if there is a deemed sale under the Code section 475, there should be a sufficient "sale or exchange" for purposes of Code section 582. Of course, the Code section 582 rules have no application to a taxpayer other than a bank. Any member of a bank holding company group that is not a bank faces the specter of capital loss treatment on any security in which it does not deal. Thus, a Section 20 Subsidiary would not be entitled to the special bank rule. A dealer that is not a bank, would not be entitled to ordinary loss treatment on securities if it identifies the security as held for investment.[350]

Any gain or loss allocable to a period during which the security is a hedge with respect to a security that is subject to the mark-to-market rule will not be covered by the automatic ordinary income rule, nor will any security that is a hedge with respect to a position, right to income, or liability that is not a security in the hands of the taxpayer.[351] Further, if the security is improperly identified, the character of any gain or loss will depend upon the proper classification.[352] A swap between two members of a consolidated group is an intercompany transaction. The gain in one entity and loss in the other normally offset each other. However, if one member is subject to Code section 475 and the other is not, there could be a mismatch because the affiliates may be subject to different timing and characterization rules.[353]

A security held by a bank that becomes worthless during the taxable year is not treated as a Code section 165 security loss, but is deductible as a Code section 166 bad debt.[354] For this rule, a security has a narrow definition. It shall include

---

[347] Reg. § 1.475(d)-1. For a bank, a debt instrument that may be classified as a capital asset will be entitled to ordinary treatment. I.R.C. § 582.

[348] I.R.C. § 582.

[349] I.R.C. § 1221. *Cf.* I.R.C. § 108(e)(7) for a recapture rule that applies to equity instruments.

[350] I.R.C. § 1236. *Stephens v. United States*, 464 F.2d 53 (8th Cir. 1970), *cert. denied*, 409 U.S. 1118 (1973).

[351] I.R.C. § 475(d)(3)(B). Regulations have been issued under I.R.C. § 1221 which have the effect of characterizing gains and losses on hedging transactions as ordinary. Reg. § 1.1221-2. *See also*, PLR 9743013, July 23, 1997.

[352] I.R.C. §§ 475(d)(3)(B)(ii) and (iii).

[353] Reg. § 1.1502-13.

[354] I.R.C. § 582(a).

only a bond, debenture, note, or certificate or other evidence of indebtedness, issued by a corporation or by a government or political subdivision thereof, with interest coupons or in registered form.[355] By shifting the debt instrument to Code section 166, a loss deduction may be taken by a bank before the instrument is disposed. Partial charge-offs are allowed under Code section 166, but not under Code section 165. Nonbank taxpayers holding "securities" must defer losses because they are allowed only under Code section 165.

(b) *Bad Debt Deductions*

For purposes of determining the amount of mark-to-market gain or loss, the mark-to-market rules must be coordinated with the bad debt deduction rules.[356] Proposed regulations provide that the tax basis of a debt must first be adjusted for worthlessness that occurred during the taxable year or during any previous taxable year.[357] Thus, if a debt has been charged off in part or in whole during the taxable year, the debt's tax basis must be reduced to the extent of the charge-off. If a debt is wholly worthless, its basis is reduced to zero, regardless of the amount charged off.

Any mark-to-market gain, determined after taking into account the basis adjusted for worthlessness, is first treated as a recovery on a bad debt to the extent of any basis reduction for worthlessness. If a bank is on the direct charge-off method, the recovery will be treated as a direct credit to income. A large bank that is in the process of recapturing its reserve will also treat the recovery as a direct credit to income. However, a large bank that has elected the cut-off method for reserve recapture will treat any recovery with respect to pre-disqualification year loans as a credit to its reserve, but recoveries with respect to loans made on or after the first day of its disqualification year will be direct credits to income.[358] A bank on the reserve method treats the recovery as a credit to its bad debt reserve.

§4.4.10 Tax-Free Acquisitions

In general, the mark-to-market rules will apply only to changes in value of the security occurring after an acquisition.[359] Thus, if a dealer's tax basis is determined, in whole or in part, by reference to the basis of that security in the hands of the person from whom the security is acquired, mark-to-market gain or loss is determined by comparing the fair market value of the security at the date of acquisition to the fair market value of the security at subsequent year-ends.[360] Gain or loss will be computed similarly with respect to any security where the dealer's tax basis is determined, in whole or in part, by reference to other property held at any time by the dealer.[361] With respect to built-in gain or loss,

---

[355] I.R.C. §§582(a) and 165(g)(2)(C). Rev. Rul. 57-167, 1957-1 C.B. 294.

[356] FSA 199909007, March 5, 1999.

[357] Prop. Reg. §1.475(a)-1(f). *See* discussion at Ch. 10, §10.4 for additional affects of mark-to-market rules on bad debt deductions. Banks that have made the conformity election may have to rely on the exclusionary rule of Reg. §1.166-2(d)(3)(iii)(B)(3) to deduct any mark down as a bad debt.

[358] I.R.C. §585(c)(4); Reg. §1.585-7.

[359] Reg. §1.475(a)-3(b)(1).

[360] Reg. §1.475(a)-3(a)(1).

[361] Reg. §1.475(a)-3(a)(2).

the general rules applicable thereto will apply without regard to the mark-to-market rules.[362]

§4.4.11 Other Mark-to-Market Rules

Code section 1256 contracts are subject to the mark-to-market rules contained in that section and are not subject to the Code section 475 mark-to-market rules.[363] The Code section 475 mark-to-market rules and not the Code section 1256 mark-to-market rules apply to hedging transactions.[364]

As a general rule, any gain or loss that is recognized when a Code section 1256 contract is marked-to-market under the special rules contained in that section is treated as a short-term capital gain or loss to the extent of 40 percent of such gain or loss, and long-term capital gain or loss to the extent of 60 percent of such gain or loss.[365]

A Code Section 1256 contract is defined as any regulated futures contract, foreign currency contract, nonequity option, dealer equity option, and dealer securities futures contract, but only if the securities futures contract or option on such contract is a dealer securities futures contract. An option, including an over-the-counter option that is a private contract not traded on a regulated exchange is a Code section 1256 contract, as are forward contracts and future contracts.[366] A forward foreign currency contract is a bilateral contract between a seller and a buyer that obligates the seller, at the time of signing, to settle his obligation to perform by either delivering the currency or making cash settlement. A futures contract has the same characteristics as a forward contract, but it is highly standardized and traded on a regulated exchange. A foreign currency option is a unilateral contract that does not require delivery or settlement unless and until the option is exercised by the holder.[367] A Code section 1256 Contract does not include any interest rate swap, currency swap, basis swap, interest rate cap, interest rate floor, commodity swap, equity swap, equity index swap, credit default swap, or similar agreement.[368]

§4.4.12 Change of Accounting Method

A dealer in securities that is required to and does change its method of accounting to comply with the mark-to-market rules will be treated as having initiated the change and as having received the consent of the IRS to the change.[369] This rule extends only to a change in method that was effected by a taxpayer who (1) became a dealer for the tax year that includes December 31,

[362] I.R.C. §382; Reg. §1.1502-13.

[363] I.R.C. §475(c)(1) and (d)(1). Conference Committee Report to Pub. L. No. 103-66 (1993).

[364] I.R.C. §§ 475(c)(1)(F) and 1256(e)(1).

[365] I.R.C. §1256(a)(3). Congress enacted I.R.C. §1256 as part of the Economic Recovery Tax Act of 1981 ("ERTA"), Pub. L. No. 97-34, sec. 503(a), 95 Stat. 327. As originally enacted, the section applied only to regulated futures contracts that required physical delivery of personal property. Section 988(a)(1)(A) and Reg. §1.988-3(a) override the characterization of capital losses specified if I.R.C. §988 also applies.

[366] *Wright v. Commissioner*, 809 F.3d 877 (6th Cir. 2016).

[367] *Summitt v. Commissioner*, 134 T.C. 248 (2010); *Garcia v. Commissioner*, T.C. Memo. 2011-85 (2011).

[368] I.R.C. §1256(b)(2)(B).

[369] Pub. L. No. 103-66 (1993), Act Sec. 13223(c)(2).

1993, by virtue of the passage of P.L. 103-66, and (2) who accounted for securities as a dealer under Code section 475 on its original return for that year.[370]

Once a taxpayer has used the Code section 475 mark-to-market method as its accounting method for securities, the taxpayer may not change that accounting method without obtaining IRS consent. The request must comply with Revenue Procedure 97-27 as modified.[371] For example, if a taxpayer accounts for securities by using the mark-to-market accounting method because the taxpayer made more than negligible sales of securities and in later years makes only negligible sales of securities, the taxpayer must obtain IRS consent to change its method of accounting for securities.[372] Consent for other changes of method to comply with Code section 475, such as election out of an exemption, must be obtained either on a taxpayer-by-taxpayer basis or as part of automatic consent contained in Revenue Procedure 97-43.

For purposes of Code sections 475(e) and 475(f), any taxpayer that makes the election to use the mark-to-market rules is treated as though it changed its method of accounting. Any adjustment required under Code Sec. 481 as a result of this change in accounting is to be taken into account ratably over four tax years. The four-year period begins with the year in which the election is first effective.[373] According to the Conference Committee Report for P.L. 105-34, Congress intended that the special rule pertaining to Code section 481 adjustments applies only to taxpayers that make the mark-to-market election for the tax year that includes the date this provision was enacted into law. Any election made in a subsequent tax year is to be governed by rules and procedures that will be established by the IRS.

§4.5 Security Investment Transactions

§4.5.1 Statement of Financial Accounting Standards No. 115

Statement of Financial Accounting Standards No. 115 (Statement No. 115) addresses the accounting and reporting for investments in equity securities that have a readily determinable fair value and for all investments in debt securities.[374] According to Statement No. 115, an institution is required, at the time of acquisition of the debt or equity security, to classify the security into one of three categories:

1. Held-to-Maturity;
2. Available for sale; or
3. Trading.

An investment is classified as Held-to-Maturity only if the reporting institution has a positive intent and ability to hold the security to maturity. A Trading

[370] Rev. Rul. 97-39, 1997-2 C.B. 62.

[371] Rev. Pro. 97-27 as modified by Rev. Proc. 97-30, Rev. Proc. 2002-19, Rev. Proc. 2002-54, Rev. Proc. 2006-11, and Rev. Proc. 2006-12.

[372] Rev. Rul. 97-39.

[373] Pub. L. No. 103-66 (1993), Act Sec. 1001(d)(4), Pub. L. No. 105-34.

[374] Statement of Financial Accounting Standards No. 115 is dated May 1993. It supersedes Statement No. 12, "Accounting for Certain Marketable Securities."

Security is one that is bought and held for the purpose of selling it in the near term. The objective of the institution in acquiring a Trading Security is to generate a profit on a short-term swing in its market value. As a general rule, mortgage-backed securities that are held for sale in conjunction with mortgage banking activities are classified as Trading Securities.[375] Available for Sale Securities are ones that are not properly classified as either Held-to-Maturity Securities or Trading Securities.

Investments in debt securities and equity securities are measured at fair value in the institution's balance sheet if they are classified as either Trading Securities or Available for Sale Securities. Any unrealized gain or loss from a Trading Security is included in the institution's earnings. Such gains or losses from Available for Sale Securities are reported as a net amount in a separate component of shareholders' equity until the gain or loss is realized.[376]

Statement No. 115 provides that at each reporting date the appropriateness of a classification shall be reassessed. Any transfer of a security between categories of investments is accounted for at fair value. If a debt security is transferred into the Held-to-Maturity category, the use of a fair value may create a premium or discount that, under amortized cost accounting, is amortized thereafter as an adjustment of yield pursuant to Statement of Financial Accounting Standards No. 91.[377] Transfers from the Held-to-Maturity category should be rare except for transfers due to certain changes in circumstances described next, and transfers into or from the Trading category also should be rare.

The following changes in circumstances may reasonably result in a reclassification of a security from Held-to-Maturity to one of the other classifications:

1. Evidence of a significant deterioration in the issuer's creditworthiness;
2. A change in tax law that eliminates or reduces the tax-exempt status of interest on a debt security (but not a change in tax law that revises the marginal tax rates applicable to interest income);
3. A major business combination or major disposition (such as sale of a segment) that necessitates the sale or transfer of a Held-to-Maturity security to maintain the enterprises existing interest rate risk position or credit risk policy;
4. A change in statutory or regulatory requirements significantly modifying either what constitutes a permissible investment or the maximum level of investments in certain kinds of securities, thereby causing an enterprise to dispose of a Held-to-Maturity security;
5. A significant increase by the regulator in the industry's capital requirements that causes the enterprise to downsize by selling Held-to-Maturity securities; and

---

[375] The mortgage banking activities are those that are described in Statement No. 65, "Accounting for Certain Mortgage Banking Activities."

[376] Statement No. 115 is effective for fiscal years beginning after December 15, 1993.

[377] Statement No. 91, "Accounting for Nonrefundable Fees and Costs Associated with Originating or Acquiring Loans and Initial Direct Costs of Leases."

6. A significant increase in the risk weights of debt securities used for regulatory risk-based capital purposes.[378]

Statement No. 115 does not apply to firms whose specialized accounting practices include accounting for substantially all investments in debt and equity securities at market value or fair value, with changes in value recognized in earnings (income) or in the change in net assets.

For purposes of this Statement, a debt security is defined as any security representing a creditor relationship with an enterprise.[379] It includes both federal and state government securities, including U.S. government agency securities, corporate bonds, convertible debt, commercial paper, all securitized debt instruments, such as collateralized mortgage obligations, Real Estate Mortgage Investment Conduits ("REMICs") and interest-only principal-only strips, and certain preferred stock. It excludes option contracts, financial futures contracts, forward contracts, and lease contracts and most loans.[380]

§4.6 Loans of Securities

In 1978 Congress added section 1058 to the Code.[381] The section is designed to provide nonrecognition treatment to parties who lend and borrow "securities" in which "the contractual obligation [to return identical securities] does not differ materially either in kind or in extent from the securities exchanged . . . ."[382] The term "securities" is defined for purposes of Code section 1058 in Code section 1236(c) as a share of stock in a corporation, a certificate of stock or interest in any corporation, a note, bond debenture, or evidence of indebtedness, or any evidence of an interest in or right to subscribe to or purchase any of these interests.[383] With the enactment of Code section 1058, Congress sought to encourage securities holders to make their securities available for loans.[384] The Senate Report accompanying the enacting legislations provided:

> "Under present law, uncertainty has developed as to the correct income tax treatment of certain securities lending transactions. As a result, some owners

[378] Statement No. 115, ¶8.

[379] Statement No. 115, Appendix C, ¶137.

[380] *Id.*

[381] Proposed regulations were issued in 1983 but never finalized or updated. Prop. Reg. §§1.1058-1 and -2, 48 Fed. Reg. 33912-01.

[382] S. Rep. No. 762, 95th Cong., 2d Sess. 7 (1978); 1978-2 C.B. 357, 361 ("Senate Report").

[383] I.R.C. §1058(a). Perhaps this definition is now too narrow, as it does not include various financial instruments currently traded on established securities markets. Notably, I.R.C. § 1058 was enacted in 1978 when there were fewer types of publicly traded property than currently in the market. Thus, Congress could revisit I.R.C. § 1058 and remove the cross-reference to I.R.C. § 1236(c), instead inserting a broader definition for securities that better reflects the diverse financial instruments that are publicly traded today. At a minimum, Congress could substitute the cross reference of I.R.C. § 1236(c) for I.R.C. § 475(c)(2) which contains a broader definition for securities as it was enacted in 1993. However, if Congress does not act, the Treasury and IRS have no authority to expand the definition of securities under I.R.C. § 1058. Instead, the Treasury and IRS could extend nonrecognition treatment for publicly traded securities falling outside the scope of I.R.C. § 1236(c) (and thus I.R.C. § 1058) via Treas. Reg. § 1.1001-1(a). For more on I.R.C. § 1058's arguably problematic definition of securities, see "Report on Tax Section of the New York State Bar Association on Certain Aspects of the Taxation of Securities Loans and the Operation of Section 1058," June 9, 2011.

[384] *See* "Report of the Tax Section of the New York State Bar Association on Certain Aspects of the Taxation of Securities Loans and The Operation of Section 1058" June 9, 2011 for a discussion of the section in light of *Samueli v. Commissioner*, 661 F.3d 399 (9th Cir. 2011); *Anschutz v. Commissioner*, 135 T.C. 78 (2010); *Calloway v. Commissioner*, 135 T.C. 26 (2010).

of securities are reluctant to enter into such transactions . . . . Because of time delays which a broker may face in obtaining securities (from the seller or transfer agent) to deliver to a purchaser, brokers are frequently required to borrow securities from organizations and individuals with investment portfolios for use in completing these market transactions. It is generally thought to be desirable to encourage organizations and individuals with securities holdings to make the securities available for such loans since the greater the volume of securities available for loan the less frequently will brokers fail to deliver a security to a purchaser within the time required by the relevant market rules."

A transfer of securities pursuant to Code section 1058 will qualify for nonrecognition of gain or loss on the transfer and return of securities, and the transferor is treated as owning the securities for all other purposes.[385] The transferor takes a substituted basis in the lending agreement; that is, the basis that the transferor had in the securities will become the basis that the transferor has in the agreement. When the securities are returned, the transferor will continue with the same tax basis. If the requirements of Code section 1058 are met, the transferor of securities is treated as the owner of the securities for all purposes, including the exclusion of interact on tax-exempt obligations.

To satisfy the conditions of Code section 1058, the parties to the transaction should enter into an agreement that has these terms:

1. It must provide for the return to the transferor of securities identical to the securities transferred;
2. It must require that all payments pursuant to the agreement be made to the transferor of amounts equivalent to all interest, dividends, and other distributions which the owner of the securities is entitled to receive during the period beginning with the transfer of the securities by the transferor and ending with the transfer of the identical securities back to the transferor;[386]
3. It must not reduce the risk of loss or the opportunity for gain of the transferor of the securities in the securities transferred;[387] and
4. It must meet such other requirements that the IRS may impose.[388] However, the IRS may not require that the agreement include any provision that is inconsistent with normal commercial practice, as permitted by the Securities Exchange Commission, as of December 31, 1974.[389]

---

[385] The IRS has provided guidance in 2008 regarding the application of I.R.C. § 1058(a) to situations involving securities loan agreements where the borrower subsequently defaults under the agreement as a result of its bankruptcy (or that of an affiliate) and, as soon as it is commercially practicable (but in no event more than 30 days following the default), the lender uses collateral provided pursuant to the agreement to purchase identical securities. Pursuant to the guidance, the purchase of the identical securities will not result in the loss of tax-free treatment under I.R.C. § 1058(a) for the lender, as long as designated conditions are met. Rev. Proc. 2008-63, 2008-42 I.R.B. 946.

[386] For a definition of "payments with respect to securities loans," *see* I.R.C. § 512(a)(5).

[387] This requirement does not speak to whether gain or loss is retained but to whether it is reduced. *Samueli v. Commissioner*, 132 T.C. 37, *aff'd*, 661 F.3d 399 (9th Cir. 2011).

[388] I.R.C. § 1958(b).

[389] I.R.C. § 1058(b); S. Rep. No. 95-762.

Whether these requirements, prescribed in Code section 1058(b) are absolute requirements or merely create a "safe-harbor" is not settled. If the transaction does not comply with Code section 1058, under an I.R.S. pronouncement that predated the enactment of that section the transaction may be treated as a nonrecognition event under Code section 1036.[390]

[390] Rev. Rul. 78-88, 1978-1 C.B. 163.

Chapter 5
Nonperforming Loans

Contents

§5.1 Tax Planning Suggestions
§5.2 Book Treatment of Delinquent Interest
  §5.2.1 Treatment
  §5.2.2 Statement of Financial Accounting Standards No. 114
§5.3 Tax Treatment of Delinquent Interest
  §5.3.1 General Rule
  §5.3.2 "All Events" Test for Nonperforming Loans
  §5.3.3 Reasonable Expectancy Standard
  §5.3.4 Banks Not Using Conformity Bad Debt Method
  §5.3.5 Loans Not Completely Charged-Off
  §5.3.6 Safe Harbor Method
  §5.3.7 Charge-Off of Accrued Interest
  §5.3.8 Banks Using Conformity Bad Debt Method
  §5.3.9 Mark-to-Market Loss
  §5.3.10 Resumption of Accrual
  §5.3.11 Payments After Non Accrual
  §5.3.12 O.I.D. on Nonperforming Loans
  §5.3.13 Open and Speculative Transactions
  §5.3.14 Coordinated Issue Papers
  §5.3.15 Code Sections 166 and 451 Contrasted
  §5.3.16 Appeals Guidelines
  §5.3.17 IRS Historical Practice
  §5.3.18 Audit Protection

§5.1 Tax Planning Suggestions

The accrual of interest on nonperforming loans is one of the most troublesome tax accounting issues with which banks have to deal.[1] Court cases and the audit experience of many banks document an unfortunate history of disputes between the IRS and taxpayers on this issue. The tremendous volume of loans elevates this issue above most other tax accounting issues.

In past years, the controversy stemmed from the inconsistency in the IRS's historical position and the position taken by taxpayers, which was to follow the book accounting treatment, an approach that does not comply with established tax principles. A recent significant development provides the bank tax planner with an opportunity to avoid this controversy.

---

[1] *See The Art of Tax Efficiency in Community Banks*, by M. Gula, J. Brew, and R. Blasi, 2007, Red Room Publishing, *http://www.mraeresources.com/bookstore/*.

The IRS's historical position was expressed in Coordinated Issue Papers promulgated by the Banking Industry Specialist and by an Appeals Settlement Guideline promulgated by the National Director of Appeals. The positions expressed in these documents often deviated from the audit practices of IRS agents. This discrepancy created considerable uncertainty for taxpayers. Moreover, these pronouncements did not appear to be based on strong statutory authority, and they did not respect the different statutory standards applicable to interest income in default and bad debts. The interest accrual standard contained in Code section 451, and not the bad debt standard prescribed in Code section 166, should be applied to interest income in default; however, the IRS coordinated issue paper applied the more onerous bad debt standard before accepting that a loan could be placed in a nonaccrual status.

In an effort to reduce the controversy surrounding this issue, the IRS announced in July 2004 that the treatment of interest on nonperforming loans was selected for its Industry Issue Resolution Program ("IIRP").[2] After considerable time and effort, the IRS in 2007 published a revenue ruling and a revenue procedure that appear to clarify its position on this issue and that prescribe a relatively clear and authoritatively supportable rule of law to nonperforming loan interest.[3]

The revenue ruling requires interest income to be accrued as long as a bank has a "reasonable expectancy of receiving future payments" on the loan. The revenue ruling then provides that if a bank elects the conformity method of accounting for bad debts prescribed in Regulation § 1.166-2(d)(3), it will be permitted to avoid tax on this accrued interest by classifying the accrued interest as a worthless debt deduction. The availability of this offsetting bad debt deduction should cause those banks that have not made the bad debt conformity election to consider doing so. The treatment of nonperforming loan interest contained in this revenue ruling appears to be applicable to all open tax years.

For purposes of determining the amount of a taxpayer's uncollected interest income that a bank has a "reasonable expectancy of receiving," the accompanying revenue procedure provides a rule of administrative convenience. This elective rule will obviate the necessity of examining each loan to determine whether there is a reasonable expectancy of receiving the accrued interest income, a process that, because of its factual dependant nature, will likely lead to audit controversy.

The elective approach appears to be available to both banks that have made the conformity bad debt deduction as well as those banks that have not done so. The alternative procedure looks to the bank's collection experience over the five years preceding the current tax year to determine the amount of interest for which a bank has a reasonable expectancy of payment. The elective approach for

---

[2] IR-2004-100, July 29, 2004. The IIRP is designed to provide clarity and consistency for complex business tax issues and reduce the compliance burden associated with them.

[3] Rev. Rul. 2007-32, I.R.B. 20007-21; Rev. Proc. 2007-33, I.R.B. 2007-21. These pronouncements were followed in 2010 by an Industry Directive that contained guidance for agents and also a sample Information Document Request. See A.9 in Appendix.

determining "reasonable expectancy" is available to taxpayers for taxable years ending after May 4, 2007.

If the "reasonable expectancy" rule for interest accrual is, in fact, applied by agents when examining banks, banks will have considerably less flexibility than they have had in the past. Moreover, it is likely to result in considerably more interest income being included in taxable income on audit, unless taxpayers voluntarily modify their treatment of interest on nonperforming loans.

Even those banks that are not customarily audited are now placed in a position of risking accuracy related penalties if they fail to adequately disclose a position contrary to the new published guidance.[4]

§5.2 Book Treatment of Delinquent Interest

§5.2.1 Treatment

Income tax treatment of delinquent interest income has frequently been in conflict with RAP and GAAP. Book accounting rules follow the bank regulatory rules for income accrual on nonperforming loans. Under federal bank regulatory rules, unless a loan made by a bank is both well secured and in the process of collection, the bank is required to suspend the recognition of uncollected accrued interest income on the loan.[5] Moreover, regulatory rules require that the bank reverse any previously recognized uncollected interest income. This treatment is mandated if any one of the following three factors is present:

1. The loan is maintained on a cash basis because of deterioration in the borrower's financial condition;
2. Payment in full of principal or interest is not expected; or
3. Payment of principal or interest has been in default for a period of 90 days or more.

With respect to the principal balance of the loan, bank regulatory rules do not require the loan to be charged-off even if accrued interest on the loan is no longer being recognized as income for regulatory financial statement purposes. Any payment received on a non-accrual loan receivable must be applied to reduce the bank's recorded investment in the loan to the extent necessary to

---

[4] I.R.C. §6662(d)(2)(B).

[5] *See* Office of the Comptroller of the Currency and Federal Financial Institution's Examination Council Call Report guidance. *Comptroller of the Currency Handbook for National Book Examiners—Commercial, International*, §205.1, p. 8 (1979). Prior to 1989, regulations of the now abolished Federal Home Loan Bank Board provided, in part, that accounting income does not include "[a]ll earned but uncollected interest on a conventional loan if any portion thereof is due but uncollected for a period in excess of 90 days," unless the balance due is secured by an approved list of assets, active collection efforts are being made, and there is a reasonable expectation of delinquent interest collection. 12 C.F.R. §563c.11(b)(1). This regulation has been repealed. The instructions to federal regulatory reporting schedule RC-N provide that "for purposes of this schedule, an asset is to be reported as being in non-accrual status if: (1) it is maintained on a cash basis because of deterioration in the financial condition of the borrower, (2) payment in full of principal or interest is not expected, or (3) principal or interest has been in default for a period of 90 days or more unless the asset is both well secured and in the process of collection." *See also* the instructions to FFIEC Schedules 031, 032, 033, and 034, at page A-57 (9-97), which provide that "deferred net fees or costs shall not be amortized during periods in which interest income on a loan is not being recognized because of concerns about realization of loan principal or interest."

eliminate any doubt as to collectibility. Therefore, the bank must characterize any payment received on a loan in nonperforming status as a payment of principal rather than a payment of the outstanding accrued interest on the loan until the remaining principal on the loan is considered to be fully collectible. State bank regulators often apply similar rules.[6]

As a general rule, it has long been the policy of federal regulators that loans should be charged off in no payment had been received for 90-days. In 1980, the FDIC published a statement that became an interagency standard that required charge-off of closed-end consumer installment credit that was 120 days delinquent and for open-end consumer credit card loans that were 180 days delinquent.[7]

For book accounting purposes, banks may be reluctant to accrue amounts into income when there has been a default, even after a partial payment is received. To do so may overstate income because the total amount that will be received will be less than the principal balance. Regardless of the terms of the loan agreement or the tax rule, it is customary in accordance with conservative accounting practices to defer the interest income until principal payments are current. Thus, loans in nonaccrual status often give rise to a deferred tax credit in the bank's reserve for taxes, and book and regulatory treatment conform.

§ 5.2.2 Statement of Financial Accounting Standards No. 114

Statement of Financial Accounting Standards No. 114 addresses the circumstances under which a creditor should measure and take into account impairment of a loan.[8] A loan is deemed impaired when "it is probable that a creditor will be unable to collect all amounts due according to the contractual terms of the loan agreement."[9] The statement amends Statement No. 5, "Accounting for Contingencies," and Statement No. 15, "Accounting by Debtors and Creditors for Troubled Debt Restructuring." Statement No. 114 is effective for financial statements for fiscal years beginning after December 15, 1994.

Starting in 2007, the sub-prime mortgage crisis caused residential mortgage lenders to modify existing sub-prime home loans through restructurings that could, arguably, be considered troubled debt restructurings ("TDRs"), which must be accounted for in accordance with Statement No. 114.[10] Prior to the sub-prime mortgage crisis, lenders had been accustomed to quickly selling bundles of mortgages on the secondary mortgage backed securities market, which effectively limited the likelihood that a lender would be forced to modify large numbers of impaired mortgages.[11] This practice became increasingly difficult during the sub-prime mortgage crisis, which forced lenders to hold mortgages

---

[6] *See, e.g.*, New York State Banking Law; I.R.C., § 109(2)(a).

[7] FDIC, "Uniform Policy for Classification of Cosumer Installment Credit Baseed on Delinquency Status." (1980).

[8] For impairment of debt and equity securities, see Statement 115-1 and 124. A brief discussion of Statement 115 is contained in Chapters 4 and 10.

[9] Statement No. 114, ¶ 8.

[10] *Application of Statement 114 to Modifications of Residential Mortgage Loans that Qualify as Troubled Debt Restructurings*, CENTER FOR AUDIT QUALITY, at 1 (2008).

[11] *Id.* at 2.

for extended periods of time, leading in turn to increased reliance on troubled debt restructuring for the modification of loans on the lenders' books.[12] With this reliance on Troubled Debt Restructuring for loan modifications came the requirement that lenders comply with Statement 114 in accounting for the modification of residential mortgages.[13]

In the early years of the crisis, lending institutions urged the FASB to reduce the scope of Statement 114 in regards to accounting for modifications to home loans. Lending institutions argued that the burdensome nature of accounting for modifications to a very large number of subprime loans made the application of Statement 114 unfeasible.[14] While some industry groups argued that the restructuring of individual residential loans was not generally within the scope of Statement 114, the FASB affirmed in its January 30, 2008, meeting that these loans could fall within the definition of a TDR, and therefore the loans must be accounted for under the requirements of Statement 114.[15]

In late 2007, the Mortgage Bankers Association ("MBA") sent two letters to the FASB requesting relief from the requirements of Statement 114 with regard to modified home loans.[16] The MBA requested that FASB promulgate alternate approaches for accounting for the modification of loans.[17] The MBA argued that when Statement 114 was first promulgated in 1993, the FASB indicated its intent to exclude residential mortgages entirely from Statement 114 by not including small balance, homogeneous loans in the scope of Statement 114 reporting requirements.[18] In effect, the MBA argued that the FASB had never intended for home loans to fall within the purview of Statement 114, and that the unforeseeable circumstances of the sub-prime mortgage crisis should be accommodated by the FASB through the modification of Statement 114.[19] Second, the MBA argued that the use of the Financial Accounting Statement 5 approach would "produce more relevant information about the amounts that lenders have at risk within their held-for-investment modified smaller-balance loan portfolios . . . ."[20] Third,

[12] *See id.*

[13] *Id.* at 2 ("[I]f any loan meets the definition of a TDR, regardless of the size of the loan, Statement 114 requires that the loan be evaluated for impairment under Statement 114.").

[14] Floyd Norris, *Banks Plead They Can't Follow the Rules*, N.Y. TIMES, January 11, 2008 ("The banks argue that [complying with Statement 114] would take too much effort, given the volume of loans likely to be restructured. 'This would be extremely time-consuming and would likely involve additional staff dedicated to this purpose,' Ms. Utermohlen said in a letter to the Financial Accounting Standards Board this week.").

[15] *Application of Statement 114 to Modifications of Residential Mortgage Loans that Qualify as Troubled Debt Restructurings*, CENTER FOR AUDIT QUALITY, at 1 (2008). *See also* Handout issued for January 30, 2008 meeting of the Financial Standards Accounting Board at 2, available at *http://www.fasb.org/jsp/FASB/Document_C/DocumentPage&cid=1218220088848* ("Statement 114 applies to all loans identified for impairment evaluation, excluding, among other loan types, large groups of smaller-balance homogeneous loans that are collectively evaluated for impairment, such as residential mortgage loans that are not classified as TDRs.").

[16] *Id.* at 1.

[17] *Id.*

[18] Handout issued for January 30, 2008 meeting of the Financial Standards Accounting Board at 3, available at *http://www.fasb.org/jsp/FASB/Document_C/DocumentPage&cid=1218220088848* ("The MBA believes that the scope exception reflects the Board's understanding that smaller-balance, homogeneous loans need to be evaluated differently than larger-balance, non-homogeneous loans.").

[19] *See id.*

[20] *Id.* at 4 (The FASB characterized MBA's argument as follows: "A Statement 114 measurement approach based on discounted cash flows would capture the difference between the interest rate prior to and after modification and would reflect the foregone future cash receipts specific to interest as an

the use of Statement 5 in reporting loan modifications would lead to a more accurate portrayal of losses because of the nature of sub-prime mortgages.[21] Finally, MBA argued that while lenders' computer systems could accommodate accounting for loan modifications under Statement 5, the approach required in Statement 114 would be technologically unfeasible.[22]

FASB's response to MBA's request was decisively opposed to any further exploration into amending Statement 114. The board reasoned that the provisions in Statement 114 were sufficiently clear, and the approach described in Statement 5 would fail to indicate interest rate concessions to homeowners.[23] Finally, the board observed:

> Statement 114 has been in effect since January 1995. Lenders are requesting relief from Statement 114's requirements for loans currently being originated; their request for relief is not limited to previously originated loans that were intended to be sold in secondary markets. The staff believes that lenders should consider the costs to comply with Statement 114's requirements when continuing to offer teaser-rate loan programs.[24]

The board recommended that further study of amendments to Statement 114 was not warranted.[25]

On October 12, 2010, the FASB issued an exposure draft of proposed changes to FAS 114.[26] The exposure draft recommended that Statement 114 be modified by precluding creditors from using the borrower's effective rate test in evaluating whether a restructuring constitutes a TDR.[27] The staff proposed four additional factors that would weigh in favor of determining that a restructuring is a TDR.[28] First, the staff recommended that when a debtor lacks access to market rate funds for debt with similar risk characteristics to the restructured debt, the creditor

(Footnote Continued)

impairment. However, the MBA believes that the lender's sacrifice of the potential future interest may not have a direct bearing on the amount of a loan's carrying value that will not be recovered. The MBA also states that measuring impairment based on collateral values or market values under Statement 114 is a fair value measurement, as opposed to a cost-based measurement, and would produce values that reflect changes in market factors that may be irrelevant to the recoverability of the loan's carrying value at a point in time.").

[21] *Id.* at 4. More specifically, the MBA argued that the nature of sub-prime mortgages made them inappropriate for Statement 114 treatment. At the time such loans were created, lenders fully expected homeowners to refinance their loans before variable interest rates reset, and long before the homeowners had paid their loans in full. Thus, calculating the value of foregone interest lost (as required under Statement 114) would provide an inaccurate picture of the actual loss sustained by the lender. In addition, MBA argued that the likely alternative to restructuring residential mortgages, foreclosure, was not taken into account when calculating foregone interest lost under Statement 114 analysis. Finally, MBA argued that the subjective nature of characterizing residential mortgages for the purpose of accounting for loan modifications under Statement 114 would make whatever calculations arrived at by the lender subject to extensive debate.

[22] *Id.* at 5.

[23] *Id.*

[24] *Id.* at 6-7 (The FASB also noted that Statement 114, as interpreted, complied with IFRS, whereas any modification of Statement 114 to accommodate lending institutions would make GAAP inconsistent with IFRS standards on this matter.).

[25] See Meeting Minutes of the Financial Accounting Standards Board on January 30, 2008, at 2-5, available at *http://www.fasb.org/jsp/FASB/Document_C//DocumentPage&cid=1218220099139*.

[26] Clarifications to Accounting for Troubled Debt Resructurings by Creditors Exposure Draft, available at *http://www.fasb.org/cs/ContentServer?site=FASB&c=Document_C& pagename=FASB%2FDocument_C%2FDocumentPage&cid=1176157634787*.

[27] *Id.* at 1.

[28] *Id.*

should consider the debt to be a troubled debt restructuring.[29] Second, when a restructuring results in an interest rate increase—whether temporary or permanent—the "contractual interest rate cannot be presumed to be at a rate that is at or above market."[30] Third, when default by a debtor is considered "probable in the foreseeable future," the debtor would still be deemed to be experiencing financial difficulty.[31] Finally, the staff clarified that even insignificant delays in contractual cash flows resulting from a restructuring may be considered a factor in discerning whether a loan modification is a troubled debt restructuring.[32] In addition, the staff recommended changing Statement 114 to provide that if the debtor fulfills the following two requirements, the restructuring should not be considered a troubled debt restructuring because they are not experiencing financial difficulty.[33] If the debtor, who is currently servicing the existing debt, could repay pre-payable debt from new creditors "at an effective interest rate equal to the current market interest rate for a non-troubled debtor," and "the creditors agree to restructure the old debt solely to reflect a decrease in current market interest rates for the debtor or positive changes in the creditworthiness of the debtor since the debt was originally issued," then the restructuring should not be considered a TDR.[34] If only one of the factors is present, then that factor "would be an indicator, but not determinative, that the debtor is not experiencing financial difficulty."[35]

(a) *Book v. Tax*

The book accounting standard for determining when a loan is impaired bears a close resemblance to the IRS's standard for discontinuance of accrual. Thus, an argument can be made that application of the Statement No. 114 provisions should satisfy an IRS auditor. At the very least, the documentation that will be prepared to classify a loan as impaired and to compute the amount of impairment will be sufficient to substantiate discontinuance of accrual of interest on the impaired portion of the loan for tax purposes.

A 1991 amendment to federal banking law requires that RAP be in accordance with GAAP.[36] The Federal Deposit Insurance Corporation Act now provides:

> Subject to the requirement of this Act and any other provision of Federal law, the accounting principles applicable to reports or statements required to be filed with Federal banking agencies by all insured depository institutions shall be uniform and consistent with generally accepted accounting principles.[37]

---

[29] *Id.* (reasoning that the restructuring should be considered at below market rate when there is no benchmark for the debtor's market rate on similar debt).

[30] *Id.* at 8 (reasoning that "the new contractual interest rate . . . could still be below market interest rates for new debt with similar terms").

[31] *Id.*

[32] *Id.*

[33] *Id.* at 11.

[34] *Id.*

[35] *Id.* The period for commenting on the proposed changes expires on December 13, 2010. Should the board adopt the staff's recommendations, modifications to Statement 114 will "be effective for interim and annual periods ending after June 15, 2011, and would be applied retrospectively to restructurings occurring on or after the beginning of the earliest period presented."

[36] Pub.L. 102-242, § 543 (1991).

[37] 12 U.S.C. § 1831(n) (1970).

If the bank's federal regulator or the FDIC determines that a GAAP rule is inconsistent with RAP objectives, the regulator may prescribe an accounting principle, for reports or statements required to be filed with the regulator, that is no less stringent than the GAAP rule. The repeal by Statement No. 118 of the income recognition rules contained in Statement No. 114 may provide federal bank regulators with leeway to retain the current arbitrary RAP nonaccrual rule.[38]

(b) ***Measuring Impairment***

According to Statement No. 114, when a loan is impaired, a creditor is required to measure the impairment based on the present value of expected future cash flows discounted at the loan's effective interest rate.[39] Alternatively, a creditor is permitted, "as a practical expedient," to measure the loan's impairment based on the loan's observable market price.[40] If a loan is collateral dependent, the fair value of the collateral may be used to measure the impairment. Moreover, if a creditor determines that foreclosure is probable, the creditor is required to measure impairment based on the fair value of the collateral. A loan is considered to be "collateral dependent" if the repayment of the loan is expected to be provided solely by the underlying collateral. This would be true in most cases of nonrecourse loans. If a creditor measures an impaired loan using a present value calculation, the estimates of expected future cash flows shall be the creditor's best estimate based on reasonable and supportable assumptions and projections.

(c) ***Income Recognition***

Statement No. 118, released by the Financial Accounting Standards Board in October 1994, eliminates the provisions in Statement No. 114 (paragraphs 17-19) that require specified methods for reporting income on an impaired loan. The amendment to Statement No. 114 permits a creditor to use existing methods for recognizing interest income. However, Statement No. 118 does not modify the provisions in Statement No. 114 that relate to the method for measuring impairment of a loan. The effective date of Statement No. 118 is concurrent with the effective date of Statement No. 114.

The income recognition methods set forth in Statement No. 114 provide that a creditor shall recognize any change in the present values of cash flows in accordance with either of the two methods described below. If there is a significant increase or decrease in the amount or timing of an impaired loan's expected future cash flows, or if actual cash flows are significantly different from the cash flows previously projected, a creditor is required to recalculate the impairment. Statement No. 114 provides that the present value of an impaired loan's expected

---

[38] The Federal Financial Institution Examination Council issued, on May 17, 1994, a request for public comment on two issues relating to Statement No. 114: whether reserve additions made by reason of Statement No. 114 would be specific reserves or general reserves, and whether banking agencies should continue to use their historical nonaccrual rule. 59 Fed. Reg. 25,656-9 (May 17, 1994).

[39] Statement No. 114, ¶13. The loan's effective interest rate is used instead of a market rate to separate impairment resulting from credit deterioration from a decline in loan value resulting from interest rate movement.

[40] *Id.*

future cash flows will change from one reporting period to the next because of the passage of time.

1. If the increase in the present value of expected future cash flows is attributable to the passage of time, it shall be reported as interest income accrued on the net carrying amount of the loan at the effective interest rate used to discount the impaired loan's estimated future cash flows. If there is any change in present value attributable to changes in the amount or timing of expected future cash flows, it shall be reported as bad-debt expense in the same manner in which impairment initially was recognized or as a reduction in the amount of bad-debt expense that otherwise would be reported.[41]
2. The entire change in present value shall be reported as bad-debt expense in the same manner in which impairment initially was recognized or as a reduction in the amount of bad-debt expense that otherwise would be reported.

Under the Statement, a creditor's recorded investment in a loan, both at origination and subsequently during the life of the loan, as long as the loan performs according to its contractual terms, is the sum of the present values of the future cash flows that are designated as interest and the future cash flows that are designated as principal, including any amount due at maturity, discounted at the effective interest rate implicit in the loan.

Because loans are recorded originally at discounted amounts, the ongoing assessment of impairment should be made in a similar manner. Thus, a loan that becomes impaired should continue to be carried at an amount that considers the present value of all expected future cash flows, in a manner consistent with the loan's measurement before it became impaired. Since the expected future cash flows from an impaired loan are usually uncertain, creditors are required to exercise significant judgment in developing the estimates of future cash flows.

The accounting procedures for impaired loans are illustrated by the following example.

Example: On December 31, 1994, XYZ Inc. issued a $1,000,000, 6-year, noninterest-bearing note to Bank A. The notes effective annual yield was 12 percent and the present value of the note was $506,631. Bank A made the following journal entry to record the loan:

Journal Entries	*Dr.*	*Cr.*
Notes receivable	$1,000,000	
Discount on notes receivable		$493,369
Cash		$506,631

At December 31, 1996, due to unfavorable economic conditions, Bank A estimated that XYZ would repay only $800,000 of the principal amount at maturity. It was thus determined that the loan met the impairment criteria under Statement No. 114.

41 *Id.* at ¶ 17.

Recording The Impairment:

Step 1. Determine the amount of the loan's present value under the new assumptions.

Present value of $800,000, due in 4 years, using the loan's effective interest rate of 12%:	$508,414

Step 2. Determine the loss due to impairment, equal to the difference between the loan's carrying amount at the date of impairment and the present value of expected future cash flows.

Carrying amount at 12/31/96	$635,518
Less: Present value of expected future cash flows	508,414
Loss from impairment	$127,104

Step 3. Record the impairment as a charge to Bad Debt Expense and a credit to a valuation allowance account.

Journal Entries	*Dr.*	*Cr.*
Bad debt expense	127,104	
Allowance for uncollectible accounts		127,104

Step 4. Record interest revenue on the loan based on the new carrying amount of $508,414. This method is permitted, but not required, by Statement No. 118, assuming that Bank A previously accounted for interest in a similar manner.

Date	*Interest revenue*	*Amortized discount*	*Carrying amount*
12/31/96			$508,414
12/31/97	$61,010	$61,010	569,424
12/31/98	68,331	68,331	637,755
12/31/99	76,531	76,531	714,286
12/31/00	85,714	85,714	800,000
Total	$291,586	$291,586	

Each year, the difference between the interest that would have been accrued under the original assumption of loan with a $1,000,000 maturity value and the interest after the loan impairment is added to the valuation allowance account. This journal entry is illustrated for the 1997 year as follows:

Journal Entries	*Dr.*	*Cr.*
Discount on Notes Receivable	76,262	
Interest revenue		61,010
Allowance for uncollectible accounts		15,252

Step 5. On 12/31/00, Bank A would make the following journal entry, assuming XYZ repaid only $800,000:

Journal Entries	*Dr.*	*Cr.*
Cash	800,000	
Allowance for Uncollectible Accounts	200,000	
Notes receivable		1,000,000

If conditions change and XYZ Inc. repays the original loan amount of $1,000,000 on 12/31/00, Bank A would reduce its Bad Debts Expense account balance by the original amount recorded ($127,104) and would increase Interest Revenue by the additional amount in the valuation allowance account ($200,000 – $127,104 = $72,896).

§5.3 Tax Treatment of Delinquent Interest

§5.3.1 General Rule

Neither GAAP nor RAP control the tax treatment of interest on non performing loans.[42] In a 1991 "Report to the Congress on the Tax Treatment of Bad Debts by Financial Institutions," conformity between the book and tax treatment of interest on loans in nonaccrual status was rejected.[43] It was reasoned that because the book standard looked to factors that were not controlling for tax purposes, conformity was inappropriate.[44]

For tax purposes, an accrual method taxpayer takes an item of income into account when all the events have occurred that fix the right to the item and the amount can be determined with reasonable accuracy.[45] Under this "all events" test, a taxpayer's right to receive income becomes fixed on the earlier of the date that: (1) payment is earned through performance; (2) payment is due; or (3) payment is actually received.[46] The right to receive interest income becomes "fixed" as it is earned over the term of the loan.[47]

§5.3.2 "All Events" Test for Nonperforming Loans

In Revenue Ruling 2007-32 the I.R.S. explains how it believes that the "all events" test should be applied to interest earned by a bank on nonperforming loans, which the ruling refers to as "non-accrual loan receivable."[48] In doing so, it clarifies the IRS's position and provides taxpayers with more certainty as to how the item will be treated on audit. An accompanying Revenue Procedure provides for an elective safe harbor method for determining the amount of interest on nonperforming loans that must be included in taxable income.[49]

Under the guidance contained in Revenue Ruling 2007-32, a bank on the accrual method of accounting is required to recognize uncollected accrued interest income if the lender has a "reasonable expectancy" that the borrower will make some payments on the loan, even if the borrower is not expected to make

---

[42] *Old Colony R. Co. v. Commissioner*, 284 U.S. 552 (1932); *Bellefontaine Federal Savings and Loan Association v. Commissioner*, 33 T.C. 808 (1960); *J.B.N. Telephone Co., Inc. v. United States*, 638 F.2d 227 (10th Cir. 1981).

[43] Department of the Treasury, Sept. 1991. The report was prepared pursuant to a directive contained in the Conference Report for the Tax Reform Act of 1986. H.R. Conf. Rep. No. 841, 99th Cong. 2d Sess. II-316 (1986).

[44] See discussion at §5.2.1.

[45] I.R.C. §446; Reg. §1.446-1(c)(1)(ii); I.R.C. §451; Reg. §1.451-1(a); Reg. §1.1275-2(a).

[46] Rev. Rul. 84-31, 1984-1 C.B. 127. An amount of accrued interest determined pursuant to §1.446-2 satisfies the "reasonable accuracy" requirement of §1.451-1(a).

[47] Rev. Rul. 72-100, 1972-1 C.B. 122, *as clarified by* Rev. Rul. 74-607, 1974-2 C.B. 149; *Atlantic Coast Line Railroad Co. v. Commissioner*, 31 B.T.A. 730, Dec. 8817 (1934); *Clifton Mfg. Co. v. Commissioner*, 43-2 U.S.T.C. ¶9539, 137 F.2d 290 (4th Cir. 1943); *Lomas & Nettleton Financial Co. v. United States*, 80-1 U.S.T.C. ¶9326, 486 F. Supp. 652 (N.D. Tex. 1980).

[48] Rev. Rul. 2007-32, 2007-1 C.B. 1278.

[49] Rev. Proc. 2007-33, 2007-1 C.B. 1289.

all payments on the loan. Only if there is no "reasonable expectancy" of payment may accrual be discontinued. Thus, banks must include in taxable income all interest on nonperforming loans if the taxpayer reasonably expects to receive payments on the debt. Apparently, when the interest accrual exceeds expected payments, accrual of the excess may be terminated.

Examining agents have been instructed to apply this new rule on audit.[50] If they do, they will be taking a more rigid position than the one they often took in the past, but the position they take will be on a sounder legal basis. In the past, examining agents struck arrangements with some banks that were not applied consistently throughout the industry. Furthermore, published pronouncements appeared to confuse the Code section 166 rules applicable to bad debt deductions with the Code section 451 rules applicable to the accrual of interest income.[51] They argued that accrual could be discontinued only when the bad debt standard for charging-off a loan was satisfied.

§ 5.3.3 Reasonable Expectancy Standard

As a general rule, whether there is a reasonable expectancy that a borrower will make payments on a loan is a question of fact, and the standard must be applied on a loan-by-loan basis. The IRS refers to the reasonable expectancy standard as an exception to the general rule of income accrual, which must be strictly construed. There is considerable judicial support for this standard.[52]

Accrual may not be discontinued if there is merely a delay in payment or if the debtor is merely encountering temporary financial difficulties.[53] There must be substantial evidence that there is no reasonable expectancy of payment and the uncertainty as to collection must be substantial.[54] The Tax Court also held that since there was insufficient evidence to show reasonable doubt that payments would be made, interest must be accrued when earned even though interest payments on the debt were deferred due to financial difficulties of the borrower.[55] The Board of Tax Appeals earlier ruled that the substantial earnings and assets of the debtors justified a reasonable expectancy of receipt on the part of the taxpayer.[56] The Tax Court has stated that "the fact that a lapse of time is contemplated before actual satisfaction is possible does not constitute the requisite doubtful collectibility."[57]

However, when a debtor repeatedly defaulted on payments in spite of numerous extensions and attempts to renegotiate, accrual could be discontinued.[58] The Board of Tax Appeals found that the debtor "was chronically suffering

---

[50] LMSB Industry Director Directive, Nonperforming Loans, LMSB-4-0110-003, March 17, 2010, with accompanying IDR. Appendix A.20.

[51] See discussion of earlier IRS pronouncements at § 5.3.14.

[52] Rev. Rul. 2007-32, 2007-1 C.B. 1278.

[53] Rev. Rul. 2007-32, I.R.B. 2007-21. *Koehring Co. v. United States*, 421 F.2d 715, 721-722 (Ct. Cl. 1970); *Harmont Plaza Inc. v. Commissioner*, 64 T.C. 632, 649 (1975), *aff'd* 549 F.2d 414 (6th Cir. 1977).

[54] *European American Bank and Trust Company v. United States*, 20 Cl. Ct. 594, 605 (1990).

[55] *Union Pacific R.R. Co. v. Commissioner*, 14 T.C. 401 (1950).

[56] *Bettendorf Co. v. Commissioner*, 34 B.T.A. 72 (1936).

[57] *Harmont Plaza Inc.*, 64 T.C. at 650.

[58] *O'Sullivan Rubber Co. v. Commissioner*, 42 B.T.A. 721, 723 (1940). *See also Electric Controls and Service Co. v. Commissioner*, T.C. Memo. 1996-486 (where the Tax Court permitted a taxpayer to avoid any interest

from financial embarrassment and the petitioner was in imminent danger, not only of not collecting the interest but of losing the principal payments" as well.[59] The Board of Tax Appeals also decided that a taxpayer was justified in discontinuing accrual when it owned a substantial portion of the stock of the debtor. The Board stated that although collection may have been possible once the debtor was in receivership, the amounts received would have been at the "sacrifice" of the taxpayer's "investment" in the debtor company and therefore not income.[60]

The Second Court of Appeals in *Corn Exchange Bank v. U.S.* held that "a taxpayer cannot be charged to have realized an income unless there exists a reason for believing that the income is likely to be paid or can be collected."[61] That court allowed an accrual basis taxpayer to discontinue accrual of interest on loans when the borrower went into receivership.[62] In *European American Bank and Trust Company v. U.S.*, the Claims Court stated that "accrual of income is not required when a fixed right to receive arises if there is not a reasonable expectancy that the claim will ever be paid."[63]

§5.3.4 Banks Not Using Conformity Bad Debt Method

Revenue Ruling 2007-32 appears to state that the "reasonable expectancy" standard for determining when accrual of interest may be discontinued applies to all banks, regardless of whether the bank elects the conformity method of accounting for bad debts set forth in Regulation section 1.166-2(d).[64] In the synopsis of the ruling it is stated, without any qualification, that "[a]n accrual method bank with a reasonable expectancy of receiving future payments on non-accruable loan receivables is required to include accrued interest in gross income in the tax year in which the right to receive the interest becomes fixed, notwithstanding bank regulatory rules that prevent accrual of interest for regulatory purposes." Furthermore, and more specifically, in the application of the "reasonable expectancy" standard to the basic facts of the ruling, it concludes: "As an accrual method taxpayer, X is required to recognize the $8000 of uncollected 2006 accrued interest as income in X's 2006 taxable year for federal income tax

(Footnote Continued)

accrual when the interest became uncollectible in the year of accrual).

[59] *O'Sullivan Rubber Co.*, 42 B.T.A. at 723.

[60] *Great Northern Ry. Co. v. Commissioner*, 8 B.T.A. 225, 257 (1927).

[61] *Corn Exchange Bank v. United States*, 37 F.2d 34 (2d Cir. 1930). *See also Cuba Railroad Company v. Commissioner*, 9 T.C. 211 (1947); *Atlantic Coast Line R.R. Co. v. Commissioner*, 31 B.T.A. 730 (1934); *Lomas & Nettlecon Financial Corp. v. United States*, 486 F. Supp. 652, 660 (N.D.Tx.1980); *American Fork & Hoe Co. v. Commissioner*, 33 B.T.A. 1139 (1936); *Koehring Company v. United States*, 421 F.2d 715 (Ct. Cl. 1970); and *Chicago & North Western Ry. v. Commissioner*, 29 T.C. 989, 996 (1958), holding that the test was whether the taxpayer would receive the income within a "reasonable time." *See also North American Oil Cons. v. Burnet*, 286 U.S. 417 (1932); *H. Liebes & Co. v. Commissioner*, 90 F.2d 932, (9th Cir. 1937).

[62] *Cf Broderick v. Anderson*, 23 F. Supp. 488 (S.D.N.Y. 1938), distinguishing *Corn Exchange Bank* and holding accrual of interest proper even after foreclosure on a mortgage because the value of the mortgage was adequately secured by lien.

[63] *European American Bank and Trust Company v. United States*, 20 Cl. Ct. 594, 605 (1990); *Jones Lumber Co. v. Commissioner*, 404 F.2d 764 (6th Cir. 1968); Rev. Rul. 80-361, 1980-2 C.B. 164. Reg. §1.166-2(d)(3); FSA 200018017, January 13, 2000. See discussion of conformity method banks a §5.3.8.

[64] Some commentators have suggested that the reasonable expectancy standard as articulated in the Rev. Rul. 2007-32 is applicable only to those banks that have adopted the conformity election. "Interest on Nonaccrual Loans: New Rules and a 'Safe Harbor' Method," by J.D. Goeller and J. E. Cederberg, Taxation and Regulation of Financial Institutions, July/August 2007, Vol. 20, No. 6.

purposes. X is also required to recognize the $24,000 of uncollected 2007 accrued interest in X's 2007 taxable year. *The result is the same regardless of whether the bank uses a conformity method of accounting provided for in § 1.166-2(d).*" [*Emphasis added.*]

§ 5.3.5 Loans Not Completely Charged-Off

The hypothetical facts of Revenue Ruling 2007-32 indicate that the lender "reasonably expects the borrower to continue making some but not all payments on the loan." During the period of default, it appears that no payments were made, and there is no indication that any of the principal on the loan was charged-off. Apparently, because no portion of the principal was charged-off, the payments that the lender reasonably expected the borrower to make would be applied by the bank to the outstanding principal balance of the loan. However, even if it is assumed that the expectation of the lender was that payments would not exceed the principal balance of the loan, the position of the IRS appears to be that interest income should be recognized. This is consistent with Treasury Regulations.

Regulation section 1.446-2(e) provides: "[E]ach payment under a loan (other than payments of additional interest or similar charges provided with respect to amounts that are not paid when due) is treated as a payment of interest to the extent of the accrued and unpaid interest . . . ." Thus, at least to the extent that the lender expects to receive what it may classify for book purposes as a payment toward the unpaid principal balance of the loan, there is an expectancy of receiving payments that must be applied for tax purposes to accrued interest income.[65] It appears that this would lead to the conclusion that only if the entire principal balance of the debt were charged-off would the bank be in a position to argue that it has no expectancy of receiving some future payments.

§ 5.3.6 Safe Harbor Method

As an alternative to looking at the facts and circumstances surrounding each loan to determine whether there is a reasonable expectancy of payment, a bank is permitted to change its method of accounting for uncollected interest to an elective safe harbor method that is based on the bank's collection experience.[66] The safe harbor method is available only to banks, not to other members of a bank holding company group that do not meet the Code section 581 definition of a "bank." It is also available only to accrual method taxpayers.

Under this safe harbor method of accounting, the amount of uncollected interest for each taxable year for which the bank is considered to have a reasonable expectancy of payment and which is included in gross income is

---

[65] A similar rule is provided for O.I.D. in Reg. § 1.1275-2(a)(1).

[66] Rev. Proc. 2007-33, 2007-1 C.B. 1289. If a bank wants to change its method of accounting for uncollected interest to the safe harbor method, the bank is required to follow the automatic change in method of accounting provisions of Rev. Proc. 2002-9 (or its successor), with the following modifications: (1) the scope limitations in section 4.02 of Rev. Proc. 2002-9 do not apply to a bank that makes the change for either its first or second taxable year ending on or after December 31, 2006; and (2) the designated automatic accounting change number for changes in method of accounting made pursuant to the revenue procedure is 108.

equal to the total accrued but uncollected interest for the year multiplied by the bank's "recovery percentage" for that year. The bank then excludes from gross income the portion of accrued but uncollected interest for which it has no reasonable expectancy of payment. The bank is not considered to have a reasonable expectancy of payment for the excess, if any, of the accrued but uncollected interest over the expected collection amount determined using the bank's recovery percentage.

The interest that is taken into account for this computation is, generally, qualified stated interest; that is, all interest income other than interest described in Regulation section 1.446-2(a)(2), which includes unstated interest relating to original issue discount, market discount, discount on short-term obligations, etc. Qualified stated interest accrues ratably over the accrual period to which it is attributable, and it accrues at the stated rate for the period.[67]

The "recovery percentage" for each taxable year is determined by dividing total payments that the bank received on loans during the 5 taxable years immediately preceding the taxable year by total amounts that were due and payable to the bank on loans during the same 5 (or fewer) taxable years. The recovery percentage cannot exceed 100 percent, and it must be calculated to at least four decimal places. With the approval of the Commissioner, a shorter period may be used if the bank has less than 6 years of collection experience. It does not appear that a period shorter than 6 years can be used merely if the bank has a significant change in its recovery experience.[68]

The opportunity to use a shorter experience period is occasionally encountered in connection with loan loss deductions. Regulation section 1.585-2(c)(1)(ii) provides for a shortened experience period "only where there is a change in the type of a substantial portion of the loans outstanding such that the risk of loss is substantially increased." The regulation also provides that "[t]he fact that a bank's bad debt experience has shown a substantial increase in not, by itself, sufficient to justify use of a shorter period."[69]

The term "total payments" includes both interest and principal payments on the loan. To the extent that the interest payments are labeled "fees," they would be treated as part of the "total payments." However, it is questionable whether amounts received for performing services would be included in "total payments" on the loan. Presumably, these are not payments "received on loans," but rather received for services.

If a bank has engaged in an acquisition or disposition during the six year period, the data used in the recovery percentage must be adjusted. In the case of

---

[67] Reg. § 1.446-2.

[68] If a bank with less than 6 years of collection experience wants to change its method of accounting for uncollected interest to the safe harbor method, the bank is required to follow the provisions of Rev. Proc. 97-27, 1997-1 C.B. 680 (or its successor), as modified and amplified by Rev. Proc. 2002-19, as amplified and clarified by Rev. Proc. 2002-54, except that the scope limitations in section 4.02(2) through (6) of Rev. Proc. 97-27 do not apply to a bank that makes the change for either its first or second taxable year ending on or after December 31, 2006.

[69] There are also special rules for new financial institutions that permit a shorter period to be used to determine their loan loss deduction. Reg. § 1.585-2(c)(2).

an acquisition by a bank of the major portion of a trade or business of a predecessor, or the major portion of a separate unit of a trade or business of a predecessor, then for any taxable year ending on or after the acquisition, the data from preceding taxable years of the predecessor attributable to the portion of the trade or business acquired, if available, must be used in determining the bank's recovery percentage.

If a bank disposes of a major portion of a trade or business, or the major portion of a separate unit of a trade or business, then for any taxable year ending on or after the disposition, the data from preceding taxable years attributable to the disposed portion of the trade or business may not be used in determining the bank's recovery percentage. However, the data is excluded only if the bank furnished the acquiring person the information necessary for the computation of the acquiring firm's recovery percentage. No special provision is made for dispositions either to entities that are not banks or to entities that do not elect the safe harbor method of accounting for interest on nonperforming loans.[70]

§5.3.7 Charge-Off of Accrued Interest

When interest is accrued into taxable income and subsequently becomes uncollectible, the bank's remedy is to take a loan loss deduction, even if the accrual and the uncollectibility occur in the same tax year.[71] It is improper to reverse the accrual during the year by reducing interest income, as is usually done on the books.[72] Thus, if during the taxable year the principal of a loan is determined to be uncollectible in whole or in part, accrual of interest is required to continue for tax purposes until it is determined that there is no reasonable expectancy to receive the interest. A loan loss deduction is the appropriate method for adjusting income once the accrued interest is determined to be uncollectible.[73]

The standards for discontinuing income accrual and for charging-off a bad debt are materially different.[74] Thus, it is quite possible that accrual can be discontinued but, because of the different standards for charging-off a loan and discontinuing accrual, in the absence of following the procedure outlined in Revenue Ruling 2007-32 the accrued interest does not qualify as a bad debt deduction.

Revenue Ruling 2007-32 permits a bad debt deduction for accrued interest, without question, to those banks that have elected the conformity method of accounting for loan losses prescribed in Regulation section 1.166-2(d).[75]

---

[70] See Reg. §1.585-4 for rules applicable to loan loss deductions when there are reorganizations and asset acquisitions.

[71] Rev. Rul. 2007-32, 2007-1 C.B. 1278.

[72] *Spring City Foundry Co. v. Commissioner*, 34 U.S.T.C. ¶1276, 292 U.S. 182 (1934); *European American Bank and Trust Co. v. United States*, 20 Cl. Ct. 594, 608 (1990). *Cf. Electric Controls and Service Co. v. Commissioner*, T.C. Memo. 1996-486.

[73] Rev. Rul. 80-361, 1980-2 C.B. 164; *see also* Rev. Rul. 81-18, 1981-1 C.B. 295.

[74] *Corn Exchange Bank v. United States*, 38-2 U.S.T.C. ¶455, 37 F.2d 34 (2nd Cir. 1938); Code §§451, 166 and 585.

[75] See discussion at §5.3.8.

The conformity method is available only to those members of the consolidated group that meet the tax definition of a "bank."[76] Thus, a mortgage company, credit card bank, or any other member of the consolidated group that does not satisfy the Code section 581 tax definition of a "bank" is not permitted to elect this conformity method for accrued interest receivable.

As an alternative, a taxpayer (any taxpayer, not only a "bank") may consider treating the accrued interest as a "security" for purposes of the Code section 475 mark-to-market rules and mark the receivable it to its fair market value at year end.[77]

For those banks that neither make the conformity election nor take a mark-to-market write down, the only alternative to discontinuing accrual is to prove that there is no reasonable expectancy that payments will be received on the loan and secure a bad debt deduction. However, the taxpayer must prove that the interest is a worthless debt. If the taxpayer does not charge-off the entire amount of the loan, it may be that the IRS will take the position that this standard will not be satisfied.

There may be an advantage to those banks who use the experience formula for determining their allowable bad-debt deductions under the reserve method and who treat the interest reversed on the books, as well as the uncollected interest that is not included in income, as a bad debt for tax purposes. By classifying the accrued interest as a bad debt, the bank's ratio used to determine the allowable bad-debt reserve balance under the experience method would be increased.[78] However, the IRS has taken the position on audit that including accrued interest receivable in a bank's bad-debt computation is a method of accounting.[79] A bank that had not previously used this method of accounting could not adopt it without first receiving permission from the IRS to change its method of accounting. Only if the taxpayer complies with the procedures contained in Revenue Procedure 2007-33, discussed below, will permission be granted.[80]

§ 5.3.8 Banks Using Conformity Bad Debt Method

A taxpayer that has made the Regulation section 1.166-2(d) bad debt conformity election may offset the accrued interest income on nonperforming loans with a bad debt deduction. A deduction is allowed for the amount of interest income on non-accrual loan receivables that is included in income with respect to a loan charged-off under the conformity method of accounting.[81]

Regulation section 1.166-2(d)(3) permits a "bank," as defined in Code section 581, to use a conformity method of accounting to determine when a debt

[76] I.R.C. § 581. See discussion in Chapter 1 of which entities satisfy the tax definition of a "bank."

[77] See discussion at § 5.3.9.

[78] The benefit would not be realized by a thrift that had used the percentage of taxable income method or an institution that is limited in its reserve addition by, for example, a decline in loans.

[79] TAM 8741006, May 21, 1987. *See* discussion of "Deduction For Worthless Debt" in Ch. 10 for comment on this Technical Advice Memorandum.

[80] Rev. Proc. 2007-33, I.R.B. 2007-21.

[81] See discussion at § 10.4.2.

becomes worthless.[82] This method is not available to any member of the bank consolidated group that is not a Code section 581 bank, but it is available to both banks that use the Code section 166 specific charge-off method for determining bad debt deductions and banks that use the Code section 585 reserve method accounting for loan losses.

Under a conformity method, debts that are classified as "loss assets" and charged-off, in whole or in part, for regulatory purposes are conclusively presumed to become worthless for federal income tax purposes at the time of the regulatory charge off. This method for determining worthlessness is a method of accounting and is permitted to be used in lieu of the other bank specific methods for determining worthlessness set forth in Regulation sections 1.166-2(d)(1) and (2). This conformity method permits a bank to recognize a bad debt deduction for the taxable year in which a debt is conclusively presumed to have become worthless.

The conformity method of accounting is available only with respect to a loan that has been charged-off. Revenue Ruling 2007-32 takes a fairy liberal interpretation of when a loan will be regarded as charged-off. It treats the reversal of the accrued interest as constituting a charge-off of the interest receivable.[83] Furthermore, the failure to recognize accrued interest for regulatory financial statement purposes is treated as tantamount to recognizing the accrued interest as income and immediately charging-off the uncollected accrued interest receivable as a loss asset. Thus, under the conformity method of accounting, the taxpayer will be entitled to claim a worthless debt deduction under Code section 166 for the reversed interest and the uncollected interest.

§5.3.9 Mark-to-Market Loss

It is possible that accrued interest receivable may qualify as a "security" for purposes of the Code section 475 mark-to-market rules.[84] As such, this item is eligible under those rules for a year-end mark to fair market value. The fair market value of accrued interest on a loan in a nonperforming status is likely to be little or nothing. Thus, taxpayers may wish to consider identifying the account into which accrued interest receivable is booked as a security which is subject to the Code section 475 mark-to-market rules. To properly mark a security to market value at year-end, the security must be properly identified when acquired. A retroactive identification is not permitted. Proper identification includes placing the security in an account that is identified as containing securities that are marked-to-market under Code section 475.[85]

---

[82] The IRS recognizes that there are various procedures that a bank may employ to classify a debt, or portion thereof, as a loss asset described in §1.166-2(d)(3)(ii)(C). Rev. Rul. 2001-59, 2001-2 C.B. 585.

[83] Reg. § 1.166-2(d)(3)(ii)(C).

[84] The term "security" is defined in I.R.C. § 475(c)(2). For a discussion of the mark-to-market rules, see Chapter 4.

[85] Rev. Rul 97-39, 1997-2 C.B. 62. See discussion in Chapter 4.

§5.3.10 Resumption of Accrual

Income accrual must be reinstated if the debtor's circumstances change such that collectibility is assured.[86] However, according to a leading case on the issue, "The Government should not tax under claim of income that which is not received during the taxable year and in all probability will not be paid within a reasonable time thereafter."[87]

The Fourth Circuit Court of Appeals in *Clifton Manufacturing Company* held that although an accrual method taxpayer is permitted to discontinue accrual on amounts where collection is sufficiently doubtful, the taxpayer must include those amounts in income if and when the circumstances change so that the doubt is removed and the likelihood of collection is restored.[88] In a reversal of roles the taxpayer, in order to shield itself by using the statute of limitations, argued that interest income should have been accrued in the year in which it was earned as opposed to the subsequent year in which it was actually received. The Commissioner attempted to demonstrate that at the time when the interest was earned there was reason to doubt that the payment would ever be collected because the debtor was in receivership. In holding for the taxpayer, the court stated that the test for inclusion is at what point in time does both the right to receive the income and the assurance of collection exist.[89] Based on the facts of the case, the court found that the test was satisfied when the debtor was returned to complete solvency.[90]

§5.3.11 Payments After Non Accrual

If accrual has been discontinued and then a payment is received, the Court of Appeals for the Federal Circuit has held that the loan contract controls in spite of the continuing question of collectibility.[91] In *European American Bank and Trust Co.* the lender chose not to declare a note due and payable. The court concluded that the lender was bound to the contract provision requiring payments to be applied to interest first, even in a case where collectibility might ordinarily be sufficiently doubtful to warrant discontinuance of accrual by an accrual method taxpayer.[92] The court went on to find that under the facts of that case, even if the contract had not included this limiting clause, there was a reasonable expectation

---

86 *Clifton Manufacturing Company v. Commissioner*, 43-2 U.S.T.C. ¶9539, 137 F.2d 290 (4th Cir. 1943). *Clifton* arose on appeal from the Tax Court, which discussed but did not decide the issue. Subsequently, in *Commissioner v. New Hampshire Fire Insurance Company*, 45-1 U.S.T.C. ¶9141, 146 F.2d 697 (1st Cir. 1945), the Tax Court indicated its approval of the Court of Appeals decision. For bank regulatory purposes, the instructions to FFIEC schedules 031, 032, 033, and 034 at page A-62 (9-97) provides that "a non-accrual asset may be restored to accrual status when (1) none of its principal and interest is due and unpaid, and the bank expects repayment of the remaining contractual principal and interest, *or* (2) when it otherwise becomes well secured and in the process of collection."

87 *Corn Exchange Bank v. United States*, 38-2 U.S.T.C. ¶455, 37 F.2d 34 (2d Cir. 1938).

88 *Clifton*, 137 F.2d at 292.

89 *Id. See also American Central Utilities Co. v. Commissioner*, 36 B.T.A. 688, 691 (1937), holding that a taxpayer's income need only include the amount of interest actually collected due to doubtfulness of collectibility.

90 *Id. See also* PLR 8650035, September 12, 1986. As discussed in this letter ruling, this exception has also been applied to situations where the borrower is in receivership, the assets are not sufficient to satisfy the debt in full, and the distribution was based on the principal amount of the debt.

91 *European American Bank and Trust Co. v. United States*, 940 F.2d 677 (Fed. Cir. 1991).

92 *Id.*

of payment. This conclusion was based on the fact that the majority of the interest had been paid and the unpaid amounts were adequately protected by collateral.[93] This conclusion is supported by Regulation section 1.446-2(e), which appears to require all payments on a loan to first be applied to accrual interest.[94]

§5.3.12 O.I.D. on Nonperforming Loans

When a default in payment has occurred, accrual of O.I.D. may be subject to the statutory O.I.D. rules and not to the general rules applicable to the accrual of interest. The statutory framework for the treatment of debt instruments having O.I.D. is contained in Code sections 1271 through 1275. Although current inclusion in income of O.I.D. is generally required, an exception is provided for certain contingent obligations. Treasury regulations provide that a payment is not contingent "merely because of the possibility of impairment by insolvency, default, or similar circumstances."[95] Debt instruments may contain both stated interest and O.I.D. Thus, the accrual rules applicable to a debt instrument with both types of interest will be different. It is the position of the IRS that holders of debt instruments having O.I.D. must accrue O.I.D. so long as they hold the debt instruments, regardless of financial condition of the issuer, because there is no "doubtful collectibility" exception to O.I.D. accrual.[96] Although the O.I.D. provisions can be viewed as an accrual method of accounting designed to place holders of debt instruments having O.I.D. on par with holders of debt instruments that pay interest currently, it is the IRS's position that it does not follow that the "doubtful collectibility" exception to Regulation section 1.451-1(a) accrual should apply to O.I.D. accrual as well.

The IRS reasoned that O.I.D. is not included in income in advance of receipt; it is included in lieu of receipt. The O.I.D. provisions treat the O.I.D. transaction as occurring in two steps: first, interest is deemed paid to the holder; second, the holder is deemed to re-lend the same amount to the issuer. This additional investment in the debt causes the holder's basis in the debt instrument to increase by an equivalent amount. As O.I.D. is accrued, the holder is, in effect, receiving current interest and extending additional credit. The IRS stated that the argument that general interest accrual rules should trump more specific rules has been considered and rejected by the Tax Court, where the Court held that the general provisions of Code sections 446 and 461 do not override the specific imputed interest rules of section 483.[97]

§5.3.13 Open and Speculative Transactions

Under limited circumstances, the timing of income may be determined under a cost recovery method that holds a transaction "open" until the full

---

[93] *Id. See also Broderick v. Anderson*, 23 F. Supp. 488, 491 (S.D.N.Y. 1938), holding no reasonable doubt as to collection in spite of financial difficulties of the debtor where the debt was adequately protected by liens.

[94] See discussion at §5.3.5.

[95] Reg. §1.1275-4(a)(3).

[96] FSA 200018017, January 13, 2000; TAM 9538007, June 13, 1995. *See also* General Counsel Memorandum 39668, 1987.

[97] *Weis v. Commissioner*, 94 T.C. 473 (1990) and *Williams v. Commissioner*, 94 T.C. 464 (1990).

amount of loan principal or tax basis is recovered.[98] The consequence of a transaction being treated as "open" is for income to be deferred.[99]

For example, it has been held that the cost recovery method is acceptable where a taxpayer establishes that there is no readily ascertainable market value for rights to collect unpaid loans purchased at a discount.[100] No part of the collections are taxed as discount or interest income until basis is fully recovered.[101] Similarly, the uncertainty of realizing acquisition discount occasioned by the speculative nature of promissory notes permits deferral of discount income.[102] However, where the speculative nature of purchased notes cannot be proven, a taxpayer is required to include discount in income on a current basis.[103]

Factors that determine whether an obligation is "speculative" include:

1. The existence of personal liability of the debtor and/or a guarantor or endorser and his financial responsibility;
2. The marketability of the obligation and its negotiability;
3. The presence or absence, at the time of acquisition, of substantial default on payments due by the obligor;
4. The terms of payment and the nature and the amount of the security for the obligation at acquisition; and
5. The size of the discount.[104]

§5.3.14 Coordinated Issue Papers

Prior to the issuance of Revenue Ruling 2007-32, it was the IRS's position that discontinuance of accrual of interest was not automatic, either upon the borrower's default in the payment of interest or when a bank regulatory agency required discontinuance of accrual.[105] The IRS position was expressed in two examination level Coordinated Issue Papers, one issued by the Commercial Bank Specialist and another issued by the Thrift Specialist, and in a Coordinated Issue Paper released by the National Director of Appeals. The examination level papers were intended to guide IRS agents examining banks and thrifts.[106] In theory, examining agents were required to apply the rules set forth in the papers; however, actual practice was often at variance with the stated policy. Moreover,

[98] *See* discussion at §1.5 for treatment of income inclusion in the absence of any payment of interest or principal.

[99] *Burnet v. Logan*, 2 U.S.T.C. ¶736, 283 U.S. 404 (1931). Loans or other debt obligations purchased at a discount are probably subject to the market discount bond rules. *See* I.R.C. §1277 and following.

[100] *E.A. Phillips v. Frank*, 61-2 U.S.T.C. ¶9712, 295 F.2d 629 (9th Cir. 1961); *Vancoh Realty Co. v. Commissioner*, 33 B.T.A. 918, Dec. 9204 (1936); *Columbia State Savings Bank v. Commissioner*, 31 B.T.A. 685, Dec. 8797 (1934).

[101] *Id.; see also Harris Trust & Savings Bank v. Commissioner*, 24 B.T.A. 498, Dec. 7236 (1931); *Appeal of Somers Lumber Co.*, 2 B.T.A. 106, Dec. 548 (1925); *Stevenson v. Commissioner*, 9 B.T.A. 552, Dec. 3172 (1927).

[102] *M. Liftin v. Commissioner*, 63-1 U.S.T.C. ¶9465, 317 F.2d 234 (4th Cir. 1963). This is not the case with O.I.D. *See* TAM 9538007, June 13, 1995.

[103] *M.L. Grinsten v. Commissioner*, 23 T.C.M. 390, Dec. 26,678(M)(1964), TC Memo. 1964-51; *Darby Investment Corp. v. Commissioner*, 63-1 U.S.T.C. ¶9396, 315 F.2d 551 (6th Cir. 1963).

[104] *W.E. Underhill v. Commissioner*, 45 T.C. 489, Dec. 27, 857 (1966).

[105] Reg. §§1.446-1(c)(2)(ii) and 1.451-1(a).

[106] *See* IRS ISP Coordinated Issue Papers on Accrual of Interest on Non Performing Loans in Appendiz at §§A.6, A.7, A.8. The commercial bank paper is one of the oldest Coordinated Issue Papers, having been issued in the 1970s. The thrift paper was issued in the 1980s. The Appeals Paper was issued in 1993.

the papers were administratively infeasible to comply with and they sought to apply inapposite law. The IRS's Market Segment Specialization Program, "Audit Technique Guide for Commercial Banking," which is now at variance with the current policy expressed in Revenue Ruling 2007-32, sets forth the procedures agents were to follow when auditing this issue.[107]

In the two examination level Coordinated Issue Papers, the IRS has stated that interest accrual must continue until:

1. The bank has been given specific written instructions by its bank regulatory agency that the loan, in whole or in part, should be charged-off. If this occurs, interest accrual can be discontinued to the extent that the loan is charged-off;

2. On loans not charged-off, the taxpayer substantiates, on a loan by loan basis, that the interest is "uncollectible."[108]

The threshold for discontinuing accrual set forth in these Coordinated Issue Papers is practically unattainable by most banks. First of all, it is unusual for a bank to receive "specific written instructions" to charge-off a loan. This is because banks customarily charge-off loans before they are ordered to do so by their regulator. If a bank waits until after its regulatory examination to determine which of its loans will be charged-off, the bank's CAMEL rating may be adversely affected.[109] Thus, banks self-monitor their loan portfolio to determine when to charge-off bad debts.

Secondly, it is not feasible for a bank "on a loan by loan basis" to substantiate that interest is uncollectible, especially for larger institutions. Because banks have literally thousands of loans, including small denomination installment and credit card loans, a loan by loan analysis would require burdensome, time consuming and costly administrative work. The automatic discontinuation of accrual policies that most banks employ, such as discontinuance of accrual after a loan is in default for a period of 90-days, avoids this costly analysis.

Beyond these practical and operational reasons for the IRS Coordinated Issue papers to be infeasible, there is a substantive tax law problem with the discontinuance of accrual thresholds they prescribe. The standard for discontinuing accrual expressed in these papers is a bad debt charge off standard, as prescribed in Code section 166, and not the Code section 451 income accrual standard.

---

[107] Audit Technique Guide for Commercial Banking, Ch. 4, located at Appendix D.

[108] *See also* TAM 8137004, May 19, 1980, which contains IRS approval of discontinuance of accrual when the taxpayer, on a loan-by-loan basis, determined that interest was uncollectible. It has been the IRS's audit policy that banks should continue to accrue interest on loans to lesser developed countries that were placed in a nonaccrual status on the books in 1987. Taxpayers have been required, on a loan-by-loan basis, to substantiate that the interest was uncollectible. According to the IRS, the fact that interest was collected on many of these loans during 1988 as part of the restructuring of the loans made it impossible for taxpayers to show that the interest was uncollectible.

[109] The CAMELS rating is a regulatory rating of a bank's capital, assets, management, earnings and liquidity and sensitivity to interest rate risk. It is the "management" component of the rating that is adversely affected when a bank is repeatedly ordered to write off loans.

§5.3.15 Code Sections 166 and 451 Contrasted

The standard of proof for discontinuing interest accrual is different from the test for charging off a bad debt. In *Corn Exchange Bank*, the Second Circuit stated that "[i]t is not necessary that there be equally as strong evidence [to discontinue interest accrual], as warrants writing off an account as a loss, as in the case of a bad debt."[110] In *European American Bank*, the Claims Court stated: "[t]he requirements necessary to establish a bad debt deduction, however, are entirely different from those necessary to accrue income."[111] Further, the Board of Tax Appeals earlier stated that a reasonable doubt as to the ability of the debtor to pay justified a bank's reporting only the amount of interest that was actually received.[112] Even the National Office of the IRS recently acknowledged this distinction. In a Field Service Advice it stated: "[a]s a general matter, the determination of the proper accrual on interest on nonperforming loans should be considered separately from the issue of whether Taxpayer is entitled to a bad debt deduction with respect to a debt instrument or whether Taxpayer is entitled to a conclusive presumption of correctness under the conformity method."[113]

Despite these established principles, in the Examination Level Coordinated Issue Papers on nonaccrual of interest the two tests have been merged.[114] The papers also appear to misconstrue judicial authority on this point when stating:

> Thus, it can be seen that there appears to be agreement on the basic law in the area . . . . What the above cases have in common is a showing of worthlessness as that term is used in Code Sec. 166(a).

Both the "charge off" test and the "uncollectible" test relate to the Code section 166 bad-debt deduction provision and not to the Code section 451 discontinuance of accrual rule. In fact, the language of the two tests prescribed in the paper is nearly identical to language contained in Regulation section 1.166-2(d). Furthermore, the "above cases" cited by the IRS include the *Corn Exchange Bank* case, which does not stand for the proposition expressed by the IRS. Of course, the test for discontinuing interest accrual has not been applied by the IRS for purposes of determining whether a loan may be charged off. The IRS has ruled that discontinuance of tax accrual will not justify a loan loss deduction.[115]

§5.3.16 Appeals Guidelines

The Appeals Settlement Guideline that addresses non performing loans is designed to provide guidance to Appeals Officers who deal with a nonaccrual of

[110] *Corn Exchange Bank v. United States*, 37 F.2d 34 (2d Cir. 1930). The Appeals Coordinated Issue Paper on accrual of interest on non-performing loans appears to pay some respect to this different standards. After summarizing the law on accrual of income, the paper states: "Certainly, if the underlying loan is properly written off, that standard has been met . . . ." *See also Bank of Kirksville v. United States*, 943 F. Supp. 1191 (W.D. Mo. 1996).

[111] *European American Bank and Trust Co. v. United States*, 20 Cl. Ct. 594, 608-609 (1990).

[112] *Atlantic Coast Line R.R. Co. v. Commissioner*, 31 B.T.A. 730, Dec. 8817 (1934). *See also Electric Controls and Service Co. v. Commissioner*, T.C. Memo. 1996-486.

[113] FSA 200018017, January 13, 2000.

[114] *See* IRS Industry Specialization Program Position Papers on Delinquent Loans at A1, 106, 107, 108.

[115] TAM 8251001, December 15, 1981.

interest issue raised in a protest filed with the IRS or a Petition filed in U.S. Tax Court.[116] In light of Revenue Ruling 2007-32, this pronouncement also must be modified. The paper is similar to that issued by the examination level paper, but it does have some significant differences. First, the paper addresses the situation in which a taxpayer has made the Regulation Section 1.166-2(d)(3) conformity election. Not surprisingly, the paper concludes that accrual can be discontinued on loans (or portions thereof) classified as "loss assets" by taxpayers who have made the conformity election.

Second, the paper revokes Revenue Ruling 81-18 and explains why it was never intended to apply to commercial banks.[117] To the contrary, Revenue Ruling 2007-32 refers extensively to Revenue Ruling 81-18. In this ruling, the taxpayer charged off, pursuant to regulations of the Federal Home Loan Bank Board ("FHLBB") then in effect, interest accrued on its accounting books that was in default for 90 days.[118] The charge-off was confirmed in writing by FHLBB examiners upon the first audit of the thrift following the charge-off.[119] The IRS concluded that the charge-off, as confirmed by the bank examiners, was conclusive evidence that the interest due and payable was uncollectible, and discontinuance of future accruals would automatically be justified.

The taxpayer did not offer any evidence of the uncollectibility of the future interest, nor did it charge-off any of the principal. The IRS's conclusion was based on its reading of Regulation section 1.166-2(d), which provides a conclusive presumption of worthlessness if (1) indebtedness is charged off in obedience to the specific orders of a bank regulator, or (2) indebtedness is charged off and the charge-off is confirmed in writing by the appropriate bank regulator upon its examination of the bank following the charge-off.[120]

The reasons given for the revocation of Revenue Ruling 81-18 are questionable. The Appeals Settlement Guideline states that the FHLBB regulation requiring the charge-off of accrued but uncollected interest when delinquency reaches

[116] Accrual of Interest on Non Performing Loans, Appeals Settlement Guideline, Appendix A.8. The Appeal Settlement Guideline was promulgated in June 1993. There are two categories of papers issued by the Appeals Office of the IRS: settlement guidelines and settlement positions. According to an explanation provided by the IRS, a "settlement guideline" is a paper that explains the basic premise behind the adjustment, explores the positions of the opposing parties (government and taxpayer), and sets out the major items of fact and law that must be known and/ or considered in order to arrive at a conclusion in the case. The paper will not have a settlement number, nor will it have a settlement range. It will not tell the appeals officer what constitutes an acceptable settlement. A "settlement position" is a paper that sets out a specific settlement for a purely legal issue. This is an issue where differences in fact either do not exist because the issue or transaction only takes one form, or differences in fact would not change the settlement because the only question is the resolution of legal dispute.

[117] Rev. Rul. 81-18, 1981-1 C.B. 295.

[118] 12 C.F.R. §563c.11(b)(1) (1997) provides that interest shall be classified uncollectible if any portion thereof is due but uncollected for a period in excess of 90 days, with certain exceptions. The regulation then provides that "[a]t least quarterly, appropriate income accounts shall be charged with the amount of uncollectible income and a corresponding amount shall be credited to an account or accounts descriptive of uncollectible income."

[119] It is understood that the Office of the Comptroller of the Currency no longer issues confirmation letters. However, some state banks continue to receive such letters from Federal Reserve Board bank examiners and state regulators.

[120] Rev. Rul. 81-18 was confirmed in a subsequently issued Technical Advice Memorandum involving two savings and loan institutions. In the latter, the IRS expressly stated that it was unnecessary for the taxpayers to charge off the underlying debt, provided that the requirements of Reg. §1.166-2(d) were met. TAM 8251001, December 15, 1981.

90-days was withdrawn effective January 1, 1989. Although this statement is accurate, thrifts continue this treatment in accordance with general regulatory accounting practices. Since there is no statutory support for a distinction in the treatment of thrifts and commercial banks (and there does not appear to be any rational justification for a distinction), the Revenue Ruling 81-18 threshold for discontinuing accrual set forth for thrifts should be applicable to commercial banks as well. The reliance placed on it in Revenue Ruling 2007-32 thus appears to be justified.

In addition to these two differences between the Examination Level Coordinated Issue Papers and the Appeals Settlement Guidelines, there is one other significant distinction. In the Appeals Settlement Guideline there appears to be more overt recognition of the difference between the standards for when a loan may be charged-off and when accrual of income may be discontinued. For example, in the Appeals Settlement Guideline, the IRS paraphrases the language from *Corn Exchange Bank* in saying that "the Court stated that the evidence need not be as strong to justify non-accrual as is needed to write off the underlying debt . . . ." Elsewhere in the Appeals Settlement Guideline, the IRS acknowledges in a backhanded way that the bad debt uncollectibility standard is not the accrual standard when it states, "How strong the showing of uncollectibility must be is not clear . . . . Certainly, if the underlying loan is properly written off, that standard has been met . . . ."

§5.3.17 IRS Historical Practice

Many revenue agents have applied a more practical and equitable approach than that specified in the Coordinated Issue Papers. It is unlikely that they will exercise this flexibility under the rules of Revenue Ruling 2007-32. What has been the practice of some revenue agents was the following:

1. On loans that are placed in nonaccrual status by a bank, the bank's treatment will not be disturbed if the loan does not return to accrual status on the books, the borrower does not repay the interest in default, or the debt is not repaid with collateral that has been foreclosed;[121]
2. On loans substantially charged off, accrual can be discontinued on the entire loan, not just the portion charged off;[122]
3. On credit card and other short-term loans, the book treatment can be followed for tax purposes; and
4. On large loans that are not covered by the first or second of the above practices, the taxpayer must, on a loan-by-loan basis, substantiate the discontinuance of accrual;[123] however, statistical sampling may be employed.

---

[121] This "look back" approach cannot be employed to convince an agent that the bank should have discontinued accrual when it did not do so.

[122] *See* the Supreme Court's opinion in *Spring City Foundry Co. v. Commissioner*, 4 U.S.T.C. ¶1276, 292 U.S. 182 (1934), where a change in the bad debt deduction statute, from permitting a deduction only when a debt became completely worthless to permitting a deduction when a debt became *partially* worthless, provides support for discontinuing accrual at least to the extent that a loan is partially worthless.

[123] Reg. §1.166-2(d). TAM 8137004, May 19, 1980.

Of course, these practices were not universal; that is, particular revenue agents applied some, all, or none of the above practices. For those banks, especially larger institutions, which followed book treatment, agents commonly employed statistical sampling techniques to arrive at the portion of interest on non performing loans that may be nonaccrual for tax purposes.

§5.3.18 Audit Protection

A bank that elects to change its method of accounting for uncollected interest to the safe harbor method provided for in Revenue Procedure 2007-33 does so under Revenue Procedure 2002-9. The latter procedure is available to banks or other taxpayers whose primary business is making or managing loss.[124] If a taxpayer elects to change its method of accounting, the election must be made for all of its loans.[125] When a taxpayer timely complies with the applicable provisions of the revenue procedure, the IRS will not require the taxpayer to change its method of accounting for the same item for a taxable year prior to the year of change.[126] Thus, audit protection will be obtained.[127]

The method of accounting for nonperforming loans required by Revenue Procedure 2002-9 was a method that appears to be contrary to the judicially approved method and to the method of accounting for interest income set forth in Treasury regulations under Code section 451.[128] According to the revenue procedure:

> "[A] taxpayer must continue accruing qualified stated interest on any nonperforming loan until either the loan is worthless under §166 and charged-off as a bad debt, or (ii) the interest is determined to be uncollectible. In order for interest to be determined uncollectible, the taxpayer must substantiate, taking into account all the facts and circumstances, that it has no reasonable expectation of payment of the interest. This substantiation requirement is applied on a loan by loan basis."[129]

Code section 481(a) provides that a taxpayer making a change of accounting method must take into account those adjustments that are determined to be necessary solely by reason of the change in order to prevent amounts from being duplicated or omitted. A taxpayer making the adjustment for nonperforming loans may be permitted to report its Code section 481(a) adjustment over a six-year spread period.[130] In effect, a Code section 481(a) adjustment represents the aggregate amount of net income or expense that would have been reported in years prior to the year of change if the taxpayer had been on the new method in such prior years. Accordingly, the amount of a taxpayer's Code section 481(a) adjustment is generally computed at the beginning of the year of change by comparing the amounts of income and/or expense the taxpayer reported under

---

[124] Revenue Procedure 2002-9, 2002-1 C.B. 327.

[125] *Id.* at §5A.01(1)(d).

[126] *Id.* at §7.

[127] Quite possibly, this revenue procedure can be used to discontinue accrual at the date of default, if the taxpayer was discontinuing accrual at a later date in accordance with its book accounting treatment of the item.

[128] *SecurityBank Minnesota v. Commissioner*, 98 T.C. 33 (1992), *aff'd.* 994 F.2d 432 (8th Cir. 1993); *Security Bank v. Commissioner*, 214 F.3d 1254 (10th Cir. 2000).

[129] Revenue Procedure 2002-9, 2002-1 C.B. 327.

[130] TAM 200134005, April 27, 2001.

its prior method and the amounts that the taxpayer would have reported if the taxpayer had used the new method in prior years.[131] In general, in order to properly compute its Code section 481(a) adjustment, a taxpayer is required to compare, for nonperforming loans outstanding at the beginning of the year of change, the amount of qualified stated interest it reported under its prior method and the amount of qualified stated interest it would have reported if it had used the new method in prior years.

The Code section 481(a) adjustment with respect to nonperforming loans, more precisely, is equal to the amount of qualified stated interest on the taxpayer's nonperforming loans outstanding as of the beginning of the year of change that, in accordance with the IRS's interpretation of the applicable law, should have been accrued under Code section 451 and Treasury regulation section 1.451-1(a), but was not accrued. Interest for which the taxpayer, as of the beginning of the year of change, has no reasonable expectation of payment is not taken into account in determining the amount of the Code section 481(a) adjustment.

[131] Reg. § 1.481-1(c)(1).

Chapter 6
Modified Debt

Contents

§6.1 Tax Planning Suggestions
§6.2 Elements of Exchange Treatment
  §6.2.1 *Cottage Savings Association*
  §6.2.2 Foundation for Regulations
  §6.2.3 *Cottage Savings* Regulations
§6.3 Measuring Gain or Loss
  §6.3.1 Statutory Rules
  §6.3.2 IRS Positions
  §6.3.3 O.I.D. Rules

§6.1 Tax Planning Suggestions

In nearly every situation when a loan or other debt instrument is renegotiated, a deemed taxable exchange occurs.[1] A taxable exchange will occur regardless of whether the transaction has any book accounting effect.[2] To a bank, taxation of a debt exchange may result in a deductible ordinary loss or an ordinary gain. For a nonbank taxpayer, the resulting gain or loss may be capital. Banks appear to have significant flexibility to determine when a taxable event will occur and to determine the amount of the gain or loss.

If a debt instrument that is acquired after issuance is modified, current Treasury regulations appear to cause phantom gain to be recognized. The gain is equal to the difference between the taxpayer's adjusted cost basis in the instrument and the instrument's amount realized, as determined under Treasury regulations. Unlike with originated debt instruments, there is no offsetting bad debt deduction to eliminate the phantom gain.

In addition to the prospect of gain or loss occurring at the time that a debt instrument is renegotiated, there are other significant tax implications. The instrument received in the exchange may properly be classified as a debt obligation with original issue discount, thus requiring the holder to take into income the discount in accordance with Code section 1272.[3] If any debt is forgiven, the creditor may be responsible for reporting the debt forgiveness to the Internal Revenue Service.

Exchange treatment for debt modifications has been accepted by the IRS for some time, and the Treasury Department has promulgated final regulations under Code section 1001 that clarify the situations when the modification of a

[1] *See The Art of Tax Efficiency in Community Banks*, by M. Gula, J. Brew, and R. Blasi, 2007, Red Room Publishing, *http://www.mraeresources.com/bookstore/*.

[2] Financial Accounting Standards Board Statement No. 114 contains financial accounting rules governing debt restructuring. *See* discussion of Statement No. 114 in Ch. 5.

[3] For a discussion of income inclusion rules applicable to O.I.D., *see* Chapter 3.

debt instrument triggers a taxable exchange. The regulations explicitly apply the deemed debt exchange rules to loans made by banks.[4] These regulations are often referred to as the "Cottage Savings Regulations" because they were issued in response to the Supreme Court's 1991 decision in *Cottage Savings Association v. Commissioner*.[5] In that case, the Supreme Court found that a taxable exchange occurred when an interest in a mortgage pool was exchanged for a comparable interest in another mortgage pool. The *Cottage Savings* regulations appear to be designed to attenuate the so called hair trigger approach that seems to be expressed in the Supreme Court's opinion for when a taxable event occurs.

Subsequent to the promulgation of the *Cottage Savings* regulations, the Treasury Department finalized other regulations under Code section 1001 that contain rules for measuring the amount of gain or loss on deemed debt exchanges.[6] These regulations appear to alter long-standing rules for determining the amount of gain or loss that arises from an exchange. Their validity may be questioned as being in conflict with the expressly applicable Code section 1001 statutory provisions. Thus, Code section 1001 and the regulations thereunder may provide taxpayer with two choices for determining the amount of recognized gain on deemed debt exchanges: the statutory rule or the rule contained in the regulations.

With the enactment in 1993 of the Code section 475 mark-to-market rules, taxpayers were offered a third choice in determining gains or losses from debt exchanges. Any "new" debt received in an exchange, at the election of a taxpayer, can be subjected to the Code section 475 rules that will require unrealized gain or loss, measured by reference to year-end market value, to be recognized. However, if the mark-to-market rules are applied, the taxpayer would be required to make annual adjustments to income for the annual unrealized gain or loss. Conversely, if the taxpayer applies the Code section 1001 rules, any difference between tax basis and the stated redemption price of the obligation would probably be accrued into income using the Original Issue Discount ("O.I.D.") rules.

This chapter discusses all issues associated with the current state of the law on debt exchanges, including the IRS's long-standing position on what constitutes a taxable exchange, how to measure gain or loss, and the effect of the final regulations. Examination of this issue begins with a discussion of the Supreme Court's opinion in *Cottage Savings*, which reveals judicial interpretation of Code section 1001.

---

[4] Reg. §1.1001-3, 61 Fed. Reg. 32,930 (June 26, 1996). This final regulation was preceded by proposed regulations published in 57 Fed. Reg. 57,034 (December 2, 1992).

[5] *Cottage Savings Association v. Commissioner*, 91-1 U.S.T.C. ¶50,187, 499 U.S. 554 (1991), *rev'g & rem'g* 89-2 U.S.T.C. ¶9662, 890 F.2d 848 (6th Cir. 1989). The regulations were prompted by *Cottage* because language in the opinion was thought to suggest a "hair trigger" test; *i.e.*, that any modification would result in a taxable exchange.

[6] Reg. §1.1001-1(g), 59 Fed. Reg. 4,799 (February 2, 1994). Statement No. 114 contains financial accounting rules governing debt restructuring. *See* discussion of Statement No. 114 in Ch. 5.

§6.2 Elements of Exchange Treatment

The substitution of a new debt instrument for the original instrument may be treated in either of two ways: (1) as a nontaxable alteration of the debt instrument, or (2) as a taxable exchange of the original instrument for the modified instrument. Most debt renegotiations will be treated as taxable events, regardless of whether an actual exchange of instruments evidencing the debt takes place, because the renegotiations will usually significantly modify the original debt instrument.

§6.2.1 *Cottage Savings Association*

In *Cottage Savings*, the Supreme Court ruled that a savings institution was allowed to deduct losses resulting from the exchange of participation interests in a group of mortgages.[7] Resolving a split between the Fifth and Sixth Circuit Courts of Appeals, the Supreme Court found that, because the mortgage loans exchanged constituted materially different properties, the exchanging institutions incurred deductible losses.

During the late 1970s, many savings and loan associations ("S&Ls") experienced considerable declines in the value of their long-term fixed-interest mortgage loans due to a dramatic increase in market rates of interest. At the time, S&Ls were regulated by the Federal Home Loan Bank Board ("FHLBB"). Under FHLBB accounting regulations, if an S&L wanted to sell its devalued mortgages and deduct the resulting losses for tax purposes, the losses would have to be recorded on the S&L's books. Such a practice would have decreased the net worth of many S&Ls to unacceptable levels, applying FHLBB standards, and could have precipitated S&L closings.

To assist S&Ls, the FHLBB issued Memorandum R-49.[8] It permitted S&Ls to avoid reporting losses from certain mortgage exchanges for regulatory and book accounting purposes, as long as the mortgages received in the exchange were substantially identical to the mortgages given. The FHLBB set forth various criteria that the mortgages had to satisfy in order to be considered substantially identical, including the requirement that the mortgages had to be single-family residential mortgages with the same terms to maturity and the same stated interest rates. Primarily for tax reasons, many S&Ls took advantage of this favorable FHLBB ruling. They formed groups or pools of mortgages which were "substantially identical" to pools being formed by other S&Ls. The substantially identical interests were then exchanged.

Although the resulting losses from the exchange went unreported for regulatory and book accounting purposes, the S&Ls took tax deductions for the difference between their tax basis in the participation interest that they gave up and the fair market value of the participation interest received. The IRS took the

[7] *Cottage Savings Association v. Commissioner*, 499 U.S. 554 (1991). This decision was followed by regulations issued under I.R.C. §1001, discussed below. Reg. §1.1001-3, 61 Fed. Reg. 32,930 (June 26, 1996). This final regulation was preceded by proposed regulations published in 57 Fed. Reg. 57,034 (December 2, 1992).

[8] Memorandum R-49, Federal Home Loan Bank Board (June 27, 1980).

position that the two pools of mortgages had to be materially different from each other for the exchange to be treated as a taxable disposition giving rise to the realization of gain or loss, and the participation interests were not materially different because they were mere economic substitutes.[9]

In *Centennial Savings Bank*, the companion case to *Cottage Savings*, the Fifth Circuit Court of Appeals accepted as the legal test, that a "material difference" was required, and found, as a fact, that the mortgage pools were materially different from one another because the obligors of the pooled mortgages (the homeowners) and the collateral securing such mortgages (the residences) were materially different.[10] Thus, the Fifth Circuit concluded that mortgages that qualified for special treatment under FHLBB rules as substantially identical could be materially different for tax purposes.

In *Cottage Savings*, the Sixth Circuit Court of Appeals did not endorse the view that the key issue was whether the exchanged properties were materially different.[11] Rather, it focused its analysis on the loss requirement of Code section 165. The Court held that although losses were realized at the time that the interests in the mortgage pools were exchanged (because the exchange was an identifiable event that fixed the amount of the decline in the value of the mortgages), the deduction was not allowable, as a matter of law, unless *actual* losses were sustained.[12] The Court found as a fact that Cottage's economic position was unchanged by the "reciprocal sales." Thus, it concluded that under such circumstances no deduction was allowable. In the Court's view, a loss is deductible only if it is specifically authorized by the Code, and Code section 165 limits deductibility to losses actually sustained.

The Supreme Court reviewed both the "material difference" and the "actual loss" tests and adopted the Fifth Circuit's position that a material difference requirement is the test to apply when determining whether gain or loss on the exchange of property is recognized. The Court focused on the appropriate criteria for evaluating material differences between properties. It rejected the IRS's economic substitute argument, which would find that properties were materially different only if they differed in economic substance. The Court viewed such a criteria as overly burdensome, as it required, in this case, a subjective examination of the attitudes of the parties, an evaluation of the secondary mortgage market, and an analysis of FHLBB considerations.

In formulating the criteria for material difference, the Court analogized groups of mortgages to groups of corporate stock. Typically, stocks are considered materially different as long as they are issued by different corporations.[13] Accordingly, a proper test for groups of mortgages was found to be one that determined the mortgages to be materially different if the holders enjoyed "legal

[9] I.R.C. § 1001(a); Reg. § 1.1001-1(a).

[10] *Centennial Savings Bank FSB v. Commissioner*, 89-2 U.S.T.C. ¶ 9612, 887 F.2d 595 (5th Cir. 1989); *San Antonio Savings Association v. Commissioner*, 89-2 U.S.T.C. ¶ 9614, 887 F.2d 577 (5th Cir. 1989).

[11] *Cottage Savings Association v. Commissioner*, 89-2 U.S.T.C. ¶ 9662, 890 F.2d 848 (6th Cir. 1989).

[12] I.R.C. § 165(a); Reg. § 1.165-1(b).

[13] *Marr v. United States*, 1 U.S.T.C. ¶ 137, 268 U.S. 536 (1925); *Phellis v. United States*, 1 U.S.T.C. ¶ 54, 257 U.S. 156 (1921).

entitlements" that were different in kind or in extent. Under this standard, the participation interests commonly exchanged by S&Ls were found to embody legally distinct entitlements because they derived from loans that were made to different obligors and were secured by different property.

§ 6.2.2 Foundation for Regulations

Although the debt modification regulations were triggered by the Supreme Court decision in *Cottage Savings,* the content of the regulations was significantly influenced by the many rulings and court decisions that preceded their issuance. Long before the finalization of regulations under Code section 1001, the IRS ruled that a taxable exchange occurs whenever there is a significant change in the material terms of an obligation.[14] Taxable exchange treatment did not depend on an amendment of the debt instrument itself.[15] Further, it was unnecessary for there to be an actual physical exchange of obligations if the changes to the terms "are so material as to amount virtually to the issuance of a new security . . . ."[16]

(a) *Change in Yield*

If an obligation's yield was significantly altered, a new debt was found to have been substituted for the old.[17] Thus, the IRS has ruled that an S&L recognized a deductible loss when a customer was granted a ten percent discount to refinance its mortgage loan. The loss was attributable to the cancellation of indebtedness.[18] Similarly, the waiver of a right under an interest adjustment clause to receive a higher rate of interest was a material change in the terms of an obligation.[19] It was found to give rise to a deemed exchange of "old" bonds for "new" bonds.

(b) *Change in Maturity Date*

In general, a change in the maturity date of a debt obligation was insufficient, in the absence of other changes in the terms, to cause a taxable event. Thus, the IRS has ruled that merely extending a note's maturity date did not constitute a taxable exchange.[20] Courts also have been reluctant to conclude that a taxable

---

[14] Rev. Rul. 73-160, 1973-1 C.B. 365. *See also* I.R.C. § 1037, which treats the surrender of certain U.S. government obligations as an "exchange," and I.R.C. § 1271, which treats the retirement of debt instruments as an exchange.

[15] Rev. Rul. 73-160

[16] *Id.*

[17] *Thomas Emery v. Commissioner,* 48-1 U.S.T.C. ¶ 9165, 166 F.2d 27 (2d Cir. 1948); General Counsel Memorandum 37002, February 10, 1977.

[18] TAM 8547001, June 26, 1985.

[19] Rev. Rul. 87-19, 1987-1 C.B. 249. *Cf.* PLR 8649046, September 9, 1986, where the substitution of one installment obligation bond and promissory note for another bond and note, with the only changes in terms being an adjustment in the interest rate, a temporary deferral of principal payments and the addition of a prepayment penalty, did not constitute a satisfaction or disposition of an installment obligation within the meaning of I.R.C. § 453B(a). Note that the rules for what constitutes an exchange or deemed exchange for purposes of I.R.C. § 453 are considerably different than those for purposes of I.R.C. § 1001.

[20] Rev. Rul. 73-160, 1973-1 C.B. 365; *see also Thomas Watson v. Commissioner,* 8 T.C. 569, Dec. 15,676 (1947); *Girard Trust Co. v. United States,* 48-1 U.S.T.C. ¶ 9209, 166 F.2d 773 (3d Cir. 1948); Rev. Rul. 60-195, 1960-1 C.B. 300. In Rev. Rul. 73-160, the IRS stressed that "there was not an actual exchange of one security for another." It is important to note that Rev. Rul. 73-160 is a restatement of earlier pronouncements in which two bonds differing in the dates of issue, of interest payments, and of maturity were held not to be substantially identical. General Counsel Memorandum 22056, 1940-2 C.B. 189. General Counsel Memorandum 22056 distinguished IT 2672, XII-1 C.B. 72 (1933). These earlier memoranda contained the following statement: "In all of these cases one issue of securities was exchanged for an entirely new and distinct issue, or securities of one issue

exchange has occurred when the maturity date is the only changed term.[21] In *Motor Products Corp. v. Commissioner*, the Board of Tax Appeals stated:

> Although they had different maturity dates, such dates were of little or no significance to petitioner as a creditor . . . . In this respect, from the standpoint of both the City and petitioner, the new bonds differed but little from the old bonds with regard to the time when they could be paid off.[22]

Similarly, where a debtor and creditor agreed to revise the amortization schedule but not extend the maturity date, the IRS ruled that no disposition occurred for purposes of Code section 1001.[23] However, where the change in the maturity date was material, exchanged bonds were not sufficiently identical obligations to permit tax deferral.[24] Coupling a change in interest rate with a change in maturity date will normally result in a taxable exchange.[25] Moreover, if the change in the maturity date causes a change in the yield of the obligation, there could be a deemed debt-exchange under the change in yield rules.

(c) *Change in Security, etc.*

When an obligation was issued with the intention that it was to serve as additional security for a debt, a taxable exchange of obligations did not occur, even if the newly issued obligation was secured.[26] The execution of a one-year agreement between a bank and a private obligor under bonds issued to provide tax-exempt financing for state development projects did not result in a reissuance of the bonds. Although the bank waived its right to accept the full amount of interest provided in the bond documents, the agreement effected a change of less than 12.5 basis points in the yield, which was found to be immaterial and insufficient to constitute a reissuance of the bonds.[27] The mere change in fair market value of a debt instrument before and after modification did not, on its own, establish that a new instrument has been issued in a taxable exchange for an old debt.[28]

(Footnote Continued)

were sold and those of an entirely new and distinct issue were purchased. In the present case, there was not an exchange of one security for another."

[21] Note that an extension of a maturity date is distinguished, in the final I.R.C. § 1001 regulations, from temporary inaction by the creditor to demand payment at the original maturity date.

[22] *Motor Products Corp. v. Commissioner*, 47 B.T.A. 983, Dec. 12,885 (1942). *See also City Bank Farmers Trust Co. v. Hoey*, 43-2 U.S.T.C. ¶ 9627, 138 F.2d 1023 (2d Cir. 1943).

[23] PLR 8714034, January 2, 1986. The revised amortization schedule resulted in less principal being paid in earlier years and more principal being paid in later years than originally called for under the terms of the bond. There was no change in the principal amount, interest rate, collateral, overall maturity dates or any other term relating to the bonds. The revision of the amortization schedule was consistent with the changes made to the obligation discussed in Rev. Rul. 73-160, 1973-1 C.B. 365. The revision also did not affect the tax-exempt status of the bonds. In PLR 8742032, July 20, 1987, the reduction in an amortization rate of a bond from ten percent to 6.5 percent, which caused a reduction in the monthly obligations, did not constitute a reissuance of the bond. Thus, the change did not constitute a deemed exchange of the outstanding obligation for a new and materially different obligation. The tax-exempt status of the interest paid on the bond was, accordingly, unaffected.

[24] *Marjorie K. Campbell v. Commissioner*, 41-1 U.S.T.C. ¶ 9359, 313 U.S. 15 (1941).

[25] Rev. Rul. 81-169, 1981-1 C.B. 429; TAM 8451012, August 23, 1984; TAM 8052023, September 25, 1980.

[26] *Robert J. Dial v. Commissioner*, 24 T.C. 117, Dec. 20,983 (1955).

[27] PLR 8932067, August 11, 1989.

[28] Rev. Rul. 81-169, 1981-1 C.B. 429.

If a new obligor is substituted for the original obligor, a taxable exchange is likely to have occurred whenever a truly different debtor becomes liable under the terms of the obligation.[29]

§6.2.3 *Cottage Savings* Regulations

The *Cottage Savings* regulations embrace the principles expressed in earlier IRS rulings and in court decisions, but they provide broader guidance, they clarify some areas of uncertainty, and they specifically apply the new rules to loans made by banks. Furthermore, the regulations ameliorate what was perceived to be the "hair-trigger" approach to determining whether a taxable exchange occurred expressed in the Supreme Court's *Cottage Savings* opinion. As a general rule, the regulations provide that any "significant modification" of a debt instrument, regardless of how the modification is effectuated, is treated as an exchange of the original instrument for a modified instrument that differs materially either in kind or extent.[30] Gain or loss realized from such an exchange is treated as recognized, except as otherwise provided in the Code.[31]

The final regulations have abandoned the strict term-based approach contained in proposed regulations to prevent the manipulation of the recognition of gain or loss.[32] In those situations not dealt with in specific debt modification situations described in the regulations, an economic significance rule will apply. Pursuant to this rule, a modification will be significant if, based on all the facts and circumstances, the legal rights or obligations being changed and the degree to which they are being changed are economically significant.[33]

The Cottage Savings regulations apply, generally, to determine whether certain securitization vehicles that hold loans qualify as Real Estate Mortgage Investment Conduits ("REMICs"), which are governed by Code sections 860A through 860G. Pursuant to those provisions, a REMIC must hold a fixed pool of real estate mortgages and related assets, and it may not have the power to vary those assets. Even if an entity initially qualifies as a REMIC, one or more significant modifications of loans held by the entity may terminate the qualification if the modifications cause less than substantially all of the entity's assets to be qualified mortgages.

However, the I.R.S. has ruled that certain loan modifications will not be significant for purposes of Regulation section 1.860G-2(b)(1), even if the modifications are significant under the rules of Regulation section 1.1001-3. In particular, under Regulation section 1.860G-2(b)(3)(i), if a change in the terms of an

[29] General Counsel Memorandum 39225, April 28, 1984; *but cf.*, PLR 8504049, October 30, 1984.

[30] Reg. §1001-3(b). Earlier cases placed emphasis on the intention of the parties. In recent cases the courts were persuaded by the collectibility of the new note. *Mellinger v. United States*, 38-1 U.S.T.C. ¶9090, 21 F. Supp. 964 (Cl. Ct. 1938); *Joe W. Scales v. Commissioner*, 18 T.C. 1263, Dec. 19,227 (1952) *(Acq.)*; *Francis Ward Paine v. Commissioner*, 25 B.T.A. 764, Dec. 7469 (1932). The regulations appear to place little emphasis on the intention of the parties.

[31] Reg. §1.1001-1(a).

[32] For a discussion of the tax treatment to a bank on the deemed exchange of debt obligations, *see* Harold L. Adrion and Ronald Blasi, *Renegotiated Debt: A Search for Standards*, Tax Lawyer, Vol. 44, Summer 1991. *See also* Rev. Rul. 89-122, 1989-2 C.B. 200, where the term-based approach was applied to determine whether a taxable exchange had occurred, but then the O.I.D. rules were used to measure the gain or loss.

[33] Reg. §1.1001-3(e).

obligation is "occasioned by default or a reasonably foreseeable default," the change is not a significant modification for purposes of Regulation section 1.860G-2(b)(1), regardless of the modification's status under Code section 1.1001-3.[34]

(a) *What is a "Modification?"*

A modification is defined as "any alteration including the addition or deletion, in whole or in part, of a legal right or obligation of the issuer or a holder whether the alteration is evidenced by an express agreement (oral or written), conduct of the parties, or otherwise."[35]

(i) General Rules. An alteration may occur automatically, it may occur by the original terms of a debt instrument, or it may occur as a result of the exercise of an option provided to the issuer or a holder. An actual physical exchange between a holder and the issuer of the original and the new instrument need not take place for there to be a modification.

(ii) Failure to Perform. The failure of either the borrower or the lender to exercise an option to change a term of an instrument is not a modification,[36] and an agreement between two or more holders (as compared with a holder and an issuer) of an instrument altering their rights and obligations under the instrument will not constitute a modification.[37] Furthermore, the failure of a borrower to perform in accordance with the terms of the loan agreement is not an alteration of the agreement.[38] Moreover, an agreement by a bank to stay collection or temporarily waive an acceleration clause or similar default right is not a modification.[39] A modification will not take place when a bank temporarily waives its right to receive full principal payment upon the borrower's default in making a scheduled payment. However, if the forbearance remains in effect for a period that exceeds (a) two years following the borrower's default and (b) an additional period during which the parties conduct good faith negotiations or during which the borrower is in a Title 11 or similar case, the agreement to forbear collection will be a modification.[40]

---

[34] Rev. Proc. 2008-47, 2008-31 I.R.B. 272 Rev. Proc. 2007-72, 2007-52 I.R.B. 1257, provided similar guidance regarding fast-track loan modifications that were effected in a manner consistent with certain principles, recommendations, and guidelines, which the American Securitization Forum ("ASF") released on December 6, 2007. In July 2008, the ASF released an updated Framework, which covers additional fast-track loan modifications.

[35] Reg. § 1.1001-3(c).

[36] Reg. § 1.1001-3(c)(5).

[37] Such an agreement may result in tax consequences to the parties, including a taxable sale to the original holder.

[38] Reg. § 1.1001-3(c)(4)(i).

[39] Reg. § 1.1001-3(d), Ex. 13.

[40] Reg. § 1.1001-3(c)(4)(ii).

(iii) Automatic Alteration. In general, an automatic alteration of a debt instrument will not be a modification. Thus, if the terms of a loan provide that the interest rate will be reset periodically based on the movement of the prime interest rate or based on some other objective market index, the change in interest rate will not be a modification.[41] For example, if a mortgage loan provides that the variable rate of interest charged on the loan will be reset annually based on the movement of the prime rate of interest, a change in the interest rate, even if by more than the greater of 25 basis points or 5 percent of the annual yield, would not result in a significant modification.[42] Similarly, if the terms of a loan provides that the interest rate is 9 percent but the rate would decrease to 8 percent if the borrower files an effective registration statement covering the loan with the Securities and Exchange Commission, the decrease in the interest rate would not be treated as a modification of the original instrument.[43]

(iv) Alteration by Operation of Original Terms. In general, an alteration of a legal right or obligation that occurs by operation of the original terms of a debt instrument will not be a modification. However, there are four situations when such an alteration will be a modification as follows:[44]

1. There is a change in the obligor.[45] If the obligor on an instrument changes, a modification occurs even if the change is pursuant to the original terms of the debt instrument. For example, if under the terms of a loan agreement with a corporate borrower an acquirer of substantially all of the corporation's assets may assume the corporation's obligations under the loan, and if substantially all of the corporation's assets are acquired by another corporation, when an acquiring corporation becomes the new obligor on the loan, the substitution of the new obligor will be a modification, even though it occurs by operation of the terms of the loan.[46]

2. The debt instrument changes from recourse to nonrecourse or vice versa.[47] If a debt instrument changes from recourse to nonrecourse or vice versa, a modification occurs even if the change is pursuant to the original terms of the debt instrument. For example, if under the terms of a loan agreement the borrower may secure release of recourse liability by placing certain government securities in trust in an amount sufficient to provide all interest and principal payments without any obligation to contribute additional securities to the trust, the release is a modification of the instrument.[48] However, if the borrower remains obligated to contribute additional securities to the trust if necessary to provide suffi-

---

41 Reg. § 1.1001-3(c)(1)(ii); Reg. § 1.1001-3(d), Ex. 1.

42 Reg. § 1.1001-3(g), Ex. 7. If the interest rate change exceeded the greater of 25 basis points or five percent of the annual yield and the change was not an automatic alteration, it would be a significant modification. Reg. § 1.1001-3(e)(2).

43 Reg. § 1.1001-3(d), Ex. 3.

44 Reg. § 1.1001-3(c)(ii).

45 Reg. § 1.1001-3(c)(2)(i).

46 Reg. § 1.1001-3(d), Ex. 4. This modification will probably not be a significant modification under an exception provided in Reg. § 1.1001-3(e)(4).

47 Reg. § 1.1001-3(c)(2)(i).

48 Reg. § 1.1001-3(d), Ex. 6.

cient amounts to satisfy payment obligations, a modification does not occur when the transfer is made.[49]

3. The debt instrument changes to an equity instrument or some other non debt instrument, other than a change pursuant to a conversion option.[50] If a debt instrument changes to an equity instrument or some other non debt instrument, other than a change pursuant to a conversion option, a modification occurs even if the change is pursuant to the original terms of the debt instrument. For example, if a debt instrument is exchanged for common stock at the option of the holder, a modification occurs.
4. The debt instrument changes pursuant to an option. In general, any other change in the terms of the instrument, with the exception of certain unilateral options discussed below, made pursuant to an option granted to an issuer or a holder will be a modification.

(v) Unilateral Alteration. A change made pursuant to an option granted to an issuer (borrower) or to a holder (lender) will not be a modification if the change is unilateral and, if the option is exercised by a holder, the alteration does not result in a deferral of, or a reduction in, any scheduled payment of interest or principal.[51] For example, if in connection with a loan to a corporation, a bank has the option to increase the interest rate by a specified amount upon a certain decline in the corporation's credit rating (which does not result in a deferral of or reduction in the scheduled payments), the increase in the interest rate is pursuant to a unilateral option and is not a modification.[52] However, if a bank has an option under the terms of a loan agreement to decrease the interest rate if market interest rates decline, the exercise of the unilateral option is a modification because it is exercised by the holder and it results in a reduction in scheduled payments of interest.[53]

An option is unilateral only if under the terms of an instrument or under applicable law three conditions are met.[54]

1. No offsetting option.[55] There does not exist at the time the option is exercised, or as a result of the exercise, a right of the other party to alter or terminate the instrument or to transfer the instrument to a person who is related to the issuer.
2. No consent.[56] The exercise of the option does not require the consent or the approval of the other party, a person who is related to the other party, or a court or arbitrator.[57] For example, if under the original terms

[49] Reg. § 1.1001-3(d), Ex. 5.

[50] Reg. § 1.1001-3(c)(2)(ii).

[51] Reg. § 1.1001-3(c)(2)(iii). For no apparent reason, the regulation prescribe a different rule for an alteration that results in an acceleration of payments by the holder. Such an alteration will not be a modification under this rule. However, it may be a modification under the general significance rule. Conversely, regardless of whether the yield on a debt instrument is increased or decreased, the safe-harbor rule applies. *See* § 6.2.3(b).

[52] Reg. § 1.1001-3(d), Ex. 9.

[53] Reg. § 1.1001-3(d), Ex. 7.

[54] Reg. § 1.1001-3(c)(3).

[55] Reg. § 1.1001-3(c)(3)(i).

[56] Reg. § 1.1001-3(c)(3)(ii).

[57] Under proposed regulations an exception to this rule was provided for situations where consent may not be unreasonably withheld. No such exception appears to be provided in the final regulations.

of the agreement the maturity date of a loan can be extended by the borrower, but only with the consent of the bank, because it requires the consent of both the borrower and the lender the option is not unilateral and the extension of the maturity date would be a modification.[58]

3. No consideration.[59] The exercise of the option does not require consideration. Consideration that, on the issue date of the instrument, is de minimis, a specified amount, or an amount that is based on a formula that uses objective financial information, and consideration that is paid to cover incidental costs and expenses relating to the exercise of the option, will not be taken into account.[60]

For example, if the borrower has a right granted under the terms of the loan agreement to defer any payment of interest until maturity, and on any payment deferred interest accrues at a specified higher interest rate, the exercise of the option by the borrower is not a modification.[61] Furthermore, if a corporation enters into a loan agreement pursuant to which interest is payable semi-annually, but the bank may grant the corporation the right to defer all or part of the interest payments, and on the interest that is deferred interest will compound at a specified rate that is higher than the stated rate of interest, the option is not a unilateral option and the exercise of the option is a modification.[62] Similarly, if a mortgagor may pay a fee that is fixed on the issue date to convert the mortgage to a fixed rate from an adjustable rate mortgage, without the consent or approval of the bank, the alteration is not a modification.[63]

(b) *When Is a Modification "Significant?"*

Only if a modification is "significant" will a taxable deemed exchange occur. Under no circumstances will a mere ministerial change in the terms of an instrument be "significant." A ministerial change includes a change in the mechanics of making a payment, such as changing the address to which payments are to be made. Furthermore, a modification that adds, deletes, or alters customary accounting or financial covenants is not a significant modification.[64]

There are four specific situations when a modification will be found to be "significant."[65] In some of these situations, a modification will be significant only if payment expectations are changed. Moreover, the regulations set forth an economic significance rule against which modifications, other than the four specific situations, are to be tested to determine whether the modification is significant.[66]

---

[58] Reg. § 1.1001-3(d), Ex. 12.

[59] Reg. § 1.1001-3(c)(3)(iii).

[60] Reg. § 1.1001-3(c)(3). The term "objective financial information" is defined in Reg. § 1.446-3(c)(4)(ii).

[61] Reg. § 1.1001-3(d), Ex. 10.

[62] Reg. § 1.1001-3(d), Ex.11.

[63] Reg. § 1.1001-3(d), Ex. 8.

[64] Reg. § 1.1001-3(e)(6).

[65] Reg. § 1.1001-3(e)(2)-(5).

[66] For an illustration of modifications to a tax-exempt obligation that were found to be significant, *see* PLR 9844021, October 30, 1998.

(i) Change in Payment Expectations. A change in payment expectations occurs if, as a result of the transaction, there is a substantial enhancement or a substantial impairment of the obligor's capacity to meet the payment obligations under the debt instrument.

- In the case of a substantial enhancement, a change in payment expectations occurs if the obligor's capacity to meet payment obligations is primarily speculative prior to the modification and, after the modification, it is adequate.[67]
- In the case of a substantial impairment, a change in payment expectations occurs if the obligor's capacity to meet payment obligations is adequate prior to the modification and, after the modification, it is primarily speculative.[68]

(ii) Economic Significance Rule. The economic significance rule provides that a modification will be significant only if, based on all facts and circumstances, the legal rights or obligations that are altered and the degree to which they are altered are economically significant.[69] The four specific situations and the general significance rule appear to be mutually exclusive, with each one applying to different situations.[70] In determining whether modifications are significant under this general rule, all modifications to the debt instrument, except those modifications subject to the four specific rules, are considered collectively.

The introduction of this rule in the final regulations appears to be an attempt to prevent manipulation by taxpayers. Thus, it appears that without this rule modifications could be made that offset each other, but which would result in a taxable event. While the economic significance rule provides the IRS with a weapon to prevent this type of abuse, the highly subjective nature of the rule may make enforcement difficult, and it leaves the rule's scope unclear.

(iii) Four Specific Situations. . The four specific situations when a modification will be found to be "significant" are as follows:

1. *Change in Yield.* A change in the annual yield of a debt instrument by the greater of one-fourth of 1 percent (25 basis points) or 5 percent of the annual yield of the unmodified instrument will be a significant modification. A change will be significant if it either increases or decreases the annual interest rate by the greater of 25 basis points or by 5 percent of the annual yield of the unmodified instrument. The annual yield of a variable rate debt instrument is the annual yield of the equivalent fixed rate debt instrument as of the date of modification.[71] A change in the yield can occur by a change in the stated rate of interest, a change in when payments are received, a change in the principal amount of the debt, or a change in a call option.[72]

---

[67] The obligor's capacity includes any source for payment including collateral, guarantees, or other credit enhancements. Reg. § 1.1001-3(e)(4)(B).

[68] Reg. § § 1.1001-3(e)(4)(vi)(A)(1) and (2).

[69] Reg. § 1.1001-3(e)(1).

[70] However, *see* Reg. § 1.1001-3(g), Ex. 1(iii) for a situation where the economic significance rule is applied to a change in yield and Reg. § 1.1001-3(e)(5)(ii)(A) where the economic significance rule is applied to the change in the nature of an instrument.

[71] Reg. § 1.1001-3(e)(2).

[72] If the principal amount of the debt is reduced, the borrower will probably have cancellation of in-

For example, if a borrower and a lender agree, at the end of the fifth year of a loan with a ten-year maturity date, to reduce the amount payable at maturity from $100,000 to $80,000, retaining the stated interest rate of ten percent payable at the end of each year, the yield on the loan after the modification drops to 4.332 percent. This change in yield resulting from the reduction in principal is a significant modification.[73]

If the holder of a debt obligation pays the issuer to waive the issuer's right to call a bond, the payment is treated as causing a change in the yield on the debt obligation. If the yield on the modified debt obligation varies from the yield on the original debt obligation by more than the greater of 25 basis points or 5 percent of the original yield, a significant modification will have occurred.[74]

Moreover, if the parties to a zero coupon bond agree that at the end of the five-year maturity date to extend the maturity date for two years and no other changes are made to the instrument, the extension of maturity date will cause a change in yield that will have to be tested to determine whether it constitutes a significant modification.[75]

Finally, if it is assumed that the terms of a mortgage loan provide that the loan could be assumed by a purchaser of the real property that secures the loan if the purchaser has a specified credit rating, but the assumption would cause the interest rate on the loan to increase from 9 percent to 9½ percent, the assumption will cause a significant modification to occur. Even if the loan is assumed by an acquirer of substantially all of the assets of the original mortgagor, the increase in interest rate would result in a significant modification because of the change in yield.[76]

2. *Change in Timing of Payments*. Any material deferral of payments due under the instrument resulting from a change in the timing and/or in the amounts of payments will be a "significant" modification. Whether a change in the timing of payments is material depends on all the facts and circumstances. Facts that will be taken into account include:[77]

- The length of deferral;
- The original term of the instrument;
- The amount of payments; and
- The time period between the modification and the actual deferral of payments.

(Footnote Continued)

debtedness income requiring information reporting on Form 1099-C. Nevertheless, the borrower may be entitled to an exclusion under § 108.

73 Reg. § 1.1001-3(g), Ex. 3. The yield after the modification is computed using an adjusted issue price of $100,000.

74 Reg. § 1.1001-3(g), Ex. 1(ii). Even though the change in yield may not exceed the safe-harbor amounts, the change to the instrument may be a significant modification under the economic significance test. Reg. 1.1001-3(g), Ex. 1(iii).

75 Reg. § 1.1001-6(g), Ex. 2. The deferral of the scheduled payment at maturity will have to be tested under the change in maturity date rule also.

76 Reg. § 1.1001-3(g), Ex. 5(iv). The change in obligor may not otherwise be significant under the "substantially all" exception to the change in obligor rules, discussed below.

77 Reg. § 1.1001-3(e)(3).

Under a safe-harbor rule, a change in the timing of payments will not be found to materially defer a payment or payments if an extension of the final maturity date of the instrument does not exceed the lesser of five years or 50 percent of the original term of the instrument.[78] For this purpose, the term of an instrument is determined without regard to any option to extend it. If payments are deferred and the deferral does not exceed the safe-harbor period, the unused portion of the period remains a safe-harbor period for any subsequent deferral of payments on the same instrument.

Thus, if a loan with a two-year term is extended for more than one year, there will be a significant modification because of the change to the payment date. However, if the extension of the final maturity date is in respect of only de minimis payments, the extension is disregarded. Furthermore, if a borrower and a lender agree, at the beginning of the eleventh year of a loan with a 20-year maturity date, to defer all remaining interest payments until maturity, the deferral would not be within the safe-harbor period. It is a significant modification because the safe-harbor period begins at the end of the eleventh year, when the interest payment for that year is deferred, and ends at the end of the sixteenth year.[79]

If the terms of a debt instrument are modified to defer one or more payments and the modification does not result in an exchange under Regulation section 1.1001-3, Regulation section 1.1275-2(j) provides rules to account for the modified debt instrument. This may occur, for example, when a borrower chooses to refinance and consolidate loans ("old debt") from two or more outstanding loans into a single loan ("new debt"). In general, if the terms of the new debt are not materially different from the terms of the old debt, substituting the new debt for the old debt does not result in a significant modification of the old debt under Regulation section 1.1001-3. Therefore, the substitution of the new debt for the old debt in the consolidation is not a realization event for federal income tax purposes.[80] However, under Regulation section 1.1275-2(j), some or all of the new debt may have original issue discount in varying amounts depending upon the terms of the old debt for which the new debt was substituted. Under Regulation section 1.1275-2(j), and solely for purposes of Code sections 1272 and 1273, the debt instrument is treated as retired and then reissued on the date of the modification for an amount equal to the instrument's adjusted

[78] Reg. § 1.1001-3(e)(3)(ii).

[79] Reg. § 1.1001-3(g), Ex. 4.

[80] The IRS has provided guidance relating to an election that will facilitate the substitution of debt instruments from two or more outstanding issues of debt with debt instruments from a new issue. The election allows certain taxpayers to treat a substitution of debt instruments as a realization event for federal income tax purposes. An electing holder does not recognize any gain or loss as a result of the deemed exchange. Instead, the holder's basis (immediately after the substitution) in the new debt is the same as the holder's adjusted basis (determined as of the date of the substitution) in the debt instruments for which the new debt was substituted. In addition, the holder's holding period for the new debt includes the holder's holding period for the old debt. If the stated redemption price at maturity of the new debt (as determined under Reg. § 1.1273-1(b)) is greater than the holder's basis (immediately after the substitution) in the new debt, the holder treats the difference as market discount on the new debt and the new debt as a market discount bond (unless the amount of the discount is a de minimis amount within the meaning of § 278(a)(2)(C)). *See* §§ 1276 and 1278 for the treatment of market discount. Rev. Proc. 99-18, 1999-1 C.B. 868, modified by Rev. Proc. 2000-29

issue price on that date. As a result, the debt instrument is retested for original issue discount based on the instrument's adjusted issue price and the remaining payments, as modified, to be made on the instrument. If the debt instrument has original issue discount as a result of the modification, both the issuer and the holder account for the original issue discount over the remaining term of the instrument.

3. *Change in Obligor.* Depending upon whether the change in obligor is a substitution or an addition or deletion of an obligor, the change may or may not be a significant modification. Generally, the substitution of a new obligor for the old obligor on a recourse debt instrument will be a significant modification, but the substitution of an obligor on a nonrecourse debt instrument will not be a significant modification.[81] There is no absolute rule that prevents a significant modification from taking place when there is a mere election to treat an entity as a regarded or disregarded entity under Treasury Regulation § 301-7701-1.

The addition or deletion of a co-obligor will generally be treated as a significant modification only if it results in a change in payment expectations.[82] Thus, the IRS ruled that the removal of a co-obligor on various debt instruments and on other debt instruments' collateral would not be considered a significant modification and, therefore, would not be treated as a taxable exchange because there was no change in payment expectations.[83] However, if the addition or deletion of a co-obligor (on either a recourse or a nonrecourse debt instrument) is part of a transaction or series of related transactions that results in the substitution of a new obligor, the alteration will be tested under the substitution of obligor rule and not under the rule that otherwise applies to the addition or deletion of a co-obligor.[84]

If the change in obligor is the result of a Code section 381(a) transaction or the acquisition of substantially all of the assets of the original obligor, and the new obligor is the acquiring corporation, the modification will not be significant if two conditions are met:

- The transaction does not result in a change in payment expectations, and
- The transaction does not result in a significant alteration.[85]

Thus, if under the terms of a recourse mortgage loan that is secured by an office building, a purchaser of the building may assume the debt and be substituted for the original mortgagor, the assumption of the loan upon purchase of the building would constitute a significant modification.[86] However, if the acquisition of the building were pursuant to a Section 381(a) transaction or a transaction where substantially all of the assets of the original mortgagor were acquired, the assumption of the debt, in the absence of any other alterations in the debt

[81] Reg. §§ 1.1001-3(e)(4), (4)(i)(A) and (4)(ii). An election under I.R.C. § 338 following a qualified stock purchase or the filing of a bankruptcy petition in a Title 11 case, by itself, does not result in the substitution of a new obligor. Reg. § 1.1001-3(e)(4)(i)(F) and (G); Reg. § 1.1001-3(g), Ex. 5(i) and (ii).

[82] *Id.*

[83] PLR 200047046, November 22, 2000.

[84] Reg. § 1.1001-3(e)(4)(iii).

[85] Reg. § 1.1001-3(e)(4)(i)(B).

[86] Reg. § 1.1001-3(g), Ex. 6.

instrument, would not be a significant modification.[87] Code section 381(a) transactions include liquidations of subsidiaries under Code section 332 and certain corporate reorganizations under Code section 361. The Type "B" reorganization is not included. For this purpose, a significant alteration is an alteration that would be a significant modification but for the fact that the alteration occurs by operation of the terms of the instrument.[88]

4. *Change in Security, Credit Enhancement, Priority, or Payment Expectations.* As a general rule, a modification will be significant if it releases, substitutes, adds or otherwise alters the collateral for, a guarantee on, or other form of credit enhancement for a recourse debt, while resulting in a change in payment expectations.[89] Furthermore, a change in the priority of a debt instrument relative to other debt of the issuer is a significant modification if it results in a change in payment expectations.[90] However, there are exceptions for similar available credit enhancements, fungible collateral, and improvements to collateral securing nonrecourse notes.

For example, if under the terms of a recourse debt instrument the debtor's obligations are secured by a letter of credit from a specified bank, and there is no option to substitute a letter of credit from a different bank, and if the specified bank's credit rating is lowered because it experiences financial difficulty, an agreement between the debtor and the creditor that a different bank can furnish the letter of credit will not be a significant modification unless the substitution results in a change in payment expectations.[91]

The substitution of a similar commercially available credit enhancement contract is not significant. However, a significant modification of a nonrecourse debt will occur if a guarantee or other form of credit enhancement is released, substituted, added or altered by a modification which alters a substantial amount of collateral.[92] However, the substitution of fungible collateral, or collateral that is otherwise of a type where the particular units pledged as security are unimportant (government securities or securities of a particular type and rating), will not be significant.[93] Furthermore, adjustments and improvements to collateral securing a nonrecourse note will not result in a significant modification.

For example, if a borrower on a nonrecourse debt instrument that is secured by a shopping center expands the shopping center by constructing an additional building on the same parcel of land and, after the construction, the improvements that secure the nonrecourse debt instrument include the new building, the

---

[87] Reg. § 1.1001-3(g), Ex. 5(iii). Even if it were a significant modification, the debt instrument is not retested to determine whether it provides for adequate stated interest. Code § 1274(c)(4) provides that if a debt instrument is assumed in connection with the sale or exchange of property, the assumption is not taken into account in determining if Code § 1274 applies to the debt instrument (unless there are other terms altered in connection with the transaction). Reg. § 1.1001-3(g), Ex. 6(iii).

[88] Reg. § 1.1001-3(e)(4)(i)(E).

[89] Reg. § 1.1001-3(e)(4)(iii) and (iv), (v), (vi).

[90] Reg. § 1.1001-3(e)(4)(v).

[91] Reg. § 1.1001-3(g), Ex. 8. The mere substitution of a letter of credit from a bank with a higher credit rating will not result in a change in payment expectations. However, if the debtor's capacity to meet payment obligations is dependent on the letter of credit and the substitution enhances that capacity, a change in payment expectations will occur.

[92] Reg. § 1.1001-3(e)(4)(iv)(B).

[93] *Id.*

addition of the building in the collateral securing the debt is not a significant modification.[94]

5. *Change in Nature of Instrument.* A modification of the nature of an instrument will constitute a signification modification if the change converts the instrument into another instrument or other property right that is not considered to be debt for federal income tax purposes.[95]

In general, federal income tax principles are used to determine the classification of a modified instrument resulting from an exchange, except as specifically provided in Regulation section 1.1001-3(f)(7). The rules provided in that regulation apply to determine whether the modified instrument received in an exchange will be classified as debt for federal income tax purposes.[96] Thus, unless there is a substitution of a new obligor or the addition or deletion of a co-obligor, all relevant factors (for example, creditor rights or subordination) other than any deterioration in the financial condition of the issuer are taken into account in determining whether a modified instrument is properly classified as debt for federal income tax purposes.

The extent to which the deterioration in the financial condition of an issuer is taken into account to determine whether a modified debt instrument will be recharacterized as an instrument or property right that is not debt[97] calls for an analysis of all of the factors relevant to a debt determination of the modified instrument at the time of an alteration or modification. However, in making this determination, any deterioration in the financial condition of the issuer between the issue date of the debt instrument and the date of the alteration or modification (as it relates to the issuer's ability to repay the debt instrument) is not taken into account, unless there is a substitution of a new obligor or the addition or deletion of a co-obligor.

Thus, any decrease in the fair market value of a debt instrument (whether or not publicly traded) between the issue date of the debt instrument and the date of the alteration or modification is not taken into account to the extent that the decrease in fair market value is attributable to the deterioration in the financial condition of the issuer and not to a modification of the terms of the instrument. If a debt instrument is significantly modified and the issue price of the modified debt instrument is determined under Regulation section 1.1273-2(b) or (c) (relating to a fair market value issue price for publicly traded debt), then any increased yield on the modified debt instrument attributable to this issue price generally is not taken into account to determine whether the modified debt instrument is debt or some other property right for federal income tax purposes. However, any portion of the increased yield that is not attributable to a deterioration in the

[94] Reg. § 1.1001-3(g), Ex. 9.

[95] Reg. § 1.1001-3(e)(5)(i). For this purpose, any deterioration in the financial condition of the obligor between the issue date of the unmodified instrument and the date of modification (as it relates to the obligor's ability to repay the debt) is not taken into account, unless in connection with the modification there is a substitution of a new obligor or the addition or deletion of a co-obligor. To determine whether an instrument is debt or equity, *see* I.R.C. § 385.

[96] *See* preamble to final regulations that add paragraph (f)(7) to Reg. § 1.1001-3. T.D. 9513, 76 FR 10063-01 (January 7, 2011).

[97] T.D. 9513, 76 FR 10063-01 (January 7, 2011). REG-106750-10

financial condition of the issuer, such as a change in market interest rates, is taken into account.[98]

A significant modification occurs if the alteration in the nature of the instrument changes the instrument from a recourse (or substantially all recourse) instrument to a nonrecourse (or substantially all nonrecourse) instrument or from a nonrecourse (or substantially nonrecourse) instrument to a recourse (or substantially recourse) instrument.[99]

If an instrument is not substantially all recourse or not substantially all nonrecourse either before or after a modification, the significance of the modification is determined under the general economic significance rule discussed above. However, a modification that changes a recourse debt instrument to a nonrecourse debt instrument is not a significant modification if the instrument continues to be secured only by the original collateral and the modification does not result in a change in payment expectations.[100]

§ 6.3 Measuring Gain or Loss

There is considerable uncertainty relating to the correct approach for measuring gain or loss on a debt exchange caused by Treasury regulation section 1-1001-1(g). Code section 1001 provides one rule and the regulation provides a second rule. Code section 475 appears to allow a third approach.

§ 6.3.1 Statutory Rules

Code section 1001(a) provides that the gain from the sale or other disposition of property is equal to the excess of the amount realized over the adjusted basis of the property. Loss from dispositions will be equal to the excess of adjusted basis over the amount realized.[101]

Code section 1001(b) provides, in pertinent part, that "[t]he amount realized from the sale or other disposition of property shall be the sum of any money received plus the fair market value of the property (other than money) received."[102] The adjusted basis of the property disposed of is usually its cost,

[98] The regulations apply to alterations of the terms of a debt instrument on or after January 7, 2011; however, a taxpayer may rely on Reg. § 1.1001-3(f)(7) for alterations of the terms of a debt instrument occurring before that date.

[99] Reg. § 1.1001-3(e)(5)(ii)(A).

[100] Reg. § 1.1001-3(e)(5)(ii)(B)(2). Fungible collateral, such as government obligations, may be substituted for other fungible collateral.

[101] If unrealized discount or accrued but untaxed interest from the original debt is reflected in a renegotiated new debt, an accrual basis bank must include in income such unrealized discount or interest (and any commission or discount charged for the extension of the debt) in the year in which the old debt is exchanged for a "new" debt. (No such income would be realized unless the new debt is collectible. *See Mellinger v. United States, Joe W. Scales* and *Francis Ward Paine, supra* note 30; *Vancoh Realty Company v. Commissioner*, 33 B.T.A. 918, Dec. 9204 (January 17, 1936). On "reorganization" exchanges of debt instruments, original issue discount (O.I.D.) must be determined by reference to I.R.C. § 1275(a)(4)). The treatment of a cash basis bank is less clear, although it would appear that the unrealized discount income would be deferred until it is actually or constructively received. (Note that the borrower making interest payments to the bank with funds borrowed from the same lender will not be deemed to have made a payment of deductible interest, unless the borrower has "unrestricted control" over the borrowed funds (*i.e.*, the lender surrenders control) and the "primary purpose" of advancing the funds was not to fund interest. *N.W. Menz v. Commissioner*, 80 T.C. 1174, Dec. 40,248 (1983); and *B.L. Battelstein v. Internal Revenue Service*, 80-1 U.S.T.C. ¶ 9225, *reh'g en banc* 80-2 U.S.T.C. ¶ 9840, 631 F.2d 1182 (5th Cir. 1980), *cert. denied*, 451 U.S. 938 (1981).

[102] I.R.C. § 1001(b).

adjusted as provided in Code section 1016.[103] Among the adjustments contained in that section are adjustments for "receipts, losses, other items, properly chargeable to capital account . . . ."[104] In the case of a loan, the adjusted basis will start out being the amount loaned. This amount will be reduced by repayments and amounts charged-off and increased by any accrued and taxed interest that has not been received.

In addition to this rule for measuring gain or loss, Code section 475 provides that a dealer in securities must take into account at its fair market value any security which is inventory. If a dealer holds any security which is not inventory at the close of any taxable year, the dealer must recognize gain or loss as if the security were sold for its fair market value on the last business day of the taxable year.[105] Thus, the Code section 475 rule applies apart from any disposition, including a deemed disposition that results from a significant modification of a debt instrument. The dealer rules may apply to a "new" debt received in a deemed taxable exchange that results from a significant modification of a debt instrument. If the dealer does not identify the "new" debt as eligible for one of the exceptions to the mark-to-market rules, gain or loss determined by reference to its fair market value at year-end would, in effect, be recognized.[106]

§6.3.2 IRS Positions

The IRS's position on the correct approach for determining the amount realized for purposes of Code section 1001(b) appears to have evolved over the past several years.[107]

(a) *Historical Position*

Historically, the IRS applied the plain meaning of Code section 1001(b) and ruled that the fair market value of property received in an exchange would determine the amount realized. It took this position in a variety of situations, including ones where debt instruments were deemed to be exchanged, as well as in situations where there was an actual exchange.[108]

However, in at least some situations, the IRS took the position that an accrual basis taxpayer was required to treat the face amount of a debt received in a taxable event as its "amount realized." For a cash method taxpayer, the fair

---

[103] I.R.C. §1011.

[104] I.R.C. §1016(a)(1).

[105] I.R.C. §§475(a)(1) and (3).

[106] I.R.C. §475(b). Note that if gain or loss is determined under the general rule of I.R.C. §1001, the new debt instrument may be an O.I.D. obligation. Any discount will have to be accrued annually in accordance with the O.I.D. rules.

[107] This discussion is concerned with the tax implications to the creditor. An exchange of debt instruments could also produce taxable gain to the debtor. I.R.C §61(a)(12) provides that gross income includes income resulting from cancellation of indebtedness. But note the exceptions dealing with loan workouts at I.R.C. §108(e)(10) and the election to exclude such income contained in I.R.C. §108(a)(1). Taxable income would never arise unless the new debt can be valued. *Dudley T. Humphrey v. Commissioner*, 32 B.T.A. 280, Dec. 8913 (1935) (non-negotiable notes); and *Robert J. Dial v. Commissioner*, 24 T.C. 117, Dec. 20,983 (1955) (negotiable notes).

[108] General Counsel Memorandum 37002, February 10, 1979; PLR 8451012, August 23, 1984; *see also Emery v. Commissioner*, 48-1 U.S.T.C. ¶9165, 166 F.2d 27 (2d Cir. 1948), and *Girard Trust Co. v. United States*, 48-1 U.S.T.C. ¶9209, 166 F.2d 773 (3d Cir. 1948), in which the IRS argued that the exchange of bonds was a taxable event giving rise to recognized gain measured by reference to the fair market value of the new bonds received. *Cf.* General Counsel Memorandum 37884, March 19, 1979. TAM 8451012.

market value of any evidence of indebtedness received in a taxable exchange of obligations was treated as the "amount realized" for purposes of computing realized gain or loss. The situation in which the face amount of a debt was treated as an accrual basis taxpayer's "amount realized" involved a taxpayer receiving a promissory note as evidence of the amount owing on the sale of property.[109]

In *Nestle Holdings*, the Tax Court rejected the IRS's distinction between the determination of the amount realized for cash and for accrual method taxpayers.[110] It stated, "Nothing in the language of the statute requires an accrual method taxpayer to compute the amount realized any differently than a cash method taxpayer; both would appear to be required to add the amount of money and the fair market value of property other than money, received on the sale or other disposition in order to arrive at the amount realized."[111]

The IRS itself appears to have limited this "face value" rule by implication when it stated in its earlier pronouncement that "the fair market value of a note received *from a solvent maker* is irrelevant in determining the amount realized from the sale of property."[112] Presumably, if the maker were insolvent, fair market value would determine the amount realized. Further, in a pre-1954 ruling, the IRS explicitly authorized the use of fair market value to measure the amount realized in a bond-for-bond exchange.[113]

In a somewhat analogous situation, Congress has explicitly mandated the use of an obligation's fair market value for purposes of determining the amount of recognized gain. Code section 356 provides that on an exchange of debt obligations in a recapitalization, the excess principal amount received is treated as boot to the extent of its *fair market value*.[114] Similarly, in exchanges involving government bonds, the IRS has ruled, without apparent distinction between cash and accrual basis taxpayers, that fair market value is to be used to measure recognized gain.[115]

---

[109] *George L. Castner, Co., Inc. v. Commissioner*, 30 T.C. 1061, Dec. 23,133 (1958); *Jones Lumber Co., Inc. v. Commissioner*, 69-1 U.S.T.C. ¶9113, 404 F.2d 764 (6th Cir. 1969) (with respect to personal property); *First Savings & Loan Association v. Commissioner*, 40 T.C. 474, Dec. 26,158 (1963) (with respect to real property). *Cf. Spring City Foundry Co. v. Commissioner*, 292 U.S. 182 (1934); Reg. § 1.453-6(a); and Rev. Rul. 79-292, 1979-2 C.B. 287.

[110] *Nestle Holdings, Inc. v. Commissioner*, 94 T.C. 803 (1990).

[111] *Id.* at 808. Assuming the accrual basis taxpayer's amount realized is determined by reference to the face value of the substituted debt, any recognized gain could be eliminated from taxable income by a loss deduction. The deduction would generally equal the amount of the excess of the face of the obligation (*i.e.*, its tax basis) over its fair market value. *See* discussion of securities loss deductions under I.R.C. § 165 and of loan losses under I.R.C. § 166 in Ch. 2.

[112] [Emphasis added]. Rev. Rul. 79-292, 1979-2 C.B. 287, 288. The holding of this ruling is questionable. The transaction under examination was not an exchange of property. Instead, it involved the sale of property. The not received appears to be properly classified as an evidence of indebtedness not as property received in an exchange.

[113] IT 2778, XIII-1 C.B. 79 (1934).

[114] I.R.C. §§ 356(a) and (d).

[115] Rev. Rul. 57-535, 1957-2 C.B. 513; Rev. Rul. 60-25, 1960-1 C.B. 283; Rev. Rul. 54-501, 1954-2 C.B. 197; and Rev. Rul. 69-263, 1969-1 C.B. 197. *See also* the discussion in the Committee Reports under I.R.C. § 1037, H. Rept. No. 1148, 86th Cong., 1st Sess. 8 (1959).

(b) *Introduction of O.I.D. Rules*

In Revenue Ruling 89-122 the IRS first expressed its substantially revised interpretation of the term "amount realized."[116] This change was not caused by any statutory change or any judicial reinterpretation of Code section 1001(b). The ruling addressed the tax consequences to banks involved in the modification of loans made to foreign countries as part of a program to reduce the amount of the foreign country's outstanding dollar denominated debt.

In the first of the two situations examined in the ruling, the modification involved the reduction in the stated rate of interest on a debt from ten percent to 6.25 percent per annum. In the second situation, the principal amount of a debt instrument was reduced from $1,000,000 to $650,000, with the other terms remaining the same. In both situations, the IRS concluded that a taxable debt exchange occurred. There can be little doubt that under then current law, or under the *Cottage Savings* regulations, a taxable exchange did, in fact, occur.

In reaching its conclusion, the IRS appeared to focus solely on the change in the terms of the instruments. In the first situation the interest rate term was changed and in the second situation the principal amount term was changed. This term based approach to identifying whether a taxable exchange occurs may possess the virtue of administrative simplicity, but it fails to properly consider economic reality. It is not inconceivable that multiple terms could be changed having offsetting effect.

The IRS's use of a term-based analysis appears to be inconsistent with their litigating position in *Cottage Savings.* As discussed earlier, in that case the IRS argued that the economic reality, not the form of the transaction, should control the analysis of whether a taxable exchange occurred. The final *Cottage Savings* regulations demonstrate an understanding of this potential problem by prescribing an economic significance rule.[117]

With respect to the measurement of the gain or loss resulting from the exchange, the IRS first stated that Revenue Ruling 79-292 should be "clarified by removing any implication created by that ruling that the amount realized included unstated interest."[118] It reasoned that the situation dealt with in the ruling did not involve a case where the face amount of the note received by the accrual basis taxpayer includes "any amount that is, in effect, recharacterized as interest under section 1274 of the Code."[119] Thus, it appears that the fair market value of the note and its face amount were the same. The IRS then introduced the O.I.D. rules into the determination of amount realized. It concluded that the amount realized would be equal to the "issue price," as determined under Code section 1274.

§6.3.3 O.I.D. Rules

Final regulations issued in 1994 under the O.I.D. sections of the Code and under Code section 1001 confirm and elaborate on the position taken in Revenue

[116] Rev. Rul. 89-122, 1989-2 C.B. 200.

[117] Reg. § 1.1001-3(e)(1). *See* discussion at § 6.2.3.

[118] Rev. Rul. 89-122, 1989-2 C.B. 200, 202.

[119] *Id.* at 201.

Ruling 89-122, by providing that in debt for debt exchanges, including debt modifications, the O.I.D. rules set forth in the Code and Regulations would be used to determine the amount realized.[120]

(a) *Regulation Section 1.1001-1(g)*

Regulation section 1.1001-1(g), promulgated after the *Cottage Savings* regulations, provides that if a debt instrument is issued in exchange for property, the amount realized attributable to the debt instrument is the issue price of the debt instrument determined under the O.I.D. rules.

The issue price of a debt instrument is determined under either Code section 1273(b) or Code section 1274. Section 1273(b)(3) generally provides that in the case of a debt instrument issued for property and part of an issue some or all of which is traded on an established securities market (often referred to as "publicly traded"), the issue price of the debt instrument is the fair market value of the debt instrument. Similarly, if a debt instrument is issued for stock or securities (or other property) that are publicly traded, the issue price of the debt instrument is the fair market value of the stock, securities, or other property.[121] If a debt instrument issued for property is not publicly traded or is not issued for property that is publicly traded, the issue price of the debt instrument is usually determined under Code section 1274, which generally results in an issue price equal to the stated principal amount of the debt instrument if the debt instrument provides for adequate stated interest. Regulations finalized in 2012 determine when property is publicly traded for purposes of determining the issue price of a debt instrument.[122] The regulations amend the preexisting regulations to clarify the circumstances that cause property to be publicly traded.[123]

A debt instrument received in an exchange or deemed exchange, if it is a traditional loan, will be treated as "property" that is not publicly offered.[124] As such, the issue price of the debt instrument is determined under Code section 1274. Code section 1274 contains two rules for determining "issue price." One rule applies when there is adequate stated interest and the other rule applies in all other situations.[125]

In the case of a debt instrument that has adequate stated interest, the issue price and, thus, the amount realized of the new instrument shall be its stated

---

[120] Reg. § 1.1274-5(c) provides an exception for cash method debt instruments that are modified in a deemed I.R.C. § 1001 exchange.

[121] "The general policy . . . is that the issue price of a debt instrument should be the fair market value as long as such fair market balance can be determined accurately and objectively. In this context, the concept of public trading is used as a standard for determining when fair market value should be deemed to be determinable in an accurate and objective manner." New York State Bar Association Tax Section, *Report on Definition of 'Traded on an Established Market' within the Meaning of Section 1273 and Related Issuers*, Report No. 1209, 8 (March 2010).

[122] T.D. 9599, 77 FR 56533-01.

[123] *See* Reg. § 1.1273-2(f).

[124] Reg. § 1.1274-1(a) provides that for purposes of I.R.C. § 1274, property includes debt instruments. I.R.C. § 1273 defines "property" to include services and the right to use property, but not money. Reg. § 1.483-1(a)(1) defines property for purposes of I.R.C. § 483 as including debt instruments and investments units, but not money, services, or the right to use property. Reg. § 1.1273-2(c)(1) includes within the definition of "property" a debt instrument. However, in Reg. § 1.1273-2(a)(1) a debt instrument which is "evidencing a loan to a natural person" is not treated as property. Instead the issue price is the amount of money loaned.

[125] I.R.C. § 1274(a).

principal amount. If interest is not "adequate," then the instrument's issue price is equal to the "imputed principal amount."

An instrument's imputed principal amount is equal to the sum of the present values of all payments due under the instrument.[126] Present value is determined by using a discount rate equal to the Applicable Federal Rate ("AFR") as of the date of the sale or exchange, compounded semiannually.[127] The AFR is determined by the Treasury Department according to the federal short-term rate, mid-term rate, and long-term rate.[128]

Whether there is adequate stated interest is dependent upon the imputed principal amount. If the stated principal amount of a debt instrument is less than or equal to the imputed principal amount of the instrument, there is adequate stated interest.[129] Thus, in theory, the issue price of a note issued in consideration for the sale or exchange of nonpublicly traded property is the portion of the face amount of the note that is not recharacterized as interest under Code section 1274. A portion of the face amount of a note is recharacterized as interest if the interest rate is inadequate. In this situation, the issue price of the instrument generally is the imputed principal amount of the instrument.[130]

To the extent that the taxpayer's adjusted basis in the old instrument exceeds the imputed principal amount of the new instrument, the taxpayer will realize a loss, which shall be recognized. If the modified instrument has adequate stated interest, a loss, if any, would be recognized equal to the excess of the taxpayer's tax basis in the old instrument over the stated principal amount of the new instrument.

Example: A loan with a stated principal amount of $90,000, a seven-year maturity, and a 7 percent interest rate, is renegotiated. The new loan has the same face amount ($90,000) but bears interest at 5 percent per annum. Annual payments of $4,500 are required in years 1 through 6 and a final payment of $94,500 is due in year 7. The present value of the new loan, assuming a discount rate of ten percent, is $66,928, as follows:

Year	*Payment at Year End*	*Present Value Using AFR 10% Compounding Semiannually*
1	$4,500	$4,081
2	$4,500	$3,702
3	$4,500	$3,358
4	$4,500	$3,046
5	$4,500	$2,506
6	$4,500	$2,506
7	$94,500	$47,729
Total Present Value		$66,927

[126] I.R.C. § 1274(b).

[127] I.R.C. § 1274(b)(2).

[128] I.R.C. § 1274(d)(1)(A) provides that the federal short-term rate applies in the case of a debt instrument with a term of not over three years; the federal mid-term rate applies in the case of a debt instrument with a term of over three years but not over nine years; and the federal long-term rate applies in the case of a debt instrument with a term of over nine years.

[129] I.R.C. § 1274(c)(2).

[130] I.R.C. § 1274(a)(2).

The present value of all payments is the imputed principal amount $66,928. Since it is less than the stated principal amount $90,000, the imputed principal amount is considered to be the issue price for purposes of making the O.I.D. computations. Thus, there is $23,072 of O.I.D. (redemption price of $90,000 minus issue price of $66,928). If the taxpayer's tax basis in the obligation is $90,000, a loss of $23,072 will be recognized.[131]

(b) *Deemed Charge-off*

Application of the O.I.D. rules to determine the amount realized on debt exchanges would result in gain if the imputed principal amount or stated principal amount, as the case may be, exceeds adjusted basis. This gain is sometimes referred to as "phantom income." This could occur, for example, if tax basis of a loan were reduced by a charge off and the debt were later significantly modified. Similarly, it could occur if the debt instruments were purchased at a market discount. The gain may be attributable to the previously claimed charge-off, although the charged-off portion of the debt remains uncollectible, or the market discount.

The Treasury Department has addressed the situation to a limited extent in regulations issued under Code section 166.[132] The regulations set forth limited circumstances under which a taxpayer will be permitted to deduct an amount of a partially worthless debt even though no amount has been charged off within the taxable year. Generally, a charge off within the taxable year is a prerequisite for a partially worthless bad debt deduction.[133] Thus, the purpose of the regulations is to preserve the portion of a taxpayer's bad debt deduction with respect to a partially worthless debt. This deemed deduction is available on to the taxpayer that charged-off the debt.

The amount of the deduction that the regulations allow is equal to the amount the taxpayer would have been entitled to deduct for partial worthlessness with respect to the modified debt if the book basis of the modified debt were increased to the same extent as the tax basis of that debt by the gain created by applying the O.I.D. rules to determine amount realized.[134] The deduction will be in the form of a deemed charge-off of the modified debt.[135]

---

[131] While the creditor realizes a loss, the issuer in the exchange may incur discharge of indebtedness income because the issue price of the new debt fell below the adjusted issue price of the old debt. *See* I.R.C. §§61(a)(12), 108(e)(10)(A); Reg. §1.61-12(c)(2)(ii). "The amount of discharge of indebtedness income is equal to the excess of the adjusted issue price over the repurchase price." Reg. §1.61-12(c)(2)(ii). I.R.C. §108(e)(10)(A) states an issuer satisfies his or her old debt, and thus faces no discharge of indebtedness income, if the new debt equals the issue price of the old debt. The "issue price" for purposes of I.R.C. §108(e)(10)(A) is also determined under I.R.C. §§1273 (publicly traded debts) and 1274 (nonpublicly traded debts). I.R.C. §108(e)(10)(B). Additionally, I.R.C. §108(a)(1) lists five major exceptions to discharge of indebtedness income, most notably §108(a)(1)(B)'s exception for insolvent taxpayers..

[132] Reg. §1.166-3.

[133] I.R.C. §166(a)(2).

[134] Reg. §1.166-3(a)(3)(iii).

[135] For a bank that has made the conformity election under Reg. §1.166-2(d)(3) only if the charge-off satisfies the "loss asset" classification will a deduction be allowed, unless the exclusionary rule of Reg. §1.166-2(d)(3)(iii)(B)(3) applies.

Example: A loan is altered resulting in a significant modification. The lender recognizes a gain of $60,000 on the deemed exchange. Previously, the lender charged off $50,000 of the loan as a partially worthless bad debt. Under the regulations the lender would have a deemed charge-off of $50,000 and $10,000 of gain from the deemed exchange of the debt. For a taxpayer using the reserve method of accounting for loan losses, the charge-off would be an adjustment to its reserve for loan losses, but the gain would be a direct credit to income.

Chapter 7
Foreclosures

Contents

§7.1 Tax Planning Suggestions
§7.2 Legal Aspects of Foreclosure
§7.3 Treatment of Gain or Loss
  §7.3.1 General Rules
  §7.3.2 Foreclosures by Thrifts: Pre-1996 Acquisitions
§7.4 Interest Income on Foreclosure
§7.5 Holding Security Property
  §7.5.1 Post-Acquisition Expenses
  §7.5.2 Post-Acquisition Income
§7.6 Disposing of Security Property
  §7.6.1 Capital Asset Treatment
  §7.6.2 Stock Acquired at Foreclosure
  §7.6.3 Interest Income at Sale
  §7.6.4 Nominee Corporations

§7.1 Tax Planning Suggestions

When a bank forecloses on security property, there are usually three stages associated with the foreclosure that will have tax implications: acquiring the property, holding the property, and disposing of the property.[1] The IRS and taxpayers have taken conflicting positions with respect to each stage.

The acquisition of real property by a bank at foreclosure may trigger phantom gain or present the opportunity for a deductible bad debt. For property acquired by a thrift at foreclosure in taxable years beginning prior to January 1, 1996, special rules were codified in Code section 595. These rules had the effect of permitting loss, but not gain, to be recognized when security property was acquired.[2] Congress later repealed Code section 595 effective for property acquired in taxable years beginning after December 31, 1995.[3] Thus, under current law, foreclosures by commercial banks and thrifts will be treated alike.

During the time that security property is held, current deductions for depreciation and other expenses relating to the property may be allowed. The IRS has taken the position that deductibility depends on whether the property is an operating asset. If it is, deductions are allowed as if the taxpayer were operating a business. Thus, expenses are deductible if they are ordinary and necessary business expenses, and depreciation allowances will be deductible if

[1] *See The Art of Tax Efficiency in Community Banks*, by M. Gula, J. Brew, and R. Blasi, 2007, Red Room Publishing, *http://www.mraeresources.com/bookstore/*.

[2] I.R.C. §595 was added to the Code by the Revenue Act of 1962, Pub. L. No. 87-834, 76 Stat. 960 (1962).

[3] Small Business Job Protection Act of 1996, §1616 (b)(8), Pub. L. No. 104-188. 110 Stat. 1755 (1996).

the property is placed in service or use. If the property is not placed in service or use, then it is the position of the IRS that all expenditures are subject to the Code section 263A UNICAP rule. As discussed below, this position appears to be contrary to the statutory language of that section, which requires property to be acquired for resale.

When security property is disposed of, the amount of gain or loss must be calculated and its character determined. The amount will be determined by reference to tax basis and the amount realized.[4] Tax basis will be equal to the fair market value of the property, assuming that the property was acquired in a taxable transaction.[5] The character will be determined under Code section 1221. Banks will want to plan for ordinary loss or capital gain on a future sale. For a taxpayer that is an S Corporation, long-term capital gains property would produce significant tax savings due to the differential between the maximum marginal rate on ordinary income and on long-term capital gains.

§7.2 Legal Aspects of Foreclosure

Generally, state laws determine property rights and obligations of the parties to a transaction, but federal law (the Internal Revenue Code) determines how those rights and obligations are taxed. Regardless of the method provided under state law for acquiring security property, the federal tax treatment usually will not vary from state-to-state. Federal banking regulations also have an effect on bank ownership of security property. In general, bank regulations regard other real estate owned ("OREO")[6] as an unsound asset that must be disposed of within 5 years from acquisition.[7]

There are at least four methods by which a creditor may acquire security property upon default by the borrower in the payment of interest or principal: (1) power of sale, (2) writ of entry, (3) strict foreclosure, or (4) foreclosure sale.[8] Under a "power-of-sale" procedure, property is sold by a sheriff at a public auction without a court order but pursuant to a power-of-sale clause in the mortgage. Power-of-sale terms are permitted to be included in mortgages in most states. Writ-of-entry and strict foreclosure procedures are unusual remedies not permitted in most states. Under the former, the mortgagee obtains a writ enti-

[4] I.R.C. § 1001(a).

[5] I.R.C. § 1012.

[6] OREO is a term described in 12 CFR §34.81.

[7] 12 USC 29. The Depository Institutions Deregulation and Monetary Control Act, Pub. L. No. 96-221, 94 Stat. 161 (1980) amended 12 USC 29 to permit banks to hold security property for up to an additional 5 years, as follows: "For real estate in the possession of a national banking association upon application by the association, the Comptroller of the Currency may approve the possession of any such real estate by such association for a period longer than five years, but not to exceed an additional five years, if (1) the association has made a good faith attempt to dispose of the real estate within the five-year period, or (2) disposal within the five-year period would be detrimental to the association. Upon notification by the association to the Comptroller of the Currency that such conditions exist that require the expenditure of funds for the development and improvement of such real estate, and subject to such conditions and limitations as the Comptroller of the Currency shall prescribe, the association may expend such funds as are needed to enable such association to recover its total investment." *cf. State v. Liberty National Bank and Trust Co.*, 427 NW 2d 307 (N.D. 1988), *cert.* denied 109 S. Ct. 393, 488 U.S. 956, which held that under limited circumstances state law prevails over federal law.

[8] The acquisition of property at foreclosure is subject to information reporting rules. I.R.C. §6050J and Reg. §1.6050J-1T. Form 1099-A must be used to satisfy these reporting requirements.

tling him or her to possession. In those few states (usually located in New England) where strict foreclosure is permitted, the creditor acquires absolute title after a specified period of time without the necessity of engaging in a judicial sale procedure.

A foreclosure sale occurs when security property is sold at a judicial sale pursuant to a court order. This is the most common method for reducing collateral to possession. If foreclosure sale proceeds are insufficient to satisfy the unpaid loan principal, in many states (California is one exception) the creditor is authorized to obtain a deficiency judgment for the balance, which can be levied against other property belonging to the mortgagor. If the foreclosure sale proceeds exceed the loan balance, the excess is paid over to the debtor, unless there are junior mortgagees (*i.e.*, second or third mortgagees) who have priority over the mortgagor. In approximately one-half of the states, the debtor has a statutory right of redemption. Pursuant to this right, the debtor is permitted to reacquire the property within a statutorily prescribed time period, usually six months to one year.

Whenever a debtor conveys security property voluntarily in satisfaction of a debt, the transaction is referred to as a deed-in-lieu-of-foreclosure. Most costs of foreclosure are avoided by this method. For this reason, debtors may prefer a deed-in-lieu of foreclosure sale. Any deficiency judgment may be reduced or any excess sale proceeds may be greater.

§7.3 Treatment of Gain or Loss

§7.3.1 General Rules

A bank that acquires real property in a foreclosure determines income or deductions by assuming two independent steps occur simultaneously: first, the debt is collected; and second, the debt is exchanged for real property.[9] If a debt is repaid in whole or in part out of the proceeds of a sale of the security property to a third party, only the first of the two steps affects the determination of income or deduction. In those states that grant a mortgagor a right to redeem property after foreclosure, the recognition of gain or loss by the lender should be deferred until the right of redemption expires because the transaction remains "open" until then.

Deductions resulting from the debt collection step are characterized as bad-debt deductions. A bank that determines its bad-debt deductions under the Code section 585 reserve method may be eligible to take the loan loss into account in determining its reasonable reserve addition under Code section 585(b)(2). In the second step, gain or loss could be recognized. Because deductions that arise from the second step are characterized as "losses," it is less likely that they may be treated as bad debt deductions. Instead, the deduction may be properly allowa-

[9] Reg. §1.166-6; Rev. Rul. 72-238, 1972-1 C.B. 65. The accounting and reporting standards for foreclosed assets are set forth in FASB Statement No. 15, "accounting for debtors and creditors for troubled debt restructurings," and FASB Statement No. 21, "accounting for the impairment of long-lived assets and for long-lived assets to be disposed of." Foreclosed assets must be reported on Schedule RC-M for regulatory purposes. FASB Statement No. 15 and No. 21.

ble under Code section 165. The character of any loss deductible under Code section 165 should be ordinary, as would be the bad debt deduction in the debt collection step.[10]

A bank appears to be able to maximize its bad-debt deductions in lieu of loss deductions by properly adjusting its bid price. Because of the advantage to a bank to do so, a bank should bid in for the security property for an amount equal to the fair market value of the security property and not the unpaid balance of the debt, if it is greater.[11] This will give rise to a bad-debt deduction equal to the difference between the adjusted basis in the property and the property's fair market value.

(a) *Step 1: Debt Collection*

If no portion of a loan has been charged off, and all interest, including delinquent interest, has been included in taxable income, the amount of any bad debt deduction taken under the specific charge-off method, or the amount of any charge to the reserve if the bank is using the reserve method of accounting for loan losses, will be equal to the excess, if any, of the amount of the debt over the amount of money and the fair market value of property received at foreclosure. The difference represents the portion of the debt that remains unsatisfied after the sale.[12]

Whenever a portion or all of the debt has been charged-off or a portion or all of the delinquent interest (included in "the amount of the debt") has not been reported, the deduction otherwise resulting from the Step 1 calculation must be adjusted. It is reduced to the extent that the amount otherwise allowed does not represent "capital" or "an item the income from which has not been returned."[13] Thus, it is reduced by any amount charged-off and by any interest that is not included in income. Accrued interest may be deductible in this step only if it has previously been included in income.[14]

Consistent with these adjustments, the IRS has illustrated the operation of this regulation by substituting tax basis for the "amount of the debt."[15] In determining tax basis in its debt, a bank subtracts from the original amount of the loan principal any repayments and specific charge-offs and adds interest that is delinquent but that has been accrued and included in taxable income.[16] Indeed, an incorrect overall result often would occur if the "amount of the debt" (the unpaid balance), without any adjustments, were used in this determination.

Example 1: The original amount loaned was $1,000x; $50x has been repaid; $100x has been charged-off; $26x interest is in default, and of that amount, $10x has been included in taxable income but not book income. The

[10] I.R.C. §582.

[11] It is not unusual for a bank to bid in for the full amount of the unpaid debt. This is often done for non tax business reasons.

[12] Reg. §1.166-6(a)(1).

[13] Reg. §1.166-6(a).

[14] Reg. §1.166-6(a)(2).

[15] Rev. Rul. 72-238, 1972-1 C.B. 65.

[16] Tax basis is increased for expenses incurred by the bank in reducing the security property to possession. *Estate of Schieffelin v. Commissioner*, 44 B.T.A. 137, Dec. 11,752 (1941).

property is sold at a foreclosure sale at its fair market value of $800. Under these assumptions, Bank X's bad-debt deduction would be $60x, as follows:

Amount of Debt		
	$1,000	
	26	
	(50)	$976
Sale Price		800
Tentative Bad Debt		176
Less:		
Amount not returned		(16)
Amount not capital		(100)
Bad Debt Deduction		$60

(b) *Step 2: Property Exchange*

In the second step, the debt and property exchange step, gain or loss is realized by a bank bidding in at a foreclosure sale if the acquired property's fair market value is different from the bid price.[17] The amount of gain or loss is calculated by comparing the adjusted amount of obligations applied toward the bid price with the fair market value of the property received. Adjustments made to the obligations applied toward the bid price must be made to reduce them to the extent that such obligations do not represent capital or an item of income that has been returned. Thus, as in the debt collection step, adjustments are made for charge-offs and delinquent interest not included in income. If a bad debt deduction is allowed in the first step, basis will be reduced by the amount of the deduction. Any gain or loss that a bank realizes on this second step will be characterized as ordinary income, since it arises from the exchange of a debt instrument, which is an ordinary asset.[18]

Example 2: The facts are the same as in Example 1. Assume also that the obligations applied toward the bid price, before adjustment for amounts not constituting capital and items not reported, amount to $800x. Thus, there is no gain or loss in Step 2.

Obligations Applied Toward Bid Price		
Amount Owed	$976	
Less:		
Charge-off	(100)	
Bad Debt in Step 1	(60)	
Amount not returned	(16)	$800
Less:		
Fair Market Value		800
Gain or (Loss)		$0

[17] Reg. § 1.166-6(b). If the debtor is granted a right to reacquire the security property, often referred to as a statutory right of redemption, the bank's deduction may be deferred until the redemption period expires or the likelihood of redemption no longer exists. *Securities Mortgage Co. v. Commissioner*, 58 T.C. 667, Dec. 31, 468 (1972).

[18] Rev. Rul. 72-238, 1972-1 C.B. 65; I.R.C. § 582.

Notice that the net effect of the transactions to the bank (steps one and two combined) is a deduction of $60x. This is the proper outcome since, if the two steps were consolidated, the Bank's tax basis in the loan would exceed the fair market value of the property received by $60x, as follows:

Tax Basis:	
Original Amount Loaned	$1,000x
Interest Accrued and Taxed	10x
Amount Repaid	(50x)
Amount Charged Off	(100x)
Tax Basis	$860x
Fair Market Value of Property Received	800x
Tax Deduction	$60x

(c) *Determining Fair Market Value*

For purposes of this calculation, fair market value "shall, in the absence of clear and convincing proof to the contrary, be presumed to be the amount for which it is bid in by the taxpayer . . . ."[19] However, a subsequent sale of the property within a short period of time following foreclosure may result in a more accurate "fair market value" than the bid price. It may constitute adequate "clear and convincing proof." Moreover, if the taxpayer has had the property appraised within a short period of time prior to foreclosure, the IRS has taken the position on audit that the appraisal establishes fair market value for tax purposes at the date of foreclosure.

In *United States v. Cartwright*, the United States Supreme Court defined the fair market value of property for federal tax purposes.[20] That definition is as follows: "The fair market value [of property] is the price at which the property would change hands between a willing buyer and a willing seller, neither being under any compulsion to buy or to sell and both having reasonable knowledge of relevant facts."[21] In *Cartwright*, the Supreme Court noted that this "willing buyer-willing seller" test of fair market value is nearly as old as the federal income, estate, and gifts taxes themselves.[22] It is the IRS's position that the foregoing definition of fair market value does not permit consideration of estimated sales costs or an estimated reduction in amount realized due to a possible distress sale.[23]

In *Community Bank v. Commissioner*, the Ninth Circuit Court of Appeals ruled that the IRS was entitled to introduce evidence of actual market value of properties purchased by the taxpayer-mortgagee at foreclosure sales.[24] The evidence could be introduced to rebut the presumption that the bid price of property acquired by a bank at foreclosure is equal to the fair market value of the

[19] Reg. § 1.166-6(b)(2). For federal banking law purposes, national banks must obtain an appraisal of OREO at the time of acquisition. 12 CFR § 34.85.

[20] 411 U.S. 546 (1973), 73-1 U.S.T.C. ¶ 12,926.

[21] *U.S. v. Cartwright*, 411 U.S. at 551, quoting Estate and Gift Tax Reg. § 20.2031-1(b).

[22] 411 U.S. at 551.

[23] TAM 200134005, April 27, 2001.

[24] *Community Bank v. Commissioner*, 87-2 U.S.T.C. ¶ 9379, 819 F.2d 940 (9th Cir. 1987).

property for purposes of determining whether the taxpayer has realized any gain from the purchase.[25]

The estimated cost to carry security property may not be taken into account for purposes of determining fair market value because taking such costs into account has the effect of allowing current deductions for future costs that may never be incurred.[26] Under Regulation section 1.461-1(a)(2) an accrual method taxpayer generally may not take into account a liability until "all the events have occurred that establish the fact of the liability, the amount of the liability can be determined with reasonable accuracy, and economic performance has occurred with respect to the liability." Allowing hypothetical sales costs to reduce fair market value would result in improper determinations of worthlessness that would, in effect, produce current deductions for costs that are uncertain and speculative. Like other costs, sales costs are taken into account only when actually incurred, in accordance with Regulation section 1.461-1(a)(2). However, in *Bank of Kirksville v. United States*, the court considered future costs to be a component of "all pertinent evidence." The court stated:

> [I]n making the determination of fair market value of collateral securing a loan by a bank, the bank may take into account all reasonable factors effecting the amount of money the bank could expect to receive if the collateral were liquidated, including a reasonable estimate of the cost of disposing of the property.[27]

§7.3.2 Foreclosures by Thrifts: Pre-1996 Acquisitions

For property acquired by a thrift prior to January 1, 1996, the two-step approach applicable to foreclosures by commercial banks was not applicable to thrifts.[28] Rather, the tax treatment of foreclosures by such institutions was controlled by Code section 595. That section, which was repealed by the Small Business Job Protection Act of 1996, governed foreclosures by any mutual savings bank (with or without capital stock), domestic building and loan association, or cooperative bank without capital stock organized and operated for mutual purposes and without profit.[29] The treatment provided by Code section 595 was mandatory, and it applied to acquired security property even after an organization no longer qualified as a thrift for tax purposes.

Furthermore, Code section 595 applied regardless of whether the thrift used the specific charge-off method or the reserve method for computing its loan loss deduction.[30] In addition, it applied to both a voluntary conveyance (deed-in-lieu-of-foreclosure), a transfer pursuant to some process of law (a judicial sale, power of sale, strict foreclosure, etc.), or an abandonment to the creditor.[31] Moreover, the provisions of Code section 595 applied regardless of whether real or personal

---

[25] Rev. Rul. 80-56, 1980-1 C.B. 154.

[26] FSA 200129003, July 20, 2001.

[27] *Bank of Kirksville v. United States*, 943 F.Supp. 1191, 1198 (W.D. Mo. 1996).

[28] Reg. §1.166-6(d).

[29] Small Business Job Protection Act of 1996, §1616(b)(8), Pub. L. No. 104-188. 110 Stat. 1755 (1996). A domestic building and loan association is defined in I.R.C. §7701(a)(19); a cooperative bank is defined in I.R.C. §7701(a)(32); and a mutual savings bank is described in I.R.C. §591(b). *See* Ch. 1.

[30] Reg. §1.595-1(a).

[31] Reg. §1.595-1(b)(2).

property was acquired or whether the loan secured by the real property was a "qualified real property loan."[32]

The acquisition of property at foreclosure that came within the purview of Code section 595 was a nonrecognition transaction.[33] Any gain or loss realized by the creditor was deferred, and the character of the acquired property was the same as the underlying debt.[34] The purpose of Code section 595 was to consolidate the acquisition and disposition of security property into one taxable event, treat the post-foreclosure receipts as payments on the indebtedness, and treat the foreclosed property as having the same characteristics as the debt for which it was security.[35] Thus, the tax consequences of a foreclosure or similar proceeding were determined upon the disposition of the acquired property.

Regulations allowed a thrift to treat the excess of the adjusted basis of property acquired at foreclosure over its fair market value as a partially worthless bad debt.[36] Thus, as a practical matter, whenever the thrift had not charged off a loan prior to foreclosure, it was permitted to do so afterwards even though, technically, no loss (or gain) was recognized on the foreclosure transaction.

The thrift took a substituted tax basis in the acquired security property equal to the tax basis in its loan, determined as of the date of acquisition of the property and increased for acquisition costs. Acquisition costs included attorneys' fees, court costs and auctioneer fees.[37] Any amount of unpaid but taxed interest income was also added to basis.[38] To the extent that a loss was deductible, a reduction in the tax basis of the acquired property was required. The effect of this treatment was to place thrifts in a similar situation as commercial banks. In effect, the first step of the commercial bank treatment of mortgage foreclosures which could give rise to a bad-debt deduction is similar to the write down in the book value of the real property for thrifts.

The acquisition date of security property was the earlier of the date when: (1) indefeasible title is acquired, (2) the bank secures the right to direct use and possession, or (3) the bank sells or otherwise disposes of the property or any interest therein.[39]

> **Example 3:** In 1995, ABC Savings Bank acquired property at foreclosure with a fair market value of $150X. Its basis in the defaulted loan (excluding capitalized interest) is $180X. Acquisition costs of $20X are incurred. Interest income unpaid but previously taxed equals $10X. No gain or loss would be recognized by ABC Savings Bank on foreclosure, and it would have a substituted basis in the acquired real estate of $210X. ($180X + $20X + $10X)

---

[32] For definition of "qualified real property loan," *see* I.R.C. § 593(d)(1). *See also* the discussion in Ch. 10.

[33] I.R.C. § 595(a) and § 7701(a)(45).

[34] I.R.C. § 595(b) and (c). *See also* the discussion of *Gibraltar Financial Corp. of Calif.*, at § 7.6.3.

[35] *First Charter Financial Corp. v. United States*, 82-1 U.S.T.C. ¶ 9222, 669 F.2d 1342, 1348 (9th Cir. 1982); S. Rep. No. 1881, 87th Cong., 2d Sess. 47 (1962), 1962-3 C.B. 703, 753-54; H.R. Rep. No. 1447, 87th Cong., 2d Sess., 1962-3 C.B. 401, 440-41.

[36] Reg. § 1.595(e)(1).

[37] I.R.C. § 595(c).

[38] Reg. § 1.595-1(d).

[39] Reg. § 1.595-1(b).

§7.4 Interest Income on Foreclosure

If the fair market value or the bid price of property acquired at foreclosure exceeds the unpaid principal of the debt and there exists accrued but untaxed interest income, such excess may suggest that unpaid interest was collectible, thereby requiring income inclusion under normal accrual rules. For thrifts acquiring security property after December 31, 1995, income inclusion also appears to be appropriate.[40]

In a situation involving a nonbank, cash-method taxpayer, the U.S. Supreme Court has held in *Midland Mutual* that interest income must be recognized to the extent that the bid price of the acquired property exceeds the unpaid principal of the debt.[41] In the event that there is no excess fair market value, courts are reluctant to find taxable interest income arising out of the transaction.[42]

> **Example 4:** In 1997, XYZ Bank acquires at foreclosure property with a fair market value of $200X. The unpaid balance of the debt is $190X, and there is accrued but untaxed interest income of $20X. Under these facts and applying the holding in *Midland Mutual*, XYZ Bank must recognize interest income of $10X and would have a basis in the acquired property of $200X, as follows:
>
> | | |
> |---|---|
> | FMV of property | $200X |
> | Unpaid balance of debt | (190X) |
> | Interest income to be recognized | $10X |
>
> If XYZ were a thrift, and the acquisition occurred prior to January 1, 1996, no interest income would be recognized by reason of the foreclosure, although such excess may indicate that the interest is collectible, and it should have been accrued prior to foreclosure

§7.5 Holding Security Property

§7.5.1 Post-Acquisition Expenses

Because the tax rules relating to carrying costs and selling expenses relating to OREO differ from bank regulatory rules and generally accepted accounting principles, an adjustment is often required to ensure that taxable income is clearly reflected for tax purposes.[43] Certainly, if there is a reduction of the

---

[40] I.R.C. §595(a); Reg. §1.595-1(a). *First Charter Financial Corp. v. United States*, 82-1 U.S.T.C. ¶9222, 669 F.2d 1342 (9th Cir. 1982). In light of the IRS's victory in *Gibraltar Financial Corp. of Calif.*, at §7.6.3, the IRS may seek to expand the court's ruling to tax the interest income at the time of foreclosure. Standing as a bar may be Reg. §1.595-1(a) and the IRS's own position in *Gibraltar*, which was that interest income is recognized at the time of sale.

[41] *Helvering v. Midland Mutual Life Insurance Co.*, 37-1 U.S.T.C. ¶9114, 300 U.S. 216 (1937).

[42] *Nichols v. Commissioner*, 44-1 U.S.T.C. ¶9269, 141 F.2d 870 (6th Cir. 1944); *Hadley Falls Trust Co. v. United States*, 40-1 U.S.T.C. ¶9352, 110 F.2d 887 (1st Cir. 1940).

[43] In general, the accounting and reporting standards for foreclosed real estate are set forth in Statement of Financial Accounting Standards No. 15, *Accounting by Debtors and Creditors for Troubled Debt Restructurings (FAS 15)*, and Statement of Financial Accounting Standards No. 144, *Accounting for the Impairment or Disposal of Long-Lived Assets (FAS 144)*. In addition, certain provisions of the American Institute of Certified Public Accountants (AICPA) Statement of Position 92-3, *Accounting for Foreclosed Assets (SOP 92-3)*, have been retained because they represented prevalent and safe and sound banking practices. The provisions retained from AICPA SOP 92-3 include that when an institution receives ORE from a borrower in full satisfaction of a loan, the long-lived asset is presumed to be held for sale, and

carrying value of a parcel of OREO that results in a charge to accounting income, or if there is a charge to accounting income for anticipated costs to carry or to sell OREO, the items must be added back to arrive at taxable income.[44]

Ordinary and necessary business expenses, real property taxes, and depreciation expense incurred while carrying acquired security property would appear to be deductible under the general rules of Code sections 162, 164, and 167, respectively. However, if the acquired security property is not an operating asset, the IRS has taken the position on audit hat all expenses incurred with respect to the property must be capitalized in accordance with the Uniform Capitalization Rules contained in Code section 263A, and also that no depreciation is allowed.[45] Thus, it appears to be the IRS's position that if a bank acquires at foreclosure an office building that is not placed in service or use, expenses such as property taxes, maintenance, security, and depreciation must be added to the bank's tax basis in the property.

Code section 263A contains the so-called uniform capitalization rules ("UNICAP" rules).[46] The UNICAP rules require certain otherwise deductible expenditures to be capitalized rather than deducted currently. The IRS has taken the position that expenses incurred with respect to security property acquired at foreclosure (or by deed in lieu of foreclosure) must be capitalized because the UNICAP rules require capitalization of any expenditures incurred with respect to "[r]eal or personal property described in section 1221(a)(1) which is acquired by the taxpayer for resale."[47] In an Information Document Request submitted to a taxpayer in 2011, the agent stated: "Generally, under Internal Revenue Code Section 236A(a)(1)(B), all direct and indirect expenses of an OREO property are required to be capitalized to the property's basis, since a bank's OREO property is "property acquired for resale" under Internal Revenue Code Section 263(b)(2)(A)."

The plain language of Code section 263A(b)(2)(A) calls for a two-part test for capitalization. The property with respect to which the expenditure is made must be "described in section 1221(a)(1)" and it must be "acquired . . . for resale." Thus, Code section 263(A) imposes an "acquired" and a "held" requirement on

(Footnote Continued)

the institution should initially record the ORE at its fair value less cost to sell. FDIC Financial Institutions Letter "Guidance on Other Real Estate" (7/1/2008).

[44] FSA 200129003, July 20, 2001. Bank may be required to write-down the book value of OREO in accordance with a "collateral evaluation policy that allows the bank to monitor the value of each panel of OREO in a manner consistent with prudent banking practice." 12 CFR § 34.85(a)(2).

[45] Regulations applicable to thrifts do not appear to draw any distinction between property placed in service or use and property which is not in that status. As discussed in the text that follows, "expenses incurred with respect to such property" have been deductible. Reg. § 1.595-1(e)(7).

[46] The UNICAP section was enacted as part of the Tax Reform Act of 1986, P.L. 99-514, § 803(a). The intent behind the provision was to prescribe a single comprehensive set of rules to govern the determination of whether costs should be capitalized from the moment of acquisition through production and disposition of property. According to the Senate Report that accompanied the legislation: "The Committee believes that, in order to more accurately reflect income and make the income tax system more neutral, a single, comprehensive set of rules should govern the capitalization of costs of producing, acquiring, and holding property . . . ." S. Rep. No. 99-313, at 140 (1986).

[47] I.R.C. § 263A(b)(2).

capitalization.[48] Property that is described in Code section 1221(a)(1) is "stock in trade of the taxpayer or other property of a kind which would properly be included in the inventory of the taxpayer if on hand at the close of the taxable year, or property held by the taxpayer primarily for sale to customers in the ordinary course of his trade or business."[49] Because property included in inventory does not include real property, to be subject to the UNICAP rules, security property that is real property must be "held" primarily for sale to customers in the ordinary course of the taxpayer's trade or business.[50]

The IRS regularly takes the position that bank security property acquired at foreclosure satisfies the test of Code section 1221(a)(1). It has ruled that real property acquired by a bank, mortgage finance company, or an insurance company in foreclosure, or by deed in lieu of foreclosure, that was not held for the production of rental income but was advertised and sold as soon as possible, is treated as held primarily for sale to customers in the ordinary course of the taxpayer's trade or business with the meaning of Code section 1221.[51]

Although it is generally advantageous for a corporate taxpayer to treat security property as a Code section 1221(a)(1) ordinary asset, there are situations when a taxpayer may wish to obtain capital asset treatment. A taxpayer that sells security property at a gain can use the capital gain to absorb expiring capital losses.[52] If the taxpayer is taxed under Subchapter S, any capital gain would flow through to the shareholders and be taxed at preferential individual capital gains rates.[53]

While the IRS has published a pronouncement with respect to the treatment of acquired security property as an ordinary asset, there is no such pronouncement with respect to the application of the UNICAP rules to security property.[54] It appears that the IRS believes that being "held by the taxpayer primarily for sale" is all that is needed for a bank's security property to satisfy the "acquired" requirement of Code section 263A.

---

[48] Treasury regulations confirm this dual requirement by providing that taxpayers who are resellers—taxpayers who acquired property and held the property for resale—must capitalize the acquisition costs, purchasing costs, handling costs, and general administrative costs of property. Treas. Reg. § 1.263A-1(d)(3)(ii); TAM 200736026. Costs that are not required to be capitalized include, among others, marketing, selling and advertising expenses. Treas. Reg. § 1.263A-1(e)(3)(iii); FSA 1992 WL 1355771.

[49] The inventory provision of the section has no application to security property. The Tax Court has consistently held that real property, land and improvements on land, cannot be accounted for as inventory. *See Homes by Ayres v. Comm'r*, 48 T.C.M. (CCH) 1050 (1984), *aff'd*, 795 F.2d 832 (9th Cir. 1986); *W.C. & A.N. Miller Dev. Co. v. Comm'r*, 81 T.C. 619 (1983); *Atl. Coast Realty Co. v. Comm'r*, 11 B.T.A. 416 (1928).

[50] For a discussion of this requirement in connection with securities dealers, see discussion of exceptions to Code section 475 recognition rules in Chapter 4.

[51] Rev. Rul. 74-159, 1974-1 C.B. 232, *superseding* Rev. Rul. 57-468, 1957 C.B. 543.

[52] I.R.C. § 1212.

[53] I.R.C. § 1366.

[54] In a 1998 Field Service Advice, the IRS addressed whether the UNICAP rule applied to a subsidiary of a thrift. 1992 WL 1355771. The subsidiary acquired foreclosed property from its parent thrift and sold the foreclosed property to unrelated third parties. *Id.* The subsidiary was found to have acquired the property by purchase for value and was required to capitalize its direct and allocable indirect costs under § 263A. *Id.* It is unclear from the FSA whether the thrift itself was required to capitalize any of its costs attributable to its acquisition of security property.

Whether property sold by a taxpayer is held primarily for sale to customers in the ordinary course of the taxpayer's trade or business is a question of fact, not a matter of law.[55] Courts look at the facts surrounding the sales activity to make the determination. For example, in *Girard Trust* the Tax Court stated, "There is no fixed formula or rule of thumb for determining whether property sold by the taxpayer was held by him primarily for sale to customers in the ordinary course of his trade or business. Each case must, in the last analysis, rest upon its own facts."[56] The Fifth Circuit has taken a similar position, stating, "Undoubtedly, in most subdivided-improvement situations, an investment purpose of antecedent origin will not survive into a present era of intense retail selling. The antiquated purpose, when overborne by later, but substantial and frequent selling activity, will not prevent ordinary income from being visited upon the taxpayer."[57] The Tax Court also has attached sometimes controlling significance to the pattern-of-substantial-sales test.[58]

Infrequent sales for significant profits tend to show property held for investment. Where a taxpayer, even though substantially engaged in a project that is ordinarily carried on as part of a business, produces and sells only a single unit of the produced property, the sale will probably result in capital gain.[59] Similarly, where the largest part, or saleable part, of a single parcel of real property is sold in a single sale, the sale may well be a sale of a capital asset.[60]

If acquired security property is found to be held by the taxpayer primarily for sale to customers in the ordinary course of the taxpayer's trade or business, it does not necessarily follow that the property was acquired for the purpose or "resale." The Ninth Circuit, in a situation where the taxpayer received parcels of property in repayment of a debt and later improved and liquidated the parcels, stated, "We fail to see that the reasons behind a person's entering into a business—whether it is to make money or whether it is to liquidate—should be determinative of the question of whether or not the gains resulting from sales are ordinary gains or capital gains."[61] The Court concluded that the taxpayer was required to treat the property as an ordinary asset at the time of sale because it held the property for sale to customers in the ordinary course of the taxpayer's trade or business even though it did not acquire the property for that purpose. The Tax Court ruled similarly, stating, "While the purpose for the acquisition must be given consideration, intent is subject to change, and the determining factor is the purpose for which the property is held . . . ."[62] The Tenth Circuit analyzed the law similarly in a situation in which the taxpayer acquired property for farming but later subdivided the property into lots when the property

---

[55] *Mathews v. Comm'r*, 315 F.2d 101, 107 (6th Cir. 1963), *aff'g* 20 T.C.M. (CCH) 1058 (1961).

[56] *Girard Trust v. Comm'r*, 22 T.C.1343, 1359 (1954).

[57] *Biedenharn Realty Co. v. United States*, 526 F.2d 409, 421 (5th Cir. 1976).

[58] *See Hancock v. Comm'r*, 78 T.C.M. (CCH) 569 (1999) (finding that the frequency and substantiality of sales is the most important factor); *Matz v. Comm'r*, 76 T.C.M. (CCH) 465 (1998) (same); *Harris v. Comm'r*, 47 T.C.M. (CCH) 760 (1983) (same).

[59] *See Reese v. Comm'r*, 615 F.2d 226 (5th Cir. 1980); *Comm'r v. Williams*, 256 F.2d 152 (5th Cir. 1958); *Gamble v. Comm'r*, 242 F.2d 586 (5th Cir. 1957).

[60] *Buono v. Comm'r*, 74 T.C. 187, 207 (1980); *see also*, *Bramblett v. Comm'r*, 960 F.2d 526 (5th Cir. 1992).

[61] *Ehrman v. Comm'r*, 120 F.2d 607, 610 (9th Cir. 1941).

[62] *Eline Realty Co. v. Comm'r*, 35 T.C. 1, 5 (1960).

became too valuable for farming operations. The Court stated, "While the purpose for which the property was acquired is of some weight, the ultimate question is the purpose for which it was held."[63]

Treasury regulations promulgated under the UNICAP rules also underscore the "resale" requirement. They provide that the type of taxpayer that is intended to be subject to the UNICAP rules is a "reseller" of property.[64]

A reseller is one who acquires property expecting to derive a profit from marking up the sales price of the property.[65] One Court stated that a dealer acquires property expecting to realize a profit,

> not because of a rise in value during the interval of time between purchase and resale, but merely because they have to hope to find a market of buyers who will purchase from them at a price in excess of their cost. This excess or mark-up represents remuneration from their labors as a middle man bringing together buyer and seller, and performing the usual services of a retailer or wholesaler of goods.[66]

Similarly, Regulation § 1.471-5 states that:

> For the purposes of this section, a dealer in securities is a merchant of securities . . . with an established place of business, regularly engaged in the purchase of securities and their resale to customers; that is, one who as a merchant buys securities and sells them to customers with a view to the gains and profits that may be derived therefrom.[67]

In *Kemon* the Tax Court applied the merchant analogy when stating, "Those who sell 'to customers' are comparable to a merchant in that they purchase their stock in trade . . . with the expectation of reselling at a profit, not because of a rise in value during the interval of time between purchase and resale, but merely because they have or hope to find a market of buyers who will purchase from them at a price in excess of their cost."[68]

In a case involving a non-bank taxpayer that acquired property at foreclosure, the Tax Court found that the taxpayer did not acquire the property primarily for resale. The case examined the application of Code section 1221(a)(1) to the taxpayer's real estate sales. The Court concluded, "The manner in which she acquired the property in question and the fact that it was not at the time acquired for resale, is not determinative of the issue presented."[69] Similarly, in *Thompson*, a

---

[63] *Mauldin v. Comm'r*, 195 F.2d 714, 717 (10th Cir. 1952); *see Dunlap v. Oldham Lumber Co.*, 178 F.2d 781, 784 (5th Cir. 1950) ("[T]his Court has pointed out that the purpose of the acquisition of the subject matter is not as controlling as is the activity of the seller or those acting for him with reference to the property while held."); *Neal T. Baker Enters. v. Comm'r*, T.C. Memo 1998-302, *8 (Westlaw) ("Thus, we must decide whether petitioner abandoned its original intent and thereafter at the time of the exchange held the property for investment."); *Howell v. Comm'r*, 57 T.C. 546, 555 (1972) ("[T]hough the property may have been acquired with the ultimate intention of reselling, this does not result in a determination that the property was held primarily for sale in the ordinary course of business."); *see also Rollingwood Corp. v. Comm'r*, 190 F.2d 263 (1951); *Hustead v. Comm'r*, 68 T.C.M. (CCH) 342 (1994).

[64] The UNICAP rule is intended to apply if property is *"acquired for resale by a retailer, wholesaler, or other taxpayer (reseller)."* Treas. Reg. § 1.263A-3(a)(1) (emphasis added).

[65] As such, a reseller for purposes of Code section 263A is analogous to a dealer in securities.

[66] *United States v. Nordberg*, No. CIV. A. 93-12681-NMG, 1996 WL 170119, *5 (D. Mass. 1986) (citations omitted).

[67] Treas. Reg. § 1.471-5(c).

[68] *Kemon v. Comm'r*, 16 T.C. 1026, 1032 (1951).

[69] *Jackson v. Comm'r*, No. 3113, 1946 WL 7149 (1946).

case involving the application of the predecessor of Code section 1221(a)(1) to the acquisition of real property acquired in satisfaction of indebtedness, the Board of Tax Appeals found that the real estate was not acquired for resale purposes, stating, "Petitioner never purchased any real estate for the purpose of selling it at a profit or holding it for investment."[70]

In generic legal advice, IRS Chief Counsel concluded that OREO held by the loan-originating bank for resale without improvement "is not 'property acquired for resale' within the meaning of Code section 263A(b)(2)(A)."[71] For a taxpayer who originates a loan that later produces OREO, the cost of holding the OREO should not be capitalized because the foreclosed property is acquired to mitigate losses from the loan originating activity. Section 263A(b)(2)(A) specifies that the capitalization rule applies to certain types of property acquired for resale. Thus, the taxpayer must do two things: acquire the property for resale and hold it for sale.[72] Clearly OREO is held for sale, but the Regulations provide that "the origination of loans is not considered the acquisition of intangible property for resale."[73] Since OREO is a product of loan origination activity, it is neither acquired for resale nor covered by section 263A. The cost of holding OREO should be currently deductible to the extent allowed by other sections of the Code.[74]

Where foreclosed property is acquired prior to January 1, 1996, and held by a thrift, regulations provided that Code section 595 "does not change the treatment . . . of expenses incurred with respect to such property."[75] An example contained in the regulations makes it clear that, with respect to maintenance expense, a current deduction was allowed.[76] Other ordinary and necessary business expenses, and other current expenses such as property taxes, appear to be deductible in the year incurred under the same theory.

With respect to depreciation, the Code has never expressly prohibited a thrift from taking a deduction with respect to security property; however, regulations provided that "no deduction for exhaustion, wear and tear, obsolescence, amortization, or depletion shall be allowed to a creditor with respect to acquired property."[77] This rule appears to derive from the provision in the Code that acquired security property "shall be considered as property having the same characteristics as the indebtedness for which such property was security."[78] The indebtedness does not qualify as "property used in the trade of business, or . . .

[70] *Thompson Lumber Co. v. Comm'r*, 43 B.T.A. 726, 728 (1941).

[71] IRS AM 2013-001, 2013 WL 1148927 (February 22, 2013). Note, this memorandum lacks precedential value.

[72] For a discussion of the statutory requirements as applied by the courts and the IRS's conflicting interpretation, see Stanley Langbein and David Lehr, *Acquisition Purpose and the OREO Expense/Capitalization Question*, TAX NOTES TODAY, February 20, 2013.

[73] Treas. Reg. § 1.263A-1(b)(13). The Regulation states that this exception does not apply to preexisting loans acquired from another person.

[74] This only applies to unimproved OREO, as described in the general legal advice memorandum, *supra*.

[75] Reg. § 1.595-1(e)(7). *First Charter Financial Corp. v. United States*, 82-1 U.S.T.C. ¶9222, 669 F.2d 1342 (9th Cir. 1982).

[76] Reg. § 1.595-1(e)(8), Ex. 2.

[77] Reg. § 1.595-1(e)(1).

[78] I.R.C. § 595 (b).

property held for the production of income," as those terms are used in Code section 167, which provides for a deduction for depreciation.

Federal banking law does not prohibit a bank from improving OREO, but there are limitations on the amount that a bank is permitted to spend on improving OREO. To the extent that capital improvements were made by the thrift to security property prior to January 1, 1996, depreciation was allowed. Such expenditures were treated as property that was not an extension of the original debt.[79] For capital improvements that amounted to less than $3,000, a thrift was permitted to elect to treat them as an extension of the debt, provided that the thrift treated all capital improvements, regardless of their amount, in a similar manner.[80] There is no current prohibition on either a commercial bank or thrift taking depreciation on OREO, including improvements thereon.

§7.5.2 Post-Acquisition Income

Rents or other income from acquired security property are taken into account as ordinary income. This is the treatment regardless of whether the bank is on the reserve method for computing loan loss deductions or the specific charge-off method. Because the loan is no longer on the bank's books, there are no adjustments to loan or reserve balances.

For a thrift that acquired security property prior to January 1, 1996, Code section 595 provided that "[a]ny amount realized . . . with respect to such property shall be treated . . . as a payment on account of such indebtedness, and loss with respect thereto shall be treated as a bad debt to which the provisions of section 166 (relating to allowance of a deduction for bad debts) apply."[81] Considerable controversy surrounds the scope of this provision and whether it requires income realized from operating security property to be credited to a thrift's reserve for bad debts.[82]

Regulations explained that "any amount realized" means an amount representing a recovery of capital.[83] Such amounts include:

1. Proceeds from the sale or other disposition of the security property;
2. Amounts repaid by the debtor;
3. Amounts repaid on behalf the debtor, such as amounts under an insurance contract with the Federal Housing Administration or a guarantee by the Veterans' Administration;

---

[79] Reg. §1.595-1(e)(3).

[80] Reg. §1.595-1(e)(3).

[81] I.R.C. §595(b).

[82] Although I.R.C. §595 (b) referred to I.R.C. §166, this reference should be read to apply to the reserve computation under I.R.C. §593 as well. Prior to the amendments made to I.R.C. §166 by the Tax Reform Act of 1986, P.L. 99-514, 100 Stat. 2085 (1986), that section allowed a deduction for a reasonable addition to a reserve for bad debts, as well as a deduction for specific charge-offs. Thus, the reference to I.R.C. §166 embraced those institutions calculating their bad-debt deductions under the reserve method. The Tax Reform Act of 1986 repealed the allowance of a deduction for a reserve addition contained in I.R.C. §166, and transferred the allowance provision to the sections which earlier only provided the rules for computing the deduction; that is, I.R.C. §§585 and 593.

[83] Reg. §1.595-1(e)(6).

4. Collections on a deficiency judgment obtained against the debtor; and
5. Amounts realized in certain nonrecognition transactions, including transfers described in Code sections 351, 354, 453, 1031, 1033, 311, and 336.

If an amount was realized with respect to acquired security property, it was first applied against and used to reduce the thrift's tax basis in the property. To the extent there was any excess of amount realized over tax basis, it was a credit to the thrift's reserve for qualifying or nonqualifying loans, as the case may be, or if the thrift was using the specific charge-off method for determining bad-debt deductions, it was included in gross income.[84] Any credit to a loan loss reserve would have the effect of reducing the thrift's loan loss deduction computed under the experience method, but there would not be a similar effect if the thrift calculated its bad-debt deduction using the percentage of taxable income method. If the amount realized from the sale or other disposition of security property was less than the thrift's tax basis in the property, the thrift was allowed either a bad-debt deduction or a charge to its reserve for qualifying or nonqualifying loans. A subsequent recovery was either a credit to the appropriate reserve or a direct credit to income.[85]

According to regulations, earnings on security property, such as rents, royalties, and similar amounts, were not a "recovery of capital." Thus, they did not qualify as "any amount realized" for purposes of the section, and they were not adjustments to the thrift's loan loss reserves if the thrift was on the reserve method for computing loan loss deductions. If the security property was an intangible earning asset, the nature of income earned on the property was unchanged by Code section 595. For example, if the acquired security property were a tax-exempt obligation, the interest income from the obligation would be exempt under Code section 103.

The treatment provided in regulations was not universally adopted by the courts. The Claims Court reasoned that because Congress prohibited depreciation deductions with respect to acquired security property, it was unlikely that it intended for earnings relating to that property to be included directly in gross income.[86] In declaring the regulation that required such treatment invalid, the court stated: "[A]nomaly is avoided if 'amount realized' in the statute and in the . . . committee report is read to include amounts realized in the form of rentals."[87]

§7.6 Disposing of Security Property

Federal banking law requires that a bank engage in "continuing and diligent efforts" to dispose of OREO.[88] The amount of any realized gain or loss on the disposition of OREO is measured in accordance with the general rule of Code section 1001. Thus, gain or loss is equal to the difference between the amount

---

[84] Reg. §1.595-1(e)(6)(i).

[85] Reg. §1.595-1(e)(6)(ii).

[86] *First Federal Savings and Loan Association of Bristol v. United States*, 81-2 U.S.T.C. ¶9681, 660 F.2d 767 (Cl. Ct. 1981).

[87] *Id.* at 769.

[88] 12 CFR §7.3025(e).

realized by the creditor and its adjusted basis in the security property.[89] The "amount realized" includes, in addition to the amount of money and the fair market value of any property other than money, any collections on deficiency judgments obtained against the debtor that were not previously recognized. Expenses incurred by a thrift in disposing of foreclosed property acquired prior to January 1, 1996 were not deductible as such. Instead, they were taken into account in computing foreclosure gains and losses, for purposes of the adjustment to the thrifts bad-debt reserve, by reducing the amount realized.[90] Under current law both commercial banks and thrifts would simply reduce the amount realized that is taken into account for purposes of determining gain or loss.

A disposition of acquired security includes not only a sale to an unrelated third party but also an intercompany distribution; however, special consolidated return rules defer recognition of gain or loss and apply to determine the character of any gain or loss.[91]

§7.6.1 Capital Asset Treatment

Normally, the character of any recognized gain or loss will depend upon the character of the property disposed of, and the gain will be capital if the property meets the Code section 1221 definition of a capital asset. Code section 1221(a) defines a capital asset in the negative. It provides that "the term 'capital asset' means property held by the taxpayer (whether or not connected with his trade or business), but does not include--."[92] Eight exceptions are then listed. Thus, unless security property were to fit within one of the exceptions, it would meet the definition of a "capital asset." Among the exceptions are two that possibly could result in recognized gain or loss being characterized as ordinary, subsections (a)(1) and (a)(2).[93]

The character of gain or loss on the sale of property has been examined by the Supreme Court in *Arkansas Best*.[94] The Court, in ruling for the Commissioner, pruned the expansive reading of Code section 1221, which evolved from the Court's earlier opinion in *Corn Products Refining Co*.[95] The latter had been interpreted by several lower courts as adding a judicial exception to the list of exceptions contained in Code section 1221 to what type of property constitutes a capital asset. *Arkansas Best* can be read as nullifying what has become known as the *Corn Product's* doctrine and as restricting the definition of a capital asset to that expressly contained in Code section 1221.

---

[89] I.R.C. §1001(a).

[90] Rev. Rul. 73-116, 1973-1 C.B. 300. *See also Allstate Savings & Loan Association v. Commissioner*, 79-2 U.S.T.C. ¶9478, 600 F.2d 760 (9th Cir. 1979); *cert. denied*, 445 U.S. 962 (1980).

[91] Reg. §1.1502-13(c)(7).

[92] I.R.C. §1221(a).

[93] These two exceptions are property "which would properly be included in the inventory of the taxpayer . . . or property held by the taxpayer primarily for sale to customers in the ordinary course of his trade or business" and "property, used in his trade or business, of a character which is subject to the allowance for depreciation provided in section 167, or real property used in his trade or business." *Id.* at §1221(a)(1)–(2).

[94] *Arkansas Best Corp. v. United States*, 88-1 U.S.T.C. ¶9210, 485 U.S. 212 (1988).

[95] *Corn Products Refining Co. v. Commissioner*, 55-2 U.S.T.C. ¶9746, 350 U.S. 46 (1955).

Following the Court's decision, considerable uncertainties arose relating to the tax treatment of common business hedges. Although *Arkansas Best* itself did not involve a business hedging transaction, the Court's narrow interpretation of its earlier decision in *Corn Products,* prompted the IRS, in individual cases, to treat various types of business hedging transactions as giving rise to capital gain or loss.

In *Federal National Mortgage Association ("FNMA"),*[96] the IRS took the position that gains and losses from the sale of regulated futures contracts, options on regulated futures contracts, and Treasury securities were capital in nature.[97] The case was decided before Code section 1221 was amended in 1999 to add subsection "7," which prescribes ordinary treatment for certain hedging transactions.[98] In *FNMA* the IRS argued that the transactions did not fit within Code section 1221(1), the only possible exception to the capital asset characterization at that time that could apply to sales of these financial instruments.

However, the Tax Court rejected the IRS's position and held that the taxpayer's business hedges gave rise to ordinary gain or loss. The taxpayer was using short positions in futures contracts, put options, and short sales of Treasury securities to hedge the spread between the rate of interest on mortgages that it held or had committed to buy and the rate of interest on indebtedness to be incurred to carry the mortgages. The Court concluded that because the hedges were integrally related to the mortgages, they also were not capital assets and were entitled to ordinary treatment. The Court cited with favor the pre-*Corn Products* cases. Although the Court's opinion could be criticized as re-introducing a judicial exception to the definition of a capital asset contained in Code section 1221, it does appear to comport with longstanding Congressional treatment of business hedges.[99]

Shortly after the Court's decision in *FNMA*, the Treasury Department undertook a comprehensive study of the tax treatment of hedging. As a result of that study, three regulations were issued: temporary regulations dealing with the character of income and loss from business hedges;[100] proposed regulations under which the temporary character regulation is proposed to be made final, along with some additional detail not included in the temporary regulation;[101] and a proposed regulation addressing the timing of hedging gains and losses.[102] Following public hearings on the proposed regulations, final regulations were adopted.[103]

In its announcement accompanying the release of the temporary regulations, the IRS stated that although it may disagree with some aspects of the *FNMA*

---

[96] *Federal National Mortgage Association v. Commissioner,* 100 T.C. 541 (1993).

[97] Not surprisingly, losses exceeded gains.

[98] The Tax Relief Extension Act of 1999, Pub. L. No. 106-170, §532(a).

[99] *See* legislative history of Internal Revenue Code of 1954 which expressly notes that hedges were ordinary under then-current law and that Congress intended to continue that treatment. H.R. Rep. No. 1337, 83d Cong. Cal. 2d Sess. A278 (1954). *See also* I.R.C. §§1256(e), 1092(e), 263(g)(3), and 1233(g).

[100] 58 Fed. Reg. 54037, October 20, 1993.

[101] 58 Fed. Reg. 54075, October 20, 1993; 59 Fed. Reg. 36394, July 18, 1994.

[102] 58 Fed. Reg. 36394, July 7, 1993.

[103] 59 Fed. Reg. 36356, July 18, 1994.

opinion, it has decided to abandon the position it took with respect to the character of many common business hedges by providing that property that is part of a hedging transaction is not a capital asset.[104]

The Tax Court's opinion in *Federal National Mortgage Association v. Commissioner,* which interpreted this section, could be relied upon as furnishing authority for ordinary treatment.[105]

(a) *Property Held For Sale: Code Section 1221(1)*

Code section 1221(a)(1) excludes from the definition of a "capital asset":

> Stock in trade of the taxpayer or other property of a kind which would properly be included in the inventory of the taxpayer if on hand at the close of the taxable year, or property held by the taxpayer primarily for sale to customers in the ordinary course of his trade or business . . . ."[106]

The IRS takes the position that all bank OREO is an ordinary asset because it is "held by the taxpayer primarily for sale to customers in the ordinary course" of the bank's trade or business. In a ruling that applied to mortgage finance companies and insurance companies as well as banks, the IRS concluded that property acquired by foreclosure or by deed in lieu of foreclosure that was not held for the production of rental income but was advertised and sold as soon as possible is an ordinary asset under Code section 1221(a)(1).[107] This position is not entirely consistent with judicial opinions.

In *Girard Trust* the Tax Court stated: "There is no fixed formula or rule of thumb for determining whether property sold by the taxpayer was held by him primarily for sale to customers in the ordinary course of his trade or business. Each case must, in the last analysis, rest upon its own facts."[108]

Thus, whether foreclosed property is a capital asset or an ordinary asset depends upon the facts surrounding the purpose for holding the property. While it is likely that the position of the IRS and taxpayers will usually be in accord (this avoids the specter of capital loss treatment when OREO is sold), if a taxpayer wishes to obtain capital gains treatment in order, for example, to absorb capital losses, the taxpayer is not precluded from establishing that the property was held not for sale but for investment.

In *Kanawha Valley Bank* the Tax Court has held that capital asset treatment is appropriate where sales of real property acquired at foreclosure were very limited in number and the bank was not permitted to engage in a general real estate sales business under applicable banking laws.[109] Where a taxpayer, even

---

[104] Temp. Reg. § 1.1221-2T(a)(1). Similar rules were provided with respect to short sales and options. Temp. Reg. § 1.1221-2T(a)(2).

[105] *Federal National Mortgage Association v. Commissioner,* 100 T.C. 541 (1993).

[106] I.R.C. § 1221(1).

[107] Rev. Rul 74-159, 1974-1 C.B. 232.

[108] *Girard Trust v. Commissioner,* 22 T.C. 1243. *See also Biedenharn Realty Co. v. United States,* 526 F.2d 409 (5th Cir. 1976), *cert. denied,* 429 U.S. 819 (1976); *Hancock v. Commissioner,* T.C. Memo. 1999-336; *Matz v. Commissioner,* T.C. Memo. 1998-334; *Harris v. Commissioner,* T.C. Memo 1983-774.

[109] *Kanawha Valley Bank v. Commissioner,* 4 T.C. 252, Dec. 14,199 (1944). *See also Redwood Empire Savings & Loan Association v. Commissioner,* 80-2 U.S.T.C. ¶ 9615, 628 F.2d 516 (9th Cir. 1980). Note that, in *Kanawha,* the Tax Court held that General Counsel Memorandum 21497, 1939-2 C.B. 187, was inconsistent with the Court's holding in *Thompson Lumber*

though substantially engaged in a project which is ordinarily carried on as part of a business, produces and sells only a single unit of the produced property, the sale will probably result in capital gain.[110] Similarly, where the largest part, or saleable part, of a single real property parcel is sold in a single sale, the sale may well be a sale of a capital asset.[111] However, the bank must be able to document that the property was held for investment.[112]

To the contrary is a 1939 General Counsel's Memorandum, in which the IRS propounded an absolute rule: In all cases, parcels of real estate acquired by a bank through foreclosure must be considered as held primarily for sale to customers in the ordinary course of a trade or business, and that the gains and losses resulting from the disposition of the parcels are to be treated as ordinary.[113]

In a Coordinated Issue Paper issued by the IRS's commercial banking industry specialist, the possibility of capital asset treatment for commercial banks was acknowledged. The IRS stated that regardless of the property involved, it is clear that:

> any analysis under Code section 1221(1) requires a dissection of subjective criteria in order to determine the purpose for which the property was held. Further, case law has clearly established that such determination is made at the time that property is disposed of and not at the time of acquisition, nor during the holding period.[114]

The Supreme Court's willingness in *Arkansas Best* to construe Code section 1221(1) in a way to avoid the character mismatches that result from treating business hedges as capital may be added support for the position that security property acquired by a bank and foreclosure, which may not precisely fit within Code section 1221(1), can be brought within the purview of that subsection in order to avoid any character mismatch.

For a thrift, regulations are clear that security property acquired prior to January 1, 1996, is an extension of the debt for which the property was security. Since a debt is an ordinary asset to a "financial institution," the security property must be treated accordingly.[115] If the thrift accounted for its loan losses under the reserve method, gain was treated as a recovery, and it was credited to the appropriate loan loss reserve (qualifying loan reserve or nonqualifying loan

(Footnote Continued)

Company v. Commissioner, 43 B.T.A. 726, Dec. 11,667 (1941).

[110] *Gamble v. Commissioner*, 242 F.2d 586 (5th Cir. 1957); *Commissioner v. Williams*, 256 F.2d 152 (5th Cir. 1958), *aff'd on remand*, 285 F.2d 582 (5th Cir. 1961); and *Reese v. Commissioner*, 615 F.2d 226 (5th Cir. 1980).

[111] *Buono v. Commissioner*, 74 T.C. 187 (1980), acq., 1981-2 C.B. 1; *Bramblett v. Commissioner*, 960 F.2d 526 (5th Cir. 1992).

[112] *Continental Illinois National Bank & Trust Co. of Chicago v. Commissioner*, 69 T.C. 357, Dec. 34,772, (1977) *Acq.*, 1978-2 C.B. 1. *See also* Rev. Rul. 78-94, 1978-1 C.B. 58.

[113] General Counsel Memorandum 21497, 1939-2 C.B. 187.

[114] *See* IRS Industry Specialization Program Coordinated Issue Paper in Appendix at § A.10. The I.R.S. reported on its website that this paper was cancelled effective June 26, 2006, because it "no longer reflects current law and is no longer needed."

[115] Reg. § 1.595-1(a). However, the IRS has unsuccessfully attempted to require the inclusion in income of uncollected interest at the date of foreclosure. *See also* I.R.C. § 582.

reserve); any loss was a charge to the appropriate reserve.[116] Under the specific charge-off method of accounting for loan losses, gain or loss will be a direct adjustment to taxable income.[117]

To the extent that gain or loss on the sale or other disposition of security property was allocable to capital improvements made after the date of acquisition, capital asset treatment may have been available to the thrifts. Regulations stated that "[t]he portion of the amount realized which is allocable to such capital improvements shall be treated under the applicable rules governing the sale or other disposition of such property and without regard to Code section 595."[118] The amount realized from the sale or other disposition was apportioned to the capital improvements and to the underlying security property in relation to their respective fair market values.[119] An allocation using relative investments or some other basis was not authorized.

(b) *Property Used In Taxpayer's Business: Code Section 1221(2)*

In addition to the possible application of the Code section 1221(1) exception to the disposition of security property, there exists the possibility of applying the Code section 1221(2) exception to what constitutes a capital asset to support a position that gain or loss should be ordinary. This latter provision excludes from capital asset characterization:

> property, used in his trade or business, of a character which is subject to the allowance for depreciation provided in section 167, or real property used in his trade or business . . . .

Because the IRS generally concedes that a commercial bank may depreciate improved real property acquired at foreclosure when it is placed in service or use, the applicability of this exception seems equally likely whenever the security property acquired is improved real property. However, the I.R.S appears to have relied exclusively on the Code section 1221(1) exception as support for its position that ordinary asset treatment is most appropriate.

The applicability of Code section 1221(2) may lend support to taxpayers who argue for the very favorable treatment afforded by Code section 1231.[120] That section prescribes capital gain treatment and ordinary loss treatment on the disposition of "property used in the trade or business," as well as certain other property. The term "property used in the trade or business" describes one of the two types of property excepted from the capital asset definition of Code section 1221(2), the other being land used in a trade or business.

(c) *Intercompany Transactions*

If security property is sold[121] by one member of a consolidated group to another member of the same group, the timing of recognition of income and the

---

[116] *First Federal Savings & Loan Association of Bristol v. United States*, 81-2 U.S.T.C. ¶9681, 660 F.2d 767 (Cl. Ct. 1981).

[117] I.R.C. §582; Reg. §1.595-1(e)(6)(i).

[118] Reg. §1.595-1(e)(3).

[119] Reg. §1.595-1(e)(3).

[120] Capital gains are recharacterized as ordinary income to the extent of recaptured depreciation. I.R.C. §§1245 and 1250.

[121] Intercompany transactions include not only sales but also the performance of services, licensing or technology, rental of property, loan of money, payment or accrual of expenditures, and the distri-

amount and character of any gain or loss is determined under the consolidated return regulations that deal with intercompany transactions.[122] For some purposes, transactions between members of a consolidated group are treated as transactions between unrelated parties, but for other purposes such transactions are treated as between divisions of the same entity. Each transaction is separately evaluated under these rules. There is no consolidation of transactions occurring during the year to determine how the rules apply to the net of all in the aggregate.[123]

The amount of any gain or loss recognized by the selling member and the buying member is determined on a separate entity basis.[124] Thus, the selling member's "intercompany item" and the buying member's "corresponding item" will be separately determined.[125] For this purpose, the buying member will take a cost basis in the item purchased from the selling member.[126]

Once the amount of gain or loss for each member is determined, the timing of recognition and the source and character of the gain or loss is determined as if the transaction were between divisions of a single corporation. For example, if a bank sells a parcel of land to a special purpose corporation, the bank calculates the amount of gain or loss on the transaction, but the recognition of the gain or loss is deferred until the property is disposed of, outside the group, by the buying member. As a division of a single corporation, the buying member is treated for this purpose as succeeding to the basis that the selling member had in the property acquired,[127] and for purposes of determining whether gain or loss is short-term or long-term, the holding period of the buying member includes the holding period of the selling member.[128] If gain or loss is determined to be attributable to a buyer-dealer after combining the activities of both the selling and buying members, then the gain deferral rules of Code section 453 will be unavailable to both members of the group, regardless of whether the selling member is not a dealer in the property sold.[129]

Applying these rules to OREO, if property were sold by one member of the consolidated group to another member, the character of any gain or loss to the selling member could change depending upon the combined activities with respect to the property by both members.[130] Thus, if the selling member were a bank that would normally recognize ordinary treatment on the sale of OREO, the character could change to capital when the activities of both the bank and the buying member were combined. This could benefit a bank that is taxed as an S corporation. Conversely, if property were capital in the hands of the bank, the

(Footnote Continued)

bution of property with respect to stock. Reg. § 1.1502-13(b)(1)(i).

[122] Reg. § 1.1502-13.

[123] Reg. § 1.1502-13(b)(1)(iii).

[124] Reg. § 1.1502-13(a)(2).

[125] After each member determines its gain or loss, there is a consolidated netting of the items. Reg. § 1.1502-22.

[126] I.R.C. § 1012.

[127] Reg. § 1.1502-13(c)(3).

[128] Reg. § 1.1502-13(c)(1)(ii).

[129] Reg. § 1.1502-13(c)(2)(i).

[130] Reg. § 1.1502-13(c)(7)(i),Ex. 1.

combination of activities of the buyer with the bank's activities could result in and gain or loss being characterized as ordinary.

§7.6.2 Stock Acquired at Foreclosure

With respect to the acquisition of stock of a debtor corporation in satisfaction of the debtor's indebtedness, Code section 108(e)(7) contains a special recapture rule. It recharacterizes the stock as Code section 1245 property and deductions taken with respect to the underlying debt as depreciation. Thus, gain, if any, on the sale of such stock is recharacterized as ordinary income to the extent of any deduction taken by the creditor under Code section 166 because the underlying debt is partially or wholly worthless.

§7.6.3 Interest Income at Sale

In *Gibraltar Financial Corp.*, the Court of Appeals for the Federal Circuit ruled that a cash basis thrift using the reserve method of accounting for loan losses recognized interest income upon the sale of security property.[131] The taxpayer argued that the excess of the amount realized over its adjusted basis in the security property sold was entirely a nontaxable credit to its bad-debt reserve. The IRS's position limited the Code section 1001 "amount realized," for purposes of the Code section 595 nonrecognition rule, to "an amount representing a recovery of capital. . . ."[132] Consequently, any amount realized with respect to interest would be outside the nonrecognition rule.[133]

The court accepted the IRS's argument, although it did so with considerable reluctance when it stated:

> Despite the *Bristol*[134] decision, as well as the *First Charter*[135] decision, both of which have indicated that Regulation 1.595-1(e)(6) is, at best, poorly drafted and clearly wrong as applied in *Bristol*, Treasury has not taken heed and revised it appropriately. That we do not approve the regulation in all respects does not, however, warrant overturning Treasury's interpretation that section 595(b) imbues the proceeds with the characteristics of the underlying indebtedness and that a gain from a sale of property that secures interest indebtedness and constitutes a payment of such interest, resulting in taxable income.[136]

§7.6.4 Nominee Corporations

Acquired security property may be placed in a separately incorporated entity. This is often done to avoid tort liability. Under state tort laws, a parent corporation may insulate itself from such liability if property is owned by a separate corporation, even a 100 percent owned subsidiary. However, if the corporation owning the property is a mere nominee, its separate legal form will

---

[131] *Gibraltar Financial Corp. of Calif. v. United States*, 87-2 U.S.T.C. ¶9445, 825 F.2d 1568 (Fed. Cir. 1987).

[132] Reg. §1.595-1(e)(6). *See also* IRS Industry Specialization Program Coordinated Issue Papers on Interest Income on Sale of Foreclosed Property at A.110 and A.111.

[133] This would not be the case if the interest were accrued into taxable income. In this case, the creditor would have a tax basis in it and it would constitute "capital."

[134] *First Federal Savings and Loan of Bristol v. United States*, 81-2 U.S.T.C. ¶9681, 660 F.2d 767 (Ct. Cl. 1981).

[135] *First Charter Financial Corp. v. United States*, 82-1 U.S.T.C. ¶9222, 669 F.2d 1342 (9th Cir. 1982).

[136] *Gibraltar Financial Corp. of Calif. v. United States*, 87-2 U.S.T.C. ¶9445, 825 F.2d 1568, 1575 (Fed. Cir. 1987).

probably be ignored for both legal liability and tax purposes. This would occur, for example, if the subsidiary acts as a mere agent for its principal, the bank. Under these circumstances, the income and expenses of the subsidiary will be properly reported by the bank, as will any gain or loss on the sale of the property. If the stock of a nominee corporation is sold, the capital asset characterization of any resulting gain or loss may be questionable.

Chapter 8
Business Expenses

Contents

§ 8.1 Tax Planning Suggestions
§ 8.2 General Rules for Taxable Year of Deduction
§ 8.2.1 Economic Performance Requirement
§ 8.2.2 Deducting Refunded Interest
§ 8.3 Capitalization of Expenditures
§ 8.3.1 General Rules
§ 8.3.2 Separate and Distinct Asset Test
§ 8.3.3 Future Benefit Test
§ 8.3.4 Loan Origination Costs
§ 8.4 Capitalization of Acquisition or Creation of Intangibles
§ 8.4.1 Overview of Capitalization Regulations
§ 8.4.2 Acquired Intangibles
§ 8.4.3 Created Intangibles
§ 8.4.4 Capitalized Transaction Costs
§ 8.4.5 Special Rules for Pooling Methods
§ 8.4.6 Accounting Method Changes
§ 8.5 Acquisition Costs
§ 8.5.1 Capitalization Regulations
§ 8.5.2 Judicial Background to Regulation Section 1.263(a)-5
§ 8.6 Debt Issuance Costs
§ 8.7 Amortization of Capitalized Costs
§ 8.8 Pre-Regulation IRS Pronouncements
§ 8.8.1 Home Equity Lines of Credit
§ 8.8.2 Origination of Mortgage Loans
§ 8.8.3 Advertising and Other Expenditures
§ 8.9 Start-Up and Expansion Expenditures
§ 8.9.1 Overview
§ 8.9.2 Start-Up Expenditures—Code Section 195
§ 8.9.3 Organizational Expenditures—Code Section 248
§ 8.9.4 Comparison of Code Sections 195 and 248
§ 8.9.5 Electing Code Section 248
§ 8.10 Business Expansion and New Product Expenditures
§ 8.10.1 Branch Pre-Opening Costs
§ 8.10.2 Branch Geographic Expansion Costs
§ 8.10.3 Training Costs
§ 8.10.4 Promotional and Selling Costs
§ 8.10.5 Advertising Costs
§ 8.10.6 Mutual Fund Costs
§ 8.10.7 Credit Card Costs
§ 8.10.8 Bailout Costs
§ 8.10.9 Expenditures Reducing Future Costs

§8.11 Year 2000 Costs
§8.12 FDIC Deposit Insurance Assessment
§8.13 FDIC Exit and Entrance Fees
§8.14 Regulatory Examination Assessment
§8.15 Farm Credit System Assessment
§8.16 Directors' and Officers' Insurance
§8.17 Premiums on Debtor's Life Insurance
§8.18 Discount for Early Mortgage Pay-off
§8.19 Supervisory Goodwill
§8.20 Net Operating Losses
§8.20.1 Pre-1987 Net Operating Losses
§8.20.2 1987-1993 Net Operating Losses
§8.20.3 Election to Forego Carryback
§8.20.4 2008-2009 Net Operating Losses
§8.21 Abandonment Losses—Customer Lists and Goodwill
§8.21.1 Abandonment Loss for Customer Lists
§8.21.2 Abandonment Loss for Supervisory Goodwill
§8.22 Covered Asset Losses

§8.1 Tax Planning Suggestions

The IRS has abandoned attempts to deny the deductibility of most loan origination expenses that taxpayer's have traditionally deducted as ordinary and necessary business expenses incurred in carrying on a trade or business.[1] In regulations under Code section 263(a), which were finalized in December 2003, the IRS conceded that amounts paid to employees, including commissions and related overhead to originate loans, are currently deductible. However, the regulations seem to require capitalization for certain amounts paid to loan brokers and other non-employees. To this extent, the regulations may be invalid.

In general, the regulations require taxpayers to capitalize amounts paid to another party to acquire any intangible from that party in a purchase or similar transaction. A nonexclusive list of acquired intangibles for which capitalization is required is set forth. With respect to created intangibles, the regulations prescribe eight categories of intangibles for which capitalization is required. The capitalization regulations provide capitalization rules that apply to nearly all assets on a financial institution's balance sheet.

The IRS had attempted to disallow expenses associated with branch expansion and certain new product expenses. Under the status of the law in the past, the IRS was unsuccessful in most of its attempts to compel capitalization. Recent IRS pronouncements indicate that current deduction of branch expansion expenses will not be challenged. The recently finalized capitalization regulations also provide some guidance on these expenditures, and, for the most part, the existing law has been adopted.

[1] *See The Art of Tax Efficiency in Community Banks*, by M. Gula, J. Brew, and R. Blasi, 2007, Red Room Publishing, *http://www.mraeresources.com/bookstore/*.

Because some banks are engaging in nontraditional banking businesses or, through bank holding company affiliates, in nondepository businesses, care should be taken to make an election under Code section 195 to preserve deductibility of any start-up expenses. The Treasury Department finalized regulations under Code section 195, which provide rules that must be followed when making an election to amortize start-up expenses. The regulations contain provisions that eliminate the possibility of what some taxpayers referred to as protective elections. Now, the election must contain specificity with respect to the activity and the expenditures. Moreover, a recent Tax Court opinion, Revenue Ruling, and two Technical Advice Memoranda provide significant guidance into what expenditures qualify as investigatory start-up expenses. The recently issued final regulations under Code section 263(a) also address business acquisition and business expansion expenditures. With the exception of establishing a rule for when an expenditure becomes a Code section 263(a) capitalizable item, Code section 195 is unaffected.

The tax treatment of start-up expenditures is quite different from the accounting treatment. Recently, the FASB issued a "Statement of Position" that outlines the accounting treatment, which calls for current expensing of both start-up as well as organization expenditures. This should always result in a Schedule M adjustment.

§8.2 General Rules for Taxable Year of Deduction

An accrual method taxpayer is allowed to deduct a liability in the taxable year in which all the events have occurred that establish the fact of the liability, the amount of the liability can be determined with reasonable accuracy, and economic performance has occurred with respect to the liability.[2] If these tests are met, an accrual method taxpayer is allowed to deduct the face amount of an accrued expense. A deduction for a contingent liability is not allowed because all of the events necessary to fix the liability will not have occurred until the contingency terminates.[3] However, the amount of a liability is determinable with reasonable accuracy even though the amount is not precisely ascertained. Courts have held that technical estimates and estimates based on industrywide experience or on the experience of the taxpayer are acceptable.[4] The book treatment of contingent liabilities may not be in accordance with the tax treatment. FASB No. 5 specifies the accounting treatment for contingent liabilities, which will not be controlling for tax purposes.[5]

§8.2.1 Economic Performance Requirement

A liability is treated as incurred for all purposes of the Code once economic performance has occurred.[6] The economic performance requirement was added

[2] I.R.C. §461(h); Reg. §1.461-1(a)(2).

[3] *C.F. Lukens Steel Co. v. Commissioner*, 442 F.2d 1131 (3d Cir. 1971).

[4] *Kaiser Steel Corp. v. United States*, 411 F.2d 235 (9th Cir. 1983). *Cf.* PLR 7831003, April 13, 1978.

[5] Reg. §1.446-1(c)(1)(ii)IC). *See* "The Tax Treatment of Acquired Contingent Liabilities," by Stevenson and Reinstein, Journal of Taxation and Regulation of Financial Institutions, May/June 2005, Vol. 18/No. 5.

[6] H.R. Rep. No. 98-432, at Part 2, 98th Cong., 2d Sess. 1255 (1984). There are exceptions to the eco-

to the Code by the Tax Reform Act of 1984.[7] Before its enactment, court decisions and IRS rulings had produced somewhat conflicting opinions as to when an amount had become a fixed liability and could be deducted.[8] Congress was concerned that the existing law could be interpreted to permit accrual method taxpayers to deduct currently expenses that were attributable to activities to be performed or amounts to be paid in the future.[9] Section 461(h) was intended to remedy this uncertainty by taking into account the time value of money and not allowing a deduction for a liability until the taxpayer performs the activities that he is obligated to perform in order to satisfy the liability, or, put another way, until economic performance occurs.[10]

(a) *Services and Property Provided to the Taxpayer*

If a liability arises out of the provision of services or property to the taxpayer by another person, economic performance occurs as the services or property are provided to the taxpayer.[11] A taxpayer may treat services or property as provided to the taxpayer as the taxpayer makes payment to the person providing the services or property, if the taxpayer can reasonably expect the person to provide the services or property within 3 1/2 months after the date of payment.[12] This rule is designed to "lessen the burden of a taxpayer incident to determining when property or services are provided to the taxpayer."[13]

> **Example:** Bank holding company subsidiary X, a calendar year, accrual method taxpayer, is a retailer of check processing machines. Y is the manufacturer. On January 15, 19X1, X agrees to pay an additional $10 per machine to Y, in exchange for advertising and promotional activities provided by Y to X. During 19X1, X buys 100 machines and pays Y the agreed upon $1000 extra. Y uses the $1000 to provide the advertising and promotional activities, but not until the year 19X3. Economic performance occurs as the services are provided, thus, X incurs $1000 of liability for the 19X3 taxable year.
>
> If X had paid the $1000 on December 15, 19X1, and Y was to perform the services before the first of April, 19X2, then X could apply the liability to the 19X1 taxable year. This would be possible because of the 3 1/2 month rule, where X would be allowed to treat the services as being provided as X makes payments, since X could expect Y to provide the services within 3 1/2 months.[14]

(Footnote Continued)

nomic performance requirement, and certain other provisions of the Code may provide alternative timing rules for certain situations and thus override section 461(h).

[7] The Tax Reform Act of 1984, Pub. L. No. 98-369, § 91(a), 98 Stat. 494 (1984).

[8] The legislative history cites some examples of the uncertainty produced pertaining to each of the two criteria used in the "all events test." *See* H.R. Rep. No. 98-432 at 1252-53 (1984).

[9] *Id.* at 1254.

[10] *Id.* at 1254-55.

[11] I.R.C. § § 461(h)(2)(A)(i) and (ii).

[12] Reg. § 1.461-4(d)(6)(ii).

[13] 55 F.R. at 23236. Some who have commented on the economic performance regulations when they were in proposed form suggested that payment by the taxpayer should, as a general rule, be treated as economic performance. The IRS and the Treasury Department concluded that such a rule would lead to income shifting between taxpayers. 57 F.R. 12411, 12413. Commentators also suggested that the 3 1/2 month rule should be expanded to 6 months, another recommendation that was not adopted.

[14] Example is adopted from Reg. § 1.461-1(d).

(b) *Use of Property by the Taxpayer*

If the liability of a taxpayer arises out of the use of property by the taxpayer, economic performance occurs as the taxpayer uses the property.[15] In general, economic performance occurs ratably over the period of time the taxpayer is entitled to the use of the property.[16] If the liability is determined by the frequency or volume of use of the property, or by the income from the property, then economic performance occurs, with respect to that portion of the liability, as the taxpayer uses the property or includes the income from the property, as the case may be.[17]

Example: Bank X agrees to lease a copier from Y for a three-year period beginning January 1, 19X1 for $6,000, and pays Y the full $6,000 when X takes delivery of the copier. X would incur $2,000 of deductible liability per taxable year. If X took delivery of the copier in the middle of 19X1, and the lease was to run for 3 years (July 1, 19X1 through June 30, 19X4), then X would incur $1,000 in 19X1, $2,000 in 19X2 and 19X3, and another $1,000 in 19X4.

Suppose that Bank X is also to pay 5 cents for every copy made, payable at the end of the lease, in addition to the base rental fee. Economic performance would be determined with respect to this amount as X uses the machine. Thus, if 2,000 copies were made in 19X1, X's liability for the 19X1 taxable year would be $1,100 ($1,000 for the base charge, determined ratably, and $100 for the variable usage, determined as the machine is used.)[18]

(c) *Services and Property Provided by the Taxpayer*

If a taxpayer is obligated to provide services or property, economic performance occurs as the taxpayer incurs costs in connection with the satisfaction of the liability.[19]

Example: Bank holding company subsidiary X sells ATM machines with a five-year warranty obligating X to repair each machine it sells. In 19X1, X sells 10 machines, and in 19X3 X repairs two of the machines that were sold in 19X1. If X incurs costs of repairing the machines of $5,000, when X repairs them, the $5,000 is treated as incurred by X in the 19X3 taxable year.[20]

(d) *Workers' Compensation, Tort Liabilities, and Other Liabilities*

Economic performance is deemed to occur when payment is made for certain liabilities, including liabilities arising under a workers' compensation claim, from a tort,[21] a breach of contract, a violation of laws, rebates and refunds, awards, prizes, and jackpots, amounts paid for insurance, and taxes (other than

---

15 I.R.C. § 461(h)(2)(A)(iii).

16 Reg. § 1.461-1(d)(3)(i).

17 Reg. § 1.461-1(d)(3)(ii). The special rules for liabilities that vary with the amount of usage or the amount of income derived from the property were added by the final regulations in response to commentator's concerns about the general ratable rules. *See* F.R. 12414.

18 Example is adopted from Reg. § 1.461-1(d).

19 I.R.C. § 461(h)(2)(B); Reg. § 1.461-4(d)(4).

20 Example is adopted from Reg. § 1.461-1(d).

21 I.R.C. § 461(h)(2)(C).

creditable foreign taxes).[22] The payment must be made to the person to which the liability is owed, and not to a trust, escrow account, *etc.*[23] Thus, when a bank pays the real property tax liability associated with property acquired at foreclosure, the liability is probably deductible when the liability is paid.[24]

(e) ***Recurring Item Exception***

An exception to the economic performance rule is provided for liabilities that are recurring in nature.[25] A liability is recurring in nature if it can generally be expected to be incurred from one taxable year to the next, such as insurance premiums.[26] Under this exception, if the liability is recurring in nature, the liability can be treated as incurred for a taxable year if the "all events" test has been met by the end of that taxable year and economic performance will occur within 8 1/2 months of the close of the taxable year or before the taxpayer files a timely return for the taxable year, whichever is earlier. The amount of the liability must also not be material, or the accrual of the liability for that taxable year must result in a better matching of the liability with the income to which it relates than would result from accruing the liability for the taxable year in which economic performance results.

§ 8.2.2 Deducting Refunded Interest

Any excess of the amount received and taxed over the amount earned for the term of the loan is deductible by the lender. However, courts differ on whether a deduction is allowed in the year that a cash basis taxpayer renounces its claim to funds and recognizes its obligation to repay them but does not actually transfer any funds in satisfaction of its obligation. The Ninth Circuit Court of Appeals in *Merrill* has allowed a deduction in this situation,[27] but in the Second and Seventh Circuits, only actual repayment in the year of receipt will give rise to a deduction.[28] Normally, there is no support for a doctrine of constructive payment.

In *Merrill,* the taxpayer agreed in 1940 to repay amounts erroneously received in 1939 and 1940 from his deceased wife's estate. The actual repayment occurred in 1943. Entries were made in 1940 on the books of the estate and the taxpayer's personal books to show the indebtedness owed to the estate. It was acknowledged by the parties that the claim of right doctrine called for inclusion in 1939 of the amounts received in that year. However, the 1940 receipts were

---

[22] Reg. §§ 1.461-4(g)(2)-(6).

[23] Reg. § 1.461-4(g)(1)(i). There are exceptions for liabilities assumed in connection with the sale of trade or business and assignments. *See* Reg. § 1.461-4(g)(1)(ii)(C) and Reg. § 1.461(g)(1)(iv). The standards for a cash basis taxpayer are to be used with regards to whether a payment has been made and to whom it was made. *See* Reg. §§ 1.461-4(g)(1)(ii)(A) and (B).

[24] *See* discussion in Chapter 7 for IRS's position on expenses associated with holding property acquired at foreclosure.

[25] I.R.C. § 461(h)(3).

[26] Reg. § 1.461-5(b)(3). The liability does not have to be incurred by the taxpayer in each taxable year, nor does it have to have been previously incurred, so long as it is reasonable to expect that it will be incurred on a recurring basis in the future.

[27] *United States v. Merrill*, 54-1 U.S.T.C. ¶9275, 211 F.2d 297 (9th Cir. 1954); *Charles Kay Bishop v. Commissioner*, 25 T.C. 969, Dec. 21,554 (1956).

[28] *Buff v. Commissioner*, 74-1 U.S.T.C. ¶9353, 496 F.2d 847 (2d Cir. 1974); and *H.B. Quinn v. Commissioner*, 75-2 U.S.T.C. ¶9764, 524 F.2d 617 (7th Cir. 1975).

held to be outside the claim of right doctrine. Because the taxpayer acknowledged the error in the year of receipt, no amount was held under a claim of right.

§8.3 Capitalization of Expenditures

§8.3.1 General Rules

Code section 162 provides, in general, that there shall be allowed as a deduction all the ordinary and necessary expenses paid or incurred during the taxable year in carrying on any trade or business. For an expenditure to be "necessary" it must be appropriate and helpful to the development of the taxpayer's business. An "ordinary" expense is one that is common and accepted in the taxpayer's trade or business.[29] It need not be habitual or even normal in the sense that the taxpayer will often incur the expense. Recurring expenses are usually "ordinary."[30]

Code section 263(a) is viewed as operating contrary to Code section 162. The former provides for capitalization of any amount "paid out for new buildings or for permanent improvements or betterments made to increase the value of any property or estate." In general, capital expenditures are amounts paid or incurred to restore, add to the value of, or substantially prolong the useful life of tangible or intangible property owned by the taxpayer. Capital expenditures also include amounts expended to adapt property to a new or different use. However, amounts paid or incurred for incidental maintenance of property, including incidental repairs, are not capital expenditures.[31] Regulations have been promulgated under Code Section 263(a) that provide detailed rules for capitalizing expenditures associated with intangible assets.[32] These regulations have particular application to financial institutions.

Although Code section 263(a) denies a current deduction for capital expenditures, other sections may allow the amount expended to be recovered through depreciation, depletion, or amortization deductions. If the asset is not subject to depreciation, depletion, or amortization, then such expenditures are recovered upon the sale of the property. If Code section 263(a) requires that an expenditure be capitalized, the amount must be added to tax basis.[33] Capital expenditures cannot be taken into account through inclusion in inventory costs or as a charge to capital accounts or basis any earlier than the tax year during which the amount is incurred within the meaning of Regulation section 1.446-1(c)(1)(ii).[34]

Code section 263A, added to the Code by the Tax Reform Act of 1986, contains a uniform capitalization rule ("UNICAP rule").[35] It requires certain direct and indirect costs of real or tangible personal property produced by the

---

[29] *Welsch v. Helvering*, 290 U.S. 111 (1933); *Commissioner v. Tellier*, 383 U.S. 687 (1966).

[30] *Encyclopedia Britannica, Inc. v. Commissioner*, 685 F.2d 212, 214 (7th Cir. 1982), *rev'g* T.C. Memo. 81-255 (1981). *See also* Rev. Rul. 89-23, 1989-1 C.B. 85.

[31] Reg. §1.263(a)-1.

[32] Reg. §1.263(a)-4. T.D. 9107, 2004-1 C.B. 447. *See* discussion below of capitalization regulations.

[33] Reg. §1.263(a)-4. No similar express addition to basis is provided for expenditures that are not currently deductible by reason of Code Sec. 195.

[34] Reg. §1.263(a)-1.

[35] Tax Reform Act of 1986, Pub. L. No. 99-514, 100 Stat. 2085 (1986). The Technical and Miscellaneous Revenue Act of 1988, Pub. L. No. 100-647, 102 Stat. 3342 (1988) contained several amendments to I.R.C. §263A.

taxpayer, and certain direct and indirect cost of intangible property acquired by the taxpayer for resale, to be capitalized.

If the UNICAP rule applies, all costs incurred by a function or department of the taxpayer that directly benefit a particular production or resale activity are allocable to those activities. In addition, indirect costs, which constitute all costs other than direct labor and material costs, must be allocated to determine the portion attributable to each of the taxpayer's activities. Direct costs include related salaries, and indirect costs would include the cost of owning and operating a building in which the activity is conducted.[36]

The origination of a loan is treated under Code section 263A as the production of intangible property for resale and not the acquisition of intangible property.[37] Property produced by the taxpayer is subject to the Code section 263A capitalization rules only if it is tangible property. Accordingly, the UNICAP rules do not apply to loans made by a bank. However, if a taxpayer purchases pre-existing loans from other parties for resale, Code section 263A would apply.

(a) ***Capitalization Examples***

The following are some examples of capital expenditures:

(1) The cost of defending or perfecting title to property, regardless of whether the property is tangible or intangible;

(2) Commissions paid in purchasing securities (commissions paid in selling securities are an offset against the selling price by reducing the Code section 1001 "amount realized," except that in the case of dealers in securities such commissions may be treated as an ordinary and necessary business expense);

(3) Amounts assessed and paid under an agreement between bondholders or corporate and individual shareholders of a corporation to be used in a reorganization of the corporation;

(4) Voluntary contributions by corporate or individual shareholders to the capital of the corporation for any corporate purpose;

(5) Amounts paid in carrying out a guaranty by a holding company in computing its taxable income in instances where the company guarantees dividends at a specified rate on the stock of a subsidiary corporation for the purpose of securing new capital for the subsidiary and increasing the value of its stockholdings in the subsidiary; and

(6) The cost of goodwill in connection with the acquisition of the assets of a going concern.[38]

(b) ***Judicial Interpretation of Code section 263(a)***

When expenditures may arguably be classified as either business expenses or capital expenditures, the IRS and the courts have often applied the Supreme

[36] *See* Reg. § 1.263-1.

[37] Reg. § 1.263A-1(b)(13); Notice 88-86, 1988-2 C.B. 401, at IV, (c).

[38] Reg. § 1.263(a)-2. *See* Code Sec. 197 for rules that apply to the amortization of goodwill.

Court's separate and distinct asset test articulated in *Lincoln Savings* or the future benefits test introduced in *INDOPCO* to determine whether an expenditure must be capitalized.[39] Under *Lincoln Savings*, if the expenditure creates for the taxpayer a separate and distinct asset then the amount must be capitalized. However, the presence or absence of a separate and distinct asset does not establish a bright-line rule for purposes of determining deductibility. What has also been important in determining the appropriate tax treatment is a taxpayer's realization of benefits beyond the year in which the expenditure is incurred.

In *INDOPCO*, the Supreme Court stated that the creation or enhancement of a separate and distinct asset is not an exclusive test for identifying a capital expenditure. Thus, although the creation of a separate and distinct asset may be sufficient in-and-of-itself to classify an expenditure as capital in nature, it is not a necessary condition. Although an "incidental future benefit" will not dictate that an expenditure be capitalized, the realization of significant future benefits may result in expenses being capitalized. Final regulations issued under Code section 263(a) that apply to intangible assets have sharply curtailed the *INDOPCO* future benefits test by prescribing an exclusive list of intangibles resulting from future benefits, the cost of which must be capitalized.[40]

(c) *Burden of Proof*

Once it is determined that a deduction is generally allowed for a particular type of expenditure, determining whether a particular expenditure is of that type is a question of fact.[41] The Supreme Court acknowledged that distinctions between ordinary and capital expenditures are of degree, not kind,[42] and the Court observed that Congress has not provided "a complete list of nondeductible (capital) expenditures."[43] Thus, whether an expenditure is capital or ordinary depends on an analysis of the specific expenditure. As stated in the often quoted language of the Supreme Court relating to capitalization rules:

> One struggles in vain for any verbal formula that will supply a ready touchstone. The standard set up by the statute is not a rule of law; it is rather a way of life. Life in all its fullness must supply the answer to the riddle.[44]

The burden of proof to sustain a deduction for loan origination or other related expenses, as with other deductions, is on the taxpayer.[45] Deductions have been referred to as exceptions to the norm of capitalization.[46] Elsewhere it has

---

[39] *Lincoln Savings and Loan Association v. Commissioner*, 403 U.S. 345 (1971); *INDOPCO, Inc. v. Commissioner*, 92-1 USTC ¶50,113, 503 U.S. 79 (1992). *See* detailed discussions below of the separate and distinct asset test and the future benefits test.

[40] Reg. §1.263(a)-4.

[41] *Plainfield-Union Water Company v. Commissioner*, 39 T.C. 333 (1962); *Pittman v. Commissioner*, 100 F.3d 1308, 1313 (7th Cir. 1996).

[42] *INDOPCO, Inc. v. Commissioner*, 92-1 U.S.T.C. ¶50,113, 503 U.S. 79 (1992).

[43] *Lincoln Savings & Loan Association v. Commissioner*, 403 U.S. 345 (1971). However, note that the Committee reports under the Tax Reform Act of 1986 state that the enactment of I.R.C. §263A was to establish a "single comprehensive set of rules [to] govern the capitalization of costs of producing, acquiring and holding property including interest expense . . . ." General Explanation of the Tax Reform Act of 1986, Staff of the Joint Committee on Taxation, May 4, 1987, pp. 508-509.

[44] *Welch v. Helvering*, 290 U.S. 111, 115 (1933).

[45] *Id.* at 116.

[46] *INDOPCO, Inc. v. Commissioner*, 92-1 U.S.T.C. ¶50,113, 112 S. Ct. 1039, 1043 (1992).

been said that deductions are a matter of legislative grace; they are strictly construed; and they are allowed only "as there is a clear provision therefore."[47]

(d) *Supremacy of Code Section 263*

Code section 161 provides that in computing taxable income there shall be allowed as deductions the items specified in Code section 162 through Code section 196, subject to the exceptions provided in Code section 261 through Code section 280H.

The limitation on the deduction allowance sections set forth in Code section 161, often referred to as the priority ordering rule, was discussed by the Supreme Court in *Idaho Power* as it pertained to the relationship between Code section 263 and the depreciation section, Code section 167.[48] There the Court stated:

> The clear import of section 161 is that, with stated exceptions set forth either in section 263 itself or provided for elsewhere . . . , an expenditure incurred in acquiring capital assets must be capitalized even when the expenditure otherwise might be deemed deductible under [Code section 161 and following].[49]

Thus, allowance of a deduction under Code section 162 is limited by the provisions of Code section 263. Code section 263 excepts from deductibility any expenditure which is a capital expenditure; that is, "[a]ny amount paid out for new buildings or for permanent improvements or betterments made to increase the value of any property or estate."[50] In other words, deductibility of an expenditure as an ordinary and necessary business expense requires that the expenditure pass the "ordinary and necessary" text of Code section 162 and that deductibility not be denied by Code section 263.

§ 8.3.2 Separate and Distinct Asset Test

In an effort to articulate a workable standard for determining when expenditures should be deductible or capitalized, in 1971 the Supreme Court crafted the so called separate and distinct asset test. This test has withstood the test of time and has been recently elevated by Treasury Regulations § 1.263(a)-4 to the position of the predominant test for capitalization of intangibles. The case in which this test first appeared was *Commissioner v. Lincoln Savings and Loan Association*.[51]

In *Lincoln Savings*, a state-chartered savings and loan institution insured by the Federal Savings and Loan Insurance Corporation ("FSLIC") made premium payments to FSLIC for the purpose of funding reserves for loan losses. To establish a "secondary reserve," Lincoln Savings was required to make additional premium payments in excess of those required to fund the "primary reserve." The secondary reserve differed from the primary reserve in that it was only to be used to cover losses to the extent that the primary reserve and other accounts of FSLIC were insufficient.

---

[47] *New Colonial Ice Company v. Helvering*, 292 U.S. 434, 440 (1934); *Deputy v. DuPont*, 308 U.S. 488, 493 (1940).

[48] *Commissioner v. Idaho Power Co.*, 74-2 U.S.T.C. ¶ 9521, 418 U.S. 1 (1974).

[49] *Id.* at 17.

[50] I.R.C. § 263(a)(1).

[51] *Commissioner v. Lincoln Savings and Loan Association*, 71-1 U.S.T.C ¶ 19476, 403 U.S. 345 (1971).

Each institution that was insured by FSLIC owned a *pro rata* share of the secondary reserve, but the institution had no property interest in the funds constituting the primary reserve. The institution's interest in the secondary reserve was assignable, but under very limited circumstances, and it was refundable to the insured institution, but only if there were a termination of insured status or a liquidation. Each year, FSLIC submitted to each insured institution that contributed to the secondary reserve a statement setting forth the institution's share of the secondary reserve and the earnings credited to that reserve account.

Lincoln Savings & Loan Association deducted the payments made to both the primary and secondary reserve as ordinary and necessary business expenses under Code section 162. The IRS allowed the deduction for the premiums made to fund the primary reserve but disallowed the deductions for the premium payments made to fund the secondary reserve. The Court took note of the separate accounting for each insured institution's share of the secondary reserve, the transferability feature of each *pro rata* share, the prospective refund feature upon termination of insured status or liquidation, and the fact that each share was productive of income to the insured institution.

The legal test applied by the Court was whether the expenditure served to create or enhance a separate and distinct capital asset with an ascertainable and measurable value. The Court found that the mandatory premium paid by Lincoln Savings to the FSLIC that funded the secondary reserve in which participating institutions had a *pro rata* share was a nondeductible capital investment in the FSLIC. It was not an "expense." The expenditure was found to create a distinct and recognized property interest in the secondary reserve. Although it is not expressly stated, the *Lincoln Savings* test is not a test of whether an expense is "ordinary" for purposes of Code section 162. Rather, it appears to be a test used to determine whether an expenditure is an "expense." Unfortunately, the Court seemingly failed to note that the expenditure in *Lincoln Savings* was probably not "ordinary" for purposes of Code section 162. The discussion of Code section 263 only served to confuse the issue.

§8.3.3 Future Benefit Test

The separate asset test crafted by the Supreme Court in *Lincoln Savings* was qualified by the Supreme Court two decades later in *INDOPCO v. Commissioner*.[52] In *INDOPCO*, the Court concluded that certain legal and investment banking fees incurred by a target corporation to facilitate a friendly acquisition were required to be capitalized under Code section 263. The Court found that the costs created significant long-term benefits for the taxpayer. Had the benefits, instead, produced only some incidental future benefit, a current deduction under Code section 162 would have been allowed.[53]

---

[52] *INDOPCO, Inc. v. Commissioner*, 92-1 U.S.T.C. ¶50,113, 503 U.S. 79 (1992).

[53] Rev. Rul. 92-80, 1992-2 C.B. 57; *Iowa-Des Moines National Bank v. Commissioner*, 592 F.2d 433 (8th Cir. 1979), *aff'g* 68 T.C. 872 (1977); *Sun Microsystems, Inc. v. Commissioner*, 66 T.C.M. 997, T.C. Memo. 1993-467.

This future benefit test appears to be a reincarnation, with some modifications, of the so-called one-year rule, earlier applied, which required capitalization of an expenditure if it created an asset with a life extending beyond the end of the tax year. Moreover, it resembles a long-standing Treasury regulation, which provides that any expenditure that results in the creation of an asset having a useful life that extends substantially beyond the close of a taxable year may not be deductible, or may be deductible only in part, for the taxable year in which incurred.[54]

In reaching its conclusion, the Court in *INDOPCO* clarified the scope of its opinion in *Lincoln Savings*. It stated that *Lincoln Savings* should not be read as holding "that only expenditures that create or enhance separate and distinct assets are to be capitalized under Section 263."[55] However, the court was careful to refrain from expressing this future benefit test as the exclusive test for capitalization. Instead, it affirmed the validity of the separate asset test,[56] the test on the basis of which most bank capitalization cases were decided prior to *INDOPCO*.[57] Oddly, the Court indicated that *Lincoln Savings* was decided under Code section 263, but it appears to have been decided under Code section 162. Because the expenditure was not an "expense" it failed the Code section 162 test.

This future benefit test has spawned considerable controversy. Indeed, the IRS itself has criticized its scope. In the preamble to the 2002 proposed regulations on the capitalization of intangible assets, the IRS stated: "A significant future benefit standard, however, does not provide the certainty and clarity necessary for compliance with, and sound administration of, the law."[58] Thus, the IRS and Treasury Department have chosen not to employ the future benefit test when determining whether expenditures to create or acquire intangibles are required to be capitalized under the new Code section 263(a) regulations. Because one of the objectives of the regulations is to reduce controversy, this was a prudent decision.

Regulation section 1.263(a)-4 has limited the scope of the significant future benefit test.[59] If a taxpayer pays an amount to acquire or to create an intangible that is not described as falling into one or more of eight categories of intangibles, or is not otherwise required to be capitalized by the regulations, the taxpayer will not be required to capitalize the expenditure even if it produces a significant future benefit for the taxpayer. Of course, the IRS is authorized to publish guidance requiring capitalization of other expenditures.[60] The regulations provide that if such guidance is published, it will apply only prospectively.[61]

---

[54] Reg. § 1.461-1(a)(1), for cash method taxpayers, and Reg. § 1.461-1(a)(2), for accrual method taxpayers.

[55] *INDOPCO, Inc. v. Commissioner*, 92-1 U.S.T.C. ¶50,113, 503 U.S. 79, 86-87 (1992).

[56] *See* Peter L. Faber, "INDOPCO: The Still Unsolved Riddle," 47 Tax Law 607 (1994) *The Tax Lawyer*, Vol. 47:3 (Spring 1994), p. 607.

[57] Among the cases that relied upon the *Lincoln Savings* test were: *NCNB Corp. v. United States*, 82-2 U.S.T.C. ¶9469, 684 F.2d 285 (4th Cir. 1982); *Central Texas Savings & Loan Association v. United States*, 84-1 U.S.T.C. ¶9471, 731 F.2d 1181 (5th Cir. 1984).

[58] "Guidance Regarding Deduction and Capitalization of Expenditures," II, C, 67 Fed. Reg. 77,701 (Dec. 19, 2002) (to be codified at 26 C.F.R. pt. 1).

[59] Reg. § 1.263(a)-4(d).

[60] Reg. § 1.263(a)-4(b)(1).

[61] Reg. § 1.263(a)-4(b)(2).

Furthermore, the regulations are clear that the IRS will not take the position that if an amount paid to acquire or to create an intangible is not required to be capitalized by the Code or by regulations, including the new intangibles regulations, the clear reflection of income requirement of Section 446(b) and the regulations thereunder will necessitate capitalization.[62]

§8.3.4 Loan Origination Costs

For several years the IRS took the position on audit that the direct costs associated with originating loans could not be currently deducted under Code section 162. Instead, such costs were required to be capitalized under Code section 263(a) as expenditures that created separate and distinct assets.[63] When this position was challenged in the courts by taxpayers, the Tax Court, in opinions that lacked careful analysis, customarily affirmed the position taken by the IRS.[64] However, the first federal appeals court that reviewed one of these Tax Court decisions reversed the Tax Court and significantly contributed to a change in the direction taken by the IRS and the Treasury Department with respect to capitalization of intangibles, in general.

(a) *Overview of PNC Bancorp Opinion*

In *PNC Bancorp*, the Third Circuit Federal Court of Appeals held that costs incurred by banks for marketing, researching, and originating loans are deductible under Code section 162 as an ordinary and necessary business expenses, and the expenses are not required to be capitalized under Code section 263.[65] The Tax Court in *PNC Bancorp* found that the expenditures were incurred in creating separate and distinct assets. Consequently, under the Tax Court opinion the banks were not entitled to deduct the expenditures under Code section 162(a).[66] Rather, they were required to be capitalized under Code section 263(a) and recovered through amortization deductions.

A two-step analysis that adhered to statutory provisions was applied by the Third Circuit in reaching its conclusion. It first examined the facts of the case to see whether the expenses were "ordinary" for purposes of the Code section 162 test. Then it turned to Code section 263 to see whether the "ordinary" expenses were required to be capitalized as incurred "for new buildings or for permanent improvements or betterments made to increase the value of any property." In so doing, it properly applied the relationship between the two sections and respected the meaning of the applicable statutory language. To the contrary, the Supreme Court in *Lincoln Savings* and in *INDOPCO*, and the Tax Court in subsequent opinions, blended the two sections thereby obscuring the plain meaning of the statutory language.

---

[62] Reg. §1.263(a)-4(b)(4)(i).

[63] In FSA 199910012, December 4, 1998, the I.R.S seemingly distinguished expenses associated with unsuccessful loan efforts (deductible) from successful loan efforts (nondeductible) and expenses incurred subsequent to a loan's origination (deductible) from those incurred prior to origination (nondeductible).

[64] Most of these opinions lacked thoughtful analysis, making them ripe for reversal.

[65] *PNC Bancorp, Inc. v. Commissioner*, 110 T.C. 349 (1998), *rev'd*, 212 F.3d 822 (3d Cir. 2000).

[66] 212 F.3d at 835.

The Third Circuit concluded that the expenses in issue were "ordinary" because they were commonly or frequently incurred in the type of business in which the taxpayer was engaged. Furthermore, the Court noted that the expenditures were "expenses" for purposes of Code section 162. Thus, *Lincoln Savings* was distinguished. Finally, it also found that the expenses did not result in permanent improvements or betterments that increased the value of the taxpayer's property. Instead, the expenditures maintained the taxpayer's existing business. Thus, the Court adhered to the statutory language of Code section 162 and Code section 263 and correctly applied the ordering rule of Code section 161. As a consequence, the Court, in accordance with statutory language and pre-*Lincoln Savings* judicial precedent, re-established the correct legal tests for deductibility and for capitalization.

(b) *Book Accounting Treatment*

In *PNC Bancorp* the taxpayer deferred certain loan origination costs over the expected life of the loans for financial accounting purposes, in accordance with SAFS 91 (hereinafter "Statement 91"). Specifically, the costs at issue included an allocable portion of the salaries and fringe benefits paid to employees for evaluating the borrower's financial condition, evaluating guarantees, collateral and other security arrangements, negotiating loan terms, preparing and processing loan documents, and closing the loan transaction. They also included amounts paid to record security interests, amounts paid to third parties for property reports, credit reports, and appraisals. None of the costs at issue were associated with loans that were not completed, nor were they costs incurred after the closing of a loan.

The loan origination costs that are required to be capitalized for book purposes by Statement No. 91 are direct costs incurred in processing a credit request, including evaluation of a borrower's financial condition, evaluating and recording guarantees and collateral, negotiating the loan's term, preparing and processing loan documents and closing the loan. According to Statement No. 91, the costs that are treated as directly related to loan origination include only that portion of employee's total compensation and payroll-related fringe benefits directly related to time spent performing those activities for that loan and other costs related to those activities that would not have been incurred but for that loan.[67]

On audit, the IRS has taken the position that the implementation of Statement No. 91 falls within accepted tax conventions for computing taxable income, at least with respect to expenses.[68] The relevance of the book accounting of an item determining the correct tax treatment is questionable. On the one hand,

---

[67] Statement No. 91 ¶6.

[68] Among the authorities cited by the IRS in support of its position are *Commissioner v. Lincoln Savings & Loan Association*, 71-1 U.S.T.C. ¶9476, 403 U.S. 345 (1971); *INDOPCO, Inc. v. Commissioner*, 92-1 U.S.T.C. ¶50,113, 503 U.S. 79 (1992); *Woodward v. Commissioner*, 70-1 U.S.T.C. ¶9348, 397 U.S. 572 (1970); and *Commissioner v. Idaho Power Company*, 74-2 U.S.T.C. ¶9521, 418 U.S. 1 (1974). In the latter case, the court found that the capitalization requirement applies not only to the acquisition of a capital asset by purchase, but also to the costs incurred to construct capital facilities. It is understood that the IRS has disallowed similar expenses incurred in originating mortgage loans, even where FAS 91 was not used.

Code section 446(a) provides that "taxable income shall be computed under the method of accounting on the basis of which the taxpayer regularly computes his income in keeping his books." However, the Supreme Court has stated uncategorically that book accounting does not control for tax purposes.[69] Nevertheless, it has also stated that where the book accounting method is mandated by a regulatory agency and the method clearly reflects income, "it is almost presumptively controlling of federal income tax consequences . . . ."[70] In the government's "Answering Brief" in *PNC Bancorp*, the IRS acknowledged that Statement No. 91 "does not provide the authority for capitalization of the costs at issue here."[71]

(c) *Announcement 93-60*

Prior to the promulgation in 1993 of the intangible capitalization regulations, the IRS temporarily suspended granting any change from a method of accounting that deducts loan origination costs when paid to a method of capitalizing loan origination costs.[72] Accompanying the suspension was an announcement that the IRS would issue a revenue procedure for lenders who wish to change their method of accounting for loan origination costs.[73] Moreover, the suspension granted taxpayers a procedure for obtaining audit protection.

Announcement 93-60 permits a taxpayer to request a change in accounting method for loan origination costs by filing the Form 3115 with the examining agent during the first 90 days of the examination or during any of the "window periods" available in Revenue Procedure 92-20.[74] A taxpayer is considered to be "under examination" as soon as the taxpayer has been contacted in any manner by a representative of the IRS for purposes of scheduling any type of examination of any of its federal income tax returns.[75]

Revenue Procedure 97-27, which superseded Revenue Procedure 92-20, eliminated the 90-day window period. Thus, there appears to be a conflict created by the provision in Announcement 93-60 permitting a taxpayer to request an accounting method change with respect to loan origination costs by filing a Form 3115 during the 90-day window period provided in Revenue Procedure 92-20 and the elimination of the window period by Revenue Procedure 97-27.

---

69 *Thor Power Tool Co. v. Commissioner*, 79-1 U.S.T.C. ¶9139, 439 U.S. 522 (1979). For a short period of time I.R.C. §56(g)(4)(F) required acquisition expenses of life insurance companies to be capitalized and amortized in accordance with the treatment generally required under generally accepted accounting principals. Sec. 701(a) of the Tax Reform Act of 1986, Pub. L. No. 99-514, §701(a), 100 Stat. 2085 (1986). In 1990, this provision was repealed and replaced by I.R.C. §848. The latter section permitted the deductibility of otherwise allowable items equal to a certain percentage of an insurance company's annual premium receipts. The deduction was spread over a 10-year period using the straight line cost recovery method.

70 *Commissioner v. Idaho Power*, 74-2 U.S.T.C. ¶9521, 418 U.S. 1 (1974).

71 *PNC Bancorp, Inc. v. Commissioner*, "Respondent's Answering Brief," 110 T.C. 349 (1998).

72 Announcement 93-60, 1993-16 IRB 9.

73 The IRS also stated in the announcement that it intended to amend Revenue Procedure 93-3, Section 5, to reflect the temporary suspension. Rev. Proc. 93-3, 1993-1 C.B. 209. In the proposed intangible capitalization regulations, procedures are described for changing a method of accounting that will take effect when the regulations are finally adopted. Prop. Reg. §1.263(a)-4(o), 67 FR 77701, December 19, 2002.

74 *Id.* §6 sets forth various "window periods." Taxpayers should not be disinclined to submit the application for accounting method change because of fear that the application may be accepted. Taxpayers are under no obligation to change their accounting method if the IRS approves the method change.

75 *Id.* §3.02. *See also* Rev. Proc. 97-27, 1997-1 C.B. 680, §3.07.

The IRS informally stated that Announcement 93-60 would be followed by agents on audit.

If a taxpayer filed Form 3115, the request for accounting method change with respect to loan origination costs will be returned to the taxpayer, except where the capitalization of loan origination cost issue was "pending" at the time that the Form 3115 was filed.[76] If a taxpayer were under examination on March 30, 1993, the publication date of the announcement, or subsequently comes under examination, the announcement permits the taxpayer to give the examining agent a copy of the returned Form 3115 that had requested an accounting method change. It is the IRS's position that this procedure does not apply to loan acquisition costs.

The provision in Announcement 93-60 permitting an accounting method change request to be filed during the 90-day window period was strictly applied by the IRS. Relief was not to be granted under Regulation section 301.9100-1(f) to permit an application to be filed outside of that period.[77] Regulation section 301.9100-3(c)(2) provides rules for accounting method regulatory elections. Under that regulation, the Commissioner has discretion to grant a reasonable extension of time to make certain regulatory elections, provided the taxpayer demonstrates to the satisfaction of the Commissioner that: (1) the taxpayer acted reasonably and in good faith; and (2) granting relief will not prejudice the interests of the government.

(d) *Intangible Regulations: IRS Concession*

There has always been significant statutory and judicial authority for taking a current deduction for both direct and indirect expense associated with originating and acquiring loans.[78] Historically, taxpayers relied on the general statutory provision of Code section 162. Taxpayers did not believe that Code section 263 disallowed the deduction because the loans that were made maintained the taxpayer in its trade or business. Confirming this interpretation of the statutory provisions are recently finalized regulations in which the IRS has conceded that most loan origination expenses, which were previously challenged on audit, are allowed to be currently deductible.[79]

Treasury regulations discussed in detail below now allow a current deduction for all employee compensation, including commissions and related over-

---

[76] This Announcement was issued during the pendency of Rev. Proc. 92-20, 1992-1 C.B. 675, and prior to the effective dates of Rev. Proc. 97-27, 1997-1 C.B. 680, which superseded Rev. Proc. 92-20. In Rev. Proc. 92-20, 1992-1 C.B. 675, 707, § 14.02 an issue is treated as "pending" if the IRS has sent the taxpayer written notification indicating that an adjustment is being or will be proposed with respect to a so-called Category A Method. A Category A Method of accounting is a method of accounting that taxpayer is specifically not permitted to use under the Code, the Regulations, or a decision of the Supreme Court of the United States. A Category A Method also includes a method of accounting that differs from a method the taxpayer is specifically required to use under the Code, the Regulations, or a decision of the United States Supreme Court. *See* Rev. Proc. 92-20, 1992-1 C.B. 675, § 3.06.

[77] PLR 9838026, June 23, 1998.

[78] In an advanced notice of rulemaking on capitalization of expenditures, released on January 17, 2002, the Treasury Department indicated that it would be appropriate to deduct loan origination costs. Reg-125638-01. Prior to this pronouncement, taxpayers considered amortization deductions under I.R.C. § 195; however newly originated loans probably cannot satisfy the new business requirement.

[79] Reg. § 1.263(a)-4.

head, associated with originating loans. Under these regulations, however, commissions paid to nonemployees must be capitalized. Other amounts paid to nonemployers need not be capitalized if they are de minimis. An amount is de minimis if it does not exceed $5000 per transaction.

§ 8.4 Capitalization of Acquisition or Creation of Intangibles

§ 8.4.1 Overview of Capitalization Regulations

Final regulations promulgated under Code section 263(a) prescribe a sweeping set of rules that affect the tax treatment of a variety of expenditures paid by taxpayers to acquire or to create intangibles, including amounts paid to facilitate these transactions.[80] In some respects, the regulations represent an abrupt departure from the position previously taken by the I.R.S. and the Treasury Department when interpreting Section 262(a), including the treatment of loan origination expenses.[81] One of the objectives of these regulations is to attenuate the controversy that has surrounded the extent to which capitalization is required of amounts paid to acquire or to create intangible assets, while adhering to established tax principles.[82]

(a) *Structure of Regulations*

The bulk of the rules are contained in regulations issued under Section 263(a), and these are divided into two parts: Regulation section 1.263(a)-4 and -5. In Regulation section 1.263(a)-4 general principles are prescribed for determining what costs must be capitalized that are paid to acquire or to create, and to facilitate the acquisition or creation of, intangible assets. Under these rules, capitalization is required of the actual cost of intangibles, including several specifically identified intangibles, and for the ancillary cost paid to effectuate the acquisition or creation of the intangible. The determination of whether an amount is paid to acquire or to create an intangible is made as of the taxable year during which the amount is paid, and not later using the benefit of hindsight.

Specifically, this regulation requires capitalization of amounts paid:

1. To acquire any intangible in a purchase or similar transaction,[83]
2. To create eight types of intangibles,[84]

---

[80] T.D. 9107, 2004-1 C.B. 447. The regulations under Reg. § 1.263(a)-4 and Reg. § 1.263(a)-5 are generally applicable to amounts paid or incurred on or after December 31, 2003. As discussed in more detail below, only amounts paid or incurred in taxable years ending on or after January 24, 2002, may be taken in to account the Section 481(a) adjustment for a change in method of accounting to comply with this section. As to the treatment of expenses incurred in relation to tangible assets, the I.R.S. has issued proposed regulations. REG-168745-03, Aug. 18, 2006.

[81] The final regulations were issued in proposed form on December 19, 2002. 67 Fed. Reg. 77,701 (Dec. 19, 2002) (to be codified at 26 C.F.R. pt. 1). They followed an Advanced Notice of Proposed Rulemaking published on January 24, 2002. 67 Fed. Reg. 3461-02 (Jan. 24, 2002) (to be codified at 26 C.F.R. pt. 1). A public hearing on the proposed regulations was held on April 22, 2003.

[82] Portions of this cost capitalization discussion is excerpted from *"New Capitalization Rules: Their Sweeping Effect on Financial Institutions"*, Journal of Taxation and Regulation of Financial Institutions, May/June 2004, Vol. 17/No. 5 by Blasi and Lee.

[83] Reg. § 1.263(a)-4(b)(1)(i).

[84] Reg. § 1.263(a)-4(b)(1)(ii); Reg. 1.263(a)-4(d). The proposed regulations eliminated the general rule that if an intangible is "enhanced" the cost of the enhancement would have to be capitalized. Instead, the final regulations specifically identify types of enhancement for which capitalization is required.

3. To create or enhance a "separate and distinct intangible asset,"[85] and
4. To facilitate an acquisition or creation of any of those acquired or created intangibles for which capitalization is required under the regulations.[86]

Regulation § 1.263(a)-4 also provides that capitalization may be required of amounts paid to create or to enhance a future benefit that is subsequently identified in guidance published by the IRS as an intangible for which capitalization is required.[87] In determining whether capitalization is appropriate for a particular category of expenditure in the future guidance, the preamble to the proposed regulations provides that consideration will be given to all relevant facts and circumstances including the probability, nature, and size of the expected future benefit. If guidance is published that identifies a future benefit as an intangible for which capitalization is required, the rule will be applied only to amounts paid on or after the date of publication of the guidance.[88]

Regulation § 1.263(a)-5 addresses amounts paid or incurred to facilitate an acquisition of a trade or business, a change in the capital structure of a business entity, and certain other similar transactions. These rules apply regardless of whether the transaction is structured as an acquisition of the entity or as an acquisition of assets (including tangible assets) constituting a trade or business.

Both the -4 and the -5 regulations provide for the use of simplifying conventions intended to promote administrability and reduce the cost of compliance with section 263(a).[89] These simplifying conventions set forth basically taxpayer-favorable rules with respect to employee compensation, overhead, and de minimis amounts. In addition, the regulations codify a 12-month rule, which permits most expenditures with a short duration to be expensed.[90]

Accompanying the regulations under Code section 263(a) are regulations that provide capitalization rules under Section 446 that apply to amounts paid with respect to debt issuance costs[91] and regulations that provide for a safe harbor amortization period under Section 167 for certain intangibles.

With very limited exceptions, the new rules do not apply to amounts paid to acquire or to create tangible assets.[92] The Treasury Department has said that they will be addressing this area in the near future. Furthermore, the regulations do not encompass intangible interests in land, such as easements, life estates, mineral interests, etc. However, the regulations do prescribe rules for capitalization of amounts paid to acquire or to create a lease of real property.[93]

(b) *Intangibles Required to be Capitalized*

There is no definition of an intangible asset that is subject to capitalization under the regulations. Instead, the regulations provide "examples" and "catego-

[85] Reg. § 1.263(a)-4(b)(1)(iii); Reg. § 1.263(a)-4(b)(3).

[86] Reg. § 1.263(a)-4(b)(1)(v).

[87] Reg. § 1.263(a)-4(b)(1)(iv).

[88] Reg. § 1.263(a)-4(b)(2).

[89] Reg. § 1.263(a)-4(e)(4); Reg. 1.263(a)-5(d).

[90] Reg. § 1.263(a)-4(f).

[91] The preamble to the final regulations makes it clear that no substantive change is intended by substituting in the final regulations the word "intangibles" for the term "intangible asset," as used in the proposed regulations.

[92] Reg. § 1.263(a)-4(a).

[93] Reg. § 1.263(a)-4(c)(1)(vi).

ries" of intangibles that are created or acquired, the costs of which must be capitalized. With respect to acquired intangibles, the general rule is that the cost of any intangible that is acquired from another party must be capitalized. To illustrate the application of this rule, the regulations provide fifteen "examples" of intangibles the cost of which has to be capitalized. The regulations also provide that the cost to create eight "categories" of intangibles are required to be capitalized. The cost of any other created intangible is not required to be capitalized.

(c) *Separate and Distinct Intangible Asset*

Although there is no definition in the regulations of the term "intangible," there is a definition of a "separate and distinct" intangible asset.[94] With respect to that type of intangible, the costs not only to create the asset but also to enhance the asset must be capitalized. Costs paid to enhance other created intangibles (such as goodwill) are not required to be capitalized.[95] This would appear to encompass advertising costs. In what must be an oversight, the regulations do not specifically provide that the cost to acquire a separate and distinct intangible asset must be capitalized. Instead, a general rule provides that the cost to acquire any intangible (presumably including separate and distinct intangible assets) must be capitalized.

For an asset to be a "separate and distinct" intangible asset it must pass a three part test: it must be a property interest that is measurable in money or money's worth; it must be property that is subject to protection under applicable state, federal, or foreign law; and it must be property that is intrinsically capable of being sold, transferred, or pledged separate and apart from a trade or business.[96] Thus, goodwill would not qualify as a separate and distinct intangible asset, but based on Tax Court discussions the core deposit intangible would. This definition is based on factors traditionally used by the courts to determine whether an expenditure serves to create or to enhance a separate and distinct asset.[97]

Five types of expenditures will not be treated as creating or facilitating the creation of a separate and distinct intangible asset:

1. Amounts paid another party to create, originate, enhance, enter into, renew or renegotiate an agreement with that party that produces rights or benefits for the taxpayer, and amounts paid to facilitate the creation, origination, enhancement, renewal or renegotiation of such an agreement,[98]

2. Amounts paid to another party to terminate an agreement with that party, and amounts paid to facilitate the termination of an agreement,

[94] Reg. § 1.263(a)-4(b)(3)(i).

[95] Reg. § 1.263(a)-4(b)(3).

[96] Reg. § 1.263(a)-4(b)(3)(i).

[97] The "separate and distinct asset" test derives from *Commissioner v. Lincoln Savings & Loan Assoc.*, 403 U.S. 345 (1971).

[98] Reg. § 1.263(a)-4(b)(3)(ii).

3. Amounts paid in performing services under an agreement, regardless of whether the amount results in the creation of an income stream,[99]
4. Amounts paid to develop computer software. However, a taxpayer is required to capitalize amounts paid to acquire computer software in a purchase or similar transaction.[100]
5. Amounts paid to develop a package design.[101]

Although amounts paid to create or to terminate contract rights generally are not a separate and distinct intangible asset, other provisions of the regulations will require such costs with respect to certain agreements to be capitalized.[102]

(d) *Intangibles Yielding Substantial Future Benefit*

The IRS and Treasury Department have chosen to refrain from requiring, as a general rule, capitalization of expenditures that create a "substantial future benefit." The future benefits test (discussed above) has spawned considerable litigation.[103] Thus, if one of the objectives of the regulations was to reduce controversy, this was a prudent decision. In fact, the IRS and the Treasury Department have noted that the separate and distinct asset standard has not historically yielded the same level of controversy as the future benefit standard.[104]

Nevertheless, the regulations do apply the future benefit test for capitalization in a limited fashion by prescribing capitalization for certain specific categories of created intangible future benefits.[105] If a taxpayer pays or incurs an amount to acquire or to create an intangible that is not described as falling into one or more of the eight categories of created intangibles or is not otherwise required to be capitalized by the regulations, the taxpayer will not be required to capitalize the expenditure even if it produces a significant future benefit for the taxpayer, unless, of course, the IRS publishes guidance requiring capitalization of the expenditure.[106] If such guidance is published, it will apply only prospectively.[107] Furthermore, the regulations are clear that the IRS will not take the position that if an amount paid to acquire or to create an intangible is not

---

[99] Reg. § 1.263(a)-4(b)(3)(iii).

[100] Reg. § 1.263(a)-4(b)(3)(iv). The Treasury Department and the IRS have stated that the regulations are not intended to affect the determination of whether computer software is acquired from another party in a purchase or similar transaction, or whether computer software is developed or otherwise self-created (including amounts paid to implement Enterprise Resource Planning (ERP) software). *See* PLR 200236028 (September 6, 2002). While the proposed regulations identify ERP implementation costs as an issue to be addressed in the final regulations, the Treasury Department and the IRS believe that rules regarding the treatment of such costs are more appropriately addressed in separate guidance dedicated exclusively to computer software issues. Taxpayers are told that until separate guidance is issued, taxpayers may continue to rely on Revenue Procedure 2000-50 (2000-2 C.B. 601). Because neither the PLR nor the Revenue Procedure adequately defines the term "software development," clarification of this essential term is critical, and it will eliminate a considerable amount of controversy.

[101] Reg. § 1.263(a)-4(b)(3)(v).

[102] *See* Reg. § § 1.263(a)-4(d)(2), (d)(6), and (d)(7).

[103] *INDOPCO, Inc. v. Commissioner*, 503 U.S. 79 (1992).

[104] "Guidance Regarding Deduction and Capitalization of Expenditures," II, C, 67 Fed. Reg. 77701 (December 19, 2002) (to be codified at 26 C.F.R. pt. 1).

[105] Reg. § 1.263(a)-4(d). *See* discussion below of "Created Intangibles."

[106] Reg. § 1.263(a)-4(b)(1).

[107] Reg. § 1.263(a)-4(b)(2).

required to be capitalized by another provision of the Code or by regulations, including the new intangibles regulations, that the clear reflection of income requirement of Section 446(b) and the regulations thereunder will not necessitate capitalization.[108]

§ 8.4.2 Acquired Intangibles

(a) *General Rule*

Regulation 1.263(a)-4(c) provides that capitalization is required of amounts paid to another party to acquire any intangible from that party in a purchase or similar transaction.[109] Under this rule, the well-established principal that requires the capitalization of the purchase price of property is merely restated. This rule does not require capitalization of any transaction costs that the taxpayer may incur to acquire the property. These costs are dealt with in the regulations as costs that "facilitate" the acquisition of an intangible,[110] and they are discussed below under the heading "Transaction Costs." Neither the twelve-month rule nor any of the simplifying conventions (both discussed below) apply to these costs.

(b) *Fifteen Examples of Acquired Intangibles Required to be Capitalized*

Consistent with the general principles, capitalization is specifically required of amounts paid to acquire a nonexclusive list of fifteen categories of intangibles. These are merely examples of the types of intangibles the cost to acquire of which will have to be capitalized. Several of the types meet the definition of an "amortizable section 197 intangible," which make them eligible for 15 year, straight-line amortization under Section 197(a). Nearly all of these intangibles will appear on the balance sheets of all financial institutions.

The fifteen examples of intangibles the cost to acquire of which must be capitalized are as follows:[111]

1. An ownership interest in a corporation, partnership, trust, estate, limited liability company, or other similar entity;
2. A debt instrument (including a loan or a portfolio of loans), deposit, stripped bond, stripped coupon (including a servicing right treated for federal income tax purposes as a stripped coupon), regular interest in a REMIC or FASIT, or any other intangible treated as debt for federal income tax purposes.
3. A financial instrument, including, but not limited to, the following six types:
    (i) A notional principal contract;
    (ii) A foreign currency contract;
    (iii) A futures contract;

[108] Reg. § 1.263(a)-4(b)(4)(i).

[109] Reg. § 1.263(a)-4(c)(1).

[110] Reg. § 1.263(a)-4(e).

[111] Reg. § 1.263(a)-4(c)(1)(i)-(xv).

(iv) A forward contract (including an agreement under which the taxpayer has the right and obligation to provide or to acquire property (or to be compensated for such property));

(v) An option (including an agreement under which the taxpayer has the right to provide or to acquire property (or to be compensated for such property)); and

(vi) Any other financial derivative.[112]

4. An endowment contract, annuity contract, or insurance contract that has or may have cash value;
5. Non-functional currency;
6. A lease;
7. A patent or copyright;
8. A franchise, trademark or tradename (as defined in Regulation §1.197-2(b)(10));
9. An assembled workforce (as defined in Regulation §1.197-2(b)(3));
10. Goodwill (as defined in Regulation §1.197-2(b)(1)) or going concern value (as defined in Regulation 1.197-2(b)(2));
11. A customer list;
12. A servicing right (for example, a mortgage servicing right that is not treated for federal income tax purposes as a stripped coupon);
13. A customer-based intangible (as defined in Regulation §1.197-2(b)(6)) or supplier-based intangible (as defined in Regulation §1.197-2(b)(7));
14. Computer software;
15. An agreement providing either party the right to use, possess or sell an intangible described in one through five above.

§8.4.3 Created Intangibles

(a) *General Rule*

Regulation 1.263(a)-4(d) provides that capitalization is required of amounts paid to create or enhance eight types of intangibles.[113] This list of eight is not illustrative. The eight created intangibles that must be capitalized are generally eligible for current deductibility under the twelve-month rule discussed below, but the simplifying conventions do not apply to the cost to create these intangibles.[114] As with the rule that applies to acquired intangibles, this provision deals with the amounts paid to create the intangible itself and not to any

---

[112] In both the advanced notice of proposed rulemaking and in the proposed regulations, the Treasury Department and the IRS included among the list of "financial instruments" a letter of credit and a credit card agreement. These two types of financial instruments have been omitted from the illustrative list of financial instruments that are subject to capitalization under this provision. They are included in the list of "financial interests" the cost of which to create must be capitalized. It can be assumed that the removal of these two items from the list of financial instruments is intended to indicate that the cost to acquire them is not to be capitalized.

[113] Reg. §1.263(a)-4(d).

[114] Reg. §1.263(a)-4(d)(1). An exception is provided for "financial interests."

amounts paid to facilitate the creation of the intangible. Facilitation expenses will be subject to the capitalization rule that deal with transaction costs, discussed below.

To prevent taxpayers from deducting expenditures based on immaterial distinctions between an expenditure and the description of any of the eight categories, the regulations state that the determination of whether an amount is paid to create an intangible is made based on all of the facts and circumstances, disregarding distinctions between the labels used in the regulations to describe the intangible and the labels used by the taxpayer and other parties to describe the transaction.[115]

For purposes of determining whether a "financial interest" is created, if a payment is made to another party by the taxpayer with only a hope or expectation of developing or maintaining a business relationship with that party and it is not contingent on the origination, renewal or renegotiation of a financial interest with that party, the amount will not be treated as paid to create, originate, enter into, renew, or renegotiate a financial interest with that party.[116] Thus, if an amount is paid to a customer or supplier with the mere hope or expectation of beginning or continuing a business relationship with the taxpayer, capitalization is not required.[117]

A taxpayer will be treated as having "renegotiated" an agreement if either: the terms of the agreement are modified, or if (a) the taxpayer enters into a new agreement with the same party (or substantially the same parties) to an agreement, (b) the taxpayer could not cancel the terminated agreement without the agreement of the other party (or parties), and (c) the other party would not have agreed to the cancellation unless the taxpayer entered into the new agreement.[118] A taxpayer will be treated as "unable to cancel a financial interest" without the consent of the other party if the taxpayer is subject to a termination penalty and the other party to the financial interest modifies the terms of the penalty. Although there is no cross reference in the Regulation 1.263(a)-4 to the regulations under Section 1001, it is likely that the latter regulations can serve as a guide for what constitutes a modification of an agreement.

(b) *Eight Types of Created Intangibles Required to be Capitalized*

The cost to create the following eight intangibles must be capitalized:

1. **Financial interests.** Capitalization is required of amounts paid to another party to create, originate, enter into, renew or renegotiate with that party any one or more of the intangibles fitting into one of the following six categories of "financial interests." Capitalization is required regardless of whether the financial interest is regularly traded on an estab-

---

[115] Reg. § 1.263(a)-4(d)(1). The preamble to the final regulations indicates that the "Treasury Department intends to construe broadly the categories of intangibles identified in the regulations in response to any narrow technical arguments that an intangible created by the taxpayer is not literally described in the categories."

[116] Reg. § 1.263(a)-4(d)(2)(ii). See also a comparable provision with respect to contract rights contained in Reg. § 1.263(a)-4(d)(d)(6)(ii).

[117] Reg. § 1.263(a)-4(d)(6)(ii).

[118] Reg. § 1.263(a)-4(d)(6)(iii). Similar rules dealing with contract rights are discussed at Reg. § 1.263(a)-4(d)(6)(iii).

lished market.[119] The six categories are not intended to be merely illustrative. The intangibles on the list are the only created financial interests for which capitalization is required.[120] Any amount that is paid to create one of the financial interest is ineligible for expensing under the twelve-month rule (discussed below). The first five intangibles on this list are nearly identical to the first five types of acquired intangibles that are required to be capitalized.

Amounts paid to create or acquire the following six financial interests must be capitalized:

(i) An ownership interest in corporation, partnership, trust, estate, LLC, or other entity,[121]

(ii) A debt instrument (including a loan), deposit, stripped bond, stripped coupon (including servicing right treated as stripped coupon), regular interest in a REMIC or FASIT, or any other intangible treated as a debt for federal income tax purposes. Thus, a commercial bank must capitalize the principal amount of any loan that is made by the bank because the amount is considered paid to another party to create a debt instrument.[122]

(iii) A financial instrument, such as: a letter of credit, a credit card agreement, a notional principal contract, a foreign currency contract, a futures contract, a forward contract, an option, and any other financial derivative,[123]

(iv) An endowment contract, annuity contract, or insurance contract that has or may have cash value[124]

(v) A nonfunctional currency[125]

(vi) An agreement providing either party the right to use, possess or sell one of the above "financial interests."[126]

2. **Prepaid expenses.** Capitalization is required of amounts paid for insurance, rent, and other intangibles which results in benefits to be received in the future.[127] This rule does not apply to the acquisition of tangible property; however, if the prepayment creates a right to receive goods in the future, it would have to be capitalized under this provision.

3. **Memberships and privileges.** Capitalization is required of expenditures paid to obtain, renew, renegotiate, or upgrade a membership or privilege; however, a taxpayer is not required to capitalize any amount paid to upgrade certification of the taxpayer's products, services, or business processes.[128] Under this provision, capitalization is not required of amounts paid to obtain benefits such as ISO 9000 certification or Underwriters' Laboratories Listing.

[119] Reg. § 1.263(a)-4(d)(2)(i).

[120] Reg. § 1.263(a)-4(d)(2)(i)(A)-(F).

[121] Reg. § 1.263(a)-4(d)(2)(i)(A).

[122] Reg. § 1.263(a)-4(d)(2)(vi), Ex. 1.

[123] Reg. § 1.263(a)-4(d)(2)(i)(C)(1)-(5).

[124] Reg. § 1.263(a)-4(d)(2)(i)(D).

[125] Reg. § 1.263(a)-4(d)(2)(i)(E).

[126] Reg. § 1.263(a)-4(d)(2)(i)(F).

[127] Reg. § 1.263(a)-4(d)(3).

[128] Reg. § 1.263(a)-4(d)(4).

4. **Certain rights obtained from a governmental agency.** Capitalization is required of amounts paid by a taxpayer to obtain, renew, renegotiate, or upgrade its rights under a trademark, trade name, copyright, license, permit, franchise, or other similar right granted by a governmental agency.[129] Thus, a corporation that pays an amount to a state to obtain a business license that is valid indefinitely must capitalize the amount as an amount paid to a governmental agency for a contract right.[130] The twelve-month rule (discussed below) can avoid capitalization in limited situations, such as when a taxpayers pays to a government agency an annual renewal fee. Furthermore, this provision will not alter the treatment of expenditures under other provisions of the Code. Thus, if an amount is deductible under Code section 174 it is not required to be capitalized under this provision.[131]

5. **Certain contract rights.** Capitalization is required of amounts (other than de minimis amounts) paid to another party to create, originate, enter into, renew, or renegotiate any of the five contract rights listed below.[132] Common to each of these is that they are reasonably certain to produce future benefits for the taxpayer. As with a created "financial interest," rules are provided that exclude any amount that is paid with a mere hope or expectation and that is not contingent on the creation of the agreement with that party from being capitalized.[133]

   Amounts paid to create the following five types of contract rights must be capitalized:

   (i) An agreement to use tangible or intangible property or the right to be compensated for the use of tangible or intangible property (lease modification payments).[134]

   (ii) An agreement for the right to provide or acquire services or the right to be compensated for services regardless of whether the taxpayer provides such services. These payments may include amounts paid for mortgage servicing rights.[135]

   A right to use property or to provide or receive services will not be created if the agreement may be terminated at will by the other party to the agreement before the end of the period prescribed by the twelve-month rule.[136] However, if the other party is "economically compelled" not to terminate the agreement until the end of the twelve-month period, the agreement will not be treated as if it is terminable at will. To determine whether a party is "economi-

[129] Reg. § 1.263(a)-4(d)(5)(i).

[130] Reg. § 1.263(a)-4(d)(5)(ii), Ex. 1.

[131] Code section 174 provides for deductibility of amounts paid to a government agency to obtain a patent from that agency.

[132] The de minimis exception that applies here is not the de minimis exception contained among the simplifying conventions, discussed below. Reg. § 1.263(a)-4(e)(4)(iii). *See also* the de minimis rule that applies to acquisitions of businesses at Reg. § 1.263(a)-5(d)(3).

[133] Reg. § 1.263(a)-4(d)(6)(ii). *See also* Reg. § 1.263(a)-4(d)(2)(ii).

[134] Reg. § 1.263(a)-4(d)(6)(i)(A).

[135] Reg. § 1.263(a)-4(d)(6)(i)(B).

[136] Reg. § 1.263(a)-4(d)(6)(iv). The twelve-month rule is provided in Reg. § 1.263(a)-4(f), and it is discussed below.

cally compelled" not to terminate an agreement, all of the facts and circumstances will be considered. An agreement will not be one that provides a taxpayer with the right to provide services if the agreement merely provides that the taxpayer will stand ready to provide services if requested and it places no obligation on the other party to request or to pay for the taxpayer's services.

(iii) A covenant not to compete, or similar agreement having substantially the same effect as a covenant not to compete. In the case of an agreement that requires the performance of services, to the extent that the amount represents reasonable compensation for services actually rendered, capitalization is not required;[137]

(iv) An agreement not to acquire additional ownership interests in the taxpayer.[138] These payments are commonly referred to as a "standstill agreements."

(v) An agreement providing the taxpayer (as the covered party) with an annuity, an endowment, or insurance coverage. This provision was added to the final regulations for the purpose of clarifying that capitalization is required when such a contract does not have or provide for cash value (e.g., a comprehensive liability policy or a property and casualty policy) if the taxpayer is the covered party under the contract.[139]

If the amount paid to another party to create, originate, enter into, renew or renegotiate with that party one of the agreements described above is de minimis, the amount does not have to be capitalized. For this purpose, de minimis means $5000 per transaction. In determining whether the $5000 threshold is exceeded, all similar agreements are taken into account. If the consideration paid is in the form of property other than money, then the amount is determined by reference to the fair market value of the property at the time of the payment.[140] The de minimis exception to the capitalization rule for all five types of contract rights does not apply to other intangibles created by the taxpayer.[141]

In general, taxpayers are required to apply this de minimis rule by accounting for specific amounts paid with respect to each agreement. However, the regulations authorize a pooling method that averages amounts paid with respect to all agreements included in a pool.[142] The pooling method is authorized only if the taxpayer reasonably expects to create, originate, enter into, renew or renegotiate at least 25 similar agreements during the taxable year. A taxpayer computes the average

[137] Reg. § 1.263(a)-4(d)(6)(i)(C). Because employment contracts are often entered into in conjunction with covenants not to compete, the regulations contain a rule similar to that contained in Reg. § 1.197-2 (b)(9).

[138] Reg. § 1.263(a)-4(d)(6)(i).

[139] Reg. § 1.263(a)-4(d)(6)(i)(E).

[140] Reg. § 1.263(a)-4(d)(v).

[141] Reg. § 1.263(a)-4(d)(6)(v).

[142] Nearly identical pooling rules are provided for transaction costs described in Reg. § 1.263(a)-4(e)(4)(iii), and with respect to twelve-month rule in Reg. § 1.263(a)-4 (f)(5)(ii). These rules are amplified by additional safe harbor pooling method rules contained in Reg. § 1.263(a)-4(h), discussed below.

amount paid with respect to all agreements included in the pool by dividing the sum of all amounts paid with respect to all agreements included in the pool by the number of agreements included in the pool.

6. **Contract terminations.** Capitalization is required of amounts paid to another to terminate three types of contracts.[143] Under this rule, a taxpayer is required to capitalize contract termination payments that permit the taxpayer to reacquire some valuable right that the taxpayer did not possess immediately prior to the termination. This capitalization rule does not apply to amounts paid to terminate a transaction described in Regulation section 1.263(a)-5 ("Amounts paid or incurred to facilitate an acquisition of a trade or business, a change in the capital structure of a business entity, and certain other transactions") where a special rule is prescribed.

   Amounts paid to terminate the following three types of contracts must be capitalized:

   (i) A lease of real or tangible personal property (payment by lessor, not lessee),[144]

   (ii) An agreement that grants another party the exclusive right to acquire or use the taxpayer's property or services or to conduct the taxpayer's business. Excluded from this capitalization rule are payments with respect to any of the six intangibles described in Regulation § 1.263(a)-4(c)(1)(i)-(iv), which include "debt instruments" and "financial instruments," and payments with respect to "financial interest" described in Regulation 1.263 (a)-4(d)(2),[145]

   (iii) An agreement that prohibits the taxpayer from competing with the other party or from acquiring property or services from a competitor of that other party.[146]

   Capitalization is not required for a payment to terminate a supply contract with a supplier, nor is capitalization required by a lessee that makes a payment to terminate a lease agreement with a lessor. In the case of the payment by the lessor, capitalization is appropriate because, in theory, the lessor reacquires the leasehold interest from the lessee.

7. **Certain benefits arising from the provision, production, or improvement of real property.** With certain exceptions, a taxpayer must capitalize amounts paid to acquire real property (a) if the taxpayer transfers ownership to the real property to another party for less than its fair market value, and (b) if the real property can reasonably be expected to produce significant economic benefits to the taxpayer after the trans-

[143] Reg. § 1.263(a)-4(d)(7). With respect to amounts paid to terminate a transaction described in Reg. § 1.263(a)-5, which relates to an acquisition of the trade or business, a change in the capital structure of the business entity, and certain other transactions, the final regulations clarify that the contract termination provisions do not apply to amounts paid to terminate the transaction.

[144] Reg. § 1.263(a)-4(d)(7)(i)(A). *Peerless Weighing and Vending Machine Corporation v. Commissioner*, 52 T.C. 850 (1969).

[145] Reg. § 1.263(a)-4(d)(7)(i)(B). *Roadway Inns of America v. Commissioner*, 63 T.C. 414 (1974).

[146] Reg. § 1.263(a)-4(d)(7)(i)(C).

fer.[147] Capitalization is also required for amounts paid to produce or to improve real property (a) if the taxpayer produces or improves the real property for an amount that is less than the fair market value of the services, and (b) if the real property can reasonably be expected to produce significant economic benefits to the taxpayer.[148]

Capitalization is not required for either of these two amounts where the taxpayer is selling the real property, is providing the real property to another as payment for some other property or service provided to the taxpayer, or is selling services to produce or improve the property.[149]

8. **Defense or perfection of title to intangible property.** A taxpayer must capitalize amounts paid to another party to defend or perfect title to intangible property if that other party challenges the taxpayer's title to the intangible property.[150] This rule is consistent with the well-established rule with respect to real property, where the issue more frequently arises. This rule does not change the current rule that allows deductibility of amounts paid to protect property against infringement or to recover profits and damages as a result of an infringement.[151] Any amounts paid to another party to terminate an agreement permitting that party to purchase the taxpayer's intangible property or to terminate a transaction described in Regulation § 1.263(a)-5 ("Amounts paid or incurred to facilitate an acquisition of a trade or business, a change in the capital structure of a business entity, and certain other transactions"), sometimes referred to as break-up fees, are not treated as amounts paid to defend or perfect title.[152]

§ 8.4.4 Capitalized Transaction Costs

(a) *General Rules*

Regulation section 1.263(a)-4(e) prescribes the rules for capitalization expenditures incurred to facilitate the acquisition or creation of an intangible. These rules do not apply to amounts paid to facilitate a borrowing.[153] With respect to the latter costs, Regulation section 1.263(a)-5(a)(9) and Regulation section 1.446-6 provide new rules that are discussed below.

Under the general rule applicable to these transaction costs, any cost required to be capitalized under the capitalization regulations is added to the tax basis of the related asset.[154] For this purpose, a transaction to acquire or to create an intangible includes all of the factual elements comprising the acquisition,

[147] Reg. § 1.263(a)-4(d)(8)(i).

[148] Reg. § 1.263(a)-4(d)(8)(i). Costs are required to be capitalized under this rule are eligible for safe harbor amortization under section 167 on a ratable basis over a 25-year period.

[149] Reg. § 1.263(a)-4(d)(8)(ii).

[150] This rule is similar to the rule that has been contained in Reg. § 1.263 (a)-2(c).

[151] *Urquhart v. Commissioner*, 215 F.2d 17 (3d Cir. 1954).

[152] Reg. § 1.263(a)-4(d)(9).

[153] Reg. § 1.263(a)-4(e)(1)(iv). *See* Regs. 1.263(a)-5 and 1.446-5 for the treatment of amounts paid to facilitate a borrowing.

[154] Reg. § 1.263(a)-4(g)(1). The costs governed by the transaction cost regulations are referred to inconsistently in the regulations as transaction costs or as facilitation costs.

creation, or enhancement of an intangible asset.[155] The purchase of multiple intangibles under a single agreement will be treated as constituting a single transaction notwithstanding the fact that the amounts paid to facilitate the acquisition are capable of being allocated among the various intangibles acquired.[156]

(b) *Date Rules*

There is a general date rule and a specific date rule for determining whether an expenditure is a capitalizable transaction cost. Under the general rule, an amount is treated as paid to facilitate a transaction if the amount is paid in the process of investigating or otherwise pursuing the transaction.

By referring to when an expenditure is incurred "in the process of investigating" the transaction, confusion could occur with Code section 195 investigatory expenditures. The latter expenditures are subject to a disallowance rule unless a valid amortization election is made. All facts and circumstances are taken into account in determining whether an amount is paid in the process of investigating or otherwise pursuing a transaction.[157] If the amount is paid to determine the value or the price of an intangible, it is paid in the process of investigation or otherwise pursuing the transaction and would have to be capitalized. The fact that the amount would or would not have been paid "but for" the transaction is a relevant factor, but not the only factor, to be considered. Under a strict "but for" standard, some transaction costs would be capitalized that are not required to be capitalized under the regulation. Thus, costs to downsize a workforce, including severance payments, or costs to integrate the operations of businesses are not required to be capitalized.

An amount paid to terminate, or to facilitate the termination of, an existing agreement will be treated as not facilitating the acquisition of another agreement under this rule.[158] Similarly, an amount paid by an open end regulated investment company to facilitate a redemption of its stock is treated as an amount that does not facilitate the acquisition of an intangible.[159]

The specific date rule applies to the six types of "financial interests" listed in Regulation 1.263(a)-4(d)(2) and the five types of "contract rights" described in Regulation § 1.263(a)-4(d)(6). It provides special guidance for when the "process of investigating or otherwise pursuing" begins. Pursuant to the special guidance, an amount is treated as not paid in the process of investigating or otherwise pursuing the creation of the financial interest or the contract right if the amount relates to activities performed before the earlier of the date the taxpayer begins preparing its bid for the agreement or the date the taxpayer begins discussing or negotiating the agreement with another party to the agreement.[160]

---

155 Reg. § 1.263(a)-4(b)(i)(ii) and (iii) and (e)(3).

156 Reg. § 1.263(a)-4(e)(3).

157 Reg. § 1.263(a)-4(e)(1)(i).

158 Reg. § 1.263(a)-4(e)(1)(ii).

159 Reg. § 1.263(a)-4(e)(1)(v).

160 Reg. § 1.263(a)-4(e)(1)(iii).

(c) *Simplifying Conventions*

In an effort to resolve much of the controversy that surrounded the deductibility of transaction costs paid to acquire or to create intangible assets and to eliminate the burden on taxpayers of allocating certain transaction costs among various intangible assets, the regulations contain simplifying conventions.[161] These are rules of administrative convenience and are not intended to be substantive rules of law. In general, under these simplifying conventions, compensation paid employees (including commissions), overhead, and de minimis costs of non-employee services (other than commissions) will be treated as amounts that do not facilitate a transaction.[162] The simplifying conventions do not apply to the actual cost of the intangible, but only to facilitation expenses.

(d) *Employee Compensation*

Salary, bonuses, and commissions paid to employees will not be treated as facilitating a transaction.[163] This rule applies regardless of the percentage of the employee's time that is allocable to transaction. Thus, capitalization is not required for compensation paid to an employee of the taxpayer who works full time on the acquisition of loans, nor is compensation paid to loan officers who originate loans, even though the regulations require the underlying intangibles to be capitalized. The Treasury Department and the IRS considered but rejected adopting a rule that would have limited the application of this simplifying conventions to taxpayers that deduct employee compensation and overhead for financial accounting purposes.

Employee compensation includes certain amounts paid to persons who may not, under the general rule of Code section 3401(c), be employees of the taxpayer.[164] Thus, a guaranteed payment to a partner in a partnership is treated as employee compensation, as is annual compensation paid to a director of a corporation. However, if the amount paid to a director is for attendance at a special meeting of the Board of Directors (or committee thereof), it will not be treated as employee compensation for purposes of this rule. Of course, it does not necessarily follow that the amount paid a director to attend a special meeting will necessarily be capitalized. In the absence of a specific rule, the general rules of Code section 162 and Code section 263(a) will control.

As a general rule, amounts paid to outside contractors for secretarial, clerical, and similar administrative services shall be treated as amounts paid to employees even though the independent contractors are not hired specifically to

[161] Reg. § 1.263(a)-4(e)(4). Simplifying conventions are also provided in Reg. 1.263(a)-5 for costs to facilitate a restructuring or reorganization of a business entity or to facilitate a transaction involving the acquisition of capital, including stock issuance, borrowing, or recapitalization. The simplifying conventions applicable to transactions described in Reg. § 1.263(a)-5 are comparable to the simplifying conventions applicable to acquisition or creation of intangibles governed by Reg. § 1.263(a)-4(e)(4). A simplifying convention that allows de minimis amounts paid to create contract rights is provided in Reg. § 1.263(a)-4(d)(6).

[162] Reg. § 1.263(a)-4(e)(4).

[163] Reg. §§ 1.263(a)-4(e)(4)(i), (e)(4)(ii)(A) and (B).

[164] Reg. § 1.263(a)-4(e)(4)(ii)(A).

facilitate a transaction.[165] Other amounts paid to outside contractors will not be considered employee compensation.[166]

In general, employees of one entity in a related group of corporations will not be treated as employees of a related member. However, in the case of an affiliated group of corporations filing a consolidated federal income tax return, a payment by one member of the group to a second member of the group for services performed by employee of the second member is treated as employee compensation if the services are performed at a time during which both members are affiliated.[167]

(e) *De Minimis Costs*

De minimis costs (other than compensation and overhead) that do not exceed $5000 do not facilitate any transaction (creating or acquiring an intangible) and therefore are not required to be capitalized.[168] The de minimis cost rule applies on a transaction by transaction basis, but a single transaction may comprise the acquisition of multiple intangible assets. If transaction costs exceed $5000, no portion of the costs is considered de minimis. For purposes of determining whether a transaction cost paid in the form of property is de minimis, the property is valued at its fair market value at the time of the payment. The regulations authorize the IRS to prescribe, in the future, a higher threshold amount.[169]

> **Example:** W corporation, a commercial bank, acquires a portfolio containing 100 loans from Y corporation. As part of the acquisition, W pays an independent appraiser a fee of $10,000 to appraise the portfolio. The fee is an amount paid to facilitate W's acquisition of an intangible. The acquisition of the loan portfolio is a single transaction within the meaning of Regulation 1.263(a)-4(e)(3). Because the amount paid to facilitate the transaction exceeds $5,000, the amount is not de minimis as defined in Regulation § 1.263(a)-4(e)(4)(iii)(A). Accordingly, W must capitalize the $10,000 fee under Regulation § 1.263(a)-4(b)(1)(v).[170] Had the appraisal fee been $4000, it would have been currently deductible.

De minimis costs do not include commissions paid to a non-employee to facilitate the acquisition of an intangible described in Regulation 1.263(a)-4(c)(1)(i) through (v). These paragraphs apply to certain acquired intangibles, including all acquired "financial instruments." De minimis costs also do not include commissions paid to non-employers that facilitate the creation, origination, entrance into, renewal or renegotiation of an intangible described in

165 Reg. § 1.263(a)-4(e)(4)(ii)(B).

166 However, with respect to transactions described in Reg. § 1.263(a)-5 ("Amounts paid or incurred to facilitate an acquisition of a trade or business, a change in the capital structure of a business entity, and certain other transactions"), capitalization is required for amounts paid to independent contractors who perform services involving the preparation and distribution of proxy solicitations and other documents seeking shareholder approval of a transactions described in those regulations. Reg. 1.263(a)-5(d)(2).

167 Reg. § 1.263(a)-4(e)(4)(ii)(B).

168 Reg. § 1.263(a)-4(e)(4)(iii)(A).

169 Reg. § 1.263(a)-4(e)(4)(iii)(A).

170 Reg. § 1.263(a)-4(e)(5), Ex. 7. Although this regulation states that capitalization is required, it is probably more accurate to say that the de minimis rule does not apply. The regulation cannot require capitalization unless it is called for by Sec. 263(a).

Regulation 1.263(a)-4(d)(2)(i). This paragraph applies to created intangibles including created "financial instruments."[171] Thus, any commissions paid by a bank to a mortgage broker to facilitate the acquisition or origination of mortgage loans will not be a de minimis cost, regardless of the amount of the payment. However, if the amount paid is not a commission, it could be treated as a de minimis cost.

Although the regulations provide that commissions paid to third parties do not qualify for treatment as a de minimis cost or as employee compensation, it does not necessarily follow that the amount paid to a third party is properly capitalized under Code section 263(a). The simplifying conventions contained in the capitalization regulations are part of the interpretive regulations promulgated under the general authority granted by Congress in Code section 7805(a). They are not the more authoritative regulations commonly referred to as legislative regulations, which are specifically authorized in a statutory provision. Thus, the capitalization regulations cannot force capitalization of an expenditure that is properly deductible under Code section 162 and not denied deductibility under Code section 263. An item is required to be capitalized under Section 263(a) only if it results in a "permanent improvement or betterment made to increase the value" of the taxpayer's property. It would appear that if a financial institution paid a commission to a loan broker to assist in the generation of a loan, under the authority of *PNC Bancorp* the amount should be currently deductible.[172]

(f) *Pooling De Minimis Costs*

Although taxpayers must generally take into account actual costs in determining whether the de minimis threshold is exceeded, the regulations authorize using an "average cost pooling method" for determining whether transaction costs are de minimis.[173] If a taxpayer reasonably expects to enter into at least 25 similar transactions during the taxable year, a taxpayer is permitted to establish a pool of similar transactions for purposes of determining the amount of transaction costs paid in the process of investigating or otherwise pursuing the transactions in the pool. The amount of transaction costs paid with respect to each transaction included in the pool will be deemed to be equal to the average transaction costs paid in the process of investigating or otherwise pursuing all transactions included in the pool.[174]

---

[171] Reg. § 1.263(a)-4(e)(4)(iii)(B).

[172] *PNC Bancorp, Inc. v. Commissioner*, 110 T.C. 349 (1988), *rev'd*, 212 F.3d 822 (3d Cir. 2000).

[173] Reg. § 1.263(a)-4(e)(4)(iii)(A) and Reg. § 1.263(a)-4(h). Nearly identical pooling rules are provided for created contract rights described in Reg. § 1.263(a)-4(d)(6)(v), and with respect to twelve-month rule in Reg. § 1.263(a)-4 (f)(5)(ii). These rules are amplified by additional safe harbor pooling method rules contained in Reg. § 1.263(a)-4(h), discussed below.

[174] Reg. § 1.263(a)-4(e)(4)(A)(iii). The average is equal to the sum of all transaction costs paid divided by the number of transactions included in the pool. In Notice 2015-82, 2015-50 I.R.B. 859, the IRS announced that it would increase the de minimis safe harbor limit provided in § 1.263(a)-1(f)(1)(ii)(D) for a taxpayer without an "applicable financial statement." For taxable years beginning on or after January 1, 2016, the Reg. § 1.263(a)-1(f)(1)(ii)(D) de minimis safe harbor limitation for a taxpayer without an AFS is increased from $500 to $2,500.

(g) *Election to Capitalize Transaction Costs*

At the election of the taxpayer, employee compensation, overhead, or de minimis costs paid in the process of investigating or otherwise pursuing a transaction that are not required to be capitalized under the simplifying conventions may be capitalized.[175] The election is provided to accommodate those taxpayers who capitalize such costs for financial accounting purposes or if it would be administratively difficult for the taxpayer to segregate these costs.

The capitalization election is made separately with regard to any or all of the three categories of costs covered by the simplifying conventions (employee compensation, overhead, and de minimis costs). The election is also made separately for each transaction, and, in the case of an affiliated group of corporations filing a consolidated return, the election is made separately with respect to each member of the group.

The election is made by treating the amounts to which the election applies as amounts that facilitate the transaction in the taxpayers timely filed original federal income tax return (including extensions) for the taxable year during which the amounts are paid. Once made, the election is binding unless consent to terminate the election is received from the Commissioner.[176]

For banks that have earlier adopted or changed their method of accounting for employee compensation and certain other costs related to originating loans to a deferral method, an accounting method change is not required. For example, if the bank is conforming its tax treatment to the accounting treatment under SFAS 91, it is not necessary to establish a separate method of accounting for employee compensation for tax purposes.

(h) *Twelve-Month Rule*

In general, a taxpayer is not required to capitalize transaction costs paid to create or to facilitate the creation of certain rights or benefits with a brief duration (the "twelve-month rule").[177] Although the twelve-month rule will simplify compliance and administration, it is not referred to in the regulations as a "simplifying convention."

This exception to the capitalization rules does not apply to amounts paid to create or to facilitate the creation of "financial interests" described in Regulation 1.263(a)-4(d)(2), which includes all six types of "financial instruments," or to an intangible described in Section 197(c) (a self-created amortizable intangible).[178] Moreover, the twelve-month rule does not apply to amounts paid to acquire any intangibles. Thus, if the amount is paid to acquire or to facilitate the acquisition of an intangible, the twelve-month rule will not permit current expensing.

---

[175] Reg. § 1.263(a)-4(e)(4)(iv). The final regulations did not adopt the earlier considered rule that would have limited the application of the simplifying conventions to taxpayers that deduct these costs for financial accounting purposes.

[176] Reg. § 1.263(a)-4(e)(4)(iv).

[177] Reg. § 1.263(a)-4(f).

[178] Reg. § 1.263(a)-4(f)(3).

The twelve-month rule is consistent with existing regulations under Sections 263(a), 446, and 461 that require taxpayers to capitalize expenditures that create an asset having a useful life substantially beyond the close of the taxable year.[179] The twelve-month rule does not in any way change the application of the Section 461 economic performance rules, which, in the case of the taxpayer using the accrual method of accounting, requires an item be incurred before taking into account through capitalization or deduction.[180]

(i) Measuring Twelve-Month Period. Capitalization is not required under the twelve-month rule if an amount is paid to create (or to facilitate the creation of) an intangible asset and the amount does not create or enhance any right or benefit for the taxpayer that extends beyond the earlier of: (a) twelve months after the first date on which the taxpayer realized the right or benefit or (b) the end of the taxable year following the taxable year in which the payment is made.[181] Any amounts paid to create rights or benefits that extend beyond the period prescribed by the twelve-month rule must be capitalized in full.

> **Example:** Financial interests. On October 1, 2005, X corporation makes a 9-month loan to B in the principal amount of $250,000. The principal amount of the loan to B constitutes an amount paid to create or originate a financial interest under Regulation § 1.263(a)-4(d)(2)(i)(B). The 9-month term of the loan does not extend beyond the period prescribed by Regulation § 1.263(a)-4(f)(1). However, as provided by Regulation § 1.263(a)-4(f)(3), the rules of this Regulation § 1.263(a)-4(f) do not apply to intangibles described in Regulation § 1.263(a)-4(d)(2). Accordingly, X must capitalize the $250,000 loan amount.[182]

(ii) Renewal Periods. For purposes of determining the duration of a right, any renewal period will be included if the facts and circumstances in existence during the taxable year in which the right is created indicate a reasonable expectancy of renewal.[183] In determining whether there is a reasonable expectancy of renewal, renewal history and the economics of the transaction are taken into account. If similar rights are typically terminated prior to renewal, evidence exists of a lack of reasonable expectancy of renewal.

---

[179] Regs. §§ 1.263(a)-2(a), 1.446-1(c)(1)(ii), and 1.461-1(a)(2)(i). *See also U.S. Freightways Corp. v. Commissioner*, 270 F.3d 1137 (7th Cir. 2001), *rev'g* 113 T.C. 329 (1999).

[180] Reg. § 1.263(a)-4(f)(1)(i).

[181] Reg. § 1.263(a)-4(f)(1) and Reg. § 1.263(a)-4(f)(8), Ex. 3; *see also* Reg. § 1.263(a)-4(l), Ex. 1.

[182] Reg. § 1.263(a)-4(f)(8), Ex. 3.

[183] Reg. § 1.263(a)-4(f)(5).

(iii) Indefinite Duration. The twelve-month rule does not apply to amounts paid to create or to facilitate the creation of an asset of indefinite duration.[184] A taxpayer will be treated as having received a license of indefinite duration granted by governmental agency if the license may be revoked only upon the taxpayer violating of the terms of the license. A right will have an indefinite duration if no period of duration is fixed by the agreement or by law. Amounts paid to create or enhance such rights are required to be capitalized and recovered through amortization, a loss deduction upon abandonment of the right, or through basis recovery upon sale.[185]

(iv) Contract Terminations. If an amount is paid to terminate one or more of the three types of contracts described in Regulation § 1.263(a)-4(d)(7)(i) (the "contract termination" rules), or if the amount is paid to facilitate the termination of such a contract, it will be treated as creating a benefit for the taxpayer that lasts for the unexpired term of the contract immediately before the date of termination.[186] If a taxpayer is permitted to terminate an agreement only after a notice period, in determining whether the twelve-month rule applies, amounts paid to terminate the agreement before the end of the notice period create a benefit for the taxpayer that lasts for the amount of time by which the notice period is shortened.

(v) Election to Capitalize. Taxpayers may elect not to apply the twelve-month rule to categories of similar transactions that may be difficult for taxpayers to identify and calculate.[187] Thus, some taxpayers who capitalize amounts for financial accounting purposes will not be required to expense the amounts for federal income tax purposes due to the twelve-month rule. Instead, taxpayers will be permitted to conform their tax treatment with their book treatment.

(vi) Pooling Method. If a taxpayer reasonably expects to enter into at least 25 similar rights during the taxable year for which the initial term does not extend beyond the twelve-month period, a taxpayer may use a pooling method in lieu of applying the reasonable expectancy of renewal test to each separate right created during the taxable year.[188]

If elected, the pool will contain similar rights for which the initial term does not extend beyond the twelve-month period. The reasonable expectancy of renewal test is then applied to the pool. Within the pool is included all amounts, other than de minimis amounts, paid to create, or to facilitate the creation of, the rights contained in the pool. Capitalization will not be required of any amounts included in the pool if less than 20 percent of the rights in the pool are reasonably expected to be renewed beyond the twelve-month period.[189]

---

[184] Reg. § 1.263(a)-4(f)(4).

[185] *See* Reg. 1.167 (a)-14(c) which provides rules for amortizing costs to obtain a right to receive a fixed amount of property or services.

[186] Reg.§ 1.263(a)-4(f)(2).

[187] Reg. § 1.263(a)-4(f)(7).

[188] Reg. § 1.263(a)-4(f)(5) (iii). Nearly identical pooling rules are provided for created contract rights under Reg. § 1.263 (a)-4(d)(6)(v) and for transaction costs described in Reg. § 1.263(a)-4(e)(4)(iii). These rules are amplified by additional safe harbor pooling method rules contained in Reg. § 1.263(a)-4(h), discussed below.

[189] Reg. § 1.263(a)-4(f)(5)(iii).

§ 8.4.5 Special Rules for Pooling Methods

A taxpayer that is permitted to adopt one or more of the pooling methods, which may be used for de minimis costs applicable to certain created contract rights described in Regulation 1.263(a)-4(d)(6)(v), de minimis transaction costs described in Regulation 1.263(a)-4(e)(4)(iii)(A), and the twelve-month rule applicable to transaction costs described in Regulation 1.263(a)-4(f)(5)(iii), is subject to the following special pooling method rules:[190]

(a) *IRS Authority*

The pooling rules are described in the regulations in very general terms. For that reason, the regulations provide that the IRS is authorized to publish guidance prescribing more specific pooling methods that apply the pooling methods to particular industries or to specific types of transactions.[191]

(b) *Accounting Method*

If a taxpayer adopts or changes to one of the pooling methods authorized by the regulations, it must use the method for the year of adoption or change and for all subsequent taxable years during which the taxpayer qualifies to use the method, unless a change to another method is required by the Commissioner, or unless permission to change to another method is granted by the Commissioner.[192]

(c) *Composition of Pool*

When defining a pool and similar transactions, agreements or rights, a taxpayer is permitted to use any reasonable method to define the pool, but the pool must contain all similar transactions, agreements or rights created during the taxable year.[193]

(d) *Distortion of Pool*

When applying the pooling method rules to de minimis amounts, an agreement or transaction will not be similar to other agreements or transactions included in the pool if the amount with respect to the agreement or transactions is reasonably expected to differ significantly from the average amount of the other agreements or transactions properly included in the pool. This restriction is designed to prevent one or more large-dollar transactions to qualify under the de minimis rule.[194]

(e) *Consistency Rule*

There is a consistency requirement for taxpayers using the pooling method for purposes of the twelve-month rule. Pursuant to that requirement, taxpayers must use the de minimis pooling method rules for purposes of determining the amount paid to create, or to facilitate the creation of, the right or benefit. Furthermore, the taxpayer must use the same pool for purposes of the de

---

[190] Reg. § 1.263(a)-4(h); Reg. § 1.263(a)-4(d)(5)(v) and Reg. § 1.263(a)-4(e)(4)(iii)(A).

[191] Reg. § 1.263(a)-4(h)(6).

[192] Reg. § 1.263(a)-4(h)(2).

[193] Reg. § 1.263(a)-4(h)(4).

[194] Reg. § 1.263(a)-4(h)(4).

minimis rules and the twelve-month rule.[195] The same pools are not required to be used under the pooling method for purposes of the twelve-month rule and the de minimis rules, as are used for depreciation purposes under Code Section 167.[196]

§ 8.4.6 Accounting Method Changes

Regulation 1.263(a)-4(p) describes rules for taxpayers to automatically change their method of accounting to conform to the capitalization regulations that deal with costs to acquire or create intangible assets.[197] These automatic accounting method change rules were further implemented in Revenue Procedure 2004-23.[198] The procedures are available for a taxpayer's first tax year ending on or after December 31, 2003.[199] In a subsequent revenue procedure, the IRS provided procedures under which a taxpayer may obtain automatic consent for the taxpayer's second taxable year ending on or after December 31, 2003.[200]

Following issuance of the advance notice of proposed rulemaking regarding capitalization of costs, some taxpayers changed to methods of accounting provided in the final regulations without I.R.S. consent. These taxpayers are not eligible to use the automatic change procedures unless they amend their prior federal income tax returns to correct unauthorized changes.

The accounting method change rules contained in Revenue Procedure 2004-23 are in addition to specific accounting method rules that permit a taxpayer to elect to retain its current accounting method for capitalized costs.[201] The procedure generally is consistent with the existing procedures for automatic changes in method of accounting set forth in Revenue Procedure 2002-9. Furthermore, the automatic change rules may be superseded by the Regulation section 1.263(a)-4 rules that contain an accounting method rule for taxpayers who elect a pooling method for certain costs. Similarly, a taxpayer may adopt a method of accounting that capitalizes costs that would otherwise be deductible under the Regulation section 1.263(a)-4 twelve-month rule.[202] If those costs are currently capitalized, no accounting method change is required.[203]

Thus, several methods may be required or permitted to be changed in order to comply with the capitalization regulations. Although Revenue Procedure

---

[195] Reg. § 1.263(a)-4(h)(5).

[196] Reg. § 1.263(a)-4.

[197] Reg. § 1.263(a)-4 and -5 contain identical automatic accounting method change rules.

[198] 2004-1 C.B. 785, March 24, 2004.

[199] In Rev. Proc. 2004-57, 2004-2 C.B. 498, the IRS allowed additional time for taxpayers to comply with the requirements of section 6.02 of Rev. Proc. 2004-23. Section 6.02 of Rev. Proc. 2004-23 requires certain taxpayers that seek to change to a method of accounting provided in Reg. §§ 1.263(a)-4, 1.263(a)-5, and Reg. § 1.167(a)-3(b) to submit a written statement containing information necessary to obtain automatic consent for the change.

[200] Rev. Proc. 2005-9, 2005-1 C.B. 303, December 13, 2004.

[201] Reg. § 1.263(a)-4(e)(4)(iv) permits taxpayers to make an irrevocable election to capitalize employee compensation, overhead, and de minimis costs, in lieu of a current deduction, which is permitted under the general rule of the regulations. If the election is made, the costs will be treated as amounts that facilitate the related transaction, and they will not be subject to the general automatic accounting change rule.

[202] Reg. § 1.263(a)-4(f)(7).

[203] There is no twelve-month rule for costs that facilitate an acquisition of a trade or business, a change in the capital structure of a business entity, and certain other similar transactions.

2004-23 provides the administrative convenience of reporting all changes on one Form 3115, Section 5.02 of the procedure provides that the resulting Code section 481(a) adjustments are not to be netted for purposes of determining the Code section 481(a) adjustment period.[204]

For a taxpayer's first taxable year ending on or after December 31, 2003, a change in a method of accounting to comply with the regulations must be made on a modified cut-off basis, taking into account, for purposes of Code section 481(a), only amounts paid or incurred in taxable years ending on or after January 24, 2002. This is the date of publication of the advance notice of proposed rulemaking in the Federal Register.[205] By prescribing a modified cut-off method, Code section 481(a) adjustments are made only for amounts paid or incurred in taxable years ending on or after the date of the advance notice of proposed rulemaking. With respect to changes to a pooling method authorized by Regulation section 1.263(a)-4 (no pooling methods are authorized under Regulation section 1.263(a)-5), a taxpayer must apply a cut-off method. This is designed to reduce the burden associated with attempting to determine which assets fit into a pool on a retroactive basis.

§ 8.5 Acquisition Costs

As a general rule the costs incurred in connection with the acquisition of the stock of another corporation or the assets of another entity are required to be capitalized either pursuant to Code section 263 or because they are not "ordinary" expenses as that term is used in Code section 162. Moreover, if the acquisition is one of the types of transactions that qualifies for tax-free treatment, in part or in whole, any acquisition costs may not be treated as acquiring a "section 197 intangible," which makes the costs ineligible for straight line amortization over 15 years.[206] However, in some situations, costs incurred when an acquisition is attempted but fails may be deducted. Moreover, the costs incurred by a target corporation that defends itself from a hostile takeover are deductible.[207] However, antitrust defense expense incurred in connection with an acquisition may have to be capitalized.[208]

§ 8.5.1 Capitalization Regulations

Regulations were adopted under Code section 263(a) to prescribe workable rules for determining whether amounts paid for intangible assets in connection with the acquisition of a business are required to be capitalized.[209] These regulations were the other significant part of the intangible capitalization regulations promulgated in December 2003.[210]

---

[204] For a detailed discussion of the accounting method change rules, *see* "*New Capitalization Rules: Their Sweeping Effect on Financial Institutions*," Journal of Taxation and Regulation of Financial Institutions, May/June 2004, Vol. 17/No. 5, by Blasi and Lee.

[205] Reg. § 1.263(a)-5(n)(3).

[206] I.R.C. § 197(e)(8).

[207] *Commissioner v. Tellier*, 383 U.S. 687 (1966); TAM 8927005, March 27, 1989.

[208] *American Stores Company v. Commissioner*, 114 T.C. 458 (2000).

[209] Reg. § 1.263(a)-5.

[210] The first part of the regulations, Reg. § 1.263(a)-4, is discussed in detail above.

Regulation section 1.263(a)-5 contains rules that require taxpayers to capitalize amounts paid to facilitate ten types of transactions, most of which relate to acquisitions of businesses. Special rules in the regulation governs the treatment of eight specific types of acquisition costs that relate to the ten types of transactions.[211] These regulations prescribe a safe haven bright-line test for determining when expenditures are capital in nature. A facilitation expense does not include an amount paid to another party for the property itself. Thus, the amount paid to the target in an asset acquisition for the assets is not an amount paid to facilitate the acquisition, nor is the cost of stock in a stock acquisition. The regulation recognizes that transaction costs that effect a change in the taxpayer's capital structure create betterments of a permanent or indefinite nature and are appropriately capitalized. As with Regulation section 1.263(a)-4, this regulation contains simplifying conventions, rules for the treatment of capitalized costs, and rules for accounting method changes.[212]

(a) *Ordering Rules*

The rules contained in Regulation section 1.263(a)-5 are to be integrated with the general rules for deduction contained in Code section 162 and the rules that deal with the treatment of "start-up" expenditures contained in Code section 195. In an acquisition that involves a taxpayer not entering a new trade or business, the rules of Regulation section 1.263(a)-5 will provide guidance for when expenditures transition from ordinary and necessary business expenses to capitalized expenses. If the transaction is one in which the taxpayer is entering a new trade or business, then the rules of this regulation will prescribe rules for when the threshold between both Code section 162 as well as Code section 195 are crossed.

(b) *Scope of Regulations*

Regulation 1.263(a)-5 is designed to provide a single set of rules for amounts paid that facilitate an acquisition of a trade or business, regardless of whether the transaction is structured as an acquisition of the entity or as an acquisition of assets (including tangible assets) constituting a trade or business.[213] If the transaction that is facilitated is described in both Regulations. 1.263(a)-4 and -5, the rules of Regulation section 1.263(a)-5 will apply.[214] However, if the transaction does not fit the description of one of the following ten transactions, then the rules contained in Regulation section 1.263(a)-4 that apply to the acquisition of intangibles in general will apply. Furthermore, any amount that is required to be capitalized by Regulations sections 1.263(a)-1, 1.263(a)-2, or 1.263(a)-4 will be treated as not facilitating a transaction that is described in Regulation section 1.263(a)-5.[215]

---

[211] Reg. § 1.263(a)-5(a)(1)-(10).

[212] Reg. § 1.263(a)-5(c)(1)-(8).

[213] The application of these capitalization rules to tangible assets is a significant change from the rule that was contained in the proposed regulations.

[214] Reg. § 1.263(a)-5(b)(2).

[215] Reg. § 1.263(a)-5(b)(2).

(c) *Hostile Acquisitions*

The regulations do not contain any special rules related to hostile acquisitions. Often, amounts that a target would pay in defending against a hostile acquisition would not be capitalized either because the costs would not be paid in investigating or otherwise pursuing the transaction with the hostile acquirer or because the costs would relate to activities performed before the bright line dates discussed below.[216] For example, if the amounts paid relate to costs paid by the target in a hostile acquisition to seek an injunction against the acquisition, they would not have to be capitalized.

(d) *Ten Types of Transactions*

Under the general rules for capitalization contained in Regulation section 1.263(a)-5, taxpayers are required to capitalize amounts paid to facilitate ten types of transactions. These transactions encompass taxable and tax-free transactions, stock and assets acquisitions, and transactions that may not actually be acquisitions, such as transactions associated with the recapitalization of a corporation.

The costs to facilitate the following ten transactions are required to be capitalized:

1. An acquisition of assets that constitute a trade or business, regardless of whether the taxpayer is the acquirer or the target;[217]
2. An acquisition by the taxpayer of an ownership interest (stock, partnership interest, etc) in a business entity.[218] If the taxpayer acquires an ownership interest in an entity conducting a trade or business, Regulation section 1.263(a)-5 will apply only if, immediately after the acquisition, the taxpayer and the entity are related within the meaning of Code section 267(b) or 707(b).
3. An acquisition of an ownership interest in the taxpayer (other than an acquisition by the taxpayer of an ownership interest in the taxpayer, whether by retention or otherwise);[219]
4. A restructuring, recapitalization, or reorganization of the capital structure of a business entity, including Code section 368 and 355 transactions;[220]
5. A transfer described in Code section 351 or 721, regardless of whether the taxpayer is the transferor or the transferee;[221]
6. A formation or organization of a disregarded entity;[222]
7. An acquisition of capital;[223]
8. A stock issuance;[224]

---

[216] In a hostile situation the target will not execute any agreement with the acquirer and the target's board of directors will not authorize the acquisition.

[217] Reg. § 1.263(a)-5(a)(1).

[218] Reg. § 1.263(a)-5(a)(2).

[219] Reg. § 1.263(a)-5(a)(3).

[220] Reg. § 1.263(a)-5(a)(4).

[221] Reg. § 1.263(a)-5(a)(5).

[222] Reg. § 1.263(a)-5(a)(6).

[223] Reg. § 1.263(a)-5(a)(7).

[224] Reg. § 1.263(a)-5(a)(8).

9. A borrowing, including an issuance of debt in an acquisition of capital, in a recapitalization, in a debt for debt exchange under Regulation section 1.1001-3, as well as any other issuance of debt;[225]

10. Writing an option.[226]

For purposes of these rules, the terms "reorganization" and "restructuring" are intended to be applied in a broad sense. Thus, they will encompass any change to an entities capital structure, and not, for example, merely a transaction that meets the Code section 368 definition of a reorganization.[227] These terms also are sufficiently broad to encompass a Code section 351 transaction and a bankruptcy reorganization. With respect to stock redemptions, the specific rule of Code section 162(k) will apply to deny a current deduction in most cases. If a divisive transaction occurs pursuant to a government mandate, capitalization of amounts paid to facilitate the divestiture is not required unless the divestiture is a condition of permitting the taxpayer to participate in a separate restructuring or reorganization transaction.

(e) *Eight Types of Costs*

In addition to requiring capitalization of any amount paid to facilitate one of the above ten transactions, Regulation section 1.263(a)-5 prescribes special rules with respect to eight types of costs, as follows:

(i) Borrowing Costs. The treatment of debt issuance costs is addressed in newly promulgated Regulation section 1.446-5, discussed below. In Regulation section 1.263(a)-5, a special rule is provided to ensure that the former regulation will control the treatment of debt issuance costs. Regulation section 1.263(a)-5 provides that any amount paid to facilitate a borrowing does not facilitate one of the ten types of transactions listed above.[228]

(ii) Asset Sale Costs. As a general rule, an amount paid to facilitate a sale of assets does not facilitate a transaction other than the sale itself, regardless of the circumstances surrounding the sale.[229] Thus, an amount paid by a target corporation that facilitates the disposition of an asset in preparation for a merger with the acquiring corporation is not to be treated as facilitating the merger, and it should not be capitalized as an amount paid to facilitate the merger. Any amount paid to effectuate the sale of assets will have the immediate effect of reducing the gain or increasing the loss on the transaction and will not be capitalized.

(iii) Mandatory Stock Distribution Costs. Special rules are provided with respect to government mandated stock distributions. In general, the costs associated with mandatory stock distributions will not be treated as facilitating a transaction described in Regulation section 1.263(a)-5.[230] This special rule acknowledges that capitalization is not required under the general principles of capitalization contained in Regulation section 1.263(a)-4.

225 Reg. § 1.263(a)-5(a)(9).
226 Reg. § 1.263(a)-5(a)(10).
227 Reg. § 1.263(a)-5(a)(4).
228 Reg. § 1.263(a)-5(c)(1).
229 Reg. § 1.263(a)-5(c)(2).
230 Reg. § 1.263(a)-5(c)(3).

Under this rule, costs associated with distributions of stock in three government mandated situations may escape capitalization:

- An amount paid in the process of investigating or otherwise pursuing a distribution of stock by a taxpayer to shareholders if the divestiture of the stock (or of properties transferred to an entity whose stock is distributed) is required by law, regulatory mandate, or court order.
- Amounts paid to organize (or facilitate the organization of) an entity that is formed for the exclusive purpose of receiving the properties required to be divested.
- An amount paid to transfer property to an entity if the taxpayer is required to divest itself of that property and if the stock of the recipient entity is distributed to the taxpayer's shareholders.[231]

(iv) Bankrupcty Reorganization Costs. In general, most amounts paid by the debtor in bankruptcy to institute or administer a bankruptcy proceeding under Chapter 11 of the Federal Bankruptcy Code will be treated as amounts paid to facilitate a "restructuring, recapitalization, or reorganization of the capital structure of a business entity," regardless of the purpose for which the proceeding is instituted.[232] Costs that must be capitalized under this provision include: amounts paid to prepare and file the petition, to obtain an extension of the exclusivity, to formulate plans of reorganization, to analyze plans of reorganization, and to contest or obtain approval of a plan of reorganization. The regulations do not distinguish between a bankruptcy proceeding that is instituted to resolve tort claims and other bankruptcy proceedings, except as discussed below.

Certain costs will not be treated as facilitating a bankruptcy reorganization under this rule. These costs are:

- An amount paid to operate the debtor's business during a Chapter 11 proceeding. Such costs are treated in the same manner as they would have been treated had the bankruptcy proceeding not been instituted.[233]
- An amount paid by the taxpayer to defend against the commencement of an involuntary bankruptcy proceeding against the taxpayer.[234]
- An amount paid to formulate, analyze, contest or obtain approval of the portion of a plan or reorganization under Chapter 11 that resolves the taxpayer's tort liability, if the amount would have been treated as an ordinary and necessary business expense under Code section 162 had the bankruptcy proceeding not been instituted.[235]

(v) Stock Issuance Costs of RIG. Amounts paid by an open-end regulated investment company to facilitate an issuance of its stock are treated as amounts that do not facilitate one of the ten transactions, unless the amounts are paid during the initial stock offering period.[236]

---

[231] Reg. § 1.263(a)-5(c)(3).

[232] Reg. § 1.263(a)-5(c)(4).

[233] *See* Rev. Rul. 77-204, 1977-1 C.B. 40, for the types of costs that are treated in this manner.

[234] Reg. § 1.263(a)-5(c)(4).

[235] Reg. § 1.263(a)-5(c)(4).

[236] Reg. § 1.263(a)-5(c)(5).

(vi) Integration Costs. Amounts paid to integrate the business operations of the taxpayer with the business operations of another entity do not facilitate a transaction, regardless of when the integration activities occur.[237]

(vii) Registrar and Transfer Agent Costs. If amounts are paid by a taxpayer to a registrar or transfer agent in connection with the transfer of the taxpayer's capital stock in one of the ten transactions, the amounts will be treated as facilitating the transaction.[238] For example, capitalization is required of an amount paid to a transfer agent for distributing proxy statements requesting shareholder approval of one of the ten listed transactions. If the payment is not with respect to a specific transaction, it will not be treated as facilitating a transaction. Thus, capitalization is not required of periodic payments to a transfer agent that maintains records of the names and addresses of shareholders who trade the taxpayer's shares on a national exchange.

(viii) Termination Costs and Mutually Exclusive Transaction. An amount paid to terminate (or to facilitate the termination of) an agreement to enter into a transaction may be treated as an amount paid to facilitate another transaction, but only in limited circumstances.[239] If an amount is paid to terminate (or to facilitate the termination of) an agreement to enter one of the ten transactions, it will be treated as facilitating another of the ten transactions only when:

- The transactions are mutually exclusive, and
- The agreement is terminated to enable the taxpayer to engage in the second transaction.[240]

The second transaction does not have to be expressly conditioned on the termination for the termination costs to be treated as facilitating a subsequent transaction. For example, an amount paid to abandon a transaction in order to enter into another transaction (both of which are among the list of ten) will be treated as facilitating the second transaction if the transactions are mutually exclusive.[241]

(f) *Simplifying Conventions*

Simplifying conventions for employee compensation, overhead, and de minimis amounts are contained in Regulation section 1.263(a)-5. These conventions are identical, in all material respects, to the simplifying conventions contained in Regulation section 1.263(a)-4.[242] The Regulation section 1.263(a)-5 simplifying conventions apply to all ten transactions. The only modifications of the Regulation section 1.263(a)-4 simplifying conventions are as follows:

---

[237] Reg. § 1.263(a)-5(c)(6).

[238] Reg. § 1.263(a)-5(c)(7).

[239] Even in the limited circumstances dealt with in the regulations, there is a question whether the rule contained in the regulations violates the "origin-of-the-claim" test established by the Supreme Court in *United States v. Gilmore,* 372 U.S. 39 (1963).

[240] Reg. § 1.263(a)-5(c)(8).

[241] Reg. § 1.263(a)-5(l), Ex. 13.

[242] Reg. § 1.263(a)-5(d)(1).

(i) Payments to Independent Contractors. Amounts paid to persons, who are not employees, for services involving the preparation and distribution of proxy solicitations and other documents seeking shareholder approval of one of the ten transactions will not be treated as an amount paid to an employee.[243] It is the position of the IRS and the Treasury Department that these are inherently facilitating services, which are commonly performed by independent contractors, and, as such, these amounts must be capitalized.

(ii) De Minimis Costs. The de minimis cost rule contained in Regulation section 1.263(a)-5 does not contain the "twenty-five similar transaction" rule contained in Regulation section 1.263(a)-4, as discussed above.[244]

(g) *Special Rules for Facilitation Costs—Generally*

(i) Facilitation Costs—Generally. In rules that are similar to rules contained in Regulation section 1.263(a)-4, Regulation section 1.263(a)-5 provides generally that an amount facilitates a transaction if it is paid in the process of investigating or otherwise pursuing the transaction, taking into account all of the facts and circumstances surrounding the transaction.[245] An amount paid to determine the value or price of a transaction is an amount paid in the process of investigating or otherwise pursuing that transaction. The fact that an amount would (or would not) have been paid "but for" the transaction is a relevant, but not determinative, factor in evaluating whether an amount is paid to facilitate a transaction.[246]

(ii) Bright-line Date Rule. With respect to certain transactions, a "bright line date" rule is provided to determine whether amounts must be capitalized because they are paid at a time when they facilitate a transaction. The transactions that are subject to this rule are referred to as covered transactions, and they comprise all acquisitive transactions. If an amount is paid prior to the bright line date, then, it appears, that the amount need not be capitalized unless the amount is "inherently facilitative." Certain costs are capitalized regardless of when they are incurred if they are "inherently facilitative."

The bright line date rule is applied to all amounts, other than inherently facilitative amounts, in lieu of a rule based on facts and circumstances.[247] It is designed to eliminate the subjectivity and controversy inherent in this area. It does not apply to spin-offs, stock offerings, and acquisitions of individual assets that do not constitute a trade or business. Thus, amounts paid in the process of investigating or otherwise pursuing these transactions must be capitalized, if at all, under general capitalization rules.

Because both the acquirer and the target must execute one of the agreements referred to in the first prong of the test, and because the second part of the test is applied independently by the acquirer and the target, the mere submission of a bid by a bidder could not trigger the bright line date. However, capitalization

---

[243] Reg. § 1.263(a)-5(d)(2)(ii).

[244] Reg. § 1.263(a)-5 (d)(2)(iii); Reg. § 1.263(a)-4(d)(5)(v); and Reg. § 1.263(a)-4 (e)(4)(iii)(A).

[245] Reg. § 1.263(a)-5(b)(1). *See* discussion of relationship between I.R.C. §§ 195 and 263 in text addressing Reg. § 1.263(a)-4.

[246] Reg. § 1.263(a)-5(b)(1).

[247] Reg. § 1.263(a)-5(e)(2).

may occur before the date that the board of directors approves a transaction if the parties have mutually agreed to pursue a transaction, notwithstanding the fact that the parties are not bound to complete the transaction. If the board of directors merely authorizes a committee or management to explore the possibility of an acquisitive transaction with another party, the capitalization threshold will not be crossed. However, the board of director's approval date will normally occur prior to the date that the board ratifies a shareholder vote in favor of the transaction.[248]

An amount (that is not an inherently facilitative amount) facilitates a transaction pursuant to the bright-line date rule only if the amount relates to activities performed on or after the earlier of either:

- The date on which a letter of intent, exclusivity agreement, or similar written communication (not including a confidentially agreement) is executed by representatives of the acquirer and the target, or
- The date on which the material terms of the transaction are authorized or approved by the taxpayer's (acquiring or target's) board of directors (or other appropriate governing officials). Where board approval is not required for a particular transaction, the bright line date for the second prong of the test is the date on which the acquirer and the target execute a binding written contract reflecting the terms of the transaction.[249]

(iii) Covered Transactions. The regulations introduced the term "covered transaction" to describe the acquisitive transactions which are subject to this bright line date rule.[250] If an amount is paid by the taxpayer in the process of investigating or otherwise pursuing a transaction that is not a "covered transaction," the bright line date rule will not control the timing of when facilitation costs are incurred. Instead, a facts and circumstances rule will apply.

A covered transaction is defined as one of three types of acquisitive transactions:

- A taxable acquisition by the taxpayer of assets that constitute a trade or business;[251]
- A taxable acquisition of an ownership interest in a business (whether the taxpayer is the acquirer in the acquisition or the target of the acquisition) if, immediately after the acquisition, the acquirer and the target are related within the meaning of Code section 267(b) or 707(b);[252]
- A reorganization described in Code section 368(a)(1)(A), (B), or (C) or in Code section 368(a)(1)(D) in which stock or securities of the corporation to which the assets are transferred or distributed in a transaction which qualifies under Code section 354 or 356 (whether the taxpayer is the acquirer or the target in the reorganization).[253]

---

[248] Reg. § 1.263(a)-5(e)(1).

[249] Reg. § 1.263(a)-5(e)(1)(i) and (ii).

[250] Reg. § 1.263(a)-5(e)(1).

[251] Reg. § 1.263(a)-5(e)(3)(i).

[252] Reg. § 1.263(a)-5(e)(3)(ii).

[253] Reg. § 1.263(a)-5(e)(3)(iii).

(iv) Inherently Facilitative Amounts. Amounts that are inherently facilitative must be capitalized, regardless of when the activity for which the payment is made is performed.[254] An amount is treated as inherently facilitative under the regulations if the amount is paid to:

- Secure an appraisal, formal written evaluation, or fairness opinion related to the transaction;[255]
- Structure the transaction, including negotiating the structure of the transaction and obtaining tax advice on the structure of the transaction (for example, obtaining tax advice on the application of Code section 368);[256]
- Prepare and review the documents that effectuate the transaction (for example, a merger agreement or purchase agreement);[257]
- Obtain regulatory approval of the transaction, including preparing and reviewing regulatory filings (for example, a filing with a federal or state bank regulator);[258]
- Obtain shareholder approval of the transaction (for example, proxy costs, solicitation costs and costs to promote the transaction to shareholders);[259] or
- Convey property between parties to the transaction (for example, transfer taxes and title registration costs).[260]

The inherently facilitative rule is not rebuttable. Because this rule does not allow for the consideration of facts and circumstances, it may be criticized as rigid and overly broad. It applies to the above list of expenditures, regardless of when they occur.[261] With respect to expenditures relating to securing fairness opinions, reviewing transaction documents, and regulatory filing, the absolute nature of this rule may be criticized as failing to recognize that many of these same expenditures affect a taxpayer's decision whether to enter into a transaction. As such, they are not treated as acquisition expenditures.

If a taxpayer incurs cost to perform general due diligence, the costs will not be inherently facilitative. Instead, the taxpayer must apply the bright line date rule to determine whether any cost must be capitalized. If an amount is required to be capitalized under these regulations, the amount cannot qualify for amortization under the Code section 195 rules for deferred start-up expenses.

(h) *Success-based Fees*

A fee that is contingent on the successful closing of any transaction to which Regulation section 1.263(a)-5 applies, not only to acquisitive acquisitions (a "success based fee"), is presumed to facilitate a transaction.[262] The presumption that applies to these success-based payments can be rebutted with evidence that clearly demonstrates that some portion of the payment is allocable to activities

[254] Reg. § 1.263(a)-5(e)(2).
[255] Reg. § 1.263(a)-5(e)(2)(i).
[256] Reg. § 1.263(a)-5(e)(2)(ii).
[257] Reg. § 1.263(a)-5(e)(2)(iii).
[258] Reg. § 1.263(a)-5(e)(2)(iv).
[259] Reg. § 1.263(a)-5(e)(2)(v).
[260] Reg. § 1.263(a)-5(e)(2)(vi).
[261] Reg. § 1.263(a)-5(e)(2).
[262] Reg. § 1.263(a)-5(f).

that do not facilitate the acquisition. Sufficient documentation must be maintained to establish that a portion of the fee is allocable to activities that do not facilitate the transaction.

Historically, the IRS has ruled, and the courts have held, that investment banker fees may be allocated among actual services provided and are not necessarily treated in their entirely as costs incurred to facilitate a transaction. In Revenue Ruling 99-23, investment banker fees are allocated based upon the types of services provided.[263] In *A.E. Staley*,[264] the Seventh Circuit directly addressed the issue of an investment banker fee that was success-based and stated:

> "We must look to all the facts of the case, including the fee arrangement, to determine the context of the expenditures and the services for which the investment bankers were paid."[265]

Adequate documentation that an amount paid is a success based fees will consist of time records and itemized invoices that identify:

- The various activities for which payment is made,
- The amount of the fee (or percentage of time) that is allocable to each of the various activities for which payment is made,
- Where the date that the activity was performed is relevant to understanding whether the activity facilitated the transaction, the amount of the fee (or percentage of time) that is allocable to the performance of that activity before and after the relevant date, and
- The name, business address, and business telephone number of the service provider. The documentation must be completed on or before the due date of the taxpayer's timely filed original federal income tax return (including extensions) for the taxable year during which the transaction closes. Inadequate documentation would be documentation that consists of a mere allocation between activities that facilitate the transaction and activities that do not facilitate the transaction.

(i) Treatment of Capitalized Cost

Regulation section 263(a)-5 does not address whether the costs that must be capitalized under that regulation have the effect of increasing the taxpayer's basis in property, or whether they should be treated as a separate intangible asset.[266] Thus, no guidance is provided as to cost recovery of capitalized costs associated with tax-free transactions, stock issuance, and amounts paid by the target in a taxable stock acquisition, as well as in certain other acquisitions to which Regulation section 1.263(a)-5(g) applies.[267]

---

[263] 1999-1 C.B. 998.

[264] *A.E. Staley Manufacturing Co. v. Commissioner*, 119 F.3d 482 (7th Cir. 1977).

[265] *Id.* at 491.

[266] Reg. § 1.263(a)-4(g)(1) does prescribe that basis be increased for costs required to be capitalized under Reg. § 1.263(a)-4.

[267] *See* discussion below under "Safe Harbor Amortization Rules" for discussion of stock issuance costs. Reg. § 1.263(a)-5(g). The treatment of costs incurred with respect to borrowings that are required to be capitalized is governed by Reg. § 1.446-5.

Under accepted tax rules, however, adjustments to basis are required when costs are capitalized in taxable acquisitive transactions, including a taxable merger or consolidation that is not described in Code section 368.[268] The target in a taxable asset acquisition is required to treat the amount paid as a reduction of the target's amount realized under Code section 1001 on the disposition of its assets.[269] Transaction costs that facilitate a stock issuance or recapitalization will not create a separate intangible asset, but they will offset the proceeds of the stock issuance.[270] With respect to stock issuance costs of an open and regulated investment company (other than those costs incurred during the initial stock offering period), capitalization is not required.[271]

For those costs not covered by the regulations, the Treasury Department and the IRS have announced that they intend to issue separate guidance to address their treatment, and in the guidance they will consider whether such amounts should be eligible for the 15-year safe harbor amortization period applicable to other intangibles that are described in Regulation section 1.167(a)-3 in Code section 197, discussed below.

(j) *Accounting Method Changes*

Regulations 1.263(a)-4 and -5 contain identical rules that permit taxpayers to automatically change their methods of accounting to conform to the new capitalization regulations.[272] For a discussion of the automatic accounting method change rules, see the discussion of those rules in connection with Regulation section 1.263(a)-4, above.

§ 8.5.2 Judicial Background to Regulation Section 1.263(a)-5

Prior to the issuance of Regulation section 1.263(a)-5, the most recent judicial view of the treatment of internal acquisition costs was expressed in the 2000 case of *Wells Fargo v. Commissioner*.[273] In *Wells Fargo*, the Court of Appeals for the Eighth Circuit reversed the Tax Court's earlier decision in *Norwest Corp.* and held that most challenged expenditures paid by a target in an acquisition were currently deductible. The Tax Court held that investigatory costs, due diligence costs, and officers' salaries incurred in connection with an acquisition of a specific bank were not deductible under Code section 162(a). Although the expenses were incurred prior to the formal decision to enter into the transaction, and were not incurred as direct costs of facilitating the acquisition, the court found that the preparatory expenses enabled the taxpayer, which was the target in the acquisition, to achieve the long-term benefits that it desired from the transaction. The Tax Court held that the expenditures were "sufficiently related to an event that produced a significant long-term benefit" and therefore were not "ordinary and necessary business expenses" that could be deducted under Code

[268] Reg. § 1.263(a)-5(g)(2)(i).

[269] Reg. § 1.263(a)-5(g)(2)(ii).

[270] Rev. Rul. 69-330, 1969-1 C.B. 51.

[271] Rev. Rul. 94-70 (1994-2 C.B. 17).

[272] Reg. § 1.263(a)-4(p) and Reg. § 1.263(a)-5(n).

[273] *Wells Fargo & Co. v. Commissioner*, 224 F.3d 874 (8th Cir. 2000). Although the caption of the case on appeal lists *Wells Fargo* as the Petition-Appellant, rather than *Norwest*, the latter entity was acquired by *Wells Fargo* after the Tax Court decision was handed down. *Norwest Corp. and Subsidiaries v. Commissioner*, 112 T.C. 89 (1999).

section 162.[274] The Tax Court noted that Norwest's focus on the timing of the investigatory fees was similar to the position argued and rejected in *Ellis Banking Corp. v. Commissioner*.[275]

In *Ellis Banking*, the taxpayer, which was the acquiring corporation in the acquisition, incurred expenses for office supplies, filing fees, travel, and accounting services in connection with its examination of a target bank's books and records. The examination was conducted pursuant to an acquisition agreement that was contingent on several terms and conditions being met, including regulatory approval. The Tax Court concluded that the expenses were nondeductible capital expenditures incurred in connection with the acquisition a capital asset because the taxpayer ultimately acquired the stock of the target bank. The Eleventh Circuit substantially affirmed the Tax Court and stated that expenses incurred to investigate a capital investment are properly allocable to the investment and must be capitalized.[276] Although the decision to acquire the target was not final at the time of the expenditures, that did not change the character of the investment. If a taxpayer abandons a project or fails to make an attempted investment, the preliminary expenditures that have been capitalized are allowed to be deducted as a loss under Code section 165.[277]

On appeal, the Eighth Circuit in *Wells Fargo* concluded that it was error for the Tax Court to require capitalization of the expenses at issue simply because they were incidentally connected with a future benefit. With respect to the salaries, the Circuit Court stated that the Tax Court should have performed "an independent and appropriate legal analysis to determine whether each of the expenditures at issue were 'ordinary.'[278] In addition to the previously cited characteristics of an 'ordinary' expense, an additional qualification is that the expense must relate to a transaction 'of common or frequent occurrence in the type of business involved.'"[279] The court noted that other courts have traditionally permitted current deductions for expenses attributable to salaries similar to those at issue. Applying the origin of the claim test, the court reasoned that the origin of the payments was not the acquisition, but rather the employment relationship between the taxpayer and its employees.

Neither the court nor the IRS seemed to be concerned with the possible application of Code section 195.[280] Although the court referred to the expenditures for which it allowed a deduction under Code section 162 as "investigatory expenses," the use of Code section 195 terminology did not appear to be intended to suggest that the section had any application. Presumably, the "carry-

---

[274] *Id.*

[275] *Ellis Banking Corp. v. Commissioner*, T.C. Memo 1981-123, *aff'd in part and rem'd in part*, 688 F.2d 1376 (11th Cir. 1982).

[276] *Ellis Banking*, 688 F.2d at 1382.

[277] *Id.*

[278] *Wells Fargo*, 224 F.3d at 886. This recommended approach is nearly identical to that taken by the Third Circuit in *PNC Bancorp, Inc. v. Commissioner*, 212 F.3d 822 (3d Cir. 2000), decided a few months earlier. There the court stated: "[w]e pursue a real-life inquiry into whether the expenditures associated with loan marketing and origination are 'ordinary' expenses incurred in the day-to-day maintenance of a bank's business," *Id.* at 828.

[279] *Wells Fargo*, 224 F.3d at 886, *citing INDOPCO*, 503 U.S. at 85-86, *quoting Deputy v. Dupont*, 308 U.S. 488, 495 (1940).

[280] TAM 8141033, June 30, 1981.

ing on" test of Code section 162 was satisfied because the acquisition did not result in the taxpayer engaging in a new trade or business.

The test that the court crafted distinguished between expenses that were directly related to the transaction and expenditures that were indirectly related to the transaction. It stated: "We conclude that if the expense is directly related to the capital transaction (and therefore, the long term benefit), then it should be capitalized. In this case, there is only an indirect relation between the salaries (which originated from the employment relationship) and the acquisition (which provides the long term benefit)."[281] Only "indirectly" did the payment of the salaries provide the taxpayer with a long term benefit.

On appeal, the outside legal expenses were conceded by the government to be largely deductible because they were attributable to the investigatory stage of the transaction. The expenses that remained in controversy were determined to be acquisition expenditures. They were found to be made after the "final decision" regarding acquisition was reached. That decision was made, according to the court, when the parties entered into their "Agreement and Plan of Reorganization." This event occurred more than six months after the acquirer and the target began to discuss a merger. It also followed by several months the time when the law firm was hired, when the target's board of directors met to consider merging into the acquirer and the appointment of the board of an ad hoc committee to perform an independent due diligence review, to obtain professional advice, and to report to back to the board as to the fairness and appraisal of the proposed transaction, and the decision of the acquirer's board to issue the additional shares of common stock to effect the transaction.

It appears that the court's opinion rests largely on the failure of the Tax Court to make an appropriate factual finding relating to the extent to which the taxpayer's employees actually worked on the acquisition. It appears that if there were a finding that a significant portion of employees' activities were acquisition related, the court may have reached a different conclusion because the salaries would be directly related to the acquisition.

§8.6 Debt Issuance Costs

Regulation section 1.446-5 contains new rules for the treatment of debt issuance costs. However, these rules are intended to make no change to the traditional rules that determine which costs associated with the issuance of debt must be capitalized. For a bank, costs associated with deposit liabilities will remain fully deductible, but borrowing outside the day-to-day banking business may be subject to these rules. By cross reference to Regulation section 1.263(a)-5, capitalized debt issuance costs are generally defined in the regulations as any amount paid to facilitate any issuance of debt, including an issuance of debt in an acquisition of capital, a recapitalization, or in a debt-for-debt exchange.[282] Regulation section 1.446-5 prescribes the original issue discount rules of the Code for amortization of debt issuance costs.[283]

[281] *Wells Fargo*, 224 F.3d at 886.

[282] Reg. § 1.263(a)-5(a)(9).

[283] Reg. § 1.446-5(a) and (b). *See* Code section 1272 *et seq.*

To determine the annual amortization deduction for debt issuance costs, original issue discount must be calculated by reducing the issue price of the debt instrument by any debt issuance costs.[284] In general, the resulting OID will be deductible over the term of the debt instrument using the constant yield method of accounting described in Regulation section 1.1272-1(b). The requirement that the constant yield method be used, instead of the straight line method that had been employed in the past by taxpayers, appears to introduce an additional compliance burden on taxpayers, which is inconsistent with one of the objectives of the new regulations.

However, if the resulting OID is de minimis, as an alternative to the constant yield method, a taxpayer is permitted to use any one of the several methods of accounting specified in Regulation section 1.163-7 that apply to de minimis OID. That regulation permits de minimis OID to be deducted at maturity, on a straight-line basis over the term of the debt instrument, or in proportion to stated interest payments.[285] Whether OID is de minimis is determined under Regulation section 1.1273-1(d).

Debt issuance costs may also have the effect of reducing bond issuance premium. As a general rule, bond issuance premium limits the amount of the taxpayer's interest deduction otherwise allowable under Code section 163.[286] It is allocated to an accrual period using the constant yield method. Bond issuance premium is defined for this purpose as the excess, if any, of the issue price of a debt instrument over its stated redemption price at maturity.[287]

§8.7 Amortization of Capitalized Costs

Accompanying Regulation 1.263(a)-4 are regulations that provide safe harbor amortization rules that will apply to most, but not to all, intangibles described in that regulation.[288] The rules permit a taxpayer to amortize an intangible over 15 years using a straight line method. Salvage value is ignored and the amortization period begins on the first day of the month in which the intangible asset is placed in service by the taxpayer. No amortization is permitted in the month in which the intangible is disposed. Loans that are purchased also may be subject to the Code section 475 mark-to-market rules. If they are, there exists the possibility that any capitalized costs may be taken into account in determining the annual mark-to-market.

The safe harbor amortization rules do not apply to debt issuance costs, which are governed by existing amortization rules contained in regulations under Section 163.[289] Furthermore, they do not apply to an amount paid to facilitate an acquisition of a trade or business, a change in the capital structure of a business entity, and certain other transactions described in Regulation

[284] *See* Code section 1273(a) for the definition of OID.

[285] Regulation §1.163-7(b)(2) requires the taxpayer who issues the debt instrument to elect the cost recovery method by reporting the de minimis OID in a manner consistent with the method chosen on the issuer's timely filed federal income tax return for the taxable year in which the debt instrument is issued.

[286] Reg. §1.163-13(a).

[287] Reg. §1.446-5(b)(3); Reg. §1.163-13(c).

[288] Reg. 1.167(b)(3).

[289] Reg. 1.163-13.

1.263(a)-5.[290] With respect to stock issuance costs and or other transaction costs involving the acquisition of capital, the preamble to the regulations provides that historical treatment will continue. As such, these costs, according to the Treasury and the IRS, will reduce the capital proceeds from the transaction and not be treated as a separate intangible asset with an amortizable life.[291]

The safe harbor amortization rule also does not apply to the following four types of intangibles:

(i) An intangible for which an amortization period or useful life is specifically prescribed or prohibited by the Code, regulations, or other published guidance.[292] Thus, a 36-month useful life is prescribed for certain computer software by Code section 167(f)(1)(A); a 15-year amortization period is prescribed for Code section 197 intangibles; and a 108 month amortization period is prescribed for mortgage servicing rights by Regulation section 1.167(a)-14(d)(1). In addition, Code section 171 prescribes rules for determining the amortization period for bond premium and Code section 178 prescribes the amortization period for costs to acquire a lease.

(ii) An intangible described that is acquired from another party or one that is a created financial interest.[293] If these intangibles are eligible for amortization, it would be under some specific provision of the Code such as Code section 197.

(iii) An intangible that has a useful life the length of which can be estimated with reasonable accuracy.[294] Such intangibles are likely to be amortizable under Regulation section 1.167(a)-3. Such intangibles include prepaid expenses, contracts with a fixed duration, and certain contract terminations. Prepaid expenses would be amortizable over the period covered by the prepayment. Further, amounts paid to induce another to enter into a contract with a fixed duration are amortized over the duration of the contract.[295]

(iv) An intangible that is a benefit arising from the provision, production, or improvement or real property.[296] In the case of this intangible, the taxpayer may treat the intangible as having a useful life equal to 25 years.

§ 8.8 Pre-Regulation IRS Pronouncements

Prior to the Supreme Court's decision in *INDOPCO* and the Code Section 263 intangible regulations, the IRS issued pronouncements that related to whether loan origination or similar expenditures were currently deductible or properly capitalized. The intangible regulations reflect the positions taken in

[290] Reg. 1.167(a)-3(2).

[291] Rev. Rul. 69-330, 1969-1 C.B. 51; *Affiliated Capital Corp. v. Commissioner*, 88 T.C. 1157 (1987).

[292] Reg. § 1.167(a)-3(b)(i).

[293] Reg. § 1.167(a)-3(b)(ii). Reg. § 1.263(a)-4(c); Reg. § 1.263(a)-4(d)(2).

[294] Reg. § 1.167(a)-3(b)(iii).

[295] It is the position of the IRS that any amounts paid by a lessor to terminate a lease contract are amortized over the remaining term of the lease.

[296] Reg. § 1.167(a)-3(b)(iv); Reg. § 1.263(a)-4.

these pronouncements but only in general. To the extent that the earlier pronouncement is inconsistent with the intangible regulations the latter will control.

§ 8.8.1 Home Equity Lines of Credit

The taxpayer, a state-chartered savings bank, incurred expenses for credit reports, filing and recording fees, attorney fees, and other related costs in connection with establishing the lines of credit. The IRS stated that an expenditure must be capitalized if it creates, enhances, or is part of the cost of acquiring or defending a tangible or intangible asset with a useful life greater than one year. It determined that the expenditures incurred to create the home equity loans were in respect of separate assets with a life greater than one year. Consequently, the costs incurred had to be capitalized. The taxpayer could recover the capitalized costs through amortization deductions upon proving the life of the loans with reasonable accuracy.

Although the simplifying convention dealing with employee compensation overrules this conclusion, even prior to these regulations it could be argued that the IRS's legal analysis of the transaction is at odds with the facts of the transaction. Unlike a loan where credit has been extended, it is often the case with home equity lines of credit that the taxpayer is acquiring nothing more than the right to draw on credit in the future. The bank selling that intangible property right appears to be entering into a loan commitment, similar to the commitment made when an option is granted. Although it is not always the case that a bank will receive a fee when a home equity line of credit is established, at least a portion of the expenses incurred by the bank to establish the line of credit would appear to relate to any commitment fee earned and not to interest that may or may not be earned depending on whether credit is drawn upon. Thus, a taxpayer could argue that the expenses incurred to sell the commitment should offset the amount realized for the sale of the commitment, or, at the very least, they should be recovered over the commitment period and not the term of any loan. In a more recent Field Service Advice, the IRS seemingly acknowledges the material differences between extending credit and committing to extend credit.[297]

The IRS's position in Technical Advice Memorandum 9024003 also appears to be at odds with the taxpayer argument that the expenses a bank incurs to extend credit are associated with the financial intermediation function of a bank. This function is similar to the activities of a dealer. As such, no separate and distinct asset is created, nor is a substantial future benefit secured by the expenditure.

§ 8.8.2 Origination of Mortgage Loans

Several years earlier in General Counsel Memorandum 35681, the IRS examined a similar issue: whether salaries, wages, office overhead, and other similar expenses incurred in connection with the origination of mortgage loans were currently deductible as ordinary and necessary business expenses, where such loans were subsequently sold to institutional investors who may retain the

[297] FSA 199910012, December 4, 1998.

taxpayer to service the loans.[298] The IRS concluded that any expenditure that was directly related to acquiring a mortgage loan was part of the cost of the loan and amortizable over its life. Any unamortized amount existing at the time a mortgage loan was sold reduced the gain on sale since the unamortized amount was included in tax basis. The IRS also concluded that salaries, rents, and other expenses incurred in originating a mortgage that were not directly attributable to the acquisition of the mortgage were ordinary and necessary expenses within the meaning of Code section 162(a).[299] The intangibles regulations draw no distinction between acquired loans and originated loans in so far as employee compensation overhead and de minimis amounts are concerned. All are allowed to be currently deducted under the simplifying conventions.

This pronouncement also predated a string of taxpayer victories relating to new credit card activities engaged in by banks. In *Iowa-Des Moines National Bank*, the Eighth Circuit Court of Appeals decided that credit evaluation and documentation costs associated with bank lending activities were currently deductible under Code section 162 and were not subject to the disallowance rule of Code section 263.[300] Taxpayers may argue that the expenses incurred in the credit card lending process are legally indistinguishable from those incurred in the mortgage or consumer lending process.

§8.8.3 Advertising and Other Expenditures

After the Supreme Court's opinion in *INDOPCO*, but prior to the intangibles regulations, the IRS had issued several pronouncements relating to the capitalization of various business expenditures. It does not appear that any of those regulations were overruled by the intangibles regulations.

In Revenue Ruling 92-80, the IRS ruled that advertising expense is currently deductible because it provides only "some future effect on business activities."[301] However, in the "unusual circumstances where advertising is directed towards obtaining future benefits significantly beyond those traditionally associated with ordinary product advertising or with institutional or goodwill advertising," such advertising costs must be capitalized. In Revenue Ruling 94-12, the IRS affirmed its longstanding position that the current deductibility of incidental repair costs is not affected by *INDOPCO*.[302] In Revenue Ruling 94-77, severance payments made by a taxpayer to its employees were found to be currently deductible; however, if severance payments were made as part of an acquisition, capitalization may be required.[303] In Revenue Ruling 96-62, the IRS ruled that training costs were currently deductible as ordinary and necessary business expenses under

[298] General Counsel Memorandum 35681, February 19, 1974.

[299] *Id.* As pointed out above, the IRS has subsequently stated that the UNICAP rules do not apply to loans made by a bank.

[300] *Iowa-Des Moines National Bank v. Commissioner*, 68 T.C. 872 (1977), *aff'd*, 592 F.2d 433 (8th Cir. 1979); *See also First National Bank of South Carolina v. United States*, 558 F.2d 721 (4th Cir. 1977); *Colorado Springs National Bank v. United States*, 505 F.2d 1185 (10th Cir. 1974).

[301] Rev. Rul. 92-80, 1992-2 C.B. 57. *See also* Reg. §§1.162-1(a) and -20(a).

[302] Rev. Rul. 94-12, 1994-1 C.B. 36.

[303] Rev. Rul. 94-77, 1994-2 C.B. 19.

Code section 162, even though they may result in some future benefit.[304] Finally, in Revenue Procedure 97-50 the IRS provided guidance involving the costs incurred to convert or replace computer software to recognize dates beginning in the year 2000.[305] In general, those costs will be deductible under the provisions of an earlier revenue procedure.[306] In a variety of other pronouncements, the IRS applied *INDOPCO* to less common situations.[307]

§ 8.9 Start-Up and Expansion Expenditures

§ 8.9.1 Overview

When a financial institution expands its business it may incur organizational expenses to establish a new incorporated entity, and it may also incur several types of other expenditures including: start-up expenses to either investigate the creation or the acquisition of a new trade or business or to actually create a new trade or business; ordinary and necessary business expenses to carry on its trade or business; expenditures that are not "ordinary;" or acquisition expenses and other capital expenditures. The Code provides for amortization deductions of organizational expenses under Code section 248 and for start-up expenses under Code section 195. It also provides for the current deduction of ordinary and necessary business expenses under Code section 162. Amounts paid to acquire or to create an asset or to facilitate the acquisition or creation of an asset must be capitalized under Code section 263.

Code sections 195 and 248 are mutually exclusive sections that allow amortization deductions for expenses that are incurred incident to the creation of a new business or the creation of a new corporation, respectively. Code section 195 applies to "start-up expenditures," and Code section 248 applies to "organizational expenditures." Although these sections allow deductions for different expenditures, the purpose for which the expenditures are incurred may be the same; that is, a corporation may be formed to contain the operations of a new business activity. For example, if a bank holding company forms a subsidiary to conduct an investment advisory business, an activity in which it previously had not been engaged, expenditures amortizable under both Code sections 195 and 248 may be incurred.

§ 8.9.2 Start-Up Expenditures—Code Section 195

(a) *Overview*

Code section 195 is a section that serves two functions: first it expressly denies a deduction for any "ordinary and necessary" business expenditure which is incurred prior to when a business is carried on. Second, it allows an amortization deduction for such "ordinary and necessary" expenditures beginning once

[304] Rev. Rul. 96-62, 1996-2 C.B. 9. *See also* Rev. Rul. 95-32, 1995-1 C.B. 8 and FSA 199918013, January 12, 1999.

[305] Rev. Proc. 97-50, 1997-2 C.B. 525.

[306] Rev. Proc. 69-21, 1969-2 C.B. 303.

[307] In addition to the items discussed in the text, *see also* TAM 9645002, June 21, 1996 (pre-opening costs), discussed below, TAM 9641004, June 25, 1996 (amortization of emergency facilities), TAM 9544001, July 21, 1995 (just-in-time manufacturing), PLR 9535011, September 1, 1995 (prudency audit expenditures), PLR 9402002, January 14, 1994 (anti-trust settlement expenditures), Rev. Rul. 95-32, 1995-2 C.B. 379 (energy conservation expenditures).

the business is carried on.[308] More precisely, Code section 195 denies a current deduction for "start-up" expenditures, but it allows taxpayers to elect to amortize such expenditures and deduct them on a *pro rata* basis beginning with the month in which the active trade or business begins.[309]

Effective for start-up expenditures paid or incurred after October 22, 2004, taxpayers are permitted to elect to deduct up to $5,000 of start-up expenditures in the tax year in which their trade or business begins.[310] The $5,000 amount must be reduced (but not below zero) by the amount by which the start-up expenditures exceed $50,000. The remainder of any start-up expenditures, those that are not deductible in the year in which the trade or business begins, must be ratably amortized over the 180-month period (15 years) beginning with the month in which the active trade or business begins. The 15-year amortization period for the start-up expenditures and organizational expenditures that are not deductible in the year in which the trade or business begins is consistent with the amortization period for section 197 intangibles.

In order to properly understand the scope and operation of Code section 195, it is necessary to determine when an expenditure is properly deductible under Code section 162 and when an expenditure is denied deduction by Code section 263. These two sections bracket the operation of Code section 195. Thus, an ordinary and necessary expense may be nondeductible in the current tax period by reason of Code section 195 if it is made in the tax year with respect to investigating the acquisition or creation of a trade or business or creating a trade or business. Similarly, an expenditure that may be otherwise eligible for amortization under Code section 195 may become ineligible for an amortization deduction by reason of Code section 263 if it is required to be capitalized under Code section 263(a). Consequently, a taxpayer must examine both ends of the Code section 195 continuum; that is, when an expenditure is no longer deductible under Code section 162 and when it must be capitalized under Code section 263. Prior to the extension in the Code section 195 amortization period, it was clear that a taxpayer should be biased in favor of Code section 195 to avoid disallowance of deduction for the item or significant deferral of deduction. Now, the significant deferral in the cost recovery deduction makes this decision more difficult.

(b) *Legislative History*

Code section 195 was enacted in 1980 in an effort to "encourage [the] formation of new businesses and decrease controversy and litigation arising

---

[308] *See* discussion of "Acquisition Costs as Start Up Expenses" in Section 8.6.2.

[309] I.R.C. § 195 was added to the I.R.C. by the Miscellaneous Revenue Act of 1980, Pub. L. No. 96-605, 94 Stat. 3521 (1980), effective with respect to amounts paid or incurred after July 29, 1980, in taxable years ending after that date. The section was amended in 1984 by the Deficit Reduction Act of 1984, Pub. L No. 98-369, 98 Stat. 494 (1984). Among the modifications made by the 1984 amendments was the addition of the word "active" to the provision defining when a trade or business begins. I.R.C. § 195(c)(2). I.R.C. § 195 was amended in 1984 to slightly expand the definition of a "start-up expenditure." Congress clarified that a start-up expenditure must be one that otherwise be deductible if incurred by an operating active trade or business.

[310] Sec. 902(a)(1) of the American Jobs Creation Act of 2004, Pub. L. No. 108-357, amending Code Sec. 195(b)(1).

under present law with respect to the proper income tax classification of start-up expenditures."[311] The legislative history of the section indicates further that Congress recognized that there were certain expenses that were necessary to starting-up a business that were ineligible for amortization under section 248 and nondeductible under Code section 162.[312] Code section 195 broadened the scope of expenditures eligible for amortization deduction to include expenses incurred in connection with creating, or investigating the creation or acquisition of, a trade or business. According to its legislative history, expenditures eligible for amortization under Code section 248 are not affected by the enactment of Code section 195.[313]

(c) *Judicial Precedent*

The enactment of Code section 195 followed considerable controversy surrounding the deductibility of start-up expenditures culminating in the Fourth Circuit's decision in *Richmond Television Corp.*[314] In *Richmond Television Corp.*, the taxpayer paid or incurred amounts for employees' salaries and training prior to a decision by the Federal Communications Commission to grant the taxpayer a television station license. The expenditures were found to be nondeductible because they did not satisfy the Code section 162(a) requirement that they be incurred while "carrying on" an active trade or business. The Court's decision turned on its factual finding that the expenditures were incurred before, not after, the taxpayer began carrying on the trade or business.

(d) *Carrying on a Trade or Business*

An expenditure is incurred while "carrying on" a trade or business if it is incurred in connection with the activities of an existing business. Even though the taxpayer may be engaged in business, to be deductible the expenditure must be incurred in connection with the business with respect to which the taxpayer was formed and historically had been operating, not a new activity that has not yet matured to active trade or business status. Expenditures incurred to investigate the creation or acquisition of, or to actually create a trade or business are, by definition, incurred prior to the time that a trade or business is "carried on." In *Wells Fargo and Co.*,[315] the court decided that the acquisition by one bank of another can give to either ordinary and necessary expenses deductible under Code section 162 or expenses that were required to be capitalized under Code section 263. The IRS did not appear to argue that Code section 195 would apply to the extent that the expenditures were not disallowed by Code section 263, presumably because a new trade or business was not being acquired.[316]

---

[311] S. Rep. No. 1036, 96th Cong., 2d Sess. 11 (1980), Miscellaneous Revenue Act of 1980, Pub. L. No. 96-605.

[312] *Id.* at 10.

[313] *Id.* at 11-12.

[314] *Richmond Television Corp. v. United States*, 65-1 U.S.T.C. ¶9395, 345 F.2d 901 (4th Cir. 1965).

[315] *Wells Fargo and Co. v. Commissioner*, 224 F.3d 874 (8th Cir. 2000).

[316] In GCM 20040302F, September 26, 2003, the Office of Chief Counsel of the IRS stated: "The word 'enter' in the Congressional definition of 'investigatory expenses' indicates that the target business is new to the taxpayer: either the taxpayer is not engaged in an existing business or is engaged in a business in a different field. Grammatically, 'business' is the object of both 'acquire' and 'enter.' The meaning of the word 'business' in this context, then, must be such that fits both verbs. It is therefore logical to conclude that the word 'business' can only

Code section 195 legislative history states, "In the case of an existing business, eligible start-up expenditures do not include deductible ordinary and necessary business expenses paid or incurred in connection with an expansion of the business."[317] These expenses are currently deductible.[318] Thus, if the expansion cost is incurred in connection with an existing business, amortization deduction under Code section 195 is not appropriate because a current deduction under Code section 162(a) would be allowed.

Start-up expenditures eligible for amortization do not include any amount with respect to which a deduction would not be allowed to an existing trade or business for the taxable year in which the expenditure was paid or incurred. Thus, to qualify for the Code section 195 amortization deduction, a "start-up expenditure" must pass both an activities (new trade or business) test and a deductibility (ordinary or necessary) test as discussed below.

(i) Relationship between Section 195 and 263. Final regulations promulgated in December 2003 under Code section 263(a) are relevant in determining whether an expenditure constitutes a start-up expenditure within the meaning of Code section 195. Under Code section 263(a), capitalization is required of certain acquisition or creation expenditures that are made "in the process of investigating or otherwise pursuing a transaction"[319] or that are inherently facilitative.[320] An amount cannot constitute a start-up expenditure if the amount is a capital expenditure under Code section 263(a). Amounts that are not required to be capitalized under the Code section 263(a) regulations may, but do not necessarily, constitute start-up expenditures.

The language in the Code section 263 regulations that describes when an amount is paid to facilitate "the acquisition or creation of an intangible (the transaction)" is unfortunately similar to the Code section 195 language that defines a "start-up expenditure." The latter provides that the term "start-up expenditure" means any amount paid or incurred in connection with "investigating the creation or acquisition of an active trade or business . . ."[321] The distinction turns on whether a transaction has begun, which triggers Code section 263, or whether the taxpayer is merely investigating whether to engage in a transaction. The threshold when a taxpayer crosses from Code section 195 to Code section 263 may be far from obvious in practice. However, the regulations under Code section 263 do provide a limited bright line rule when by providing, "An amount paid to determine the value or price of an intangible is an amount paid in the process of investigating or otherwise pursuing the transaction."[322] Of course, if the taxpayer is investigating whether to engage in a transaction that

(Footnote Continued)

mean a business in a field different from the acquirer's. Thus, the Congressional definition of 'investigatory expenses' appears to imply that §195 only applies to acquiring a business in a different field."

[317] H.R. Rep. No. 1278, 96th Cong. 2d Sess. 11 (1980); S. Rep. No. 1036, 96th Cong. 2d Sess. 12 (1980).

[318] *Id.*

[319] Reg. §1.263(a)-4(e)(1)(i) and (iii); Reg. §1.263(a)-5(e)(1)(i) and (ii).

[320] Reg. §1.263(a)-5(e)(2).

[321] I.R.C. §195(c)(1)(A)(i).

[322] Reg. §1.263(a)-4)(e)(1)(i).

involves the same trade or business of the taxpayer, Code section 195 would not be implicated.

(ii) Acquisition of Stock. The legislative history underlying Code section 195 provides that "although investigatory expenses attributable to the acquisition of corporate stock generally will not be eligible for amortization, the investigatory expenses are eligible for amortization under Code section 195 if in substance the taxpayer is investigating a transaction involving the acquisition of the assets of a trade or business, even though one of the steps of the transaction involved the acquisition of the stock."[323] Under at least two circumstances, a stock acquisition will be treated as an asset acquisition.

If the stock of the target is acquired and the target is liquidated, the acquisition will be treated as an asset acquisition, and any investigatory expenses that are "ordinary and necessary" will be eligible for amortization under Code section 195. A stock acquisition also will be treated as an asset acquisition if the target is not liquidated but "the acquired corporation becomes a member of an affiliated group which includes the taxpayer incurring the investigatory expenses and a consolidated income tax return is filed for that group."[324] In such situations, the taxpayer will be treated as having acquired the trade or business assets of the acquired entity, rather than having made a portfolio investment, and the expenses will be eligible for amortization under Code section 195.

As discussed above, only those investigatory expenditures made prior to the date when capitalization is required under Code section 263(a) are eligible for amortization under Code section 195. Therefore, if a taxpayer engages in a "pure" stock acquisition, the only start-up expenses eligible for amortization are the initial investigatory expenses made prior to that date. However, if the stock acquisition will be treated as an asset acquisition, any expenses incurred after the that date can be treated as costs to acquire the assets which are eligible to be depreciated and deducted over time under Code section 197 or 167. Depending on the type of assets acquired, the depreciation deduction period may be shorter than the 15-year amortization period prescribed in Code section 195.

(iii) Activities Test. To meet the activities test, the expenditure must be paid or incurred in connection with one or more of the following three activities:

1. Investigating the creation or acquisition of an active trade or business,[325] or
2. Creating an active trade or business,[326] or
3. An activity engaged in for profit or for the production of income before the day on which the active trade or business begins, in anticipation of such activity becoming an act of trade or business.[327]

---

323 TAM 9901004, January 8, 1999, FN 2; H.R. Rep. No. 1278, 96th Cong. 2d Sess. 12 (1980); S. Rep. No. 1036, 96th Cong., 2d Sess. 13 (1980).

324 *Id.*

325 I.R.C. § 195(c)(1)(A)(i).

326 I.R.C. § 195(c)(1)(A)(ii).

327 I.R.C. § 195(c)(1)(A)(iii).

Investigatory expenses are those costs incurred in reviewing a prospective business prior to reaching a final decision to acquire or enter into the business.[328] If the expenditure is incurred in the course of a general search for, or an investigation of, an active trade or business, it is an investigatory cost. Among the types of expenditures that would qualify as investigatory costs are expenses incurred for the analysis or survey of potential markets, products, labor supply, transportation facilities, and so on.

It had been the IRS's position that an expenditure that is paid or incurred in order to determine whether to enter a new business and which new business to enter will qualify as a start-up expenditure.[329] This "whether-and-which" test provided in Revenue Ruling 99-23 was designed to distinguish costs to investigate the acquisition of a new trade or business (which are amortizable under section 195) from costs to facilitate the acquisition (which are capital expenditures under section 263(a) and are not amortizable under section 195).[330] Under this test, costs incurred to determine whether to acquire a new trade or business, and which new trade or business to acquire, were treated as investigatory costs. Costs incurred in the attempt to acquire a specific business were treated as costs to facilitate the consummation of the acquisition.

In the recently issued regulations under Code section 263(a), the IRS abandoned the "whether-and-which" test in favor of the date rules discussed above. The preamble to the proposed version of the Code section 263(a) regulations promulgated in December 2002 stated that the "whether-and-which" test "has created controversy between taxpayers and the IRS."[331] Accordingly, the final regulations do not adopt the standard contained in the Revenue Ruling 99-23 for purposes of determining capitalization under Code section 263.

Presumably, the abandonment of the "whether and which" test for purposes of determining whether an expenditure must be capitalized under Code section 263(a), also signals its abandonment for purposes of determining whether an expenditure does not qualify as a Code section 195 "start-up" expense. Instead, the date rules contained in the Code section 263(a) regulations should be consistently applied as both the reference for determining when an expenditure is not eligible for Code section 195 amortization and for determining when an expenditure is required to be capitalized under Code section 263.

In many acquisitions, both the acquiring corporation and the target may incur start-up expenditures. The dates when expenditures begin to qualify as start-up expenses and when they cross the Code section 263(a) threshold could differ for each party to an acquisition. It could be that the acquiring firm does not inform the target of its intention to acquire until after the former makes its decision. Furthermore, the acquiring firm may incur expenditures that are for services different than those incurred by the acquiring firm. Thus, to determine when the Code section 263 threshold is crossed there must be an independent analysis of when the Code section 263 is reached by each party.

---

[328] S. Rep. No. 1036, 96th cong., 2d Sess. 11 (1980).

[329] Rev. Rul. 99-23, 1999-1 C.B. 998.

[330] Rev. Rul. 99-23, 1999-1 C.B. 998.

[331] Preamble to Prop. Reg. § 1.263(a)-4, at V, B.

Costs incurred to conduct industry research and review public financial information are typically general investigatory expenses under Code section 195. However, if the expenditure relates to appraisals of the target's assets and an in-depth review of the target's books and records to establish the purchase price, it is a capital expenditure that would not be eligible for amortization under Code section 195.[332] Costs to evaluate competitors to the target firm may be investigatory costs depending on the purpose for which they are incurred. If they are incurred to assist the acquiring firm in determining whether to acquire a business and which business to acquire, they would qualify as investigatory costs. They would not qualify if the costs were incurred to establish the purchase price or for any other purpose after the decision to acquire the target occurred.[333] One indication of when the decision to acquire a firm has been made is when the acquirer's board of directors approves the material terms of the acquisition.[334] Regardless of when they were acquired, if the costs are incurred for the purpose of drafting documents needed to secure regulatory approval of the acquisition, the costs are not investigatory costs. They are, instead, costs that fall under the Regulation Section 1.263(a) -5 definition of inherently facilitative costs and must be capitalized.[335]

Investigatory expenses qualify for the Code section 195 amortization deduction only if they are incurred in connection with investigating the creation or acquisition of an active trade or business. Expenditures attributable to an investment would not be eligible for amortization, and whether an activity is an investment activity or a business activity will not be determined solely on the basis of whether property used in the activity would qualify as a Code section 1231 asset. A taxpayer will be considered to have entered into an active trade or business only if the taxpayer has an equity interest in, and actively participates in the management of, the trade or business. Thus, if the investigatory expenses are incurred with respect to the acquisition of common stock, the taxpayer would usually be considered to have acquired an investment interest rather than a qualifying trade or business interest. However, the legislative history to Code section 195 makes it clear that if, in substance, a transaction is the acquisition of the assets of a trade or business, the investigatory expenses are eligible for amortization even though one of the steps in the transaction involved the acquisition of stock.[336] The legislative history also provides that a corporate taxpayer is treated as having acquired the assets of a trade or business if: (a) it acquires the stock of another corporation; (b) the acquired corporation becomes a member of an affiliated group that includes the acquiring taxpayer who incurs the investigatory expenses, and (c) a consolidated income tax return is filed for the group.[337]

---

[332] Rev. Rul. 99-23, 1999-1 C.B. 998; *Ellis Banking Corp. v. Commissioner*, T.C. Memo 1981-123, *aff'd in part and rem'd in part*, 688 F.2d 1376 (11th Cir. 1982).

[333] *Id.*

[334] Reg. § 1.263(a)-5(e)(1)(i).

[335] Reg. § 1.263(a)-5(e)(2)(iv).

[336] It does not seem unreasonable to take the position that depreciation on assets acquired prior to when an active trade or business begins but which are used in the investigation or creation of that business may be treated as I.R.C. § 195 expenditures.

[337] H.R. Rep. No. 1278, 96th Cong., 2nd Sess. 12 (1980); S. Rep. No. 1036, 96th Cong., 2nd Sess. 13 (1980).

Expenses qualify as "creating an active trade or business" if they are incurred subsequent to a decision to acquire or establish a particular business and prior to the time that the business begins. Such costs include advertising, salaries and wages paid to employees for being trained and to their instructors, travel and other expenses incurred in lining up prospective distributors, suppliers or customers, and salaries or fees paid or incurred for executives, consultants, and or similar professional services preparatory to commencing business.[338]

(iv) Deductibility Test. To meet the deductibility test, start-up expenditures must be both "ordinary and necessary," as that term is used in Code section 162,[339] and their deductibility must not be denied because they are expenditures that constitute "permanent improvements or betterments made to increase the value of any property or estate," within the meaning of Code section 263.[340] Thus, the expenditures must be appropriate and helpful ("necessary"); they must be related to a situation that is not unique in the existence of the classification of entities of which the taxpayer is one ("ordinary"); and they may not create a separate and distinct asset with a life extending substantially beyond the end of the taxable year or provide a substantial future benefit.

The expenditure must be one which would be allowable as a deduction for the taxable year in which paid or incurred if it were paid or incurred in connection with the operation of an existing active trade or business in the same field as the trade or business with respect to which it was paid or incurred.[341] Excluded from the definition of a "start-up expenditure" is any amount with respect to which a deduction is allowable under Code section 163 (interest), Code section 164 (taxes), or Code section 174 (research and experimental expenditures).[342]

The IRS has held that expenditures incurred by a target bank in connection with the acquisition are not start-up expenditures eligible for amortization under Code section 195 when they are expenses of acquisition in the nature of Code section 263 expenditures. Such expenditures are not allowable as a current deduction if paid or incurred in connection with an existing active trade or business in the same field as the acquired business. Accordingly, the expenditures do not meet the requirement for start-up expenditures under Code section 195(c)(1)(B).[343]

---

[338] It does not seem unreasonable to take the position that depreciation on assets acquired prior to when an active trade or business begins, but which are used in the investigation or creation of that business, may be treated as I.R.C. § 195 expenditures.

[339] *Welch v. Helvering*, 290 U.S. 111 (1933).

[340] *INDOPCO, Inc. v. Commissioner*, 92-1 U.S.T.C. ¶ 50,113, 503 U.S. 79 (1992); *Commissioner v. Lincoln Savings and Loan Ass'n*, 403 U.S. 345 (1971); *Commissioner v. Tellier*, 383 U.S. 687 (1966); *Encyclopedia Britannica v. Commissioner*, 685 F.2d 212 (7th Cir. 1982). Reg. § 1.461-1(a).

[341] *Duecaster v. Commissioner*, 60 T.C.M. 917, Dec. 46,902(M)(1990), T.C. Memo. 1990-518.

[342] I.R.C. § 195(c)(1). Note that depreciation is not listed among nonstart-up expenditures.

[343] TAM 9825005, March 20, 1998.

(e) *Electing Code Section 195*

Regulations issued under Code section 195(d) provide strict rules and procedures for electing to amortize start-up expenditures.[344] Pursuant to Code section 195, an election to amortize start-up expenditures must be made not later than the time prescribed by law for filing the return for the taxable year in which the active trade or business begins (including extensions thereof). The regulations confirm that an election to amortize start-up expenditures must be made by attaching a statement to the taxpayer's income tax return. A taxpayer that is uncertain as to the year in which the active trade or business begins need not file an election for each possible tax year. Rather, a Code section 195 election for a particular trade or business will be effective if the trade or business becomes active in the year for which the election is filed or in any subsequent year. Furthermore, the regulations allow taxpayers who have made timely elections to file a revised statement with a subsequent return to include certain start-up expenditures not described in the original statement.

Although the regulations may appear to grant taxpayers some flexibility, in at least one important respect, taxpayers will be operating under a significant constraint. According to the regulations, the required statement must:

> set forth a description of the trade or business to which the expenses relate with sufficient detail so that expenses relating to the trade or business can be identified properly for the taxable year in which the statement is filed and for all future taxable years to which it relates. The statement also shall include the number of months (not less than 60) over which the expenditures are to be amortized, and to the extent known at the time the statement is filed, a description of each start-up expenditure incurred (whether or not paid) and the month in which the active trade or business began (or was acquired). A revised statement may be filed to include any start-up expenditures not included in the taxpayer's original election statement, **but the revised statement may not include any expenditures for which the taxpayer had previously taken a position on a return inconsistent with their treatment as start-up expenditures.** The revised statement may be filed with a return filed after the return that contained the election. [Emphasis added.][345]

Thus, the availability of what some taxpayers commonly referred to as a protective Code section 195 election has been eliminated. The requirement that the trade or business must be identified with "sufficient detail so that expenses relating to the trade or business can be identified properly for the taxable year" places taxpayers in the position of having to identify the start-up activity with some precision. Under the regulations, a taxpayer would apparently not make a valid election if the statement merely provided that if the taxpayer had any start-up expenditures, the taxpayer elected to amortize those expenditures under Code section 195. Much more precision is required. Furthermore, the prohibition against amortizing additional expenditures that are treated "inconsistent with

[344] Reg. § 1.195-1 *et seq.* Announcement 81-43, 1981-1 I.R.B. 52, earlier described the time and manner for making the election. The regulations are effective with respect to elections filed on or after December 17, 1998.

[345] Reg. § 1.195-1(c). The amortization period is no longer 60 months. Effective for start-up expenditures paid or incurred after October 22, 2004, a 180-month amortization period must be used.

their treatment as start-up expenditures" appears to prohibit a reclassification of previously deducted items. On audit, the only issue should be whether the taxpayer has identified all expenditures that relate to the activity.

The amortization period must commence with the month in which business begins. The determination of when a business begins that is not acquired is to be made by reference to the existing provisions for the amortization of organizational expenditures contained in Code section 248 and, with respect to partnerships, Code section 709.[346] Generally, a business will be deemed to have begun if the activities of the corporation have advanced to the extent necessary to establish the nature of its business operations.[347] An acquired trade or business is treated as beginning with the month in which a taxpayer acquires it.

(f) *Book Accounting*

The Financial Accounting Standards Board released a Statement of Position ("SOP") that requires costs of start-up activities and organizational costs to be expensed as incurred. The SOP applies to all non-governmental entities and is effective for financial statements for fiscal years beginning after December 15, 1998.[348] Excepted from the scope of the SOP are: costs of acquiring or constructing long-lived assets and getting them ready for their intended uses; costs of acquiring or producing inventory; costs of acquiring intangible assets; costs related to internally developed assets; costs that are within the scope of Financial Accounting Standards Board Statement No. 2, "accounting for research and development costs," and FASB Statement No. 71, "accounting for the effects of certain types of regulation"; costs of fundraising incurred by not-for-profit organizations; costs of raising capital; costs of advertising; costs incurred in connection with existing contracts as stated in ¶ 75d of SOP 81-1, "accounting for performance of construction-type and certain production-type contracts."[349]

Because the book accounting treatment requires current expensing of start-up and organizational expenditures, but the tax accounting requires deferral, a Schedule M adjustment must be made to reconcile the book treatment with the tax treatment. IRS agents may expect to see such adjustments for taxpayers that are expanding their activities.

§ 8.9.3 Organizational Expenditures—Code Section 248

(a) *Legislative History*

Code section 248 was enacted to allow an amortization deduction for expenses incurred on behalf of a corporation prior to the date the corporation begins business and incident to its creation.[350] Mere organizational activities, such

---

[346] Senate Committee Report on the Miscellaneous Revenue Act of 1980, Pub. L. No. 96-605, § 102 (1980).

[347] Reg. § 1.248-1(a)(3).

[348] The bank regulatory rule is found at FFIEC 031, 032, 033, and 034 at page A-64 (9-97), which provides that "pre-opening expenses such as salaries and employment benefits, rent, depreciation, supplies, directors' fees, training, travel, postage, and telephone are *not* considered organizational costs and should not be capitalized. In addition, allocated internal costs (*e.g.*, management salaries) shall not be capitalized as organizational costs.

[349] Statement of Position 98-5 (April 3, 1998).

[350] Section 248 was added to the law with the enactment of the Internal Revenue Code of 1954, P.L. 591. *See* H.R. Rep. No. 1337, 83rd Cong., 2d Sess. 4056 (1954).

as the obtaining of a corporate charter, are not alone sufficient to demonstrate that the corporation began business. However, if a corporation acquires operating assets that are necessary to the type of business that it will engage in, this will probably constitute the beginning of business. These costs are nondeductible because they are not "ordinary;" that is, because they are "chargeable to capital account."[351] Amortization of Code section 248 expenditures had previously been allowed only when their useful life could be determined by establishing a limited term of existence, which was unlikely in the majority of cases where the corporate life is perpetual. As a result, under pre-Code section 248 law, organization expenses could be recovered only in the year of corporate liquidation. The legislative history of Code section 248 indicates that by allowing corporations to amortize such expenditures, the tax accounting would more closely conform to the general business accounting used for such costs.[352]

For organization expenses paid or incurred after October 22, 2004, corporations may elect to deduct up to $5,000 (but not below zero) of organizational expenditures for the tax year in which the corporation begins business.[353] The $5,000 amount must be reduced by the amount by which the organizational expenditures exceed $50,000. The corporation may deduct any remainder of organizational expenditures ratably over the 180-month period beginning with the month in which the corporation begins business.

(b) ***Operation of Section 248***

Code section 248 provides that to be eligible for an amortization deduction for organizational expenditures, the expenditure must be:

1. Incident to the creation of the corporation;
2. Chargeable to capital account; and
3. Of a character which, if expended incident to the creation of a corporation having a limited life, would be amortizable over such life.[354]

§ 8.9.4 Comparison of Code Sections 195 and 248

The following lists are expenditures for which an amortization deduction is allowed under Code section 195, allowed under Code section 248, and those expenditures that are not deductible under either section.

(a) ***Code Section 248 Expenditures***

Expenditures that have been found to be amortizable under Code section 248 include expenditures for:[355]

- Legal services incident to the organization of the corporation, excluding drafting the corporate charter, by-laws, and terms of original stock certificates,

[351] I.R.C. § 248(b)(2).

[352] *Id.*

[353] The American Jobs Creation Act of 2004 Act Sec. 902(b), amending Code Sec. 248(a). *See also* Act Sec. 902(c)(1), amending Code Sec. 709(b)(1)-(3) and Act Sec. 902(c)(2), amending Code Sec. 709(b); Act Sec. 902(d).

[354] I.R.C. § 248(b).

[355] Reg. § 1.248-1(b)(2).

- Necessary accounting expenses,
- Expenses of temporary directors of the corporation,
- Fees paid to the State of incorporation, and[356]
- Expenses related to organizational meetings of directors and stockholders, including drafting of minutes.

(b) ***Code Section 195 Expenditures***

Expenditures that have been found to be amortizable under Code section 195, but not under Code section 248, include expenditures for:[357]

- Consulting fees for analysis or survey of potential markets, products, labor supply, transportation facilities,
- Advertising expenses,
- Salaries and wages of employees who are being trained for new business, along with instructors' salaries,
- Travel and other expenses for lining-up prospective distributors, suppliers, and customers, and
- Professional services in setting up books and records for start-up activity.

(c) ***Neither Code Section 195 Nor 248 Expenditures***

Expenditures that have been found not to be amortizable under either Code section 195 or section 248 include expenditures for:[358]

- Issuing shares of stock or other securities, such as commissions, professional fees, printing costs, etc.,
- Expenses connected with reorganizing a corporation,
- Acquisition costs of stock or assets of a trade or business,[359]
- Expenses associated with transferring assets to a corporation, and
- Investment banking fees and other costs associated with a friendly takeover.[360]

§8.9.5 Electing Code Section 248

Legislative history indicates that Congress expects that the election procedures of Code section 195 and Code section 248 to be similar.[361] The election to amortize start-up expenditures must be made no later than the time prescribed for filing the federal tax return (including extensions) for the taxable year in which the trade or business begins.[362] The election to amortize organizational expenditures applies only with respect to such expenditures incurred before the

[356] H.R. Rep. No. 1337, 83d Cong. 2d Sess. 4201 (1954); Reg. §1.248-1(b)(2).

[357] S. Rep. No. 1036, 96th Cong., 2d Sess. 11 (1980); H.R. Rep. No. 1337, 83d Cong. 2d Sess. 4201 (1954); Reg. §1.248-1(b)(3).

[358] Reg. §1.248(b)(3), S. Rep. No. 1036, 96th Cong., 2d Sess., 11 (1980).

[359] *Ellis Banking Corp. v. Commissioner*, 82-2 U.S.T.C. ¶9630, 688 F.2d 1376 (11th Cir. 1982).

[360] *INDOPCO, Inc. v. Commissioner*, 503 U.S. 79 (1992). *But cf. Victory Markets v. Commissioner*, 99 T.C. 648 (1992).

[361] S. Rep. No. 1036, 96th Cong., 2d Sess. 14 (1980).

[362] I.R.C. §195(d)(1); Reg. §1.195-1(a); I.R.C. §248(b); Reg. §1.248-1(c).

end of the taxable year in which the corporation begins business.[363] Once an amortization period is selected, it may not be changed. The selected period must be used in computing taxable income for the taxable year in which the election is made and for all subsequent taxable years.[364] For example, if a bank trains its employees to improve their ability to market the bank's products and services, then the expenditures are currently deductible, even though the training may have some future benefit. Moreover, training that has the effect of reducing future operating and capital costs, but which does not result in the creation or acquisition of an assets, also is currently deductible.[365] Furthermore, training expenditures (as well as other expenditures) that are incurred to build a workforce for a new division are currently deductible.[366]

§ 8.10 Business Expansion and New Product Expenditures

Expenses incurred to expand a firm's geographic presence and its product line have been frequently challenged by the IRS on grounds that the expenditures are not "ordinary and necessary," they are not incurred in "carrying on" a trade or business, or they are Code section 263 capital expenditures. Several cases have considered the deductibility of these expenditures incurred by banks and in nearly all situations, a current Code section 162 deduction was allowed. The final regulations under Code section 263(a) that address the capitalization of intangibles appear to adopt the judicial principles articulated in several of these case.

§ 8.10.1 Branch Pre-Opening Costs

As a general rule, costs incurred by a bank for the purposes of opening new branches are currently deductible. Such costs are recurring, and they qualify as costs incurred in "carrying on" a trade or business. They do not result in the acquisition or creation of an intangible asset. As the Seventh Circuit has stated and the IRS has acknowledged, "the distinctions between recurring expenditures and nonrecurring expenditures provides a crude demarcation in determining whether an expenditure should be capitalized or deducted currently."[367] Furthermore, such costs typically generate short-term benefits. Employee training costs that may be incurred in connection with opening a new branch usually generate short-term benefits because of the high rate of employee turn-over and the fact that the training occurs in connection with the same functions performed by existing employees.[368]

§ 8.10.2 Branch Geographic Expansion Costs

If a taxpayer incurs costs to geographically expand the locations at which it operates its existing business, it will likely incur Code section 162 ordinary and

[363] Reg. § 1.248-1(a)(2).

[364] I.R.C. § 195(d)(2).

[365] Rev. Rul. 95-32, 1995-1 C.B. 8.

[366] FSA 199918013, January 12, 1999.

[367] *Encyclopedia Britannica, Inc. v. Commissioner*, 685 F.2d 212 (7th Cir. 1982); TAM 9645002, November 8, 1996; Rev. Rul. 89-23, 1989-1 C.B. 85. The Tax Court has recently concluded that the recurring nature of an expenditure is to be viewed as controlling in determining whether an expenditure is an ordinary and necessary business expense. *PNC Bancorp, Inc. v. Commissioner*, 110 T.C. No. 27 (1988).

[368] *Fidelity Associates, Inc. v. Commissioner*, T.C. Memo 94-142 (1994); *Sun Microsystems, Inc. v. Commissioner*, T.C. Memo 93-467 (1993).

necessary business expenses and not nondeductible "start-up" or Code section 263(a) expenditures.[369] However, with respect to the treatment of the preliminary costs incurred to obtain approval of a bank regulatory agency to establish a new branch, it is the IRS's position that such expenses are not deductible because they create a separate and distinct asset. Regulation section 1.263(a)-4(d)(5)(i) provides generally that capitalization is required of amounts paid by a taxpayer to obtain, renegotiate, or upgrade its rights under a license, permit or similar right granted by a governmental agency.[370]

In Technical Advice Memorandum 8141033, the IRS considered the deductibility of certain costs incurred in establishing four new branch facilities as part of an expansion program of an existing savings and loan association. The taxpayer under examination established that the purpose of opening the new branches was to better serve the needs of its existing customers and also to attract new customers located in areas where the taxpayer had traditionally not been competitive. The IRS found that the business activity of the taxpayer was the same both before and after the new branches were opened, and the activity was conducted in the same manner at the taxpayer's main office as at the new branches. Thus, the IRS concluded that the expenses incurred were deductible as Code section 162 ordinary and necessary business expenses incurred in carrying on an existing trade or business. They were not "start-up" costs, nor were they expenditures that were denied deductibility under Code section 263. A current deduction was also allowed for promotional expenditures, such as expenditures for advertising, printing and merchandise distributed to customers.[371]

In *NCNB Corp. v. United States*[372] and *Central Texas Savings and Loan Association v. United States*,[373] two federal circuit courts reached opposite conclusions on whether a Code section 162 deduction would be allowed when a bank expands its branch network.

NCNB Corp. was decided at the trial court level prior to the issuance of Technical Advice Memorandum 8141033, discussed above, but it was finally decided by the Fourth Circuit after the Technical Advice Memorandum was

---

[369] TAM 8141033, June 30, 1981. The IRS may argue that a new physical location is a new trade or business. For this position to be feasible, the taxpayer could not have been "carrying on" the trade or business prior to establishing the new location.

[370] In GCM 20040302F, September 26, 2003, the Office of Chief Counsel of the IRS stated: "In enacting § 195, Congress did not contemplate ordinary and necessary business expenses paid or incurred in connection with the expansion of an existing business. Congress noted that these expenses were already deductible under the then existing law . . . . Congress was only concerned with those that were ordinary and necessary yet could not be deducted under § 162 because they were not paid or incurred in carrying on a business."

[371] *Id.* In the Technical Advice Memorandum, the IRS did state that some of the promotional expenditures produced benefits that extended to later years. Because this Technical Advice Memorandum was issued prior to the Supreme Court's opinion in *INDOPCO*, in which the Court clarified that the separate asset test was not the exclusive test for determining capitalization. Instead, as discussed above, the future benefit test should be regarded as an alternative to the separate asset test. Concerning the merchandise distributed to customers *see* Reg. § 1.162-20(a)(2).

[372] *NCNB Corp. v. United States*, 82-2 U.S.T.C. ¶9469, 684 F.2d 285 (4th Cir. 1982). NCNB North Carolina National Bank was renamed NationsBank.

[373] *Central Texas Savings and Loan Assoc. v. United States*, 84-1 U.S.T.C. ¶9471, 731 F.2d 1181 (5th Cir. 1984).

issued. The case involved the deductibility of expenditures similar to the preliminary expenditures discussed in the Technical Advice Memorandum.

During the six-year period, 1965 to 1970, NCNB incurred approximately $1,000,000 of expenditures associated with a branch expansion program. It deducted the expansion costs as ordinary and necessary business expenses. These expenditures consisted of approximately $200,000 of external costs for consultants, attorneys and governmental fees, and $800,000 for allocated internal costs. The expenditures included costs for two types of studies, "metro studies" and "feasibility studies," and also for costs associated with applications to the Comptroller of the Currency.

The metro studies were long-range planning reports which contained recommendations and strategies for NCNB in various regions of the state. The studies concerned both existing facilities and opportunities to expand into new geographic areas. They were prepared both internally and by outside consultants. The feasibility studies focused on specific proposed branch locations. These studies typically followed the metro study in time and evaluated the economics of various expansion options. The applications to the Comptroller of the Currency were for the purpose of obtaining the statutorily required authorization before a national bank may open new branch offices. Costs associated with these applications included the application fee itself, internal staff time to prepare the application, outside legal fees and related expenses connected with the application.

The Fourth Circuit identified the principal issue as being whether the expenditures were "ordinary and necessary," not whether they were incurred in "carrying on" an existing trade or business. This latter requirement contained in Code section 162 was assumed to have been met for the apparent reason that the Court found that "all of these expenses were connected with NCNB's developing and operating a statewide network of branch banking facilities."[374] Apparently, although the taxpayer was expanding its business into "new territories,"[375] the business that the taxpayer was expanding was one in which the taxpayer was already "carrying on."

The Court noted that the permission sought from the Comptroller of the Currency was only to "establish and operate" a new branch.[376] As such, it was factually different from many other government licenses: it did not grant an exclusive territorial franchise; it was not transferable; the branch bank was not readily saleable as such; and the branch had no value except as was inherent in its tangible and real assets.[377] Further, the Court noted the "long-established policy" of the Comptroller of the Currency to require national banks to charge to current operations all expenditures relating to the development and expansion of banking services.[378] This required regulatory accounting policy was "presump-

[374] 684 F.2d at 289.

[375] *Id.* at 290.

[376] 12 U.S.C. § 36(c) (1997).

[377] This language is similar to that used to describe one of the characteristics of goodwill.

[378] Letter from Comptroller of the Currency to Assistant Secretary for Tax Policy, United States Treasury Department, Aug. 21, 1972.

tively controlling" for federal income tax purposes.[379] For these reasons, the Court concluded that the expenditures in question were incurred to maintain a statewide branch network, and they did not create or enhance any separate and identifiable asset.[380]

In *Central Texas Savings and Loan Association*, the taxpayer also incurred various expenses to expand its branch system.[381] The Fifth Circuit concluded that the expenditures incurred to establish its new branches were nondeductible. In a well-reasoned opinion that could be said to articulate the position expressed eight years later by the Supreme Court in *INDOPCO*, the Court concluded that a multifaceted test should be applied. It found that while the period over which benefits flowing from an expenditure are realized may not be controlling in all cases, it nonetheless remains a prominent, if not predominant, characteristic of a capital item.[382]

Along with this nascent future benefit test, the Court considered whether the expenditures were incurred in "carrying on" an existing trade or business. It reasoned that, "It would seem anomalous to say that if a taxpayer purchases or merges with a savings and loan in another city, it must capitalize the investigative and start up costs; but if it establishes a new office these same costs may be deducted under Section 162(a)."[383]

The Court then turned to whether the expenditures were capital in nature. It found that the permit received from the bank regulator was a one-time payment that gave the taxpayer the right to operate for an indefinite period of time. The benefit secured by the permit extended beyond the taxable year in which it was paid or incurred. The permit granted a separate right to do business in a new territory in which the taxpayer had a right to receive new accounts for new customers in a new market. Thus, it found that *Central Texas* acquired a property interest in its branch offices. It gained the right to challenge the entry of competitors into the market, and it was an easily valued right at the time the permit was acquired. The taxpayer was found to have obtained a separate and identifiable business right that was exercised in a separate office, by a separate staff, in an exclusive territory. Finally, the Court concluded that the current deduction of investigatory and start-up expenses was an inaccurate reflection of the timing of when the benefits or income of the taxpayer is realized. Because the expenses procured a future benefit, the tax treatment should reflect this "longevity" by deferring any deduction.[384]

---

[379] *NCNB*, 684 F.2d 285 at 292. *See also Commissioner v. Idaho Power Co.*, 74-2 U.S.T.C. ¶9521, 418 U.S. 1 (1974).

[380] *NCNB* was decided under the *Lincoln Savings* separate asset test. The *NCNB* court stated that "costs incurred in expanding a business are not considered capital costs unless they meet the *Lincoln Savings and Loan* 'separate and distinct additional asset' test." *NCNB*, 684 F.2d at 291 (1982). Thus, the Court rejected the panel decision, 651 F.2d 942, 962-63 (4th Cir. 1981) in which the panel concluded that "benefits from the expenditures in question extended beyond the individual accounting years and thus the taxpayer could not deduct them as current expenses in the years incurred."

[381] *Central Texas Savings and Loan Assoc. v. United States*, 84-1 U.S.T.C. ¶9471, 731 F.2d 1181 (5th Cir. 1984).

[382] *Id.* at 1882.

[383] *Id.*

[384] *Id.* at 1884. Although I.R.C. § 195 was enacted prior to the decision in *Central Texas*, the taxable years before the Court predated the effective date (June 29, 1980) of that section. The Court refrained from deciding whether the branch opening expendi-

The Treasury Department and the IRS have now acknowledged that the future benefits test is not a workable tool for determining whether an expenditure should be capitalized. As a result, in the final regulations under Code section 263(a), they have chosen to abandon the test in favor of an exclusive list of eight types of created intangibles that are required to be capitalized. It does not appear that any of the types listed would have prevented the taxpayers in NCNB or Central Texas from currently deducting most of the expenditures they paid to expand their branch system, with the possible exception of those expenditures to obtain permission from bank regulators for branch expansion.

More recently, in a non-bank audit, but in a situation that could be analogized to a branch bank expansion, the IRS allowed a current deduction for numerous pre-opening expenses associated with expanding the taxpayers' existing business including: internal payroll expense; maintenance, service, and supplies; utilities and occupancy; communication; office, non-selling, and janitorial supplies; selling supplies; equipment rental; relocation; recruiting; travel; security; freight and postage; and personnel in training.[385] The IRS reasoned that the costs had a recurring nature, and they appeared to generate predominantly short-term benefits. The taxpayer under examination was undertaking the opening of stores as part of a long-term expansion program. The stores were operationally indistinguishable from one another and from the taxpayer's other established stores.

§ 8.10.3 Training Costs

As a general rule, amounts paid or incurred for training, including the costs of trainers and routine updates of training materials, are generally deductible as business expenses under Code section 162.[386] This is true even though the costs may provide some future benefit.[387] Training costs must be capitalized only in the unusual circumstance where the training is intended primarily to obtain future benefits significantly beyond those traditionally associated with training provided in the ordinary course of a taxpayer's trade or business.[388]

(Footnote Continued)

tures would meet the requirement contained in I.R.C. § 195(b)(2) that they must be those that would be deductible if they were paid in connection with the expansion of an existing business.

[385] TAM 9645002, June 21, 1996. *See also Fidelity Associates, Inc. v. Commissioner*, T.C. Memo. 94-142 (1994); *Sun Microsystems, Inc. v. Commissioner*, T.C. Memo. 93-467 (1993).

[386] Rev. Rul. 96-62, 1996-1 C.B. 9; FSA 199918013, May 7, 1999.

[387] *INDOPCO Inc. v. Commissioner*, 503 U.S. 79, 87 (1992). *See, e.g., Cleveland Electric Illuminating Co. v. United States*, 7 Cl. Ct. 220 (1985) (deduction for costs of training employees to operate new equipment in an existing business); Rev. Rul. 58-238, 1958-1 C.B. 90, 91 (deduction for costs of training employees that relate to the regular conduct of the employer's business); *see also Ithaca Industries, Inc. v. Commissioner*, 97 T.C. 253, 271 (1991) (deduction for costs of training new employees to keep the assembled workforce unchanged), *aff'd*, 17 F.3d 684 (4th Cir.), *cert. denied*, 115 S. Ct. 83 (1994).

[388] *See, e.g., Cleveland Electric*, 7 Cl. Ct. at 227-29 (capitalization of costs for training employees of an electric utility to operate a new nuclear power plant, which were akin to start-up costs of a new business, was required). Rev. Rul. 96-62, 1996-2 C.B. 9.

§8.10.4 Promotional and Selling Costs

In *Lykes Energy, Inc. v. Commissioner of Internal Revenue,*[389] the Tax Court did not permit a natural gas company to deduct certain promotional and selling expenditures made to increase its customer base. The court used sweeping language which suggests a new test for determining when an expense is considered "ordinary" for purposes of Code section 162(a). In *Lykes*, the Tax Court held that only those expenses that "relate primarily" to income generated from a sale in the current year are "ordinary" and deductible under Code section 162(a). Thus the courts held promotional or selling expenses unrelated to a specific sale in the current year must be capitalized under Code section 263(a).[390]

Promotional and selling expenses not tied to a specific sale were found to increase the taxpayer's customer base. The gaining of new customers yielded a significant future benefit to the taxpayer that was more than incidental. The only deductible expenditures allowed by the Tax Court were for subsidies paid to customers to induce them to purchase energy saving appliances. Promotional and selling expenditures not tied to a specific sale, such as energy conservation audits and the costs to install gas lines and appliances, were not deductible. The projected revenue stream resulting from the selling and promotional expenditures was found to yield significant future benefits that justified capitalization. Although the language in *Lykes* is broad and does not appear to limit its ruling to the specific facts and circumstances of the case, it ignores existing Treasury Regulations and Revenue Rulings and therefore may not apply in many circumstances. Furthermore, the Tax Court's opinion is unclear as to whether the expenditures were not deductible because they were not "ordinary" or because they were with respect to "permanent improvements and betterments."

Under the final Code section 263(a) regulations, whether promotion, selling, and advertising expenditures are required to be capitalized will not be determined under the *INDOPCO* future benefits test, as such.[391] In most situations, these expenditures will be currently deductible because they neither create a separate and distinct intangible asset, are not one of the future benefits that must be capitalized under the regulations, nor do they constitute the acquisition of a trade or business. Furthermore, most internal costs (employee compensation and overhead) and de minimis external costs (excluding commissions) are deductible under certain simplifying conventions.

§8.10.5 Advertising Costs

Regulation section 1.162-1(a) specifically provides that advertising and other selling expenses are deductible business expenses. In Revenue Ruling 92-80, the IRS held that *INDOPCO* did not affect the treatment of advertising costs as ordinary and necessary business expenses that are generally deductible under Code section 162(a).[392] Regulation section 1.162-20(a)(2) provides that expenditures for institutional or goodwill advertising which keep the taxpayer's name

---

[389] *Lykes Energy, Inc. v. Commissioner,* 77 T.C.M. 1535 (1999).

[390] *Id.*

[391] *See* Reg. § 1.263(a)-4 generally.

[392] Rev. Rul. 92-80, 1992-2 C.B. 57.

before the public are generally deductible as ordinary and necessary business expenses, provided the expenditures are related to the patronage the taxpayer might reasonably expect in the future. Even though advertising may have some future effect on business activities, only when advertising is directed towards obtaining future benefits significantly beyond those traditionally associated with ordinary product advertising, or institutional or goodwill advertising, must the cost of advertising be capitalized.[393] Perhaps when advertising goes beyond "traditional" advertising because the taxpayer seeks to obtain significant future benefits, *i.e.* by increasing its customer base, the advertising expenses become "promotional" and would be capitalized under the *Lykes* analysis. In any event, Regulation 1.263(a)-4 no longer requires the future benefits test to be applied to these items.

What constitutes an advertising expenditure is not necessarily always clear. The term advertising is not a term of art for federal income tax purposes.[394] *The American Heritage Dictionary of the English Language* defines advertising as "the activity of attracting public attention to a product or business as by paid announcements in print or on the air."[395] The current textbook definition is the 1948 definition of the American Marketing Association, which provides, "Any paid form of non-personal presentation and promotion of ideas, goods, or services by an identified sponsor, which involves the use of mass media."[396]

In *RJR Nabisco Inc.* the IRS attempted unsuccessfully to draw a distinction between advertising expenditures that create an advertising campaign and expenditures that execute the campaign. To the IRS, the former are long-term oriented and the latter contribute to income earned in the current accounting period. Although the court rejected this distinction, the reasoning advanced is somewhat questionable. It appears that on the one hand the court acknowledged that the distinction had merit. Nevertheless, it rejected the IRS's argument on the authority of Revenue Ruling 92-80 and Regulation sections 1.162-1 and -20.[397] The court stated:

> Although the case law admits the possibility of allocation between the short- and long-term benefits of advertising expenditures and, thus, would provide a basis for the Commissioner to insist that a taxpayer prove the portion of his advertising expenditures allocable to current benefits, the authorities previously cited, section 1.162-20(a)(2), Income Tax Regs., and Rev. Rul. 92-80, supra, establish that the Secretary and the Commissioner, respectively, have eschewed that approach with respect to ordinary business advertising, even if long-term benefits (*e.g.* goodwill) are the taxpayer's primary objective.[398]

---

[393] *Id.*

[394] T.C. Memo. 252 (1998). 76 T.C.M. (CCH) 71 (1998).

[395] *The American Heritage Dictionary*, 3rd edition (1992).

[396] American Marketing Association.

[397] The IRS earlier ruled that "salaries and advertising are less directly and significantly productive of intangible assets having a value extending beyond the taxable years in which they were paid or incurred. Such expenditures may, therefore, be treated as ordinary and necessary business expenses deductible under section 162 of the Code." Rev. Rul. 68-561, 1968-2 C.B. 117.

[398] 76 T.C.M. (CCH) 71, 82.

This statement is made despite the court acknowledging that "Rev. Rul. 92-80, *supra,* may raise some question of just what are benefits traditionally associated with ordinary product advertising or with institutional or goodwill advertising, there is no doubt that such traditional benefits include not only patronage but also the expectancy of patronage (*i.e.*, goodwill)."[399]

§ 8.10.6 Mutual Fund Costs

In a Securities and Financial Industry Coordinated Issue Paper, the IRS concluded that the costs incurred by investment advisors to obtain management contracts by creating new mutual funds are required to be capitalized under Code section 263(a).[400] The costs in question were incurred before the management contracts were entered into. The contracts were between an investment advisor and a mutual fund, and they determined the investment advisor's responsibilities with respect to management fund assets. It was believed to be extremely unlikely that the management contract would be terminated or not renewed. Instead, they were expected to remain in force as long as a particular fund remains in operation.

The IRS analogized the expenditures incurred that result in the creation of a mutual fund with the expenditures discussed in *INDOPCO*, which were found to create a significant long-term benefit for the taxpayer. The existence of the fund was found to confer a significant long-term benefit on the investment advisor because the advisor expected to realize significant economic benefits from long-term contractual relationships with the fund.[401] The IRS also concluded that the relationship between the investment advisor and the mutual fund was a separate and distinct asset with an expected life of more than one year.

Amounts paid to create this type of intangible asset now appear to be governed by Regulation 1.263(a)-4(d). As such, unless the expenditure creates one of the eight intangibles listed in that regulation, the cost to create it would not be capitalized. Although it cannot be said with certainty, it does appear that the cost to create the mutual funds fit within the description of amounts paid to create a "financial interest." As such, it would have to be capitalized as an intangible listed in Regulation section 1.263(a)-4(d). Alternatively, if the amount paid is treated as acquiring a separate and distinct asset, then the likelihood of capitalization is greater. The scope of Regulation 1.263(a)-4(c) is considerably broader than Regulation 1.263(a)-4(d).

Regardless of whether the expenditures may be encompassed within the intangibles regulations, the language contained in the coordinated issue paper suggests a significant expansion of the traditional scope of Code section 263. When stating that the costs should be capitalized because the taxpayer "expects to realize significant economic benefits from long-term contractual relation-

[399] *Id.*

[400] A similar issue was resolved in favor of the taxpayer by the Tax Court in *Iowa-Des Moines National Bank v. Commissioner*, 69 T.C. 872 (1977), *aff'd*, 592 F.2d 433 (8th Cir. 1979). The Eighth Circuit did not address the issue because it was not the subject of the appeal by the IRS.

[401] *First National Bank of South Carolina v. United States*, 77-2 U.S.T.C. ¶9526, 558 F.2d 721 (4th Cir. 1977).

ships," the IRS is coming quite close to a position that would require capitalization of the costs incurred to create goodwill. It is accepted that goodwill comprises the expectation of continued patronage, which produces an economic benefit from the customer relationship.

The position expressed in the coordinated issue paper was adopted by the Tax Court in *FRM Corp.*[402] In that case, the adjustment at issue was the taxpayer's expenditures incurred in creating and entering into separate contracts to manage 82 new regulated investment companies "(RICs)". The expenditures were incurred to develop the concept for each of the 82 new RICs, to develop the initial marketing plan, to draft the management contract, to form the RICs, to obtain the board of trustees' approval of the contract, and to register the RIC with the SEC and the various states in which the RIC would be marketed.

In its opinion, the Tax Court stated that an expenditure is capital if it "creates or enhances" a separate and distinct asset. However, it noted that the existence of a separate and distinct asset is not necessary in order to classify an expenditure as capital in nature. Another consideration in making such a determination is whether the expenditure provides the taxpayer with a long-term benefit. The Court noted that the Supreme Court has observed that grounding tax status on the existence of an "asset" would be unlikely to produce a bright-line rule "given that the notion of an 'asset' is itself flexible and amorphous."[403]

The Tax Court found that the contract between the taxpayer and the new RICs generally provided fund management services in exchange for remuneration. Both the taxpayer and the RIC realistically expected the relationship to continue indefinitely and, thus, the relationship had an expected life of more than one year. In addition to potential future revenue from the individual contracts with each new RIC, the new RICs were expected to and, in fact, did produce synergistic benefits to the taxpayer's entire family of funds. It was this type of benefit that banks often argued were generated from a core deposit intangible asset when one was acquired in a taxable asset acquisition.

The taxpayer in *FMR* argued that there were numerous court decisions which support the principal that the costs of expanding or preserving an existing business are deductible expenses rather than capital expenditures. The Tax Court observed that many of the cases cited by the taxpayer relied on a "separate and distinct asset" test. However, under post-*INDOPCO* law, the creation of a separate and distinct asset was not, according to the Court, a condition to capitalizing expenses.

The taxpayer also argued that the legislative history accompanying the 1980 enactment of Code section 195 confirmed that Congress explicitly recognized that business expansion costs were currently deductible. The Court countered by finding that Code section 195 allows taxpayers to amortize "start-up" expenses only when such expenses, "if paid or incurred in connection with the operation of an existing active trade or business . . . would be allowable as a deduction for

[402] *FMR Corp. & Subs. v. Commissioner*, 110 T.C. 402 (1988).

[403] *Id.*

the taxable year in which paid or incurred."[404] Code section 195, according to the Court, did not create any new class of deductible expenditures for existing business.

In conclusion, the Court found that the petitioner contemplated and received significant long-term benefits as a result of the expenditures it incurred in the creation of the 82 RICs during the years in issue. The future benefits derived from these RICs were not merely incidental. Accordingly, it held that the expenditures did not qualify for deduction as "ordinary and necessary" business expenses under Code section 162. Furthermore, the Court found that the evidence failed to reveal any basis for determining a useful life. Therefore, it found that the taxpayer failed to meet its burden of establishing a limited life for the future benefits obtained from the expenditures it incurred during the years in issue.

§8.10.7 Credit Card Costs

In *Colorado Springs National Bank v. United States,*[405] the Tenth Circuit Court of Appeals concluded that the cost of becoming a member of the Mountain States Bankcard Association ("MSBA") was a nondeductible capital expenditure; however, certain other expenditures incurred by the bank to establish the credit card product were deductible under Code section 162(a) as ordinary and necessary business expenses incurred in carrying on a trade or business.[406] Regulation 1.263(a)-4(d) could be construed as adopting the holding of this case by listing a "credit card agreement" among the created intangibles, the cost of which must be capitalized.[407]

The MSBA was a nonprofit corporation formed to handle the Master Charge program through the Interbank Card Association ("ICA"). ICA was a nationwide clearing house for Master Charge cards. The fee paid to MSBA was a one-time, nonrefundable payment that could not be separately transferred. However, if the bank were sold, the Master Charge franchise or license could be transferred along with the bank. The payment of this fee was found to obtain an intangible property right. As such, it was found to be a nondeductible capital expenditure.

In some situations, the costs of establishing a credit card product may be in conjunction with costs to establish a credit card system. In *First National Bank of South Carolina,*[408] the Fourth Circuit Court of Appeals concluded that payments by the bank of an assessment to Atlantic State's Bankcard Association, Inc. ("ASBA"), a nonprofit association incorporated by the taxpayer and 21 other banks entering the credit card market, were deductible as ordinary and necessary expenses.

---

[404] *Id.*

[405] *Colorado Springs National Bank v. United States,* 74-2 U.S.T.C. ¶19809, 505 F.2d 1185 (10th Cir. 1974).

[406] A similar issue was resolved in favor of the taxpayer by the Tax Court in *Iowa-Des Moines National Bank v. Commissioner,* 69 T.C. 872 (1977), *aff'd,* 592 F.2d 433 (8th Cir. 1979). The Eighth Circuit did not address the issue because it was not the subject of the appeal by the IRS.

[407] Reg. §1.263(a)-4(d)(2)(1)(C)(2). The term "credit card agreement" is not defined in the regulation. Could it mean instead the agreement between the issuer and the card holder?

[408] *First National Bank of South Carolina v. United States,* 77-2 U.S.T.C. ¶9526, 558 F.2d 721 (4th Cir. 1977).

Prior to the date that ASBA began operations, it incurred substantial pre-operational expenses, including salaries, office and equipment rentals, general office expenses, advertising costs and fees paid to a consulting firm. Each member of the cooperative venture was assessed an amount of the expenses calculated on the basis of the participating banks total deposits. The ASBA began operations in 1969, and the taxpayer deducted the expenses in 1968, the year in which they were paid or incurred by ASBA.

The Court noted that membership in ASBA was not a separate and distinct asset created or enhanced by the payments in question. The members of the association owned no stock in the association, had no interest in ASBA's assets, and were not entitled to any distribution of its profits. Membership was non-transferable, and upon dissolution, ASBA's assets were required to be paid over to a tax-exempt charitable organization.

Credit card pre-operational costs are usually currently deductible under Code section 162. Thus, the taxpayer in *First National Bank of South Carolina* incurred deductible pre-operational costs associated with its participation in the Master Charge system, some of which were incurred prior to when the business became operational.[409] The costs fell into six categories:

1. Computer costs incurred to keypunch and insert its customer account data into the MSBA computer;
2. Computer service and assessment fees paid to MSBA, including a new merchant fee for the addition of each merchant to the system, a card-holder fee for the addition of each cardholder to the system, and a maintenance fee for computer operation;
3. Advertising and promotional costs paid to familiarize the public with the Master Charge system;
4. Credit bureau reports secured by the taxpayer to ascertain the credit risks present in the extension of credit to cardholders;
5. Travel, education, and entertainment expenses of employees reimbursed by the taxpayer for attendance at MSBA meetings held to motivate the employees and familiarize them with the Master Charge system;
6. Temporary clerical services required by the taxpayer to augment its existing staff.

[409] *First National Bank of South Carolina v. United States*, 558 F.2d 721 (4th Cir. 1977). *See also, Iowa-Des Moines National Bank v. Commissioner*, 68 T.X. 872 (1977), *aff'd*, 592 F.2d 433 (8th Cir. 1979).

(i) *"Ordinary" Expenses.* The Court concluded as a factual matter that the taxpayer's expenses incurred in connection with its entry into the Master Charge system had no extrinsic or marketable value, created no property interest; produced nothing corporeal or saleable, and were recurring. In short, they did not create "a distinct and recognized property interest."[410] The expenditures merely introduced a more efficient method of conducting an old business; they were for the continuation of an existing business and for the preservation and improvement of existing income. Thus, they were "ordinary" expenditures.[411]

(ii) *"Necessary" Expenses.* The Court next turned to the question whether the expenses were "appropriate and helpful" so that the "necessary" test of Code section 162(a) was met.[412] The expenditures were placed into three general categories: computer costs, credit check costs, and promotional costs. The Court found that the computer costs were incurred to establish a function which at one time was performed by individuals. The expenses incurred in connection with credit checks were not unlike the risk determination expenses that had historically been incurred by the taxpayer in connection with its banking business. The promotional expenditures, which included expenses for promotion, solicitation, training, and advertising, were found to accomplish little more than encouraging the sale and use of an old product, the financing of consumer transactions, in a new package, credit cards. Accordingly, the Court concluded that the three categories of expenses met the "necessary" requirement contained in Code section 162(a); that is, they were appropriate and helpful in the conduct of taxpayer's existing trade or business.

(iii) *"Carrying On" an Existing Business.* Although it recognized that a bank has the power to issue credit cards, the IRS argued that bank credit cards constituted a new "area" or "line" of business designed to return a "future benefit." The Court rejected this argument, citing with approval the Second Circuit Court of Appeal's decision in *Briarcliff Candy Corporation*.[413] In *Briarcliff Candy Corporation* the taxpayer incurred various promotional expenses before an agency system established by franchise agreements became operative. The Court ruled that "expenditures by an already established and going concern in developing a new sales territory are deductible under Section 162 . . . ."[414] The Court reasoned that the bank had long been established, and it merely adopted a new method, the use of credit cards and computers, to conduct an old business, the financing of computer transactions. Thus, it found the "carrying on" requirement of Code section 162(a) to be satisfied.

---

[410] *Lincoln Savings v. Commissioner*, 71-1 U.S.T.C. ¶9476, 403 U.S. 345, 355 (1971).

[411] Shortly after the Fourth Circuit's decision in *First National Bank of South Carolina*, the Eighth Circuit Court of Appeals held that similar expenditures were ordinary and necessary incurred in carrying on an existing trade or business. The expenditures in question were paid by the taxpayer to other banks and to a credit information providing corporation in connection with its entry into the Master Charge system. The Court stated that the "most significant factor" was that the payment was for a service that could have been performed by personnel employed by the taxpayer. *Iowa-Des Moines National Bank v. Commissioner*, 79-1 U.S.T.C. ¶9198, 592 F.2d 433 (8th Cir. 1979).

[412] *Commissioner v. Tellier*, 66-1 U.S.T.C. ¶9319, 383 U.S. 687, 689 (1966).

[413] *Briarcliff Candy Corp. v. Commissioner*, 73-1 U.S.T.C. ¶9288, 475 F.2d 775 (2d Cir. 1973).

[414] *Id.* at 782. This statement is also support for current deductibility of branch expansion expenses.

(iv) ***Book Accounting Effect.*** In reaching its conclusion the Court took notice of the bank regulatory accounting requirement that costs incurred to develop and implement a credit card program must be charged to expense rather than capital.[415] Although it found that this accounting rule was a factor to consider, it concluded that compulsory accounting rules of a regulatory agency do not control tax consequences. The Court also took notice of applicable federal statutes that constrain the powers that may be exercised by a bank.[416] Under rulings by the Comptroller of the Currency interpreting these provisions, a bank is authorized to issue credit cards.[417] Moreover, it noted that the Federal Reserve Board recognizes that bank credit cards are "bank services."[418]

§ 8.10.8 Bailout Costs

The IRS and the Tax Court have sought to prescribe rules to govern the taxation of costs incurred in maintaining the financial viability of business units. These so called bailout costs are generally deductible as ordinary and necessary business expenses.

In Technical Advice Memorandum 200247004, the IRS has determined that the cost incurred by a bank to bailout a proprietary mutual fund was a deductible expenditure.[419] This pronouncement reverses the IRS position on this issue contained in an earlier Field Service Advice issued to a revenue agent examining the same taxpayer.[420]

The bailout took the form of a cash transfer in an amount approximately equal to the losses incurred by the fund. The IRS determined that the taxpayer did not realize significant long-term benefits from the new capital that it transferred to the fund.

Under the Code section 263(a) final regulations, the rational for the IRS's conclusion is questionable. The *INDOPCO* future benefits test has been greatly attenuated, and it appears that capitalization is not required under those regulations because the bailout costs do not create a separate and distinct intangible asset, they are not one of the eight future benefits that must be capitalized, and they are not made for the purpose of facilitating the acquisition of a trade or business.

In the pronouncement, the IRS reasoned that the contributions were made to avoid damage to the taxpayer's goodwill and reputation, to avoid potential mutual fund shareholder litigation and/or shareholder redemptions, to stem the loss of the bank customers, and to defend its core retail franchise.

The IRS noted that, generally, expenditures made to protect or promote a taxpayer's business and which do not result in the acquisition of a separate and distinct asset are deductible under Code section 162 as ordinary and necessary

[415] August 21, 1972 letter to Assistant Secretary for Tax Policy, U.S. Treasury Department.

[416] 12 U.S.C. § 24, Seventh (2006).

[417] Comptroller's manual for national banks, paragraphs 7.7376(b) and 7.7378.

[418] 12 CFR § 219.104(d).

[419] TAM 200247004, July 29, 2002.

[420] FSA 199938018, June 25, 1999. The technical advice memorandum was issued to an appeals officer.

business expenses.[421] Furthermore, the IRS observed that it is well established that expenses incurred to protect, maintain, or preserve a taxpayer's business, even though not in the normal course of such business, may be deductible as ordinary and necessary business expenses.[422]

Thus, the IRS concluded that the payments made to protect goodwill, to prevent lawsuits, to prevent redemptions, and to protect the core business of a taxpayer would all seem to fall within the category of payments which are made to protect and preserve a taxpayer's business.[423] Such analysis applies even though the protection of the taxpayer's business and reputation, along with the protection of its future income stream (from the mutual fund fees) did produce long term benefits. Furthermore, this analysis applies even though the transfer of the cash was not made in the normal course of the taxpayer's business because of the unusual situation of the structured securities mutual funds and the interest rate increases in the taxable years under examination. As such, the payments made by the taxpayer were allowed to be deductible under Code section 162 as ordinary and necessary business expenditures.

In reaching this conclusion the IRS commented on other expenditures. It acknowledged that capitalization is not required for every expenditure that produces some future benefit, including the costs of training, trainers, and routine updates of training materials, even though they may have some future benefit. The Code section 263 regulations also acknowledge this providing an exclusive list of categories of intangible that are required to be capitalized. Expenditures with respect to intangibles that are not enumerated need not be capitalized.[424]

The technical advice memorandum also attaches importance to the duration of the benefit of an expenditure and its financial significance. However, the Treasury Department curtailed this analysis in the Code section 263(a) regulations by suggesting that the duration of an expenditure that creates or enhances an intangible asset, the benefits from which do not extend beyond the end of the next tax year, is insufficient to require capitalization.[425] Moreover, a de minimis rule provides that if an expenditure in the nature of a transaction cost associated with an intangible asset does not amount to more than $5000 per transaction, no

---

[421] *Van Iderstine Co. v. Commissioner*, 261 F.2d 211 (2d Cir. 1958) (payments made to suppliers to ensure a continuing supply of raw materials were deductible); *T.J. Enterprises, Inc. v. Commissioner*, 101 T.C. 581 (1993) (expenses incurred to protect, maintain, or preserve a taxpayer's business generally do not result in significant future benefits); *Snow v. Commissioner*, 31 T.C. 585 (1958), *acq*, 1959-2 C.B. 7 (payments made to protect and supplement the taxpayer's income from its existing law business were deductible).

[422] *Associated Milk Producers, Inc. v. Commissioner*, 68 T.C. 729, 742 (1977); *see United States v. E.L. Bruce Co.*, 180 F.2d 846 (6th Cir. 1950); *L. Heller & Son, Inc. v. Commissioner*, 12 T.C. 1109 (1949); *Catholic News Publishing Co. v. Commissioner*, 10 T.C. 73 (1948); *Miller v. Commissioner*, 37 B.T.A. 830, 832- 833 (1938).

[423] Rev. Rul. 56-359, 1956-2 C.B. 115, 116. *See also* Rev. Rul. 79-283, 1979-2 C.B. 80 (payments made by a member of a savings and loan association league to a disaster fund for victims of natural disasters who have property mortgaged with the members of the league are deductible because the payments were made to prevent injury to the taxpayer's business).

[424] *See, e.g., Cleveland Electric Illuminating Co. v. United States*, 7 Cl. Ct. 220 (1985) (deduction for costs of training employees to operate new equipment in an existing business); Rev. Rul. 96-62, 1996-2 C.B. 9 (*INDOPCO* decision does not affect the treatment of training costs as business expenses, which are generally deductible under Code § 162).

[425] Reg. § 1.263(a)-4(f).

capitalization is required under a de minimis rule.[426] These two limitations on the *INDOPCO* future benefits test are clearly intended to ease the administrative burden associated with applying that judicially crafted test. The two rules under the Regulations—the twelve-month and de minimis rules—reveal the intent of the IRS to ease the administrative burden caused by the *INDOPCO* ruling.

Unlike the regulations, however, the memorandum seems to introduce a third limitation on the future benefits test that is fact based and is likely to create some administrative challenges. This third limitation seems to add a "primary" limitation on the capitalization of expenditures. The memorandum states: "Taxpayer's transfer of $x to two of its structured securities mutual funds primarily protected, maintained, and preserved its business. Such payments only secondarily provided long term benefits, which were not significant in quality or duration within the meaning of *INDOPCO*." Thus, if an expenditure is of insufficient duration or dollar amount or if the expenditure only secondarily provides long term benefits, it is not required to be capitalized under the *INDOPCO* future benefit test.

Of course, the objective of tax rules should not be to strive for ease of administration at the expense of equitable application of the tax laws. So, for this reason, the introduction of a primary/secondary analysis may be called for. However, it will remain to be seen whether taxpayers, courts, and the IRS will be willing to further develop this subjective analysis for determining whether *INDOPCO*'s future benefit test is passed. A likely place for this to be officially described will be in the regulations that are eventually promulgated pursuant to the proposed regulations.

§ 8.10.9 Expenditures Reducing Future Costs

As a general rule, any amounts paid or incurred for the purpose of reducing or eliminating expenses, such as damages paid to secure relief from an unprofitable contract, are currently deductible as ordinary and necessary business expenses.[427] However, if the expenditure relates to the reacquisition of a property interest, deduction may be denied under Code section 263.

(i) ***Lease Termination Payments.*** As a general rule, the cost incurred by a lessee to terminate a lease, whether on real or personal property, is allowed to be currently deducted as an ordinary and necessary business expense under Code section 162. Such expenditures are in the nature of damages that are paid in order to secure relief from an unprofitable contract. Moreover, a deduction may be allowed for abandoning a leasehold interest under Code section 165. However, an abandonment does not result simply from cessation of use, and the mere diminution in value of property is also not enough to establish an abandonment loss.[428]

---

[426] Reg. § 1.263(a)-4(e)(4)(iii)(A).

[427] *Cassatt v. Commissioner*, 137 F.2d 745, 749 (3d Cir. 1943); Rev. Rul. 95-32, 1995-1 C.B. 8.

[428] FSA 200048002, May 22, 2000.

If a lease termination fee is associated with entering into a new lease or securing a significant future benefit, the lessee may be required to capitalize the payment. Thus, the cost associated with terminating a lease on a branch location for the purpose of entering into a lease on another location may be required to be capitalized into the cost of the new lease under Code section 263. The requirement that the cost be capitalized is dependent on there being established an interrelationship between the two sites. The requirement for capitalization will be present even if the terminated site was leased and the acquired site is purchased.[429] Similarly, if a bank pays a lease termination fee in connection with the acquisition of the assets of another bank, the fee may have to be capitalized as part of the cost of the acquisition of an identifiable property right.

If the amount paid is not for the purpose of entering into another lease, but, instead, for the purpose of relieving the taxpayer from an onerous contract, the expenditure would be deductible. Thus, a taxpayer may be permitted to deduct the excess of the cost of a building that the taxpayer was renting over its market value as a business expense if the taxpayer can demonstrate that the rent was excessive.[430]

A similar rule applies with respect to personal property. Thus, the charge incurred by a lessee in terminating a lease of a mainframe computer and simultaneously initiating a new lease of a more powerful mainframe computer with the same lessor is not deductible in the year incurred. It must be capitalized and amortized over the term of the new lease. This assumes that there is an interrelationship and continuity of rights between the two leases. Any rollover charge is required to be treated as a cost of acquiring the second lease. The same treatment would result if the properties covered by the two leases were not identical, but merely similar in that both are mainframe computers used for the same purposes in the taxpayer's business.[431]

In appropriate circumstances, a payment to a lessor may be bifurcated between the amount that is paid for the purpose of terminating an unprofitable contract or onerous lease and the amount paid for the purpose of acquiring a capital asset. An allocation may be permitted where the amount paid for the two purposes is ascertainable.[432]

A similar capitalization rule has applied to a lessor before the promulgation of regulations under Code section 263(a) in December 2003. Under case law, an amount paid by the lessor for the cancellation of a lease prior to the expiration of

[429] PLR 9607016, February 16, 1996; *Cassett v. Commissioner*, 137 F.2d 745 (3d Cir. 1943); Rev. Rul. 69-511, 1969-2 C.B. 23; PLR 9615028, April 12, 1996.

[430] *Cleveland Allerton Hotel v. Commissioner*, 166 F.2d 805 (6th Cir. 1948). *Cf. Millinary Center Building Corp. v. Commissioner*, 21 T.C. 817 (1954), *rev'd on other grounds*, 221 F.2d 322 (2d Cir. 1955), *aff'd* 350 U.S. 456 (1956). *See also* PLR 199918022, May 7, 1999.

[431] *U.S. Bancorp v. Commissioner*, 111 T.C. 231 (1998); *Pig & Whistle Co. v. Commissioner*, Dec. 3198, 9 B.T.A. 668 (1927); *Phil Gluckstern's, Inc. v. Commissioner*, Dec. 21,521(M), T.C. Memo. 1956-9.

[432] PLR 199918022, May 7, 1999. *Cf. U.S. Bancorp. v. Commissioner*, 111 T.C. 231 (1998).

its term is not an ordinary and necessary business expense deductible in full during the taxable year. Instead, it is a capital expenditure that must be amortized over the unexpired term of the canceled lease.[433] However, if the cost of cancellation was integrally related to entering into a new lease, the cost of cancellation must be amortized over the term of the new lease.[434]

Under the final Code section 263(a) regulations, if the payment is made by the lessor to the lessee, capitalization is generally required and amortization of the amount capitalized is permitted over the unexpired term of the old lease. The rational for the capitalization rule is to require capitalization of termination payments that enable the taxpayer to reacquire some valuable right it did not possess immediately prior to the termination.[435] The rule in the regulation does not require capitalization in cases where the taxpayer, as a result of the termination, does not reacquire a right for which capitalization is appropriate. Thus, the rule does not require a taxpayer to capitalize a payment to terminate a supply contract with a supplier, and does not require a lessee to capitalize a payment to terminate a lease agreement with a lessor.

(ii) *Program Implementation Costs.* The costs that are incurred to implement a program that was designed to reduce the taxpayer's future operating costs, as well as capital costs, may be treated as ordinary and necessary business expenses. The IRS ruled that when a public electric utility incurred costs to inform its customers how they would be able to promote energy conservation and energy efficiency the costs were deductible.[436] The costs were deductible under Code section 162 as ordinary and necessary business expenses because they were appropriate and helpful in carrying on the taxpayer's business and were commonly and frequently incurred by utilities. Moreover, the costs were not required to be capitalized under Code section 263 because they were not for a "permanent improvement or betterment."

---

[433] Reg. § 1.263(a)-4(d)(7)(i)(A), *Henry B. Miller v. Commissioner*, 10 B.T.A. 383 (1928).

[434] *Wells Fargo Bank & Union Trust Co. v. Commissioner*, 163 F.2d 521 (9th Cir. 1947).

[435] *See Peerless Weighing and Vending Machine Corp. v. Commissioner*, 52 T.C. 850 (1969). Capitalization also is required for payments by a taxpayer to terminate an agreement that provides another party the exclusive right to acquire or use the taxpayer's property or services or to conduct the taxpayer's business. *See Rodeway Inns of America v. Commissioner*, 63 T.C. 414 (1974). Finally, capitalization is required for payments to terminate an agreement that prohibits the taxpayer from competing with another or from acquiring property or services from a competitor of another. Prop. Reg. § 1.263(a)-4(d)(7).

[436] Rev. Rul. 95-32, 1995-1 C.B. 8.

(iii) Severance Pay. In general, amounts paid or accrued as severance payments to employees are treated as amounts paid on account of injuries received by employees with the consequence that the payments are proper deductions as ordinary and necessary expenses.[437] Treasury regulations provide that "[a]mounts paid or accrued within the taxable year for dismissal wages, unemployment benefits, guaranteed annual wages, vacations, or a sickness, accident, hospitalization, medical expense, recreational, welfare, or similar benefit plan, are deductible under Code section 162(a) if they are ordinary and necessary expenses of the trade or business."[438] However, such amounts are not generally deductible under Code section 162(a) if, under any circumstances, they may be used to provide benefits under a stock bonus, pension, annuity, profit-sharing, or other deferred compensation plan of the type referred to in Code section 404(a). In such an event, the extent to which these amounts are deductible from gross income shall be governed by the provisions of Code section 404 and the regulations issued thereunder.

§ 8.11 Year 2000 Costs

The expenditures that a bank incurs to modify its computer systems to accommodate four-digit years should be currently deductible under Code section 162 as an ordinary and necessary business expense.[439] These costs are in the nature of repairs or other costs incurred to maintain property. Alternatively, Code section 174 may allow a current deduction for "year 2000" costs if they qualify as research and development expenditures. However, the IRS has stated that year 2000 costs will not satisfy the definition of "qualified research" for purposes of the credit provided in Code section 41 for increasing research activities. The tax treatment of these expenditures is consistent with the required accounting treatment, which calls for treating them as period costs.

§ 8.12 FDIC Deposit Insurance Assessment

Each financial institution that participates in the Federal Deposit Insurance Corporation's ("FDIC") insurance program is generally assessed a semiannual charge (premium) equal to its liability for deposits multiplied by the applicable

---

[437] Rev. Rul. 94-77, 1994-2 C.B. 19.

[438] Treas. Reg. § 1.162-10.

[439] Rev Proc. 97-50, 1997-2 C.B. 525; Rev. Proc. 69-21, 1969-2 C.B. 303.

rate.[440] The annual assessment is deductible as an ordinary and necessary business expense.[441]

Normally, there are two assessments each calendar year. The assessment for the semiannual period January 1 through June 30 is due on or before January 31 of the first assessment period. The assessment amount is computed by multiplying a bank's average assessment base for the prior semiannual period by one-half the annual assessment rate. The rate is provided by the Federal Deposit Insurance Corporation ("FDIC") to banks prior to the end of the prior assessment period. The average assessment base for the first semiannual period is the average of the deposits shown on a bank's quarterly Report of Condition for September 30 and December 31 of the preceding calendar year. Under FDIC regulations, a bank is permitted to prepay, on December 30 of a taxable year, its first quarterly payment for the semiannual period beginning on January 1. During the month of January, the bank is required to file with the FDIC a certified statement reporting its average assessment base.

It is the IRS's position that the liability to pay the deposit insurance assessment is not established until January of the year following the December 30 payment.[442] It is not until then that the taxpayer has a fixed and absolute or unconditional liability and the FDIC provides the insurance. For the liability to be fixed the taxpayer has to be in existence on the January 1 following the year of payment. Thus, payment does not serve to fix the liability. The liability must be fixed independently as a consequence of the "all events" test being satisfied.[443] Regardless of how statistically certain the liability is, the taxpayer may not deduct an estimate of an anticipated expense.[444] Moreover, economic performance will not occur until the year of examination. The "recurring item" exception

[440] The applicable rates are set forth in 12 U.S.C. §1817(b)(1)(C) or (D) (1994). Congress established the FDIC in 1933 to insure bank deposits, *see Lebron v. National R.R. Passenger Corp.*, 513 U.S. 374, 388 (1995); *FDIC v. Godshall*, 558 F.2d 220, 221 (4th Cir. 1077), and it established the Federal Savings and Loan Insurance Corporation (FSLIC) in 1934 to insure savings association deposits, *see United States v. Winstar Corp.*, 518 U.S. 839, 844 (1996). Savings associations were required to participate in the FSLIC insurance system but could withdraw from the FSLIC insurance fund by converting from a Federal to a State charter. *See Great W. Bank v. Office of Thrift Supervision*, 916 F.2d 1421, 1423 (9th Cir. 1990). *See United States v. Winstar Corp., supra* at 845-846; *Great W. Bank v. Office of Thrift Supervision, supra* at 1423. On August 9, 1989, Congress enacted the Financial Institutions Reform, Recovery and Enforcement Act of 1989 (FIRREA), Pub. L. No. 101-73, 103 Stat. 183, as an emergency measure to prevent the collapse of the savings association industry. *See* H. Rep. 101-54(I) at 307 (1989); *see also* H. R. Rep. No. 101-222 at 393 (1989); *United States v. Winstar Corp., supra* at 856. In relevant part, FIRREA abolished the FSLIC, transferred to the FDIC the responsibility of insuring the deposits at savings associations, and established the BIF and the SAIF. FIRREA gave the FDIC responsibility for regulating both the insurance fund it had traditionally administered (now known as the BIF) and the insurance fund formerly regulated by the FSLIC (now known as the SAIF). *See* FIRREA §§202, 215, 103 Stat. 188, 252. FIRREA imposed on SAIF (as opposed to BIF) participants higher deposit premiums and a higher degree of supervision in an attempt to ensure the SAIF's strength. *See generally* 12 U.S.C. §1817 (1994).

[441] 12 U.S.C. §1811 (1993). Any amount assessed against a participant in the Savings and Loan Assistance Fund ("SAIF") is deposited into the SAIF and is available to the FDIC for use with respect to any SAIF participant. 12 C.F.R. §327.

[442] TAM 199924060, March 5, 1999.

[443] *See United States v. General Dynamics Corp.*, 481 U.S. 239, 243 (1987) (holding, "[i]t is fundamental to the 'all events' test that, although expenses may be deductible before they have become due and payable, liability must first be firmly established). Further, the Supreme Court in *United States v. Hughes Properties, Inc.*, confirmed that, "to satisfy the all-events test, a liability must be 'final and definite in amount,' must be 'fixed and absolute,' and must be 'unconditional'" (citations omitted). 476 U.S. 593, 600 (1986).

[444] *General Dynamics Corp.*, 481 U.S. at 243.

will not afford taxpayers the opportunity to deduct an item before the "all events" test is met.

The FDIC, in November 2009, amended its assessment regulations to require prepayment on December 30, 2009 of quarterly risked-based assessments for the fourth quarter of 2009 through 2012. This prepayment is not entirely deductible when paid. Instead, the prepayment had to be capitalized as "prepaid expenses."[445] Furthermore, these prepayments fail to satisfy Regulation section 1263(a)-4(f)'s "12-month rule" that provides exceptions to capitalization for rights or benefits lasting only a brief duration. Under the rule, a taxpayer is not required to capitalize amounts paid to create (or to facilitate the creation of) any right or benefit for the taxpayer that does not extend beyond the earlier of—(i) 12 months after the first date on which the taxpayer realizes the right or benefit; or (ii) The end of the taxable year following the taxable year in which the payment is made. Because these prepayments covered the subsequent 13 quarters, they surpassed the 12-month window and had to be capitalized in accordance with Regulation section 1.263(a)-4(d)(3).[446]

§8.13 FDIC Exit and Entrance Fees

It has been the IRS's position that FDIC exit and entrance fees are not deductible as ordinary and necessary business expenses because they create a significant long term benefit for the taxpayer. This position has not been affirmed by the Tax Court.

Exit and entrance fees are imposed because congress anticipated that participants in the Savings Association Insurance Fund ("SAIF") would try to convert to the Bank Insurance Fund ("BIF") in order to escape the higher SAIF premiums and regulatory costs. Thus, Congress included in the Financial Institutions Reform, Recovery and Enforcement Act of 1989 ("FIRREA")[447] certain control measures to prevent an exodus from SAIF.[448] First, FIRREA required that entrance and exit fees be paid to the respective funds whenever there is a conver-

---

[445] Treas. Reg. §1.263(a)-4(d)(3). In Treas. Reg. §1.263(a)-4(d)(3)(ii), Ex. 1, the IRS takes the position an accrual method taxpayer who prepays three years of insurance coverage must capitalize that expense. This example is analogous to prepayment of assessments.

[446] It is unlikely the IRS would allow an institution to divide up the prepayment period into segments that each fit within the 12-month window just to gain the benefit of Treas. Reg. §1.263(a)-4(f)'s 12-month exception to capitalization. The IRS disapproves of such scheming. Even so, Treas. Reg. §1.263(a)-4(f)(5) holds the duration of a right includes any renewal period if all of the facts and circumstances in existence during the taxable year in which the right is created indicate a reasonable expectancy of renewal. Thus, even if a taxpayer were successful in separating the prepayments into segments that each fit within the 12-month window, the prepayments would nevertheless still be excluded from the 12-month exception because there remains a "reasonable expectancy of renewal" of the assessments. In fact, renewal was essentially automatic since the FDIC required prepayment of quarterly assessments from 2009-2012. Therefore, the taxpayer institution must capitalize its prepayments in these scenarios.

[447] The FDIC adopted an interim rule prescribing the amount of exit fees and amending previously prescribed entrance fee rules in March 1990. 55 FR 10,406. The previously prescribed entrance fee rule was published in 54 FR 40,377, October 2, 1989. For conversion transactions occurring before January 1, 1997, the exit fee amount is determined jointly by the FDIC and the Treasury Department. After that date, the exit fee is determined solely by the FDIC. The FDIC and the Treasury Department have agreed that the amount of the fee shall be determined by multiplying the dollar amount of deposits transferred from SAIF to the Bank Insurance Fund ("BIF") by 0.90%.

[448] 12 U.S.C. §1815(d)(2)(E) and (F) (1994).

sion transaction between a BIF participant and a SAIF participant.[449] A higher exit fee was placed on financial institutions leaving the SAIF for the BIF in order to discourage SAIF-insured institutions from insuring their deposits with BIF.[450] Second, FIRREA imposed a 5-year moratorium beginning on August 9, 1989, to replace the expired moratorium imposed by the Competitive Equality Banking Act of 1987 ("CEBA").[451] Under the FIRREA moratorium, SAIF-insured institutions were generally unable to enter into conversion transactions, which essentially prevented them from converting to BIF-insured institutions and essentially ensured mandatory SAIF participation for savings associations during the moratorium's duration.

FIRREA imposed two exceptions to the moratorium. First, the FDIC could allow certain conversion transactions involving the acquisition of a depository institution that was in default or in danger of default. A financial institution that utilized this exception was required to pay an exit fee to the fund that insured the assumed deposit liabilities before the transaction and an entrance fee to the fund that insured the assumed deposit liabilities after the transaction.[452]

Under the second exception to the moratorium, certain conversion transactions could be consummated through a merger or consolidation.[453] One alternative under this exception is for the institution to engage in an "Oakar" transaction.[454] In an Oakar transaction, a BHC that controls a savings association merges or consolidates the assets and liabilities of the acquired savings association with, or transfers such assets and liabilities to, a subsidiary bank which is a BIF member. The acquired deposits that were insured at the SAIF insurance rates are identified and continue to be treated as deposits subject to SAIF insurance. These deposits are referred to as the "adjusted attributable deposit amount," which is an amount equal to the sum of the acquired deposits plus a prescribed increase in deposits. The increase is determined by reference to the annual rate of growth of deposits of the acquiring institution.[455]

Because the deposit liabilities of the SAIF-insured institution and certain percentage of future deposits always remained assessable by the SAIF, the financial institution utilizing this exception was not required to pay the exit and entrance fees as to the conversion transaction.[456] The institution, however, could not during the moratorium period stop paying SAIF assessments on the ascertained percentage of the future deposits. The institution could switch the insurance coverage on those deposits, if it so desired, after the moratorium expired,

[449] 12 U.S.C. § 1815(d)(2)(E) (1994). The amount of the entrance fee is an approximate amount which the FDIC determines is necessary to prevent dilution of the fund to which the resulting or acquiring member belongs. Thus, in a conversion from a SAIF member to a BIF member, the calculation will be made by reference to the amount needed to prevent dilution of the BIF fund. The amount of the entrance fee is determined by multiplying total deposits transferred from SAIF to BIF by the BIF "reserve ratio."

[450] 12 U.S.C. § 1815(d)(2)(F) (1994).

[451] Pub. L. No. 100-86, 101 Stat. 552. *See* 12 U.S.C. § 1815(d)(2)(A)(ii) (1994).

[452] 12 U.S.C. § 1815(d)(2)(C), (E) (1994).

[453] 12 U.S.C. § 1815(d)(3) (1994); *see also* FIRREA § 206(a)(7), 103 Stat. 196.

[454] 12 U.S.C. § 1815(d)(3)(A) (2006).

[455] 12 U.S.C. § 1815(d)(3)(B) and (C) (2006). An earlier version of this provision specified a fixed percentage increase in deposits in lieu of the rate of growth of deposits of the acquiring institution, whichever was greater.

[456] 12 U.S.C. § 1815(d)(3)(B), (G) (1994).

but only if the FDIC approved the switch and the institution paid the requisite exit and entrance fees. Congress provided explicitly that any entrance fee was imposed to prevent dilution of the reserves of the fund that began insuring the assumed deposit liabilities as a result of the transaction.[457] The pertinent legislative history does not contain an explicit explanation of Congress' intent as to the imposition of the exit fee.

A type of transaction that does not result in the combination of SAIF and BIF deposits under the auspices of a single depository institution is often referred to as a "Sasser" transaction. In this transaction, a SAIF member converts to a commercial bank charter, but it elects to remain a SAIF member and pay SAIF assessments.[458] Neither a Sasser nor an Oakar transaction is considered to be a "conversion transaction." The only difference between a Sasser and an Oakar is that in the former the resulting depository remains a member of SAIF, while in an Oakar, only that portion of deposits acquired by the BIF member are subject to SAIF insurance premiums.

In *Metrobank v. Commissioner*, the IRS argued that exit and entrance fees paid by the taxpayer provided the taxpayer with a significant long-term benefit that was required to be capitalized.[459] The IRS did not assert that either fee created or enhanced a separate and distinct capital asset. However, the Tax Court rejected this argument and stated that it was unable to find as a fact that the taxpayer's payment of either fee produced a significant future benefit requiring capitalization. It reasoned that whether a benefit is significant to the taxpayer who incurs the underlying expense rests on the duration and extent of the benefit, and a future benefit that flows incidentally from an expense may not be significant. Any benefit that the taxpayer derived from insuring the assumed deposit liabilities with BIF, rather than SAIF, was found to be insignificant when weighed against the primary purpose for the payment of the fees. That purpose, as explained by the court, was, in the case of the exit fee, to protect the integrity of the SAIF for the direct benefit of the FDIC and the potential benefit of the SAIF's participants, one of which was not the taxpayer, by imposing upon the taxpayer a final premium for the insurance coverage that the assumed deposit liabilities had received while insured by the SAIF before their assumption. The primary purpose of the entrance fee was to protect the integrity of the BIF by charging an additional first-year premium for insurance coverage on the assumed deposit liabilities.

Prior to the *Metrobank* decision, the IRS issued two pronouncements that indicate its position on the deductibility of exit and entrance fees.[460] In one situation, the facts indicate that a member of BIF acquired the assets and assumed the liabilities of a SAIF member that was in danger of default.[461] The

---

[457] H. R. Rep. No. 101-54(I), at 325.

[458] 12 U.S.C. § 1815(d)(2)(G) (2006).

[459] 116 TC 211 (2001). Unless these fees fit within one of the eight types of expenditures described in Reg. § 1.263(a)-4(d), even if the expenditures created a future benefit it would not have to be capitalized.

[460] PLR 9348003, August 30, 1993.

[461] 12 U.S.C. § § 1815(d)(2)(C) and (D) (2006) provide that conversion transactions are permitted in only limited situations, but including a situation in which a SAIF member is "in default or in danger of default."

acquiring BIF member elected to transfer the insured deposits of the SAIF member from SAIF to BIF in a "conversion transaction." In connection with the transfer of the insured deposits, the acquiring institution incurred an exit and entrance fee.[462]

The taxpayer took the position that both the exit fee and the entrance fee were currently deductible as ordinary and necessary business expenses incurred in carrying on its trade or business. It reasoned that neither fee created a significant benefit that extends beyond the year. The exit fee provided no benefit, according to the taxpayer, because it merely enabled the deposits to leave the SAIF. Moreover, the entrance fee provided no benefit because, according to the taxpayer, it already was a member of BIF. The entrance fee did not, it was argued, enhance its membership benefits in BIF.

In a Technical Advice Memorandum issued shortly after the Private Letter Ruling, the IRS was confronted with a similar conversion transaction; however, there the taxpayer sought to allocate the fees (less a small amount that it attributed to goodwill) to its purchase price allocated to core deposits.

The IRS concluded that:

- The exit and entrance fees were a single cost associated with the conversion transaction;
- The combined amounts must be capitalized; and
- No amortization deduction was permitted under Code section 167(a).

The IRS reasoned that the exit and entrance fee must be capitalized because the cost was for a benefit that extends beyond the taxable year.[463] The IRS found that the two fees should be analyzed as a single payment because the FDIC will always assess both when a conversion transaction occurs. It analogized the fees to the costs incurred by a lessor when canceling one lease for the purpose of entering into a new lease. According to judicial authority, the entire cost to the lessor must be aggregated and capitalized.[464]

The IRS reasoned that because the one-time payment of an exit fee and an entrance fee to the FDIC enabled the acquiring institution to obtain, for its newly acquired and future deposits, the benefit of a separate and identifiable membership in BIF for future years, the payment must be capitalized. It analogized the fee to the fee that is paid by a taxpayer to become a member of a stock exchange. In such case, the payment enables the taxpayer to obtain the benefits of a separate and identifiable membership for future years.[465]

The taxpayer argued that if the fees must be capitalized, the cost may be recovered over the life of the deposits that were acquired. It reasoned that the amount of the fees were based on the amount of deposits transferred and the

[462] These fees are imposed pursuant to 12 U.S.C. § 1815(d)(2)(E) (2006) to prevent possible dilution of SAIF and BIF caused by member financial institutions leaving or entering these funds.

[463] *INDOPCO, Inc. v. Commissioner*, 503 U.S. 79 (1992).

[464] *Wells Fargo Bank & Union Trust Co., Trustee v. Commissioner*, 163 F.2d 521 (9th Cir. 1947); *Montgomery Co. v. Commissioner*, 54 T.C. 986 (1970).

[465] *Harman v. Commissioner*, 72 T.C. 362 (1979).

costs incurred to acquire the deposits were the type of intangible expenditure similar to the core deposit intangible for which depreciation is allowable.[466]

The IRS responded that the right to obtain insurance or membership in the FDIC is not tied to specific deposits transferred. Further, the benefits of the transferred membership or right to BIF insurance do not have a limited life. The benefits attached to a constant percentage of the acquiring institutions deposits. The loss or addition of any particular deposit from customer movement does not affect the membership benefits or the right to insurance. The IRS analogized this situation with the treatment of an assembled workforce, which might be subject to attrition or expansion through the departure of employees and the hiring of others.[467] In this case, judicial authority concludes that the asset would not be depleted due to the passage of time or as a result of use.[468] The IRS concluded that the two intangibles are separate assets.[469] While the value of the core deposit might be subject to attrition, the benefits of the transferred membership from SAIF to BIF do not deplete due to time or use.[470]

§8.14 Regulatory Examination Assessment

Bank regulators assess banks a fee to cover the cost of the regulatory examination.[471] The regulatory examination assessment fee is deductible as an ordinary and necessary business expense.

Under federal bank regulatory rules, the assessment fee is payable on or before January 31 and July 31 of each year.[472] The fee is payable with respect to the six-month period beginning 30 days prior to each payment date, and it is based on total assets shown in the bank's quarterly Consolidated Report of Condition for the period immediately preceding the payment date. For example, the semiannual assessment for the first six months of the taxable year will be based on the Consolidated Report of Condition submitted for the fourth quarter reporting period ending December 31.

The IRS has ruled that the semiannual assessment is not payable until the year of the examination, even though it is based on the report of condition for the quarter ending on December 31 of the immediately preceding calendar year.[473] Thus, even if the liability is paid in the preceding calendar year, all of the events that determine the fact of the liability, a prerequisite for deduction prescribed by Code section 461, will not have occurred in that taxable year.

§8.15 Farm Credit System Assessment

The payment of a one-time assessment to the Farm Credit System Financial Assistance Corporation (FAC) for the purchase of FAC stock by a bank in the farm credit system is deductible under Code section 162.[474] The IRS noted that

---

[466] *Citizens and Southern Corp. v. Commissioner*, 91 T.C. 463 (1988), *aff'd*, 900 F.2d 266 (11th Cir. 1990).

[467] An assembled workforce is an I.R.C. §197 intangible eligible for 15-year, straight line amortization.

[468] *Ithaca Industries v. Commissioner*, 97 T.C. 253 (1991).

[469] PLR 9348003, December 3, 1993.

[470] TAM 9402006, January 14, 1994.

[471] 12 U.S.C. §482 (1994).

[472] 12 C.F.R. §8.2.

[473] Rev. Rul. 80-230, 1980-2 C.B. 169.

[474] PLR 9333005, May 7, 1993.

the FAC Stock itself lacked many of the characteristics found typically among other equity investments. It was nontransferable and nonredeemable, it did not represent a share in the equity of FAC, and it did not entitle the owner to any voting rights. It noted that in the legislative history to the Agricultural Credit Act of 1987,[475] which established FAC, the "stock purchase" was characterized as an assessment, and FAC is described as an entity under government control.

The IRS found that because the taxpayer did not acquire an interest in property when it purchased the FAC stock, the FAC stock was not stock for tax purposes. The IRS distinguished the facts of *Lincoln Savings* by noting that in *Lincoln Savings*, each insured institution owned a *pro rata* share of a secondary reserve funded by the premium payments. The FSLIC maintained separate accounting for each insured institution's share of the secondary reserve and submitted to each contributing institution an annual report disclosing the share amount and interest credited to each institution's respective account. Citing *INDOPCO*, the IRS concluded that because the taxpayer did not derive a significant long-term benefit from its purchase of FAC stock, and because the expenditures satisfied all requirements contained in Code section 162, a current deduction was allowed.

§ 8.16 Directors' and Officers' Insurance

In general, the cost of directors' and officers' liability insurance is currently deductible under Code section 162.[476] However, the cost of pre-paid insurance that provides more than one year of protection must be capitalized and amortized over the life of the policy.[477] In some situations, however, an expenditure for insurance that may otherwise be currently deductible is required to be capitalized if it is incurred in connection with a merger or acquisition.

In Technical Advice Memorandum 9402004, the IRS analyzed a transaction in which a taxpayer purchased an additional five years of directors' and officers' insurance coverage. The cost was nearly five times the normal cost of D & O insurance. The purchase took place just prior to a merger, and the sales price of the taxpayer's stock was reduced to reflect the expenditure.

The IRS denied the taxpayer a current deduction for the expenditure, but permitted amortization over the five-year life of the policy. Contrary to what the examining agent argued, the IRS concluded that the premium payment did not have its origin in the taxpayer's merger transaction. The IRS reasoned that the treatment of the cost of the insurance was not affected by *INDOPCO* because any future benefit from the expenditure was incidental to the merger transaction.[478]

---

[475] Agricultural Credit Act of 1987, Pub. L. No. 100-233, 101 Stat. 1568.

[476] Rev. Rul. 69-491, 1969-2 C.B. 22.

[477] Reg. § 1.461-4(g)(8), Ex. 6(ii). Rev. Rul. 70-413, 1970-2 C.B. 103.

[478] In this ruling, the IRS also concluded that certain costs attributable to financial advice, legal, accounting, internal payroll and other transaction costs related to six unsuccessful potential purchases could not be deducted as an abandonment loss.

§ 8.17 Premiums on Debtor's Life Insurance

The premiums paid by a bank on an insurance policy on a borrower's life is eligible for deduction under Code section 162 as an ordinary and necessary business expense if the premiums are paid incident to the protection of loan collateral.[479] Even though there is no express agreement covering the bank's right of reimbursement for premiums paid, the implied right of the bank to be reimbursed out of a policy that is assigned as security for a loan will justify the deduction. The deduction is allowed despite local law not granting the bank any cause of action against the debtor personally for the premium payments. To sustain the deduction, the bank must show that the unpaid debt exceeds the cash surrender value of the policy. If in a subsequent taxable year the bank recovers any portion of the deducted premiums, the amount recovered is includible in gross income, except to the extent excludible under Code section 111.

§ 8.18 Discount for Early Mortgage Pay-off

The discount from the amount of an outstanding loan that a bank may grant a borrower for the purpose of encouraging the borrower to repay the loan before the maturity date may be deducted as a loss under Code section 165.[480] However, to be allowable as a deduction under Code section 165, a loss must be evidenced by "closed and completed transactions," fixed by identifiable events, and actually sustained during the taxable year.[481]

If the amount of the discount is an incentive for the borrower to enter into a new loan, the discount would not be currently deductible because the two transactions cannot properly be deemed as separate and independent transactions.[482] Instead, it would be added to the bank's tax basis in the new loan.

Whether the discount is deductible or added to tax basis depends upon whether the old loan and the new loan are interrelated. If the borrower has the option of simply repaying the old loan and not take out a new loan, the transactions do not appear to be interrelated. Furthermore, if the terms of the new loan are not more favorable to the borrower receiving the discount than to other borrowers, the discount appears to relate to the cancellation of the old loan and not an incentive to enter into a new loan.

§ 8.19 Supervisory Goodwill

It is the IRS's position that a taxpayer may not depreciate under Code section 167 the tax basis of supervisory goodwill over its useful life.[483] Taxpayers have argued that the contractual "right to use" the purchase method of accounting, along with the resultant purchased goodwill, results in an asset on its books properly identified as supervisory goodwill. This supervisory goodwill, it is

---

[479] Rev. Rul. 75-46, 1975-1 C.B. 55; *Dominion National Bank v. Commissioner*, 26 B.T.A. 421 (1932), *acq.* XI-2 C.B. 3 (1932).

[480] *Burbank Liquidating Corporation v. Commissioner*, 39 T.C. 999 (1963), *aff'd (and rev'd on other grounds)*, 335 F.2d 125 (9th Cir. 1964). PLR 8447001, June 26 1985.

[481] Reg. § 1.165-1(b).

[482] *The 12701 Shaker Boulevard Company v. Commissioner*, 36 T.C. 255, 258 (1961), *aff'd*, 312 F.2d 749 (6th Cir. 1963).

[483] CCA 200210053, December 11, 2001.

reasoned, qualifies as other property for purposes of Code section 597 and is a form of financial assistance provided by the Federal Savings and Loan Insurance Corporation ("FSLIC") under section 406(f) of the National Housing Act.[484] As such, the asset is properly excluded from income pursuant to Code section 597(a).

Relying on *Newark Morning Ledger Co.* and Code section 597, which provides an exclusion for certain federal financial assistance received in the form of money or other property, it could be argued that a taxpayer has an ascertainable tax basis in its supervisory goodwill and that the asset, with the enactment of the Financial Institutions Reform, Recovery and Enforcement Act of 1989 ("FIRREA"), has a limited useful life.[485]

These arguments were rejected by the IRS, which determined that "supervisory goodwill" does not qualify as "money or other property" for purposes of Code section 597.

In a lengthy IRS Settlement Guideline,[486] the following conclusions were reached:

1. Supervisory goodwill does not qualify as "money or other property" under Code section 597 because it is not financial assistance provided by the Federal Savings and Loan Insurance Corporation under § 406(f) of the National Housing Act.
2. A taxpayer cannot establish a tax basis in supervisory goodwill because thrift acquisitions were tax-free transactions and the acquiring taxpayer took a carryover basis in the acquired assets.
3. Because a taxpayer does not have a tax basis in supervisory goodwill, it is not entitled to Code section 165 losses based upon worthlessness, abandonment or confiscation. Moreover, even if a taxpayer were able to establish a tax basis in supervisory goodwill, that taxpayer must affirmatively establish that it met the other requirements of Code section 165 for the loss as claimed in the tax years for which the amended returns were filed.
4. Because a taxpayer cannot establish a tax basis in supervisory goodwill, it is not entitled to deductions under Code section 167 for depreciation or amortization with respect to supervisory goodwill. Even if a taxpayer could establish a tax basis in supervisory goodwill, that taxpayer must affirmatively establish that it satisfied *Newark Morning Ledger's* requirements before it would be entitled to such deductions.
5. Even if a taxpayer could satisfy the *Newark Morning Ledger's* requirements with respect to supervisory goodwill, the taxpayer is not entitled to deductions under Code section 167 with respect to supervisory goodwill that result from the taxpayer's use of an amended return to effectuate a retroactive change in method of accounting.

---

[484] 12 U.S.C. § 1729(f) Repealed. Pub. L. No. 101-73, Title IV, § 407, Aug. 9, 1989, 103 Stat. 363.

[485] *Newark Morning Ledger Co. v. U.S.*, 507 U.S. 546 (1993).

[486] *See* Appendix § A.17 *IRS Settlement Guideline Supervisory Goodwill.*

§ 8.20 Net Operating Losses

In general, an NOL may be carried back two years and carried over 20 years to offset taxable income in such years.[487] NOLs offset taxable income in the order of the taxable years to which the NOL may be carried. The alternative minimum tax rules provide that a taxpayer's NOL deduction cannot reduce the taxpayer's alternative minimum taxable income ("AMTI") by more than 90 percent of the AMTI.[488]

Nonbank members of an affiliated group in which a bank is an includible corporation do not qualify for any bank-specific net operating loss treatment merely by reason of their affiliation with a bank, even if the bank is the common parent corporation.[489] Taxation as a bank is available only to those entities that meet the tax definition of a bank.[490] Similarly, if an affiliated group elects to file a consolidated return, the special bank tax rules are applied only to bank members of the group. For this reason, intercompany allocations take on an importance uncommon for members of a nonbank group filing a consolidated return.

Generally, the adjustments necessary to take into account the bank modifications to the C corporation tax rules present no unique difficulties when a consolidated return is filed. However, as discussed below, in the past careful consideration had to be given to the effect of the application of the special bank net operating loss rule in the context of a consolidated return in which a bank and nonbank corporation join.[491] For tax years beginning after 1993, banks are subject to the same net operating loss deduction rules that are applicable to nonbanks. Thus, the general rule prescribed in Code section 172(a) that allows net operating losses to be carried back two years and carried forward twenty years will apply to a bank.

§ 8.20.1 Pre-1987 Net Operating Losses

For taxable years beginning before January 1, 1987, and ending after December 31, 1975, Code section 172(b)(1)(F) provided that commercial banks and thrifts were allowed to carry back net operating losses to each of the ten taxable years preceding the loss year and then to carry forward any remaining NOL to each of the five subsequent taxable years. Most other C corporations were permitted only a 3-year carryback, but they were granted a 15-year carryforward.

§ 8.20.2 1987-1993 Net Operating Losses

The Tax Reform Act of 1986 set forth different net operating loss carryback rules for commercial banks and thrifts.[492] These rules differed from those availa-

[487] I.R.C. § 172(b). Limitations may apply to an NOL from an acquired corporation. *See* Ch. 11.4.

[488] I.R.C. § 56(d).

[489] *See* I.R.C. § 1504(a) for the definition of an "affiliated group."

[490] I.R.C. § 581. *See also* Ch. 1.

[491] *See* TAM 8527004, March 19, 1985, as to bank and nonbank NOLs. *See* PLRs 8512012, December 17, 1984 and 8544070, August 7, 1985, for treatment of a merged bank NOL.

[492] The Tax Reform Act of 1986, Pub. L. No. 99-514, § 903; I.R.C. § 172(b)(1)(L)[K] and (M)[L].

ble to most other C corporations. In addition to segregating the treatment of commercial banks and thrifts, the net operating losses of commercial banks are required to be bifurcated into the portion of the loss attributable to loan losses and the portion of loss from other sources.[493] The amendments made by the Tax Reform Act of 1986 to the bank NOL rules apply to taxable years beginning after December 31, 1986, and before January 1, 1994, except for a retroactive change in the thrift net operating loss rules, as discussed below.

(a) *Commercial Banks*

Any portion of a net operating loss incurred by a commercial bank that used the charge-off method for deducting bad debts incurred in any taxable year beginning after December 31, 1986, and before January 1, 1994, that is attributable to a wholly or partially worthless bad-debt deductible under Code section 166(a) is granted a 10-year carryback and a 5-year carryforward.[494] Because thrifts generally used the reserve method, the 10-year rule did not apply to thrifts unless the thrift used the specific charge-off method.[495] Thus, the 1987-1993 rule with respect to any net operating loss attributable to a loan loss deductible under the specific charge-off method is identical to the pre-1987 rule governing the entire portion of any bank's net operating loss.

The balance of any 1987-1993 net operating loss incurred during a six-year transition period was subject to the net operating loss rules applicable to most other C corporations.[496] Thus, any non bad-debt net operating loss from this period was treated as a net operating loss carryback to the two preceding taxable years and a net operating loss carryover to each of the 20 taxable years following the taxable year of loss.[497]

The consequence of subjecting non bad-debt net operating losses to the general C corporation rules was to reduce the carryback period by 7 years (from 10 to three years) and extend the carryover period by 10 years (from five to 15 years), a net increase of three taxable years to which a non bad-debt net operating loss may be carried.[498]

To determine the portion of any net operating loss attributable to a bad-debt deductible under Code section 166(a), the net operating loss for the loss year determined without regard to the amount allowed as determined under Code section 166(a) is subtracted from the total net operating loss for the loss year.[499] This calculation may result in less than the total loan loss deduction being subtracted from the total net operating loss, since the total net operating loss may be less than the bad-debt deduction for the year. This would occur, for example,

[493] I.R.C. § 172(b)(1)(L)[K].

[494] I.R.C. § 172(b)(1)(D). The portion of the NOL attributable to bad debts is determined under I.R.C. § 172(g).

[495] *Id.; see also* General Explanation of the Tax Reform Act of 1986, Prepared by the Joint Committee on Taxation (the "Bluebook"), at 567-8.

[496] I.R.C. § 172(b)(1)(A) and (B).

[497] The Taxpayer Relief Act of 1997. Pub. L. No. 105-34, § 1082(b), added I.R.C. § 172(b)(1)(F) for taxable years beginning after August 5, 1997 as provide for the 2-year back and 20-year forward carryover rules. For taxable years beginning prior to August 6, 1997, I.R.C. § 172 provided for a 3-year back and 15-year forward carryover of net operating losses.

[498] For most commercial banks, a longer carryback period is preferable to an extended carryover period. This may not be the case with thrifts.

[499] I.R.C. § 172(g).

if the bank had taxable income before the loan loss deduction. Consequently, the amount of the net operating loss carried back ten years may be less than the bank's bad-debt deduction for the loss year.

Once the loss is bifurcated, each portion is carried back to the appropriate year. Thus, the portion attributable to the bad debt is carried first to the tenth taxable year preceding the loss year; the portion attributable to the non bad-debt loss is carried to the third preceding taxable year.

(b) ***Thrifts***

A net operating loss of a thrift using the reserve method for taxable years beginning after December 31, 1986, was subject to the general C corporation rules, which allow a two-year carryback and a 20-year carryforward.[500] No segregation of the net operating loss attributable to bad debts and non bad debts is made as required for commercial banks.

A net operating loss for any taxable year beginning after December 31, 1981, and before January 1, 1986, was afforded a special carryover rule. Such a net operating loss could be carried back to each of the 10 taxable years preceding the loss year and carried over to each of the eight taxable years following the loss year.[501]

§ 8.20.3 Election to Forego Carryback

Code section 172(b)(3) generally allows both banks and other C corporations to make an irrevocable election to forego carrying back an NOL and instead to carry forward the loss. It must be made by the due date (including extensions of time) for filing the taxpayer's return for the loss year. The election is irrevocable, and it is the IRS's position that it may not be made on an amended return.[502]

When a consolidated return is filed, the common parent is treated as the agent of the group and, as such, is responsible for making all elections.[503] Accordingly, if one member of the group desires to elect to have the carryback period waived, the common parent of the group must make the election to forego the carryback period, and the election applies to all members of the group. Separate elections may not be made for individual members.[504] The IRS would doubtlessly require a commercial bank member of a consolidated group to waive its carryback period and be limited to the carryover period if the common parent elected to forego its two-year carryback period and instead carry forward losses for 20 years. As a practical matter, the IRS's position would substantially reduce the value of the waiver provision to nonbank taxpayers that join with a bank in a consolidated return.

---

[500] I.R.C. §§ 172(b)(1)(M) and (L).

[501] I.R.C. § 172(b)(1)(L). Rev. Rul. 89-78, 1989-1 C.B. 80.

[502] This election was added to the I.R.C. by § 806(c) of the Tax Reform Act of 1976, Pub. L. No. 94-455. (In Temp. Reg. § 7.0, the procedure for making the election on an amended return for any taxable year ending before December 31, 1976, for which a return had been filed before January 31, 1977, was set forth.) Amendments made to I.R.C. § 172 by the Tax Reform Act of 1986 did not alter the elective carryforward rules.

[503] Reg. § 1.1502-77(a).

[504] TAM 8145027, July 31, 1981.

§ 8.20.4 2008-2009 Net Operating Losses

The Worker, Homeownership, and Business Assistance Act of 2009 ("WHBAA")[505] provides a taxpayer with an election to increase the present-law carryback period for an "applicable net operating loss"[506] from two years to any whole number of years elected by the taxpayer that is more than two and less than six.[507] An "applicable net operating loss" is defined as a taxpayer's net operating loss for a taxable year ending after December 31, 2007, and beginning before January 1, 2010. Because most banks and bank holding company groups are calendar year taxpayers, this means for calendar years 2008 and 2009. A taxpayer that has an applicable net operating loss and has elected to apply the special carryback rule can use a carryback period of three, four, or five years for *one* of the two years' NOLs, but not NOLs from both 2008 and 2009.[508]

Taxpayers that elect the special carryback rule are limited in the amount of net operating loss that can be carried back to the fifth taxable year preceding the NOL year.[509] Such carryback losses cannot "exceed 50 percent of the taxpayer's taxable income (computed without regard to the net operating loss for the loss year or any taxable year thereafter) for such preceding taxable year."[510] Alternative minimum tax NOLs ("ATNOLs") would be subject to the same elective carryback period. The carryover period for applicable NOLs remains at 20 years regardless of whether the taxpayer elects to use an extended carryback period.

WHBAA provides for certain transitional rules. For an NOL for a taxable year ending before the enactment of the WHBAA: (1) any election to waive the carryback period under either Code section 172(b)(3) or 810(b)(3) "with respect to such loss may . . . be revoked before the due date (including extensions of time) for filing the return for the taxpayer's last taxable year beginning in 2009"; (2) any application for a tentative carryback adjustment under Code section 6411(a) "with respect to such loss [is] treated as timely filed if filed before [the] due date" (including extensions of time) for filing the return for the taxpayer's last taxable year beginning in 2009.[511]

In general, the amendments made to the carryback rules for NOLs apply to NOLs arising in tax years ending after December 31, 2007.[512] The transitional rules apply with respect to elections and applications for tentative tax adjustments related to NOLs for tax years ending before November 6, 2009.[513] None of

[505] Worker, Homeownership, and Business Assistance Act of 2009, Pub. L. No. 111-92, § 13(a), 123 Stat. 2984.

[506] IRC § 172(b)(1)(H)(ii).

[507] IRC § 172(b)(1)(H)(i)(I).

[508] IRC § 172(b)(1)(H)(iii)(I). Any "eligible small business" that made an election pursuant to the WHBAA as of the day before enactment of the act can elect to apply the special carryback rule to net operating losses from both 2008 *and* 2009. IRC § 172(b)(1)(H)(v)(I). An "eligible small business" is defined as a "corporation or partnership which meets the gross receipts test of Code section 448(c) for the taxable year in which the loss arose (or, in the case of a sole proprietorship, which would meet such test if such proprietorship were a corporation)," except that in applying Code section 448(c), $15,000,000 is substituted for $5,000,000 each place it appears. IRC § 172(b)(1)(H)(v)(II).

[509] IRC § 172(b)(1)(H)(iv)(I).

[510] IRC § 172(b)(1)(H)(iv)(I). This limitation does not apply to any eligible small business that made an election pursuant to WHBAA as of the day before enactment of the act IRC § 172(b)(1)(H)(iv)(III).

[511] Pub. L. No. 111-92, § 13(e)(4).

[512] Pub. L. No. 111-92, § 13(e)(1).

[513] Pub. L. No. 111-92, § 13(e)(4).

the amendments established by WHBAA apply to any financial institution that provided an equity interest or warrant to the federal government pursuant to the Emergency Economic Stabilization Act of 2008.[514]

§ 8.21 Abandonment Losses—Customer Lists and Goodwill

Code section 165 allows a deduction for any loss sustained during the taxable year and not compensated for by insurance or otherwise. To be allowable as a deduction under Code section 165, a loss must be evidenced by closed and completed transactions and fixed by identifiable events.[515] Only a bona fide loss is allowed to be deducted. Substance and not mere form shall govern in determining a deductible loss.[516]

In order to take a deduction under Code section 165 for an abandonment of property, there must be (1) an intention on the part of the owner to abandon the asset, and (2) an affirmative act of abandonment.[517] The intention to abandon standing alone is not sufficient to establish a recognition event; instead, there must be an affirmative act of abandonment.[518] As a result, there is arguably an inherent requirement for an abandonment loss that the taxpayer, rather than some other party, take the action to abandon permanently the property in question. Further, an abandonment does not result simply from cessation of use.[519] A loss incurred in a business and arising from the sudden termination of the usefulness of any nondepreciable property may be deductible where the business is discontinued or where the property is permanently discarded from use in the business for the taxable year in which the loss is actually sustained.[520]

In general, the amount of loss allowable as a deduction under Code section 165(a) may not exceed the adjusted basis for determining loss from the sale or other disposition of the property involved,[521] and proper adjustment must be made for any insurance or other compensation received.[522] If an event occurs which could result in a loss, and, in the year of the event, there exists a claim for reimbursement with respect to which there is a reasonable prospect of recovery, no portion of the loss with respect to which reimbursement may be received is sustained until it can be ascertained with reasonable certainty whether or not the reimbursement will be received.[523]

Whether a reasonable prospect of recovery exists with respect to a claim for reimbursement of a loss is a question of fact to be determined upon an examina-

---

[514] Pub. L. No. 111-92, § 13(f)(1); Emergency Economic Stabilization Act of 2008, Pub. L. No. 110-343, 122 Stat. 3765.

[515] *United States v. S.S. White Dental Manufacturing Co.*, 274 U.S. 398, 401 (1927).

[516] Reg. § 1.165-1(b).

[517] *A.J. Industries, Inc. v. United States*, 503 F.2d 660, 670 (9th Cir. 1974); *Citron*, 97 T.C. at 209; *CRST, Inc. v. Commissioner*, 92 T.C. 1249, 1257 (1989), *aff'd*, 909 F.2d 1146 (8th Cir. 1990).

[518] *See Brountas v. Commissioner*, 692 F.2d 152 (1st Cir. 1982), *cert. denied*, 462 U.S. 1106 (1983); *Beus v. Commissioner*, 261 F.2d 176, 180 (9th Cir. 1958); *Citron*, 97 T.C. at 210; *Zurn v. Commissioner*, T.C. Memo. 1996-386.

[519] *See Beus*, 261 F.2d at 180; *Citron*, 97 T.C. at 210.

[520] Reg. § 1.165-2(a).

[521] Reg. § 1.165-1(c)(1). As provided in Reg. § 1.1001-1 the adjusted basis for determining the gain or loss from the disposition of property is the cost or other basis prescribed in section 1012 or other applicable provisions of subtitle A of the Code.

[522] Reg. § 1.165-1(c)(4).

[523] Reg. § 1.165-1(d)(2)(i).

tion of all facts and circumstances. Whether or not such reimbursement will be received may be ascertained with reasonable certainty, for example, by a settlement of the claim, by an adjudication of the claim or by an abandonment of the claim. The determination of whether reasonable certainty as to reimbursement exists is an objective inquiry into the facts and circumstances surrounding the loss as of the close of the taxable year in which the deduction is claimed.[524]

§8.21.1 Abandonment Loss for Customer Lists

An abandonment loss may be taken with respect to intangible assets.[525] However, case law has established that goodwill may not be abandoned until the business to which it relates ceases to operate.[526] Otherwise, the transaction is not considered to be a closed and completed transaction within the meaning of Regulation section 1.165-1(b). Exceptions arise when the taxpayer abandons a portion of its business that has "distinct transferable value."[527]

If the intangible asset is an "amortizable section 197 intangible," however, Code section 197 provides that no loss shall be recognized by reason of a disposition or the worthlessness if the asset if it were acquired in a transaction or series of related transactions and if one or more other amortizable section 197 intangibles acquired in the transaction is retained.[528] An "amortizable section 197 intangible" includes goodwill, going concern value, deposit base and other customer based intangibles.[529]

Customer lists are closely associated with goodwill, yet judicial authority exists for allowing an abandonment loss even though the underlying business of the taxpayer is not terminated.[530] Of course, in those situations when Code section 197 applies, the judicial rule is preempted.

In *Metropolitan Laundry*, the cost attributable to an abandoned customer lists was found to be deductible.[531] The court stated:

---

[524] *Boehm v. Commissioner*, 326 U.S. 287, 292-93 (1945); *Ramsey Scarlett & Co. v. Commissioner*, 61 T.C. 795, 811 (1974), *aff'd*, 521 F.2d 786 (4th Cir. 1975); *Brown v. Commissioner*, T.C. Memo. 1996-284.

[525] *Parmelee Transportation Co. v. United States*, 351 F.2d 619 (Ct. Cl. 1965). *See Massey-Ferguson, Inc. v. Commissioner*, 59 T.C. 220 (1959), *acq.* 1973-2 C.B. 2; *Solar Nitrogen Chemicals, Inc. v. Commissioner*, T.C. Memo. 1978-486.

[526] *Thrifticheck Service Corp. v. Commissioner*, 33 T.C. 1038 (1960), *aff'd*, 287 F.2d 1 (2d Cir. 1961); *Illinois Cereal Mills, Inc. v. Commissioner*, T.C. Memo. 1983-469, *aff'd*, 789 F.2d 1234 (7th Cir.), *cert. denied*, 479 U.S. 995 (1986); *Danco Products, Inc. v. Commissioner*, T.C. Memo. 1962-52.

[527] *Metropolitan Laundry Co. v. United States*, 100 F. Supp. 803 (N.D. Cal. 1951). In *Metropolitan Laundry*, the taxpayer was permitted an abandonment loss on a portion of a customer list that was attributable to a specific geographic area. The taxpayer had purchased the customer lists of several laundry businesses in San Francisco and Oakland. During World War II, the government seized the taxpayer's San Francisco plant for military purposes. After the war, the taxpayer had trouble reestablishing its business and abandoned its San Francisco routes while it continued its operations in Oakland.

[528] I.R.C. §197(f)(1); Reg. §1.197-2(g)(1)(i)(B) provides: "The abandonment of an amortizable section 197 intangible, or any other event rendering an amortizable section 197 intangible worthless, is treated as a disposition of the intangible . . . ."

[529] I.R.C. §197(c) and (d).

[530] *See Metropolitan Laundry*, 100 F. Supp. at 806.

[531] The Tax Court has followed *Metropolitan Laundry* holding that "if there is a clearly identifiable and severable asset, its abandonment entitles the taxpayer to a loss deduction." *Massey-Ferguson*, 59 T.C. at 225. Specifically, *Massey-Ferguson* allowed an abandonment loss for a line of business the taxpayer had purchased from another party and operated at a distinct location, even though the taxpayer continued to manufacture similar products under a different trade name at another location.

> It may be granted that good will cannot exist in the abstract, apart from a going business, and that, generally speaking, the good will of a business cannot be entirely disposed of or destroyed while the business continues. But certainly a going concern can dispose of its business in a particular area or in respect to a particular product or service along with incidental good will without abandoning its entire business . . . . So also, certain types of concerns can dispose of their business and good will apart from their physical properties . . . . And, in either instance, so long as the business and the good will disposed of may be assigned a distinct transferable value, the transaction may properly be recognized, for tax purposes, as a closed one.[532]

§ 8.21.2 Abandonment Loss for Supervisory Goodwill

The IRS concluded that a bank's supervisory goodwill arising from the acquisition of failed thrifts was not deductible as an abandonment loss under Code section 165.[533] Supervisory goodwill is the excess of the purchase price (which included liabilities assumed by the acquirer) over the fair market value of the assets acquired from the failing thrift. The case involves an intangible that has been characterized by the Supreme Court as goodwill.[534] The bank in question filed an amended return claiming a Code section 165 abandonment loss for the year that supervisory goodwill became worthless because of certain provisions in the Financial Institution's Reform, Recovery and Enforcement Act of 1989 ("FIRREA").[535] The IRS concluded that most of the value ascribed to supervisory goodwill was derived from loans that had declined in value because of rising interest rates.[536] It also found that tax basis was properly ascribed to the loans and other assets from which the supervisory goodwill was derived and not in the supervisory goodwill itself. In its claim for refund, the bank also asserted that it should have assigned a tax basis to the goodwill created at the time it acquired the failed thrifts.[537]

At the time the bank acquired the thrift, Code section 597(a) provided that the gross income of a domestic building and loan association did not include any amount of money or other property received from the Federal Savings and Loan

[532] 100 F. Supp. at 806-07 (citations omitted).

[533] FSA 200013006, December 29, 1999. *See also* FSA 200028001, March 22, 2000, where the IRS also concluded that a transferee takes a substituted basis in assets acquired pursuant to a "G" reorganization, and the taxpayer had no basis in supervisory goodwill.

[534] *See Winstar*, 518 U.S. at 848-49.

[535] Pub. L. No. 101-73, 103 Stat. 183 (1989), (codified at various sections of 12 and 15 U.S.C.). Regulatory capital requirements were set forth in 12 C.F.R. § 563.13. During the years in issue, the savings and loan industry was in crisis, and the FSLIC lacked the funds necessary to liquidate all of the failing thrifts. Accordingly, the FSLIC arranged mergers between healthy thrifts and failing thrifts. As an inducement for these mergers, the FSLIC allowed the acquiring thrifts to count supervisory goodwill toward regulatory capital reserve requirements and to amortize the goodwill over as much as 40 years. The concept of supervisory goodwill was merely part of an accounting regime designed to induce healthy thrifts to acquire failing thrifts. Because the FSLIC had insufficient funds to make up the difference between a failed thrift's liabilities and assets, banks had to be offered a "cash substitute" to induce a healthy thrift to assume a failed thrift's obligations. *United States v. Winstar Corp.*, 518 U.S. 839, 849-56 (1996).

[536] *See Winstar*, 518 U.S. at 851-52.

[537] Supervisory goodwill is not listed in section 406(f) of the National Housing Act. Furthermore, the IRS believes that it does not resemble any type of financial assistance listed in section 406(f), *e.g.* capital contributions, deposits, asset purchases, assumption of liabilities and loans. The types of transactions listed in section 406(f) imply that something of value, either cash or an asset, changes hands between the FSLIC and the acquiring thrift. With respect to supervisory goodwill, no money or assets are received by the thrift from the FSLIC.

Insurance Corporation ("FSLIC") pursuant to section 406(f) of the National Housing Act, regardless of whether any note or other instrument was issued in exchange.[538] Further, Code section 597(b) provided that such payments would not reduce the basis of the recipient's assets.

§8.22 Covered Asset Losses

The Financial Institutions Reform, Recovery and Enforcement Act of 1989 (the "Act")[539] repealed certain tax rules that were originally enacted in the Economic Recovery Tax Act of 1981, extended by the Tax Reform Act of 1986, and re-extended and modified by the Technical and Miscellaneous Revenue Act of 1988.[540] These rules generally permitted the relevant supervisory authority to arrange mergers of Financially Troubled Institutions with healthy institutions at a tax-subsidized cost. The repeal of these provisions is effective for acquisitions occurring on or after May 10, 1989. The Act also clarifies the effective date of the TAMRA provisions as they apply to Agency assisted transactions involving financially troubled banks.

Prior to the effective date of the Act, sections 368(a)(3)(D) and 382(1)(5)(F) of the Internal Revenue Code provided special rules regarding the availability of tax-free reorganization status for, and the applicability of the loss limitation rules of section 382 following, certain Agency supervised restructurings of financial institutions described in section 581 or section 591. Section 597 generally provided that Agency assistance paid to or on behalf of a Financially Troubled Institution was excluded from gross income, but required the reduction of certain tax attributes in an aggregate amount equal to 50 percent of the amount of assistance received. Repeal of these prior law rules generally subjects such transactions to the generally applicable rules of sections 368 and 382 and generally requires that Federal financial assistance be accounted for as gross income, as described more fully below.[541]

These provisions had the effect of permitting an acquiring institution to realize tax benefits attributable to a particular item even though FSLIC assistance is received with respect to such item. For example, if the acquiror received coverage for capital losses incurred on the disposition of identified assets of the acquired institution, the acquiror was entitled to deduct such loss for federal income tax purposes, notwithstanding that it was reimbursed for the loss by the FSLIC, and that the FSLIC payment was tax free. Similarly, if payments were made by the FSLIC to an acquiror pursuant to a yield guarantee, such assistance did not have to be reported as taxable income by the acquiror.

---

[538] 12 U.S.C. §1729(f) (1982) and Repealed. Pub. L. No. 101-73, Title IV, §497, Aug. 9, 1989, 103 Stat. 363. The FSLIC was created pursuant to 12 U.S.C. §1725. The statute referred to formation and operation of the FSLIC under the direction of the FHLBB for the purpose of providing insurance for savings and loan accounts. In addition to providing deposit insurance, the FSLIC was authorized to provide assistance from its assets to insolvent savings associations. This assistance included capital contributions, deposits, asset purchases, assumption of liabilities and loans. National Housing Act §406(f), 12 U.S.C. §1729(f) (1982). The FSLIC was abolished by FIRREA, and its functions were transferred to the Federal Deposit Insurance Co.

[539] Pub. L. No, 101-73, section 1401.

[540] Pub. L. No. 100-647, 102 Stat. 3342 ("TAMRA"). TAMRA extended the sunset of the FSLIC-specific tax provisions to December 31, 1989, but cut by fifty percent the tax benefits for FSLIC-assisted acquisitions occurring after December 31, 1988.

[541] Cumulative Bulletin Notice 89-102, 1989-2 C.B. 436, October 2, 1989.

Chapter 9
Interest Expense

Contents

§9.1 Tax Planning Suggestions
§9.2 Allowance of Deduction
  §9.2.1 Deducting Dividend Payments on TARP-Preferred Stock
§9.3 Timing of Deduction
  §9.3.1 General Rule
  §9.3.2 Special Rule for Thrifts
  §9.3.3 When Crediting Takes Place
  §9.3.4 Savings Certificates and O.I.D.
§9.4 Deferred Interest Expense
  §9.4.1 Prepaid Interest by a Thrift
  §9.4.2 Market Discount Bonds
  §9.4.3 UNICAP Rule
§9.5 Disallowed Interest Expense
  §9.5.1 Overview of Automatic Disallowance Rules
  §9.5.2 Overview of General Disallowance Rule
  §9.5.3 The TEFRA Disallowance
  §9.5.4 The TRA '86 Disallowance Rule
  §9.5.5 Qualified Tax-Exempt Obligations
  §9.5.6 Interest Expense
  §9.5.7 Acquisition Date
  §9.5.8 Consolidated Disallowance
  §9.5.9 Tax Basis of Assets and Tax-Exempts
§9.6 S Corporation Banks
§9.7 Registration-Required Obligations

§9.1 Tax Planning Suggestions

There are interest expense deferral rules and dissallowance rules that override the general rule that allows a deduction for all interest expense.[1] One interest expense dissallowance rule applies to all taxpayers, including banks. Two other disallowance rules apply only to banks, but under limited circumstances the IRS has extended the bank rules so that they apply to assets held by nonbank members of a consolidated group.

The disallowance rule that applies to all taxpayers becomes operative only upon a showing of a purpose by the taxpayer to use borrowed funds to purchase or carry tax-exempt securities. This rule will not apply to a bank unless a borrowing is not in connection with its day-to-day banking business, or unless it

[1] *See The Art of Tax Efficiency in Community Banks,* by M. Gula, J. Brew, and R. Blasi, 2007, Red Room Publishing, *http://www.mraeresources.com/bookstore/.*

can be traced to an investment in tax-exempt obligations. However, under the bank specific rules, a relationship between a borrowing and an investment does not have to be established to disallow interest expense on all types of borrowings. The bank specific rules disallow interest using a formula that allocates interest expense to tax-exempt obligations. If there are multiple bank members within an affiliated group, the portion of disallowed interest expense may vary from bank to bank. Thus, tax-exempts should be held by the bank member, which is subject to the smallest disallowance ratio. If the entity owning the obligation is not a bank, the automatic interest expense disallowance rules are generally inapplicable. Thus, the yield on tax-exempt obligations will increase if a nonbank member of a bank holding group owns the obligations. However, historical rules that require a nexus between the tax-exempt obligation and the borrowing continue to apply. Moreover, a recent Revenue Ruling and a U.S. Tax Court decision indicate that under certain circumstances the historical disallowance rule can be applied on a consolidated basis.

Statutory provisions contain an exception to the 100 percent interest expense disallowance rule applicable to banks for certain qualified tax-exempt obligations. Holding this type of tax-exempt obligation can increase the after-tax yield on tax-exempt obligations held by a bank. On audit, banks are required to prove that the obligations they are holding are, in fact, qualified tax-exempt obligations.

Whether all, only a portion, or none of the interest expense that is allocable to tax-exempt obligations held by a bank is automatically disallowed depends upon the acquisition date of the obligation. In the situation where tax-exempt obligations are acquired as part of the acquisition of the assets of another bank, the form of the acquisition could affect the disallowance rule. For example, if an acquisition is tax-free, the acquirer may be entitled to more favorable rules than if the tax-exempt obligations were acquired in a taxable transaction. Thus, this is a potential cost of a taxable transaction.

Interest expense is also subject to various deferral rules. In particular, taxpayers should be aware that the Uniform Capitalization rule of Code section 263A may require that interest expense be deferred to the extent that it is allocable to the construction of real property. If a bank builds a new headquarters location or any other facility, a portion of its interest expense, including the interest that it pays to depositors, may have to be capitalized into the cost of the structure.

§9.2 Allowance of Deduction

Interest is commonly defined as the amount received for the use, or forbearance, or detention of money.[2] In other words, it is rent paid for the use of property. Regardless of what the parties to the transaction call the payment, if it is for the use of money it is treated as interest for federal income tax purposes. Interest is deductible only if there is an underlying obligation to pay both interest and principal. The obligation must be enforceable and must have economic substance.

[2] *Fall River Electric Light Company v. Commissioner*, 23 B.T.A. 168 (1931); *Ripple v. Mortgage & Acceptance Corporation*, 137 S.E. 156; 193 N.C. 422 (1927); *Baird v. Meyer et al.*, 215 N.W. 542; 55 N.D. 930 (1927); *Kishi v. Humble Oil & Refining Co.*, 10 F.2d 356 (1925).

Interest can be deducted only by the debtor, the taxpayer who is liable on the debt. The taxpayer must be primarily liable for the debt, so payments made when a taxpayer is jointly liable qualify, but payments made as guarantor or endorser do not. A special rule permits the deduction of interest by a person who is not directly liable on a bond when the bond is secured by a mortgage on property of which the person is the legal or equitable owner.

Usually, payments that are characterized as interest are interest in fact; however, in some instances payments that are called interest are actually disguised rent, dividends, purchase price payments, or principal. Although such mischaracterized payments are not deductible as interest, they may be allowed as some other deduction (e.g., an ordinary and necessary business deduction under Code section 162).

The following items are generally outside the definition of interest and cannot be deducted as such:

1. Commitment fees as standby charges (fees that are incurred to have business funds made readily available over a period of time, but not for the actual use of funds). If the funds are ultimately borrowed, a part of the fee may be deducted in each tax year over the life of the loan;
2. Penalties and fines on the income tax deficiencies of individuals;
3. Service charges;
4. Down payments;
5. Preferred stock "interest," i.e., dividends;
6. Intra-company interest charges that do not represent debt to another "person."

Conversely, some payments that are not called interest are, in fact, deductible as interest, such as:

1. Repurchase premium (a price paid in excess of the adjusted issue price of a debt instrument);[3]
2. Commitment fees for the actual use of loans including points and other pre-paid interest (although such interest must generally be deducted ratably over the life of the loan, and there are special rules for points paid in connection with the purchase of a residence);
3. Prepayment penalties on loans;
4. Late payment charges (when a fee is not for service);
5. Interest paid on most publicly offered debt obligations, i.e., bonds, notes, etc., issued in registered form;
6. Early withdrawal penalties on certificates of deposit, savings accounts, etc;
7. Imputed interest on no-interest or below market loans.

[3] Reg. § 1.163-7(c).

Interest expense is deductible by banks under the general rule of Code section 163, which allows a deduction for all interest paid or accrued within the taxable year on indebtedness.[4] This rule is made expressly applicable to banks by regulations, which state, "In the case of banks and loan or trust companies, interest paid within the year on deposits, such as interest paid on moneys received for investment and secured by interest-bearing certificates of indebtedness issued by such bank or loan or trust company, may be deducted."[5]

Code section 591(a) expressly allows an equivalent deduction for thrifts operating in mutual form which pay dividends on deposits. It provides that, in the case of mutual savings banks, cooperative banks, domestic building and loan associations and other savings institutions, a deduction is allowed for dividends paid to depositors or credited to their accounts as dividends or interest if such amounts may be withdrawn on demand subject only to the customary notice of intention to withdraw. However, only "dividends" otherwise qualifying for deduction under Code section 591 that are allocable to the withdrawable portion of "stock accounts" will be deductible as interest equivalents under that section. Any portion of credited dividends allocable to the minimum paid-in capital of stock accounts is to be treated as a nondeductible distribution.[6]

Code section 591 prevails over the general interest deductibility rule of Code section 163.[7] However, with respect to original issue discount, regulations under Code section 591 provide that Code section 163, and not Code section 591, controls the deductibility of amounts with respect to certificates of deposit (irrespective of term) and other deposit arrangements issued after May 27, 1969.[8]

No deduction is permitted for interest paid or accrued on loan arrangements that lack economic substance apart from anticipated tax consequences.[9] A transaction between related parties is generally subject to special scrutiny, as use of legal formalities may give the appearance of substance where it would otherwise be lacking.[10] Thus, a taxpayer will not be allowed a deduction for interest paid on a loan to an affiliated company on the grounds that: (1) no valid indebtedness was created because the loan was a fictitious sham lacking in substance; and (2) the taxpayer had no business purpose for borrowing the money other than to reduce its taxes.

---

[4] I.R.C. § 163(a) (2000). I.R.C. § 171(e) treats bond premium as interest expense deductible under that section by the holder of a bond. *See* Reg. § 1.446-2 for rules for determining the amount of interest that accrues during an accrual period and the portion of a payment that consists of accrued interest.

[5] Reg. § 1.163-1(c).

[6] Rev. Rul. 70-121, 1970-1 C.B. 141.

[7] *Hudson City Savings Bank v. Commissioner*, 53 T.C. 70, Dec. 29,800 (1969).

[8] Reg. § § 1.163-4, 1.591-1(b).

[9] *Knetsch v. United States*, 364 U.S. 361, 366 (1960); *Goldstein v. Commissioner*, 364 F.2d 734, 740 (2d Cir. 1966).

[10] *Riverpoint Lace Work, Inc. v. Commissioner*, 13 T.C.M. (CCH) 463, 466 (1954) (citations omitted); *Shaffer Terminals, Inc. v. Commissioner*, 16 T.C. 356, 362 (1951), (*citing Higgins v. Smith*, 308 U.S. 473 (1940), aff'd per curiam, 194 F.2d 539 (9th Cir. 1952)).

§9.2.1 Deducting Dividend Payments on TARP-Preferred Stock

In the fall of 2008, the Treasury Department instituted the Capital Purchase Program ("CPP"), one of the purposes of which was to enhance the liquidity of financial institutions. CPP was within the Troubled Asset Relief Program ("TARP") of the Emergency Economic Stabilization Act ("Stabilization Act").[11] The Stabilization Act was designed to ensure the liquidity of the national financial system.[12] The Treasury was instructed to structure TARP in a manner that would result in the least cost to taxpayers.[13] To do so, assisted institutions issued "senior preferred stock" to the government in exchange for funds that were designed to improve bank capital levels.[14] The purpose of characterizing the capital infusion as equity was to ensure that under bank regulatory rules, it would qualify as Tier 1 capital.

The senior preferred stock had debt-like characteristics.[15] It was required to pay cumulative[16] quarterly dividends at a fixed rate that increased after five years. While the stock remained outstanding, the assisted institutions were constrained on executive compensation, the redemption of common stock, and the repurchase of other preferred stock. The preferred stock was non-voting. Moreover, "[t]here is no fixed date on which the banks must redeem the preferred stock . . . . This is necessary for the investment to qualify as "Tier 1" capital under regulatory requirements."[17]

It is uncertain whether the equity form of the senior preferred stock will outweigh its debt-like qualities and prevent dividend distributions from being treated as deductible interest expenses. In general, the deductibility of distributions as interest should depend upon the substance of the instrument.[18] Courts have developed a thirteen-factor test for distinguishing debt from equity.[19] While

---

[11] Pub. L. No. 110-343, 122 Stat. 3765, *codified* at 12 U.S.C. § 5201 *et seq*.

[12] 12 U.S.C. § 5201.

[13] 12 U.S.C. § 5213(1).

[14] Banks organized as Subchapter S corporations issued senior debt instead. The contract for Subchapter S financial institutions issuing senior debt is largely equivalent to the contract for preferred stock, apart from the mechanical difference of issuing debt rather than stock. Notably, the senior debt was subordinated to other senior debt, the quarterly interest payments could be deferred for up to twenty quarters, and there were limits in place similar to the preferred stock contract. The senior debt had a 30-year term. The Treasury used standardized contract terms for the exchanges, and all contracts are available to the public. See U.S. Department of the Treasury, Program Documents (October 5, 2012), http://www.treasury.gov/initiatives/financial-stability/TARP-Programs/bank-investment-programs/cap/Pages/documents.aspx.

[15] Preferred stock, defined in Code section 305, and in contrast to common stock, is "(i) limited and preferred as to dividends and does not participate in corporate growth to any significant extent, and (ii) has a fixed redemption price." I.R.C. §305(e)(5)(B). Participation in growth is defined elsewhere in the Code as "real and meaningful likelihood of the shareholder actually participating in the earnings and growth of the corporation." I.R.C. §351(g)(3)(A).

[16] Missed dividend payments accrue.

[17] Office of Financial Stability, U.S. Dep't of the Treasury, Troubled Asset Relief Program: Two Year Retrospective (2010).

[18] Jonathan Prokup and Dustin Covello, *Rethinking the Tax Treatment of Government Assistance to Financial Institutions in Light of Treasury's 2008 Capital Purchase Program*, Tax. & Reg. of Fin. Inst., Jan.-Feb. 2012, at 5, 11 (noting that the preferred stock has three characteristics indicative of a "debt-like nature . . . 1) the existence of an implicit maturity/redemption date for the Preferred Stock, (2) the government's extraordinary remedies for default [nationalization of the bank], and (3) the existence of a coupon-dividend rate that was more consistent with debt than stock.")

[19] *Estate of Mixon v. U.S.*, 464 F.2d 394, 402 (5th Cir. 1972) (holding that a capital contribution by certain stockholders of a bank was a loan to the institution).

the label or form of the instrument is a factor to consider, it, alone, is never controlling. The intent of the parties is an important factor to consider.

The paramount goal of the CPP was to furnish banks with funds that would qualify as Tier 1 Capital for regulatory purposes. Tier 1 capital is a class of assets held by a financial institution for the purposes of the minimum capital requirements set by bank regulators. The definition of Tier 1 capital includes "noncumulative perpetual preferred stock," but not debt.[20] Thus, an infusion of funds that was structured as a loan would not qualify as Tier 1 capital. Because the CPP's preferred stock was cumulative, it did not qualify as Tier 1 capitals under then existing banking regulations. As an apparent accommodation bank regulators issued a ruling that "the preferred stock issued to Treasury . . . is considered to be senior perpetual preferred stock issued to Treasury under the TARP" that may be included in Tier 1 capital.[21]

The Treasury and the bank regulators went to great lengths to ensure that the CPP funds were received by the financial institutions in a form that satisfied capital requirements. This may indicate that the intent of the CPP was less to take an equity position than to provide useful capital to financial institutions while also minimizing taxpayer risk. Viewed in this light, the designation of the CPP instruments as preferred stock may have been a pragmatic compromise between substantive risk minimization and formalistic capital requirements, but a compromise that has spawned uncertainty as to whether the distributions on the preferred stock are, in fact, deductible interest payments.

§9.3 Timing of Deduction

For a commercial bank, the timing of a deduction for interest expense depends upon whether the bank has adopted the cash method or the accrual method of accounting. For a thrift, Code section 591 governs whether and when a deduction for the interest equivalent—dividends—can be taken.

§9.3.1 General Rule

Interest expense is deductible by a bank in the year in which it is paid or accrued, depending upon the method of accounting employed by the bank.[22]

A cash method bank is allowed an interest expense deduction when interest is actually paid.[23] Proper crediting to a depositor's account will normally constitute "payment" by a cash method bank. In *Fourth Financial Corporation*, the Tax Court held that a current deduction was available to a cash method bank for amounts paid toward its interest liability even though the amount paid was subject to an agreement to refund the interest if it became "excess interest."[24]

---

[20] *Cf.* FDIC's Minimum Capital Requirements, 12 C.F.R. § 325.2(v).

[21] 74 Fed. Reg. 26082 fn. 4, June 1, 2009. The senior debt of Subchapter S banks is also included in Tier 1 capital. *Id.* at fn. 5.

[22] I.R.C. § 461 (2000); Reg. § 1.461-1(a)(2).

[23] Reg. § 1.461-1(a)(1).

[24] *Fourth Financial Corporation & Consol. Subsidiaries v. Commissioner*, 49 T.C.M. 1485, Dec. 42,087(M) (1985), T.C. Memo. 1985-232. *See* discussion of CAP loans in Chapter 2, which address the treatment of this transaction from the lender's viewpoint. *See also Stevens Bros. Foundations, Inc. v. Commissioner*, 39 T.C. 93 (1962), *rev'd on another issue*, 324 F.2d 633 (8th Cir. 1963); *Sherman v. Commissioner*, 18 T.C. 746 (1952).

"Excess interest" was defined as the amount paid, computed at a floating rate, that exceeded interest computed at a fixed rate. The reimbursement, if any, was made at the end of the loan's term. The court reasoned that for the deduction to be disallowed the lender must be assured of both the right to reimbursement and the amount of reimbursement must be reasonably determined. In this case, the lender was found not to have a fixed right to reimbursement.[25]

An accrual method bank deducts interest expense in the taxable year in which all the events have occurred that determine the fact of the liability and in which the amount thereof can be determined with reasonable accuracy.[26] However, the IRS has ruled that this "all-events" test is not satisfied if the depositor has a right to withdraw its account balance before the interest is properly credited.[27]

Code section 461(h) provides that, in determining whether an accrual method taxpayer has incurred an amount of interest expense during a taxable year, all the events that establish the taxpayer's liability for such amount will not be deemed to have occurred at any time earlier than the time when economic performance occurs.[28] With respect to interest expense, economic performance occurs as the interest cost economically accrues; that is, as time passes, since by definition interest is an amount paid for the use of money.[29]

§9.3.2 Special Rule for Thrifts

For mutual savings banks, cooperative banks, domestic building and loan associations and other savings institutions chartered and supervised as a savings and loan or similar associations, Code section 591 contains the rules for determining both whether and when a deduction is allowed for interest or "dividends" paid to or credited to the account of depositors or holders of accounts, deposits or withdrawable stores.[30] Pursuant to that section, a deduction is allowed in the taxable year in which an amount paid or credited to the account of a depositor or holder of an account is withdrawable on demand, subject only to customary notice of intention to withdraw.[31] Thus, "dividends" credited to a depositor's account on December 31, 20X1, but not made available for withdrawal by the account owners until the first business day of 20X2, are deductible in 20X2. A practice of allowing early withdrawal of otherwise nonwithdrawable

[25] The IRS has taken a position on both sides of this issue. Their positions appear to be in conflict. *See* discussion of "Receipt of Prepaid Interest" at Ch. II, in particular. *Continental Illinois Corp. v. Commissioner*, 998 F.2d 513 (7th Cir. 1993), *cert. denied*, 510 U.S. 1041 (1994).

[26] Reg. §1.461-1(a)(2). The IRS has been working on a regulations project that would set forth rules for proper accrual of interest and discount on troubled debt. "Resource constraints" have impeded the promulgation of those rules.

[27] *Peoples Bank and Trust Company v. Commissioner*, 69-2 U.S.T.C. ¶9566, 415 F.2d 1341 (7th Cir. 1969); Rev. Rul. 67-352, 1967-2 C.B. 176.

[28] Section 91 of the Deficit Reduction Act of 1984 added subsection "h" to I.R.C. §461. Act §44(b)(3) provides that the effective date of this provision is "after June 8, 1984." This provision was added to the Code to ameliorate the controversy involving whether an expense relating to a future obligation satisfies the all-events test in a year significantly earlier than the year in which the taxpayer must fulfill the obligation. Deficit Reduction Act of 1984, Pub. L. No. 98-369, 98 Stat. 494 (1984).

[29] Reg. §1.461-4(e).

[30] Reg. §1.591-1(a)(2). A "mutual savings bank" includes any bank that is subject to and operates under federal or state laws relating to mutual savings banks. I.R.C. §591(b) (2000).

[31] I.R.C. §591(a) (2000).

amounts does not accelerate the deduction.[32] Similarly, a depositor's dividend check mailed by a thrift on December 31 would result in the amount being deductible in the subsequent year.[33]

§9.3.3 When Crediting Takes Place

An entry on magnetic tape or on an internal computer listing showing the amount of interest earned constitutes "crediting" to a depositor's account by both a commercial bank and a thrift.[34] However, merely making an entry to a reserve account established on the depository's books does not entitle the bank to a current interest expense deduction.[35]

§9.3.4 Savings Certificates and O.I.D.

(a) *Timing of Deduction*

Accrual basis treatment is mandated for cash basis banks with respect to original issue discount ("O.I.D.") obligations.[36] O.I.D. obligations include any bond, debenture, note, certificate, or other evidence of indebtedness issued by a corporation at a discount.[37] The historical rule that requires a cash basis taxpayer to defer its interest expense deduction until a discounted obligation is paid at maturity no longer applies.[38] However, a cash basis bank may deduct accrued interest on short-term obligations only when paid.[39] For this purpose, a "short-term" obligation is a taxable bond, debenture, note, certificate, or other evidence of indebtedness with a fixed maturity date not more than one year from the issue date.[40]

(b) *Amount of Deduction*

For corporate debt, including bank deposit liabilities, issued after May 27, 1969, and before July 2, 1982, a *pro rata* amount of O.I.D. is deductible as interest over the life of the obligation.[41] For obligations issued after July 1, 1982, the amount of the interest accrual is determined by applying a constant rate to the loan balance.[42] Thus, under pre-July 2, 1982, rules, the issuer of a note with discount was entitled to substantially larger deductions in the early years of a debt instrument's term as compared to deductions allowed issuers of notes not issued at a discount. The 1982 changes were designed to correct this disparity.

---

[32] *Hancock County Federal Savings & Loan Association of Chester*, 32 T.C. 869, Dec. 23,672, (1959), *acq.*, 1959-2 C.B.

[33] Rev. Rul. 66-232, 1966-2 C.B. 236; Reg. §1.591-1(a)(2).

[34] *See* Rev. Rul. 81-142, 1981-1 C.B. 371, with respect to entries on tape; and PLR 8025163, March 27, 1980, with respect to entries on an internal computer listing.

[35] *Peoples Bank and Trust Co.*, 69-2 U.S.T.C. ¶9566, 415 F.2d 1341 (7th Cir. 1969); *Hudson City Savings Bank v. Commissioner*, 53 T.C. 70, Dec. 29,800 (1969); PLR 7829021, April 19, 1978.

[36] I.R.C. §§163(e), 1272 (2000). *See also* Rev. Rul. 83-60, 1983-1 C.B. 39; Rev. Rul. 78-37, 1978-1 C.B. 54.

[37] I.R.C. §1275(a) (2000); I.R.C. §163(e); Reg. §1.163-3(d).

[38] Rev. Rul. 59-260, 1959-2 C.B. 137.

[39] I.R.C. §163(e)(2)(c) (2000).

[40] I.R.C. §1283(a)(1) (2000). It is the IRS's position that a loan made by a bank fits within the definition of a "short-term obligation." *Security Bank of Minnesota v. Commissioner*, 93-1 U.S.T.C. ¶50,301, 994 F.2d 432 (8th Cir. 1993).

[41] Reg. §1.163-4. If a bank is not organized as a corporation, it is unclear whether this rule would apply.

[42] I.R.C. §§163(e)(2), 1272(a)(3) (2000).

Example: Bank T issues a $100,000, 8% certificate of deposit in 19X0 with a five-year maturity date. Interest is payable annually. Because the market rate of interest is 10%, Bank T must issue the debt at a discount of $7,582. Interest expense is computed as follows:

Year	*Nominal Interest Deduction*	*O.I.D. Interest Deduction*	*Total Interest Deduction*	*Tax Basis to Depositor*
19X0				$92,418
19X1	$8,000	$1,242	$9,242	93,660
19X2	8,000	1,366	9,366	95,026
19X3	8,000	1,503	9,503	96,529
19X4	8,000	1,653	9,653	98,182
19X5	8,000	1,818	9,818	100,000

Maturity Value of Bond	$100,000
Less: PV of Maturity Value 10%	62,092
PV of Interest Payments	30,326
Discount on Bond	$7,582

The O.I.D. expense deduction is computed as follows: ([Tax basis of debt× (Market interest rate – Stated interest rate)] – (Stated interest rate×Remaining O.I.D.).) For example, with respect to 19X1, the O.I.D. interest expense deduction would be $1,242 ([$92,418×(10% – 8%)] – (8%×7,582)).[43]

(c) *Early Withdrawal*

With respect to savings certificates, the IRS has ruled that a deduction is allowed under Code section 591 for interest computed at a rate that assumes the certificate is held until maturity.[44] The possibility that the interest rate may be reduced if an early withdrawal occurs does not preclude deductions based on a higher rate. In addition, the IRS has reasoned that changes in Federal Reserve Board Regulation Q do not necessitate a change in the tax treatment of O.I.D. on a deposit contract with a commercial bank.[45] Thus, the reduction or elimination

[43] In the case of a typical balloon payment loan, the interest deduction (O.I.D. plus nominal interest) exceeds actual interest payments during the term of the loan. In the case of a typical self-amortizing loan, interest expense deductions and actual payments will be equal.

[44] Rev. Rul. 73-221, 1973-1 C.B. 298, *superseding* Rev. Rul. 69-147, 1969-1 C.B. 165.

[45] Rev. Rul. 78-37, 1978-1 C.B. 54; Rev. Rul. 83-60, 1983-1 C.B. 39. Prior to its amendment on July 5, 1973, Regulation Q of the Board of Governors of the Federal Reserve, 12 CFR §217.4 (1973), provided that a time deposit could be paid before maturity only in an emergency when it was necessary to prevent great hardship to the depositor. The emergency provision was deleted under the Regulation Q amendment effective July 6, 1973, by rules promulgated by the Depository Institutions Deregulation Committee ("DIDC"). The DIDC was established by the Depository Institutions Deregulation Act and Monetary Control Act of 1980, Pub. L. No. 96-221, §203, 94 Stat. 132, 142 (1980), (codified as 12 U.S.C. §3502 (2000)). Beginning on that date and continuing until September 30, 1983, a time deposit could be paid before maturity without any necessity for the depositor to prove hardship, but the depositor was subject to a premature withdrawal penalty. The bank was permitted by the amended Regulation Q to pay interest on premature withdrawals on the amount withdrawn at a rate not to exceed the maximum rate prescribed for a savings deposit during the period the funds had remained on deposit, less three months interest. 12 CFR §217.4(d) (1974). The three-month penalty provision was reduced to one month for certain deposit arrangements by amendment of 12 CFR §1204.103, effective October 1, 1983. 48 Fed. Reg. 38457, 38458 (August 24, 1983). For time deposits entered into after April 1, 1986, the one-month penalty is no longer imposed by federal banking regulations. The Depository Institutions Deregulation and Monetary Control Act of 1980 mandated that, on March 31, 1986, the DIDC

of any premature withdrawal penalty will not, by itself, alter the deductibility of interest.[46]

The possibility of renegotiation by the parties to permit early redemption of a time deposit, such as a certificate of deposit, is not a contingency sufficient to prevent the current accrual of the interest deduction for an accrual method commercial bank.[47] Moreover, a full-interest expense deduction is allowed notwithstanding the fact that, as a customary condition of withdrawal, the depository has the right to retain or recover a portion of the total amount invested in, or credited as earnings or interest, as a fine, penalty, forfeiture, or other withdrawal fee.[48] Thus, a current deduction would be allowed notwithstanding the fact that:

1. The taxpayer would, by not withdrawing the earnings until a later date, receive a higher rate of earnings than would be payable if the earnings were withdrawn during the taxable year;
2. The earnings may be withdrawn only upon a withdrawal of all or part of the deposit or account; and
3. A notice of intention to withdraw must be given in advance of withdrawal.[49]

§9.4 Deferred Interest Expense

§9.4.1 Prepaid Interest by a Thrift

(a) *Deferral Rule*

Under Code section 461(e), thrifts are expressly prevented from accelerating interest expense deductions.[50] Regardless of whether interest is actually paid or merely credited to a depositor's account, it is not currently deductible to the extent it relates to a period greater than 12 months.[51] Any interest expense not currently deductible by reason of Code section 461(e) is deferred to, and may be taken as a deduction in, a later taxable year or years to the extent that it does not result in total interest expense deductions representing a period of more than 12 months.[52] Any excess is then permitted to be taken into account ratably in each of the 10 taxable years beginning with the disallowance year, if the event causing disallowance was not motivated by tax avoidance.[53] The amount allowed under the 10-year rule may be added to the amount spread under the twelve-month

(Footnote Continued)

be terminated. Pub. L. No. 96-211, §210, 94 Stat. 132, 145 (1980) (codified as 12 U.S.C. §3509 (2000)). In accordance with that requirement, the regulations of the DIDC were revoked and removed from the Code of Federal Regulations. However, many banks continue to impose the penalty as a matter of their own policy.

[46] Reg. §1.163-4.

[47] Rev. Rul. 71-63, 1971-1 C.B. 143, *as amplified by* Rev. Rul. 76-308, 1976-2 C.B. 133.

[48] Reg. §1.591-1(b).

[49] The rule for income inclusion conforms with the rule for deductibility. Rev. Rul. 73-221, 1973-1 C.B. 293, *superseding* Rev. Rul. 69-147, 1969-1 C.B. 165.

[50] I.R.C. §461(3) (2000) was added to the Code in 1962, Pub. L. No. 87-876, §2(a), effective with respect to taxable years ending after December 31, 1962.

[51] It has been the IRS's position that interest expense deductions must be spread over the term of Federal Home Loan Bank Board advances if paid out of the advances. If paid with "fresh funds," then a current deduction is allowed to a cash basis thrift.

[52] I.R.C. §461(e) (2000); Reg. §1.461-1(e)(3)(i).

[53] Reg. §1.461-1(e)(3)(ii).

rule even though the combined amounts exceed deductions representing total interest for twelve months.

Violation of the twelve-month rule may occur inadvertently if the bank changes:

1. The time of crediting "dividends" (as defined in Code section 591);
2. The period with respect to which credits are made; or
3. Its annual accounting period, thereby creating a short taxable year.

If the payor-bank pays dividends or interest in a short taxable year, the deferral rules apply to the short taxable year in a manner consistent with the application of the rules to a twelve-month period.[54]

(b) *Exceptions to Deferral Rule*

There are several exceptions to the deferral rule. In general, the deferral rule does not apply to a thrift: (1) in the year in which it liquidates; (2) when it pays "grace dividends or interest" to a terminating depositor or shareholder; or (3) if violation of the rule is the result of federal or state bank regulators requiring certain changes in the bank's annual accounting period or dividend, interest payment or crediting dates.[55] However, if the liquidation follows, or is a part of, an acquisition of the interest-paying bank's assets and the acquiring corporation, pursuant to Code section 381(a), takes into account the acquired entities' corporate tax attributes, the deferral rule may apply.[56] In this situation, the acquiring corporation succeeds to and is allowed to take into account the balance of the interest deferral on the same basis as is the acquired bank.[57]

§9.4.2 Market Discount Bonds

(a) *General Rule*

Under certain circumstances, interest expense deductions are deferred, in part or in whole, with respect to any "market discount bond" ("MDB") acquired after July 18, 1984.[58]

Market discount usually arises when the fair market value of a debt instrument declines after issuance and before acquisition in the secondary market. This decline could be the result of several factors, including a decline in the creditworthiness of the obligor, an increase in the prevailing market rates of interest, etc. Financial institutions that purchase debt after origination are likely to acquire instruments with market discount.[59] Whenever "market discount" exceeds "net direct interest expense," there will be no current deduction allowed for the interest expense allocable to the bond. Conversely, to the extent that net direct interest expense exceeds market discount, the interest expense is deductible.

[54] Reg. §§1.461-1(e)(1), (2), Ex. 1-3.

[55] Reg. §1.461-1(e)(3)(ii).

[56] Reg. §1.461-1(e)(1)(ii). Note that I.R.C. §381(a) does not pertain to stock-for-stock exchanges defined in I.R.C. §368(a)(1)(B).

[57] Reg. §1.461-1(e)(3)(iii).

[58] I.R.C. §1277 (2000). Bank regulatory strictures impose limits on the total amount of corporate bonds that may be owned by banks. Thus, banks typically do not hold significant amounts of MDBs.

[59] For a discussion of the timing and character of income from the disposition of market discount bonds, *see* Chapter 3.

(b) *Legislative History*

The MDB rule was added to the Code by the Deficit Reduction Act of 1984.[60] It was designed to address two problems. According to legislative history, "When a taxpayer makes a leveraged purchase of a market discount bond, the taxpayer effectively converts the ordinary income that is offset by current interest deductions to capital gains that [are] taxed on a deferred basis and at preferential rates."[61] Code section 1276, enacted as part of the attack on MDBs, characterizes what would otherwise be capital gain as ordinary income to the extent of accrued market discount. The Tax Reform Act of 1986 essentially repealed for corporations one of the two reasons for the MDB rules, the capital gains preference.[62] However, the recognition given to the time value of money suggests that the mismatching of deductions and income alone would support the MDB rule.[63]

(c) *MDB Defined*

A MDB is any taxable bond with a maturity date of more than one year in which the taxpayer has a tax basis, immediately after acquisition, that amounts to less than the bond's stated redemption price at maturity.[64] For this purpose, a "bond" means any bond, debenture, note, certificate, or other evidence of indebtedness.[65] The term is not dependent upon the instrument being in registered form or with coupons attached.

(d) *Allocable Interest Expense*

Code section 1277(a) provides that "net direct interest expense," which is allocated to a MDB, is deductible during the taxable year only to the extent that such expense exceeds the portion of the market discount allocable to the days during the taxable year on which the bond was held by the taxpayer. A bank's "net direct interest expense" is the excess of the interest expense allocable to the bond over the amount of interest, including O.I.D., currently includible in income.[66]

Interest expense allocable to an MDB is the amount of interest paid or accrued during the taxable year on indebtedness that is incurred or continued to purchase or carry MDBs.[67] For purposes of determining whether interest is "incurred or continued to purchase or carry" a market discount bond, banks are subject to a special rule. Unlike all other taxpayers, banks must allocate interest expense to MDBs using the mechanical rules of Code section 291.[68] Under the Code section 291 rules, total interest expense is allocated to MDBs using a

---

[60] Deficit Reduction Act of 1984, Pub. L. No. 98-369, 98 Stat. 491 (1984).

[61] Staff of J. Comm. on Taxation, 98th Cong., General Explanation of the Revenue Provisions of the Deficit Reduction Act of 1984, p. 93 (Comm. Print 1984).

[62] Tax Reform Act of 1986, Pub. L. No. 99-514, §§301(a) (individuals), 311(a) (corporations), 100 Stat. 2085 (1986).

[63] *See, e.g.*, I.R.C. §1272 (2000).

[64] I.R.C. §1278(a) (2000).

[65] I.R.C. §1278(a)(3) (2000).

[66] I.R.C. §1277(c) (2000).

[67] *Id.*

[68] I.R.C. §291(e)(1)(B)(ii) (2000).

fraction, the numerator of which is the bank's average adjusted tax basis in the bond and the denominator of which is the bank's average adjusted tax basis in all assets.[69] Thus, the rule that must be employed for determining the amount of interest expense allocable to MDBs is the same as the special bank interest expense disallowance rule contained in Code section 265(b). For taxpayers other than banks, such as a bank holding company, interest expense is allocated to MDBs under provisions that are identical to the Code section 265(a) rule, which disallows interest expense only if there is a nexus between the borrowing and the investment in the tax-exempt obligation.[70] Thus, the after-tax yield on a MDB may be increased if a non-bank member of a bank holding company group owns the obligation.

Example: A bank's total interest expense is $800,000, and its tax basis in all assets is $10,000,000. Interest expense allocated to an MDB bond with a tax basis of $500,000 is $40,000 ([500,000 ÷ 10,000,000]×800,000).

(e) *Deducting Deferred Interest Expense*

To the extent that any portion of a bank's interest expense deduction is deferred under Code section 1277, it is allowed as a deduction in the taxable year in which the bond is disposed of, regardless of whether gain or loss is realized at the time of disposition.[71] However, if the bond is disposed of in a nonrecognition transaction, the deductible amount is limited to the amount of recognized gain.[72] Any excess deferred interest expense is disallowed.

An election may be made to deduct previously disallowed interest expense to the extent of the current year's "net interest income."[73] Net interest income is the excess of the taxable interest on the MDB (including O.I.D.) includible in gross income over interest expense paid or accrued during the taxable year on indebtedness incurred or continued to purchase or carry the bond.[74] Here, too, the rule of Code section 291 is applied to determine related interest expense.

§9.4.3 UNICAP Rule

Code section 163(a) allows taxpayers a current deduction for all interest "paid or accrued within the taxable year on indebtedness."[75] Code section 263A sets forth the Uniform Capitalization Rules (UNICAP rules), which require taxpayers, including banks, to capitalize all direct and indirect costs related to the production[76] of specified property.[77] The property that may trigger capitalization is real or tangible personal property produced by the taxpayer and real or personal property that the taxpayer holds in inventory or that is held primarily for sale to customers in the ordinary course of the taxpayer's trade or business.[78] Interest expense on "eligible debt," including loans secured to construct specified

[69] *See* Rev. Rul. 90-44, 1990-1 C.B. 52 for guidance on applying the I.R.C. §291 disallowance rule.

[70] *See* the discussion of I.R.C. §§265(2) and 291 at §9.5.

[71] I.R.C. §1277(b)(2) (2000).

[72] I.R.C. §1277(b)(2)(B) (2000).

[73] I.R.C. §1277(b) (2000).

[74] I.R.C. §1277(b)(1) (2000).

[75] I.R.C. §163(a).

[76] Code section 263A(g)(1) defines "produce" to mean, "construct, build, install, manufacture, develop, or improve."

[77] I.R.C. §263A.

[78] I.R.C. §263A(b).

property, is among the indirect costs that must be capitalized. Treasury regulations define eligible debt as including "all outstanding debt (as evidenced by a contract, bond, debenture, note, certificate, or other evidence of indebtedness)."[79]

Only interest paid or incurred during the property's production period need be capitalized under the UNICAP rules.[80] Additionally, for property that falls within Code section 263A(f)'s scope, it must have a long useful life, an estimated production period exceeding two years, or an estimated production period exceeding one year and a cost exceeding $1,000,000.[81] Lastly, Regulation section 1.263A-8(a)(1) establishes the avoided cost method as the vehicle for determining the amount of interest that must be capitalized under Code section 263A(f).[82]

(a) *Separateness of Taxpayers and Consolidated Returns*

Code section 7701(a)(14) defines "taxpayer" as "any person subject to any internal revenue tax"[83] and Code section 7701(a)(1) defines "person" to "mean and include an individual, a trust, estate, partnership, association, company or corporation."[84] Thus, a corporation remains a separate taxable entity" apart from the income tax consequences of its shareholders.[85]

Despite a corporation's status as a separate taxable entity, the Code allows affiliated corporations (referred to in the Code as an "affiliated group") to file a consolidated return as a single taxable entity subject to the provisions of Chapter 6.[86] An affiliated group comprises a parent "includible corporation" (the term "includible corporation" is defined in Code section 1504(b))[87] and at least one subsidiary where the parent owns stock worth no less than 80 percent of the voting power and stock worth no less than 80 percent of the subsidiary's value.[88]

The regulations espouse two noteworthy tax advantages for affiliated groups to file a consolidated return. First, Regulation section 1.1502-11(a) grants corporations "the ability to combine the income and loss of each member of an affiliated group into a single taxable income. Thus, net operating losses of one member of the group can be used to offset the taxable income of another member."[89] Secondly, Regulation section 1.1502-13(a) treats intercompany transfers of an affiliated group as "transactions between divisions of a single corporation" for purposes of a consolidated return.[90]

---

[79] I.R.C. § 263A(f). *See also* TAM 200009004, March 3, 2000 (finding the interest on a "bank's customer deposit account arrangements constitute[d] debt . . . subject to the interest capitalization requirements of section 263A(f) and section 1.263A-9" because the bank used the customer deposit accounts to fund the construction of a new main office facility).

[80] I.R.C. § 263A(f)(1)(A).

[81] I.R.C. § 263A(f)(1)(B).

[82] The avoided cost method is discussed further in § 9.4.3(e) below.

[83] I.R.C. § 7701(a)(14).

[84] I.R.C. § 7701(a)(1).

[85] *Moline Properties v. Commissioner of Internal Revenue*, 319 U.S. 436, 439 (1943).

[86] I.R.C. § 1501.

[87] The term "includible corporation" excludes all tax-exempt corporations under Code section 501 (I.R.C. § 1504(b)(1)), Code section 801 insurance companies (I.R.C. § 1504(b)(2)), foreign corporations (I.R.C. § 1504(b)(3)), and S corporations (I.R.C. § 1504(b)(8)).

[88] I.R.C. § 1504(a).

[89] Martin J. McMahon, Jr., Understanding Consolidated Returns, 12 FLA. TAX REV. 125, 129 (2012).

[90] *Id.* at 130.

While notable tax benefits exist for affiliated corporations to file a consolidated return, Code section 269 authorizes the Secretary to disallow those tax benefits when the parent acquires subsidiaries for the principal purpose of "eva[ding] or avoid[ing] . . . Federal income tax by securing the benefit of a deduction, credit, or other allowance which such . . . corporation would not otherwise enjoy."[91] Courts in multiple jurisdictions have affirmed the Secretary's authority to deny consolidation benefits to corporations ostensibly seeking to reduce its taxable income by acquiring loss-burdened subsidiaries.[92] Therefore, a parent corporation must show a business-motivated reason for acquiring subsidiaries for the group to ensure access to these tax advantages. When the Code denies affiliated corporations the ability to file a consolidated return as a single taxable entity, those corporations must file as separate entities.[93] Lastly, corporations are the only entities eligible to file consolidated returns.[94] Partnerships and trusts, for example, are limited to filing as separate entities.[95]

(b) *Intercompany Transactions and Code Section 482*

The application of the UNICAP rules to intercompany transactions where an affiliated group files a consolidated return is unsettled. The plain language of Code section 263A(f) and the regulations thereunder require a subsidiary to capitalize the interest expense on a loan the subsidiary secured from the parent to pay for the subsidiary's production costs.[96] Whether the parent must capitalize its interest expenses on its own debt, either related or unrelated to the loan or on its capital contribution to the subsidiary, has yet to receive substantial consideration. While Code section 482 authorizes the Secretary to reallocate "gross income, deductions, credits or allowances" between members of an affiliated group "to

---

[91] I.R.C. § 269.

[92] *See e.g., Hall Paving Co. v. United States*, 471 F.2d 261, (5th Cir. 1973) (finding "the legislative history of section 269 itself indicates Congress intended to discourage one corporation from buying another corporation when the main reason is to take advantage of the other corporation's operating loss"); *Borge v. Commissioner of Internal Revenue*, 405 F.2d 673, 678 (2d Cir. 1968)(affirming Tax Court's ruling "that 'the principal purpose for which [petitioner acquired control of a subsidiary]' was evasion of Federal income tax within the meaning of section 269" and thus the Commissioner was reasonable in disallowing petitioner's deductions on the subsidiary's losses); *Elko Realty Company v. Commissioner*, 29 T.C. 1012, 1025-26 (1958), *aff'd per curiam*, 260 F.2d 949 (3d Cir. 1958) (holding Commissioner was correct to disallow the losses of two corporations the petitioner acquired primarily to secure a deduction on its consolidated return).

[93] There are several reasons why affiliated corporations would be prohibited from filing a consolidated return. For one, the parent company may not own the necessary 80% stock in its subsidiary. Or perhaps the parent is a section 501 tax-exempt corporation or S corporation and thus not one of the necessary "includible corporations" detailed under Code section 1504(a)'s "affiliated group" definition. Furthermore, a parent corporation may not be able to take advantage of the tax benefits of a consolidated return if the parent acquired a subsidiary principally for tax avoidance.

[94] I.R.C. § 1504(a)(1)(A) provides, "The term 'affiliated group' means – (A) 1 or more chains of includible *corporations*..." (emphasis added). Of course, married individuals are permitted to file a joint tax return.

[95] Even though partnerships are not themselves subject to income taxation (I.R.C. § 701), they must still compute their own taxable income. I.R.C. § 703(a). However, "[o]nce [the partnership's]income is ascertained and reported, its existence may be disregarded since each partner must pay tax on a portion of the total income as if the partnership were merely an agent or conduit through which the income passed." *United States v. Basye*, 410 U.S. 441 (1973). See also Reg. § 1.703-1(a): "A partnership is required to state separately in its return the items described in section 702(a)(1) through (7) and, in addition, to attach to its return a statement setting forth separately those items described in section 702(a)(8) which the partner is required to take into account separately in determining his income tax."

[96] Reg. § 1.263A-9(g)(5)(iii), Ex.

prevent the evasion of taxes,"[97] the Service in a 1987 Technical Advice Memorandum concluded Code section 482 allocations were not appropriate "in the absence of evidence of non-arm's length transactions."[98] Thus, where a parent with its own obligations makes an arm-length loan to a subsidiary for production (construction) purposes, Code section 482 ought to play no role in determining whether the parent must capitalize its interest expenses under Code section 263A(f).

(c) *Judicial Analysis of Intercompany Transactions under Code Section 265(a)(2)*

The Tax Court in *H. Enterprises International, Inc. v. Commissioner*[99] did address and ultimately disallow[100] interest expense deductions involving intercompany transactions; however, these disallowances fell under Code section 265(a)(2).[101] In H. Enterprises, the subsidiary (Waldorf Corp.) borrowed from an outside lender and then distributed those funds to its parent (H. Enterprises International).[102] Later, the parent purchased investments, among them tax-exempt obligations.[103] The parent and subsidiary filed Code section 1504 consolidated returns and the subsidiary claimed deductions for its interest expense on the loans it secured from the outside lender.[104] The Service determined deficiencies in the returns arguing the subsidiary could not deduct the interest expense because the subsidiary distributed the borrowed funds to the parent for the purpose of allowing the parent to purchase tax-exempt obligations.[105] H. Enterprises filed for summary judgment arguing Code section 265(a)(2)'s interest expense disallowance did not apply because the borrowing and tax-exempt purchases were performed by separate entities and that, despite their affiliation, Code section 265(a)(2) must treat the parent and subsidiary as separate taxpayers.[106]

In denying H. Enterprise's contention that Code section 265(a)(2) cannot apply to either parent or subsidiary when one borrows and the other purchases tax-exempt securities, the Tax Court noted, "there is no provision [in Code section 265] that the borrower be the same as the person who acquires the tax-exempt securities."[107] This reasoning was not novel,[108] but it is questionable. For one, while the Code allows affiliated groups to file a consolidated return, the regulations specify that each entity calculate its own separate taxable income.[109]

---

[97] I.R.C. § 482.

[98] TAM 8740001, March 23, 1987.

[99] 105 T.C. 71 (1995).

[100] 75 T.C.M. (CCH) 1948 (1998), *aff'd* 183 F.3d 907 (8th Cir. 1999).

[101] I.R.C. § 265(a)(2) denies a deduction for "interest on indebtedness incurred or continued to purchase or carry obligations the interest on which is wholly exempt from the taxes imposed by this subtitle." There were other tax issues brought before the Tax Court in *H. Enterprises* involving Code section 246A which will not be discussed.

[102] *H. Enterprises*, 105 T.C. at 74-75.

[103] *Id.* at 75-76.

[104] *Id.* at 73-74.

[105] *Id.* at 76-77.

[106] *Id.* at 72.

[107] *H. Enterprises*, 105 T.C. at 79.

[108] TAM 8740001, March 23, 1987 (holding "Section 265(2) of the Code can be applied in the related party context in circumstances where either the proceeds of indebtedness are used for, and are directly traceable to, the purchase of tax-exempt obligations, or where tax-exempt obligations are used as collateral for indebtedness").

[109] Reg. § 1.1502-11(a)(1). Regulation section 1.1502-13 on intercompany transactions does lists situations where an affiliated group has to ascertain its taxable income as a collective group instead of separately. The regulation even frequently discusses Code section 265. However, the regulation deals

Thus, the court's reading into Code section 265(a)(2) an implication that the borrower need not be the same "taxpayer" as the purchaser of tax-exempts conflicts with the consolidated return regulations requiring affiliated corporations to determine their taxable income separately.

The *H. Enterprises* court next looked to Code section 7701(f)'s tax avoidance provision[110] as authorization for Section 265(a)(2) capturing a parent and subsidiary's actions in a single taxable transaction.[111] The Tax Court also found Code section 7701(f)'s legislative history persuasive.[112] Citing Code section 7701(f) and its legislative history, the court concluded "the provisions of sections . . . 265(a)(2) . . . may in appropriate circumstances be used when one member of an affiliated group is the borrower and another member the purchaser of . . . tax-exempt securities."[113]

The *H. Enterprises* court applied Code section 7701(f) in its reasoning despite H. Enterprise's objection that the Secretary had not (and still has not) promulgated regulations under that section thereby rendering the section inactive.[114] After reviewing cases offered by each party, the court determined the lack of regulations under Code section 7701(f) was not fatal because Code section 7701(f) did not, unlike other sections, include a clause limiting its applicability "only to the extent prescribed by regulations."[115] However, Code section 7701(f), by its plain language, seemingly stands dormant, waiting to be awakened by the Secretary's issuing regulations. Nevertheless, H. Enterprises found Code section 7701(f) and its legislative history persuasive in its ultimate ruling that Code

(Footnote Continued)

with scenarios where the transactions are solely between the members of the affiliated group filing the consolidated return. In the facts of *H. Enterprises*, however, the subsidiary sought to deduct interest expense on a loan it secured from an entity *outside* of its affiliated group.

110 Code section 7701(f), enacted in 1984, instructs the Secretary to "prescribe such regulations as may be necessary or appropriate to prevent the avoidance of those provisions of this title which deal with – (1) the linking of borrowing to investment, or (2) diminishing risks, through the use of related persons, pass-thru entities, or other intermediaries." For more discussion on Code section 7701(f) and its legislative history see § 9.5.8(a) discussion on "Consolidated Disallowance."

111 *H. Enterprises*, 105 T.C. at 79.

112 *Id.* Specifically, the Service pointed the Tax Court to a House Conference report that stated, "Nor is any inference intended that any particular provision under present law or as amended the Conference Agreement (e.g., sec. 265(2) or 246A), by its own terms, is not applicable in the case of related parties, pass-through entities, or other intermediaries." H. Conf. Rept. 98-861, at 1042 (1984).

113 *H. Enterprises*, 105 T.C. at 81. In so finding, the Tax Court denied H. Enterprise's summary judgment motion as a material fact existed as to whether there was a valid business purpose in the subsidiary's distributions to the parent. *H. Enterprises*, 105 T.C. at 85-86. At trial, H. Enterprises argued the subsidiary's distributions constituted a valid business purpose excluding Code section 265(a)(2)'s applicability (Id. at 76-77); however, the Tax Court and Eighth Circuit agreed with the Service that the distribution was for the purpose of buying tax-exempts and enforced Code section 265(a)(2) to disallow the interest deductions. *H. Enterprises*, 75 T.C.M. (CCH) at 6; H. Enterprises, 183 F.3d at 908.

The court also looked to *Drybrough v. Commissioner*, 42 T.C. 1029 (1964) where that Tax Court found 265(a)(2) disallowance when a husband incurred indebtedness, transferred funds to his wife, and the wife purchased tax-exempt obligations in her name alone. H. Enterprises attempted to distinguish the case as involving spouses instead of affiliated corporations and cited to the famed *Moline Properties, Inv. v. Commissioner* United States Supreme Court case standing for the proposition that corporations are separate taxable entities. In reply, the Tax Court cited its own precedent holding "the '*Moline Properties* rule' should not be taken out of context and mechanically applied to an entirely different type of question." *H. Enterprises*, 105 T.C. at 80.

114 *H. Enterprises*, 105 T.C. at 81.

115 *Id.* at 84.

section 265(a)(2) may be enforced even when the borrower and purchaser of tax-exempts is not the same entity.[116]

(d) *H. Enterprises Unpersuasive Authority in 263A(f) Intercompany Transaction Analysis*

The Service might cite to H. Enterprises as persuasive authority to deny interest expense deductions under 263A(f) where the borrower and producer of property are different, albeit affiliated, entities. However, *H. Enterprises* remains weak precedent given its questionable use of Code section 7701(f). In addition to Code section 7701(f)'s apparent dormancy absent regulations, the House Conference Report *H. Enterprises* alluded to specifically cited Code section 265, but never mentioned Code section 263A. Therefore, that legislative history loses its usefulness in relation to Code section 263A because it does not explicitly contemplate 263A.

Moreover, the facts in *H. Enterprises* showed an unequivocal "linking of borrowing to investment" which Code section 7701(f) lists as one of its two hooks to applicability. H. Enterprises admitted as much, yet claimed valid business purposes for the subsidiary's distribution to the parent.[117] And where there was a clear "linking of borrowing to investment" at least triggering an initial Code section 7701(f) analysis in H. Enterprises, there would not be that clear "link" where a parent has outside debt unrelated to its loan or capital contribution to a subsidiary for production purposes. Thus, how Code section 263A(f) handles the parent's interest expenses in those situations cannot derive its conclusions from either Code section 7701(f) or H. Enterprises. Without Code section 7701(f), the H. Enterprises ruling rests solely on its statutory construction of Code section 265(a)(2)'s dealing with interest on the purchase of tax-exempt securities,[118] which would hardly be helpful for a court construing Code section 263A(f)'s interest expense deferral on debt secured for the production of property. The two sections have little to do with one another.

Further dividing Code sections 265 and 263A is the regulation's separate treatment of each for consolidated return purposes. As aforementioned, the avoided cost method applies where a member of a consolidated group capitalizes interest under Code section 263A(f) from a loan of another member of that group.[119] Consequently, the intercompany transaction rules laid out in Regulation section 1.1502-13 do not apply to the interest on these intercompany loans.[120] The

---

[116] Not all scholars agree. Tax attorney and adjunct professor Phillip Gall posits that, "although it may appear that the court applied phantom section 7701(f) regulations, the court actually concluded that sections 246A and 265(a)(2) themselves applied where one person did the borrowing and a related person did the investing." Phillip Gall, *Phantom Tax Regulations: The Curse of Spurned Delegations*, 56 TAX LAW 413, 429 (2003). Gall concludes *H. Enterprises* is a "misunderstood decision" so much so that "subsequent decisions rel[ied] on the case as if it had" applied "phantom regulations against the taxpayer." Id. at 425, 430. Gall then discussed the generation-skipping transfer tax case *Estate of Neumann v. Commissioner* as an example of a Tax Court case that erroneously relied upon *H. Enterprises. Id.* at 430.

[117] *See* fotnote 40 above.

[118] *See* footnote 28 above. Indeed Phillip Gall argues this is the proper understanding of *H. Enterprises.*

[119] Reg. § 1.263A-9(g)(5)(i).

[120] *Id. See also* Reg. § 1.263A-9(g)(5)(iii), Ex. i..

intercompany transaction regulations reciprocate this yielding to the avoided cost method.[121]

Code section 7701(f) stands seemingly lifeless absent regulations and has a legislative history that envisions its application to Code section 265 but not 263A. Even if Code section 7701(f) is applicable absent those regulations, the section never gets off the ground where a parent has debts unrelated to the loan or capital contribution it makes to a subsidiary for production costs because there is no "linking of borrowing to investment."[122] An *H. Enterprises* decision, without Code section 7701(f), is limited to its construction of Code section 265(a)(2) and thus not all that useful in construing Code section 263A(f). Moreover, Code section 482 should never enter a Code section 263A(f) analysis where the transactions between parent and subsidiary were conducted at arms-length. As a result, the UNICAP's treatment of interest expenses involving intercompany transactions continues to remain foggy.

(e) *Conclusions and the Avoided Cost Method*

To analyze the issue of whether a corporation must capitalize its interest expenses under Code section 263A(f) on its debts either related or unrelated to the loan or capital contribution the parent made to the subsidiary it is helpful to break down the issue into separate scenarios along a continuum. At one end is the situation where a parent has no borrowings or debts and lends funds or makes a capital contribution to the subsidiary for production purposes. Here, there is no question whether the parent must capitalize interest expense under 263A(f) because the parent does not even have any interest expense to either deduct or capitalize. The subsidiary likewise has no interest expense when it is the recipient of a capital contribution, but does have interest expense it must capitalize when it secures a loan from the parent. The plain language of Code section 263A(f) requires the subsidiary to capitalize this interest expense on a loan secured to produce property provided all the other elements of Code section 263A(f)(1) are met.[123]

Complexity arises when the parent does have debts on its books and makes a loan or capital contribution to the subsidiary. If the parent's debts are unrelated to the loan or capital contribution it makes to the subsidiary, then the Service has little authority to require the parent to capitalize its interest expense. This parent's interest expense cannot reasonably be said to be "allocable to property which is"[124] "produced by the taxpayer"[125] because the parent did not enter into its obligations for the purpose of then lending funds to the subsidiary for production costs.

---

[121] Reg. § 1.1502-13(k)(2). There is an exception: if "for any year, the aggregate amount of interest income" from an intercompany loan "for all members of the group with respect to all units of designated property exceeds the total amount of interest that is deductible for that year by all members of the group with respect to debt of a member owed to nonmembers (group deductible interest) after applying section 263A(f), the intercompany transaction provisions of the consolidated return regulations are applied to the excess." Reg. § 1.263A-9(g)(5)(ii).

[122] I.R.C. § 7701(f)(1).

[123] *See* footnotes 5 and 6 and accompanying text above. *See also* Reg. § 1.263A-9(g)(5)(iii), Ex.

[124] I.R.C. § 263A(f)(1)(B).

[125] I.R.C. § 263A(b)(1).

The regulations, echoing the Code, holds that, "[g]enerally, any interest that the taxpayer theoretically would have avoided if accumulated production expenditures (as defined in § 1.263A–11) had been used to repay or reduce the taxpayer's outstanding debt must be capitalized under the avoided cost method."[126] This broad language first appears to capture the parent's interest expense in this hypothetical since the parent could be using the money it loaned or distributed to the subsidiary to pay off the parent's own debts.

However, Regulation section 1.263A-9(a)(2)(i) also narrows the scope of the avoided cost method's applicability holding that for each unit[127] of designated property,[128] the avoided cost method requires the capitalization of the "traced debt amount"[129] and the "excess expenditure amount."[130] The regulations then define traced debt "as the outstanding eligible debt (as defined in paragraph (a)(4) of this section) that is allocated, on that date, to accumulated production expenditures with respect to the unit of designated property under the rules of § 1.163–8T."[131] In other words, interest payments that are indirect costs of producing designated property and that are due during the measurement period must be capitalized.[132] Even so, where a parent has debts unrelated to a loan or capital contribution the parent makes to the subsidiary, the parent's obligations are not traced debt because the debt is not "allocated. .. to accumulated production expenditures with respect to the unit of designated property" being constructed by the subsidiary.[133] The parent did not secure loans for the purpose of funding the subsidiary's property production efforts. Thus, the parent should not have to capitalize under Code section 263A(f). Furthermore, neither the H. Enterprises decision nor Code section 7701(f) holds any authority for requiring the parent to

---

[126] Reg. § 1.263A-9(a)(1). Again, the regulations establish the avoided cost method as the means for determining the amount of interest that must be capitalized under Code section 263A(f). See footnote 9 and accompanying text above.

[127] Reg. § 1.263A-10 states "a unit of real property includes any components of real property owned by the taxpayer or a related person that are functionally interdependent and an allocable share of any common feature owned by the taxpayer or a related person that is real property even though the common feature does not meet the functional interdependence test." The regulations go on to provide an example of the construction of a four-house subdivision where the homes are all served via a perimeter road. "Under the principles of paragraph (b)(1) of this section, each planned house (including attributable land) is part of a separate unit of real property (house unit). Under the principles of paragraph (b)(3) of this section, the perimeter road (including attributable land) constitutes a common feature with respect to each planned house (i.e., benefitted property)." Reg. § 1.263A-10(6), Ex. 1. Importantly, "[d]esignation of each unit of property is required to properly determine the accumulated production costs that directly benefit or are incurred by reason of the production of that unit, as well as to determine when the production period begins and ends." James R. Hamill, *Capitalization of Interest Related to Real Estate Development Activities*, 40 WGL-RETAX 60, 61 (First Quarter, 2013).

[128] Regulation section 1.263A-8 defines "designated property" as property produced by the taxpayer that is real property or tangible personal property, provided that the latter is either property with a class life of at least 20 years, property with an estimated production period exceeding two years, or property with an estimated production period exceeding one year and an estimated production cost exceeding $1,000,000. Alternatively, Reg. § 1.263A-8(b)(4) lists a de minimis rule whereby designated property does not include property which has a production period of no more than 90 days *and* the total production expenditures do not exceed $1,000,000 divided by that number of production period days.

[129] *See* Reg. § 1.263A-9(b)(1): "[I]nterest must be capitalized with respect to a unit of designated property in an amount (the traced debt amount) equal to the total interest incurred on the traced debt during each measurement period (as defined in paragraph (f)(2)(ii) of this section) that ends on a measurement date described in paragraph (f)(2)(iii) of this section."

[130] Reg. § 1.263A-9(a)(2)(i).

[131] Reg. § 1.263A-9(b)(2).

[132] *See* Reg. § 1.263A-9(b)(3), Ex.

[133] Reg. § 1.263A-9(b)(2).

capitalize under this hypothetical. Again, the subsidiary will be capitalizing its interest expense on the loan it secured from the parent in accordance with Code section 263A(f)'s plain language.

When the parent secures a loan from an outside lender for the purpose of then distributing those funds to galvanize a subsidiary's specific construction project, the parent is more likely to be required to capitalize this interest expense under Code section 263A(f) if the parent made a capital contribution to the subsidiary. This scenario forms the other end of the spectrum comprising the most risky move for the parent if the parent wishes to deduct its interest expense. Consequently, the parent's obligations could be considered traced debt because the debt is "allocated . . . to accumulated production expenditures with respect to the unit of designated property" being constructed by the subsidiary.[134] The parent borrowed for the purpose of then distributing those funds to the subsidiary for production costs, which composes a transaction the avoided cost method is designed to capture. Additionally, the Service could cite to Code section 7701(f) now, its effectiveness notwithstanding, because there is a "linking of borrowing to investment." The parent borrowed for the very purpose of investing those funds in the subsidiary's construction campaign. Thus, the parent should probably plan on capitalizing its interest expense in this scenario. Similarly, if the parent has related debt but issues a loan to the subsidiary instead of a capital contribution, then either the parent or the subsidiary must capitalize under 263A(f). Both have interest expenses that fall under Code section 263A(f)'s capitalization requirements, however, only one entity needs to capitalize.

The table below summarizes these conclusions:

	Parent makes a **loan** to Subsidiary for production purposes.	Parent makes a **capital contribution** to Subsidiary for production purposes.
Parent has **no** outstanding debts or obligations.	No interest expense for Parent; Subsidiary must capitalize its interest expense.	No interest expense for either Parent or Subsidiary.
Parent has outstanding debts or obligations **unrelated** to its distributions to Subsidiary.	Parent does not have to capitalize its interest expense; Subsidiary must capitalize its interest expense.	Parent does not have to capitalize its interest expense; Subsidiary has no interest expense.
Parent has debts or obligations **related** to its distributions to Subsidiary.	Either Parent or Subsidiary must capitalize its interest expense.	Parent must capitalize its interest expense; Subsidiary has no interest expense.

As the table illustrates, there is only one scenario where both the parent and subsidiary may be subject to the UNICAP rules with respect to capitalizing its interest expenses: where the parent secures a loan from an outside lender for the purpose of then loaning those funds to the subsidiary. Due to fundamental tax principles, the Service is unlikely to be able to mandate both the parent and subsidiary to capitalize their interest expenses. Thus, the parent and subsidiary must decide when filing their consolidated return which one should take the deduction and which one should capitalize.

---

[134] *Id.*

§ 9.5 Disallowed Interest Expense

§ 9.5.1 Overview of Automatic Disallowance Rules

The Code contains two automatic interest expense disallowance rules applicable only to banks.[135] Code Section 291 applies generally with respect to tax-exempt obligations acquired by a bank after December 31, 1982, and before August 8, 1986. It disallows 20 percent of the interest expense that is allocable to such obligations using a mathematical formula. No tracing of the borrowed funds to the investment in tax-exempt obligations is required to trigger this disallowance rule. Code section 265(b) disallows 100 percent of the interest expense allocable to tax-exempt obligations acquired by a bank after August 7, 1986, using a similar formula. The issue date of the tax-exempt obligation has no bearing on which disallowance rule applies.

After the enactment of Code Section 291 by the Tax Equity and Fiscal Responsibility Act of 1982[136] and the revisions to Code Section 265 made by the Tax Reform Act of 1986,[137] it became irrelevant whether the taxpayer invested in the tax-exempt obligations for the purpose of deriving tax-exempt income therefrom; that is, under current law no nexus need be established between the borrowing and the tax-exempt investment before a bank's interest expense is disallowed.[138] For taxable years beginning before 1983, the rule then contained in 1954 Code section 265(2) subjected banks (as well as other taxpayers) to interest expense deduction disallowance only in the unlikely event that a nexus was established between borrowings and tax-exempt obligations.[139]

The special bank rules do not generally apply to the subsidiaries of banks. When a bank is the owner of a single-member LLC—a disregarded entity—the bank rules do not apply to the LLC.[140] Also, in rare instances an S corporation bank may have a non-bank subsidiary, a QSub.[141] While the special bank rules do not generally apply to non-bank QSubs, Code sections 291(a)(3), (e)(1)(B), and 265(b) may be applied to non-bank QSubs if the IRS publishes guidance to that effect.[142]

---

[135] Interest expense incurred with respect to debt-financed acquisitions is nondeductible under I.R.C. § 279. This section contains the same language as that contained in I.R.C. § 265(a) (I.R.C. § 265(2), prior to amendment by the Tax Reform Act of 1986, Pub. L. No. 99-514, 100 Stat. 2085 (1986)), which requires that a nexus be established between the borrowing and the use of the funds.

[136] Pub. L. No. 97-248, § 204, 96 Stat. 324, 423 (1982).

[137] Pub. L. No. 99-514, 100 Stat. 2085 (1986).

[138] *Denman v. Slayton,* 2 U.S.T.C. ¶ 678, 282 U.S. 514 (1931). In *Denman,* the Supreme Court concluded that the section was not violative of the Constitution, since it did not tax indirectly what could not be taxed directly. The court rejected the taxpayer's contention that the disallowance section acted as a "back-door" to impose a tax on tax-exempt income.

[139] The 1954 code rule is now found in I.R.C. § 265(a)(2) (2000).

[140] Treas. Reg. § 301.7701-2(c)(2)(ii). However, this treatment does not apply to Code sections § § 864(c), 882(c), and 884.

[141] I.R.C. § 1361(b). For further discussion on QSubs, *see* Ch. 1.6.4.

[142] Treas. Reg. § 1.1361-4(a)(3)(i). *But cf.* Rev. Rul. 90-44, 1990-1 C.B. 54 (applying I.R.C. § 265(b) to any "financial institution" in addition to banks as defined in I.R.C. § 585).

§ 9.5.2 Overview of General Disallowance Rule

Statutory disallowance of interest expense deductions with respect to indebtedness traceable to tax-exempt obligations has been in the federal income tax laws since 1917.[143] This rule, now embodied in Code section 265(a), continues to apply to the nonbank members of a bank holding company group, including the bank holding company itself and all other taxpayers.[144] Moreover, the general disallowance rule continues to apply to banks, but only in unusual situations. If interest is disallowed under the general disallowance rule it is not taken into account for purposes of applying the specific bank disallowance rule of Code section 265(b).[145]

(a) *De Minimis Exception*

The general disallowance rule has one exception that could provide significant relief for nonbank members of a bank holding company group. Revenue Procedure 72-18 relieves a taxpayer from the application of the general interest disallowance rule if the taxpayer's investment in tax-exempt obligations is "insubstantial."[146] An investment in tax-exempt obligations shall be presumed insubstantial only when during the taxable year the average amount of the tax-exempt obligations (valued at their adjusted tax basis) does not exceed two percent of the average total assets (valued at their adjusted tax basis) held in the active conduct of the taxpayer's trade or business. According to the Revenue Procedure, this *de minimis* rule does not apply to dealers in tax-exempt obligations. For this purpose, it should be assumed that the determination of whether a taxpayer is a dealer for purposes of Code section 475 is not conclusive. The taxpayer must in fact be a dealer in tax-exempt obligations.[147] According to Revenue Procedure 72-18, a dealer is a person who "buys securities and sells them to customers with a view to the gains and profits that may be derived therefrom".

In determining what constitutes assets that are held in the active conduct of the taxpayer's trade or business, it is unclear what assets of a bank holding company are taken into account. Although it could be argued that the stock that

[143] The original limitation on the deduction of interest relating to tax-exempt securities was contained in § 1201(1) of the Revenue Act of 1917 for individuals and in § 1207(2) of that Act for corporations. Revenue Act of October 3, 1917, Pub. L. No. 65-50, §§ 1201(1), 1207(2), 40 Stat. 300, 330, 334-335 (1917). These two sections allowed a deduction for all interest paid within the year on indebtedness "except on indebtedness incurred for the purchase of obligations or securities the interest upon which is exempt from taxation as income under this title." H.R. Rep. No. 64-4280 at. 300, 330 (1917). A discussion of the interest expense disallowance rule is contained in "Ineffective and Inequitable: The Section 265(a) Interest Disallowance," *Wake Forest Law Review*, Vol. 25, No. 4, p. 811 (1990).

[144] Rev. Rul. 81-200, 1981-2 C.B. 81. *See also* Rev. Rul. 72-523, 1972-2 C.B. 242.

[145] I.R.C. § 265(b)(6) (2000).

[146] Rev. Proc. 72-18, 1972-1 C.B. 740. A statutory version of this de minimis exception was enacted for tax-exempt obligations issued during 2009 and 2010. I.R.C. § 265(b)(7); American Recovery and Reinvestment Tax Act of 2009, Pub. L. No. 111-5, § 1501(a).This rule is discussed below in conjunction with the disallowance rule enacted in the Tax Reform Act of 1986. Pub. L. No. 99-514, § 902(a).

[147] A portion of the deduction that a mortgage company pays on funds borrowed from its parent bank holding company was disallowed in Rev. Rul. 81-200, 1981-2 C.B. 81.

the holding company owns represents the business of the holding company, there may be more support for a contrary position.[148]

(b) *Administrative Difficulties*

Without any major change, the statutory language disallowing interest expense was, for all years prior to 1983, substantially the same as 1954 Code section 265(2). That section provided that no deduction was allowed for "[i]nterest on indebtedness incurred or continued to purchase or carry obligations the interest on which is wholly exempt from the taxes imposed by this subtitle." However, it was recognized early on that this disallowance section presented grave administrative difficulties.[149] The judicially mandated requirement that a "nexus" be established between the borrowing and the investing in tax-exempt obligations imposed a subjective test for determining whether interest expense should be disallowed.[150]

(c) *Application to Banks*

Clarification of Code section 265(a)'s application to banks was provided in the form of a series of revenue procedures. The IRS took the position that the general disallowance was not intended to apply to interest expense incurred by banks "in the ordinary course of their day-to-day business unless there are circumstances demonstrating a direct connection between the borrowing and the tax-exempt investment."[151] The IRS also ruled that no connection would be inferred when borrowed funds were invested by a bank in certain "short-term" financial obligations. However, this exemption for short-term bank borrowings did not extend to nonbank subsidiaries of a bank or to a bank holding company.[152] For this purpose, an obligation was treated as "short-term" if it had a maturity date of not more than three years.[153] A bank deposit for a term in excess of three years "will be treated as short-term where there is no restriction on withdrawal other than reduction, forfeiture or recapture in whole or in part of interest otherwise payable over the term."[154]

Obligations that were exempt by administrative pronouncements from the disallowance rule of 1954 Code section 265(2) included: (1) bank deposits (including interbank deposits and certificates of deposit); (2) short-term notes; (3) short-term Eurodollar deposits and borrowings; (4) federal funds transactions (as well as other day-to-day and short-term interbank borrowings); and (5) repurchase agreements and borrowings directly from the Federal Reserve to meet reserve requirements.[155]

---

[148] In *Arkansas Best Corp. v. Commissioner*, 485 U.S. 212 (1988), the Supreme Court ruled that the disposition of bank stock by its holding company gave rise to a capital loss. The bank stock was not an ordinary asset.

[149] H.R. Rep. 65-767, at, 10 (1918).

[150] *Wisconsin Cheeseman, Inc. v. United States*, 68-1 U.S.T.C. ¶9145, 388 F.2d 420 (7th Cir. 1968). For a discussion of the "foreseeability test" in establishing a "sufficiently direct relationship" between borrowings and investments, *see Earl Drown Corp. v. Commissioner*, 86 T.C. 217, Dec. 42,890 (1986).

[151] Rev. Proc. 83-91, 1983-2 C.B. 618, *modifying* Rev. Proc. 70-20, 1970-2 C.B. 499.

[152] Rev. Rul. 81-200, 1981-2 C.B. 81. *See also* discussion of I.R.C. §7701(f) at §9.15. Moreover, the other "bank" rules do not apply to nonbank members of an affiliated group that includes a bank.

[153] Rev. Proc. 70-20, 1970-2 C.B. 499.

[154] Rev. Proc. 70-20, 1970-2 C.B. 499, §3.11.

[155] *Id.*

The IRS also ruled that, even if tax-exempt obligations were pledged to secure borrowings of Treasury tax and loan funds, there would be no interest expense disallowance.[156] With respect to interest expense on capital notes, there would be no disallowed interest expense if the borrowing was "for the purpose of increasing capital to a level consistent with generally accepted banking practice . . . or to finance bank building construction or for similar improvements."[157] This line of authority may be useful to bank holding companies that hold tax-exempt obligations.

In *New Mexico Bancorporation and Subsidiaries,* the IRS challenged the deductibility of interest expense relating to the issuance of repurchase agreements.[158] The Tax Court held in favor of the taxpayer, and Revenue Procedure 70-20 was amended to conform with the court's decision.[159] Subsequent to that decision, the IRS ruled that even interest on repurchase agreements collateralized by tax-exempt obligations would be fully deductible.[160]

Notwithstanding the historical rule that bank borrowings in the normal course of a trade or business were not in the proscribed borrowings class, it was the IRS's position that "unusual facts and circumstances outside of the normal course of business may demonstrate a direct connection between the borrowing and the investment in tax-exempt securities."[161] Thus, the provisions of 1954 Code section 265(2) were found to apply where a bank issued certificates of deposit to a state government in a direct and clearly connected exchange for tax-exempt obligations.[162]

If a bank borrows from the Federal Home Loan Bank and those funds can be clearly traced to investments in tax-exempt obligations, the bank should expect to have its interest expense disallowed by the IRS. When determining whether the borrowed funds are traceable to investments in tax-exempt obligations, statements made by the bank's management that the purpose of the borrowing was for the purpose of investing in tax-exempt obligations may be sufficient to establish the nexus.

§9.5.3 The TEFRA Disallowance

(a) *Scope of Disallowance Rule*

The Tax Equity and Fiscal Responsibility Act of 1982 ("TEFRA") contained the first statutory amendment to the required "nexus" test of 1954 Code section 265(2).[163] TEFRA singled out banks, but not other members of a bank holding company group or any other taxpayer, for application of a statutory rule that automatically disallows interest expense.[164]

---

156 Rev. Proc. 78-34, 1978-2 C.B. 535.

157 Rev. Proc. 70-20, 1970-2 C.B. 499, §3.10.

158 *New Mexico Bancorporation & Subsidiaries,* 74 T.C. 1342, Dec. 37,283 (1980).

159 Rev. Proc. 83-91, 1983-1 C.B. 618.

160 PLRs 8327016, April 1, 1983 and 8329020, April 20, 1983.

161 Rev. Proc. 83-91, 1983-2 C.B. 618.

162 Rev. Rul. 67-260, 1967-2 C.B. 132, *modified by* Rev. Rul. 71-163, 1971-1 C.B. 106.

163 Tax Equity and Fiscal Responsibility Act of 1982, Pub. L. No. 97-248, §204, 96 Stat. 324, 423 (1982).

164 I.R.C. §291(e)(1)(B) (2000).

(b) *Legislative History*

The legislative history accompanying TEFRA lists three reasons for the enactment of Code section 291.[165] First, tax preferences should be subject to careful scrutiny in light of the federal budget deficit that existed at that time. Second, the passage of the Accelerated Cost Recovery System made some corporate tax preferences less necessary. Third, a cutback of corporate tax preferences would address concern about the inequity of the tax system.[166]

(c) *Operation of Disallowance Rule*

Code section 291(a)(3) provides that "[t]he amount allowable as a deduction with respect to any financial institution preference item shall be reduced by 20 percent."[167] The term "financial institution preference item" includes, among other items, that portion of total interest expense allocable to tax-exempt obligations acquired after December 31, 1982, and before August 8, 1986.[168] The amount of interest expense allocable to tax-exempt obligations acquired during this period is equal to a bank's total interest expense otherwise deductible multiplied by a fraction, the numerator of which is the average adjusted basis of tax-exempt obligations acquired during that period and the denominator of which is the taxpayer's average adjusted basis for all assets.[169] This computation is on a bank-by-bank basis if there is more than one bank in a consolidated group.

> **Example:** One-tenth of Bank H's tax basis in its assets comprises tax-exempt obligations acquired after December 31, 1982, and before August 8, 1986. Thus, 2 percent (.20×.10) of Bank H's total interest expense that would otherwise be deductible is disallowed by Code section 291.

---

[165] I.R.C. § 291(e)(1)(B) (2000). The inclusion of a bank's interest expense relating to tax-exempt obligations among the list of "corporate preference items" in I.R.C. § 291 resulted from the enormous criticism directed at the IRS following the issuance of Rev. Proc. 80-55, 1980-2 C.B. 849. The pronouncement was an attempt by the IRS to apply I.R.C. § 265(2) to one type of day-to-day banking activity. Critics from the banking community and municipalities alleged that if the pronouncement were allowed to become effective, it would have a major adverse impact on the municipal bond market. *See, e.g., Wall Street Journal*, Dec. 22, 1980, at 10, col. 1. Before the pronouncement became effective, it was revoked. Rev. Proc. 81-16, 1981-1 C.B. 688. However, accompanying the revocation was an announcement that the IRS would study the issue of whether banks should be treated differently than other taxpayers under 1954 I.R.C. § 265(2). When the Administration proposed in February 1982 that the add-on-minimum tax be repealed and a new minimum tax be imposed, it listed as one of the new preference items the interest a bank deducts that can be attributed to tax-exempt obligations. The Administration's proposals were revised, and the I.R.C. § 291 scale-back in deductions with respect to "corporate preference items" was enacted.

[166] S. Rep. No. 97-494, at 446 (1982).

[167] As initially enacted, the cut-back was 15-percent. It was increased to 20 percent in the Deficit Reduction Act of 1984, Pub. L. No. 98-369, sec. 68(a), 98 Stat. 588.

[168] The IRS has released interim guidance on reissuance standards for tax-exempt bonds that will apply until regulations are issued. Under the interim guidance, certain changes to a qualified tender bond will not be treated as a modification causing reissuance or retirement. Notice 2008-41, 2008-15 I.R.B. 742, March 25, 2008. Also, the IRS will allow government issuers to purchase their own tax-exempt auction rate bonds on a temporary basis without having it result in a reissuance or retirement of the purchased bond under certain circumstances. Special rules for purposes of applying the arbitrage investment restrictions of Code Sec. 148 are also provided. The IRS also supplemented Notice 2008-41 with Notice 2008-88, I.R.B. 2008-42, October 1, 2008.

[169] An exception to this general disallowance rule permits a taxpayer "under regulations prescribed by the Secretary" to use a different method for determining the amount of disallowed interest expense. To date, no regulations have been issued. I.R.C. § 291(e)(1)(B)(i) (2000).

§9.5.4 The TRA '86 Disallowance Rule

(a) *Scope of Disallowance Rule*

The Tax Reform Act of 1986 amended Code section 265 by adding Code section 265(b).[170] The change eliminated the historical requirement contained in Code section 265(c) that borrowed funds be traced to tax-exempt investments. Proportional disallowance was seen as a way of placing financial institutions on an equal footing with other taxpayers.[171]

Pursuant to the amended provisions of Code section 265, banks became subject to an automatic interest expense disallowance rule for all interest expense allocable to wholly tax-exempt obligations acquired after August 7, 1986.[172] The effect of the 1986 provision was to increase the interest expense automatically disallowed by the TEFRA Code section 291(e) rule to 100 percent for tax-exempt obligations acquired after August 7, 1986.

Tax-exempt obligations acquired prior to August 8, 1986, and after 1982 remained subject to the 20-percent disallowance rule of Code section 291(e). Pursuant to a transition rule, tax-exempt obligations acquired after August 7, 1986, and before 1987 were subject to the 20-percent disallowance for the taxable year ending in 1986 only. Thereafter, they are subject to the 100-percent disallowance rule.[173] The acquisition date of an obligation is the date on which the holding period begins for the obligation in the hands of an acquiring bank.[174]

To improve the marketability of tax-exempt bonds, a temporary de minimis safe harbor exception to the 100-percent disallowance rule was enacted in 2009.[175] Under the safe harbor, the portion of interest expense that is allocable to investments in tax-exempt obligations does not include investments in tax-exempt obligations bonds issued during 2009 and 2010 to the extent that these investments constitute less than two percent of the average adjusted bases of all the assets of the financial institution.[176] The portion of any obligation not taken into account under this rule is treated as having been acquired on August 7, 1986.[177] Accordingly, the 20-percent deduction disallowance for interest on debt used by a bank to carry tax-exempt obligations applies.[178] If a bank's non QTEO tax exempt obligations exceed the two-percent threshold, only the excess is subject to the 100-percent disallowance rule.

---

170 Tax Reform Act of 1986, Pub. L. No. 99-514, §902(a), 100 Stat. 2085, 2380 (1986). 1954 I.R.C. §265 (2) became I.R.C. §265(a) (2000).

171 Staff of J. Comm. on Taxation 99th Cong., General Explanation of the Tax Reform Act of 1986 (Comm. Print 1987). In fact, it was unlikely that other taxpayers were denied interest expense deductions under the general disallowance rule.

172 I.R.C. §265(b), (b)(4) (2000). A "tax-exempt obligation" also includes shares of stock of a regulated investment company which, during the taxable year of the holder, distributes exempt interest dividends. I.R.C. §265(b)(4)(B) (2000).

173 This rule is not contained in the I.R.C. It is set forth in the effective date section of the Act and the related Conference Committee Report. The Tax Reform Act of 1986, Pub. L. No. 99-514, §902(a), 100 Stat. 2085, 2380 (1986); H.R. Rep. No. 99-841, pt. 2, at 334 (1986) (hereinafter Conference Committee Report).

174 Conference Committee Report, pt. 2, at 333; I.R.C. §1223.

175 American Recovery and Reinvestment Tax Act of 2009, Pub. L. No. 111-5, § 1501(a).

176 I.R.C. §265(b)(7)(A) and (B).

177 I.R.C. §291(e)(1)(B)(4).

178 I.R.C. §291(a)(3).

Example: The Second National Bank acquires $50 million in Springfield municipal bonds issued in 2009, which is less than two percent of the bank's average adjusted basis for all its assets. The 100-percent disallowance rule does not apply, but the 20-percent disallowance rule does. However, if two percent of the bank's average adjusted basis for all its assets is $40 million, then the excess ($10 million) of the bonds' value ($50 million) over this two-percent threshold is subject to the 100-percent disallowance. The first $40 million, which does not exceed the two-percent threshold, is subject to the 20-percent disallowance rule.

A refunding bond (whether a current or advance refunding) is treated as issued on the date of the issuance of the refunded bond (or in the case of a series of refundings, the original bond).[179] Accordingly, the safe harbor will not apply to bonds issued to retire or fund bonds issued prior to 2009.

Example: The City of Springfield originally issued bonds in 2006, and would now like to use refunding bonds to take advantage of the current lower interest rates. If Springfield issues refunding bonds in 2009, the issuance will not qualify for the safe harbor. If, however, it originally issues bonds in 2009, and later wants to issue refunding bonds with respect to 2009 bonds, the refunding bonds will be treated as issued in 2009, and thereby may qualify for the safe harbor.

(b) *Legislative History of 1986 Act*

According to the legislative history of the Tax Reform Act of 1986, Code section 265 was changed for two reasons. First, the pre-1986 version of Code section 265 discriminated in favor of financial institutions by allowing them to deduct interest payments regardless of tax-exempt holdings. Second, Congress believed that the pre-1986 version of Code section 265 allowed a financial institution to eliminate its tax liabilities by investing one-third or less of its assets in tax-exempt obligations.[180]

(c) *Operation of Disallowance Rule*

In describing the modifications to Code section 265, Congress stated that "[t]he amount of interest allocable to tax-exempt obligations generally is to be determined as it is for purposes of the 20 percent reduction in preference items under present law . . . ."[181] Thus, the portion of total interest expense otherwise deductible that is allocable to wholly tax-exempt obligations is computed as it is for purposes of the TEFRA disallowance. As such it is equal to total interest expense multiplied by a fraction, the numerator of which is the average adjusted tax basis of tax-exempt obligations acquired after August 7, 1986, and the denominator of which is the average adjusted basis of all assets.[182]

---

[179] I.R.C. § 265(b)(7)(C).

[180] Tax Reform Act of 1985, Report of the Committee on Ways and Means, H.R. Rep. No. 99-426, at 588 (1985).

[181] *Id.* at 589. Similar language is contained in I.R.C. § 1277(c), with respect to market discount bonds.

[182] I.R.C. §§ 265(b)(2), 291(e)(1)(B)(iii) (2000), as amended by the Tax Reform Act of 1986, Pub. L. No. 99-514, 100 Stat. 2085 (1986). With respect to the parallel situation addressed in I.R.C. § 265(b), it is provided that tax-exempt obligations "acquired" after August 7, 1986, pursuant to a direct or indirect written commitment entered into before September

The disallowance rule is applied before any provision requiring capitalization of interest expense, such as Code section 263 (Capital Expenditures) and Code section 266 (Carrying Charges). Thus, tax basis may not be increased by disallowed interest expense, which would convert the disallowance rule into a deferral rule. Tax basis is reduced by the outstanding principal amount of any indebtedness taken into account for purposes of the Code section 265(a) disallowance rule.[183] Interest does not fail to be treated as wholly exempt solely by reason of being included in alternative minimum taxable income.[184]

§ 9.5.5 Qualified Tax-Exempt Obligations

A permanent exception to the 100 percent automatic interest expense disallowance rule of Code section 265(b) is provided for any Qualified Tax-Exempt Obligation ("QTEO") acquired after August 7, 1986.[185] Pursuant to this exception, a QTEO shall be treated, for purposes of the 100-percent disallowance rule, as having been acquired on August 7, 1986, which subjects related interest expense to the Code section 291(e) 20-percent interest expense disallowance rule.

A QTEO is a tax-exempt obligation designated by the issuer to be treated as a "qualified" tax-exempt obligation for purposes of Code section 265(b).[186] However, it does not include a Code section 141 "private activity bond."[187] The statute is explicit in providing that a qualified Code section 501(c)(3) private activity bond is not a private activity bond for purposes of Code section 265(b)(3)(B).[188] Thus, if the proceeds from the issue of such bond are to be "owned by a 501(c)(3) organization or a governmental unit" and if certain other requirements are met, it may be a QTEO.

Characterization of a bond as a QTEO is subject to two $10 million limitations, which are applied by treating the issuer and all subordinate entities as a single issuer, as follows:[189]

1. No bond may be treated as a QTEO if the issuer reasonably anticipates that the total amount of QTEOs issued during the calendar year (including refundings) will exceed $10 million;[190] and

(Footnote Continued)

25, 1985, are treated as if acquired before August 8, 1986.

183 I.R.C. § 265(b)(4) (2000).

184 I.R.C. § 59(i) (2000).

185 I.R.C. § 265(b)(3) (2000).

186 On audit, the I.R.S. often requests proof that an obligation that has been treated by the taxpayer as a QTEO is, in fact, a QTEO. Taxpayers are able gather appropriate proof by searching for municipal bonds by CUSIP number on the web site for the Municipal Securities Rulemaking Board, EMMA.msrb.org..

187 I.R.C. § 265(b)(3)(B) (2000). Although the Committee Reports accompanying the addition of I.R.C. § 265(b) describe a "private activity bond" as including these obligations, the statute appears to grant no room for other types of bonds to be included within the definition. Conference Committee Report, pt. 2, at 333-4. Private activity bonds are defined in I.R.C. § 145 (2000). *See also* Staff of J. Comm. on Taxation, 100th Cong., Description of the Technical Corrections Act of 1987, at 74-77 (Comm. Print 1987).

188 *See* I.R.C. § 145 (2000) for definition of "Qualified 501(c)(3) bond." I.R.C. § 265(b)(3)(B) (2000).

189 I.R.C. § 265(b)(3)(E) (2000). The issuer reports the issuance to the IRS on Form 8038, which must be filed by the 15th day of the second calendar month after the close of the calendar quarter in which the bond was issued.

190 I.R.C. § 265(b)(3)(C) (2000).

2. No bond issued may be designated a QTEO beyond the first $10 million so designated during any calendar year.[191]

For obligations issued during 2009 and 2010, the limit for the small issuer exception is increased from $10 million to $30 million, and the small issuer exception applies to a pooled financing issue if all of the ultimate borrowers in such issue would separately qualify for the exception.[192]

Any obligation issued as a part of a pooled financing issue is to be treated as a qualified tax-exempt obligation if the requirements for the exception are met with respect to each qualified portion of the issue. This determination is made by treating each qualified portion as a separate issue. The rule in Code section 265(b)(3)(F) that requires composite issues to qualify for the exception as a whole as well as in its parts does not apply.[193] A qualified portion is the portion of the proceeds which are used with respect to each qualified borrower under the issue. A qualified borrower is a state or political subdivision thereof or a tax-exempt Code section 501(c)(3) organization.

Example: The proceeds from a $100 million pooled financing issued in 2009 are used to make four equal loans of $25 million to four qualified borrowers. The issue can qualify for the small issuer exception. However, if (1) more than $30 million were loaned to any qualified borrower, (2) any borrower were not a qualified borrower, or (3) any borrower would, if it were the issuer of a separate issue in an amount equal to the amount loaned to such borrower, fail to meet any of the other requirements of Code Sec. 265(b)(3), the entire $100 million pooled financing issue would fail to qualify for the exception.[194]

A "subordinate governmental entity" includes any entity deriving its issuing authority from another entity or which is subject to substantial control by another entity.[195] The legislative history indicates that a "subordinate" entity would include a sewer or solid waste authority created by a city or county in order to issue bonds for that city or county.[196]

An entity is not a subordinate entity, merely because of geographic inclusion in a larger entity such as a city or county, if two conditions are met:

1. The smaller (included) entity derives its power independently of the larger entity; and

2. The smaller (included) entity is not subject to control by the larger entity.[197]

Furthermore, the $10 million limitation is determined by looking through an issuing entity when the entity is acting on behalf of another political subdivision. Thus, a joint housing finance corporation was found to have issued three

---

191 I.R.C. § 265(b)(3)(D) (2000).

192 I.R.C. § 265(b)((3)(G).

193 I.R.C. § 265(b)((3)(G)(iii).

194 Joint Committee on Taxation, Description of Title I of H.R. 598, the American Recovery and Reinvestment Tax Act of 2009 (JCX-5-09), January 21, 2009.

195 Conference Committee Report, pt 2, at 334.

196 *Id.*

197 *Id.*

separate issues of "qualified tax exempt obligations" on behalf of its three member counties for purposes of the $10 million limit on QTEOs.[198] The housing finance corporation was found to be an instrumentality of its three member counties. Prior to the issuance of the bonds by the housing corporation, the three member counties irrevocably agreed to allocate all of the proceeds of the issuance to one of the three counties. Similarly, a statutorily created agency, whose function was to buy and sell securities and to make loans to qualified entities, was treated as merely the nominal purchaser of financial assets and the nominal issuer of obligations.[199]

The provisions regarding composite issues, aggregation of issues, and refunding obligations are effective as of June 30, 1987, or as if included in the Tax Reform Act of 1986, if the issuer so elects. All other provisions are effective as if included in the Tax Reform Act of 1986.[200]

§ 9.5.6 Interest Expense

For purposes of the interest expense disallowance rules contained in Code section 265(b) and in Code section 291(e), the term "interest expense" means the total deductible interest for the taxable year.[201] It includes certain amounts not designated as interest, such as amounts deductible under Code section 591 with respect to deposits, investment certificates, or withdrawable shares, and amounts of original issue discount.

The IRS has ruled that neither service fees nor payments made pursuant to notional principal contracts, nor a commitment fee paid to obtain a line of credit, should be treated as interest for purposes of section 265(a)(2).[202] In the case of the service fees, the IRS gave three reasons for not treating them as interest expense. First, neither the predecessors of section 265(a)(2) nor their legislative histories indicate that Congress intended the term "interest" to have any meaning other than its original meaning. Second, when Congress wanted the term "interest" under section 265(a)(2) to apply to certain expenses that might not be interest under the usual meaning of that term it has done so explicitly. Third, under section 265(a)(1), Congress specifically intended not to disallow deductions for non-interest expenses (other than section 212 expenses) related to such obligations.[203]

In the case of interest rate swap transactions, if the up-front payment is not significant, the periodic payments and the up-front payments will not be treated as interest expenses.[204] The IRS concluded that these payments are not interest expense because they are not "compensation for the use or forbearance of money . . . ," as no amount is actually loaned.[205] A fee paid in consideration for a

---

[198] PLR 9805032, January 30, 1998.

[199] PLR 199909043, March 5, 1999.

[200] I.R.C. § 265(b)(3), as amended by the Technical and Miscellaneous Revenue Act of 1988, Pub. L. No. 100-647, § 1009(b)(3)(A), 102 Stat. 3342, 3446 (1988).

[201] For rules relating to intercompany interest paid within a consolidated group of corporations, *see* Reg. § 1.1502-13(g)(5), Eg. 1.

[202] FSA 200037034, June 15, 2000.

[203] S. Rep. No. 73-558, 1939-1 (Part 2) C.B. 586, 606 (1934).

[204] PLR 98240026, June 12, 1998.

[205] Deputy v. du Pont, 308 U.S. 488, 498 (1940).

lender's agreement to make a loan at a specified date and at a specified rate of interest is not interest because the commitment fee earned is an amount paid for the right to draw on credit in the future.[206]

Total deductible interest for the taxable year subject to the disallowance rule may not be reduced by interest expense directly traceable to the purchase of any asset. Under the authority granted by Code section 7701(f), the IRS is considering a rule that would permit taxpayers to trace proceeds of borrowings to specific taxable investments or other specific uses, but would apply a pro rata approach to determine the use of proceeds of borrowings that are not traceable to a specific use.[207] However, if interest expense is indirectly allocated to a tax-exempt obligation pursuant to the provisions of Code section 265(a), that interest becomes nondeductible and, thus, is excluded from the total amount of interest expense for purposes of applying the disallowance rules of Code section 291(e) or 265(b).

The interest expense incurred by a bank in acquiring an unrelated bank's excess reserves (the purchase of federal funds) is not permitted to be excluded from the calculation of interest expense allocable to indebtedness on tax-exempt obligations.[208] The bank's contention that it could establish an alternative means of determining interest expense that is allocable to indebtedness on tax-exempt obligations was rejected. The IRS's position is that the Code does not impose any obligations on it to provide for, or allow, computations of interest allocable to tax-exempt securities other than the statutory method.

§9.5.7 Acquisition Date

For purposes of Code sections 265(b) and 291(e), a taxpayer's holding period of tax-exempt obligations is determined under Code section 1223, which generally provides that the holding period begins on the day after the date of purchase.[209] If a taxpayer has a tacked holding period because the taxpayer's holding period is determined by reference to the holding period of a transferor, the acquisition is not treated as a new acquisition for purposes of the interest expense disallowance rules.

With respect to transfers of tax-exempt obligations between members of an affiliated group, Code section 1502 and the regulation thereunder apply. Pursuant to those rules, obligations purchased in a deferred intercompany transaction are treated as acquired on the date of the purchase transaction.[210] Further, tax-exempt obligations acquired in a Code section 351 corporate formation, a Code section 118 contribution to capital by a shareholder, or a Code section 368 reorganization will not be treated as new acquisitions.[211] Thus, there will be tacked holding periods in respect of tax-exempt obligations transferred in these transactions.[212] The assets and interest expense of a newly formed subsidiary in a

---

[206] Rev. Rul. 70-540, 1970-2 C.B. 101 (Situation 3), obsoleted by Rev. Proc. 94-29, 1994-1 C.B., 616 (Apr. 4, 1994).

[207] Advance Notice of Proposed Rulemaking, 69 Fed Reg. 25534 (May 7, 2004).

[208] TAM 8838004, June 8, 1988.

[209] Conference Committee Report, pt 2, at 333.

[210] *See* Reg. §1.1502-13 which addresses intercompany transactions.

[211] *Id.*

[212] I.R.C. §1223 (2000).

Code section 351 transaction will be treated as assets and interest expense of the transferor-shareholder-bank for purposes of applying the disallowance rules.[213]

Tax-exempt obligations acquired after August 7, 1986, pursuant to a plan of merger entered into prior to September 25, 1985, will be treated as acquired prior to August 8, 1986.[214] Consequently, any tax-exempt obligations that were held by the target prior to August 8, 1986, will not be treated as obligations purchased after August 7, 1986, for purposes of Code sections 265(b) and 291(e)(1)(B) by virtue of a Code section 338 election by the parent. Any tax-exempt obligations that were held by the target and that were purchased prior to August 8, 1986, remain subject to the provisions of Code sections 265 and 291(e)(1)(B) to the same extent that they were subject to those provisions previously.[215]

If a tax-exempt obligation is significantly modified after it is acquired, the modification could trigger a deemed taxable exchange, causing a redating of the holding period.[216] Since the waiver of a right under an interest rate adjustment clause to receive a higher rate of interest results in a material change in the terms of an obligation, it has been found to constitute a deemed exchange under Code section 1001 of old bonds for new bonds. If such deemed exchange occurs after August 7, 1986, a bank holder is precluded from deducting any of its interest expense that is allocable to the new tax-exempt bonds under the provisions of Code section 265(b).[217] If the deemed exchange occurred prior to August 8, 1986, but after December 31, 1982, in respect of an obligation originally acquired prior to January 1, 1983, the 20 percent disallowance rule would apply.

§ 9.5.8 Consolidated Disallowance

The weight of authority now indicates that the general interest expense disallowance rule of Code section 265(a)(2), under limited circumstance, can be applied on a consolidated basis to disallow interest expense paid or incurred by one member of a consolidated group with respect to the tax-exempt obligations held by another member of the group. Moreover, the IRS has taken the position on audit that the bank specific rules of Code sections 265(b) and 291(e) also can be applied on consolidated basis.

(a) *Statutory Rule*

Code section 7701(f) was enacted in 1984, just two years after the TEFRA bank-specific interest expense disallowance rule was enacted. It was added to the Code for the purpose of preventing avoidance of sections such as Code sections 265 (prior to its 1986 amendment) and 291 by a taxpayer who attempts to artificially separate borrowing from tax-exempt investments.[218] The section requires the Treasury Department to promulgate regulations designed to prevent the avoidance of sections that link borrowing to investment, or that deal with

---

213 PLR 9205013, October 31, 1991.

214 Section 902(f)(2) of the Tax Reform Act of 1986, Pub. L. No. 99-514, 100 Stat. 2085, 2382 (1986) contains this transitional rule.

215 PLR 8737033, June 15, 1987. *See also* PLR 8738030, June 22, 1987. I.R.C. § 338(h)(2) (2000).

216 *See generally* the discussion of renegotiated debt, and Prop. Reg. § 1.1001-3 in Ch. 6.

217 Rev. Rul. 87-19, 1987-1 C.B. 249.

218 Deficit Reduction Act of 1984, Pub. L. No. 98-369, 98 Stat. 494 (1984).

diminishing risks through the use of "related persons, pass-through entities, or other intermediaries."[219] A "related person" includes any corporation, 80 percent or more of the value of the outstanding stock of which is owned (directly or indirectly) by or for such corporations.[220] To date, no regulations have been issued.

In 2004, the I.R.S. and Treasury Department issued an advance notice of proposed rulemaking in which they solicited comments and suggestions regarding the scope and details of regulations that may be proposed under Code section 7701(f) to address the application of Code sections 265(a)(2) and 246A.[221] The advance notice did not specifically refer to Code sections 265(b) or 291(e), the two bank specific disallowance rules.

The advance notice indicates that the Treasury and I.R.S. are considering a rule that would permit taxpayers to trace proceeds of borrowings to specific taxable investments or other specific uses, but would apply a pro rata approach to determine the use of proceeds of borrowings that are not traceable to a specific use. This would differ from a general rule requiring a pro rata allocation of borrowings among all available uses, such as the rule in Code section 265(b) applicable to financial institutions.

The Conference Report under Code section 7701(f) states that Congress intended Code section 7701(f) to authorize regulations under Code section 265(2) (now Code section 265(a)(2)). However, Congress did not intend this authority to be used to adopt regulations that would "cause interest on borrowings by an affiliated company to be disallowed in any case where such interest would not be disallowed under present law if the operations of the corporations were carried on as separate divisions of a single corporation."[222] Therefore, a deduction would not be disallowed merely because one corporation borrows in the ordinary course of business operations and an affiliated bank, insurance company, or similar business holds tax-exempt obligations.[223] There, the required nexus would not appear to be present.

---

[219] The Tax Reform Act of 1986 contains a special effective date for I.R.C. § 7701(f) as it may apply to 1954 I.R.C. § 265(2), the predecessor to 1986 I.R.C. § 265(a). Pub. L. No. 99-514, § 1804(b)(2), 100 Stat. 2085, 2798-99 (1986). According to the effective date provision, I.R.C. § 7701(f) will apply to "term loans" made after July 18, 1984, and to "demand loans" outstanding after that date unless repaid before September 18, 1984. July 18, 1984, is the effective date unless repaid before September 18, 1984. July 18, 1984, is the effective date for many of the provisions contained in the Deficit Reduction Act of 1984, Pub. L. No. 98-369, 98 Stat. 494 (1984). Any loan renegotiated after July 18, 1984, is treated as a loan made after that date. A "demand loan" is a loan defined in I.R.C. § 7872(f), except that it does not include a nontransferable loan conditioned upon future services. A "term loan" is any loan other than a "demand loan." I.R.C. § 7872(f) (2000).

[220] The General Explanation of the Tax Reform Act of 1984 Prepared by the Staff of the Joint Committee on Taxation, at 146, states that "related person" is to be defined in accordance with the rules contained in I.R.C. § 1239.

[221] Request for Comments, 69 Fed. Reg. 25534 (May 7, 2004).

[222] H.R. Rep. No. 98-861 at 1041-42 (1984), 1984-3 (Vol. 2) C.B. 295.

[223] *See* 130 Cong. Rec. S4511 (April 12, 1984) (colloquy between Sen. Percy and Sen. Dole).

(b) *Judicial Analysis*

In *H. Enterprises International, Inc. v. Commissioner,*[224] the Tax Court concluded that interest expenses of an affiliate could be disallowed under Code section 265(a)(2) if the borrowing could be traced to a related taxpayer's investments in tax-exempt obligations. The Court stated that "[i]n our view, the provisions of sections . . . and *265(a)(2),* particularly when considered in conjunction with section 7701(f), may in appropriate circumstances be used when one member of an affiliated group is the borrower and another member the purchaser of the portfolio stock or tax-exempt securities. The legislative history of section 7701(f) specifically states that no inference is intended that any particular provision under present law is not applicable in the case of related parties."[225]

The Tax Court reasoned that interest expense of one member of an affiliated group could be disallowed under Code section 265(a)(2) when another member of the group owned tax-exempt obligations because the section did not prohibit such a consolidated disallowance. The Court stated: "There is no provision that the borrower be the same as the person who acquires the tax-exempt securities."[226]

More recently, in *PSB Holdings, Inc. v. Commissioner* the Tax Court limited the scope of its opinion in *H. Enterprises.*[227] The court ruled in favor of the taxpayer when deciding the issue whether a bank must include the tax-exempt obligations purchased and owned by its subsidiary in the calculation of the bank's average adjusted bases of tax-exempt obligations under Code sections 265(b)(2)(A) and 291(e)(1)(B)(ii)(I).

The bank in that case organized a wholly owned subsidiary to consolidate and improve the efficiency of managing, safekeeping, and operating its securities investment portfolio and to reduce the state tax liability of the bank's holding company group. During a period of approximately ten years, the bank trans-

---

[224] *H. Enterprises International, Inc. v. Commissioner,* 105 T.C. 71 (1985). *See also H. Enterprises International, Inc. v. Commissioner,* 75 T.C.M. 1948 (1998), *aff'd* 183 F.3d 907 (8th Cir. 1999).

[225] *H. Enterprises International, Inc. v. Commissioner,* 105 T.C. 71, 81 (1985). H. R. Rep. No. 98-861, at 1041-1042 (1984). GCM 39667, I-077-86, September 30, 1987, provides that §265(2) may be applied to related parties. However, in view of the enactment of §7701(f) and the Conference report statement that present law was unclear, the GCM recommends limiting the application of §265(2) for years prior to the effective date of §7701(f) to situations where the proceeds of indebtedness are used for and are directly traceable to the purchase of tax-exempt obligations, or where tax-exempt obligations are used as collateral for indebtedness. *See* sections 3.02 and 3.03 of Rev. Proc. 72-18, 1972-1 C.B. 740.

[226] This reasoning is quite shocking! It may be reasonable if it were not axiomatic that the statutory rules contained in the Code that deny a deduction (as well as those that allow a deduction) are to be applied in the determination of the taxable income of a taxpayer. I.R.C. § 161 provides: "In computing taxable income under section 63, there shall be allowed as deductions the items specified in this part, subject to the exceptions provided in part IX (sec. 261 and following, relating to items not deductible)." All affiliated taxpayers do not aggregate their I.R.C. §163 interest expense deductions and their I.R.C. § 265(a)(2) interest expense disallowance, even if a consolidated tax return is filed. Thus, Reg. § 1.1502-11 provides: "The consolidated taxable income for a consolidated return year shall be determined by taking into account—(1) The separate taxable income of each member of the group . . . ." Furthermore, Reg.§ 1.1502-12 provides: "The separate taxable income of a member . . . is computed in accordance with the provisions of the Code covering the determination of taxable income of separate corporations . . . ." The Court appears to have overlooked this fundamental principal in what could only be seen as a results oriented opinion.

[227] 129 T.C. No. 15 (Nov. 2007).

ferred to its subsidiary cash, tax-exempt obligations, taxable securities, and loan participations, including substantially all of the bank's long-term investments. The cash totaled $18,460 and was transferred to the subsidiary upon its organization in exchange for all of its common stock. The tax-exempt obligations and taxable securities totaled $38,141,487, and the loan participations totaled $27,710,909; these three categories of assets were transferred to the subsidiary as paid-in capital. No security or tax-exempt obligation of any kind was transferred by the bank to its subsidiary during the years under examination.

At the time of the transfers, no liabilities encumbered the transferred securities or obligations, and the subsidiary did not assume any liability of the bank. The subsidiary did not sell any tax-exempt obligation or taxable security before maturity, and all such obligations and securities received from the bank matured by the end of the years under audit. The subsidiary did not own any other asset.

On the consolidated returns filed for the bank's affiliated group, the bank included all of the tax-exempt obligations that were purchased by the bank and that were outstanding as of the end of the year in the bank's calculation of the numerator. Some of those obligations were owned by the subsidiary during the year, having been earlier transferred by the bank to the capital of the subsidiary. The IRS claimed that all tax-exempt obligations purchased and owned by the subsidiary must be included in the bank's interest expense disallowance fraction.

The court held that the amount of a bank's interest expense allocated to tax-exempt interest, and thus rendered nondeductible, is computed by multiplying the otherwise allowable interest expense by a fraction, the numerator of which equals "the taxpayer's" average adjusted basis of tax-exempt obligations.[228] The fraction's denominator equals the average adjusted basis of all assets of "the taxpayer."[229]

The court reasoned that the statute referred to the tax-exempt obligations and assets owned by the bank alone or, in other words, by the "taxpayer" for whom the subject calculation is performed. It did not read that text to provide that a bank must include in its tax-exempt obligations any tax-exempt obligation purchased and owned by another taxpayer, whether the taxpayers are related or not. It reasoned:

> ". . . the statutes use the term "taxpayer" in the singular, and well-established law treats [the bank] and [its subsidiary] as separate taxpayers notwithstanding the fact that they join in the filing of a consolidated return. [footnotes omitted] Nor do the consolidated return regulations, as applicable here, change this result. Those regulations require that [the bank] calculate its net income separately from [its subsidiary's] net income."[230]

(c) *Non Bank Rules: IRS Pronouncements*

The audit position taken by the IRS in *H. Enterprises* and adopted by the Tax Court and the appellate court has been refined and formally adopted by the IRS in Revenue Ruling 2004-47.[231] That ruling holds that the interest expense of one

---

[228] I.R.C. §§265(b)(2)(A), 291(e)(1)(B)(ii)(I).

[229] I.R.C. §§ 265(b)(2)(B), 291(e)(1)(B)(ii)(II).

[230] I.R.C. §1.1502-11(a)(1).

[231] Rev. Rul. 2004-47, I.R.B. 2004-21.

member of an affiliated group may be disallowed when that member makes either a capital contribution or a loan to another member of the group from funds borrowed from an unrelated lender. In the ruling, the recipient of the loan or the capital contribution is a dealer in tax-exempt securities to whom the borrowed funds are directly traceable.[232]

In the ruling four situations are described, three of which result in interest expense disallowance under Code section 265(a)(2). To arrive at the interest expense disallowance, the investment of one member of an affiliated group ("S") is linked to the borrowing of another member of the group ("P") to determine whether there was a proscribed purpose of the borrowing. The four situations could be summarized as follows:

Situation #	*Consolidated Return*	*How Transferred to "S"*	*Transfer Directly Traceable*	*Interest Disallowed*
1	No	Cont. to Cap.	Yes	Yes-P
2	Yes	Cont. to Cap.	Yes	Yes-P
3	No	Cont. to Cap.	No	No
4	No	Loan	Yes	Yes-S

In all situations, P borrows funds from an unrelated bank, the borrowing is not directly traceable to the purchase of tax-exempt obligations by S, and S is a dealer in tax-exempt obligations. In situations 1, 2, and 3, the borrowed funds are contributed to the capital of S, but in the fourth situation the borrowed funds are loaned to S. In Situations 1, 2, and 4 when interest expense is disallowed, the approach used in Revenue Procedure 72-18 was employed to determine the amount of the disallowance.[233] As such, if P borrows funds from L (an unrelated bank) and contributes the funds to the capital of S (a dealer in tax-exempt securities), a portion of P's interest expense deduction is likely to be disallowed on audit.

The result in the ruling obtains regardless of whether the borrowed funds are directly traceable to the dealer's purchasing or carrying of tax-exempt obligations. If the funds P borrows are not directly traceable to S, then P's interest expense would not be disallowance. Thus, if P borrowed funds from L but there is no direct evidence that the borrowed funds were contributed or loaned to S, none of P's interest expense deduction would be disallowed.

In determining what portion of interest expense is disallowed, the ruling requires taxpayers to multiply interest on borrowed funds that are not directly traceable to tax-exempt obligations by the allocation formula set forth in Revenue Procedure 72-18.[234] The portion of disallowed interest expense is determined by

[232] If a taxpayer is merely a dealer in securities for purposes of Code § 475, the taxpayer will not necessarily be a dealer in tax-exempt securities for purposes of this disallowance rule, even if the taxpayer holds tax-exempt securities.

[233] Rev. Proc. 72-18, 1972-1 C.B. 740. *See also Leslie v. Commissioner*, 413 F.2d 636 (2d Cir. 1969) *cert denied*, 396 U.S. 1007 (1970), where this formula was earlier employed by the Second Circuit to deny a portion of the interest expense deduction to a dealer in securities.

[234] Rev. Proc. 72-18, 1972-1 C.B. 740, Section 7. The allocation formula contained in this revenue procedure was earlier utilized by the Second Circuit in *Leslie, Commissoner* 413 F.2d 636 (2nd Cir. 1969). The formula is similar to that contained in Code § 265(b) and in Code § 291(e), which are exclusively applicable to banks.

calculating a disallowance fraction, the numerator of which is the average adjusted basis of the taxpayer's tax-exempt obligations and the denominator of which is the average adjusted tax basis of the taxpayer's total assets. In the examples above, it is S's tax-exempt obligations and total assets that comprise the disallowance fraction. If there is a loan to S from P, S's interest expense is multiplied by the fraction, but if the borrowed funds are contributed to the capital of S, then it is the interest expense of P that is multiplied by the fraction.

In a situation involving a taxable year prior to the enactment of Code section 7701(f), the Chief Counsel of the IRS concluded that Code section 265(2) could be applied in a related party context in circumstances where the proceeds of indebtedness are used for, and are directly traceable to, the purchase of tax-exempt obligations, or where tax-exempt obligations are used as collateral for indebtedness.[235] The opinion held that Code section 7701(f) does not preclude this rule in such circumstances prior to its effective date. The legislative history under the Tax Deficit Reduction Act of 1984[236] stated that, at the time, the application of Code section 265(2) to related parties was unclear.[237]

Regulations issued under Code section 7701(f) may provide that a bank or other taxpayer may not avoid Code section 265 by incurring long-term indebtedness that is used to acquire tax-exempt obligations transferred to a nonbank affiliate.[238] However, the section is not intended to disallow interest expense deductions by a corporation if the interest would not otherwise be disallowed to the payor.[239] Thus, tax-exempt obligations acquired in the market by a bank holding company, with its own funds, would not appear to be subject to the 100 percent disallowance rule. Similarly, "a deduction would not be disallowed merely because one corporation borrows in the ordinary course of its business and an affiliated bank, insurance company, or similar business holds tax-exempt obligations."[240]

The IRS reiterated some of the arguments that it made in *H. Enterprises* in a Field Service Advice relating to a similar situation. In Field Service Advice 200129009, the borrower was the parent, which made a capital contribution to its

[235] General Counsel Memorandum 39667, March 13, 1987.

[236] H.R. Rep. 98-861, at 1041 (1984).

[237] Taxpayers should consider the possible application of I.R.C. § 482. However, in PLR 8740001, March 23, 1987, the IRS concluded that allocations under I.R.C. § 482 are not appropriate where there are only arm's length transactions.

[238] These regulations would fall into the category of "legislative regulations," which would limit their application to transactions occurring after their adoption. However, the IRS will be inclined to apply them retroactively to the date of enactment of I.R.C. § 7701(f) (2000).

[239] I.R.C. §§ 265(b) and 291(e) contain automatic interest expense disallowance rules for banks. For taxable years beginning prior to 1987, a transfer of tax-exempt obligations by a bank to its subsidiary would not cause any related interest expense to be disallowed. The nexus requirement of 1954 I.R.C. § 265(2) (prior to its amendment by the Tax Reform Act of 1986, Pub. L. No. 99-514, 100 Stat. 2085 (1986)), as limited in numerous revenue rulings in its application to banks, would not have disallowed any interest expense if a bank concurrently held tax-exempt obligations. I.R.C. § 7701(f) does not prohibit what may be done directly if it is done indirectly.

[240] The General Explanation of the Tax Reform Act of 1984 Prepared by the Staff of the Joint Committee on Taxation, at 146 (footnotes omitted). *See also* Joint Committee on Taxation Staff Description (JCS-15-87) of the Technical Corrections Bill of 1987 (H.R. 2636, at 1350), released June 15, 1987, at 74. I.R.C. § 7701 was generally effective on the date of its enactment (July 18, 1984). Regulations issued under the broad authority of I.R.C. § 7701(f) should be effective no earlier than the date of their issuance. I.R.C. § 7805(b) (2000).

subsidiary.[241] However, in *H. Enterprises*, the borrower was a subsidiary that distributed the borrowed funds to its parent, which then invested in the tax-exempt obligations. The IRS found as a matter of fact that the purpose of the loan in the field service advice was to provide an insurance subsidiary of the taxpayer, whose business involved the holding of tax-exempt securities, with additional capital. Consequently, the proscribed purpose of Code section 265(a)(2) was not present.[242] However, in reaching its decision, the IRS also concluded that Code section 265(a)(2) can be applied to disallow interest expenses to the consolidated group where a parent incurs the debt and a subsidiary holds the tax-exempt securities. The parent may deduct the interest expense only if the parent can substantiate that it needed additional capital for a valid business purpose (*i.e.*, a purpose other than meeting ordinary and recurring business expenses), rather than to purchase or carry tax-exempt securities. Furthermore, although regulations have not been issued under Code section 7701(f), the field service advice held that Code section 265(a)(2) can apply in situations such as where one member of a consolidated group incurs or continues debt and another member acquires or holds tax-exempt obligations.

(d) *Bank Rules: IRS Pronouncements*

According to the IRS, a bank that creates a wholly-owned subsidiary to manage, invest, and reinvest the bank's investment assets may have to treat the subsidiary's assets and interest expense as those of the bank for purposes of applying Code sections 265(b) and § 291(e) in order to clearly reflect the income of the bank and the subsidiary.

In TAM 200428027, a subsidiary was formed with the exchange of securities owned by a bank for the stock of a subsidiary.[243] The bank later transferred cash to the subsidiary as additional capital. Virtually all of the tax-exempt obligations that the bank transferred to the subsidiary matured, and the tax-exempt obligations held by the subsidiary at the time of the audit had been purchased either from cash that the subsidiary received from the bank or from earnings and proceeds of assets that the subsidiary received from the bank. No liabilities or debts were transferred to the subsidiary. For book accounting and also for the

---

241 FSA 200129009, February 22, 2001.

242 This case appears to be factually similar to PLR 8438003 (May 24, 1984), where the taxpayer was a holding company and was the parent company of an affiliated group of insurance corporations. In that ruling, the subsidiaries were approaching the limit of policies that they could issue based on their then-existing surplus levels. Accordingly, the taxpayer issued long-term debentures, and a portion of the proceeds were contributed to the capital of the subsidiaries to increase their surplus levels. The ruling determined that the totality of the circumstances did not establish a sufficiently direct relationship between the borrowing and the investment in tax-exempt securities to justify disallowing the interest expense. Similarly, in PLR 8745024 (Aug. 7, 1984), the interest expense of a loan was not disallowed where a capital contribution was made to a subsidiary in order to raise a surplus. The taxpayer was a holding company that held all the outstanding stock of two property and casualty insurance companies. The ruling also determined that under separate entity taxable income computations prescribed by the consolidated return regulations, I.R.C. §265(a)(2) would not apply to match borrowing by one member of the consolidated group to another member's tax-exempt securities. The ruling was issued before Congress enacted I.R.C. §7701(f). I.R.C. §7701(f) is effective for term loans made after July 18, 1984, and demand loans outstanding on July 18, 1984 (and not repaid before September 18, 1984). *See* Pub. L. No. 99-514, §1804(b)(2), 100 Stat. 2085, 2798 (1986).

243 TAM 200428027, July 9, 2004. *See also* 200434021, Aug. 20, 2004, and TAM 200434029, Aug. 20, 2004, for similar treatment of interest expense.

bank regulatory purposes, the subsidiary's assets and liabilities were consolidated with those of the bank.

The IRS acknowledged that there was a valid non tax business reason for forming the subsidiary. The bank created the subsidiary to improve the efficiency of managing investment assets that the bank did not expect to need for its immediate, day-to-day operations.

Apparently supporting the conclusion that the tax-exempts of the subsidiary should be consolidated with the bank's assets were the facts indicating that there was very significant overlap among the senior executives and Board members of the subsidiary, the bank, and the bank's parent company ("BHC").

The subsidiary had three members of its Board of Directors. One individual was the subsidiary's Chairman of the Board, Chief Executive Officer and President. This individual also held those same positions in the bank's parent company ("BHC"), and that individual held the positions of Chairman of the Board and Chief Executive Officer of the bank. Another member of the subsidiary's Board was the subsidiary's Secretary/Treasurer. This individual also was the Senior Vice President and Secretary of BHC and an Executive Vice President and the Secretary of the bank. The third member of the subsidiary's Board of Directors was the subsidiary's Vice President. This individual also held the positions of President and Chief Operating Officer of the bank.

Furthermore, there was very significant similarity between the investment policies and decision making in the subsidiary and the bank. The subsidiary's Chairman of the Board (also the bank's Chairman of the Board) made all of the investment decisions for the subsidiary and the bank. The investment policy established by the bank's Board of Directors applies to both the bank and the subsidiary. According to this written investment policy, all of the bank's and the subsidiary's securities transactions were subject to monthly review by the bank's Board of Directors and were required to be executed through securities dealers approved by the bank's Board. The investment policy generally did not distinguish between the investment portfolios of the bank and the subsidiary but, rather, treated them as a single portfolio.

The subsidiary also paid substantial dividends to the bank; it borrowed some funds from the bank (on which the subsidiary paid interest to the bank); and the subsidiary leased office space in the bank's headquarters building.

In the TAM, the Service concludes that it has the authority to compel a consolidation of the subsidiary's assets, including its tax-exempt holdings, and its interest expense with the bank in order to "clearly reflect the income of the financial institution or to prevent the evasion or avoidance of taxes." The guidelines contained in Revenue Ruling 90-44 were the apparent support for the conclusion reached in the TAM.[244] These guidelines include the following statement on the treatment of related taxpayers:

---

[244] 1990-1 C.B. 54.

> "If one or more financial institutions are members of an affiliated group of corporations (as defined in section 1504 of the Code), then, even if the group files a consolidated return, each such institution must make a separate determination of interest expense allocable to tax-exempt interest, rather than a combined determination with the other members of the group."
>
> "However, in situations involving taxpayers which are under common control and one or more of which is a financial institution, in order to fulfill the congressional purpose underlying section 265(b) of the Code, the District Director may require another determination of interest expense allocable to tax-exempt interest to clearly reflect the income of the financial institution or to prevent the evasion or avoidance of taxes."

It is possible that taxpayers will challenge the application of the disallowance rule in this situation because of the paucity of authority for any broad application of the rule. A revenue ruling has limited value, at best, as precedent, especially if it appears to run counter to a specific statutory provision. It may be argued that the disallowance rules were carefully crafted to apply only to those taxpayers who met the statutory definition of a bank. Furthermore, while the IRS is granted authority by Code section 446(b) to ensure that income is clearly reflected, that authority does not extend to reallocating income simply to maximize reported tax liability within a consolidated group. Provisions are contained in the consolidated return regulations that call for a separate computation of taxable income for the various members of a consolidated group. Finally, the resolution of this issue should turn on the facts of the particular case. No rule of law can be established that requires consolidation in all situations.

(e) *Consolidated Exclusion*

Regulation section 1.1502-13(c)(6)(i) currently provides for an exclusion from the income of one member of a consolidated group that earns interest from a loan to another member of the group when the borrower has interest expense disallowed by Code section 265(a)(2). The exclusion provided in Regulation section 1.1502-13(c)(6)(i) is proposed to be curtailed.

The rule of Proposed regulation section 1.265-2(c) will reduce the exclusion whenever:

a) One member of a consolidated group ("P") incurs or continues indebtedness to a nonmember of the group ("B"),

b) The borrowed funds are directly traceable to an intercompany loan extended by P to a member of the group ("S"), and

c) Section 265 (a)(2) applies to disallow a deduction for all or a portion of S's interest-expense on the intragroup loan.

The modification of the exclusion is designed to ensure that the net effect of these transactions for the group should be a disallowance of a deduction for interest expense under Code section 265(a)(2) and an exclusion under Code section 103. It does this by requiring that all or a portion of P's interest income on the intercompany obligation to S not be excluded under Regulation section 1.1502-13(c)(6)(i).

§ 9.5.9 Tax Basis of Assets and Tax-Exempts

The term "average adjusted tax basis" as it applies to total assets and to tax-exempt obligations has the same meaning in Code sections 265(b) and 291(e).[245] Moreover, the identical term is used in Code section 585 to define a "large bank."[246] Although there is no explicit connection between Code section 585 and the two interest expense disallowance sections, it would seem to be reasonable to conclude that the identical term used in sections that have application only to banks and, in the case of Code section 585(c) and Code section 265(b), that were enacted at the same time, should have the same meaning.

For purposes of determining the amount of "total assets," the statutory provisions are not explicit in stating that only assets that appear on the books of the taxpayer are taken into account.[247] Nevertheless, it would be unusual for there to be an unbooked asset in which the taxpayer had a tax basis. Thus, the notional principal amount of a swap is not included in the asset base for purposes of this calculation.[248] Furthermore if the taxpayer has created goodwill, the goodwill would not have a tax basis. Conversely, acquired goodwill would be an asset that would have to be taken into account for purposes of the interest expense disallowance rule.

Tax basis is computed under the general rules of Code section 1016, and the "average" of total assets and of tax-exempt obligations is computed applying guidance contained in the legislative history accompanying the Tax Reform Act of 1986, in regulations, and in IRS rulings.[249]

According to the legislative history accompanying the Tax Reform Act of 1986,

> [t]he average adjusted basis of the assets of a bank or controlled group is the average of the adjusted basis of the assets for each period of time falling within the taxable year the bank is required to report for regulatory purposes.[250]

Averaging rules contained in issued regulations under Code section 585 are similar to rules contained in Revenue Ruling 90-44; however, there are some subtle differences that may be significant to some taxpayers. It is reasonable to assume that the rules contained in regulations under Code section 585 could be applied to compute the average of total assets for purposes of the interest expense disallowance rules. The regulations are a more recent consideration of the computation method, as they were issued four years after the ruling. These regulations have been issued only after receiving careful consideration during the normal comment period afforded proposed regulations.

According to the Code section 585 regulations, the averaging interval, in general, is the last day of the regular period for which the institution must report

245 H.R. Rep. No. 99-426 at 589 (1985).

246 I.R.C. § 585(c) (2000); Reg. § 1.585-5(b).

247 H.R. Rep. No. 99-426, at 577 (1985).

248 Rev. Rul. 90-44, 1990-34 IRB 8; Conference Committee Report, at pt. 2, 334; Reg. § 1.585-5(c).

249 Reg. § 1.585-5(c)(3).

250 PLR 9824026, June 12, 1998.

to its primary federal regulatory agency.[251] If the institution does not have a reporting responsibility to a federal regulatory agency, then its primary State regulatory agency is substituted for its primary federal agency. Alternatively, if the institution is required to report to its federal regulatory agency more frequently than quarterly, then it may choose the last day of the calendar quarter as its report date.[252] Thus, it may use an interval that is less frequent than the reporting interval, but not less frequent than quarterly.

In Revenue Ruling 90-44, the average of the bases of tax-exempt obligations is determined by averaging the month ending balances of those obligations.[253] Although the average basis of all assets is generally determined by averaging the quarter ending balances, at the election of the taxpayer, the average of all tax-exempt obligations and all assets may be computed on a more frequent basis; that is, weekly, or even daily for all assets. A taxpayer may not compute the average adjusted tax basis of tax-exempt obligations and total assets on a less frequent basis than monthly and quarterly, respectively, without receiving special permission from the IRS. Moreover, a taxpayer may not compute such averages for any taxable year on a less frequent basis than it used in the preceding taxable year.

In addition to the flexibility of selecting dates for computing averages, if the taxpayer elects, the adjusted tax basis of total assets may be estimated for the first three quarters of the taxable year using the book basis of total assets at the end of each quarter. No such estimate may be used for tax-exempt obligations. An election to use the estimation method does not bind the taxpayer to use the estimation method in a subsequent taxable year. However, if the taxpayer switches from the estimation method to the actual method, the estimation method may not be elected in any subsequent quarter or year. An illustration from Revenue Ruling 90-44 of this estimation method follows.

Estimate of Tax Bases of Total Assets

1st Quarter Estimate=$B \times (R + {}^{1}/_{4}Y)$

2nd Quarter Estimate=$B \times (R + {}^{1}/_{2}Y)$

3rd Quarter Estimate=$B \times (R + {}^{3}/_{4}Y)$

Where:

B=Total book bases of all assets held by the taxpayer at the end of the quarter;

R= "Tax/book ratio" as of the close of the preceding taxable year; and

Y=The result (whether positive or negative) obtained when R is subtracted from the "tax/book ratio" as of the close of the current taxable year.

---

[251] Reg. § 1.585-5(c)(2). The primary federal regulatory agencies are as follows: the OCC for nationally chartered banks; the OTS for nationally chartered thrifts; the FDIC for state chartered banks and thrifts; the Federal Reserve Board for banks chartered by a foreign country.

[252] Reg. § 1.585-5(c)(2)(i).

[253] Rev. Rul. 90-44, 1990-1 C.B. 54. Regulations under I.R.C. § 585 are not concerned with tax-exempt obligations, only total assets.

For purposes of determining R and Y, a taxpayer's "tax/book ratio" is the ratio of (1) the total tax bases of all of the taxpayer's assets to (2) the total book bases of those assets.

Example: Assume that the adjusted tax bases of a calendar year taxpayer's total assets are $450z on December 31, 1989, and $480z on December 31, 1990. Also assume that the book bases of those assets are $500z on December 31, 1989; $520z on March 31, 1990; $540z on June 30, 1990; $560z on September 30, 1990; and $600z on December 31, 1990. Applying the estimation method shown in the taxpayer's "tax/book ratio" as of the close of 1989, (*R*) is 0.9 (450z/500z). The taxpayer's "tax/book ratio" as of the close of 1990 is 0.8 (480z/600z).

Thus, *Y* is 20.1. The estimated adjusted tax bases of the taxpayer's total assets are as follows:

1st Quarter $=B\ (R + {}^{1}/_{4}\ Y)$
$=\$520z\ [0.9 + {}^{1}/_{4}(-0.1)]$
$=\$455z$
2nd Quarter $=B\ (R + {}^{1}/_{2}\ Y)$
$=\$540z\ [0.9 + {}^{1}/_{2}(-0.1)]$
$=\$459z$
3rd Quarter $=B\ (R + {}^{3}/_{4}\ Y)$
$=\$560z\ [0.9 + {}^{3}/_{4}(-0.1)]$
$=\$462z$

An election to use this method of estimating quarterly total asset bases must be made no later than the taxpayer's first taxable year ending after May 14, 1990. If a taxpayer makes this election and subsequently uses the actual adjusted tax bases of its total assets for any of the first three quarters of any taxable year, the taxpayer may not use the estimation method for any subsequent quarter in that year or any subsequent year.

§9.6 S Corporation Banks

In 1996, Code section 1361 was amended to allow banks to elect to be treated as S corporations and to allow an S corporation to elect to treat a wholly owned subsidiary as a QSub.[254] In effect, these amendments permit a bank holding company to elect S Corporation status and for it to elect to treat its bank subsidiary as a QSub. When a QSub election is made, the subsidiary is treated, for tax purposes, as no longer existing as a separate corporation and all of its assets, liabilities, items of income, deductions, and credits are treated as those of the parent S corporation.[255]

These amendments precipitated some uncertainty associated with whether the bank specific disallowance rule contained in Code section 265(b), and by

[254] Small Business Job Protection Act of 1996, Pub. L. No. 104-188, sec. 1315, 110 Stat. 1785; I.R.C. § 1361(b)(1), (2), and (3)(A).

[255] I.R.B. § 1361(b)(3).

cross reference Code section 291(e), applied to a Qsub bank after it has been in that status for three consecutive years.[256]

Code section 1363(b) provides that the income of an S corporation shall be computed in the same manner as in the case of an individual.[257] Because Code section 291 is applicable only to a corporation, the cross reference in Code section 265(b) to Code section 291 would appear to be inapplicable to a bank that is treated as an S corporation.[258] Code section 1363(b)(4) provides a limited exception to this general rule. It states that Code section 291 will apply as if the S corporation was a C corporation for any of the 3 immediately preceding taxable years. Thus, beginning in the fourth years after S corporation status is achieved, it appears that the bank would escape interest expense disallowance under Code section 291.

In 1997, the I.R.S. issued Notice 97-5 alerting taxpayers that the interaction between the QSub deemed liquidation rule and special banking rules may create unintended and inappropriate results. In that notice taxpayers were also informed that Treasury was working with Congress on an appropriate technical correction.[259] In the same year, Congress enacted a technical correction to Code section 1361(b)(3)(A) to address Treasury's concern.[260] The amendment added the introductory "Except" language to Code section 1361(b)(3)(A) emphasized below:

> In general.—Except as provided in regulations prescribed by the Secretary, for purposes of this title—
>
> (i) a corporation which is a qualified subchapter S subsidiary shall not be treated as a separate corporation, and
>
> (ii) all assets, liabilities, and items of income, deduction, and credit of a qualified subchapter S subsidiary shall be treated as assets, liabilities, and such items (as the case may be) of the S corporation. [Emphasis added.]

Thus, the technical correction to Code section 1361(b)(3)(A) granted the Secretary the authority to issue regulations providing exceptions to the QSub deemed liquidation rule. In January 2000, the final version of Regulation section 1.1361-4(a)(3) was promulgated. It provides:

> (3) Treatment of banks.—(i) In general.—If an S corporation is a bank, or if an S corporation makes a valid QSub election for a subsidiary that is a bank, any special rules applicable to banks under the Internal Revenue Code continue to apply separately to the bank parent or bank subsidiary as if the deemed liquidation of any QSub under paragraph (a)(2) of this section had not occurred (except as other published guidance may apply section 265(b) and section 291(a)(3) and (e)(1)(B) not only to the bank parent or bank subsidiary

[256] *See* "Regulations Overstep Authority: Application of Special Bank Rules to Banks," by R. W. Blasi and J. J. Ensminger, Vol. 9, No. 2, *Business Entities*, March/April 2007.

[257] *See* discussion of "Separate Treatment of Bank" in section dealing with "Q Sub and Corporate Structure" contained in Chapter 1, above. A bank may be treated as an S corporation either because it is an S corporation or because it is a Q Sub.

[258] Statutory provisions that prescribe special tax treatment for a "bank" appear to apply only to corporations: IRC 581. Moreover, the rule contained in IRC § 1363(b) must be read in conjuction with IRC § 1371, which provides coordination of Subchapter S with Subchapter C, "Corporate Distributions and Adjustments."

[259] 1997-1 C.B. 352.

[260] Taxpayer Relief Act of 1997, Pub. L. No. 105-34, sec. 1601, 111 Stat. 1086.

> but also to any QSub deemed to have liquidated under paragraph (a)(2) of this section). For any QSub that is a bank, however, all assets, liabilities, and items of income, deduction, and credit of the QSub, as determined in accordance with the special bank rules, are treated as assets, liabilities, and items of income, deduction, and credit of the S corporation. For purposes of this paragraph (a)(3)(i), the term bank has the same meaning as in section 581. (Emphasis added.]

On audit the IRS has taken the position that the Code section 291 bank interest expense disallowance rules continue to apply to banks even after the three year period expires.[261] Citing Regulation section 1.1361-4(a)(3)(i), the IRS has argued that Code section 291, as well as all other special bank tax rules, will continue to apply to the bank regardless how long it has been treated as an S corporation. These regulations may be regarded as legislative regulations by reason of an amendment to Code section 1361(b)(3) made by the Taxpayer Relief Act of 1997.[262]

The IRS position was expressed in Proposed regulation section 1.1363-1 that was issued in 2006 and then withdrawn in 2011.[263] It provided:

> (2) Treatment of banks. Section 1363(b) (concerning computation of an S corporation's taxable income) does not affect an S corporation's status as a bank within the meaning of section 581, and **it does not prevent the application to such an S corporation bank of any special rule applicable to banks under the Internal Revenue Code**, such as sections 582(c) and 291(a)(3) and (e)(1)(B). *See §1.1361–4(a)(3) regarding application under subchapter S of the special rules applicable to banks. Further, section 1363(b)(4) causes section 291 to apply to an S corporation if the S corporation (or any predecessor) was a C corporation for any of the three immediately preceding taxable years, but section 1363(b)(4) does not prevent section 291 from applying to an S corporation to which section 291 otherwise applies. [Emphasis added.]*[264]

The preamble to the proposed regulation seems to rely primarily on Regulation section 1.1361-4(a)(3) for its support. Even apart from the doubtful authority for a new regulation founded on merely an earlier promulgated regulation, if the IRS believes that the proposed regulation is dependent on that regulation for its support, the foundation for the proposed regulation appears to be weak. Code section 1361(b)(3) and the regulations thereunder are not addressed to the issue which is the focus of the proposed regulations. Code section 1361(b)(3) address how to determine the separate income of an S corporation and its qualified subchapter S corporation subsidiary after the deemed liquidation of the subsidiary takes place. Code section 1361(b)(3) and the regulations thereunder do not purport to resolve the issue of whether the income of the S corporation or its subsidiary will be determined under individual or corporate income tax rules.

The effective date of the proposed regulations is August 24, 2006, the date when the regulations were first proposed. However, the potential of audit adjustments in open years could increase the tax liability of S Banks in taxable

---

[261] See Office of Chief Counsel Memorandum No. AM 2006-005, Oct. 2, 2006, in which the IRS's litigating position is set forth.

[262] Pub. L. No. 105-34, §1601(c)(3).

[263] Announcement 2011-75, Nov. 28, 2011.

[264] REG-158677-05, 71 Fed. Reg. 50007 (Aug. 24, 2006).

years beginning as early as 2000. For some S Corporation banks, that was the first year in which the election to become an S Corporation became effective.

In *Vainisi v. Commissioner* the Tax Court agreed with the IRS's interpretation of the law; however, the Seventh Circuit reversed the Tax Court.[265] The Tax Court attached little or no significance to the statutory rule of Code section 1363(b) that requires the income of an S corporation to be computed in the same manner as in the case of an individual. It rejected the taxpayer's argument that Regulation section § 1.1361-4(a)(3) was an invalid exercise of regulatory authority.[266]

The Seventh Circuit concluded that the Treasury Department had ample time in which to decide whether, what it referred to as "the favored treatment of S and QSub banks," was appropriate. It stated: "The Internal Revenue Service thinks it a bad idea, the Tax Court thinks it a bad idea, but the institutions authorized to correct the favored treatment of these banks-Congress by statute, and the Treasury Department (we are assuming without deciding), as Congress's delegate, by regulation-have thus far left it intact. True, the Treasury has *proposed* to subject all subchapter S banks, no matter how long they have enjoyed that status, to section 291, with its 80 percent rule . . . . But the proposal has been in limbo for years, its validity questioned on the ground that it contradicts section 1363(b)(4)."[267]

An additional issue relating to the treatment of banks relates to whether Code section 265(b) is incorporated by the reference in Code section 1363(b)(4) to Code section 291. The language of Code section 1363(b)(3) refers only to Code section 291. However, it is only by reason of the cross reference in Code section 265(b) to Code section 291 that application of the latter is of any real concern.[268] Code section 265(b)(3)(A) provides that "[a]ny qualified tax-exempt obligation acquired after August 7, 1986, shall be treated for purposes of paragraph 2 and section 291(e)(1)(B) as if it were acquired on August 7, 1986." If the obligation is treated as acquired on that date, then it would be subject to the TEFRA 20 percent disallowance rule contained in Code section 291. Some may argue that it is not the same to say that Code section 291 will only apply during the first three years of the entities treatment as an S corporation as it is to say that Code section 265(b)(3)'s special rule for QTEO's will only apply during the first three years of the entities treatment as an S corporation.

Of course, regardless of the application of the Code section 1363(b) three year rule, the 100 percent disallowance of Code section 265(b) will apply to any bank that is treated as an S corporation.

§ 9.7 Registration-Required Obligations

As a general rule, interest expense (including original issue discount) on "registration-required obligations" is not deductible unless the obligation is in

[265] 130 T.C. No. 1 (Jan. 2009). *rev'd* 599 F.3d 567 (7th Cir. 2010).

[266] By making this argument, the taxpayer may have inadvertently diminished focus on the significance of I.R.C. § 1363(b).

[267] 599 F.3d 567, 572. Citations omitted.

[268] On its own, IRC § 291 is applicable to banks, but the application is quite limited these days. It applies only to tax-exempt obligations acquired after December 31, 1982 and before August 8, 1986.

registered form.[269] This disallowance of interest expense applies to interest paid on obligations issued after December 31, 1982; however, with respect to tax-exempt obligations, the effective date of this provision is July 1, 1983.[270]

Issuers may not reduce earnings and profit for disallowed interest expense, and they incur liability for an excise tax equal to one percent of the principal amount for each year from the date of issue to the maturity date.[271] Certificates of interest in a mortgage pool should be treated as registration-required obligations, although the mortgage obligations held in the pool do not fit the definition.[272]

Exempt from the definition of registration-required obligations are, among others, certain obligations issued to foreign persons.[273] The applicability of this exemption is made on an obligation-by-obligation basis, and it will apply only if both of the following conditions are satisfied:

1. The arrangements are reasonably designed to ensure that the obligation will be sold (or resold in connection with the original issue) only to a person who is not a U.S. person. If an obligation is offered for sale outside the United States, and it need not be registered under the Securities Act of 1933 (Act) because it is intended for distribution to persons who are not U.S. persons, then it will not be a "registered required obligation."[274]
2. The obligation is not in registered form and (a) interest is payable only outside the United States and it possessions, and (b) there appears on the face of the obligation a statement that any U.S. person who holds the obligation will be subject to "limitations under the U.S. income tax laws."[275] Regulations provide that the quoted phrase specifically encompasses the limitations contained in Code section 165(j). Thus, no deduction will be allowed for a loss on an unregistered "registration-require obligation," and any gain on sale or disposition of such obligation shall be characterized as ordinary income.[276]

---

[269] I.R.C. § 163(f) (2000). For special rules pertaining to obligations issued to foreign persons, see Reg. § 1.163-5(c). *See also* I.R.C. § 149 (2000), which deals with registration requirements on tax-exempt bonds.

[270] Transition rules and effective dates are found in Pub. L. No. 97-248, § 310(b)(2), 965 Stat. 324, 596 (1982). *See also* I.R.C. § 103(j) (2000) for a special rule.

[271] I.R.C. §§ 312(m), 4701 (2000). *See also* I.R.C. § 165(j) for denial of deduction for losses on registration-required obligations.

[272] T.D. 8046, 1985-2 C.B. 61; Temp. Reg. 1.163-5T(d), published in the *Federal Register* on September 2, 1983. Temp. Reg. § 1.163-5T was superseded by temporary regulations published in the *Federal Register* on August 22, 1984, which regulations were later amended and adopted as final on December 16, 1986 (Reg. § 1.163-5). The final regulations do not contain any explicit rule relating to pass-through certificates.

Prior to the amendments, Reg. § 1.163-5T(d) provided, "(d) *Pass-through certificates*—(1) A pass-through or participation certificate evidencing an interest in a pool of mortgage loans which under Subpart E of Subchapter J of the Code is treated as a trust of which the grantor is the owner . . . is considered to be a 'registration-required obligation' under section 163(f)(2)(A) and this section if the pass-through certificate is described in section 163(f)(2)(A) and this section, without regard to whether any obligation held by the fund or trust to which the pass-through certificate relates is described in section 163(f)(2)(A) and this section."

[273] I.R.C. § 163(f)(2)(B) (2000). A foreign person is defined in I.R.C. §§ 7701(a)(1),(5) and (30) as a natural person (an individual) who is not a citizen or resident of the United States and a trust, estate partnership, or corporation that is not created or organized in the United States or under the law of the United States or of any state.

[274] If the obligation is sold to U.S. persons (within or without the United States) on the basis of the exemption of § 4(2) of the Securities Act of 1933, it shall not be treated as intended for foreign persons. Reg. § 1.163-5.

[275] I.R.C. § 163(j) (2000). For a discussion of what constitutes interest payable outside the U.S., *see* Reg. § 1.163-5.

[276] I.R.C. § 165(j) (2000); Reg. § 1.165-12.

Chapter 10
Bad-Debt Deductions

Contents

§10.1 Tax Planning Suggestions
Basic Rules
§10.2 Deduction for Worthless Debt
§10.2.1 Available Methods
§10.2.2 Amount of Deduction
§10.2.3 What Constitutes a "Bad Debt"?
§10.3 Direct Charge-Off Method
§10.3.1 Establishing Worthlessness
§10.3.2 The Meaning of "Charge-Off"
§10.4 Presumptions of Worthlessness
§10.4.1 Industry Directive
§10.4.2 Bank Specific Rules
§10.4.3 Historical Presumption
§10.4.4 The Conformity Election
§10.4.5 Rebutting Conclusive Presumption
§10.5 Involuntary Charge-Off
§10.6 Recoveries
Reserve Methods
§10.7 Allowable Reserve Methods
§10.7.1 Electing a Reserve Method
§10.7.2 Legislative History of Code Section 585
§10.7.3 Pre-1987 Rules
§10.7.4 Post-1986 Rules—Overview
§10.7.5 Commissioner's Discretion Revoked
§10.7.6 Eligible Taxpayers
§10.7.7 Minimum Reserve Addition
§10.7.8 Alternative Formula Within Code Section 593
§10.7.9 Recoveries
§10.7.10 Establishing and Maintaining Reserves
§10.7.11 Acceptable Bookkeeping for Reserves
§10.8 The Experience Method
§10.8.1 Moving-Average Formula
§10.8.2 Reserve Restoration—General Rule
§10.8.3 Reserve Restoration—Decline in Loan Balance
§10.8.4 Shorter Experience Period
§10.8.5 "Loans" Defined
§10.8.6 Extraordinary Loan Losses
§10.9 Percentage of Taxable Income Method
§10.9.1 Loans That Are Qualifying
§10.9.2 Loans That Are Nonqualifying
§10.9.3 Specially Computed Taxable Income

§10.9.4 Applicable Percentages
§10.9.5 Limitations on Reserve Additions
§10.9.6 Limitations on Reserve Additions (Pre-1987 Law)
§10.10 Commercial Bank Bad-Debt Reserve Recapture
§10.10.1 "Large Bank" Defined
§10.10.2 Code Section 481(a) Adjustments
§10.10.3 Advantages/Disadvantages of Recapture Methods
§10.10.4 Financially Troubled Banks
§10.11 Thrift Bad-Debt Reserve Recapture
§10.11.1 Applicable Excess Reserves—Large Bank
§10.11.2 Applicable Excess Reserves—Small Bank
§10.11.3 Acquisitions and Dispositions
§10.11.4 Residential Loan Requirement
§10.12 Tax Preference Issues
§10.12.1 Alternative Minimum Tax
§10.12.2 Corporate Preference Item

§10.1 Tax Planning Suggestions

Although the tax treatment of bad debts has historically been the most fruitful method to engage in tax planning by banks, the statutory amendments accompanied by changes in regulations now significantly limit taxpayer flexibility. For reserve method banks, those banks that are not "large banks" or S Banks, the available methods for determining a reasonable reserve deduction have been constrained by statutory amendments.[1] Now, only one approach, the "experience method," may be used and, Treasury regulations attempt to require a minimum reserve addition, even though case law, statute, and the IRS's historical position afford taxpayers considerably more flexibility. For banks on the specific charge-off method, the IRS's attempt to encourage taxpayers to conform tax deductions to book charge-off and to link the treatment of nonperforming loans and bad debts is designed to further limit tax planning options.

The Treasury Department has promulgated regulations, revenue rulings, and industry directives that liberalize rules for determining when a debt will be accepted as "worthless" or as conclusively presumed "worthlessness." These rules tend to conform tax deductions to book or regulatory charge-offs. There are obvious advantages, and some not so obvious disadvantages, to making the

[1] For financial accounting purposes, nearly all banks are on the reserve method for determining loan loss deductions. On June 16, 2016, the Financial Accounting Standards Board issued Accounting Standards Update 2016-13 that will significantly alter the determination of the accounting allowance. When it is fully implemented, it will probably require earlier recording of credit losses on loans and other financial instruments held by financial institutions. It requires an organization to measure all expected credit losses for financial assets based on historical experience, current conditions, and reasonable, and supportable forecasts. Thus, forward-looking information will be used to determine credit loss estimates. The effective date of the new rule will be staggered. Large banks must apply the rule beginning January 1, 2019. Small banks have an additional two years to implement the rule. The determination of the Schedule M adjustment for loan losses will be significantly altered by the Update.

required elections to conform tax deductions for bad debts to book charge-offs. However, the conformity elections continue to contain several areas of uncertainty.

Critical to the computation of a reasonable reserve addition is an appreciation of what may be included in the loan base and what is a charge-off. Guidance is found in IRS rulings, detailed regulations and judicial opinions. Although Congress intended the book balance of loans to be the starting point for the tax loan base, numerous modifications are required to arrive at the computation of the tax reserve addition. In many, but not all situations, it is advantageous for a taxpayer to ensure that the loan base and net charge-off are maximized.

The Treasury Department has promulgated regulations providing guidance for determining when an institution becomes a large bank and whether it retains a large bank taint after certain corporate distributions or reorganizations. Further, a bank that becomes a "large bank" may elect to select among three methods to take into account its historical reserve balance. Depending on the method selected, a bank's income can be accelerated or deferred.

Historically, the loan loss reserve methods available to thrifts were considerably more favorable than those available to commercial banks. However, recently enacted legislation terminated the historical distinction between commercial bank and thrift bad debt deduction rules. Nevertheless, thrifts are afforded bad debt reserve recapture rules that are more favorable than those available to commercial banks. A thrift is permitted to avoid recapture of a portion of its reserve for so long as a thrift remains a "bank," as that term is defined in Code section 581.

This chapter will discuss all aspects of the computation of a bank's loan loss deduction under the direct charge-off method and the reserve method. It will point out the opportunities for tax planning that inhere in the reserve method and even in the direct charge-off method. The elections available to avoid challenges to the deductibility of book charges-offs and for alternative recapture methods will be discussed, with a focus on the advantages and disadvantages associated with them. All of the intricacies of the reserve method will be explored, and the areas of IRS challenge will be revealed. Problems raised by the IRS position on nonaccrual loans and by the new mark-to-market rules will be set forth.

Basic Rules

§ 10.2 Deduction for Worthless Debt

§ 10.2.1 Available Methods

In general, partially or wholly worthless bona fide debts are deductible by commercial banks under either the specific charge-off method provided for in Code section 166 or the reserve method provided for in Code section 585. For taxable years beginning January 1, 2010 through 2014, a bank or a bank subsidiary may elect to apply a Directive published in 2014 that permits book tax conformity on worthlessness.[2] For taxable years beginning on or after January 1, 1987, those commercial banks that meet the definition of a "large bank" are prohibited from using the reserve method.[3] For taxable years beginning before January 1, 1996, thrifts were permitted to elect the Code section 166 specific charge-off method or the Code section 593 reserve method, regardless of the size of the institutions. The Small Business Job Protection Act of 1996 repealed Code section 593 effective for taxable years beginning after 1995.[4] Thus, at present, thrifts and commercial banks are subject to the same loan loss deduction rules.

§ 10.2.2 Amount of Deduction

The amount of any deduction under the specific charge-off method is limited to the taxpayer's tax bases in the bad debt,[5] and, with respect to debts recoverable only in part, the deduction is also limited by the amount charged-off.[6] A partially or wholly worthless debt may be deducted prior to when it is due.[7] "Tax bases" equals the adjusted tax bases determined under Code section 1011, which is used to determine gain or loss from the sale or other disposition of property.[8] Thus, it will be equal to the amount of funds advanced, plus capitalized interest (that is, interest that has been included in taxable income but not received and added to the debt), less any amounts repaid and any amounts charged-off.[9] If a loan is subject to the mark-to-market rules of Code section 475, any mark down does not reduce tax basis, but it has the effect of a charge-off, the calculation of future marks.[10]

The IRS has taken the position that a lending institution's inclusion of accrued interest receivable in the tax basis of loans for purposes of its bad-debt computation, when it had not previously included such interest in the base used to compute the annual addition to its reserve, constituted an unauthorized change in method of accounting.[11] However, the facts of the ruling indicate that this conclusion was reached because some portion of the taxpayer's bad-debt deduction in years prior to the change may have been based on the accrued interest receivable. This would cause a shifting of deductions between years, which would involve the proper time for taking a deduction. A change in a material item occurs when such a shifting occurs. If the taxpayer were successful in establishing that no deduction was taken for accrued interest receivable prior to its inclusion in the loan base, an impermissible accounting method change would not have been made.

---

[2] LB&I Directive "Related to § 166 Deductions for Eligible Debt and Eligible Securities," LB&I-04-1014-008, Oct. 24, 2014. *See* Directive at Appendix A.23.

[3] I.R.C. § 585(c) (2000). An exception is provided for those banks that elect to be subject to the rules prescribed in subchapter S. IRC. § 1361(B)(2).

[4] P. L. 104-188, § 1616, 110 Stat. 1755, 1854 (1996).

[5] Reg. § 1.166-1(d); TAM 8232010, April 26, 1982.

[6] I.R.C. § 166(a)(2) (2000).

[7] Reg. § 1.166-1(c).

[8] Reg. § 1.166-1(d). I.R.C. §§ 166(b), 1001(a) (2000). Note that this tax bases rule applies to deductions taken under the specific charge-off method and not to deductions taken under the reserve method. Reg. § 1.166-1(d).

[9] I.R.C. § 1011 (2000); Reg. § 1.166-1(d)(1); TAM 8232010, April 26, 1982.

[10] I.R.C. § 475(a) (2000).

[11] TAM 8741006, May 21, 1987. Example (3) of Reg. § 1.466-1(e)(2)(iii) provides that a change in underlying facts is not a change in a method of accounting.

§ 10.2.3 What Constitutes a "Bad Debt"?

A "bad debt" must first be a "bona fide debt," defined as one "which arises from a debtor creditor relationship based on a valid and enforceable obligation to pay a fixed or determinable sum of money."[12] If there is an understanding that payment on a debt need not be made, no bad-debt deduction will be allowed.[13] Moreover, if there is no reasonable basis for believing that a debt will be repaid at the time it is created, a subsequent bad-debt deduction will not be allowed on the theory that the debt was worthless when acquired.[14] Banks, unlike other taxpayers, are not subject to the provisions that deny a bad-debt deduction for losses that arise from loans to political parties.[15] Interest that has been earned but not received is a debt that is usually accounted for separately from the underlying loan.

(a) *Renegotiated Debt*

In a transaction that results in an exchange between the debtor and creditor, the distinction between a loss deduction and a bad-debt deduction depends upon whether the debtor and the creditor agree to the modification of the debt or whether the creditor determines unilaterally that the debt is partially worthless.[16] If a bank independently determines that a loan is partially worthless, and if it charges-off the worthless portion before the exchange of the debt pursuant to an agreement to restructure, the deduction would be properly taken as bad-debt under Code section 166. Otherwise, a loss on the sale or exchange of the debt instrument is allowed under Code section 165.

(b) *Guarantor Payments*

A taxpayer who is a guarantor, endorser, or indemnitor of (or other secondary obligor upon) a debt obligation is generally entitled to a bad debt deduction if the issuer defaults and the taxpayer pays interest or principal in discharge of part or all of the taxpayer's obligation as a guarantor, endorser, or indemnitor of the obligation.[17] However, a deduction is not allowed where the agreement between the taxpayer and the primary obligor provides for a right of subrogation, reimbursement or other similar right against the issuer until the taxable year in which the right against the issuer becomes worthless.[18] Thus, the deduction is allowed only if and when the new debt obligation to the taxpayer-guarantor, which is the right of reimbursement, becomes worthless.[19] A right of subrogation or reimbursement may be present regardless of whether these rights are ex-

---

[12] Reg. § 1.166-1(c).

[13] *Farmers & Merchants National Bank of Nocona, Tex. v. Commissioner*, 10 B.T.A. 709, Dec. 3549 (1928). Advances by one member of a controlled group to another member of the group could be treated as equity contributions and not as debt. All of the indicia of the arrangement must be examined in light of the authorities that are employed to evaluate whether an instrument is debt or equity. I.R.C. §§ 385, 956, Reg. § 1.956-2T(d)(2); TAXES - The Tax Magazine, "Tax Issues of Intragroup Open Accounts and Cash Management," Dec. 1, 2012.

[14] *Eckert v. Burnet*, 2 U.S.T.C. ¶714, 283 U.S. 140 (1931); *Bank of Wyoming v. Commissioner*, 22 B.T.A. 1132, Dec. 6860 (1931).

[15] I.R.C. § 271(a) (2000).

[16] TAM 9253003, January 1, 1993.

[17] Reg. § 1.166-9(a).

[18] Reg. § 1.166-9(e).

[19] *Putnam v. Commissioner*, 352 U.S. 82, 85 (1956); *Intergraph Corporation v. Commissioner*, 106 T.C. 312 (1996).

pressly stated in the guaranty agreement.[20] Furthermore, no treatment as a worthless debt is allowed with respect to a payment made by the taxpayer if, on the basis of the facts and circumstances at the time the obligation was entered into, the payment constituted a contribution to capital by a shareholder.[21]

A guarantor's bad debt deduction is conditioned on an irrevocable economic outlay by the taxpayer. Both a payment in discharge of the guarantor's liability and the worthlessness of any right of subrogation are required for a bad debt deduction. Payment is a precondition to a guarantor bad debt deduction because it is the event that creates the debtor-creditor relationship between the guarantor and the debtor and it is the worthlessness of that debt that provides the basis for the guarantor's bad debt deduction. Upon the payment by the guarantor of the debt, the debtor's obligation to the creditor becomes an obligation to the guarantor, not a new debt, but, by subrogation, the result of the shift of the original debt from the creditor to the guarantor who steps into the creditor's shoes. Payment does not include the furnishing of a note or other indebtedness of the taxpayer.[22]

(c) *Theft and Other Losses*

Not all instruments labeled by a creditor bank as "loans" will be treated as "bona fide debts." If a bank incurs a loss on an instrument that is not "debt," the loss may be deductible under Code section 165 as a theft loss. A "theft" loss includes, but is not limited to, larceny, embezzlement, and robbery.[23] Thus, arrangements labeled "loans" made upon order of a bank president to a company in which he had a financial interest and which was insolvent when the "loan" was made gave rise to "loss" deductions under Code section 165.[24] Similarly, the IRS has ruled that a nonrecoverable overdraft resulting from a fraudulent check-kiting scheme was properly deductible as a Code section 165 theft loss.[25] However, where no evidence of fraud was found, bank loans made to, and overdrafts by, officers of a bank evidenced by promissory notes, even though inadequately secured, were treated as bad debts.[26]

(d) *Securities Losses*

As a general rule, a bank is allowed a deduction for a bad debt evidenced by a security, including a debt security defined in Code Section 165(g)(2)(C), that has become partially or wholly worthless.[27] Code section 582(a) explicitly authorizes banks to deduct such losses on debts as "bad debts" under Code section 166 (a) and (b).[28] Thus, no sale or exchange need occur with respect to a security loss for a bad-debt deduction to be allowed. For purposes of Code section 582, a

---

[20] *Id.*

[21] Reg. § 1.166-9(c).

[22] *See* PLR 2014 50011 (September 10, 2014) in which the IRS held that a payment into a segregated bank account to be held for the benefit of certain creditors satisfied the requirements of Reg. § 1.166-9.

[23] Reg. § 1.165-8(d).

[24] *Eckert v. Burnet*, *supra* note 14; *Bank of Wyoming v. Commissioner*, 22 B.T.A. 1132, Dec. 6860 (1931). *See also* Rev. Rul. 71-381, 1971-2 C.B. 126.

[25] Rev. Rul. 77-215, 1977-1 C.B. 51; I.R.C. § 165(h) (2000).

[26] *Austin v. Helvering*, 35-1 U.S.T.C. ¶9238, 77 F.2d 373 (D.C. Cir. 1935); *Porter v. United States*, 27 F.2d 882 (9th Cir. 1928).

[27] I.R.C. § 166(e) (2000). Rev. Rul. 66-321, 1966-2 C.B. 59.

[28] I.R.C. § 582(a) (2000); Reg. §§ 1.166-1(g)(2) and 1.582-1(a).

security is defined as a "bond, debenture, note, or certificate, or other evidence of indebtedness, issued by a corporation or by a government or political subdivision thereof, with interest coupons or in registered form."[29] Notwithstanding this special rule, bad debts that are not "loans" may be precluded from inclusion in the computation of a bank's addition to its loan loss reserve.[30]

Subject to the special rule applicable to bank subsidiaries discussed below, for taxpayers that do not meet the Code section 581 definition of a "bank," such as a mortgage company or a leasing company, debt instruments that meet the Code section 165 definition of a "security" are deductible under Code section 165. As such, there does not appear to be any authority for taking a partial worthless deduction while the security is held. To recognize a loss, the taxpayer must engage in an event that qualifies as a sale or exchange. Acceleration of built-in losses may be available if the taxpayer marks the security to market under the provisions contained in Code section 475. In the latter section, the definition of a security is much broader. Taxpayers that do not meet the definition of a "bank" also are confronted with the possibility that any recognized loss is characterized as capital. Because Code section 582 does not treat losses incurred by nonbanks as ordinary, such taxpayers must refer to the general characterization rules contained in Code section 1221 to characterize the bad debt loss. This appears to be the case even if the security is marked-to-market. If the debt instrument does not meet the Code section 165 definition of a security, then the holder may be able to accelerate its deduction and convert what may have been a capital loss into an ordinary loss deduction by claiming a bad debt deduction for a partially worthless debt under Code section 166(a)(2).

There is a special rule for determining worthlessness of certain debt securities, held by most bank subsidiaries. This rule permits the bank subsidiary to treat as "worthless" for bad debt purposes any debt security, other than securities defined in Code section 165(g)(2)(C), if the security was charged-off on the books of the entity. For the security to be treated as partially or wholly worthless, an accounting entry or set of accounting entries for the taxable year must reduce the security's carrying value and result in a realized loss or a charge to the statement of operations that is recorded on the subsidiary's "applicable financial statement" for that year.[31]

If a security is sold to a third party, any gain or loss is not taken into account as a bad debt or as a recovery. Gain or loss is income or loss arising from the sale of an asset, which is characterized as ordinary if the security is sold by a bank.[32] This treatment also would apply when a debt is significantly modified under the

[29] I.R.C. §§165(g)(2)(C), 166(e) (2000); Reg. §1.166-1(g)(2). Note that for noncorporate taxpayers, a bad-debt deduction is allowed for a worthless "business" bad debt not evidenced by a "security." A "business" bad debt is one created or acquired in connection with a trade or business of the taxpayer or a debt incurred in the taxpayer's trade or business, I.R.C. §166(d) (2000). *See* discussion of "wash sale" rule at Ch. 4.

[30] The IRS has ruled that a separate reserve may not be established for securities losses. PLR 7921016, February 12, 1979.

[31] *See* LB&I Directive Related to § 166 Deductions for Eligible Debt and Eligible Securities, LB&I-04-1014-008, Oct. 24, 2014. Directive at Appendix A.23.

[32] I.R.C. §582(c) (2000).

so called *Cottage Savings* regulations.[33] A mark-down under the Code section 475 mark-to-market rules may consist of a bad debt loss and also a loss from the disposition of the security.[34]

The Seventh Circuit Court of Appeals has decided that a write-down of bonds held in a bank's dealer inventory, valued at the lower of cost or market, was not permitted to be treated as a bad debt and recoveries were direct credits to income and not credits to a bank's bad-debt reserve.[35] However, in reaching its conclusion the court appeared to be influenced by the fact that approximately 40 percent of the bonds that gave rise to the deduction and recovery were U.S. Treasury Bonds. It stated, "Any allegation that they were worthless or even partially so is a non sequitur."[36] Similarly, a portion or all of write-downs under the Code section 475 mark-to-market rules also may not qualify as bad debts because the decline in value may be attributable to interest rate movement, not to credit worthiness of the issuer. However, if the write-down is attributable to partial or complete worthlessness, a bad-debt deduction is appropriate.[37] Since a taxpayer may have only one method of accounting for loan losses, deducting loan losses under Code section 475 is improper.

*(e) **Other-Than-Temporary Impairments***

In 2009 the Financial Accounting Standards Board issued a Staff Position on Statements 115 and 124 containing guidance for holders of investments in debt or equity securities. The guidance is to be employed to determine whether a holder of such securities should recognize an impairment loss. FAS 115-2 and 124-2 amend previous pronouncements dealing with impairment losses on debt securities. In general, FAS 115-2 and 124-2 provide for a three step analysis for whether an investment is impaired, whether the impairment is other than temporary, and how to measure the amount of an impairment loss.

Although Code section 446 provides that "[t]axable income shall be computed under the method of accounting on the basis of which the taxpayer regularly computes his income in keeping his books," it is well settled that neither regulatory accounting principles nor generally accepted accounting principles determine the permissible or required method of accounting for items for tax purposes.[38]

If the tax requirements for worthlessness are not satisfied, then an impairment loss that is recorded on the accounting books and records of an entity is not deductible for tax purposes. Among the tax requirements before a partially worthless debt may be deductible is the necessity that the debt be charged-off on the books of the taxpayer.[39] Special rules (discussed below) contained in a Directive permit banks, and in certain cases bank subsidiaries, to treat debts as worthless if they are charged-off on the entities books and if certain other

[33] Reg. § 1.166-3; Reg. § 1.1001-3.

[34] Prop. Reg. § 1.475(a)-1(f).

[35] *Union Trust Co. of Indianapolis v. United States*, 49-1 U.S.T.C. ¶ 9188, 173 F.2d 54 (7th Cir. 1949), *cert. denied*, 337 U.S. 940 (1949).

[36] *Id.* at 56.

[37] Prop. Reg. § 1.475(a)-1(f).

[38] *Thor Power Tool Company v. Commissioner*, 79-1 U.S.T.C. ¶ 9139, 439 U.S. 522 (1979).

[39] Reg. § 1.166-3(a)(2).

conditions are satisfied.[40] These rules may not be satisfied if a loan or other debt instrument is classified on the entities accounting books as "impaired." Moreover, banks that elect the conclusive presumptions of worthlessness contained in Regulation section 1.166-2(d)(3) are subject to special requirements that may not be satisfied by conforming to GAAP guidelines for impairment losses.[41]

(f) Interrelationship Between Code Sections 166, 582, and 585

The Tax Reform Act of 1986 repealed the provision contained in Code section 166(c) allowing a deduction for a reasonable addition to a reserve for bad debts. Prior to the effective date of the Tax Reform Act repeal of Code section 166(c), a reference in Code section 582(a) to Code section 166(c) extended the securities loss rule to banks computing bad-debt deductions under the reserve method. It appeared that securities losses were accounted for under the reserve method, even though "securities" were not loans for purposes of the Code section 585 reserve computation.

This would yield a strange result regardless of whether the bank previously established a reserve balance for securities. However, the allowance of a deduction for bad debts for reserve method banks was shifted by the Tax Reform Act of 1986 to Code section 585. Although Code section 582(a) does not explicitly do so, it should be read as continuing to apply the securities loss rule to banks deducting bad debts under Code section 585, although such losses may not be taken into account in the computation of the Code section 585 reserve addition.

(g) Interrelationship Between Code Sections 165 and 166

Although the provisions of Code sections 165 and 166 may overlap, they are mutually exclusive. When an item appears to be deductible under both sections, the latter will control.[42] Thus, it has been held that a bad-debt deduction under Code section 166 with respect to a loan is not converted into a Code section 165 loss when the debtor's notes are taken in payment of the loan.[43] Similarly, where a mortgagee (1) foreclosed on a mortgage, (2) bid for the property at an amount greater than its value but less than the debt, and (3) secured a deficiency judgment for the balance, the amount of the judgment, when ascertained to be worthless and charged-off, was held to be a bad debt and not a Code section 165 loss.[44]

Whether an item is properly deductible under Code section 165 or under Code section 166 could affect the computation of a bank's loan loss deduction under the reserve method. If an item is a charge to a banks reserve for bad debts in the year of worthlessness, it will have the effect of possibly increasing the banks allowable reserve balance in future years. This is the case for both commercial banks and thrifts; however, for thrifts that had used the percentage of taxable income method for computing bad-debt deductions, no benefit would have been realized.

---

[40] *See* Directive at Appendix A.23.

[41] Reg. § 1.166-2(d).

[42] *Spring City Foundry Co. v. Commissioner*, 4 U.S.T.C. ¶ 1276, 292 U.S. 182 (1934).

[43] *D.P. Harris Hardware & Mfg. Co. v. Commissioner*, 24 B.T.A. 752, Dec. 7269 (1931), *aff'd per curiam*, 71 F.2d 1004 (2d Cir. 1934).

[44] *Doris Havemeyer v. Commissioner*, 45 B.T.A. 329, Dec. 12,112 (1941).

Deducting an economic loss under Code section 166 instead of under Code section 165 also had an effect on net operating loss deductions. For those banks using the specific charge-off method for determining their bad-debt deduction, a special 10-year carryback (and 5-year carryforward) period had been allowed. This rule permitted that portion of a net operating loss deduction attributable to bad-debt deductions, taken under the Code section 166(a) specific charge-off method, to be carried back 10 years and carried forward 5 years. This special carryback/carryover rule was available only for taxable years beginning before January 1, 1994. For taxable years prior to its repeal, it was unavailable to thrifts using the Code section 593 reserve method. These institutions are now subject to a 3-year carryback period and a 20-year carryover period.[45]

(h) Nonbank Bad Debts

Losses on debt securities, as well as other (equity) worthless securities, are deductible by nonbank members of a bank holding company group under Code section 165, and for partially worthless securities, it appears that the deduction is allowed only when a realization event occurs.[46] The Code section 582(c) characterization rule for debt securities also does not apply to nonbank members of a bank holding company group.

(i) Loan v. Joint Venture

In determining whether the intention to repay a loan exists, traditional loan documents such as promissory notes and security agreements should first be examined. If no promissory note exists, no collateral is pledged, and no loan repayment terms or interest obligation exists, amounts withdrawn from a corporation may be reclassified as constructive dividends or as compensation for services or for the use of property.

An agreement to fund a project may be classified as a joint venture and not a loan, regardless of whether the advance of funds is evidenced by a promissory note and whether an obligation to pay exists outside the profits from the project itself.[47] Factors that are taken into account when analyzing whether a loan exists include whether principle and interest are to be paid from the project's profits or from another source. A court is free to re-characterize an agreement describing an advance as a loan to find something other than a debtor and creditor relationship exists. "The contract must be judged by its true character rather than by the form" the parties chose to give it.[48]

Thus, an advance of funds to a limited partnership may be recast as an equity interest and not a debt depending upon whether the partners have a

---

[45] I.R.C. § 172(b)(1)(D) (2000). Other special carryback periods have been allowed to thrifts and to all commercial banks in prior years. *See* discussion in Ch. 8.

[46] Reg. §§ 1.166-1(g)(1), 1.165-5. Under I.R.C. § 165, the term "securities" generally encompasses both debt and equity instruments.

[47] *Hartman v. Commissioner*, 17 T.C.M. 1020 (1958), T.C. Memo. 1958-206.

[48] *Id.* at 1023.

personal liability to repay the loan, whether the loan was non-recourse, and whether there existed enough security for the loan.[49] If these factors are coupled with the right of the "lender" to convert the "loan" into a percentage of interest in the profits of the partnership, the funds would probably be deemed to be a capital contribution.

A similar reclassification may arise where the taxpayer had an unrestricted privilege of withdrawal, no loan documentation existed, there were no bona fide loan repayments, no maturity date was set for repayment, and no provision existed for the event of default that would require repayment. In this situation, withdrawals from a closely held corporation were held to be constructive dividends, not loans.[50]

§ 10.3 Direct Charge-Off Method

Under the Code section 166 direct charge-off method, bad-debt deductions are allowed:

1. For debts that become wholly worthless during the taxable year;[51] and
2. When the Secretary is satisfied that a debt is recoverable only in part and in an amount not in excess of the part charged-off within the taxable year.[52]

Example: Bank A, a calendar year taxpayer, made a $5,000 loan to Y Corporation on July 1, 19X6. The loan was to be repaid in full, with interest at an annual rate of 10 percent, on June 30, 19X7. An unpredictable shift in consumer demand caused Y Corporation to declare bankruptcy on December 12, 19X6. Bank A determined in 19X6 that it would recover only $2,000 of the loan and, therefore, charged-off $3,000 in the tax year ended December 31, 19X6. In early 19X7, and before it filed its 19X6 tax return, Bank A determined that it would not recover any of the loan proceeds. It then charged-off the remaining loan balance, $2,000, plus accrued and taxed interest. Under the direct charge-off method, Bank A is limited to a deduction of $3,000 for the tax year ended December 31, 19X6. The balance of its

[49] Rev. Rul. 72-350, 1972-2 C.B. 394.

[50] *Crowley v. Commissioner*, 962 F.2d 1077 (1st Cir. 1992).

[51] I.R.C. § 166(a) (2000); Reg. § 1.166-3.

[52] The deduction of partially worthless debts was first allowed by The Revenue Act of 1921, ch. 136 § 214(a)(7), 42 Stat. 227, 240 (1921). I.R.C. § 166(a)(2) (2000) appears to provide that the IRS has authority to allow or disallow a deduction even if the debt is partially worthless and has been charged-off in the taxable year. It would be an abuse of discretion if the IRS applied this provision unreasonably. Reg. § 1.166-3(a)(2). This regulation was promulgated on July 31, 1959. It does not vary in any substantial respect from Reg. § 118, Section 39.23(k)-1 promulgated under Section (k) of the Internal Revenue Code of 1939. Curiously, contained in both the 1986 House and Senate proposals to amend I.R.C. § 166 was a provision that would have denied a deduction for wholly worthless debts until it was charged-off on the taxpayer's books, as is the case for partially worthless debts. *See* H.R. Rep. No. 99-426, at 640 (1985) (the House Ways and Means Committee Report). However, the Conference agreement did *not* include a provision limiting the deduction of wholly worthless business debts to the amount written off on the taxpayer's books. Conference Committee Report, H.R. Rep. No. 99-841, pt. 2 at 315. *See* discussion following of involuntary charge-offs for exception to rule that deduction is limited to amount charged-off within the taxable year. An exception is provided for loans transferred to an Allocated Transfer Risk Reserve. Rev. Rul. 92-14, 1992-1 C.B. 94.

bad debt, $2,000 plus taxed interest, would be deductible in the taxable year ended December 31, 19X7.[53]

A taxpayer that is using the specific charge-off method is not precluded from claiming a tax deduction attributable to the partial worthlessness of a loan merely because that taxpayer had not taken similar deductions previously.[54] Similarly, the IRS will not foreclose a reserve method taxpayer from taking a charge-off to its reserve for an otherwise allowable loan loss based on partial worthlessness merely because it has not established such a practice in the past. The crucial determination in both situations is whether the taxpayer has established a currently recognizable loss based on partial worthlessness.

A loss that results from the sale of a debt instrument may not be deducted as a charge-off. However, if a taxpayer is merely considering whether to sell a debt instrument, it should be entitled to a deduction for partial worthless if it charges-off the debt before entering into a sale. If the charge-off was made after the sale was entered into, the loss deduction is not converted into a charge-off.[55] Furthermore, a loss that results from the partial extinguishment or retirement of a debt instrument may not be deductible under Code section 166.[56] Code section 1271 provides that: "[a]mounts received by the holder on retirement of any debt instrument shall be considered as amounts received in exchange therefor."[57] If the debt instrument is one to which Code section 1271 applies, the rules that are applicable to sales or exchange of property that are contained in Code sections 1001 (measuring gain or loss) and 165 (allowing a deduction for losses on sales and exchanges) will apply.

§ 10.3.1 Establishing Worthlessness

Worthlessness is required to be established before a bad debt deduction may be taken.[58] The mere act of charging-off a debt does not establish worthlessness.[59] There are two conclusive presumptions of worthlessness contained in Treasury regulations that relieve a bank from the burden of proving that a debt has become partially or wholly worthless.[60] In addition, the IRS has issued a Directive instructing IRS examiners of banks and bank subsidiaries using the specific charge-off method not to challenge a bank or bank subsidiary's bad debt deductions if the entity elects to conform its tax deductions to its book charge-offs and to file a "Certification Statement" to that effect.[61] Otherwise, establishing worthlessness in whole or in part is a question of fact, and the determination will turn

---

[53] A possibility exists that the full loss may be deductible in 19X7. Reg. § 1.166-2(d)(2).

[54] FSA 200129003, July 20, 2001.

[55] *Mitchell v. Commissioner*, 187 F.2d 706 (2d Cir. 1951).

[56] *McCain v. Commissioner*, 311 U.S. 527 (1941).

[57] There are several exceptions to the general rule of I.R.C. § 1271 contained in the statute and the regulations. For example, in addition to the exceptions provided in I.R.C. §§ 1271(a)(2)(B) and 1271(b), and I.R.C. § 1271(a)(1) does not apply to a debt instrument that is publicly offered, a debt instrument to which I.R.C. § 1272(a)(6) applies, and certain private placement debt instruments. Reg. § 1.1271-1(a)(2).

[58] For special rules that deal with intercompany worthless debts, *see* Treas. Reg. § 1.1502-13(b) and (g). *See also* I.R.C. § 2679f)(2) that defers the deduction of losses between members of a consolidated group.

[59] *Findley v. Commissioner*, 25 T.C. 311 (1995), *aff'd*, 236 F.2d 959 (3d Cir. 1956).

[60] *Riss v. Commissioner*, 478 F.2d 1160, 1168 (8th Cir. 1973).

[61] *See* "LB&I Directive Related to § 166 Deductions for Eligible Debt and Eligible Securities,"

on "all pertinent evidence, including the value of the collateral, if any, securing the debt and the financial condition of the debtor."[62]

The Supreme Court observed: "The taxing act does not require the taxpayer to be an incorrigible optimist."[63] The Fourth Circuit stated similarly that the taxpayer "is required only to exercise good faith and to establish as a basis for his deduction facts upon which a prudent business man would act."[64] The I.R.S. may not ignore a taxpayer's "soundly exercised business judgment."[65] However, "[t]he Commissioner's determination will not be disturbed unless it is plainly arbitrary or unreasonable, indicating an abuse of discretion."[66]

A deduction is appropriate where "the surrounding circumstances indicate that a debt is worthless and uncollectible and that legal action to enforce payment would in all probability not result in the satisfaction of execution on a judgment."[67] To satisfy this burden of proof, a taxpayer may present evidence that an identifiable event has occurred which negates any possibility of potential future recovery of the debt.[68] Identifiable events include a debtor's bankruptcy, insolvency, sale of assets, disappearance, death, refusal to pay or abandonment of business.[69] Courts have denied a bad debt deduction where there is evidence that the debtor made payments toward the principal or interest during the year at issue.[70] Similarly, a creditor's continuation of loans or the advancement of additional monies to debtor are factors which may negate a finding of worthlessness.[71]

When a debt becomes worthless must be determined from the facts and circumstances known, or which reasonably could have been known, at the end of the year of asserted worthlessness.[72] Facts subsequent to the taxable year "may be used only to evaluate the soundness of [the taxpayer's] decision that the debt was worthless in [that year] and not as evidence of the fact of worthlessness."[73]

(Footnote Continued)

LB&I-04-1014-008, Oct. 24, 2014. Appendix A.23, hereof.

[62] Reg. §1.166-2(a). *Production Steel, Inc. v. Commissioner*, 39 T.C.M. 77, Dec. 36,299(M) (1979), T.C. Memo. 1979-361. In the Conference Committee Report to the Tax Reform Act of 1986, Congress ordered the Treasury Department to issue a report by January 1, 1988, regarding the appropriate criteria to be used to determine if a debt is worthless. H.R. Rep. No. 99-841, pt. 2 at 315. *See* Dept. of the Treasury, Report to the Congress on the Tax Treatment of Bad Debts by Financial Institutions 19-24 (1991).

[63] *United States v. S.S. White Dental Mfg. Co.*, 274 U.S. 398, 403, 47 S.Ct. 598, 600, 71 L.Ed. 1120 (1927); Reg. § 1.166-2(b).

[64] *Murchinson National Bank v. Commissioner*, 50 F.2d 1056 (4th Cir. 1931).

[65] *Portland Mfg. Co*, 56 TC 58 (1971), *acq*, 1972-1 C.B 1; *Bank of Kirksville v. United States*, 943 F. Supp. 1191 (W.D. Mo. 1996); *The Austin Co., Inc. v. Commissioner*, 71 T.C. 955, Dec. 35,908 (1979).

[66] *Brimberry v. Commissioner*, 588 F.2d 975 (5th Cir. 1979).

[67] Treas. Reg. § 1.166-2(b).

[68] *Dustin v. Commissioner*, 53 T.C. 491, 501 (1969); *Minneapolis St. Paul & S. Ste. M. R.R. v. U.S.*, 164 Ct. Cl. 226, 240-41 (1964); *Findley v. Commissioner*, 25 T.C. 311, 319, *aff'd*, 236 F.2d 959 (3d Cir. 1956); *Dallmeyer v. Commissioner*, 14 T.C. 1281, 1291 (1950).

[69] *Cole v. Commissioner*, 871 F.2d 64, 67 (7th Cir. 1989); *Dustin*, 53 T.C. at 503.

[70] *Cole*, 871 F.2d at 68; *Appalachian Trail Co. v. Commissioner*, T.C. Memo. 1973-119, 32 T.C.M. 520, 522; *Clemens v. Commissioner*, T.C. Memo. 1969-235, 28 T.C.M. 1225, 1231, *aff'd*, 453 F.2d 869 (9th Cir. 1971).

[71] *See, e.g., Riss*, 478 F.2d at 1166; *Simon v. Commissioner*, T.C. Memo. 1978-485, 37 T.C.M. 1849-67, 1849-70.

[72] *Estate of Mann v. U.S.*, 731 F.2d 267 (5th Cir. 1984).

[73] *Hubble v. Commissioner*, 42 T.C.M. 1537, 1546 (1981); *Sollitt Construction Co. v. United States*, 1 Cl.Ct. 333 (1983).

Although the facts that exist during the tax year determine worthlessness, a taxpayer that suffered a partial bad debt loss is permitted to either take an immediate deduction or to defer the deduction.[74] Specific authorization for the deferral of a deduction is allowed to banks under Treasury regulations.[75]

Treasury regulation § 1.166-2 requires consideration of all pertinent evidence and provides that a deduction is warranted if the surrounding circumstances indicate that the debt is uncollectible. The IRS acknowledges that no precise test exists for determining whether a debt is worthless.[76] Furthermore, it is not uncommon that no single factor or event clearly demonstrates whether a debt has become worthless. Usually, a series of factors or events in the aggregate establishes whether the debt is worthless. The IRS has ruled that among the factors indicating worthlessness include: a debtor's serious financial reverses, insolvency, lack of assets, continued refusal to respond to demands for payment, ill health, death, disappearance, abandonment of business, bankruptcy, a debt's unsecured or subordinated status, and expiration of the statute of limitations.[77] However, factors suggesting that the debt is not worthless include the availability of collateral or third party guarantees, a debtor's earning capacity, payment of interest, a creditor's failure to press for payment, and a creditor's willingness to make further advances.

Bankruptcy is generally an indication of the worthlessness of at least part of any unsecured and unpreferred debt;[78] however, even when bankruptcy occurs, factors such as insurance, collateral, and guarantees are to be taken into account in determining at least the amount of worthlessness. The requirement that the taxpayer bears the burden of proving that a debt became worthless in the particular year in which the deduction was taken is not set aside when the Code section 166 deduction arises in the context of a bankruptcy proceeding.[79] Insolvency is one indication of the worthlessness of a debt.[80] However, if a business is on the decline, if it has failed to make a profit, or if the loan is merely difficult to collect, a bad debt may not be justified.[81]

When a bank's deduction is later disallowed for a bad debt that has been charged-off in the deduction year, a deduction will be allowed in the subsequent year in which the debt becomes partially worthless, notwithstanding the failure to charge-off the debt in the proper year of deduction.[82] However, the allowable

[74] *Findley v. Commisioner*, 25 T.C. 311, 319, *aff'd*, 236 F.2d 959 (3d Cir. 1956); *E. Richard Meining Co. v. Commisioner*, 9 T.C. 976, 978 (1947), *acq.* 1948-1 C.B.2. *The Capital National Bank of Sacramento v. Commissioner*, 16 T.C. 1202 (1951); *E. Richard Meinig Co.*, 9 T.C. 976 (1947); *Moock Electric Supply Co.*, 41 B.T.A. 1209 (1940); *Blair v. Commissioner*, 91 F.2d 992 (2d Cir. 1937). *See also* preamble to Prop. Reg. § 1.475(a): "In addition, computing the mark-to-market adjustment as if the debt's basis had been adjusted to reflect worthlessness preserves a taxpayer's ability to postpone claiming a deduction for partial worthlessness until the debt becomes wholly worthless." 60 FR 397-01.

[75] Reg. § 1.166-2(d)(2). *See* discussion of the involuntary charge-off rule below.

[76] Rev. Rul. 2001-59, 2001-51 I.R.B. 585.

[77] *Id.*

[78] Reg. § 1.166-2(c). *LaStaiti v. Commissioner*, 41 T.C.M. 511, Dec. 37,449(M) (1980), T.C. Memo. 1980-547.

[79] *In re Landbank Equity Corp.*, 92-2 U.S.T.C. ¶ 50,464, 973 F.2d 265 (4th Cir. 1992).

[80] *Roth Steel Tube Co. v. Commissioner*, 620 F.2d 1176, 1181 (6th Cir. 1980), *aff'g* 68 T.C. 213 (1977).

[81] *Riss v. Commissioner*, 56 T.C. 388, 407 (1971), abrogated by 57 T.C. 455 (1971) *aff'd in part and remanded*, 478 F.2d 1160 (8th Cir. 1973).

[82] Reg. § 1.166-3(a)(2)(ii).

deduction will be limited to the amount charged-off in the disallowance year plus any amount charged-off in the deduction year. A special seven-year statute of limitations applies to deductions attributable to bad debts.[83]

§10.3.2 The Meaning of "Charge-Off"

A deduction is allowed for a partially worthless debt only if the debt is changed-off.[84] No such prerequisite is required for wholly worthless debts.[85] Code section 166(a)(2) requires that the charge-off occurs "within the taxable year."[86] The purpose of a charge-off is "to require that some record be made of the ascertainment of worthlessness."[87] If the debt is on the taxpayer's accounting books then when it is eliminated from the taxpayer's books a charge-off occurs. For audit purposes, the IRS has stated that a charge-off "means an accounting entry or set of accounting entries for a taxable year that reduces the basis of the . . . debt when the . . . debt is recorded in whole or part as a Loss Asset on the Bank or Bank Subsidiary's Applicable Financial Statement for that year."[88] The manner in which a debt is eliminated from the taxpayer's books is not prescribed in the statute or in Treasury regulations.

Judicial opinions have stated that any reasonable method may be employed to charge-off the debt.[89] In *Commissioner v. MacDonald Engineering Co.*, the Seventh Circuit stated:

> "There is no fixed mode of charge-off. The principal reason for the requirement is to prevent a taxpayer from taking advantage of the loss for tax purposes while continuing to carry the item on his books as an asset for other purposes. Anything which manifests the intent to eliminate an item from assets is sufficient to constitute a charge-off."[90]

The Board of Tax Appeals earlier established a similar principal. It stated that:

> "The fundamental purpose in requiring the charge-off is to evidence the worthlessness of the debt, . . . and this end is accomplished and the charge-off effected by the elimination of the bad debt from the taxpayer's assets. If the debt is in fact ascertained to be worthless, it should no longer be treated or considered as an asset. The effective elimination of the debt as an asset meets the statutory requirement as to charge-off."[91]

---

[83] I.R.C. §6511(d)(1) (2000).

[84] I.R.C. § 166(a)(2).

[85] I.R.C. § 166(a)(1).

[86] Limited exceptions are permitted. *American Finance & Morgage Co. v. Commissioner*, 22 BTA 32, (1931); *O. S. Stapley Co. v. Commissioner*, 13 BTA 557 (1928).

[87] *Fraser v. Commissioner*, 6 BTA 997 (1927); *Pate v. Commissioner*, 13 BTA 1236 (1928).

[88] *See* LB&I Directive Related to § 166 Deductions for Eligible Debt and Eligible Securities, LB&I-04-1014-008, Oct. 24, 2014 located at Appendix A.23 hereof.

[89] *Perry v. Commissioner*, 22 BTA 13 (1931); *Malden Trust Co. v. Commissioner*, 110 F.2d 751 (1st Cir. 1940); *Planters National Bank v. Commissioner*, 18 BTA 705 (1930); *First Nat'l Bank v. Commissioner*, 26 BTA 370 (1932).

[90] 102 F.2d 942 (7th Cir. 1939). *See also Fairless v. Commissioner*, 67 F.2d 475, 478 (6th Cir. 1933) (holding, "[i]t was clearly the purpose of the Congress to condition allowance of deduction for bad debts upon the perpetuation of evidence that they were ascertained to be worthless within the taxable year, and upon some specific act of the taxpayer clearly indicating their abandonment as assets").

[91] *Ewald & Co. v. Commissioner*, 18 BTA 1130 (1930).

A charge-off usually results in a reduction of tax basis in a debt. Reduction in tax basis results in either a direct deduction against income (the "specific charge-off method") or an indirect deduction against income by means of a deductible addition to a reserve for bad debts (the "reserve method"). For a taxpayer that uses the reserve method of accounting for bad debts, a charge-off occurs when there is recording or "charging" that worthlessness against its tax reserves, which has the result of reducing its reserve for bad debt losses. Thus, the term "charge-off" may refer to more than one step in the bad debt process and may have a different meaning and tax consequence depending on the context.[92]

Included among the acceptable procedures for eliminating a portion or all of a debt from a taxpayer's booked assets may be the establishment of a specific reserve or contra-asset account,[93] although this does not appear to be generally accepted for commercial banks under current IRS regulations. However, regulations permit a thrift to treat as a charge-off an allowance for loan losses in the amount of 100 percent of the portion of the debt classified as loss.[94] Commercial banks may find support for treating a contra-asset as a charge-off in *Brandtjen & Kluge.*[95] In that case the Tax Court held that an entry to a fund designed to absorb anticipated losses, rather than eliminating an amount from the asset account itself, satisfied the statutory requirement of the charge-off. The entry appeared to be similar to a contra-asset entry. The Tax Court found that the book entries were limited to one specific indebtedness, were intended to accomplish a charge-off, and were described in terms indicating a sustained loss, rather than an anticipated loss, in the one specific account.

Regulations that deal with modified also lend support to the position that a formal charge-off is required to evidence worthlessness. If originated debt is significantly modified, a "deemed charge-off" is allowed. The amount of the deemed charge-off is measured by comparing the taxpayer's tax basis of the debt to the greater of the fair market value of the debt or the amount of the debt recorded on the taxpayer's books reduced as appropriate for a specific allowance for loan losses.[96] The latter rule does not appear to be limited to thrifts; however, the deemed charge-off rule is not available to purchased debt, as contrasted with originated debt.[97]

The IRS in private and public rulings also acknowledged that a "charge-off" is not limited to a taxpayer's physical act of charging off a debt.[98] However, a taxpayer must take some "affirmative action" to remove the worthless portion of the asset from its books as an indication that the debt is actually worthless.[99] Thus, the I.R.S. has ruled that the reversal of accrued interest constitutes a

---

[92] FSA 200129003, issued on July 20, 2001.

[93] *Brandtjen & Kluge, Inc. v. Commissioner,* 34 T.C. 416, Dec. 24,213 (1960), *acq.* 1960-2 C.B. 3.

[94] Reg. § 1.166-2(d)(4)(ii).

[95] *Brandtjen & Kluge v. Commissioner,* 34 T.C. 416, Dec. 24,213 (1960), *acq.,* 1960-2 C.B. 3.

[96] Reg. § 1.166-3(a)(3)(iii).

[97] Reg. § 1.166-2(d)(4)(ii). *See also* Preamble to Prop. Reg. § 1.475(a)-1(f) which states: "The basis of the marked-to-market debt is treated as having been reduced by the amount of any book or regulatory charge off (including the establishment of a specific allowance for loan losses) . . . ."

[98] PLR 9338044, June 30, 1993 issued Sept. 24, 1993.

[99] *Southern Pacific Transportation Co. v. Commissioner,* 75 T.C. 497, 563 (1980). What constitutes such action is a matter that is likely to be controversial.

charge-off of the interest receivable for purposes of the bad debt conformity election.[100] Similarly, the failure to recognize accrued interest for regulatory financial statement purposes was determined to be tantamount to recognizing the accrued interest as income and immediately charging-off the uncollected accrued interest receivable as a loss asset.[101] If the actions taken by the taxpayer indicate an abandonment and removal from the taxpayer's books of a portion of a loan, even though the actual charge-off on the books of the taxpayer does not occur until a subsequent taxable year, a "charge-off" could be found to have been made.[102]

Treasury regulations under the bad debt conformity election provide that the conclusive presumption of worthlessness is secured for any charge-off of part or all of a debt that corresponds to the bank's classification of the debt as a "loss asset."[103] Implicit in this requirement is that the debt be eliminated to the extent of the "loss" classification from the regulatory books of the taxpayer. Although there is no statutory charge-off requirement for wholly worthless debts, Treasury regulations under the bad debt conformity election appear to require a charged-off, regardless of whether the debt is partially or wholly worthless.

The charge-off requirement may be satisfied by a regulatory charge-off even when there is no charge-off on accounting books. The possibility of a regulatory charge-off where there is no book charge-off was acknowledged in the preamble to proposed regulations promulgated under Code section 475, the mark-to-market section of the Code. There, the Treasury Department stated:

> "The basis of the mark-to-market debt is treated as having been reduced by the amount of **any book or regulatory charge-off** (including the establishment of a specific allowance for a loan loss) for which a deduction could have been taken, without regard to whether any portion of the charge-off is, in fact, deducted or charged to a tax reserve for bad debts." [Emphasis added.][104]

The Code section 475 mark-to-market rule requires a dealer in securities to write down to fair market value any security held by the dealer that is not identified as held for investments, not held for sale, or a hedge of one of these two classifications of securities. The mark may, in part, be with respect to a portion of a debt security charged-off during the year or that becomes wholly worthless during the year. If this occurs, to the extent of worthlessness, the mark is treated as a bad debt deduction.[105]

With respect to credit card loans, it is customary for a bank to completely eliminate the loan from its books and not partially charge-off the loan. As such, it appears that there is no statutory requirement that credit card loans treated this way be charged-off to be allowed a deduction under Code section 166. (A charge-off requirement is imposed only on partially worthless debts.[106]) Moreover, credit card debts are typically treated as "loss assets" pursuant to federal regulatory

---

[100] Rev. Rul. 2007-32, 2007-21 I.R.B. 1278; Reg. § 1.166-2(d)(3)(ii)(C).

[101] *Id.*

[102] *Id.*

[103] Reg. § 1.166-2(d)(3)(ii)(A)(1).

[104] 60 FR 397-01 (January 4, 1995).

[105] Prop. Reg. § 1.475(a)-2(f). *See also* discussion in Ch. 4.

[106] I.R.C. § 166(a)(2).

guidelines.[107] In a Chief Counsel Advice, the IRS has stated that a "charge-off" of these loans takes place pursuant to "automatic charge-off procedures" set forth in the Comptroller of the Currency Handbook for National Bank Examiners.[108]

§ 10.4 Presumptions of Worthlessness

There are five methods by which a bank may establish the worthlessness of its bad debts. Regulation section 1.166-2(a) provides for a facts and circumstances test. This test is available to all taxpayers, including all members of a bank holding company group. It is the method employed by most banks. Alternatively, all banks are permitted to elect one of two special rules that provide for conclusive presumptions of worthlessness prescribed in Regulations sections 1.166-2(d)(1) and (2). These rules may be used only by a bank and not by any other member of the bank holding company group, including subsidiaries of a bank unless the subsidiary is a "regulated corporation" as that term is used in Regulation section 1.166-2(d)(1).[109] The fourth method is contained in a Directive issued in 2014.[110] It permits some, but not all, banks and bank subsidiaries to avoid any audit adjustment to bad debt deductions if the conditions contained in the Directive are met.[111] The fifth method is the reserve method prescribed in Code section 585(a) available only to banks that are not "large banks" or that have not elected to be treated as S Banks. Each of these methods is discussed in detail below.

§ 10.4.1 Industry Directive

The IRS Commissioner for Large Businesses and the International Division issued an Industry Directive in 2014 that contained guidance for IRS bank examiners. It instructs them not to challenge the bad debt deductions claimed for certain debts including bad debts with respect to certain debt "securities" claimed by banks and bank subsidiaries, if the taxpayer (a) employs the specific charge-off method for determining its bad debt deduction (b) satisfies certain book and regulatory conformity requirements contained in the Directive, and (c) properly executes a "Certification Statement." The Directive also instructs examiners not to challenge the inclusion in a bank or a bank subsidiary's bad debt deduction of certain estimated selling costs.[112]

---

[107] Uniform Retail Credit Classification and Account Management Policy of the Federal Institutions Examination Council require such loans to be eliminated from the books of the bank after the loan has been delinquent for a period of 180 days.

[108] Chief Council Advise 200045030 (November 27, 2000).

[109] There is no definition of the term "regulated corporation" in the Code or regulations. It is unclear whether the term applies to bank subsidiaries and other members of the bank holding company group.

[110] In Notice 2013-35, 2013-24 I.R.B. 1240, May 20, 2013 the IRS requested comments on Reg. § 1.166-2(d)(1) and (3), the "conclusive presumption" regulations. The Directive is the result of that Notice.

[111] *See* "LB&I Directive Related to § 166 Deductions for Eligible Debt and Eligible Securities" LB&I-04-1014-008, Oct. 24, 2014. *See* Directive at Appendix A.23.

[112] The Directive contains no definition of the term "selling costs." Because banks customarily include in their bad debt deductions estimates of future costs to carry property, such as the cost of utilities, insurance, maintenance, and property taxes, as well as legal and brokerage fees, these should qualify as "selling costs" for purposes of the Directive. It appears that a taxpayer must add the selling costs to the amount charged-off on the loan to receive the audit protection offer by the Directive. Separately deducting selling costs as operating expenses will not be sufficient.

An examining agent is permitted to continue to challenge bad debt deductions to the extent that the charge-off of the debt is not credit-related. For example, if a bank writes-down a loan to reflect its fair market value, that portion of the write-down that is related solely to an increase in the market interest rate on a similar debt will likely be disallowed.[113]

The Directive promulgates an administrative rule (without following the required procedures associated with promulgating regulations) that provides those taxpayers to which the Directive applies an alternative method for determining the worthlessness of a debt, in addition to the methods currently provided in regulations.[114] The Directive was prompted, in part, by "concerns" that changing regulatory bad debt standards have created some uncertainty with the application of the bank specific conclusive presumption regulations under Code section 166.[115] It also is designed to relieve examiners from the burden of attempting to determine on audit whether the debts claimed by a taxpayer as worthless satisfy bad debt criteria currently prescribed in regulations.

(a) *Taxpayers to Whom Directive May Apply*

The audit protection the Directive affords is available on an entity-by-entity basis. It applies only to qualifying banks and subsidiaries of qualifying banks that use the specific charge-off method for determining bad debt deductions.[116] The Directive is not available to other members of the bank's affiliated group even though these other entities are permitted to use only the specific charge-off method for determining their bad debt deductions. It appears that a bank subsidiary is permitted to obtain the protection of the Directive even though its parent bank that qualifies for the audit protection of the Directive does not choose to do so, and vice versa.

(b) *Qualifying Banks*

The Directive applies only to those banks that are described in Regulations section 1.166-2(d)(4) and that use the specific charge-off method to determine bad debt deductions. That regulation provides that the term bank is defined by reference to Code section 581. The latter is the only Code section that defines a "bank," although other sections define a "financial institution" in much the same way.[117] The term bank also includes any corporation that would be a bank within the meaning of Code section 581 except for the fact that it is a foreign corporation, but only with respect to loans the interest on which is effectively connected

[113] The Directive contains detailed "Implementation" rules at paragraph "D." See Directive in Appendix A.23 hereof.

[114] This Directive appears to be short-circuiting the normal Administrative Procedure Act requirements associated with promulgating regulations by saying that it ". . . is not an official pronouncement of law, and cannot be used, cited, or relied on as such. In addition, nothing in this Directive should be construed as affecting the operation of any other provision of the Code, regulations or guidance thereunder." *See* Directive at Appendix A.23 at "I."

[115] Even though the Directive refers only to the "conclusive presumption regulations contained in Reg. § 1.166-2(d)(2)," when mentioning the "concerns" that contributed to promulgation of the Directive, the Directive also applies to banks that determine worthlessness under the facts and circumstances test of Reg. § 1.166-2(d)(1).

[116] Bank subsidiaries are not permitted to use the reserve method of accounting for bad debts. I.R.C. § 585(a).

[117] *See, e.g.*, IRC § 265(b)(5). *See* discussion of the definition of the term "bank" for tax purposes contained in Ch. 1 hereof.

with the conduct of a banking business within the United States. In addition, the term bank includes a Farm Credit System institution that is subject to supervision by the Farm Credit Administration.[118]

The Directive will not apply to most banks that are not "large banks." Code section 585(c)(1) allows banks that are not "large banks" to elect the reserve method of accounting for bad debts.[119] Those banks that are not "large banks" are allowed by Code section 585(a) to deduct a reasonable addition to a reserve for bad debts, unless the bank elects to be taxed under the provisions of Subchapter S. S banks may not use the reserve method of accounting for bad debts, and thus would qualify under the Directive.[120]

(c) *Qualifying Bank Subsidiaries*

The Directive will apply to "bank subsidiaries" if the bank parent meets the definition of a bank contained in the Directive and if the bank and the bank subsidiary use the specific charge-off method.[121] If a bank uses the reserve method for deducting loan losses, the bank subsidiary is not permitted to use the Directive even though the subsidiary uses the specific charge-off method. The specific charge-off method is the only method for determining worthless available for nearly all bank subsidiaries.

For purposes of the Directive, the term "bank subsidiary" means an entity that:

(a) Is not a bank, but conducts businesses that a the parent bank may conduct,

(b) Is a member of the same affiliated group as the parent bank (within the meaning of Code section 1504(a)(1)), determined without regard to the exception for S corporations contained in Code section 1504(b)(8) (or would be a member of the same affiliated group as parent bank after the application of the partnership rule that appears below),

(c) Bears the same relationship to the parent bank that the members of an affiliated group bear to their common parent under Code section 1504(a)(1), and

(d) Is under the supervision of parent bank's regulator.

For purposes of this definition (including for purposes of determining whether a partnership would be an "includible corporation" within the meaning of Code section 1504(b)), any partnership whose interests are wholly and directly

---

[118] *See* discussion in Ch. 1 of the meaning of the term "bank" for purposes of I.R.C. § 581. *See* I.R.C. § 861 *et seq.* for the treatment of "effectively connected" income.

[119] The term "large bank" is defined in Code section 585(c)(2) to mean a bank:

> ". . . if, for the taxable year (or for any preceding taxable year beginning after December 31, 1986)-- (A) the average adjusted bases of all assets of such bank exceeded $500,000,000, or (B) such bank was a member of a parent-subsidiary controlled group and the average adjusted bases of all assets of such group exceeded $500,000,000."

[120] I.R.C. § 1361(b)(2)(A).

[121] Although it is generally understood that nonbanks are not permitted to use the two conclusive presumption of worthlessness, Reg. § 1.166-2(d)(1) permits its conclusive presumption of worthlessness to apply to not only banks but also to any "other corporation which is subject to supervision by Federal authorities, or by State authorities maintaining substantially equivalent standards . . . ."

owned by the parent bank, by a bank wholly owned by the parent bank, and/or one or more subsidiaries of the parent bank shall be treated as if it were a corporation; however, a partnership shall not be treated as wholly and directly owned by the parent bank and/or one or more bank subsidiaries if any interests in such partnership are owned by one or more entities in which the partnership, directly or indirectly, owns an interest.

As a general rule, a bank subsidiary is usually subject to the same supervision and oversight by bank regulators as the parent bank. Thus, a bank subsidiary will qualify under the Directive because it is under the supervision of the parent bank's regulator. For purposes of the Directive, a "bank regulator" means the bank regulator responsible for the supervision of the bank and its subsidiaries. A bank subsidiary will be under this supervision if it is regulated by either the Office of the Comptroller of the Currency, the Federal Reserve Board, the Federal Deposit Insurance Corporation, the Office of Thrift Supervision (prior to its merger with the Office of Comptroller of the Currency), the Farm Credit Administration, any successor to any of the foregoing entities, or state authorities maintaining substantially equivalent standards as these Federal regulatory authorities.

The Directive's definition of a "bank subsidiary" appears to exclude an Edge Act bank, an entity that is a bank subsidiary and that receives a federal charter as a bank for federal regulatory purposes to conduct a banking business limited to international banking from branches in the United States. Presumably, an Edge Act bank would be treated for purposes of the Directive as a "bank" and not a "bank subsidiary," even though Edge Act banks are usually bank subsidiaries.[122]

(d) *Bad Debt Deductions That May Not Be Challenged*

The charged-off debts that will be insulated from challenge by the Directive include both "eligible debts" and "eligible debt securities." An "eligible debt" means any debt (whether originated or acquired) reported in the taxpayer's balance sheet or other "applicable financial statement" that:

- Is a bond, debenture, note, or other evidence of indebtedness, issued by a corporation or by a government or political subdivision there, with interest coupons or in registered form,[123]
- Is not subject to the mark-to-market rules applicable to dealers in securities set forth in Code section 475, and
- Is either within the scope of Accounting Standards Codification (ASC) 450 or ASC 310-40 under U.S. GAAP, or the predecessors or successors of such accounting standards, or would be subject to such accounting standards (or such predecessors or successors) if such debt were accounted for under U.S. GAAP (for example, accounted for under International Financial Reporting Standards).

---

[122] An Edge Act bank is defined in 12 U.S.C. § 611 *et seq.* (2000).

[123] It seems unnecessary for the Directive to do so, but it excludes from the concept of eligible debt and eligible debt security "a share of stock, a right to subscribe for, or to receive, a share of stock in a corporation," instruments that are not debts.

An "eligible debt security" means any debt security reported in the taxpayer's "applicable financial statement, other than a debt security classified as a trading security, that:

- Is not a bond, debenture, note, or other evidence of indebtedness, issued by a corporation or by a government or political subdivision, with interest coupons or in registered form, unless the debt securities are held by a bank,[124]
- Is not subject to the mark-to-market rules applicable to dealers in securities set forth in Code section 475, and
- Is either within the scope of ASC 320 under U.S. GAAP, or the predecessors or successors of such accounting standard, or would be subject to such accounting standard (or such predecessors or successors) if such debt were accounted for under U.S. GAAP (for example, accounted for under International Financial Reporting Standards). Debt securities classified as trading securities are excluded from the definition of "eligible debt securities."

(e) Charge-Off and Financial Statement Requirement

The directive does not obviate the necessity of a debt being properly charged-off. To charge-off a debt an accounting entry or set of accounting entries must be made for a taxable year that reduces the basis of the debt at the time that the debt is recorded in whole or part as a "loss asset" on the taxpayer's "applicable financial statement" for that year.[125] Similarly, a charge-off of debt security means an accounting entry or set of accounting entries for a taxable year that reduces the debt security's carrying value and results in a realized loss or a charge to the statement of operations (as opposed to recognition of an unrealized loss) that is recorded on the taxpayer's "applicable financial statement" for that year.

An "applicable financial statement" means a financial statement that must be filed by a bank and/or bank subsidiary with the Securities and Exchange Commission or one that must be provided to a bank regulator. Thus it includes the taxpayer's Form 10-K. It may also include a financial statement, such as a call report, that must be provided to the Office of the Comptroller of the Currency, the Federal Reserve Board, the Federal Deposit Insurance Corporation, the Office of Thrift Supervision (prior to its merger with the OCC), and the Farm Credit Administration, including any successor to these governmental entities. Financial statements furnished to state authorities that maintain substantially equivalent standards as these federal regulatory authorities will also satisfy the definition of "applicable financial statement."

(f) Effect on "Worthlessness" Regulations

The Directive prescribes slightly different rules for examiners to follow depending upon whether the taxpayer availed itself on its return of the general

[124] IRC § 582(a) permits a bank to apply the bad debt rules to these debt securities.

[125] *See* discussion of "loss asset" in section below that discusses the conformity election.

facts and circumstances test for determining worthlessness contained in Regulation section 1.166-2(a) or one of the two conclusive presumptions available only to banks (and not to most bank subsidiaries) contained in Regulation section 1.166-2(d). Regardless of which method is employed, an examiner may not challenge the inclusion in the bank or bank subsidiary's bad debt deduction estimated selling costs to the extent such estimated selling costs are included in the charge-off reported in the bank or bank subsidiary's "applicable financial statement."

(g) *Banks and Bank Subsidiaries Using Facts and Circumstances*

If a bank or bank subsidiary determines its bad debt deduction under the general facts and circumstances method (which is probably the only method contained in the regulations allowed to be used by most bank subsidiaries), an examiner may not challenge bad debt deductions for eligible debts, eligible debt securities, and selling costs if the deduction is the same amount as the amount of the credit-related impairment portion of its charge-off of the eligible debt, eligible debt security, and selling costs reported on the taxpayer's "applicable financial statement." In no event, however, may the post-deduction tax basis of eligible debt be less than the post-charge-off book basis of the eligible debt as increased by any portion of the charge-off not related to credit impairment, nor may the post-deduction tax basis of eligible debt securities be less than the post-charge-off carrying amount of the eligible debt securities as increased by any portion of the charge-off not related to credit impairment.

(h) *Banks Electing Conclusive Presumption of Worthlessness: Reg. § 1.166-2(d)(1)*

For banks that elect the conclusive presumption of worthlessness method for determining worthlessness contained in Regulation section1.166-2(d)(1), examiners may not challenge bad debt deductions for eligible debts, eligible debt securities, or selling costs if the deductions are equal to the sum of: (a) the amount of the credit-related impairment portion of its charge-off as reported on its "applicable financial statement;" and (b) the portion of the charge-off in excess of the credit-related impairment that was taken pursuant to a specific order or written confirmation (as described in Regulation section 1.166-2(d)(1)) by a bank regulator as reported on its "applicable financial statement."[126]

Examiners also may not challenge the bad debt deductions regardless of whether a bank or bank subsidiary presents a specific order by a bank regulator or confirmation letter as described in Regulation section 1.166-2(d)(1).[127] However, the properly executed "Certification Statement" (described below) from the bank or the bank subsidiary is required. The Certification Statement requires the

---

[126] It is unusual for bank regulators to order charge-offs and to issue confirmation letters. For that reason, banks seldom qualify for the conclusive presumption of worthlessness contained in Reg. § 1.166-2(d)(1).

[127] The provision in the Directive that relieves a bank or a bank subsidiary from the need to "present" the order or letter is confusing. It seems to be saying that even though the bank qualified under Reg. § 1.166-2(d)(1) by having an ordered charge-off or receiving a confirmation letter, the order or letter does not have to be provided.

taxpayer to provide "the portion of the Charge-off charged-off pursuant to a specific order or written confirmation by a Bank Regulator."[128]

As with the facts and circumstances test, examiners are instructed to ensure that the post-deduction tax basis of eligible debt are not less than the post-charge-off book basis of the eligible debt as increased by any portion of the charge-off not related to credit impairment and reduced by any amount of the charge-off in excess of the credit-related impairment that was taken pursuant to a specific order or written confirmation (as described in Regulation section 1.166-2(d)(1)) by a bank regulator, and that the post-deduction tax basis of eligible debt securities are not less than the post-charge-off carrying value of the eligible debt securities as increased by any portion of the charge-off not related to credit impairment and reduced by any amount of the charge-off in excess of the credit-related impairment that was taken pursuant to a specific order or written confirmation (as described in Regulation section 1.166-2(d)(1)) by a bank regulator.

(i) Banks Making Conformity Election of Reg. §1.166-2(d)(3)

If a bank makes the conformity election for determining worthlessness provided in Regulation section 1.166-2(d)(3), examiners may not challenge a bank's bad debt deduction for eligible debt, eligible debt securities, and selling costs regardless of whether the express determination requirement as described in Regulation section 1.166-2(d)(3)(iii)(D) is satisfied.[129]

(j) Taxable Years to Which Directive Applies

At the election of the taxpayer, the Directive may be applied no earlier than a taxpayer's 2010 taxable year and no later than a taxable year that begins in 2014.[130] Once the Directive is elected, it must be consistently applied to all future years.[131]

If a bank or bank subsidiary chooses to follow the provisions of the Directive, it may implement any applicable changes by filing amended returns or

[128] *See* "Certification Statement" at paragraph "G" appended to Directive at Appendix A.23.

[129] Reg. § 1.166-2(d)(3) provides that the conclusive presumption of worthlessness of that regulation is not available unless the taxpayer "meets the express determination requirement. . . ." Reg. § 1.166-2(d)(3)(i). It is unclear how a taxpayer may determine the worthlessness under Reg. § 1.166-2(d)(3) if it does not satisfy the express determination requirement. Reg. § 1.166-2(d)(3)(C) provides: "(1) In general--A bank's election under this paragraph (d)(3) is revoked automatically if, in connection with any examination involving the bank's loan review process by the bank's supervisory authority as defined in paragraph (d)(3)(iii)(D) of this section, the bank does not obtain the express determination required by that paragraph.".

[130] If a bank or bank subsidiary makes the election, it may file amended returns to implement the Directive or it may make the changes in its current taxable year. If it is under examination, the IRS will decide whether it is appropriate to change the amount of bad debt deduction for open taxable years under examination to be consistent with this Directive or to allow the taxpayer to file amended returns.

[131] An ambiguous provision in the Directive could be read to restrict a bank from changing from the facts and circumstances method to the historical presumption of worthlessness method. The statement in the Directive reads: "For each taxable year beginning after the Adjustment Year, the amount of the bad debt deduction under § 166 for Eligible Debt and Eligible Debt Securities should be determined as provided in C.1 for Banks and Bank Subsidiaries described in section C.1, and as provided in section C.2 for Banks and Bank Subsidiaries described in section C.2." The reference to "C.1" is to those banks that use the facts and circumstances method, and the reference to "C.2" is to those banks that use the historical presumption method.

making the changes in its current taxable year. If the taxpayer is under examination, the examiner, in consultation with the taxpayer, may decide whether to change the amount of bad debt deduction for the open taxable year(s) under examination to be consistent with the Directive or to allow the taxpayer to file amended returns.

§10.4.2 Bank Specific Rules

A bank or "other corporation which is subject to supervision by Federal authorities or by State authorities maintaining equivalent standards" is afforded special treatment with respect to bad debts (hereinafter, the "bank" specific rules).[132] The bank specific rule currently contained in Regulation section 1.166-2(d)(1) has its origin in a 1921 Treasury Decision that promulgated regulations providing for a rebuttable presumption that debts charged off in whole or in part "in obedience to the specific order or in accordance with the general policy of" bank supervisors were worthless for purposes of the bad debt deduction.[133] The Board of Tax Appeals concluded in 1925, however, that this rebuttable presumption did not afford banks with any advantage over other taxpayers because the bank examiner's treatment did not conclusively determine the appropriate tax treatment.[134] This rebuttable presumption was converted to a conclusive presumption in a 1936 amendment to the regulations.[135]

Regulations now afford banks two conclusive presumptions of worthlessness. One shall be referred to herein as the historical presumption of worthlessness because it has been a long-standing component of bad-debt regulations.[136] The other presumption is relatively new and will be referred to as the conformity election. If the criteria necessary for either of these presumptions is met, bad debts covered by the elections will be conclusively presumed to be worthless and deductible in the year of worthlessness. The presumptions apply to only the bank members of a bank holding company group, not to nonbank members. Thus, a mortgage company or even a credit card bank that does not meet the definition of a "bank" contained in Code section 581 may not employ the special bank tax rules.[137]

---

[132] Reg. §1.166-2(d)(1).

[133] Treasury Decision 3262 promulgated regulations under the bad debt provisions of the 1921 Revenue Act.

[134] *Murchison National Bank*, 1 B.T.A. 617 (1925). The Board of Tax Appeals persisted in this opinion despite a ruling to the contrary by the Fourth Circuit. In *Citizens National Bank of Orange v. Commissioner*, 74 F.2d 604 (4th Cir. 1935) the court held that "[t]here should be at least some semblance of coordination between the several branches of government in dealing with the taxpayer . . . Otherwise the banks would be compelled to keep two sets of books, or, as directed by the bank examiner, and the other for purposes of making a tax return. *Id.* at 605.

[135] T.D. 4633 (XV-1 C.B. 118).

[136] In Notice 2013-35, 2013-24 I.R.B. 1240, May 20, 2013, the IRS used the term "Specific Order Method" to refer to the historical presumption. This is somewhat misleading because the historical presumption allowed a conclusive presumption when there was no specific order as well as when there was a specific order. *See* discussion below of historical presumption.

[137] In Notice 2013-35, 2013-24 I.R.B. 1240, the IRS requested comments on the type of entities that are permitted, or should be permitted, to apply a conclusive presumption of worthlessness. In particular, comments were requested on "Which corporations are regulated by a Federal or State entity that reviews and makes determinations about worthlessness of debt assets in a manner consistent with the tax standards for worthlessness under section 166, and which of these entities should be covered by revised conclusive presumption rules?" I.R.C §582, the second section in Subchapter H, applies to "financial institutions," a term that includes entities that are not within the scope of the bank regulations under I.R.C. §166.

§ 10.4.3 Historical Presumption

Under the historical presumption of worthlessness, a debt will be conclusively presumed to be worthless in whole or in part, as the case may be, if:

1. It is charged-off in whole or in part in obedience to the specific orders of a federal regulator or a state regulator maintaining substantially equivalent standards; or
2. It is charged-off and the charge-off is "confirmed" during a regulator's first examination of the bank subsequent to the charge-off. Confirmation must be in writing and must provide that the loan charged-off would have been subject to specific regulatory order if the examination had been made on the date of the charge-off.[138]

Once the presumption applies, neither a bank regulator's expression of doubt as to the worthlessness of loss nor its later retraction of the order to charge-off the loan will reverse the conclusive presumption.[139] However, the conclusive presumption obviates only the necessity of proving that the loan is partially or totally worthless, not the requirement that the loan must be charged-off.[140] Also, to be entitled to this presumption the deduction must be taken in the year of charge-off.

The Office of the Comptroller of the Currency ("OCC"), the principal regulator of national banks, and most state bank regulatory agencies have refrained from issuing confirmation letters for several years.[141] However, the Federal Reserve Board continues to authorize its examiners to issue such letters.[142] When such letters are given, the IRS ruled that the requirement that the charge-off be confirmed "in writing" is satisfied when a write-down, in obedience to a bank regulator's oral instructions, is later confirmed in writing.[143] Further, a loan classified as a loss on a bank examiner's written report and charged-off by the bank in obedience to that report will satisfy the requirement that the charge-off is in obedience to a "specific order" of a bank regulator.[144] Such "specific order" obviates the necessity for "confirmation." Both the order and the confirmation letter may be obtained from state or federal bank regulators. Neither the "order" nor the "confirmation letter" requirement is satisfied with a letter from a bank regulator that merely describes loans as "low-quality assets" that should be removed from the taxpayer's books prior to a merger.[145]

---

[138] Reg. § 1.166-2(d)(1). 25 Fed. Reg. 11402 (Nov. 26, 1960). IRS Internal Audit Guideline No. 242 states that examining agents may not challenge the deductibility of ordered or confirmed charge-offs. *See* Appendix B.

[139] Rev. Rul. 80-180, 1980-2 C.B. 66.

[140] Reg. § 1.166-2(d)(1).

[141] The "confirmation letter" should not be confused with the "express determination letter" required when the conformity election is made.

[142] Board of Governors of Federal Reserve System, Division of Banking Supervision and Regulation, SR 92-39 (FIS), Oct. 30, 1992, *See also* SR-73-225, Sept. 7, 1973.

[143] Rev. Rul. 66-335, 1966-2 C.B. 58.

[144] Rev. Rul. 79-214, 1979-2 C.B. 90; Rev. Rul. 66-335, 1966-2 C.B. 58. *See also* Rev. Rul. 81-18, 1981-1 C.B. 295 where charge-offs made in accordance with regulations of the Federal Home Loan Board were "in obedience" to bank regulatory orders. The regulatory regulation dealt with in this ruling has been repealed. *See* discussion of Coordinated Issue Paper promulgated by the Appeals Office in 1993, discussed in Ch. 5, "Loans in Default" and located at Appendix A106.

[145] *Idaho First Nat. Bank and its Subsidiaries v. Commissioner*, T.C. Memo. 1990-499 (1990).

(a) Shared National Credit Review

A Shared National Credit Examination is an examination of large participation loans shared by more than one federally insured bank that is based on standards and practices of the three agencies, the OCC, the Federal Deposit Insurance Corporation ("FDIC"), and the Federal Reserve, with auditors participating in the examination. A Shared National Credit Review is a list of ratings of those large participation loans that is compiled annually. Typically, the ratings are compiled in May of any year with a follow up of some loans later in the year. The rating list is compiled based on a review of the participation loans that is subject to the same standards for asset review as the supervisory authorities would apply in examining an individual bank. The rating list, with individual write ups, is treated by the OCC as similar to an examination report and, consequently, is confidential.

A bank that charges-off a loan pursuant to a Shared National Credit Review is treated as charging-off a debt pursuant to a specific order within the meaning of that regulation.[146] However, a Shared National Credit Review is not sufficient to constitute a subsequent confirmation order. According to the IRS, a subsequent confirmation order confirms both the timing and the amount of the charge-off and gives the IRS assurance that no events have transpired between the time of the charge-off and the subsequent confirmation that would have caused the worthlessness of the debt. When a taxpayer charges-off a debt before receiving a Shared National Credit Review in the same taxable year, it is not entitled to the conclusive presumption of worthlessness. Nonetheless, the IRS has stated that a Shared National Credit Review is evidence of worthlessness that may be used to establish that the taxpayer properly deducted the amounts charged-off.

(b) Allocated Transfer Risk Reserve

A transfer of certain international loans to an Allocated Transfer Risk Reserve ("ATRR"), established and maintained under federal banking regulations, satisfies the requirement that the charge-off be "in obedience" to bank regulatory orders.[147] An ATRR is a separate reserve account established and maintained on the bank's accounting books pursuant to the International Lending Supervision Act of 1983.[148] According to that Act, the special reserve is required whenever the appropriate federal bank regulator determines that "the quality of such banking institution's assets has been impaired by a protracted inability of public or private borrowers in a foreign country to make payments on their external indebtedness . . . ."[149]

Under regulations issued by bank regulatory agencies, factors to be considered in determining whether an ATRR is required for any loan include whether

[146] TAM 9253003, September 22, 1992, issued Jan. 1, 1993.

[147] Rev. Rul. 92-14, 1992-1 C.B. 94, *amplifying and superseding* Rev. Rul. 84-94, 1984-1 C.B. 34.

[148] Domestic Housing and International Recovery and Financial Stability Act of 1983, Pub. L. No. 98-181, § 905, 97 Stat. 1153, 1279 (1983).

[149] *Id.;* § 905(a)(1)(A); *see also* 12 C.F.R. §§ 20.8, 211.42, 351.1 (2000) for regulations promulgated by federal banking agencies (Comptroller of the Currency, Board of Governors of the Federal Reserve System, Federal Deposit Insurance Corporation).

no definite prospects exist for the orderly restoration of debt service and whether:

1. The obligors have failed to make full interest payments on external indebtedness;
2. The obligors have failed to comply with the terms of any restructuring indebtedness; or
3. A foreign country has failed to comply with any International Monetary Fund or other suitable adjustment program.[150]

§ 10.4.4 The Conformity Election

(a) Background to Regulation

As with the historical presumption and the audit directives, the conformity election gives a bank greater certainty in the tax treatment of its bad debts by providing for a conclusive presumption of worthlessness based on the application of a single set of standards for both regulatory and tax purposes.[151] It was added to regulations following a Treasury Department study that found there to be sufficiently similar standards for worthlessness in federal regulatory guidelines and in Treasury regulations. It does not accept conformity merely between book accounting for loan losses and tax accounting.[152] Instead, the conformity is between regulatory classification and the tax classification of a debt.

The Treasury Department's study states:

> The breadth of circumstances taken into account in classifying commercial and real estate loans for regulatory purposes is comparable to the inquiry that would be appropriate for a finding of worthlessness for purposes of section 166. Although the classification of consumer installment loans and credit card plans depends on a single fact, length of delinquency, the unsecured (or as may be the case with consumer loans secured by household items, undersecured) nature of these loans may cause that single fact to be an adequate measure of worthlessness for tax purposes. In any event, the high volume of such loans and their comparatively low face value would make an in-depth inquiry into all relevant facts and circumstances a very burdensome task for the lending institution. In the absence of persuasive evidence, such as an unusually high recovery rate for such loans, that the automatic charge-off criteria for these types of high volume loans results in overstated losses, it is appropriate to permit the regulatory loss classification to determine the worthlessness of such debts for tax purposes.[153]

---

[150] By virtue of the renegotiation process, foreign loans are often saved from falling into default as to interest or principal. However, it is possible that a loan is "in default" if the borrower fails to remit foreign withholding tax receipts due the lender under the terms of the loan agreement. Although a default may be averted by renegotiation, a material change in the terms of a debt could constitute a taxable exchange. *See* discussion in Ch. 6, "Modified Debt."

[151] The election is not available to any non-bank members of the bank's consolidated group.

[152] The Attachment to the Industry Director Guidelines on the conformity election located in the Appendix at § A.21 appears to incorrectly suggest book/tax conformity instead of regulatory/tax conformity.

[153] *See Dept. of the Treasury, Report to the Congress on the Tax Treatment of Bad Debts by Financial Institutions* 19-24 (1991). *See also Federal Financial Institutions Examination Council, Policy Statement on Allowance for Loan and Lease Losses, Methodologies and Documentation for Banks and Savings Institutions,* (2001), which was designed to provide guidance on the design and implementation of allowance the loan and lease loss methodologies and supporting documentation practices. See also SEC Staff Accounting Bulletin: No. 102, 66 Fed. Reg. 36467 (July

The preamble to Treasury regulation § 1.166-2(d)(3), the regulation that implements the conformity election, states:

> The Treasury Department's study on the appropriate-criteria to be used in determining whether a debt is worthless for Federal income tax purposes concludes that the regulatory criteria governing the charge-off of debts by banks are sufficiently similar to the criteria for worthlessness under section 166 to make regulatory criteria and examination by the regulatory authorities an acceptable surrogate for an independent investigation by the Internal Revenue Service.[154]

The "regulatory criteria governing the charge-off of debts" has been modified on several occasions since the promulgation of the final conclusive presumption regulations. In 2004 the Uniform Agreement on the Classification of Assets and Appraisal of Securities Held by Banks and Thrifts that was in effect when the conclusive presumption regulations were adopted was amended.[155] This document outlines the standards that bank regulatory examiners are to apply when classifying "securities" during examinations.

The principal changes made by the revised agreement issued on June 15, 2004 include:

- Revising security classifications to ensure consistency with generally accepted accounting principles (GAAP); the loss classification applies when depreciation in a security is other than temporary.
- Eliminating the automatic classification of sub-investment-grade debt securities when a national bank has developed an accurate, robust, and documented credit risk management framework to analyze its securities holdings.
- Providing examiners the flexibility to depart from classifications implied by nationally recognized statistical rating organizations; examiners may classify an investment-grade security, or "pass" a non-investment-grade security, depending upon applicable facts and circumstances.
- Outlining expectations for the analysis and ongoing monitoring of non-rated securities.
- Eliminating the preferential classification treatment for municipal general obligations.

Whether a bank should make the conformity election will depend on several factors. If the bank has had its loan losses challenged on audit or suspects that they will be challenged, the election should be seriously considered. Moreover, if a bank has tax exposure from not including in income interest income on nonperforming loans, the conformity election will likely avoid an adjustment on

(Footnote Continued)

12, 2001), which expresses certain of the views of the staff of the SEC on the development, documentation, and application of a systematic methodology as required by Financial Reporting Release No. 28 for determining allowances for loan and lease losses in accordance with general accepted accounting principles.

[154] T.D. 8396, 1992-1 C.B. 95.

[155] The Uniform Agreement in effect when the 1991 conformity regulation was promulgated was first issued in 1979. OCC Banking Circular 127, dated April 26, 1991, was used to implement the 1979 Agreement.

audit.[156] However, if it is unlikely that this will occur, the potential problems associated with the election may dissuade some taxpayers from making the election. Moreover, a taxpayer that makes the election loses a degree of flexibility in its annual bad debt deduction.

(b) *Conclusive Presumption*

Under the Specific Order Method, a debt will be conclusively presumed to be worthless if the following five requirements are met:

1. The debt instrument is owned by a bank as defined in Code section 581;
2. An election is made to apply the conformity method;
3. The "express determination requirement" is met;
4. The debt is charged-off, in whole or in part, for regulatory purposes during the taxable year;
5. The charge-off results from either a specific order of the bank's federal or state supervisory authority or the charge-off corresponds to the bank's classification of the debt, in whole or in part, as a "loss asset."[157]

The IRS does not have the authority to question a bank's loan loss classification standards when a bank makes a conformity election and has received an express determination letter.[158]

(c) *Eligible Taxpayers*

For purposes of this presumption, a "bank" includes a bank defined in Code section 581, a foreign corporation, but only with respect to its loans that are effectively connected with its U.S. trade or business,[159] or a Farm Credit Institution.[160] The reference to Code section 581 has the effect of applying the provisions to thrifts as well as to commercial banks.

Although the regulations do not expressly so provide, a bank that determines its bad-debt deduction under the reserve method provided for in Code section 585 is entitled to make the conformity election.[161] The regulations providing for the conformity election were issued under Code section 166, not Code section 585, and no cross reference is contained in the regulations to banks that determine their loan loss deduction under the reserve method. This apparent oversight can be explained by a failure on the part of the Treasury Department to take into account the fact that the Tax Reform Act of 1986 repealed the provision that had been contained in Section 166(c) of the Internal Revenue Code of 1954, which allowed a deduction for a reasonable reserve addition.[162]

---

[156] Rev. Rul. 2007-32, 2007-1 C.B. 1278.

[157] Reg. § 1.166-2(d)(3). *See also* Temp. Reg. 1.166-2T. For insight on the application of the conformity election, *see* "Industry Director Guidelines on Auditing Bank Bad Debt Conformity Election" contained in the Appendix to this volume.

[158] CCA 200045030 (2000).

[159] I.R.C. § 864(c) (2000).

[160] Reg. § 1.166-2(d)(4)(I).

[161] FSA 200129003, July 20, 2001.

[162] The Tax Reform Act of 1986 repealed I.R.C. § 166(c) and shifted the allowance provision to I.R.C. §§ 585 and 593.

(d) *Historical Presumption Contrasted*

The first alternative under the conformity election is nearly identical to the historical presumption, discussed previously. However, it does not appear to explicitly embrace the confirmation letter component of that presumption. Yet, the more general language of the conformity election presumption, that the charge-off "results from a specific order," instead of the language in the Specific Order Method that it is "[i]n obedience to the specific orders," appears to indicate that the confirmation letter alternative is embraced by the conformity election.[163] Moreover, in a recent Field Service Advice, a confirmation letter appeared to satisfy the "specific order" requirement.[164]

The ordered charge-off requirement in the first alternative does not mandate that the order be in writing. In the Specific Order Method there is a writing requirement in respect of the confirmation letter but not the ordered charge-off alternative. Although the express determination letter (discussed below) must be obtained from the institution's federal regulator, an effective order (or confirmation letter) may be received from the institution's federal or state regulator.

(e) *Loss Asset Defined*

A "loss asset" is a debt (or portion thereof) that is assigned to a class that corresponds to a loss asset classification under standards set forth in the "Uniform Agreement on the Classification of Assets and Appraisal of Securities Held by Banks and Thrifts" or similar guidance issued by the Office of the Comptroller of the Currency, Federal Deposit Insurance Corporation, Federal Reserve Board, Farm Credit Administration, or Office of Thrift Supervision.[165]

The Office of the Comptroller of the Currency, along with the FDIC, Federal Reserve and Office of Thrift Supervision, promulgated the most recent version of the "Uniform Agreement on the Classification of Assets and Appraisal of Securities Held by Banks" in 2009. It provides that there are three classification units for assets in Bank and Thrift regulatory examinations: "substandard", "doubtful", and "loss".[166] A classification of "loss" is appropriate when the asset is considered uncollectible and of such little value that its continuance as a bankable asset is not warranted.[167] Once an asset has been classified, the quality of the asset/security must also be appraised by ranking it along a continuum ranging from "investment quality debt securit[y]" to "sub-investment quality debt securit[y] with 'other-than temporary impairment, including defaulted debt securities.'" The Uniform Agreement instructs examiners to rely on nationally recognized statistical ratings organizations ("NRSROs") in making their determinations as to

---

[163] As mentioned in the discussion of the historical presumption, confirmation letters are generally not provided by bank regulators.

[164] FSA 199912005, March 26, 1999.

[165] Reg. § 1.166-2(d)(4)(ii)(C). *See* Uniform Agreement in Appendix at § A.19.

[166] Uniform Agreement on the Classification of Assets and Appraisal of Securities Held by Banks, at 1, available at http://www.federalreserve.gov/board docs/srletters/2004/SR0409a1.pdf.

[167] *Id.* The Uniform Agreement goes on to provide, "This classification does not mean that the asset has absolutely no recovery or salvage value, but rather it is not practical or desirable to defer writing off this basically worthless asset even though partial recovery may be effected in the future. Amounts classified Loss should be promptly charged off." *See also* Comptroller of Currency, "Allowance for Loan and Lease Losses," Comptroller's Handbook 10, 19 (1996).

the quality of debt securities. Generally speaking, investment quality debt securities will be marketable obligations that are not speculative, and generally score in the four highest rating categories provided by NRSROs. Sub-investment quality debt securities are mainly speculative investments, including those that have been rated below the four highest rating categories.

The precursor to the current "Uniform Agreement on the Classification of Assets and Securities Held by Banks" was originally introduced by the Office of the Comptroller of the Currency in 1979 and was amended in 1991, 2004, and 2009.[168] When the regulatory conformity election was promulgated, the 1991 version of the Uniform Agreement was in effect.[169]

Under the 1991 Uniform Agreement, a bank was required to classify a debt instrument as a loss asset when the asset was "considered uncollectible and of such little value that [its] continuance as a bankable asset is not warranted."[170] A debt that is classified as a loss asset may still have recovery or salvage value, but it is not practicable for the bank to defer writing off the debt.[171]

The 2004 Uniform Agreement made several substantive changes to how debts are classified. It instructed banking regulatory examiners to use ratings published by nationally recognized statistical ratings organizations as a "proxy" for the supervisory classification definitions and it provided examiners with the discretion to depart from these ratings when classifying assets.[172] Most significantly, however, the 2004 Uniform Agreement required a creditor to assess whether a decline in value below the amortized cost of a security is a "temporary" or "other-than-temporary" impairment ("OTTI").[173] If the security has OTTI, the bank should recognize a loss equal to the full difference between the debt's fair value and its amortized cost.[174]

The 2009 amendments to the Uniform Agreement further refined the rules relating to OTTI by requiring banks to recognize the amount of OTTI related to the *credit* loss of a debt security in earnings and recognize the total OTTI related to all other factors in comprehensive income.[175]

---

[168] *See* Attachment to O.C.C. BC-127, 1979 WL 27069; Attachment to O.C.C. BC-127 (Rev.), 1991 WL 434633 (revising the 1979 Uniform Agreement); Attachment to O.C.C. Bulletin 2004-25; O.C.C. Bulletin 2009-11. The 1979 and 1991 agreements were substantially similar in most respects. This discussion will only concern the 1991 agreement, however, because the Treasury regulations base the Conclusive Presumptions on the 1991 agreement.

[169] The IRS incorrectly refers to this method as the "Book Conformity Method." *See* I.R.S. Notice 2013-35, 2013 WL 2156283. This method does not create conformity with book accounting, however. It would more appropriately be termed the "Regulatory Conformity Method."

[170] Attachment to O.C.C. BC-127 (Rev.), 1991 WL 434633. The three classification units are designated as "Substandard," "Doubtful," and "Loss." *Id.*

[171] *Id.*

[172] Attachment to O.C.C. Bulletin 2004-25. It is unclear whether examiners were exercising discretion before the 2004 Bulletin was issued. The 2004 Agreement does not appear to have changed the classification definitions, it simply provided examiners with considerable discretion in classifying assets.

[173] *Id.* "Impairment" is the amount by which amortized cost exceeds fair value. *Id.*

[174] *Id.* The 2004 Agreement appears to only apply to debt securities. The Agreement exclusively uses the words "debt securities" and not "loans" or "debt instruments." Additionally, the subject line of the Bulletin stated "Classification of Securities," further indicating that the changes in the 2004 Agreement may only apply to debt securities, not other debt instruments.

[175] O.C.C. Bulletin 2009-11. Generally, OTTI "related to all other factors" includes interest rate fluctuations and other non-credit related components

In Notice 2013-35, the I.R.S. expressed concern that changes in banking regulatory loss classification standards that have occurred since the adoption of the 1991 conformity regulations have undermined the initial intention of the regulations.[176]

The phrase "or similar guidance" contained in the Treasury regulation § 1.166-2(d)(3) may include the supervisory authority's manuals, handbooks and guidebooks as they relate to the loan loss classification standards of high volume consumer installment loans and credit card plans when those documents include a standard similar to the "Uniform Agreement on the Classification of Assets and Securities Held by Banks" and the documents require the standard apply in a uniform manner. The loss standards in the handbook for examiners employed by the Comptroller of the Currency, as well as the handbooks for examiners employed by the Office of Thrift Supervision, Federal Reserve Board, and Federal Deposit Insurance Corporation currently satisfy the requirements in Treasury regulation § 1.166-2(d)(3) (ii)(C). The Comptroller of the Currency Handbook for National Bank Examiners provides specific regulatory criteria for determining whether a loan should be classified as a loss asset.

High-volume loans, such as consumer installment loans, credit card plans, and check credit plans are subject to automatic charge-off procedures. The conclusive presumption of worthlessness standard can apply to such loans that are classified as a regulatory loss asset after the applicable period passes.[177] Consumer installment paper that is delinquent 120 days or more and credit card debt that is delinquent 180 days or more are considered loss assets for regulatory purposes.[178]

To the extent that interest on a loan placed in nonaccrual status is reversed from book income or not accrued on the books, it may never be classified as a "loss" asset. Moreover, if a debt is significantly modified, the deemed charge-off that may result would probably not qualify as a "loss" asset.[179] However, as

(Footnote Continued)

affecting market value. The 2009 Agreement also appears to only apply to debt securities. The Bulletin sought to alert bankers to recent guidance released by the Financial Accounting Standards Board that "amend[ed] the existing OTTI guidance in U.S. generally accepted accounting principles (GAAP) for debt securities." *Id.* (emphasis added).

[176] *See* I.R.S. Notice 2013-35. ""[T]he standards and processes applied by a regulator must result in loan classifications that are 'similar enough to the criteria for worthlessness under section 166 to make regulatory criteria and examination by regulatory authorities an acceptable surrogate for independent investigation by the Internal Revenue Service.'" *Id.* (citations omitted). The IRS requested comments on the Conclusive Presumption regulations in response to the changes following the 1991 Uniform Agreement. In that Notice the IRS also requested comment on what entities should be considered "other corporations" for purposes of this regulation. A previous IRS directive advised examiners not to challenge an insurance company's bad debt deduction on mortgage backed securities if the company met certain conditions. *See* I.R.S. Large Business & International Division, Control No. LB&I-4-0721-009 (July 30, 2012).

[177] CCA 200045030, September 27, 2000, issued Nov. 9, 2000.

[178] Comptroller of the Currency, Handbook for National Examiners—Commercial, International §§ 209.1, 211.1, 212.1 (1990). These provisions provide for exceptions to the automatic charge-off procedure when significant amounts are involved and the bank can demonstrate that repayment will be made irrespective of delinquency status. Alternatively, these procedures do not preclude the classification of assets delinquent for a lesser period when classification is warranted. Although citations are to the OCC Handbook, comparable standards apply to institutions supervised by the FRB, the FDIC, and the OTS.

[179] Of course, if the charge-off were "ordered," a conclusive presumption would apply.

discussed below, if the conformity election is made, the IRS will permit interest on loans in a nonperforming status to be treated as a loss asset.[180]

Because only loans that are classified as "loss assets" may be deductible, if a bank charges-off on its accounting books a portion of a loan which is classified as "doubtful" or "substandard," no deduction would appear to be allowed for such charge-off under the conformity method.[181] The act of charging-off the loan does not satisfy the requirement that the loan be classified as a "loss asset." The Treasury Department considered, but rejected, extending the conformity presumption to loans that are classified as substandard or doubtful, and in a recent Field Service Advisory this position was reaffirmed.[182] Thus, the bank must ensure that a loan is classified as "loss" to the extent of the charge-off.

(f) Classifying Loans as Loss Assets

The IRS has ruled that there are several procedures that are permitted to be used by a bank to classify loans (or portions of loans) as loss assets.[183] Among the acceptable procedures are these: an officer or employee may record or memorialize on a form the determination that a loan (or loan portion) is a loss asset; loan or credit committee reports or internal credit rating reports also can demonstrate that a loan has been classified as a loss asset; and, if officers and employees are authorized to charge off loans (or loan portions) only if the loans (or loan portions) are loss assets, then the charge-offs of the loans (or loan portions) demonstrate that the loans (or loan portions) have been classified as loss assets. Thus, if under a resolution adopted by a bank's board of directors, the bank's officers and employees are authorized to charge-off loans (or portions of loans) only when the charge-off is required under the loan loss classification standards issued by the bank's supervisory authority, loans so charged-off will be treated as loss assets for purposes of the conformity election, regardless of whether the bank's officers and employees take any additional steps to record or memorialize the charge-offs.

If loans are erroneously classified as loss assets by the bank's officers and employees, the erroneous classification may be overlooked by the IRS.[184] Thus, if a bank charged off for regulatory purposes certain credit card debts that were not required to be charged off under applicable regulatory loan loss standards, but the bank otherwise charged off only loans required to be charged off under the loan loss standards, the conclusive presumption of worthlessness will apply to the credit card debts that the bank erroneously charged off for regulatory purposes during the taxable year income tax return.[185]

---

[180] Rev. Rul. 2007-32, 2007-21 I.R.B. 1278.

[181] *See* preamble to final regulations, 57 Fed. Reg. 6291 (Feb. 24, 1992); *See also* preamble to final regulations adopted on October 18, 1993, 58 Fed. Reg. 53656 (Oct. 18, 1993). *See also* FSA 199912005, March 26, 1999.

[182] *See* § 10.3.2.

[183] Rev. Rul. 2001-59, 2001-2 C.B. 585. For elaboration of the Rev. Rul. 2001-59, *see* Industry Director Guidelines on Auditing Bank Bad Debt Conformity Election and Attachment in Appendix at § § A.20 and A.21.

[184] CCA 200045030 (2000).

[185] Rev. Rul. 2001-59, Holding 2; 2001-51 I.R.B. 585, 586.

(g) Charge-Off

The general principles associated with what constitutes a charge-off should be applicable to the conformity method.[186] In addition, regulations do provide that the term "charge-off" includes a specific allowance for loan losses in the amount of 100 percent of debts classified by the Office of Thrift Supervision as "loss."[187] The IRS also has ruled that if a bank makes the conformity election the reversal of interest on loans in a nonperforming status, referred to as the accrued interest receivable, constitutes a charge-off of the interest receivable as a loss asset for purposes of § 1.166-2(d)(3)(ii)(C).[188] The ruling also provides that, if a bank stops the accrual of interest on nonperforming loans, the bank will be treated as recognizing the accrued interest as income and immediately charging-off the uncollected accrued interest receivable as a loss asset.

Treasury regulations appear to require that the conformity method will apply only if a debt is charged-off, either pursuant to a specific order from a bank regulator or because the loan was classified as a "loss asset" under regulatory rules. This requirement goes beyond the language of Code section 166(a), which imposes a charge-off requirement only when debts are partially worthless. The so called automatic charge-off procedure described in Chief Counsel Advice 200045039 seems to ameliorate the requirement, at least for wholly worthless installment and credit card loans. Furthermore, the regulations appear to be careful not to state that the required charge-off is required for book accounting purposes. In fact, they describe the required charge-off as one that is "for regulatory purposes."[189]

Because the election will have no effect on debts not subject to regulatory loss classification standards or that have been totally charged-off prior to the year the conformity election is effective, the rigidity of the election may be avoided in certain situations. Regulation 1.166-2(d) provides:

> With respect to debts that are not subject to regulatory loss classification standards or that have been totally charged off prior to the year [the conformity election was made], bad debt deductions are determined under the general rules of section 166.[190]

(h) Making the Election

The conformity election is a bank-by-bank election. It need not be made by all "bank" members in an affiliated group if one member wishes to make the election. Thus, a thrift or a commercial bank member may make the election while another commercial bank or thrift, which is a member of the same affiliated group, may choose not to make the election. The election constitutes the adoption of a method of accounting, but advanced permission to make the election is automatically granted if an election has not been previously made. Consent will not be automatically granted if a previous election has been revoked. No Code section 481(a) adjustments are required or permitted, because

---

186 *See* discussion above.

187 Reg. § 1.166-2(d)(4)(ii).

188 Rev. Rul. 2007-32, 2007-1 C.B. 1278.

189 Reg. § 1.166-2(d)(2)(3)(ii)(B).

190 Reg. § 1.166-2(d)(3)(iii)(B)(3).

amounts will not be duplicated or omitted by reason of the accounting method change.[191]

For all banks besides new banks, the conformity election is made by attaching a completed Form 3115 to the bank's timely filed return. The bank must also satisfy the express determination requirement for the year of election. The election is made by a new bank when it adopts its overall method of accounting by attaching a statement to its return, which provides that the express determination requirement is satisfied for the year of the election.

*(i) **Express Determination Requirement***

To satisfy the express determination requirement, the bank's federal supervisory authority must expressly determine that the bank maintains and applies loan loss classification standards consistent with regulatory standards.[192] This requirement is satisfied only if, in connection with the supervisor's most recent examination involving the bank's loan review process, a signed and dated letter is obtained from the examiner in charge that contains the following statement:

> In connection with the most recent examination of [NAME OF BANK], by [NAME OF SUPERVISORY AUTHORITY], as of [EXAMINATION DATE], we reviewed the institution's loan review process as it relates to loan charge-offs. Based on our review, we concluded that the bank, as of that date, maintained and applied loan review and loss classification standards that were consistent with regulatory standards regarding loan charge-offs.
>
> This statement is made on the basis of a review that was conducted in accordance with our normal examination procedures and criteria, including sampling of loans in accordance with those procedures and criteria. It does not in any way limit or preclude any formal or informal supervisory action (including enforcement actions) by this supervisory authority relating to the institution's loan review process or the level at which it maintains its allowance for loan and lease losses.[193]

Final regulations permitting the conformity election clarified the scope of the express determination requirement contained in earlier proposed regulations.[194] Also accompanying the final regulations was a revenue procedure that clarified an earlier revenue procedure which set forth the required language for the express determination letter.[195]

---

[191] Reg. § 1.166-2(d)(3)(iii)(B).

[192] The federal supervisory authority is as follows: the Office of the Comptroller of the Currency for national banks; the Federal Deposit Insurance Corporation for state banks; the Federal Reserve Board for foreign banks; and the Office of Thrift Supervision for thrifts.

[193] Rev. Proc. 92-84, 1992-2 C.B. 489, *modifying and superseding* Rev. Proc. 92-18, 1992-1 C.B. 684. Regulations promulgated on October 15, 1993, amended an earlier version of final Reg. § 1.166-2(d)(3) to require that a bank's supervisory authority expressly determine that the bank maintains and applies "loan loss classification standards," rather than "loan review and loss classification standards" that are consistent with regulatory standards.

[194] Regulations granting the conformity election were proposed on May 29, 1991. 56 Fed. Reg. 24154 (May 29, 1991). Those regulations were finally adopted on February 24, 1992. 57 Fed. Reg. 6291 (Feb. 24, 1992). Temporary regulations clarifying the scope of the express determination letter and extending the transitional period were issued on October 2, 1992. 57 Fed. Reg. 45568 (Oct. 2, 1992). The Temporary regulations were modified and adopted on October 18, 1993. 58 Fed. Reg. 53656 (Oct. 18, 1993).

[195] Rev. Proc. 92-84, 1992-2 C.B. 489 *modifying and superseding* Rev. Proc. 92-18, 1992-1 C.B. 684. Concurrent with the release of the final regulations was a notice which allowed certain banks, on an amended return for a taxable year ending on or after December 31, 1991, to elect to use the conform-

Once the letter is obtained, it will satisfy the express determination requirement for all tax years until the bank's next federal regulatory examination. An immaterial individual deviation from regulatory standards will not preclude a finding that a bank maintains and applies loan classification standards that are consistent with regulatory standards.[196]

For taxable years ending before completion of the first examination of the bank by its supervisory authority and ending after 1991 that involve the bank's loan review process, the express determination requirement is met if the Form 3115 *or* the statement includes a declaration that the bank maintains and applies loan classification standards that are consistent with the regulatory standards of its appropriate federal banking supervisor.[197]

(j) Revoking the Election

The conformity election may be revoked in three ways:

1. Automatically;[198]
2. By the IRS;[199] or
3. Voluntarily.[200]

In general, if a bank does not obtain an express determination letter each time it is examined by its primary federal bank regulator, the election is automatically revoked as of the beginning of the taxable year of the election or, if later, the earliest taxable year that tax may be assessed.[201] When a letter is issued, it covers all tax years until the next federal supervisory examination of the bank's loan review process.[202]

> **Example:** Thrift makes a conformity election on a timely filed return for its tax year 19X1. It is not examined by the Office of Thrift Supervision until 19X3, when it obtains an express determination letter. When the thrift was next examined, in 19X5, it did not receive an express determination letter. The conformity election is effective for 19X1 through 19X4. The election is automatically revoked in 19X5.

A bank which has its method of accounting changed under this automatic revocation rule must attach a completed Form 3115 to its return for the year of revocation on which form is typed or legibly printed on the top of the first page the following words: "REVOCATION OF § 1.166-2(d)(3) ELECTION."[203] If the original return has been filed for the year of revocation, an amended return must

(Footnote Continued)

ity method of accounting. Notice 93-50, 1993-2 C.B. 336. The final regulations apply generally to taxable years ending on or after December 31, 1991.

[196] *See* preamble to Reg. § 1.166-2(d)(3), 58 Fed. Reg. 53656 (Oct. 18, 1993).

[197] Notice 93-50, 1993-2 C.B. 336.

[198] Reg. § 1.166-2(d)(3)(iv)(C).

[199] Reg. § 1.166-2(d)(3)(iv)(D).

[200] Reg. § 1.166-2(d)(3)(iv)(E).

[201] The "express determination letter" must be obtained in connection with the first examination involving the bank's loan review process that occurs after October 1, 1992, if a bank makes an election under a transitional rule. In all other situations, the bank must obtain the letter before making a valid election. I.R.C. § 6501 provides, in general, that tax may be assessed within three years of the due date, including extensions, of a return.

[202] Reg. § 1.166-2(d)(3)(iv)(C)(2).

[203] Reg. § 1.166-2(d)(3)(iv)(C)(4).

be filed for that year.[204] Amended returns also must be filed for any intervening years subsequent to the year of revocation for which original returns have been filed. If this procedure is followed, the bank will be deemed to receive the consent of the Commissioner to change its method of accounting for bad debts from the conformity election presumption to the general rule of the historical presumption.[205]

The Commissioner *may* revoke the conformity election if the bank fails to follow the method or if the bank has taken charge-offs and deductions substantially in excess of those warranted by either reasonable business judgment or regulatory standards of the bank's supervisor. If the Commissioner revokes the election, the revocation is effective at the beginning of the taxable year for which the Commissioner determines the bank's violation occurred.[206]

A bank may voluntarily revoke the conformity election if the bank applies for, and receives, consent to revoke from the Commissioner. The application is made on a timely filed Form 3115 on which is typed or legibly printed on the top of page one the following words: "REVOCATION OF § 1.166-2(d)(3) ELECTION."[207] Generally, the voluntary revocation is effective for the taxable year in which the Form 3115 is filed. However, if the bank has had its election automatically revoked and has not changed its method in accordance with the requirements applicable to automatic changes, the voluntary change is effective when the automatic change is effective.[208]

(k) Consequences of Revocation

Regulation section 1.166-2(d)(3) provides that the conformity election may be revoked "if the Commissioner determines that a bank has taken charge-offs and deductions that, under all facts and circumstances existing at the time, were substantially in excess of those warranted by the exercise of reasonable business judgement in applying the regulatory standards of the bank's supervisory authority . . . ." Furthermore, an examining agent may consider revoking the election if the taxpayer takes deductions for bad debt on loans that have not been classified as loss assets and charged off for regulatory purposes in the same tax year.[209] If the taxpayer is found not to be in compliance with the regulations because of the taxpayer's intentional improper use of the conformity method, the IRS believes that revocation is the sole remedy. This position appears to be more severe than the revocation rule that is expressed in the regulations. Regulation section 1.166-2(d)(3)(ii)(B) provides that "[a] pattern of charge-offs in the wrong year, however, *may* result in revocation of the bank's election by the Commissioner . . . ." [Emphasis added.]

In other circumstances, such as when a bank has inadvertently treated a very small number of loans as loss assets that, in fact, were not classified and charged

---

[204] *Id.*

[205] Reg. § 1.166-2(d)(3)(iv)(C)(3).

[206] Reg. § 1.166-2(d)(3)(iv)(D).

[207] Reg. § 1.166-2(d)(3)(iv)(E). Automatic consent is not granted to revoke the election.

[208] Reg. § 1.166-2(d)(3)(iv)(E).

[209] FSA 200018017, January 13, 2000, issued May 5, 2000. *See also* Reg. § 1.166-3(d)(iv)(D).

off that way, the IRS believes that it may be appropriate to consider making a correction to the conformity method. Moreover, the IRS has taken the position that when a bank that claimed a bad debt deduction for all loans charged to a specific allowance and classified as substandard, doubtful, or loss, no deduction was allowable for the categories other than for the loss loans.[210] Presumably, the IRS did not find that there was intentional improper use of the conformity method.

If the conformity election is revoked, there is some uncertainty surrounding the impact on the bank. Regulation section 1.166-2(d)(3)(iv)(A) and (B) provide that revocation of an election constitutes a change in method of accounting, and the change does not require or permit Section 481 adjustments. Furthermore, there is no change in the tax basis of the banks existing loan, and bad debt deductions in the year of change and thereafter are determined under the "new method." It is clear that the IRS believes that the accounting method change required by the revocation is accomplished on a cutoff basis as of the first day of the earliest open year under examination. However, because of the possibility of duplication or omission of deductions, there may have to be some type of Code section 481 adjustment.

Beyond this guidance, the effect of revocation is not explicitly stated. Of course, without a valid conformity election in place, the taxpayer would be unable to avail itself of the conclusive presumption of worthlessness that accompanies the conformity election. Yet, it seems that the historical conclusive presumption of worthlessness in Regulation section 1.166-2(d)(1) may be available to the taxpayer. The historical conclusive presumption may, itself, be of no use because to apply it requires either an ordered charge-off or a confirmation letter. Neither of these criteria is likely to be satisfied in most situations. The involuntary charge-off rule of Regulation section 1.166-2(d)(2), however, is likely to be available. Unfortunately, that rule does not provide a bank with a conclusive presumption of worthlessness, but it may grant some flexibility in the year in which a bad debt deduction may be deducted.

Even without a conclusive presumption of worthlessness, it is conceivable that, for some taxpayers under audit, the revocation may have less dire consequences than if the IRS kept the election in place but disallowed the deduction for loans not classified as loss assets. Thus, if the taxpayer is able to substantiate the worthlessness of the loans classified as doubtful or substandard, claimed deductions should be allowed despite the loss of the conclusive presumption of worthlessness.

For loans properly placed in the loss category, the IRS will probably not be successful in challenging bad debt deductions even without a conclusive presumption of worthlessness. This assumes the taxpayer can demonstrate actual, partial or complete worthlessness. Statistical sampling should be helpful. Of course, taxpayers should maintain adequate books and records to substantiate

[210] FSA 199912005, December 11, 1998, issued Mar. 26, 1999.

worthlessness. In addition to losing the deduction, failure to maintain adequate books and records may subject the taxpayer to understatement penalties.

§10.4.5 Rebutting Conclusive Presumption

Because the IRS can claim that the taxpayer has taken charge-offs substantially in excess of those warranted by reasonable business judgment, the conclusiveness of the presumption is in question.[211] Moreover, courts are sometimes unwilling to rigidly adhere to the "conclusive" presumption of worthlessness contained in the regulations. It has been held that the presumption of worthlessness may be subordinate to the Code section 166 provision requiring "worthlessness" before a bad-debt deduction is allowed.[212]

In the situation of a loan that is classified under federal bank regulatory standards as "other real estate," the IRS has ruled that there is no conclusive presumption of worthlessness when the amount that the Comptroller of the Currency requires to be charged-off is not based on the bad-debt criteria of Code section 166.[213] Thus, it is possible that real estate acquired by a thrift in satisfaction of a defaulted debt was also subject to this treatment prior to the repeal of the special thrift foreclosure rules contained in Code section 595. Although Code section 595(b) provided that such property shall have the same characteristics as the underlying loan for purposes of Code sections 166 and 1221, the IRS's position on "other real estate" owned that is in fact a loan may affect the Code section 595(b) characterization for purposes of Code section 166.

§10.5 Involuntary Charge-Off

The statutory requirement that a bad debt deduction be allowed "not in excess of the part charged-off within the taxable year" has been modified by regulations.[214] In what is referred to as the involuntary charge-off rule, taxpayers are given the flexibility of deducting in a taxable year, as a partially worthless bad debt, an amount charged-off in a prior taxable year.[215] However, the conclusive presumption of worthlessness applies only to debts that are deducted in the same taxable year that the charge-off is taken. Thus, if the deduction and charge-

[211] In the "Explanation of Provisions" accompanying the proposed regulations under I.R.C. §166 the IRS stated, "This rule is designed to limit the application of the conclusive presumption to debts that generally would be worthless under general tax principles." 56 Fed. Reg. 24154 (May 29, 1991). The aggressiveness of bank examiners varies from time to time. During the early 1990s, the Office of the Comptroller of the Currency required banks to establish reserves with respect to loans to certain borrowers regardless of whether the loan was in default. What appeared to guide regulators was the general economic health of the segment of the industry in which the borrower was a member. Thus, performing loans to real estate developers in certain areas of the country were viewed as doubtful of collection. The IRS may refuse to accept the application of the presumption of worthlessness to loans classified as loss assets or charged-off under such policy.

[212] *Central National Bank of Richmond v. Commissioner*, 1 T.C. 244, Dec. 12,905 (1942). In this case, the court was construing an earlier version of I.R.C. §166(a), which required, as a condition to a deduction, that a debt "becomes worthless within the taxable year." Section (k) of the Revenue Act of 1938 was amended by Section 124 of the Revenue Act of 1942. *Id.* at 249.

[213] Rev. Rul. 84-95, 1984-2 C.B. 53.

[214] Reg. §1.166-2(d).

[215] The Preamble to Prop. Reg. § 1.475(a) states: "In addition, computing the mark-to-market adjustment as if the debt's basis had been adjusted to reflect worthlessness preserves a taxpayer's ability to postpone claiming a deduction for partial worthlessness until the debt becomes wholly worthless." 60 FR 397-01.

off do not occur in the same taxable year, the burden of proving worthlessness falls on the taxpayer. However, a taxpayer does not have the flexibility to retroactively change the year in which it deducted a partially worthless debt in order to increase its loan basis in a subsequent year if the taxpayer already claimed a deduction on its original return for the earlier year.[216]

In accordance with the involuntary charge-off rule, a deduction is allowed for a partially worthless bad debt in a year subsequent to the charge-off year if the earlier charge-off is considered "involuntary." However, even in this situation no deduction is allowed in a year if the debt did not become worthless, in whole or in part, in the subsequent year.[217] The involuntary charge-off rule appears to have no application to nonbank taxpayers who, apparently, may not deduct partially worthless bad debts in excess of the amount charged-off during the taxable year.[218]

A charge-off will be considered "involuntary" with respect to wholly worthless bad debts only if the taxpayer establishes that the debt became wholly worthless in the later taxable year in which the deduction is claimed.[219] In the case of a partially worthless bad debt, the taxpayer must establish that it became partially worthless subsequent to the taxable year in which the involuntary charge-off occurred, and to the extent that the deduction exceeds the amount charged-off in the earlier year, a charge-off must take place in the deduction year.[220]

> **Example:** Assume that a debtor declared bankruptcy on February 12, 19X7. In obedience to a regulator's order, Bank A charged-off $3,000 of the $5,000 loan on December 31, 19X6 but took no deduction for the tax year then ended. Assuming that the bankruptcy was sufficient for the bank to establish that the debt became worthless in 19X7, a $5,000 deduction in 19X7 would be allowed if Bank A charges-off $2,000, the amount by which the deduction ($5,000) exceeds the amount charged-off in the earlier year ($3,000). The earlier year's charge-off would be considered "involuntary."

There is some uncertainty concerning the application of the involuntary charge-off rule when a bank deducts in a year following the initial charge-off year an amount which includes that portion of the debt which became worthless in the initial charge-off year. Assuming the facts of the immediately preceding example, except that it is clear that the loan became partially worthless in 19X6 to the extent of $3,000, the issue is whether the deduction for the 19X6 worthlessness may be deferred at the bank's option until 19X7.[221]

---

[216] FSA 200024004.

[217] *Malden Trust Co. v. Commissioner*, 39 B.T.A. 190, Dec. 10,574, (1939) *aff'd*, 40-1 U.S.T.C. ¶9353, 110 F.2d 751 (1st Cir. 1940).

[218] Reg. §1.166-3(a)(2). *See also Denver and Rio Grande Western R.R. Co. v. Commissioner*, 32 T.C. 43, Dec. 23,537 (1959), *acq.*, 1959-2 C.B. 3, *aff'd*, 60-2 U.S.T.C. ¶9540, 279 F.2d 368 (10th Cir. 1960).

[219] Reg. §1.166-2(d)(2)(I).

[220] Reg. §1.166-2(d)(2)(ii); *Keller v. Commissioner*, 29 T.C.M. 369 (1970), Dec. 30,043(M), T.C. Memo. 1970-079.

[221] In the preamble to Prop. Reg. §1.475(a), it is stated: "Computing the mark-to-market adjustment as if the debt's basis had been adjusted to reflect worthlessness preserves a taxpayer's ability to postpone claiming a deduction for partial worthlessness until the debt becomes wholly worthless." 60 Fed. Reg. 397 (Jan. 4, 1995).

The involuntary charge-off rule appears to be designed to afford taxpayers some flexibility to defer bad-debt deductions, especially taxpayers on the specific charge-off method. The description in regulations of the rule as an "involuntary" charge-off rule suggests that the charge-off would not be taken but for the order from a bank regulator. Presumably, the taxpayer determines that the charge-off was not warranted and, thus, the deduction was not appropriate in the year the charge-off was taken on the books. This interpretation is consistent with the proviso in the regulations that a deduction is allowed in the subsequent year in which the taxpayer establishes that the debt becomes partially or wholly worthless, as the case may be.[222]

§ 10.6 Recoveries

Any amount attributable to the recovery of an amount that resulted in the reduction of taxes in an earlier year must be taken into income in the year of recovery.[223] Recoveries during the taxable year of any portion of a bad debt previously charged-off and deducted by a taxpayer using the direct charge-off method are includible in gross income in the recovery year.[224] A bank using the reserve method would credit bad debt recoveries to the loan loss reserve.

However, if an amount is received on a debt that has been partially or wholly charged-off and there is interest outstanding on the debt, it is possible that the amount received will first be treated as interest income to the extent of the unpaid interest. Regulation section 1.446–2(e) provides: "[E]ach payment under a loan (other than payments of additional interest or similar charges provided with respect to amounts that are not paid when due) is treated as a payment of interest to the extent of the accrued and unpaid interest . . . ." This interest characterization rule applies to all payments made on a loan regardless of whether the uncollected accrued interest was not previously recognized as income or whether the uncollected accrued interest was previously recognized as income and subsequently deducted as a worthless debt under the taxpayer's method of accounting.[225]

For a bank or thrift employing the Code section 585 experience method for computing bad-debt deductions, crediting recoveries to the reserve will usually have the effect of reducing the tax deduction in the recovery year. Further, it will cause the taxpayer's experience factor to be reduced, which will usually result in smaller tax deductions in subsequent years. A thrift that employed the percentage of taxable income method would not adjust taxable income in the recovery year.

---

[222] Reg. § 1.166-2(d)(2). The author understands that the IRS accepts the more flexible approach.

[223] I.R.C. § 111 (2000). *See also* Corlew, *The Tax Benefit Rule, Claim of Right Restorations, and Annual Accounting: A Cure for the Inconsistencies*, 21 Vand. L. Rev. 995 (1968); Plumb, *The Tax Benefit Rule Today*, 57 Harv. L. Rev. 129 (1943).

[224] Reg. § 1.166-1(f); *see also Estate of William H. Block v. Commissioner*, 39 B.T.A. 338, Dec. 10,585 (1939). For example, recovery income was recognized by a bank when a charged-off note deducted as a charitable contribution was later collected by the charitable donee of the note. *First Wisconsin Bankshares Corp. v. United States*, 74-1 U.S.T.C. ¶ 9164, 369 F. Supp. 1034 (D. Wisc. 1973). *See also Allen v. Trust Co. of Georgia*, 50-1 U.S.T.C. ¶ 9213, 180 F.2d 527 (5th Cir. 1950); *Continental Illinois National Bank & Trust Co. of Chicago v. Commissioner*, 69 T.C. 357 (1977), Dec. 34,772, *acq.*, 1978-2 C.B.1

[225] Rev. Rul. 2007-32, 2007-21 I.R.B. 1278.

An exclusion from income is provided for items "attributable to the recovery during the taxable year of any amount deducted in any prior taxable year to the extent such amount did not reduce income subject to tax."[226] This rule "permits the exclusion of the recovered item from income so long as its initial use as a deduction did not provide a tax savings . . . ."[227] Thus, where a taxpayer recovers previously deducted bad debts but such deductions did not result in a tax benefit, it is entitled to exclude the recoveries from gross income.[228] This could occur when the charge-off occurred during a year when a thrift employed the percentage of taxable income method. Moreover, there is no taxable recovery of an item if, with respect to the item in a prior year, a deduction was not taken because of a mistake.[229] Similarly, an erroneous deduction improperly allowed that gives rise to a tax benefit in a prior year will not give rise to income in a subsequent year when the item is recovered.[230]

The burden of proof is on the taxpayer to show that the prior allowance of a bad-debt deduction did not result in a tax benefit.[231] In the absence of a specific statutory provision to the contrary, courts have held that, in order to be entitled to the recovery exclusion, the debt must be charged-off and recovered by the same entity.[232]

Reserve Methods

§ 10.7 Allowable Reserve Methods

Historically, most banks have employed the reserve method of accounting for loan losses because of the flexibility it afforded and because allowable tax deductions often exceeded the amount that would otherwise be allowable under the specific charge-off method. The Tax Reform Act of 1986 amended the Code to prohibit large commercial banks from using the reserve method.[233] Moreover, it reduced the generosity traditionally afforded to the reserve method available to thrifts, and it required those commercial banks that were permitted to continue to use the reserve method to base their reserve additions on actual experience. Amendments to the Code effective in 1988 eliminated the percentage of eligible loans method previously available for those banks permitted to use the reserve method. The Small Business and Job Protection Act of 1996 repealed the special reserve addition rules available to thrifts, with the consequence that thrifts will receive the same treatment for loan losses as commercial banks.[234]

---

[226] I.R.C. § 111(a) (2000); Reg. § 1.111-1.

[227] *Alice Phelan Sullivan Corp. v. United States*, 67-2 U.S.T.C. ¶ 9570, 381 F.2d 399 (Ct. Cl. 1967); *see also* Bittker and Kanner, *The Tax Benefit Rule*, 26 UCLA L. Rev. 265 (1978).

[228] *Fairbanks, Morse & Co. v. Harrison*, 46-1 U.S.T.C. ¶ 9217, 63 F. Supp. 495 (D.C. Ill. 1946).

[229] *First National Bank v. Commissioner*, 55-1 U.S.T.C. ¶ 9448, 221 F.2d 959 (2d Cir. 1955), *cert. denied*, 350 U.S. 887 (1955).

[230] *Streckfus Steamers, Inc. v. Commissioner*, 19 T.C. 1, Dec. 19,234 (1952).

[231] *Citizens National Bank & Trust Co. v. Commissioner*, 4 T.C.M. 703, Dec. 14,657(M) (1945).

[232] *First National Bank in Houston v. Scofield*, 53-1 U.S.T.C. ¶ 9186, 201 F.2d 219 (5th Cir. 1953); *National Bank of Commerce of Seattle v. Commissioner*, 12 T.C. 717, Dec. 16,950 (1949). Note that I.R.C. § 381(c)(12) provides an exception to this general rule. It allows the carryover of bad debts to a successor entity under limited circumstances.

[233] Tax Reform Act of 1986, Pub. L. No. 99-514, 100 Stat. 2085 (1986).

[234] The Small Business and Job Protection Act of 1996, Pub. L. No. 104-188, § 1616, 110 Stat. 1755, 1854 (1996).

§ 10.7.1 Electing a Reserve Method

(a) Elective Status

A plain reading of Code section 585(a) may suggest that the reserve method of accounting for loan losses is mandatory for all banks, except large banks, who must use the specific charge-off method. However, both the House and the Conference Committee Reports under the Tax Reform Act of 1986 clarify the elective status of Code section 585. The House Report states, "The committee seeks to balance these concerns by providing for the continued *availability* of reserves for bad debts for smaller banks, *as under present law,* while *requiring* larger banks to compute their losses from bad debts using the specific charge-off method."[235] [Emphasis added.] Moreover, in taxable years after the general repeal of the reserve method, the IRS has granted permission to commercial banks to change their method of accounting from the reserve method of Code section 585 to the Code section 166 specific charge-off method.

(b) Binding Effect of Election

Regulations have been promulgated under the 1954 Code section 166(c) that set forth the rules for electing the reserve method.[236] For taxable years beginning on or after January 1, 1987, these regulations have been supplemented by regulations issued under Code section 585, which deal with the treatment and the accounting for reserves.[237] Under the Code section 166 regulations, once an election is made to employ the reserve method, it is binding until permission to change is granted by the Commissioner. The election must be made on the income tax return for the first taxable year for which the bank is entitled to a bad-debt deduction.[238] However, the Sixth Circuit Court of Appeals has held that a savings and loan association's notation on a return that it elected to charge-off bad debts as they occurred was not binding on the taxpayer.[239] The court stated that the "election initially made was done in error." It pointed to the fact that the bank experienced no actual bad debts prior to the years for which the reserve method was employed.

(c) Special Procedure to Elect Reserve Method

As a general rule, the procedures set forth in Code section 446(e) and the regulations thereunder must be followed in order to request permission to change methods of accounting for bad debts.[240] However, the IRS has promulgated a special rule for changing from the specific charge-off method to the reserve method of accounting for bad debts.[241] This procedure overrides the general rule of Code section 446, and it is the exclusive procedure for effectuating the changes. If the provisions of the revenue procedure are followed, the consent of the Commissioner to change the method of accounting for loan losses will be deemed to have been given.

---

[235] H.R. Rep. No. 99-426 at 577 (1985).

[236] Reg. § 1.166-1(b).

[237] Reg. § 1.585-3(b).

[238] Reg. § 1.166-1(b).

[239] *Toledo Home Federal Savings and Loan Association v. United States,* 63-2 U.S.T.C. ¶9522, 318 F.2d 292 (6th Cir. 1963).

[240] Reg. § 1.166-1(b)(3).

[241] Rev. Proc. 85-8, 1985-1 C.B. 495.

An application to change a method of accounting for bad debts is made by filing Form 3115 in duplicate. The original must be attached to a timely filed tax return, and a copy must be filed with the National Office of the IRS. For commercial banks, the copy must be filed no later than 60 days *after* the end of the tax year in which the initial balance of the reserve is determined and, for thrifts, the copy must be filed at least 30 days *prior* to the close of the year of change.

Regulations provide that commercial banks changing their method of accounting for bad debts from the specific charge-off method to the reserve method must compute the initial balance of the reserve at the close of the year of change and deduct the initial balance over a period of 10 years or over a shorter period as may be approved by the Commissioner.[242] In the case of a thrift that had been allowed to determine bad debt deductions under Code section 593, regulations provide that to change bad-debt methods, an application for permission to change must be filed at least 30 days prior to the close of the taxable year for which the change is to be effective.[243]

(d) Code Section 481 Adjustments

As a condition to obtaining permission to change accounting methods, a bank or thrift must agree that Code section 481 adjustments will be taken into account. These adjustments are necessary to prevent amounts from being duplicated or omitted when the taxpayer computes its taxable income under a method of accounting different from the method used to compute taxable income during the year preceding the taxable year of change. For banks, the determination of the amount of these adjustments and the period in which they are taken into income is to be made under the aforementioned revenue procedure and in accordance with the regulations under Code section 585.[244]

As a general rule, the period over which Code section 481(a) adjustments are to be taken into account may not exceed six taxable years. A cooperative bank may take the Code section 481(a) adjustments into account in the year of change. Any portion of any net operating loss arising in the year of change or in any subsequent year in the adjustment period that is attributable to a negative Code section 481(a) adjustment may not be carried to the three tax years preceding the year of change to which Code section 172 otherwise would require a net operating loss first to be carried.[245]

In the case of a commercial bank, Code section 481(a) adjustments are not computed as of the beginning of the year of change, but rather determine the amount of the reserve for bad debts under Regulation section 1.585-2(d). The amount of the Code section 481(a) adjustment is an amount determined by dividing the total net losses on bad debts for the five taxable years preceding the taxable year of change by the sum of the amount of outstanding loans at the close

[242] Reg. §§1.585-2(d)(2) and (3).

[243] Reg. §1.593-1(a).

[244] Reg. §§1.585-2(d), 1.593-1(b). *See* special rules for reserve recapture discussed later in this chapter.

[245] Rev. Proc. 97-37, 1997-2 C.B. 455 modified by Rev. Proc. 97-18 1997-1 C.B. 642.

of those same tax years, and then multiplying the amount of outstanding loans at the close of the taxable year preceding the year of change by the resulting decimal amount.[246]

§10.7.2 Legislative History of Code Section 585

Prior to 1969, the first tax year to which Code section 585 applied, the Treasury Department allowed commercial banks to maintain more generous bad-debt reserves than were available to most taxpayers.[247] For the purpose of granting commercial banks some protection from catastrophic losses, the IRS allowed commercial banks to establish a bad-debt reserve equal to 2.4 percent of outstanding loans not insured by the Federal Government.[248] If banks were required to apply the same bad-debt reserve rules to which other taxpayers were subject, they would, on average, have been allowed a bad-debt reserve of 0.2 percent or less of outstanding noninsured loans.[249] According to legislative history, Code section 585 was added to the Code to "bring the bad-debt reserves allowed for banks into line with the bad-debt reserves allowed for business taxpayers generally."[250]

To accomplish this goal, Code section 585, after a phase-in period, provided that banks generally were permitted reserve additions not to exceed the amount called for on the basis of their own experience as indicated by loan losses for the current year and the 5 preceding tax years.[251] To protect banks against unusually large bad-debt losses, the number of years that banks, as well as taxpayers in general, are permitted to carry back net operating losses is 2 years.

The Tax Reform Act of 1986, amended Code section 585 in several ways, including limiting its application to banks which were not "large banks."[252] According to the legislative history of the Act, Code section 585 was changed for three reasons: first, the reserve method allowed deductions before the losses actually occur in contravention of the "all-events" test of Code section 451; second, the reserve method allowed deductions larger than the actual present value of the losses; and, third, there was a concern that many large banks were taking advantage of the reserve method to drastically reduce their Federal income tax liabilities. To avoid adverse impact on banks with gross assets of less than $500 million from the repeal of the reserve method, they were permitted to continue to use the reserve method to determine bad-debt losses.[253] The special 10-year net operating loss deduction was repealed effective for taxable years beginning after January 1, 1994.

---

[246] *Id.* at §5.02(3). As a general rule, the total adjustment period shall not exceed six taxable years.

[247] H. R. Rep. No. 91-413, pt. 1, at 120 (1969).

[248] Rev. Rul. 65-92, 1965-1 C.B. 112, superseded and modified.

[249] H. R. Rep. No. 91-413, pt. 1, at 121.

[250] *Id.*

[251] I.R.C. §446 (2000); Reg. §1.585-2.

[252] H.R. Rep. No. 99-426, pt. 5 at, 574 (1986). *See* §10.10.1 for the definition of a "large bank."

[253] H.R. Rep. No. 99-426, pt. 5, at 577 (1986). The House of Representatives Report does not indicate what the adverse impact would be or how that impact will differ for large banks.

§ 10.7.3 Pre-1987 Rules

For tax years beginning prior to 1987, a commercial bank or thrift was permitted on its first return for which it was entitled to a bad-debt deduction, to elect to compute its bad-debt deductions by deducting either specific debts as they become worthless, or by deducting a reasonable addition to a reserve for bad debts. The reasonable addition to the commercial bank or thrift reserve was deductible under Code section 166(c). The amount of any deductible reserve addition for all commercial banks was computed under Code section 585, using either the percentage of eligible loans method or the experience method, and the reasonable addition for thrifts was computed under Code section 593 using either the percentage of taxable income method or the method available to commercial banks.

A taxpayer's use of a particular computational formula (for example, the percentage of taxable income method to compute its maximum addition to the reserve for qualifying real property loans) does not bind the taxpayer to use that same computational formula either for that tax year or for subsequent tax years.[254] Thus, for example, where a taxpayer carries back a net operating loss to an earlier tax year, the taxpayer may recompute the amount of its addition to its reserve in that carry back year.[255] However, it is the IRS's position that a shift from one special reserve method to another special reserve method is one instance of a change in circumstances that will rise to the level of an accounting method change.[256]

The percentage of eligible loans method was an available alternative for computing reserve additions by those commercial banks which were not "large banks" and by thrifts with respect to qualifying real property loans for taxable years beginning before 1988.[257] However, "large banks" were prohibited from using the method in taxable years beginning after 1986. In general, the percentage of eligible loans method permitted a reserve addition equal to the amount necessary to increase the reserve balance before the addition, to the balance permitted, determined by multiplying "eligible loans" by a statistically specified percentage. For most years, this method allowed reserve additions in an amount substantially in excess of the amount that would be allowed based on actual experience.

For taxable years beginning before January 1, 1988, a thrift was permitted to determine the addition to its loan loss reserve for qualifying real property loans under the percentage of eligible loans method, as well as under the percentage of taxable income method and the experience method. However, the amount otherwise allowable as an addition to its reserve for qualifying real property loans had

[254] Reg. § 1.593-6A(a)(1).

[255] Rev. Rul. 79-123, 1979-1 C.B. 215; FSA 200129003, July 20, 2001.

[256] Rev. Rul. 85-171, 1985-2 C.B. 148 (a change in method occurs when a taxpayer switches from the I.R.C. § 593 reserve method to the I.R.C. § 585 reserve method even though the experience formula used under I.R.C. § 593 is calculated by reference to I.R.C. § 585).

[257] I.R.C. § 585(b)(2)(A) (2000). The Revenue Reconciliation Act of 1990 provided for the elimination from the I.R.C. of I.R.C. § 585(b)(2) percentage of eligible loan method. Pub. L. No. 101-508, § 11801(a)(26), 104 Stat. 1388-521 (1990).

to be reduced by the addition to its reserve for nonqualifying loans.[258] The Tax Reform Act of 1986 eliminated the use of the percentage of eligible loans method for both thrifts and commercial banks.[259]

§10.7.4 Post-1986 Rules—Overview

For taxable years beginning after December 31, 1986, "large banks" (as well as most other taxpayers) are restricted to the specific charge-off method for deducting bad debts provided for in Code section 166(a). Commercial banks that are not "large banks" may continue to deduct a reasonable addition to a reserve for bad debts under Code section 585, in lieu of any deduction under Code section 166(a). Thrifts were permitted to compute their loan loss deduction under either the direct charge-off method or under the reserve method of Code section 593. The special Code section 593 rules were repealed effective for taxable years beginning on or after January 1, 1996.

The Tax Reform Act of 1986 also repealed Code section 166(c), which allowed the deduction for a reasonable reserve addition.[260] It inserted into Code sections 585 and 593 provisions allowing a bad-debt deduction for reasonable reserve additions for commercial banks and thrifts, respectively. Previously, these sections were limited to providing the rules for computing the amount of the reasonable reserve addition. The commercial bank rules for computing reasonable reserve additions are expressly integrated into the Code section 593 reserve calculation method previously available to thrifts.[261]

Although Code section 585(a) could be read to require all banks, other than "large banks," to use the reserve method to determine bad-debt deductions, this is not the accepted interpretation. In fact, the IRS grants permission to banks which are not "large banks" to change their method of accounting for bad debts from the Code section 585 reserve method to the Code section 166(a) specific charge-off method.[262] Of course, the reserve method is a method of accounting, and a change to the specific charge-off method is permitted only with permission from the IRS.

§10.7.5 Commissioner's Discretion Revoked

Prior to the Tax Reform Act of 1986, use of the reserve method was expressly made subject to "the discretion of the Secretary."[263] The extent of the grant of the

---

[258] I.R.C. §593(b)(3) (1982), prior to amendment by the Tax Reform Act of 1986, Pub. L. No. 99-514, 100 Stat. 2085 (1986).

[259] The Tax Reform Act of 1986, Pub. L. No. 99-514, §901, 100 Stat. 2085, 2375 (1986).

[260] Prior to repeal, I.R.C. §166(c) provided, "In lieu of any deduction under subsection (a), there shall be allowed (in the discretion of the Secretary) a deduction for a reasonable addition to a reserve for bad debts." Tax Reform Act of 1986, Pub. L. No. 99-514, §805(a), 100 Stat. 2085, 2361 (2000).

[261] I.R.C. §593(b). As will be discussed later in this chapter, thrifts may use the commercial bank experience method as an alternative to the thrifts' percentage of taxable income method, but they are subject to special limitations. Regulations under I.R.C. §§166 and 582 have not been modified to recognize this change, and old case law should be read in light of then applicable law. I.R.C. §585(a)(2) (2000).

[262] The accounting method change may have been made to permit the bank a longer net operating loss carryback period. Under pre-1994 rules a ten-year carryback was permitted for losses attributable to bad-debt deductions taken under the specific charge-off method.

[263] I.R.C. §166(c) (1982), prior to repeal by the Tax Reform Act of 1986, Pub. L. No. 99-514, 100 Stat. 2085 (1986).

Secretary's discretion was the subject of the Federal Circuit's opinion in *Beneficial Corporation and Subsidiaries*.[264] The issue resolved by the court was whether the Commissioner's discretion under Code section 166(c) allowed him, when assessing "reasonable addition to a reserve for bad debts," to focus only on that portion of outstanding debts expected to become worthless in the next taxable year. The court found that the accounting concept of reserve for bad debts was the only available approach in 1921 (the time of the enactment of Code section 166(c)). Further, Code section 166(c) gave the Commissioner discretion not to change the concept but to work with it, for example, in determining which entities should be allowed to use it and in approving the various figures used.

The amendments made by the Tax Reform Act of 1986 to Code section 166 have removed the authority of the Secretary to determine whether a bank may use the reserve method.[265] Prior to the amendments, Code section 166(c) provided, in part, that "there shall be allowed (in the discretion of the Secretary or his delegate) a deduction for a reasonable addition to a reserve for bad debts." For taxable years beginning after December 31, 1986, the statutory language grants the Secretary no discretion to determine whether a bank may elect the reserve method, nor to determine the amount of the deduction.[266]

§ 10.7.6 Eligible Taxpayers

The Code section 585 loan loss reserve rules apply to loans made by a "bank" defined in Code section 581 (other than a "large bank").[267] The Code section 585 rules also expressly apply to loans made by a foreign corporation engaged in banking if interest from its loans are treated as effectively connected with the conduct of a banking business in the United States.[268]

The Code section 585 reserve method is available to banks that employ the cash method of accounting as well as to those who use the accrual method.[269] However, it is not available to a production credit association, which is an entity that is organized for the purpose of making loans to farm owners and operators, because this entity is not a "bank" for this purpose.[270]

---

[264] *Beneficial Corporation and Subsidiaries v. United States*, 814 F.2d 1570 (Fed. Cir. 1987), 87-1 U.S.T.C. ¶ 9240, *rev'g and rem'g*, 85-2 U.S.T.C. ¶ 9778, 9 Cl. Ct. 119 (1985).

[265] However, I.R.C. § 166(a)(2) provides that, with respect to partially worthless debts, the Commissioner continues to have discretion to determine whether the debt is partially worthless.

[266] Although the regulations under I.R.C. § 593 acknowledge the requirement that the adoption of the pre-1986 I.R.C. § 166(c) reserve method "shall be subject to the approval of the Commissioner . . . ," no similar statement has been contained in the regulations under I.R.C. § 585. Reg. § 1.593-1(a). There apparently is no significance to the omission, however, since both the statute and the regulations under I.R.C. § 166(c) have made selection of the reserve method subject to IRS approval. I.R.C. § 166(c) (1982), prior to repeal by the Tax Reform Act of 1986, Pub. L. No. 99-514, 100 Stat. 2085 (1986); Reg. § 1.166-1(b)(1).

[267] The term "bank" includes a thrift. A "thrift" embraces three types of banks: a mutual savings bank, a domestic building and loan association, and a cooperative bank without capital stock organized and operated for mutual purposes and without profit. A state stock cooperative bank was entitled to compute its bad debt resume under the methods available to thrifts. PLR 9836030, September 4, 1998. The thrift bad debt rules had been contained in I.R.C. § 593(a)(1); Reg. § 1.593-4. "Domestic building and loan associations" and "cooperative banks" are defined in I.R.C. §§ 7701(a)(19) and (32) (2000).

[268] I.R.C. § 585(a)(2)(B) (2000); Reg. § 1.585-1(b).

[269] Rev. Rul. 74-604, 1974-2 C.B. 60. *See* discussion of the limitations on use of the cash method in Ch. 2.

[270] Rev. Rul. 81-172, 1981-1 C.B. 39; TAM 8001006, September 26, 1979.

In order for the Code section 585 reserve method to be available, it is not enough that an entity meet the bank regulatory definition of a commercial bank or a thrift. The entity must also meet the tax test. For example, under pre-1996 law a savings and loan association was not permitted to use the Code section 593 reserve method if its business did not qualify, during the years in question, as actually acquiring the savings of the public and investing in loans.[271] If it was found to be primarily a lending agent for others, it would not pass the tax test.[272] Furthermore, a taxpayer which failed to meet the tax definition of a thrift was treated as a "bank" for tax purposes, where a substantial part of the taxpayer's business consisted of receiving deposits and making loans or exercising fiduciary powers similar to those of a national bank.[273] Thus, where the taxpayer was disqualified from computing its bad-debt reserve under Code section 593, it was probably entitled to compute its bad-debt reserve additions under Code section 585,[274] unless it was a "large bank."[275]

§ 10.7.7 Minimum Reserve Addition

Regulations have been adopted that mandate a minimum reserve addition under Code section 585 for commercial banks.[276] Similar regulations were proposed in 1983 for thrifts under Code section 593, but they were revoked in 2000.[277] Moreover, the IRS has recently ruled that a negative reserve balance will terminate the taxpayer's reserve method of accounting for loan losses.[278] From a plain reading of the statute it appears that commercial banks and thrifts are permitted to make a reserve addition in any amount that does not exceed the maximum amount, including zero or any amount between zero and the maximum. Both Code section 585 and 593 provide that reserve additions "shall be an amount determined by the taxpayer which shall not exceed . . . ."

The IRS has ruled publicly that a reserve addition equal to less than the maximum was allowed in taxable years prior to the promulgation of the minimum addition regulation.[279] It stated that "[a] bank is not required to take as a tax deduction its maximum permissible annual reserve addition for each taxable year, and unused portions of [amount] . . . may be used in a subsequent year."[280]

---

271 I.R.C. § 7701(a)(19) (2000).

272 *See* discussion of what entities qualify as commercial banks and as thrifts in Ch. 1. *Permanent Savings and Loan Association v. Commissioner*, 77-2 U.S.T.C. ¶ 9625, 439 F. Supp. 917 (S.D. Ohio 1977).

273 I.R.C. § 581 (2000).

274 PLRs 8701040, October 8, 1987, and 8652014, September 24, 1986.

275 I.R.C. § 585(c) (2000). The IRS has ruled that the change in computing bad-debt reserve additions from I.R.C. § 593 to I.R.C. § 585 is a change in method of accounting. Rev. Rul. 85-171, 1985-2 C.B. 148; General Counsel Memorandum 39469 (Jan. 20, 1983). This is consistent with the IRS's expansive view of what constitutes an accounting method. A further illustration of the IRS's position on accounting methods is contained in final regulations under I.R.C. § 166, which provide for the so-called conformity election.

276 Reg. § 1.585-2(a)(2). This regulation was originally scheduled to apply retroactively to all tax years beginning after July 11, 1969. In a News Release dated July 17, 1977, the IRS deferred the effective date to taxable years beginning on or after January 1, 1977. TIR-1740.

277 65 Fed. Reg. 42900 (July 12, 2000). According to the IRS, the proposed regulations were withdrawn because under a subsequent amendment to the underlying statute, subsections (a), (b), (c), and (d) of Code § 593 does not apply to taxable years beginning after December 31, 1995. *See* proposed amendments to Reg. §§ 1.593-1 and 1.593-11, 48 Fed. Reg. 56083 (Dec. 19, 1983).

278 TAM 9847004, November 20, 1998.

279 Rev. Rul. 66-26, 1966-1 C.B. 41 (Guideline 8), *supplementing* Rev. Rul. 65-92, 1965-1 C.B. 112. *See also* Rev. Rul. 59-83, 1959-1 C.B. 52.

280 *Id.*

In at least two private rulings, it was held that a $1 addition (when a much larger deduction was allowable) claimed in years prior to the promulgation of the minimum addition rules was permissible.[281] Moreover, in at least one private letter ruling, the IRS has allowed a thrift to defer its entire reserve addition pending final adoption of the proposed minimum addition regulation that was proposed for thrifts.[282]

At one time, the IRS resisted taxpayers' attempts to retroactively increase reserve balances, and courts supported this position.[283] For example, in *Rio Grande Building & Loan Association,* the Tax Court agreed with the government that a savings and loan association could not "retroactively enlarge its reserve accounts for prior years, albeit that the increased amounts would have been reasonable and allowable as deductions if timely made."[284]

More recently, the Tax Court has held that Code section 593 "grants wide latitude and complete discretion to taxpayers to decide the amount of available reserves they wish to claim in any year, not to exceed the statute's limit."[285] In so holding, the Court declared Regulation Section 1.593-6(a)(3) invalid. The last sentence of that regulation, which was the focus of the Court's deliberations, provided "a taxpayer may not subsequently reduce the amount claimed in the return . . . for the purpose of obtaining a larger deduction in a later year."[286] This regulation, which was later withdrawn, had the effect of prohibiting a thrift from reducing its bad-debt deduction on an amended return.[287] The Tax Court reasoned that the Treasury Department "does not possess statutory authority"[288] to determine the amount of reserve permitted to the taxpayer "because the statute vests the election solely within the discretion of taxpayers."[289] The court also stated that "[s]ection 593 and the regulation do not limit this selection or election to the time of filing the original return."[290] [Footnote omitted.] In conclusion, the Court stated that "so long as a taxable year remains open, it would not seem to make a difference when a taxpayer determined to increase or forego some portion of a potential reserve allowance."[291]

The decision indirectly challenges the validity of any Treasury Department minimum addition regulation by reaffirming the statutory rule that the reasona-

---

281 TAM 8009003, May 21, 1979, and 8031062, November 30, 1979.

282 PLR 8807046, November 23, 1987. It is unclear whether the IRS would permit a taxpayer to deduct a negative reserve balance in a subsequent year. The author understands that this issue is being considered by the IRS. It may be that a taxpayer which voluntarily allows its reserve balance to fall into a negative balance could be treated as having changed from the reserve method of accounting for loan losses.

283 *American National Bank of Austin v. United States,* 74-2 U.S.T.C. ¶9572, 497 F.2d 40 (5th Cir. 1974).

284 *Rio Grande Building & Loan Association v. Commissioner,* 36 T.C. 657 (1961).

285 *The Home Group, Inc. v. Commissioner,* 91 T.C. 265, 273, Dec. 44,994 (1988).

286 Reg. § 1.593-6(a)(3) as it existed for taxable years beginning before July 12, 1969.

287 Reg. § 1.593-6(a) was altered by T.D. 7549, filed May 17, 1978, 1978-1 C.B. 185. Among the changes was the elimination of the last sentence of Reg. § 1.593-6(a)(3). The regulation section for taxable years beginning after July 11, 1969, had no similar regulatory restriction. *See* Reg. § 1.593-6A(a)(1), applicable to taxable years beginning after July 11, 1969.

288 *The Home Group, Inc. v. Commissioner,* 91 T.C. 265, 270, Dec. 44,994 (1988).

289 *Id.*

290 *Id.*

291 *Id.*

ble reserve addition is *"determined by the taxpayer to be a reasonable addition."*[292] [Emphasis added.] Since language identical to that found in Code section 593 prior to its repeal in 1996 is contained in Code section 585, the attempt, in the minimum addition regulation applicable to commercial banks, to remove the historical flexibility accorded commercial banks also may be declared invalid if brought before a court.[293] Apparently, only judicial action will determine the fate of the commercial bank minimum addition rule, since the IRS apparently displays no propensity to withdraw the regulation.

§10.7.8 Alternative Formula Within Code Section 593

Once the reserve method is elected, the adoption of one of the two available alternatives for computing reserve additions under Code section 593 (experience method or percentage of taxable income method), did not constitute adopting a method of accounting.[294] According to regulations, "use of a particular method for a taxable year is not a binding election by the taxpayer to apply such method either for the taxable year or for subsequent taxable years."[295] Moreover, a taxpayer was permitted to change both its method and the amount of its deduction after filing its return as long as the year remains open and the taxpayer remains on the reserve method. In Regulation section 1.593-6(a)(3), and in its post-1969 counterpart Regulation section 1.593-6A(a)(1), express authorization is set forth for the recomputation after the taxpayer's return is filed of a thrift's bad-debt deduction "under whichever method the taxpayer selects . . . irrespective of the method initially applied for the taxable year."[296]

As a general rule, a thrift was permitted to change its method for computing reserve additions under Code section 593 on an amended return without obtaining IRS consent, and adjustments were permitted to be made retroactively to correct clerical errors.[297] The IRS has ruled that a mutual savings bank, a domestic building and loan association, or a cooperative bank may increase loan loss reserves for a taxable year in which an audit adjustment is made with respect to some other item of income or expense.[298]

Thrifts with net operating loss carrybacks have been permitted to change from the method used on their returns as originally filed to a different method even when the carryback year was closed.[299] Thus, if a thrift claimed a bad-debt

---

[292] I.R.C. §593(b)(1)(B) (2000).

[293] I.R.C. §585(b) (2000). The language of I.R.C. §585, preceding by several years the enactment of I.R.C. §593, was probably the source of the I.R.C. §593 language. *See also Winter & Hirsch v. United States*, 78-1 U.S.T.C. ¶9249, 571 F.2d 11 (Ct. Cl. 1978).

[294] Reg. §§1.593-6A(a)(1)(ii), 1.585-1(a). *Cf.* General Counsel Memorandum 39760 (Sept. 27, 1988) revoking General Counsel Memorandum 39276 (May 16, 1984).

[295] Reg. §§1.585-1(a), 1.593-6A(a); Rev. Rul. 79-123, 1979-1 C.B. 215 (with respect to thrifts).

[296] *The Home Group, Inc. v. Commissioner*, 91 T.C. 265, Dec. 44,994 (1988). *See also* Rev. Rul. 79-123, 1979-1 C.B. 215 and TAM 8453002, May 24, 1984; 8442003, June 20, 1984; 8442002, June 20, 1984; 8437007, May 24, 1984.

[297] Rev. Rul. 79-123, 1979-1 C.B. 215 (from percentage of eligible loan to experience method). In Rev. Rul. 75-560, 1975-2 C.B. 73, the taxpayer intended, but erroneously did not claim, maximum additions under the percentage method. In Rev. Rul. 75-445, 1975-2 C.B. 74, a change from the percentage to the experience method was permitted.

[298] Rev. Rul. 70-5, 1970-1 C.B. 142.

[299] TAM 8442002, June 20, 1984; 8442003, June 20, 1984; 8435015, May 24, 1984; and 8437007, May 24, 1984. I.R.C. §650(a) provides, in general, for a three-year statute of limitations on assessment and collections. I.R.C. §6511(a) provides for a three-year stat-

deduction in a closed year based on the percentage of taxable income method, and that deduction is later reduced by a net operating loss carryback, the thrift may use an alternative method for computing its bad-debt deduction for the carryback year.[300] A deduction was not barred under the alternative method to the extent it was available in the carryback year and did not exceed the deduction originally computed and taken under the percentage of taxable income method. The alternative deduction was "attributable to" the carryback within the meaning of Code section 6511(d)(2).[301]

The use of an alternative method that would produce a lower reserve addition than that originally claimed was barred when it could create a deficiency in a closed year. It was not permissible because the change in the method of computing the reserve addition would not be attributable to the carryback. Of course, if the statute of limitations on assessments and collections and on credits and refunds has not expired, there is no bar to any change in the reserve additions or method of calculation.[302] The IRS has permitted such change on audit, and at least one private letter ruling has been issued to that effect.[303]

In a ruling that some may find difficult to reconcile with these regulations and with Code section 593 (prior to its repeal), the IRS has taken the position that the integration of a thrift's bad-debt reserve account into an acquiring commercial bank's reserve account pursuant to Code section 381(c)(4) constitutes a change in an accounting method.[304] The IRS reasoned that a change from the use of the Code section 593 reserve method to the Code section 585 reserve method was a change in a material item and, therefore, a change in a method of accounting. Special rules apply to loans that are subject to the mark-to-market rules.[305]

§10.7.9 Recoveries

Because a taxpayer employing the reserve method for determining bad-debt deductions does not deduct bad debts, recoveries are not directly included in income.[306] Instead, they result in a credit to the bad-debt reserve.[307] Regulations provide that a bad debt previously charged to a reserve is not a "Section 111 item" entitling it to exclusion from income to the extent it did not result in a reduction of any tax in a prior year.[308]

In general, recoveries must be credited against the reserve even if to do so would increase the reserve balance above the balance allowable under Code

(Footnote Continued)

ute of limitations on claims for credit or refund of overpayments.

[300] General Counsel Memorandum 39760 (Sept. 27, 1988). *Empire Case Goods Company v. Commissioner*, 8 T.C.M. (CCH) 686 (1949); General Counsel Memorandum 34436 (Feb. 18, 1971).

[301] General Counsel Memorandum 38292 (Feb. 22, 1980).

[302] General Counsel Memorandum 36301 (June 6, 1975); 33820 (May 10, 1969); and 33640 (Oct. 2, 1967).

[303] TAM 8023017, February 26, 1980.

[304] Rev. Rul. 85-171, 1985-2 C.B. 148; General Counsel Memorandum 39469 (Jan. 20, 1983).

[305] *See* discussion in Ch. 4.

[306] Reg. §1.166-1(f), "Recoveries of Bad Debts," states, in part, "This paragraph shall not apply, however, to a bad debt which was previously charged against a reserve by a taxpayer on the reserve method of treating bad debts."

[307] Reg. §1.585-3(a).

[308] Reg. §1.111-1(a)(1).

section 585. This could have the effect of preventing the taxpayer from making a reserve addition in a subsequent year. However, the IRS has held that an insurance recovery for a loss suffered from an improper diversion of funds which would have constituted gross income would not be a credit to a thrift's loan loss reserve since a reserve addition with respect to the item was never taken.[309] Instead, the recovery is a direct credit to income.[310] Further, a nonbank taxpayer using the reserve method of accounting for bad debts was required to use the specific charge-off method for recovery of an extraordinary item that was previously charged to its reserve.[311] The IRS ruled that because only the normal losses that arise in the ordinary course of a taxpayer's trade or business may be charged to a reserve, "the recovery of an extraordinary loss should not be handled through the bad-debt reserve . . . ."[312] The IRS reasoned that to permit a recovery to be credited to the reserve would result in a distortion of income in the year of crediting and in subsequent years.

Regulations provide and the IRS has ruled that, for a bank, a recovery of an extraordinary loss is not to be treated differently than other recoveries.[313] The IRS reasoned that in light of explicit regulations providing that if a bank establishes a reserve, any bad debt in respect of the loan must be charged to that reserve. Even "rare and unpredictable" losses and recoveries not arising out of the bank's "normal day-to-day operations" must be charged to the reserve.[314] An extraordinary large recovery that is credited to the reserve will prevent the taxpayer from taking reserve additions until the allowable reserve balance is brought into line with the actual reserve balance before addition. An exception to this general rule for banks using the reserve method is allowed for international loans transferred to an Allocated Transfer Risk Reserve.[315]

Prior to the repeal of Code section 593 in 1996, thrifts normally established three reserves: a reserve for qualifying loans, a reserve for nonqualifying loans, and a supplemental reserve.[316] Recoveries must be credited to the reserve that was originally charged for the bad-debt loss.[317] If the loss was charged to more than one reserve, the credit for the recovery must be apportioned among the reserves originally charged in the ratio that the amount of the bad debt charged against such reserve bears to the total amount of such bad debt charged against the reserves.[318]

§ 10.7.10 Establishing and Maintaining Reserves

(a) General Rules

As a condition to the use of the reserve method, permanent reserve records must be established and maintained.[319] The regulations under Code section 585

309 Rev. Rul. 74-34, 1974-1 C.B. 35.

310 I.R.C. § 111 could not be relied upon to exclude the item from income.

311 Rev. Rul. 74-409, 1974-2 C.B. 61.

312 *Id.*

313 Reg. § 1.585-3(a). TAM 7943021, 1979; 7945011, July 24, 1979; and 8009003, May 21, 1979.

314 TAM 8009003, May 21, 1979. Reg. § 1.585-3(a).

315 Rev. Rul. 92-14, 1992-1 C.B. 94, *amplifying and superseding* Rev. Rul. 84-94, 1984-1 C.B. 34.

316 I.R.C. § 593(c) (2000).

317 Reg. § 1.593-7(c)(3)(ii).

318 Reg. § 1.593-7(c)(3)(iii).

319 Reg. § § 1.585-3(b), 1.593-7(a)(2).

state that a reserve for loan losses must be "established and maintained in the manner provided under Code section 166." However, neither the latter section nor the regulations thereunder contain any procedures for establishing and maintaining loan loss reserves.[320]

Thus, the Tax Court has held:

> "Although the Code section does not expressly state that the amount sought to be deducted as a reserve for bad debts must be reflected on the books of the taxpayer, the regulations implementing the Code state a clear and obvious requirement to do so. We think the regulation sets forth a reasonable administrative requirement and is in no sense inconsistent with the provisions of the Code. A reserve for bad debt deductions is not a statutory deduction, allowed irrespective of any bookkeeping entries establishing a reserve. In this respect it is unlike a true bad debt deduction where a taxpayer may deduct a worthless debt without maintaining any books of account."[321]

In general, reserve balances are maintained by making certain adjustments. The opening reserve balance is reduced by charge-offs, increased by recoveries, and increased by the reserve addition. Specific rules were set forth for establishing and maintaining reserves in Code section 593 prior to its repeal and in regulations under both Code sections 585 and 593.[322]

Code section 585 requires the establishment and maintenance of a single reserve for loan losses.[323] Thrifts were required to establish and maintain separate loan loss reserves for qualifying loans (qualifying reserve), nonqualifying loans (nonqualifying reserve) and, under certain circumstances, a supplemental reserve.[324] The supplemental reserve was established to account for certain bad-debt losses incurred prior to 1952, when thrifts first became taxable.[325]

(b) Retroactive Reserve Adjustments

Statutory provisions relating to the reserve method and regulations thereunder do not contain any express rule with respect to retroactive adjustments to a reserve for bad debts. As a reasonable addition to a reserve is based on an estimate of future losses, to permit the reasonable addition to be changed to take into account events that occurred after the end of the tax year would appear to distort the theory of reserve accounting Recognition of this is seemingly the basis for Treasury regulations under Code section 166 that provide:

> "**(1) Relevant Factors**. What constitutes a reasonable addition to a reserve for bad debts shall be determined in the light of the facts existing at the close of the taxable year of the proposed addition. The reasonableness of the addition will vary as between classes of business and with conditions of business prosperity. It will depend primarily upon the total amount of debts outstanding as of the close of the taxable year, including those arising currently as well as those arising in prior taxable years, and the total amount of the existing reserve.

---

[320] Reg. § 1.585-1(a).

[321] *Rio Grande Bldg. & Loan Ass'n v. Commissioner*, 36 T.C. 657 (1961).

[322] I.R.C. § 593(c) (2000); Reg. §§ 1.585-3(b), 1.593-7.

[323] Reg. § 1.585-1(a); Reg. § 1.593-1. It appears that the earliest version of Reg. § 1.593-1 was promulgated in 1953 as Reg. § 39.23(k)-5. Treasury regulations were subsequently renumbered. *See* TD 6500 (1960). *But see* the discussion of the cut-off method for "large banks" later in this chapter.

[324] I.R.C. § 593(c) (2000).

[325] Reg. § 1.593-7(b).

> **(2) Correction of errors in prior estimates**. In the event that subsequent realizations upon outstanding debts prove to be more or less than estimated at the time of the creation of the existing reserve, the amount of the excess or inadequacy in the existing reserve shall be reflected in the determination of the reasonable addition necessary in the current taxable year."[326]

Thus, a distinction should be drawn between adjusting the reserve for facts that exist at the close of the taxable year and facts that occur subsequent to the close of the taxable year, even if the latter facts demonstrate that the addition to the reserve was inadequate. If a fact exists at the close of the taxable year but the taxpayer was unaware of the fact or misunderstood the fact, there does not appear to be a restriction on a retroactive adjustment to correct for the error.[327] For this reason, Treasury regulations had expressly allowed a retroactive reserve adjustment to take into account an adjustment on audit to the taxpayer's taxable income on which the reserve addition had been based.[328]

Similarly, the Second Circuit held that a taxpayer was permitted to increase its reserve addition when the taxpayer was unaware of facts that justified a greater addition. However, the Tax Court had held that even if the taxpayer demonstrated that it intended to take the maximum reserve addition, but failed to do so because of what appeared to be an oversight, the taxpayer was not permitted to retroactively increase its reserve addition.[329] In this case, on the taxpayer's originally filed return for the year in question, the taxpayer failed to transfer the entire amount of its allowable addition to a reserve account on its regular books of account because it misunderstood the reserve accounting requirement.

(c) Negative Reserve Balance

Although the language of Code sections 585 and 593 appears to grant commercial banks and thrifts, respectively, the option to defer bad-debt deductions, the IRS believes that if that deferral causes a bad debt reserve to fall into a negative position at the end of a tax year, the taxpayer would no longer be on the reserve method of accounting.[330] Moreover, if the taxpayer allowed the reserve to fall into a negative position, the IRS would treat the taxpayer as not having a method of accounting because the accounting practice was arbitrary or random. Furthermore, the change in its method of accounting would be considered to have been made without receiving prior consent from the Commissioner, as is generally required prior to making a change in the accounting method for an

[326] Reg. § 1.166-4(b).

[327] *AmBase Corp. v. U.S.*, 731 F.3d 109 (2d Cir. 1913). *See also* Rev. Rul. 70-5, 1970-1 C.B. 142 and General Counsel Memorandum 33820 (May 10, 1968) 1968 WL 16122.

[328] Reg. § 39.23(k)-5(b)(3), Reg. § 118, Ex. 2.

[329] *Rio Grande Bldg. & Loan Ass'n v. Commissioner*, 36 T.C. 657 (1961). *See also Rogan v. Commercial Discount Co.*, 149 F.2d 585, 589 (2d Cir. 1945) where the court held that "Ignorance of the law does not warrant a taxpayer's failure to ascertain worthlessness and charge off a debt or make reasonable addition therefor in its bad debt reserve within the taxable year, as required by statutes, regulations and the authorities." *Cf. Abraham Sultan*, 22 B.T.A. 889, 892 (1931) where the court Board held that the taxpayer was permitted to correct a technical error.

[330] TAM 9847004, July 24, 1998.

item of income or expense. This position of the IRS does not appear to be consistent with earlier pronouncements allowing bank taxpayers wide latitude in determining reserve additions. Furthermore, it conflicts with case law that has struck down attempts by the IRS to require minimum reserve additions.[331]

§ 10.7.11 Acceptable Bookkeeping for Reserves

Strict conformity with reserve nomenclature and adjustment procedures is not necessary to be entitled to the loan loss deduction under the reserve method.[332] As the Tax Court concluded with respect to thrifts, neither the irregular nomenclature, the original extraneous balance in the taxpayer's bad-debt reserve, nor the taxpayer's failure to charge bad debts against the reserve are fatal to a bad-debt deduction under the Code section 593 reserve method.[333]

Requirements for establishing and maintaining reserves are satisfied if a reserve account is made a permanent part of a bank's regular books of account. A reserve account must be established and maintained to ensure that if, upon the taxpayer's liquidation, there remains a balance in the reserve account, or the reserve is invaded for other purposes, the taxpayer pays income taxes in relation to this amount.[334] The amount represents deductions in prior years, which never actually represented bad debts.

A permanent subsidiary ledger containing an account of the reserve also will be considered a part of the regular books of account if the ledger contains sufficient information to permit the reconciliation of the balance in the account with the balance of the reserve for losses on loans for financial statement purposes.[335]

There is no requirement that reserves for bad debts for financial statement purposes be conformed with reserves for tax purposes.[336] Further, it is generally unnecessary that a reconciliation be made between the tax return and the accounting books.[337] However, the IRS has ruled that adjustments to a subsidiary reserve ledger for book purposes, which do not adjust the tax reserve, require a reconciliation.[338] Reserve records also must reflect any changes in the amount initially added to the reserve and the amount finally determined by the taxpayer to be a reasonable addition.[339]

Regulations governing commercial banks provide that the taxpayer include on its federal income tax return (or amended return) a schedule showing the

---

[331] *See* discussion of minimum reserve addition at § 10.7.7.

[332] Rev. Rul. 71-133, 1971-1 C.B. 70; *Centralia Fed. Savings & Loan Association v. Commissioner*, 78-2 U.S.T.C. ¶ 9833, 586 F.2d 723 (9th Cir. 1978).

[333] *Centralia Fed. Savings & Loan Association v. Commissioner*, 66 T.C. 599 (1976). *See also Levelland Savings & Loan Association v. United States*, 421 F.2d 243 (5th Cir. 1970); *Colorado County Federal Savings & Loan Association v. Commissioner*, 36 T.C. 1167 (1961), *aff'd*, 309 F.2d 751 (5th Cir. 1962); *Rio Grande Building & Loan Association v. Commissioner*, 36 T.C. 657 (1961).

[334] *Rio Grande Building and Loan Association v. Commissioner*, 36 T.C. 657, 663 (1961).

[335] Reg. § 1.593-7(a)(2).

[336] Rev. Rul. 76-245, 1976-1 C.B. 175. Note that wholly worthless bad debts may be deducted under I.R.C. § 166 or charged to the I.R.C. § § 585 and 593 reserves without being charged off on the accounting books.

[337] *Security Fed. Sav. & Loan Association of St. Augustine v. United States*, 72-2 U.S.T.C. ¶ 9545, 346 F. Supp. 908 (M.D. Fla. 1972).

[338] Rev. Rul. 77-128, 1977-1 C.B. 159.

[339] Reg. § 1.593-5(b)(2).

computation of the amount of the reserve addition and the method selected to determine the reserve addition.[340] A thrift that is a mutual savings bank using the percentage of taxable income method for determining its reasonable addition with respect to "qualifying" real property loans was required to file a statement that shows: (1) the amount of Code section 7701(a)(19)(C) assets as of the close of the taxable year; (2) a "brief description" of all other assets; and (3) a description of the method used for determining such amounts.[341]

The IRS has ruled that the record-keeping requirement has not been satisfied where the taxpayer charges the amount of a stock dividend to a subsidiary ledger tax adjustment account maintained for book purposes and controlled to its single appropriated reserves and undivided profits general ledger account.[342] However, controlling subsidiary ledger bad-debt reserve accounts to undivided profits and surplus accounts in the general ledger satisfies the reconciliation requirement.[343]

The IRS and the courts have held that thrifts could satisfy the "permanent record" requirement if their federal income tax returns become part of the taxpayer's permanent records.[344] Similarly, the use of supervisory accounts as required to be maintained by the Federal Home Loan Bank Board reflected on a supplementary schedule affixed to the taxpayer's tax return setting forth the three required tax reserves for thrifts met the record-keeping requirement.[345] However, it has been held that the bookkeeping requirement is not met by filing amended tax returns or crediting a lump sum representing cumulative reserves for past years in a single journal entry.[346]

Additions to a thrift's reserves for qualifying and nonqualifying loans were required to be credited to their respective reserves "by the close of the taxable year, or as soon as practicable thereafter."[347] Thus, it has been held that failure to timely establish the separate reserves for qualifying real property loans, nonqualifying loans and supplemental reserves precluded a bad-debt deduction.[348] The Tax Court has ruled that the "[o]rdinary business practices necessitate the allowance of a reasonable time after the close of the year for . . . the adjusting entries, including the entries for the various reserve accounts."[349] Similarly, the taxpayer

---

340 Reg. § 1.585-3(b).

341 Reg. § 1.593-6A(b)(2)(i). The consequence of failure to comply with these record-keeping requirements are unstated.

342 Rev. Rul. 79-198, 1979-1 C.B. 215; *see also* Rev. Rul. 56-404, 1956-2 C.B. 326.

343 Rev. Rul. 68-475, 1968-2 C.B. 259.

344 Rev. Rul. 77-333, 1971-2 C.B. 244; *Security Fed. Sav. & Loan Association of St. Augustine v. United States*, 72-2 U.S.T.C. ¶ 9545, 346 F. Supp. 908 (M.D. Fla. 1972). However, regulations under I.R.C. § 593 contain no such explicit authorization.

345 Rev. Rul. 78-226, 1978-1 C.B. 192; *see also Home Savings v. Commissioner*, 80 T.C. 571, Dec. 39,984 (1983). The supervisory duties of the Federal Home Loan Bank Board were transferred to the Office of Thrift Supervision by the Financial Institutions Reform, Recovery, and Enforcement Act of 1989, Pub. L. No. 101-73, 103 Stat. 183 (1989).

346 *Annapolis Federal Savings & Loan Association v. Commissioner*, 31 T.C.M. 1206, Dec. 31,627(M) (1972), T.C. Memo. 1972-243.

347 Reg. § 1.593-5(b); *see also* Rev. Rul. 66-26, 1966-1 C.B. 41 (Guideline 1). Rules relating to the establishment and maintenance of reserves have been contained in regulations for some time. I.R.C. § 39.23(k)-5(b)(3) (2000), Regs. 118, interpreting section 23(k)(1) of the 1939 code states, in part: "The establishment of such [bad debt] reserve and all adjustments made thereto must be reflected on the regular books of account of the institution at the close of the taxable year, or as soon as practicable thereafter."

348 *Silverton Loan and Building Company v. United States*, 76-1 U.S.T.C. ¶ 9393, 412 F. Supp. 17 (S.D. Ohio 1976).

349 *Rio Grande Bldg. & Loan Association v. Commissioner*, 36 T.C. 657, Dec. 24,938 (1961).

must actually make a book entry for the taxable year of the credit to the appropriate reserve, and such entry cannot be made substantially after the due date for filing the taxpayer's return.[350] Reflecting the reserve additions at a date four and one-half months after the filing of the taxpayer's return for the taxable year was found to be within a reasonable time of the close of the year when the delay was due to illness of the taxpayer's accountant.[351] In the event that a bank transfers a portion of its outstanding loans to another bank in a Code section 351 transaction, the transferred loans must be accounted for by reducing the transferor bank's loan balance at the beginning of the year of transfer.[352]

§ 10.8 The Experience Method

Under current law commercial banks and thrifts that are not "large" institutions may compute their allowable reserve balance by employing the experience method.[353] Prior to the repeal of Code section 593 in 1996, thrifts on the reserve method of accounting for loan losses were required to use the experience method of Code section 585 to account for losses on nonqualifying loans and, with respect to qualifying real property loans they were permitted alternatively, to employ either the experience method or the percentage of taxable income method of Code section 593.

Under the experience method, the allowable reserve addition is equal to an amount determined by the taxpayer not to exceed the amount necessary to increase the balance of the reserve for loan losses at the close of the taxable year, after adjustments for net charge-offs, equal to the greater of:

1. A reserve balance determined under a moving-average approach;[354] or
2. A reserve balance determined by reference to the base year amount.[355]

These alternatives are not methods of accounting. Accordingly, no permission need be obtained from the Commissioner before a change may be made from the moving-average method to the base-year method, or vice versa. Contrary to the tax reduction strategy that had been applied when using the now repealed percentage of eligible loans method, by maximizing the balance of total loans, bad-debt experience is not necessarily increased.

§ 10.8.1 Moving-Average Formula

Under the moving-average alternative, the maximum reserve addition is equal to the current year-end loan balance multiplied by a fraction, the numerator of which is the sum of net charge-offs for the taxable year and the preceding

---

[350] *Newport Federal Savings & Loan Association v. United States*, 66-2 U.S.T.C. ¶9702, 259 F. Supp. 82 (E.D. Ark. 1966); *Colorado County Federal Savings & Loan Association v. Commissioner*, 36 T.C. 1167, Dec. 25,055, (1961), *aff'd per curiam*, 62-2 U.S.T.C. ¶9847, 309 F.2d 751 (5th Cir. 1962); *Commercial Savings and Loan Association v. Commissioner*, 53 T.C. 14, Dec. 29,772 (1969).

[351] *Peoples Federal Savings & Loan Association v. United States*, 71-1 U.S.T.C. ¶9138, 320 F. Supp. 179 (D. S.C. 1971); *Levelland Savings & Loan Association v. United States*, 70-1 U.S.T.C. ¶9197, 421 F.2d 243 (5th Cir. 1970). *But cf. Rio Grande Bldg. & Loan Association v. Commissioner*, 36 T.C. 657, Dec. 24,938 (1961); *Colorado County Fed. Sav. & Loan Association, id.*, in which the Tax Court held that the entry must be made by the time the taxpayer filed its return.

[352] Rev. Rul. 80-270, 1980-2 C.B. 200.

[353] I.R.C. § 585(b)(2) (2000).

[354] I.R.C. § 585(b)(2)(A) (2000).

[355] I.R.C. § 585(b)(2)(B) (2000).

five taxable years, and the denominator of which is the sum of the year-end loan balances for those six years.[356]

Example: Bank Z is a commercial bank that has elected the reserve method of accounting for bad debts. Its reserve balance at 12/31/X6 is $5,100,000. For its taxable year ended 12/31/X7, Bank Z's maximum allowable reserve addition under the moving-average approach is $5,400,000, computed as follows:

TY	*Net Charge-Offs*	*Loans Outstanding*
19X2	$ 4,000,000	$ 650,000,000
19X3	4,090,000	700,000,000
19X4	4,235,000	770,000,000
19X5	5,170,000	930,000,000
19X6	5,005,000	950,000,000
19X7	5,000,000	1,000,000,000
	$27,500,000	$5,000,000,000

A. The bank's experience ratio, the ratio of net charge-offs to total loans outstanding for the six-year period, expressed as a percentage, is:

$$\frac{27{,}500{,}000}{5{,}000{,}000{,}000} = 0.55\%$$

B. The allowable reserve balance is:

$$\$1{,}000{,}000{,}000 \times .0055 = \$5{,}500{,}000$$

C. The reserve balance before addition is:

Opening Reserve Balance	$5,100,000
19X7 Net C/O's	(5,000,000)
Balance before Addition	$100,000

D. The allowable addition for 19X7 under moving-average formula is:

$$\$5{,}500{,}000 - 100{,}000 = \$5{,}400{,}000$$

§ 10.8.2 Reserve Restoration—General Rule

As a general rule, if the base-year reserve balance is greater than the balance allowable under the moving-average formula, a bank is permitted a reserve addition not to exceed the amount necessary to increase its reserve balance to the base-year amount.[357]

[356] I.R.C. § 585(b)(2)(A) (2000). In *Beneficial Corp and Subsidiaries v. United States*, 814 F.2d 1570 (Fed. Cir. 1987); 87-1 U.S.T.C. ¶ 9240, *rev'g and rem'g* 85-2 U.S.T.C. ¶ 9778, 9 Cl. Ct. 119 (1985), the Federal Circuit ruled that this moving-average formula could be modified when calculating a reserve addition with respect to long-term receivables. The moving-average formula was established in *Black Motor Co. v. Commissioner*, 42-1 U.S.T.C. ¶ 9265, 125 F.2d 977 (9th Cir. 1942), a case that dealt with short-term financing. The lag inherent in the formula yields a distorted reserve balance whenever the amount of receivables, or actual bad debts, significantly changes over a short period of time.

[357] I.R.C. § 585(b)(2)(B) (2000). This rule is limited, however, whenever loans at the close of the taxable years are less than loans outstanding at the close of the base year. I.R.C. § § 585(b)(2) and (b)(2)(A).

For taxable years beginning before 1988, the "base year" is the last taxable year before the most recent adoption of the experience method. For taxable years beginning after 1987, the base year is the last taxable year beginning before 1988.[358] Thus, these days, for calendar year banks the base year will be 1987.

Example: Assuming the following facts for Bank X, a calendar-year taxpayer:

Taxable Year-End	*Loans*	*Reserve Balance*
(Base year)	$475,000,000	$5,700,000
19X7	1,000,000,000	100,000[359]

Under the reserve restoration approach, the reserve addition for 19X7 is $5,600,000 computed as follows:

Base year reserve balance	$5,700,000
Less current year reserve balance	100,000
19X7 allowable reserve addition	$5,600,000

§ 10.8.3 Reserve Restoration—Decline in Loan Balance

If loans at the close of the taxable year have declined from the loans outstanding at the close of the base year, the otherwise allowable addition under the reserve restoration alternative will be limited.[360] The reserve balance for the taxable year under this approach is limited to the current year-end loans multiplied by the ratio, the numerator of which is the base year reserve balance and the denominator of which is loans outstanding at the close of the base year.

Example: Assume the same facts as in the original example, except that loans outstanding and the reserve balance for 19X7 are $425,000,000 and $5,700,000, respectively. The addition under the reserve restoration for 19X7 is $5,000,000, as follows:

A. Base year reserve limitation:

$$\$425,000,000 \times \frac{\$5,700,000}{\$475,000,000} = \$5,100,000$$

B. Current year reserve balance before addition $100,000

C. Allowable reserve addition $5,000,000

§ 10.8.4 Shorter Experience Period

There are several reasons why the moving average alternative, as it is contained in Code section 585, is inappropriate for commercial banks and thrifts, including: (a) the ratio is based on statistics some of which are six years old that may yield an allowable reserve balance that will be significantly out of line with a reserve balance that is computed using more current data; (b) there will be a

358 I.R.C. §§ 585(b)(2) and (b)(2)(A) (2000).

359 After adjustments for net charge-off, but before any addition.

360 I.R.C. § 585(b)(2)(B)(ii) (2000).

significant lag between the time when loan losses increase or decrease and when the change is reflected in the allowable reserve balance; (c) if a bank's loans are increasing, the use of year-end loan balances with net charge-offs that occur during the year will have the effect of understating the bank's bad debt experience ratio.[361]

To address certain of these shortcomings, regulations indicate that permission will be granted to use less than six-years for computing the experience ratio in two circumstances:[362]

1. When there has been a change in the risk of loss inherent in a substantial portion of the loan portfolio; or
2. When the entity is a new bank.

(a) Change in Risk of Loss

Regulations provide that permission to use less than six years will usually be granted when:

1. There has been a change in the type of a substantial portion of the loans outstanding;
2. The risk of loss on the bank's loans is substantially increased by reason of that change; and
3. The taxpayer furnishes the IRS with specific evidence that loans, outstanding at the close of the taxable years for the short period requested, are not comparable in nature and risk to loans outstanding at the close of the six taxable years.[363]

The "change" in type includes both a material change in the mix of a bank's loan portfolio (for example, from agricultural loans to industrial loans), as well as a material expansion of the bank's loan portfolio to include loans to a new class of borrowers (*e.g.*, the addition of consumer-installment loans to a portfolio of commercial loans).[364] Thus, the IRS has ruled that a mutual savings bank was permitted to use a shorter experience period when it experienced unusually large losses resulting from its entry into the credit card business and when its portfolio of consumer and commercial loans substantially increased.[365]

Regulations also state that a "decline in the general economic conditions in the area, which substantially increase the risk of loss is a relevant factor which may be considered." However, the experience period may not be shortened when a bank opens a new branch in a high unemployment area thereby causing a higher rate of loan losses.[366] Further, the fact that an institution's bad-debt experience has shown substantial increase is not, by itself, sufficient to justify the use of a shorter period.

---

[361] "The Black Motor Bad Debt Formula," *The Journal of Taxation*, Jules I. Whitman, John W. Gilbert, and Peter J. Picotte, II, Dec. 1971, p. 369.

[362] Reg. § 1.585-2(c)(1)(ii).

[363] *Id.*

[364] *Id.*

[365] PLR 8919035, May 12, 1989 (credit card loans and unsecured lending); PLR 8929061, July 21, 1989 (consumer loans); PLR 8425059, March 20, 1984.

[366] PLR 8427025, March 30, 1984.

A request for permission to use a period shorter than the required six years must be submitted at least 30 days *before* the end of the taxable year.[367] If permission to use a shorter period for computing the moving average is granted, none of the excluded years may be taken into account for any future year's moving-average computation.

(b) New Banks

A new bank, or one with less than six years of bad debt and loan history, will not have available to it the normal six "authorization years" of its own data to compute its allowable reserve addition under the experience method. Regulations specifically authorize, without permission or approval first being obtained from the IRS, for a new bank to use "comparable bank" bad-debt experience during "comparison years" to determine the maximum reserve addition under the experience method.[368] The loans of the new bank for the six-year period shall be six times the average loans outstanding of the new bank during the "authorization years."

A "comparable bank" is a term which describes a bank, as defined in Code section 581, and an institution which would otherwise meet the Code section 581 definition of a "bank," except that the institution is a foreign corporation, and that is located within the same Federal Reserve District as the taxpayer.[369] The "comparison years" are consecutive taxable years containing 12 completed months of the comparable bank, the last year of which ends within 12 months immediately preceding the beginning of the first taxable year of the taxpayer. Comparison years will be limited to six minus the number of "authorization years" of the taxpayer.[370]

The "authorization years" of a taxpayer are the years, containing 12 complete months, between the first day of the first full taxable year of the taxpayer for which it, or any predecessor, was authorized to do business as a financial institution, and the taxable year.[371] Regulations indicate that the authorization years are those "*between*" the first day of the full taxable year of the taxpayer and the current tax year. Although this appears to exclude from the calculation of allowable reserve balance the current tax year and the first full tax year of the taxpayer, to do so would be illogical. To eliminate two full years of the taxpayer's actual experience would result in the unnecessary use of additional "comparable bank" data for years in which the taxpayer has accurate individual experience.

Total bad debts for purposes of the six-year experience factor will equal the sum of the taxpayer's net bad debts during its authorization years plus the net bad debts determined using the experience of the comparable bank.[372] The net bad debts using the experience of the comparable bank shall be equal to the net bad debts of the comparable bank during the comparison years multiplied by a fraction, the numerator of which is the average loans outstanding of the taxpayer

[367] Reg. § 1.585-2(c)(1)(ii).

[368] Reg. § 1.585-2(c)(2).

[369] Reg. § 1.585-2(e)(7). *See* listing of the twelve Federal Reserve Districts in Appendix E.

[370] Reg. § 1.585-2(e)(6).

[371] Reg. § 1.585-2(e)(5).

[372] Reg. § 1.585-2(c)(2)(ii).

during the authorization years and the denominator of which is the average loans outstanding of the comparable bank during the comparison years.

Example: Assume that "Bank" is a calendar year taxpayer authorized to conduct business on September 15, 1993. The current tax year is 1995. Also, assume the following:

Bank's Authorization Years		*Bad Debts*		*Loans Outstanding*
19X4		$350		$22,000
19X5		450		18,000
	TOTAL:	$800	AVERAGE:	$20,000

Comparable's Comparison Years		*Bad Debts*		*Loans Outstanding*
19X3		$300		$20,000
19X2		500		30,000
19X1		500		22,000
19X0		200		28,000
	TOTAL:	$1,500	AVERAGE:	$25,000

The first day of the first full taxable year for which Bank was authorized to conduct business was January 1, 19X4. Because the current tax year is preceded by less than five authorization years, Bank is subject to the "new financial institution" rules contained in the regulations, and it must determine its bad-debt experience using comparable bank data.

To compute Bank's allowable reserve balance for 19X5, bad debts and loans for the six-year period ending December 31, 19X5 must be determined. Loans for the period will be equal to six times the average loans outstanding during the authorization years. Bad debts for the period will equal the sum of Bank's bad debts during its authorization years and bad debts determined by employing the experience of the comparable bank selected ("Comparable") during the comparison years, 19X0-X3.

The sum of Bank's loans outstanding is $120,000, which is the average loans outstanding for Bank's authorization years, $20,000, multiplied by six.[373]

The portion of Comparable's bad debts that will be added to Bank's bad debts is $1200, which is the ratio of Bank's average loans outstanding, $20,000, to Comparable's average loans outstanding, $25,000, multiplied by Comparable's bad debts during the comparison years, $1500.

This portion of Comparable's bad debts, $1200, is then added to Bank's bad debts, $800, and divided by Bank's total loans for the six-year period, $120,000, to determine Bank's loss ratio, 0.016667.

---

[373] If there were one authorization year, then the loans outstanding during that year would be multiplied by six.

If Bank has $18,000 in loans outstanding at the end of the cur-rent tax year, Bank's allowable reserve balance will be $300 (.016667×$18,000).

Comparable bank data gradually ceases to be applicable as the institution develops bad-debt experience of its own.[374] Thus, each time that the institution completes 12 months of its own experience, a year of comparable bank data ceases to be taken into account for purposes of developing the institution's experience ratio.

It is seldom clear what constitutes, in reality, a "comparable bank." Although regulations define a "comparable bank" as "*all* the financial institutions" in the taxpayer's Federal Reserve District, regulations also indicate that a new financial institution should use data from "a comparable bank."[375] The legislative history to Code section 585 states that a taxpayer may calculate bad-debt reserves "on the basis of an industrywide average."[376] However, using data from all financial institutions in the taxpayer's Federal Reserve District may yield a distorted experience ratio.

By using data from select banks in the District, the taxpayer would be able to choose banks that conduct similar business. It is quite possible that selective data from a few banks, and not "all" banks, would produce more accurate indicia of the new bank's likely experience ratio. For example, if the Federal Reserve District contains several money center banks which have substantial credit card portfolios and less developed country debt, an inflated experience factor may be applied. Similarly, if the new institution is located in a town which historically had high personal and corporate bankruptcies relative to the banks in most other towns located within the District, more local specific data would produce a more accurate experience factor.

Regulations appear to permit use of the experience of thrift institutions located within the District.[377] Since the types of loans that a thrift is authorized to make may closely resemble those of a new commercial bank, thrift data would be relevant in establishing a bank's experience factor. Moreover, since thrifts are expressly authorized to use the Code section 585(b) experience method, the reference in the regulations to the Federal Reserve District should be read as Federal Home Loan Bank District when developing a substituted experience factor for a new thrift.

§ 10.8.5 "Loans" Defined

The Code section 585 computation rules are applicable to all "loans" made by a bank that accounts for loan losses under the reserve method.[378] The amount of a debt that may be treated as a "loan" for purposes of the reserve computation is the portion in which the taxpayer has a tax basis. Thus, a "loan" will equal the original amount loaned, plus accrued and taxed interest that has not been

---

[374] Reg. § 1.585-2(e)(6).

[375] Reg. § 1.585-2(c)(2)(ii)(A)(2).

[376] H.R. Rep No. 91-413, at 121 (1986).

[377] A "comparable bank" is a "bank" as defined in I.R.C. § 581, which includes a thrift. *Department of Banking and Consumer Finance v. Clarke*, 809 F.2d 266 (5th Cir. 1987).

[378] Reg. § 1.585-3.

received, minus any charge-off. In addition, proposed regulations issued under Code section 475 provide that the tax basis of any loan that is subject to the mark-to-market rules must be adjusted for mark-to-market gain or loss.[379] Gains will increase tax basis, and losses will reduce tax basis. However, the proposed regulations provide that for purposes of the computation of a bank's reserve for bad debts, the tax basis of a loan may not be increased above the actual amount that the borrower owes the bank.[380]

§ 10.8.6 Extraordinary Loan Losses

Bad debts on loans may not be deducted under the direct charge-off method if the reserve method applies.[381] Although the IRS has ruled that, under limited circumstances, an extraordinary bad debt experienced by a mercantile firm could be accounted for outside the firm's bad-debt reserve, no such treatment appears to be allowable for banks.[382]

For taxable years beginning prior to January 1, 1987, losses on securities that became wholly or partially worthless could be accounted for under the reserve method if they were segregated in a separate reserve and not included in the reserve for loan losses.[383] The IRS also ruled that the losses incurred by a bank with respect to deposits made in another bank may be deducted only under Code section 166 specific charge-off method and not under the reserve method. The IRS reasoned that these losses are rare and unpredictable and do not arise in the normal course of the depositing bank's business of making loans and providing banking services.[384] Authority for this position is not provided.

It appears to be the IRS's position that deductions for securities losses by a bank on the reserve method should be taken under the specific charge-off method.[385] Certain loans, if "packaged," may be treated as securities. If the taxpayer regularly makes mortgage loans with the intention of aggregating them, the taxpayer should note the possibility that they may be reclassified as securities. It is not appropriate to establish a separate reserve for these "securities." If such debts become wholly or partially worthless they should be accounted for under the specific charge-off method.

Pursuant to authority expressly granted in Code section 585(b)(3) the Treasury Department has promulgated regulations which define the term "loan."[386]

---

[379] Prop. Reg. § 1.475(a)-1(g)(1), 60 Fed. Reg. 397, (January 4, 1995). Portions of the proposed regulations under I.R.C. § 475 have been finalized, but this regulation was reserved. The Code does not provide for this adjustment to tax basis. *See* I.R.C. § 475(a) (2000).

[380] *Id.* This rule appears to ignore the fact that most mark-to-market gain or loss will be the result of interest rate movements. It is unclear why a taxpayer is required to decrease its loan balance for the full amount of mark-down, but not to increase the loan balance for the full amount of mark-up.

[381] Reg. § § 1.585-2 and 1.593-7(c)(2).

[382] Rev. Rul. 74-409, 1974-2 C.B. 61.

[383] TAM 7921016, February 12, 1979; General Counsel Memorandum 25605, 1948-1 C.B. 38; Rev. Rul. 66-26, 1966-1 C.B. 41.

[384] Rev. Rul. 68-3, 1968-1 C.B. 75.

[385] PLR 7921016, February 12, 1979. *See* discussion of securities losses at § 10.2. If a bank has made the conformity election under Reg. § 1.166-2(d)(3), losses on loans that are not subject to regulatory loss classification standards may be deducted under the specific charge-off method. Reg. § 1.166-2(d)(3)(iii)(B)(3). *See* discussion of conformity election at § 10.4.

[386] Reg. § 1.585-2(e)(2). These regulations probably have the status of legislative regulations, which imbue them with authority greater than normal in-

Regulations under Code section 585 define a "loan" as a debt (as that term is used in Code section 166), including, but not limited to:

1. An overdraft in one or more deposit accounts by a customer in good faith whether or not other deposit accounts of the same customer have balances in excess of the overdraft;[387]
2. A bankers acceptance purchased or discounted by a bank; that is, an acceptance made by the bank which purchased or discounted the acceptance and not one made by the originating bank;[388] and
3. A loan participation to the extent that the taxpayer bears a risk of loss.[389]

A bona fide debt is one that "arises from a debtor-creditor relationship based on a valid and enforceable obligation to pay a fixed or determinable sum of money."[390] If the loan is sold subject to an agreement by the selling bank to repurchase it if the borrower defaults, the risk of loss on the loan remains with the selling bank, and the purchasing bank may not include the loan in its loan base for bad-debt calculation purposes. Such a transaction more closely resembles a collateralized borrowing by the "selling" bank.

(a) *Insured Loans—Mortgage Backed Certificates*

A taxpayer bears the "risk of loss" on a loan if the taxpayer has credit outstanding. Thus, a bank has a risk of loss on a bona fide loan even though it is fully guaranteed or insured by the federal government.[391]

The IRS appears to have modified its earlier position relating to whether a taxpayer could bear a "risk of loss" with respect to a federally guaranteed instrument. In 1988 the IRS ruled privately that federally guaranteed mortgage certificates insured by the Federal Home Loan Mortgage Corporation ("FHLMC"), the Federal National Mortgage Association ("FNMA"), or the Government National Mortgage Association ("GNMA") were loans outstanding for purposes of computing additions to a bank's loan loss reserve under the experience method, "but only to the extent Taxpayer bears a risk of loss."[392] Such pass-through mortgage-backed certificates represent proportional ownership of underlying mortgages. More recently, the IRS privately ruled that such certificates

(Footnote Continued)

terpretive regulations promulgated under I.R.C. §7805(a). The term "loan" also is defined in I.R.C. §593(d) for purposes of computing a thrifts reserve for loan losses. By implication, a "loan" includes all debts defined as qualifying loans and nonqualifying loans. All debts meeting the I.R.C. §593 definition of a "loan" should meet the I.R.C. §585 definition as well, and vice versa.

[387] Reg. §1.585-2(e)(2)(i)(A).

[388] Reg. §1.585-2(e)(2)(i)(B). By "accepting" the draft drawn on it the bank extends credit as it would in the case of a check drawn at the bank. For regulatory definition and rules relating to bankers acceptances, *see* 12 U.S.C. §372.

[389] Reg. §1.585-2(e)(2)(i)(C); PLR 8903001, August 31, 1988. Mortgage-backed pass-through certificates purchased by a taxpayer are "loan participations" within the meaning of Reg. §1.585-2(e)(2)(i)(C). TAM 8822001, February 3, 1988; Rev. Rul. 84-10, 1984-1 C.B. 155.

[390] Reg. §1.166-1(c). *See* §10.1 for discussion of what constitutes a "debt." In TAM 200439041, September 24, 2004, the IRS concluded that rights to service mortgages owned by others may not be included in loans outstanding for purposes of determining the balance of its bad debt reserve under §585.

[391] PLR 8928002, March 22, 1989; Rev. Rul. 84-10, 1984-1 C.B. 155.

[392] PLR 8822001, February 3, 1988.

are properly includable in a bank's total outstanding loans for purposes of computing its bad-debt deduction under the experience method.[393]

(b) *REMICs, GNMAs*

The IRS has privately ruled that although a Real Estate Mortgage Investment Conduit ("REMIC") interest is referred to as, and may appear in the form of, a mortgage-backed security, it qualifies as a "loan" for purposes of the experience method calculation.[394] Further, for purposes of the calculation of a thrifts addition to its reserve, a regular or residual interest in a REMIC is generally treated as a qualifying real property loan[395] as is a certificate issued by the FNMA, the FHLMC, and the GNMA.[396]

(c) *Eligible Loans*

For purposes of the experience method computation of "loans," the provisions contained in the Code and in regulations relating to the items that constituted "eligible loans" for purposes of the repealed percentage of eligible loans method are instructive. For taxable years beginning before 1988, this was an alternative method for determining a commercial bank and thrift's allowable reserve balance. In fact, the IRS has privately ruled that "the definition of the term 'eligible loan' provides useful guidance as to what constitutes a 'loan' for purposes of section 585 of the Code."[397]

Unless expressly excluded, each of the following loans that were not "eligible" loans should be included in the loan base for purposes of the current experience method calculation:[398]

1. A loan to a bank or to a domestic branch of a foreign corporation conducting a banking business in the United States. Such loans include repurchase transactions or other similar transactions;[399]
2. A loan in the form of a deposit in another bank, including funds available on or after a stated date or period of time;[400]
3. A "sale" of federal funds; that is, an unsecured overnight loan by one bank to another of funds deposited in a Federal Reserve Bank;[401]
4. A loan to or guaranteed by the United States, a possession or instrumentality thereof, or a state or a political subdivision thereof;[402] and

---

[393] PLR 9423002, January 25, 1994; Rev. Rul. 70-545, 1970-2 C.B. 7, at 8; Rev. Rul. 77-349, 1977-2 C.B. 20.

[394] PLR 9423002, January 25, 1994.

[395] I.R.C. § 593(d)(4) (2000).

[396] Rev. Rul. 84-10, 1984-1 C.B. 155; Rev. Rul. 71-399, 1971-2 C.B. 433; Rev. Rul. 74-169, 1974-1 C.B. 147.

[397] PLR 9423002, January 25, 1994.

[398] I.R.C. § 585(b)(4) (2000); Reg. § 1.585-2(e)(3). I.R.C. § 585(b)(4) (2000) was repealed by the Omnibus Budget Reconciliation Act of 1990, Pub. L. No. 101-508, § 11801(c)(12)(D), 104 Stat. 1388 (1990).

[399] I.R.C. § 585(b)(4)(A)(B); Reg. § 1.585-3(ii)(A). Rev. Rul. 68-3, 1968-1 C.B. 75.

[400] I.R.C. § 585(b)(4)(C) (2000); Reg. § 1.585-3(ii)(B).

[401] I.R.C. § 585(b)(4)(F) (2000); Reg. § 1.585-3(ii)(C). PLR 9423002, January 1, 1994. The lending bank is usually making available to the borrowing bank excess reserves of liquid assets maintained to satisfy reserve requirements. Some banks also use federal funds as a limited source of funds or as an investment opportunity.

[402] I.R.C. § 585(b)(4)(D) (2000); Reg. § 1.585-3(ii)(D).

5. A loan secured by a deposit in the lending bank over which the lending bank has control.[403]

Two types of loans excluded from eligible loans are also excluded from "loans" for purposes of the experience calculation:

1. A loan evidenced by a "security" as defined in Code section 165(g)(2)(C);[404] and
2. Commercial paper, including short term promissory notes that may be purchased on the open market.[405]

(d) Loans to Banks

This category includes any loan to a domestic bank or to a domestic branch of a foreign bank, including a sale or a loan of federal funds, the purchase of certificates of deposit and the placing of other deposit arrangements and repurchase transactions (such as agreements to resell).[406] In this respect, the IRS has ruled that a mortgage loan to a nominee of a bank was excludable from the lender's eligible loan base.[407] If the bank assumes the risk of loss pursuant to a repurchase agreement entered into with another bank, the arrangement qualifies as a "loan."[408] The Tax Court has held that a loan to a trust managed by the trustee bank's trust department qualifies as an eligible loan, although trust department overdrafts do not.[409] The sale of Federal funds is, essentially, a short-term loan between banks.[410]

(e) Loans to Governments

This category includes any loan made to, or guaranteed or insured by, the federal government, a possession or instrumentality thereof or by any state government or political subdivision thereof.[411] However, loans contingently guaranteed by the federal government or an instrumentality thereof are not considered "guaranteed." Loans collateralized with federal, state or local governmental obligations also are not considered "guaranteed."[412]

The mere fact that a loan generates tax-exempt income does not automatically classify it as a loan to, or guaranteed or insured by, a state government or a municipality. In *First Wisconsin Bankshares Corp.*, the District Court held that there was a sufficient risk of loss to justify inclusion of such a loan in the bank's

[403] I.R.C. § 585(b)(4)(C) (2000); Reg. § 1.585-3(ii)(E).

[404] I.R.C. § 585(b)(4)(E) (2000).

[405] I.R.C. § 585(b)(4) (2000).

[406] Rev. Rul. 68-524, 1968-2 C.B. 83.

[407] Rev. Rul. 77-216, 1977-1 C.B. 52.

[408] TAM 8147004, July 24, 1979.

[409] *First National Bank of Chicago v. Commissioner*, 64 T.C. 1001 (1975), Dec. 33,408. (Nonacq.), 1978-2 C.B. 3, *rev'd*, 77-1 U.S.T.C. ¶9117, 546 F.2d 759 (7th Cir. 1976), *cert. denied*, 431 U.S. 914, (1977).

[410] PLR 9423002, June 10, 1994.

[411] Rev. Rul. 68-630, 1968-2 C.B. 84, *clarifying* Rev. Rul. 65-92, 1965-1 C.B. 112; Rev. Rul. 77-216, 1977-1 C.B. 52, *amplifying* Rev. Rul. 68-630, 1968-1 C.B. 84. With respect to certain government insured mortgage-backed pass-through certificates, *see* PLRs 8822001, February 3, 1988; 8928002, March 22, 1989; and 9423002, January 25, 1947.

[412] *First Wisconsin Bankshares Corporation v. United States*, 74-1 U.S.T.C. ¶9164, 369 F. Supp. 1034 (D. Wisc. 1973); TAM 8214016, December 30, 1981. Thus, the IRS has announced that a regulation will be proposed under I.R.C. § 103, which will provide that state and local obligations issued before December 31, 1985, and guaranteed by letters of credit insured by the FDIC will not be treated as federally guaranteed obligations solely by reason of the federally insured collateral.

eligible loan base even though there was a close relationship between the state government and the borrower of the funds.[413] Normally, a loan to a school district, or a fire or police department will be considered made to a state political subdivision.[414] Moreover, in a ruling under Code section 103, the IRS has stated that a not-for-profit corporation formed by a fire district was an "exempt person" within the meaning of Code section 103(b). Thus, the interest paid to a bank was exempt from federal income tax.[415] Given the minimal risk of loss described in the ruling, the loan would probably be excludable from the bank's eligible loan base. However, if a loan is made to a state university or to certain industrial development authorities, it will be considered an eligible loan.[416]

(f) Loans Secured by Deposits

A loan secured by a deposit includes any loan to a customer that is secured by a deposit in any bank (foreign or domestic) provided that the lending bank has control over the withdrawal of such deposit. A deposit for this purpose includes a "holdback" (pledged collateral that has been reduced to cash) and loan payments that are maintained in a separate account.[417] Mortgage escrow accounts for taxes and insurance are not considered collateral for this purpose.[418]

A deposit is security for a loan only if the deposit is of such a nature that in the event of default the deposit could be subjected to the satisfaction of the loan.[419] A bank will be deemed to have control over the deposit only when withdrawal of the deposited funds can be accomplished with the consent of the lender. Merely because the bank requires a minimum, average, or compensating deposit balance as a condition for the loan will not normally constitute control by the bank over the funds.[420]

(g) Arrangements That Are Not Loans

Expressly excluded from "loans" are the following items:[421]

1. *Unrecognized Discount.* Discount or interest receivable reflected in the face amount of an outstanding loan and which has not been included in gross income.[422]
2. *Commercial Paper.* Commercial paper, including short-term promissory notes which may be purchased on the open market.[423]

---

413 *Id.*

414 Rev. Rul. 77-164, 1977-1 C.B. 52. *See also* I.R.C. § 7871(d) in which Indian tribal governments are treated as states for certain purposes.

415 PLR 8601040, October 7, 1985, *citing* Rev. Rul. 82-26, 1982-1 C.B. 476.

416 TAM 7905009, September 27, 1978; Rev. Rul. 77-165, 1977-1 C.B. 21.

417 Reg. § 1.585-2(e)(3)(iii)(B).

418 Rev. Rul. 74-584, 1974-2 C.B. 177; *Richmond Hill Savings Bank v. Commissioner*, 57 T.C. 738, Dec. 31,294 (1972).

419 Reg. § 1.585-2(e)(3)(iii)(A).

420 Reg. § 1.585-2(e)(3)(iii)(C).

421 Reg. § 1.585-2(e)(2); I.R.C. § 593(d)(3).

422 Reg. § 1.585-2(e)(2)(ii)(A).

423 *Id.*

3. *Securities.* A debt evidenced by a bond, debenture, note, or other evidence of indebtedness, issued by a corporation or by a government or political subdivision thereof, with interest coupons or in registered form.[424]
4. *Distortion Loans.* Any loan that is entered into or acquired for the primary purpose of enlarging an otherwise available bad-debt deduction.[425]
5. *Pending Loans.* Loans that have been contractually committed to the extent that funds have not been disbursed to the borrower or disbursed on behalf of the borrower.[426]
6. *Illegal Loans.* Any transaction that is in violation of a federal or state statute that governs the activities of a financial institution.[427]
7. *ATRR Loans.*[428] That portion of certain international loans that are charged to either an allocated transfer risk reserve ("ATRR") or against the allowance for possible loan losses are excluded from the bank's loans for purposes of computing the bank's reasonable addition to its reserve for bad debts.[429]
8. *Security Property.* A commercial bank or a thrift for tax years beginning on or after January 1, 1996 may not treat as a "loan" any property acquired at foreclosure, deed-in-lieu of foreclosure or similar means.[430]
9. *Loans to Affiliates.* Any loan by a bank that is made to a member of the bank's affiliated group with which a consolidated return is filed is considered to be a loan to an affiliate.[431] Regulations do not provide that a loan to an affiliate is excluded from the loan base. A deduction for bad debts with respect to such loans must be deferred until one of the triggering events described in Regulation section 1.1502-14(d)(2) and (3) occurs.[432] One of the more common "triggering events" is when the borrowing entity ceases to be a member of the affiliated group. Of course, to treat the loss as a bad-debt deduction, even at the time one of the triggering events occurs, is conditioned upon the existence of a bona fide debt. If advances to a subsidiary are intended to enlarge the bank's stock investment, they will be treated as capital contributions and not loans.[433]
10. *Noncustomer Loans.* Any loan that is not incurred in the course of a bank's normal customer loan activity is deemed to be a noncustomer loan.

---

[424] Reg. § 1.585-2(e)(2)(ii)(C). This is not the definition of a "security" employed in I.R.C. § 475.

[425] Reg. § 1.585-2(e)(2)(ii)(D).

[426] Reg. § 1.585-2(e)(2)(ii)(E).

[427] Reg. § 1.585-2(e)(2)(ii)(F).

[428] Rev. Rul. 92-14, 1992-1 C.B. 93.

[429] *Id.*

[430] I.R.C. § 595 (2000); PLR 8903001, August 31, 1988. For security property acquired prior to 1996, thrifts may treat "security property" as a loan. I.R.C. § 595.

[431] Rev. Rul. 76-430, 1976-2 C.B. 183.

[432] *First National Bank in Little Rock v. Commissioner*, 83 T.C., 202, Dec. 41, 422 (1984).

[433] *Fairbanks, Morse & Co. v. Harrison*, 46-1 U.S.T.C. § 9217, 63 F. Supp. 495 (DC Ill. 1946). *See also* the characteristics of debt and equity instruments as set forth in I.R.C. § 385.

Under intercompany consolidated return regulations, a bank's deduction under section 585 for an addition to its reserve for bad debts with respect to an intercompany obligation is not taken into account and is not treated as realized until:

1. The intercompany obligation becomes a non-intercompany obligation; or
2. The redemption or collection of less than the recorded amount of the intercompany obligation (and the corresponding charge-off against the reserve), whichever occurs first.[434]

Example: On January 1 of 19X1, Affiliate borrows $100 from Bank in return for Affiliate's note providing for 10% of interest annually at the end of each year and repayment of $100 at the end of 19X5. For 19X3, Bank claims a $40 partial bad-debt deduction under section 166(a)(2) on a separate entity basis. Affiliate is never insolvent within the meaning of section 108(d)(3).

Affiliate is treated as satisfying its note for $60 immediately before Bank's bad-debt deduction, and reissuing a new note to Bank with a $60 issue price and a $100 stated redemption price at maturity.[435] Thus, Affiliate takes into account $40 of discharge of indebtedness income, and Bank takes into account a corresponding $40 of ordinary loss.[436]

§ 10.9 Percentage of Taxable Income Method

Special loan loss deduction rules for thrifts were established in 1951, when the exemption from federal income taxation granted to thrifts was repealed. The exemption from taxation was founded on the notion that these institutions were in effect doing business with themselves (i.e., the member's money was being used for loans to members). Accordingly, there was no profit on which to impose an income tax.[437] These special rules were repealed in 1996, effective for taxable years beginning on or after January 1, 1996.

In its original form, thrifts were allowed to deduct additions to their bad debt reserves, which were so generous that they remained virtually tax exempt until amendments were made in 1962. During the first decade of taxation, thrifts could make reserve additions in whatever amount the institution deemed appropriate so long as the amount did not exceed the taxable income of the institution, or the institution's total reserves and surplus did not exceed 12 percent of its deposits or withdrawable accounts at the close of the year. The 1962 amendments established the provisions of Code section 593 in a form that remained nearly the same for the following 35 years. Under current law, thrift institutions are treated as commercial banks. Thus, any large thrift institution is prohibited from using the reserve method of accounting for bad debts and must claim deductions for partially or wholly worthless bad debts under the specific charge-off method contained in Code section 166. A thrift institution that qualifies as a small bank would be permitted to use the experience method contained in Code section 585 or the specific charge-off method.

[434] Reg. § 1.1502-13, 58 Fed. Reg. 18011, April 15, 1994.

[435] Reg. § 1.1502-13(g)(3).

[436] Reg. § 1.1502-13(g)(6) Ex. 3.

[437] Report of Committee on Ways and Means, H.R. Doc. No. 87-1447, at 436 (1962).

The percentage of taxable income ("PTI") method was instituted as an acceptable method for determining loan loss deductions in respect of qualifying real property loans.[438] In respect of nonqualifying loans, thrifts were permitted to use the experience method available to commercial banks. As structured in 1962, Code section 593 provided that a reserve addition for "qualifying real property loans" was allowed in an amount equal to specially computed taxable income multiplied by a statutory percentage.[439] This method was available only for those taxable years when a thrift's holdings of Code section 7701(a)(19)(C) assets amount to 60 percent or more of total assets.[440] An entity satisfied the Code section 7701(a)(19) test but was unable to use the PTI method if its assets did not include the requisite percentage of qualifying real property loans.

This requirement replaced a more stringent provision applicable to tax years beginning prior to 1987. Under that provision, the PTI method (and Code section 593, in general) was applicable only to organizations which met the tax definition of a mutual savings bank, a domestic building and loan association, or a cooperative bank without capital stock organized and operated for mutual purposes and without profit.[441] To meet the tax definition of a domestic building and loan association or a cooperative bank, a three-part test was required to be passed.[442] The 60 percent asset test was one of the three components of that test, but the organization also had to pass a business operations and a supervisory component.[443]

In those circumstances where less than 60 percent of thrift's total assets consisted of Code section 7701(a)(19)(C) assets (*e.g.*, certain real property loans, cash and taxable government securities), a thrift was not permitted to compute its reserve addition under Code section 593.[444] However, since the thrift would no longer be "an organization to which section 593 applies," it was permitted to qualify as a bank for purposes of Code section 585. As such, it would have available to it the experience and, with respect to taxable years beginning before 1988, the percentage of eligible loan methods applicable to commercial banks. Should the thrift meet the Code section 585 definition of a "large bank" not only would the reserve method of that section be unavailable, but reserve recapture would be triggered.

Although the PTI method allowed a bad-debt deduction irrespective of actual loss experience, it was subject to several limitations. Moreover, whenever

[438] Thrifts also were permitted to use the percentage of eligible loans method for qualifying real property loans. This method was repealed, effective for taxable years after 1987, by the Tax Reform Act of 1986.

[439] I.R.C. §593(b)(2).

[440] *See* discussion of I.R.C. §7701(a)(19)(c) (2000) assets in Ch. 1.

[441] I.R.C. §593(a) (2000) prior to amendment by Pub. L. No. 99-514, §901(b)(1).

[442] Reg. §§301.7701-13A; 301.7701-14. A definition of a mutual savings bank is not contained in the code or regulations.

[443] I.R.C. §7701(a)(19) (2000); Reg. §301.7701-13A. *See* discussion in Ch. 1.

[444] I.R.C. §593(a)(2) (2000). For taxable years beginning before January 1, 1987, failure to pass the 60% test meant only that the thrift could not calculate its reserve addition under the percentage of taxable income method. The experience and percentage of eligible loan methods remained available. A detailed definition of I.R.C. §7701(a)(19)(C) (2000) assets is contained in Ch. 1.

it was used, a thrift was required to reduce by eight percent any dividends received deduction otherwise allowed.[445] Finally, use of the PTI method was more likely to result in the thrift incurring an alternative minimum tax liability.[446]

§10.9.1 Loans That Are Qualifying

A "qualifying real property loan" is a "loan," as that term was used in Code section 585 for purposes of the experience method, which was secured by an interest in qualifying real property.[447] The term "qualifying real property" means any real property which was either "improved real property," or property which became "improved real property" from the proceeds of the loan. Regulations expressly provided that the following property not commonly considered to be a "loan" was treated as a "loan" for purposes of Code section 593:

1. Certain mortgage transactions referred to as redeemable ground rents (defined in Code section 1055(c)), which was owned by the taxpayer; and
2. Any property (real or personal) acquired by the taxpayer in a transaction in which the institution bids in or otherwise reduces to ownership or possession any property which was security for the payment of any indebtedness.[448]

No mention is made of whether these two items will constitute "qualifying real property loans." However, it would appear that if the mortgage transaction in respect of the "redeemable ground rents" case or the security property were in respect of preexisting qualifying real property loan, then these items would be treated as qualifying real property loans.

Improved real property which satisfies the definition of qualifying real property is defined as:

1. Land on which is located any building the value of which is substantial in relation to the land and which is permanent in nature. A permanent building includes a house, mobile unit, apartment house, office building, hospital, shopping center, warehouse, garage, or other similar permanent structure.
2. Any building lot or site without any building or permanent structure, which by reason of installations and improvements that have been completed in keeping with applicable government requirements and with general practice in the community, is a building lot or site ready for the construction of any building of a permanent nature described in "1" above.

---

[445] I.R.C. §596 (2000) and Reg. §1.596-1(c); Reg. §§1.1502-26(a)(3) and (a)(4). I.R.C. §§243, 244 and 245 allow a deduction for dividends received.

[446] I.R.C. §57(a)(4) provided that an "item of tax preference" includes, for a thrift, the excess of its deduction for a reasonable addition to its reserve for bad debts in excess of the amount that would have been allowable had the institution maintained its bad-debt reserve for all taxable years on the basis of actual experience. I.R.C. §57(a)(4) was repealed in 1996. Pub. L. No. 104-188, Title I, §1616(b)(3), August 20, 1996, 110 Stat 1856.

[447] I.R.C. §593(d)(1) (2000). Notice that fewer types of real property loans are taken into account for purposes of calculating I.R.C. §7701(a)(19)(C) assets than qualify as real property loans for purposes of computing the reserve for "qualifying real property loans." A loan to purchase an interest in a cooperative apartment is a loan secured by an interest in real property. Rev. Rul. 89-59, 1989-1 C.B. 317; PLRs 8825039, March 22, 1988 and 8830065, May 4, 1988.

[448] This is an I.R.C. §595(a) transaction, as that section provided before its repeal in 1996.

3. Any income producing "real property" that, because of its state of improvement, generates income sufficient to maintain the property and also to retire the loan in accordance with the terms of the loan agreement.
4. A mobile unit which is permanently fixed to real property.

As a general rule, state law will determine whether property is "real" or "personal."[449] However, regardless of state law, a mobile unit which is permanently fixed to real property shall be treated as "real property" for purposes of this provision. Among the circumstances when a mobile unit will be treated as "permanently fixed" to real property during the taxable year will be when the unit is placed upon a foundation at a site with wheels and axles removed, affixed to the ground by means of straps, and connected to water, sewer, gas, and electric facility.[450]

A loan is "secured" by an interest in real property if real property is specific security for the payment of the loan. It will be treated as such only if the instrument securing the loan provides that, in the event of default, the property could be subjected to the satisfaction of the loan with the same priority as a mortgage or deed of trust in the jurisdiction in which the property is situated.[451]

A taxpayer has an "interest" in real property under the laws of the jurisdiction in which the property is situated if the interest constitutes either:

1. A fee interest in the property, or an ownership interest in the case of a mobile unit;
2. A leasehold interest in the property extending or renewing automatically for a period of at least thirty years, or at least ten years beyond the date scheduled for the final payment on the loan secured by the interest;
3. A leasehold interest in improved residential property consisting of a structure or structures containing, in the aggregate, no more than four family units. The interest must extend for a period of at least two years beyond the date for the final payment on the loan secured by the interest; or
4. A leasehold interest in property held subject to a redeemable ground rent as defined in Code section 1055(c).

As a general rule, a regular or residual interest in a REMIC is a qualifying real property loan. However, if less than 95 percent of the REMIC's assets are qualifying real property loans, then the thrift's investment in the REMIC will be treated as a qualified real property loan only to the extent thereof.[452]

---

449 Reg. § 1.593-11(b).
450 *Id.*
451 Reg. § 1.593-11(b)(2).
452 I.R.C. § 593(d)(4) (2000), added by the Tax Reform Act of 1986, Pub. L. No. 99-514, 100 Stat. 2085 (1986).

§ 10.9.2 Loans That Are Nonqualifying

The term "nonqualifying loan" encompasses any loan that is not a "qualifying real property loan."[453] Thus, consumer installment loans, such as auto or commercial loans, would be nonqualifying loans. A nonqualifying loan also includes any loan:

1. Evidenced by a security. For this purpose a "security" is any bond, debenture, note, or certificate, or other evidence of indebtedness, issued by a corporation or by a government or political subdivision thereof, with interest coupons or in registered form;[454]
2. Made to a government or political subdivision or instrumentality thereof;[455]
3. Made to a bank;[456]
4. Made to a member of a thrift's affiliated group, as defined in Code section 1504(a) (but substituting a 50 percent "voting and value" test for Code section 1504's 80 percent test) without regard to the exclusions for certain corporations listed in Code section 1504(b);[457]
5. Secured by a deposit in, or share of, the taxpayer, determined as of the close of the taxable year;[458] or
6. Made and repaid or disposed of within a 60-day period spanning two taxable years, unless it is established that the transaction had a bona fide business purpose.[459]

§ 10.9.3 Specially Computed Taxable Income

The allowable reserve addition, prior to the repeal of Code section 593, that was permitted under the PTI method was equal to 8 percent multiplied by specially computed taxable income.[460] Specially computed taxable income was equal to taxable income as otherwise computed,[461] with the following adjustments:[462]

---

[453] I.R.C. § 593(d)(2).

[454] I.R.C. § 165(g)(2)(C) (2000); Reg. § 1.593-11(b)(5)(i). Although regulations describe a "security" as a "loan," such item is not treated as a "loan" for purposes of the experience method, as well as the PTI method. Reg. § 1.585-2(e)(2)(ii)(C).

[455] Reg. § 1.593-11(b)(5)(ii). Since an insured note of the Farmer Home Administration of the Department of Agriculture represents a governmental obligation, it cannot be treated as a "qualifying loan." Rev. Rul. 78-407, 1978-2 C.B. 185. A guaranteed mortgage participation certificate issued by the FHLMC is neither a loan "evidenced by a security" nor a loan "made to a government." Rev. Rul. 90-7, 1990-1, C.B. 153; Rev. Rul. 84-10, 1984-1 C.B. 155; Rev. Rul. 80-96, 1980-1 C.B. 317; Rev. Rul. 74-300, 1974-1 C.B. 169; Rev. Rul. 74-221, 1974-1 C.B. 365; Rev. Rul. 72-376, 1972-2 C.B. 647, *amplifying* Rev. Rul. 71-399, 1971-2 C.B. 433. PLRs 8918026, February 2, 1989; 8822048, March 4, 1988; 8822001, February 3, 1988; 8724035, March 16, 1987; 8625004, February 7, 1986; 8620019, February 7, 1986; 8428091, April 12, 1984; and 8425036, March 19, 1984. Similarly, neither a pledge account mortgage included in an FHLMC mortgage pool (Rev. Rul. 81-203, 1981-2 C.B. 137), nor an interest in mortgages pooled by a commercial bank (Rev. Rul. 77-349, 1977-2 C.B. 20; PLRs 8434039, May 21, 1984 and 8430112, April 27, 1984) is disqualified as being a loan evidenced by securities.

[456] Reg. § 1.593-11(b)(5)(ii).

[457] *Id.*

[458] Reg. § 1.593-11(b)(5)(iii).

[459] I.R.C. § 593(d)(1)(A)-(D) (2000); Reg. § 1.593-11 (b)(5)(iv).

[460] I.R.C. § 593(b)(2)(A) (2000).

[461] I.R.C. § 63 (2000). Taxable income is reduced by any mark-to-market gain or loss. Prop. Reg. § 1.475(a)-1(g)(2).

[462] I.R.C. § 593(b)(2)(D)(v). I.R.C. § 593(b)(2)(E)(iv) (2000), prior to amendment by the Tax Reform Act of 1986, Pub. L. No. 99-514, 100 Stat. 2085 (1986). For

1. *Nondeductible Distributions.* Certain nondeductible distributions to shareholders in redemption of their stock, or in partial or complete liquidation are excluded from gross income, to the extent such distributions are included in the thrift's gross income under Code section 593(e).[463]
2. *Reserve Additions.* Any deduction allowable for an addition to a reserve for bad debts is not taken into account.[464]
3. *Net Gains.* Net gains (long- or short-term) from sales or exchanges of corporate stock or of tax-exempt obligations are excluded from gross income.[465]
4. *Dividends Received.* Dividends eligible for the deduction under one of the dividends received deduction sections, that exceed the dividends-received deduction (determined without regard to Code section 596) multiplied by eight percent, are excluded from gross income.[466]
5. *Net Operating Losses and Other Deductions.* Regulations provide that taxable income, computed for purposes of the PTI method shall also be reduced by:
   (a) Any deduction the amount of which is computed upon, or may be subject to a limitation computed upon, the amount of taxable income, such as the charitable contribution deduction (but not the net operating loss deductions);[467] and
   (b) For taxable years beginning after December 31, 1977, any amount referred to in (a) above, plus all other allowable deductions not taken into account in computing taxable income, including the net operating loss deduction allowed under Code section 172 and the capital loss carryback deduction allowed under Code section 1212.[468]

Those portions of regulations that required taxable income to be reduced by net operating loss carrybacks have been repeatedly declared invalid by the Tax

(Footnote Continued)

taxable years in which a capital gains rate differential applied, a portion of the capital gains rate differential was excluded from gross income. Note the significance of properly classifying gains. Specially computed taxable income is reduced by the *entire* amount of net gain from the sale of corporate stock or tax-exempt obligations but only a portion of other gains. *See* Rev. Rul. 77-265, 1977-2 C.B. 203.

[463] I.R.C. § 593(b)(2)(D)(i) (2000); Reg. § § 1.593-6A (b)(5)(i), and 1.593-10.

[464] I.R.C. § 593(b)(2)(D)(ii); Reg. § 1.593-6A (b)(5)(ii). This add-back included reserve additions allowed under I.R.C. § 166(c) for taxable years beginning prior to 1987, regardless of whether they were taken under I.R.C. § 593.

[465] I.R.C. § 593(b)(2)(D)(iii) (2000); Reg. § 1.593-6A (b)(5)(iii).

[466] For example, if Bank H received $10,000 in eligible dividends during 1990, without regard to I.R.C. § 596, the bank is allowed a dividends-received deduction of $8,000. The amount by which gross income is decreased is $9,360 (10,000 – [8,000 × .08]); For taxable years beginning prior to 1987, the "applicable percentage" was substituted for "eight percent." Sections allowing dividends received deductions are contained in I.R.C. § § 243-247.

[467] Reg. § 1.593-6A(b)(5)(vi).

[468] Reg. § 1.593-6A(b)(5)(vii). Several Technical Advice Memoranda were issued which addressed the relationship between the taxable income calculation for purposes of the PTI method and the net operating loss carryback rules. These include: 8813001, December 10, 1987; 8809002 (no date given); 8806005 (no date given); 8453002, May 24, 1984; 8442003, June 20, 1984; 8442002, June 20, 1984; 8437007, May 24, 1987; and 8242001, March 30, 1982. *See also* General Council Memorandum 39701, June 30, 1987; and 39760, September 27, 1988. *See also* ISP Coordinated Issue Paper on Validity of Regulation Section 1.593-6A(b)(5)(vi) at A. 111.

Court and by one federal district court.[469] By invalidating these provisions, the Tax Court reinstated the approach to computing a thrift's taxable income under the PTI method that existed for 20 years before the invalidated provisions were adopted in 1978. Thus, net operating losses did not reduce "taxable income" for purposes of the PTI calculation. The holdings of the Tax Court at first relieved thrifts from the dilemma of considering whether to change their method for computing bad-debt deductions from the PTI method to the Code section 585(b) experience method.[470] However, the Sixth, Seventh and Ninth Circuits have reversed the Tax Court, affirming the validity of the regulations.[471] Following these reversals, the Tax Court has begun to apply the rulings of the appeals courts.[472]

6. *Consolidated Losses.* With respect to a thrift that joins in a consolidated return, its taxable income may be reduced by certain losses of other group members. Under the consolidated return regulations, a thrift's separate taxable income computed for purposes of PTI method was reduced by losses of other thrift members of the group[473] determined by including a bad-debt deduction under the experience method (as provided in Code section 593(b)(1)) and by certain losses of nonthrift members.[474] The losses of nonthrift members that reduced a thrift's separate taxable income were losses attributable to "functionally related activities."[475]

A loss is related to an activity of a nonthrift which is "functionally related" if it is either:

1. Attributable to providing assets or services (leasing office space, providing computer or financial services) to the thrift;[476] or
2. Derived from Code section 7701(a)(19)(iii)-(xi) assets, but only if such assets comprise 5 percent or more of the gross assets of the nonthrift.[477]

---

[469] *Pacific First Federal Savings Bank v. Commissioner*, 94 T.C. 101, Dec. 46,401 (1970); *Georgia Federal Bank v. Commissioner*, 98 T.C. 105, Dec. 47,977 (1992); *Leader Federal Savings and Loan Association v. Commissioner*, 62 T.C.M. 201, Dec. 47,481(M), T.C. Memo. 1991-334; *Peoples Federal Savings & Loan Association of Sydeny v. Commissioner*, 59 T.C.M. 85, Dec. 46, 453(M), T.C. Memo. 1990-129. *Bell Federal Savings and Loan Association v. Commissioner*, T.C. Memo 1991-368 (1991); *First Federal Savings Bank of Washington v. United States*, 766 F. Supp. 897 (D. Wash. 1991). The decision in this case would be appealable to the Ninth Circuit, which has earlier ruled in favor of the government. *See also* "Must Bad Debt Reserves Be Recomputed for an NOL Carryback?" McCahill and Heath, *Journal of Bank Taxation* No. 3, p. 15 (1992).

[470] *See* General Counsel Memorandum 39760, September 27, 1988, which deals with constraints imposed by the IRS on a thrift's ability to switch computation methods. It also allows thrifts to avoid a recalculation of earnings and profits, which, pursuant to the I.R.C. §312 rules, begins with "taxable income." PLR 8571043, September 23, 1987.

[471] *Pacific First Federal Savings and Loan Association v. Commissioner*, 92-1 U.S.T.C. ¶50,099, 961 F.2d 800 (9th Cir. 1992), *rev'g*, 94 T.C. 101, Dec. 46,401, *cert. denied*, 506 U.S. 872 (1992); *Peoples Federal Savings & Loan Association of Sydney v. Commissioner*, 91-2 U.S.T.C. ¶50,541, 948 F.2d 289 (6th Cir. 1991). *Bell Federal Savings and Loan Association v. Commissioner*, 40 F.3d 224 (7th Cir. 1995).

[472] *Central Pennsylvania Savings Association v. Commissioner*, 104 T.C. 384 (1995); *Cheltenham Federal Savings and Loan Association v. Commissioner*, T.C. Memo 1995-149 (1995); *Fredericksburg Federal Savings and Loan Association v. Commissioner*, T.C. Memo 1995-166 (1995). *See also* "Three Strikes and You're Out: Tax Court Gives Up After Third Reversal," 83 *Journal of Taxation* 320 (1995). *See also* "Did IRS Amend Regulations Out of Pique?," 79 *Journal of Taxation* 262 (1993).

[473] Reg. § 1.1502-42(f)(1)(i).

[474] Reg. § 1.1502-42(f).

[475] Reg. § 1.1502-42(g).

[476] Reg. § 1.1502-42(g)(1)(i).

[477] Reg. § 1.1502-42(g)(1)(ii).

The amount of loss from a functionally related activity that reduces a thrift's separate taxable income may not exceed the nonthrift's adjusted separate taxable loss.[478] Adjustments that must be made to the nonthrift's separate taxable income include apportioning the:

1. Charitable contribution deduction;
2. Dividends received reduction;
3. Net capital loss deduction; and
4. Net Code section 1231 loss deduction.[479]

The "functionally related" losses of a nonthrift that would otherwise be offset against the taxable income of a thrift are reduced to the extent of the nonthrift's income reported in prior years and attributable to functionally related activities.[480]

§ 10.9.4 Applicable Percentages

Specially computed taxable income used to determine a thrift's bad debt deduction under the repealed PTI method was multiplied by the "applicable percentage" to determine the reserve addition. The applicable percentage for the years 1969 to 1995 are:[481]

%	*For a Taxable Year Beginning in*
8	1987-1995
40	1979-1986
41	1978
42	1977
43	1976
45	1975
47	1974
49	1973
51	1972
54	1971
57	1970
60	1969

The "applicable percentage" was as high as 100% in 1952. The early percentage has the effect of completely exempting thrifts from federal income tax to which they first were subject in 1952. Credit unions remain expressly exempt from federal income tax I.R.C. § 501(c)(14).

§ 10.9.5 Limitations on Reserve Additions

Under pre-1996 law, the reserve addition for nonqualifying loans was permitted to be computed only under the Code section 585(b)(3) experience method, which included both the moving average formula and the base year restoration

[478] Reg. §§ 1.1502-42(g)(2) and (e).

[479] Reg. §§ 1.1502-42(e)(1) and (e)(3).

[480] Reg. § 1.1502-42(f)(4)(iv). The income allowed to offset the loss is reduced to the extent that it offset loss in a prior year. Reg. § 1.1502-42(f)(4)(iv)(B).

[481] I.R.C. § 593(b)(2)(A).

approach.[482] The addition to the reserve for qualifying real property loans was permitted to be computed under the Code section 585(b)(3) experience method or the Code section 593 PTI method. However, two limitations were imposed on deductions with respect to reserve additions for qualifying real property loans.

First, the addition to the reserve for qualifying real property loans, regardless of whether it is computed under the PTI method or the experience method, could not be greater than the larger of:

1. The addition determined under the Code section 585(b)(3) experience method;[483] or
2. The addition which, when added to the addition to the reserve for nonqualifying loans, equals the amount by which 12 percent of the total deposits or withdrawable accounts[484] of depositors (*i.e.*, amounts placed with the thrifts for deposit or investment) at the *close* of the taxable year exceeds the sum of its surplus, undivided profits, and reserves at the *beginning* of the year.[485]

Example: Assume that for Bank A the addition to its reserve for nonqualifying loans is $22,000. Further assume:

Reserve addition under the experience method	$30,000
Opening reserve balance	$55,000
Total deposits and withdrawable accounts	$2,500,000
Surplus, undivided profits and reserves	$250,000

Thus, the reserve addition for qualifying loans may not exceed $72,000, which is greater of:

1. $30,000, the reserve addition under the experience method; or
2. $72,000, computed as follows ([0.12 × 2,500,000] – $250,000) + $22,000.

Second, the addition to the reserve for qualifying real property loans computed under the PTI method could not exceed the amount necessary to increase the balance of the reserve for qualifying loans at the close of the taxable year to 6 percent of qualifying loans outstanding at such time.[486] This limitation did not apply to reserve additions for qualifying real property loans computed under the Code section 585(b)(3) experience method. No similar limitation applied to reserve additions with respect to qualifying loans, which were made under the experience method.

(a) Deposits and Withdrawable Accounts

For purposes of the 12 percent limitations, deposits and withdrawable accounts are the aggregate of "amounts placed with an institution for deposit or investment" and interest (or dividends deductible under Code section 591)

[482] I.R.C. §§585(b)(3) and 593(b)(1)(A) (1994).

[483] I.R.C. §593(b)(1)(B)(i) (1994).

[484] Reg. §1.1052-42 provides that for this purpose the total deposits or withdrawable accounts of affiliated thrifts are excluded from a thrift's own total of these amounts.

[485] I.R.C. §593(b)(1)(ii) (2000).

[486] I.R.C. §593(b)(2)(C) (2000).

credited to a depositor's (or owner's) account that is withdrawable on demand and outstanding on the bank's books at the close of the taxable year.[487]

Deposits and withdrawable accounts do not include any permanent non-withdrawable capital stock represented by shares or earnings credited thereon.[488] The term "deposits and withdrawable accounts" is also used in regulations under Code section 7701(a)(19) for purposes of defining an entity that qualifies as a "domestic building and loan association."[489] However, it is not only "deposits and withdrawable accounts" but also "other obligations" which can be used to satisfy the Code section 7701(a)(19) test.

The items that qualify as "other obligations" are notes, bonds, debentures, or other obligations or other securities (except capital stock), issued by the institution in conformity with rules and regulations of the Federal Home Loan Bank Board or substantially equivalent rules of a state law or supervisory authority.[490] Regulations under Code section 7701(a)(19) provide that certain advances made by a Federal Home Loan Bank are not "other obligations," for purposes of satisfying the business activities test.[491]

The IRS has ruled that where the "investment" of a preferred shareholder was in substance a "deposit or with drawable share," the par value of the stock was includible in the deposit base for purposes of the reserve addition.[492] Thus, the label ascribed to the arrangement is not controlling. Mortgage escrow deposits (including amounts retained for the payment of taxes, water charges, insurance, *etc.*) that are (1) segregated on the bank's book, (2) treated for book accounting purposes as "assets," and (3) subject to the general risk of the bank's business are also included among the "deposits" for this purpose.[493] Similarly, in *Richmond Hill Savings Bank*, mortgage escrow deposits were treated as "deposits" although they were found not to secure certain real property loans."[494] Moreover, the Tax Court has held that unless the thrift's cash position is increased or the customer is permitted to withdraw funds, a deposit or withdrawable account is not present.[495]

(b) Surplus, Undivided Profits and Reserves

A thrift's "surplus, undivided profits, and reserves" is equal to the excess of its assets over liabilities.[496] "Assets" are equal to the sum of money plus the adjusted bases of property other than money held by the taxpayer.[497] "Liabilities"

---

487 Reg. § 1.593-1(d)(3). *See also* the pre-1970 regulation at Reg. § 1.593-6(f)(3). These regulations are applicable to post-1970 years. Reg. § 1.593-6(e).

488 *Id.*

489 Reg. § 301.7701-13A(c)(2).

490 *Id.*

491 It is not inconceivable that such advances could be classified as "deposits." The FHLB is no longer the lender of last resort for thrifts. This function has been transferred to the Federal Reserve Bank. The FHLB now operates more like a financial intermediary.

492 Rev. Rul. 55-391, 1955-1 C.B. 306.

493 Rev. Rul. 55-435, 1955-2 C.B. 540.

494 *Richmond Hill Savings Bank v. Commissioner*, 57 T.C. 738 (1972); *see also* Rev. Rul. 74-548, 1974-2 C.B. 177.

495 *First Savings & Loan Association v. Commissioner*, 40 T.C. 474, Dec. 26,158 (1963).

496 Reg. §§ 1.593-1(d)(2) and 1.593-6(f)(1). The definition of "surplus, undivided profits and reserves" contained in Regulations which construe the pre-1970 rules applicable to reserve additions for losses on qualifying real property loans is applicable to post-1969 years. Reg. § 1.593-6A(e).

497 Reg. §§ 1.593-1(d)(2)(ii) and 1.593-6(f)(2). Post-1969 regulations do not provide that the

include the amount of "total deposits or withdrawable accounts" determined in accordance with the rules set forth above, as well as all other liabilities.[498] A liability is taken into account only if it is "fixed and determined, absolute and not contingent."[499] Assets and liabilities are determined in accordance with the taxpayer's method of accounting and under provisions required to be followed in determining earnings and profits.[500]

§ 10.9.6 Limitations on Reserve Additions (Pre-1987 Law)

Prior to amendments made by the Tax Reform Act of 1986, a thrift was entitled to a deduction under the percentage of the PTI method equal to 40 percent of taxable income. This deduction was available, however, only where a certain percentage of the thrifts assets were "qualified." If the requisite percentage of qualified assets was not present, the percentage of taxable income that was allowed as a deduction was reduced. The amendments made by the Tax Reform Act of 1986 included a substantial reduction in the percentage of taxable income that was allowed as a deduction, from 40 percent to 8 percent. Because of this reduction, the limitations discussed below were eliminated.

(a) Pre-1987 Reduction in Applicable Percentage

For taxable years beginning before 1987, the "applicable percentage" of taxable income was reduced from what it otherwise might have been, depending on the type of entity and the percentage of its total assets that are described in Code section 7701(a)(19). For mutual savings banks either (1) without capital stock or (2) not subject to, and operating under, federal or state laws relating to mutual savings banks, if Code section 7701(a)(19)(C) assets amounted to less than 72 percent of total assets, the "applicable percentage" was reduced by 1.5 percentage points for each percentage point of such difference.[501] Asset balances used to compute the "applicable percentage" were determined either at the close of the taxable year or, at the option of the taxpayer, on the basis of a monthly, quarterly or semiannual asset average.[502]

Example 1: In 1986, Bank Y, a mutual savings bank without capital stock, had 65 percent of its assets qualified as Code section 7701(a)(19)(C) assets. Its taxable income percentage was determined as follows:

Applicable percentage before adjustment	40.0%
Less: (72 – 65) × 0.015	10.5%
Taxable income percentage	29.5%

For mutual savings banks with capital stock represented by shares and which operated under and were subject to federal or state laws relating to mutual

(Footnote Continued)

pre-1970 regulation definition of "total assets," Reg. § 1.593-6(f)(2), will apply to post-1969 years. *See* Reg. § 1.593-6(e).

[498] Reg. § 1.593-1(d)(2)(iii).

[499] *First Savings and Loan Association v. Commissioner*, 40 T.C. 474, 483, Dec. 26,158 (1963).

[500] I.R.C. §§ 312 and 446 (2000).

[501] I.R.C. § 593(b)(2)(B) (1982), prior to amendment by the Tax Reform Act of 1986, Pub. L. No. 99-514, 100 Stat. 2085 (1986).

[502] Reg. § 1.593-6A(b)(2)(i) (1982).

savings banks, if Code section 7701(a)(19)(C) assets amounted to less than 82 percent of total assets, the "applicable percentage" was reduced by three quarters of 1 percent for each percentage point of such difference.[503]

Example 2: In 1986, Bank Y, a mutual savings bank with capital stock, had 75 percent of its assets qualified as Code section 7701(a)(19)(C) assets. Its taxable income percentage was determined as follows:

Applicable percentage before adjustment	40.00%
Less: (82 – 75) × .0075	5.25%
Taxable income percentage	34.75%

(b) *Pre-1987 Qualifying Reserve Additional Reduction*

For taxable years beginning prior to 1987, the addition under the PTI method, to a thrift's (mutual savings bank with or without stock) reserve for qualifying loans was also reduced from the amount otherwise allowable by a portion of the amount of the reserve addition computed under the Code section 585(b)(3) experience method whenever the thrift held assets not described in Code section 7701(a)(19)(C).[504] For a mutual savings bank without stock, the reserve addition for qualifying loans determined under the PTI method was reduced by the excess of the reserve addition for nonqualifying loans over such reserve addition multiplied by the ratio that 28 percent bore to the percentage of the thrift's assets that were not Code section 7701(a)(1)(C) assets.

Example 1: In 1986, Bank Z, a mutual savings bank without capital stock, had 65 percent of its assets qualifying as Code section 7701(a)(19)(C) assets and taxable income after adjustments of $50,850. Its applicable percentage was therefore reduced from 40 percent to 29.5 percent.

Addition under PTI method before reduction and limitations ($50,850 × 29.5%)	$15,000
Less: Excess of nonqualifying reserve addition, $2,000 over such addition multiplied by 28/35	(400)
Qualifying loan addition under PTI method	$14,600
Nonqualifying loan addition	2,000
Total additions	$16,600

For thrifts with capital stock, the reserve addition for qualifying loans[505] was reduced by the excess of the reserve addition for nonqualifying loans over such reserve addition multiplied by the ratio that 18 percent bore to the percentage of the thrift's assets that were not Code section 7701(a)(19)(C) assets.

Example 2: In 1986, Bank Z, a mutual savings bank with capital stock, had 75 percent of its assets qualifying as Code section 7701(a)(19)(C) assets

[503] I.R.C. § 593(b)(2)(B) (1982), prior to amendment by the Tax Reform Act of 1986, Pub. L. No. 99-514, § 901, 100 Stat. 2085 (1986).

[504] I.R.C. § 593(b)(2)(C) (1982), prior to amendment by the Tax Reform Act of 1986, Pub. L. No. 99-514, 100 Stat. 2085 (1986).

[505] *See* I.R.C. § 593(b)(1)(A) (1982), prior to amendment by the Tax Reform Act of 1986, Pub. L. No. 99-514, 100 Stat. 2085 (1986).

and taxable income (after adjustments) of $57,550. The applicable percentage is reduced from 40 percent to 34.75 percent.

Addition under PTI method before reduction and limitations ($57,550 × 34.75%) .	$20,000
Less: Excess of "nonqualifying" reserve addition, $3,000, over such addition multiplied by 18/25	(840)
Qualifying loan addition under PTI method	$19,160
Nonqualifying loan addition	3,000
Total addition	$22,160

§10.10 Commercial Bank Bad-Debt Reserve Recapture

§10.10.1 "Large Bank" Defined

Banks that are "large banks" may not use the Code section 585 reserve method for determining their bad-debt deduction.[506] Any bank that is prohibited from continuing to use the reserve method of accounting for loan losses because it becomes a "large bank" is treated as having changed, in the "disqualification year," its method of accounting with regard to its calculation of its losses on bad debts. The necessitated change in method of accounting is considered to have been initiated by the bank, and it is considered to have been made with the consent of the Secretary.[507]

A bank is a "large bank" if at the end of its taxable year or at the end of any preceding taxable year beginning after December 31, 1986:[508]

1. The average adjusted bases of all assets of the bank exceed $500 million; or
2. The bank is a member of a parent-subsidiary controlled group and the average adjusted bases of all assets of such group exceed $500 million.[509]

As a general rule, once a bank is a large bank it remains as such, even though its assets may drop below the large bank threshold.[510] Regulations provide that if a corporation acquires the assets of a large bank, the acquiring entity, in general, will be treated as a large bank for any taxable year ending after the date of the acquisition in which it is a bank.[511] This rule applies in three situations:

1. When more than 50 percent (by vote or value) of the outstanding stock of the acquiring institution is owned by a transferor-large bank and a significant portion of a large bank's assets are acquired;[512]

---

[506] I.R.C. §585(c) (2000).

[507] I.R.C. §§585(c)(3)(A)(i) and (ii) (2000). Reg. §1.585-6(a). However, the automatic change in accounting procedures contained in Rev. Proc. 2002-9, 2002-3 I.R.B. 327, do not apply. *See* Sec. 11 of Appendix to that Rev. Proc.

[508] If a bank exceeded the allowable asset size for a taxable year beginning prior to January 1, 1987, but not thereafter, it would not be a large bank for purposes of the I.R.C. §585 definition.

[509] Reg. §1.585-5(b).

[510] Reg. §§1.585-5 through 1.585-8, 58 FR 68753, correction at 59 FR 15502, April 1, 1994.

[511] Reg. §1.585-5(b)(2).

[512] Reg. §1.585-5(b)(2)(ii). Stock of the acquiring institution will be considered owned by the transferor-large bank if the stock is owned by any member of a parent-subsidiary controlled group of which the transferor-large bank is a member, or by any related party within the meaning of I.R.C. §§267(b) or 707(b), or by any person that received the stock in a transaction to which I.R.C. §355 applies.

2. When there is a transfer to which Code section 381(a) applies, but only if immediately after the acquisition, the acquiror's principal method of accounting for bad debts determined under Regulation Section 1.381(c)(4)-1(c)(2) with respect to its banking business is the specific charge-off method;[513] or
3. In the case of a transfer between parties that are related before or after the acquisition and the principal purpose of the acquisition is to avoid treating the acquired assets as those of a large bank.[514]

(a) *Disqualification Year*

The disqualification year is the first taxable year beginning after December 31, 1986, for which the bank is no longer permitted to use the reserve method by reason of it being a "large bank."[515] If a bank becomes a large bank because its stock is acquired by a large bank, the disqualification year of the acquired bank is its first taxable year ending after the date of acquisition.[516] The acquired bank would be entitled to make its own election regarding which of the recapture methods will be used.

(b) *Adjusted Tax Bases*

Taxpayers determine the amount of "average total assets" by using the actual tax bases of assets held by the institution or group, determined under Code sections 1012, 1016, and other applicable sections, at each "report date" within the taxable year.[517] Alternatively, regulations permit estimation of the tax bases of assets held on the certain report dates, based on amounts recorded on books and records maintained for financial reporting purposes. The amounts of actual or estimated tax bases of assets on the various report dates are added together and divided by the number of the report dates within the taxable year to determine the average.[518]

The term "average adjusted bases for all assets" contained in Code section 585(c)(2)(A) also appears in Code sections 265(b)(2)(B) and 291(e)(1)(B)(ii)(II). The latter two sections are bank-specific sections dealing with disallowed interest expense.[519] To provide guidance to bank taxpayers in determining the average

---

[513] Reg. § 1.585-5(b)(2)(iii). For purposes of this rule, a transferor-large bank will be considered to use the specific charge-off method for all of its loans immediately before the acquisition. An acquiring institution will be considered to use the reserve method for all of its loans immediately before the acquisition. All banking businesses of the acquirer immediately after the acquisition will be treated as one integrated business.

[514] Reg. § 1.585-5(b)(d)(iv) (2000). The transferor bank and the acquiring institution will be considered to be related parties if they are members of the same parent subsidiary controlled group or are related parties within the meaning of I.R.C. §§ 267(b) or 707(b).

[515] I.R.C. § 585(c)(5)(B) (2000); Reg. § 1.585-5(d). Regulation under I.R.C. § 585 are unclear on whether a short taxable year ending on the day of acquisition is treated as a "disqualification year."

[516] Reg. § 1.585-5(d)(3).

[517] Reg. § 1.585-5(c)(3)(i). H.R. Rep. No. 99-426, at 577 (1985). *See also* the *General Explanation of the Tax Reform Act of 1986* (the "Blue Book"), prepared by the staff of the Joint Committee on Taxation, at 551. *See also* Reg. § 1.585-5(c)(3).

[518] Reg. § 1.585-5(c)(4)(i); Reg. § 1.585-1(c)(1). *See also* the *General Explanation of the Tax Reform Act of 1986* (the Blue Book), prepared by the staff of the Joint Committee on Taxation, at 578.

[519] The term's inclusion in I.R.C. § 291 preceded its later use in I.R.C. §§ 265 and 585. *See* discussion in Ch. 9, of "Interest Expense."

adjusted bases for all assets under those sections, the IRS has issued similar guidance.[520]

In determining the average adjusted bases of all assets held by a parent-subsidiary controlled group, interests held by one member of the group in another member are to be disregarded.[521] This is done in order to prevent the bases of the group's assets from being inflated by double counting.[522]

(c) *Report Date*

Regulations generally define a "report date" as the last day of the regular period for which the institution must report to its primary federal regulatory agency, or, if it does not have a federal regulatory agency, its primary state regulatory agency.[523] An institution's report date will be no less frequent than the last day of each calendar quarter; however, an institution may choose as its report date the last day of any regular interval in the taxable year that is more frequent than quarterly, such as bimonthly, monthly, weekly, or daily.[524] If a bank is required to report more frequently than quarterly, it may choose the last day of the calendar quarter as its report date. The first or last day of an institution's short taxable year, in the case of a short taxable year that does not otherwise include a report date, is the institution's report date for that year.[525]

(d) *Affiliated Corporations*

All corporations includible in the group under the parent-subsidiary, brother-sister, combined group, and insurance company ownership tests of Code section 1563(a)(1), (2), (3), and (4), respectively, are included without regard to their status under Code section 1563(b)(2) as an "excluded member" of a controlled group and regardless of whether the corporation meets the definition of a commercial bank.[526] A "parent-subsidiary" controlled group exists where one or more chains of corporations are connected through stock ownership with a common parent corporation, 80 percent or more of the voting power or value of the stock of each corporation in the group is owned by one or more corporations in the group, and the common parent owns at least 80 percent of the voting power or value of the stock of one of the other corporations in the group.[527]

If a bank is a member of a parent-subsidiary controlled group for only part of a taxable year the determination of "large bank" status is made on the basis of the group's average total assets for the portion of the year that the institution is a member of the group, and only the report dates that are included in that portion of the year are taken into account.[528] For a parent subsidiary controlled group, the

---

[520] Rev. Rul. 90-44, 1990-1 C.B. 54.

[521] Reg. § 1.585-5(c)(3).

[522] I.R.C. § 585(c)(5)(A).

[523] Reg. § 1.585-5(c)(2).

[524] Reg. § 1.585-5(c)(2)(i).

[525] Reg. § 1.585-5(c)(2)(iii).

[526] *Id. See also* the *General Explanation of the Tax Reform Act of 1986* (the "Blue Book"), prepared by the staff of the Joint Committee on Taxation, at 551, also expressly includes foreign corporations. Reg. § 1.585-5(d)(2).

[527] I.R.C. § 585(c)(5) (2000) and I.R.C. §§ 1563(a)(1)(A) and (B) (2000).

[528] Reg. § 1.585-5(c)(2)(iii).

report date for any one bank member of the group must be applied to all members of the group.[529]

(e) *Estimating Tax Basis*

Tax basis for interim report dates may be estimated. The method for estimating the tax basis of assets of an institution or a group requires the use of actual tax basis for report dates that are the first and the last day of the taxable year.[530] What will be estimated will be the tax basis of assets on the intervening report dates. Whenever the tax basis of assets is estimated, an institution or group member must estimate the tax basis for all assets (other than cash) held on that report date and on all other interim report dates during the year.[531] The estimate must reflect any change in the ratio between an asset holder's tax basis and its "book basis" of assets occurring during the year, and it must assume that the change in the ratio occurs ratably throughout the year. "Book basis" is determined by reference to the holder's books and records maintained for financial reporting purposes. An asset holder's "tax/book ratio" is the ratio of:

> (Total tax basis of all of the holder's assets (other than cash))/(Total book basis of those assets).

The estimated adjusted tax basis of assets of an institution or group on the intervening report dates during the year is determined by multiplying the book bases of assets on each of those report dates by the sum of the tax/book ratio at the close of the preceding taxable year and a fraction of the difference between the tax/book ratio at the end of the current taxable year and at the tax/book ratio at the end of the preceding taxable year. The fraction will be either one-quarter, one-half or three-quarters, depending on which of the three intervening report dates is being estimated. The following example will illustrate the method for estimating tax bases.

> **Example 1:** Bank A, a calendar year taxpayer, reports to its primary regulator on the last day of each calendar quarter. The adjusted tax bases of all of A's assets (other than cash) at the close of the preceding taxable year is $450 million, and the book bases of those assets on that date is $500 million. At the end of the current taxable year, the adjusted tax bases of all of Bank A's assets is $480 million and the book bases of those assets on that date is $600 million. Thus, Bank A's tax/book ratio at the close of the preceding taxable year is 0.9 and at the close of the current taxable year it is 0.8. During the intervening 3 quarters, Bank A's book bases for all assets are $520 million, $540 million and $560 million, respectively. The estimated adjusted tax bases of Bank A's assets on the 3 report dates occurring during the taxable year are as follows:

Bases	*End Preceding Year*	*End Current Year*
Actual Adjusted Tax	$450 M	$480 M
Book Basis	$500 M	$600 M
Tax/Book Ratio	0.9	0.8

---

529 Reg. § 1.585-5(c)(2)(ii).

530 Reg. § 1.585-5(c)(4).

531 *Id.*

Intervening Report Date Calculations:

March 31:	$520 M × [0.9 + 1/4 (0.8 – 0.9)]=	$455 M
June 30:	540 M × [0.9 + 1/2 (0.8 – 0.9)]=	459 M
September 30:	560 M × [0.9 + 3/4 (0.8 – 0.9)]=	462 M

$$\text{Average total assets} = \frac{\text{Sum of actual and estimated tax bases}}{\text{Number of report dates}}$$

$$= \frac{450 + 455 + 459 + 462 + 480}{5}$$

$$= \$461.2 \text{ M}$$

Example 2: Assume the basic facts of Example 1 and also that in year 2 various transactions during the year involving the sale of heavily depreciated assets and the purchase of new long-life assets create an increase in book bases of $150 M and an even greater increase, $195 M, in tax bases. These transactions cause an increase in the tax/book ratio for the year of 0.1. The report date amounts exceed the $500 M threshold for all four quarters.

Bases	*End Preceding Year*	*End Current Year*
Actual Adjusted Tax	$480 M	$675 M
Book Basis	$600 M	$750 M
Tax/Book Ratio	0.8	0.9

Intervening Report Date Calculations:

March 31:	$650 M × [0.8 + 1/4 (0.9 – 0.8)] =	$536.25 M
June 30:	700 M × [0.8 + 1/2 (0.9 – 0.8)] =	595.00 M
September 30:	725 M × [0.8 + 3/4 (0.9 – 0.8)] =	634.375 M

$$\text{Average total assets} = \frac{\text{Sum of actual and estimated tax bases}}{\text{Number of report dates}}$$

$$= \frac{480 + 536.25 + 595 + 634.375 + 675}{5}$$

$$= \$584.125 \text{ M}$$

Example 3: Assume the facts of the preceding examples and that various transactions occur during Year 3 involving the sale of new or relatively new long-life assets thus leaving the bank with those older assets on which the bank has taken more depreciation; *i.e.*, book value reduced by $200 M while tax bases reduced by $262.5 M. These transactions cause a decrease in the tax/book ratio for the year of 0.015. The report date amounts exceed the $500 M threshold for the first half of the year.

Bases	*End Preceding Year*	*End Current Year*
Actual Adjusted Tax	$675 M	$412.5 M
Book Basis	$750 M	$550 M
Tax/Book Ratio	0.9	0.75

Intervening Report Date Calculations:

March 31:	$\$700\ M \times [0.9 + {}^1/_4\,(0.75 - 0.9)] =$	$603.75 M
June 30:	$650\ M \times [0.9 + {}^1/_2\,(0.75 - 0.9)] =$	536.25 M
September 30:	$600\ M \times [0.9 + {}^3/_4\,(0.75 - 0.9)] =$	472.50 M

$$\text{Average total assets} = \frac{\text{Sum of actual and estimated tax bases}}{\text{Number of report dates}}$$

$$= \frac{675 + 603.75 + 536.25 + 472.5 + 412.5}{5}$$

$$= \$540\ M$$

Example 4: Continue to assume the facts of the preceding examples and that various transactions occur during Year 4 involving the sale of partially-depreciated short-life assets with book value of $100 M and tax bases of $52.5 M, resulting in the increase in tax/ book ratio for the year of 0.05. The report date amounts remain below the $500 M threshold for the entire year.

Bases	*End Preceding Year*	*End Current Year*
Actual Adjusted Tax	$412.5 M	$360 M
Book Basis	$550 M	$450 M
Tax/Book Ratio	0.75	0.8

Intervening Report Date Calculations:

March 31:	$\$525\ M \times [0.75 + {}^1/_4\,(0.8 - 0.75)] =$	$400.3125 M
June 30:	$500\ M \times [0.75 + {}^1/_2\,(0.8 - 0.75)] =$	387.50 M
September 30:	$475\ M \times [0.75 + {}^3/_4\,(0.8 - 0.75)] =$	374.0625 M

$$\text{Average total assets} = \frac{\text{Sum of actual and estimated tax bases}}{\text{Number of report dates}}$$

$$= \frac{412.5 + 400.3125 + 387.5 + 374.0625 + 360}{5}$$

$$= \$386.875\ M$$

Example 5: Continuing with these scenarios various transactions occur during the first half of Year 5 involving the acquisition of assets, and during the last half of the year involving the sale of assets, about which these figures do not reveal to the reader any tax basis information. The assumption behind the estimated tax bases calculations is that the change in the tax bases is ratable, consistent with the change in the tax/book ratio. As illustrated in the previous examples, this assumption may be false depending on the age and type of assets transferred. Actual tax bases for the interim quarters may be substantially different from the impression given by the estimates. The question is, Does it matter or does it all "come out in the wash?" It depends on what you do with these calculations. If you use them to value or sell a bank or a portion thereof, then it should matter. If they are simply used to satisfy a regulatory requirement wherein the government keeps tabs on the solvency of the bank, then it may not be as critical. Any significant changes in the book values for the intervening quarters should give a reader some indication that a more in-depth analysis may be required.

Bases	*End Preceding Year*	*End Current Year*
Actual Adjusted Tax	$360 M	$510 M
Book Basis	$450 M	$600 M
Tax/Book Ratio	0.8	0.85

Intervening Report Date Calculations:

March 31:	$550 M × [0.8 + 1/4 (0.85 – 0.8)] =	$446.875 M
June 30:	650 M × [0.8 + 1/2 (0.85 – 0.8)] =	536.25 M *
September 30:	575 M × [0.8 + 3/4 (0.8 5 – 0.8)] =	481.5625 M

* *Amount exceeds $500 M threshold.*

$$\text{Average total assets} = \frac{\text{Sum of actual and estimated tax bases}}{\text{Number of report dates}}$$

$$= \frac{360 + 446.875 + 536.25 + 481.5625 + 510}{5}$$

$$= \$466.9375\text{ M}$$

Because the average total assets of Bank A during the taxable year do not exceed $500 million, Bank A is not treated as a large bank for purposes of Code section 585.

(f) Large Bank Resulting from Transfer

As discussed above, there are at least three transfer situations when an acquiring corporation that is not a large bank will be treated as a large bank after acquiring the assets of a large bank, regardless of whether the average adjusted tax bases of its assets exceed $500 million. They are as follows:

1. A large bank transfers a significant portion of its assets directly or indirectly to another corporation, and after the transfer more than 50 percent by vote or value of the outstanding stock of the acquiror is owned by the transferor large bank or a related entity;[532]
2. Immediately after a Code section 381(a) transaction an acquiror's principal method of accounting for bad debts with respect to its banking business is the specific charge-off method;[533] or
3. The transferor and the acquiror are related parties before *or* after the acquisition and the principal purpose of the acquisition is to avoid treating the acquired assets as large bank assets.[534]

For purposes of the first of these transfer situations, stock of an acquiror is considered owned by a transferor bank if: (a) the stock is owned by any member of the parent-subsidiary controlled group of which the bank is a member, (b) by any related party, or (c) by any person that received the stock in a distribution of stock of a controlled corporation. A "parent-subsidiary controlled group" includes all of the members of a parent-subsidiary controlled group of corporations described in Code section 1563(a)(1). Thus, it contains one or more chains of

532 Reg. § 1.585-5(b)(2).
533 Reg. § 1.585-5(b)(2)(iii).
534 Reg. § 1.585-5(b)(2)(iv).

corporations connected through stock ownership with a common parent corporation if stock possessing at least 80 percent of the total combined voting power or 80 percent of the total value of assets of all classes of stock of each corporation is owned by the common parent corporation and one or more of the other corporations.[535] The members of the controlled group of corporations are determined without regard to whether any member is one of the "excluded members" described in Code section 1563(b)(2), a foreign entity, or a commercial bank. A transferor bank and an acquiror also shall be considered to be related parties for purposes of this rule if they are related within the meaning of Code sections 267(b) or 707(b).[536]

For purposes of acquisitions to which Code section 381(a) applies, the principal method of accounting for bad debts shall be determined under Code section 381(a), assuming that: (a) the transferor large bank is considered to use the specific charge-off method for all of its loans immediately before the acquisition; (b) the acquiror is considered to use the reserve method for all of its loans immediately before the acquisition; and, (c) all banking business of the acquiror immediately after the acquisition are treated as one integrated business.[537]

An "integrated business" continues to employ the same methods of accounting used by the parties to a transaction described in Code section 381(a) to the extent the same methods of accounting were employed by the parties in the integrated business.[538] If different methods of accounting were employed on the date of distribution or transfer by the parties with respect to the integrated trade or business, the acquiring corporation is required generally to adopt the principal method of accounting of the parties. The principal overall method of accounting of an integrated business is determined by making a comparison of the total adjusted tax bases of assets immediately preceding the date of distribution or transfer and the gross receipts for a representative period, usually the most recent period of twelve consecutive calendar months ending on or prior to the date of distribution or transfer.[539]

For purposes of the third transfer situation, a transferor bank and an acquiror are considered to be related parties if they are members of the same parent-subsidiary control group or they are related parties within the meaning of Code sections 267(b) or 707(b).[540]

In the case of a stock acquisition that meets the requirements of Code section 338 for a "qualified stock purchase" in which a corporation that is not a large bank acquires the stock of a large bank, and in which the acquiring corporation makes an election under Code section 338 to treat the stock purchase as an asset

---

535 I.R.C. §§ 1563(a)(1)(A) and (B) (2000).

536 I.R.C. § 267(b) (2000) lists 12 persons that shall be considered related for purposes of the disallowance of loss rule contained in I.R.C. § 267(a) (2000). I.R.C. § 707(b) (2000) describes the persons with respect to whom no deductions shall be allowed in respect of losses from sales or exchanges of property, directly or indirectly, between those persons and certain partnerships.

537 Reg. § 1.585-5(b)(iii).

538 Reg. § 1.381(c)(4)-1(b)(3).

539 Reg. § 1.381(c)(4)-1(c)(2).

540 *See* discussion above in connection with first transfer for definition of "parent-subsidiary control group" and "related parties."

acquisition, the acquired entity shall be treated as a new corporation. The acquired bank's prior membership in a parent-subsidiary controlled group which had average total assets in excess of $500 million will not cause the acquired bank to be treated as a large bank for taxable years ending after the date of its sale by its former parent-subsidiary controlled group. Of course, the acquired institution could be treated as a large bank if it becomes a member of a large bank group or if it has average total assets in excess of $500 million or it is treated as a large bank as a result of one of the three types of transfers described above.[541]

§ 10.10.2 Code Section 481(a) Adjustments

In order to prevent amounts from being duplicated or omitted by reason of the change in accounting method, a bank's bad-debt reserve balance that exists on the last day of the taxable year before the disqualification year is required to be taken into account in computing taxable income beginning in the year of change unless the "cut-off" method is elected.[542] The reserve balance at the close of the taxable year immediately preceding the disqualification year shall be the amount of the net Code section 418(a) adjustment.[543] However, since the inclusion of adjustments in income for the year of change might result in telescoping income for several years into one taxable year, Code section 585(c)(3) provides relief for the taxpayer. Unlike the normally mandated three-year ratable spread of Code section 481(a) adjustments, Code section 585(c)(3) provides for a four-year spread at a rate which defers most recapture income.[544]

One of the following three methods of accounting for the existing reserve balance and future charge-offs and recoveries must be adopted if a bank is required to have changed its method of accounting for loan losses:

1. The deferral method;
2. The accelerated method; or
3. The cut-off method.

(a) Deferral Method

Under the deferral method, a large bank is required to recapture its bad-debt reserve by taking into income its net Code section 481(a) adjustment at the rate of 10 percent of the reserve balance in the disqualification year, and 20, 30, and 40 percent in the next three years, respectively.[545] The rate of recapture is adhered to regardless of actual charge-offs or recoveries. While reserve recapture is occurring, and for subsequent years, the bank is on the specific charge-off method for bad debts and recoveries.

Example: In 1998, Bank became a "large bank." Its reserve balance at year-end 1997 is $650,000 and bad-debt deductions for 1998 and 1999,

541 Reg. § 1.585-5(b)(3), Ex. 4.

542 *See also* the *General Explanation of the Tax Reform Act of 1986* (the "Blue Book"), prepared by the staff of the Joint Committee on Taxation, at 578, providing that it is the reserve balance which existed on the last day of the taxable year before the disqualification year that is the amount that must be recaptured.

543 Reg. § 1.585-6(b)(3).

544 I.R.C. § 481(b)(1) (2000).

545 I.R.C. § 585(c)(3); Reg. § 1.585-6(b) (2000).

respectively are $165,000 and $140,000. Reserve recapture and bad-debt deductions for 1998 and 1999 will be as follows:

	1998	*1999*
Reserve recapture	$65,000	$130,000
Bad-debt deductions	165,000	140,000
Net income	($100,000)	($ 10,000)

During 2000 and 2001, income will include 30 percent and 40 percent, respectively, of the reserve balance and net charge-offs will be deducted.

(b) *Accelerated Method*

The accelerated method permits a bank to elect to include in income any amount in excess of 10 percent of its net Code section 481(a) adjustment in the year of change, 2/9 of the remainder of the reserve balance in the first succeeding year (after reduction for the amount included in income in the first taxable year), 3/9 in the second succeeding taxable year, and 4/9 of the remainder in the third succeeding taxable year.[546]

The flexibility granted by this method is available only in the disqualification year. No amount greater or less than 2/9, 3/9 and 4/9 of the balance remaining after the first year's recapture may be included in income in the second, third and fourth years, respectively. This method, however, allows the entire reserve to be recaptured in the disqualification year, an option that may be attractive if the taxpayer had expiring net operating losses, anticipates a tax rate increase, or wishes to absorb a net operating loss that may be limited by consolidated return rules such as the separate return limitations rules.

The election to accelerate must be made no later than the due date, including extensions, for filing the taxpayer's return for the disqualification year, and once it is made, it is binding on the taxpayer.[547]

Example: Assume the facts of the immediately preceding example, except that Bank elected the accelerated method and recaptured 30 percent of its reserve balance in the disqualification year. Its reserve recapture and bad-debt deductions in 1998 and 1999 would be as follows:

	1998	*1999*
Reserve recapture	$195,000	$101,111
Bad-debt deductions	165,000	140,000
Net income	$30,000	($ 38,889)

During 2000 and 2001, income will include 3/9 and 4/9 of the reserve balance remaining after the first year's recapture and net charge-off will be deducted.

[546] I.R.C. § 585(c)(3)(A)(iii) (2000); Reg. § 1.585-6(b)(2).

[547] Reg. § 1.585-8. The election is made by attaching a statement to the tax return for the taxable year it is to be effective. Consent to revoke the election may be granted by the Commissioner.

(c) *Cut-Off Method*

Under the elective cut-off approach, there will be no recapture of the reserve balance. Two accounts are created by a bank electing to use the cut-off method: an account for pre-disqualification year loans, and an account for loans made on or after the first day of the disqualification year.[548] If the amount of any pre-disqualification year loan is increased during or after the disqualification year, the amount of the increase is not treated as part of the pre-disqualification year loan balance.[549] Pre-disqualification year loans are those loans on the bank's books on the last day of the taxable year immediately preceding the disqualification year.

All charge-offs and recoveries with respect to the pre-disqualification year loans will be adjustments to the loan loss reserve account and not direct credits or charges to income.[550] Included in any charge to the reserve will be any losses resulting from pre-disqualification year loans, including losses that result from the sale or other disposition of these loans. In general, recoveries on these loans are additions to the reserve.[551]

If the reserve balance at the close of any year exceeds the balance of the bank's outstanding pre-disqualification year loans at such time, the excess must be included in income in the year the excess occurs.[552] In the event that loan losses charged to the reserve reduce the balance of the reserve to zero, the bank will be treated as if it is on the specific charge-off method with regard to subsequent charge-offs or recoveries on pre-disqualification year loans.[553] Thus, the bank will have items of income and expense in the year of the charge-off (loss) or recovery.[554]

Example 1: Assume the facts of the basic example, except that Bank elects the cut-off method. Also assume that the 1998 and 1999 net charge-offs were attributable to loans as follows:

	1998	*1999*
Loans made prior to disqualification year	$150,000	$40,000
Loans made in disqualification year	$15,000	$100,000
	$165,000	$140,000

On Bank's 1998 and 1999 income tax returns, no portion of the reserve would be recaptured. Bank will be allowed a bad-debt deduction of $15,000 and $100,000 in 1998 and 1999, respectively.

548 *See also* the *General Explanation of the Tax Reform Act of 1986* (the "Blue Book"), prepared by the staff of the Joint Committee on Taxation, at 552-3.

549 Reg. § 1.585-7(b)(2).

550 I.R.C. § 585(c)(4); Reg. § 1.585-7(a) (2000).

551 Reg. § 1.585-7(a)(1).

552 I.R.C. § 585(c)(4) (2000); Reg. § 1.585-7(a).

553 Reg. § 1.585-7(a)(1).

554 H.R. Rep. No. 99-841, pt. 2 at 328 (1986).

Example 2: Continue to assume the facts of the basic example and that the bank elects the cut-off method. Also, assume 1998 and 1999 net charge-offs as follows:

	1998	*1999*
Loans made prior to disqualification year	$250,000	$450,000
Loans made in disqualification year	$50,000	$100,000
	$300,000	$550,000

On Bank's 1998 and 1999 income tax returns, no portion of the reserve would be recaptured. Bank will be allowed a bad-debt deduction of $50,000 and $150,000 in 1998 and 1999, respectively. Of the $150,000 bad-debt deduction in 1999, $50,000 is attributable to loans in existence on the first day of the disqualification year. This deduction is allowed because charge-offs on these reserves historically exceed the reserve balance by this amount. In subsequent years, all net charge-offs will be deductible.

Although the Staff of the Joint Committee of Taxation, in their explanation of the Tax Reform Act of 1986, provided that the election to use the cut-off method is to be made on a taxpayer-by-taxpayer basis, and not a bank-by-bank basis, Congress made it clear by a 1988 amendment to Code section 585 that the election to use the cut-off method may be made on a bank-by-bank basis.[555] This has been confirmed in regulations.[556]

(d) Disposing of Loans

As a general rule, if a bank sells or otherwise disposes of any of its loans on or after the first day of its disqualification year, the bank's obligation to recapture its reserve is not effected.[557] The bank must continue to recapture its reserve, and the disposition does not affect the amount of its Code section 481(a) adjustment. However, if the bank ceases to engage in the business of banking before it has recaptured its full reserve, it must include in income the remaining amount of its Code section 481(a) adjustment in the taxable year in which it ceases to engage in the banking business.[558]

---

[555] Technical and Miscellaneous Revenue Act of 1988, Pub. L. No. 100-647, 102 Stat. 3342 (1988) amending I.R.C. §585(c) by adding at the end thereof subparagraph "(C)." §1009(a)(2)(A). Compare the parent level election of I.R.C. §585(c)(3)(B) applicable to financially troubled banks.

[556] Reg. §1.585-8(d).

[557] Reg. §1.585-6(c)(1).

[558] Reg. §1.585-6(c)(2). Pursuant to I.R.C. §446(e) and Reg. §1.446-1(e), the IRS has published uniform standards for accounting method changes that include guidance on when a taxpayer is considered to have ceased to engage in business for purposes of I.R.C. §481(a). *See* Rev. Proc. 97-27, 1997-21 I.R.B. 10.

(i) Code Section 381(a) Transactions: General Rule. If a bank transfers loans in a Code section 381(a) transaction in which the transferor bank is not treated as ceasing to engage in the business of banking, the unrecaptured balance of the transferor's net Code section 481(a) adjustment carries over to the acquiror.[559] A Code section 381(a) transaction is a liquidation of a subsidiary (Code section 332) or certain corporate reorganizations (Code sections 368(a)(1)(A), (C), (D), (F), (G)). The acquiring corporation must complete the four-year recapture procedure begun by the transferor, using the same recapture method. The transferor's taxable year that ends on or includes the date of acquisition shall be treated as one year within the four-year recapture period, and the acquiror's first taxable year ending after the date of the acquisition shall be treated as the immediately following taxable year for purposes of the four-year recapture period. If the acquiring institution is not a large bank and uses the reserve method of accounting for bad debts, the positive Code section 481 adjustment may be offset by a new negative Code section 481 adjustment attributable to the reserve addition.[560] The transfer of loans also may result in a "large bank" taint being carried over to the acquiror.

(ii) Code Section 381(a) Transaction: Cut-Off Election. In the case of a Code section 381(a) transaction in which a bank using the cut-off approach transfers outstanding pre-disqualification year loans to another corporation, the acquiring corporation is treated as the transferor.[561] As a general rule, the transferor's bad-debt reserve immediately before the transaction will carry over to the acquiring institution; the acquiring institution shall take as its balance of outstanding pre-disqualification year loans immediately after the Code section 381(a) transaction the balance of these loans that it receives in the transaction; and the acquiring institution assumes all the transferor's rights and obligations under the elective cut-off approach.[562]

An institution acquiring pre-disqualification year loans in a Code section 381(a) transaction from a bank that has elected the cut-off method will not continue to account for the loans under that method if the acquiring institution is not a "large bank" immediately after the Code section 381(a) transaction and if it uses the reserve method of accounting for bad debts.[563] Instead, the transferor's reserve balance immediately before the transaction will carry over to the acquiring institution. A negative Code section 481(a) adjustment will be required if the allowable reserve balance, computed under the Code section 585(b)(2) six-year moving average method, for the loans received in the transaction exceeds the balance of the reserve that is transferred.[564]

If a principal purpose of the Code section 381(a) transaction in which a significant amount of pre-disqualification year loans is transferred is to avoid the provisions of the cut-off approach, including the denial of a deduction for losses

[559] Reg. § 1.585-6(c)(3).

[560] Reg. § 1.585-6(c)(3).

[561] Reg. § 1.585-7(d)(2).

[562] Reg. § 1.585-7(d)(2)(i).

[563] Reg. § 1.585-7(d)(2)(ii).

[564] The negative I.R.C. § 481(a) (2000) adjustment is taken into account as required under I.R.C. § 381. The moving average method is more fully described in Reg. § 1.585-2(c)(1)(ii).

on pre-disqualification year loans, the IRS may disregard the disposition, or it may treat the replacement loans as pre-disqualification year loans.[565] If the loans are treated as pre-disqualification year loans, no deduction shall be allowed under the specific charge-off method with respect to the loans. However, if a bank sells pre-disqualification year loans and uses the proceeds to originate new loans, this anti-avoidance rule will not apply.

§ 10.10.3 Advantages/Disadvantages of Recapture Methods

The decision to select the accelerated or the cut-off method in lieu of the deferral method will be influenced by several factors. If the taxpayer wishes to accelerate deductions or minimize taxable income, the deferral method is normally preferred. Reserve recapture income will be less than the income from the accelerated method and deductions from actual charge-offs are likely to exceed the income inclusion in the disqualification year. In unusual circumstances, the cut-off method could result in less taxable income in early years. This may occur when charge-offs in early years on loans held at the beginning of the disqualification year are less than the amount required to be recaptured if the deferral method were utilized.

> **Example:** Assume the facts of the basic example (reserve balance is $650,000) except that charge-offs during the disqualification year are $200,000, $50,000 of which are in respect to loans made prior to the disqualification year. Under these facts the elective cut-off method would result in net deductions of $50,000. Under the deferral method, net income of ($100,000) would result, as follows:

	Method	
	Deferral	*Cut-off*
Disqualification year:		
Reserve recapture	$100,000	
Bad-debt deductions	$200,000	$150,000
Net income	($100,000)	($150,000)

To defer recapture of the reserve under the cut-off method (*e.g.*, when the predisqualification year loans drop to an amount below the reserve balance), consideration should be given to acquiring long-term maturity loans prior to the disqualification year. To the extent that the loans remain on the books and exceed the reserve balance at the beginning of the disqualification year, the reserve will not be recaptured.

§ 10.10.4 Financially Troubled Banks

As a general rule, for each taxable year in which a "large bank" is "financially troubled," reserve recapture is suspended if either the accelerated method or the deferral method is used.[566] If the bank has elected the cut-off method, it

565 Reg. § 1.585-7(b)(3).

566 I.R.C. §§ 585(c)(3)(A)(iii)(I) and (c)(3)(B)(ii) (2000); Reg. § 1.585-6(d)(1). H.R. Rep. No. 99-841, at 329 (1986). I.R.C. § 585(c)(3)(C) permits the suspension of reserve recapture to be taken into account for purposes of determining installment payments of estimated tax under I.R.C. § 6655(e)(2)(A) (2000).

must continue to account for charge-offs and recoveries without regard to its financially troubled status.[567] Regulations provide that if an election is made by the financially troubled bank in the process of recapturing its reserve, it may elect to recapture any percentage greater than 10 percent of its loan loss reserve in its "election year" which is either:

1. The disqualification year,
2. The first taxable year after the disqualification year in which the bank is not financially troubled, or
3. Any taxable year between the disqualification year and the first taxable year after the disqualification year in which the bank is not financially troubled.[568]

This election may be especially attractive to those banks with net operating losses that would otherwise be carried over to years subsequent to the disqualification year. The election applies only to a bank which is financially troubled in its disqualification year.[569] It is not available if the bank is not financially troubled in the disqualification year but becomes financially troubled in a subsequent year. Moreover, the election permits reserve recapture in only one year, the election year, and that year may not be a year after the first taxable year after the disqualification year in which the bank is not financially troubled. If a bank is financially troubled after the election year, reserve recapture must be suspended and no election may be made to include any portion of the reserve balance in income in that year or any subsequent year.[570]

Example 1: Assume that Bank's disqualification year is 19X0 and during that year, Bank becomes financially troubled. Assume also that 19X4 is the first taxable year in which Bank is not financially troubled. Thus:

19X0 Disqualification year/financially troubled

19X1 Intervening year

19X2 Intervening year

19X3 Intervening year

19X4 Not financially troubled

Under these circumstances, Bank may elect to recapture any percentage of its net Code section 481(a) reserve that is greater than 10 percent in *one* of

[567] *Id.* It appears that the special rules relating to financially troubled banks should apply if a bank that elected the cut-off method is required to recapture its reserve by reason of the reserve balance exceeding pre-disqualification year loans.

[568] The I.R.C. does not appear to grant the flexibility to recapture in any intervening year. I.R.C. § 585(c)(3)(B)(ii). The legislative history of the provision appears to allow reserve recapture in any year in which the bank is financially troubled. H.R. Rep. No. 99-841, at 329 (1986).

[569] I.R.C. § 585(c)(3)(B)(ii) (2000); Reg. § 1.585-6(d)(2). Although elections generally must be made by attaching a statement to the return for the disqualification year, in the case of an election that is in respect of the "election year," the statement must be attached to the return for that year. Reg. § 1.585-8(a). The statement must contain the following information: (a) the name, address and taxpayer identification number of the electing bank; (b) a statement that the election is being made to include in income more than 10 percent of the bank's net section 481(a) adjustment under Reg. § 1.585-6(d)(2); and (c) the percentage being elected. Reg. § 1.585-8(b).

[570] Reg. § 1.585-6(d)(2).

the following years: 19X0, 19X1, 19X2, 19X3, or 19X4. In the nonelection years that Bank is financially troubled, Bank may not recapture reserve.

Example 2: Assume the same facts as in Example 1, and that Bank elects to recapture in 19X1.

19X0 Disqualification year/financially troubled

19X1 Intervening year/election to recapture year 1

19X3 Intervening year

19X4 Not financially troubled

19X5 Recapture year 2

Since Bank is financially troubled for the years following its election (19X2, 19X3, and 19X4), Bank may not recapture its reserve in those years and Bank may not include those years in its future application of the reserve recapture rules. Additionally, the election year, 19X1, will be treated as the disqualification year. Therefore, an election to include in income more than 10 percent of the net Code section 481(a) adjustment will be available only for 19X1. Recapture must resume in 19X5.

Example 3: Assume the same facts as in Example 1, except that Bank becomes financially troubled in 19X1.

19X0 Disqualification year/recapture year 1

19X1 Financially troubled

19X2 Intervening year

19X3 Intervening year

19X4 Not financially troubled

19X5 Recapture year 2

The bank must begin to recapture its reserve during 19X0. The election is not available. Thus, recapture will be suspended while Bank is financially troubled and Bank must resume recapture in 19X5.

A bank is "financially troubled" for any taxable year if its "nonperforming loan percentage" exceeds 75 percent.[571] A bank's nonperforming loan percentage is determined by dividing the average of its nonperforming loan balance by the average of its equity.[572] Although the Conference Committee Report under the Tax Reform Act of 1986 indicates that the average balances are to be determined by reference to the balances of nonperforming loans and equity "at each time during the taxable year that the bank is required to report for regulatory purposes," the statute appears to require quarterly averages regardless of how frequently the bank files its regulatory reports of condition.[573] Regulations attempt to reconcile these two rules by providing that, as a general rule, quarter ending numbers are to be used; however, a bank may, for all years, determine its

[571] I.R.C. § 585(c)(3)(B)(iii) (2000); Reg. § 1.585-6(d)(3).

[572] I.R.C. § 585(c)(3)(B)(iv).

[573] H.R. Rep. No. 99-341, at 329 (1986).

nonperforming loan percentage on the bases of loans and equity at the close of each "report date."[574]

The quarters for a short year of at least three months are the same as those of the bank's annual accounting period, except that quarters ending before or after the short year are disregarded. If the short taxable year consists of less than three months, the first or last day of the taxable year is treated as the last day of its only quarter. Tax bases in loans are not taken into account for purposes of computing the nonperforming loan percentage.[575]

Nonperforming loans are those considered to be nonperforming by the bank's primary federal regulatory agency.[576] For this purpose, a loan is any extension of credit that is defined and treated as a loan under standards prescribed by the Federal Financial Institutions Examination Council ("FFIEC"). They include:

1. Loans that are past due as to interest or principal 90 days or more and that are still accruing,
2. Loans in nonaccrual status, and
3. Renegotiated troubled debt determined to be such under the standards (as of October 22, 1986) of the FFIEC.[577]

Under these rules, a troubled debt restructuring that is, in substance, a foreclosure or repossession is not considered a loan. If a debt is evidenced by a security issued by a foreign government, it is treated as a loan if the security is issued as an integral part of a restructuring of one or more troubled loans to the foreign government, to an agency of the foreign government, or to an instrumentality of the foreign government. Moreover, if a deposit with the central bank of a foreign country is made under a deposit facility agreement that is entered into as an integral part of a restructuring of one or more troubled loans to the foreign country's government, agency, or instrumentality, it shall be treated as a loan for this purpose.[578] A loan will not be considered to be "nonperforming" merely because it is past due, if it past due less than 90 days.[579]

For purposes of this computation, a troubled bank's equity equals its assets minus its liabilities, as determined for federal regulatory purposes.[580] No part of the reserve for loan loss balance is included in the equity balance.[581]

Both non-performing loans and equity balances are determined on a "financial group" basis if the bank is a member of a parent-subsidiary controlled group.[582] All banks that are members of the same parent-subsidiary controlled

---

[574] Reg. § 1.585-6(d)(3)(i). For purposes of determining a bank's "report date" the "alternative report date" provided for in Reg. 1.585-5(c)(2)(i)(B) is not taken into account. Thus, if a bank chose as its report date the last day of any regular interval in the taxable year that is more frequent than quarterly, it is not taken into account for determining its nonperforming loan percentage. Of course, most banks will have a quarter ending report date.

[575] Reg. § 1.585-6(d)(3)(i).

[576] Reg. § 1.585-6(d)(3)(iii)(A).

[577] *Id.*

[578] Reg. § 1.585-6(d)(3)(iii)(B).

[579] Reg. § 1.585-6(d)(3)(iii).

[580] Reg. § 1.585-6(d)(3)(iv).

[581] *Id.*

[582] I.R.C. § 585(c)(3)(B)(iv) (2000). Reg. § 1.585-6(d)(3)(ii) and I.R.C. § 1563(a)(1) (2000).

group must determine their "financial group" under one of two alternatives, and whichever alternative is selected, it must be applied by all bank members in the same group. Under the first alternative, a bank's financial group shall consist of all banks (and comparable foreign financial institutions) that are members of the parent-subsidiary controlled group of which the bank is a member.[583] Under the second approach, a bank's "financial group" shall consist of all members of the parent-subsidiary control group of which the bank is a member.[584]

For purposes of these calculations, any equity interest that a member of a bank's financial group holds in another member of the group is not counted in determining equity, and any loan that a member of a bank's financial group makes to another member of the group is not counted in determining non-performing loans. All bank members in the same parent-subsidiary control group must determine their non-performing loan percentage for all years that they are members of the group on the basis of loan and equity balances at the close of each quarter of the taxable year or they all must determine the percentage on the base of the close of each "report date."[585]

§ 10.11 Thrift Bad-Debt Reserve Recapture

A thrift that is required to change its method of accounting for bad debt by reason of the repeal of Code section 593 must recapture a portion of its reserves for loan losses.[586] Guidance for thrift institutions that became ineligible to maintain bad-debt reserves under Code section 593 prior to the repeal of the section had been provided in proposed regulations.[587] Prior to the issuance of the proposed regulations, the IRS ruled that a change from the Code section 593 method to Code section 585 is a change in the treatment of a material item and, therefore, is a change in a method of accounting.[588] If the change in the accounting for bad debts is the result of an acquisition of a thrift by a large commercial bank, the commercial bank may be required to take into account the entire amount of the thrift's reserve balances in the year of acquisition.[589]

The repeal of Code section 593 requires a thrift institution to change its method of accounting for bad debts and treat such change as a change in a method of accounting initiated by the taxpayer and having been made with the consent of the Secretary of the Treasury.[590] Any Code section 481(a) adjustment required to be taken into account with respect to the accounting method change is taken into account ratably over a six-taxable year period beginning with the first taxable year beginning after December 31, 1995.[591] The amount of the Code section 481(a) adjustment will be equal to the "applicable excess reserves" of the thrift.[592]

---

583 Reg. § 1.585-6(d)(3)(ii)(B)(2). The entities that are combined for this purpose are "financial institutions" within the meaning of I.R.C. § 265(b)(5) (2000).

584 Reg. § 1.585-6(d)(3)(ii)(B)(3).

585 Reg. § 1.585-6(d)(3)(iii). For this purpose, the alternative report date, if elected, is not taken into account.

586 I.R.C. § 593(g) (2000).

587 Prop. Reg. §§ 1.593-12 through 1.593-14, 57 Fed. Reg. 1232-01, January 13, 1992; correction at 57 Fed. Reg. 6060-01, February 19, 1992.

588 Rev. Rul. 85-171, 1985-2 C.B. 148.

589 FSA 199944014, November 5, 1999.

590 I.R.C. § 593(g)(1)(B) (2000).

591 I.R.C. § 593(g)(1)(C) (2000).

592 I.R.C. § 593(g)(1)(C)(i) (2000).

An important exception may apply in the case of a tax-free reorganizations occurring prior to the effective date of Code section 593(g). That section applies to taxable years beginning after December 31, 1995. It is the IRS's position that a target entity that determines its bad debt reserves under Code section 593 may be required to recapture its entire reserve balance and the additional tax resulting from the recapture will be taken into account by the acquiring corporation.[593]

Code section 381(c)(4) provides that the acquiring corporation in a reorganization to which Code section 368(a)(1) applies shall use the method of accounting used by the transferor corporation unless the acquiring corporation and the transferor used different methods. In that instance, the acquiring corporation shall use the method prescribed by regulations. In accordance with Treasury regulation section 1.381(c)(4)-1(a)(1) (ii), the acquiring corporation shall take into account the dollar balances of those accounts of the transferor corporation which represent reserves in respect of which the transferor has taken a deduction for taxable years ending on or before the date of transfer. The amount of the adjustment necessary to reflect a method change, the manner in which the reserves are to be taken into account, and the tax attributable to such reserves shall be determined and computed under Code section 481, subject to the rules provided in Treasury regulation section 1.381(c)(4)-1(c) and (d).[594]

Treasury regulation section 1.381(c)(4)-1(c)(2) (iii) sets forth rules for determining the principal method of accounting for bad debts when the transferor and the acquiring corporation use different methods. Treasury regulation section 1.381(c)(4)-1(c)(1) provides that when an acquiring corporation must use a different method of accounting for an acquired business than its transferor did, the adjustments necessary to reflect such change and any resulting increase or decrease in tax are determined as if the transferor had initiated a change in method of accounting on the date of transfer. The increase or decrease in tax shall be taken into account by the acquiring corporation. In other words, a transferor should prepare its final return using its old method of accounting. The transferor would then compute a hypothetical tax based on the assumption that it had changed its accounting method for its final year. The acquiring corporation would then take into account directly the increase or decrease in tax which would be imposed on (a) the income that would have been reported by the transferor under the new method, plus (b) the Code section 481(a) adjustment that would have resulted had the change actually been made by the transferor.[595]

If Code section 593(g) did apply, an acquired entity would be required to recapture only its "applicable excess reserves." Under Code section 593(g)(1)(C) such reserves would have been taken into account ratably over the six-taxable year period beginning with the first taxable year beginning after December 31, 1995.

---

[593] FSA 200022009, February 17, 2000.

[594] *See also* Rev. Rul. 85-171, 1985-2 C.B. 148.

[595] GCM 39,436, I-279-84 (Nov. 1, 1985).

§ 10.11.1 Applicable Excess Reserves—Large Bank

The applicable excess reserves for a thrift that is a "large bank," as that term is defined in Code section 585(c)(2), in an amount equal to the excess, if any, of the balance as of the close of its last taxable year beginning before January 1, 1996, of the thrift's reserve for losses on qualifying real property loans, for losses on non-qualifying loans, and its supplemental reserve for losses on loans, over the lesser of (a) the balance of such reserves as of the close of the taxpayers last taxable year beginning before January 1, 1988, the thrift's base year, or (b) the balance of such reserves reduced in some manner as under Code section 585(b)(2)(B)(ii) for a decline in loans from the base year loan balance.[596] Thus, for purposes of determining the Code section 481(a) adjustment, the reserve balance with respect to the thrift's base year is not taken into account for purposes of determining the Code section 481(a) adjustment. However, the balance contained in these three reserves as of December 31, 1987, will continue to be subject to the reserve recapture rules that are contained in Code section 593(e).

If a thrift becomes a large bank in a taxable year after its first taxable year beginning after December 31, 1995, and if it elects the cut-off method provided in Code section 585(c)(4), the reserve held by the thrift as of the first day of the disqualification year is reduced by the reserve balance taken into account for purposes of determining the Code section 481(a) adjustment arising from the conversion of the thrift to commercial bank status. Thus, if the taxpayer elects the cut off method, net bad debts will be charged against the reserve balance as of the first day of the disqualification year reduced by the reserve balance that is not recaptured when the thrift converts to a bank charter.[597]

§ 10.11.2 Applicable Excess Reserves—Small Bank

If a thrift becomes a bank that is not a large bank as defined in Code section 585(c)(2), for its first taxable year beginning after December 31, 1995, the thrift will generally recapture only a portion of the post-1988 reserve balance increase. The "applicable excess reserves" that will be recaptured will be an amount equal to the balances contained in the thrift's three reserves as of the close of the last taxable year beginning before January 1, 1996, over the greater of the balance of the reserves as of the close of the taxpayer's last taxable year beginning before January 1, 1988, or the balance in a hypothetical reserve.[598] The hypothetical reserve balance is equal to a reserve balance as of the close of the thrift's last taxable year beginning before January 1, 1996, assuming that the thrift computed additions to the hypothetical reserve for all taxable years under the moving average experience method contained in Code section 585(b)(2)(A).[599] If a thrift that is not a large bank continues on the experience method contained in Code section 585, it will establish as its opening reserve balance as of the beginning of the first taxable year beginning on or after January 1, 1996, this hypothetical

[596] I.R.C. § 593(g)(2)(A) (2000).

[597] I.R.C. § 593(g)(5)(B) (2000).

[598] I.R.C. § 593(g)(2)(B) (2000).

[599] I.R.C. § 593(g)(2)(B)(i) (2000).

reserve balance or its reserve balance at the close of its base year, 1987, whichever is greater.[600]

Thus, a large thrift is required to recapture its post-1987 increase in its bad-debt reserve while a thrift that becomes a small bank generally is required to recapture only its post-1987 additions to its bad-debt reserves that were attributable to the use of the percentage of taxable income method taken during that post-1987 period. For small thrifts as with large thrifts, there is a proportional scale back of the base year amount that is not subject to recapture whenever there is a decline in loan balances since December 31, 1987. The scale back rule applies to all pre-1988 reserves, including the supplemental reserve.

If a thrift is not a large bank for its first taxable year beginning after December 31, 1995, but becomes a large bank in a subsequent taxable year, a special rule is provided to avoid duplication of reserve recapture. For purposes of determining the net Code section 481(a) adjustment that would have to be taken into account when a thrift becomes a large bank, only the excess of the reserve for bad debts as of the close of the last taxable year before the disqualification year over the balance that is taken into account under the reserve recapture rule applicable by reason of the conversion of a thrift to a commercial bank is taken into account. Thus, the four-year spread of adjustments required by Code section 585(c)(3), applicable when a bank becomes a large bank, is reduced by the thrift's balance in its reserves as of the close of the thrift's last taxable year beginning before January 1, 1988.[601]

§ 10.11.3 Acquisitions and Dispositions

In the case of an acquisition of the assets of the thrift in certain nonrecognition transactions, including liquidations of subsidiaries and certain corporate reorganizations, the acquiring corporation shall succeed to and take into account, as of the close of the day of distribution or transfer, the balance of the applicable excess reserves and the balance taken into account by the thrift of such reserves as of the close of the thrifts last taxable year beginning before January 1, 1988.[602]

If a thrift transfers a portion of its loan portfolio, but it continues to conduct a banking business within the meaning of Code section 581, Code section 593(g)(6) will not require any portion of the suspended reserve or the thrift's supplemental reserve to be recaptured.[603] Suspended reserves will be recaptured whenever a thrift ceases to be a bank.[604] The suspended reserves will normally equal the reserve balance as of the close of the last taxable year beginning before January 1, 1988. Suspended reserves also are recaptured upon certain distributions to shareholders.[605] Code section 593(g)(8) confers on the IRS authority to prescribe regulations that may be necessary to carry out the intention of Code sections 593(g) and (e), including regulations providing for the application of

[600] I.R.C. § 593(g)(2)(B)(ii) (2000).
[601] I.R.C. § 593(g)(5)(A) (2000).
[602] I.R.C. § 593(g)(6) (2000).
[603] PLR 199937032, June 22, 1999.
[604] I.R.C. § 593(g)(3) (2000).
[605] I.R.C. § 593(e) (2000).

these sections in the case of acquisitions, mergers, spinoffs, and other reorganizations.[606]

§ 10.11.4 Residential Loan Requirement

For the first taxable year beginning after December 31, 1995, or for the following taxable year, reserve recapture may be suspended if a taxpayer met a "residential loan requirement," computed on a controlling group basis.[607] A taxpayer meets the residential loan requirement for any taxable year if the principal amount of the taxpayer's residential loans made during the taxable year is not less than the "base amount" for the year. Thus, all taxpayers will recapture applicable excess reserves within six, seven, or eight years, depending upon the availability of the residential loan requirement.

The term "residential loan" is defined as any loan described in Code section 7701(a)(19)(C)(v), but only if such loans are incurred in acquiring, constructing, or improving the property described in that Code section.[608] Refinancings and home equity loans are not taken into account, except to the extent that the proceeds of the loan are used to acquire, construct, or improve qualified residential property.[609] Code section 7701(a)(19)(C)(v) describes one type of asset that will satisfy the 60 percent asset test for purposes of defining a domestic building and loan association. The loans described in that section are:

1. Loans (including redeemable ground rents, as defined in Code section 1055) secured by an interest in residential real property or real property used primarily for church purposes;
2. Loans secured by an interest in real property which, or from the proceeds of the loan, will become residential real property or real property used primarily for church purposes; and
3. Loans made for the improvement of residential real property or real property used primarily for church purposes.

Residential real property includes single or multifamily dwellings, facilities in residential developments dedicated to public use, or property used on a nonprofit basis for residents, and mobile homes not used on a transient basis.

The "base amount" is the average of the principal amounts of the residential loans made by the taxpayer during the six most recent taxable years beginning before January 1, 1996.[610] At the election of the taxpayer, the high and low years in this six-year period are not taken into account in computing the average. The election to omit the highest and lowest years may be made only for the first taxable year beginning after December 31, 1995, and, if it is made for such taxable year, it will apply to all succeeding taxable years unless revoked with the consent of the Secretary of the Treasury.

---

[606] No regulations have been issued under I.R.C. § 593(g)(8) (2000).

[607] *See* I.R.C. § 1563(a)(1) (2000) for definition of a parent-subsidiary controlled group.

[608] I.R.C. § 593(g)(4)(C) (2000).

[609] *General Explanation of the Tax Reform Act of 1986* (the "Blue Book"), prepared by the staff of the Joint Committee on Taxation, at 254.

[610] I.R.C. § 593(g)(4)(D) (2000).

§ 10.12 Tax Preference Issues

§ 10.12.1 Alternative Minimum Tax

Code section 55 imposes a 20 percent alternative minimum tax (AMT) on AMT income.[611] AMT income is taxable income computed for the taxable year under Code section 63 (regular taxable income), with certain adjustments.[612] Taxable income is adjusted by Code sections 56 and 58 and increased by the Code section 57 items of tax preference.[613]

Prior to its amendment by the Revenue Reconciliation Act of 1990, Code section 57 listed among the "items of tax preference" for commercial banks and thrifts, the amount by which the deduction allowable for the taxable year for a reasonable addition to a reserve for bad debts exceeds the amount that would have been allowable had the institution maintained its bad-debt reserve for all taxable years on the basis of actual experience.[614] This preference item applied to thrifts employing the percentage of taxable income method as well as to commercial banks.

The Revenue Reconciliation Act of 1990 amended Code section 57(a)(4) to delete any reference to "financial institutions to which section 585 applies."[615] No change was made to the reference to thrifts determining their bad-debt deductions under Code section 593.[616] Thus, a commercial bank will no longer be exposed to the possibility of a minimum tax on any portion of its bad-debt deduction.

Regulations under Code section 57 state that:

> [T]he determination of the amount which would have been allowable had the institution maintained its reserve for bad debts on the basis of actual experience is the amount determined under Code section 585(b)(3)(A) and the regulations thereunder.[617]

Thus, the reference for computing the Code section 57 item of tax preference is the reserve addition determined under the moving average approach of the experience method.

An institution will "maintain" its bad-debt reserve by first computing an opening reserve balance for the bank's first taxable year ending in 1970.[618] This will equal the amount which bears the same ratio to loans outstanding at the beginning of the taxable year as:

---

611 I.R.C. § 55(b)(1)(A) (2000).

612 I.R.C. § 55(b)(2) (2000).

613 I.R.C. § § 55(b)(2)(A) and (B) (2000).

614 I.R.C. § 57(a)(4) (2000).

615 Pub. L. No. 101-508, 104 Stat 1388 (1990), § 11,001 *et seq.* at Sec. 11801(c)(12)(A). In the event that a thrift determines its reserve addition under the reserve restoration approach, there appears to continue to be AMT exposure.

616 A production credit association is neither a commercial bank nor a domestic building and loan association. Accordingly, this item of tax preference has no application to production credit associations. Rev. Rul. 81-172, 1981-1 C.B. 39; PLR 8001006, September 26, 1979.

617 Reg. § 1.57-1(g)(4).

618 Reg. § 1.57-1(g)(4).

1. Total net bad debts sustained during the 5 preceding taxable years bears to;
2. The sum of loans outstanding at the close of such 5 years.[619]

§ 10.12.2 Corporate Preference Item

For taxable years beginning after December 31, 1982, but before January 1, 1987, commercial banks and thrifts were subject to a reduction in the otherwise allowable deduction permitted for reserve additions taken under Code sections 585 or 593. Code section 291 provided that such deductions are "corporate preference items" subject to a 20 percent reduction.[620] The Tax Reform Act of 1986 amended Code section 291 to delete the reference to financial institutions to which Code section 593 applies. Thus, for taxable years beginning after December 31, 1986, thrifts were not subject to the 20 percent cutback in their bad-debt deductions.[621] The Omnibus Budget Reconciliation Act of 1990 repealed the 20 percent cutback for commercial banks effective November 5, 1990.[622]

---

[619] Special rules are provided for selecting a period shorter than 6 taxable years, for new banks, and for short-taxable years. Reg. § 1.57-1(g)(4)(i) and (ii).

[620] I.R.C. § 291(e)(1)(A) (1982), prior to amendment by the Tax Reform Act of 1986, Pub. L. No. 99-514, § 901(d)(4)(C), 100 Stat. 2085 (1986).

[621] The Tax Reform Act of 1986, Pub. L. No. 99-514, § 901(b)(4), 100 Stat. 2085 (1986).

[622] Omnibus Budget Reconciliation Act of 1990, Pub. L. No. 101-508, § 1180(c)(12)(B), 104 Stat. 1388 (1990).

Chapter 11
Acquisitions

Contents

§11.1 Tax Planning Suggestions
§11.2 Interstate Opportunities for Banks and BHCs
§11.2.1 Permissible Interstate Bank Activities
§11.2.2 Permissible Interstate BHC Activities
§11.3 Taxable Acquisitions
§11.3.1 Taxation of Selling Corporation
§11.3.2 Cost Recovery Rules to Acquiring Corporation
§11.3.3 Cost Recovery: Code Section 197 Intangibles
§11.3.4 Code Section 197 Intangible Assets
§11.3.5 Code Section 197 Intangibles: Exceptions
§11.3.6 Code Section 197 Intangibles: Dispositions
§11.3.7 Loan Premium
§11.3.8 Qualified Stock Purchase
§11.4 Limitation on Loss Carryovers
§11.4.1 Code Section 382 Limitation
§11.4.2 Loss Corporations
§11.4.3 Pre-change Loss and Post-change Year
§11.4.4 Entity
§11.4.5 Short Tax Year
§11.4.6 Net Operating Loss Carryovers; Built-in Gain and Loss
§11.4.7 Net Unrealized Built-in Gain and Loss
§11.4.8 Taxable Year of Net Unrealized Built-in Loss
§11.4.9 Recognized Built-in Gain or Loss
§11.4.10 Threshold Requirement
§11.4.11 Calculating RBIL and RBIG
§11.4.12 Ownership Changes
§11.4.13 Owner Shift Involving Five-percent Shareholders
§11.4.14 Equity Structure Shift
§11.4.15 Multiple Transactions
§11.4.16 Testing Periods
§11.4.17 Stock Ownership Rules
§11.4.18 Disregarded Stock
§11.4.19 Options
§11.4.20 Worthless Stock
§11.4.21 Mutual Funds
§11.4.22 Separate Accounting
§11.4.23 Seized Financial Corporations
§11.4.24 Capital Contributions
§11.4.25 Recapitalized Financial Institutions
§11.5 Tax-Free Acquisitions
§11.5.1 Overview

§11.5.2 Type A Reorganizations
§11.5.3 Acquisitions with Solely Voting Stock—Type B and Type C Reorganizations
§11.5.4 Type D Reorganizations
§11.5.5 Charter Stripping of Type C and D Reorganizations
§11.5.6 Type E Reorganizations
§11.5.7 Type F Reorganizations
§11.5.8 Type G Reorganizations
§11.6 Federal Financial Assistance
§11.6.1 Federal Financial Assistance, Defined
§11.6.2 Principles Used in Prescribing Regulations
§11.6.3 Income Inclusion of FFA
§11.6.4 Transfers of Property by Institution
§11.6.5 Bridge Banks and Residual Entities
§11.6.6 Taxable Transfers
§11.6.7 Limitation on Collection of Income Tax
§11.6.8 Miscellaneous Rules
§11.6.9 Phantom Income from Loan Modifications

§11.1 Tax Planning Suggestions

The tax treatment of an acquisition by a bank or a bank holding company ("BHC") will vary depending on whether the transaction is structured as either a taxable purchase or as falling within one of the types of tax-free reorganizations defined in Code section 368.[1] Because acquisitions of banks often occur only after a time-consuming regulatory process is completed, the tax advisor is usually afforded ample opportunity to plan for the transaction.

Many nontax factors, such as the geographic and business characteristics of the target company, influence the tax structure of the acquisition. However, the tax interests of the parties to the transaction also should affect its design. Moreover, tax planning should evaluate the possibilities for actions that may affect the computation of the tax liability of the target firm for its tax year in which the acquisition takes place.

As a result of the economic crisis of 2008, the Treasury Department significantly altered the rules on Code section 382 that controlled the ability of net operating losses and certain built-in losses to survive an ownership change of a bank. The changes greatly liberalized the ownership change rules so as to permit acquiring institutions to utilize the losses of target institutions. The Treasury Department rules were soon thereafter nullified by legislative action.

Federal and state legal and regulatory rules impose restrictions on acquisitions by banks and BHCs, especially with respect to acquisitions of non-financial entities. In 1999, however, Congress amended federal banking laws to greatly expand a bank or bank holding companies permitted activities.[2] This develop-

[1] *See The Art of Tax Efficiency in Community Banks*, by M. Gula, J. Brew, and R. Blasi, 2007, Red Room Publishing, *http://www.mraeresources.com/bookstore/*.

[2] Financial Modernization Act, Pub. L. No. 106-102 (1999).

ment has accelerated the pace of bank acquisitions, and it will raise significant issues associated with the current deductibility of expansion or acquisition costs.

In the case of a taxable acquisition, one of the primary tax planning objectives of the acquiring corporation is to maximize the amount of purchase price allocated to depreciation or amortizable assets and to attempt to recover cost over the shortest possible period. In 1993, Congress enacted federal income tax rules designed to reduce controversies that had been associated with the deductibility of certain intangible assets. While the new rules expand the portion of purchase price that will be deductible, opportunities and pitfalls remain.

Although the discussion that follows is divided into two broad acquisition categories, taxable purchase acquisitions and tax-free reorganizations, it is not unusual for there to be a close resemblance between the substance that results from certain taxable purchases and certain tax-free transactions. For example, a Type A merger may be tax-free if the requisite continuity-of-interest is maintained. However, a very similar transaction may be treated as a cash merger or a taxable purchase of stock. Careful planning is needed to ensure the expected tax treatment of mergers because they often involve taxable boot.

§ 11.2 Interstate Opportunities for Banks and BHCs

§ 11.2.1 Permissible Interstate Bank Activities

Historically, the McFadden Act of 1927 and state branch banking laws confined branch banking by national banks to the state in which the bank's head office was located.[3] The Banking Act of 1933 established parity between the branching rights of state and national banks by an amendment to the McFadden Act that permitted a national bank to branch within the state in which it is located to the same extent as a bank chartered in that state.[4] Moreover, the Federal Reserve Act subjects state member banks to "the same limitations and restrictions" on branching as national banks and requires Federal Reserve Board ("FRB") approval of new branches.[5] Although the Federal Deposit Insurance Act does not restrict branch locations, it requires an insured state member bank to receive Federal Deposit Insurance Corporation ("FDIC") approval before establishing and operating a new branch.[6]

Under Office of the Comptroller of the Currency ("OCC") regulations, a national bank may establish an operating subsidiary to "engage in activities which are part of or incidental to the business of banking . . . ."[7] The Garn-St.

---

[3] 12 U.S.C. § 36(c), 44 Stat. 1244 (1927); *Securities Industry Ass'n v. Comptroller*, 577 F. Supp. 252 (D.D.C. 1983). The constraints on branch banking contained in 12 U.S.C. § 36 do not apply to thrifts. In 1911, Attorney General George Wickersham issued an opinion to the effect that the National Bank Act prohibited full-service branching by national banks. 29 Ops. Atty. Gen. 81 (1911).

[4] 48 Stat. 162 (1933).

[5] 12 U.S.C. § 321 (2000). A "member bank" is a bank that is a member of the Federal Reserve System.

[6] 12 U.S.C. § 1828(d)(1) (2000).

[7] 12 C.F.R. §§ 5.34, 7.7376, *rescinded* Oct. 18, 1983, 48 FR 48452, and *merged into* 12 C.F.R. § 5.34(c). Thrifts also may form service corporations. 12 U.S.C. § 1464(c)(4)(B) (2000). Prior to the Savings and Loan Holding Company Act, Pub. L. No. 90-255, 82 Stat. 5 (1968), the thrift service corporation was the primary vehicle used by thrifts to geographically expand and diversify.

Germain Depository Institutions Act of 1982 permits a bank to form a "bank service corporation," which may perform clerical services for a bank at any location, both within and without the bank's home state.[8] In addition, banks may own international banking subsidiaries ("Edge Act" Corporations) that are not subject to the McFadden Act and that may branch interstate.[9] Finally, the OCC has interpreted the National Bank Act[10] as permitting national banks to operate loan production offices outside the national bank's home state, on the condition that the loans originated in these offices "are approved and made at the main office or a branch office of the bank or at an office of the subsidiary located on the premises of, or contiguous to, the main office of the bank."[11]

The Rigle-Neil Interstate Banking and Branching Efficiency Act of 1994 (the "Branch Banking Act of 1994") greatly liberalizes the rules pertaining to interstate expansion of banks.[12] Beginning June 1, 1997, an adequately capitalized bank with necessary management skills may merge or consolidate with an out-of-state bank.[13] States were permitted to apply these merger rules prior to June 1, 1997, and prior to that date they also were permitted to entirely opt out of this provision. Thus, interstate mergers of banks, themselves, may presently take place. Interstate expansion through *de novo* branches is permitted only if a state expressly authorizes such activity by an out-of-state bank.[14] Once a bank has a branch in a state, it will be permitted to establish additional branches in the state to the same extent that a bank chartered in the state may branch.

Branching by acquisition is not permitted if the resulting bank controls 10 percent of the deposits of the nation, or 30 percent of the deposits of a single state. In addition, if state law provides that a bank must be of a minimum age in order to be bought by an out-of-state holding company, a bank is permitted to branch into that state only by acquiring an existing bank that conforms to the state's minimum age requirements, and then it may convert it into branches. State laws enacted after the date of enactment of the Branch Banking Act of 1994 requiring banks to be of a minimum age apply only up to a maximum of five years.

Until the Branch Banking Act of 1994 takes full effect, the Comptroller of the Currency may permit a national bank to relocate its main office across state lines or across other geographic restrictive boundaries, such as county lines, and maintain its former main office location as a branch site as long as the new main office is not more than 30 miles from the old main office. This action, which was validated by the Branch Banking Act of 1994, reduces for many banks the significance of the branch banking provisions contained in the Branch Banking Act of 1994.

---

[8] Garn-St. Germain Depository Institutions Act of 1982, Pub. L. No. 97-320, 96 Stat. 1469 (1982), as codified, 12 U.S.C. § 1861 *et seq.* Permissible services are listed in 12 U.S.C. §§ 1863-64. This Act also permits otherwise prohibited interstate bank acquisitions when the specter of a bank failure is present.

[9] 12 U.S.C. § 611 *et seq.* (2000).

[10] Ch. 58, 12 Stat. 665 (1863).

[11] National Bank Act, 12 U.S.C. §§ 24 and 81 (2000); Comptroller of the Currency Interpretive Ruling 7.7380. Loan production offices may be "branches," *but see Independent Bankers Ass'n of America v. Heimann*, 627 F.2d 486 (D.C. Cir. 1980).

[12] The Rigle-Neil Interstate Banking and Branching Efficiency Act of 1994, Pub. L. No. 103-328, 108 Stat. 2338 (1994).

[13] *Id.* at § 102.

[14] *Id.* at § 103.

§ 11.2.2 Permissible Interstate BHC Activities

Acquisitions by a BHC are also subject to legal and regulatory restraints, although not the same restraints to which national banks are subject. The Bank Holding Company Act of 1956 ("BHC Act") defines the activities in which BHCs may engage.[15] Pursuant to that Act, a BHC is defined as any company that has control over any bank or over any company that is or becomes a bank holding company.[16] A "company" is any corporation, partnership, business trust, association, or similar organization, or any other trust, except a short-term trust or the typical family trust.[17] A bank is an "insured bank" as defined in section 3(h) of the Federal Deposit Insurance Act and any domestic institution that *both* accepts demand deposits or deposits that the depositor may withdraw by check or similar means ("NOW accounts") *and* is engaged in the business of making commercial loans.[18] The definition of a "bank" for purposes of the Change in Bank Control Act, Federal Deposit Insurance Act, or any state's bank holding company statute does not determine whether an institution is a "bank" for purposes of the Bank Holding Company Act.[19] A bank holding company "controls" a bank if it owns or controls 25 percent or more of any class of voting stock of a bank or a bank holding company.[20] The BHC Act may become an anachronism if the financial services industry moves toward a universal banking model. Under such a model the parent corporation of a banking group is a bank, not a BHC. The historical utility of the BHC Act has been to provide a means for circumventing limitations on bank securities underwriting activities and limits on interstate expansion. With changes in Federal Reserve Board ("FRB") policy, and provisions contained in the Branch Banking Act of 1994, the BHC structure is losing much of its value.[21]

---

[15] 12 U.S.C. §§ 1841-1850 (2000). The Bank Holding Company Act of 1956, c. 240, 70 Stat. 133 (1956) was the first comprehensive regulation of multibank holding companies. It is administered by the Board of Governors of the Federal Reserve System. Thrifts form holding companies for many of the same reasons that motivate commercial banks to do so. *See* 12 U.S.C. § 1730a, which contains the Savings and Loan Holding Company Amendments Act of 1967, Pub. L. No. 90-255, 82 Stat. 5 (1968). The Garn-St. Germain Depository Institutions Act of 1982, *supra* note 8, allowed thrifts to convert from a mutual to a federal stock charter, thereby permitting them to enter the commercial paper and other securities markets for capital. Note also that there is not the same explicit statutory prohibition against thrifts being involved in general commerce activities as exists for commercial banks (12 U.S.C. § 24(7)), and thrifts are not subject to the severe constraints applicable to commercial bank involvement in securities activities. 12 U.S.C. § 377, Repealed, Pub. L. No. 106-102, Title I, § 101(a), Nov. 12, 1999, 113 Stat. 1341. *Cf. Investment Company Institute v. FDIC*, 815 F.2d 1540 (D.C. Cir. 1987).

[16] 12 U.S.C. § 1841(a)(1) (2000).

[17] 12 U.S.C. § 1841(b) (2000).

[18] 12 U.S.C. § 1841(c) (2000), as amended by the Competitive Equality Banking Act of 1987, Pub. L. No. 100-86, § 101, 101 Stat. 552 (1987).

[19] Change in Bank Control Act of 1978, Pub. L. No. 95-630, 92 Stat. 3641, Title 6 (1978), 12 U.S.C. § 1817(j) (2000); Federal Deposit Insurance Corporation Act, ch. 967, 64 Stat. 873 (1950), 12 U.S.C. § 1828; Bank Holding Company Act, ch. 240, 70 Stat. 133 (1956), 12 U.S.C. §§ 1841 *et seq.* (2000).

[20] 12 U.S.C. § 1841(a)(2). The Bank Holding Company Act of 1956, *supra* note 15, authorizes the Federal Reserve Board to make determinations that actual control over the management or policies of a bank is present independent of whether the 25 percent test is met. 12 U.S.C. § 1841(a)(2)(C) (2000).

[21] For the largest of banks, the BHC is often used as a funding vehicle, because it, and not a bank, has access to the commercial paper market.

As amended by the Douglas Amendment, the BHC Act has prohibited a BHC from organizing or acquiring a bank subsidiary outside its home state unless specifically authorized by statute in such other states.[22] Nevertheless, a BHC is prohibited from engaging in nonbank activities or from acquiring or retaining voting shares of any company that is not a bank, with only limited exceptions.[23]

When the BHC Act was passed, no state specifically authorized interstate BHC expansion.[24] Currently most states have such authorizing statutes. By the early 1990s, approximately 49 states and the District of Columbia permitted some form of interstate banking, and 39 states permitted some variation of statewide intrastate branching.[25] The Constitutionality of these "compacts" was addressed by the U.S. Supreme Court, which ruled that a regional confederation that permitted out-of-state BHCs with principal offices located in one of the other states to acquire an in-state bank did not violate the commerce or compact clause of the Constitution, provided that reciprocal privileges were accorded the other states' banks.[26]

The BHC Act also permits BHCs to engage at any location (within or without its home state) in activities that the FRB has determined to be "so closely related to banking or managing or controlling banks as to be a proper incident thereto."[27] The FRB has determined that the following activities are permissible for a BHC to engage in: lending, industrial banking, trust company activities, investment or financial advising, leasing, community development, data processing, insurance, underwriting credit related activities, courier services, managing consulting for depository institutions, consumer payment instruments, real estate appraising, arranging real estate equity financing, brokerage activities, underwriting and dealing in government obligations and money market instruments, foreign exchange advisory and transactional services, and futures commission merchant activities.[28] Moreover, a BHC may create a subsidiary to solicit loans for its banking corporation affiliate, and it may create operations subsidiaries that provide services to its bank subsidiary.[29] BHCs also are authorized by statute to

[22] 12 U.S.C. § 1842(d)(1) (2000). The Douglas Amendment was added on the floor of the Senate. Its entire legislative history is confined to the Senate Debate. 102 Cong. Rec. 6858 (1956). The Douglas Amendment was, in effect, repealed, effective Sept. 29, 1995, by the Rigle-Neil Interstate Banking and Branching Efficiency Act of 1994. Pub. L. No. 103-328, 108 Stat. 2338 (1994).

[23] 12 U.S.C. § 1843 (2000). *See also* FRB Reg. Y, 12 C.F.R. § 225.21(a). This constraint dates back to the Banking Act of 1933, often referred to as the Glass-Steagall Act. Ch. 89, 48 Stat. 162 (1933). *See also* 12 U.S.C. §§ 24, 377, and 378.

[24] *Northeast Bancorp, Inc. v. The Board of Governors of the Fed. Reserve Sys.*, 472 U.S. 159,163 (1985).

[25] Conference of State Bank Supervisors, "A Profile of State Chartered Banking," 14th ed. 1992, Tables II.I and II.II.

[26] *Northeast Bancorp., supra* note 24. *See also* 99 Harv. L. Rev. 283 (1985); 27 B.C. L. Rev. 821 (1986); 18 Loy. L.A. L. Rev. 993 (1985).

[27] 12 U.S.C. § 1843(c)(8). The 1970 version of 12 U.S.C. § 1843(c)(8), as passed by the House, contained a list of permissible activities. The House-Senate Conference Committee removed the list and adopted the above-quoted language.

[28] 12 C.F.R. § 225.4(a). A listing of impermissible activities is set forth at 12 C.F.R. § 225.126.

[29] Bank Holding Company Act § 4(c)(1)(C), *supra* note 15, 12 U.S.C. § 1843(c)(1)(C) (2000); 12 C.F.R. § 225.22. *See also* 12 C.F.R. § 250.141.

make noncontrolling investments in companies that do not conduct a banking business.[30]

The Branch Banking Act of 1994 makes major changes in the regulatory constraints imposed on banks and on bank holding companies in respect of interstate expansion.[31] Beginning September 29, 1995, a BHC with adequate capital and management skills may acquire an existing bank in any state.[32] States may not opt-out of this provision of the Branch Banking Act. An interstate acquisition would not be permitted, however, if the BHC, after the acquisition, would control more than 10 percent of the deposits in the country or more than 30 percent of the deposits in the host state.[33] In addition, any state laws requiring banks to be of a minimum age in order to be bought by an out-of-state holding company will continue to apply. State laws enacted after the date of enactment requiring banks to be of a minimum age will apply only up to a maximum of five years.

§11.3 Taxable Acquisitions

§11.3.1 Taxation of Selling Corporation

(a) *Distribution or Sale of Property*

Under current law, a corporation that sells its assets, even if in complete liquidation, recognizes gain or loss.[34] Similarly, a liquidating distribution to shareholders of assets will trigger recognized gain or loss to the distributing corporation as if the property were sold to the shareholder at its fair market value.[35] An exception is provided for property distributed to a parent corporation in complete liquidation of a subsidiary.[36] In an effort to prevent abuse of the recognition rule, a loss is usually not recognized to a liquidating corporation on the distribution of property to a related person.[37] The general recognition rule does not apply to distributions in pursuance of a plan of reorganization.[38]

(b) *Liabilities*

If property distributed in a complete liquidation is subject to a liability, the fair market value of the property is deemed to be no less than the amount of the liability.[39] Thus, gain will be recognized to the distributing corporation when the amount of a liability exceeds the value of the property that secures it. Similarly, if the amount of a liability assumed by shareholders of a liquidating corporation exceeds the fair market value of the distributed property, the liquidating corporation will recognize gain to the extent any assumed liabilities exceed the adjusted basis of the property. In a sale that is not associated with a liquidation,

[30] 12 U.S.C. §1843(c)(6) (2000).

[31] The Rigle-Neil Interstate Banking and Branching Efficiency Act of 1994, Pub. L. No. 103-328, 108 Stat. 2338 (1994).

[32] *Id.* at §101.

[33] An initial acquisition in a state is not subject to the 30 percent rule. Under limited circumstances the 30 percent rule may be waived by the Federal Reserve Board and by state regulators.

[34] I.R.C. §§61 and 1001.

[35] I.R.C. §336.

[36] I.R.C. §§332 and 337.

[37] I.R.C. §336(d).

[38] I.R.C. §§336(c) and 361(c)(4).

[39] I.R.C. §336(b).

liabilities assumed by the purchaser, or where property transferred is subject to a liability, the amount of the liability will be included in the amount realized for purposes of measuring gain or loss.[40]

(c) *General Utilities Doctrine*

The Tax Reform Act of 1986 amended the Code to require recognition of gain on a corporate liquidation.[41] The recognition rule applies to transactions occurring after July 31, 1986 (and for Code section 338 deemed asset purchases in which the acquisition date is after 1988).[42] It causes many taxable asset acquisitions to be more costly than under prior law to the acquired firm and its shareholders. It overrides over a half century of judicial and statutory law that permitted nonrecognition of gain by a corporation on certain distributions of appreciated property.[43] The nonrecognition rule originated from the U.S. Supreme Court's decision in *General Utilities.*[44]

Although *General Utilities* involved a dividend distribution of appreciated property by an ongoing business, the "General Utilities Doctrine" had come to be applied in a broader sense to refer to the nonrecognition treatment accorded in certain situations to liquidating as well as nonliquidating distributions to shareholders and to liquidating sales. In its 1954 revision of the Internal Revenue Code, Congress codified the result in *General Utilities* by enacting Code section 311(a) (nonrecognition of gain or loss on nonliquidating distributions of property with respect to stock), Code section 336 (nonrecognition of gain or loss to corporation on distributions of property and partial or complete liquidation), and Code section 337 (nonrecognition of gain or loss on sale of property in complete liquidation of the corporation).

§ 11.3.2 Cost Recovery Rules to Acquiring Corporation

(a) *Purchase Price Allocation*

In a taxable asset acquisition, both the purchaser and the seller must allocate the purchase price among the transferred assets. For the seller, the allocation is to determine the amount of gain or loss and whether capital or ordinary income is recognized. For the buyer, the allocation will determine the cost that will be recoverable by tax savings from deductions for amortization or depreciation. Tax basis allocated to assets that are not depreciable or amortizable will reduce gross income only when the asset is sold or otherwise disposed. Because of the importance of time value of money considerations, the objective of an acquiring entity is to ensure that the maximum allowable amount of purchase price is allocated to assets having costs that are recoverable through a capital allowances (depreciation or amortization) or other income offset (for example, tax basis in loans) as soon after the acquisition as possible.

---

[40] *Crane v. Commissioner*, 331 U.S. 1 (1947).

[41] Tax Reform Act of 1986, Pub. L. No. 99-514, 100 Stat. 2085 (1986).

[42] I.R.C. § 336, as amended by the Tax Reform Act of 1986, Pub. L. No. 99-514, 100 Stat. 2085 (1986).

[43] *General Utilities & Operating Co. v. Helvering*, 296 U.S. 200 (1935); I.R.C. of 1954 §§ 311, 336, and 337.

[44] *Id.*

(b) *Cost Recovery Table*

Table 11.1 illustrates the relative present values of after-tax savings derived from a $1,000 purchase price being allocated to assets with different recovery periods, depreciation methods, and applicable conventions.

Thus, if $1,000 of purchase price is allocated to nonresidential real property, the present value of the tax savings, assuming a 40 percent combined federal and state tax rate a recovery period of 39 years and a 5 percent discount rate, will be $17.81. If the same amount were properly allocated to computer software, the present value, at the same discount rate and assuming a 36-month recovery period, would more than double to $37.13. This chart also reveals the percentage of cost recovered for various classes of assets.

Table 11.1 Present Value of Tax Savings from Depreciating the Cost of Various Assets—Per $1,000 of Asset Value

			Percentage of Cost Savings per $1,000 Discount Rates		
Property Type	**Asset Life**	**Deprec. Method**	**3%**	**5%**	**7%**
Nonresidential real property	39 yrs.[a]	S/L[b]	23.68	17.81	13.99
Automobiles	5 yrs.[c]	200%[d]	37.31	35.71	34.22
Equipment	7 yrs.[e]	200%[f]	36.40	34.31	32.43
Computer software	36 mos.[g]	S/L[h]	38.23	37.13	36.10
Mortgage servicing rights	108 mos.[i]	S/L[j]	35.07	32.30	29.87
Section 197 intangibles	15 yrs.	S/L	31.83	27.67	24.28

[a] *I.R.C. § 168(c).*
[b] *I.R.C. § 168(b)(3)(A). Based on mid-month convention. I.R.C. § 168(d)(2).*
[c] *I.R.C. § 168(c); § 168(e)(3)(B).*
[d] *I.R.C. § 168(b)(1). Based on mid-year convention. I.R.C. § 168(d)(1).*
[e] *I.R.C. § 168.* Equipment not described elsewhere in the code section is given a 7-year asset life. I.R.C. § 168(e)(3)(C). Qualified technological is defined in the section 168(i)(2) and given a 5-year asset life. I.R.C. § 168(e)(3)(B)(iv).
[f] *I.R.C. § 168(b)(1). Based on mid-year convention. I.R.C. § 168(d)(1).*
[g] *I.R.C. § 167(f)(1).* Modified for tax years 2008-2012 by I.R.C. § 168(k)(1) to permit an increased cost recovery deduction.
[h] *Id.*
[i] *I.R.C. § 167(f)(3).*
[j] *Id.*

(c) *Determining Purchase Price*

A purchase and sale agreement must be analyzed to determine the price paid for all acquired assets. The price that is paid for an asset or a group of assets often consists of money, the fair market value of property, and liabilities assumed or to which property that is purchased are subject.[45] Fair market value is defined as the price arrived at by a willing buyer and a willing seller, neither being under any compulsion to buy or to sell.[46] No single method of determining fair market value is appropriate in all circumstances. Three commonly accepted methods are the reproduction cost method, the capitalization of earnings method, and the comparable sales method.

For purposes of determining the amount of liabilities assumed (as in the case of determining the assets acquired), items not listed on the acquired company's

[45] I.R.C. §§ 1012 and 1001(b).

[46] Reg. § 20.2031-1(b).

balance sheet must be taken into account. Thus, the cost associated with an unfavorable long-term lease assumed by the acquiring corporation, even though not listed among balance sheet liabilities, may be treated as a component of the purchase price.[47]

(d) ***Allocating Purchase Price***

As a general rule, Code section 167 allows a depreciation deduction for a reasonable allowance for the exhaustion, wear and tear, and obsolescence of cost allocated to property used in a trade or business or held for the production of income.[48] Regulations define the term "property" to include both tangible and intangible property:

> If an intangible asset is known from experience or other factors to be of use in the business or in the production of income for only a limited period, the length of which can be estimated with reasonable accuracy, such an intangible asset may be the subject of a depreciation allowance. Examples are patents and copyrights.[49]

Code section 168 provides rules for determining the annual depreciation deduction allowed by Code section 167. It specifies the depreciation method, applicable recovery period, and applicable conventions.[50] The depreciation method, which will determine the rate of cost recovery, will vary depending on the recovery period of the property to the acquiring corporation.[51] Of course, to the extent that cost is properly allocated to assets, the cost of which is not recoverable through depreciation or amortization deductions (*e.g.*, land), a tax benefit will be derived only at the time that the asset is disposed of.

Prior to the Tax Reform Act of 1986,[52] there was no statutorily mandated scheme for allocating purchase price among assets in a taxable asset acquisition. The acquirer and the acquired entity were free to use any method of allocation that resulted in a fair allocation of purchase price to the various assets acquired. Occasionally, the parties to a purchase and sale agreement would agree to a specific allocation of the purchase price among the assets and reflect the allocation in the sales contract. The Tax Court has stated, "specific allocation in the purchase agreement or in negotiations leading thereto may be the best evidence of the purchaser's basis in each asset."[53]

If the parties made a specific contractual allocation taking into account the fair market value of the assets, courts and the IRS have accepted a stated

---

[47] Conversely, a favorable lease has been treated as an unlisted amortizable asset to which purchase price may be attributed. *KFOX, Inc. v. United States*, 75-1 U.S.T.C. ¶9253, 510 F.2d 1365 (Ct. Cl. 1975); *Maurice Mittleman v. Commissioner*, 7 T.C. 1162 (1946).

[48] I.R.C. § 167(a).

[49] Reg. § 1.167(a)-3.

[50] I.R.C. § 168(a).

[51] Reg. § 1.167(a)-1(b). Note for taxable years beginning before 1987, the reduced investment credit available with respect to three-year class property relative to five-year class property substantially reduced the attractiveness of more accelerated depreciation. Also consider the effect of the $125,000 limitation on the dollar amount of acquired used property eligible for the investment tax credit.

[52] Tax Reform Act of 1986, Pub. L. No. 99-514, 100 Stat. 2085 (1986).

[53] *Banc One Corporation v. Commissioner*, 84 T.C. 476 (1985). The allocation of acquisition costs to assets acquired and the price at which acquired assets are recorded on the books of the acquirer is dealt with in Securities and Exchange Commission Staff Bulletin No. 61 (May 6, 1986) and Accounting Principles Board Opinion No. 16.

allocation with appropriate regard to value, provided the parties have adverse tax interests with respect to the allocation.[54] The IRS will normally adhere to a contractual allocation of purchase price unless it is "devoid of economic realities of the transaction."[55] Although the parties are generally prohibited from challenging the allocation for tax purposes,[56] courts have decided that neither the parties to the transaction nor the IRS will be bound in all cases by a contractual allocation apportionment.[57] Moreover, taxpayers have been permitted to set aside an express allocation contained in the contract for sale, but only in limited situations. The repeal of the preferential taxation of capital gains by the Tax Reform Act of 1986 substantially reduces the desire of a seller to allocate purchase price to capital assets. Thus, less significance should now be attached to a contractual allocation.

In the absence of a contractual purchase price allocation, the purchase price (less cash and cash equivalents) must be allocated among the noncash assets in proportion to their respective fair market values on the date of the acquisition.[58] With respect to *sales* of a basket of assets, regulations provide:

> When a part of a larger property is sold, the cost or other basis of the entire property shall be equitably apportioned among the several parts, and the gain realized or loss sustained on the part of the entire property sold is the difference between the selling price and the cost or other basis allocated to such part.[59]

A similar rule is provided in regulations for basis allocations when property is *purchased*:

> In the case of the acquisition . . . of a combination of depreciable and nondepreciable property for a lump sum . . . the basis for depreciation cannot exceed an amount which bears the same proportion to the lump sum as the value of the depreciable property at the time of acquisition bears to the value of the entire property at that time.[60]

---

[54] *Black Industries, Inc. v. Commissioner*, T.C. Memo. 1979-061, 38 T.C.M. 242 (1979).

[55] *First Northwest Industries of America v. Commissioner*, 70 T.C. 817 (1978); *Particelli v. Commissioner*, 54-1 U.S.T.C. ¶9383, 212 F.2d 498 (9th Cir. 1954). In *Black Industries, Inc.*, *supra* note 54, the Tax Court observed that the parties did not, as a practical matter, have adverse tax interests. Thus, it was justified in "carefully scrutinizing the merits of the allocation."

[56] *Ullman v. Commissioner*, 59-1 U.S.T.C. ¶9314, 264 F.2d 305 (2d Cir. 1959); *Commissioner v. Danielson*, 67-1 U.S.T.C. ¶9423, 378 F.2d 771 (3d Cir. 1967); *cert. denied*, 389 U.S. 858 (1967); *Thorndson v. Commissioner*, 72-1 U.S.T.C. ¶9333, 457 F.2d 1022 (9th Cir. 1972); *J. Leonard Schmitz v. Commissioner*, 51 T.C. 306, Dec. 29,250 (1968), *aff'd sub nom.*, 72-1 U.S.T.C. ¶9333, 457 F.2d 1022 (9th Cir. 1972).

[57] *Leslie S. Ray Ins. Agency Inc. v. United States*, 72-2 U.S.T.C. ¶9552, 463 F.2d 210 (1st Cir. 1972); *David Ullman v. Commissioner*, 29 T.C. 129 (1957), *aff'd*, 59-1 U.S.T.C. ¶9314, 264 F.2d 305 (2d Cir. 1959); *J. Leonard Schmitz v. Commissioner*, 51 T.C. 306 (1968), *aff'd sub nom.*, 72-1 U.S.T.C. ¶9333, 457 F.2d 1022 (9th Cir. 1972). *But cf. Commissioner v. Danielson*, 67-1 U.S.T.C. ¶9423, 378 F.2d 771 (3d Cir. 1967), *cert. denied*, 389 U.S. 858 (1967).

[58] *Winn-Dixie Montgomery, Inc. v. United States*, U.S.T.C. ¶9488, 444 F.2d 677 (5th Cir. 1971). The three accepted methods of determining fair market value are the reproduction cost method, the capitalization of earnings method, and the comparable sales method. *See* H.R. Rep. No. 99-3838 at 356 (1986).

[59] Reg. § 1.61-6(a).

[60] Reg. § 1.167(a)-5.

(e) *Second-Tier Allocation*

A variation to the fair market value allocation method was the second-tier allocation method, a method that is no longer permitted.[61] It results in the allocation of an amount of purchase price in excess of fair market value to the basis of each of the assets acquired. Pursuant to this method, each acquired asset, including goodwill and going-concern value, was separately valued and allocated purchase price up to fair market value. Then, any premium paid for the basket of assets (purchase price in excess of fair market value) is allocated to all assets (other than cash and cash equivalents) in proportion to the relative fair market values of the acquired assets.

(f) *Mandatory Allocation Rule: Code Section 1060*

Code section 1060 provides a mandatory method for purchase price allocation in certain types of acquisitions.[62] It requires both the buyer and seller to use the residual method for computing the transferee's tax basis and the transferor's gain or loss.[63] The section requires that consideration received for assets in any "applicable asset acquisition" be allocated among assets acquired in the same manner as amounts are allocated to assets under Code section 338(b)(5).[64] The term "applicable asset acquisition" means any direct or indirect asset acquisition of a trade or business in which the transferee's basis in the assets is determined wholly by reference to the consideration paid for such assets.[65]

Proposed and temporary regulations issued under Code sections 338 and 1060 require the acquirer to use the residual allocation method to determine the tax basis of assets acquired when a Code section 338 election is made or deemed to be made; that is, a stock purchase that is treated as a purchase of assets for tax purposes.[66] However, the Code section 338 rules do not, by their terms, apply to actual asset acquisitions. In the absence of the reference in Code section 1060 to Code section 338, the residual method would not be a statutorily mandated method.

According to Code section 1060's legislative history, it was enacted for at least four reasons:[67]

1. Congress sought to eliminate the "second-tier allocation" that some taxpayers had used to allocate the premium or purchase price in excess of the fair market value of the tangible and intangible assets to Code section 1231 assets, increasing the basis of those assets.[68]
2. It was intended to reduce the conflicts between taxpayers and the IRS concerning the valuation of goodwill or going-concern. Code section

---

[61] Reg. 1.338(b)-2T(c)(1).

[62] Reg. § 1.1060-1T(a)(1).

[63] Tax Reform Act of 1986, Pub. L. No. 99-514, § 641, 100 Stat. 2085 (1986), redesignated I.R.C. § 1060 as I.R.C. § 1061 and added new I.R.C. § 1060. I.R.C. § 1060(a)(1) and (2). Acquisitions subject to the I.R.C. § 338 residual allocation rule are those that are completed after May 6, 1986, unless they are completed pursuant to a binding contract in effect on that date and at all times thereafter.

[64] I.R.C. § 1060(a); Reg. § 1.1060-1T(d)(1).

[65] I.R.C. § 1060(c).

[66] Reg. § 1.338(b)-2T; Reg. § 1.1060-1T(d)(1).

[67] H.R. Rep. No. 99-841 (1986) (hereinafter referred to as Conference Committee Report).

[68] *Id.*; Reg. § 1.1060-1T(e).

1060 was designed to reduce controversies by requiring the use of one standard method for all taxpayers.

3. Congress was concerned with the "difficult and uncertain assumptions" that were required by the application of the highly subjective formula valuation method.
4. The section was designed to eliminate the potential for abuse when the buyer and the seller use conflicting methods for purchase price allocation resulting in a "whipsaw of the government."

However, Congress noted that with the elimination of favorable tax treatment of capital gains and the repeal of the rule which had allowed for nonrecognition of corporate level gain in liquidating sales or distributions, the buyer and seller would be less likely to have competing tax interests.

(g) *Residual Allocation: Code Section 338*

Under the residual allocation method, adjusted grossed-up basis is allocated among four "Classes" of assets.[69] The adjusted grossed-up basis is the amount for which the new target entity is deemed to have purchased all of its assets in a deemed purchase under Code section 338.[70] A deemed purchase takes place when the purchasing corporation makes an election under Code section 338. When the election is made, the target corporation is treated as having sold all of its assets at the close of the acquisition date at fair market value in a single transaction, and it is treated as a new corporation (new target company) which purchased all of the assets as of the beginning of the day after the acquisition date.[71]

The adjusted grossed-up basis is first reduced by the amount of cash, demand deposits and similar accounts in banks, savings and loan associations (and other similar depository institutions), and other items designated by the IRS as Class I assets. The remaining adjusted grossed-up basis is allocated among Class II assets of the target held at the beginning of the day after the acquisition date in proportion to their relative fair-market values at such time, then among Class III assets and finally to Class IV assets.[72]

Class II assets are certificates of a deposit, U.S. government securities, readily marketable stock and securities, foreign currency, and other items designated as Class II assets by the IRS.[73] Class III assets are all tangible and intangible (whether or not depreciable, depletable, or amortizable) assets of the target, other than those that meet the definition of Class I, II, and IV assets.[74] Class IV assets are intangible assets in the nature of goodwill and going-concern value.[75] The basis allocated to goodwill and going-concern value is the excess of the total purchase price over the aggregate basis allocated to assets in Class I, II, and III.

---

69 Reg. § 1.338(b)-2T(b); Reg. § 1.1060-1T(d).

70 Reg. § 1.338(b)-1(a).

71 I.R.C. § 338(a).

72 Reg. §§ 1.338(b)-2T(b)(1) and (2); Reg. § 1.1060-1T(d).

73 Reg. § 1.1060-1T(d)(1).

74 Reg. § 1.338(b)-2T(b)(2)(iii); Reg. § 1.1060-1T(d)(2).

75 Reg. § 1.1060-1T(d)(2)(iii).

The residual method does not eliminate the necessity of first arriving at the fair market value of the assets other than goodwill and going-concern value. For this, as well as most other purposes of the Code, the time-honored definition of fair market value is "the price at which the property would change hands between a willing buyer and a willing seller, neither being under any compulsion to buy or to sell and both having reasonable knowledge of relevant facts."[76] The fair market value of an asset is its gross fair market value; that is its value determined without regard to mortgages, liens, pledges, or other liabilities.[77]

Cash equivalents are ascribed a fair market value basis.[78] Cash equivalents include receivables guaranteed by the seller, but exclude other receivables, inventories, prepaid expenses, stock, and securities.[79]

§ 11.3.3 Cost Recovery: Code Section 197 Intangibles

(a) *Background to Code Section 197*

The addition to the Code, by the Omnibus Budget Reconciliation Act of 1993, of Code section 197 greatly increases the probability that an acquiring corporation will recover, over time, the corporation's marginal tax rate multiplied by the cost of depreciable or amortizable acquired assets.[80] Code section 197 allows an amortization deduction with respect to any "amortizable section 197 intangible."[81] With the addition of this provision to the Code, the tax treatment was brought into closer alignment with the book accounting rule.[82] Among the more significant effects of the section is the abrogation of the longstanding proscription on the deductibility of goodwill and going-concern value.[83] It does not relieve the taxpayer of its burden to establish a basis in the asset. The taxpayer has to establish a basis to a "reasonable degree of certainty."[84]

The legislative history of Code section 197 indicates that the reasons for the provision is to eliminate disputes concerning:

---

[76] Reg. § 20.2031-1(b).

[77] Reg. § 1.338(b)-2T(a)(2).

[78] *Victor Meat Co., Inc. v. Commissioner*, 52 T.C. 929 (1969); Rev. Rul. 55-79, 1955-1 C.B. 370; Rev. Rul. 69-539, 1969-2 C.B. 141.

[79] *Bixby v. Commissioner*, 58 T.C. 757 (1972); Rev. Rul. 66-290, 1966-2 C.B. 112.

[80] Omnibus Budget Reconciliation Act of 1993, Pub. L. No. 103-66, 107 Stat. 312, (1993). *See also* "Internal Revenue Code Section 197: A Cure for the Controversy Over the Amortization of Acquired Intangible Assets," 49 U. Miami L. Rev. 731 (1995).

[81] I.R.C. § 197(a). For taxpayers with taxable income of less than $10,000,000, the cost recovered equals their tax rate multiplied by the purchase price. The Treasury Department has issued proposed regulations under I.R.C. §§ 167(f) and 197 relating to the amortization of certain intangible property. 62 Fed. Reg. 2336 (January 16, 1997).

[82] In January 2014, the Financial Accounting Standards Board issued Accounting Standards Update No. 2014-02, "Intangibles—Goodwill and Other (Topic 350)," which allows an accounting alternative to Statement No. 142, "Goodwill and Other Intangible Assets," issued June 2001.

[83] Regulations have long recited the judicially accepted rule: "An intangible asset, the useful life of which is not limited, is not subject to the allowance for depreciation. No deduction for depreciation is allowable with respect to goodwill." Reg. § 1.167(a)-3. It is in large measure because of this nondeductibility rule that the "second-tier allocation" method described above was developed.

[84] In *Washington Mutual, Inc. v. United States*, 130 Fed. Cl. 653 (Fed. Cl. 2017), the taxpayer was unsuccessful in its attempt to allocate basis to government assistance provided to a federally chartered mutual savings bank prior to the taxpayer's acquisition of the bank with assistance of the Federal Deposit Insurance Corporation and its right to maintain deposit-taking branches in connection with acquisitions of thrift institutions it made with assistance of the Federal Savings and Loan Insurance Corporation.

1. Whether an amortizable intangible asset exists;
2. The portion of purchase price that should be properly allocable to the asset; and
3. The amortization method and recovery period for any purchase price properly allocated to the intangible asset.[85]

Among the developments that prompted the enactment of Code section 197 was the U.S. Supreme Court's decision in *Newark Morning Ledger*.[86] In that case, the Court held that a taxpayer was able to prove that a particular intangible asset could be valued and that the asset had a limited useful life, which could be ascertained with reasonable accuracy even though the asset appeared to reflect the expectancy of continued patronage. Thus, the Court permitted an amortization deduction for an asset that substantially resembled goodwill. For bankers, the decision in *Newark Morning Ledger* was interpreted as confirming the treatment accorded by the U.S. Tax Court in *Citizens and Southern Corp.* and its progeny that the core deposit intangible, an asset that embodied the essence of goodwill, was entitled to amortization deductions.[87]

As described in more detail below, a "section 197 intangible" includes goodwill and going-concern value, as well as many other intangible assets, including "deposit base."[88] Goodwill and going-concern value were, under pre-Code section 197 law, either nonamortizable or the focus of substantial controversy.[89] In theory, the cost of goodwill or going-concern value was not recoverable through depreciation or amortization allowances because these assets were regarded as assets the useful lives of which could not be determined with reasonable accuracy.[90]

Goodwill was viewed by some courts as an asset, such as land, the life of which is perpetual.[91] The assumption that goodwill had no determinable useful life has been criticized as simplistic since it ignored business reality and violates fundamental tax equity.[92] The treatment of *purchased* goodwill also was inconsistent with the tax treatment of costs associated with *creating* or *maintaining* goodwill. As a general rule, costs incurred in creating or maintaining goodwill

---

[85] Text of technical explanation of HR 4287, "Tax Fairness and Economic Growth Act of 1992," introduced Feb. 20, 1992, by the House Ways and Means Committee Chairman Dan Rostenkowski and House Majority Leader Richard Gephardt, at 217.

[86] *Newark Morning Ledger Co. v. United States*, 507 U.S. 546 (1993). The book accounting treatment of goodwill underwent a significant change, effective January 1, 2002, with the adoption of FAS 141 and 142, which provide, in general, that goodwill shall not be amortized.

[87] *Citizens and Southern Corp. & Subsidiaries v. Commissioner*, 91 T.C. 463 (1988), *aff'd*, 900 F.2d 266 (11th Cir. 1991), *published in full at* 919 F.2d 1492, (11th Cir. 1990).

[88] I.R.C. §§ 197(d)(1)(C)(iv) and (2)(B).

[89] I.R.C. § 197(d).

[90] As a general rule, the useful life of an asset for cost recovery purposes is established based on the taxpayer's own experience with similar property or, if its own experience is inadequate, based upon the general experience in the industry. Reg. § 1.167(a)-1(b).

[91] The Eighth Circuit stated that goodwill has an "unlimited" life. *Donrey, Inc. v. Commissioner*, 87-1 U.S.T.C. ¶ 9143, 809 F.2d 534 (8th Cir. 1987).

[92] *See* Note, "Amortization of Intangibles: An Examination of the Tax Treatment of Purchased Goodwill," 81 Harv. L. Rev. 859 (1968); Donaldson, "Goodwill and Other Intangibles in Business Acquisitions," 31 N.Y.U. Inst. on Fed. Tax. 291 (1973); and APB Op. No. 17, *Intangibles* (1970), which assumes that intangibles have a limited life.

are recognized as current expenses, which are deductible as ordinary and necessary business expenses under Code section 162.[93]

(b) ***Scope of Code Section 197***

For a Code section 197 intangible to be amortizable, it must be acquired by the taxpayer after August 10, 1993, the date of the enactment of Code section 197,[94] and it must be held in connection with the conduct of a trade or business or an activity described in Code section 212.[95] The section applies to an asset that would otherwise qualify as a Code section 197 intangible if the asset is deemed to be acquired by reason of the taxpayer making an election under Code section 338. Although the asset must be "held" in connection with the conduct of a trade or business or a Code section 212 activity, in some, but not all, cases it need not be "acquired" as part of the acquisition of a trade or business to qualify as a Code section 197 intangible. However, a Code section 197 intangible that is created by the taxpayer will not be eligible for the amortization deduction unless it is created in connection with a transaction (or series of related transactions) that involve the acquisition of a trade or business or a substantial portion thereof and it fits one of the limited exceptions applicable to self-created intangibles.[96]

Code section 197 takes precedence over other amortization sections. Thus, no depreciation or amortization deduction is allowed with respect to any Code section 197 intangible, other than that permitted under Code section 197.[97] However, the Code section 197 amortization rule will not generally apply to any amount that is otherwise currently deductible under provisions of the Code in effect prior to the enactment of Code section 197. An exception to this rule is made in the case of amounts paid or incurred under certain covenants not to compete or under certain other arrangements that have substantially the same effect as covenants not to compete, and certain amounts paid or incurred on account of the transfer of a franchise, trademark, or tradename.

(c) ***Retroactive Application of Code Section 197***

On March 10, 1994, proposed and temporary regulations were issued for making an election to retroactively apply the Code section 197 intangibles provisions.[98] The regulations became effective March 13, 1994. An election under the regulations must be made on a timely filed return for the year that includes August 10, 1993. It applies to property acquired after July 25, 1991, and on or before August 10, 1993.[99] Once made, the election applies to all property acquired during this period by the taxpayer or taxpayers under common control with the electing taxpayer. In order to apply Code section 197 retroactively, taxpayers

---

[93] *Dunn and McCarthy, Inc. v. Commissioner*, 43-2 U.S.T.C. ¶9688, 139 F.2d 242 (2d Cir. 1943). However, the IRS has held that the premium paid for the assets of a bank that, according to the taxpayer, were acquired to protect the latter's business reputation and goodwill, were not deductible. TAM 8009007, November 14, 1979.

[94] The Omnibus Budget Reconciliation Act of 1993, Pub. L. No. 103-66, §13261, 107 Stat. 312 (1993).

[95] I.R.C. §197(c)(1).

[96] I.R.C. §199(c)(2). H.R. 4287, "Tax Fairness and Economic Growth Act of 1992," at 218.

[97] *Id.*

[98] Reg. §1.197-1T; 59 Fed. Reg. 11922, March 15, 1994.

[99] After August 10, 1993, I.R.C. §197 is effective.

must file amended returns. In situations where taxpayers are owed a refund, interest on back taxes will be payable.

(d) ***Settlement Offers Relating to Code Section 197***

On February 9, 1994, the Internal Revenue Service announced a settlement initiative for most of the intangibles issues pending in the controversy systems. It was estimated at that time that approximately $15,000,000,000 of taxes were at issue. Under the settlement initiative, a taxpayer was required to agree to adjust the basis of its amortized intangibles by the greater of a 50 percent cost recovery adjustment or 15 percent minimum concession adjustment. In general, the offer was limited to audits begun prior to April 1, 1994, and to controversies with the IRS at the time the Omnibus Budget Reconciliation Act of 1993 was enacted.

In certain cases, the IRS would not extend an offer. Determinations not to extend an offer in a specific case were to be made only after review by a National Office committee. In addition, taxpayers with acquisitions eligible for the retroactive provisions of Code section 197 were not offered the terms of the settlement offer. Generally, the terms of the retroactive election were more favorable than the terms of the settlement offer. However, a taxpayer may elect the retroactive provisions of Code section 197 for all intangibles acquired after July 25, 1991, and elect the settlement initiative program for all acquisitions on or before July 25, 1991. Field offices began making offers to taxpayers on April 1, 1994.

A taxpayer is not required to accept an offer. If the offer is rejected, the final result in a case could be either more or less favorable than the settlement offer, depending on the merits of the taxpayer's position. Before making the offer, the IRS will engage in normal audit procedures to determine the correct acquisition purchase price and the allocation between tangible and intangible assets.

§ 11.3.4 Code Section 197 Intangible Assets

(a) ***Identifying and Valuing Goodwill and Going-Concern Value***

Under pre-Code section 197 law, goodwill or going-concern value could exist either when specifically identified as an acquired asset or when there is determined to be a purchase premium; that is, an excess of purchase price over the fair market value of other specifically identified acquired assets.[100] The "excess" or residual method has long been recognized by the courts as an acceptable method for both determining the existence of goodwill and arriving at the amount of purchase price that should be allocated to it.[101] However, in *R.M. Smith, Inc.*, the Third Circuit indicated that a determination under the residual method is not conclusive as to the value of the intangible assets acquired.[102]

---

[100] The latter approach to identifying the presence of goodwill and going-concern value is referred to as the "residual" or "gap" method and is mandated by I.R.C. § 1060 for "applicable asset acquisitions."

[101] *Philadelphia Steel & Iron Corp. v. Commissioner* 65-1 U.S.T.C. ¶9308, 344 F.2d 964 (3d Cir. 1965); *Jack Daniel Distillery v. United States*, 67-2 U.S.T.C. ¶9499, 379 F.2d 569 (Ct. Cl. 1967). *See also Banc One, supra* note 53, in which the Tax Court held that "[s]ince petitioner has not proven that the value of those loans exceeded their face amounts, this case represents the paradigm for application of the residual method." 84 T.C. 476, 502 (1985).

[102] *R.M. Smith, Inc. v. Commissioner*, 79-1 U.S.T.C. ¶9179, 591 F.2d 251 (3d Cir. 1979).

Whenever there is such excess purchase price, it normally has been the IRS's position that goodwill and/or going-concern value exists, even if the parties did not intend these assets to be transferred.[103] Moreover, the IRS has taken the position that in the case of a failing banking institution in which the acquiring bank does not wish to acquire, nor does it actually acquire, the acquired institution's trade name goodwill may be evident under the residual method. The Tax Court has held that when a failed bank's assets are not acquired, no goodwill may be transferred, stating that "[the taxpayer] reached the none-too-difficult conclusion that a bank which has failed and had been closed had no goodwill to offer."[104]

Notwithstanding the absence of excess purchase price and any specific identification of goodwill as an acquired asset, the IRS has, in certain instances, maintained that goodwill has been acquired.[105] It has taken the position that when there is excess earning power of the assets acquired over the reasonable earnings on the acquired tangible assets, such excess may be attributable to goodwill.[106] By capitalizing the excess earning power, the cost thereof is thereby determined. However, the Tax Court has stated that "[just] as high earnings alone do not prove the existence of goodwill, . . . lack of profitability does not in itself prove the absence of any intangible value."[107]

Purchase price in excess of the price of acquired assets other than goodwill or going-concern value will not necessarily establish the presence of goodwill or going-concern value if the acquiring firm is able to establish that the tangible assets were purchased for a bargain consideration.[108] Such would be the case if the fair market value of the acquired assets (not including goodwill) exceeds the consideration paid for them.[109] To the extent that this bargain element is allocable to tangible assets, what is, by default under the residual method, treated as goodwill becomes tax deductible basis.[110]

Because the valuation of goodwill and going-concern value is often more difficult than the valuation of certain other types of intangibles, and, certainly, most tangible assets, alternative methods for valuing goodwill and going-concern value are often employed. The two most commonly used methods are the

---

[103] *Copperhead Coal Co., Inc. v. Commissioner*, 17 T.C.M. 30, Dec. 22,815(M), T.C. Memo. 1958-9 (1958), *aff'd*, 60-1 U.S.T.C. ¶9108, 272 F.2d 45 (6th Cir. 1960).

[104] *Midlantic National Bank v. Commissioner*, 46 T.C.M. 1464, Dec. 40,477(M), T.C. Memo. 1983-581.

[105] Rev. Rul. 68-608, 1968-2 C.B. 327.

[106] *Id.*

[107] *Appeal of C.F. Hovey Co.*, 4 B.T.A. 175, Dec. 1473 (1926) (footnotes omitted).

[108] *Poncin Corp. v. Commissioner*, 27 B.T.A. 328, Dec. 7861 (1932); *Means v. Commissioner*, 29 B.T.A. 590, Dec. 8326 (1933); *A.N. McQuown v. Commissioner*, 12 T.C.M. 654, Dec. 19,727 (1953).

[109] It is generally accepted that the bargain element is not recognized gain to the purchaser. Note that a taxpayer would have a heavy burden of proof to carry in view of the presumption that an arm's length sale establishes the value of the item sold. Practically, this is a doctrine of extremely limited applicability outside of a family or other clearly related transaction context.

[110] But note the potentially negative impact this treatment could have on the allocation of purchase price. To the extent that longer lived assets attract the bargain element, the smaller *proportion* of purchase price allocated to assets the cost of which would be recovered over a shorter time may result in a smaller *amount* of cost being so allocated. It is unclear how the single-step purchase price allocation rule contained in I.R.C. § 1060 would be applied in the context of a bargain purchase.

formula method and the residual method.[111] The formula approach capitalizes earnings in excess of a fair rate of return on net tangible assets.[112] According to the IRS the formula approach may be used to determine fair market value of intangible assets of a business only if there is no better approach available for making the determination.[113] Under the residual method, the value of goodwill and going-concern value will equal the excess of the purchase price of all assets over the aggregate fair market values of the tangible assets and the identifiable intangible assets other than goodwill and going-concern value.

(b) *Goodwill*

The legislative history to Code section 197[114] provides that the term "goodwill" means, for purposes of the section, "the value of a trade or business that is attributable to the expectancy of continued customer patronage, whether due to the name of a trade or business, the reputation of a trade or business, or any other factor."[115] This definition derives from long accepted judicial opinions on the definition of goodwill. The Fifth Circuit has said that the nature of goodwill is the expectancy that "the old customers will resort to the old place."[116] The Ninth Circuit stated that "the essence of goodwill is the expectancy of continued patronage, for whatever reason."[117] As more eloquently expressed for the U.S. Supreme Court by Justice Story, goodwill is

> [T]he advantage or benefit, which is acquired by an establishment, beyond the mere value of the capital stock, funds, or property employed therein, in consequence of the general public patronage and encouragement which it receives from constant or habitual customers, on account of its local position, or common celebrity, or reputation for skill or affluence, or punctuality or from other accidental circumstances or necessity, or even from ancient partialities or prejudices.[118]

---

[111] A.R.M. 34, 2 C.B. 31 (1920), *superseded by* Rev. Rul. 68-609, 1968-2 C.B. 327.

[112] The formula approach is defined in Rev. Rul. 68-609 as follows: "A percentage return on the average annual value of the tangible assets used in a business is determined, using a period of years (preferably not less than 5) immediately prior to the valuation date. The amount of the percentage return on tangible assets, thus determined, is deducted from the average earnings of the business for such period and the remainder, if any, is considered to be the amount of the average annual earnings from the intangible assets of the business for the period. This amount (considered as the average annual earnings from intangibles), capitalized at a percentage of, say, 15 to 20 percent, is the value of the intangible assets of the business determined under the single 'formula' approach."

[113] A.R.M. 34, A.R.M. 68, O.D. 937, and Rev. Rul. 65-122, *superseded by* Rev. Rul. 68-609, 1968-2 C.B. 327.

[114] I.R.C. § 197(d)(1)(A). For financial accounting purposes, FAS 147 provides that effective in 2002 goodwill arising from financial institution business combinations may no longer be amortized in accordance with FASB Statement 72. The tax amortization required by I.R.C. § 197 will likely create a long-lived deferred tax liability under FAS 109. *See also* the requirements of the Securities and Exchange Commission ("SEC") contained in SAB 42A in which the SEC staff confirms that 25 years is the maximum period over which goodwill may be amortized for financial institution combinations initiated after September 30, 1982, the effective date of FASB Statement 72.

[115] H.R. 4287, "Tax Fairness and Economic Growth Act of 1992," at 219; P.D. Leak, "Commercial Goodwill," Sir Isaac Pitman & Sons, Ltd. (London, 1921), at 2. *See also Herndon v. Commissioner*, 21 T.C.M. 1013 (1962). In at least one case, the Tax Court has rejected the IRS's contention that "the expectation of future profit" or the acquisition of an asset that may attract customers is goodwill. *Indiana Broadcasting Corp. v. Commissioner*, 41 T.C. 793, *rev'd on other grounds*, 65-2 U.S.T.C. ¶9620, 350 F.2d 580 (7th Cir. 1965).

[116] *Commissioner v. Killian*, 314 F.2d 852, 855 (5th Cir. 1963).

[117] *Boe v. Commissioner*, 62-2 U.S.T.C. ¶9699, 307 F.2d 339, 343 (9th Cir. 1962).

[118] *Metropolitan National Bank of New York v. St. Louis Post Dispatch*, 149 U.S. 436, 446 (1893).

Goodwill has been seen as:

1. The earnings of a firm in excess of those considered normal for a given type of firm;
2. A group of intangible assets the separate elements of which are indistinguishable (*e.g.*, trade name, valuable employees, office locations, ability to solicit customers, customer structure and monopolistic situation);
3. The excess of the fair market value of the total firm over the sum of the fair market values of the component parts of the firm (*i.e.*, the premium paid); and
4. The advantage that an established business has over a new business (including the avoidance of branch start-up costs).[119]

The IRS has ruled that goodwill attributable to a segment of the taxpayer's business and sold, with related assets, by a taxpayer qualified as a capital asset under Code section 1221.[120] Taxpayer and its subsidiaries were in the business of providing services through three separate business divisions. Taxpayer decided to dispose of two of its divisions. The disposition of these two divisions occurred primarily in one tax year and was fragmented into numerous transactions that involved the sale of stock and assets. Because each sale was structured as either an asset sale or a stock sale to which an election under Code section 338(h)(10) was made, all of the sales were treated as asset sales. Each sale generated taxable gain, and in each sale the residual sale price in excess of fair market value of all other assets was allocated to goodwill and going concern value in accordance with Code sections 338 and 1060.

(c) ***Going-Concern Value***

The presence of goodwill is often confused with the existence of going-concern value. This is due in large part to the similarity in the tax treatment they receive: both goodwill and going-concern value constitute nonamortizable assets.[121] However, courts have long recognized going-concern value to be an asset separate and distinct from goodwill.[122] The distinction between the two is an important one since, even in the absence of goodwill, purchase price can be allocated to a nondeductible asset—going-concern value.[123]

Going-concern value is defined as the additional element of value of a trade or business that attaches to property by reason of its existence as an integral part

---

119 *VGS Corp. v. Commissioner*, 68 T.C. 563 (1965). Note that with the enactment of I.R.C. § 195 (Miscellaneous Revenue Act of 1980, Pub. L. No. 96-605, § 102(a), 94 Stat. 3521 (1980)), effective with respect to amounts paid or incurred after July 29, 1980, the term "start-up costs" has taken on a special and more precise meaning. *See* definition of "start-up expenditures" in I.R.C. § 195(c).

120 PLR 200243002, July 16, 2002.

121 I.R.C. § 197(d)(1)(B); *Computing & Software, Inc. v. Commissioner*, 64 T.C. 223 (1975).

122 *Los Angeles Gas & Electric Corp. v. Railroad Comm'n*, 289 U.S. 287, 313 (1933).

123 *Black Industries v. Commissioner*, 38 T.C.M. 242, T.C. Memo. 1979-61; *VGS Corp. v. Commissioner*, 68 T.C. 563, Dec. 34,519 (1977); *Concord Control Inc. v. Commissioner*, 35 T.C.M. 1345, T.C. Memo. 1976-301, *aff'd and rem'd*, 80-1 U.S.T.C. ¶9248 (6th Cir. 1980). The I.R.C. § 1060 allocation rule embraces going-concern value as well as goodwill. *See* "General Explanation of the Tax Reform Act of 1986," prepared by the Joint Committee on Taxation, May 4, 1987 at 355-360, *supra* note 106.

of a going concern.[124] This definition embraces the value that is attributable to a firm's ability to continue to function and generate income without interruption even though a change in ownership occurs. It also includes any value attributable to the use or availability of an acquired business that would arise, for example, when net earnings are realized that would not otherwise be received during any period where the acquired trade or business is not available or operational.

Going-concern value may exist whenever a business is transferred without business operations being interrupted. It represents the start-up costs that the buyer would otherwise have to incur if the business were begun *de novo*.[125] As distinguished from goodwill, going-concern value constitutes "the additional element of value which attaches to property by reason of its existence as an integral part of a going concern."[126] Factors indicating that the target's going-concern value has *not* been purchased include:

1. The reluctance to retain employees of the acquired firm;
2. Substitution of the acquiring firm's methods and procedures in conducting business;
3. Disposition of the acquired firm's office supplies and furnishings; and
4. Operation of the acquired business under a different name and at a different location.

(d) *Workforce*

A "section 197 intangible" includes any value placed on employees or any of their attributes including: the value associated with having a workforce, agency force, or assembled workforce in place; the experience, education, or training of a workforce which comprises the "composition" of a workforce; and the terms and conditions of employment, whether contractual or otherwise.[127] If some portion of the total purchase price is properly allocated to an existing employment contract or other relationship with an employee or consultant, including a "key employee" contract, it will be treated as part of the cost allocated to the "workforce."[128] This should not be confused with any purchase price that is allocated to a covenant not to compete that is entered into in connection with an acquisition of an interest in a trade or business.[129]

(e) *Information Base*

A "section 197 intangible" includes the intangible value of any technical manuals, training manuals or programs, data files, accounting or inventory control systems or other business books and records, operating systems and any other information base including lists or other information with respect to

[124] H.R. 4287, "Tax Fairness and Economic Growth Act of 1992," at 219.

[125] *Midlantic National Bank v. Commissioner*, 46 T.C.M. 1464, Dec. 40,477(M), T.C. Memo. 1983-581.

[126] *VGS Corp. v. Commissioner*, *supra* note 119.

[127] I.R.C. § 197(d)(1)(C)(I). *See* "Industry Specialization Program Coordinated Issue Paper, Amortization of Assembled Workforce," (Revised February 19, 1996), for IRS exam position for taxable years prior to enactment of I.R.C. § 197.

[128] H.R. 4287, "Tax Fairness and Economic Growth Act of 1992," at 219.

[129] I.R.C. §§ 197(d)(1)(E) and 197(f)(3).

current or prospective customers. Thus, it includes the portion of purchase price allocated to acquiring any customer lists, subscription lists, insurance expirations, patient or client files, or lists of advertisers.[130]

(f) *Know-How*

A "section 197 intangible" includes any patent, copyright, formula, process, design, pattern, know-how, format, or similar item. The term "know-how" includes computer software. However, exceptions are provided for certain "off-the-shelf" software (discussed below).[131]

(g) *Customer-Based Intangibles*

A "section 197 intangible" includes any "customer based intangible."[132] This encompasses deposit base and similar items.[133] The legislative history of Code section 197 indicates that the term "customer based intangible" includes that portion of any purchase price of an acquired financial institution that is attributable to the checking accounts, savings accounts, escrow accounts, and other similar items of the acquired financial institution.[134] The value of an acquired firm's "core deposit intangible" ("CDI") is inherent in the expectancy that demand and savings account deposits will be maintained for a period of time following their acquisition.

Taxpayers have successfully argued that when a bank is acquired, the acquirer assumes an identifiable group of deposit accounts, which remain open for a period of time with little, if any, need for further marketing efforts.[135] These accounts eventually close because depositors' circumstances change with time. Individuals relocate to other communities, change jobs, marry, and die. Busi-

---

[130] H.R. 4287, "Tax Fairness and Economic Growth Act of 1992," at 220.

[131] I.R.C. §§197(d)(1)(C)(iii) and 197(e)(3). *See* discussion below of computer software at § 11.3.5(c).

[132] *See* "Industry Specialization Program Coordinated Issue Paper, Customer Based Intangibles," (Revised February 19, 1996) for the IRS exam position for taxable years prior to the enactment of I.R.C. §197.

[133] I.R.C. §197(d)(2)(B).

[134] What constitutes a "financial institution" is not defined in the Code or in the legislative history; however, a similar term is used in I.R.C. §§582, 267 and 291. For purposes of all three sections, the term is defined to include both a commercial bank and a thrift. The broadest definition of the term "financial institution" is contained in I.R.C. §582(c)(2). There it provides that the term includes a "bank," any mutual savings bank (with or without capital stock represented by shares), cooperative bank, domestic building and loan association and other savings institution chartered and supervised as savings and loan or similar associations under federal or state law, any small business investment company operating under the Small Business Investment Act of 1958, and any business development corporation. I.R.C. §582(c)(2)(A). The term "financial institution" is defined in Section 265(b)(5) as a financial institution defined in I.R.C. §582(c)(2), as well as any institution that accepts deposits from the public in the ordinary course of its trade or business and which is subject to federal or state supervision as a financial institution. The I.R.C. §291 definition means any bank defined in I.R.C. §581 which includes commercial banks, domestic building and loan associations, mutual savings banks, and cooperative banks without capital stock organized and operated for mutual purposes and without profit which pass the 60 percent asset test of I.R.C. §7701(a)(19).

[135] *Citizens and Southern Corporation & Subsidiaries v. Commissioner*, 91-1 U.S.T.C. ¶50,043, 919 F.2d 1492 (11th Cir. 1990), *aff'g* 91 T.C. 463, Dec. 45,036 (1988). *See also AmSouth Bancorporation v. United States*, 88-1 U.S.T.C. ¶9232, 681 F. Supp. 698 (D.C. Ala. 1988); *Colorado National Bankshares, Inc. v. Commissioner*, 60 T.C.M. 771, Dec. 46,875(M), T.C. Memo. 1990-495; *Iowa Trust & Savings v. Commissioner*, 97 T.C. 496, Dec. 47,735 (1991); *Peoples Bancorporation & Subsidiaries v. Commissioner*, 63 T.C.M. 3028, Dec. 48,226(M), T.C. Memo. 1992-285; *Newark Morning Ledger v. United States*, 91-2 U.S.T.C. ¶50,451, 945 F.2d 555 (3d Cir. 1991); *Ithaca Industries Inc. v. Commissioner*, 97 T.C. 253, Dec. 47,536 (1991); and *Trustmark Corporation & Subsidiaries v. Commissioner*, 67 T.C.M. 2764, T.C. Memo. 1994-184.

nesses are sold, reorganize and fail; their personnel changes; they relocate; and their owners retire or die. Any of these factors may lead to an account's closing. In addition, an account may terminate because it has been acquired by a competing bank as the result of customer dissatisfaction or the perceived greater attractiveness of the competing bank.

Although it is usually impossible to predict the useful life of a particular account, statistical analysis may be useful to predict the percent of acquired accounts that would remain open at periodic future intervals. Consequently, taxpayers take the position that if they are able to determine a useful life for the value attributable to the deposit liabilities, the cost allocated thereto is deductible as amortization under Code section 167.

Taxpayers have claimed that either the net earnings from the deposit liabilities or the cost saved from the use of below mark funds determine the value of the CDI. The deposit relationship may also serve as an entree for the acquiring bank to provide additional profit-generating services such as safe deposit box leases, installment, mortgage and other loans, and trust services. There are "rules of thumb" used in the banking industry to value the premium paid for a deposit base. For example, in *Midlantic*, the taxpayer cited an industry custom used in the 1970s of valuing the premium to be paid for a deposit base as an amount equal to 6 to 7 percent of the total deposit base.[136]

The Office of the Comptroller of the Currency ("OCC") defines "core deposits" as the deposit base of demand and savings accounts which, while usually not legally restricted, is generally based on stable customer relationships that the bank can expect to maintain for an extensive period of time.[137] Elsewhere, it has been defined as the present value of the future net income stream associated with a bank's deposits.[138] Common to these definitions is the recognition that the assumption of a deposit base avoids incurrence of the prolonged advertising and business development costs associated with generating a deposit base.[139]

It was the IRS's position that any value attributable to a bank's core deposits was not sufficiently distinguishable from goodwill or going-concern value to allow a deduction for amortization. It argued that any projected earnings that a taxpayer attributes to the assumed deposit liabilities are attributable to profits expected from all of the acquired bank's business dealings, including existing customers and others who would become customers of the bank. A premium is paid for an acquired bank because of the expectation that earnings on booked assets will continue as a result of the acquired firm's goodwill. The IRS argues further that a customer's deposit relationship is only one part of a multifaceted

---

136 *Midlantic National Bank v. Commissioner*, 46 T.C.M. 1464, Dec. 40,477(M), T.C. Memo. 1983-581.

137 *See* Office of the Comptroller of the Currency Circular No. 164, Dec. 29, 1981.

138 *See* IRS Industry Specialization Program Coordinated Issue Papers on Core Deposit Intangibles at Appendix A.113 and A.114.

139 For a short period of time (1982-85), the OCC permitted national banks to capitalize and amortize the value of the customer deposit relationships. OCC Circular 164. A similar policy was adopted by the FDIC on March 5, 1982. Under a "Final Rule" issued in 1985, the CDI may not be treated as an asset for capital adequacy or lending limit purposes.

relationship between the bank and the customer. Other aspects of the total relationship include a variety of loan contacts.

In contrast to the value ascribed to a deposit relationship is the value paid for the right to solicit customers. In an IRS Coordinated Issue Paper on core deposits, it is stated:

> The treatment of costs to acquire the right to solicit the former depositors of a failed bank *in order to develop a new deposit base* must be distinguished from the treatment of costs incurred to acquire a pre-existing deposit base of both a going-concern bank and, in most cases, of a failing bank where the doors never close but the signs of ownership merely change from one day to the next.[140]

The IRS has acquiesced to the opinion in *Midlantic*. In that case, the court reasoned that the cost of a right to solicit depositors of a failed bank is recoverable through the allowance for amortization, since it is separate and distinct from goodwill or going-concern value.[141] The "right" in that case was purchased by Midlantic and evidenced by a binding contract. The Tax Court found that the right had an ascertainable value and an identifiable useful life. Rigorous exactitude was not needed to establish either of these factors. Only reasonable accuracy in forecasting useful life and reasonable certainty and approximation are needed to prove the entitlement to depreciation and rate of depreciation.[142]

(h) *Supplier-Based Intangibles*

A "supplier-based intangible" is defined as any value resulting from the future acquisitions of goods or services pursuant to relationships in the ordinary course of business with suppliers of goods or services to be used or sold by the taxpayer.[143] The relationships may be either contractual or based on simply the course of dealing between the parties. The legislative history of the section indicates that term "supplier-based intangible" includes that portion of the purchase price of an acquired trade or business that is attributable to the existence of a favorable relationship with persons that provide distribution services, the existence of a favorable credit rating, or the existence of favorable supply contracts. A "distribution service" includes favorable shelf or display space at a retail outlet.

Since the term "supplier-based intangible" describes relationships with suppliers of goods or services to be used or sold by the taxpayer, it is unclear why

---

[140] IRS Industry Specialization Program Coordinated Issue Papers in Appendix at §§A.14 and A.15.

[141] *Midlantic National Bank v. Commissioner*, 46 T.C.M. 1464, Dec. 40,477(M), T.C. Memo. 1983-581. *See also Houston Chronicle Publishing Co. v. United States*, 73-2 U.S.T.C. ¶9537, 481 F.2d 1240 (5th Cir. 1973); *cert. denied*, 414 U.S. 1129 (1974); *Holden Fuel Oil Co. v. Commissioner*, 73-2 U.S.T.C. ¶9514, 479 F.2d 613 (6th Cir. 1973); *Super Food Services, Inc. v. United States*, 69-2 U.S.T.C. ¶9558, 416 F.2d 1236 (7th Cir. 1969); *Savings Assurance Agency, Inc. v. Commissioner*, 22 T.C.M. 200, Dec. 25,976(M), T.C. Memo. 1963-52, *appeal dismissed*, (6th Cir. 1963). In *Savings Assurance*, the court held that an insurance policy expiration list had a distinct value apart from the creator of the list, who, incidentally, was deceased. Note that it is the position of the New York State Department of Taxation and Finance that a customer list transferred by computer to an acquiring firm is tangible personal property subject to sales tax.

[142] Similarly, the Tax Court has allowed an amortization deduction for the cost of the right to use acquired escrow deposits. *First Pennsylvania Banking and Trust Corp. v. Commissioner*, 56 T.C. 677, Dec. 30,859 (1971).

[143] I.R.C. § 197(d)(3).

distribution services that appear to relate to products that will be sold or distributed by the taxpayer are included within the scope of this provision. It would appear that they would, more appropriately, be included within the scope of a "customer-based intangible."

(i) *Licenses and Permits*

Any license, permit, or other right granted by a governmental unit is a "section 197 intangible."[144] A governmental unit includes any agency or instrumentality of a governmental unit, and a right will be included within the scope of this provision even if the right is granted for an indefinite period or it is reasonably expected to be renewed for an indefinite period.[145] Examples of what constitutes a license or permit include a liquor license, a taxi cab medallion or license, an airport landing or take-off right, a regulated airline route, and a television or radio broadcasting license. It appears to be immaterial whether the license or permit is acquired in connection with the acquisition of a trade or business. Thus, the issuance or renewal of a license or permit or other right granted by a governmental unit would be considered the acquisition of such license or permit for purposes of this provision.[146] A banking franchise may be a "license or permit" granted by a governmental unit.

(j) *Covenants-Not-to-Compete*

Any covenant not to compete entered into in connection with an acquisition of an interest in a trade or business is a "section 197 intangible."[147] Any other employment arrangements having substantially the same effect as a covenant not to compete will be treated as a covenant not to compete to the extent that it has substantially the same effect. The inclusion of any covenant not to compete or similar arrangement in the definition of a "section 197 intangible" is not overcome by the general rule excluding self-created intangibles from the definition of an "amortizable section 197 intangible."[148]

An arrangement that requires a former owner of an interest in a trade or business to continue to perform services that benefit the trade or business will be treated as having "substantially the same effect" as a covenant not to compete, but only to the extent that the amount paid to the former owner under the arrangement exceeds the amount that represents reasonable compensation for the services actually rendered by the former owner.[149] Similarly, if a former owner provides the business with property or permits the business to use property, it shall be considered to have "substantially the same effect" as a covenant not to compete, but only to the extent that the amount paid to the former owner for the services or use of the property exceeds an amount that represents reasonable compensation for the services or property provided by the former owner. Determining the excess is likely to present substantial valuation issues.

---

[144] I.R.C. § 197(d)(1)(D).

[145] H.R. 4287, "Tax Fairness and Economic Growth Act of 1992," at 221.

[146] I.R.C. § 197(f)(4)(B).

[147] I.R.C. § 197(d)(1)(E).

[148] I.R.C. § 197(c)(2)(A).

[149] IRS Industry Specialization Program Coordinated Issue Paper "Covenants Not to Compete," February 19, 1996.

This capitalization rule will apply regardless of whether the acquisition is of the assets of a trade or business, of the stock in a corporation, or an interest in a partnership. Further, if any amount that is allocated by the taxpayer to a covenant not to compete or similar arrangement represents additional consideration for the acquisition of stock in a corporation, such amount is not taken into account as a Code section 197 intangible, but, instead, is included in the acquiror's tax basis in the stock.[150]

Any amount paid or incurred pursuant to a covenant not to compete, or any other employment arrangement having substantially the same effect as a covenant not to compete, is treated as chargeable to capital account.[151] As such, it is to be amortized ratably over the 15-year period specified for "section 197 intangibles." Any amounts that are paid or incurred under such an agreement after the taxable year in which the agreement is entered into must be amortized ratably over the remaining months in the 15-year amortization period that applies to the agreement.[152]

A covenant not to compete or similar arrangement may not be treated as disposed of or as becoming worthless before the disposition of the entire interest in the trade or business (or substantial portion thereof) in connection with which such covenant or other arrangement was entered into.[153] For purposes of the disposition rule, all members of the same controlled group of corporations are treated as a single taxpayer.[154] However, this nonrecognition rule will apply only if, after the disposition, a member of the same control group as the corporation retains other Code section 197 intangibles that were acquired in the same transaction or a series of related transactions as the "section 197 intangible" that was disposed of. The legislative history indicates that the Treasury Department should promulgate rules for taking into account the amount of any loss that is not recognized due to this nonrecognition rule, and it suggests that the disposing corporation should be allowed to amortize the loss over the remaining portion of the 15-year amortization period.[155]

(k) *Franchises, Trademarks, and Tradenames*

The inclusion of franchises, trademarks and tradenames in the definition of a "section 197 intangible" is not overcome by the general rule excluding self-created intangibles from the definition of an "amortizable section 197 intangible."[156] For purposes of this provision, the term "franchise" includes an agreement which gives one of the parties to the agreement the right to distribute, sell, or provide goods, services, or facilities within a specified area.[157]

---

[150] H.R. 4287, "Tax Fairness and Economic Growth Act of 1992," at 222.

[151] I.R.C. § 197(f)(3).

[152] H.R. Conf. Rep. 103-213 at. 678-679 (1993).

[153] I.R.C. § 197(f)(1)(B).

[154] I.R.C. § § 197(f)(1)(C) and 41(f)(1)(A).

[155] H.R. Conf. Rep. No. 103-213 at 685.

[156] I.R.C. § 197(c)(2)(A).

[157] I.R.C. § § 197(f)(4)(A) and 1253(b)(1).

The acquisition of a franchise, trademark,[158] or tradename[159] includes any renewal of the agreement, but only with respect to the costs incurred in connection with the renewal.[160] Any costs incurred in connection with the issuance (or an earlier renewal) of a franchise, trademark, or tradename are to continue to be taken into account over the remaining portion of the amortization period that began at the time of such issuance (or earlier renewal).[161]

Certain contingent amounts that are paid or incurred on account of the transfer of a franchise, trademark or tradename are not treated as Code section 197 intangibles if they conform to the description of "contingent payment" contained in Code section 1253(d)(1).[162] In accordance with this provision, a payment shall be currently deductible under Code section 162(a) by the transferee of a franchise, trademark or tradename if it is paid or incurred on account of a transfer, sale, or other disposition of a franchise, trademark or tradename if the payment meets the following requirements:

1. It is contingent on the productivity, use or disposition of a franchise, trademark, or tradename, and
2. It is paid as a part of series of payments—
   (a) Which are payable not less frequently than annually throughout the entire term of the transfer agreement, and
   (b) Which are substantially equal in amount (or payable under a fixed formula).[163]

All other contingent (as well as fixed) amounts paid for the transfer of a franchise, trademark, or tradename shall be treated as a Code section 197 intangible.

§ 11.3.5 Code Section 197 Intangibles: Exceptions

There are several items, as set forth in Code section 197, which are expressly excepted from the definition of a "section 197 intangible."[164] In addition, a "section 197 intangible" does not include certain interests or rights that are not acquired in a transaction (or series of related transactions) involving the acquisition of assets constituting a trade or business or a substantial portion thereof.[165]

(a) *Financial Interests*

The term "section 197 intangible" does not include any interest in a corporation, partnership, trust, or estate, or any interest under an existing futures contract, foreign currency contract, notional principle contract, or other similar

[158] According to 15 U.S.C. § 1127 (2000): "The term 'trademark' includes any word, name, symbol, or device, or any combination thereof—

(1) Used by a person, or

(2) Which a person has a bona fide intention to use in commerce and applies to register on the principle register established by [15 U.S.C. § 1127], to identify and distinguish his or her goods, including a unique product, from those manufactured or sold by others and to indicate the source of the goods even if that source is unknown."

[159] The term tradename means any name used by a person to identify his or her business or vocation. 15 U.S.C. § 1127 (2000).

[160] I.R.C. § 197(f)(4)(B). H.R. 4287, "Tax Fairness and Economic Growth Act of 1992," at 222.

[161] *Id.*

[162] I.R.C. § 197(f)(4)(C).

[163] I.R.C. § 1253(d)(1)(B).

[164] I.R.C. § 197(e).

[165] I.R.C. § 197(e)(4).

financial contract.[166] The exclusion for any such interest means that its cost, whether or not such interests are regularly traded on an established market, shall be treated as under the law in existence prior to the enactment of Code section 197.

(b) *Interests in Land*

A "section 197 intangible" does not include any interest in land.[167] The term "any interest in land" is defined broadly to include any fee interest, life estate, remainder, easement, mineral rights, timber rights, grazing rights, riparian rights, air rights, zoning variances, as well as other similar rights with respect to land.[168]

(c) *Computer Software*

Computer software that is readily available for purchase by the general public, is subject to a non-exclusive license, and has not been substantially modified will not be treated as a Code section 197 intangible. Other computer software will qualify as a "section 197 intangible."[169]

Unlike under pre-1993 law, the Code now explicitly provides for the period over which amortization deductions are permitted with respect to computer software and the rate of cost recovery. If a depreciation deduction is allowed with respect to computer software under Code section 167, and not Code section 197, the deduction is computed using the straight-line method and a useful life of 36 months.[170] Also eligible for the more rapid amortization deductions allowed under Code section 167 is other computer software that is not acquired in a transaction (or series of related transactions) involving the acquisition of assets constituting a trade or business or substantial portion thereof.[171] The 36 month period begins with the month that the computer software is placed in service. For purposes of this exclusion, the term "computer software" is defined as "any program designed to cause a computer to perform a desired function. Such term shall not include any database or similar item unless the database or item is in the public domain and is incidental to the operation of otherwise qualifying computer software."[172] Thus, any cost that is taken into account as part of the cost of computer hardware or other tangible property continues to be taken into account as under prior law.[173]

---

166 I.R.C. §§ 197(e)(1)(A) and (B). H.R. 4287, "Tax Fairness and Economic Growth Act of 1992," at 223. The House Report provides: "[A] temporal interest in property, outright or in trust, may not be used to convert a Section 197 intangible into property that is amortizable more rapidly than ratably over the [15 year] period specified in the bill." H.R. 4287 "Tax Fairness and Economic Growth Act of 1992," at 223.

167 I.R.C. § 197(e)(2).

168 H.R. 4287, "Tax Fairness and Economic Growth Act of 1992," at p. 223. An airport landing or takeoff right is not treated as an interest in land nor is any regulated airline route, or a franchise to provide cable television services.

169 I.R.C. § 197(e)(3). *See* Prop. Reg. § 1.197-2(c)(4); 62 Fed. Reg. 2336, January 16, 1997.

170 I.R.C. § 167(f)(1).

171 I.R.C. § 197(e)(3)(A)(ii).

172 I.R.C. § 197(e)(3)(B).

173 H.R. 4287, "Tax Fairness and Economic Growth Act of 1992," at 224.

(d) *Leases*

A "section 197 intangible" does not include any interest under an existing lease of tangible property.[174] For purposes of the exclusion relating to leases it is irrelevant whether the existing lease establishes the acquiring entity as lessor or lessee. Further, it is irrelevant whether the lease is of real or of personal property.[175] Moreover, a sublease shall be treated in the same manner as a lease of the underlying property involved.[176]

The cost of acquiring an interest as a lessor under a lease of tangible property, where the interest as lessor is acquired in connection with the acquisition of the tangible property, is to be taken into account as part of the cost of the tangible property.[177] Thus, if a taxpayer acquires a building that is leased to tenants operating retail stores, the portion, if any, of the purchase price of the building that is attributable to the favorable attributes of the leases is to be taken into account as a part of the basis of the building and is to be taken into account in determining the depreciation deduction allowed with respect to the building.[178] As under the law in existence prior to the enactment of Code section 197, the cost is amortized over the term of the lease including all renewal options if less than 75 percent of the cost is attributable to the period of the term of the lease remaining on the date of its acquisition.[179]

If the acquirer acquires an interest as a lessee under a lease of tangible property along with any other intangible property (either in the same transaction or series of related transactions), the portion of the total purchase price that is allocable to the interest as a lessee is not to exceed the excess of:

1. The present value of the fair market value rent for the use of the tangible property for the term of the lease, over
2. The present value of the rent reasonably expected to be paid for the use of the tangible property for the term of the lease.[180]

(e) *Debt Instruments*

A "section 197 intangible" will not include any interest under indebtedness that was in existence on the date that the interest was acquired.[181] The interest that is excluded may be one in which the acquirer is either a creditor or a debtor. Thus, if the acquirer is a debtor that assumes an existing indebtedness that has a below market interest rate, the value attributable to this asset is not treated as a

---

174 I.R.C. § 197(e)(5).

175 H.R. 4287, "Tax Fairness and Economic Growth Act of 1992," at 225.

176 I.R.C. § 197(f)(6).

177 *Id.*

178 H.R. 4287, "Tax Fairness and Economic Growth Act of 1992," at 225, 226.

179 I.R.C. § 178(a). Reg. § 1.162-11(a).

180 H.R. 4287, "Tax Fairness and Economic Growth Act of 1992," at 226. The legislative history indicates that "[i]n no event is the present value of the fair market value rent for the use of the tangible property for the term of the lease to exceed the fair market value of the tangible property as of the date of acquisition. The present value of such rent is presumed to be less than the value of the tangible property if the duration of the lease is less than the economic useful life of the property."

181 I.R.C. § 197(e)(5)(B).

Code section 197 intangible. Similarly, if the acquirer is a creditor that pays a premium for acquiring the right to receive an above market rate of interest under a debt instrument, the premium is taken into account under Code section 171 and not as "section 197 intangible."[182]

Under Code section 171, the amount of the premium is amortized on a yield to maturity basis over the remaining term of the debt instrument. If the interest under any existing indebtedness is properly classified as a deposit base or similar item that qualifies for inclusion in the definition of a "section 197 intangible" as a "customer-based intangible," it is not excluded by reason of this exception.[183]

(f) *Mortgage Servicing Rights*

A "section 197 intangible" does not include any right to service indebtedness which is secured by residential real property that is acquired separately from the acquisition of a trade or business.[184] The cost properly allocated to such right may be recoverable as a depreciation deduction under Code section 167(a). However, the rate of cost recovery and the period over which cost is recovered are expressly provided for in the Code. The cost associated with mortgage servicing rights shall be recoverable using the straight-line method and a useful life of 108 months. Mortgage servicing rights that are acquired in a transaction (or series of related transactions) involving the acquisition of assets constituting a trade or business or a substantial portion thereof are not excluded from the definition of a "section 197 intangible."[185]

(g) *Transaction Costs*

The term "section 197 intangible" does not include any fees for professional services and any transaction costs incurred by parties to a transaction with respect to which any portion of the gain or loss is not recognized under the corporation organization and reorganization sections of the Code.[186] This exception is designed to prevent amortization deductions with respect to amounts that are required to be capitalized as transaction costs under the law in effect before the enactment of Code section 197.[187]

---

[182] Although the legislative history of the 1993 act provides that the term "interest" under any existing indebtedness includes mortgage servicing rights to the extent that the rights are stripped coupons described in I.R.C. § 1286, Congress amended the Code itself to explicitly provide for a limited exclusion from the term "Section 197 intangible" for mortgage servicing rights. I.R.C. § 197(e)(7). Rev. Rul. 91-46, 1991-2 C.B. 358. *See* discussion of mortgage servicing rights below and in Ch. 2.

[183] I.R.C. § 197(d)(2)(B).

[184] I.R.C. § 197(e)(7). *See* Prop. Reg. § 1.197-2(11). 62 Fed. Reg. 2335 (January 16, 1997).

[185] I.R.C. § 167(f)(3). The Taxpayer Relief Act of 1997, Pub. L. No. 105-34 § 1086(a) amended I.R.C. § 167(g) to provide that the income forecast method may not be used for any amortizable I.R.C. § 197 intangible. The Treasury Department issued temporary regulation § 1.1286-1T, which treats the amount of O.I.D. on purchased mortgages as equal to zero if the O.I.D. is less than the de minimis amount of O.I.D. prescribed in I.R.C. § 1273(a).

[186] I.R.C. § 197(e)(8). *See also* I.R.C. §§ 351-384.

[187] H.R. Conf. Rep. No. 213, 103rd Cong., 1st Sess (1993).

(h) ***Trade or Business Not Acquired***

There are several exceptions to what constitutes a "section 197 intangible" that apply only if the intangible property acquired is not acquired in a transaction (or series of related transactions) that involves the acquisition of assets that constitute a trade or business or a substantial portion of a trade or business.[188] The legislative history of Code section 197 indicates that Congress "anticipated that the Treasury Department will exercise its regulatory authority to require any intangible property that would otherwise be excluded from the definition of the term 'section 197 intangible' to be taken into account as a section 197 intangible under circumstances where the acquisition of the intangible property is, in and of itself, the acquisition of an asset which constitutes a trade or business or a substantial portion of a trade or business."[189]

To determine whether a group of assets will constitute a trade or business, the standard of Code section 1060 will apply. Thus, a group of assets will constitute a trade or business if the assets are of such a character that goodwill or going concern value could, under any circumstances, attach to the assets.[190] Only those assets acquired in a transaction (or series of related transactions) by a taxpayer (and persons related to the taxpayer) from the same person (and any related person) are to be taken into account in determining whether a taxpayer has acquired an intangible asset in a transaction (or series of related transaction) that involves the acquisition of assets that constitute a trade or business or a substantial portion of a trade or business.[191] If any employee relationships continue after the acquisition, or if a covenant not to compete is entered into in connection with the acquisition, an inference may be drawn that the transferred assets constitute a trade or business or a substantial portion of a trade or business.[192]

In any event, the determination of whether acquired assets constitute a substantial portion of a trade or business is to be based on all the facts and circumstances, including the nature and the amount of the assets acquired as well as the nature and the amount of the assets retained by the transferor. The value of the assets acquired relative to the value of the assets retained by the transferor shall not be determinative of whether the acquired assets constitute a substantial portion of a trade or business.[193] The exception for interests or rights acquired separately is worded in such a way that it will exclude certain interests or rights from the classification of a "section 197 intangible," but it does not suggest that if the right is acquired as part of an acquisition of assets constituting a trade or business or a substantial portion thereof that the interest or right will be treated as a "section 197 intangible."

---

[188] I.R.C. § 197(e)(4).

[189] H.R. 4287, "Tax Fairness and Economic Growth Act of 1992," at 222, 223.

[190] H.R. 4287, "Tax Fairness and Economic Growth Act of 1992." This House Report indicates that the acquisition of a franchise, trademark, or tradename will constitute the acquisition of a trade or business or a substantial portion of a trade or business.

[191] *Id.*

[192] *Id.*

[193] H.R. Conf. Rep. No. 103-213, at 678-679 (1993).

(i) ***Quick Reference Tables***

Table 11.2 sets forth those assets that are Code section 197 intangibles regardless of whether they are acquired as a part of a trade or business.

Table 11.3 sets forth those assets that are Code section 197 intangibles only if acquired in a transaction that involves the acquisition of assets that constitute a trade or business or a substantial portion of a trade or business. Each of these items is discussed in detail.

Table 11.4 sets forth those assets that are not Code section 197 intangibles, regardless of whether they are acquired as part of a business, or separate from a business unless they meet certain defined exception rules.

Table 11.2

General Item	Definitions and Examples
Goodwill and going concern	*Goodwill: The value of a business that is attributed to the expectancy of continued customer patronage.* *Going concern: The value of a trade or business that results from the ability to continue to function and generate income without interruption.*
Workforce	*Workforce in place, the composition of a workforce, the terms and conditions of employment, an existing employment contract and any other value placed on employees.*
Information base	*Examples: Intangible value of technical manuals, training manuals or programs, data files, and accounting or inventory control systems, and the cost of acquiring customer lists, subscription lists, insurance expirations, patient or client files, or lists of advertisers.*
Customer-based intangibles	*Examples: Customer base, circulation base, undeveloped market or market growth, insurance in force, mortgage servicing contracts, investment management contracts, or other relationships with customers that involve the future provision of goods or services.* *
Supplier-based intangibles	*The value resulting from the future acquisition of goods or services pursuant to relationships in the ordinary course of business with suppliers of goods or services to be used or sold by the taxpayer. Example: a favorable relationship with persons that provide distribution services, a favorable credit rating, or a favorable supply contract.*
Licenses, permits, and other rights granted by governmental units	*Examples: A liquor license, a taxi-cab medallion, an airport landing or takeoff right, a regulated airline route, a broadcasting license or the renewal of any such license.*
Franchises, trademarks, and tradenames and the renewal costs of franchises, trademarks, and tradenames	*Franchise: Any agreement that provides a party to the agreement the right to distribute, sell, or provide goods, services, or facilities, within a specified area.*

* *For financial institutions, this item includes deposit base and similar items. I.R.C. § 197(d)(2)(B).*

Table 11.3

General Item	Definitions and Examples
Certain interests in film, sound recordings, videotapes, books or other similar property	
Certain rights to receive tangible property or services under a contract	*Example: A supply or requirements contract.*
Certain interests in patents and copyrights	
Covenants not to compete and other similar arrangements	*For this item, a trade or business includes the stock of a corporation that is engaged in a trade or business or an interest in a partnership that is engaged in a trade or business.*
Computer software generally	*Any program that is designed to cause a computer to perform a desired function, but not any data base or other similar item regardless of the form in which it is maintained or stored. See Table 11.4 for software that is not an I.R.C. § 197 intangible, however acquired.*
Financial interests *	*A mortgage servicing contract, credit card servicing contract or other contract to service indebtedness issued by another person, and any interest under an assumption reinsurance contract.*

* *The following financial interests are not I.R.C. § 197 intangibles however acquired: interest under an existing futures contract, foreign currency contract, notional principal contract, interest rate swap, cost of acquiring stock, partnership interests, interests in a trust or estate, or other similar interests.*

Table 11.4

General Item	Definitions and Examples	Exceptions
Interests in land	*Examples: a fee interest, life estate, remainder, easement, mineral rights, grazing rights, riparian rights, air rights, zoning variations, and any other similar rights with respect to land.*	*Not excluded: an airport landing or takeoff right, a regulated airline route, or a franchise to provide cable television services.*
Computer software	*Computer software that (1) is readily available for purchase by the general public; (2) is subject to nonexclusive license; and (3) has not been substantially modified.*	*See Table 11.3 for computer software that may be treated as an I.R.C. § 197 intangible.*
Interests under leases of tangible property and debt instruments	*Interest as a lessor or lessee under an existing lease of tangible property (whether real or personal) and any interest (whether as a creditor or debtor) under any indebtedness that was in existence on the date that the interest was acquired.*	*Not excluded: a deposit base or similar item that is included in the definition of a "customer based intangible" as defined in Table 11.2.*

§11.3.6 Code Section 197 Intangibles: Dispositions

If any amortizable Code section 197 intangible is disposed of in a transaction or series of related transactions, gain or loss is recognized; however, if one or more other amortizable Code section 197 intangibles acquired in such transaction or series of related transactions are retained, no loss may be recognized on the disposition.[194] For purposes of this rule, any Code section 197 intangible that becomes worthless shall be treated as if it were disposed of.[195] The adjusted basis of the retained Code section 197 intangibles are increased by the amount of the unrecognized loss. The basis adjustment is equal to the product of:

1. The amount of the loss that is not recognized solely by reason of this nonrecognition rule, and
2. A fraction, the numerator of which is the adjusted basis of the intangible as of the date of the disposition and the denominator of which is the total adjusted basis of all such retained Code section 197 intangibles as of the date of the disposition.[196]

If a Code section 197 intangible is transferred in certain specified nonrecognition transactions, a carryover rule applies to the Code section 197 intangible taint. Thus, the transferee in such transaction is treated as the transferor for purposes of applying the amortization rules with respect to the amount of the adjusted basis of the transferee that does not exceed the adjusted basis of the transferor in the Code section 197 intangible immediately before the transfer.[197] The transactions which will result in a carryover of the Code section 197 intangible taint are any transaction described in Code sections 332, 351, 361, 721, 731, 1031, or 1033.[198] Moreover, the carryover rule will apply to any transaction between members of the same affiliated group during any taxable year for which a consolidated return is made by such group.[199]

§11.3.7 Loan Premium

The excess of the amount paid for a loan over its net book value is defined as "loan premium." A loan's net book value is equal to its face amount (the amount of the original loan, less repayments) plus any interest that has been taxed but not received, less any portion of the loan that has been charged off.[200] Loan premium is not a Code section 197 intangible; however, it is an amortizable asset.

(a) *Deducting Loan Premium*

In *Commissioner v. Seaboard Finance Company*, the taxpayer was permitted to amortize and deduct that portion of the purchase price allocated to acquired loans in excess of their net book value.[201] The taxpayer was found to have

194 I.R.C. § 197(f)(1)(A)(i).

195 I.R.C. § 197(f)(1)(A). Legislative history indicates that "the abandonment of a section 197 intangible or any other event that renders a section 197 intangible worthless is to be considered a disposition of a section 197 intangible." H.R. Conf. Rep. No. 103-213 at 685 (1993).

196 *Id.*

197 I.R.C. § 197(f)(2).

198 I.R.C. § 197(f)(2)(B)(i).

199 I.R.C. § 197(f)(2)(B)(ii).

200 *See* discussion of accrual of interest on loans in Ch. 2.

201 *Commissioner v. Seaboard Finance*, 23 T.C.M. 1512, Dec. 26,979(M), T.C. Memo. 1964-253, *aff'd*, 66-2 U.S.T.C. ¶ 9707, 367 F.2d 646 (9th Cir. 1966).

sustained its two-part burden of proof by (1) demonstrating that a premium was paid for the loans and not for goodwill or going-concern value, and (2) establishing the useful lives of the loans.

What appeared to persuade the court was the preacquisition process employed by the taxpayer to arrive at premiums paid for the loans.[202] Detailed testimony and other evidence was presented by the taxpayer at trial to describe the process known in the industry as "spreading," which was used by the taxpayer to determine the value and useful life of each loan receivable. This process demonstrated that the acquired loan contracts were not fungible, and it provided the information used to arrive at the amount offered for the loans.

The court also found that the taxpayer did not attach any significant value to whatever goodwill might have resided in the personnel employed by the seller, the seller's office locations, or the seller's trade name. However, seven factors were identified as indicating that part of the purchase price was paid for goodwill:

1. Loans were renewed from two to three times on the average;
2. Over 10 percent of Seaboard's new business came from former customers who previously repaid their loans;
3. Customers acquired by Seaboard were sold, or solicited for the purchase of, life insurance and for the use of a special check program;
4. Some of the contracts between Seaboard and the sellers contained covenants not to compete;
5. Start-up costs were avoided;
6. Many of the loan companies acquired were old established businesses; and
7. The acquired companies had a "customer structure."

Since neither party offered evidence in support of the specific amount to be allocated to goodwill, the court, applying the so-called *Cohan* rule, allocated 30 percent of the purchase price to goodwill.[203]

What distinguishes *Seaboard* from those cases in which taxpayers have not prevailed is that in *Seaboard* the calculation was used to determine the price offered for the loans. In other cases, an *ex post* determination of loan premium was pointed to as ineffectual in establishing deductible loan premium. Thus, in *Banc One Corp.*, the court stated that "[the taxpayer] did not utilize the loan 'values' as determined by [its accounting firm] in negotiating an acquisition price with [the old bank]. The loan spreading performed by [the firm]was merely a postacquisition means of allocating the purchase price among the acquired assets."[204] Similarly, in *Southern Bancorporation*, the court stated that "SBC's attempt to increase the basis of the loan portfolios is wholly *post hoc.* A purchaser must prove the purchase price; that is, the cost, at the time of sale . . . . SBC

---

[202] *Id.*

[203] *Cohan v. Commissioner*, 2 U.S.T.C. ¶489, 39 F.2d 540 (2d Cir. 1930).

[204] *Banc One Corporation v. Commissioner*, 84 T.C. 476, Dec. 4 (1985).

introduced no evidence to prove that it intended to pay an enhanced value for the loan portfolios *at the time of sale.*"[205]

(b) ***Loan Premium and Customer-Based Intangible***

Because loan premium may be attributable, at least in part, to deposit balances, it may be difficult to separate the loan premium from a Code section 197 intangible. Thus, if it is established that loan premium is attributable in whole or in part to the deposit balances maintained by the acquired bank's borrowers, it appears to be appropriate to allocate a portion of premium to the value of the customer-based intangible.[206] For example, if "compensating balances" were required to be maintained as a condition for receiving a reduced interest rate on a loan, a portion of the value of the premium may be attributable to the related deposit balances. This relationship suggests that some portion of the value of at least the linked deposits would enhance the value of the loans.

Conversely, it may be argued that the absence of any commitment to maintain deposits as a condition for receiving the loan or receiving a reduced interest rate would indicate that the value of the deposit balances relate entirely to the customer based intangible. Thus, whether the value of the deposit balance is attributable to loans or to a separate asset will depend upon a careful examination and analysis of the customer relationship as a whole. An improper allocation could affect the period over which cost is recovered. For example, cost allocated to mortgage loan premium may be recovered over a longer period than cost allocated to commercial loan premium, and cost allocated to an amortizable Code section 197 intangible would be recovered over 15 years, which would probably be a longer period than the recovery period of loans.

§ 11.3.8 Qualified Stock Purchase

(a) ***General Characteristics***

If the stock of one corporation is acquired by another corporation within a 12-month acquisition period (a qualified stock purchase), and if an election is made under Code section 338, then the transaction will be treated as a deemed acquisition of the assets of the acquired corporation. As with an actual acquisition of assets, the purchase price must be allocated to the assets deemed acquired in accordance with the provisions of Code section 1060. Further, the provisions of Code section 197 will apply to determine the amortization of any Code section 197 intangibles.

A qualified stock purchase is usually an alternative to a merger that qualifies as a Type A reorganization[207] or to a stock-for-stock acquisition that qualifies as a Type B reorganization.[208] In the case of a qualified stock purchase that resembles a Type A reorganization, the transaction will be taxable because it does not

[205] *Southern Bancorporation v. United States*, 83-1 U.S.T.C. ¶9400, *rev'd and rem'd*, 84-1 U.S.T.C. ¶9396, 732 F.2d 374 (4th Cir. 1984), *cert. denied*, 469 U.S. 1207 (1985).

[206] *Banc One Corporation v. Commissioner*, 84 T.C. 476, Dec. 4 (1985); *Commissioner v. Seaboard Finance*, 23 T.C.M. 1512, Dec. 26,979(M), T.C. Memo. 1964-253, *aff'd*, 66-2 U.S.T.C. ¶9707, 367 F.2d 646 (9th Cir. 1966).

[207] PLR 9436057, June 15, 1994.

[208] PLR 9508009, November 21, 1994.

satisfy the continuity-of-interest requirement. In the case of a qualified stock purchase that resembles a Type B reorganization, the transaction will be taxable because it does not satisfy the solely for voting stock requirement.[209]

A qualified stock purchase followed by an Code section 338 election will result in the acquired corporation being treated as having sold all of its assets at the close of the acquisition date at fair market value in a single transaction.[210] The acquired corporation is also treated as a new corporation beginning on the day after the acquisition date that purchases all of the assets that were deemed sold by the old corporation.[211] Any gain that results from the deemed sale of assets from the old corporation to the new corporation is reported on the return of the old corporation. Thus, any income is offset to the extent of the acquired corporation's net operating loss. Similarly, if the acquired corporation is a member of a consolidated group, the consolidated net operating loss of the acquired corporation's consolidated group will offset the gain on the deemed sale of assets.

(b) *Illustration: Cash Merger*

A qualified stock purchase may involve the following steps:

1. A bank subsidiary (Bank) distributes cash to its Parent BHC;
2. BHC forms an interim bank (I-Bank) to which the cash is contributed in exchange for the I-Bank stock;
3. I-Bank merges into the target bank (Target) with each share of Target's stock outstanding being canceled and each of Target's shareholders receiving cash for their shares;
4. Target merges into Bank with Bank being the surviving corporation and Target's existence terminating. Thus, the transaction would appear as diagramed on Table 11.5.

---

[209] *See* discussion of Type A reorganizations at § 11.8, and Type B reorganizations at § 11.9.

[210] I.R.C. § 338(a)(1).

[211] I.R.C. § 338(a)(2).

Table 11.5 Code Section 338: Qualified Stock Purchase

BEFORE:

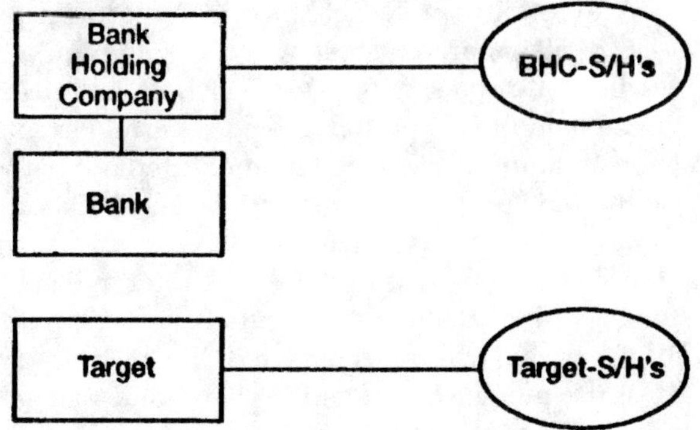

TRANSACTION: Creation of I-Bank; cash merger of I-Bank into Target and merger of Target into Bank

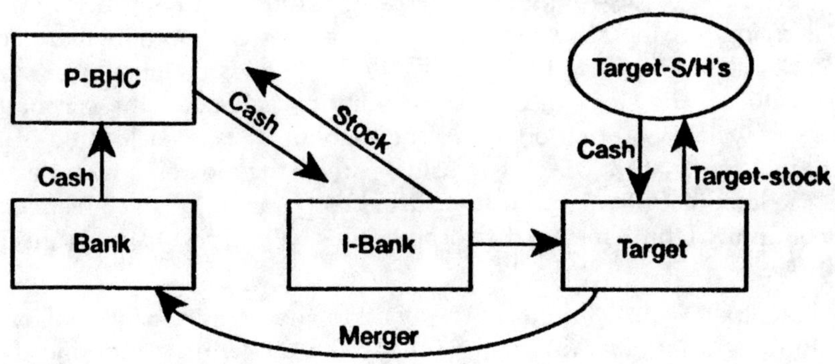

AFTER:

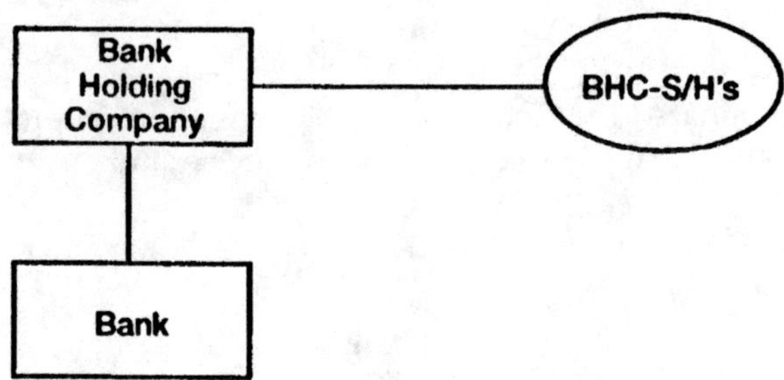

(c) ***Tax Treatment of Parties***

The formation of the I-Bank and the merger of I-Bank into Target is disregarded for federal income tax purposes. The transaction, instead, will be treated as a sale by the shareholders of Target of their Target stock to Bank in exchange for cash.[212] The purchase by BHC of all of Target's stock will constitute a qualified stock purchase within the meaning of Code section 338.[213] Each of Target shareholders will realize and recognize gain or loss on the receipt of cash in exchange for their shares of Target stock in an amount measured by the difference between the cash received and each shareholder's adjusted basis in Target stock surrendered in the exchange.[214] No gain or loss is recognized by BHC, the Bank, the I-Bank, or Target as a result of the stock purchase affected by the interim merger.[215] The BHC's basis in Target stock acquired will equal the purchase price paid for Target shareholder's stock.[216] The BHC will be considered the historic shareholder of Target for purposes of the merger of Target into Bank and will satisfy the continuity-of-interest requirement with respect to the merger of Target and Bank. Consequently, the merger of Target into the Bank will be treated as a Type A reorganization.

§ 11.4 Limitation on Loss Carryovers

Limitations are imposed by Code Section 382 on the use of pre-change tax losses of purchased "loss corporations."[217] The limitations apply in the event of a substantial change in the stock ownership of the loss corporation that occurs during a specified time period. Generally, if the ownership of more than 50 percent in value of the stock of a "loss corporation" changes, the corporation becomes a "new loss corporation," and the amount of taxable income of any "post-change year" that may be offset using "pre-change losses" cannot exceed the Code Section 382 limitation. Further, if the corporation fails to meet certain business continuity requirements, the corporation's NOL carryforwards are eliminated entirely.

On September 30, 2008, and in response to the volatile condition of the banking industry, the I.R.S. issued Notice 2008-83, which announced the following:

> For the purposes of section 382(h), any deduction properly allowed after an ownership change (as defined in section 382(g)) to a bank with respect to losses on loans or bad debts (including any deduction for a reasonable addition to a reserve for bad debts) shall not be treated as a built-in loss or a deduction that is attributable to periods before the change date.[218]

The notice effectively eliminated the Code section 382 limitation on built-in losses from loans and bad debt for banks which undergo an ownership change.[219]

---

212 Rev. Rul. 73-427, 1973-2 C.B. 301; Rev. Rul. 78-250, 1978-1 C.B. 83.

213 I.R.C. § 338(d)(3); Reg. § 1.338-2(b)(2)(ii), Ex. 2.

214 I.R.C. § 1001.

215 Rev. Rul. 73-427, 1973-2 C.B. 301.

216 I.R.C. § 1012.

217 I.R.C. § 382(a). There are similar rules for carryforwards of other items, such as tax credits, etc. *See* I.R.C. § 383.

218 2008-42 I.R.B. 905, 2008-2 C.B. 905.

219 I.R.C. § 382(h) and (m). I.R.C. § 582(a) provides that debts that are evidenced by a security are subject to the I.R.C. § 166 bad debt rules. Reg. § 1.585-2(e)(2) clarifies that a "loan means debt as

These built-in losses, which were previously treated as pre-change deductions subject to the Section 382 limitation, were then treated as post-change deductions subject to the ordinary deduction rules of Code sections 165 and 166. This new treatment allowed the acquiring bank to reduce its tax obligation. Note, however, that Notice 2008-83 did not eliminate the Code section 382 limitation on NOLs.

Subsequently, the Treasury Department issued Notices 2009-38 and Notice 2010-2, both of which relate to Code section 382 treatment of carryover losses by corporations in which the Treasury Department has acquired instruments pursuant to the Emergency Economic Stabilization Act of 2008 (EESA).[220]

Notice 2009-38 set forth guidelines relating to the calculation of when an ownership change in the corporation would occur for the purpose of ascertaining whether Code section 382 limitations on carryover losses must be applied.[221] The Notice applied to instruments other than warrants acquired by the Treasury Department through programs other than TARP CAP, and provided that debt instruments and preferred stock acquired by the Treasury Department would not be treated as stock for any purpose under Code section 382. Accordingly, when calculating whether an ownership change has taken place under Code section 382(h), a corporation may generally treat instruments held by the Treasury Department as stock options, and the stock itself will be considered outstanding for the purpose of calculating ownership percentages.[222] As a result, large-scale acquisitions of instruments in corporations by the Treasury Department would not generally affect the determination of whether a corporation has undergone an ownership change.[223]

In Notice 2010-2, the Treasury Department revisited its treatment of Code section 382 by expanding the treatment of instruments held by the Treasury Department to include warrants issued to the Treasury Department.[224] In addition, Notice 2010-2 provides that if a sale of stock held by the Treasury Department creates a public group, the public group's increase in ownership of stock due to the purchase will not be considered as having increased for the purposes calculating ownership percentages pursuant to Code section 382(h).[225] However, any sale or disbursement of stock from any source other than the Treasury

(Footnote Continued)

the term debt is used in section 166." Reg. § 1.585-2(e)(2). I.R.C. § 165(g)(2) defines a security as stock, the right to stock, or "a bond, debenture, note, or certificate, or other evidence of indebtedness, issued by a corporation or by a government or political subdivision thereof, with interest coupons or in registered form." Therefore, losses from loans include losses on mortgage-backed and asset-backed securities.

[220] *Emergency Economic Stabilization Act of 2008*, Pub. L. No. 110–343, 122 Stat 3765 (codified as amended in scattered sections of the U.S.C.).

[221] *Id.* (Under Reg. § 1.382-2T(a), an ownership change occurs when "[the corporation] is a loss corporation on a testing date and, immediately after the close of the testing date, the percentage of stock of the corporation owned by one or more 5-percent shareholders has increased by more than 50 percentage points over the lowest percentage of stock of such corporation owned by such shareholders at any time during the testing period.").

[222] *But see id.* (excluding stock purchased by the Treasury Department through CPP and S Corp. CPP from treatment as stock options).

[223] In addition, I.R.S. Notice 2009-38, 2009-18 I.R.B. 901, specifically exempted these transactions from statutory protections against intentional avoidance of loss limitations under I.R.C. § 382(l)(1).

[224] *See generally* I.R.S. Notice 2010-2, 2010-2 I.R.B. 251.

[225] *Id.*

Department to the public group will not be subject to exemption from Code section 382.[226]

Critics claimed that the Treasury Department overstepped its authority in issuing the Notices without consulting Congress, and the Notices were revoked in Section 1261 of the American Recovery and Reinvestment Act of 2009.[227] Congress found that the Treasury Department was not authorized to "provide exemptions or special rules that are restricted to particular industries or classes of taxpayers."[228] However, Congress grandfathered the provisions of Notice 2008-83 for bank acquisitions and for binding contracts for bank acquisitions occurring on or before January 16, 2009.[229]

§11.4.1 Code Section 382 Limitation

The Code Section 382 limitation is applied annually and generally equals the value of the stock of the loss corporation immediately before the ownership change multiplied by a prescribed percentage rate.[230] This limitation applies to limit the use of both net operating losses and certain built-in losses (whether capital or ordinary in character) recognized by the loss corporation after an ownership change. Such limitation for a tax year may be increased by certain items such as an unused limitation for a prior tax year or certain built-in gains recognized during the recognition period.

§11.4.2 Loss Corporations

A "loss corporation" is any corporation that is entitled to an NOL carryforward or has an NOL for the tax year in which an ownership change occurs.[231] Additionally, the term includes any corporation with a net unrealized built-in loss, except to the extent to be provided in regulations. A "new loss corporation" is a corporation that is a loss corporation after an ownership change, while an "old loss corporation" is a corporation that was a loss corporation before an ownership change. The same corporation may be both "old" and "new" loss corporations. Also, the predecessor or successor corporation of a loss corporation and the loss corporation are treated as one entity.[232] For example, if a new loss corporation liquidates and distributes its property to another corporation in a Code Section 332 transaction, the acquiring corporation will be treated as a new loss corporation.

§11.4.3 Pre-change Loss and Post-change Year

A pre-change loss is any NOL carryforward to the tax year that ends with the ownership change or in which the change occurs. It also includes any NOL of the old loss corporation for the year ending with the change that is allocable to the pre-change period in a tax year. The allocation is done, except as provided by regulations, on a daily pro rata basis. A post-change year is any tax year ending after the change date.

---

[226] I.R.S. Notice 2010-2(E).

[227] American Recovery and Reinvestment Act of 2009, Pub. L. No. 111-5, 123 Stat. 115, Section 1261.

[228] *Id.* Section 1261(a)(1).

[229] *Id.*, Section 1261(b).

[230] I.R.C. § 382(b)(1).

[231] I.R.C. § 382(k)(1). Reg. §1.382-2(a)(1).

[232] I.R.C. § 382(l)(8).

§11.4.4 Entity

For purposes of aggregating stock ownership, an entity includes corporations, estates, trusts, associations, companies, partnerships, or similar organizations.[233] A group of persons who have a formal or informal understanding among themselves to make a coordinated acquisition of stock is also an entity. Accordingly, a group of persons must be aggregated into a separate public group where, under a plan, the group owns five percent or more of a loss corporation's stock in the aggregate, even though each member of the group individually owns less than five percent of the stock. Any shift of ownership by the group must be considered in determining whether an ownership change has occurred. However, creditors who participate in the formulation of a plan for an insolvency proceeding or a bankruptcy reorganization and receive stock in exchange for debt do not constitute an entity.[234]

§11.4.5 Short Tax Year

The Code Section 382 limitation for any post-change year that is less than 365 days is the amount that bears the same ratio to the Code Section 382 limitation determined under Code Section 382(b)(1) as the number of days in the post-change year bears to 365. The Code Section 382 limitation, as so determined, is adjusted as required by Code Section 382 and the regulations thereunder. This rule does not apply to a 52-53 week tax year that is less than 365 days unless a return is required under Code Section 443 (relating to short periods) for such year.[235]

If a loss corporation has two (or more) ownership changes, any losses attributable to the period preceding the earlier ownership change are treated as pre-change losses with respect to both ownership changes. Thus, the later ownership change may result in a lesser Code Section 382 limitation with respect to such losses. The application of this rule cannot result in a greater limitation. The amount of taxable income for any post-change year that can be offset by pre-change losses may not exceed the Code Section 382 limitation for the ownership change, reduced by the amount of taxable income offset by pre-change losses subject to any earlier ownership change or changes.[236]

§11.4.6 Net Operating Loss Carryovers: Built-in Gain and Loss

There are limitations on the use of built-in loss of an old loss corporation and relief for built-in gain of such a corporation. In general, if the old loss corporation has net unrealized built-in loss, any such loss recognized within the five-year period beginning on the change date and ending at the close of the fifth post-change year (the "recognition period") is treated as a pre-change loss and, as such, is subject to the Section 382 limitation. On the other side of the coin, if a loss corporation has net unrealized built-in gain, the Section 382 limitation is increased by any such gain recognized within the recognition period.[237]

---

233 Reg. § 1.382-3(a)(1).

234 Reg. § 1.382-3(a)(1).

235 Reg. § 1.382-5(c).

236 Reg. § 1.382-5(d).

237 I.R.C. § 382(h)(1).

If there is an installment sale of a built-in gain asset either before or during the recognition period and income is reported under the installment method, Code Section 382 will continue to apply to gain recognized from the installment sale after the recognition period.[238] Similar treatment is provided for a gain recognized on the disposition of such installment obligation. This rule applies to a situation where a corporation transfers a built-in gain asset to an affiliated corporation where gain is deferred under consolidated return regulations[239] and, before the expiration of the recognition period, the affiliated corporation sells the built-in gain asset and reports income from the sale under the installment method. Thus, the recognized gain will cause an increase in the Code Section 382 limitation for the year of payment, provided that such an increase is otherwise permitted if, solely for purposes of such recognized gain, the recognition period is extended through the date of the last installment payment (or the date of the disposition of the installment obligation).

§ 11.4.7 Net Unrealized Built-in Gain or Loss

A net unrealized built-in gain (NUBIG) is the amount by which the fair market value of the corporation's assets just prior to the ownership change exceeds the aggregate adjusted basis of those assets at that time. Similarly, a net unrealized built-in loss (NUBIL) is the amount by which the aggregate adjusted basis of the assets exceeds the fair market value of those assets.[240] In computing either of these amounts, the value of the corporation's assets does not include (1) cash or cash items or (2) marketable securities that have not declined or appreciated substantially in value.[241] It also includes intangible assets, such as goodwill. If a redemption or other corporate contraction occurs in connection with an ownership change, the determination of NUBIG or NUBIL is made after taking the redemption or contraction into account.

§ 11.4.8 Taxable Year of Net Unrealized Built-in Loss

To address difficulties associated with determining the tax year in which a NUBIL accrues to a loss corporation which is a component member of a controlled group, Treasury Regulation § 1.382-8(b)(2) sets forth an irrebuttable presumption that certain built-in losses are attributable to a period before a particular tax year. The presumption applies to a loss corporation that had an ownership change prior to the first day of the tax year at issue that caused its NUBILs to become subject to a Code Section 382 limitation. Under the presumption, any built-in loss in such an asset is considered to be attributable to a period prior to the tax year at issue to the extent that the built-in loss in that asset existed on the previous change date.

§ 11.4.9 Recognized Built-in Gain or Loss

Recognition of built-in gain or loss triggers the relief or limitation, respectively, provided under these rules. Recognized built-in gain ("RBIG") is any gain recognized during the recognition period from the disposition of an asset to the

---

[238] Notice 90-27, 1990-1 C.B. 336.

[239] Reg. § 1.1502-13.

[240] I.R.C. § 382(h)(3).

[241] I.R.C. § 382(h)(3)(B)(ii).

extent that the new loss corporation can establish that (1) the asset was held by the old loss corporation immediately before the change date and (2) the gain is no larger than the amount by which the fair market value of the asset on the change date exceeds the asset's adjusted basis on that date.[242] The increase in the Section 382 limitation cannot exceed the NUBIG reduced by RBIG for prior years ending in the recognition period.

Temporary regulations clarify that prepaid income is not RBIG for purposes of Code Section 382(h). Prepaid income is defined as any amount received prior to the change date that is attributable to performance occurring on or after the change date. Examples of prepaid income include, but are not limited to, income received prior to the change date that is deferred under the Code Section 455 prepaid subscription income rules.[243]

Recognized built-in loss (RBIL) is any loss recognized during the same period except to the extent that the new loss corporation establishes that (1) the asset was not held by the old loss corporation immediately before the change date and (2) the loss is larger than the amount by which the asset's adjusted basis exceeds its fair market value on the change date.[244] Such losses are subject to the limitation (i.e., treated as pre-change losses) for any year only to the extent that they do not exceed the NUBIL reduced by RBIL for prior years ending in the recognition period. If a deduction is denied for any RBIL in any post-change year, the loss is carried forward to subsequent years under rules similar to the NOL carryforward rules and is subject to limitation as a pre-change loss.[245]

In the case of one transaction, or a series of related transactions during any 12-month period, in which 80 percent or more (by value) of the stock of a corporation is acquired, the fair market value of the corporation's assets, for purposes of determining NUBIL, cannot exceed the grossed up amount paid for the stock, as adjusted for the corporation's debt and other relevant items.[246]

Built-in depreciation may be included in a new corporation's RBILs. Thus, the RBILs that arise out of a new corporation's disposition of an asset include depreciation, amortization, or depletion for the excess of an asset's adjusted basis on the date of an ownership change over the asset's fair market value on that date.

§11.4.10 Threshold Requirement

The treatment of built-in gain and loss often requires the valuation of a corporation's assets. To alleviate the difficulty of accurately valuing assets (including goodwill and other intangible assets), a threshold requirement states that the NUBIG or NUBIL of an old loss corporation is zero unless such gain or loss

---

[242] I.R.C. § 382(h)(2)(A).

[243] Reg. §1.451-5, or Rev. Proc. 2004-34, 2004-1 C.B. 991 (or any successor revenue procedure). This rule applies to loss corporations that have undergone an ownership change on or after June 14, 2007. Its applicability, however, expires on June 14, 2010 (Temp. Reg. § 1.382-7T). The IRS has indicated that the I.R.C. § 338 approach described in Notice 2003-65, 2003-2 C.B. 747, will be applied consistently with these temporary regulations (T.D. 9330, 2007-31 I.R.B. 239).

[244] I.R.C. § 382(h)(2)(A).

[245] I.R.C. § 382(h)(4).

[246] I.R.C. § 382(h)(8).

exceeds the lesser of $10,000,000 or 15 percent of the fair market value of the old loss corporation just before the ownership change.[247]

§ 11.4.11 Calculating RBIL and RBIG

The IRS has issued guidance setting forth two alternative approaches for the identification of built-in items for purposes of Code Section 382(h), the Code Section 1374 approach, and the Code Section 338 approach.[248] Taxpayers can rely on this guidance pending the issuance of regulations implementing Code Section 382(h). Taxpayers may use either the Code Section 1374 approach or the Code Section 338 approach, but not elements of both. Although the approaches serve as safe harbors, they are not the exclusive methods by which a taxpayer may identify built-in items; other methods will be examined on a case-by-case basis.[249]

(a) *The Code Section 1374 Approach*

Under the Code Section 1374 approach, the amount of gain or loss recognized during the recognition period on the sale or exchange of an asset owned on the change date is RBIG or RBIL, respectively, subject to the limitations described in Code Section 382(h)(2)(A) or (B). The sum of the RBIG or RBIL (including deductions that are treated as RBIL, as described below) attributable to an asset cannot exceed the unrealized built-in gain or loss in that asset on the change date. With respect to gain from sales reported under the Code Section 453 installment method, the Code Section 1374 approach follows the Code Section 1374 regulations.[250]

In cases other than sales and exchanges, the Code Section 1374 approach generally relies on the accrual method of accounting to identify income or deduction items as RBIG or RBIL, respectively. Under this approach, items of income or deduction properly included in income or allowed as a deduction during the recognition period are considered "attributable to periods before the change date" under Code Section 382(h)(6)(A) and (B) and, thus, are treated as RBIG or RBIL, respectively, if an accrual method taxpayer would have included the item in income or been allowed a deduction for the item before the change date.[251]

In general, the Code Section 1374 approach does not treat income from a built-in gain asset during the recognition period as RBIG because such income

---

247 I.R.C. § 382(h)(3)(B).

248 Notice 2003-65 modifies Notice 87-79, 1987-2 C.B. 387, in which the IRS has announced that it anticipates that regulations under I.R.C. § 382 would permit income from a discharge of indebtedness that is integrally related to a transaction resulting in an ownership change to be allocated to the pre-change period.

249 Notice 2003-65, 2003-2 C.B. 747.

250 *See* Reg. § 1.1374-4(h)) and Notice 90-27, 1990-1 C.B. 336, which treat built-in gain recognized from installment sales that occur before or during the recognition period as RBIG, even if recognized after the recognition period. In addition, as set forth in Notice 90-27, if a corporation transfers a built-in gain asset to an affiliated corporation, the gain is deferred under the consolidated return regulations, and, before the close of the recognition period, the affiliated corporation sells the built-in gain asset in a sale reportable under the installment method, such deferred gain is RBIG when such gain is taken into account by the selling or distributing member, and will cause an increase in the Section 382 limitation for the taxable year of payment, even if the gain is taken into account after the recognition period.

251 However, for purposes of determining whether an item is RBIL, I.R.C. § 461(h)(2)(C) and Reg. § 1.461-4(g) (concerning certain liabilities for which payment is economic performance) do not apply (*see* Reg. §§ 1.1374-4(b)(1) and (2)).

did not accrue before the change date. The Code Section 1374 approach departs from the tax accrual rule and the regulations under Code Section 1374 in its treatment of amounts allowable as depreciation, amortization, or depletion (collectively, "amortization") deductions during the recognition period. In accordance with the second sentence of Code Section 382(h)(2)(B), except to the extent the loss corporation establishes that the amount is not attributable to the excess of an asset's adjusted basis over its fair market value on the change date, these amounts are treated as RBIL, regardless of whether they accrued for tax purposes before the change date. A loss corporation may use any reasonable method to establish that the amortization deduction amount is not attributable to an asset's built-in loss on the change date. One acceptable method is to compare the amount of the amortization deduction actually allowed to the amount of such deduction that would have been allowed had the loss corporation purchased the asset for its fair market value on the change date. The amount by which the amount of the actual amortization deduction does not exceed the amount of the hypothetical amortization deduction is not RBIL.

Finally, the Code Section 1374 approach generally treats as RBIG or RBIL any income or deduction item properly taken into account during the first 12 months of the recognition period as discharge of indebtedness income (COD income) that is included in gross income or as a bad debt deduction under Code Section 166 if the item arises from a debt owed by or to the loss corporation at the beginning of the recognition period.[252] Any reduction of tax basis under Code Secs. 108(b)(5) and 1017(a) that occurs as a result of COD income realized within the first 12 months of the recognition period is treated as having occurred immediately before the ownership change for purposes of determining whether a recognized gain or loss is an RBIG or an RBIL under Code Section 382(h)(2). However, the reduction of tax basis does not affect the loss corporation's NUBIG or NUBIL under Code Section 382(h)(3).[253]

(b) *The Code Section 338 Approach*

The other approach that may be used to identify items of RBIG and RBIL is the Code Section 338 approach.[254] This approach identifies such items generally by comparing the loss corporation's actual items of income, gain, deduction, and loss with those that would have resulted if a Code Section 338 election had been made with respect to a hypothetical purchase of all of the outstanding stock of the loss corporation on the change date (the hypothetical purchase). As a result, unlike under the Code Section 1374 approach, under the Code Section 338 approach, built-in gain assets may be treated as generating RBIG even if they are not disposed of at a gain during the recognition period, and deductions for

---

[252] *See* Reg. § 1.1374-4(f).

[253] As suggested above, the treatment of COD income under the I.R.C. § 1374 approach differs from the treatment of that item as described in Notice 87-79, which treats COD income that is "integrally related to an ownership change" but is recognized after the ownership change as RBIG. Taxpayers that otherwise follow the I.R.C. § 1374 approach may apply the rules described in Notice 87-79, rather than the rules included in the I.R.C. § 1374 approach, to COD income for ownership changes that occur before September 12, 2003, but may not rely on the rules described in Notice 87-79 for ownership changes that occur on or after September 12, 2003.

[254] Notice 2003-65, 2003-2 C.B. 747.

liabilities, in particular contingent liabilities, that exist on the change date may be treated as RBIL.

For purposes of identifying those items that would have resulted had a Code Section 338 election been made with respect to the hypothetical purchase, after the hypothetical purchase, the loss corporation is treated as using those accounting methods that the loss corporation actually uses. With respect to gain from sales reported under the Code Section 453 installment method, the Code Section 338 approach treats built-in gain recognized from installment sales that occur before or during the recognition period as RBIG, even if recognized after the recognition period.[255]

The Code Section 338 approach assumes that, for any taxable year, an asset that had a built-in gain on the change date generates income equal to the cost recovery deduction that would have been allowed for such asset under the applicable Code Section if an election under Code Section 338 had been made with respect to the hypothetical purchase. Therefore, with respect to an asset that had a built-in gain on the change date, the Code Section 338 approach treats as RBIG an amount equal to the excess of the cost recovery deduction that would have been allowable with respect to such asset had an election under Code Section 338 been made for the hypothetical purchase over the loss corporation's actual allowable cost recovery deduction. The cost recovery deduction that would have been allowed to the loss corporation had an election under Code Section 338 been made with respect to the hypothetical purchase will be based on the asset's fair market value on the change date and a cost recovery period that begins on the change date. The excess amount is RBIG, regardless of the loss corporation's gross income in any particular taxable year during the recognition period.

For loss corporations with a NUBIL, the Code Section 338 approach treats as RBIL certain deductions of the loss corporation. In particular, with respect to an asset that has a built-in loss on the change date, the Code Section 338 approach treats as RBIL the excess of the loss corporation's actual allowable cost recovery deduction over the cost recovery deduction that would have been allowable to the loss corporation with respect to such asset had an election under Code Section 338 been made with respect to the hypothetical purchase. The Code Section 338 approach treats a deduction for the payment of a liability that is contingent on the change date as RBIL to the extent of the estimated liability on the change date.

Under the Code Section 338 approach, COD income that is included in gross income and that is attributable to any pre-change debt of the loss corporation is RBIG in an amount not exceeding the excess, if any, of the adjusted issue price of

---

[255] Notice 90-27, 1990-1 C.B. 336. In addition, the I.R.C. § 338 approach follows Notice 90-27 in cases in which a corporation transfers a built-in gain asset to an affiliated corporation, the gain is deferred under the consolidated return regulations, and, before the close of the recognition period, the affiliated corporation sells the built-in gain asset in a sale reportable under the installment method. In such cases, the deferred gain is RBIG when it is taken into account by the selling or distributing member, even if the gain is taken into account after the recognition period.

the discharged debt over the fair market value of the debt on the change date. The Code Section 338 approach treats a reduction of tax basis under Code Sections 108(b)(5) and 1017(a) that occurs during the recognition period as having occurred immediately before the ownership change for purposes of Code Section 382(h)(2) to the extent of the excess, if any, of the adjusted issue price of the debt over the fair market value of the debt on the change date. However, the reduction of tax basis does not affect the loss corporation's NUBIG or NUBIL under Code Section 382(h)(3).[256]

§ 11.4.12 Ownership Changes

There are two kinds of ownership changes that can trigger the income limitation on corporate NOL carryforwards: (1) an owner shift involving a "five-percent shareholder" and (2) any "equity structure shift." The limitations are applicable if, immediately after an ownership change of either type, the percentage of stock of the new loss corporation owned by one or more five-percent shareholders has increased by more than 50 percentage points (by value) over the lowest percentage of the old loss corporation's stock owned by the same shareholders at any time during the testing period, which generally is the three-year period ending on the day of the shift.

The determination of stock ownership percentages is made by comparing the fair market value of stock owned by a person to the fair market value of a corporation's outstanding stock.[257] Any change in proportionate ownership resulting solely from market fluctuations in the relative fair market values will be ignored.

Loss corporations must determine whether an ownership change has occurred immediately after an ownership shift or equity shift has occurred.[258] Such a determination must also be made if an option for stock in a loss corporation is either (1) transferred to, or by, a five-percent shareholder (or a shareholder who would be a five-percent shareholder if the option were exercised), or (2) issued by the corporation, a first-tier entity that owns five-percent or more of the corporation, or a higher tier entity that owns five-percent or more of a first-tier entity or other higher-tier entity.[259] No determination has to be made if an equity structure shift does not also result in an ownership shift, or if a transfer of stock has been made either (1) in trust, (2) to a spouse, (3) to satisfy a person's right to a pecuniary bequest, (4) as a gift, (5) due to a divorce or separation, or (6) due to someone's death.[260]

To ensure that the IRS is informed of ownership changes, loss corporations are required to file a statement with their income tax return for each tax year in which they are a loss corporation in which an ownership change occurs.[261]

---

[256] As with the I.R.C. § 1374 approach, taxpayers that otherwise follow the I.R.C. § 338 approach may apply the rules described in Notice 87-79, rather than the rules included in the I.R.C. § 338 approach to COD income for ownership changes that occur before September 12, 2003, but may not rely on the rules of Notice 87-79 for ownership changes that occur on or after September 12, 2003.

[257] Reg. § 1.382-2T(f)(18)(i).

[258] Temp. Reg. § 1.382-2T(a)(1).

[259] Temp. Reg. § 1.382-2T(a)(2)(i), Temp. Reg. § 1.382-2T(f)(9) and (14).

[260] Temporary Reg. § 1.382-2T(a)(2)(i)(B).

[261] Reg. § 1.382-11(a).

§11.4.13 Owner Shift Involving Five-Percent Shareholders

An owner shift involving a five-percent shareholder consists of any change in the ownership of a corporation's stock that results in a change in the percentage of stock in the corporation owned by any person who is a five-percent shareholder before or after the change. For purposes of determining whether an ownership change has occurred, all shareholders holding less than five percent of the corporation's stock are aggregated and treated as one five-percent shareholder. The change in a shareholder's percentage share of stock must be determined by comparing how much stock he holds on the test date for ownership change with the lowest percentage of stock he held during the three-year testing period.[262] If a shareholder holds a 10-percent interest at the beginning of the testing period, sells his entire interest at midpoint, and purchases a 10-percent interest before the test date, there has been an ownership change of 10 percent in his interest.

Owner shifts include purchases or dispositions of loss corporation stock by a five-percent shareholder, and any of the following transactions if they affect the percentage ownership of a five-percent shareholder: (1) transfers to controlled corporations; (2) redemptions or recapitalizations; (3) issues of loss corporation stock; and, (4) equity structure shifts.[263] Transfers of shares between persons who are not five-percent shareholders are not considered.

Example 1: Assume that on January 1, Minus Corp. is publicly traded and no shareholder owns five percent or more of the stock. On September 1, A, B and C, who previously were not shareholders (and to whom no stock was attributed because of any relationship with a shareholder), each buy one-third of Minus Corp.'s stock. An ownership change has occurred because A, B, and C each became five-percent shareholders who in the aggregate increased their holdings by more than 50 percent from what they were at any time in the three years prior to September 1.

The following persons or entities are treated as five-percent shareholders.[264]

1. Individuals who directly or indirectly (i.e., through ownership in an entity) own five percent or more of the stock in a loss corporation.
2. Shareholders, whether individuals or entities, who own less than a five-percent indirect interest in a loss corporation but hold their interest through an entity that owns a five-percent or more interest in the corporation. These shareholders are treated as members of a "public group."
3. Individuals or entities who own less than a five-percent direct interest in a loss corporation but who are treated as a public group. They are treated as a public group even if the cumulative interest of the group never reaches five percent. A public group in category (2) that fails to reach the five-percent level is treated as part of the public group in category (3).

---

[262] Temp. Reg. §1.382-2T(c).

[263] Temporary Reg. §1.382-2T(e)(1).

[264] *See* Temp. Reg. §1.382-2T(f)(9), (11), (13), and (14), Temp. Reg. §1.382-2T(g)(1), and Temporary Reg. §1.382-2T(j).

There are several situations in which a category (3) group may be split into two public groups, each of which is treated as a five-percent shareholder.[265] This will occur if (1) there is an equity structure shift that qualifies as a tax-free reorganization, (2) there has been a nontaxable exchange of the loss corporation's stock for property, (3) the loss corporation has sold property to acquire its own stock (e.g., cash redemption), (4) there is a deemed acquisition of stock in the loss corporation because an individual or entity owns a right to acquire the stock (e.g., convertible debentures), or (5) an entity or individual who owns a five-percent or more direct interest in a loss corporation transfers a direct ownership interest to a member of a category (3) group. One public group will be composed of persons who were shareholders prior to one of these transactions, while the other public group (i.e., the new public group) will be made up of persons who became shareholders as a result of the transaction (e.g., an individual who becomes a shareholder as a result of an equity shift). If more than one of these transactions has occurred and, therefore, has caused the formation of several new public groups in the same tax year, public groups with less than a five-percent ownership interest in a loss corporation may be combined.

In determining whether an owner shift involving five-percent shareholders occurred, the IRS ruled that an investment advisor who had the power to acquire, hold, vote and dispose of the common stock of the parent of an affiliated group, but did not have economic ownership, was not the economic owner of the stock. Further, affiliated organizations that were the economic owners did not constitute an entity, within the meaning of Treasury Regulation § 1.382-3(a)(1), because neither their investment adviser's power over the stock nor the fact that the organizations had common officers or directors resulted in the creation of an entity.[266]

§ 11.4.14 Equity Structure Shift

An equity structure shift is any tax-free reorganization other than a Type "D" or Type "G" reorganization (unless in the Type "D" or Type "G" reorganizations substantially all of the assets of the transferor are acquired and the transferor corporation distributes the stock, securities, and other property it receives) or a "F" reorganization involving a mere change in form or identity of one corporation. In order to determine whether an equity structure shift has resulted in an ownership change, the rule for aggregating less-than-five-percent shareholders in the case of an owner shift (see above) applies separately to each group of shareholders of each corporation involved in the equity structure shift.

Example 2: Assume that Minus Corp. and Piranha Corp. are both publicly traded corporations and that no shareholder owns as much as five percent of either corporation. Assume further that on January 1, Minus merges into Piranha, which survives the merger, and that no shareholder of

[265] Temp. Reg. § 1.382-2T(j)(2) and (3).

[266] IRS Letter Ruling 9725039.

post-merger Piranha owns as much as five percent of its stock. During the merger, the former Minus shareholders receive 30 percent of Piranha's stock, and the remaining Piranha stock is owned by Piranha shareholders. Because the percentage of stock held by former Minus shareholders is more than 50 percentage points less than their prior holdings (100 percent of Minus - 30 percent of Piranha), there has been an ownership change.

Example 3: Assume the same facts as in Example 2, above, except that former Minus shareholders receive 70 percent of Piranha stock. In this case, no more ownership change would have occurred because the decrease in the holdings of the Minus shareholders is only 30 percent.

§11.4.15 Multiple Transactions

Because the occurrence of an ownership change is determined by reference to stock ownership during a testing period, a series of transactions consisting of both owner shifts involving five-percent shareholders and equity structure shifts may constitute an ownership change. In determining whether such a change results from a transaction following an owner shift or equity structure shift that did not itself cause a change, stock acquisitions following the initial shift are treated as made proportionately from all shareholders just prior to the acquisition, unless a different proportion is established.

Example 4: Assume that Minus Corp. and Grab Corp. are both widely held and that no shareholder of either corporation owns as much as five percent of the corporation's stock. On January 1, the corporations merge in a tax-free transaction and Grab shareholders receive 49 percent of Minus Corp.'s stock. On July 1, Mr. Bart, an individual who never owned stock in either corporation, purchases five percent of Minus Corp.'s stock from Minus Corp. shareholders who held the stock prior to the merger.

The merger does not constitute an ownership change because Minus Corp. shareholders held 51 percent of the stock after the merger; thus, the aggregate interests of these shareholders has not declined (during the testing period) by more than 50 percentage points from their 100-percent ownership during the pre-merger portion of the testing period. However, Mr. Bart's purchase constitutes an owner shift because he owns at least five percent after the purchase. Further, this purchase results in a more than 50-percent owner shift because he and Grab Corp. shareholders own 54 percent of Minus Corp.'s stock, and this is more than 50 percentage points greater than the zero-percent interests of these shareholders during the portion of the testing period prior to the merger and the purchase.

§11.4.16 Testing Periods

If there has been an ownership change, the testing period for a subsequent ownership change does not begin before the first day following the testing period, generally three years ending on the day of any owner shift involving a five-percent shareholder or equity structure shift, for the first ownership change. Under a special rule, the testing period is shortened if losses arise after the three-year period begins, and does not begin before the earlier of the first day of either

(1) the first tax year from which there is a carryforward to the first tax year ending after a test day, or (2) the tax year in which the test date occurs.[267] But, if the loss corporation has a net unrealized built-in loss on a test day, the shorter period may not be claimed unless the corporation establishes the tax year in which the loss first accrued. Then the testing period may not start before the earlier of either the first day of the tax year in which the loss first accrued, or the first day in categories (1) and (2) above.

§ 11.4.17 Stock Ownership Rules

On the test date for determining stock ownership, a loss corporation must determine the stock ownership of (1) individual shareholders who own a direct interest of five percent or more in the corporation, (2) entities that own a five-percent or more direct interest (i.e., first-tier entities), (3) entities that own a five-percent or more direct interest in a first-tier entity or other higher-tier entity, and (4) individuals who own a five-percent or more direct interest in a first-tier or higher-tier entity.[268]

To ease a corporation's burden in establishing a five-percent shareholder's identity, the IRS permits a loss corporation whose stock is registered with the Securities and Exchange Commission under Rule 13d-1(d) of Regulation 13D-G to rely on information contained in Schedules 13D and 13G filed with the commission. A corporation may not rely on these schedules if it has identifying information that is inconsistent with information on the schedules. In establishing the identity of owners of first-tier or higher-tier entities, a corporation may rely on a statement signed by an officer, director, partner, trustee, or executor under penalties of perjury. The statement may not be used if an entity has either a direct or indirect ownership interest in the corporation of 50 percent or more or if the corporation knows that the statement is false.

Generally, the constructive ownership rules of Code Section 318 regarding attribution of stock ownership to and from family members, estates, trusts, partnerships and corporations apply in determining stock ownership for purposes of the NOL limitations. All family members are treated as one shareholder for purposes of the NOL carryforward limitations. Stock owned by a corporation is attributed to a corporation shareholder on a pro rata basis even if the shareholder does not own 50 percent or more of the corporation's stock, as is required under Code Section 318.[269] Stock attributed from a partnership, estate, trust or corporation to a partner, beneficiary or shareholder is not treated as being held by the entity.[270]

Because stock owned by an entity such as a corporation or a partnership is attributed to its shareholders or partners, if a corporation makes a pro rata distribution of an interest in a loss corporation to its shareholders, that distribution does not need to be taken into account in determining whether there has been an ownership change. The same would be true for similar distributions

---

[267] Reg. § 1.382-2T(d).

[268] Reg. § 1.382-2T(k)(3).

[269] Reg. § 1.382-2T(h)(2)(i)(B).

[270] Reg. § 1.382-2T(h)(2)(i)(A) and Reg. § 1.382-2T(h)(3).

from partnerships, estates and trusts. Because the regulations under Code Section 318 except qualified trusts from the general rules of attribution, distributions of interests in a loss corporation from a qualified trust do not give rise to an ownership change. The Code Section 382 regulations specifically provide that such a distribution does not cause the distribution date to be a testing date. In addition, for testing dates on or after the date of a distribution from a qualified trust, the distributed ownership interest is treated as having been acquired by the distributee on the date and in the manner acquired by the trust, and not as having been acquired or disposed of by the trust. Further, in determining which ownership interests have been distributed, the loss corporation must account for all dispositions of such interests by the qualified trust either by specifically identifying the ownership interests disposed of or by using a FIFO method.[271]

Holders of stock options that have not been exercised will be treated as owners of the stock on the testing date for ownership changes if the exercise of these options would create an ownership change.[272] An option to acquire an option, a warrant, a convertible debt instrument, an instrument other than debt that is convertible into stock, a put, a stock interest subject to risk of forfeiture, and a contract to acquire or sell stock are treated as options to acquire stock. Among the options that may not be treated as exercised are options on stock that have been held by the same five-percent shareholder for at least three years and that are actively traded on an established securities market, and options that are exercisable only upon death, complete disability or incompetency.[273]

The actual exercise of an option may be ignored if it occurs immediately before or after an ownership change. Even if the entire option is not exercised, it will be treated as fully exercised. If an option is exercised within 120 days after the day on which the option is treated as exercised, a loss corporation may elect to recognize only the stock that is actually purchased through the exercised option. Loss corporations may file amended returns to change their carryforward limitation if an option that has been treated as exercised lapses without being exercised, or if the owner of an option irrevocably forfeits his right to exercise the option. Options do not have to be treated as exercised if on the testing date for ownership change the pre-change losses of a loss corporation are *de minimis* (i.e., the losses are less than double the corporation's carryforward limitation).

Stock transferred by gift, from a decedent, pursuant to a divorce or separation instrument (as defined in the rules of Code Section 71 relating to alimony), or in satisfaction of a pecuniary bequest is not taken into account in determining whether an ownership change has occurred. The person holding such stock is treated as owning it during the time that it was held by the person from whom it was acquired. Furthermore, the same type of stock ownership that is disregarded if stock is owned directly must be disregarded if it is owned constructively.[274]

---

[271] Reg. § 1.382-10; *see also* T.D. 9269, 2006-30 I.R.B. 92, and T.D. 9063, 2003-2 C.B. 510.

[272] I.R.C. § 382(l)(3)(A) and (k)(6)(B), and Reg. § 1.382-2T(h)(4).

[273] Reg. § 1.382-2T(h)(4)(x).

[274] I.R.C. § 382(l)(3)(A)(v).

§ 11.4.18 Disregarded Stock

Certain preferred, nonparticipating stock is not taken into account in determining whether an ownership change has occurred, though it is a factor in determining the value of a loss corporation. Thus, stock is disregarded if it (1) does not entitle its holder to vote, (2) is limited and preferred as to dividends and does not participate in corporate growth to any significant extent, (3) has redemption and liquidation rights that do not exceed paid-in capital by more than a reasonable redemption premium, and (4) is not convertible to any other class of stock.

Stock is also disregarded if (1) the only reason that it fails to fall within the foregoing categories is that a holder is entitled to vote because of dividend arrearages,[275] or (2) the stock is not likely to participate in a corporation's future growth, an ownership change occurs as a result of the stock being disregarded, and the amount of a corporation's pre-change losses is not *de minimis* (i.e., its pre-change loss is double the amount of its carryforward limitation, namely the pre-change value of its stock multiplied by the long-term tax-exempt rate). On the other hand, disregarded stock may be treated as stock if it stands to significantly participate in a corporation's growth, the treatment results in an ownership change, and a corporation's pre-change losses are not *de minimis*.[276] This stock is also counted in calculating the pre-change value of a loss corporation.

§ 11.4.19 Options

Stock options can affect whether a loss corporation has an ownership change that would subject it to the annual limitation on the use of certain losses.[277] An option is treated as exercised on the date of its issuance or transfer if, on that date, it satisfies either an ownership, control or income test.[278]

The ownership test is satisfied if a principal purpose of the issuance, transfer or structuring of an option is to avoid or ameliorate the impact of an ownership change by providing the holder of the option, prior to its exercise or transfer, with a substantial portion of the attributes of ownership of the underlying stock.[279]

The control test requires that a principal purpose of the issuance, transfer or structuring of an option is to avoid or ameliorate the impact of an ownership change and that the holder of the option, and any persons related to the option holder, have, in the aggregate, more than a 50-percent direct and indirect ownership interest in the loss corporation.[280]

An option meets the income test if a principal purpose of its issuance, transfer or structuring is to avoid or ameliorate the impact of an ownership change by facilitating the creation of income or value prior to its exercise or transfer.[281]

---

275 Reg. § 1.382-2T(f)(18)(i).

276 *See* Reg. § 1.382-2T(f)(18).

277 Temp. Reg. § 1.382-2T(h)(4) and Reg. § 1.382-4.

278 Reg. § 382-4(d)(2)(i).

279 Reg. § 1.382-4(d)(3).

280 Reg. § 1.382-4(d)(4).

281 Reg. § 1.382-4(d)(5).

An option is also treated as exercised if a principal purpose of its issuance or transfer is abusive, although the review under this standard is not limited to the transfer, issuance, or structuring purposes.[282] Evidence of an abusive principal purpose must be determined based on a series of factors that exemplify circumstances that may be probative under the ownership, control, and income tests. The weight to be accorded these factors is dependent on the facts and circumstances, and a presumption is not created because of the presence or absence of any of these factors.

The following options are not treated as exercised under the ownership, control or income tests: (1) typical contracts to acquire stock that are closed on a change date within one year after they are entered into, (2) options that are part of security arrangements in typical lending transactions, (3) certain compensatory options, (4) certain options exercisable only upon death, disability, mental incompetency, or retirement, and (5) certain rights of first refusal.[283]

Included in the definition of options are certain interests that are similar to an option, such as warrants, convertible debt instruments, contracts to acquire or sell stock,[284] private placement memorandum,[285] and agreements to redeem stock.[286]

§ 11.4.20 Worthless Stock

The net operating losses of an old loss corporation may not be carried over to a new loss corporation if the stock of a 50-percent shareholder in the old loss corporation had been treated by the shareholder as worthless during the testing period.[287] The shareholder must have owned 50-percent or more of the stock at any time during the three-year period that ends on the last day of the tax year in which the stock is treated as worthless. This rule prevents a double tax benefit -- one from the worthless stock deduction that may be claimed by the shareholder, another from the deductions for net operating loss carryovers that the new loss corporation may claim against its income.[288] Worthless stock is excluded from a determination of whether the old loss corporation has undergone an ownership change. The shareholder is treated as if he did not own his worthless old loss corporation stock in the tax year in which the stock became worthless. Rather, he is treated as having acquired his stock on the first day of the next tax year. Consequently, there is no ownership change, and no old loss corporation net operating loss to carry forward.

§ 11.4.21 Mutual Funds

An open-end regulated investment company (mutual fund) is not subject to the segregation of stock ownership rules regarding the issuance or redemption of stock that is redeemable upon demand of the shareholder if that issuance or redemption occurs in the ordinary course of business.[289]

---

[282] Reg. § 1.382-4(d)(6).

[283] Reg. § 1.382-4(d)(7).

[284] Reg. § 1.382-2T(h)(4)(v); IRS Letter Ruling 9345045.

[285] IRS Letter Ruling 9330027.

[286] IRS Letter Ruling 9113032.

[287] I.R.C. § 382(g)(4)(D).

[288] I.R.C. § 165(g)(2).

[289] Reg. § 1.382-3(k) and Temp. Reg. § 1.382-2T(j)(2)(iii)(A).

§11.4.22 Separate Accounting

Pre-change losses that are succeeded to and taken into account by an acquiring corporation in a Code Section 381(a) tax-attribute-carryover transaction (i.e., subsidiary liquidations under Code Section 332 and certain Code Section 368 reorganizations) must be accounted for separately from losses and credits of the acquiring corporation.[290] The separate tracking of owner shifts of the stock of an acquiring corporation with respect to the net operating loss carryovers and other attributes ends when a fold-in event occurs. A fold-in event is either an ownership change of the distributor or transferor corporation in connection with, or after, the transaction to which Code Section 381(a) applies, or a period of five consecutive years following the Code Section 381(a) transaction during which the distributor or transferor corporation has not had an ownership change. Starting on the day after the earlier of the change date (but not earlier than the day of the Code Section 381(a) transaction) or the last day of the five consecutive year period, the losses and other attributes of the distributor or transferor corporation are treated as losses and attributes of the acquiring corporation for purposes of determining whether an ownership change occurs with respect to such losses.[291]

§11.4.23 Seized Financial Corporations

In response to the federal government's takeover of Fannie Mae, Freddie Mac and other financial corporations, Treasury and the IRS stated that they will preserve these entities' tax losses under Code Section 382(m) in future regulations. Loss preservation will be accomplished by disregarding the testing dates that generally would have applied after a takeover.[292] An earlier similar announcement was made immediately after the government seized control of Fannie Mae and Freddie Mac.[293]

Regulations will be issued that provide that the date as of the close of which the U.S. government directly or indirectly owns a more-than-50-percent interest in a loss corporation will not be considered a testing date for purposes of determining whether an ownership change has occurred under Code Section 382. The loss corporation will be required to determine whether there is a testing date (and, if so, whether there has been an ownership change) on any date as of the close of which the U.S. does not own a more-than-50-percent interest in the corporation. A more-than-50-percent interest is stock with more than 50 percent of the total value of all stock classes (excluding Code Section 1504(a)(4) preferred stock), or more than 50 percent of the combined voting power of all voting stock, or an option to acquire such stock.

---

290 Reg. §1.382-2(a)(1)(iii).

291 Reg. §1.382-2(a)(1)(iv)(ii).

292 Notice 2008-84, 2008-41 I.R.B. 855, September 26, 2008.

293 Notice 2008-76, 2008-2 C.B. 768. Guidance under new Notice 2008-84 is couched in more general terms, leaving open its application to other government bailout situations that may now arise. The government announced in Notice 2008-76 that it would issue regulations applying I.R.C. § 382(m) to Fannie Mae and Freddie Mac.

§ 11.4.24 Capital Contributions

Capital contributions to a loss corporation will not automatically be treated as a device to avoid the limits on the net operating losses used by an acquiring corporation.[294] In general, Code Section 382(l)(1) presumes that a capital contribution to the loss company made within two years of the acquisition is part of a plan to avoid or increase the NOL limit. However, in Notice 2008-78 the IRS indicated that it would issue regulations removing the anti-stuffing presumption and providing the four safe harbors.

Notice 2008-78 states that a capital contribution shall not be presumed to be part of a plan to avoid the NOL limits solely because it was made within two years of the date the loss corporation was acquired. Whether a capital contribution is part of a plan depends on the facts and circumstances, unless the contribution is covered by one of the four safe harbors.

The first two safe harbors are based on the amount of stock received for the capital contribution and the absence of an agreement to acquire the company. The first safe harbor applies if:

- The contribution is not made by a controlling shareholder or a related party;
- No more than 20 percent of the value of the loss corporation's stock is issued for the contribution;
- At the time of the contribution, there was no agreement or substantial negotiations to acquire the corporation; and
- The ownership change occurs more than six months after the contribution.

The second safe harbor applies if:

- A related party acquires no more than 10 percent of the value of the loss corporation's stock for the contribution, or the contribution is made by an unrelated party;
- At the time of the contribution, there was no agreement or substantial negotiations to acquire the corporation; and
- The ownership change occurs more than a year after the contribution.

The third safe harbor applies to contributions in exchange for stock issued in connection with the performance of services, or in exchange for stock acquired by a retirement plan, that are covered by Code Section 355 safe harbors involving spinoffs.

The fourth safe harbor applies to contributions made to a new loss corporation that does not have assets with a net unrealized built-in loss, and before the first year the corporation has a carryforward of NOLs, capital losses, excess credits or excess foreign taxes.[295]

---

[294] Notice 2008-78, 2008-41 I.R.B. 851, September 26, 2008.

[295] Taxpayers can rely on Notice 2008-78 for an ownership change occurring in a tax year ending on

§11.4.25 Recapitalized Financial Institutions

The IRS announced that it intends to issue regulations on the application of Code Section 382 when Treasury recapitalizes financial institutions under the Emergency Economic Stabilization Act of 2008.[296] The law authorizes Treasury to purchase preferred shares in financial institutions.[297]

The ownership represented by the shares acquired by Treasury will not be considered to have caused Treasury's ownership in the loss corporation to increase over its lowest percentage owned on any earlier date. With certain exceptions, these shares are considered outstanding for purposes of determining the percentage of loss corporation stock owned by other five-percent shareholders on a testing date. The IRS further explained that for all federal income tax purposes, any preferred stock of a loss corporation acquired by Treasury shall be treated as stock described in Code Section 1504(a)(4). Any warrant to purchase stock of a loss corporation shall be treated as an option and not as stock.

For purposes of measuring shifts in ownership by any five-percent shareholder on any testing date occurring on or after the date on which the loss corporation redeems shares of its stock held by Treasury, the shares so redeemed shall be treated as if they had never been outstanding. Furthermore, any capital contribution by Treasury to a loss corporation will not be considered to have been made as part of a plan, a principal purpose of which was to avoid or increase any Code Section 382 limitation.

§11.5 Tax-Free Acquisitions

§11.5.1 Overview

If an acquisition qualifies as a "reorganization," each "party to the reorganization" is afforded tax-free treatment.[298] Thus, a shareholder of a corporation that engages in a transaction that meets the definition of a reorganization will be entitled to nonrecognition of gain or loss.[299] The shareholder will take a substituted basis in stock received where the basis of stock received in an exchange will equal the basis of any stock given in the exchange.[300] There will be a tacked holding period causing the holding period of stock received to include the holding period of stock given in the exchange.[301]

A corporation that is a "party to a reorganization," will recognize no gain or loss on the issuance of its stock,[302] nor on the receipt of property.[303] The tax basis it takes in any assets acquired will be a carryover basis. The carryover basis will be equal to the tax basis that the acquired entity had in those assets, increased by any gain recognized by the acquired entity on the transfer.[304] There will be a

(Footnote Continued)

or after September 26, 2008. The notice will apply until the IRS issues additional guidance.

296 Pub. L. No. 110-343.

297 Notice 2008-100, 2008-44 I.R.B. 1081, October 14, 2008.

298 I.R.C. §§354, 355, 361, and 1032.

299 I.R.C. §354.

300 I.R.C. §358.

301 I.R.C. §1223(1).

302 I.R.C. §§361 and 1032.

303 I.R.C. §361.

304 I.R.C. §362.

tacked holding period for the property received by the acquiring corporation. As a result, the period that the property was held by the acquired corporation will be added to the period the property is held by the acquiring corporation,[305] and the tax attributes of the acquired corporation will usually carryover to the acquiring corporation.[306] Gain or loss will not be recognized if a realization event has not occurred, despite the transaction not qualifying as a reorganization.[307]

The theory underlying tax-free reorganization treatment was expressed by the U.S. Supreme Court when it stated that no gain or loss should be recognized when "a formal distribution, directly or through exchange of securities, represents merely a new form of the previous participation in an enterprise involving no change of substance in the rights and relations of interested parties one to another or to the corporate assets."[308] Although a transaction that results in a shareholder "cashing out" in whole or in part will usually be taxable to all parties, under certain of the "types" of reorganizations taxable income, referred to as "boot," may be received by one or more parties to the reorganization without the transaction failing to qualify as tax-free with regard to other parties.[309] Moreover, even for the shareholder who receives part boot in the exchange, the transaction may be tax-free with respect to the amount of nonboot consideration received.[310]

To meet the definition of a reorganization, an acquisition must pass three judicial tests in addition to meeting the technical Code section 368 definition. The judicial tests are:

1. The continuity-of-proprietary-interest test;[311]
2. The continuity-of-business-enterprise test;[312] and
3. The business-purpose test.[313]

Further, there must be a plan of reorganization, but one can be inferred from surrounding facts and circumstances.[314] These tests are designed to ensure that the spirit of the reorganization statute is not subordinated to the transaction's form.[315] The continuity-of-proprietary-interest test is often the most challenging of the three tests to meet in a bank acquisition. Accordingly, it is discussed in detail.[316]

---

305 I.R.C. § 1223(2).

306 I.R.C. § 381.

307 There are certain exceptions to this statement, most notably the recognition of unrealized gain or loss required by I.R.C. § 475.

308 *Bazley v. Commissioner*, 47-1 U.S.T.C. ¶9288, 331 U.S. 737 (1947). I.R.C. § 368(a). *See also* S. Rep. No. 398, 68th Cong., 1st Sess., 14 (1924), in which it is stated "Congress . . . adopted the policy of exempting from tax the gain from exchanges made in connection with a reorganization, in order that ordinary business transactions [would] not be prevented on account of the provisions of the tax law." This statement was quoted by the dissent in *Paulsen, infra* note 315.

309 I.R.C. § 368(a)(2)(B).

310 I.R.C. § 356.

311 Reg. § 1.368-1(c). This test does not apply to Type E or F reorganizations occurring on or after February 25, 2005. Reg. § 1.368-1(b).

312 Reg. § 1.368-1(d). This test does not apply to Type E or F reorganizations occurring on or after February 25, 2005. Reg. § 1.368-1(b).

313 Reg. §§ 1.368-1(c) and 1.368-2(g).

314 *C.T. Investment Co. v. Commissioner*, 37-1 U.S.T.C. ¶9151, 88 F.2d 582 (8th Cir. 1937).

315 *Gregory v. Helvering*, 35-1 U.S.T.C. ¶9043, 293 U.S. 465 (1935); *Paulsen v. Commissioner*, 85-1 U.S.T.C. ¶9116, 469 U.S. 131 (1985).

316 *See* Type A reorganization, *infra.*

(a) *Types of Tax-Free Reorganizations*

The seven types of reorganizations, each qualifying for tax-free treatment, are:

1. A statutory merger or consolidation (Type A), including forward and reverse triangular mergers;
2. A stock-for-stock exchange (Type B);
3. A stock-for-asset exchange (Type C);
4. A division of one corporation into one or more corporations, or an asset acquisition by a single corporation that is temporarily controlled by the acquired corporation prior to the acquired corporation's liquidation (Type D);
5. A recapitalization (Type E);
6. A change in identity, form, or place of organization (Type F); and
7. Certain bankruptcy reorganizations or similar recapitalization (Type G).

(b) *Continuity-of-Business-Enterprise Test*

Although the continuity-of-business-enterprise test is far more difficult to pass under rulings and regulations issued by the IRS since 1979, it seldom creates an impediment to reorganization status in bank acquisitions.[317] Under current regulations, continuity-of-business-enterprise will exist only when:

1. The transferee continues to conduct the transferor's "historic business;" or
2. The transferee uses a "significant portion" of the transferor's business assets in a business following the acquisition.[318]

The continuity-of-business-enterprise test does not apply to the acquiring company's historic business.[319] Further, it requires only one of the significant lines of business of the target company to be continued.[320] Thus, a merger will satisfy the continuity-of-business-enterprise test despite an acquiring bank holding company selling one of the two businesses of a merged bank holding company.[321] However, this test is not met when the acquired entity sells all of its assets prior to the acquisition and acquires assets that are better suited to the acquiring entity's business.[322]

---

[317] Rev. Rul. 79-434, 1979-2 C.B. 155. Prior to this ruling, the business enterprise test was more of a formality. *See Bentsen v. Phimey*, 62-1 U.S.T.C. ¶9257, 199 F. Supp. 363 (D.C. Tex. 1962). *See also* the Preamble to the 1980 Regulations, *reprinted at* 1981-1 C.B. 134.

[318] Reg. § 1.368-1(d). This test is similar to the I.R.C. § 382 requirement for carryover of a target firm's NOLs. Perhaps the acquisition of a thrift that, following the acquisition, is converted to a nonbank bank (one that does not make loans) may violate this rule if substantial asset sales have occurred. Consider also the acquisition of a commercial bank that, following the acquisition, converts to a thrift in order to engage in a broader range of nontraditional banking activities.

[319] Rev. Rul. 81-25, 1981-1 C.B. 132. Note the applicability of the continuity rule in a Type G reorganization, discussed *infra*.

[320] Reg. § 1.368-1(d)(3)(ii).

[321] Rev. Rul. 85-198, 1985-2 C.B. 120.

[322] Rev. Rul. 87-76, 1987-2 C.B. 84.

(c) *Business-Purpose Test*

The business purpose test is usually satisfied, unless the transaction is "a mere device that puts on the form of a corporate reorganization as a disguise for concealing its real character, and the object and accomplishment of which is the consummation of a preconceived plan having no business or corporate purpose . . . ."[323] A transaction undertaken solely for tax avoidance will not satisfy this test.[324] Seldom does this test disqualify a bank acquisition from qualifying as a tax-free reorganization.

(d) *Continuity-of-Interest Test*

In order for there to be a valid tax-free reorganization, there must be "a continuance of interest on the part of the transferor in the properties transferred."[325] For advance ruling purposes, the IRS requires that a minimum of 50 percent of the consideration given be stock (voting or nonvoting, common or preferred) of the acquiring corporation.[326] If an excessive amount of boot is utilized, the transaction will fail to qualify as tax-free and all parties, not only the party receiving the boot, will be taxed. This requirement may not be satisfied if it is met at the time of the reorganization but then is followed by "sales, redemptions or other dispositions that are part of the plan of reorganization."[327] To the extent that cash is paid for dissenting shares, the required continuity-of-interest is thereby reduced.

§ 11.5.2 Type A Reorganizations

(a) *Type A: General Rules*

A Type A reorganization is defined as a statutory merger or consolidation effectuated in accordance with federal or state corporation laws.[328] Defining this reorganization by reference to something other than federal tax statutes is a unique characteristic of the Type A reorganization, and it carries with it distinct advantages over most of the other types of reorganizations.[329]

---

[323] Reg. § 1.368-1(c). *See also* Prop. Reg. § 1.355-2(b); *Rafferty v. Commissioner*, 72-1 U.S.T.C. ¶ 9101, 452 F.2d 767 (1st Cir. 1972), *cert. denied*, 408 U.S. 922 (1972). Further, a reorganization must be "undertaken for reasons germane to the continuance of the business of a corporation." Reg. § 1.368-2(g). *See also* I.R.C. § 269.

[324] *Gregory v. Helvering*, 293 U.S. 465 (1934).

[325] *Cortland Specialty Co. v. Commissioner*, 3 U.S.T.C. ¶ 980, 60 F.2d 937 (2d Cir. 1932), *cert. denied*, 288 U.S. 599, 53 S. Ct. 316 (1932); *Pinellas Ice & Cold Storage Co. v. Commissioner*, 3 U.S.T.C. ¶ 1023, 287 U.S. 462, 53 S. Ct. 257 (1933); *LeTulle v. Scofield*, 40-1 U.S.T.C. ¶ 9150, 308 U.S. 415 (1940).

[326] Rev. Proc. 77-37, 1977-2 C.B. 568. The Supreme Court has ruled that the retention of an equity interest in the resulting entity by 38 percent of the target's shareholders satisfies this requirement, but the IRS in a private ruling concluded that a 34 percent continuity was insufficient. *John A. Nelson Co. v. Helvering*, 296 U.S. 374 (1935); TAM 7905011, October 23, 1978. It would be erroneous to conclude that a mechanical percentage test is controlling, since both the courts and the IRS examine all surrounding facts and circumstances.

[327] Rev. Rul. 66-23, 1966-1 C.B. 67. Retention for five years is generally accepted by the IRS Rev. Proc. 77-37, 1977-2 C.B. 568. *Cf.* Rev. Rul. 75-95, 1975-1 C.B. 114, in which the IRS ruled that a post-transaction transfer of stock to a voting trust did not terminate continuity. *See also* Rev. Rul. 76-528, 1976-2 C.B. 103. In Rev. Rul. 66-23, 1966-1 C.B. 67, the IRS ruled that acquired stock should be held for a significant (three-year) period of time. *See also McDonald's Restaurants of Ill., Inc. v. Commissioner*, 82-2 U.S.T.C. ¶ 9581, 688 F.2d 520 (7th Cir. 1982), in which stock held for only six months did not satisfy the continuity-of-interest rule.

[328] I.R.C. § 368(a)(1)(A); Reg. § 1.368-2(b)(1).

[329] *But see* discussion of Type G reorganizations, *infra*.

A merger is a transaction where the acquiring entity obtains ownership of the acquired firm's assets and succeeds to its liabilities by operation of law. For example, a transaction pursuant to the National Banking Act[330] in which a wholly owned bank subsidiary of a BHC merged into an existing bank and the existing bank survived under its old charter qualified as a Type A reorganization.[331] A consolidation is the combination of two firms into a newly organized entity.

If the transaction satisfies the continuity-of-interest requirement, the acquiring corporation is permitted to utilize non-voting stock, cash or other property, and the transaction will not be disqualified from Type A reorganization status. Of course, to the extent that boot is received, the transaction will not be tax free. The use of other than a relatively small amount of such consideration will normally prevent an acquisition from qualifying under one of the other types of reorganizations.[332] Thus, the only restraint placed on the type of consideration that can be utilized in a Type A reorganization results from the application of the continuity-of-interest doctrine.

Type A reorganizations also permit the acquiring corporation to transfer, or "drop down," a portion of the assets of the acquired corporation to a controlled subsidiary and to use stock of its parent instead of its own stock to acquire the assets or stock of the target company in a triangular merger.[333]

(b) ***Type A: Disadvantages***

Among the more significant nontax disadvantages associated with the Type A reorganization is the grant, under most state merger and consolidation statutes, to dissenting shareholders of appraisal rights.[334] In addition, merger statutes frequently require a favorable vote of shareholders holding a majority of the stock of both the acquiring and acquired corporations.[335] Moreover, since under state merger laws the acquired corporation's liabilities (both known and unknown) are assumed by operation of law by the acquiring corporation, this form of reorganization is undesirable for most bank acquisitions of failing institutions, especially if fraud was a contributing factor to the failure.[336]

A merger may also necessitate a change in the acquired or acquiring entity's tax accounting methods.[337] Where different overall methods of accounting are employed by the acquiring and merged companies, the acquiring corporation will be required to use the "principal method of accounting" employed by the merged entities. Total assets and total gross receipts are to be considered when determining which entity's method is dominant.

---

330 Ch. 58, 12 Stat. 665 (1863).

331 Rev. Rul. 84-104, 1984-2 C.B. 94; 12 U.S.C. § 215 (1918).

332 Although I.R.C. § 368(a)(2)(B) contains a boot relaxation rule for Type C reorganizations, it has limited practical application. *In contrast, see* the flexibility granted under Type G.

333 I.R.C. § 368(a)(2)(C).

334 This disadvantage is removed if the parties engage in a forward triangular reorganization, discussed below.

335 The necessity of a shareholder meeting at which the vote is taken may interfere with the delicate timing to which many bank acquisitions are subject. However, since bank and thrift acquisitions typically require regulatory approvals, which often take months to obtain, there is usually ample time to get shareholder approval.

336 Many bank failures result from illegal acts performed by their managers. Failed or failing banks are often the target in bank acquisitions.

337 I.R.C. § 381(c)(4).

(c) *Type A: Merger of Mutual Associations*

Until the late 1970s, most savings and loan associations and savings banks were organized in mutual form. By the early 1990s, less than 20 percent continued to operate in mutual form.[338] Under applicable state and federal laws, the equity owners of mutual associations are the depositors, who typically have voting and other rights to share in the residual equity of the association in proportion to their account balances.

Changes were made in federal and state banking laws to permit mutuals to adopt a stock corporation structure. Frequently, mutuals convert to stock corporations to raise needed equity capital. The absence of shareholders has raised particularly challenging continuity-of-interest issues when mutual associations merge or convert.

As confirmed in rulings issued by the IRS, when two mutual savings and loan associations merge, and the depositors in the target mutual savings and loan association receive equivalent deposits in the resulting mutual savings and loan association, the transaction satisfies the continuity-of-interest test and usually otherwise qualifies as a Type A reorganization.[339] A merger of a mutual savings and loan into a stock savings and loan also qualifies as a tax-free Type A reorganization.[340] Further, where the shareholders of an acquired building and loan association received passbook accounts as well as equity interests for equal passbook accounts and equity interests in the acquiring building and loan association, a Type A reorganization occurs.[341]

The receipt of the proprietary interests in the acquiring savings and loan association in exchange for the proprietary interest which the share account holders have in the acquired mutual savings and loan association will satisfy the continuity-of-interest requirement for a statutory merger.[342] A proprietary interest includes the right to vote on matters affecting the association, the right to share in current earnings, and the right to share in its assets upon liquidation. The share account holders' passbooks evidence this interest. Thus, the members of a mutual savings and loan association have a dual relationship to the association: they possess a proprietary interest and withdrawable deposits that are the equivalent of cash.[343]

The continuity-of-interest requirement may also be satisfied in those situations in which the share account holders are granted no vote under the laws under which the association is incorporated.[344] This is also true if under the state regulations concerning the liquidation of the mutual association, there are no

---

[338] "Annual Statistical Digest—1991," Board of Governors of the Federal Reserve System; FDIC, "Statistics on Banking," A Statistical Profile of the U.S. Banking Industry (1993).

[339] Rev. Rul. 69-3, 1969-1 C.B. 103; *Paulsen v. Commissioner*, 83-2 U.S.T.C. ¶9537, 716 F.2d 563 (9th Cir. 1983), *rev'g* 78 T.C. 291 (1982), *aff'd*, 85-1 U.S.T.C. ¶9116, 469 U.S. 131 (1985).

[340] Rev. Rul. 69-646, 1969-2 C.B. 54.

[341] *Id.* In this ruling, the target company owners received "free (savings) share passbooks" and "guaranty shares" of the acquiring firm. The ruling held that this exchange of passbooks in one association for passbooks of the other was an equity-for-equity exchange that satisfied the continuity-of-interest requirement.

[342] Reg. § 1.368-1(b).

[343] Rev. Rul. 66-290, 1966-2 C.B. 112.

[344] Rev. Rul. 78-286, 1978-2 C.B. 145.

explicit rules granting a right to the share account holders in the assets upon liquidation. The share account holders were the only parties specially entitled by law to share in the earnings of the mutual association.

When an exchange of "equivalent" equity interests does not occur, the requisite continuity-of-interest may not be present. The IRS has consistently taken the position that tax-free reorganization treatment is not available where a mutual savings and loan association acquires all of the assets and liabilities of a stock savings and loan association in a transaction in which savings accounts were received by the acquired corporation's shareholders in exchange for their stock.[345]

The "equivalent" interests theory adopted by the IRS was not embraced by the courts prior to the Ninth Circuit's decision in *Paulsen*.[346] For example, the Claims Court found that a merger of a stock savings and loan association into a mutual association qualified as a Type A reorganization.[347] The court reasoned that, while the savings accounts received by the target shareholders in the exchange had substantially fewer equity characteristics than the stock surrendered, they did represent the only equity interests in the resulting entity.

In *Paulsen*, in a decision that was later affirmed by the U.S. Supreme Court,[348] the Ninth Circuit reversed the Tax Court and concluded that savings accounts received in exchange for stock were "cash equivalents" rather than equity and, thus, could not be treated as stock for purposes of satisfying the continuity-of-interest requirement.[349] The court stated that the deposit accounts received did not "partake sufficiently of equity characteristics" to represent a continued proprietary interest on the part of the acquired firm's stockholders.[350]

The Supreme Court followed a line of reasoning similar to that employed by the Circuit Court in concluding that the stockholders were taxable on their receipt of deposit accounts in the resulting entity because the continuity-of-interest requirement had not been satisfied. The Court stated: "In exchange for their guaranty stock in [the target], they received essentially cash with an insubstantial equity interest."[351] However, the Supreme Court did acknowledge

[345] Rev. Rul. 69-6, 1969-1 C.B. 104. The transaction will also fail to qualify as a stock for asset reorganization under the provisions of I.R.C. §368(a)(1)(C). *See Home Savings & Loan Ass'n v. United States*, 75-1 U.S.T.C. ¶9423, 514 F.2d 1199 (9th Cir. 1975), *cert. denied*, 423 U.S. 1015 (1975).

[346] *Paulsen v. Commissioner*, 83-2 U.S.T.C. ¶9537, 716 F.2d 563 (9th Cir. 1983), *rev'g* 78 T.C. 291 (1982), *aff'd*, 85-1 U.S.T.C. ¶9116, 469 U.S. 131 (1985).

[347] *Capital Savings & Loan Ass'n v. United States*, 79-2 U.S.T.C. ¶9648, 607 F.2d 970 (Cl. Ct. 1979). *See also Everett v. United States*, 71-2 U.S.T.C. ¶9629, 448 F.2d 357 (10th Cir. 1971).

[348] *Paulsen v. Commissioner*, 83-2 U.S.T.C. ¶9537, 716 F.2d 563 (9th Cir. 1983), *rev'g* 78 T.C. 291 (1982), *aff'd*, 85-1 U.S.T.C. ¶9116, 469 U.S. 131 (1985).

[349] *Id. See also Westside Federal Savings & Loan Ass'n of Fairview Park v. United States*, 74-1 U.S.T.C. ¶9315, 494 F.2d 404 (6th Cir. 1974); *First Federal Savings & Loan Ass'n v. United States*, 78-1 U.S.T.C. ¶9398, 452 F. Supp. 32 (D.C. Ohio 1978); *Rocky Mountain Federal Savings & Loan Ass'n v. United States*, 79-2 U.S.T.C. ¶9560, 473 F. Supp. 779 (D.C. Wyo. 1979).

[350] *Paulsen*, 716 F.2d at 570. *See also Minnesota Tea Co. v. Helvering*, 38-1 U.S.T.C. ¶9050, 302 U.S. 609.

[351] *Paulsen*, 469 U.S. at 140. In *Paulsen*, a vigorous dissent was written by Justice O'Connor in which Chief Justice Berger joined. It took issue with the majority's bifurcation of the mutual share accounts into debt and equity interests. Justice Powell did not participate in the decision. Note that from the exchanging depositor's point of view, the 1980 revision of the installment sales rule has all but eliminated the significance of the Court's holding. Under I.R.C. §453, it may now be possible to structure a deposit account to defer the recognition of gain until the account matures. However, at the

that the transaction conformed with the literal requirements of the Type A reorganization.[352] The Court distinguished the *Paulsen* fact pattern from the merger of two mutuals and from the merger of a mutual into a stock corporation where stock is received for deposit accounts. In those transactions, the Court acknowledged that the transaction could be tax-free.

(d) *Type A: Illustration*

The typical merger of mutuals often involves the following steps:

1. In accordance with a merger plan and state or federal law relating to mergers, an acquiring mutual absorbs all of the assets and assumes all of the liabilities of an acquired mutual;
2. The acquiring mutual issues to each share account holder of the acquired mutual a share account equal to the same dollar amount of deposit in the acquired mutual. The share account is typically evidenced by a passbook; and
3. The acquired mutual ceases to exist, and the acquiring mutual carries on the business operations of the combined associations.

Thus, the transaction will appear as shown in Table 11.6.

(Footnote Continued)

corporate level, the decision impacts the ability of the acquiring firm to carry over the target's tax basis and corporate tax attributes. Also, there is at present the possibility of gain or loss to the corporation on revaluation of its assets. A direct merger should result in mark-to-market on all assets, recapture of reserves, and loss of tax attributes. "Two-step" acquisitions should produce a different result.

[352] Although the Supreme Court's decision in *Paulsen* expressly settled the taxation of the individual shareholders, the corporate taxation also may have been indirectly resolved, since there cannot be a Type "A" Reorganization at the corporate level without continuity-of-interest.

Table 11.6 Type A: Merger of Mutuals

BEFORE: Two Unrelated Mutual Savings & Loan into Loan Association

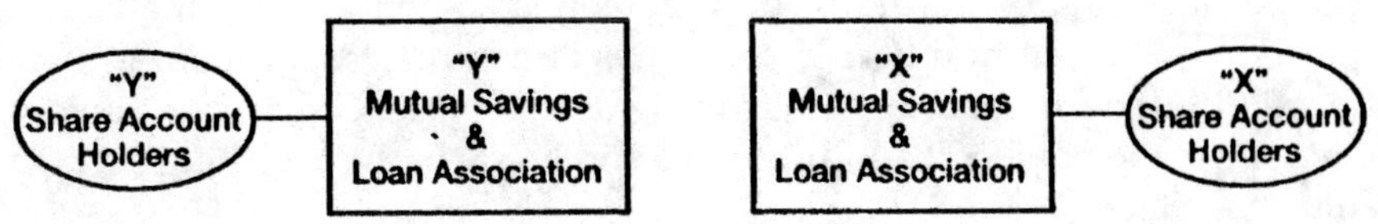

TRANSACTION: Statutory Merger of "X" into"Y"

On the date of the merger, the assets of X will vest in, and the liabilities of X will be assumed by Y by operation of law. Each Share Account Holder of X will be issued a share account of Y represented by a passbook in an equal amount.

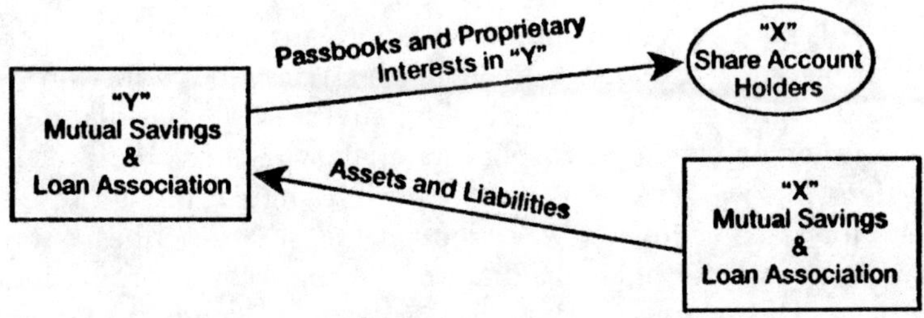

AFTER: Single ("Y") Mutual Savings & Loan

(e) *Type A: Tax Treatment of Parties*

(i) Nonrecognition of Gain or Loss. When a merger of mutuals qualifies for tax-free status as a Type A reorganization,[353] the parties to the reorganization recognize no gain or loss from the transaction. The term "party to a reorganization" includes a corporation resulting from a reorganization and, in the case of an acquisition by one corporation of properties of another corporation, both corporations.[354] Further, no gain or loss is recognized to the share account holders on the receipt of the passbook and proprietary interests in the acquiring savings and loan association.[355]

(ii) Tax Basis. Consistent with the characterization of the transaction as tax-free, the tax basis of the share account holders in their interest in the acquiring savings and loan association is the same as their basis in their share account in the acquired savings and loan association.[356] The acquiring savings association takes a basis in the assets, transferred by operation of law from the acquired savings association, equal to the basis of those assets in the hands of the acquired savings and loan association.[357]

(f) *Triangular Mergers*

Subsets of the Type A reorganization are the forward triangular merger and reverse triangular merger.[358] Code section 368(a)(2)(D) describes a forward triangular merger as the merger of a target company into a subsidiary of the controlling corporation, which is the corporation that issues stock to the acquired firm's shareholders. In several respects, the forward triangular merger resembles a Type C stock-for-asset acquisition. Section 368(a)(2)(E) describes a reverse triangular merger as a merger of a subsidiary of the controlling corporation into the target company. This acquisition has similarities to a Type B stock-for-stock acquisition.

The Code imposes an explicit requirement on both forms of triangular mergers (which is not imposed on statutory mergers under Code section 368(a)(1)(A)) as to the portion of the acquired firm's assets that must be acquired and held by the acquiring firm after the acquisition. In the case of a forward triangular merger, "substantially all" of the properties of the acquired corporation must be acquired in the merger.[359] Following a reverse triangular merger, the resulting corporation must hold substantially all of its own properties and the properties of the target corporation.[360]

For advance ruling purposes, the IRS requires a showing that the acquiring corporation receive at least 90 percent of the fair market value of the net assets and at least 70 percent of the fair market value of the gross assets held by the acquired corporation immediately before the transfer.[361] However, assets of the

[353] I.R.C. § 361.

[354] I.R.C. § 368(b).

[355] I.R.C. § 354.

[356] I.R.C. § 358.

[357] I.R.C. § 362(b).

[358] I.R.C. §§ 368(a)(2)(D) and (E), respectively.

[359] I.R.C. § 368(a)(2)(D).

[360] I.R.C. § 368(a)(2)(E).

[361] Reg. § 1.368-2(b)(2) provides that the term "substantially all" has the same meaning when applied to triangular mergers as it does for purposes

target firm used (1) to pay its reorganization expenses; (2) to purchase the stock of any dissenting shareholders; and (3) to pay cash in lieu of fractional shares will not be considered assets held by the target firm prior to the merger for purposes of determining whether the "substantially all" test is met.[362]

(g) *Forward Triangular Merger: General Characteristics*

Use of the forward triangular reorganization removes the shareholder approval disadvantage associated with the basic Type "A" reorganization because, under state merger laws, shareholders of the acquiring parent corporation usually need not approve the acquisition. However, approval by the target corporation shareholders continues to be required, and they may exercise their right to dissent.

Situations in which banks and bank holding companies have utilized the forward triangular reorganization include:

1. The formation of a bank holding company;[363]
2. The merger of an existing bank (T) into a newly formed subsidiary (S) of a newly formed bank holding company (P);[364]
3. The merger of two existing banks (T1 and T2) into newly formed subsidiaries (S1 and S2) of a newly formed bank holding company (P);[365] and
4. The merger of a one-bank holding company into a newly formed subsidiary of another one-bank holding company.[366]

In a forward triangular merger, the subsidiary of the controlling corporation must acquire "substantially all" of the properties of the target company through the issuance of the controlling corporation's stock. No stock of the acquiring subsidiary corporation may be used to effectuate the merger.[367]

(h) *Forward Triangular Merger: Illustration*

In a rudimentary forward triangular merger, a Target corporation (T) is merged into a Subsidiary (S) of the Parent corporation (P) whose stock is exchanged for the stock of the Target company (T).[368] (Table 11.7).

(Footnote Continued)

of I.R.C. § 368(a)(1)(C). Rev. Proc. 77-37, 1977-2 C.B. 568.

[362] Rev. Rul. 77-307, 1977-2 C.B. 117; PLR 8539045, June 28, 1985; Prop. Reg. § 1.368-2(j).

[363] Rev. Rul. 78-397, 1978-2 C.B. 150; TAM 8243009, July 22, 1982; PLRs 8243150, July 28, 1982; 8243159, July 28, 1982; and 8243166, July 28, 1982.

[364] PLR 8533073, May 22, 1985.

[365] PLR 8534073, May 29, 1985. *See also* PLR 8534049, May 24, 1985, for the merger of a target bank into a subsidiary of a widely held bank holding company.

[366] PLR 8533072, May 22, 1985.

[367] I.R.C. § 368(a)(2)(D)(i). PLR 9020015, May 18, 1990.

[368] The IRS currently treats liquidation accounts as a second class of stock that prevents holding company formations from qualifying as either forward or reverse triangular mergers. Although the IRS has held that such reorganizations are I.R.C. § 351 transactions, this is of no comfort if a thrift with a holding company desires to acquire a converted thrift using the parent's stock.

Table 11.7 Forward Triangular Merger

BEFORE:

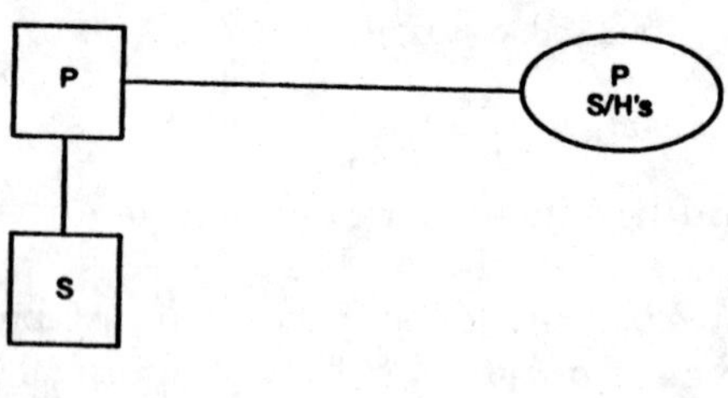

TRANSACTION:

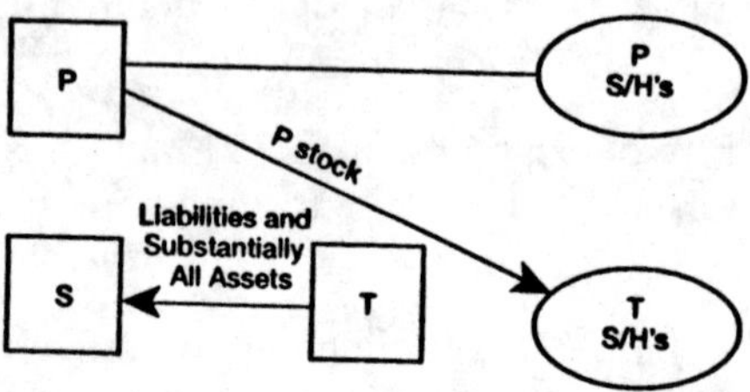

AFTER:

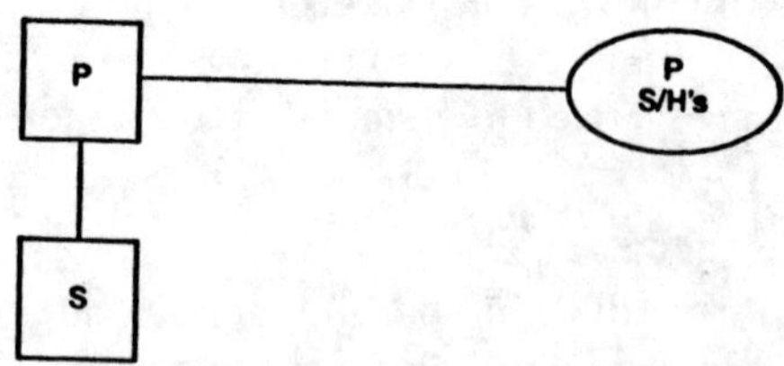

(i) *Forward Triangular Merger: Tax Treatment of Parties*

(i) Nonrecognition of Gain or Loss. Because the above transaction qualifies as a forward triangular merger, no gain or loss is recognized by Target, Parent, or Subsidiary, since each is "a party to a reorganization."[369] Further, no gain or loss is recognized by Target upon the transfer of substantially all of its assets to Subsidiary in exchange for Parent's common stock and the assumption of Target's liabilities by Subsidiary.[370] A subsequent drop down of Target's assets to a second-tier subsidiary of a newly formed subsidiary will not result in the loss of tax-free status.[371] Finally, no gain or loss is recognized by either Parent or Subsidiary upon the acquisition by Subsidiary of substantially all of the assets of Target in exchange for Parent's common stock, and the assumption of Target's liabilities.[372] The shareholders of Target who receive solely Parent stock will recognize no gain or loss on the exchange for their stock.[373]

(ii) Tax Basis and Holding Period. Consistent with the characterization of the transaction as a tax-free reorganization, the basis of the assets of Target that are acquired by Subsidiary will be the same in the hands of Subsidiary as the basis of such assets in the hands of Target immediately prior to the exchange.[374] Further, the basis of Subsidiary's common stock in the hands of Parent will be increased by an amount equal to the basis of Target's assets in the hands of Subsidiary and decreased by the sum of the amount of the liabilities of Target assumed by Subsidiary and the amount of liabilities to which the assets of Target are subject. The holding period of the assets of Target received by Subsidiary will, in each instance, include the period for which such assets were held by Target.[375]

The basis that the shareholders will take in Parent stock will be the same as the basis of Target stock surrendered in the exchange,[376] and the holding period of the Parent stock received by the shareholders of Target will include the period during which Target stock surrendered was held, provided the stock of Target is a capital asset in the hands of the shareholders of Target on the date of the exchange.[377]

---

[369] I.R.C. §§ 368(a)(1)(A), 368(a)(2)(D), and 368(b).

[370] I.R.C. §§ 361 and 357(a).

[371] Rev. Rul. 69-617, 1969-2 C.B. 57; PLR 8534082, May 30, 1985.

[372] Rev. Rul. 57-278, 1957-1 C.B. 124.

[373] I.R.C. § 354(a)(1).

[374] I.R.C. § 362(b).

[375] I.R.C. § 1223(2).

[376] I.R.C. § 358(a)(1).

[377] I.R.C. § 1223(1).

(iii) Tax Attributes. Subsidiary will succeed to and take into account the earnings and profits, or any deficit in earnings and profits, of Target as of the date of transfer.[378] Any deficit in the earnings and profits of Target or Subsidiary will be used only to offset the earnings and profits accumulated after the date of transfer. Subsidiary also will take into account, as of the date of the proposed transfer, the items of Target described in Code section 381(c).[379] If any shareholder of Target dissents to the merger and receives solely cash in exchange for stock, the cash will be treated as having been received by the shareholder as a distribution in redemption of stock subject to the provisions and limitations contained in Code section 302. A newly formed subsidiary into which the target bank merges is required to use the same method of tax accounting as the target bank, and under Code section 381, it succeeds to all of the target bank's tax attributes, including its bad-debt reserves, investment tax credits, and job credits.[380]

(iv) Dividend Income. In those circumstances in which boot is received, a forward triangular reorganization may generate dividend income to Target company's shareholders.[381] However, circular cash flows coupled with stock transfers among a bank, the bank holding company, the subsidiary into which the bank is merged, and the incorporators, instituted solely to meet minimum state capitalization requirements, and that result in the original shareholders of the merged bank holding all the stock of the holding company, which holds all the stock of the subsidiary, are disregarded for purposes of qualifying the transaction as a formed triangular merger.[382] The Eighth Circuit Court of Appeals held that, in determining whether a distribution has the effect of a dividend, the distribution should be viewed as though it were made by the transferee corporation.[383] However, it is the IRS's position that a distribution should be treated as having been made by the acquired (transferor) corporation, and that the determination of whether the receipt of stock or cash by target company's shareholders has the effect of a dividend should be determined in accordance with the rules set forth in Revenue Ruling 75-83.[384]

(j) *Reverse Triangular Merger: General Characteristics*

In a reverse triangular merger, voting stock of a controlling corporation is transferred to a newly formed subsidiary, and the subsidiary is then merged into

---

[378] I.R.C. § 381(c)(2).

[379] Reg. § 1.381(b)-1(b). These adjustments are subject to conditions and limitations of § § 381, 382, 383, and 384, and the regulations thereunder.

[380] I.R.C. § 368(a)(2)(E). I.R.C. § § 381(c)(1) and (26); Reg. § 1.381(c)(4)-1(a)(1); PLR 8534027, May 22, 1985. Note that under I.R.C. § 382(b)(6), prior to amendment by Pub. L. No. 99-514, the NOLs of the target company in most forward triangular mergers were not reduced. Moreover, the IRS has ruled that a new bank emerging from a forward triangular reorganization is eligible to deduct excess charitable contributions made by the merged bank in accordance with I.R.C. § 381(c)(19). PLR 8511017, December 12, 1984. With respect to the deductibility of contributions made by a merged bank to its retirement plan, *see* PLRs 8526062, April 4, 1985, and 8524062, March 20, 1985.

[381] I.R.C. § 356(a).

[382] Rev. Rul. 78-397, 1978-2 C.B. 150; *cf.* Rev. Rul. 74-546, 1974-2 C.B. 142. It is unclear whether funds dropped down into a subsidiary that becomes a holding company will be treated as a dividend for tax purposes, potentially triggering the operation of I.R.C. § 593(e).

[383] *Wright v. United States*, 73-2 U.S.T.C. ¶ 9583, 482 F.2d 600 (8th Cir. 1973).

[384] Rev. Rul. 75-83, 1975-1 C.B. 112.

the target company.[385] Unlike a forward triangular merger, which has to meet only the general Type A continuity-of-interest requirements, a reverse triangular merger must meet an 80 percent "solely for voting stock" requirement similar to that required in a Type B reorganization.[386] Moreover, cash provided by an acquiring bank holding company to pay dissenting target shareholders will not be included in Target's assets for purposes of determining whether substantially all Target's assets are held by the surviving corporation after the merger.[387] Cash used to capitalize a Subsidiary that is merged into Target and later returned to the Parent will be ignored for tax purposes and not treated as a dividend.[388]

A reverse triangular merger is especially attractive when a Target company possesses valuable licenses (*e.g.*, a bank charter) or whenever its assets may not be freely transferred. For these reasons, the reverse triangular merger has been utilized in numerous bank acquisitions including:

1. A "consolidation," under federal banking law, of a wholly owned bank subsidiary of a bank holding company with an existing target bank;[389]
2. A merger of a newly formed subsidiary of a newly formed bank holding company into an existing bank;[390] and
3. A merger of an interim banking subsidiary into the target bank holding company to accomplish the acquisition by a publicly traded bank holding company.[391]

(k) *Reverse Triangular Merger: Illustration*

In a reverse triangular merger, Subsidiary (S) merges into Target (T) and Parent company's (P) stock is exchanged for the outstanding stock of Target company (T).[392] (Table 11.8)

---

[385] I.R.C. §368(a)(2)(E) was enacted to permit a triangular reorganization similar to I.R.C. §368(a)(2)(D), but where the surviving corporation is the acquired corporation.

[386] I.R.C. §368(a)(2)(E).

[387] Rev. Rul. 77-307, 1977-2 C.B. 117; PLR 8537048, June 17, 1985.

[388] PLR 8544044, August 1, 1985. This could have significance for state tax purposes. Under some state tax laws, dividends may be includible in taxable income. However, the federal characterization of a distribution will normally control state tax treatment.

[389] Rev. Rul. 84-104, 1984-2 C.B. 94.

[390] PLR 8535024, May 31, 1985.

[391] PLR 8537048, June 17, 1985.

[392] PLRs 8533025, May 21, 1985; 8533075, May 22, 1985; 8243159, July 28, 1982; and 8243166, July 28, 1982. *See also A. M. Everett v. United States*, 69-2 U.S.T.C. ¶9663, *aff'd*, 71-2 U.S.T.C. ¶9629, 448 F.2d 357 (10th Cir. 1971).

Table 11.8 Reverse Triangular Merger

BEFORE:

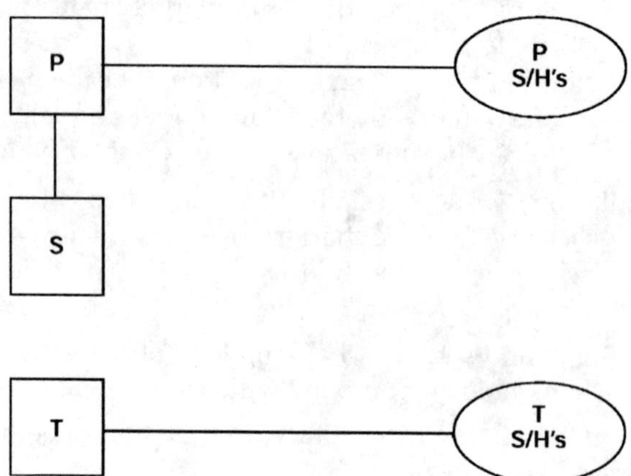

TRANSACTION:

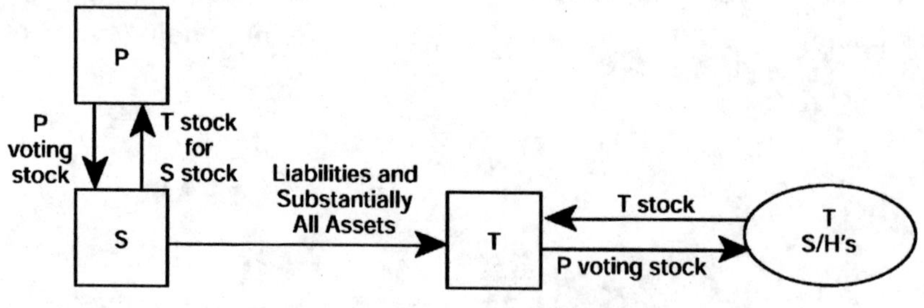

AFTER:

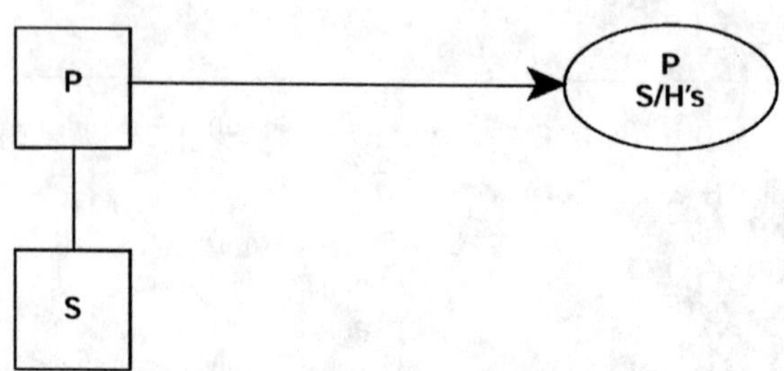

(l) *Reverse Triangular Merger: Tax Treatment of Parties*

(i) Nonrecognition of Gain or Loss. The above transaction will qualify as a reorganization because it meets the requirements for a reverse triangular merger.[393] Accordingly, no gain or loss is recognized to Subsidiary upon the transfer of its assets to Target in exchange for Target stock,[394] and no gain or loss is recognized to Target upon the receipt of the assets of Subsidiary in exchange for Target stock.[395] No gain or loss is recognized to Parent upon the receipt of the Target common stock solely in exchange for Subsidiary stock,[396] and no gain or loss will be recognized to Target shareholders upon the receipt of Parent stock.[397]

If any shareholder of Target dissents to the transaction and receives solely cash in exchange for Target stock, the cash will be treated as having been received by the shareholder as a distribution in redemption of Target stock subject to the provisions and limitations of Code section 302.

(ii) Tax Basis and Holding Period. The tax basis of Subsidiary's assets in the hands of Target will be the same as the basis of those assets in the hands of Subsidiary immediately prior to the transaction.[398] The holding period of the assets of Subsidiary in the hands of Target will include the period during which the assets were held by Subsidiary.[399] The basis of the Parent stock received by Target shareholders is the same as the basis of the Target stock surrendered in exchange therefore,[400] and the holding period of the Parent stock received by Target shareholders will include the holding period of the Target stock surrendered in exchange therefore, provided the Target stock was held as a capital asset on the date of the exchange.[401]

(iii) Tax Attributes. Target will succeed to and take into account the items of Subsidiary described in section 381(c).[402] Target will also succeed to and take into account the earnings and profits, or deficit in earnings and profits of Subsidiary as of the date of transfer. Any deficit in earnings and profits of Subsidiary or Target will be used only to offset the earnings and profits accumulated after the date of transfer.[403]

§ 11.5.3 Acquisitions with Solely Voting Stock—Type B and Type C Reorganizations

(a) *General Rules*

A Type B reorganization is an acquisition in which solely voting stock is exchanged for target's stock and, immediately after the exchange, the acquiring corporation has control of the target firm.[404] A Type C reorganization is an acquisition in which solely voting stock (common or preferred) is exchanged for

393 I.R.C. §§ 368(a)(1)(A) and (2)(2)(E).

394 I.R.C. § 361(a).

395 I.R.C. § 1032(a).

396 I.R.C. § 354(a)(1).

397 I.R.C. § 354(a)(1).

398 I.R.C. § 362(b).

399 I.R.C. § 1223(2).

400 I.R.C. § 358(a)(1).

401 I.R.C. § 1223(1).

402 I.R.C. § 381(a). *But see* limitations specified in I.R.C. §§ 381, 382, 383, and 384.

403 I.R.C. § 381(c)(2) and Reg. § 1.381(c)(2)-1.

404 I.R.C. § 368(a)(1)(B).

substantially all of the acquired firm's properties.[405] Whether stock is "voting" is generally determined by whether the holder is entitled to vote for the corporation's directors.[406] Voting stock of a corporation in control of the acquiring corporation may be used to acquire the target firm's stock, in the case of a Type B reorganization, or to acquire properties, in the case of a Type C reorganization.[407]

The rigidity of the "solely" for voting stock requirement substantially reduces the attractiveness of both the Type B and Type C reorganizations as means of acquisitions. Nevertheless, a Type B reorganization is successfully used to adopt BHC structures.[408]

(b) *"Solely" Requirement*

The "solely" for voting stock requirement is strictly construed by both the IRS and the courts.[409] However, there is a "boot relaxation rule" for Type C reorganizations, which permits up to 20 percent of the aggregate consideration in a C reorganization to be boot. This rule requires any liabilities of the target company that are assumed or otherwise transferred to the acquiring corporation to be treated as boot if any consideration other than voting stock is employed. Because deposit liabilities are counted, the boot relaxation rule seldom ameliorates the constraint imposed by the "solely" requirement in the case of an acquisition of a bank.

Where a target corporation contributed cash to a fund required to be established under state law for payment to its dissenting shareholders, the IRS ruled that the transaction qualified as a Type B reorganization.[410] It has also been held that the initial payment by a bank of cash for shares of a newly formed BHC that was returned in redemption of the initially issued shares will be ignored in an otherwise qualified Type B reorganization.[411] Moreover, the IRS has ruled that the payment of cash in lieu of fractional shares to an exchanging shareholder will not be treated as boot, subject to the boot relaxation rules.[412]

(c) *"Substantially All" Requirement*

In a Type C reorganization, "substantially all" of the properties of a target corporation must be acquired solely for voting stock.[413] What constitutes "substantially all" for this purpose is not defined in the Code, nor is there a safe harbor test set forth in the regulations. The IRS has ruled that the "nature, amount, and purpose" of retained assets of the acquired corporation are to be considered.[414] In *Commissioner v. First National Bank of Altoona*, the Third Circuit determined that 86 percent of total net worth was substantially all of the assets of

---

[405] I.R.C. § 368(a)(1)(C).

[406] Rev. Rul. 69-129, 1969-1 C.B. 218.

[407] I.R.C. § 368(a)(2)(B).

[408] PLRs 8535040, June 4, 1985; 8535005, May 28, 1985; and 8535008, May 28, 1985. It also has been approved in other BHC subsidiary acquisitions. *See, e.g.*, PLRs 8541105, July 18, 1985; and 8544071, August 7, 1985.

[409] *See* Dailey, "The Voting Stock Requirement of B and C Reorganizations," 26 Tax L. Rev. 725 (1971).

[410] Rev. Rul. 68-285, 1968-1 C.B. 147.

[411] Rev. Rul. 78-397, 1978-2 C.B. 150; PLR 8535040, June 4, 1985.

[412] Rev. Rul. 66-365, 1966-2 C.B. 116.

[413] Note that I.R.C. § 368(a)(2)(B) contains a boot relaxation rule that has limited application.

[414] Rev. Rul. 57-518, 1957-2 C.B. 253. *See also Arctic Ice Machine v. Commissioner*, 23 B.T.A. 1223 (1931); *Smothers v. United States*, 1981-1 U.S.T.C. ¶ 9368, 642 F.2d 894 (5th Cir. 1981).

the target company.[415] Conversely, in *National Bank of Commerce of Norfolk*, a federal district court concluded that the substantially all test was not met where only 81 percent of the target bank's assets were acquired.[416] For advance ruling purposes, at least 90 percent of the fair market value of the net assets and 70 percent of the fair market value of the gross assets of the target must be acquired.[417]

In analyzing the substantially all requirement, courts have focused primarily on the operating assets of the target.[418] The IRS has ruled that, for this purpose, it will not include among the target company's assets any cash provided by a parent corporation as part of a plan of reorganization, the sole purpose of which is to purchase the stock of dissenting shareholders of the target company.[419] As in the case of a triangular merger, a dropdown of "substantially all" of the target's assets to a subsidiary of the acquiring corporation will not disqualify the acquisition as a Type C reorganization.[420]

(d) *Overlap with Triangular Type A*

Many of the characteristics of Types B and C reorganizations are reflected in the optional subsets of the Type A—the forward triangular merger and reverse triangular merger.[421] The forward triangular merger contains many of the advantages, but few of the disadvantages, of the Type C reorganization. Indeed, a Type C reorganization is often referred to as a practical merger, since the corporation whose assets are acquired must generally be liquidated immediately after the acquisition.[422] If a subsidiary is used in a Type A reorganization, under the triangular merger described in Code section 368(a)(2)(D), there is the same "substantially all" asset requirement as is found with the Type C reorganization. The reverse triangular merger and the Type B reorganization are similar except for the more rigid "solely for voting stock" requirement of the Type B reorganization.

(e) *"Control" Requirement*

In the case of a Type B reorganization, voting stock must be used to acquire control of the target company. "Control" is defined as "the ownership of stock possessing at least 80 percent of the total combined voting power of all classes of stock entitled to vote and at least 80 percent of the total number of all other classes of stock of the corporation."[423] The IRS has ruled that the 80 percent

[415] *Commissioner v. First National Bank of Altoona*, 39-2 U.S.T.C. ¶9568, 104 F.2d 865 (3d Cir. 1939).

[416] *National Bank of Commerce of Norfolk v. United States*, 58-1 U.S.T.C. ¶9278, 158 F. Supp. 887 (D.C. Va. 1958).

[417] Rev. Proc. 77-37, 1977-2 C.B. 568.

[418] *See, e.g., Smothers v. United States*, 81-1 U.S.T.C. ¶9368, 642 F.2d 894, 900 (5th Cir. 1981), in which the court stated, "Properly interpreted, therefore, the assets looked to when making the 'substantially all assets' determination should be all the assets, and only the assets, necessary to operate the business . . . ."

[419] Rev. Rul. 77-307, 1977-2 C.B. 117; PLR 8427072 (1984).

[420] Rev. Rul. 73-16, 1973-1 C.B. 186; Rev. Rul. 70-224, 1970-1 C.B. 79; Rev. Rul. 64-73, 1964-1 C.B. (Part 1) 142; PLR 8541105, July 18, 1985.

[421] I.R.C. §§368(a)(2)(D) and (E).

[422] I.R.C. §368(a)(2)(G).

[423] I.R.C. §368(e).

requirements are met only if this level of control is obtained in respect of each class of stock.[424]

Control need not be obtained in a single transaction.[425] An exchange of stock that increases the acquiring corporation's percentage ownership to the requisite level (creeping acquisitions) is therefore permitted so long as previously acquired target stock was acquired for voting stock. Moreover, control can be obtained in a bootstrap transaction in which the acquired corporation redeems a portion of its stock prior to the exchange.[426] Thus, prior redemptions of up to 20 percent of stock are permitted if the balance is acquired for voting stock. Where the acquiring corporation already controls the target, the acquisition of additional shares for voting stock of the parent will qualify as a Type B reorganization despite the failure to "acquire" control in such transaction.

(f) *Type B: Illustration*

Table 11.9 is a diagram of an acquisition of a BHC group that satisfies the Type B requirements.

[424] Rev. Rul. 59-259, 1959-2 C.B. 115.

[425] I.R.C. § 368(a)(1)(B).

[426] Rev. Rul. 68-285, 1968-1 C.B. 47. *Cf.* I.R.C. § 368(a)(2)(E) in which neither of these techniques for obtaining control is permitted. However, regulations promulgated under I.R.C. § 368(a)(2)(E) allow the redemption of the target company's stock.

Table 11.9 Type B: Acquisition of BHC

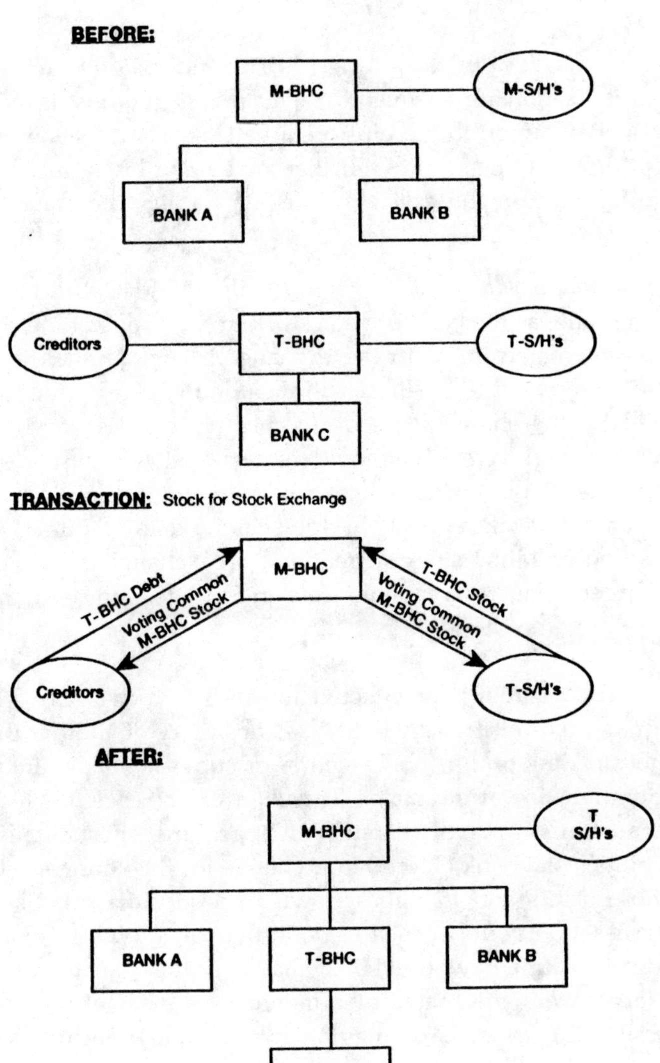

(g) *Type B: Tax Treatment of Parties*

(i) Nonrecognition of Gain or Loss. Because this acquisition was accomplished solely with voting stock of the acquiring M-BHC and the other requirements of the Type B reorganization are assumed to be met, no gain or loss is recognized by the acquiring M-BHC upon the receipt of Target's stock and solely in exchange for acquiring M-BHC voting stock.[427] Further, no gain or loss is recognized to the shareholders of Target on the exchange of their Target common stock for the voting common stock of M-BHC.[428]

(ii) Tax Basis and Holding Period. The basis that M-BHC will have in Target stock will be the same as the basis of such stock in the hands of the shareholders of the Target immediately prior to the exchange,[429] and the holding period of Target stock to be received by M-BHC will include the period during which the stock was held by the shareholders of Target.[430] The basis of M-BHC voting common stock received by the shareholders of Target will be the same as the basis of Target stock surrendered in the exchange,[431] and the holding period of M-BHC voting common stock received by the shareholders of Target will include the holding period of Target stock surrendered in exchange therefore, provided the shares of Target stock are as capital assets on the date of the exchange.[432]

(h) *Type C: Illustration*

A Type C reorganization is an effective means by which a BHC can acquire a bank.[433] This may occur even if the BHC is a subsidiary of another BHC. Such a structure is not uncommon for money-center or super-regional banks operating multiple corporations in various states. Thus, if a BHC (S-BHC), which itself is a subsidiary of a common parent (Parent BHC), acquires substantially all of the assets and liabilities of a bank (Target) in exchange for the voting stock of Parent, and drops those assets and liabilities down to a subsidiary bank of S- BHC (Bank), the transaction could meet the definition of a Type C reorganization. Further, tax-free treatment would be available if the transfer of assets and liabilities of Target were effectuated by a merger of the Target into Bank.[434] This may be necessitated because bank regulatory provisions preclude a BHC from acquiring directly the assets (including the charter) and liabilities of a bank. Finally, the IRS has ruled that the transfer of certain of the acquired assets and related liabilities to a newly formed subsidiary of S-BHC (Newcorp), also to accommodate restrictions imposed by bank regulatory provisions on the Bank acquiring those assets and liabilities, would not necessarily prevent the acquisition from qualifying for tax-free treatment. The acquisition by Newcorp (in the form of a purchase and assumption of liabilities) was limited to assets, the

427 I.R.C. § 1032(a).

428 I.R.C. § 354(a)(1).

429 I.R.C. § 362(b).

430 I.R.C. § 1223(2).

431 I.R.C. § 358(a)(1).

432 I.R.C. § 1223(1).

433 PLR 9409033, March 4, 1994.

434 Rev. Rul. 64-73, 1964-1 C.B. 142.

approximate value of which was equal to the amount of the liabilities assumed, and the assets transferred to Newcorp did not exceed 30 percent of the fair market value immediately before the transfer of the gross assets acquired from Target.[435]

Thus, a valid Type C reorganization using Parent stock in which assets and liabilities are dropped down into two subsidiaries may appear as diagrammed in Table 11.10.

[435] Reg. § 1.368-2(b)(2); Prop. Reg. § 1.368-2(j); Rev. Rul. 77-307, 1977-2 C.B. 117.

Table 11.10 Type C: Acquisition by BHC

BEFORE:

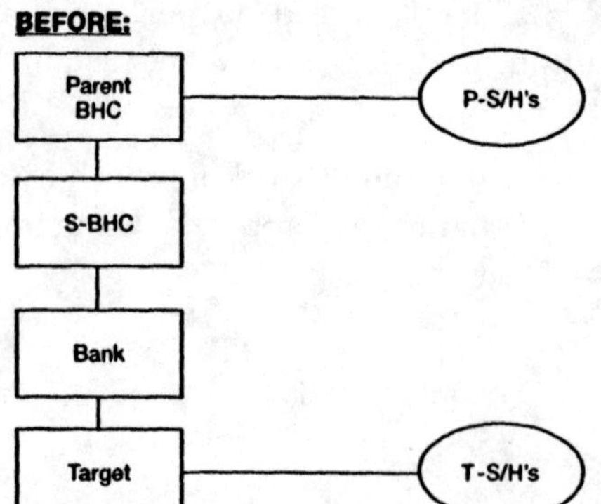

TRANSACTION: New Co. is formed. State A BHC directs substantially all of the assets of Target to be transferred to Bank in exchange for voting common stock of Parent. The transfer is effecuated as a merger. A portion of Target's assets are transferred to State A S&L, along with an equal amount of liabilities.

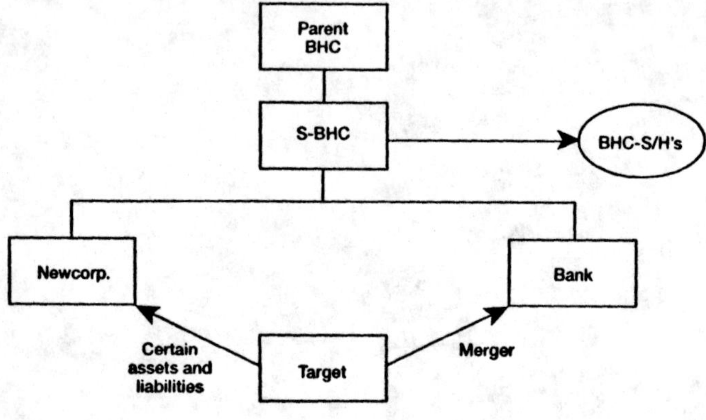

AFTER:

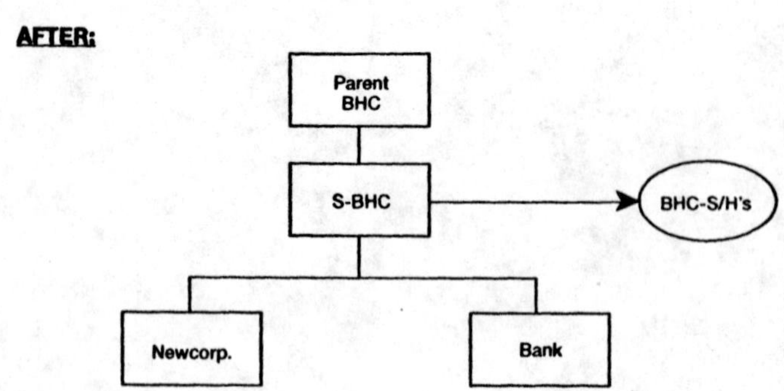

(i) *Type C: Tax Treatment of Parties*

(i) Nonrecognition of Gain or Loss. Because the transaction qualifies as a Type C reorganization, no gain or loss is recognized by Target on the transfer of substantially all of its assets and liabilities solely in exchange for Parent's voting common stock.[436] Moreover, no gain or loss will be recognized by Parent or Bank on the receipt of the assets of Target in exchange for the stock.[437] Target will recognize no gain or loss on the distribution to its shareholders of any property in pursuance of the plan of reorganization.[438] Moreover, no gain or loss will be recognized by the shareholders of Target upon the receipt of Parent voting stock solely in exchange for their shares of Target to common stock.[439] S-BHC also will recognize no gain or loss upon the transfer to Bank and to Newcorp of the assets and liabilities of Target in constructive exchange for the shares of Bank and Newcorp stock.[440]

(ii) Tax Basis and Holding Period. Consistent with the characterization of the transaction as a reorganization, the basis of Parent voting common stock received by the shareholders of Target will be the same as the basis of Target common stock surrendered in exchange therefore,[441] and the holding period of Parent voting common stock received will include the holding period of Target common stock surrendered provided Target common stock was held as a capital asset by the shareholders of Target on the date of exchange.[442] The holding period of the assets of Target that are deemed to be received by S-BHC will include the holding period during which the assets were held by Target,[443] and the basis of the assets in the hands of S-BHC will be the same as the basis of the assets in the hands of Target immediately prior to the exchange.[444]

The holding period of Target assets received by Bank and Newcorp will include the period during which the assets were considered held by S-BHC,[445] and the basis of the assets of Target transferred by S-BHC to Bank and to Newcorp will be the same as the basis of those assets in the hands of S-BHC immediately prior to the transfer.[446]

The basis of the stock of S-BHC in the hands of Parent will equal the basis of such stock immediately prior to the transaction, increased by the basis of Target assets acquired by S-BHC in the transaction and decreased by the amount of Target liabilities assumed in the transaction and the amount of liabilities to which Target assets are subject. The basis of Bank and Newcorp stock in the hands of S-BHC will equal the basis of such stock immediately prior to the transaction, increased by the basis of Target assets transferred to Bank and Newcorp in the transaction and decreased by the amount of Target liabilities assumed in the

[436] I.R.C. §§357(a) and 361(a).

[437] Rev. Rul. 57-278, 1957-1 C.B. 124.

[438] I.R.C. §§361(c)(1) and (2).

[439] I.R.C. §354(a)(1).

[440] I.R.C. §§357(a) and 368(a)(2)(C).

[441] I.R.C. §358(a)(1).

[442] I.R.C. §1223(1).

[443] I.R.C. §1223(2).

[444] I.R.C. §362(b).

[445] I.R.C. §1223(2).

[446] I.R.C. §362.

transaction by Bank and Newcorp and the amount of liabilities to which the transferred assets are subject.[447]

(j) *Type C: Sale versus Reorganization*

To qualify as a Type C reorganization, the transaction may not be a disguised sale of assets by Target to the acquiring corporation followed by the purchase of the acquiring corporation's stock by some of the Target firm's shareholders. In *Central National Bank of Lincoln, Nebraska*, the Board of Tax Appeals determined that an acquisition of assets was independent of a contemporaneous acquisition of the stock of the transferee.[448] Thus, the transaction was held to constitute a taxable sale and not a tax-free Type C reorganization.[449]

(k) *Corporate Formation versus Type B*

A transaction that fails to qualify as a Type B reorganization may still qualify for wholly or partially tax-free treatment under Code section 351 as a transfer to a corporation controlled by the transferor. Code section 351 conditions tax-free treatment on the transferor receiving nothing other than stock of the transferee and the transferor being in "control" of the transferee immediately after the transaction. For this purpose, "control" is defined, as it is for purposes of the Type B reorganization, as the ownership of stock possessing at least 80 percent of the total combined voting power of all classes of stock entitled to vote and at least 80 percent of the total number shares of all other classes of stock of the corporation.[450] The formation of a BHC structure qualifies as a Code section 351 transfer, although it may fail to qualify as a Type B reorganization.[451]

(l) *Corporate Formation: Illustration*

When a mutual savings and loan association wishes to establish a mutual holding company, the typical transaction may qualify under Code section 351. It often involves the following steps:

1. A mutual savings and loan association (Mutual) will incorporate a stock savings and loan association (Stock) to which it will transfer all of its assets. In exchange therefore, Stock will assume all of Mutual's liabilities and issue to Mutual voting common stock;
2. Stock will make a public offering of its stock to employee stock benefit plans, directors, officers, employees, depositors, borrowers, and other investors;
3. Mutual will amend its charter causing it to become a mutual holding company.

Thus, the transaction will appear as shown in Table 11.11.

---

[447] I.R.C. § 358(d)(1).

[448] *Central National Bank of Lincoln, Nebraska v. Commissioner*, 29 B.T.A. 719, Dec. 8354 (1934). *See also State Bank of Bloomington v. Commissioner*, 11 B.T.A. 66, Dec. 3717 (1928); *Cullen F. Thomas v. Commissioner*, 14 B.T.A. 1341, Dec. 4771 (1929).

[449] *See also National Bank of Commerce in Memphis v. United States*, 50-1 U.S.T.C. ¶9233, 180 F.2d 356 (6th Cir. 1950), *cert. denied*, 340 US 822 (1950).

[450] I.R.C. § 368(c).

[451] PLR 8539084, July 3, 1985.

Table 11.11 Code Section 351: Mutual Holding Company Formation

BEFORE:

Mutual Savings and Loan Association is controlled by its Board of Directors, who are elected periodically by its Share Account Holders and certain eligible borrowers.

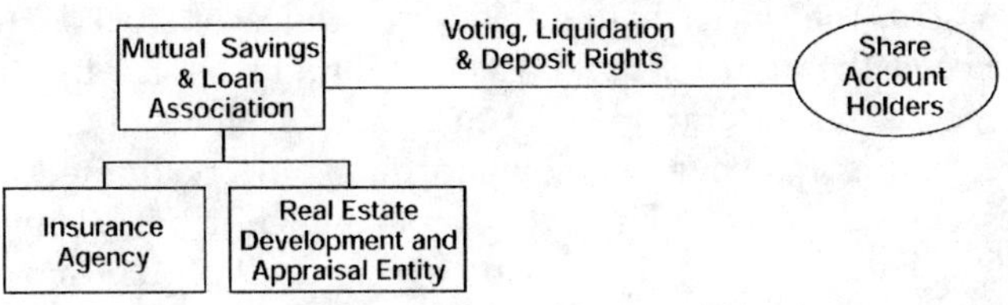

TRANSACTION: Incorporation/Charter Amendment/Asset and Liability Transfer

Mutual Savings & Loan incorporates a Stock Savings & Loan and transfers all of its assets to Stock Savings & Loan in exchange for common stock and for Stock Savings & Loan assuming all of Mutual Savings & Loan deposit and other liabilities. Mutual Savings & Loan amends its charter causing it to become a Mutual Holding Company. Stock Savings & Loan, in a public offering, sells some of its common stock to depositors, employees, and other investors, with Mutual Holding Company retaining "control."

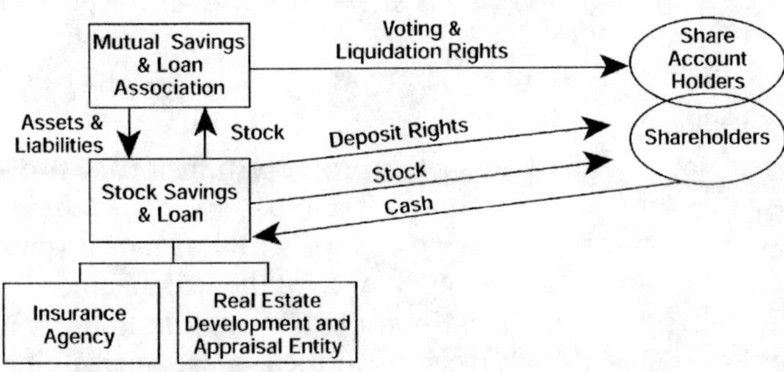

AFTER:

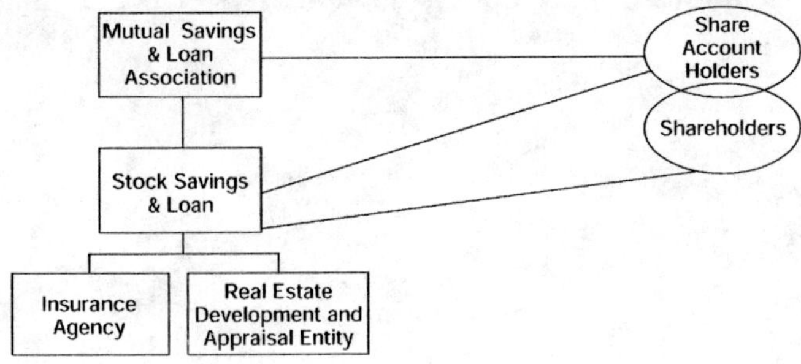

(m) *Corporate Formation: Tax Treatment of Parties*

(i) Nonrecognition of Gain or Loss. Because this transaction qualifies for tax-free status under Code section 351, no gain or loss will be recognized by Mutual on the transfer of its assets to Stock. Stock will recognize no gain or loss upon its receipt of property from Mutual in exchange for the issuance of stock.[452] If the liabilities of Mutual exceed the adjusted tax basis of Mutual's assets, the transferor is considered to receive consideration other than stock.[453] Thus, the transaction would lose tax-free status. However, taxable income would be limited to the amount that liabilities exceed basis.[454] Finally, Mutual will not be required to include any amount of its bad debt reserve in income as a result of the transfer of its loans. This is conditioned upon Mutual meeting the requirements for establishing a reserve for loan losses under Code section 593(a), immediately before the transaction and for Stock to meet those requirements immediately after the transaction.

(ii) Tax Basis and Holding Period. Consistent with the characterization of the transaction as tax-free, the transferor's tax basis in the stock received from the transferee will be the same as the basis of the property transferred, reduced by the amount of the liabilities assumed by the transferee or to which assets transferred as taken subject.

The tax basis which Mutual had in the property transferred to Stock will carry over to the latter provided that Stock establishes a bad debt reserve as discussed next.[455] In determining the taxpayer's basis in the loans it transfers, the amount of its bad debt reserve shall be netted against the loan balance.[456] Further, the tax-free status will result in a tacked holding period; that is the transferrers holding period in the common stock received in the transaction will include the period during which the property transferred was held, provided that such property was a capital asset or a Code section 1231 asset on the date of the exchange.[457]

---

[452] I.R.C. § 1032.
[453] I.R.C. § 357.
[454] I.R.C. § 351(b).
[455] I.R.C. § 362(a).
[456] Rev. Rul. 78-280, 1978-2 C.B. 139.
[457] I.R.C. § 1223(1).

(iii) Tax Attributes. Stock must establish a bad-debt reserve under Code section 593. The opening balance of Stock's bad-debt reserve must be equal to the reserve balance maintained by Mutual immediately before the transaction. The establishment of this initial reserve balance is not considered a deductible addition to a bad debt reserve by Stock. Each component of the initial reserve balance will be the same for Stock as for Mutual. Thus, the amount of the amounts of the qualifying, nonqualifying, supplemental, and pre-1952 reserves of Mutual will carry over to Stock.[458] A reserve addition will be permitted for the taxable year that includes the transaction. Also carried over will be Mutual's base year amount immediately before the transfer,[459] and Mutual's loans and bad debts for the five years preceding the transfer shall be treated as the loans and bad debts of Stock for purposes of calculating the six-year moving average amount.[460] The earning and profits of Mutual will remain with the institution when it converts to Mutual Holding Company and they will not be adjusted to reflect the transfer of its assets for stock.[461]

§ 11.5.4 Type D Reorganizations

(a) *General Characteristics*

A Type D reorganization is defined as a transaction in which assets are transferred to a corporation controlled by the transferor or by its shareholders and stock or securities of the transferee are distributed under Code section 354 or 355. Type D reorganizations encompass both divisive reorganizations (Code section 355) and nondivisive reorganizations (Code section 354).[462]

In a divisive Type D reorganization, one corporation transfers part of its assets to a controlled corporation in exchange for the controlled corporation's stock. Immediately thereafter, the transferor corporation distributes the controlled corporation's stock in a spin-off, split-off, or split-up, as those terms are described in Code sections 355 and 356.

A nondivisive Type D is similar to a divisive Type D, except that there is a transfer of substantially all of the assets of one corporation to a controlled corporation, followed by the liquidation of the transferor.[463] Thus, a transaction that fits the nondivisive Type D definition is the equivalent of a reincorporation with no change in the ownership of the transferor's business.

If a transaction would otherwise qualify under both the Type C and the Type D rules, it must conform with the more restrictive rules applicable to Type D reorganizations.[464] However, if a transaction qualifies under both the Type D and Type F rules, the IRS has ruled that it is to be treated as a Type F reorganization.[465] While the transaction will be tax-free regardless of which rules apply, the classification may have an effect on the tax treatment of boot as well as the carryover of corporate tax attributes.[466]

---

[458] Rev. Rul. 78-280, 1978-2 C.B. 139.

[459] I.R.C. § 585(b)(2)(B).

[460] I.R.C. § 585(b)(2)(A).

[461] Reg. § 1.312-11.

[462] I.R.C. § 368(a)(1)(D).

[463] I.R.C. § 354.

[464] I.R.C. § 368(a)(2)(A).

[465] Rev. Rul. 57-276, 1957-1 C.B. 126.

[466] *See* discussion of Type F reorganizations, *infra*.

(b) *BHC Reorganization*

Neither form of Type D reorganization is usually suitable for a corporate acquisition; however, a Type D reorganization does provide an effective method for a BHC to extend its business activities into another state. For example, in order to circumvent State A's banking law restrictions on an out-of-state bank operating within the state's borders, a BHC operating in State B may cause its State B bank subsidiary to spin off a segment of its operating assets to a sister corporation organized in State A. The IRS has ruled that such a transaction qualifies as a tax-free reorganization under the Type D rules, thereby affording nonrecognition treatment to the corporations involved.[467]

A Type D reorganization also is appropriate to separate the banking from the nonbanking businesses of a one-bank BHC. Thus, if a one-bank BHC that conducts a nonbanking and a banking business, directly and indirectly through subsidiaries, wishes to separate these activities, the Type D divisive reorganization often may be suitable. A somewhat typical transaction could involve the distribution of the non-banking business to certain shareholders and the banking business to others.[468]

(c) *Illustration*

Assume that the stock of a One-Bank BHC (O-BHC) was owned jointly by the A Group of shareholders (A-Group) and the B Group of shareholders (B-Group). A-Group was desirous of expanding the banking business by converting O-BHC into a multi-bank holding company (M-BHC), and B-Group wished to conduct and develop the non-banking business conducted, in part, by O-BHC and by subsidiary (S-1). To effectuate the reorganization of O-BHC, the shareholders and O-BHC agreed to a divisive Type D reorganization that resulted in the formation of a new subsidiary of O-BHC (S-2) to which the nonbanking business conducted directly by O-BHC is transferred and the transfer of other property, liabilities, and stock as depicted next (Table 11.12).

---

[467] PLR 8544038, August 1, 1985. *See also* PLR 8612063, December 24, 1985, in which the IRS ruled that a spin-off of a bank mortgage subsidiary qualified as tax-free under I.R.C. § 355.

[468] PLR 9434022, August 26, 1994.

Table 11.12 Type D: Divisive Reorganization

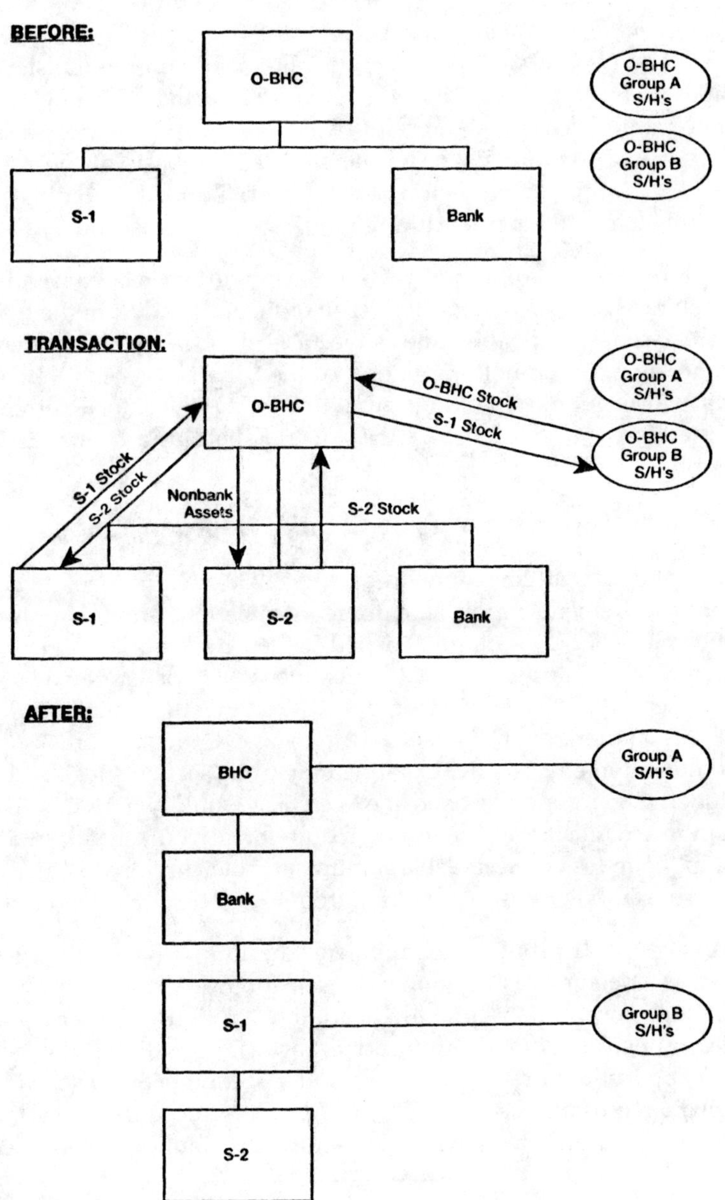

(d) ***Tax Treatment of Parties***

(i) Nonrecognition of Gain or Loss. Because the transaction qualifies as a Type D reorganization, O-BHC will recognize no gain or loss on the transfer of assets and liabilities and upon the distribution of stock.[469] Further, S-1 and S-2 will also recognize no gain or loss on the receipt of O-BHC's assets.[470] The basis of each asset received by S-1 and S-2 will be the same as the basis of the asset in the hands of O-BHC immediately before the transfer,[471] and the holding period of each asset will include the period during which the asset was held by O-BHC.[472]

The members of A-Group and B-Group also will not recognize any gain or loss upon the receipt of any property.[473] The basis of the stock in the hands of B-Group and A-Group will be the same as the basis of the stock of D surrendered in exchange therefore.[474] The holding period of the S-1 stock received by members of B-Group will include the holding period of the O-BHC stock surrendered in exchange therefore, provided the O-BHC stock is held as a capital asset on the date of distribution.[475]

§ 11.5.5 Charter Stripping of Type C and D Reorganizations

In 1989, the IRS in Revenue Procedure 89-50, determined "whether the distribution requirements applicable to reorganizations described in sections 368(a)(1)(C) and 368(a)(1)(D) [are] satisfied" when the "target corporation does not dissolve under state law so that the value of its corporate charter can be realized."[476] Regarding Type C Reorganizations, the IRS noted Code section 368(a)(2)(G)(ii) authorized the Secretary to waive Code section 368(a)(1)(C)'s distribution requirement. The IRS examined the Code section's legislative history and concluded Congress envisioned the Secretary would waive the distribution requirement in circumstances where the requirement would result in a substantial hardship. "The loss of a valuable nontransferable charter was considered to constitute a substantial hardship resulting from the distribution requirement."[477]

In waiving the distribution requirement, the IRS will treat the distribution requirement as a deemed distribution of "assets followed by a contribution to the capital of a new corporation" provided certain conditions are met.[478] Moreover, the IRS determined it was also appropriate to treat "the distribution of section 354(b)(1)(B) applicable to reorganizations under section 368(a)(1)(D) as satisfied under similar circumstances."[479] Finally, the IRS reproduced these "certain conditions under which it ordinarily will rule that the distribution requirement appli-

---

[469] I.R.C. §§ 361(a), 357(a), and 361(c).

[470] I.R.C. § 1032(a).

[471] I.R.C. § 362(b).

[472] I.R.C. § 1223(2).

[473] I.R.C. § 355(a)(1).

[474] I.R.C. § 358(a)(1); Reg. § 1.358-1(a).

[475] I.R.C. § 1223(1).

[476] Rev. Proc. 89-50.1989-2 C.B. 631. Again, reorganization treatment is vital because "[n]o gain or loss shall be recognized to a corporation if such corporation is a party to a reorganization and exchanges property, in pursuance of the plan of reorganization, solely for stock or securities in another corporation a party to the reorganization." I.R.C. § 361(a).

[477] *Id.*

[478] *Id.*

[479] *Id.*

cable to reorganizations under sections 368(a)(1)(C) and 368(a)(1)(D) of the Code has been satisfied.[480]

When state bank regulators or other local government agencies refuse to approve the bank charter transactions described in Rev. Proc. 89-50, the reorganizing corporation must get more creative. In Private Letter Ruling 200645006, a government agency did not allow a bank holding company to transfer a corporate entity that only held a state bank charter.[481] Specifically, Holdings 1, a bank holding company, was the parent of Acquiring, a State A Bank with a State A bank charter. Holdings 2, also a bank holding company, was the parent of Target, a State A Bank with a State A bank charter. Holdings 1 acquired Holdings 2. As a result, Holdings 1 had two State A bank charters. Not needing the extra charter, Holdings 1 wished to merge the operations of Acquiring and Target and then sell Target's bank charter to Foreign Bank, a corporation that operated in State B.

The government agency disallowed Holdings 1 permission to transfer the bank charter in accordance with Rev. Proc. 89-50. Instead, government agency required Holdings 1 to effectuate the following transaction: Holdings 1 contributed Acquiring to Holdings 2 and then caused Holdings 2 to transfer Target to Foreign Bank in exchange for cash. Holdings 2 received "cash in the amount equal to the sum of (i) the book value of Target ("Amount 1") and (ii) the value of the Target bank charter and any required minimum capital ("Amount 2")."[482] Acquiring then took that Amount 1 cash and bought back all of Target's assets now held by Foreign Bank with the exception of the bank charter. Thus, Acquiring kept Amount 1 and Holdings 1 was able to dispose of the extra bank charter.

The IRS ruled Acquiring engaged in a Type D Reorganization with Target when Acquiring obtained substantially all of Target's assets "solely in constructive exchange for Acquiring common stock and the assumption by Acquiring of the liabilities of Target, followed by the constructive distribution of Acquiring common stock in liquidation of Target."[483] The IRS ruled that there was no recognized gain or loss upon these transactions except with respect to the amount Foreign Bank paid for Target's State A bank charter. This private letter ruling demonstrates the IRS' willingness to maneuver around a local or state agency's refusal to approve Rev. Proc. 89-50 type transactions and allow reorganization treatment for merging entities that have to reallocate subsidiary assets to sell an extra bank charter.

(a) *Charter Stripping and Code Section 338(h)(10)*

There are other vehicles a corporation could employ to secure favorable tax treatment when seeking to sell an extra bank charter. For example, a corporation with a charter (P) acquires target (T) that has a charter of its own and P wants to sell T's charter. P wants to liquidate T, but would lose T's charter that is attached to T's stock. Thus, P will order T to distribute all operating assets to P except for minimum capital requirements T needs to retain its bank status. P then sells T to

[480] *Id.* The four conditions are listed in §3 of the Rev. Proc.

[481] PLR 200645006, November 10, 2006.

[482] *Id.*

[483] *Id.*

Acquirer (A) who only seeks to purchase T for the remaining charter. Both P and A could make a joint Code section 338(h)(10) election.[484] Code section 338(h)(10)(A) states:

> [I]f (i) the target corporation was, before the transaction, a member of the selling consolidated group, and (ii) the target corporation recognizes gain or loss with respect to the transactions as if it sold all of its assets in a single transaction, then the target corporation shall be treated as a member of the selling consolidated group with respect to such sale, and (to the extent provided in regulations) no gain or loss will be recognized on stock sold or exchanged in the transaction by members of the selling consolidated group.[485]

Thus, T, in this example, would not recognize any gain or loss on the distribution of its assets to P.[486] At the same time, the sale of the charter through the sale of the remainder of T to A would be a taxable transaction.

§ 11.5.6 Type E Reorganizations

(a) *General Rules*

A Type E reorganization involves the "recapitalization" (*i.e.*, reshuffling) of the capital structure of an existing corporation.[487] Although this type of reorganization generally involves only one corporation, the IRS has ruled that where a number of banks and bank holding companies exchange their stock for debt the transaction could qualify as a Type E reorganization.[488]

A Type E reorganization often involves an exchange of debt for newly issued stock. As a general rule, when a taxpayer's debts are satisfied at less than their face amount, income from discharge of indebtedness may be realized.[489] However, a corporation does not realize cancellation of indebtedness income when its debts are satisfied with its own stock, notwithstanding that the value of the stock is less than the face value of the debt.[490]

The Tax Reform Act of 1984 modified this rule for transactions initiated pursuant to contracts or options entered into on or after June 7, 1984.[491] As amended, Code section 108(e)(10) provides that a debtor corporation realizes gross income from discharge of indebtedness when it satisfies its debt with stock having a fair market value less than the principal amount of the debt. Exceptions are provided where the discharge occurs pursuant to a Title 11 (bankruptcy) case, to the extent the debtor is insolvent, and subject to certain loan workout situations.[492] Moreover, since corporate debt constitutes "qualified business indebtedness" within the meaning of Code section 108(a)(1)(C), the debtor corporation

---

[484] I.R.C. § 338(h)(10) holds that "an election may be made under which if– (i) the target corporation.

[485] I.R.C. § 338(h)(10)(A).

[486] *See also*, PLR 200447004, November 19, 2004; PLR 9735038, August 29, 1997.

[487] *Helvering v. Southwest Consolidated Corp.*, 42-2 U.S.T.C. ¶9630, 129 F.2d 1019 (5th Cir. 1942).

[488] PLRs 8142072, July 22, 1981; and 9031009, May 3, 1990.

[489] I.R.C. § 108.

[490] Rev. Rul. 70-271, 1970-1 C.B. 166; *Commissioner v. Capento Securities Corp.*, 44-1 U.S.T.C. ¶9170, 140 F.2d 382 (1st Cir. 1944); Rev. Rul. 59-227, 1959-1 C.B. 80; *Tower Bldg. Corp. v. Commissioner*, 6 T.C. 125, Dec. 14,947 (1946) (Acq.).

[491] Deficit Reduction Act of 1984, Pub. L. No. 98-369, 98 Stat. 494 (1984). *See* Conference Report on H.R. Rep. No. 98-861 at 4170 (1984), for additional transition rules under I.R.C. § 108(e)(10).

[492] I.R.C. § § 108(e)(10)(B) and (C).

may elect to reduce the basis of its depreciable assets and thereby defer income recognition.[493]

With respect to a debt-equity "swap" executed before July 18, 1984 (prior to the effective date of Code section 108(e)(10)), the IRS has ruled that application of the stock-for-debt exception to the rule requiring cancellation of indebtedness income was not limited to insolvent debtors. Moreover, the ruling held that the debt-equity "swap" will not be recast as a retirement of the taxpayer's outstanding debt for cash or other property. Thus, the taxpayer was not required to recognize cancellation of indebtedness income for the stock-for-debt exchange. The step transaction doctrine was not applied to treat the taxpayer as having retired its outstanding debt for cash because the underwriter was merely acting as an intermediary (agent) for the taxpayer.[494]

(b) *Mutual Conversion*

The Type E reorganization could apply to a conversion of a mutual savings bank to a stock bank.[495] In such a conversion, the mutual distributes to depositors who maintained deposit accounts at mutual their *pro rata* share of mutual's adjusted surplus and rights to purchase shares of the stock savings bank that will be issued in the conversion. Each depositor is permitted to elect to have his or her *pro rata* share of mutuals surplus deposited in an account with the stock savings bank, paid by check, or allocated to a subscription for shares of the stock savings bank.

§ 11.5.7 Type F Reorganizations

(a) *General Rules*

The Type F reorganization involves the "mere change in identity, form, or place of organization of one corporation, however effected."[496] In its current form the statute prevents the combination of identically owned brother-sister operating corporations or parent-subsidiary operating corporations from qualifying as a Type F reorganization. This amendment was designed to deny the more favorable net operating loss ("NOL") carryback rules applicable to Type F reorganizations to acquisitive reorganizations involving commonly controlled corporations.[497]

It is permissible for more than one corporation to be used to accomplish the change, so long as not more than one operating company is involved. Further, the reincorporation of an operating company in another state is a Type F

---

[493] I.R.C. § 108(b)(5). In a proposed IRS Industry Specialization Program Coordinated Issue Paper drafted by the Commercial Bank Industry Specialist Group, it is stated that when debentures are retired in an exchange for stock of a lower fair market value, the bank may recognize a taxable gain (however, the IRS has withdrawn this position paper). *See* draft at Appendix A1.115.

[494] PLR 8735006, May 18, 1987. I.R.C. § 108(e)(10), added by Pub. L. No. 99-514, requires cancellation of indebtedness income to be recognized by solvent corporate taxpayers for transactions effectuated after July 17, 1984.

[495] PLR 9207028, November 19, 1991.

[496] I.R.C. § 368(a)(1)(F). The words "one corporation" were added to the statute by the Tax Equity and Fiscal Responsibility Act of 1982. Tax Equity and Fiscal Responsibility Act of 1982, Pub. L. No. 97-248, 96 Stat. 324 (1982).

[497] General Explanation of the Revenue Provisions of the Tax Equity and Fiscal Responsibility Act of 1982, H. Res. 4961, 141.

reorganization, even though an interim (*i.e.*, nonoperating) corporation is, by necessity, employed.[498] The continuity-of-interest and business-enterprise tests do not apply to Type F reorganizations occurring on or after February 25, 2005.[499]

The Type F rules have been applied to prevent the bail-out of corporate earnings and profits by means of a liquidation-reincorporation type transaction.[500] In general, taxpayers retaining property distributed in such transactions will be treated as having received taxable boot if their ownership in the new corporation is substantially the same as it was in the old corporation, and the acquiring corporation will have a carryover tax basis in the assets it receives.

(b) *Illustration*

The typical conversion of a mutually organized thrift (*i.e.*, a thrift without stock or stockholders that is "owned" by its depositors) into a stock thrift may qualify as a Type F reorganization.[501] Thus, when a mutual savings and loan association wishes to convert to a stock savings and loan association and sell all of its stock to a recently formed BHC, the typical transaction often involves the following steps:

1. The mutual savings and loan association (Mutual) will convert to a stock savings and loan association (Stock);
2. All of the stock of the new Stock will be acquired by the BHC;
3. The BHC will issue shares of its common stock through the issuance of non-transferrable subscription rights without cost to eligible account holders and certain other depositors, BHC's employee stock ownership plan, trustees, officers and employees of Stock and, if necessary, a public offering. In exchange for a portion of the proceeds from the stock offering, the BHC will purchase 100 percent of the stock issued by Stock;
4. Stock will establish a liquidation account for the benefit of all eligible account holders who maintained accounts in Mutual as of a certain record date. The liquidation account balance will initially be an amount equal to the net worth of Mutual. Each eligible account holder will have a related in choate interest in a portion of the liquidation account balance; and
5. All voting rights in Stock will rest exclusively in its sole shareholder, the BHC, and the voting rights in the BHC will rest exclusively in the holders of the BHC's common stock.

---

[498] H.R. Rep. No. 760, 97th Cong., 2d Sess. 541 (1982).

[499] Reg. § 1.368-1(b).

[500] *J. E. Davant v. Commissioner*, 66-2 U.S.T.C. ¶ 9618, 366 F.2d 874 (5th Cir. 1966); *Reef Corp. v. Commissioner*, 66-2 U.S.T.C. ¶ 9716, 368 F.2d 125 (5th Cir. 1966).

[501] Rev. Rul. 80-105, 1980-1 C.B. 78; PLR 200021043, February 25, 2000; PLR 9528013, July 14, 1995. *See also* PLRs 8549026, September 9, 1985; 8535051, June 4, 1985; and 8542018, July 18, 1985, covering the conversion of a state-chartered mutual savings and loan association to a state-chartered stock savings and loan association. *See also* PLR 8534063, May 28, 1985, for conversion of a federal mutual savings and loan association to a federal stock savings and loan. Note that subscription offerings and public offerings may not be treated as part of the Type "F" reorganization. *See also* PLRs 8534063, May 28, 1985; 8539078, July 3, 1985; and 8824036, June 17, 1988; Rev. Rul. 80-105, 1980-1 C.B. 78.

Thus, the transaction will appear as shown in Table 11.13.

Table 11.13 Type F: Mutual Conversion

BEFORE:

TRANSACTION: Mutual Converts to Stock Savings & Loan; Stock Acquired by BHC

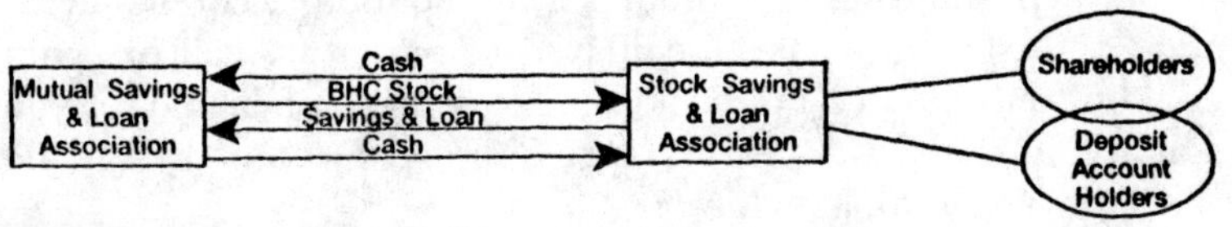

AFTER: Bank Holding Company is parent corporation of Stock Savings & Loan

(c) *Tax Treatment of Parties*

(i) Nonrecognition of Gain or Loss. Both Mutual and Stock are each considered to be "a party" to a Type F reorganization. No gain or loss will be recognized by Mutual when it converts its charter to a stock savings and loan association or by Stock upon the receipt of money from the BHC in exchange for shares of its common (or preferred) stock.[502] Further, no gain or loss will be recognized by the BHC on its receipt of money in exchange for shares of its common stock or upon the issuance to eligible account holders and others of subscription rights to purchase BHC stock or upon the lapse of those rights.[503] Neither the receipt nor the exercise of any subscription rights will result in gain or loss to the account holders.[504] Finally, the creation of a liquidation account by Stock will not affect Mutual or Stock's taxable income, section 593 bad-debt reserves, or section 593(e) distributions to shareholders.[505]

Gain, if any, will be realized by the eligible account holders upon the exchange of their interest in Mutual for liquidation accounts in Stock and subscription rights to purchase the BHC's common stock. This gain will be recognized, but only in an amount not in excess of the fair market value of the liquidation accounts and subscription rights received. Normally, the liquidation accounts will have a nominal value.[506]

(ii) Tax Basis and Holding Period. Consistent with the characterization of this transaction as a tax-free reorganization, the tax basis in the assets of the Mutual will be carried over to the Stock,[507] and the holding period of the assets of Mutual will be tacked to the holding period of Stock.[508] The holding period of the BHC common stock acquired through the exercise of subscription rights will commence on the date on which the rights are exercised.[509] The holding period of the common stock purchased pursuant to the public offering will commence on the date following the date on which the stock is purchased.[510]

---

[502] I.R.C. § 1032(a).

[503] *Id.*

[504] Rev. Rul. 56-572, 1956-2 C.B. 182. The IRS has consistently ruled that subscription rights received by eligible account holders qualify as tax-free distributions of stock rights under I.R.C. § 305. However, this position is not applicable to subscription rights received by borrower-members or to rights to acquire holding company stock. As a practical matter, the subscription rights have *de minimis* value, since they are designed only to ensure that the borrower-member is not frozen out of a public offering. Subscription rights received by directors and employers are normally compensatory in nature. Accordingly, they should be analyzed under the provisions of I.R.C. § 83. Since they have no readily ascertainable market value and the stock acquired pursuant to their exercise is acquired at current market value, both their receipt and exercise would be nontaxable.

[505] A "liquidation account" is required to be established and maintained under Federal Home Loan Bank Board regulations (12 C.F.R. § 563b.3(c)(13)) for the benefit of certain pre-conversion account holders of the converting institution. The liquidation account is used to establish the priority of those holding an interest in the account in the event of liquidation to the converting institution's assets. 12 C.F.R. § 563b.3(f)(3). The amount in the account represents the converting institution's regulatory capital or network as of the latest practical date prior to conversion. A liquidation account has both debt and equity features, and, thus, the interest therein may be regarded as a hybrid instrument.

[506] *Paulsen v. Commissioner*, 469 U.S. 131, 139 (1985), quoting *Society For Savings v. Bowers*, 349 U.S. 143 (1955); *but see* Rev. Ruls. 69-3, 1969-1 C.B. 103, and 69-648, 1969-2 C.B. 54, which indicate that the interests received may rise to the level of "stock" and, thus, I.R.C. § 354 may apply.

[507] I.R.C. § 362(b).

[508] I.R.C. § 1223(2).

[509] I.R.C. § 1223(6).

[510] Rev. Rul. 70-598, 1970-2 C.B. 168.

The eligible account holders will take as a tax basis in the savings accounts in Stock a substituted basis which will equal the basis they had in the accounts in Mutual.[511] The tax basis that each eligible account holder will have in the liquidation account of Stock will equal the cost of such property; that is, the fair market value of the proprietary interest in Stock received in exchange for the proprietary interest in Mutual. Therefore, the basis of each account holder's interest in the liquidation account and the basis in the subscription rights are zero.[512] However, the basis in the subscription rights may be increased by any gain recognized on their receipt. The tax basis of the BHC stock to its shareholders will equal the purchase price of the stock, increased (in the case of stock acquired pursuant to the exercise of subscription rights) by the basis, if any, of the subscription rights exercised.

(iii) Tax Attributes. Stock will be treated as if no reorganization took place for purposes of Code section 381. Thus, the taxable year of Mutual will not end on the effective date of the conversion, and the tax attributes of Mutual will be taken into account by Stock as if there had been no reorganization.[513] Accordingly, the part of the taxable year of Mutual that occurred before the effective date of the conversion will be included in the taxable year of Stock after the conversion.[514] The conversion of Mutual into stock form will not diminish the accumulated earnings and profits of Stock available for subsequent distribution of dividends, regardless of any book entries that may be made for the creation of the liquidation account,[515] and Stock will succeed to and take into account the earnings and profits or any deficit in earnings and profits of Mutual.

Stock also will succeed to and take into account immediately after the transaction the bad-debt reserves of Mutual no portion of the bad-debt reserves will be required to be recaptured by Mutual. The creation of the liquidation account on the records of Stock will have no effect on its taxable income, deductions or additions to reserves for bad debts, or distributions to shareholders under Code section 593(e).

(d) *NOLs*

The rules under Code section 381 applicable to the carryover of corporate tax attributes in Type F reorganizations are substantially more generous than those applicable to other types of reorganizations. The principal benefit available in a Type F reorganization is that the transferor's taxable year will not be terminated at the time of reorganization, thereby permitting post-reorganization NOLs to be carried back to pre-reorganization years if the requirements of Code section 382(b) are satisfied.[516]

---

[511] I.R.C. §1012.

[512] Rev. Rul. 71-233, 1971-1 C.B. 113.

[513] Reg. §1.381(b)-(1)(a)(2).

[514] Rev. Rul. 57-276, 1957-1 C.B. 126.

[515] I.R.C. §316; Reg. §§1.312-11(b) and (c).

[516] Note that in *Bercy Industries Inc. v. Commissioner*, 81-1 U.S.T.C. ¶9303, 640 F.2d 1058 (9th Cir. 1981), the court extended the rationale of I.R.C. §381(b)(3) to a triangular merger effected under I.R.C. §368(a)(2)(D) to permit the carryback of post-merger losses to premerger years, notwithstanding the clear language in I.R.C. §381(b)(3) limiting its application to Type F reorganizations.

In the case of a charter conversion merger, the IRS has ruled that, since the liquidation accounts are not stock within the purview of Code section 382(c), the NOLs of the target mutual may not be carried over.[517] This type of transaction has been variously treated by the IRS as a Type F reorganization (in which the thrift is converted into stock form) followed by a Type A reorganization (in which the stock thrift is merged into the acquiring corporation), or a Type A reorganization (in which case the conversion is treated as an integral part of the merger). Under prior law, the converted mutual's NOLs were "scaled down" to zero in the merger, since the "shareholders" of the converted mutual immediately before the merger (the liquidation account holders or the depositors, depending on whether the transaction was viewed as being one or two reorganizations) ended up with a liquidation account in the acquiring entity rather than "stock."

A liquidation account has generally been regarded by the IRS as equity for purposes of the reorganization sections, and the IRS has taken the position that it does not constitute nonvoting stock that is limited and preferred as to dividends for purposes of the consolidated return affiliation test.[518]

§ 11.5.8 Type G Reorganizations

(a) *General Rules*

Code section 368(a)(1)(G) was added to the Code by the Bankruptcy Tax Act of 1980[519] in order to facilitate the rehabilitation of financially troubled businesses. Prior to 1980, the availability of tax-free status in bankruptcy reorganizations depended upon conformity with the stringent rules relating to insolvency reorganizations contained in then-existing Code sections 371-374, which have since been repealed.[520]

The Economic Recovery Tax Act of 1981 ("ERTA") amended Code section 368(a)(1)(G) to clarify its application to financially troubled thrift institutions, to which Code section 593 applies.[521] The 1981 amendments eliminated the requirement for the acquired corporation to undergo formal receivership or similar

---

[517] PLR 8552068, September 30, 1985. Under the 1976 amendments to I.R.C. § 382, which were to have become effective January 1, 1986, I.R.C. § 382(b)(6)(A) replaced old I.R.C. § 382(b)(3) and utilized the term "stock" to describe the required ownership interest. Had this remained in the law, it would have resulted in a typical conversion eliminating the mutual's NOL. Private Letter Rulings issued by the IRS indicated that this provision (I.R.C. § 382(b)(3)) would apply in the case of a thrift conversion qualifying as a Type F reorganization. *See, e.g.*, PLR 8535051, June 4, 1985. Under the pre-1976 rules, I.R.C. § 382(b) would not operate to reduce a thrift's NOL carryover. Moreover, under such rules there would be no reduction in NOL carryovers even when there had been a change in control of the thrift (such as when the stock was sold to an investor), since there must be both a change in ownership and a change in the acquired firm's trade or business for I.R.C. § 382(a) to scale down NOL carryovers. I.R.C. § 382(a)(1)(C), prior to amendment by Pub. L. No. 99-514. Note that I.R.C. § 382(a)(2) may not apply to a change in control based on a converted mutual's sale of new stock, since that may be a I.R.C. § 351 transaction that is not a "purchase" and therefore not subject to I.R.C. § 382(a).

[518] PLR 8509083, December 5, 1984. Such preferred stock does not qualify as "stock" for purposes of the definition of an affiliated group. I.R.C. § 1504(a)(4).

[519] Bankruptcy Tax Act of 1980, Pub. L. No. 96-589, 94 Stat. 3389 (1980).

[520] H.R. Res. 96-5043, § 4 (1979); The Bankruptcy Tax Act of 1980, Pub. L. No. 96-589, 94 Stat. 3389 (1980); replaced existing I.R.C. §§ 371 and 372.

[521] Economic Recovery Act of 1981, Pub. L. No. 97-34, 95 Stat. 172 (1981). *See also* Rev. Proc. 82-13, 1982-1 C.B. 447. A "financially troubled thrift" to which I.R.C. § 593 applies is a mutual savings bank, domestic building and loan association, and a cooperative bank without capital stock and operated for mutual purposes and without profit.

proceedings and for the shareholders and creditors of the acquired corporation to receive stock in the reorganization.[522] These amendments also relaxed the rules concerning the acquisition of substantially all assets,[523] net operating loss carryovers, and the treatment of amounts received by a troubled thrift as assistance from the Federal Savings and Loan Insurance Corporation ("FSLIC").[524]

The Tax Reform Act of 1986 repealed the ERTA amendments to Code section 368, which exempted the acquisition of financially troubled thrifts from the otherwise applicable general reorganization rules.[525] The repeal is effective for acquisitions and mergers occurring after December 31, 1988.[526] Thus, the continuity-of-interest rules will apply to reorganizations of troubled thrifts occurring after that date, although in a relaxed form.

(b) *Pre-1989 Rules*

Under the rules in effect until 1989, no "stock or securities" of the transferee needed to be issued in a Type G reorganization. However, the other judicial requirements generally applicable to reorganizations (the "continuity-of-business-enterprise" and the "business purpose" tests) continued to apply to Type G reorganizations of thrift institutions.

Regulation section 1.368-1(b) and Code section 368(a)(3)(D)(ii), as in effect until 1989, provided for a waiver of the continuity-of-interest rule if three requirements are met:

1. The requirements of subparagraphs (A) and (B) of Code section 354(b)(1) are met with respect to the acquisition of the assets of the transferor;
2. Substantially all of the liabilities of the transferor immediately before the transfer become, as a result of the transfer, liabilities of the transferee; and
3. The Federal Home Loan Bank Board ("FHLBB") certifies that the grounds set forth in section 1464(d)(6)(A)(i), (ii), or (iii) of Title 12, United States Code, exist with respect to the transferor or will exist in the near future in the absence of action by the Board.

---

[522] In place of a formal receivership or "similar proceeding," the thrift must obtain certifications regarding its financial condition from the FDIC or FHLBB.

[523] I.R.C. §§368(a)(2)(D), 354(b)(1)(A), and 354(b)(1)(B). In the case of troubled thrifts, the legislative history of I.R.C. §368(a)(3)(D), prior to amendments made by The Tax Reform Act of 1986, indicated that this requirement was intended to be interpreted liberally and in light of the overriding intent of the section, which is to "facilitate" reorganizations of troubled thrifts. *See, e.g.*, S. Rep. No. 96-1035 (1980), *reprinted in* 1980 U.S.C.C.A.N., 7077, 7021. Thus, reorganizations of troubled thrifts could qualify for Type G treatment even if substantial amounts of assets are sold to raise cash to pay off creditors and to enhance the thrift's attractiveness to potential acquirers.

[524] I.R.C. §382(b)(7), prior to amendment by Pub. L. No. 99-514, 100 Stat. 2085 (1986). In addition, thrifts receiving FSLIC payments were relieved from the I.R.C. §362(c)requirement that basis in property be reduced by the amount of any nonshareholder (FSLIC) contributions to capital.

[525] Pub. L. No. 99-514, §904(a), 100 Stat. 2085 (1986).

[526] Pub. L. No. 99-514, §1804(g)(2), 100 Stat. 2085 (1986). The Tax Reform Act of 1986 also repealed the exclusion from gross income of a domestic building and loan association of any money or other property received from the FSLIC pursuant to Sec. 406(f) of the National Housing Act (12 U.S.C. §1729(f) Repealed. Pub. L. No. 101-73, Title IV, 409, Aug. 9, 1989, 103 Stat. 363). Pub. L. No. 99-514, §904(b)(1), 100 Stat. 2085 (1986). The repeal of the special treatment of these payments is effective for payments after 1988, unless such payments are made pursuant to an acquisition or merger occurring on or before that date. Pub. L. No. 99-514, §904(c), 100 Stat. 2085 (1986).

In waiving the continuity-of-interest rule, Congress was attempting to facilitate mergers of troubled thrifts into stronger institutions.[527] If the foregoing requirements were met, tax-free treatment as a Type G reorganization was permitted regardless of whether (a) the acquiring firm was a bank, thrift, or other company with or without stock and the target was a mutual without stock, or (b) the account holders of the target mutual receive stock in the acquiring company.[528]

The reference to "board certification" in Code section 368(a)(3)(D) was to a determination by the FHLBB or FSLIC (or comparable state authority if there is no federal jurisdiction) that the thrift is insolvent (*i.e.*, liabilities exceed assets) or, absent regulatory intervention, would soon become insolvent; its assets are substantially dissipated because of unsafe or unsound practices or because of violations of law; or the thrift is in an unsafe or unsound condition to transact business.[529] The legislative history of the ERTA amendment to the Type G reorganization rules makes it clear that certification is inappropriate where the thrift purposely has placed itself in a condition that would otherwise support certification.[530] The final requirement of a thrift Type G reorganization is that the transferee assume "substantially all" of the transferor's liabilities. This requirement is intended to ensure that the FSLIC is relieved of responsibility for customer deposit liabilities of the transferor.

(c) *Current Rules*

A Type G reorganization is defined as a transfer by one corporation of all or part of its assets to another corporation in a Title 11 bankruptcy or similar case, but only if, in pursuance of the plan, stock or securities of the corporation to which the assets are transferred are distributed in a transaction that qualifies under Code sections 354, 355, and 356. In order for a transaction to qualify as a Type G reorganization, "substantially all" of the assets of the target entity must be acquired. For purposes of the Type G reorganization provisions, a case under Title 11 (of the United States Code) is a proceeding under the Bankruptcy Act of 1980. The term "similar case" includes receivership, foreclosure or similar proceeding before either a federal or a state court.

---

[527] *See* Staff of Joint Committee on Taxation, "General Explanation of the Economic Recovery Tax Act of 1981," August 1, 1981, at 153.

[528] PLR 8551064, September 27, 1985. In Rev. Proc. 85-34, 1985-2 C.B. 433, *modifying* Rev. Proc. 85-22, 1985-1 C.B. 183, the IRS announced that it would resume issuing advance rulings or determination letters on the issue of whether the conversion of a financial institution from mutual to stock qualifies for tax-free treatment under I.R.C. §§368(a)(1)(G) and 368(a)(3)(D), without regard to whether the stock of the converted financial institution is acquired by a financial institution to which either I.R.C. §585 or I.R.C. §593 applies.

[529] 12 U.S.C. §1964(d)(6)(A)(i), (ii) and (iii). Where the Federal Home Bank Board or the FSLIC do not have jurisdiction, certification would be obtained from appropriate state agencies. I.R.C. §368(a)(3)(D)(ii)'s omission of a reference to the FDIC is inadvertent. It has caused, for example, New York mutual savings banks to seek certification from the New York Banking Department (rather than the FDIC) in order to qualify an acquisition or conversion under the Type G reorganization provisions.

[530] H.R. Conf. Rep. No. 97-215 (1981).

Example: Mortgage Company has been declared insolvent in a Title 11 proceeding. It transfers all of its assets to a BHC in exchange for stock and debt of BHC. Mortgage Company then distributes the BHC stock and debt to its security holders. Pursuant to Code sections 361 and 368(a)(1)(G), Mortgage Company will recognize no gain or loss on the exchange. Similarly, Code section 354(a) will prevent the exchanging security holders from recognizing any realized gain or loss. Code sections 381 and 382(b) will permit BHC to succeed to Mortgage Company's tax history.

In order for a transaction to qualify as a Type G reorganization, "substantially all" of the assets of the target entity must be acquired. In the case of Type G reorganization, the substantially all requirement is less restrictive than in the case of other forms of acquisitive reorganizations. Consistent with the intent of the bankruptcy law, the requirement is to be interpreted to facilitate the reorganization of companies in distressed situations.[531]

Example: Prior to the transfer to the acquiring corporation, payments to creditors and asset sales occurred in order to leave the debtor corporation with more manageable operating assets with which to continue in business. This transaction is not precluded from satisfying the substantially all test.[532]

In many respects, the Type G reorganization resembles a Type D reorganization, but it does have several important differences. Unlike the Type D reorganization, in a Type G reorganization neither the transferor nor its shareholders need control the transferee immediately after the reorganization. Moreover, a Type G reorganization may involve either the division of a failing enterprise or its acquisition by an unrelated corporation. Whenever a reorganization would otherwise qualify under both the Type G rules and another subdivision of Code section 368(a)(1), the Type G rules have exclusive jurisdiction.[533]

The Type G reorganization also can more easily satisfy the continuity-of-interest doctrine that must be satisfied by all forms of corporate reorganizations. In the case of other reorganizations, the IRS requires that shareholders of the acquired corporation receive an equity interest in the acquiring corporation as consideration for at least 50 percent of the value of their equity in the acquired corporation. In a Type G reorganization, creditors are considered shareholders for purposes of the continuity-of-interest requirement. Thus, the continuity-of-interest requirement may be met where creditors of a bankrupt corporation have a continuing interest in the acquiring corporation in the form of stock ownership but the shareholders retain no equity interest.

Example: In a Type G reorganization, Banc Corp. acquires the assets of Debtor Corp., which is insolvent. As part of the acquisition, Banc Corp. transfers $100,000 of Banc Corp. stock and $100,000 of securities for the assets of Debtor. The Banc Corp. stock and the securities are distributed to Debtor's security holders. Under the Type G reorganization provisions, the security holders of Debtor are considered as owners. Thus, since at least 50

[531] S. Rep. No. 96-1035 (1980).

[532] *Id.*

[533] I.R.C. § 368(a)(3)(C).

percent of the consideration received by the security holders was in the form of Banc Corp. stock, the continuity-of-interest requirement has been satisfied.

Acquisitive Type G reorganizations can be effected in a variety of ways, including:

1. The acquisition of assets and the assumption of substantially all of the liabilities of an entity by a newly formed subsidiary of the acquiring corporation;[534]
2. A triangular merger of a subsidiary of the acquiring corporation with the target;[535]
3. An acquisition of the failing corporation's assets followed by a drop-down of those assets;[536] and
4. A direct merger (often termed a "supervisory merger") of a troubled entity into the acquiring corporation (or a newly formed subsidiary of the acquiring corporation).[537]

(d) ***Carryforward of Losses***

If a transaction qualifies as a Type G reorganization, it will be eligible for all of the tax benefits normally flowing from qualification as a tax-free reorganization. This includes the carryover of corporate tax attributes provided by Code section 381;[538] however, the Code section 382 limitation on NOL carryforwards and built-in losses will apply to a Type G acquisition or merger.

§ 11.6 Federal Financial Assistance

Code section 597 contains the rules for determining the tax treatment of federal financial assistance (hereinafter "FFA"). It was enacted as part of the Economic Recovery Tax Act of 1981 in response to the then-emerging savings and loan crisis.[539] As originally enacted, Code section 597 provided that money or other property provided to a domestic building and loan association by the Federal Savings and Loan Insurance Corporation ("FSLIC") was excluded from the recipient's gross income,[540] and that such recipient was not required to make a downward adjustment to the basis of its assets.

The Technical and Miscellaneous Revenue Act of 1988 modified Code section 597 by requiring taxpayers to reduce certain tax attributes by one-half of the amount of financial assistance received from the FSLIC or the Federal Deposit Insurance Corporation ("FDIC").[541] Thus, troubled financial institutions could still receive half of such financial assistance without any corresponding reduction in tax attributes. These rules continued to allow the FSLIC and the FDIC to

[534] PLR 8535054, June 5, 1985.

[535] I.R.C. §§ 368(a)(2)(D) and 368(a)(2)(E).

[536] I.R.C. § 368(a)(2)(C).

[537] PLRs 8534054, June 5, 1985; and 8551064, September 27, 1985. Acquisitive Type G reorganizations also encompass supervisory conversions followed by a transfer of stock to the acquirer.

[538] I.R.C. § 381(a)(2). *See also* I.R.C. § 381(c)(4).

[539] Pub. L. No. 97-34.

[540] I.R.C. § 118

[541] Pub. L. No. 100-647.

arrange acquisitions of troubled financial institutions by healthy financial institutions at a tax-subsidized cost.[542]

The Financial Institutions Reform, Recovery, and Enforcement Act of 1989 ("FIRREA") further amended Code section 597 by providing that FFA would be treated as taxable income.[543] Thus, the FIRREA amendments repealed the special provisions enacted in ERTA. The change was made because "Congress believed that . . . [the]1981 Act rules were inconsistent with the policies of normal tax rules that otherwise would apply to . . . [depository] institutions. Moreover, the Congress believed that these special rules were unfair since they provided beneficial treatment to a select class of beneficiaries."[544] In essence, Congress believed that a tax subsidy no longer was necessary because the provisions of FIRREA that deem FFA to be included in the troubled financial institution's income at the time the institution's assets are sold or transferred generally would cause the FFA inclusion to be offset by the institution's losses.[545]

In 1995, the Treasury Department and the IRS issued the current set of regulations that provided comprehensive guidance for banks and domestic building and loan associations, including their affiliates, and a financial institution that acquires the troubled institution's assets and liabilities in a transaction facilitated by the Resolution Trust Corporation, the FDIC, any similar instrumentality of the U.S. government, and any predecessor or successor of the foregoing (including the FSLIC).

The current regulations reflect certain principles derived from the legislative history of FIRREA.[546] First, FFA generally is treated as ordinary income of the troubled institution that is being compensated for its losses through the provision of assistance. Second, an institution should not get the tax benefit of losses for which it has been compensated with FFA. Third, the timing of the inclusion of FFA should, where feasible, match the recognition of the institution's losses. Finally, the income tax consequences of the receipt of FFA as part of a transaction in which a healthy institution acquires a troubled institution should not depend on the form of the acquisition (for example, the income tax consequences should not differ depending on whether the stock or the assets of a troubled institution are acquired).

§11.6.1 Federal Financial Assistance, Defined

According to Code section 597(c) and the regulations issued thereunder, FFA is money or property provided by the Federal Deposit Insurance Corporation (hereinafter "FDIC")[547] pursuant to banking law that is either:

---

542 Notice 89-102, 1989-2 C.B. 436.

543 Pub. L. No. 101-73, Section 1401.

544 Jt. Comm. Gen. Exp. Tax Reform Act of 1986, Pub. L. No. 99-514, Pt. 3, Title IX.

545 *Id.* at 27.

546 Proposed regulations promulgated will modify and clarify the treatment of transactions in which FFA is provided to such institutions. REG-140991-09, 80 FR 28872-01 (May 20, 2015).

547 I.R.C. §597(c)(1) includes in the definition of FFA money or other property provides by the Federal Savings and Loan Insurance Corporation or Resolution Trust Corporation. These entities are no longer in existence. The insurance of domestic building and loan associations, which had been provided for by the Federal Savings and Loan Insurance Corporation, is not provided for by the FDIC. The Resolution Trust Corporation was created to assist in the liquidation of failed domestic and

1. Received by a financially troubled bank or domestic building and loan association described in Code section 7701(a)(19)(A)-(B) (hereinafter, "thrift institution"),[548] or
2. Provided to another bank or thrift institution to facilitate the acquisition of the financially troubled bank or thrift institution.[549]

FFA can take several forms, including loss guarantees and net worth assistance. The former means an agreement pursuant to which a banking agency guarantees or agrees to pay an institution a specified amount upon the disposition or charge-off (in whole or in part) of specific assets, or an agreement pursuant to which an institution has a right to put assets to the banking agency at a specified price, or a similar arrangement.[550] Net worth assistance means money or property (including an agency obligation to the extent it has a fixed principal amount) that the agency provides as an integral part of a taxable transfer, other than FFA that accrues after the date of the taxable transfer.[551] The issuance of a note or other obligation by the institution or any of its affiliates has no effect on whether the money or property provided by the FDIC is considered FFA.[552]

Supervisory goodwill is not treated by the IRS as FFA even though it was recognized as a regulatory intangible. It was created under special accounting rules used by the now defunct Federal Home Loan Bank Board ("FHLBB") during the 1980s in connection with acquisitions of insolvent savings and loan associations and other similarly chartered institutions ("thrifts"), the deposits of which were insured by the Federal Savings and Loan Insurance Corporation ("FSLIC"), another entity that is no longer in existence.[553] The IRS also does not recognize supervisory goodwill as an asset having tax basis.

In 2008, the Treasury Department issued Notice (2008-101) that announced that no amount furnished by the Treasury under the Troubled Asset Relief Program established by the Emergency Economic Stabilization Act of 2008[554] will be treated as the provision of FFA within the meaning of Code section 597.[555] The Notice provided further that any future contrary guidance will not apply to transactions with the Treasury or to securities issued by financial institutions to the Treasury prior to the publication of that guidance, or to securities insured pursuant to binding written contracts entered into prior to that date.[556]

(Footnote Continued)

building and loan associations during the banking crisis of the early 1990's.

[548] I.R.C. § 597(d).

[549] I.R.C. § 597(c).

[550] Reg. § 1.597-1(b).

[551] *Id.*

[552] *Id.*

[553] *See* "Supervisory Goodwill—LMSB Coordinated Issue" in Appendix at § A.19 and "Supervisory Goodwill—Settlement Guidelines" in Appendix at § A.18.

[554] Pub. L. No. 110-343.

[555] Notice 2008-101, 2008-44 I.R.B. 1082.

[556] The rules set forth in Reg. §§ 1.597-1 through -6 are generally effective for tax years ending on or after April 22, 1992. However, the rules contained in Notice 89-102 apply to FFA in connection with an agency-assisted acquisition that occurred before April 22, 1992. Reg. § 1.597-7. Taxpayers may also rely on the provisions of Prop. Reg. §§ 1.597-1 through -6 to the extent that the provisions were relied on prior to December 21, 1995. Reg. § 1.597-7(d)(2). Transitional rules are also provided for FFA received or accrued on or after May 10, 1989, if the assistance relates to an acquisition that occurred before that date. Reg. § 1.597-8.

§11.6.2 Principles Used in Prescribing Regulations

Regulations sections 1.597-1 through -8 generally reflect the following principles derived from the FIRREA:

1. FFA is treated as ordinary income of the institution;[557]
2. The FFA inclusion, if possible, should match recognition of the institution's losses;[558]
3. If possible, the income tax consequences of an assisted acquisition should not depend on its form;[559] and
4. The IRS will not collect tax on FFA if it determines that a federal insurer would bear the burden of the tax.[560]

§11.6.3 Income Inclusion of FFA

Generally, FFA is includible in the income of the failed institution when received or accrued, in accordance with the institution's method of accounting.[561] FFA that is provided directly or indirectly to a shareholder of the institution is treated as directly received by the institution, "to the extent money or property is transferred [by the shareholder] to the institution pursuant to an agreement with Agency." When FFA is provided in the form of property, the institution's basis in the property is its fair market value or the issue price of an agency obligation (an agency obligation is a debt instrument issued by the agency to the institution).[562]

Congress intended that FFA income "generally will be offset by the net operating losses and built-in losses of the financially troubled institution."[563] Treasury regulations prescribe rules that attempt to ensure that in certain cases, the current inclusion of FFA income matches the recognition of the institution's losses.[564] The limitation on the current inclusion of FFA is based on a formula that approximates the tax benefits currently available or previously used. The deferral formula applied depends upon whether the institution has continuing equity.

A less favorable deferral formula is available to institutions with continuing equity than to those without continuing equity. The formula requires that the institution recapture deferred FFA even if built-in losses remain unrealized. An institution has continuing equity if, on the last day of the tax year, the institution is not a bridge bank, not in agency receivership, or not treated as a new entity.[565] The continuing equity deferral provisions generally apply to a limited number of "open bank" resolutions not subject to the deemed taxable transfer rules.

The amount of FFA includible in income by an institution with continuing equity is limited to the sum of:

---

557 Reg. §1.597-1(b).

558 Reg. §1.597-2 (a). The term "institution" is defined to mean an entity that is, or immediately before being placed under agency control was, a bank or domestic building and loan association within the meaning of I.R.C. §597 (including a bridge bank). Reg. §1.597-1(b).

559 Reg. §1.597-3(a).

560 Reg. §1.597-6(a).

561 Reg. §1.597-2 (a)(1).

562 Reg. § 1.597-2 (b) and -3(c)(2).

563 H.R. Conf. Rep. No. 101-222, at 463 (1989).

564 Reg. §1.597-2 (c).

565 Reg. §1.597-1 (b).

1. The excess of the institution's liabilities over the adjusted basis of its assets at the beginning of the tax year (representing losses already recognized);
2. The institution's taxable loss for the tax year, without regard to FFA or net operating or capital loss carryovers, (or, if greater, that of the consolidated group of which the institution is a member); and
3. Net operating losses available to the institution or its consolidated group in excess of the amount in (1), above.[566]

The amount of FFA includible in income by an institution without continuing equity is limited to the sum of:

1. The excess of the institution's liabilities over the adjusted basis of its assets at the beginning of the tax year (representing losses already recognized); and
2. The institution's taxable loss for the tax year (without regard to FFA or net operating or capital loss carryovers) in excess of the amount in (1), above.[567]

An institution with or without continuing equity must maintain a deferred FFA account in the first tax year that it receives FFA that is not included in income.[568] The opening balance in that account is the FFA not included in income. The account is decreased for deferred FFA recapture, additional deferred FFA recapture by an institution with continuing equity, and any optional recapture of deferred FFA.

An institution will generally recapture deferred FFA as it recognizes losses in subsequent tax years. However, an institution with continuing equity must recapture deferred FFA ratably over six years regardless of whether it recognizes its built-in losses during that time.[569] The IRS believes that the six-year time period "is a reasonable safeguard against indefinite deferral of FFA income."[570] An accelerated recapture option is available to any institution not under agency control.[571]

Example: United Bank is an institution without continuing equity because it is in agency receivership. At the beginning of its calendar tax year, it has assets with a total adjusted basis of $100 million and total liabilities of $120 million. The bank's deductions do not exceed its gross income for the tax year. During the tax year, the agency provides it with $30 million in FFA. United Bank must include in income $20 million, which represents the amount of liabilities ($120 million) that exceed the total adjusted basis of the assets at the beginning of the tax year United Bank must establish a deferred FFA account for the remaining $10 million in FFA.[572]

---

566 Reg. § 1.597-2 (c)(3).

567 Reg. § 1.597-2 (c)(2).

568 Reg. § 1.597-2(c)(4).

569 Reg. § 1.597-2(c)(4)(iii) and (iv).

570 60 Fed. Reg. 66091, 66092 (December 21, 1995), T.D. 8641.

571 Reg. § 1.597-2(c)(4)(v).

572 Reg. § 1.597-2(e), Ex. 1.

§ 11.6.4 Transfers of Property by Institution

The transfer by the institution of property to the FDIC or other agency (or an entity under agency control) results in a taxable sale or exchange.[573] The institution is treated as realizing an amount equal to the property's fair market value for purposes of determining gain or loss under Code section 1001. If, however, the property is subject to a loss guarantee, the amount realized is the greater of the property's fair market value or the guaranteed value or price at which the property can be put at the time of transfer. An adjustment to FFA is required where the fair market value of the property transferred exceeds the consideration received from the agency.[574] The adjustment to FFA and deferred FFA is made by reducing in the following order:

1. The amount of FFA otherwise includible in income for the tax year (before application of Regulation section 1.597-2(c); and
2. The balance in the deferred FFA account maintained under Regulation section 1.597-2(c)(4).[575]

An agency and an institution may enter into a loss guarantee agreement under which the agency agrees to pay the institution a stated amount upon the disposition or charge-off of specific assets.[576] When the institution transfers property subject to a loss guarantee to the agency, the amount realized is the greater of:

1. The property's fair market value, or
2. The guaranteed value or price at which the property can be put at the time of transfer.

When the institution sells the property to a third party, FFA received from the agency is included in the amount realized. The amount realized, however, is limited to the greater of the fair market value of the property or the guaranteed value or price at which the property can be put at the time of the transfer.[577]

§ 11.6.5 Bridge Banks and Residual Entities

An institution is under FDIC or similar agency control if the agency is the conservator or receiver or if the agency has the right to appoint any of the institution's directors.[578] A bridge bank is organized by an agency to hold assets and liabilities of another institution and to continue the operation of that institution's business pending its acquisition or liquidation.[579] A residual entity is the entity that remains after the institution transfers its deposit liabilities to a bridge bank.[580] A bridge bank (or other institution under agency control) is treated as a corporation within the meaning of Code section 7701(a)(3) even if the agency owns stock of the institution.[581]

---

573 Reg. § 1.597-2(d).

574 Reg. § 1.597-2(d)(4).

575 Reg. § 1.597-2(d)(5)(i).

576 Reg. § 1.597-1(b).

577 Reg. § 1.597-2(d)(1)(ii) and (2).

578 Reg. § 1.597-1(b).

579 *Id.*

580 *Id.*

581 Reg. § 1.597-4(b).

(a) ***Treatment of Bridge Banks and Residual Entity***

As a general rule, the bridge bank and its associated residual entity are treated as the successor entity to the transferring institution if the transfer includes deposit liabilities.[582] The transferring institution recognizes no gain or loss when it transfers deposit liabilities to the bridge bank. The bridge bank takes a carryover basis in any transferred assets and succeeds to the other tax attributes, including the deferred FFA account, if any, of the transferor. The associated residual entity retains its basis in any assets it continues to hold.[583] The bridge bank also succeeds to and takes into account the transferring institution's tax year. After the transfer, the bridge bank and any residual entities are treated as a single unit for income tax purposes and must file a combined income tax return. The bridge bank is responsible for filing all income tax returns and information returns for the single entity until either is acquired by new owners.[584]

(b) ***Members of Consolidated Groups***

Unless an election is made to disaffiliate (see below), agency control of an institution does not terminate the institution's membership in a consolidated group.[585] This allows FFA to be included in the income of the institution or consolidated group, at least to the extent that the group benefited from the losses. If an institution is a member of a consolidated group immediately before it transfers deposit liabilities to the bridge bank, the bank succeeds to the institution's status in the group. Upon a bank's succession to an institution's status as a subsidiary member, the bank's stock is treated as held by the shareholders of the transferring institution and the stock basis or excess loss account of the institution carries over to the bridge bank.

A consolidated group with a subsidiary under agency control may elect not to include the subsidiary institution in its affiliated group. To make the election, the consolidated group must send a written statement by certified mail to the affected institution on or before the later of 120 days after its placement in agency receivership or May 31, 1996. The consolidated group must include a copy of any election statement and accompanying certified mail receipts with its first federal income tax return filed after the election.[586] There is a five-year consistency requirement for the treatment of all subsidiary institutions in agency receivership.[587]

A deemed election, subject to a toll charge, is imposed if members of a consolidated group deconsolidate a subsidiary institution in contemplation of agency control or the receipt of FFA. A conclusive presumption of contemplation arises if either event occurs within six months after deconsolidation. A deemed election is also imposed when deposit liabilities are transferred to a bridge bank

[582] Reg. § 1.597-4(d). Special rules apply to bridge banks that receive deposit liabilities from two or more transferors. Reg. § 1.597-4(d)(2).

[583] Reg. § 1.597-4(e).

[584] *Id.*

[585] Reg. § 1.597-4(f).

[586] *See* Reg. § 1.597-4(g)(5)(i) for the required form of the election.

[587] Reg. § 1.597-4(g)(5)(i)(B).

by two or more institutions that are not members of the same consolidated group.[588]

After disaffiliation, an institution is generally treated as a new corporation that obtains a carryover basis in its assets. The institution is allowed to retain carryback losses, but not carryover losses.[589] The disaffiliation election does not terminate the single entity treatment of a bridge bank and its residual entities. In addition, the new corporation is treated as holding a receivable in the amount of a "toll charge," which offsets the inclusion of the future FFA.[590] The toll charge is "the excess of the institution's liabilities over the adjusted bases of its assets immediately before the institution is placed in agency receivership (or [immediately before] a deemed election [to deconsolidate].)"[591] The toll charge is treated as income for the institution, not its member shareholders because the IRS believes the toll charge represents "accelerated FFA income."[592]

Following disaffiliation, the consolidated group owns stock in a nonmember corporation. The stock held in the disaffiliated institution is treated as worthless if the institution's liabilities exceed the fair market value of its assets.[593]

§11.6.6 Taxable Transfers

Regulation section 1.597-5 provides uniform rules for taxable transfers that standardize the federal income tax consequences of various forms of acquisitions, including actual and deemed asset acquisitions, that occur in connection with FFA transactions.

A taxable transfer involving an actual asset acquisition is a transaction where there is a transfer to other than a bridge bank of:

1. Deposit liabilities in connection with which FFA is provided, or
2. Assets for which the agency has a financial obligation, such as when assets are covered by loss guarantees.[594]

In a typical taxable asset acquisition, the actual transferee referred to as "acquiring" assumes all of a failed institution's deposit liabilities in exchange for FFA and the failed institution's assets.[595]

A deemed taxable asset acquisition occurs when there is a transaction where there is a transfer of stock and:

1. FFA is provided in connection with the transfer,[596]
2. the institution is a bridge bank, or
3. the institution has a balance in its deferred FFA account.[597]

---

[588] Reg. § 1.597-4(g)(6).

[589] Reg. § 1.597(4)(g)(4)(v).

[590] Reg. § 1.597-4(g)(4).

[591] Reg. § 1.597-4(g)(3).

[592] 60 Fed. Reg. 66091, 66092 (December 21, 1995), T.D. 8641.

[593] Reg. § 1.597-4(g)(2)(v).

[594] Reg. § 1.597-5(a)(1).

[595] Reg. § 1.597-1(b).

[596] The IRS has stated, "The phrase "in connection with" should be interpreted broadly." 60 Fed. Reg. 66091, 66093 (December 21, 1995), T.D. 8641.

[597] Reg. § 1.597-5(b).

All transactions in which an institution or a consolidated subsidiary under agency control leaves its group, joins a new group, or has a 50 percent or greater shift in ownership are treated as taxable transfers.[598] The deemed transferee is the "new entity".[599] As discussed below, the same rules governing the receipt of net worth assistance and allocation of amount realized and basis cover all taxable transactions (as outlined below).

(a) *Net Worth Assistance*

Net worth assistance is any money or property provided at the time of acquisition as an integral part of an acquisition of the stock or assets and liabilities of the target institution.[600] In a taxable acquisition, net worth assistance is treated as an asset received by the target immediately before the acquisition and then sold to the new entity or the acquiring entity.[601]

For an actual asset acquisition, "the amount realized in the taxable transfer is determined under Code section 1001(b) by reference to the consideration paid for the assets."[602] For a deemed asset acquisition, "the amount realized is the sum of the grossed-up basis of the stock acquired . . . plus the amount of liabilities assumed or taken subject to . . . , plus other relevant items."[603] The basis of the stock is adjusted by the amount of stock acquired and the acquiror's basis in the stock.[604] The amount realized is allocated among the assets transferred in the taxable transfer under the rules set forth in Regulation sections 1.338-2(b), 1.338-2(c)(1), and 1.338-2(c)(2).[605] When allocating the basis of an asset covered by a Loss Guarantee, the fair market value is equal to "the greater of the asset's highest guaranteed value or the highest price at which the asset can be put."[606] The stock of a subsidiary is treated as a Class II asset for purposes of the Code sections 338 and 1060 allocation rules when the fair market value of the Class I and II assets exceed the subsidiary's liabilities.[607]

(b) *Treatment of New Entity and Acquiring*

The purchase price for the assets acquired in a taxable transaction is the cost of the assets acquired determined under Temporary Regulation section 1060-1T(c)(1), now Regulation section 1.1060-1(c)(1).[608] FFA is not included in the purchase price.[609] In the case of a deemed asset acquisition, the purchase price and basis for the assets acquired is grossed up in a manner similar to that described in Code section 338. The purchase price is calculated in the same manner as the amount realized, described above.[610] No basis is allocable to agency assistance such as Loss Guarantees.[611] If the fair market value of an asset

---

[598] Reg. § 1.597-5(b)(2).
[599] Reg. § 1.597-1(b).
[600] *Id.*
[601] Reg. § 1.597-5(c)(1).
[602] Reg. § 1.597-5(c)(2).
[603] Reg. § 1.597-5(c)(2).
[604] *Id.*
[605] Reg. § 1.597-5(c)(3).
[606] Reg. § 1.597-5(c)(3)(ii).
[607] *Id.*
[608] Reg. § 1.597-5(d)(2).
[609] Reg. § 1.597-5(d)(1).
[610] Reg. § 1.597-5(d)(1) and (2).
[611] Reg. § 1.597-5(d)(2)(ii).

exceeds the purchase price, the basis in the asset equals the fair market value. The additional basis is recaptured as ordinary income over six tax years.[612]

> **Example:** United Bank is an institution in agency receivership. At the beginning of its calendar year it has $200 million in liabilities, including deposit liabilities and assets with an adjusted basis of $100 million. United Bank also has no income or loss for the calendar year and is not a member of a consolidated group. During the calendar year, the agency causes United Bank to transfer six branches, with assets having an adjusted basis of $1 million and $120 million of deposit liabilities, to Associated Bank. In connection with the transfer, the agency provided $121 million in cash that was FFA to Associated Bank. The transaction is a taxable transaction in which United Bank is treated as having received $121 million in net worth assistance before the transfer and then transferring the branches with a basis of $1 million and the $121 in net worth assistance in exchange for Associated Bank's assumption of $120 million in liabilities. United Bank realizes a $2 million loss on the transfer. The portion of the $121 million of FFA includible in United Bank's income is limited by $100 million in excess liabilities and the $2 million loss for the tax year. United Bank must establish a deferred FFA account for the remaining $19 million of FFA. ($121 million net worth assistance reduced by the total of $100 million of excess losses and $2 million of loss for the year.) Associated Bank must allocate the $120 million purchase price for the assets acquired from United Bank among those assets.[613]

§ 11.6.7 Limitation on Collection of Income Tax

Income tax attributable to either the receipt of FFA or the gain on a taxable transfer cannot be collected from an institution without continuing equity if the agency would bear the burden of the tax. A taxpayer must specify on the front page of Form 1120, to the left of the space provided for "Total Tax," the amount of income tax for the year potentially not subject to collection.[614]

The collection of a failed institution's income taxes from a transferee in a taxable transfer is also limited in certain cases. A failed institution's income taxes cannot be collected from the acquiring entity, which is the purchaser of the institution's assets in an actual taxable transfer.[615] Taxes may, however, be collected from the new entity, which is the resulting corporation in a deemed taxable transfer, provided that the institution's previous equity interests remain outstanding in the new entity or are reacquired or exchanged for consideration.[616] The IRS believes that it "should remain a creditor if all other creditors have retained their interest . . . "[617]

---

[612] Reg. § 1.597-5(d)(2)(iii).

[613] Reg. § 1.597-5(f), Ex. 1.

[614] Reg. § 1.597-6(a)and (c). The rules in Reg. § 1.597-6 supersede the I.R.C. § 7507 rules for assessment and collection of income tax attributable to FFA. Reg. § 1.597-6(f).

[615] Reg. § 1.597-6(e)(1).

[616] Reg. § 1.597-6(e)(2).

[617] 60 Fed. Reg. 66091, 66093 (December 21, 1995), T.D. 8641.

§ 11.6.8 Miscellaneous Rules

(a) *Ownership of Assets*

An institution is treated for tax purposes as the owner of all assets covered by a loss guarantee, yield maintenance or cost to carry or cost of funds reimbursement agreement, regardless of whether the agency would otherwise be treated as the owner under general tax principles.[618] The rule eliminates the burden of determining the tax ownership of covered assets under common-law standards.

(b) *Debt and Equity Interests*

A corollary to the rule that disregards any debt instrument or stock rights issued by an institution when determining FFA disregards these interests when received by the agency. For example, an institution could issue warrants to an agency in connection with the provision of FFA. The amounts paid by the institution to redeem the warrants are treated as repayment of FFA, rather than as the cost of redeeming the warrants. If the agency sells the instrument to a third party, the sales price is treated as a repayment to the agency by the issuer. Additionally, the instrument is treated as having been newly issued by the issuer to the holder at that time.[619]

(c) *Additional Rules*

Rules are also provided for determining the issue price of an agency obligation issued in connection with an acquisition, the status as successor of certain entities for purposes of the Code section 597 regulations, the treatment of FFA and gain on taxable transfers under the loss disallowance rules of Regulation section 1.1502-20 and losses and deductions with respect to covered assets. An anti-abuse rule is also provided.[620]

§ 11.6.9 Phantom Income from Loan Modifications

Shared loss agreements, also known as loan guarantees, are among the tools available to the FDIC for the resolution of failed banks. They are employed to facilitate the purchase of assets in compliance with the least-cost provision that governs FDIC resolution actions.[621] The terms of any shared loss arrangement are set by the purchase and assumption agreement entered into with the acquiring bank, but generally the FDIC agrees to reimburse 80 percent of losses on covered assets.[622] The determination of when a loan becomes a loss asset is based on criteria set by the bank's chartering authority or the Financial Accounting Standards Board.

While shared loss agreements are designed to facilitate the transfer of troubled assets, it is not unusual for the distressed debt of a financially troubled institution to be sold in a taxable transaction at a purchase price substantially

618 Reg. § 1.597-3(a).

619 Reg. § 1.597-3(b).

620 Reg. § 1.597-3(c) through (g).

621 12 C.F.R. § 360.1.

622 A list of recent failed banks and the corresponding purchase and assumption agreements is available at http://www.fdic.gov/bank/individual/failed/banklist.html.

below the face value of the debt instrument. In an effort to maximize its return on the loans, the acquiring institution often modifies the terms of the loans. Under current Treasury Regulations, these modifications usually trigger a deemed debt exchange that qualifies as a taxable event that may result in income for the purchaser/creditor even though the actual value of the loan has not significantly changed at the time of the modification. This income is commonly referred to as phantom income.

(a) *Treatment of Loan Modifications*

Whenever a debt instrument is significantly modified, a deemed taxable exchange takes place.[623] The gain or loss on the exchange is determined by assuming that the amount realized is equal to the "issue price" of the debt instrument determined under Code sections 1273 and 1274.[624] For a debt instrument with adequately stated interest, the issue price is the stated principal amount of the debt instrument.[625] If the interest is not adequately stated, the issue price is the imputed principal amount of the debt instrument.[626]

(b) *Production of Phantom Income*

The effect of the debt modification Regulations on the production of phantom income is illustrated in the following example.

> **Example:** Bank A purchases a loan from Bank B. The loan has a six percent interest rate and a five-year term. The face value of the loan is $1,000, but the fair market value of the loan (the cost to Bank A) is $300. There is a built-in loss of $700 for the loan. To assist the borrower in avoiding default, Bank A modifies the terms of the loan to a four percent interest rate and an eight-year term. A deemed taxable exchange has occurred. There is a $700 gain (phantom income) on the exchange because the adjusted basis of the loan, $300, is less than the $1,000 amount realized, assumed to be the debt instrument's issue price under Regulation section 1.1001-1(g).

This gain is a construct of the Regulations. The likelihood that the loan modification will result in the holder of the debt realizing the face amount of the debt remains doubtful.

(c) *Eliminating Phantom Income*

The Code contains two possible ways to eliminate this phantom income. If conditions are satisfied a taxpayer may either claim a Code section 166 bad debt deduction or take a deduction for a Code section 475 mark down.

Section 166(a)(2) provides a taxpayer with a deduction for partially worthless debts up to the amount of the debt charged-off during the tax year. In general, partially worthless bona fide debts are deductible by commercial banks

---

[623] Reg. § 1.1001-3(b). *See* Ch. 6.

[624] Reg. § 1.1001-1(g).

[625] Reg. § 1.1274-2(b)(1). Adequately stated interest is defined as "a single fixed rate of interest that is paid or compounded at least annually, and that rate is equal to or greater than the test rate . . . ." Reg. § 1.274-2(c)(1).

[626] Reg. § 1.1274-2(b)(2). Imputed principal amount is defined as "the sum of the present values, as of the issue date, of all payments, including payments of stated interest, due under the debt instrument . . . ." Reg. § 1.274-2(c)(1).

under the specific charge-off method provided for in Code section 166.[627] The amount of any deduction under this section is limited to the adjusted basis in the bad debt, which is generally equal to the cost of a purchased debt instrument,[628] and by the amount charged-off.[629] A bad debt deduction may be taken only when worthlessness has been established. While the mere act of charging-off a debt does not establish worthlessness,[630] regulations now afford banks two conclusive presumptions of worthlessness, the historical presumption and the conformity election. The historical presumption is available when a debt is charged-off in obedience to specific orders from a regulator, or when a charge-off is "confirmed" by a regulator.[631] The presumption afforded by the conformity election is available when a bank satisfies the "express determination" requirement the debt is classified as a "loss asset," and when the debt is charged-off for regulatory purposes during the taxable year.[632]

Example: In the preceding example, Bank A acquired a loan with a face value of $1,000 but a fair market value and purchase price of $300. When Bank A modified the loan, there was a $700 gain creating phantom income. With this gain, Bank A has a new adjusted basis of $1,000 (the $300 cost of the loan and the $700 gain). Bank A may take a $700 Code section 166(a)(2) deduction if the loan has been partially charged-off during the tax year. If either of the conclusive presumptions applies, the deduction could not be challenged on audit.

Code section 475 requires a year-end mark-to-market adjustment to the fair market value of securities, leading to the recognition of income or a loss deduction. Loans, as well as the debt instruments are "securities" for this purpose.[633] There are limitations on the applicability of section 475. The recognition provision does not apply to securities identified as held for investment, not held for sale, or held as a hedge of a non-security.[634] In addition, the holder of the security must be a dealer in securities.[635] In general, the amount of gain or loss recognized under Code section 475(a)(2) when a debt instrument is marked to market is the difference between the adjusted basis and the fair market value of the debt. Because of the potential overlap of the provisions in Code sections 166 and 475, the mark-to-market rules must be coordinated with the bad debt deduction rules.[636]

---

[627] For those banks that are not "large banks," as defined in I.R.C. § 585(c) or banks that are taxable under Subchapter S, a deduction for bad debts is allowed under the reserve method. I.R.C. § 585.

[628] The adjusted basis is determined by I.R.C. § 1011(a), which refers to the determination of basis described in I.R.C. § 1012(a).

[629] I.R.C. § 166(a)(2).

[630] *Findley v. Commissioner*, 25 T.C. 311 (1995), *aff'd* 236 F.2d 959 (3d Cir. 1956).

[631] Reg. § 1.166-2(d)(1).

[632] Reg. § 1.166-2(d)(3). *See* Ch. 10 for a discussion of bad-debt deductions.

[633] Reg. § 1.475(c)-2(a)(2).

[634] I.R.C. § 475(b)(1)(A) through (C).

[635] I.R.C. § 475(a)(1).

[636] FSA 199909007, March 5, 1999. *See* Ch. 4 for a discussion of Code section 475.

Example: As in the previous example, Bank A's modification of a loan created a $700 gain from phantom income. With a mark-to-market adjustment through Code section 475, Bank A will have a $700 mark down of the loan to its assumed fair market value. To the extent that the mark down is attributable to worthlessness, the deduction is taken under Code section 166. If one of the two conclusive presumptions applies, the deduction may not be challenged on audit.

Chapter 12
Business Tax Credits

Contents

§12.1 Research and Development Credit
§12.1.1 Expenditures Eligible for Credit
§12.1.2 Expenditures Ineligible for Credit
§12.1.3 Internal Use Software
§12.1.4 *Norwest Corp.*
§12.1.5 Calculating the R&D Credit
§12.1.6 Research and Experimental Expenditures as Tax Preference Items
§12.1.7 Election to Claim Accelerated Research Credit in Lieu of Bonus Depreciation
§12.2 Low-Income Housing Credit
§12.2.1 Applicable Percentage
§12.2.2 Low-Income Housing Credit: Qualified Basis
§12.2.3 Low-Income Unit
§12.2.4 Low-Income Housing Project
§12.2.5 Credit Period
§12.2.6 Additional Credit
§12.2.7 Disposition of Building
§12.2.8 Tenant's Right to Acquisition
§12.2.9 Agency Authorization
§12.2.10 Housing Use Agreement
§12.2.11 Maximum Allocable Credits
§12.2.12 Allocation Authority
§12.2.13 Acquisition of Existing Buildings
§12.2.14 Recapture of Credit
§12.3 New Markets Tax Credit
§12.3.1 Overview
§12.3.2 Qualified Equity Investment
§12.3.3 Qualified Community Development Entity
§12.3.4 Low-Income Community
§12.3.5 Low-Income Community Investment
§12.3.6 Qualified Active Low-Income Community Business
§12.3.7 Allowance Date
§12.3.8 Recapture of Credit

§12.1 Research and Development Credit

Code section 41 allows for a 20 percent[1] credit for expenditures incurred to increase research activities ("R&D credit").[2] Computer software development

[1] The credit percentage is reduced if an alternative method of computation is employed. I.R.C. §41(c)(4) and (5) (2008).

[2] The R&D credit was first enacted in the Economic Recovery Tax Act of 1981, Pub. L. No. 97-34, and allowed for a credit equal to 25 percent of the excess of qualified research expenditures incurred in

expenditures can qualify as research expenses and, thus, may be eligible for the credit if they meet the criteria of qualified research expenses.[3] Under limited circumstances, if a bank develops an internal computer driven accounting, management, or customer accessible system, the related costs may be eligible for the R&D credit. Such eligible expenses could include in-house expenses of the taxpayer for wages and supplies attributable to qualified research, time-sharing costs for computer use in qualified research, and 65 percent[4] of amounts paid by the taxpayer for qualified research conducted on the taxpayer's behalf.[5]

§ 12.1.1 Expenditures Eligible for Credit

To be eligible for the R&D credit, the research expenditure must satisfy the expensing definition contained in Code section 174(a) for research or experimental expenditures.[6] If the expenditure does not qualify for Code section 174 treatment as a deduction, it will not qualify for a credit under Code section 41. However, the requirements of Code section 174 are not as restrictive as those contained in Code section 41. While a taxpayer would normally prefer to qualify for the credit, a deduction under Code section 174 may be available even if the additional requirements of Code section 41 are not met.

Regulations accompanying Code section 174 state that the term "research or experimental expenditures" include "all such costs incident to the development of an experimental or pilot model, a plant process, a product, a formula, an invention, or similar property, and the improvement of already existing property of the type mentioned."[7] Although software development costs are not expressly identified as an expenditure that is deductible under Code section 174, Revenue Procedure 69-21 allows such expenditures to be accorded similar treatment.[8] The Revenue Procedure states that "costs of developing software . . . in many respects so closely resembles the kind of research and experimental expenditures that fall within the purview of [Code § 174] as to warrant accounting treatment similar to that accorded such costs under that section."[9]

(Footnote Continued)

the current year over the average from the three previous years. It has been modified on several occasions. The provisions, which were scheduled to terminate on December 31, 2009, have been extended and now apply to qualified research expenses paid or incurred on or before December 31, 2011. I.R.C. § 41(h)(i)(B) as amended by the Tax Relief, Unemployment Insurance Reauthorization, and Job Creation Act of 2010, and the Emergency Economic Stabilization Act of 2008.

[3] *See The Art of Tax Efficiency in Community Banks*, by M. Gula, J. Brew, and R. Blasi, 2007, Red Room Publishing, *http://www.mraeresources.com/bookstore/*.

[4] Sixty-five could be increased to 75 percent for amounts paid by the taxpayer for qualified research, if paid to a qualified research consortium, and the research is conducted on behalf of the taxpayer and one or more "unrelated taxpayers," as determined under I.R.C. § 52. I.R.C. § 41(b)(3)(C).

[5] I.R.C. § 41(b) (2008). *See also* Reg. §§ 1.41-2(b),(c),(d), and (e). Proposed regulations take a restrictive view of the availability of the credit for internal use software. Prop. Reg. § 1.41-4(c)(6), 66 FR 66362 (December 26, 2001). Portions of the proposed amendments to Reg. § 1.41-4 were adopted by T.D. 9104 on December 31, 2003; however, Prop. Reg. § 1.41-4(c)(6), pertaining to internal use computer software, was specifically not adopted.

[6] I.R.C. § 41(d)(1)(A) (2008). *See also* Reg. § 1.41-4(a)(2)(i), as amended by T.D. 9104 (December 31, 2003). I.R.C. § 174(a) allows an amortization deduction for research and experimental expenditures.

[7] Reg. § 1.174-2(a)(1).

[8] Rev. Proc. 69-21, 1969-2 C.B. 303.

[9] *Id.*

In addition to satisfying the Code section 174 test, for an expenditure to qualify for the R&D credit it must satisfy three other requirements.[10] First, the research must be undertaken for the purpose of discovering information that is technological in nature, the application of which is intended to be useful in the development of a new or improved business component of the taxpayer.[11] This requirement has two prongs: first, the research activities must be undertaken for the purpose of discovering information ("discovery test"), and that information must be technological in nature ("technological in nature requirement"); second, the intent for the research must be to aid in developing a new or improved business component. Computer software is considered a "business component" if it is held for sale, lease, or license, or if it is used by the taxpayer in its trade or business, and thus may satisfy the second prong.[12] The "discovery test" is not as easily met due to different formulations of the test that may apply to a given taxpayer.[13] Under the current regulations, research activities related to the development or improvement of computer software of the taxpayer are undertaken for the purpose of discovering information if the research is intended to eliminate uncertainty concerning the development or improvement of the computer software.[14] Uncertainty exists if the information available to the taxpayer does

---

[10] In *Newark Corp. v. Commissioner*, the court applied seven tests to determine whether expenditures qualify for the I.R.C. §41 credit. *See* discussion of *Norwest Corp.* at §12.1.4.

[11] I.R.C. §41(d)(1)(B). *See also* Reg. §1.41-4(a)(2)(ii), as amended by T.D. 9104.

[12] I.R.C. §41(d)(2)(B).

[13] Regulatory activity in the research credit area has been lively over the past few years, which makes it difficult to know which rules to apply. In 2000, the IRS released significant changes to the final regulations defining what constitutes qualified research, effective for expenditures made on or after January 3, 2001. Reg. §1.41-4, amended by T.D. 8930, 66 F.R. 280 (January 3, 2001). Soon thereafter, the IRS stated that it would review the regulations and amend them by means of proposed regulations, Notice 2001-19, 2001-1 C.B. 784, which were issued within a year. The 2001 proposed regulations were designed to be more taxpayer-friendly and were made effective for expenditures in tax years that end on or after December 26, 2001. Prop. Reg. §1.41-4, 66 FR 66362 (December 26, 2001). Taxpayers were allowed to rely on the proposed amendments until new final regulations were issued. Notice of Proposed Rulemaking REG-112991-01 (December 26, 2001). New final regulations were issued on December 31, 2003, and published in the Federal Register on January 2, 2004, that adopted portions of the 2001 proposed regulations with changes. These final rules generally apply to tax years ending on or after December 31, 2003, but the IRS will not challenge return positions that are consistent with the new final regulations for tax years ending before that date. Reg. §1.41-4(a)(3), amended by T.D. 9104 (December 31, 2003). The latest amendments, however, did not adopt the rules on internal-use software, which remain in proposed form. Taxpayers have a choice to rely on the provisions relating to internal-use software embodied in the 2001 proposed regulations, or the provisions embodied in T.D. 8930, 66 FR 280 (January 3, 2001). However, a taxpayer that relies upon the internal-use software rules of T.D. 8930 must also apply the stricter "discovery test" as set forth in T.D. 8930. Announcement 2004-9.

Specifically, the stricter "discovery test" set forth in Reg. § 1.41-4, as amended by T.D. 8930, held, "research is undertaken for the purpose of discovering information only if it is undertaken to obtain knowledge that exceeds, expands, or refines the common knowledge of skilled professionals in a particular field of science or engineering." However, the current regulations issued in 2003, as amended by T.D. 9104, hold, "research must be undertaken for the purpose of discovering information that is technological in nature. Research is undertaken for the purpose of discovering information if it is intended to eliminate uncertainty concerning the development or improvement of a business component." Reg. § 1.41-4(a)(3). Thus, the new regulations abrogate the stricter "discovery test" in T.D. 8930 and establish the more taxpayer friendly standard discussed above. *See*, 66 FR 66362 declaring, "these proposed regulations do not retain from TD 8930" its "discovery test." Again, the taxpayer has a choice of which test to apply. *See*, *FedEx Corp v. United States*, No. 08-2423, 2009 WL 2032905, at *6 (W.D. Tenn. 2009) (holding taxpayer could "rely on the 'discovery' test set forth in the Proposed Regulations and the 2003 Final Regulations").

[14] Reg. §1.41-4(a)(3)(i), as amended by T.D. 9104 (December 31, 2003).

not establish the capability or method for developing or improving the computer software, or the appropriate design of the computer software.[15]

The information sought to develop or improve computer software meets the "technological in nature" requirement if the process of experimentation used to discover such information fundamentally relies on principles of the physical or biological sciences, engineering, or computer science.[16] Thus, research does not rely in the principles of computer science merely because a computer is employed. However, the requirement that the research be undertaken for the purpose of discovering information that is technological in nature no longer requires that the taxpayer seek to obtain information that exceeds, expands or refines the common knowledge of skilled professionals in the field of the particular research area.[17] As a result, the fact that the information is known to others will not disqualify the research.[18] Instead, the current regulations define research activities by focusing on the actual process of experimentation, as defined in the Regulations, used to discover the information sought.[19] In addition, success in developing new or improved computer software is not necessary to satisfy this requirement and the issuance of a patent (other than a patent for design) is conclusive evidence that a taxpayer has satisfied this requirement.[20]

Before the current final regulations were issued, the Tenth Circuit had interpreted Code section 41 as requiring the taxpayer to discover new information that is applied toward the development of a product in order for the activity to be qualified research. Mere evidence that a new product was developed did not indicate that qualified research was conducted.[21] The Seventh Circuit required an even higher standard when it held that enhancement of existing software did not constitute qualified research. The research had to expand or refine existing principles of computer science and the resulting information had to be of broad effect.[22] However, the standards for the discovery requirement that were set by the Seventh and Tenth Circuits followed the strict "discovery test" set forth in T.D. 8930, and therefore may no longer apply in situations covered by the current, and more liberal, final regulations.

---

[15] *Id. But see* Reg. § 1.41-4(a)(5), as amended by T.D. 9104, indicating the requisite uncertainty can never exist without uncertainty regarding the appropriate design of the business component.

[16] Reg. § 1.41-4(a)(4), as amended by T.D. 9104. A taxpayer may employ existing technologies and may rely on existing principles of the physical or biological sciences, engineering, or computer science to satisfy this requirement. *Id.*

[17] Reg. § 1.41-4(a)(3)(ii), as amended by T.D. 9104. However, the requirement that a taxpayer seek to obtain knowledge that exceeds, expands, or refines the common knowledge of skilled professionals in a particular field of science or engineering is reinstated if the taxpayer chooses to rely upon the internal-use software rules of T.D. 8930. Announcement 2004-9.

[18] Prior to amendment by T.D. 9104, Reg. § 1.41-4(a)(3), in order to satisfy the discovery and technological in nature requirements, research had to be undertaken for the purpose of discovering information that was beyond the knowledge that should be known to skilled professionals. Reg. § 1.41-4(a)(3), as amended by T.D. 8930, 66 F.R. 280 (January 3, 2001); Prop. Reg. § 1.41-4, 66 FR 66362 (December 26, 2001).

[19] T.D. 9104 (December 31, 2003).

[20] Reg. § 1.41-4(a)(3)(ii) and (iii), as amended by T.D. 9104 (December 31, 2003). *See also* Prop. Reg. § 1.41-4(c)(6)(vii), Ex 3, 66 FR 66362.

[21] *Tax and Accounting Software Corporation v. U.S.*, CA-10, 301 F.3d 1254 (10th Cir. 2002), *cert. denied*, June 2, 2003.

[22] *Eustace v. Commissioner*, 312 F. 3d 905 (7th Cir. 2002); *United Stationers, Inc. v. United States*, 982 F. Supp. 1279 (N.D. Ill. 1997), *cert. denied*, June 21, 1999.

Second, Code section 41 requires that substantially all of the activities of the research constitute elements of a process of experimentation for a qualified purpose.[23] Research is treated as conducted for a qualified purpose if it is related to a new or improved function, a new or improved performance, or reliability or quality of a business component.[24] However, research relating to style, taste, cosmetic, or seasonal design factors is not treated as conducted for a qualified purpose, and is thus not eligible.[25] "Substantially all" activities constitute elements of a process of experimentation if 80 percent or more of the research activities are such activities.[26]

The process of experimentation must involve the evaluation of more than one alternative designed to achieve a result where the capability or the method of achieving that result, or the appropriate design of that result is uncertain at the outset.[27] The process involves (1) the identification of uncertainty concerning the development or improvement of a business component, (2) the identification of one or more alternatives intended to eliminate that uncertainty, and (3) the identification and the conduct of a process of evaluating the alternatives (through, for example, modeling, simulation, or a systematic trial and error methodology).[28] A process of experimentation must fundamentally rely on the principles of the physical or biological sciences, engineering or computer science.[29] A taxpayer may undertake a process of experimentation if there is no uncertainty concerning the taxpayer's capability or method of achieving the desired result so long as the appropriate design of the desired result is uncertain as of the beginning of the taxpayer's research activities.[30] However, the mere existence of uncertainty regarding the development or improvement of a business component (e.g., its design) does not indicate that all of a taxpayer's activities undertaken to achieve that new or improved business component constitute a process of experimentation, even if the taxpayer, in fact, does achieve the new or improved business component.[31]

---

[23] I.R.C. § 41(d)(1)(C) (2008). *See also* Reg. § 1.41-4(a)(2)(iii), as amended by T.D. 9104. The 2001 proposed regulations clarified the definition of a process of experimentation, effective for expenditures made in tax years that end on or after December 26, 2001. Prop. Reg. § 1.41-4, 66 FR 66362 (December 26, 2001). Taxpayers were allowed to rely on the proposed amendments until new final regulations were issued. Notice of Proposed Rulemaking REG-112991-01 (December 26, 2001). New final regulations were issued on December 31, 2003, and published in the Federal Register on January 2, 2004, that adopted portions of the 2001 proposed regulations with changes. These final rules generally apply to tax years ending on or after December 31, 2003, but the IRS will not challenge return positions that are consistent with the new final regulations for tax years ending before that date. T.D. 9104 (December 31, 2003).

[24] I.R.C. § 41(d)(3)(A) (2008). *See also* Reg. § 1.41-4(a)(5)(ii), as amended by T.D. 9104.

[25] I.R.C. § 41(d)(3)(B) (2008). *See also* Reg. § 1.41-4(a)(5)(ii), as amended by T.D. 9104.

[26] Reg. § 1.41-4(a)(6), as amended by T.D. 9104. This requirement is applied separately to each business component. I.R.C. § 41(d)(2)(A). *See also* Reg. § 1.41-4(a)(6), as amended by T.D. 9104.

[27] Reg. § 1.41-4(a)(5), as amended by T.D. 9104, expanding the uncertainty requirement to include uncertainty as to the appropriate design. *See* discussion below.

[28] *Id. But see Eustace v. Commissioner*, 312 F. 3d 905 (7th Cir. 2002), holding "simple" trial and error did not satisfy the experimentation requirement under the previous regulations, as set forth in T.D. 8930, and suggesting the application of the current regulations would not change the result.

[29] *Id.*

[30] *Id.* In contrast, Reg. § 1.41-4(a)(5), as originally adopted by T.D. 8930, provided that a process of experimentation does not include the evaluation of alternatives to establish the appropriate design of a business component if the capability and method for developing or improving the component is not uncertain.

[31] *Id. See also* preamble to T.D. 9104.

Example: Jetco Co. manufactures sprockets and wants to change the color of its blue sprocket to green. Jetco obtains samples of green paint from a supplier and determines that it must modify its painting process to accommodate the green paint because the green paint has different characteristics from other paints Jetco has used. The company obtains detailed data on the green paint from its paint supplier. Jetco also consults with the manufacturer of its paint spraying machines and determines that it must acquire new nozzles that are designed to operate with paints similar to the green paint it wants to use. Jetco installs the new nozzles on its paint spraying machines and tests the nozzles to ensure that they work as specified by the manufacturer of the paint spraying machines. These activities to modify the painting process do not constitute qualified research under either the 2001 proposed regulations[32] or the current final regulations.[33] As analyzed under the current regulations, Jetco did not conduct qualified research because it did not conduct a process of evaluating alternatives in order to eliminate uncertainty regarding the modification of its painting process. Further, its testing of the nozzles for the paint spraying was merely routine testing or inspection for quality control.[34]

Before the current regulations were adopted, the Seventh Circuit held in *Eustace v. Commissioner* that a process of experimentation has the scientific sense of forming and testing hypotheses rather than the lay sense of trial and error. Thus, improvements to a software program were not a process of experimentation because the programmers knew from the start that the upgrades were technologically feasible.[35] However, the court in *Eustace* was operating under the earlier final regulations which stated that a process of experimentation cannot consist of the evaluation of alternatives to establish the appropriate design of a business component when the capability and method for developing or improving the business component are not uncertain.[36] The court acknowledged the current regulations in their form as proposed regulations at that time, but refused to apply them, stating they were not legally binding and inapplicable to expenses incurred in years ending before December 21, 2001.[37] As an aside, the court opined that the application of the proposed regulations would likely make no difference in the result; however, the matter was never directly addressed and ruled upon.[38] Therefore, a more relaxed standard of experimentation may apply in situations covered by the current regulations.

Legislative history indicates that engineers who design a new computer system or who design improved or new integrated circuits for use in a computer or other electronic products are engaged in qualified research because the design of those items is uncertain at the outset and can only be determined through a process of experimentation relating to specific design hypotheses and decisions.[39]

---

[32] Prop. Reg. § 1.41-4(a)(8), Ex 2, 66 FR 66362 (December 26, 2001).

[33] Reg. § 1.41-4(a)(8), Ex 2, amended by T.D. 9104.

[34] Reg. § 1.41-4(a)(8), Ex 2, amended by T.D. 9104.

[35] *Eustace v. Commissioner*, 312 F. 3d 905 (7th Cir. 2002).

[36] Reg. § 1.41-4(a)(5), as added by T.D. 8930, 66 F.R. 280 (January 3, 2001).

[37] *Eustace v. Commissioner*, 312 F. 3d at 908.

[38] *Eustace v. Commissioner*, 312 F. 3d at 908.

[39] H.R. Rep. No. 99-841, pt. 2 at 72 (1986).

But see special restrictions relating to internal-use software discussed below at §12.1.3.

Third, the taxpayer must incur the research expenditures in the course of carrying on a trade or business.[40] This test is similar to the test used for business expense deductions under Code section 162.[41] Generally, expenditures must be directly connected with or pertain to a trade or business of the taxpayer that is being carried on at the time the expenses are paid or incurred.[42] This requirement is disregarded if the taxpayer incurs in-house research expenses for the primary purpose of using the results in the active conduct of a future trade or business of the taxpayer.[43]

§12.1.2 Expenditures Ineligible for Credit

Several categories of expenditures are ineligible for credit under Code section 41. First, any expenditures that do not qualify for Code section 174 amortization deduction do not qualify for the R&D credit.[44] In addition, research expenditures do not qualify for the credit if the research is either:

1. Conducted after the beginning of commercial production of the business component,[45]
2. Related to the adaptation of an existing business component to a particular customer's requirements,[46]
3. Related to the duplication of an existing business component from a physical examination of the component itself or certain other information,[47] or
4. Related to certain management function or techniques, efficiency surveys, market research or development, routine data collection or routine quality control.[48]

Furthermore, expenditures attributable to research that is conducted outside the United States do not enter into the credit computation,[49] and the credit is not available for research in the social science, arts, humanities,[50] or for research that is funded by any grant, contract, or otherwise by another person or governmental entity.[51] Special limitations also are imposed on internal use software.

---

[40] I.R.C. §41(b)(1) (2008). *See also* Reg. §1.41-2(a)(1). This test is more restrictive than that used under I.R.C. §174, which requires only that the expense be paid or incurred by the taxpayer "in connection with his trade or business."

[41] Reg. §1.41-2(a)(1).

[42] *Id.*

[43] I.R.C. §41(b)(4) (2008). *See also* Reg. §1.41-2(a)(2).

[44] I.R.C. §41(d)(1)(A) (2008).

[45] I.R.C. §41(d)(4)(A) (2008). *See also* Reg. §1.41-4(c)(2)(i) and (ii), listing certain activities which are deemed to occur after the beginning of commercial production of a business component.

[46] I.R.C. §41(d)(4)(B) (2008). *See also* Reg. §1.41-4(c)(3), as amended by T.D. 9104.

[47] I.R.C. §41(d)(4)(C) (2008). *See also* Reg. §1.41-4(c)(4), as amended by T.D. 9104

[48] I.R.C. §41(d)(4)(D) (2008). *See also* Reg. §1.41-4(c)(5), as amended by T.D. 9104.

[49] I.R.C. §41(d)(4)(F) (2008). *See also* Reg. §1.41-4(c)(7), as amended by T.D. 9104.

[50] I.R.C. §41(d)(4)(G) (2008). *See also* Reg. §1.41-4(c)(8), as amended by T.D. 9104.

[51] I.R.C. §41(d)(4)(H) (2008). *See also* Reg. §1.41-4(c)(9), as amended by T.D. 9104.

§ 12.1.3 Internal Use Software

Special rules apply to internal use software.[52] Internal use software is defined as software that is developed by or for the taxpayer primarily for internal use by the taxpayer,[53] such as software used for general and administrative functions or in providing non computer services, such as accounting, consulting, or banking services.[54] General administrative functions include payroll, bookkeeping, financial management and reporting, personnel management, sales and marketing, fixed asset accounting, inventory management, and cost accounting.[55] The proposed regulations apply a bright-line rule and presume all computer software is developed primarily for the internal use of the taxpayer unless the software is developed to be commercially sold, leased, licensed, or otherwise marketed for separately stated consideration to unrelated third parties.[56] Computer software that is developed primarily for the taxpayer's internal use remains such even though the taxpayer subsequently sells, leases, licenses, or otherwise markets the computer software for separately stated consideration to unrelated third parties.[57] Examples of software ineligible for the credit are software developed to streamline ordering operations and pricing; to eliminate redundancy of data; to forecast inventory levels; to improve shipping operations; and to improve performance and reliability in warehouse productivity.

---

[52] I.R.C. § 41(d)(4)(E) (2008), providing that, except to the extent provided by regulations, research with respect to internal-use software is not qualified research under section 41(d). However, the regulations in this area are less than stable. *See* footnote 13. Specifically, the current final regulations issued on December 31, 2003, with T.D. 9104, did not adopt the portion of the 2001 proposed regulation on internal-use computer software (Prop. Reg. § 1.41-4(c)(6)), which would have amended the final regulations under T.D. 8930 dealing with internal-use software, but instead reserved this portion in the final regulation. Until further guidance is published in the Federal Register, taxpayers are allowed to rely upon all provisions in the 2001 proposed regulations relating to internal-use software, or alternatively to rely upon all provisions relating to internal-use software in T.D. 8930 (66 F.R. 280), with respect to internal-use software for taxable years beginning after December 31, 1985. However, relying upon the provisions in T.D. 8930 for internal-use software may affect other aspects of determining the credit. The IRS has since requested further comments from the public on the proposed rules for internal-use software in Announcement 2004-9 indicating changes in the regulations in this area will likely continue. This book will apply the internal-use software regulations as embodied in the 2001 proposed regulations, as they appear to more closely reflect the current legislative conception of qualified research in this area.

In 2009, a United States District Court held that the Service's silence on the "internal-use software" test in the 2003 Final Regulations meant that the test still conformed with the more lax standard provided in the 2001 Proposed Regulations, and not the standard in the Service's 2004 Announcement. *FedEx Corp. v. United States*, 2009 U.S. Dist. LEXIS 59856, at *15-16 (W.D. Tenn. 2009). With this case as authority, taxpayers may argue for a research tax credit on software that is "innovative in that the software is intended to *result in a reduction in cost, improvement in speed, or other improvement that is substantial and economically significant*," and not software that is "innovative in that the software is intended to be *unique or novel and is intended to differ in a significant and inventive way from prior software implementations or methods*." *Compare* 66 Fed. Reg. 280, at 293 (Jan. 3, 2001) (pertaining to the former quote—language of the 2001 Final Treasury Regulation at § 1.41-4(c)(6)(vi)(A)) (emphasis added), *with* Prop. Treas. Reg. § 1.41-4(c)(6)(iv)(A), 66 Fed. Reg. 66362, at 66371 (Dec. 26, 2001) (pertaining to the latter quote) (emphasis added).

[53] I.R.C. § 41(d)(4)(E) (2008).

[54] Prop Reg. § 1.41-4(c)(6)(iv), REG-112991-01. *See also* H.R. Rep. No. 99-841, pt. 2 at 73 (1986).

[55] Prop. Reg. § 1.41-4(c)(6)(iv), 66 FR 66362 (December 26, 2001). *See also* Announcement 2004-9.

[56] Prop. Reg. § 1.41-4(c)(6)(iv), 66 FR 66362 (December 26, 2001). If a taxpayer chooses to apply the internal use software provisions contained in T.D. 8930 rather than those in Prop. Reg. § 1.41-4(c)(6), the definition of internal-use software is based on the software's use "internally" or "in providing non computer services."

[57] Prop. Reg. § 1.41-4(c)(6)(iv), 66 FR 66362.

Under the 2001 proposed regulation, for tax years beginning on or after the December 31, 1985, research with respect to computer software that is developed by or for the taxpayer primarily for the taxpayer's internal use is eligible for the research credit only if the research satisfies the general requirements of qualified research, and one of the following conditions is met:

1. The taxpayer develops the software for use in an activity that constitutes qualified research (other than the development of the internal-use software itself);
2. The taxpayer develops the software for use in a production process that satisfies the qualified research requirements;
3. The taxpayer develops the software for use in providing computer services[58] to customers; or
4. The software satisfies the high threshold of innovation test.[59]

These requirements do not apply to the development costs of a new or improved package of computer software and hardware developed together by the taxpayer as a single product (or to the costs to modify an acquired computer software and hardware package), of which the software is an integral part, that is used directly by the taxpayer in providing services in its trade or business to customers. In these cases, eligibility for the research credit is to be determined by examining the combined software-hardware product as a single product.[60]

Currently, financial institutions that develop internal-use software used to deliver a service to customers and software that includes an interface with customers or the public fail to fall under any of the first three conditions, and therefore must satisfy the high threshold of innovation test.[61] Computer software satisfies the high threshold of innovation test only if the taxpayer can establish that;

1. The software is innovative in that the software is intended to be unique or novel and is intended to differ in a significant and inventive way from prior software implementations or methods;[62]

[58] Computer service for this purpose is a service offered by a taxpayer to customers conducting business with the taxpayer primarily for the use of the taxpayer's computer or software technology. Prop. Reg. § 1.41-4(c)(6)(v)(A), 66 FR 66362 (December 26, 2001). A taxpayer does not provide a computer service merely because customers interact with the taxpayer's software. For purposes of this section, a noncomputer service is a service offered by a taxpayer to customers who conduct business with the taxpayer primarily to obtain a service other than a computer service, even if such other service is enabled, supported, or facilitated by computer or software technology.

[59] Prop. Reg. § 1.41-4(c)(6)(v), 66 FR 66362.

[60] Prop. Reg. § 1.41-4(c)(6)(i) through (iii), 66 FR 66362.

[61] Preamble to Prop. Reg. § 1.41-4, 66 FR 66362 (December 26, 2001). In Announcement 2004-9, the IRS stated that the majority of commentators responding to the proposed regulation believed the definition of internal-use software should not include such software.

[62] This first prong remains uncertain because it was included in Prop. Reg. § 1.41(c)(6)(vi)(A) but not adopted in the final 2003 regulations. Instead, the relevant section for internal use software is "reserved." Reg. § 1.41-4(c)(6). Thus, taxpayers can and have successfully argued for the application of the easier to satisfy prong issued in the 2001 regulations as originally adopted by T.D. 8930. That prong held, "[t]he software is innovative in that the software is intended to result in a reduction in cost, improvement in speed, or other improvement, that is substantial and economically significant." Reg. § 1.41(c)(6)(vi)(A). Further, in *FedEx Corp. v. United States*, a district court held the petitioner was correct in relying on the high threshold of innovation test in Reg. § 1.41(c)(6)(vi)(A)–(C), as originally adopted by

2. The software development must entail significant economic risks; that is, substantial resources are committed with substantial uncertainty as to their recovery within a reasonable period because of technical risk. If the only substantial uncertainty is whether the project for which the software is developed will produce the desired efficiency, it does not thereby entail significant economic risks. The risk must relate to whether the software can, in fact, be developed;
3. The software cannot be commercially available.[63]

If each of these three criteria is met, along with the general requirements for all research expenditures, internal-use software will be eligible for the credit. However, the IRS has announced that costs paid or incurred to convert or replace computer software to recognize dates beginning in the year 2000 will probably not qualify for the credit.[64]

§ 12.1.4 *Norwest Corp.*

In *Norwest Corp*, the Tax Court analyzed eight internal use software development activities of the taxpayer and concluded that only one of them qualified for the tax credit provided by Section 41 of the Code for research and development activities.[65] The court was operating under the 1997 proposed regulations relating to internal-use software, Prop. Reg. § 1.41-4(e)(5), 62 F.R. 83 (January 2, 1997), which predated the enactment of the 2001 final regulations under T.D. 8930, 66 F.R. 280 (January 3, 2001), as well as the current regulations defining "qualified research," as enacted under T.D. 9104 on December 31, 2003 and the 2001 Prop. Reg. § 1.41-4, 66 FR 66362 (December 26, 2001), relating to internal-use software. As a result, the "discovery test" and the "process of experimentation test" reflect what appears to be a stricter standard than that embodied in the current regulations, and therefore, one would expect a court applying the current regulations to facts similar to *Norwest Corp.* to expand upon the software development research activities the court found to qualify for the credit.[66] In reaching its conclusion, the Court applied seven tests:

1. The Section 174 Test. The Section 174 Test requires that the research expenditures qualify as expenses under Section 174.
2. The Discovery Test. The Discover Test requires that the research be undertaken for the purpose of discovering information which is technological in nature.

(Footnote Continued)

T.D. 8930, since "the only regulations that the Treasury has issued pursuant to its delegated rulemaking authority that address the 'internal use software' exception are the 2001 Final Regulations." No. 08-2423, 2009 WL 2032905, at *6 (W.D. Tenn. 2009).

[63] Prop. Reg. § 1.41-4(c)(6)(vi), issued with Notice of Proposed Rulemaking REG-112991-01 (December 26, 2001). *See also* Announcement 2004-9. However, software developed as a part of an integrated hardware-software product does not fall under the special rules relating to internal-use software and is examined in combination with the hardware product instead. Prop. Reg. § 1.41-4(c)(6)(iii), 66 FR 66362 (December 26, 2001).

[64] Rev. Proc. 97-50, 1997-2 C.B. 525. *See also* footnote 62 and its discussion of *FedEx Corp. v. United States*.

[65] *Norwest Corp. v. Commissioner*, 110 T.C. 454 (1998).

[66] *Id. See also* Prop. Reg. § 1.41-4, 66 FR 66362 (December 26, 2001), and T.D. 8930 (January 3, 2000).

3. The Business Component Test. The Business Component Test (which is actually part of the Discovery Test) requires that the research be undertaken for the purpose of discovering information the application of which is intended to be useful in the development of a new or improved business component of the taxpayer.
4. The Process of Experimentation Test. The Process of Experimentation Test requires that substantially all of the activities which constitute elements of a process of experimentation relate to a new or improved function, performance, reliability, or quality.
5. The Innovativeness Test. The Innovativeness Test requires that the software be innovated such that the software results in a reduction in costs, or improvement in speed, that is substantial and economically significant.
6. The Significant Economic Risk Test. The Significant Economic Risk Test requires that the software development involve significant economic risk such that the taxpayer commits substantial resources to the development and also there is substantial uncertainty, because of technical risk, that such resources would not be recovered within a reasonable period.
7. The Commercial Availability Test. The Commercial Availability Test requires that the software not be commercially available for use by the taxpayer as where the software cannot be purchased, leased, or licensed and used for the intended purpose without modifications that would satisfy tests "e" and "f".

The court observed that the higher threshold of technical advancement and functional improvement in the development of internal use software vis-a-vis other fields of research is consistent with the general rule that qualified research under Section 41 excludes internal use software development. It found that Congress sought to limit the development of internal use software under Code section 41 only to those endeavors that ventured into unchartered territory. With respect to the court's decision in *United Stationers, Inc. v. United States,*[67] the Tax Court concluded that it would not rely on or otherwise refer to *United Stationers* in evaluating the case because of the lack of a detailed record from which it could compare the facts in the case at Bar to the facts addressed by the District Court.

The IRS conceded that all eight of the sample internal use software activities may be treated as expenses under Code section 174. Thus, the Section 174 Test was satisfied with respect to all of the activities. The Court found that only the computer software development costs incurred to create the strategic banking system ("SBS") met all of the other tests and therefore qualified for the Section 41 credit. It found that the SBS project was a massive effort at developing an integrated banking system that could interact with several other systems and handle a tremendous volume of data. The SBS Customer Module project involved the discovery of information which was technological in nature and

[67] *United Stationers v. United States,* 982 F. Supp. 1279 (N.D. Ill. 1977).

expanded principals of computer science—namely, the ability to create a customer-based system that could integrate with other banking systems and handle large volumes of data. The SBS system was found to be an innovative effort that had the potential to result in substantial efficiency and significant economic benefit to the taxpayer. The system also involved significant economic risk to the three entities that participated in the development of the project. According to the court, the project, at the time, represented a concerted effort at advancing the state of technology in the field of computer science, thereby pushing existing technology to new heights.

The research credit is the sum of (1) the incremental research credit which is equal to 20 percent of the increase in *qualified research expenses* for the current tax year over a *base amount* for that year unless one of two alternate computation methods are elected, (2) the basic research payment credit which is equal to 20 percent of allowable "basic research payments" paid by a corporation to universities (and certain nonprofit scientific organizations) and (3) effective for amount paid or incurred after August 8, 2005, a credit equal to 20 percent of qualifying energy research consortium payments.[68]

Incremental credit base amount. For purposes of the 20 percent incremental research credit described in item (1), the base amount is computed by multiplying the taxpayer's fixed-base percentage by the taxpayer's average gross receipts for the four preceding tax years. A taxpayer's fixed-base percentage is the ratio that its total qualified research expenditures for 1984 through 1988 bears to its total gross receipts for that period (subject to a maximum ratio of 16 percent). Start-up companies, however, are currently assigned a fixed-base percentage of three percent.

Qualified research expenses. Qualified research expenses consist of (1) in-house research expenses and (2) contract research expenses.[69]

In-house research expenses consist of amounts paid or incurred for:

1. Employee wages for qualified services (i.e., for conducting qualified research);
2. Supplies used in the conduct of qualified research; and
3. The right to use computers in the conduct of qualified research.[70]

Contract research expenses generally only include 65 percent of any amount paid or incurred by a taxpayer to persons other than taxpayer employees for qualified research. The applicable percentage increases to 75 percent for payments to a qualified research consortium for qualified research conducted for the taxpayer and one or more unrelated persons. The applicable percentage is 100 percent for amounts paid to eligible small businesses, universities, and federal laboratories for qualified research that is energy research.[71]

Two alternative methods for computing incremental research credit. A taxpayer may elect to compute an "alternative incremental credit," in lieu of the standard

[68] I.R.C. § 41(a).

[69] I.R.C. § 41(b)(1).

[70] I.R.C. § 41(b)(2).

[71] I.R.C. § 41(b)(3).

calculation for the incremental credit described above.[72] The Tax Relief and Health Care Act of 2006 also create an alternative simplified credit calculation that may be elected in place of the standard incremental credit calculation. This simplified credit method may be elected for tax years ending after 2006.[73]

§ 12.1.5 Calculating the R&D Credit

The R&D credit can be calculated in three different ways.[74] The standard calculation of the credit is equal to 20 percent of the amount by which the taxpayer's qualified research expenditures for the current taxable year exceed its base amount.[75] The base amount for the taxable year is determined by multiplying a "fixed base percentage" by the average annual gross receipts of the taxpayer for the four taxable years preceding the "credit year," the taxable year for which the credit is being determined.[76] The taxpayer's base amount cannot be less than 50 percent of its qualified research expenses for the credit year.[77] The "fixed base percentage" is the percentage which the aggregate qualified research expenses of the taxpayer for all taxable years beginning after December 31, 1983, and before January 1, 1989, is of the aggregate gross receipts of the taxpayer for that period.[78] This fixed base percentage cannot exceed 16 percent.[79] Special rules apply for start-up companies that do not have gross receipts for four previous years.[80]

Taxpayers may elect to compute the portion of the credit for increased qualified research[81] under one of two alternative methods, the AIRC or the ASC,[82] depending on the year the expense was paid or incurred. The AIRC, or the "Alternative Incremental Research Credit", is available for qualifying expenses incurred in any tax year beginning after June 30, 1996, but is not available for tax years beginning after December 31, 2008.[83] Under the AIRC, the taxpayer uses a lower credit rate (instead of 20 percent) and a base amount computed with fixed-base percentages as follows:

- A credit rate of three percent applies for tax years ending after December 31, 2006 (2.65 percent for prior tax years beginning on or after July 1, 1999) to the extent that a taxpayer's current-year research expenses are greater than 1 percent, but less than 1.5 percent, of the average annual gross

[72] However, this election cannot be made applicable to tax years beginning after December 31, 2008. I.R.C § 41(h)(2), as amended by the Emergency Economic Stabilization Act of 2008 (Pub. L. No. 110-343).

[73] Pub. L. No. 109-432.

[74] I.R.C. §§ 41(c)(1), (c)(4), and (c)(5), as amended by the Tax Relief Extension Act of 1999, Pub. L. No. 106-170, Act § 502 (December 17, 1999), and the Tax Relief and Health Care Act of 2006, Pub. L. No. 109-432, Division A, Act § 104(b)(1) (December 20, 2006).

[75] I.R.C. § 41(a)(1) (2008).

[76] I.R.C. § 41(c)(1) (2008).

[77] I.R.C. § 41(c)(2) (2008).

[78] I.R.C. § 41(c)(3)(A) (2008).

[79] I.R.C. § 41(c)(3)(C) (2008); *Norwest Corp. v. Commissioner*, 110 T.C. 454 (1998).

[80] I.R.C. § 41(c)(3)(B) (2008).

[81] I.R.C. § 41(a)(1) (2008).

[82] The ASC was added to I.R.C. § 41 and the AIRC was amended by the Tax Relief and Health Care (TRHCA) Act of 2006, Pub. L. No. 109-432; the AIRC was repealed by the Emergency Economic Stabilization Act of 2008, Pub. L. No. 110-343 (October 3, 2008).

[83] I.R.C. § 41(c)(4)(B) (2008); I.R.C. § 41(h)(2), as amended by the Emergency Economic Stabilization Act of 2008, Pub. L. No. 110-343 (October 3, 2008); Reg. § 1.41-1(a), 8(b)(1). The election applies to the first tax year and all subsequent years through December 31, 2008, unless revoked with the IRS's consent.

receipts of the taxpayer for the 4 taxable years preceding the tax year in which the credit is sought.

- A credit rate of four percent applies for tax years ending after December 31, 2006 (3.2 percent for prior tax years beginning on or after July 1, 1999) to the extent that a taxpayer's current-year research expenses are greater than 1.5 percent, but less than 2 percent of the average used above.
- A credit rate of five percent applies for tax years ending after December 31, 2006 (3.75 percent for prior tax years beginning on or after July 1, 1999) to the extent that a taxpayer's current-year research expenses are greater than 2 percent of the average annual gross receipts of the taxpayer for the 4 taxable years preceding the tax year in which the credit is sought.[84]

The ASC, or the "Alternative Simplified Credit," is available for qualifying expenses incurred in tax years ending after December 31, 2006.[85] Taxpayers electing to use the ASC can claim an amount equal to 12 percent of the amount by which the qualified research expenses exceeds 50 percent of the average qualified research expenses for the three preceding tax years.[86] The credit under this method increases to 14 percent for tax years ending after December 31, 2008.[87] If the taxpayer has no qualified research expenses for any of the preceding three tax years, then the credit is equal to six percent of the qualified research expenses for the current tax year.[88]

A taxpayer who has already elected to use the AIRC or the ASC may not in subsequent years elect to use the other of the two alternative computation methods without the consent of the IRS.[89] However, a transitional rule allows a taxpayer to revoke a prior election that was made to use the AIRC method if the taxpayer elects to use the ASC method for the tax year that includes January 1, 2007. If the simplified method is elected for this tax year, the prior election to use the incremental credit method is deemed revoked with IRS consent.[90]

The amount of the simplified credit for a 2006-2007 fiscal year taxpayer is computed by adding (1) the credit calculated under the standard incremental computation method of Code section 41(a)(1) or the alternative incremental credit method of Code section 41(c)(4) using the rates in effect prior to their increase by the Tax Relief and Health Care Act, Pub. L. No. 109-432, and multiplied by a fraction that is the number of days in the tax year before January

---

[84] I.R.C. § 41(c)(4)(A), as amended by Pub. L. No. 106-170 and Pub. L. No. 109-432. For tax years beginning before July 1, 1999, the percentage rates are as follows: tier one, 1.65 percent; tier two, 2.2 percent; and in tier three, 2.75 percent. I.R.C. § 41(c)(4)(A), prior to amendment by Pub. L. No. 106-170.

[85] I.R.C. § 41(c)(5)(C), as added by Pub. L. No. 109-432; Reg. § 1.41-1(a); Temporary Reg. § 1.41-8T(b)(5). As with the AIRC, an election to calculate the research credit using the ASC is effective for all succeeding tax years unless revoked with the consent of the IRS.

[86] I.R.C. § 41(c)(5)(A), as added by Pub. L. No. 109-432.

[87] I.R.C. § 41(c)(5)(A), as amended by Pub. L. No. 110-343.

[88] I.R.C. § 41(c)(5)(B), as added by Pub. L. No. 109-432.

[89] T.D. 9528. A taxpayer cannot elect the AIRC or ASC on a late or amended return, but would be allowed to claim the regular research credit under Code section 41(a). The taxpayer may make or revoke the election by obtaining the consent of the Commissioner.

[90] Act § 104(c)(2) of The Tax Relief and Health Care Act of 2006, Pub. L. No. 109-432 (December 20, 2006).

1, 2007, over the total number of days in the tax year and (2) the credit calculated using the new simplified method and multiplied by a fraction that is the number of days in the tax year after December 31, 2006, over the total number of days in the tax year.[91]

Taxpayers with a 2006-2007 fiscal year who have been using the standard computation method may elect to compute the research credit under both the alternative incremental credit method and the alternative simplified credit method for a 2006 - 2007 fiscal year.[92] Such a taxpayer would compute the research credit using the alternative incremental credit method for the portion of the tax year prior to January 1, 2007 (using the lower percentage rates in effect prior to enactment of Pub. L. No. 109-432) and the alternative simplified credit method for the portion of the tax year after December 31, 2006. The alternative incremental credit election will then be treated as revoked for all tax years after the 2006-2007 fiscal tax year.[93]

When the taxpayer claims the R&D credit, any Code section 174 deduction must be reduced by 100 percent of the credit determined for the taxable year.[94] However, the taxpayer can elect to take a reduced R&D credit and not reduce the Code section 174 deduction.[95] In this situation, the R&D credit is reduced by the amount of tax saved by not reducing the deduction. The reduced credit is the credit before reduction minus the product of the credit and the maximum corporate tax rate.[96]

Standard research credit computation under I.R.C. §41(c)(1), Example: Assume that Bank A is an accrual basis, calendar year taxpayer. For the respective taxable years, Bank A had the following gross receipts and qualified research expenses:

Tax Year	Gross Receipts	Qualified Research Expenses
1984	$225,000	$40,000
1985	250,000	50,000
1986	260,000	52,000
1987	275,000	60,000
1988	280,000	58,000
1992	301,000	72,000
1993	296,000	67,000
1994	309,000	75,000
1995	314,000	80,000
1996	308,000	76,000

If Bank A claims the R&D credit on its 1996 tax return, that year would be the "credit year." Aggregate qualified research expenses for the tax years beginning after December 31, 1983, and before January 1, 1989, is $260,000 and aggregate gross receipts for the same period is $1,290,000. The percent-

91 Act § 104(c)(4) of Pub. L. No. 109-432.

92 Act § 104(c)(4)(B)(ii) of Pub. L. No. 109-432.

93 Act § 104(c)(4)(B)(iii) of Pub. L. No. 109-432.

94 I.R.C. § 280C(c)(1) (2008).

95 I.R.C. § 280C(c)(3)(A) (2008).

96 I.R.C. § 280C(c)(3)(B) (2008).

age which the qualified research expenses are of the gross receipts is 20.16. Because the maximum allowed percentage is 16 percent, Bank A's fixed base percentage is 16 percent.

Bank A's base amount is equal to its fixed base percentage (16%) multiplied by the average annual gross receipts for the 4 years preceding the credit year ($305,000), yielding a base amount of $48,800. Since this amount is greater than 50 percent of the qualified research expenses for the credit year, this is Bank A's base amount. Bank is allowed a credit of $5,440, as follows:

Credit year R&D qualified research expenses	$76,000
Base amount	48,800
	27,200
Credit percentage	0.20
Allowable credit	$5,440

AIRC computation under I.R.C. § 41(c)(4), Example: Assume that bank A from the previous example elects to compute its credit for tax year 2007 using the AIRC method, and further assume the average annual gross receipts for the four preceding years, 2003 through 2006, equals $305,000 and the qualified research expenses for 2007 equal $76,000.

Tier 1 credit using 2007 percentages: $45.75 ($1,525 × 3%). The $1,525 figure is the difference between a base amount computed using a fixed-base percentage of 1.5% ($4,575 ($305,000 × 1.5%)) and a base amount computed using a fixed-base percentage of 1% ($3,050 ($305,000 × 1%)).

Tier 2 credit using 2007 percentages: $61.00 ($1,525 × 4%). The $1,525 figure is the difference between a base amount computed using a fixed-base percentage of 2% ($6,100 ($305,000 × 2%)) and a base amount using a fixed-base percentage of 1.5% ($4,575 ($305,000 × 1.5%)).

Tier 3 credit using 2007 percentage: $3,495 (($76,000 - $6,100) × 5%). The tier 3 credit is 5% of the total qualified research expenditures for the fiscal year ($76,000) in excess of the $6,100 base amount computed using a fixed-base percentage of 2%.

Thus, the allowable credit equals:

Tier 1 = $45.75

Tier 2 = $61.00

Tier 3 = $3,495

Allowable credit = $3,601.75

ASC computation under I.R.C. § 41(c)(5), Example: Assume that Bank A from the previous two examples elects to compute its credit for tax year 2007 using the ASC method, still assuming Bank A has qualified research expenses for 2007 equal to $76,000. Bank A has incurred the following research expenses over the last three years:

Generally, Bank A is required to reduce any deduction taken under Code section 174 by 100 percent of the amount of the R&D credit in subsequent taxable years. Most other C corporations are permitted only a 3-year carryback, but they are granted a 15-year carryforward.

2004 $67,000

2005 $75,000

2006 $80,000

The average qualified research expenses for the three preceding years equals $74,000, and 50% of that is $37,000. The credit year qualified research expenses ($76,000) exceed 50% of the average qualified research expenses for the three preceding years by $39,000. Twelve percent of the $39,000 equals the allowable credit for the year, giving Bank A a credit of $4,680, as follows:

Credit year R&D qualified research expenses	$76,000
50% of averaged qualified research expenses for 3 preceding years	37,000
	39,000
Credit percentage	0.12
Allowable credit	$4,680

For tax years ending after December 31, 2008, the credit percentage is increased to 14%, increasing the allowable credit using the above figures to $5,460. If Bank A had no qualified research expenses for any of tax years 2004 through 2006, the credit is equal to 6% of the qualified research expenses for the credit year 2007, equaling $4,560.

§ 12.1.6 Research and Experimental Expenditures as Tax Preference Items

The excess of the amount deducted by expensing research and experimental expenditures over the amount that would be deductible using ten-year amortization beginning with the tax year in which the expenditures were made is a tax preference item for noncorporate taxpayers. The excess amount is treated as an adjustment in calculating a noncorporate taxpayer's alternative minimum taxable income. The excess is not a tax preference item for a corporation.[97]

There is no tax preference item for amounts paid or incurred for either corporate or noncorporate taxpayers when the taxpayer elects ten-year amortization[98] or amortizes research and experimental expenditures over at least 60 months.[99]

Individual taxpayers who materially participate in activities giving rise to research and experimental expenditures may deduct those expenses currently without making the alternative minimum tax adjustment.[100] This rule also applies

[97] I.R.C. § 56(b)(2)(A)(ii) (2008).

[98] I.R.C. § 59(e) (2008).

[99] I.R.C. §§ 56(b), (c), 57, 59(e)(6) (2008).

[100] I.R.C. § 56(b)(2)(D) (2008). Material participation has the same definition as it does for purposes of the passive loss limitation. I.R.C. § 469(h) (2008).

to activities carried out through a sole proprietorship, partnership or S corporation.[101]

§ 12.1.7 Election to Claim Accelerated Research Credit in Lieu of Bonus Depreciation

As a result of the Housing Assistance Tax Act of 2008, Pub. L. No. 110-289, a corporation may elect to claim a credit for a portion of its unused research and development credits and its alternative minimum tax (AMT) credits that are attributable to tax years beginning before January 1, 2006, instead of taking the 50 percent Code section 168(k) bonus depreciation deduction on any "eligible qualified property."[102] Eligible qualified property is property which is acquired after March 31, 2008, and is eligible for the Code section 168(k) bonus depreciation allowance.[103] An electing corporation must use the MACRS straight-line method to depreciate any eligible qualified property placed in service in the tax year of the election and in any later tax year.[104] The credit is approximately equal to 20 percent of the bonus depreciation amount that could have been deducted but may not exceed the lesser of (1) 6 percent of the corporation's unused pre-2006 credit amounts or (2) $30 million.[105] Since the credit is refundable, corporations benefiting most from the election are those with a net operating loss that would otherwise receive no immediate tax savings by claiming bonus depreciation.[106]

The accelerated credit election is made for the first tax year of the corporation that ends after March 31, 2008.[107] The election (including any allocation of the bonus depreciation amount between pre-2006 research and AMT credits) is revocable only with IRS consent.[108]

Eligible qualified property is defined the same as "qualified property" is in Code section 168(k)(2) except that "March 31, 2008" is substituted for "December 31, 2007" wherever it appears in that section.[109] Thus, in general, eligible qualified property is property that is eligible for bonus depreciation under Code section 168(k), except that it must be acquired after March 31, 2008 (rather than after December 31, 2007) and placed in service before January 1, 2009 (before January 1, 2010 in the case of property with a long production period and certain noncommercial aircraft). In the case of eligible qualified property with a longer production period, only adjusted basis attributable to manufacture, construction, or production after March 31, 2008, and before January 1, 2009, is taken into

[101] H.R. Rep. No. 247, 101st Cong., 1st Sess. 226 (1989).

[102] I.R.C. § 168(k)(4), as added by the Housing Assistance Tax Act of 2008, Pub. L. No. 110-289 (July 30, 2008); Joint Committee on Taxation, Technical Explanation of the Housing Assistance Tax Act of 2008, JCX-63-08 (July 23, 2008).

[103] I.R.C § 168(k)(4)(D) (2008), as added by Pub. L. No. 110-289.

[104] I.R.C. § 168(k)(4)(A)(ii) (2008), as added by Pub. L. No. 110-289.

[105] I.R.C. § 168(k)(4)(C) (2008), as added by Pub. L. No. 110-289.

[106] I.R.C. § 168(k)(4)(F) (2008), as added by the Housing Act.

[107] I.R.C. § 168(k)(4)(A) (2008), as added by Pub. L. No. 110-289.

[108] I.R.C. § 168(k)(4)(G) (2008), as added by Pub. L. No. 110-289.

[109] I.R.C. § 168(k)(4)(D)(i) (2008), as added by Pub. L. No. 110-289.

account in computing the bonus depreciation amount for purposes of this provision.[110]

The I.R.S. recently issued Revenue Procedure 2008-65, which provides guidance for making the election provided under Code section 168(k)(4), as added by the Housing Assistance Tax Act of 2008.[111] This revenue procedure clarifies the rules regarding the effects of making the Code section 168(k)(4) election, the property eligible for the election, and the computation of the amount by which the business credit limitation and AMT credit limitation may be increased if the election is made. The Internal Revenue Service (IRS) and Treasury Department intend to publish future guidance regarding the time and manner for making the Code section 168(k)(4) election, for allocating the credit limitation increases allowed by the election, and for making the election to apply Code section 3081(b) of the Housing Act by certain automotive partnerships, and regarding the procedures applicable to partnerships with corporate partners that make the Code section 168(k)(4) election.[112]

§ 12.2 Low-Income Housing Credit

Code section 42 provides for a Low-Income Housing Credit ("LIHC").[113] The LIHC is claimed as one of the components of the general business credit under Code section 38 and, as such, is subject to the general provisions of that credit, including the Code section 39 carryback and carryforward rules. The amount of the LIHC for any taxable year in the credit period is equal to the "applicable percentage" of the "qualified basis" of each "qualified low-income building." The LIHC credit period is ten years. A taxpayer's basis in the investment that qualifies for the credit is not reduced by the amount of LIHC claimed.

The credit, which is nonrefundable, is available to the owner of newly constructed or substantially rehabilitated qualified low-income housing.[114] It is available on a per unit basis with respect to low-income units in qualified low-income buildings in qualified low-income housing projects.

A qualified low-income building must satisfy the Code section 42 requirements for the compliance period, which comprises the 15 tax years beginning with the first tax year of the credit period.[115] To qualify for the credit, the owner of a low-income building must be subject to a long-term low-income housing use agreement with a housing agency.[116]

Low-income housing credit tax benefits are available to taxpayers investing in low-income housing even though an investment would not otherwise provide a potential for economic return.[117]

---

110 I.R.C. § 168(k)(4)(D)(ii) (2008), as added by Pub. L. No. 110-289.

111 Rev. Proc. 2008-65, 2008-44 I.R.B. 1082 (October 10, 2008).

112 *See* I.R.C. § 168(k)(4)(G)(ii) (2008), as added by Pub. L. No. 110-289.

113 The credit was originally enacted in The Tax Reform Act of 1986, Pub. L. No. 99-514. The Omnibus Budget Reconciliation Act of 1993, Pub. L. No. 103-66, permanently extended the credit.

114 I.R.C. § 42(a) (2000).

115 I.R.C. § 42(i)(1) (2008).

116 I.R.C. § 42(h)(6) (2008).

117 This is because the low-income housing credit is not subject to the rules under I.R.C. § 183 that limit tax benefits for nonprofitable activities. Reg. § 1.42-4(a).

However, the low-income housing credit may be limited or disallowed under other provisions or principles of tax law including the following:[118] (1) limitation based on the amount of tax liability;[119] (2) limitation on investment interest;[120] (3) limitation based on the amount at risk;[121] (4) limitation on passive activities;[122] (5) a sham or economic substance analysis;[123] and (6) an ownership analysis.[124]

The amount of a low-income housing credit from a rental real estate passive activity is generally limited to the tax attributable to the passive activity.[125] However, for individuals, a $25,000 exemption from such limitation is provided for the deduction equivalent amount of credits attributable to rental real estate activities.[126] For purposes of such exemption regarding an individual engaged in rental real estate activities, the low-income housing credit is treated as arising from rental real estate activities in which the individual materially participates.[127]

In Revenue Ruling 2004-82 the IRS issued guidance that addresses various issues dealing with the Code section 42 low-income housing credit.[128] In a question-and-answer format, the ruling covers issues concerning eligible basis and qualified basis; first-year, low-income units; extended low-income housing commitments; Home Investment Partnership Act loans; vacant units; record-keeping and retention; and tenant income documentation.[129]

In Revenue Procedure 95-28, the IRS issued guidance establishing the process under which it will grant temporary relief from certain requirements of Code section 42 for owners of low-income housing and housing credit agencies in major disaster areas.[130] The procedure covers carryover allocation relief, recapture relief, and compliance monitoring relief and is effective for major disaster declarations issued on or after January 1, 1995.

The IRS suspended certain requirements for low-income housing credit projects under Code Sec. 42 as a result of the destruction caused by Hurricane Katrina. The suspension of the requirements allowed owners of low-income housing credit projects to provide temporary housing for displaced individuals who resided in jurisdictions designated for Individual Assistance in Alabama,

---

118 Reg. § 1.42-4(b).

119 I.R.C. § 38(c) (2008).

120 I.R.C. § 163(d) (2008).

121 I.R.C. § 465 (2008).

122 I.R.C. § 469 (2008).

123 *See K.F. Knetsch v. United States*, 364 U.S. 361, 60-2 USTC ¶ 9785 (1960).

124 *See Frank Lyon Co. v. United States*, 435 US 561, 78-1 USTC ¶ 9370 (1978).

125 I.R.C. § 469 (2008).

126 I.R.C. § 469(i) (2008).

127 I.R.C. § 469(i)(6)(B) (2008). The portion of the $25,000 deduction equivalent amount attributable to the low-income housing credit component of a passive activity credit is not subject to an adjusted gross income phaseout rule for property placed in service after 1989. I.R.C. § 469(i)(3)(C). For property held through a partnership or a pass-through entity, an interest in the partnership or entity must be acquired after 1989 in order to be excluded from the phaseout rule. Act Sec. 7109(b)(2) of the Omnibus Budget Reconciliation Act of 1989, Pub. L. No. 101-239.

128 Rev. Rul. 2004-82, 2004-35 I.R.B. 350.

129 Revenue Procedure 2005-37, 2005-28 I.R.B. 79, establishes a safe harbor under which housing credit agencies and project owners may meet the requirements of I.R.C. § 42(h)(6)(B)(j) as described in Q&A 5 of Rev. Rul. 2004-82, concerning extended low-income housing commitments.

130 Rev. Proc. 95-28, 1995-1 C.B. 704 (May 31, 1995).

Louisiana and Mississippi.[131] Also, for calendar years 2006, 2007, and 2008, the population component of the state housing credit ceiling was modified to allow for increased ceilings for the GO Zone.[132] Certain GO Zone tax-exempt bond financed properties placed in service anytime during 2006 through 2010 received favored treatment beyond that which was accorded low-income housing in a difficult development area, allowing for more generous basis treatment which in turn yielded more generous credits.[133] Similar relief was provided with respect to Hurricane Rita and Hurricane Wilma.[134]

The Housing Assistance Tax Act of 2008, Pub. L. No. 110-289, includes a multitude of changes intended to improve access of individuals and families to low-income housing. The changes include a temporary increase to the limit on the annual amount of the federal low-income housing credit that may be allocated by each state. The legislation also includes numerous proposals to simplify the technical rules relating to the low-income housing credit. The Act authorizes and instructs the Comptroller General of the United States (the head of the Government Accountability Office (GAO)) to analyze the changes made by the Act to the low-income housing credit. The report is required to include an analysis of the distribution of credit allocations before and after the effective date of the changes. The report is required to be submitted to Congress no later than December 31, 2012.[135]

§ 12.2.1 Applicable Percentage

The low-income housing credit for any tax year in the ten-year credit period is equal to the applicable percentage (i.e., the credit rate) multiplied by the qualified basis of each low-income housing building.[136] For qualified low-income buildings placed in service after 1987, the "applicable percentage" is the appropriate percentage issued by the IRS for the month in which the building is placed in service.[137]

However, for buildings placed in service after July 30, 2008, and before December 31, 2013, the applicable percentage for new construction or rehabilitation (item (1) below) is set at 9 percent if 9 percent is greater than the applicable monthly percentage that would otherwise apply.[138]

1. For newly constructed units or rehabilitation expenditures exceeding specified minimum amounts per low-income unit that are not federally subsidized, the applicable percentage is computed so that the present value of the 10 annual credit amounts at the beginning of the credit

---

[131] Suspended requirements relate to applicable income limitations under I.R.C. § 42(g)(1), the available unit rule under I.R.C. § 42(g)(2)(D)(ii), the non-transient rule under I.R.C. § 42(i)(3)(B)(i), and the requirement to make reasonable attempts to rent vacant units to low-income individuals. Notice 2005-69, 2005-40 I.R.B. 622 (September 9, 2005).

[132] I.R.C. §§ 1400N(c)(1)(A) and (B).

[133] I.R.C. § 1400N(c)(3), as amended by the Small Business and Work Opportunity Act of 2007, Pub. L. No. 110-28, (May 25, 2007); I.R.C. § 42(d)(5)(B), as redesignated by the Housing Assistance Tax Act of 2008, Pub. L. No. 110-289 (July 30, 2008).

[134] Notice 2006-11, 2006-7 I.R.B. 457 (February 1, 2006).

[135] Housing Assistance Tax Act of 2008, Pub. L. No. 110-289, § 3004(h).

[136] I.R.C. § 42(a) (2008).

[137] I.R.C. § 42(b)(1), as amended by the Housing Assistance Tax Act of 2008, Pub. L. No. 110-289.

[138] I.R.C. § 42(b)(2) (2008), as amended by Pub. L. No. 110-289.

period equals 70 percent of the qualified basis of the low-income units.[139] However, for buildings placed in service after July 30, 2008, and before December 31, 2013, the applicable percentage used in computing the credit rate is set at 9 percent if 9 percent is greater than the applicable percentage based on a value of 70 percent of qualified basis.[140] Presently, the monthly applicable percentage computed by the IRS for months after July 2008 are approximately 8 percent. Accordingly, the 9 percent rate applies for these months and will result in a present value in excess of 70 percent of qualified basis.

2. For newly constructed units or rehabilitation expenditures exceeding specified minimum amounts per low-income unit that are federally subsidized, the applicable percentage is computed so that the present value of the 10 annual credit amounts at the beginning of the credit period equals 30 percent of the qualified basis of the low-income units.[141]

A taxpayer may elect the applicable percentage for the month in which the taxpayer and housing credit agency agree on a housing credit amount for the building, or in the case of a building financed primarily with tax-exempt bonds subject to the Code section 146 volume cap, the applicable percentage for the month in which the tax-exempt obligations are issued, if such month is earlier than the month the building is placed in service. A taxpayer may irrevocably elect to determine the low-income housing credit percentage applicable to a building in advance of the date such building is placed in service.

The present value determination is made as of the last day of the first year of the 10-year period by using a discount rate. The discount rate is 72 percent of the average of the federal mid-term rate and the annual federal long-term rate applicable under Code section 1274(d)(1) for the month in which the building is placed in service. In lieu of using the month in which the building is placed in service, a taxpayer may use the month in which the taxpayer and the housing credit agency enter into an agreement with respect to such building as to the housing credit dollar amount to be allocated to the building. When tax-exempt bonds are issued for a building financed with tax-exempt bonds for which no credit allocation from a credit agency is required, it is compounded annually. For such purpose, it is assumed that the low-income housing credit is received on the last day of such year.[142] A formula for making such computation is provided in Revenue Ruling 88-6.[143]

---

[139] I.R.C. § 42(b)(1)(B) (2008), as amended by Pub. L. No. 110-289.

[140] I.R.C. § 42(b)(2) (2008), as amended Pub. L. No. 110-289. The credit percentage for rehabilitation expenditures exceeding a prescribed minimum amount so as to be treated as a new building is determined when rehabilitation is completed and the rehabilitated property is placed in service. These rehabilitation expenditures are treated as a separate new building that is placed in service at the end of the 24-month period for which such expenditures may be aggregated for purposes of the credit. I.R.C. § 42(e).

[141] I.R.C. § 42(b)(1)(B) (2008), as amended by Pub. L. No. 110-289. This rate also applies to the cost of acquiring certain existing low-income units (including rehabilitation expenditures below the minimum rehabilitation requirement for such units incurred before the close of the first year of the credit period).

[142] I.R.C. § 42(b)(1)(C) (2008).

[143] Rev. Rul. 88-6, 1988-1 C.B. 3.

(a) *Subsidized Buildings*

For buildings placed in service on or before July 30, 2008, a new building is treated as federally subsidized if at any time during the tax year (or a prior tax year) the proceeds of a tax-exempt obligation or below-market federal loan are (or were) used directly or indirectly to fund such building or the operation thereof.[144] If an election is made to reduce eligible basis by the outstanding balance of a below-market federal loan (or tax-exempt obligation), then such loan (or the proceeds of such obligation) is not treated as a federal subsidy.[145] Such election is made on Form 8609 (Rev. December 2007), Part II, Line 9a, not later than the income tax return due date. A federal loan guarantee, such as FHA insurance, does not constitute such a subsidy. Tax-exempt financing or a below-market loan used to provide construction financing for a building is not treated as a federal subsidy if such loan is repaid and any underlying obligation is redeemed before the building is placed in service.[146]

A below-market federal loan is a loan funded with federal funds if the interest rate payable on such loan is less than the applicable federal rate under Code section 1274(d)(1) on the date that the loan is made.[147] Such term does not include below-market HUD block grants made under sections 106 through 108 of the Housing and Community Development Act of 1974. Moreover, a below-market loan under the Affordable Housing Program (Sec. 721 of the Financial Institutions Reform, Recovery, and Enforcement Act of 1989) is not made from federal funds and is not a below-market federal loan for purposes of Code section 42(i)(2)(D) prior to being stricken by Pub. L. No. 110-289. Thus, a building financed with such loan proceeds is not considered a federally subsidized building, solely by reason of such loan, for purposes of determining the applicable low-income housing credit rate.[148]

Assistance received for a building under the HOME Investment Partnerships Act (as in effect on August 10, 1993) or the Native American Housing Assistance and Self-Determination Act of 1996 (as in effect on October 1, 1997) is not considered a below-market federal loan, provided that at least 40 percent (at least 25 percent for a building located in a city described in Code section 142(d)(6)) of the residential units in the building are occupied by individuals earning 50 percent or less of the area median gross income (the "special set-aside").[149] However, such assistance does bar an increase in eligible basis to 130 percent for buildings located in high cost areas.[150]

The special set-aside rule is applied on a building-by-building basis even if a taxpayer elects to treat the buildings as part of a multiple building project and a

---

[144] I.R.C. § 42(i)(2)(A), prior to amendment by Pub. L. No. 110-289.

[145] I.R.C. § 42(i)(2)(B), prior to amendment by Pub. L. No. 110-289.

[146] I.R.C. § 42(i)(2)(C), prior to amendment by Pub. L. No. 110-289.

[147] I.R.C. § 42(i)(2)(D), prior to being stricken by Pub. L. No. 110-289.

[148] Reg. § 1.42-3.

[149] I.R.C. § 42(i)(2)(E), prior to being stricken by Pub. L. No. 110-289.

[150] Although this provision is intended to apply after August 10, 1993, a technical correction may be needed to achieve this result because of an apparent typographical error in Pub. L. No. 103-66, Act Sec. 13142(b)(6)(C), confusing the full-time-student and HOME amendments.

HOME loan is provided with respect to the project. The rent restriction that applies for all low-income units in the project is based upon the rent restriction contained in the minimum set aside elected by the taxpayer.[151]

Effective for buildings placed in service after July 30, 2008, below market federal loans are no longer treated as a federal subsidy for purposes of determining whether a new building or substantial rehabilitations to an existing building are eligible for the 70 percent present value low-income housing credit rate. As a result, a new building or substantial rehabilitations to an existing building are considered federally subsidized only if, at any time during the tax year or any prior tax year, there is or was outstanding any obligation, the interest of which is exempt from tax under Code section 103, the proceeds of which are or were used (directly or indirectly) with respect to the building or its operation.[152] As before, if an election is made to reduce eligible basis by the outstanding balance of a tax-exempt obligation, then the proceeds of the obligation is not treated as a federal subsidy and the election is made on Form 8609 (Rev. December 2007), Part II, Line 9a, not later than the income tax return due date.[153] Tax-exempt financing used to provide construction financing for a building is not treated as a federal subsidy if the underlying obligation is redeemed before the building is placed in service.[154]

(b) *Election of Appropriate Percentage Month*

A taxpayer (with the consent of the housing credit agency) may irrevocably elect to determine the low-income housing credit percentage applicable to a building in advance of the date such building is placed in service.[155] Under this election, the applicable credit percentage is the percentage for the month in which:

- a "binding commitment" is received from the credit agency as to the housing credit dollar amount to be allocated to the building, or
- tax-exempt bonds are issued for a building that is 50 percent or more financed by tax-exempt bonds subject to the volume cap of Code section 146 and for which no credit allocation from a credit agency is required.

(i) Binding Commitment

An agreement is considered "binding" if there is a written binding contract that specifies the housing credit dollar amount to be allocated to the building and the type of building to which the housing credit dollar amount applies (newly constructed, existing, or substantially rehabilitated). Such contract must be binding on the agency, the taxpayer, and all successors in interest. It must also be dated and signed by the taxpayer and the agency during the month these requirements are met. If the binding agreement is also a carryover allocation

[151] Rev. Rul. 2004-82, Q&A 6. *See* Rev. Rul. 2004-82 for rules that apply when a building is funded in part with tax-exempt obligations and a HOME loan was provided with respect to the building.

[152] I.R.C. § 42(i)(2)(A), as amended by the Housing Assistance Tax Act of 2008, Pub. L. No. 110-289.

[153] I.R.C. § 42(i)(2)(B) (2008), as amended by H.R.3221.

[154] I.R.C. § 42(i)(2)(C) (2008), as amended by Pub. L. No. 110-289.

[155] I.R.C. § 42(b)(1) (2008), as amended by Pub. L. No. 110-289.

under Code section 42(h)(1)(E)-(F), the state housing credit ceiling is reduced by the amount allocated by the agency to the taxpayer in the year the carryover allocation is made.[156] There must be a written election that is signed by the taxpayer and contains a specific reference to the applicable Code section and the binding agreement.

A taxpayer may not make an election for a building if an election has previously been made for a different month. Therefore, if a second binding agreement is entered into after a first binding agreement is rescinded, the taxpayer must apply to the building the appropriate percentage for the elected month of the rescinded binding agreement. However, if no prior election was made with respect to the rescinded binding agreement, the taxpayer may elect the appropriate percentage for the month of the new binding agreement.[157]

The election applies to any increase in the credit amount allocated for a building, whether the increase occurs in the same or in a subsequent year. However, if the binding agreement pertains to substantial rehabilitation, a taxpayer may make an election even though a prior election is in effect for a prior allocation of credit for a building undergoing substantial rehabilitation that was previously placed in service.[158]

The housing credit dollar amount eventually allocated to a building may be more or less than the amount specified in the binding agreement. The applicable percentage may be less than, but not greater than, the appropriate percentage for the month the building is placed in service or the month elected by the taxpayer. Whether the appropriate percentage is the appropriate percentage for the 70 percent present value credit or the 30 percent present value credit is determined when the building is placed in service.[159]

(ii) Tax-Exempt Bonds

For purposes of tax-exempt bond-financed buildings described above, there must be a written election that is signed by the taxpayer, contains a specific reference to the applicable Code section, and specifies the aggregate basis of the building and the land on which the building is located that is financed by such tax-exempt bonds, the month in which such bonds were issued, and that such

---

[156] Reg. § 1.42-8(a)(2). The election statement must be notarized on the last page of the election statement no later than the fifth day after the month in which the binding agreement was made. The original notarized election statement must be given to the housing credit agency no later than the fifth day of the month following the month in which the binding agreement was made. The taxpayer should retain a copy of the binding agreement and the election statement. Reg. § 1.42-8(a)(6), as amended by T.D. 9110. Effective for forms filed after January 6, 2004, it is no longer necessary to file an additional copy of the binding agreement and election statement with Form 8609 for the first tax year in which the credit is claimed (Reg. § 1.42-8(a)(6)(i), prior to amendment by T.D. 9110; Reg. § 1.42-12); however, for such forms, the agency must retain the original of the binding agreement and election statement and, to the extent required by Schedule A of Form 8610 (Carryover Allocation of Low-Income Housing Credit), account for the binding agreement and election statement on that schedule. Reg. § 1.42-8(a)(6)(ii), as amended by T.D. 9110. For forms filed on or before January 6, 2004, the agency was required to include the original binding agreement and election statement with Form 8610 when filed with the IRS and retain copies. Reg. § 1.42-8(a)(6)(ii), prior to amendment by T.D. 9110; Reg. § 1.42-12.

[157] Reg. § 1.42-8(a)(4)(i).

[158] Reg. § 1.42-8(a)(4)(ii).

[159] Reg. § 1.42-8(a)(5).

month is the month elected for the appropriate percentage regarding the building.[160]

If a substantially bond-financed building is financed with tax-exempt bonds issued in more than one month, the taxpayer may elect the appropriate percentage for any month in which the bonds are issued. Once made, the election applies for the building even if all bonds are not issued in that month.[161] Further, the credit allowable for a substantially bond-financed building is limited to the amount necessary to ensure the project's feasibility. Therefore, in making the Code section 42(m)(2) determination, an agency may use an applicable percentage that is less than, but not greater than, the appropriate percentage for the month elected or placed in service.[162]

(iii) Agency Authorization

A taxpayer who is otherwise eligible to take the low-income housing credit must, in most cases, obtain authority from an appropriate state or local agency before taking the credit. A housing credit agency may authorize all or part of the credit to which the taxpayer is otherwise entitled, and the taxpayer may not claim a credit in excess of the credit dollar amount allocated to his project. Taxpayers planning to claim a credit for a qualified low-income housing project financed by tax-exempt bonds subject to the volume cap provided by Code section 146 are not required to obtain this credit authority.[163] In allocating a housing credit dollar amount to a building, the housing credit agency must specify the applicable percentage and the maximum qualified basis.[164]

§ 12.2.2 Low-Income Housing Credit: Qualified Basis

Qualified basis is the portion of "eligible basis" allocable to low-income housing units in the building. The allocation is made by multiplying the "eligible basis" by the lesser of the "unit fraction" or the "floor space fraction." The unit fraction of a building is the number of low-income units in the building divided by the total number of residential units in the building. The floor space fraction is

---

[160] The election statement must be notarized on the last page of the election statement no later than the fifth day after the month in which the bonds are issued. The original notarized election statement must be given to the state housing credit agency no later than the fifth day of the month following the month in which the bonds are issued. The taxpayer should retain a copy of the election statement. Reg. § 1.42-8(b)(4)(i), as amended by T.D. 9110. For forms filed after January 6, 2004, a taxpayer is no longer required to file an additional copy of the election statement with Form 8609 for the first tax year that the credit is claimed (Reg. § 1.42-8(b)(4)(i), prior to amendment by T.D. 9110; Reg. § 1.42-12(a)(3)); however, for such forms, the agency retains the original election statement and a copy of Form 8609 that reflects the election statement. The agency must file an additional copy of the Form 8609 with the agency's Form 8610 that reflects the calendar year the Form 8609 is issued. Reg. § 1.42-8(b)(4)(ii), as amended by T.D. 9110; Reg. § 1.42-12(a)(3). For forms filed on or before January 6, 2004, the agency should retain a copy of the election statement. It should file the original election statement and the corresponding Form 8609 with the agency's Form 8610 that reflects the year the Form 8609 was issued. Reg. § 1.42-8(b)(4)(ii), prior to amendment by T.D. 9110.

[161] Reg. § 1.42-8(b)(2).

[162] Reg. § 1.42-8(b)(3).

[163] Form 8609 is used to obtain a housing credit allocation from the housing credit agency. The authorized housing credit agency must complete Form 8609, Part I, Allocation of Credit, and forward a copy to the owner of the building when an allocation of credit is made. The agency must also file the original Form 8609 with a completed Part I and Form 8610 not later than February 28 after the close of the calendar year in which the allocation of credit is made.

[164] I.R.C. § 42(h)(7)(D) (2008).

the total floor space of the low-income units in the building divided by the total floor space of all residential units in the building.[165]

A manager-occupied unit is considered residential rental property because it is a facility reasonably required for a project. Because it is classified in this manner, such unit is not a residential rental unit. Residential rental property includes residential rental units, facilities for use by the tenants, and other facilities reasonably required by the project. A residential rental unit has a narrower meaning in that it is merely one component of residential rental property. Consequently, the adjusted basis of a manager-occupied unit is includible in eligible basis, but such unit is not included in either the numerator or the denominator of the applicable fraction of eligible basis in determining the qualified basis to which the credit rate is applied.[166]

Certain nonhousing areas of a building that provides transitional housing are includible in qualified basis. Qualified basis is increased by the lesser of the portion of eligible basis of such building as is used throughout the year to provide supportive services designed to assist tenants in locating and retaining permanent housing, or 20 percent of the qualified basis of the building.[167]

(a) *Eligible Basis*

Eligible basis for both new and certain existing buildings is determined as of the close of the first tax year of the credit period and equals the adjusted basis of such property.[168] The eligible basis of an existing building is zero unless it meets certain existing building requirements, discussed below.[169] Expenditures incurred before the close of the first tax year in the credit period are includible in eligible basis. Eligible basis is determined before any adjustments to basis are made for depreciation allowable during the first tax year.

Effective for buildings placed in service after July 30, 2008, the eligible basis of a building does not include any costs financed with the proceeds of a federally funded grant.[170] Prior to amendment by the Housing Act, Code Sec. 42(d)(5)(A) provided that if during any tax year of a building's compliance period, a grant that is funded with federal funds is made with respect to a building or its operations, the eligible basis of the building for that tax year and all succeeding tax years is reduced by the portion of the grant that is federally funded. The eligible basis of a building placed in service on or before July 30, 2008, must also be reduced by any cost for which an election was made to deduct rehabilitation expenditures under former Code Sec. 167(k), as in effect on November 4, 1990.[171] The change by the Housing Act means that (1) federal grants do not reduce eligible basis in situations where the grant is not included in the eligible basis and (2) the exclusion (formerly reduction) from eligible basis applies whether or not the grant is made during the building's compliance period. Federal rental

---

165 I.R.C. § 42(c)(1)(A)-(D) (2008).

166 Rev. Rul. 92-61 (1992).

167 I.R.C. § 42(c)(1)(E) (2008).

168 I.R.C. § 42(d)(1) and (d)(2)(A) (2008).

169 I.R.C. § 42(d)(2)(B) (2008).

170 I.R.C. § 42(d)(5)(A), as amended by the Housing Assistance Tax Act of 2008, Pub. L. No. 110-289; Reg. § 1.42-16(a).

171 Former I.R.C. § 42(d)(5)(B), prior to repeal by the Housing Assistance Tax Act of 2008, Pub. L. No. 110-289.

assistance payments made pursuant to the following Acts or programs are not considered federal grants that must require a reduction in the building's eligible basis: (1) rental assistance payments made under section 8 or qualifying rental assistance payments (to cover operating costs) under section 9 of the United States Housing Act of 1937 and (2) rental assistance programs or methods designated by the IRS through the Federal Register or in the Internal Revenue Bulletin.[172] Application and allocation fees paid by a builder to a housing credit agency are not included in eligible basis.[173]

A payment is made pursuant to a qualified rental assistance program under section 9 of the Housing Act of 1937 to the extent that the payments are made to a building owner pursuant to a contract with a public housing authority with respect to units that the owner has agreed to maintain as public housing units in the building. In addition, such units must be occupied by public housing tenants (units may be considered "occupied" during periods of short-term vacancy not to exceed 60 days). The payments may not exceed the difference between the rents received from a building's public housing tenants and a pro rata portion of the building's actual operating costs allocable to the public housing units. For this purpose, operating costs may not include such costs as developer's fees or the principal or interest of any debt incurred with respect to any part of the building.[174]

The eligible basis of a new building or the eligible basis of rehabilitation expenditures for an existing building undergoing substantial rehabilitation that is located in a difficult-to-develop area or qualified census tract is 130 percent of such eligible basis claimed for depreciation purposes.[175] A building is eligible for the increased in basis whether or not it is federally subsidized.[176] However, buildings placed in service on or before July 30, 2008, which receive assistance provided under the HOME Investment Partnerships Act or the Native American Housing Assistance and Self-Determination Act that is not considered part of a below-market loan by reason of Code section 42(i)(2)(E)(i), are not eligible for the increase to buildings in high cost areas.[177] Difficult-to-develop areas are areas designated by the Secretary of HUD that have high construction, land, or utility costs relative to area median gross income. The portions of metropolitan statistical areas which may be designated as a difficult development area may not exceed an aggregate area having 20 percent of the population of the metropolitan statistical areas. A similar rule applies to nonmetropolitan areas.[178]

Effective for buildings placed in service after July 30, 2008, state housing credit agencies may designate a building as located in a difficult development area if the enhanced credit resulting from the increase in eligible basis is necessary for the building to be financially feasible as part of a qualified low-income

---

172 Reg. § 1.42-16(b).

173 Rev. Rul. 2004-82, 2004-35 I.R.B. 350.

174 Reg. § 1.42-16(c).

175 I.R.C. § 42(d)(5)(B), as redesignated by Pub. L. No. 110-289.

176 Announcement 91-112.

177 I.R.C. § 42(i)(2)(E)(i), prior to being stricken by the Housing Assistance Act of 2008, Pub. L. No. 110-289.

178 I.R.C. § 42(d)(5)(B)(iii), as redesignated by Pub. L. No. 110-289.

housing project.[179] A difficult development area designated by a state housing agency is not subject to the limitation that only 20 percent of the population of each metropolitan or nonmetropolitan statistical area may be designated as such.

The designated building does not need to be located in a difficult development area. If the designation is made, however, the building is treated as if it is located in such an area. As a result, its eligible basis is 130 percent of the eligible basis that would otherwise apply.

A building is not eligible for designation under this provision if:

- Any amount of the eligible basis of the building is financed by an obligation bearing interest that is tax-exempt under Code section 103;
- The obligation is taken into account in determining the state volume cap on private activity bonds under Code section 146; and
- The principal payments of the financing are applied within a reasonable period to redeem the obligations used to finance the building.[180]

In the case of property placed in service during 2006, 2007, or 2008, the Gulf Opportunity Zone, the Rita GO Zone, and the Wilma GO Zone are treated as difficult development areas and are not be taken into account when applying the 20-percent population limit on difficult development areas. This special rule applies only to housing credit dollar amounts allocated during the period beginning on January 1, 2006, and ending December 31, 2008, and buildings placed in service during such period to the extent that the rule limiting the allowable credit to the credit allocated to the building (Code section 42(h)(1)) does not apply by reason of Code section 42(h)(4), which relates to buildings financed with tax-exempt bonds.[181]

A qualified census tract is a census tract designated by HUD, for the most recent year for which census data is available on household income in such tract, in which 50 percent or more of the households have an income that is less than 60 percent of the area median gross income for such year, or which has a poverty rate of at least 25 percent. If there is insufficient census tract data, this rule is applied on the basis of enumeration districts.[182] Not more than 20 percent of the population of metropolitan or nonmetropolitan areas may qualify for such designations.

Where non low-income units are above the average quality standard of the low-income units in a building, the portion of the adjusted basis allocable to the above-average units is not included in the eligible basis.[183] An exception is provided whereby eligible basis includes a portion of the basis of housing units where the cost is disproportionate to that of the low-income units.[184] For such exception to apply, an election must be made to exclude the excess cost from eligible basis and the cost per square foot of the disproportionate unit must not

[179] I.R.C. § 42(d)(5)(B)(v), as added by the Housing Assistance Tax Act of 2008, Pub. L. No. 110-289.

[180] I.R.C. § 42(d)(5)(B)(v), as added by the Housing Assistance Act of 2008, Pub. L. No. 110-289.

[181] I.R.C. § 1400N(c)(3) (2008).

[182] I.R.C. § 42(d)(5)(B)(ii), as redesignated by Pub. L. No. 110-289.

[183] I.R.C. § 42(d)(3)(A) (2008).

[184] I.R.C. § 42(d)(3)(B) (2008).

exceed 15 percent of the average cost per square foot of the low-income units. The cost of the entire disproportionate unit is excluded from eligible basis if such limit is exceeded.

For purposes of the eligible basis rules, an existing building must meet the following requirements:

1. The building is acquired by purchase;
2. The date of acquisition by the taxpayer is at least 10 years after the date the building was last placed in service;
3. The building was not previously placed in service by the taxpayer or a person related to the taxpayer when the building was previously placed in service; and
4. A credit would generally be allowed for substantial rehabilitation expenditures made concerning such building.[185]

In order for a building to be acquired by purchase for purposes of the low-income housing credit, the building cannot be acquired from a related person and cannot be acquired by one component member of a controlled group from another component member of the same controlled group. For buildings placed in service after July 30, 2008, a person is related to the taxpayer if the person bears a relationship to the taxpayer that is described in the general limitations on losses between related parties,[186] except that the family of an individual includes only the individual's spouse, ancestors, and lineal descendants. For buildings placed in service on or before July 30, 2008, a person is related to the taxpayer if the person bears a relationship to the taxpayer that is described in the general limitations on losses between related parties or between partners and partnerships, except that 10-percent ownership rules apply, instead of 50-percent, and the family of an individual includes only the individual's spouse, ancestors, and lineal descendants.[187]

For purposes of requirement (2), above, if a buyer has a carryover basis in a nontaxable exchange, placement in service is not counted in determining when the building was last placed in service.[188] Other exceptions are provided under which a placement in service is disregarded if it results from (a) death, (b) acquisition by a governmental unit or certain Code section 501(c)(3) or Code section 501(c)(4) organizations whose acquisition of the property was at least 10 years after it was previously placed in service, (c) a foreclosure of a purchase money security interest occurring at least 10 years after the previous placed-in-service date, provided that the property is resold within 12 months after the date

---

[185] I.R.C. § 42(d)(2)(B), as amended by Pub. L. No. 110-289.

[186] I.R.C. § 267(b), or between partners and partnerships (I.R.C. § 707(b)). A controlled group has the meaning given it for purposes of the rules limiting multiple benefits to controlled groups, except that the 80-percent-or-more test is replaced by a more-than-50-percent test. I.R.C §§ 42(d)(2)(B)(i), 179(d)(2) and (d)(7).

[187] A controlled group has the meaning given it for purposes of the rules limiting multiple benefits to controlled groups, except that the 80-percent-or-more test is replaced by a more-than-10-percent test. I.R.C § 42(d)(2)(D)(iii), prior to amendment by Pub. L. No. 110-289; I.R.C. § 179(d)(2) and (d)(7).

[188] I.R.C. § 42(d)(2)(D)(i), as redesignated by Pub. L. No. 110-289.

such building is placed in service by such person after foreclosure, or (d) a single-family residence of an individual who owned and used such residence for no other purpose than as a principal residence.

For buildings placed in service on or before July 30, 2008, the date of acquisition must be 10 years or more after the later of the date the building was last placed in service or the date of the most recent nonqualified substantial improvements.[189] For purposes of this requirement, nonqualified substantial improvements are capital improvements made within a two-year period if the capital costs of the improvements are at least 25 percent of the adjusted basis of the building (computed without regard to depreciation) at the beginning of the period if five-year depreciation (former Code section 167(k)), as in effect on November 4, 1990 was elected or ACRS applied to the improvement. The date of such substantial improvement is the last day of the 24-month substantial improvement period.[190]

The 10-year holding period is automatically waived for any federally or state-assisted building placed in service after July 30, 2008.[191] For purposes of this exception, a federally-assisted building is any building which is substantially assisted, financed, or operated under Section 8 of the United States Housing Act of 1937, Section 221(d)(3), 221(d)(4), or 236 of the National Housing Act, Section 515 of the Housing Act of 1949, or any other housing program administered by the Department of Housing and Urban Development or by the Rural Housing Service of the Department of Agriculture. A state-assisted building is any building which is substantially assisted, financed or operated under any state law with purposes similar to those of the federal laws referred to in the definition of federally-assisted building.[192]

Additionally, on application by the taxpayer, the IRS may waive the 10-year holding period rule with respect to any building acquired from an insured depository institution in default (as defined in Section 3 of the Federal Deposit Insurance Act) or from a receiver or conservator of such an institution.[193]

For federally assisted buildings placed in service on or before July 30, 2008, the IRS may waive the 10-year holding period rule if necessary:

- To avert an assignment of a mortgage secured by property to the Department of Housing and Urban Development or the Farmers Home Administration;
- To avert a claim against a federal mortgage insurance fund;[194]

---

[189] I.R.C. § 42(d)(2)(B)(ii), prior to amendment by Pub. L. No. 110-289.

[190] I.R.C. § 42(d)(2)(D)(i), prior to repeal by Pub. L. No. 110-289.

[191] I.R.C. § 42(d)(6)(A) (2008), as amended by Pub. L. No. 110-289.

[192] I.R.C. § 42(d)(6)(C) (2008), as amended by Pub. L. No. 110-289.

[193] I.R.C. § 42(d)(6)(B) (2008), as amended by Pub. L. No. 110-289.

[194] I.R.C. § 42(d)(6)(A), prior to amendment by Pub. L. No. 110-289. A statement from HUD or the FHA containing information on the waiver and federal agency action specified in Regulation § 1.42-2(c)(3) is required.

- For certain low-income buildings where the mortgage may be prepaid within one year;[195] and
- For a building acquired from a failed financial institution or from a receiver or conservator of such an institution if such acquisition is necessary to avert an expenditure of federal funds by a federal agency or regulatory authority.[196]

An application for a waiver must be filed with the IRS by a taxpayer who has purchased the building or who has a binding contract to purchase the building. The application may be filed at any time after a binding contract has been executed, but no later than 12 months after the acquisition of the building. Such application must contain the information specified in Regulation Section 1.42-2(d)(1). A waiver is effective when granted in writing by the IRS and it must be attached to the taxpayer's income tax return for the first tax year in which the low-income credit is claimed.[197] A waiver may be granted only if no prior owner was allowed a low-income housing credit for such building.[198]

If there are multiple owners, a single application for a waiver is sufficient provided that all of the owners are identified. A single waiver application may be filed for a project consisting of multiple buildings as long as the information required for each federally assisted building is identified by building address. A waiver application may be filed for specific buildings that are federally assisted in a project consisting of multiple buildings that are not all federally assisted.[199]

A person who acquires an existing low-income building in a transfer occurring before the end of the prior owner's 10-year credit period would not satisfy the eligible basis rules and could not include such building in eligible basis. An exception is provided for the acquisition of an existing building or an interest therein before the end of the prior owner's compliance period for such building. In such case, the buyer steps into the shoes of the transferor and may take the credits to which the transferor would have been entitled had he retained the property.[200] Under this exception, the four requirements indicated above for existing buildings do not apply.

For purposes of requirement (4), above, no credit is generally allowed for the acquisition of an existing building unless there is a substantial rehabilitation of low-income units and common areas. This requirement also applies to rehabilitation expenses that are treated as a separate new building.

---

[195] I.R.C. § 42(d)(6)(C), prior to amendment by Pub. L. No 110-289. The mortgage on the federally assisted building must be eligible for prepayment under the Emergency Low-Income Housing Preservation Act of 1987 or under the Housing Act of 1949 within one year after the date of application for such waiver. The appropriate federal official must certify that the building would be converted to market use absent the waiver. A waiver of the right to prepay such mortgage must also be executed. A federally assisted building is one that is substantially assisted, financed, or operated under section 8 of the United States Housing Act of 1937, section 221(d)(3) or 236 of the National Housing Act, or section 515 of the Housing Act of 1949. I.R.C. § 42(d)(6)(B), prior to amendment by Pub. L. No. 110-289.

[196] I.R.C. § 42(d)(6)(C), as amended by Pub. L. No. 110-289.

[197] Reg. § 1.42(d)(4) and (5) (2008).

[198] I.R.C. § 42(d)(6)(A) (2008).

[199] Reg. § 1.42-2(d)(3).

[200] I.R.C. § 42(d)(7) (2008).

Two exceptions are provided from the "substantial rehabilitation" requirement for the acquisition of existing buildings.[201] Under one exception, an election may be made to have a building acquired from a governmental unit or agency qualify for the credit if rehabilitation expenditures average at least $2,000 per low-income unit (even if such amount is less than 10 percent of the unadjusted basis of the building). However, the 30-percent present value applicable credit rate must be used to compute such credit on both the existing portion of such building and on the qualified rehabilitation expenditures.

A second exception applies to a federally assisted building if the mortgage on the building is eligible within one year of the application for waiver for prepayment under the Emergency Low Income Housing Preservation Act of 1987 or under the Housing Act of 1949 and the appropriate federal official certifies that the building will be converted to market use absent the waiver. However, for such building to qualify for the credit, rehabilitation expenditures must result in qualified basis of at least $2,000 per low-income unit. Further, the right to repay the mortgage must be waived. The credit for the acquisition cost of such building is computed under the 30-percent present value applicable credit rate. The credit for the substantial rehabilitation expenditures regarding such buildings that are not federally subsidized is computed under the 70-percent present value applicable credit rate.

The adjusted basis of an existing building excludes the portion of basis determined by reference to the basis of other property held by the buyer.[202] In computing the adjusted basis of any building, a taxpayer may not take into account basis allocable to the portion of the property that is not residential rental property. Common areas and facilities may be taken into account, however, provided that the same or comparable areas or facilities may be used by low-income and nonlow-income tenants alike. For such purpose, adjusted basis is determined without regard to depreciation.

(b) *At-Risk Rules*

The amount of qualifying basis for which a credit can be taken is subject to an at-risk limitation similar to the at-risk rules in the case of nonrecourse financing.[203] An exception is provided for lenders related to the buyer of the low-income housing property. Another exception is provided for financing (including seller financing) that does not exceed 60 percent of the basis of the property and that is provided by charitable and social welfare organizations whose exempt purpose includes fostering low-income housing. Further, if the rate of interest for any financing qualifying for this exception is below the applicable federal rate (AFR) at the time the financing is incurred minus one percentage point, then the qualified basis to which such financing relates is reduced to reflect the present value of the payments of principal and interest, using the AFR as the discount rate.

---

[201] I.R.C. § 42 (d)(2)(B)(iv) and I.R.C. § 42 (f)(5)(B)(ii) (2008).

[202] I.R.C. § 42(d)(2)(C) (2008).

[203] I.R.C. § 49(a)(1) (2008) other than subparagraphs (D)(ii)(1) and (D)(iv)(1) thereof. I.R.C. § 49(a)(2) and (b)(1).

Such financing must be repaid by the earlier of: (a) the maturity date of the obligation; (b) the 90th day after the close of the compliance period; or (c) the date of refinancing or disposition of the building.[204] Income tax liability is increased by the applicable portion of the credit plus interest if there is a failure to fully repay such financing in the year that such failure occurs.[205] The applicable portion of the credit is the aggregate decrease in the credits allowed for all prior tax years that would result if the eligible basis were reduced by the amount of financing not repaid. Interest runs from the return due date for the first tax year for which the credit was allowable through the return due date for the year in which such failure occurs and is payable at the underpayment rate.

For purposes of treating certain nonrecourse financing provided by a qualified nonprofit organization from whom the owner did not acquire such property as an amount at risk, the deadline for full repayment of such financing in (b), above, is delayed to the 90th day after the earlier of the date the building ceases to be a qualified low-income building or the date that is 15 years after the close of the compliance period.[206]

§ 12.2.3 Low-Income Unit

(a) *Qualification Rules*

A low-income unit is a unit that is rent-restricted and occupied by individuals that meet the applicable income limitation.[207] No unit is treated as a low-income unit unless it is suitable for occupancy (meets state or local health, safety, and building rules) and is used other than on a transient basis. For purposes of computing the credit in the first credit period, a unit may be treated as a low-income housing unit in the month in which it is initially occupied, even if a tenant moves in on the last day of the month.[208] Month-to-month leasing of a single-room occupancy, low-income unit is not treated as a transient use and does not disqualify such unit. The use of certain transitional housing for the homeless for a period of not more than 24 months does not constitute a transient use.[209]

A unit is not disqualified from being a low-income unit because it is occupied by students if the unit is occupied (1) by a student receiving assistance under title IV of the Social Security Act, (2) by a student in government-supported job training programs, (3) by a student that has previously been under the care and placement of a state agency responsible for administering a foster care program,[210] (4) entirely by full-time students who are single parents and

[204] I.R.C. § 42(k)(2)(D) (2008).

[205] I.R.C. § 42(k)(4) (2008).

[206] I.R.C. § 42(k)(2)(D) (2008).

[207] I.R.C. § 42(i)(3)(A) (2008).

[208] Rev. Rul. 2004-82, 2004-35 I.R.B. 350. The entire building, however, must have been in service for the full month. *Id.* at Q&A 4.

[209] I.R.C. § 42(i)(3)(B) (2008).

[210] Specifically relating to a plan under part B or part E of title IV of the Social Security Act (effective for determinations made after July 30, 2008).

their children,[211] or entirely by full-time students who are married and file a joint return.[212]

No unit in a building that has four or fewer units qualifies as a low-income unit if the owner or a related person occupies a residential unit in the building.[213] However, 80 percent of the qualified basis of an owner-occupied building with four or fewer units is eligible for the low-income housing credit if the acquisition or rehabilitation of the building occurs as part of a development plan sponsored by a state or local government or qualified nonprofit organization.[214] For this purpose, any unit not rented for at least 90 days is treated as occupied by the owner as of the first day that it is not rented.

Residential rental units must be held for use by the general public in order to qualify for the credit, and compliance with this requirement is determined in a manner consistent with the nondiscrimination housing policy of the Department of Housing and Urban Development (HUD).[215] Accordingly, units that are provided only for members of a social organization or that are provided by an employer for employees do not qualify for the credit.[216] Only those rental units that are not for use by the general public, and not the entire building, are ineligible for the credit.[217]

The general public use requirement has been clarified to permit occupancy restrictions and tenant preferences, without losing eligibility for the low-income housing credit.[218] Specifically, low-income housing projects will not fail to meet the general public use requirement due to occupancy restrictions or preferences in favor of tenants (1) with special needs, (2) who are members of specified group under a federal program or state program or policy that supports housing for such specified group, or (3) who are involved in artistic or literary activities.

(b) *Available Unit Rules*

Units initially qualified as low-income units are not disqualified by subsequent increases in tenant income above the applicable income limitation if the unit continues to be rent-restricted. However, if the income of a tenant exceeds 140 percent of the qualifying income limitation, and if any comparable or smaller size units are rented to a new resident that has income exceeding such income limitation, the unit ceases to be treated as a low-income housing unit.[219] The gross rent restriction continues to apply to such unit until the tenant vacates the unit. In the case of a project containing more than one low-income building, the available unit rule applies separately to each building.[220]

---

[211] This exception is limited to only those single parents who are not a dependent of another individual with a child or children who is or are not the dependent of another individual other than of his or her parents.

[212] I.R.C. § 42(i)(3)(D), as amended by the Housing Assistance Act of 2008, Pub. L. No. 110-289.

[213] I.R.C. § 42(i)(3)(C) (2008).

[214] I.R.C. § 42(i)(3)(E) (2008).

[215] HUD Handbook 4350.3.

[216] Reg. § 1.42-9.

[217] Reg. § 1.42-9.

[218] I.R.C. § 42(g)(9), as added by the Housing Assistance Tax Act of 2008, Pub. L. No. 110-289, effective for buildings before, on, or after July 30, 2008.

[219] I.R.C. § 42(g)(2)(D); Reg. § 1.42-15(c) (2008).

[220] Reg. § 1.42-15(e).

A comparable unit is one that is comparably sized or smaller than an over-income unit, measured by the same method that is used to determine qualified basis for the credit year in which the comparable unit became available. In the case of deep rent-skewered projects, any low-income unit is a comparable unit.[221]

The available unit rule requires the owner of a low-income building to rent to qualified residents *all* comparable units that are available or subsequently become available in the same building in order to treat an over-income unit as a low-income unit. This is so even though Code section 42(g)(2)(D) refers to the rental of the "next available unit." Thus, the owner must continue to rent any available comparable unit to a qualified resident until the percentage of low-income units in a building (excluding the over-income units) is equal to the percentage of low-income units on which the credit is based. If a building has more than one over-income unit, renting any available comparable unit to a qualified resident preserves the status of all over-income units as low-income units. However, if any available comparable unit is rented to a nonqualified resident, all over-income units for which the available unit was a comparable unit lose their status as low-income units.[222] A unit is not considered available if a unit is subject to a contractual arrangement that is binding under local law, i.e., if a unit is reserved for a prospective tenant under an agreement binding under state law.[223]

When a current resident moves to a different unit in the same building, the newly occupied unit adopts the status of the vacated unit. Thus, if a current resident moves from an over-income unit to a vacant unit within the same building, the newly occupied unit is treated as an over-income unit. The vacated unit takes on the same status that the newly occupied unit had immediately before it was occupied by the current resident.[224]

An owner who moves a tenant to a unit in another building in the same project may not treat both the vacated unit and the newly occupied unit as low-income units if the vacated unit remains unoccupied. The vacated (unoccupied) unit ceases to be treated as a low-income unit when it is vacated. Also, an owner who makes reasonable attempts to rent vacant low-income units may rent a subsequently vacated market-rate unit before the low-income units without violating the vacant unit rule. Nor is the vacant unit rule violated if, prior to renting a market-rate unit, the owner enters into a binding contractual arrangement with a low-income individual that obligates the owner to lease and rent a similar vacant low-income unit to that individual (i.e., the unit is subject to a "reservation").[225]

For deep rent skewed projects, the next available unit rule applies only for tenants whose incomes rise above 170 percent of the threshold amount.[226] However, the continued qualification of a unit ceases if the new tenant's income exceeds 40 percent of the area median gross income. The gross rent paid by a

[221] I.R.C. § 1.42-15(a) (2008).

[222] Reg. § 1.42-15(f).

[223] Reg. § 1.42-15(c).

[224] Reg. § 1.42-15(d).

[225] Rev. Rul. 2004-82, Q&A 8-10.

[226] I.R.C. § 42(g)(2)(D)(ii) (2008).

tenant may exceed 30 percent of the applicable income limit to the extent required under the applicable federal housing program statute.[227]

Designation of an insignificant portion of the gross rent of a low-income housing unit for use towards the purchase of the unit by the tenant after expiration of the minimum compliance period does not prevent such property from being treated as residential rental property if such portion is refundable to the occupant upon cessation of occupancy of the unit. However, such amounts paid to a lessor are includible in gross rent for purposes of determining whether the unit is rent-restricted.[228]

For tax years beginning on or after July 28, 2008,[229] in determining whether gross rent does not exceed 30 percent of the applicable income limitation for purposes of determining whether a unit is a rent-restricted unit, utility allowances are included in gross rent under the following rules:[230]

1. A building that receives assistance from the Rural Housing Service (RHS) must use the utility allowance determined under the method prescribed by the RHS for all rent-restricted units.[231] If any tenant in the building receives RHS rental assistance payments, the RHS utility allowance also applies to all rent-restricted units (even if some tenants receive rental assistance payments from the Department of Housing and Urban Development (HUD).[232]

2. A building that has its rents and utility allowances reviewed by HUD on an annual basis must use HUD utility allowances for all rent-restricted units unless the building or any tenant receives RHS assistance.[233]

3. If a building is neither an RHS-assisted nor a HUD-regulated building and no tenant receives RHS assistance, the applicable utility allowance for any rent-restricted units occupied by tenants receiving HUD tenant assistance is the applicable Public Housing Authority (PHA) utility allowance established for the Section 8 Existing Housing Program.[234]

4. If a rent-restricted unit is not subject to one of the preceding rules, the PHA utility allowance applies unless (a) a local utility company estimate has been obtained by an interested party and that estimate applies to the rent-restricted unit; (b) the building owner obtains an agency estimate; (c) the building owner calculates a utility estimate using the HUD Utility Schedule Model; (d) the building owner obtains a utility estimate from a qualified professional using the Energy Consumption Model. A utility

[227] I.R.C. § 42(g)(2)(E) (2008).

[228] I.R.C. § 42(g)(6); for further applicable rules I.R.C. § 42(g)(4) (2008), *see* I.R.C. § 142(d)(2)(B) through (d)(7) (2008).

[229] A taxpayer may rely on these rules before the beginning of the building owner's tax year beginning on or after July 28, 2008, provided that any utility allowances calculated under these rules are effective no earlier than the first day of the building owner's tax year beginning on or after July 28, 2008. Reg. § 1.42-12(a)(4).

[230] I.R.C. § 42(g)(2) (2008).

[231] Reg. § 1.42-10(b)(1).

[232] Reg. § 1.42-10(b)(2).

[233] Reg. § 1.42-10(b)(3).

[234] Reg. § 1.42-10(b)(4)(i).

estimate based on (a), (b), (c), or (d) applies to all rent-restricted units of similar size and construction in the building.[235]

In the case of a project in which operations are beginning, a building owner is not required to review the utility allowances, or implement new utility allowances, until the earlier of the date the building has achieved 90 percent occupancy for a period of 90 consecutive days or the end of the first year of the credit period.[236] Thereafter, a building owner must review at least annually the basis on which utility allowances have been established and must update the applicable utility allowance. The review must take into account any changes to the building such as any energy conservation measures that affect energy consumption and changes in utility rates.[237]

For tax years beginning before July 28, 2008, in determining whether gross rent does not exceed 30 percent of the applicable income limitation for purposes of determining whether a unit is a rent-restricted unit, utility allowances are included in gross rent under the following rules:

- A HUD-regulated building where neither the building nor the tenants receive Farmers' Home Administration ("FmHA") assistance (a building that has its rents and utility allowances reviewed by HUD on an annual basis) must use HUD allowances for all rent-restricted units.[238]
- A building that receives or is occupied by one or more tenants who receive FmHA assistance must use FmHA utility allowances for every rent-restricted unit in the building. These allowances must be used even if the building is also occupied by tenants who receive HUD assistance.[239]
- A building that is neither FmHA-assisted nor HUD-regulated and that has only tenants receiving HUD and not FmHA tenant assistance must use the applicable Public Housing Authority ("PHA") utility allowances established for the Section 8 Existing Housing Program for the rent-restricted units occupied by those tenants.[240]
- A building that is neither FmHA-assisted nor HUD-regulated, and whose rent-restricted units do not fall within any of the above rules, must use the applicable PHA utility allowance. Local utility company estimates may be used under certain circumstances.[241]

These utility allowance rules must be followed throughout the 15-year compliance period for a building. A 90-day period is allowed for an owner to

---

[235] Reg. §1.42-10(b)(4)(ii). If this default rules applies, a building owner may use different options for different utilities and is also free to change the options used for calculating utilities. However, if an Agency determines that a building owner has understated the utility allowances for the building under the particular option chosen and as a result the building's units lose their rent-restricted status, the Agency must report the noncompliance on Form 8823, Low-Income Housing Credit Agencies Report of Noncompliance or Building Disposition. T.D. 9420. Rules regarding the appropriate use of the estimates allowed under the default rule are found under Reg. §1.42-10(b)(4)(ii).

[236] Reg. §1.42-10(c)(1).

[237] Reg. §1.42-10(c)(2).

[238] Reg. §1.42-10(b)(3), prior to amendment by T.D. 9420.

[239] Reg. §1.42-10(b)(1) and (2), prior to amendment by T.D. 9420.

[240] Reg. §1.42-10(b)(4)(i), prior to amendment by T.D. 9420.

[241] Reg. §1.42-10(b)(4)(ii), prior to amendment by T.D. 9420.

begin using a new allowance when there is a change in the applicable allowance.[242]

The cost of mandatory services provided by nursing homes, hospitals, or retirement homes to low-income tenants is includible in rent in determining whether the 30 percent gross rent limitation is satisfied and is also includible in qualified basis. A limited exception applies to existing federally assisted projects for the elderly and handicapped that are authorized to provide a mandatory meals program.[243] The provision of continual nursing, medical, or psychiatric care is presumed to be mandatory service. A service is optional if payment for the service is not required as a condition of occupancy.[244]

To be treated as a qualified low-income building, the building must be part of a qualified low-income housing project at all times during the period beginning on the first day in the compliance period that the building is part of such project and ending on the last day of the compliance period regarding such building. The building also must be subject to depreciation under the MACRS rules.[245] An election may be made to treat a building as not part of a project after the compliance period of such building.[246]

For buildings placed in service prior to July 30, 2008, the term "qualified low-income building" does not include any building with respect to which moderate rehabilitation assistance is provided, at any time during the compliance period, under § 8(e)(2) of the U.S. Housing Act of 1937—other than assistance under the Stewart B. McKinney Homeless Assistance Act.[247] The repeal will allow developers of low-income housing projects to obtain rehabilitation assistance during the compliance period so that they can maintain and upgrade qualified buildings without having the building disqualified for the low-income housing credit and triggering recapture of the credit amounts claimed.

§ 12.2.4 Low-Income Housing Project

A qualified low-income housing project is any project for residential rental property that meets a "minimum set-aside" test and a "rent restriction" test.

(a) *Minimum Set-Aside*

Twenty percent or more of the units in the project must be occupied by tenants whose incomes are 50 percent or less of the area median gross income, adjusted for family size ("20-50 test"), or at least 40 percent of the units in the project must be occupied by tenants whose incomes are 60 percent or less of the area median gross income, adjusted for family size (40-60 test). In determining whether a building meets the minimum set-aside requirement regarding low-income tenants, the combined income of all occupants of an apartment, whether

[242] Reg. § 1.42-10(c), prior to amendment by T.D. 9420.

[243] 24 C.F.R. § 278.

[244] Reg. § 1.42-11.

[245] I.R.C. § 42(c)(2) (2008).

[246] I.R.C. § 42(g)(5) (2008).

[247] I.R.C. § 42(c)(2), last sentence prior to being stricken by the Housing Assistance Act of 2008, Pub. L. No. 110-289.

or not legally related, is compared to the appropriate percentage of the median family income for a family with the same number of members.[248]

The owner must irrevocably elect on Form 8609 to come under either the 20-50 or the 40-60 test not later than the income tax return due date.[249] A building is treated as a qualified low-income building only if the project (of which the building is a part) meets the minimum set-aside not later than the close of the first year of the credit period for such building.[250]

The measurement of area median gross income applied for residential rental property located in qualified rural area is modified in the case of projects subject to the low-income housing credit allocation limits.[251] For this purpose, a qualified rural area is defined as any open country, or any place, town, village, or city which is not part of an urban area and which: (1) has a population not in excess of 2,500 inhabitants; or (2) has a population in excess of 2,500 but not in excess of 10,000 if it is rural in character; or (3) has a population in excess of 10,000 but not in excess of 20,000, and is not contained within a standard metropolitan statistical area and has a serious lack of mortgage credit for lower and moderate-income families.[252]

The 20-50 test will be satisfied for a rural project if 20 percent or more of the residential units are both rent restricted and occupied by individuals whose income is 50 percent or less of the greater of area median gross income or national nonmetropolitan median income. For the 40-60 test, 40 percent of the rural residential rental properties must be rent restricted and occupied by individuals whose income is 60 percent or less of the greater of area median gross income or the national nonmetropolitan median income. The income limitation tests are unchanged if the rural residential rental property construction was financed by tax-exempt bonds and not subject to the low-income housing credit allocation limits.

In the case of property placed in service during 2006, 2007, or 2008 in the Gulf Opportunity Zone, and which is also located in a nonmetropolitan area, the minimum set aside requirement is applied by substituting "national nonmetropolitan median gross income" for "area median gross income."[253]

A low-income housing project is treated as consisting of one building unless each building that is considered to be part of such project is identified by the end of the first year of the project period (the end of the first calendar year in which an allocation could be made for the first building placed in service as part of the project).[254] Each building is assigned a separate building identification number, and a separate Form 8609 is required for each building. For this purpose, scattered site low-income housing is treated as one project if 100 percent of the dwelling units are qualified low-income units and there is a common plan of

[248] Rev. Rul. 90-89, 1990-2 C.B. 8.

[249] I.R.C. § 42(g)(1) (2008).

[250] I.R.C. § 42(g)(3)(A) (2008).

[251] I.R.C. § 42(i)(8), as added by the Housing Assistance Tax Act of 2008, Pub. L. No. 110-289, effective for determinations made after July 30, 2008.

[252] § 520 of the Housing Act of 1949, 42 U.S.C. § 1490.

[253] I.R.C. § 1400N(c)(4) (2008).

[254] I.R.C. § 42(g)(3)(D) (2008).

financing.[255] For multiple building projects, a building and subsequent buildings are treated as part of a qualifying low-income project if, within 12 months of the placed-in-service date of the prior building, the project meets the set-aside requirement regarding the prior building and any subsequent buildings placed in service within the 12-month period.[256]

The income level at which a family is considered a low-income family and the area median gross income may be adjusted for areas with unusually low family income or high housing costs relative to family income in a manner consistent with section 8 of the United States Housing Act of 1937. Such determinations include adjustments for family size.[257] The determination as to whether the income of a resident of a unit in a project exceeds the applicable income limit (under the 20-50 test or the 40-60 test, above) must be made at least annually on the basis of the current income of the resident.[258]

(b) *Rent Restriction*

The gross rent charged to a tenant in a qualified low-income unit may not exceed 30 percent of the imputed income limitation attributable to such unit.[259] A gross rent restriction established for a low-income unit need not be reduced by a subsequent decline in area median income. Under the imputed income limitation, the gross rent restriction is keyed to the size of the unit rather than actual family size. Each unit is presumed to house a certain number of people based upon the number of bedrooms in the unit. A studio apartment is presumed to house one person. For a unit with one or more bedrooms, each bedroom is presumed to house 1.5 persons.[260] Thus, the imputed income limitation applicable to a unit is the income limitation that would apply under (1), above, to individuals deemed to occupy the unit under such presumptions.

> **Example:** A three-bedroom low-income unit is assumed to house 4.5 persons (three bedrooms multiplied by 1.5 persons per bedroom). If the qualifying low-income figure for a family of four is $19,000, and the low-income figure for a family of five is $21,000, to qualify as a low-income family eligible to rent this three-bedroom unit, a family of five must have an income not exceeding $21,000, and a family of four must have an income not exceeding $19,000. However, the gross rent restriction for such unit is $6,000 (30 percent of $20,000, the average of the applicable income limitations for a family of four and a family of five ($19,000 + $21,000 = $40,000 divided by 2)).

---

[255] I.R.C. § 42(g)(7) (2008).

[256] I.R.C. § 42(g)(3)(B) (2008).

[257] I.R.C. § 142(d)(2)(B) (2008).

[258] I.R.C. § 142(d)(3)(A) (2008). Safe harbors have been provided under which the IRS will treat a residential unit in a building as a low-income unit under I.R.C. § 42(i)(3)(A) if the incomes of the individuals occupying the unit are at or below the applicable income limitation under I.R.C. § 42(g)(1) or I.R.C. § 142(d)(4)(B)(i) before the beginning of the first tax year of the building's credit period under I.R.C. § 42(f)(1), but their incomes exceed the applicable income limitation at the beginning of the first tax year of the building's credit period. The revenue procedure is effective for tax years ending on or after November 24, 2003. Rev. Proc. 2003-82, 2003-47 I.R.B. 1097.

[259] I.R.C. § 42(g)(2)(A) (2008).

[260] I.R.C. § 42(g)(2)(C) (2008).

Gross rent includes utilities paid by the tenant, other than telephone expenses, but does not include payments under section 8 of the U.S. Housing Act of 1937 or similar assistance payments received on behalf of the tenant. Moreover, gross rent does not include rental payments to the owner of the unit to the extent such owner pays an equivalent amount to the Farmers' Home Administration under § 515 of the Housing Act of 1949.[261]

Fees for supportive services that are paid to the owner of the unit by a government program or Code section 501(c)(3) organization are excludable from gross rent. To qualify for such exclusion the fees must be paid under a program that provides assistance for rent, and the amount of the assistance provided for rent must not be separable from the amount of the assistance provided for supportive services.[262] Supportive services include services provided under a planned program that are designed to enable residents of a residential rental property to remain independent and avoid placement in a hospital, nursing home, or intermediate care facility for the mentally or physically handicapped, and to assist residents in transitional housing to obtain permanent housing.

§ 12.2.5 Credit Period

The credit is claimed over a credit period that comprises the 10 tax years beginning with the tax year in which the low-income housing is placed in service.[263] An irrevocable election is available to start the credit period in the tax year after the housing is placed in service, provided that the housing is qualified low-income housing as of the close of the first year of such period.[264] The first-year credit must be reduced to reflect the time during the year that any low-income housing is unoccupied. The reduced portion of the first-year credit may be claimed in the eleventh tax year (the tax year following the credit period).

§ 12.2.6 Additional Credit

An additional credit resulting from an increase in qualified basis as of the close of any tax year in the compliance period after the first year of the credit period is subject to similar treatment, provided that the building is qualified low-income housing as of the close of the first year of such period. The compliance period is the period of 15 taxable years beginning with the first taxable year of the credit period with respect thereto.[265] The additional credit, which is allowed for that year and all remaining years in the credit period, is the increase in qualified basis multiplied by two-thirds of the applicable percentage for such building.[266]

§ 12.2.7 Disposition of Building

If there is a disposition of a building or an interest therein during the tax year, the low-income housing credit is allocated between the seller and the purchaser on the basis of the number of days during such year that the building

[261] I.R.C. § 42(g)(2)(B)(iv) (2008).

[262] I.R.C. § 42(g)(2)(B) (2008).

[263] I.R.C. § 42(f) (2008).

[264] I.R.C. § 42(f) (2008).

[265] I.R.C. § 42(i)(1) (2008).

[266] I.R.C. § 42(f)(3) (2008).

or interest was held.[267] In essence, this rule applies in the situation where the buyer steps into the shoes of the transferor, uses the credit period of the latter, and may take credits to which the transferor would have been entitled had he retained the property. The buyer and seller of a project may agree to use the exact number of days each owned the property or the mid-month convention to allocate the credit for the month of a disposition.[268]

§ 12.2.8 Tenant's Right to Acquisition

No income tax benefit regarding a qualified low-income building may be denied by reason of a right of first refusal held by the tenants of the building (including tenant cooperatives, resident management corporations, qualified nonprofit organizations, and governmental agencies) to purchase the property after the close of the compliance period.[269] However, the purchase price must not be less than the sum of the principal amount of outstanding indebtedness secured by the building (other than indebtedness incurred within a five-year period ending on the date of the sale to the tenants) and taxes attributable to such sale.

§ 12.2.9 Agency Authorization

A taxpayer who is otherwise eligible to take the low-income housing credit must, in most cases, obtain authority from an appropriate state or local agency before taking the credit. A housing credit agency may authorize all or part of the credit to which the taxpayer is otherwise entitled, and the taxpayer may not claim a credit in excess of the credit dollar amount allocated to his project. Taxpayers planning to claim a credit for a qualified low-income housing project financed by tax-exempt bonds subject to the volume cap provided by Code section 146 are not required to obtain this credit authority.

Form 8609 is used to obtain a housing credit allocation from the housing credit agency. The authorized housing credit agency must complete Form 8609, Part I, Allocation of Credit, and forward a copy to the owner of the building when an allocation of credit is made. The agency must also file the original Form 8609 with a completed Part I and Form 8610 not later than February 28 after the close of the calendar year in which the allocation of credit is made. In allocating a housing credit dollar amount to a building, the housing credit agency must specify the applicable percentage and the maximum qualified basis.[270]

§ 12.2.10 Housing Use Agreement

A credit is denied to otherwise qualified property unless the owner of the building is subject to an enforceable 15-year "extended low-income housing commitment."[271] To qualify, the agreement must be between the taxpayer and the housing agency and it must contain the following provisions:

---

[267] I.R.C. § 42(f)(4) (2008).

[268] Conference Committee Report to the Revenue Reconciliation Act of 1993, Pub. L. No. 103-66.

[269] I.R.C. § 42(i)(7) (2008).

[270] I.R.C. § 42(h)(7)(D) (2008).

[271] I.R.C. § 42(h)(6)(A) and (D) (2008). A housing agency may require a longer low-income housing use agreement.

- A requirement that the low-income portion of the building for each tax year in the extended use period will not be less than the applicable portion specified in the agreement. Certain prohibitions are placed on the eviction of tenants and rent increases, throughout the entire use period plus three years.[272]
- Low-income individuals have the right to enforce the requirements and prohibitions in the agreement in state court.
- There may not be a disposition of any part of the low-income portion of the building unless the entire building is sold to the buyer.
- A prohibition against refusal to lease a unit to a holder of a voucher or certificate of eligibility under section 8 of the Housing Act of 1937 (on or after August 10, 1993).
- The commitment is binding on all successors of the taxpayer.
- The agreement is properly recorded as a restrictive covenant.[273]

If the owner is unable to transfer the property at the end of the initial 15-year compliance period for continued low-income use, the allocating agency, upon written demand of the owner's intent to dispose of the property, is allowed one year to find an eligible buyer at a specified price. Factors considered in determining the sale price include: outstanding indebtedness, investor equity contributions adjusted for inflation, other capital contributions, and cash distributions. Such period may be triggered by the owner any time after the 14th year of the compliance period.[274]

During the one-year period, the housing credit agency must establish a qualified contract to acquire the building at a specified price that consists of two components. The sale price of the non low-income portion of the building is fair market value. The sale price of the low-income portion of the building is an amount not less than the applicable fraction (specified in the low-income housing commitment) of the sum of: (1) the outstanding indebtedness secured by, or with respect to, the building; (2) the adjusted investor equity in the building (adjusted for inflation); and (3) any other capital contributions reduced by cash distributions from (or available from) the project.[275]

The term "adjusted investor equity" means the aggregate amount of cash invested in the project plus an amount equal to the cash invested multiplied by the cost-of-living adjustment for the calendar year.[276] The cost-of-living adjust-

---

272 Rev. Rul. 2004-82, Q&A 5 clarifies that the prohibitions do not simply apply during the three-year period following termination of the low-income housing commitment. Taxpayers are given a one-year period to correct an agreement which does not properly reflect this rule following a Housing Agency's determination that agreement is not in compliance under I.R.C. §42(h)(6)(J). Housing Agencies were required to complete a review of all agreements by December 31, 2004. The IRS has established a safe harbor under which housing credit agencies and project owners may meet the requirements of I.R.C. §42(h)(6)(B)(i) as described in Q&A 5, concerning extended low-income housing commitments. Rev. Proc. 2005-37, 2005-28 I.R.B. 79.

273 I.R.C. §42(h)(6)(B) (2008). If it is determined that an extended low-income housing agreement is not in effect at the beginning of a tax year, such determination shall not affect prior years and it shall be disregarded if such failure is corrected within one year from the date of the determination. I.R.C. §42(h)(6)(J) (2008).

274 I.R.C. §42(h)(6)(I) (2008).

275 I.R.C. §42(h)(6)(F) (2008).

276 I.R.C. §42(h)(6)(G) (2008).

ment utilized in computing adjusted investor equity is determined under Code section 1(f)(3), as modified by Code section 42(h)(6)(G). The adjustment is the percentage (if any) by which the CPI for the preceding calendar year exceeds the CPI for a base calendar year. This is determined by dividing the index amount for the preceding calendar year by the index amount for the base calendar year. The base calendar year is the calendar year with or within which the first tax year of the credit period ends.

This cost-of-living adjustment may not exceed five percent. If the CPI for any calendar year (as defined in Code section 1(f)(4)) exceeds the CPI for the preceding calendar year by more than five percent, the CPI for the base calendar year must be increased by such excess in order to limit the adjustment to a maximum of five percent.

If no buyer is found, the property may be converted to market rate use with the qualification that existing low-income tenants may not be evicted within three years after the end of the compliance period.[277]

§ 12.2.11 Maximum Allocable Credits

Effective after December 31, 2000, for a calendar year, a state housing agency is entitled to allocate credits to taxpayers in a total amount equal to the sum of the following:

1. The unused state housing credit ceiling (if any) of such state for the preceding calendar year (the unused carryforward component);

2. The greater of: (1) the state's population multiplied by the credit rate, adjusted annually for inflation, or (2) $2,000,000, adjusted annually for inflation.[278] The population component (i.e., the state's population for any calendar year) is determined pursuant to Code section 146(j).[279] The $2,000,000 amount is a minimum volume cap for small population states. For 2007, the inflation-adjusted credit rate is $1.95 and the $2,000,000 minimum volume cap for small states is $2,275,000.[280] For calendar years 2008 and 2009, the credit rate and minimum volume cap for small states are increased by $.20 and 10 percent rounded to the next lowest multiple of $5,000, respectively, after inflation adjustments are taken into account.[281] For 2008, the inflation-adjusted credit rate is $2.00 and the inflation-adjusted minimum volume cap for small states is $2,325,000. With the temporary increase in the volume cap, the credit rate is $2.20 and the minimum volume cap for small population states is $2,555,000;

3. The amount of state housing credit ceiling returned in the calendar year (the returned credit component);

---

[277] I.R.C. § 42(h)(6)(E) (2008).

[278] I.R.C. § 42(h)(3)(C) and (H) (2008); Reg. § 1.42-14(a)(1) and (2).

[279] I.R.C. § 142(h)(3)(G) (2008); Reg. § 1.42-14(c).

[280] Rev. Proc. 2006-53.

[281] .R.C. § 42(h)(3)(I), as added by the Housing Assistance Tax Act of 2008, Pub. L. No. 110-289.

4. The amount (if any) allocated to such state from other states by the Secretary from a national pool of unused credit (the national pool component), reduced by;
5. The amount of a grant (if any) to such state under section 1602 of the American Recovery and Reinvestment Tax Act of 2009.[282]

For purposes of item (1), the unused carryforward component of the state housing credit ceiling is the unused state housing credit ceiling, if any, of the state for the preceding calendar year. The unused housing credit ceiling for the preceding calendar year is the excess of (a) the sum of the amounts described in items (2)-(4), above, for the preceding calendar year, over (b) the aggregate housing credit dollar amount allocated for the preceding year (reduced by any housing credit dollar amounts allocated in the preceding year from any unused carryforward component).[283]

The returned credit component for a calendar year (item (3)) is equal to the housing credit dollar amounts that were allocated to projects (1) that failed to meet the 10-percent basis test described in Code section 42(1)(E)(ii) on a date after the close of the calendar year in which the allocation was made or did not become qualified low-income housing projects within the period required by Code section 42 or the terms of the allocation; or (2) with respect to which an allocation was cancelled by mutual consent of the housing credit agency and the allocation recipient.[284]

A building that receives a post-June 30, 2008 carryover allocation is not qualified within the required period if the taxpayer does not meet the 10-percent basis requirement by the date that is six months after the date the allocation was made (as described in Reg. § 1.42-6(a)(2)(ii)).[285]

Effective on or before December 31, 2000, for a calendar year, a state housing agency is entitled to allocate credits to taxpayers in a total amount equal to the sum of the following:

- $1.25 multiplied by the state's population;
- The "unused state housing credit ceiling" (if any) of such state for the preceding calendar year. The unused housing credit ceiling for any calendar year is the excess of the sum of the following two amounts, above, over the aggregate housing credit dollar amount allocated for the year.
- The amount of state housing credit ceiling returned in the calendar year; and
- The amount (if any) allocated to such state from other states by the Secretary.[286]

[282] I.R.C. § 42(h)(3)(C) (2008); Reg. § 1.42-14(a)(1). I.R.C. § 42(i)(9)(a) (2009), as amended by the American Recovery and Reinvestment Act of 2009, Pub. L. No. 111-5, 123 Stat. 115, § 1404. The basis of a qualified low-income building shall not be reduced by the amount of any grant under section 1602 of the American Recovery and Reinvestment Tax Act of 2009. I.R.C. § 42(i)(9)(b) (2009).

[283] I.R.C. § 42(h)(3)(C) (2008), flush language; Reg. § 1.42-14(b), as amended by T.D. 9110.

[284] I.R.C. § 42(h)(3)(C) (2008), flush language; Reg. § 1.42-14(d)(1).

[285] Reg. § 1.42-14(d)(2)(iv)(A).

[286] I.R.C. § 42(h)(3)(C) (2000), prior to amendment by Pub. L. No. 106-554 and Pub. L. No. 107-147.

Once the amount of credit that an agency has to allocate in a calendar year has been determined, each allocation to a qualified low-income housing project reduces the remaining allocable credit by the housing credit dollar amount so allocated. If an agency goes over its limit, the credit shall be reduced for the most recent projects for which allocations were made.[287]

A state is required to allocate at least 10 percent of its allocable credits to qualified low-income housing projects. For this purpose, a "qualified low-income housing project" is a project in which a qualified nonprofit organization owns an interest in the project (directly or through a partnership) and materially participates (within the meaning of Code section 469(h)) in the development and operation of the project throughout the compliance period. For this purpose, a qualified nonprofit organization is one that: (1) is described in Code section 501(c)(3) or Code section1(c)(4) and is exempt from tax under Code Sec. 501(a), (2) is determined by the state housing credit agency not to be affiliated with or controlled by a for-profit organization, and (3) has, as one of its exempt purposes, the fostering of low-income housing.[288]

§ 12.2.12 Allocation Authority

Various guidelines are provided to state housing credit agencies for initiating plans with specified criteria for allocating credits among projects, allocating only necessary credits, and making project evaluations.[289] The criteria to be considered include: project location; housing needs characteristics; project characteristics (including whether the project uses existing housing as part of a community revitalization plan); sponsor characteristics; tenant populations with special needs; tenant populations of individuals with children; and projects intended for eventual tenant ownership. For allocations made after December 31, 2008, the selection criteria set forth in a qualified allocation plan must also include the energy efficiency of the project and the historic nature of the project.[290] In addition, the state's allocation plan must give preference to housing projects that serve the lowest-income tenants and are obligated to serve qualified tenants for the longest periods. It must also give preference to projects that are located in qualified census tracts and the development of which contributes to a concerted community revitalization.[291] Generally, housing agencies must consider the reasonableness of the development and operational costs of a project as a factor in determining the proper amount of credits to be allocated to it.[292]

Each state's allocation authority may be divided among the various units in the state by the governor or the state legislature. Unless a building is exempt from a housing credit allocation requirement because it is financed by certain tax-exempt bonds, the owner must receive a housing credit allocation from a qualified allocation of a state or local housing agency in order to obtain such credit.[293]

---

[287] I.R.C. § 42(h)(7)(B) (2008).

[288] I.R.C. § 42(h)(5) (2008); Reg. § 1.42-14(h).

[289] I.R.C. § 42(m) (2008).

[290] I.R.C. § 42(m)(1)(C), as amended by Pub. L. No. 110-289.

[291] I.R.C. § 42(m)(1)(B) (2008).

[292] I.R.C. § 42(m)(2)(B) (2008).

[293] I.R.C. §§ 42(h)(1)(A), 42(h)(4)(B), 42(m)(1)(A), 42(m)(1)(B)(iii) and 42(m)(1)(D) (2008).

For qualified allocation plans, housing credit agencies must include a procedure for monitoring and reporting noncompliance to the IRS after 1991. In certain states, such as Illinois, constitutional home rule cities have the right to make their own credit allocations as if they were a state. The minimum credit that such cities may allocate (unless they yield the authority to the state) is their proportionate share, based on population, of the state's total credit.

In calendar years 2006, 2007, and 2008, the State housing credit ceiling of a State, any portion of which is located in the Gulf Opportunity Zone (Alabama, Louisiana, and Mississippi), is increased by the lesser of:

1. the aggregate housing credit dollar amount allocated by the State housing credit agency to buildings located in the Gulf Opportunity Zone in the applicable calendar year, or
2. the product of $18.00 multiplied by the portion of the State's population which was in the Gulf Opportunity Zone at the time of the disaster (869,544 for Alabama, 3,153,293 for Louisiana, and 1,968,283 for Mississippi).[294]

In 2006 only, the State housing credit ceiling of Texas and Florida are each increased by an additional $3,500,000.[295]

A state housing credit agency may correct certain administrative errors and omissions regarding allocations and recordkeeping within a reasonable time after their discovery.[296] A mistake that results in a document which inaccurately reflects the intent of the agency (or the affected taxpayer) when the document is originally completed is an administrative error or omission. Misinterpretations of the applicable rules and regulations are not included in this category.

Administrative errors or omissions include the following: mathematical errors; inconsistent entries; omissions of required information; failure to track the housing credit dollar amount an agency has allocated or that remains to be allocated in the current calendar year (for example, a failure to include in its state housing credit ceiling a previously allocated credit dollar amount that was returned by a taxpayer); and other items identified by the IRS.

Correctable administrative errors do not include an agency's allocation of a particular calendar year's low-income housing credit dollar amount made after the close of that calendar year or the use of an incorrect population amount in calculating a state's housing credit ceiling for a calendar year.

Prior IRS approval is required if (1) a correction is not made before the close of the calendar year of the error or omission, and (2) the correction is a numerical change to the housing credit dollar amount allocated for a building or project, affects the determination of any component of the state's housing credit ceiling

---

[294] I.R.C. § 1400N(c)(1) (2008); Instructions to Form 8610, Rev. December 2006; Notice 2006-21 (providing a list of counties and parishes in the GO-Zone). In determining the unused state housing credit ceiling for any calendar year, any increase in the state ceiling for Alabama, Louisiana, and Mississippi is treated as an increase in the population component of the state ceiling described in I.R.C. § 42(h)(3)(C)(ii). I.R.C. § 1400N(c)(1)(C).

[295] I.R.C. § 1400N(c)(2) (2008).

[296] Reg. § 1.42-13(b).

under Code section 42(h)(3)(C), or affects the state's unused housing credit carryover that is assigned to the IRS under Code section 42(h)(3)(D). A request for IRS approval must contain the information specified in Regulation § 1.42-13(b)(3)(iv) and an agreement to IRS conditions.

Although the procedure for correcting certain administrative errors and omissions is effective February 24, 1994, an agency may elect to apply this procedure to earlier administrative errors and omissions.[297] Any reasonable method used to make a correction prior to the effective date is considered proper provided that it is consistent with Code section 42.

§ 12.2.13 Acquisition of Existing Buildings

The credit period for an acquired existing building may not begin before the first tax year of the credit period for substantial rehabilitation expenditures made regarding such building.[298] This rule is a corollary to the requirement that no new credit is created by the acquisition (churning) of an existing building unless specified substantial rehabilitation expenditures are incurred. However, an acquisition credit is provided for certain acquisitions of federally assisted buildings that are not allowed a credit for rehabilitation expenditures.[299]

A federally assisted building qualifies for such credit where:

- A waiver of the 10-year holding period requirement for existing buildings is granted in the acquisition of such building, and
- A low-income housing credit would be allowed for rehabilitation expenditures regarding such building if the qualified basis attributable to such expenditures, when divided by the number of low-income units in the building, is at least $2,000 per unit. In such case, the credit period for the federally assisted building does not begin before the tax year that would be the first tax year of the credit period for rehabilitation expenditures regarding such building.

Effective for buildings placed in service after July 30, 2008, the $2,000 per-unit limitation is increased to $4,000 per-unit (adjusted for inflation beginning in calendar-year 2010.[300] The increased limit applies to substantially tax-exempt bond financed buildings which receive a tax-exempt bond allocation after July 30, 2008 (provided the requirements of Code section 42(h)(4) are satisfied and no state credit allocation is required).[301]

§ 12.2.14 Recapture of Credit

An owner of a qualified low-income housing project loses his entitlement to the credit and is required to recapture part of the credits taken on the project if it ceases to meet qualification requirements at any time within a 15-year period beginning with the first credit year.[302] Where there is a reduction in the qualifying

---

[297] Reg. § 1.42-13(d).

[298] I.R.C. § 42(f)(5)(A) (2008).

[299] I.R.C. § 42(f)(5)(B) (2008).

[300] I.R.C. § 42(f)(5)(B)(ii), as amended by the Housing Assistance Act of 2008, Pub. L. No. 110-289.

[301] Act § 3003(h)(2) of Pub. L. No. 110-289.

[302] I.R.C. § 42(j)(1) (2008).

basis, but the project remains a qualified low-income housing project, the loss of credit and recapture is limited to that portion of the credit allocable to the reduction in qualifying basis.

The Departments of Treasury, Justice and Housing and Urban Development entered into an agreement that is designed to ensure that low-income tax housing credit projects are in compliance with the Fair Housing Act. Under the agreement, Justice and HUD will provide notice to the IRS and state housing finance agencies of enforcement actions brought under the Fair Housing Act involving tax-credit property owners. The IRS, in turn, will notify involved property owners that a finding of discrimination could result in the loss of tax credits.[303]

(a) *Recapture Events*

Recapture is required in any year during the 15-year recapture period if, at the close of the year, any of the following events occur:

- The project fails to meet the minimum set-aside requirement that at least 20 percent of the units in the project must be 50-percent units or that at least 40 percent of the units must be 60-percent units (see below);
- The gross rent charged to tenants of the low-income units exceeds 30 percent of the qualifying income levels for those units;
- The project obtains financing from federal subsidies or from the proceeds of tax-exempt bonds;
- The owner disposes of his interest in the project (with exceptions noted below); or
- There is a decrease in the qualifying basis of the project (even though the minimum set-aside requirement continues to be met).

Recapture events (1) through (4), above, require recapture of the credit claimed with respect to the qualifying basis of the entire project. Recapture event (5) requires recapture only with respect to the units that go out of compliance; no recapture is required with respect to the units that continue in compliance. There is no recapture for certain insignificant changes in qualified basis by reason of changes in floor space of low-income housing units.[304]

Taxpayers may apply to the IRS to waive recapture where a low-income housing project fails to comply with the low-income tenant occupancy requirements (recapture event (1), above) because of a de minimis error on or after August 10, 1993.[305]

(b) *Recapture Amount*

An owner is required to pay additional tax for the year of a recapture event in an amount equal to the "accelerated portion" of the credit paid in earlier years with interest from the dates the recaptured credit was claimed at the overpay-

[303] Treasury Department News Release LS-835, August 14, 2000.

[304] I.R.C. § 42(j)(4)(F) (2008).

[305] I.R.C. § 42(g)(8)(A) (2008).

ment rate established under Code section 6621.[306] The accelerated portion of a credit is the aggregate of the credit taken over the aggregate credit that would have been allowable if the credit had been spread over 15 years rather than 10 years.[307] In the absence of previous recapture events, credits are recaptured in the following amounts:

If the recapture event occurs in:	*The recapture fraction is:*
Years 2 through 11	1/3
Year 12	4/15
Year 13	3/15
Year 14	2/15
Year 15	1/15

Because the credit for additions to the qualifying basis of a project is computed at two-thirds the regular credit rate, there is no accelerated portion of the credit. There is, therefore, no recapture when later reductions in qualifying basis occur except to the extent that the reductions exceed such additions to the qualifying basis.[308]

Example 1: East Side Housing Corp. constructs and places in service a qualifying low-income housing project in 1999. East Side claims credits beginning in that year based on an allocation of 30 percent of the basis of the project to 50 percent units (that is, East Side has elected to come under the 20-50 test) and 30 percent of the units are occupied by tenants earning 50 percent or less of the area median income). In 2003, vacancies in a number of 50 percent units are filled with tenants with nonqualifying incomes (see "Increases in tenant income," below) and, as a result, only 25 percent of the basis of the project is properly allocable to 50 percent units. Because the project continues to meet the minimum set-aside requirement, full recapture is not required. One-third of the credit claimed in 1999 through 2002 that was allocable to the 5 percent of basis and that is no longer eligible for the credit is recaptured together with interest, however.

Example 2: Assume the same facts as in Example 1, above. In 2004, additional vacancies in 50 percent units were filled with tenants with non-qualifying income and, as a result, only 15 percent of the basis of the project was properly allocable to 50 percent units. The project no longer complies with the minimum set-aside, so full recapture is required. The recapture amount equals one-third of the total of all the credits taken in 1999 through 2003 that was allocable to the 25 percent of the basis of the project that represented units that qualified as 50 percent units until 2004. The credits relating to the 5 percent of basis that were recaptured in 2003 are not taken into account.

Example 3: In 1997, Prosperity Acres Development Co. constructed and placed in service a qualifying low-income housing project. Twenty-five

[306] I.R.C. § 42(j)(2) (2008).

[307] I.R.C. § 42(j)(3) (2008).

[308] I.R.C. §§ 42(f)(3) and 42(j)(4)(C) (2008).

percent of the basis of the project was allocable to 50 percent units in that year. In 2004, the number of 50 percent units increased so that 35 percent of the basis of the project was allocable to such units. Prosperity Acres, therefore, began to take an additional credit for the additional 10 percent of qualifying basis computed at two-thirds of the credit percentage. In 2004, vacancies in a number of 50 percent units were filled with tenants with nonqualifying incomes and, as a result, only 30 percent of the basis of the project was properly allocable to 50 percent units. Although there is a decrease in the qualifying basis of 5 percent, there is no recapture in 2004 because that 5 percent is allocable to later additions to the qualifying basis. If, in 2004, the qualifying basis had fallen to 20 percent, 1/3 of the credit claimed in 1997 through 2003 with respect to 5 percent of the qualifying basis (plus interest) would be recaptured. The first 10 percent of the reduction would be attributable to additions to qualifying basis and exempt from recapture.

To the extent credits allowable on a project are not taken because of limitations on the general business credit or because no tax is due against which the credit can be applied, no recapture is required. An adjustment of carryovers, however, must be made.[309] No recapture is required for reductions in qualified basis caused by a casualty loss to the extent that the loss is restored by reconstruction or replacement within a reasonable period to be established by the IRS.[310]

(c) *Recapture-Increases in Tenant Income*

For purposes of the recapture rules, no unit may be treated as losing its status as a low-income unit solely because of increases in the incomes of unit tenants. Once a unit qualifies as a low-income unit it continues to qualify as such until the tenant's income exceeds 140 percent of the qualifying income level applicable to low-income units. Even then, the unit continues to qualify as a low-income unit so long as the owner continues to fill vacancies in comparable or smaller units with tenants who qualify as low-income unit tenants. That unit will not continue to qualify as a low-income unit, however, if any vacancy in a comparable or smaller unit is filled by a tenant who does not so qualify.[311]

"Deep rent skewed projects" are subject to a special rule in this respect. A taxpayer may elect to have a qualified low-income housing project treated as a deep rent skewed project if 15 percent or more of the low-income units in the project are occupied by tenants whose incomes are 40 percent or less of the area median gross income, gross rents are no more than 30 percent of the qualifying income level for such units, and the gross rent for each low-income unit does not exceed one-half of the average rent of units of comparable size that are not occupied by tenants who meet the applicable income limit. No such unit will be disqualified unless the tenant's income increases to more than 170 percent of the

[309] I.R.C. § 42(j)(4)(A) (2008).

[310] I.R.C. § 42(j)(4)(E) (2008).

[311] I.R.C. § 42(g)(2)(D) (2008).

qualifying income level and a comparable unit in the project is rented to a tenant who does not so qualify.[312]

The Conference Committee Report to the Tax Reform Act of 1986 (Pub. L. No. 99-514) indicates that, for purposes of the minimum set-aside requirement, vacant units formerly occupied by low-income tenants may continue to be treated as occupied by such low-income tenants provided that reasonable attempts are made to rent the unit and that no other units in the project of comparable or smaller size are rented to nonqualifying individuals.

(d) *Recapture-Early Disposition*

Early disposition of the building by the owner is one of the recapture events. For low-income housing credit recapture purposes, a large partnership (35 or more partners (counting a husband and wife as one partner)) is subject to recapture at the partnership level, unless an irrevocable election is made not to treat the partnership as the taxpayer.[313] Such election is made on Form 8609, Part II, Line 10b, no later than the income tax return due date. Thus, unless such election is made, no change in ownership is deemed to occur that would result in a recapture event provided that, within a 12-month period, at least 50 percent (by value) of the original ownership is unchanged.

Unless such election is made, the amount of the credit is treated as allowed to the partnership. Also, the tax benefit rule of Code section 42(j)(4)(A) is inapplicable in such case.[314] Any increase in tax resulting from such recapture is allocated among the partners in the same manner as partnership taxable income.

(e) *Recapture Bond*

For interests in buildings disposed of after July 30, 2008, the requirement to post a bond upon disposition of an interest in a qualified low-income building to avoid the recapture of previously claimed low-income housing credit amounts has been repealed. Thus, the recapture of credit amounts from previous years upon disposition of an interest in a building will not occur if it is reasonable to expect the building to continue to operate as a qualified low-income building for the remainder of the compliance period even though no bond is posted.[315]

However, since no bond is being posted under the new rules, if a building (or interest therein) is disposed of during the compliance period and there is any reduction of the qualified basis of the building which results in an increase of the amount that would be recaptured in the year of disposition or any subsequent year, then the period for assessment of any deficiency related to the increase in tax will be three years. The three-year statute of limitations begins on the date the taxpayer notifies the IRS of the reduction of the basis. The assessment may be made within the three-year period notwithstanding any other provision that would prevent the assessment.[316]

---

[312] I.R.C. § 142(d)(4) (2008).

[313] I.R.C. § 42(j)(5) (2008).

[314] I.R.C. § 42(j)(5)(A) (2008).

[315] I.R.C. § 42(j)(6)(A), as amended by the Housing Assistance Tax Act of 2008, Pub. L. No. 110-289.

[316] I.R.C. § 42(j)(6)(B), as amended by Pub. L. No. 110-289.

Projects that have previously had a disposition of an interest in a building and have purchased a recapture bond to avoid recapture can elect to not require the recapture bond if it is reasonable to expect that the building will continue to be operated as a qualified low-income building for the remaining compliance period. This election could provide significant savings from having to make the annual payments for the cost of the bonds.[317]

For pre-August 1, 2008, dispositions, no recapture is required on the disposition of a building (or interest therein) within the 15-year compliance period if the taxpayer furnished a bond in an amount and for a period required by the IRS and it is reasonably expected that the building will continue to be operated as a qualified low-income building for the remainder of the 15-year compliance period.[318] Form 8693, "Low-Income Housing Disposition Bond," is filed by taxpayers seeking to avoid recapture.

Revenue Procedure 99-11, 1999-1 C.B. 275, established a collateral program as an alternative to providing a surety bond for taxpayers to avoid or defer recapture of the low-income housing tax credits under Code section 42(j)(6). Under this program, taxpayers may establish a Treasury Direct Account and pledge certain United States Treasury securities to the Internal Revenue Service as security.

The purpose of a surety bond (or alternatively, the establishment of a Treasury Direct Account) is to secure the departing owner's potential liability for credit recapture should the building not continue to be operated as a qualified low-income housing project during the compliance period. The departing owner's obligation under the bond must be secured by a surety authorized under Treasury Department Circular 570, Companies Holding Certificates of Authority as Acceptable Sureties on Federal Bonds and as Acceptable Reinsuring Companies (published annually as of July 1 in the Federal Register).

For recapture purposes, the departing owner is deemed to continue to own such property or interest and retain a qualified basis. However, the taxpayer will not be treated as claiming any additional low-income housing credit with respect to the interest for any period after the disposition of the interest. If the qualified basis regarding the departing owner's deemed interest decreases after the disposition occurs due to a subsequent recapture event, the bond may be forfeited in whole or in part.

If a decrease in qualified basis occurs, the amount of the bond forfeited generally is the sum of:

- The credit recapture amount computed under Code section 42(j) regarding the deemed interest (including interest at the overpayment rate through the date the return is due, without regard to extensions, for the year in which the recapture event causing the forfeiture occurs), plus

[317] Act § 3004(i)(2), of Pub. L. No. 110-289. As noted above, the bond requirement for pre-August 1, 2008, dispositions is eliminated if an election is made and it is reasonable to expect that the building will continue to be operated as a qualified low-income building for the remaining compliance period.

[318] I.R.C. § 42(j)(6), prior to amendment by Pub. L. No. 110-289.

- Interest on such amount at the underpayment rate provided in Code section 6621(a)(2) from the date the return is due, without regard to extensions, for the year in which the event causing the forfeiture occurs, through the date that the government collects the proceeds of the bond.[319]

A recapture bond must be maintained for a period of at least 58 months after the end of the compliance period for a low-income housing credit building. The minimum amount for a recapture bond is determined by tables and depends on the bond factor for the month of disposition and the first year of the building's credit period.

The IRS intends to issue regulations that will provide a de minimis rule for certain partners. Under this rule, a partner in a small partnership that owns an interest in a qualified low-income building may elect to avoid or defer recapture upon the disposition of an interest in such partnership without furnishing a bond until the partner has made a disposition, in the aggregate, exceeding one-third of such partner's greatest total interest at any point in time.

Taxpayers who have disposed of less than 50 percent of their interest (direct or indirect) in a qualified low-income building before Revenue Ruling 90-60 was published may continue to defer recapture on previous dispositions without furnishing a bond until there is a disposition of an additional interest in such building. A written binding contract to dispose of an interest in a qualified low-income building is considered a disposition as of the date that such contract is executed.

§ 12.3 New Markets Tax Credit

§ 12.3.1 Overview

The Community Renewal Relief Act of 2000 provides that a taxpayer who holds a "qualified equity investment" in a "qualified community development entity" ("CDE") on a "credit allowance date" during a tax year is entitled to the New Markets Tax Credit ("NMTC").[320] The NMTC, which is part of the Code section 38 general business credit and is subject to those rules, is intended to spur investment in low-income or economically disadvantaged areas.[321]

The American Jobs Creation Act of 2004 made several adjustments in the definition of low-income community for purposes of the new markets tax credit.[322] In place of the provision authorizing the Secretary to designate areas within a census tract as low-income communities, the Secretary is authorized to prescribe regulations under which targeted populations, which may or may not be within a single census tract, may be treated as low-income communities. In

[319] Rev. Rul. 90-60, 1990-2 C.B. 3.

[320] Pub. L. No. 106-554 (2000).

[321] The Comptroller General of the United States is instructed to present no later than the 31st of January 2004, 2007 and 2010 a report on its audit of the new markets tax credit program. Act Sec. 121(g) of Pub. L. No. 106-554 (2000). The report issued in 2004 discussed progress in implementation of the NMTC program, but indicated further actions were needed to monitor compliance. GAO-04-326 (January 30, 2004). The report issued in 2007 links the NMTC program to an apparent increase in investments in low-income investments, but indicates that compliance can be improved. GAO-07-296 (January 31, 2007).

[322] Pub. L. No. 108-357 (2004).

response, the IRS and the Treasury Department released Notice 2006-60, which announced the regulations for Section 45D would be amended to provide guidance on how an entity meets the requirements to be a qualified active low-income community business when its activities involve certain targeted populations under Code Section 45D(e)(2).[323] Final regulations were issued with only minor clarifying changes to the language and guidance provided in Notice 2006-60.[324] These regulations apply to tax years ending on or after December 5, 2011 and may be applied to tax years ending before December 5, 2011 for designations made after October 22, 2004. Taxpayers can continue to rely upon Notice 2006-60 for prior tax years.[325] The American Jobs Creation Act also expanded the definition of low-income communities to include a census tract with a population of fewer than 2,000 which is located within an empowerment zone and which is contiguous with one or more low-income communities. In addition, a census tract located in a county that is not in a metropolitan area and that has lost 10 percent of its population in the 20-year period ending with the last census will be a low-income community if the poverty rate is at least 20 percent and the median family income does not exceed 85 percent (rather than the usual 80 percent) of the statewide median family income.

There are national calendar year limitations for the amount of investments that can be used to claim the NMTC.[326] The amount gradually increases from $1 billion in 2001 to $3.5 billion beginning in 2006 and 2007 to $5 billion in 2008 and 2009, and most recently to $3.5 billion in 2010 and 2011.[327] If the yearly limitation is not fully allocated, the excess is carried over and added to the next calendar year's limitation. However, no amount can be carried beyond the year 2014.[328] The Secretary of the Treasury is authorized to allocate these investments to CDEs.[329]

In response to the devastation of Hurricane Katrina in July 2005, an additional allocation of the NMTC is provided in an amount equal to $300 million for 2005 and 2006, and $400 million for 2007, to be allocated among qualified CDEs to make qualified low-income community investments within the Gulf Opportunity (GO) Zone. To qualify for this allocation, a qualified CDE must have as a significant mission the recovery and redevelopment within the GO Zone. The carryover of any unused additional allocation is applied separately from the carryover with respect to allocations made under the carryover rules of Code Sec. 45D(f)(3).[330]

Taxpayers may claim the NMTC on a credit allowance date in an amount equal to the applicable percentage of the taxpayer's qualified equity investment in a CDE. The credit allowance date for any qualified equity investment is the

[323] Notice 2006-60, 2006-29 I.R.B. 82 (June 30, 2006).

[324] T.D. 9560 (December 5, 2011).

[325] *Id.*

[326] I.R.C. § 45D(f)(1) (2008).

[327] I.R.C. § 45D(f)(1)(A)-(G) (2012), as amended by the Tax Relief, Unemployment Insurance Reauthorization, and Job Creation Act of 2010, Pub. L. No. 111-312, 124 Stat. 3296, § 733(a)(3).

[328] I.R.C. § 45D(f)(3) (2008).

[329] I.R.C. § 45D(f)(2) (2008).

[330] I.R.C. § 1400N(m), added by the Gulf Opportunity Zone Act of 2005, Pub. L. No. 109-135 (2005).

date on which the investment is initially made and each of the 6 anniversary dates thereafter. The applicable percentage is 5 percent for the first 3 credit allowance dates and 6 percent for the remaining credit allowance dates, for a total credit of 39 percent.[331] The taxpayer's basis in the qualified investment is reduced by the amount of the credit (other than for purposes of calculating the capital gain exclusion under Code sections 1202, 1400B, and 1400F).

The final regulation on the new markets tax credit,[332] regulation section 1.45D-1, applies on or after December 28, 2004, and may be applied by taxpayers before December 20, 2004. However, Regulation section 1.45D-1(d)(5)(ii), relating to the definition of substantial improvements and the requirement that each lessee must be a qualified business, applies to qualified low-income community investments made on or after February 28, 2005.[333] The final regulation replaces Temporary Regulation section 1.45D-1T, generally effective December 22, 2004. That regulation generally applied on or after December 26, 2001.[334]

The final regulations clarify the application of the substantially-all requirement; establish a six-month cure period for correcting noncompliance; provide guidance on when a distribution by a Community Development Entity to an investor will not be treated as a redemption requiring the investor to recapture credits previously taken; and clarify when a business, or a portion of a business, will be eligible for new markets tax credit financing.

At this time, there is one pending Notice of Proposed Rulemaking to amend the final regulation; the proposed regulations further revise and clarify certain rules relating to recapture of the NMTC.[335] The proposed regulations under REG-149404-07 would provide clarity with regard to when a recapture of the credit is triggered by certain partnership distributions or termination of a partnership interest of a CDE formed as a partnership, as well as clarifying that the reasonable expectations rule of Regulation section 1.45D-1(d)(6)(i) applies when a CDE makes an investment in or loan to another CDE.

The new markets credit is allowed for a percentage of a qualified equity investment in a qualified community development entity (CDE) held by taxpayer during the tax year. The maximum annual amount of qualified equity investments is capped at $2.0 billion per year for calendar years 2004 and 2005, and at $3.5 billion per year for calendar years 2006 and 2007, $5 billion for 2008 and 2009, and $3.5 billion for 2010 through 2019. Amounts that are not allocated in one year are added to the succeeding year's limitation and may be carried forward through calendar year 2024.[336]

---

[331] Taxpayers are able to claim the new markets tax credit in the event the CDE in which the qualified equity investment is made becomes bankrupt. Reg. § 1.45D-1(g)(4).

[332] Reg. § 1.45D-1 adopted by T.D. 9171.

[333] Reg. § 1.45D-1(h).

[334] However, certain amendments to the Temp. Reg. by T.D. 9116 generally applied on or after March 11, 2004, but could be applied by taxpayers before March 11, 2004. Temp. Reg. § 1.45D-1T(h), as amended by T.D. 9116.

[335] Notice of Proposed Rulemaking, REG-142339-05 (September 24, 2008); Notice of Proposed Rulemaking, REG-149404-07 (August 11, 2008).

[336] I.R.C. § 45D(f).

§ 12.3.2 Qualified Equity Investment

The new markets credit is allowed for a percentage of a qualified equity investment in a qualified community development entity (CDE) held by taxpayer during the tax year. The maximum annual amount of qualified equity investments is capped at $2.0 billion per year for calendar years 2004 and 2005, and at $3.5 billion per year for calendar years 2006 and 2007, $5 billion for 2008 and 2009, and $3.5 billion for 2010 through 2019. Amounts that are not allocated in one year are added to the succeeding year's limitation and may be carried forward through calendar year 2024.[337]

A qualified equity investment is defined as the cost of any stock in a corporation or any capital interest in a partnership (including amounts paid directly to, or on behalf of the CDE, such as underwriter's fees[338]) that is a CDE, which meets the following three requirements:

(1) The investment is acquired on the original issue date solely in exchange for cash, including cash derived from a loan, including a nonrecourse loan.[339] An investment will maintain its characterization for subsequent purchasers, allowing the credit to continue to be claimed.[340]

(2) Substantially all of the cash is used to make qualified low-income community investments. The substantially-all requirement is treated as satisfied for an annual period if either the direct-tracing calculation under Regulation section 1.45D-1(c)(5)(ii), or the safe harbor calculation under Regulation section 1.45D-1(c)(5)(iii), is performed every six months and the average of the two calculations for the annual period is at least 85 percent (reduced to 75 percent in the seventh year of the credit).[341] The use of the direct-tracing calculation (or the safe harbor calculation) for an annual period does not preclude the use of the safe harbor calculation (or the direct-tracing calculation) for another annual period. Cost basis of the assets, as determined under Code section 1012, is used for this purpose.[342]

If a CDE makes a qualified low-income community investment from a source of funds other than a qualified equity investment (for example, a line of credit from a bank), and later uses proceeds of an equity investment in the CDE to reimburse or repay the other source of funds, the equity investment may not be treated as financing the qualified low-income community investment on a direct-tracing basis. In these circumstances, the proceeds of the equity investment are not "used . . . to make" the qualified low-income community investment as required by Code section 45D(b)(1)(B). However, the regulations provide an example demonstrating that, in this situation, the substantially-all requirement may be satisfied under the safe harbor calculation.

---

[337] I.R.C. § 45D(f).

[338] Reg. § 1.45D-1(b)(4).

[339] Rev. Rul. 2003-20, 2003-6 I.R.B. 465.

[340] I.R.C. § 45D(b)(4) (2008). Reg. § 1.45D-1(c)(7).

[341] Reg. § 1.45D-1(c)(5). For the first annual period, the substantially all requirement is treated as satisfied if either the direct-tracing calculation, or the safe-harbor calculation, is performed on a single testing date and the result of the calculation is at least 85 percent.

[342] I.R.C. § 45D(b)(3) (2008) and Reg. § 1.45D-1(c)(5)(iii).

(3) The investment is designated by the qualified CDE for NMTC purposes.[343] A taxpayer's investment must be treated as invested in a qualified low-income community investment no later than 12 months after the taxpayer pays the cash to the CDE.[344] Moreover, an investment does include any equity investment issued by a CDE more than five years after the date the CDE receives an allocation.[345] In general, an equity investment in an entity is not eligible to be designated as a qualified equity investment if it is made before the entity enters into an allocation agreement with the Secretary of the Treasury.[346]

Two exceptions permit certain equity investments made before the receipt of a NMTC allocation under Code section 45D(f)(2) to be designated as qualified equity investments under Code section 45D(b)(1)(C).[347]

First, an exception is made for an equity investment if: (a) the equity investment is made on or after April 20, 2001; (b) the designation of the investment as a qualified equity investment is made for a credit allocation received pursuant to an allocation application submitted to the Secretary no later than August 29, 2002; and (c) the investment otherwise satisfies the statutory and regulatory requirements for a qualified equity investment.[348]

The second exception is made for an allocation application submitted after August 29, 2002, if: (a) the investment is made on or after the date the Secretary publishes a Notice of Allocation Availability (NOAA) in the Federal Register; (b) the designation of the investment as a qualified equity investment is made for a credit allocation received pursuant to an allocation application submitted to the Secretary under that NOAA; and (c) the investment otherwise satisfies the statutory and regulatory requirements for a qualified equity investment.[349] For equity investments falling under either exception, if the CDE does not receive an allocation pursuant to an allocation application submitted no later than August 29, 2002 or under the NOAA, whichever is required, the investment cannot be designated as a qualified equity investment.[350]

Such equity investments designated as qualified equity investments under either exception are treated as initially made on the effective date of the relevant CDE's allocation agreement.[351]

---

[343] I.R.C. § 45D(b) (2008) and Reg. § 1.45D-1(c).

[344] Reg. § 1.45D-1(c)(5)(iv). However, an otherwise qualifying equity investment invested within 12 months may nonetheless be designated as qualified, though such designation would otherwise be prohibited under Regulation § 1.45D-D(c)(3)(i) simply because no allocation agreement has been entered into, if the investment fits into one of the two exceptions under Regulation § 1.45D-D(c)(3)(ii).

[345] Reg. § 1.45D-1(c)(4).

[346] I.R.C. § 45D(b)(6) (2008) and Reg. § 1.45D-1(c)(3)(i).

[347] Reg § 1.45D-1(c)(3)(ii). The regulations incorporate Notice 2003-9 (2003-5 I.R.B. 369), which permits certain equity investments made on or after April 20, 2001, to be designated as qualified equity investments, and Notice 2003-56 (2003-34 I.R.B. 396), which permits certain equity investments made on or after the date the Treasury Department publishes a Notice of Allocation Availability to be designated as qualified equity investments. The revised regulations also incorporate Notice 2002-64 (2002-41 I.R.B. 690), which provides guidance on federal tax benefits that do not limit the availability of the new markets tax credit. The IRS and Treasury Department continue to study how the low-income housing credit under I.R.C. § 42 may limit the availability of the new markets tax credit.

[348] Reg. § 1.45D-1(c)(3)(ii)(A).

[349] Reg. § 1.45D-1(c)(3)(ii)(B).

[350] Reg. §§ 1.45D-1(c)(3)(ii)(A) and (B); Notice 2003-56, 2003-34 I.R.B. 396.

[351] Reg. § 1.45D-1(c)(3)(iv).

The stock or equity interest cannot be redeemed (or otherwise cashed out) by the CDE for at least seven years. If an entity fails to be a CDE during the seven-year period following the taxpayer's investment, or if the equity interest is redeemed by the issuing CDE during that seven-year period, then any credits claimed with respect to the equity interest are recaptured (with interest) and no further credits are allowed.[352]

§ 12.3.3 Qualified Community Development Entity

A CDE is any domestic corporation or partnership:[353]

1. whose primary mission is serving or providing investment capital for low-income communities or persons (the "primary mission test"),
2. that maintains accountability to residents of low-income communities through representation on any governing or advisory boards of the entity (the "accountability test"), and
3. that is certified by the Secretary of the Treasury as a CDE.[354]

To be certified as a CDE, an entity applies to the Community Development Financial Institutions Fund (the "Fund"). Both non-profit and for-profit entities may be certified. However, only for-profit entities are eligible to compete for, and receive, an allocation of authority to issue qualified equity investments with respect to which investors will be able to claim the credit.[355] In April of 2001, the Fund issued guidance that provided general information on how an entity may apply to become certified as a CDE, how a CDE may apply to receive an allocation of NMTC's, the competitive procedure through which such allocations will be made, and the actions that will be taken to ensure that proper allocations are made to appropriate entities.[356] On December 19, 2001, the Fund issued specific guidance on how an entity may apply to become certified as a CDE.[357]

The Fund reviews CDE certification applications on a rolling basis.[358] In allocating the credits, the Fund gives priority to entities with records of having successfully provided capital or technical assistance to disadvantaged businesses or communities, as well as to entities that intend to invest substantially all of the

[352] In the situation described under Reg. § 1.45D-1(d)(6)(ii)(C) where a CDE must redeem the entire investment or loan originally made to a qualified low-income community business due to unforeseen financial difficulties, the CDE can avoid the recapture event result from the redemption to the extent the CDE reinvests the requisite amount in a qualified low-income community investment within 12 months of the redemption. Reg. § 1.45D-1(d)(6)(ii)(C)(3)(ii).

[353] Although the statute only mentions domestic corporations and partnerships, limited liability companies, when classified as a partnership for federal income tax purposes, can also meet the requirements of a CDE. Rev. Rul. 2010-17.

[354] These requirements are deemed to be met by any specialized small business investment companies ("SSBIC" s) as defined in I.R.C. § 1044(c)(3) (2008) and any community development financial institution as defined by Section 103 of the Community Development Banking and Financial Institution Act of 1994 (12 U.S.C. § 4702 (2000)) (I.R.C. § 45D(c)(2) (2008)). CDE certification applications and other NMTC forms and program information may be downloaded from the Fund's website (*http://www.cdfifund.gov*).

[355] Treasury Department News Release PO-214 (April 23, 2001).

[356] Treasury Department News Release PO-214 (April 23, 2001).

[357] Treasury Department News Release PO-881 (December 19, 2001). The Fund has since issued supplemental guidance for applicants available at https://federalregister.gov/a/2012-15282.

[358] Treasury Department News Release PO-881 (December 19, 2001).

proceeds from their investors in businesses in which persons unrelated to the CDE hold the majority of the equity interest. A record of having successfully provided capital or technical assistance to disadvantaged businesses or communities could be demonstrated by the past actions of the CDE itself or an affiliate (e.g., in the case where a new CDE is established by a nonprofit organization with a history of providing assistance to disadvantaged communities).

CDE certification applications must be submitted prior to the deadline for the submission of an application for a NMTC allocation. The filing deadlines for both are published in the Notice of Allocation Availability. However, the deadline for filing CDE certification applications is 30 days prior to the submission of NMTC allocation applications. The CDFI Fund is providing NMTC program allocation application deadline extensions to qualified organizations whose principal place of business is located in counties where FEMA has issued a major disaster declaration as of July 7, 2005 (i.e., as a result of Hurricane Katrina). Furthermore, the allocation applications will be modified to give additional consideration to organizations that commit to target their investment activities to such counties.[359] An emphasis on placing investments in underserved rural communities was incorporated into the 2008 NMTC allocation round.[360]

A CDE applicant may submit the certification application on behalf of itself or on behalf of itself and one or more of its subsidiaries. However, the application must demonstrate how each meets the primary mission test and the accountability test.

A CDE certification will last for a period of 15 years unless it is revoked or terminated by the Fund. To maintain its certification, a CDE must certify annually during this period that it has continued to meet CDE certification requirements.[361]

If a CDE fails to sell equity interests to investors up to the amount authorized within five years of the authorization, then the remaining authorization is canceled. The Treasury Department can authorize another CDE to issue equity interests for the unused portion. No authorization can be made after 2014.

§ 12.3.4 Low-Income Community

In general, a low-income community is any population census tract that:

1. Has a poverty rate of at least 20 percent, or
2. If not located within a metropolitan area, the median family income does not exceed 80 percent of the statewide median family income, or
3. If located within a metropolitan area, the median family income does not exceed 80 percent of the greater of the statewide median family income or the metropolitan area median family income.[362]

---

[359] Treasury Department News Release JS-2712 (September 9, 2005).

[360] Treasury Department News Release HP-744 (December 21, 2007).

[361] Treasury Department News Release, PO-214 (April 23, 2001). A discussion of the evaluation process is contained in the April 23, 2001 guidance.

[362] I.R.C. § 45D(e)(1) (2008). For possessions of the United States, the possession-wide median income is to be used to make the above determination in-

As discussed above, the American Jobs Creation Act added to the definition of low-income communities a census tract located in a high migration rural county if the poverty rate is at least 20 percent and the median family income does not exceed 85 percent (rather than the usual 80 percent) of the statewide median family income. A high migration rural county is a county that is not in a metropolitan area and that has lost 10 percent of its population in the 20-year period ending with the last census.[363] Also, for investments made after October 22, 2004, a census tract with a population of less than 2,000 is treated as a low-income community if it is:

1. Within an empowerment zone, and
2. Contiguous to one or more low-income communities.[364]

Prior to October 23, 2004, the Secretary of the Treasury was authorized to designate an area within a census tract as a low-income community if:

1. The boundary of the area was continuous,
2. The area would have satisfied either the poverty rate or median income requirements discussed above if it were a census tract, and
3. There was inadequate access to investment capital in the area.[365]

The IRS has issued regulations designating "targeted populations" that qualify as low-income communities, including rules for determining which entities are qualified active low-income community businesses with respect to such populations.[366] Proposed regulations have been issued and are currently pending.[367] A targeted population is defined as individuals or an identifiable group of individuals who (1) are "low-income persons" or (2) otherwise lack adequate access to loans or equity investments.[368] A targeted population is not required to be within a single census tract.[369]

The guidance provides that, for purposes of Code section 45D(e)(2), an individual is a "low-income person" if the individual's family income, adjusted for family size, is not more than (A) for metropolitan areas, 80 percent of the area median family income; and (B) for non-metropolitan areas, the greater of (i) 80 percent of the area median family income; or (ii) 80 percent of the statewide nonmetropolitan area median family income.[370]

(Footnote Continued)

stead of statewide median income. Flush language after I.R.C. § 45D(e)(1)(B)(ii) (2008).

[363] I.R.C. § 45D(e)(5), as added by the American Jobs Creation Act of 2004, Pub. L. No. 108-357, effective for investments made after December 31, 2000.

[364] I.R.C. § 45D(e)(4), as added by Pub. L. No. 108-357.

[365] I.R.C. § 45D(e)(2), prior to amendment by Pub. L. No. 108-357.

[366] I.R.C. § 45D(e)(2), as amended by Pub. L. No. 108-357, T.D. 9560 (December 5, 2011). *See* § 12.3.6 below for further discussion of qualified active low-income community businesses with respect to targeted populations.

[367] Notice of Proposed Rulemaking REG-142339-05 (September 24, 2008); Notice 2006-60, 2006-29 I.R.B. 82 (June 30, 2006).

[368] 12 U.S.C. § 4702(20).

[369] Final regulations now apply to tax years ending on or after December 5, 2011 and may be applied to tax years ending before December 5, 2011 for designations made after October 22, 2004. Taxpayers can continue to rely upon Notice 2006-60 for prior tax years. T.D. 9560 (December 5, 2011).

[370] *Id.*

A low-income community targeted population also includes individuals or an identifiable group of individuals who lack adequate access to loans or equity investments.[371] Notice 2006-60 limits this group to GO Zone targeted populations. These are individuals who were displaced from their principal residence as a result of Hurricane Katrina and/or lost their principal source of employment as a result of Hurricane Katrina. The individual's principal residence or principal source of employment, as applicable, must have been located in a population census tract within the GO Zone that contains one or more areas designated by FEMA as flooded, having sustained extensive damage, or having sustained catastrophic damage as a result of Hurricane Katrina.[372]

§ 12.3.5 Low-Income Community Investment

A qualified low-income community investment includes the following four types of investments:

1. Any capital or equity investment in, or loan to, any qualified active low-income community business. A loan is treated as made by a CDE to the extent the CDE purchases the loan from the originator (whether or not the originator is a CDE) within 30 days after the date the originator makes the loan if, at the time the loan is made, there is a legally enforceable written agreement between the originator and the CDE which (a) requires the CDE to approve the making of the loan either directly or by imposing specific written loan underwriting criteria and (b) requires the CDE to purchase the loan within 30 days after the date the loan is made.

A loan by an entity is treated as made by a CDE, even if the entity is not a CDE at the time it makes the loan, so long as the entity is a CDE at the time it sells the loan.[373]

2. Under limited situations, a purchase from another CDE of any loan made by the CDE which is a qualified low-income community investment. The purchase of a loan by the ultimate CDE from a second CDE that purchased the loan from the originating CDE (or from another CDE) is treated as a purchase of the loan by the ultimate CDE from the originating CDE, provided that each entity that sold the loan was a CDE at the time it sold the loan. A loan purchased by the ultimate CDE from another CDE is a qualified low-income community investment if it qualifies as a qualified low-income community invest ment either at the time the loan was made or at the time the ultimate CDE purchases the loan.

3. Financial counseling or other services (i.e., advice provided by the CDE relating to the operation or organization of a trade or business) provided to businesses located in, and residents of, low-income communities, and

---

371 I.R.C. § 45D(e)(2) (2008).

372 Notice 2006-60, 2006-2 C.B. 82, and Prop. Reg. § 1.45D-1(d)(9)(ii), REG-142339-05 (September 24, 2008). *See also* I.R.C. § 1400N(m), added by the Gulf Opportunity Zone Act of 2005, Pub. L. No. 109-135.

373 Reg. § 1.45(d)(1)(ii)(B) (2008), incorporating Notice 2003-68 (2003-41 I.R.B. 824).

4. Any equity investment in, or loan to, any qualified CDE.[374] Investments are permitted through multiple tiers of CDEs. For example, some CDEs have reasons relating to bank regulatory requirements for lending to bank holding company CDEs that invest in bank subsidiary CDEs. In accordance with Notice 2003-64, an investment is permitted through two additional CDEs. If the investment is in another CDE, the investment would qualify only to the extent that the recipient CDE uses the proceeds: (1) for either an investment in, or a loan to, a qualified active low-income community business, or financial counseling and other services; and (2) in a manner that would constitute a qualified low-income community investment if it were made directly by the CDE making the equity investment or loan.[375]

§12.3.6 Qualified Active Low-Income Community Business

A qualified active low-income community business (QALICB) is defined as any corporation, nonprofit corporation, or partnership that meets specific requirements for the tax year.[376] A proprietorship or portion of a business can also qualify, provided the requirements would have been met if the entity was incorporated.[377]

In general, a qualified business can generally be any trade or business. However, certain types of businesses are excluded including, for example, any trade or business consisting predominantly of the development or holding of intangibles for sale or license or consisting of the operation of a commercial or private golf course, country club, massage parlor, hot tub facility, suntan facility, racetrack, gambling or any store the principal business of which is the sale of alcoholic beverages for consumption off premises. A trade or business with a principal activity of farming (within the meaning of Code section 2032A(e)(5)(A) or (B)) is also not eligible to be treated as a qualified business.[378] Additionally, the rental of real estate is limited to the rental of nonresidential real estate where substantial improvements have been added to the property.[379] As adopted by T.D. 9171, Regulation section 1.45D-1(d)(5) includes a definition of substantial improvements. The term substantial improvements means improvements the cost basis of which is at least equal to 50 percent of the cost basis of the land on which the improvements are located and the costs of which are incurred after the date that the CDE makes the investment or loan. In addition, a CDE's investment in or loan to a business engaged in the rental of real property is not a qualified low-income community investment to the extent any lessee of the real property is not a qualified business.[380] The purchase and holding of unimproved real estate is not a qualified active business.

---

[374] I.R.C. §45D(d)(1) (2008); Reg. §1.45D-1(d)(1); Reg. §1.45D-1(d)(7).

[375] Reg. §1.45D-1(d)(1)(iv).

[376] I.R.C. §45D(d)(2) (2008) and Reg. §1.45D-1(d)(4).

[377] I.R.C. §45D(d)(2)(B) and I.R.C. §45D(d)(2)(C) (2008); Reg. §1.45D-1(d)(4)(ii) and Reg. §1.45D-1(d)(4)(iii).

[378] Reg. §1.45D-1(d)(5).

[379] I.R.C. §45D(d)(3) (2008) and Reg. §1.45D-1(d)(5).

[380] This definition and the requirement that each lessee be a qualified business apply to qualified low-income community investments made on or after February 28, 2005. Reg. §1.45D-1(h)(2).

To ensure that the investments benefit businesses located in low-income communities, an entity must demonstrate that it maintains accountability to residents of low income communities through their representation on any governing board of the entity or on any advisory board to the entity.[381] Currently, an entity wishing to meet the accountability test should maintain a minimum of 20 percent of the members of the governing or advisory board(s) as representative of the low income community.[382] However, there is no requirement that employees of the business be residents of the low-income community.

Generally, for QALICB status, the corporation or partnership must:

1. Have at least 50 percent of its total gross income derived from the active conduct of a qualified business within any low-income community,
2. Use a substantial portion (at least 40 percent) of its tangible property within any low-income community,
3. Have a substantial portion (at least 40 percent) of the services of its employees performed in any low-income community,
4. Have less than five percent of the average of the aggregate unadjusted bases of its property attributable to collectibles, unless the collectibles are held primarily for sale in the ordinary course of business, and
5. Have less than five percent of the average of the aggregate unadjusted bases of its property attributable to nonqualified financial property as defined in Code section 1397(C)(e).[383]

For purposes of item (2), above, an entity is treated as engaged in the active conduct of a trade or business if, at the time the CDE makes a capital or equity investment in, or loan to, the entity, the CDE reasonably expects that the entity will generate revenues (or, in the case of a nonprofit corporation, receive donations) within 3 years after the date the investment or loan is made.[384]

With respect to item (3), a corporation or a partnership may be a QALICB only if a substantial portion of the services performed for such entity by its employees are performed in a low-income community.[385] Regulation section 1.45D-1(d)(4)(i)(C) defines substantial portion for this purpose as at least 40 percent of such services. If an entity has no employees, the entity is deemed to satisfy the services test (as well as the requirement in item (1), above, that at least 50 percent of the total gross income of the entity be derived from the active conduct of a qualified business within a low-income community) if at least 85 percent of the use of the tangible property of the entity (whether owned or leased) is within a low-income community.

An entity is treated as QALICB if the CDE reasonably expects at the time it makes the investment in, or loan to, the entity, that the entity will satisfy the requirements to be a qualified active low-income community business (i.e., items

[381] I.R.C. § 45D(c)(1)(B) (2008).

[382] Treasury Department News Release, PO-881, December 19, 2001. *See also* New Markets Tax Credit Program 2008 Application Workshop (January 2008) at *www.cdfifund.gov*.

[383] I.R.C. § 45D(d)(2)(A) (2008) and Reg. § 1.45D-1(d)(4)(i).

[384] Reg. § 1.45D-1(d)(4)(iv)(A).

[385] I.R.C. § 45D(d)(2)(A)(iii) (2008).

(1) - (5), above) throughout the entire period of the investment or loan.[386] However, if the CDE controls or obtains control of the entity at any time during the 7-year credit period, the entity is treated as a QALICB only if the entity satisfies the applicable requirements throughout the entire period the CDE controls the entity.[387] Control is defined as direct or indirect ownership (based on value) or control (based on voting or management rights) of 50 percent or more of the entity.[388] Prior to adoption of Temporary Regulation section 1.45D-1T(d)(6)(ii)(B) by T.D. 9116, a 33 percent or more test applied. However, if an unrelated entity had a higher percentage of control than the CDE, the CDE was not deemed to control the entity even if its ownership percentage was 33 percent or greater.

If a CDE satisfies the reasonable expectation test at the time it invests in an entity but later acquires control of the entity due to unforeseen financial difficulties of the entity, the CDE's acquisition of control may be disregarded for a 12-month period. If under these circumstances control is acquired before the seventh year of the 7-year credit period, then by the end of the 12-month period, the controlled entity must satisfy the requirements for QALICB status (items (1) - (5), above) or the CDE must sell and reinvest its investment in another qualified low-income community investment.[389]

Nonqualified financial property (item (5), above) is debt, stock, partnership interests, options, futures contracts, forward contracts, warrants, notional principal contracts, annuities, and similar property.[390] Reasonable amounts of working capital held in cash, cash equivalents, or debt instruments with a term of 18 months or less are not disqualified financial property. The proceeds of a capital or equity investment to or a loan by a CDE that will be expended for construction for real property within 12 months after the date the investment or loan is made are treated as a reasonable amount of working capital.[391] Accounts or notes receivable acquired in the ordinary course of trade or business for services rendered or from the sale of inventory are not nonqualified financial property.[392]

§ 12.3.6.1 Qualified Active Low-Income Community Business for Targeted Populations Generally

A qualified active low-income community business (QALICB) for a low-income targeted population is a corporation (including a nonprofit corporation) or a partnership engaged in the active conduct of a qualified business if:

1. At least 50 percent of the corporation's or partnership's total gross income for any tax year is derived from sales, rentals, services, or other transactions with individuals who are low-income persons;
2. At least 40 percent of the corporation's or partnership's employees are individuals who are low-income persons; or

[386] Reg. § 1.45D-1(d)(6)(i).

[387] Reg. § 1.45D-1(d)(6)(ii)(A).

[388] Reg. § 1.45D-1(d)(6)(ii)(B).

[389] Reg. § 1.45D-1(d)(6)(ii)(C).

[390] I.R.C. § 45D(2)(A)(v) (2008); I.R.C. § 1397C(e) (2008); Reg. § 1.45D-1(d)(4)(i)(E)(1)(i).

[391] Reg. § 1.45D-1(d)(4)(i)(E)(2).

[392] Reg. § 1.45D-1(d)(4)(i)(E)(1)(ii).

3. At least 50 percent of the corporation or partnership is owned by individuals who are low-income persons.[393]

The determination of whether an employee is a low-income person is made when the employee is hired.[394] The determination of whether a corporation or partnership is owned by a low-income person is made at the time the qualified community development entity (CDE) makes the qualified low-income community investment (QLICI) in the corporation or partnership.[395]

A corporation or partnership is automatically excluded from QALICB status if it is located in a population census tract for which the median family income exceeds 120 percent of:

1. in the case of a tract not located within a metropolitan area, the statewide median family income, or
2. in the case of a tract located within a metropolitan area, the greater of statewide median family income or metropolitan area median family income (120-percent-income restriction).[396]

This 120-percent-income restriction does not apply to a corporation or partnership located within a population census tract outside of a metropolitan area with a population of less than 2,000, or within a metropolitan population census tract with a population of less than 2,000 and more than 75 percent of the tract is zoned for commercial or industrial use.[397]

The 120-percent-income restriction is also violated if 50 percent or more of a corporation's or partnership's total gross income is derived from activities outside of a qualifying population census tract, 40 percent or more of its tangible property (including leased property) is used outside of a qualifying census tract, and 40 percent or more of the services performed by employees of the corporation or partnership are performed outside of the qualifying census tract. The corporation or partnership is considered to have the non-qualifying gross income amount if it has non-qualifying tangible property usage or non-qualifying services performance of at least 50 percent instead of 40 percent. If the corporation or partnership has no employees, the 120-percent-income restriction is violated if at least 85 percent of the use of the tangible property of the corporation or partnership (whether owned or leased) is within one or more non-qualifying population census tracts.[398]

The rental to others of real property for low-income targeted populations that otherwise satisfies the requirements to be a qualified business will be treated as located in a low-income community if at least 50 percent of the corporation's or partnership's total gross income is derived from rentals to individuals who are

---

[393] The IRS has issued regulations designating "targeted populations" that qualify as low-income communities, including rules for determining which entities are qualified active low-income community businesses with respect to such populations. I.R.C. § 45D(e)(2), as amended by the American Jobs Creation Act of 2004, Pub. L. No. 108-357. T.D. 9560 was issued on December 5, 2011 with only minor clarifying changes to Notice 2006-60.

[394] T.D. 9560 (December 5, 2011).

[395] *Id.*

[396] *Id.*

[397] *Id.*

[398] *Id.*

low-income persons and/or to a QALICB that meets the requirements for low-income targeted populations by reason of the 50 percent or 40 percent tests in items (1) and (2), above.[399]

§ 12.3.6.2 Qualified Active Low-Income Community Business for GO Zone Targeted Populations

Under Sec. 3.04 of Notice 2006-60, a QALICB for the GO Zone Targeted Population, with respect to any tax year, is a corporation (including a nonprofit corporation) or a partnership engaged in the active conduct of a qualified business if:

1. at least 50 percent of the corporation's or partnership's total gross income for any tax year is derived from sales, rentals, services, or other transactions with the GO Zone Targeted Population, low-income persons as defined above, or some combination thereof;
2. at least 40 percent of the corporation's or partnership's employees consist of the GO Zone Targeted Population, low-income persons as defined above, or some combination thereof; or
3. at least 50 percent of the corporation or partnership is owned by the GO Zone Targeted Population, low-income persons as defined above, or some combination thereof.[400]

A corporation or partnership cannot qualify as a QALICB unless it is located in a population census tract within the GO Zone that contains one or more areas designated by FEMA as flooded, having sustained extensive damage, or having sustained catastrophic damage as a result of Hurricane Katrina (qualifying population census tract).[401]

A corporation or partnership is considered located in a qualifying population census tract if:

1. at least 50 percent of the total gross income of the corporation or partnership is derived from the active conduct of a qualified business within one or more qualifying population census tracts (gross income requirement);
2. at least 40 percent of the use of the tangible property of the corporation or partnership (whether owned or leased) is within one or more qualifying population census tracts (use of tangible property requirement); and
3. at least 40 percent of the services performed for the corporation or partnership by its employees are performed in one or more qualifying population census tracts (services performed requirement).[402]

The gross income requirement is satisfied if the corporation or partnership meets either the use of tangible property requirement or the services performed

---

[399] *Id.*

[400] Notice 2006-60, 2006-2 C.B. 82, and Prop. Reg. § 1.45D-1(d)(9)(ii)(C), REG-142339-05.

[401] Notice 2006-60, 2006-2 C.B. 82, and Prop. Reg. § 1.45D-1(d)(9)(ii)(C)(2)(i), REG-142339-05.

[402] Notice 2006-60, 2006-2 C.B. 82, and Prop. Reg. § 1.45D-1(d)(9)(ii)(C)(2)(ii)(A), REG-142339-05.

requirement of at least 50 percent instead of 40 percent.[403] Furthermore, if the corporation or partnership has no employees, it is deemed to satisfy the services performed requirement as well as the gross income requirement if at least 85 percent of the use of the tangible property of the entity (whether owned or leased) is within a qualifying population census tract.[404]

A corporation or partnership or partnership cannot be treated as a QALICB under section 3.04 of Notice 2006-60 if it is located in a population census tract for which the median family income exceeds 200 percent of:

1. in the case of a tract not located within a metropolitan area, the statewide median family income, or
2. in the case of a tract located within a metropolitan area, the greater of statewide median family income or metropolitan area median family income (200-percent-income restriction).[405]

The 200-percent-income restriction does not apply to a corporation or partnership located within a population census tract with a population of less than 2,000 if the tract is not located in a metropolitan area.[406] It also does not apply to a corporation or partnership located within a population census tract with a population of less than 2,000 if the tract is located in a metropolitan area and more than 75 percent of the tract is zoned for commercial or industrial use.[407]

For purposes of the 200-percent-income restriction, a corporation or partnership is considered located in a population census tract for which the median family income exceeds 200 percent of the applicable median family income if:

1. at least 50 percent of the total gross income of the corporation or partnership is derived from the active conduct of a qualified business within one or more non-qualifying population census tracts (non-qualifying gross income amount);
2. at least 40 percent of the use of the tangible property of the corporation or partnership (whether owned or leased) is within one or more non-qualifying population census tracts (non-qualifying tangible property usage); and
3. at least 40 percent of the services performed for the corporation or partnership by its employees are performed in one or more non-qualifying population census tracts (non-qualifying services performance).[408]

A corporation or partnership is considered to have the non-qualifying gross income amount (item (1)) if it has non-qualifying tangible property usage (item

---

[403] Notice 2006-60, 2006-2 C.B. 82, and Prop. Reg. § 1.45D-1(d)(9)(ii)(C)(2)(ii)(B), REG-142339-05.

[404] Notice 2006-60, 2006-2 C.B. 82, and Prop. Reg. § 1.45D-1(d)(9)(ii)(C)(2)(ii)(C), REG-142339-05.

[405] Notice 2006-60, 2006-2 C.B. 82, and Prop. Reg. § 1.45D-1(d)(9)(ii)(D)(1)(i), REG-142339-05.

[406] Notice 2006-60, 2006-2 C.B. 82, and Prop. Reg. § 1.45D-1(d)(9)(ii)(D)(1)(ii), REG-142339-05.

[407] Notice 2006-60, 2006-2 C.B. 82, and Prop. Reg. § 1.45D-1(d)(9)(ii)(D)(1)(iii), REG-142339-05.

[408] Notice 2006-60, 2006-2 C.B. 82, and Prop. Reg. § 1.45D-1(d)(9)(ii)(D)(2)(i), REG-142339-05.

(2)) or non-qualifying services performance (item (3)) of at least 50 percent instead of 40 percent.[409]

If the corporation or partnership has no employees, it is considered to have the non-qualifying gross income amount (item (1)) as well as non-qualifying services performance (item (3)) if at least 85 percent of the use of the tangible property of the corporation or partnership (whether owned or leased) is within one or more non-qualifying population census tracts.[410]

The rental to others of real property for the GO Zone Targeted Population that otherwise satisfies the requirements to be a qualified business is treated as located in a low-income community if at least 50 percent of the corporation's or partnership's total gross income is derived from rentals to the GO Zone Targeted Population, low-income persons as defined above, or some combination thereof and/or to a QALICB that meets the requirements for the GO Zone Targeted Population.[411]

§ 12.3.7 Allowance Date

The allowance date is the date on which the investment is initially made, and the first six anniversary dates thereafter. The amount of the new tax credit for the first three allowance dates is five percent of the amount paid for the qualified equity investment in the CDE as of the original issue date. The tax credit increases to 6 percent for each of the four remaining allowance dates.[412] Thus, the total allowable credit (taken either by the original purchaser or a subsequent holder), claimed over seven annual allowance dates, is 39 percent of the qualified investment. If a recapture event occurs during the seven years from the original issue date of the qualified equity investment in a qualified CDE, then the new markets tax credit must also be recaptured.[413]

§ 12.3.8 Recapture of Credit

If during the seven years from the original issue date of the qualified equity investment in a CDE a recapture event occurs with respect to the investment, then the NMTC must be recaptured.[414] A recapture event occurs when:

1. The entity ceases to qualify as a CDE,

2. The proceeds cease to be used as required, or

3. There is a redemption of the investment by the CDE.[415]

A recapture event can also result if it is determined by the IRS that a principal purpose of a transaction, or a series of transactions, is to achieve a result that is inconsistent with the purposes of the NMTC.[416] Additionally, a recapture event can result where there is a failure of the substantially-all requirement as mentioned in § 12.3.3. The recapture event can be avoided if the commu-

[409] Notice 2006-60, 2006-2 C.B. 82, and Prop. Reg. § 1.45D-1(d)(9)(ii)(D)(2)(ii), REG-142339-05.

[410] Notice 2006-60, 2006-2 C.B. 82, and Prop. Reg. § 1.45D-1(d)(9)(ii)(D)(2)(iii), REG-142339-05.

[411] Notice 2006-60, 2006-2 C.B. 82, and Prop. Reg. § 1.45D-1(d)(9)(ii)(E), REG-142339-05.

[412] I.R.C. § 45D(a)(2) (2008).

[413] I.R.C. § 45D(g) (2008).

[414] I.R.C. § 45D(g) (2008) and Reg. § 1.45D-1(e).

[415] I.R.C. § 45D(g)(3) (2008).

[416] Reg. § 1.45D-1(g)(1).

nity development entity corrects the failure within six months after the date it was aware or reasonably should have been aware of the failure.[417]

The recapture penalty can be severe. The recaptured credit will increase the tax for the year in an amount equal to the amount of credits claimed plus interest for the resulting underpayment. The interest will not be deductible as such or as a reasonable and necessary business deduction. Furthermore, no other credits may be taken against the addition to tax caused by the credit recapture.[418] The underpayment interest begins to accrue from the due date of the return without extensions for each year that the credits were claimed. Finally, the recapture amount is treated as an increase in the tax after the regular tax and the alternative minimum tax liabilities are determined.

The CDE must provide notice to each holder, including all prior holders, of the investment that a recapture event has occurred. The notice must be provided within 60 days after the CDE becomes aware of the recapture event.[419]

---

[417] Reg. § 1.45D-1(e)(6).

[418] I.R.C. § 45D(g)(2) (2008).

[419] Reg. § 1.45D-1(g)(2)(i)(B).

Appendices

Appendix A IRS Banking Industry Issue Papers

§ A.1 Interest on Cap Loans (Discussed at § 2.6.3)
§ A.2 Premature Withdrawal Penalties (Discussed at § 2.14)
§ A.3 Deferred Loan Fees—Composite Method (Discussed at § 2.6.2)
§ A.4 Deferred Loan Fees—Loan Liquidation Method (Discussed at § 2.6.2)
§ A.5 Mortgage Buy-Down Fees (Discussed at § 2.7.2)
§ A.6 Nonperforming Loans (Commercial Bank)—Accrued Interest (Discussed at § 5.3.14)
§ A.7 Nonperforming Loans—Accrued Interest (Thrift) (Discussed at § 5.3.14)
§ A.8 Nonperforming Loans—Accrued Interest (Commercial Bank)—Appeals (Discussed at § 5.3.14)
§ A.9 Nonperforming Loans, LMSB Industry Directive with IDR (Discussed at § 5.3.2)
§ A.10 Foreclosures: Gain or Loss on Foreclosures (Discussed at § 7.6.1)
§ A.11 Foreclosures: Interest Income on the Sale of Foreclosed Debt (Discussed at § 7.6.3)
§ A.12 Foreclosures: Interest Income on the Sale of Foreclosed Debt—Appeals (Discussed at § 7.6.3)
§ A.13 Validity of Treasury Regulations Section 1.593-6A(b)(5)(vi)
§ A.14 Core Deposit Intangibles (Commercial Bank) (Discussed at § 11.3.4(g))
§ A.15 Core Deposit Intangibles (Thrift) (Discussed at § 11.3.4(g))
§ A.16 Debt-Equity Swaps
§ A.17 Gross Up of Net Foreign Loans
§ A.18 Supervisory Goodwill—Settlement Guideline (Discussed at § 11.6.1)
§ A.19 Supervisory Goodwill—LMSB Coordinated Issue (Discussed at § 11.6.1)
§ A.20 Bad Debts: Industry Director Guidelines on Auditing Bank Bad Debt Conformity Election (Discussed at § 10.4.2(f))
§ A.21 Bad Debts: Attachment to Industry Director Guidelines on Auditing Bank Bad Debt Conformity Election (Discussed at § 10.4.2(f))

§ A.22 Bad Debts: Uniform Agreement on Classification of Securities (Discussed at § 10.4.2(e))

§ A.23 LB&I Directive Related to § 166 Deductions for Eligible Debt and Eligible Securities

§ A.24 Mark-to-Market: I.R.C. § 475 Field Directive on Valuation

Appendix B **Audit Technique Guide for Commercial Banking**

APPENDIX A
IRS Banking Industry Issue Papers

§ A.1 INTEREST ON CAP LOANS

§ A.1.1 Issue

Whether interest received in excess of a maximum amount (CAP) is interest income to be recognized each year of the loan.

§ A.1.3 Facts, Law and Arguments

Some loan agreements contain provisions that during the term of the loan interest will be charged at a fluctuating rate usually in relation to the prime rate, but limit the total interest charged over the life of the loan to a specific maximum amount. This maximum amount is called the "CAP" amount. Other provisions of the loan instrument usually provide that at the maturity date the total interest collected will be adjusted to the CAP amount with either an additional charge or a refund. There are usually several qualifications which must be met over the life of the loan for this CAP agreement to be effective. One of these is that if the principal is paid before the maturity, then all interest collected by the lender in excess of the CAP amount is forfeited by the borrower. Many lenders are placing the excess of the interest charged over the CAP amount collected during the term of the loan in a liability account (e.g., Reserve for Interest Collected Over CAP to Be Refunded to Customers, *etc.*) and deferring the reporting of this income.

Section 1.451-1 of the Regulations states that under the accrual method of accounting, income is includible in gross income when all the events have occurred which fix the right to receive such income and the amount thereof can be determined with reasonable accuracy. This rule was further defined in Rev. Ruling 70-540 (1970-2 C.B. 101).

Rev. Ruling 66-347 (1966-2 C.B., 196) covers the year of recognition of income received without restriction as to its disposition, use, or enjoyment even though it has been received subject to a contingent liability to return part of it. This ruling holds that the income has to be reported in the year of receipt and a deduction taken only when a refund is made.

Section 1.461-1(a)(2) of the Regulations states, in part, that under the accrual method of accounting, an expense is deductible for the taxable year in which all the events have occurred that determine the fact of liability.

Another question to be answered is whether the income received in excess of the CAP amount is included in current income even though it might be subject to a possible forfeiture at some later undetermined date. The answer to this question is found in the following cases:

1. *Corliss v. Bowers* [2 U.S.T.C. 525], 281 US 376 (8 AFTR 10910) This case established the rule that income received unrestricted as to use is current income. In part it was stated, "if a man disposes of a fund in such a way that another is allowed to enjoy the income which it is in the power of the first to appropriate, it does not matter whether the permission is given by assent or by failure to express dissent. The income that is subject to a man's unfettered command and that he is free to enjoy at his own option may be taxed to him as his income, whether he sees fit to enjoy it or not."
2. *Brown v. Helvering* [4 U.S.T.C. ¶1223], 291 US 193 (13 AFTR 851) In this case the taxpayer, an insurance agent, received override commissions which could be subject to refund in future years due to policy cancellations. No deduction or postponement of taxing the full override commissions [was] allowed. In part the court stated ". . . since the events necessary to create the liability do not occur during the taxable year" no deduction was allowed. "The liability . . . arising from expected future cancellation was not deductible from gross income because it was not fixed and absolute . . . experience taught also that we are not dealing with certainties."

§A.1.5 Examiner's Position

The IRS may characterize an excess payment as (1) prepaid interest (includible in income) or (2) interest income considered as current income subject to a risk or forfeiture. Thus, whether an excess payment is determined to be prepaid interest or interest income which is considered current income subject to a risk of forfeiture, the excess payments should be included in income when received and any amount actually determined to be refundable to the borrower should be deducted only when the liability to be refunded is finally determined.

§ A.2 PREMATURE WITHDRAWAL PENALTIES

§ A.2.1 Issue

Is the penalty for the premature withdrawal of a savings certificate income from the discharge of indebtedness and thus excludable from income pursuant to IRC sec. 108?

§ A.2.2 Facts

Federal Regulations governing financial institutions that issue savings certificates with term of maturity varying from 6 months to 10 years require a holder to forfeit an amount as a penalty for withdrawal of the funds before the stated term of maturity. The amount of this premature withdrawal penalty is prescribed by the Depository Institutions Deregulation Committee (DIDC), which was established by the Depository Institutions Deregulation Act of 1980, section 203, 12 U.S.C. section 3502.

The regulation provided a premature withdrawal penalty that may cause, in effect, a forfeiture of principal, as well as interest. If the deposited funds were withdrawn before a sufficient amount of interest was earned, then a portion of the principal must be forfeited to pay the prescribed penalty.

Under the normal terms of the thrift's contracts with its savings certificate holders, interest at a fixed rate is paid or credited to accounts of the holder either monthly or quarterly at the holder's option. The interest is withdrawable on demand and without penalty. The thrift's contracts also contain the terms of the penalties required by the DIDC regulation for premature withdrawal. Should a holder incur a premature withdrawal penalty after withdrawing interest earned, a corresponding reduction is made in principal returned to the holder.

For income tax purposes some financial institutions report their income attributable to premature withdrawal penalties as income from the discharge of indebtedness under section 108 of the Code. As a result a thrift will exclude the amount of the penalties from its gross income and elect to reduce, under sec. 1017, the basis of its depreciable property by the amount excluded.

§ A.2.3 Law & Discussion

Although Treasury Regulations concerning a discharge of indebtedness appeared as early as 1918, prior to 1931 the courts rejected the Commissioner's position that a discharge of an indebtedness produces income to the debtor. The landmark decision which established the rule that a discharge of indebtedness produces income to the debtor is *United States v. Kirby Lumber Co.*, 284 U.S. 1 (1931). "The *Kirby* holding essentially rationalized that a reduction in debt (liabilities) without a corresponding reduction of assets causes income by unencumbering the assets and providing an economic gain or realizable event." *Colonial Savings Association and Subsidiaries v. Commissioner*, 85 T.C. 855, affirmed by the U.S. Court of Appeals (7th Circuit), 88-2 USTC 9458 (8-10-88). Not until well after the *Kirby* decision was the rule codified as IRC sec. 61(a)(12) by the Internal Revenue Code of 1954.

Historically IRC sections 108 and 1017 provided relief for bankrupts and insolvent entities by deferring the recognition of income on a discharge of indebtedness which may have been trapped in nonliquid assets. "In extending this relief to any taxpayer-debtor with income from discharge of indebtedness [i.e., to corporate debtors, IRC sec. 108(1)(a)(C)], Congress did not express an intent to expand the circumstances under which a discharge of indebtedness might occur. *Estate of Delman v. Commissioner*, 73 T.C. 15,31-40 (1979)." *Colonial*, 85 T.C. at 863.

Rev. Rul. 83-60, 1983-1 C.B. 39 takes the position that in the present fact pattern the debtor-financial institution repays in full the loan from the creditor-depositor. The premature withdrawal penalty is a separate contractual relationship in which the creditor-depositor must pay an amount equal to the penalty in exchange for the right to withdraw the funds before maturity.

The most important point to remember here is that consideration passes from the debtor-financial institution to the creditor-depositor in exchange for the premature withdrawal penalty. The consideration is that the debtor-financial institution gives up the right to use, or invest, the funds until the maturity date of the savings certificate. The economic relationship, as argued by the government and outlined in Rev. Rul. 83-60, is that the premature withdrawal penalty is a substitute for profits the financial institution would have received if it were allowed to retain the money until the maturity date of the savings certificate. The premature withdrawal penalty is liquidated damages that the financial institution receives in consideration for the loan being repaid before the maturity date.

Rev. Rul. 83-60 states, in part:

> Not every indebtedness that is cancelled results in gross income being realized by the debtor "by reason of" cancellation of indebtedness within the meaning of section 108 of the Code. If a cancellation of indebtedness is simply the *medium* for payment of some other form of income, section 108 does not apply.

The form, or "medium," in which the penalty occurs is as a set-off against the creditor-depositor's account. The payment could just as easily have been of the form: debtor-financial institution repays the entire amount of the indebtedness, without the set-off, and then the creditor-depositor pays the penalty. The result in both cases is the same. The mere fact that the financial institution chose to net the two steps should not prejudice the overall impact. The Service's position reflects the substance of what occurs.

§ A.2.4 Conclusion

A premature withdrawal penalty is not income from a discharge of indebtedness, and must therefore be included in gross income pursuant to IRC sec. 61.

§ A.3 DEFERRED LOAN FEES—COMPOSITE METHOD*

§ A.3.1 Issue

May an accrual basis savings and loan association defer loan fees (points) charged to a borrower when originating a mortgage?

§ A.3.2 Facts

One of the primary functions of a savings and loan association is the origination of mortgage loans. It is typical of these loans that a lender would charge the borrower "points." The point charge represents an amount paid for the use or forebearance of money. Consequently, "points" is an interest levy which is an addition to that shown on the mortgage note. "Points" is typically referred to on pertinent loan documents as the "service charge." During the late 1960's and early 1970's, many of the savings and loan associations requested and received permission from the National Office to change their method of accounting for points from full inclusion in taxable income in the year of closing to a ratable inclusion over a period of years. The approval to change this method was generally made based upon the associations' characterization of loan charges as fees discounted from the face amount of the loan rather than as charges paid from the separate funds of the borrower. For tax purposes, most associations using this method report the deferred loan fees using a straight line amortization with a five to ten year spread.

§ A.3.3 Law

Section 1.451-1 of the Income Tax Regulations provides the general rule that under the accrual method of accounting, income is includible in gross income when all the events have occurred which fix the right to receive such income and the amount thereof can be determined the reasonable accuracy.

Revenue Ruling 70-540; 1970-2 C.B. 101 considers several different factual situations in which amounts are charged to the borrower as points (stipulated to constitute interest under Revenue Ruling 69-188; 1969-1 C.B. 54) in a residential mortgage lending transaction. In situation (1) of the ruling, the amount of either the cash or accrual method of accounting the "points" is fully includible in the year of settlement.

In situation (2) of Revenue Ruling 70-540, the lender agrees to lend the borrower the points in addition to the balance of the purchase price. At settlement the borrower executes a note payable equal to the balance of the purchase price plus the point charge. The ruling holds in this situation that the amount of those discounted "points" is includible in income only when payments of the note are received.

Situation (2) of Revenue Ruling 70-540 is a case in which the agreement of both parties to finance the points is made clear by the form of the transaction, in that the points are added to an already agreed upon loan amount. However, it is

---

* The treatment of deferred loan fees has been modified by Treasury Regulations issued under the O.I.D. sections of the Code. *See* the discussion of Points at Chapter 3.3.

contended that the principle illustrated in situation (2) is not limited to add-on transactions, since a net disbursement transaction is not inconsistent with an agreement to finance points. Instead of an add-on of the points, the typical transaction involves a disbursement of a previously agreed upon loan amount net of points. Since this situation also is consistent with payment of the points at closing, this creates a purported ambiguity that an add-on transaction does not.

Under Revenue Ruling 70-540 the rule as to year(s) of inclusion is well established and easily applied once the terms between the lender and borrower are established. The terms of the agreement between the borrower and lender must be determined by the documents which are prepared in connection with the loan. If these documents to not fix the time of payment, it is appropriate to look beyond the documents to the circumstances under which the loan agreement was made, including the common understanding of the parties and the established practice in the industry. The documents typically examined include the Standard Residential Sales Contract and the "Good Faith Estimate" provided to the borrower at time of application. The settlement statement (RESPA), which is given to the borrower typically at closing, specifi cally lists the point charge under the column headed "Paid from Borrower's Funds at Settlement." Taxpayers usually use the Regulation Z form given to the borrower to argue that points are financed or discounted from the principal amount of the loan. However, the standard procedure for determining "Amount Financed" per the Regulation Z form is to list "points" and other charges as reduction from the "Amount of Loan." This reduction is a mandatory part of the computation designed to disclose the true cost of the loan rather than to identify the source of funds utilized to pay "point" charges. In fact, "point" charges would be listed as a reduction in the "Amount of Loan" whether or not the charges were paid separately. Other documents normally included in a mortgage file are:

1. New loan funding voucher
2. Borrower's escrow instructions
3. Lender's escrow instructions
4. Uniform Settlement Statement: HUD-1
5. HUD guide for home buyers

All documents listed above can be used to determine whether the "points" are actually being financed.

§ A.3.4 Discussion

Several questions must be addressed to determine whether "points" can be deferred or should be included as income at the time the loan is made:

1. Did the loan amount change from the initial application, when the closing costs were merely estimates to the close of escrow?
2. Did the borrower's payments into escrow change between the initial application and the closing of escrow?

3. How did the association compute the points to be paid by the borrower? If these fees are in fact financed then the points should be computed on an amount less than the actual loan.
4. Was the borrower's understanding as to how these fees were being paid? To be considered financed, it must be mutually understood by the borrower and lender that the points are being financed.
5. If the taxpayer also is treating the odd days interest as being financed and deferring the income, the loan statement given the borrower in the initial year (specifically the first such statement issued before the first mortgage payment) will show whether or not the odd days interest is being added to the interest paid column.

By analyzing and reviewing the loan files, we should be able to show whether or not loan fees and odd days interest are paid by the borrower up front (from fresh money secured outside of the loan).

§ A.3.5 Conclusion

Loan origination fees (points) charged by a primarily accrual basis lender to a borrower in obtaining residential real estate mortgage loans should be included in the income of the lender when the amount becomes fixed and determinable pursuant to Section 451 of the Internal Revenue Code unless: 1) a clear understanding exists between the borrower and lender that the fees are in fact being financed, and 2) the loan documents confirm this agreement.

§ A.4 DEFERRED LOAN FEES—LOAN LIQUIDATION METHOD*

§ A.4.1 Issue

May a cash basis savings and loan association defer loan fees (points) charged to a borrower when originating a mortgage?

§ A.4.2 Facts

One of the primary functions of a savings and loan association is the origination of mortgage loans. It is typical of these loans that a lender would charge the borrower "points." The point charge represents an amount paid for the use or forebearance of money. Consequently, "points" is an interest levy which is an addition to that shown on the mortgage note. "Points" is typically referred to on pertinent loan documents as the "service charge." During the late 1960's and early 1970's, many of the savings and loan associations requested and received permission from the National Office to change their method of accounting for points from full inclusion in taxable income in the year of closing to a ratable inclusion over a period of years. The approval to change this method was generally made based upon the associations' characterization of loan charges as fees discounted from the face amount of the loan rather than as charges paid from the separate funds of the borrower. For tax purposes, most associations using this method report the deferred loan fees based upon payments received on mortgages using a specified formula.

§ A.4.3 Law

Section 1.451-1 of the Income Tax Regulations provides the general rule that under the cash receipts and disbursements method of accounting, items of income are includible in gross income when actually or constructively received.

Revenue Ruling 70-540; 1970-2 C.B. 101 considers several different factual situations in which amounts are charged to the borrower as points (stipulated to constitute interest under Revenue Ruling 69-188; 1969-1 C.B. 54) in a residential mortgage lending transaction. In situation (1) of the ruling, the amount of the "points" is paid at settlement to the lender by the borrower with funds not originally obtained from the lender. In such a case the ruling holds that under either the cash or accrual method of accounting the "points" are fully includible in the year of settlement.

In situation (2) of Revenue Ruling 70-540, the lender agrees to lend the borrower the points in addition to the balance of the purchase price. At settlement the borrower executes a note payable equal to the balance of the purchase price plus the point charge. The ruling holds in this situation that the amount of those discounted "points" is includible in income only when payments on the note are received.

Situation (2) of Revenue Ruling 70-540 is a case in which the agreement of both parties to finance the points is made clear by the form of the transaction, in

* The treatment of deferred loan fees has been modified by Treasury Regulations issued under the O.I.D. sections of the Code. *See* the discussion of Points at Chapter 3.3.

that the points are added to an already agreed upon loan amount. However, it is contended that the principle illustrated in situation (2) is not limited to add-on transactions, since a net disbursement transaction is not inconsistent with an agreement to finance points. Instead of an add-on of the points, the typical transaction involves a disbursement of a previously agreed upon loan amount net of points. Since this situation also is consistent with payment of the points at closing, this creates a purported ambiguity that an add-on transaction does not.

Under Revenue Ruling 70-540 the rule as to year(s) of inclusion is well established and easily applied once the terms between the lender and borrower are established. The terms of the agreement between the borrower and lender must be determined by the documents which are prepared in connection with the loan. If these documents do not fix the time of payment, it is appropriate to look beyond the documents to the circumstances under which the loan agreement was made, including the common understanding of the parties and the established practice in the industry. The documents typically examined include the Standard Residential Sales Contract and the "Good Faith Estimate" provided to the borrower at time of application. The settlement statement (RESPA), which is given to the borrower typically at closing, specifically lists the point charge under the column headed "Paid from Borrower's Funds at Settlement." Taxpayers usually use the Regulation Z form given to the borrower to argue that points are financed or discounted from the principal amount of the loan. However, the standard procedure for determining "Amount Financed" per the Regulation Z form is to list "points" and other charges as reduction from the "Amount of Loan." This reduction is a mandatory part of the computation designed to disclose the true cost of the loan rather than to identify the source of funds utilized to pay "point" charges. In fact, "point" charges would be listed as a reduction in the "Amount of Loan" whether or not the charges were paid separately. Other documents normally included in a mortgage file are:

1. New loan funding voucher
2. Borrower's escrow instructions
3. Lender's escrow instructions
4. Uniform Settlement Statement—HUD-1
5. HUD guide for home buyers

All documents listed above can be used to determine whether the "points" are actually being financed.

§ A.4.4 Discussion

Several questions must be addressed to determine whether "points" can be deferred or should be included as income at the time the loan is made:

1. Did the loan amount change from the initial application, when the closing costs were merely estimates to the close of escrow?
2. Did the borrower's payments into escrow change between the initial application and the closing of escrow?

3. How did the association compute the points to be paid by the borrower? If these fees are in fact financed, then the points should be computed on an amount less than the actual loan.
4. What was the borrower's understanding as to how these fees were being paid? To be considered financed, it must be mutually understood by the borrower and lender that the points are being financed.
5. If the taxpayer also is treating the odd days interest as being financed and deferring the income, the loan statements given the borrower in the initial year (specifically the first such statement issued before the first mortgage payment) will show whether or not the odd days interest is being added to the interest paid column.

By analyzing and reviewing the loan files, we should be able to show whether or not loan fees and odd days interest are paid by the borrower up front (from fresh money secured outside of the loan).

§ A.4.5 Conclusion

Loan origination fees (points) charged by a primarily cash basis lender to a borrower in obtaining residential real estate mortgage loans should be included in the income of the lender when the fees are actually or constructively received pursuant to Section 451 of the Internal Revenue Code unless: (1) a clear understanding exists between the borrower and lender that the fees are in fact being financed, and (2) the loan documents confirm this agreement.

§ A.5 MORTGAGE BUY-DOWN FEES*

§ A.5.1 Issue

Should buy-down fees, also known as mortgage writedowns, received at the time of loan origination be considered current income by a savings and loan association or may they be deferred over the period of the buy-down?

§ A.5.2 Facts

A buy-down is a subsidy which is paid by the seller of real property to the lender for a portion of the interest that the buyer of the property would normally pay. The seller arranges a buy-down to facilitate the sell of its property. Buy-downs will normally occur when the economy is in a period of high interest rates, when the buyer-borrower is unable or unwilling to buy the property at the prevailing interest rates, but is able or willing to purchase the property at a lower rate. When this occurs the seller can negotiate with a financial institution for a buy-down of the interest rate. To accomplish this the seller will deposit into a savings account at the applicable thrift a sum of money sufficient, after considering the interest to be earned on the account, to cover the difference in monthly payments between the prevailing rate and the buy-down rate for the period of time agreed to in the buy-down agreement. This period of time may range anywhere from 12 to 60 months. Per the buy-down agreement, this deposit is non-refundable to the seller, even on early payoff or refinancing of the loan. Each month an amount equal to the difference between the two interest rates is transferred out of the savings account and added to the buyer's monthly payment, the resulting payment yields the required interest rate.

When the thrift receives this non-refundable deposit it immediately establishes a deposit liability for the full amount. The normal procedure is then to amortize the buy-down into income on a monthly basis. An example of this type of transaction is reflected in Exhibit A.

In the industry these buy-down loans are also known as teaser-loans and seller assisted loans. The liability account might also be classified as mortgagor funds.

§ A.5.3 Law

Section 1.446-1(c)(1)(i) of the regulations provides that a cash basis taxpayer must include in gross income all income actually or constructively received.

Section 1.446-1(c)(i)(ii) provides that under an accrual method, income is to be included for the taxable year when all the events have occurred which fix the right to receive such income.

* The treatment of mortgage buy-down fees has been modified by Treasury Regulations issued under the O.I.D. sections of the Code. *See* the discussion of Points at Chapter 3.3.

Buy-Downs
Exhibit A

Purchase/Sale Price	$100,000
Downpayment	20,000
Loan Amount	80,000
Mortgage Interest	15%
Buy-down Interest*	12%
Mortgage Term	30 yrs.
Buy-down Term	5 yrs.
Mortgage Payment Required at 15% (30 years)	1,011.56
Buy-down Payment at 12%	822.89
Difference	188.67
Deposit to Buy-down Account	8,392.48
Interest Buy-down Account	6%

The book entry upon receiving this buy-down payment from the seller might look as follows:

Dr.	Cash	8,392.48
Cr.	Interest Received in Advance on Buy-downs (Deposit Liability)	8,392.48

As the first payment is made by the borrower the book entry would be:

Dr.	Cash	822.89
Dr.	Interest received in Advance *etc.*	188.67
Cr.	Mortgage Receivable (est.)	25.26
Cr.	Interest Income (est.)	986.30

For tax purposes however, the entries should be as follows:

Dr.	Cash	8,392.48
Cr.	Interest Income	8,392.48
Dr.	Cash	822.89
Cr.	Mortgage Receivable (est. amt.)	25.26
Cr.	Interest Income	797.63

Sec. 451 of the Code states that the amount of gross income shall include any amount of gross income for the taxable year in which received by the taxpayer, unless, under the method of accounting used in computing taxable income, such amount is to be properly accounted for as of a different period.

Section 1.451-2 of the income tax regulations provides that constructive receipt includes income that the taxpayer does not actually possess, but which is so much within its control and disposition as to amount to actual receipt.

In *J.A. Mele*, 61 T.C. 358, Dec. 32,260 (acq.) the Tax Court held that interest prepaid for five years on a purchase-money promissory note was accruable as income when received was not to be prorated over the five-year period.

Similarly, in *Bjornsen Investment Corp.*, D.C. 81-1 USTC ¶ 9528, the court held that prepaid interest received by an accrual basis taxpayer in connection with a 20-year real estate contract was taxable in full at the time of receipt. Under the purchase agreement, no portion of the prepaid interest was returnable.

The leading case with respect to the timing of prepaid income regulations is *American Automobile Association v. United States*, 367 U.S. 687 (1961). There the

Association, an accrual basis taxpayer, received income consisting of prepaid annual membership dues. In return the Association provided travel information, emergency road service, and other travel related services to its members. For the year in which it received a dues payment, the Association would recognize as income only that portion of the payment corresponding to the remaining months of that year. The IRS, exercising its discretion under the predecessor to IRC section 446(b), refused to accept the Association's method of accounting for such income. The IRS contended that to reflect income clearly, the Association's method should recognize each dues payment entirely in the year of receipt.

The Supreme Court ruled for the Government. The Court noted that once the Association received a dues payment, there was no restriction upon the Association's use of the money. It further noted that the Association's services, and therefore its expenses of producing the income, were available to members on demand rather than on a fixed schedule. The Court ruled that because income was deferred without regard to any fixed schedule of expenses or services, the taxpayer's method of accounting failed the clear reflection of income test.

§ A.5.4 Discussion

It is well established in law that income is taxable to a cash basis taxpayer when received and to an accrual basis taxpayer when earned. As reported above the courts have held that an accrual basis taxpayer has earned income when it has unrestricted rights to that income. In the situation described here the association has actual unrestricted use of the funds. Per the buy-down agreement the funds are non-refundable. The fact that the association for accounting/bookkeeping purposes records the receipt of these funds as a deposit liability does not in fact establish a liability to the seller, the nonrefundable provision guarantees the opposite. In fact, the association has the unrestricted use of these funds from the moment the loan origination closes.

Deferral and amortization into income over the term of the buy-down agreement can only be justified if the associations' right to the funds were seriously restricted. This requirement is not present in this situation.

§ A.5.5 Conclusion

The receipt of these funds triggers their taxability. The association has unrestricted use of the funds.

§ A.6 NONPERFORMING LOANS—ACCRUED INTEREST (COMMERCIAL BANK)*

§ A.6.1 Issue

Whether an accrual basis bank should continue to accrue interest on delinquent loans placed in a non-accrual status.

§ A.6.2 Facts, Law and Arguments

The bank is on the accrual method of accounting and has an ongoing policy of not accruing into income interest on loans which they deem are nonperforming but have not as yet been written off as bad debts. Nonperforming loans are those loans which as a result of the inability of the borrower to meet the contractual terms of the loans are delinquent and are placed on a non-accrual basis. A non-accrual basis means that even though the loans still remain on the books, the taxpayer stops accruing interest income on these loans. Three general criteria, though not all conclusive, used by banks, to determine if a loan is delinquent are:

1. The loan account is considered delinquent when payments have not been received after [a] predetermined number of days (i.e., 30, 60, 90 days, *etc.*). The principal is placed in non-accrual status but no part of the loan is charged to the Reserve for Bad Debts.
2. A partial write off is made to the reserve account and the balance of the loan account is placed in non-accrual status.
3. The loan account is in the process of being restruct[ur]ed or renegotiated.

Section 451(6) of the Code states "The amount of any item of gross income shall be included in the gross income for the taxable year in which received by the taxpayer, unless under the method of accounting used in computing taxable income, such amount is to be properly accounted for as of a different period."

Regulation [§]1.451(a) states " . . . Under an accrual method of accounting, income is includible in gross income when all the events have occurred which fix the right to receive such income and the amount thereof can be determined with reasonable accuracy . . . ".

The taxpayers have stated that under state banking law interest income should not be accrued on loans where the principal and/or interest is past due for a stated number of days. Revenue Ruling 68-220, 1968-1 C.B.—194, generally provides, in part, that where an administrative agency requires a method of accounting as to a particular item, this accounting treatment is not controlling for Federal Income Tax purposes.

In *Greer-Robbins Co. v. Commissioner* [41-1 USTC ¶9406], 119 F.2d 92 (9th Cir. 1941), it was held that in determining whether interest is of doubtful collectibility, the burden of proof was on the taxpayer to show the bad debt character

* The treatment of accrued interest on nonperforming loans has been modified by Rev. Rul. 2007-32, I.R.B. 2007-21. *See* the discussion of Nonperforming Loans in Chapter 5.

of the accrued interest. Letter Ruling 7944014 held that delinquent loans should have been accrued in income under the Accrual Method of Accounting. This letter ruling further states "A taxpayer may not have to accrue interest income . . . if there exists no reasonable expectation at the time of accrual that the items of income . . . will be . . . collected. Such an expectation must be judged by the facts. *Broderick v. Anderson* [38-1 USTC ¶9263], 23 F. Supp. 488 (S.D. N.Y. 1938). Furthermore, taxpayers have the burden of proof that such items of interest income . . . are not collectible . . . ".

It is to be noted that a technical advice applicable to one taxpayer can not be specifically applied to another taxpayer. However, where the facts involved in each case are basically the same, the rationale and statutes in a given technical advice may be followed in the case of another taxpayer.

Revenue Ruling 77-135, although dealing with interest income and interest expense regarding graduated payment mortgages, further elaborates on the above section of the regulation as follows:

. . . with respect to the accrual basis taxpayer, all the events that fix the right to receive income occur when (1) the required performance occurs, (2) payment therefore is due, or (3) payment therefore is made, whichever happens earliest.

In applying this rule to the accrual of interest income, performance occurs when the lender allows the borrower to use the lenders [sic]money. When the lender has done this for any one day, one day's performance has occurred and one day's interest accrues (assuming that payment has not already been made).

In view of the above citations it is clear that an accrual basis taxpayer who has a right to receive income is obligated to accrue into income all amounts due with respect to loans negotiated with debtors.

It is also to be noted that the right to receive income (upon the sale or [of] property) was decided in a Supreme Court case, *Spring City Foundry Co. v. Commissioner* 292 [4 USTC ¶1276], U.S. 182 (134), where income was held to include in gross income, notwithstanding that said receivable later became uncollectible by reason of the debtor's bankruptcy in the same year. The court in said case went on to hold that the taxpayers [sic] remedy was through an appropriate bad debt deduction. However, it was clear that at the time of the sale, the receivable was presumably worth its face amount or an amount substantially equal thereto. The event of worthlessness even though in the same year was a subsequent transaction. In effect, two separate transactions are involved; the first dealing with an income inclusion and the second dealing with a possible writeoff of said interest income receivable subsequently thereto.

The above conclusions appear to be inconsistent with the conclusions reached in *Corn Exchange Bank v. Commissioner* and in *Margarite Hyde Suffolk & Berbs v. U.S.* Supra, and the distinction between these cases appears to be reconciled in *Atlantic Coast Line Railroad Co. v. Comm.* [Dec. 8817], 31 BTA 730 (1934) at 749-751. The court having determined as a matter of fact that the taxpayer had no reasonable expectation of payment of interest on certain notes, held that the interest was not required to be accrued. The court stated "The meaning of the language used by the Supreme Court (in Spring City) must be sought in the light of the facts of that case at the time that (Spring City's) right to receive arose; it is not shown that the debtor was insolvent or that the debt was not good and collectible. The fact that the obligation later became worthless, in part even though within the same taxable year, is therefore immaterial, as stated by the Court. The question then became [one]of the deduction which might be taken according to Sec. 166 of the Code. But where the obligation is worthless at the time the right to receive arises, as in the instant case, the right to receive is without substance and there is in fact nothing to accrue. Accrual of a worthless item is in fact nothing to accrue. Accrual of a worthless item in such circumstances obviously results in a distortion of gross income and in our opinion the Court did not intend its reasoning to be so applied as to reach the same result on a materially different state of facts."

Thus it can be seen that there appears to be agreement on the basic law in the area, however it is not believed that merely because an account becomes 30 days or more past due there is little or no likelihood of collection in the future. What the above cases have in common is a showing of worthlessness as that term is used in Section 166(a) of the Code.

This issue was recently covered in Revenue Ruling 80-361. In accordance with this ruling, if and when a loan becomes uncollectible the interest should be accrued to the point of uncollectibility. Accrued interest receivable should be treated as accrued interest on a bad debt pursuant to Section 166 of the Code and charged to the reserve account.

§ A.6.3 Examiner's Position

It is recommended that the taxpayer should continue to accrue interest on all loans they have substantiated that one of the following requirements have been met. The meeting of these requirements must be on a loan by loan basis and subject to audit verification by the IRS:

1. If the bank, which is subject to supervision by federal authorities, or by state authorities maintaining substantially equivalent standards, or regulatory agency has given written specific instructions by a regulatory agency that a loan, in whole or part, should be charged off as a bad debt, then on the amount so charged no further interest should be accrued. Interest should continue to be accrued up until the date the account is so charged off. Previously accrued but uncollected interest relating to the amount written off should be charged to the reserve account.
2. On loans not charged off the taxpayer must on a loan by loan basis substantiate that the interest is uncollectible in accord with Revenue Ruling 80-361.

It is the taxpayer's responsibility to present to the examiner a schedule showing the detailed specifics of how the non-accrued interest was arrived. Usually the annual report will contain just a summary figure of this amount. It is only by working with a detailed schedule will we be able to do a proper audit of this area.

§ A.7 NONPERFORMING LOANS—ACCRUED INTEREST (THRIFT)*

§ A.7.1 Issue

Whether an accrual basis savings and loan should continue to accrue interest on delinquent loans placed in a non-accrual status.

§ A.7.2 Facts, Law and Argument

The savings and loan is on the accrual method of accounting and has an ongoing policy of not accruing into income interest on loans which they deem are nonperforming but have not as yet been written off as bad debts. Nonperforming loans are those loans which, as a result of the inability of the borrower to meet the contractual terms of the loans, are delinquent and are placed on a non-accrual basis. A non-accrual basis means that even though the loans still remain on the books, the taxpayer stops accruing interest income on these loans. Three general criteria, though not all conclusive, used by institutions to determine if a loan is delinquent are:

1. The loan account is considered delinquent when payments have not been received after a predetermined number of days (e.g., 30, 60, 90 days, *etc.*). The principal is placed in non-accrual status but no part of the loan is charged to the reserve for bad debts.
2. A partial write-off is made to the reserve account and the balance of the loan account is placed in non-accrual status.
3. The loan account is in the process of being restructured or renegotiated.

Section 451(a) of the Code states "The amount of any item of gross income shall be included in the gross income for the taxable year in which received by the taxpayer unless, under the method of accounting used in computing taxable income, such amount is to be properly accounted for as of a different period."

Regulation 1.451-1(a) states ". . . Under an accrual method of accounting, income is includible in gross income when all the events have occurred which fix the right to receive such income and the amount thereof can be determined with reasonable accuracy . . .".

Revenue Ruling 68-220, 1968-1 C.B. 194, provides in part that where an administrative agency requires a method of accounting as to a particular item, this accounting treatment is not controlling for Federal Income Tax purposes.

In *Greer-Robbins Co. v. Commissioner*, 119 F.2d 92 (9th, Cir. 1941) it was held that in determining whether interest is of doubtful collectibility, the burden of proof was on the taxpayer to show the bad debt character of the accrued interest. Letter Ruling 7944014 held that delinquent loans should have been accrued in income under that accrual method of accounting. This letter ruling further states that "A taxpayer may not have to accrue interest income . . . if there exists no reasonable expectation at the time of accrual that the items of income . . . will be

* The treatment of accrued interest on nonperforming loans has been modified by Rev. Rul. 2007-32, I.R.B. 2007-21. *See* the discussion of Nonperforming Loans in Chapter 5.

. . . collected. Such an expectation must be judged by the facts. *Broderick v. Anderson*, 23 F. Supp. 488 (S.D.N.Y. 1983). Furthermore, taxpayers have the burden of proof that such items of interest . . . are not collectible . . . ".

It is to be noted that a technical advice applicable to one taxpayer cannot be specifically applied to another taxpayer. However, where the facts involved in each case are basically the same, the rationale and statutes in a given technical advice may be followed in the case of another taxpayer.

Revenue Ruling 77-135, 1977-1 C.B. 133, although dealing with interest income and interest expense regarding graduated payment mortgages, further elaborates on Regulation 1.451-1(a) as follows:

". . . with respect to the accrual basis taxpayer, all the events that fix the right to receive income occur when (1) the required performance occurs, (2) payment therefore is due, or (3) payment therefore is made, whichever happens earliest."

In applying this rule to the accrual of interest income, performance occurs when the lender allows the borrower to use the lender's money. When the lender has done this for any one day, one day's performance has occurred and one day's interest accrues (assuming that payment has not already been made).

In view of the above citations it is clear that an accrual basis taxpayer who has right to receive income is obligated to accrue into income all amounts due with respect to loans negotiated with debtors.

It is also to be noted that the right to receive income (upon the sale of property) was decided in a Supreme Court Case, *Spring City Foundry Co. v. Commissioner*, 292 U.S. 182 (1934), where income was held to be included in gross income, notwithstanding that said receivable later became uncollectible by reason of the debtor's bankruptcy in the same year. The court in that case went on to hold that the taxpayer's remedy was through an appropriate bad debt deduction. However, it was clear that at the time of the sale, the receivable was presumably worth its face amount or an amount substantially equal thereto. The event of worthlessness, even though in the same year, was a subsequent transaction. In effect, two separate transactions are involved: the first dealing with an income inclusion and the second dealing with a possible writeoff of said interest income receivable subsequently thereto.

The above conclusions appear to be inconsistent with the conclusions reached in *Corn Exchange Bank v. U.S.*, (CA-2), 2 USTC 455; 37 F.2d 34 and in *Suffolk & Berks, Marguerite H.*, 40 BTA 1121, Dec. 10,925 (Acq). The distinction between these cases appears to be reconciled in *Atlantic Coast Line Railroad Co. v. Comm.*, 31 BTA 730 (1934) at 749-751. The Court, having determined as a matter of fact that the taxpayer had no reasonable expectation of payment of interest on certain notes, held that the interest was not required to be accrued. The court stated "The meaning of the language used by the Supreme Court in (Spring City) must be sought in the light of the facts of that case at the time (Spring City's) right to receive arose; it is not shown that the debtor was insolvent or that the debt was not good and collectible. The fact that the obligation later became worthless in part, even though within the same taxable year, is therefore immaterial, as stated by the Court. The question then turned to the deduction which might be taken according to Sec. 166 of the Code. But where the obligation is worthless at the time the right to receive arises, as in the instant case, the right to receive is without substance and there is in fact nothing to accrue. Accrual of a worthless item in such circumstances obviously results in a distortion of gross income and in our opinion the Court did not intend its reasoning to be so applied as to reach the same result on a materially different state of facts."

Thus it can be seen that there appears to be agreement on the basic law in the area, however it is not believed that merely because an account becomes 30 days or more past due that there is little or no likelihood of collection in the future. What the above cases have in common is a showing of worthlessness as that term is used in Section 166(a) of the Code.

This issue was covered in Revenue Ruling 80-361, 1980-2 C.B. 164. In accordance with that ruling, if and when a loan becomes uncollectible, the interest should be accrued to the point of uncollectibility. The accrued interest receivable, if not collected, should be treated as accrued interest on a bad debt pursuant to Section 166 of the Code and charged to the reserve account.

It is recommended that the taxpayer should continue to accrue interest on all loans until they have substantiated that one of the following requirements have been met. The meeting of these requirements must be on a loan by loan basis and subject to audit verification by the IRS:

1. If a savings and loan which is subject to supervision by Federal authorities, or by State authorities maintaining substantially equivalent standards, has been given written specific instructions by a regulatory agency that a loan, in whole or part, should be charged off as a bad debt, then on the amount so charged no further interest should be accrued. Interest should continue to be accrued up until the date the account is so charged off. Previously accrued but uncollected interest relating to the amount written off should be charged to the reserve account.
2. On loans not charged off, the taxpayer must, on a loan by loan basis, substantiate that the interest is uncollectible in accord with Revenue Ruling 80-361.

§ A.7.3 Conclusion

The mere use of a general cut-off method established by the thrift regulators does not meet the tax requirement that uncollectibility be shown on a loan by loan basis. It is the taxpayer's responsibility to present to the examiner a schedule showing the detailed specifics of how the non-accrued interest was derived. Usually the annual report will contain just a summary figure of this amount. It is only by working with a detailed schedule that we will be able to do a proper audit of this area.

§ A.8 NONPERFORMING LOANS—ACCRUED INTEREST (COMMERCIAL BANK)—APPEALS*

§ A.8.1 Issue

Whether an accrual basis bank or savings and loan should continue to accrue interest on delinquent loans placed in non-accrual status.

§ A.8.2 Examination Division's Position

Examination Division's position papers recommend that interest on all loans should continue to accrue until one of two conditions exist:

1. "If a [financial institution] which is subject to supervision by Federal authorities, or by State authorities maintaining substantially equivalent standards, has been given written specific instructions by a regulatory agency that a loan, in whole or part, should be charged off as a bad debt, then on the amount so charged no further interest should be accrued. Interest should continue to be accrued up until the date the account is so charged off."
2. "On loans not charged off, the taxpayer must, on a loan by loan basis, substantiate that interest is uncollectible in accord with Revenue Ruling 80-361."

§ A.8.3 Discussion

Before getting into a discussion of the merits of this issue, it is first advisable to define the circumstances under which the issue arises.

The examination position papers refer to non-performing loans as "delinquent loans placed in non-accrual status." "Non-accrual status" means that the financial institution has ceased accruing income for financial statement purposes. The use of the word "delinquent" would seem to imply that there has been an actual delinquency in the payment of principal or interest or both. That will usually be the case, but not always. As explained in the examination division position papers, financial institutions may treat a loan as non-performing not only when there has been an actual delinquency in payments, but also when a partial write-off has been made (perhaps because the market value of the security has fallen) or the loan is in the process of being restructured or renegotiated.

Regulation 1.451-1(a) states ". . . Under an accrual method of accounting income is includible in gross income when all the events have occurred which fix the right to receive such income and the amount thereof can be determined with reasonable accuracy . . . "

The regulations are silent with respect to the treatment of an income amount that is uncollectible at the time the right to receive the income becomes fixed. The courts, however, have established a judicial exception to the accrual rules where

* The treatment of accrued interest on nonperforming loans has been modified by Rev. Rul. 2007-32, I.R.B. 2007-21. *See* the discussion of Nonperforming Loans in Chapter 5.

an income amount is uncollectible at the time the right to receive that amount becomes fixed.

In *Spring City Foundry Co.*, 292 U.S. 182, 4 USTC ¶1276 (1934), the issue involved the accruability of sales income with respect to goods sold between March and September of 1920. A petition in bankruptcy was filed against a debtor of the taxpayer on December 23, 1920; the taxpayer eventually got 27 1/2 cents on a dollar three years later. In ruling that the taxpayer must include the sales income in full in its 1920 return the Supreme Court enunciated three principles:

1. It is the *right* to receive and not the actual receipt that determines the inclusion of the amount in gross income.
2. If the accounts receivable subsequently become uncollectible, then a separate question arises as to deductibility.
3. It does not matter that the subsequent claim of loss relates to an item of gross income which had accrued in the same year, since the accrual of income and the subsequent claim of loss are two independent events.

This case was not on the books very long before it was distinguished in *Atlantic Coast Line Railroad Co.*, 31 BTA 730 (1934), aff'd on other issues, 81 F.2d 309, 36-1 USTC %% 9067, CA-4. In that case the issue involved accrual of interest in 1928, 1929 and 1930 on notes executed between 1912 and 1922. The debtor's financial condition was precarious—it had paid some of the interest due (which had been included in income by the taxpayer), but most had not been paid.

The Board of Tax Appeals sustained the taxpayer's non-accrual of the unpaid interest, distinguishing *Spring City Foundry Co.* thusly:

> "But where the obligation is worthless at the time the 'right to receive' arises, as in the instant case, the right to receive is without substance and there is in fact nothing to accrue. Accrual of a worthless item in such circumstances obviously would result in distortion of gross income, and in our opinion the Court did not intend its reasoning to be so applied as to reach the same result on a materially different state of facts."
>
> The Government has accepted the rationale of *Atlantic Coast Line Railroad Co.* in Revenue Ruling 80-361, 1980-2 C.B. 164. The facts posited in that ruling were that in the latter part of the same year that a loan was made the debtor become insolvent due to sudden and severe financial reverses. The ruling held that (1) the creditor must accrue interest income up to the time of insolvency (2) it may treat the accrued but unpaid interest as a bad debt if the requirements of Section 166 are satisfied, and (3) it need not accrue any further interest income after insolvency.

In summary, the applicable legal standard with respect to the nonaccrual issue is that income need not be accrued if, at the time the right to receive the income becomes fixed, the amount due is uncollectible. It uncollectibility is determined after the right to receive the income becomes fixed, the income must be accrued and the taxpayer may be allowed a corresponding loss deduction for the bad debt at a later point in time once uncollectibility is determined. However, once uncollectibility is determined with respect to an obligation, then any amounts that subsequently become fixed under that obligation need not be accrued unless collectibility is reestablished.

The next question that arises is how strong the proof of uncollectibility must be in order to warrant non-accrual treatment at the time of right to receive.

In *Corn Exchange Bank*, 37 F.2d 34, 2 USTC ¶455, CA-2, the Court stated that the evidence need not be as strong to justify non-accrual as is needed to write off the underlying debt and indicated that the standard to be met was that "in all probability the income will not be received." The Court also seemed to indicate that hindsight evidence is relevant by stating that " . . . a taxpayer should not be required to pay a tax when it is reasonably certain that such alleged accrued income will not be received and when, in point of fact, it never was received."

In *Georgia School-Book Depository, Inc.*, 1 T.C. 463 (1943) the Court noted that postponement of payment is not enough; there must also be a showing of improbability of payment. In ruling for the Government in that case the Court was also influenced by the fact that the taxpayer continued to sell books to the debtor (the State of Georgia).

The standard enunciated in *Union Pacific Railroad Co.*, 14 T.C. 401, 410 (1950) was that " . . . there exists reasonable grounds for believing, at the time the right to receive income becomes fixed, that such income will never be received . . . ". In ruling that the taxpayer had not met that exception to the standard for accrual of bond interest the Court was obviously influenced by the fact that such interest was paid in subsequent years.

The most recent case to address an accrual of interest income issue is *European American Bank and Trust Co.*, 90-2 USTC ¶50,333, Cls. Ct., aff'd 92-1 USTC ¶50,026, CA-FC. The facts in the case were quite complex and need not be recited. The important point to note is that this case adopted and well summarized the prior law (much of which is quite old). In so doing it stressed that a taxpayer does not have an easy task in justifying non-accrual of income:

"The concept of uncollectibility, originating in a 'reasonable expectancy of payment' criterion, is well established in case law. The 'reasonable expectancy of payment' exception is strictly construed. For accrual of income to be prevented, uncertainty as to collection must be substantial, and not simply technical in nature. For this exception to accrual of income to apply, substantial evidence must be presented to establish there was no reasonable expectancy of payment."

Factors that the court mentioned as relevant to this question were the value of the collateral and the financial condition of the debtor.

Most banks and savings and loan institutions will probably not be able to or want to substantiate their non-accrual of interest income on a loan by loan basis. It is administratively burdensome to do so and those loan files may not have the updated information necessary—the value of the collateral if a non-recourse loan and the debtor's financial condition as well if a recourse loan. They would much prefer to have a rule that would allow them to non-accrue for federal income tax purposes whenever the regulatory agencies force them to non-accrue for financial statement purposes.

Of course, it is long established that the accounting requirements of regulatory agencies are not controlling in the application of the revenue laws (*Old Colony R. Co.*, 284 U.S. 552, 3 USTC ¶880 (1932); *Bellefontaine Federal Savings and Loan Association*, 33 T.C. 808 (1960); *J.B.N. Telephone Co., Inc.*, 638 F.2d 227, 81-1 USTC ¶9151, CA-10;)

Nevertheless, the Commissioner is authorized to promulgate regulations permitting a taxpayer to elect conformity with particular regulatory treatment. Regulations 1.166-2(d) do just that with respect to the worthlessness of debts payable to financial institutions:

"(d) Banks and other regulated corporations—(1) Worthlessness presumed in year of charge-off. If a bank or other corporation which is subject to supervision by Federal authorities, or by State authorities maintaining substantially equivalent standards, charges off a debt in whole or in part, either—

(i) In obedience to the specific orders of such authorities, or

(ii) In accordance with established policies of such authorities, and, upon their first audit of the bank or other corporation subsequent to the charge-off, such authorities confirm in writing that the charge-off would have been subject to such specific orders if the audit had been made on the date of the charge-off, then the debt shall, to the extent charged off during the taxable year, be conclusively presumed to have become worthless, or worthless only in part, as the case may be, during such taxable year . . . "

The principles of this section of the regulations were extended to charge-offs of accrued but uncollected interest and accruability of interest in Rev. Rul. 81-18, 1981-1 C.B. 295. In that Ruling the facts were that a savings and loan association entered into a one-year installment loan on October 3, 1978. Interest was due on the last day of each month, but the debtor failed to make the interest payments for October 31, November 30, and December 31. The taxpayer accrued the interest income for 1978, but wrote it off as a bad debt on January 30, 1979. This charge-off was made pursuant to FHLB regulations. FHLB auditors, upon their first audit of the taxpayer after the charge-off, confirmed in writing that the charge-off was made in accordance with their established policies.

The Service ruled that not only would taxpayer be permitted to deduct the charge-offs of accrued but unpaid interest, but that taxpayer need not accrue any 1979 interest. The latter holding was based on the rationale that one need not accrue income which is presumed uncollectible on the date the right to receive income arises.

An important point to note with respect to this section of the regulations and this ruling is that they specifically require (1) an order to write off by the regulators or (2) a confirmation in writing in the next audit that the charge-off would have been subject to such specific orders if the audit had been on the date of the charge-off.

Revenue Ruling 81-18 leaves something to be desired inasmuch as it cites the FHLB regulations, but does not fully explain them. The ruling appears to rely on the general FHLB regulatory requirement that accrued but unpaid interest more than 90 days past due be classified and accounted for as uncollectible income. The impression created by the ruling, however, is that the write-off of previously accrued interest is automatic pursuant to the FHLB regulations once the single factor of 90 days delinquency has been established.

The ruling does state in its facts that the regulations pertain to "conventional" loans, but does not define that term. The FHLB regulations basically provide that a "conventional" loan is one which is not insured or guaranteed.

More importantly, the ruling does not disclose that if the loan is a home loan, interest should continue to be regarded as collectible if (1) the total owed does not exceed 90 percent of the appraised value of the security (2) active collection efforts are being made and (3) there is a reasonable expectation of delinquent-interest collection.

It is noted that the FHLB regulation requiring the charge-off of accrued but uncollected interest at the time delinquency reaches 90-days was withdrawn effective January 1, 1989. According to the "Report to the Congress on the Tax Treatment of Bad Debts by Financial Institutions" no other federal regulator of depositary institutions has promulgated such a regulation.

The Section 166 bad debt regulations were amended on February 21, 1992, adding 1.166-2(d)(3) and (4). These amendments basically permit a bank or savings and loan association to make a "conformity election" to deduct bad debts if those debts have been classified as "loss assets" for regulatory purposes.

Treasury Decision 8396, accompanying the publication of the amended regulations, refers to interest on non-performing loans thusly:

> "Several commentators requested that the conformity presumption be extended to the nonaccrual of interest on nonperforming loans. This issue is beyond the scope of these regulations. For an in-depth analysis of the appropriateness of applying a tax-book conformity standard to interest accruals on nonperforming loans, see Report to the Congress on the Tax Treatment of Bad Debts by Financial Institutions."

The report referred to above concludes that "it is not appropriate to adopt a conclusive presumption that accrued but unpaid interest on loans that are placed in nonaccrual status for regulatory purposes be considered uncollectible for tax purposes." The reason behind this conclusion derives from the two differing criteria. It is appropriate to omit accrual of interest if the right to that interest is a worthless right. But the regulatory classification of "nonperforming" generally is based on delinquency, not ultimate worthlessness.

In this respect it is noted that there is no regulation in the commercial banking area equivalent to the now rescinded FHLB regulations. The "Report to the Congress on the Tax Treatment of Bad Debts by Financial Institutions" does note that both Office of the Controller of the Currency guidance and Federal

Financial Institutions Examination Council Call Report forms require that institutions not accrue on their required quarterly reports interest income on nonperforming loans. Although the time period for determining "nonperforming" status is also 90 days, there is no automatic write-off of previously accrued but uncollected interest.

To summarize, the law is fairly well established that income need not be accrued if it can be shown that it is uncollectible at time of accrual. How strong the showing of uncollectibility must be is not clear. The language used by the courts ranges from "reasonable grounds for believing . . . that such income will never be received" (*Union Pacific Railroad Co.,* supra.) to "in all probability the income will not be received." (*Corn Exchange Bank,* supra). Certainly, if the underlying loan is properly written off, that standard has been met (Revenue Ruling 80-361, supra).

The federal tax laws are not controlled by regulatory agency rules as to when income should be accrued. Of course, the Internal Revenue Service may choose to allow taxpayers to rely on regulatory rules if it so wishes. The Service has done that in the following three situations:

1. The original bad debt regulations permit the write-offs of debts in accordance with regulatory standards if the write-off is in obedience to specific orders or the first subsequent audit confirms the write-off.
2. The February, 1992 amended regulations also permit the write-off of debts classified as "loss assets" if done in accordance with a valid "conformity election."
3. Revenue Ruling 81-18 permits the non-accrual of future interest if previously accrued interest has been written off in accordance with that section of the bad debt regulations permitting such a write-off based on regulatory standards.

If either of the first two situations exist, then taxpayer should be permitted to non-accrue in accordance with the principles of Revenue Ruling 80-361.

If the third situation exists, then taxpayer should similarly be entitled to non-accrue, but the following caveats are in order:

1. The taxpayer must be a savings and loan association. FHLB regulations do not apply to banks.
2. The time of accrual must be prior to January 1, 1989, when the FHLB regulations were withdrawn.
3. The loans must be conventional loans.
4. The Federal Home Loan Bank Board must have ordered the write-off of the previously accrued interest or upon the first subsequent audit confirmed in writing that it would have so ordered had the audit been made on the date of the charge-off. This is more than a perfunctory requirement (at least with regard to home loans), since the FHLB requirements

do not depend solely on 90 days delinquency, but also on the value of the security, collection efforts, and probability of recovery. But even if the requirement of an FHLB order or confirmation is regarded as perfunctory, that should not matter. The IRS did not have to issue Revenue Ruling 81-18 permitting reliance on regulatory standards and can impose whatever conditions it wants on qualification.

§A.9 NONPERFORMING LOANS, LMSB INDUSTRY DIRECTIVE WITH IDR

IRS LMSB Industry Director Directive #1 (LMSB-4-0110-003) on Tier II Issue:

March 17, 2010

SUBJECT: Tier II Issue - Non-Performing Loans Directive #1

This memorandum provides direction to the field for this Tier II Issue to effectively utilize resources in the identification and examination of the accrual of interest income on non-performing loans.

§A.9.1 Background/Strategic Importance

The issue of non-performing loans was the subject of a Coordinated Issue Paper (CIP) dated October 31, 1991. On May 21, 2007, Rev. Rul. 2007-32, 2007-1 C.B. 1278, and Rev. Proc. 2007-33, 2007-1 C.B. 1289 were issued regarding the position of the IRS on the tax treatment of interest income on non-performing loans. Subsequently, the issue of non-performing loans was designated a Tier II Issue by LMSB. The Issue Owner Executive (IOE) is Rosemary Sereti, Acting Director, Field Operations (Manhattan), Financial Services. IRM 4.51.1.3 requires issue coordination under direction of the IOE.

In recognition of the strategic importance of this Tier II issue, Financial Services created an Issue Management Team (IMT) to improve Service-wide coordination of the issues that arise from non-performing loans. The IMT was formed to help identify, develop, and resolve cases with these issues. A primary purpose of the IMT is to ensure that when these issues are identified for audit, they are examined fairly and consistently for all taxpayers. The IMT also plays a key role in providing guidance and technical support to the field on issue development and resolution.

§A.9.2 Issue

This Tier II issue typically involves when a regulated bank can stop accruing interest on non-performing loans for tax purposes. In addition, we need to be concerned with the treatment of accrued but unpaid interest and the application of any subsequent payments after a bank places a loan in non-accrual status for regulatory purposes.

§A.9.3 Overview

The timing of when a regulated bank can stop accruing interest on non-performing loans for tax purposes involves a difficult and time consuming loan-by-loan analysis, which was previously the subject of a Coordinated Issue Paper. Factually, interest should only stop accruing on non-performing loans for tax purposes when, at the time the interest becomes due, that interest is determined to be uncollectible or the underlying loan is determined to be worthless. In addition to when a regulated bank can stop accruing interest on non-performing loans for tax purposes, we need to be concerned on audit with the treatment of accrued but unpaid interest and the application of any payments after a loan is placed in non-accrual status for regulatory purposes, since some regulated banks may be following regulatory accounting for tax. Specifically, once a loan is placed in non-accrual status for regulatory purposes, some regulated banks may be reversing any accrued but unpaid interest for both regulatory and tax purposes, instead of continuing to include this interest in income as required for tax purposes. Also, some regulated banks may be applying any subsequent payments on their non-accrual loans to principal, instead of applying these subsequent payments first to any outstanding interest as required for tax purposes.

On May 21, 2007, Rev. Rul. 2007-32, 2007-1 C.B. 1278, and Rev. Proc. 2007-33, 2007-1 C.B. 1289, were published to deal with the above issues. Specifically, Rev. Rul. 2007-32 reaffirms the Service's position of what the tax law is regarding the accrual of interest on non-performing loans by regulated banks. Also, under the facts of this revenue ruling, a regulated bank under the conformity election for bad debts as provided for in Treas. Reg. Sec. 1.166-2(d), stops accruing interest on loans placed in non-accrual status for regulatory purposes and gets a bad debt deduction for previously accrued but unpaid interest, when that interest is reversed for regulatory accounting purposes. Under Rev. Proc. 2007-33, regulated banks can now elect a safe harbor method of accounting where they can limit the amount of unpaid interest on non-performing loans they have to accrue for tax purposes based on a "recovery percentage".

§ A.9.4 Discussion

Rev. Rul. 2007-32 requires that an accrual method bank with a "reasonable expectancy" of receiving future payments on a loan must include accrued interest (determined under Treas. Reg. Sec. 1.446-2(a)(2)) in gross income for the taxable year in which the right to receive the interest becomes fixed, notwithstanding bank regulatory rules that prevent accrual of the interest for regulatory purposes (i.e. loan placed in non-accrual status for regulatory purposes). This ruling also states that when an income item is properly accrued and subsequently becomes uncollectible, a taxpayer's remedy is by way of a bad debt deduction under section 166, rather than through elimination (i.e. reversal) of the accrual. Furthermore, this tax rule is applicable even when the item of income is accrued and becomes uncollectible during the same taxable year. *Spring City Foundry Co. v. Commissioner*, 292 U.S. 182 (1934).

Rev. Rul. 2007-32 also states Treas. Reg. Sec. 1.446-2(e) generally provides that each payment made on a loan is treated first as a payment of interest to the extent of any accrued interest that is uncollected on the date the payment becomes due. Similarly, the interest characterization provided for in Treas. Reg. Sec. 1.446-2(e) would apply to a payment on a loan for which the uncollected accrued interest was previously recognized as income for federal income tax purposes and subsequently deducted as a worthless debt under the taxpayer's method of accounting.

Finally, Rev. Rul. 2007-32 provides guidance as to the period in which a regulated bank that has elected the conformity method of accounting for bad debts under Treas. Reg. Sec. 1.166-2(d)(3) can treat uncollected accrued interest as worthless for tax purposes. Specifically, under the facts of this revenue ruling, a regulated bank under the conformity election can stop accruing interest on any loans placed in non-accrual status for regulatory purposes and is entitled to a bad debt deduction for previously accrued but unpaid interest, when that interest is reversed for regulatory accounting purposes. Furthermore, this treatment of accrued but unpaid interest would apply to loans placed in non-accrual status for regulatory purposes, even if the underlying loan, itself, cannot be charged off as a bad debt for tax purposes at that time.

Rev. Proc. 2007-33 provides the exclusive procedure by which an accrual method regulated bank may obtain the Commissioner's consent to change its method of accounting for uncollected interest (other than interest described in Treas. Reg. Sec. 1.446-2(a)(2)) to the safe harbor method provided in the revenue procedure. Specifically, under Rev. Proc. 2007-33, regulated banks can now elect a safe harbor method of accounting where they limit the amount of unpaid interest on non-performing loans they have to accrue for tax purposes based on a "recovery percentage".

§ A.9.5 Issue Tracking

Cases identified having this issue should use the following UIL and IMS Issue Tracking Codes:

- UIL Code – 451.11-03 – Accrued Interest on Non-Performing Loans
- IMS Issue Tracking Code – 2370 – Non-Performing Loans

§ A.9.6 Risk Analysis

This issue of non-performing loan should be considered on all examinations where the taxpayer is a regulated bank, which utilizes the accrual method for tax accounting purposes. Due to the current economic conditions, non-performing loans are likely to be present on all regulated banks. During the risk analysis process, examiners should become familiar with Rev. Rul. 2007-32 and Rev. Proc. 2007-33.

Once examiners have made a determination that the issue warrants further consideration, materiality thresholds should be established. If the issue is selected for examination, agents should contact the Banking Technical Advisor for advice and assistance to ensure consistent and uniform treatment of this issue.

§ A.9.7 Audit Techniques

In the consideration of income tax returns of regulated banks, the following techniques should be considered:

- Schedule M-3 should be reviewed to determine if there is an adjustment increasing taxable income for the accrual of interest on non-performing loans.
- The CAS should be contacted to develop a strategy to identify payments made by customers.
- Examiners should issue an IDR which contains the questions presented on Attachment A to this Memorandum.

§ A.9.8 Contacts

Any questions regarding this Directive may be addressed to the Commercial Banking Technical Advisors, Jeffrey Kammerman and William Coe or to Banking Industry Counsel, Vincent Guiliano.

This Directive is not an official pronouncement of law or the position of the Service and can not be used, cited, or relied upon as such.

Attachment A – IDR for Non-Performing Loans
cc: Commissioner, LMSB
Deputy Commissioner, Operations, LMSB
Division Counsel, LMSB
Chief, Appeals
Directors, Field Operations, LMSB
Director, Pre-Filing Technical & Guidance
Director, Performance, Quality, Analysis & Support, LMSB

§ A.9.9 Attachment A—IDR for Accrual of Interest on Non-Performing Loans

For each of the years under examination, please provide the following information:

1. Have you elected the safe harbor method of accounting for uncollected interest as provided in Rev. Proc. 2007-33? If so, when and how was the election made? Also, please provide a detailed explanation and supporting schedules of how you determined the "recovery percentage".
2. Have you elected the conformity method of accounting for bad debts under Treas. Reg. Sec. 1.166-2(d) (3)? If so, when and how was the election made?
3. Please provide a written explanation of the bank's tax policy regarding the accrual of interest on non-performing loans placed in non-accrual status for regulatory purposes. For example, did you stop accruing interest for tax purposes whenever the underlying loan was placed in non-accrual status for regulatory purposes? Also, how did you treat any accrued but unpaid interest for tax purposes once the underlying loan was placed in non-accrual status?
4. Please provide a written explanation of the bank's tax policy regarding the application of any subsequent payments on non-performing loans between uncollected accrued interest and principal. For example, is any payment on a non-performing loan for tax purposes first applied to any uncollected accrued interest, whether or not that accrued interest has previously been deducted as a bad debt?
5. Please provide a complete list of all year end account balances, both book and tax, for unpaid interest on each non-performing loan.
6. For each non-performing loan identified in question 5, please provide detailed information including whether and when that loan was placed

in non-accrual status for regulatory purposes, type of loan, borrower, collateral and balance of loan principal.

7. For each loan placed in non-accrual status for regulatory purposes during the year under examination, please provide the current status of that loan, such as was it written off, now current or renegotiated.
8. Please provide a written explanation of any Schedule M-3 differences in accrued interest income reported for book and tax, including the amounts resulting from each issue.

§A.10 FORECLOSURES: GAIN OR LOSS ON FORECLOSURES*

§A.10.1 Issues

Whether the gain or loss realized on the disposal of

a) real property received through foreclosures or deeds in lieu of foreclosure, or

b) securities/equities (stocks, bonds, warrants, *etc.*) received as part of a workout or restructuring of debt is ordinary or capital gain or loss.

§A.10.2 Facts, Law and Argument

One of the primary functions of a commercial bank is the making of loans. The interest income generated from these loans is a significant source of a bank's income. Upon default of a loan or continued non payment of interest on a loan, usually one of the following events could occur:

A) When payments are late or the borrower has trouble in meeting the terms, both parties may agree to renegotiate the loan. As part of this renegotiation or workout, the bank could receive stock or securities, warrants or options to purchase stock or securities. In return, the borrower usually pays less interest and has more time to pay the loan.

B) The bank, at time of default on the loan instrument, may acquire the collateral by either a foreclosure or deed in lieu of foreclosure. The property thus acquired is then disposed of by the bank as soon as a sale can be arranged. However, it is not uncommon for the bank to: (a) expend money to "fix up" the property; (b) in the case of uncompleted projects, to expend construction funds to complete; or (c) to rent it out until a purchaser can be found.

The basis of the property is not in question since that is the fair market value determined at the time of foreclosure.

Code [sec.] 1221 defines a capital asset to be any property held by a taxpayer except certain enumerated items. Of importance here is the exception at Code 1221(1) which provides basically for the exclusion of three types of property from the capital asset definition: (1) stock in trade, (2) property of a kind which is properly includible in a taxpayer's inventory, and (3) property held previously to sell to customers in the ordinary course of a taxpayer's trade or business.

Revenue Ruling 72-238 (1972-1 C.B., 65) involved a bank, which issued mortgage loans as a regular part of its banking business, foreclosing on a loan. The gain on the foreclosure sale was held to be ordinary income as gain arising from the ordinary operation of the banking business. Reliance was placed on IRC section 1221(4) and *Corn Products Refining Co. v. Commissioner* [55-2 USTC ¶9746], (350 U.S. 46, 51, 52 (1955) Ct. D. 1787, C.B. 1955-2, 511.

---

* This coordinated issue paper was withdrawn by the IRS effective June 26, 2006 because, according to the IRS website, the paper "no longer reflects current law and is no longer needed."

Revenue Ruling 74-159 (1974-1 C.B., 232) brings into play another aspect in dealing with this issue by addressing itself to the purpose for which the bank acquired the property. In arriving at its conclusion it stated:

> In the instant case none of the properties sold was a rental or income producing property in the hands of the bank. As in the *Mauldin* and *Brown* cases, the type and scope of the taxpayer's activities indicate that the taxpayer is in the business of selling such properties to customers in the ordinary course of such business.

Therefore, Revenue Ruling 74-159 held that the transactions came under the meaning of Section 1221 of the Code and any gain or loss on the sale thereof is ordinary rather than capital. While the ruling concludes that the property there in question was held primarily for sale to customers in the ordinary course of its trade or business within the meaning of Code [Sec.] 1221(1), the determination was made not as a matter of law but rather rested on a factual analysis, limited to the facts and circumstances of the particular case.

Further, the purpose for acquisition must now be viewed as a starting point in analyzing the issue and may not be viewed as solely determinative. In the case law that follows, each of these cases in substance reduces itself to an examination of the reason for which property is *held at the time of disposition.*

The Tax Court in *Gerard Trust Corn Exchange Bank* [Dec. 20,585], 22 T.C. 1343 (1954), addressed the issue as follows:

> The present case cannot be disposed of simply upon the narrow ground that the taxpayer is a bank or a lending institution selling property acquired by foreclosure or by deed in lieu of foreclosure. On the contrary, consideration must be given to other factors which have been recognized as significant. As stated in *Mauldin v. Commissioner,* supra, 195 F.2d at page 716:
>
> "There is no fixed formula or rule of thumb for determining whether property sold by the taxpayer was held by him primarily for sale to customers in the ordinary course of his trade or business. Each case must, in the last analysis, rest upon its own facts. There are a number of helpful factors, however, to point the way, among which are the purpose for which the property was acquired, whether for sale or investment; and continuity and frequency of sales as opposed to isolated transactions.*** (citing and reviewing many decisions.)"

Similar statements were made in the case of *Albert Winik,* supra, 17 T.C. at pages 541-542, 544. Among other cases expressing and applying the same rule are: *Martin Dressen* [Dec. 18,821], 17 T.C. 1443, 1447 (1952); *Thomas E. Wood* [Dec. 18,070], 16 T.C. 213, 226 (1951); *W.T. Thrift, Sr.,* 15 T.C. 366, 369 (1950); and *Boomhower v. United States* [48-1 USTC ¶9133], 74 F. Supp. 997 (1947).

Factually, we can imagine several scenarios: The bank acquiring property in a foreclosure or workout may within some reasonable short period of time sell the property. Particularly when dealing with real property which banks are generally precluded from holding as an investment, this situation would probably yield ordinary gain or loss.

A second scenario would have the bank deciding to utilize the property in its basis, e.g., a branch bank or as rental property. It would seem in such a situation the property would be considered as Code section 1231(b) property.

A final scenario is where the bank transfers (in some fashion) property to an investment account. Here, the result would be seem [sic] to suggest capital treatment.

In essence, it is a question of the facts and circumstances of each individual case. While the purpose for acquisition is not determinative it is, again, our starting point. Factually, it would seem that the banks acquire property in these situations in a transaction that is a normal and regular part of the everyday business of the bank. *It is necessary for the bank to establish a change in position,* e.g., a shift to an investment account, in order that capital gain treatment be justified.

It should also be stressed that while banks may well establish that their purpose for holding property was investment related, a simple passage of time, is not sufficient proof.

§ A.10.3 Examiner's Position

It is clear that regardless of the property involved, any analysis under Code [Sec.] 1221(1) requires a dissection of subjective criteria in order to determine the purpose for which the property was held. Further, case law has clearly established that such determination is made at the time the property is disposed of and not at the time of acquisition, nor during the holding period. But, because this type of property is acquired in the ordinary course of business, a clear investment motive for holding property at time of disposal must be established or the *Corn Products* doctrine will prevail and ordinary income will result.

§A.11 FORECLOSURES: INTEREST INCOME ON THE SALE OF FORECLOSED DEBT

Whether a savings and loan institution must include in gross income gain from the sale of foreclosed property to the extent there was interest which was unpaid at the time of foreclosure which had not been previously accrued.

§A.11.1 Examination Division's Position

Examination Division's position is that such gain must be included in income.

§A.11.2 Discussion

The tax treatment of the foreclosure and subsequent sale or disposition of property by a savings and loan institution is governed by IRC section 595. The basic rules set forth in that section are that (1) foreclosure is a non-taxable event and (2) any amount realized upon sale or disposition is accounted for as a payment on account of the indebtedness and any loss is treated as a bad debt. For reserve method taxpayers, such gain or loss is accounted for through adjustments to the bad debt reserve.

The Service took the position in Revenue Ruling 75-251, 1975-1 CB 175, that the portion of the gain realized upon a foreclosure sale representing the interest (as opposed to capital) characteristic of the property represents interest income in the year received.

The Service's position has been upheld in *First Charter Financial Corp.*, 669 F.2d 1342, 82-1 USTC par. 9222, CA-9 and *Gibraltar Financial Corp.*, 825 F.2d 1568, 87-2 USTC par. 9445, CA-FC, reversing 10 Cls. Ct. 31, 86-1 USTC par. 9405.

Although this issue normally arises with respect to cash basis taxpayers, it could arise with respect to an accrual basis taxpayer which had not accrued the unpaid interest. Footnote 2 in *Gibraltar Financial Corp.*, supra, indicates that the same result would obtain.

§ A.12 FORECLOSURES: INTEREST INCOME ON THE SALE OF FORECLOSED DEBT—APPEALS

§ A.12.1 Issue

Whether a cash basis savings and loan must include in gross income gain from the sale of foreclosed property to the extent it represents accrued but unpaid interest (See last page for application to accrual basis taxpayers).

§ A.12.2 Facts

This issue is addressed in Rev. Rul. 75-251, 1975-1 C.B. 175. This Revenue Ruling was validated by *Gibralter Financial Corporation of California,* 60 AFTR 2d 87-5318 and *First Charter Financial Corporation,* 669 F.2d 1342 (9th Cir. 1982).

The fact pattern is as follows. A cash basis taxpayer who uses the reserve method, for bad debts, pursuant to IRC Sections 166(c) and/or 593(a), takes possession or ownership of property securing the payment of a debt after a borrower defaults. The foreclosure or similar process by which the taxpayer takes possession or ownership of the property is governed by state law. The borrower's indebtedness includes both unpaid principal and accrued but unpaid interest. The taxpayer then disposes of or sells the property at a gain in excess of its basis in the property. The taxpayer's basis in the property is defined in IRC section 595 as the "basis of the indebtedness for which such property was security (determined as of the date of the acquisition of such property) properly increased for costs of acquisition." Treas. Reg. Section 1.595-1(d) states that the taxpayer's basis in the property includes the amount of any accrued but unpaid interest on the indebtedness but only if the taxpayer has included the accrued but unpaid interest in its gross income. A cash method taxpayer would not have included the accrued but unpaid interest in its gross income, therefore its basis in the property would not include the accrued but unpaid interest.

§ A.12.3 Applicable Law

IRC Section 595 controls the tax consequences of a foreclosure and subsequent sale of property by a 593(a) organization. It states in full:

(a) Nonrecognition of Gain or Loss as a Result of Foreclosure. In the case of a creditor which is an organization described in section 593(a), no gain or loss shall be recognized, and no debt shall be considered as becoming worthless or partially worthless, as the result of such organization having bid in at foreclosure, or having otherwise reduced to ownership or possession by agreement or process of law, any property which was security for the payment of any indebtedness.

(b) Character of Property. For purposes of sections 166 and 1221, any property acquired in a transaction with respect to which gain or loss to an organization was not recognized by reason of subsection (a) shall be considered as property having the same characteristics as the indebtedness for which such property was security. Any amount realized by such organization with respect to such property shall be treated for purposes of this chapter as a payment on account of such indebtedness, and any loss with respect thereto shall be treated as a bad debt to which the provisions of section 166 (relating to allowance of a deduction for bad debts) apply.

(c) Basis. The basis of any property to which subsection (a) applies shall be the basis of the indebtedness for which such property was secured (determined as of the date of the acquisition of such property), properly increased for costs of acquisition.

(d) Regulatory Authority. The Secretary shall prescribe such regulations as he may deem necessary to carry out the purposes of this section.

The Senate Finance Committee Report states that 595 was included in the Revenue Act of 1962, Pub. L. No. 87-834, Sec. 6, to eliminate the often erratic results that were produced by treating the foreclosure as a taxable event. Pursuant to IRC Sec. 595, a foreclosure is not a taxable event, and "amounts received by [a 595(a) organization]subsequent to the foreclosure are to be treated as payments on the indebtedness." S. Rep. No. 1881, 87th Cong., 2nd Sess. 47, reprinted in 1962 U.S. Code Cong. & Admin News 3297, 3550 (1962). In effect, IRC sec. 595 collapses the "foreclosure, purchase, and resale of property into a single transaction for tax purposes." *First Charter,* 669 F.2d at 1347, citing *Allstate Savings & Loan Association,* 68 T.C. 310, 317 (1977), *aff'd* 600 F.2d 760 (9th Cir. 1979), *cert. denied,* 445 U.S. 962 (1980).

IRC sec. 595(b) states that property in the hands of a sec. 593(a) organization has the same "characteristics as the indebtedness for which such property was security" and "any amount realized" is considered "payment on account of such indebtedness." The Senate Finance Committee Report explains the consequences of this by stating:

> When the property is ultimately sold or disposed of, the difference between the amount realized and the original or previously reduced debt is to be treated as ordinary loss or income and [sic or] is to be charged, or credited as the case may be, against the reserve for losses on qualifying real property loans. Because the foreclosed property is to have the same characteristics as the indebtedness, where property is rented by the mutual thrift institution after foreclosure, no depreciation deduction is to be permitted.

S. Rep. No. 1881, 87th Cong., 2nd Sess. 47, reprinted in 1962 U.S. Code Cong & Admin News 3297, 3550.

As explained by the Senate Finance Committee Report, upon the sale of the foreclosed property, a taxpayer who uses the reserve method for bad debts would charge, or credit, his reserve depending on whether the gain from the sale was less than, or greater than, his basis in the property.

§ A.12.4 Argument

The issue arises when the proceeds from the sale are in excess of a cash method taxpayer's basis and there is accrued but unpaid interest on the original indebtedness. The Service's position is that for a cash method taxpayer the proceeds in excess of basis, to the extent of the accrued but unpaid interest on the original indebtedness, must be included in gross income. *Gibraltar,* 825 F.2d at

1570; *First Charter*, 669 F.2d at 1347; Rev. Rul. 75-251. A gain in excess of the cash method taxpayer's basis plus accrued but unpaid interest would be credited to the taxpayer's reserve for bad debts as explained by the Senate Finance Committee Report. Essentially a portion of the gain is being carved out for inclusion in gross income to the extent it represents accrued but unpaid interest.

§ A.12.5 Application to Accrual Basis Taxpayers

It should be noted that an accrual method taxpayer would normally have included the unpaid interest in gross income as it accrued, and as a consequence the taxpayer would have increased its basis in the property under Treas. Reg. Sec. 1.595-1(d). If all accrued interest has already been included in gross income, recovery of the interest upon the sale of foreclosed property cancels out the increase in basis so no credit is assigned to the bad debt reserve.

If an accrual basis taxpayer did not accrue the interest income prior to the foreclosure, they would be in the same position as a cash method lender and would be required to carve out the interest portion as reportable gross income. This position is supported by the Gibraltar decision.

Footnote 2 of that decision refers to the body of case law which deemed a lender to have received ordinary income to the extent of accrued but unpaid interest upon the acquisition of property in a foreclosure which developed prior to the enactment of section 595. It states: "This body of case law did not apply to an accrual basis mortgagee who had already reported the interest as income prior to the foreclosure, which would generally be the case. If the interest income were not properly accruable (e.g. because collection was too uncertain) an accrual method lender would be on the same footing as a cash method lender. See *Corn Exch. Bank v. United States*, 37 F.2d 34, 35." *Gibraltar Financial Corporation*, 60 AFTR 2d 87-5318 at 5321.

The Court further stated "Section 595 applies not only to the reserve method taxpayers of section 593, but also to non-reserve method taxpayers. We see no policy reason that requires overturning the treatment of recovered interest when that was the situation under section 593 prior to the 1962 amendments." *Gibraltar Financial Corporation*, 60 AFTR 2d 87-5318 at 5322.

§ A.13 VALIDITY OF TREASURY REGULATIONS SECTION 1.593-6A(B)(5)(VI)

§ A.13.1 Issue

Is Treasury Regulations section 1.593-6A(b)(5)(vi) a valid regulation?

§ A.13.2 Facts

In 1978 the regulations under section 1.593-6A(b)(5) were revised. This revision contained the current provisions which require a recomputation of the bad debt deduction in the event of a NOL carryback.

§ A.13.3 Law Discussion

IRC section 593 permits a savings & loan to deduct for tax purposes a reasonable addition to a reserve for bad debts. Section 593(b) provides that this shall include a reasonable addition to the reserve for losses on qualifying real property loans. That section sets forth several alternative methods of calculating the deductible amount. Under the percentage of taxable income method the savings & loan is permitted to deduct a statutory percentage of taxable income. In 1969 the percentage was 60% and gradually decreased to 40% in 1979. The current 8% rate began in 1987.

Section 593(b) also states that "taxable income," for purposes of the bad debt deduction computation, shall be computed by excluding several types of income, including grain arising from the sale of stock and certain dividends. Section 593 does not make any explicit reference to a NOL carried back from a subsequent year or the effect of such NOL on the taxable income computation. Treas. Reg. section 1.593-6A(b)(5)(vii), however, specifically provides that for years beginning after 1977, taxable income under IRC section 593(b) shall be adjusted for a NOL carryback, requiring recomputation of the bad debt deduction. Regulation 1.593-6A(b)(5)(vi), moreover, provides that for years beginning before 1978, such bad debt deduction must similarly be recomputed in the event of a NOL carryback, unless such NOL originates in a year prior to 1979.

IRC section 593(b)(2) provides for a bad debt computation based on "taxable income." Regulations section 1.593-6A(b)(5) provides exceptions to the regular definition of taxable income but neither section provides a definition of taxable income. Section 63 of the IRC provides the necessary definition. It defines "taxable income" as gross income minus the deductions allowed by Chapter 1 of the Internal Revenue Code, which includes the NOL deduction set forth in IRC section 172. Congress made a comprehensive revision to section 1.593-6A(b)(5) in 1969 (which included an exhaustive list of exceptions to taxable income for section 593 purposes) but did not include a provision for NOL's. The revised regulations published in 1978 which call for a recomputation of the bad debt deduction in the event of a NOL carryback are therefore consistent with the Code and the intent of Congress.

§ A.13.4 Conclusion

Regulation section 1.593-6A(b)(5)(vi) is a valid regulation. Accordingly, if there is an NOL carryback originating after 1978, the savings & loan must adjust taxable income by such NOL carryback and recompute the bad debt deduction for the carryback year based upon the adjusted taxable income.

§ A.14 CORE DEPOSIT INTANGIBLES (COMMERCIAL BANK)

§ A.14.1 Issue

Should the excess purchase price paid for a bank over the tangible assets acquired be treated as goodwill/going concern value or as an amortizable intangible asset called core deposit intangible?

§ A.14.2 Recommended Position

As a general rule the core deposit intangible is indistinguishable from goodwill/going concern value.

§ A.14.3 Facts, Law & Argument

The Office of the Comptroller of the Currency (O.C.C.) issued circular #164 on December 29, 1981 which provides that national banks could, under appropriate circumstances, capitalize and amortize the value of the customer deposit relationships. A similar policy was adopted by the FDIC on March 5, 1982. Banks intending to record such assets must obtain prior approval from the Comptroller of the Currency and the S.E.C.

The O.C.C. defines *Core Deposits* as the deposit base of demand and savings accounts which, while usually not legally restricted, are generally based on stable customer relationships that the bank can expect to maintain for an extensive period of time, often many years. Jumbo certificates of deposit ($100,000 denomination or more) are normally excluded from the definition as they are considered more indicative of a borrower rather than customer relationship.

The *Core Deposit Intangible* is the present value of the future net income stream associated with a Bank's deposit.

Accountants characterize goodwill as the potential of a business to earn above normal profits. Conceptually, goodwill is the present value of the expected future excess earnings. Goodwill arises as a result of such factors as customer acceptance, efficiency of operation, location, internal competency and financial standing.

In *Herndon v. Commissioner* [Dec. 25,596(M)], 21 TCM (1962), the Tax Court stated that "goodwill" may refer to the expectation that customers of an established business will continue their patronage.

"Going concern value" is related to the ability of an established business, fully equipped and staffed, to generate earnings without interruption because of a change in ownership (*Winn-Dixie Montgomery Inc. v. United States* [71-1 USTC ¶ 9488], 444 F.2d 667-5th Cir. 1971). It is an intangible asset that exists as a value enhancement for the assemblage of a business and is not depreciable. (*Cornish et al. v. United States* [65-2 USTC ¶ 9508], 348 F.2d 175)

In *Rev. Rul. 74-456,* the government held that, generally, customer and subscription lists (when considered as mass, indivisible assets) location contracts, insurance expirations, *etc.* represent the customer structure of a business, whose value lasts until an indeterminate time in the future. Such assets are in the nature of goodwill or otherwise have indeterminate lives. The ruling assumes that a mass asset is really one asset the loss of any part of which is offset in a continuing manner by additions there to; the "regenerative theory." It should be noted that bankers themselves liken core deposit to customers lists.

In *First National Bank of Omaha v. Commissioner,* T.C. Memo 1975-67, the Court in its citation of *First Pennsylvania Banking and Trust Co.* [Dec. 30,859], 56 TC 677, noted: "If, however, the purchaser has not paid for mortgage servicing rights but rather has purchased goodwill, going concern value, business organizations, *investor and borrower relationships,* (emphasis added) opportunities for future business and income and similar intangibles, he is not entitled to a deduction for amortization."

In contrast, in *Midlantic National Bank v. Commissioner* [Dec. 40,477(M)], 46 TCM 1464, the Tax Court factually determined that no goodwill or going concern value was acquired in the transaction and that the solicitation right acquired from the FDIC was a separate asset. But in this case, the acquiror bid for the right to solicit the failed bank's depositors as they were being paid off by the FDIC. As accounts attributable to the solicitation rights were closed, the taxpayer de ducted amounts allocated to that account. The court essentially treated the solicitation rights as customer lists where amortization may be allowed. However, the treatment of costs to acquire the right to solicit the former depositors of a failed bank *in order to develop a new deposit base* must be distinguished from the treatment of costs incurred to acquire a pre-existing deposit base of both a going concern bank and, in most cases, of a failing bank where the doors never close but the signs of ownership merely change from one day to the next. Here, none of the amount paid to acquire the deposit base would be depreciable because there is no wasting asset in an ongoing stream of customers and their deposits.

In *Southern Bancorporation Inc. v. United States* [84-1 USTC ¶9396], (4th cir 1984) the circuit court rejected the taxpayer's post hoc upward revaluation of the loan portfolio it acquired and found the premium paid to acquire a failing bank was attributable to its going concern value. Although the bid was figured as a percentage of the largest deposits, the taxpayer did not pursue its argument that it acquired "cheap money," which it believed was an amortizable asset.

The Court noted that the taxpayer had failed to show that it intended to pay an enhanced value for the loan portfolio at the time of acquisition. The court was persuaded by the evidence offered by the government which indicated that the loans in aggregate were worth less, not more, than face, and that the premium was paid to obtain the going concern value of the largest branches.

In *Banc One* (84 TC 476; Dec. 41,985), the Court rejected the taxpayer's method of estimating the useful life of the core deposits primarily because the information relied upon by the taxpayer to compute the deposit lives was based upon hindsight. The deposit base studies submitted by the taxpayer relied upon events occurring after the date of acquisition and, therefore, post hoc valuations of the core deposit base could find no legal support for amortization. Although the Court did recognize that reasonable approximations are appropriate in establishing the useful life of an asset, the date used must be contemporaneous and not post hoc. No opinion was expressed, therefore, as to whether core deposit intangibles are properly amortizable since the issue was otherwise decided.

§ A.14.4 Conclusion

Based on the cited authorities our position should be that the so called core deposit intangible is not sufficiently distinguishable from goodwill/going concern value to allow a deduction for amortization.

§ A.15 CORE DEPOSIT INTANGIBLES (THRIFT)

§ A.15.1 Issue

Should the excess purchase price paid for a savings and loan association over the tangible assets acquired, be treated as goodwill/ going concern value or as an amortizable intangible asset called core deposit intangibles.

§ A.15.2 Recommended Position

As a general rule, the core deposit intangible is indistinguishable from goodwill/going concern value.

§ A.15.3 Discussion

There have been many mergers and acquisitions in the thrift industry in recent years. Some financial institutions have been acquired for as much as 2 1/2 times book value. Rather than identify the entire purchase premium as goodwill, savings and loan institutions have allocated this premium to other amortizable intangibles.

One of the most prominent of these intangible assets is the "core deposit intangible." The Comptroller of the Currency has defined "core deposit intangible" as the deposit base of demand and savings accounts which, while not usually legally restricted, are generally based on stable customer relationships that the financial institution can expect to maintain for an extensive period of time, often many years. [Jumbo Certificates of deposit, $100,000 denominations or more, are normally excluded from this definition as they are considered more indicative of a borrower-type, rather than a customer relationship.]

Historically, intangible assets have been amortized for book purposes by both banks and thrifts. National banks were allowed to capitalize and amortize the value of customer deposit relationships "under appropriate circumstances" by the Comptroller of the Currency on December 21, 1981 (Circular #164). The F.D.I.C. adopted a similar policy on March 5, 1982.

The Internal Revenue Code also allows amortization of intangible assets. Treas. Reg. 1.167a-1 provides that depreciation of an intangible asset is allowable if that asset has a limited useful life which can be estimated with reasonable accuracy, an ascertainable value, and is separate and distinct from goodwill. No depreciation deduction is allowed for goodwill.

Accountants characterize goodwill as the potential of a business to earn above normal profits. Conceptually, goodwill is the present value of the expected future excess earnings. Goodwill arises as a result of such factors as customer acceptance, efficiency of operation, location, internal competency and financial standing.

The United States District Court for the Northern District of Alabama has ruled in favor of the Service on the core deposit issue. In *AmSouth Bancorporation and Subsidiaries,* 88-1 USTC 9232 (2-25-88), the Court specifically ruled that the bank was not entitled to depreciate the customer deposit base it acquired through the purchase of the assets and liabilities of another financial institution. The Court ruled that the customer deposit base is inseparable from goodwill.

The courts have also spoken at length to the question of what constitutes goodwill. In *Boe v. Commissioner*, 307 F.2d 339 (9th Cir. 1962), the court stated that . . . the essence of goodwill is the expectancy of continued patronage, for whatever reason . . . at 343. The Tax Court has defined goodwill as the probability that old customers will resort to the 'old place' without contractual compulsion. *Brooks v. Commissioner*, 36 TC 1128, at 1133. (1961). This definition has also been used in the Fifth and Seventh Circuits. See: *Commissioner v. Killiam*, 314 F.2d 852, 855 (5th Cir. 1963) and *Karan v. Commissioner*, 319 F.2d 303, 306 (7th Cir. 1963).

In Revenue Ruling 74-456, the government held that, generally, customer and subscription lists (when considered as mass, indivisible assets), location contracts, insurance expirations, *etc.*, represent the customer structure of a business, whose value lasts until an indeterminate time in the future. Such assets are in the nature of goodwill or otherwise have indeterminate lives. The ruling assumes that a mass asset is really one asset, the loss of any part of which is offset in a continuing manner by additions thereto; the "regenerative theory." It should be noted that bankers themselves like core deposits to customers lists.

The Tax Court in *First National Bank of Omaha v. Commissioner*, TC Memo 1975-67, 34 TCM 360 (1975) citing to *First Pennsylvania Banking and Trust*, 56 TC 677 (1971), noted "If, however, the purchaser has not paid for mortgage servicing rights, but rather has purchased goodwill, going concern value, business organizations, *investor and borrower relationships* (emphasis added), opportunities for future business and income and similar intangibles, he is not entitled to a deduction for amortization." at 364.

In contrast, the Court in *Midlantic National Bank v. Commissioner*, TC Memo 1983-581, 46 TCM 1464 (1983) factually determined that no goodwill or going concern value was acquired in a transaction involving the acquisition of the right to solicit the customers of an insolvent bank, which was obtained separately from the F.D.I.C. The petitioner successfully bid for the right to solicit the depositors of a failed financial institution as those depositors were being paid off by the F.D.I.C. When an account attributable to that particular solicitation was subsequently closed, the petitioner deducted an amount allocated to the acquisition of that account.

The Tax Court determined that the solicitation right that petitioners acquired was the approximate equivalent of an acquired customer list, and allowed the deductions. However, the treatment of costs to acquire the right to solicit *former* depositors of another, failed institution, in order to *develop a new deposit base* in another separate institution is distinguishable from the treatment of costs incurred to acquire a preexisting deposit base in a going-concern thrift which is made part of the taxpayer's network of financial institutions. This would also be the case when the failed institution is not closed, but rather the signs of ownership merely changed from one day to the next. In these cases, the amounts paid to acquire the deposit base would not be amortizable or depreciable because there is no wasting asset but rather an ongoing stream of customers and deposits.

In *Southern Bancorporation, Inc. v. United States*, 732 F.2d 374 (4th Cir. 1984) the circuit court rejected the taxpayer's post hoc upward revaluation of the loan portfolio it acquired, and found the premium paid to acquire a failing bank was attributable to its going concern value. Although the bid to acquire the failed institution was calculated as a percentage of the largest deposits, the taxpayer did not pursue its argument that, it had acquired "cheap money," which it believed was an amortizable asset. The Court noted that the taxpayer had failed to show that it intended to pay an enhanced value for the loan portfolio at the time of acquisition. The Court was persuaded by the evidence offered by the government which indicated that the loans in aggregate were worth less, not more, than face, and that the premium was paid to obtain the going concern value of the largest branches.

This decision was subsequently appealed and the decision of the Tax Court was affirmed by the 4th Circuit on 5-16-88. Refer to 88-1 USTC 9344.

The Tax Court in *Banc One Corp. v. Commissioner*, TC 476 (1985) also held that the petitioner was not entitled to deduct depreciation for core deposits. The Court rejected the taxpayer's method of estimating the useful life of the core deposits primarily because the information relied upon in the computation was based on hindsight. The taxpayer submitted deposit base studies which relied upon events occurring after the acquisition date. The Court ruled that evidence of experience subsequent to the year in issue could be used as *corroboration* for establishing a useful life, but it could not be used to *support* the computation. Since the Court rejected the computation, and thus decided the issue, it expressed no opinion as to whether core deposit intangibles are properly amortizable.

§ A.15.4 Conclusion

Based on the arguments and authorities cited above, our position should be that the so-called "core deposit intangible" is not sufficiently distinguishable from goodwill/going concern value to allow a deduction for amortization.

§A.16 DEBT-EQUITY SWAPS

Authors Note: The IRS draft paper below, prepared by the IRS Banking Industry Group, discusses whether a bank can retire its debentures in exchange for its common stock, realize a book gain on the swap, and treat the exchange as a tax-free reorganization. It concludes that a bank generally may retire its debentures through the issuance of its stock (a debt-equity swap) and claim tax-free treatment for the exchange. However, where a brokerage firm acts in an agency and underwriting capacity for the bank, the substance of such a transaction can result in the bank realizing and recognizing a taxable gain on the sale of its debentures equal to the difference between the face value of the debentures that are retired and the fair market value of the stock used to retire those debenture. This is true notwithstanding the fact that the swap may have been structured to indicate that the brokerage firm was acting as a principal in the exchange. While this draft paper has been withdrawn and is not under consideration as a coordinated issue, it is the author's opinion that it illustrates the IRS's analysis of this issue.

§A.16.1 Issue

Whether a bank can retire its debentures in exchange for its common stock and thereby realize a book gain on the swap (debt-equity swaps), while treating the exchange as a non-taxable reorganization per I.R.C. Sections 368(a)(1)(E) and 361(a).

§A.16.2 Facts, Law & Arguments

The fact pattern described below is typical of the debt-equity swap transaction. The bank exchanges its own debentures, the face amount of which is in excess of its fair market value, plus accrued interest, for shares of its common stock having a fair market value less than the face amount of the debentures. Prior to the transaction, the bonds are owned by other, unrelated banks.

The exchange is arranged by a brokerage/investment banking firm who is paid a fee for "rounding up" the bonds. The brokerage firm is also given a preferential rate on the exchange rate of the stock for the bonds. The stock is valued on the day of the exchange at 95% of its fair market value whereas the bonds are valued at their full cost to the brokerage firm. In other words, the brokerage firm is receiving stock at a discount for 5% from its fair market value.

The results of this exchange is as follows: 1) the bond holders sold their debentures to the brokerage firm and realized and recognized a loss on the difference between the face amount of the bonds and the discounted fair market value; 2) the brokerage firm earned a set fee plus an additional amount for rounding up the bonds and turning them over to the bank for their common stock valued at 95 cents on the dollar. As part of the transaction, the bank registered this stock with the Securities Exchange Commission so that it was freely marketable by the brokerage firm; 3) the bank was able to retire its debentures through the issuance of common stock thereby realizing a book gain amounting to the difference between the face value of the debentures and the fair market value of the stock.

> The bank treated this exchange as a non-taxable reorganization per I.R.C. 368(a)(1)(E) and 361(a).
>
> A good starting point for an analysis of the exchange would be Treasury Regulations Section 1.368-1(b).
>
> Under the general rule, upon the exchange of property, gain or loss must be accounted for if the new property differs in a "material particular," either in kind or in extent from the old property. The purpose of the reorganization provisions of the Code is to except from the general rule certain specifically described exchanges incident to such readjustments of corporate structures made in one of the particular ways specified in the Code, as are required by business exigencies and which effect only a readjustment of *continuing interest* in property under modified corporate forms. Requisite to a reorganization under the Code are a continuity of the business enterprise under the modified corporate form, and . . . a *continuity of interest* therein on the part of those persons who . . . were the owners of the enterprise prior to the reorganization (Emphasis Added).

The latter part of this regulation requires continuity both on the part of the corporation and on the part of the securities holder. There is no doubt we have continuity on the corporate part, as the bank survived the exchange with only a minor difference to its corporate structure. However, there is no continuity on the part of the security holders. These security holders cashed in their investment by selling the bonds to the brokerage firm. The common stock which was exchanged for the bonds was sold to *other parties* who had nothing to do with the bonds before this transaction.

The U.S. Supreme Court defined a recapitalization as the "reshuffling of a capital structure within the framework of an existing corporation." *Helvering v. Southwest Consol. Corp.* 315 U.S. 194 (1942). The framework of an existing corporation means changes within the interest of existing bond holders and shareholders; it does not encompass the wholesale deletion of a class of bond holders and substitution of new stockholders in their place.

Apparently in this case the bank takes the position that the *brokerage firm* is the debenture holder and the *brokerage firm* exchanges the bonds for stock thereby downgrading their status from creditor to shareholder. In this case continuity of interest would be present as the old bond holder and new shareholder are the same person-namely, the brokerage firm. However, the facts of this case argue against considering the brokerage firm a party to the reorganization. It is obvious that the brokerage firm had no intention of retaining the stock after it was exchanged for the bonds as the Plan of Reorganization calls for the stock to be registered with the S.E.C. for it to be freely marketable and contemplates the use of other underwriters to dispose of the stock.

Furthermore the bank agreed to issue the certificates to whomever the brokerage firm said they would be issued to. It is questionable whether the brokerage firm was ever listed as a shareholder or bond holder on the books of the corporation.

Revenue Ruling 66-23 (C.B. 1966-1) sheds some light on holding period requirements after a reorganization saying that "unrestricted rights of ownership for a period of time sufficient to warrant the conclusion that such ownership is definite and substantial" will suffice, and that "ordinarily, the Service will treat five years of unrestricted . . . ownership as a sufficient period" for continuity of interest purposes. Furthermore, the ruling notes that "a preconceived plan or arrangement" to dispose of the acquiring corporation's stock would cause trouble, at least if more than 50% of the stock is disposed of by the transferor's shareholders under the plan. The leading treatise on corporate taxation adds that "it seems to be generally acceptable that shareholders of the transferor are relatively free to sell part or all of the stock received by them in the exchange if they are under no binding obligation to do so, without fear of breaking the reorganization, al though it is arguable that a preconceived plan for such a sale would be fatal even without a formal commitment." Bittker and Eustice, *Federal Income Taxation of Corporations and Shareholders*, Par. 14-11 at 5.

Everything done by the brokerage firm in this transaction more resembles the dealings of an underwriter rather than of a true investor. They earned a profit by performing a service, indeed they were guaranteed a profit. A bona fide investor, on the other hand ties his/her profits or losses to the fortunes of the company he/she invests in. The reorganization provisions were drafted with the investor in mind—to exempt from tax mere changes in the form of investment—not to exempt from tax two separate purchase and sale transactions. The brokerage firm was paid a fee for doing so. The brokerage firm was practically insulated from loss on the transaction as the exchange value of the bonds was based upon the fair market value of the bonds on the exchange date. The brokerage firm also received interest on the money advanced by them to purchase the bonds. In addition, the liquidation of damages provision was written so as to reimburse the brokerage firm for the cost of the bonds plus any out of pocket expenses. Clearly it appears that the brokerage firm was merely performing a service for the bank in the purchase of these debentures.

The bulk of the brokerage firm's fee was to be earned on the sale of the stock which was valued in the exchange at 95 ¢ on the dollar. The brokerage firm would earn their 5 ¢ per share fee on the later sale of the stock at full market value. This is precisely the function of an underwriter.

The Securities Act of 1933 defines an underwriter as "any person who has purchased from an issuer with a view to . . . the distribution of any security." 15 *U.S.C.A.* Section 77b. Whatever work characterizes the actions of the brokerage firm—be it agent, broker or underwriter, it is certainly to be distinguished from the actions of an investor, or principal who is one who invests for his/her own account and takes on the risk of loss and other burdens or benefits of ownership. It is for this latter type of individual that the reorganization provisions were designed to protect. Since the brokerage firm is not a bona fide principal, the exchange of bonds for stock is not a qualified reorganization, and the bank should be taxed on their gain from cancellation of indebtedness income. This brings us to a discussion of whether I.R.C. Section 1032 exempts the bank from recognizing their gain.

Section 1032 of the IRC says "No gain or loss shall be recognized to a corporation on the receipt of money or other property in exchange for stock of such corporation." But this section should not be applied to the instant situation. In the case at hand, the brokerage firm was function ing as agent of the bank in both the acquisition of its debentures and then in a separate transaction, the sale of its stock.

Typically, a statement included in the exchange agreement between the bank and the brokerage firm states, "All acquisitions . . . all exchanges . . . and all distributions by the brokerage firm . . . are for the brokerage firm's own account and not for the account of the issuer: and no principle-agent [sic] relationship is created between the issuer and the brokerage firm by any of the provisions of this agreement."

Despite the extract quoted above, the agreements also in essence require the bank to guarantee that the brokerage firm is made whole in case of any loss. This is not the assurance given to a brokerage house when they buy debentures for their own account. If the brokerage firm and the bank were in fact two independent parties, then why is the bank guaranteeing that the brokerage firm will not incur any loss? This relationship between the bank and the brokerage house seems on its face to negate any assertion of independence. If the brokerage firm was acting on its own then it should have taken all risks when it purchased the debentures from the holders. In a stock for debentures exchange, the bank should have been required to issue the stock—not to pay up in cash. The essence of the entire transaction, involved the purchase for retirement of bonds at a discount and the subsequent stock sale.

When the brokerage firm purchased the debentures for less than its face value, the bank had income as defined by IRC 61(a)(12).

In defining gross income IRS Section 61(a) says "Gross income means all income . . . including (12) Income from discharge of indebtedness." Regs 1.61-12(c)(3) is exactly on point ". . . bonds are issued by a corporation and subsequently repurchased by the corporation at a price which is exceeded by the issue price . . . the amount of such excess is income for the taxable year." This reg addresses itself to the situation at hand.

When taking into account the substance over form doctrine, we find that the entire agreement was set up for the brokerage firm to acquire the bank's debentures and then sell the bank's stock. Had this been a true swap, the bank should have given the stock to the brokerage firm to distribute before the brokerage firm acquired any of the bank's debentures.

§ A.16.3 Examiner's Position

Although a bank may retire its debentures through the issuance of its stock (a debt—equity swap) and claim that the exchange should be treated as a nontaxable I.R.C. Section 368(a)(1)(E) reorganization, based upon the facts above, it is held that:

1. The brokerage firm is acting in an agency and underwriting capacity for the bank in the above transactions, although the swap is structured to show that the brokerage firm is acting as a principal and, therefore
2. The substance of the transaction resulted in the bank realizing and recognizing a taxable gain on the sale of their debenture equal to the difference between the face value of the debentures that are retired and the fair market value of the stock used to retire those debentures.

§A.17 GROSS UP OF NET FOREIGN LOANS

§A.17.1 Issue

1. Whether an amount equal to the foreign withholding taxes paid by borrowers pursuant to "net" loan agreements must be included in gross income of the lender in the taxable year in which the obligation of the borrower to pay such taxes arose.
2. If the foreign withholding tax is creditable and included in the income of the lender, whether such taxes recognized for purposes of inclusion in the lender's gross income are also considered documented for purposes of the foreign tax credit in accordance with Section 905 of the IRC.
3. Whether the accrued income can be reduced by a deduction or otherwise to reflect a reduction in the corresponding amount of foreign tax credits allowed the lender.

§A.17.2 FACTS, LAW AND ARGUMENT

The bank, a domestic corporation, during the year under examination negotiated foreign loans on a net basis whereby any foreign taxes due thereon were to be paid and be the responsibility of the debtor. The type or form of the loan varies but the ultimate result is that the borrower pays the bank the full interest rate stated in the contract, not reduced by any foreign taxes. Any foreign taxes due are, under the loan agreement, the responsibility of the borrower.

Under the laws of the foreign countries of the borrowing companies, the bank is the "technical taxpayer" of the relevant taxes and has a liability to pay income tax on the amount of interest received with respect to such loans and that in the event of the failure of a borrower to pay such tax, the lender must pay the tax. Typically, the foreign borrower is obligated to submit to the lender documentation proving payment of the tax. Failure to provide such evidence is an event leading to default. The failure to submit documentation may reflect the fact that (1) the foreign borrower failed to discharge the lender's tax liability, (2) the borrower merely neglected to submit the documentation, or (3) there never was a foreign tax liability.

In a Technical Advice issued on March 22, 1979, concerning this issue, it was held that: (1) the lender is entitled to claim a foreign tax credit for the tax paid by a borrower pursuant to a "net" loan agreement under which interest is received by the lender without deduction for the tax; (2) The tax assumed by the borrower is includible in gross income of the lender as additional interest income in the taxable year in which the lender accrued its tax obligation; and (3) The tax, includible in the gross income of the lender as additional interest income, remains to be properly documented, in accordance with section 905 of the Code and section 1.905-2 of the Income Tax Regulations, because such documentation is independent of and not satisfied by the inclusion of additional income with respect to such tax. In addition, the Technical Advice, citing *Acme Coal Co. v. United States* [2 USTC ¶597], 44 F.2d 95 (Ct. Cl. 1970), provided in the rationale that if the amount of income accrued by the lender differs from the amount of the actual tax liability ultimately assumed and paid, an adjustment to income for the year of accrual is to be made.

In some instances, the lender has taken the position that one only has to include as additional income that amount that will match foreign taxes documented as paid for foreign tax credit purposes (the "paper" system). Initially, the lender only includes in its tax return for the year in which the foreign tax liability accrues such income amount and corresponding foreign tax credits that can be documented at that time. If it receives additional documentation for the foreign taxes in later years, on audit or by claim, the lender submits the additional documentation and claims additional income and credits for the earlier year in which the foreign tax liability properly accrued.

Section 451(a) of the Code provides a general rule that the amount of any item of gross income shall be included in the gross income for the taxable year in which received by the taxpayer, unless, under the method of accounting used in computing taxable income, such amount is to be properly accounted for as of a different period.

Section 1.451-1(a) of the regulations provides, in part, that under an accrual method of accounting, income is includible in gross income when all the events have occurred which fix the right to receive such income and the amount thereof can be determined with reasonable accuracy.

Section 461(a) of the Code provides, in part, that the amount of any deduction or credit shall be taken for the taxable year which is the proper taxable year under the method of accounting used in computing taxable income.

Section 1.461-1(a)(2) of the regulations provides, in part, that under an accrual method of accounting, an expense is deductible for the taxable year in which all the events have occurred which determine the fact of the liability and the amount thereof can be determined with reasonable accuracy.

Section 166(a)(1) of the Code allows a deduction for any debt that becomes worthless within the taxable year. Section 166(c) provides, in lieu of deduction under section 166(a), that there shall be allowed (in the discretion of the Secretary) a deduction for a reasonable addition to a reserve for bad debts.

Section 1.166-1(c) of the regulations provides that only a bona fide debt qualifies for purposes of section 166 of the Code and defines a bona fide debt as a debt that arises from a debtor-creditor relationship based upon a valid and enforceable obligation to pay a fixed or determinable sum of money.

Section 1.166-2(a) of the regulations provides, in part, that in determining whether a debt is worthless in whole or in part the district director will consider all pertinent evidence, including the financial condition of the debtor.

Section 1.166-2(d) of the regulations provides that if a bank, which is subject to supervision of federal authorities, charges off a debt in whole or in part in obedience to the specific orders of such authority, then the debt shall to the extent charged off and deducted for federal income tax purposes, be conclusively presumed to be worthless during the taxable year.

If one discharges the tax liability of another, the taxpayer who is liable for the tax realizes additional income. *Old Colony Trust v. Commissioner* [1 USTC ¶408], 279 U.S. 716 (1929). An accrual basis taxpayer must accrue additional income for taxes assumed by another at the time such taxes are properly accruable and the obligation is assumed, and not at a time in the future when the assumed tax liability is ultimately satisfied. Rev. Rul. 57-106, 1957-1 C.B. 242, as modified by Rev. Rul. 78-258, 1978-1 C.B. 239; *Commissioner v. Terre Haute Electric Co.* [3 USTC ¶1176], 67 F.2d 697 (7th Cir. 1934). In accordance with the all events test of section 1.461-1(a) of the regulations, an expense is deductible when all the events have occurred which determine the fact of the liability, and the amount of the liability can be determined with reasonable accuracy. With respect to the facts previously cited, the fact and the amount of the lender's liability for foreign taxes is known when the liability is fixed and the tax payment becomes due; generally this occurs when the interest is paid to the lender or, in some countries, when the interest payment is due. Therefore, the lender must accrue additional income at the time its assumed foreign tax liability is accruable by it under section 1.461-1(a) of the regulations (*i.e.*, when the liability is fixed to pay the tax), and not when the liability is ultimately satisfied by the borrower. In addition, in order to receive a foreign tax credit for the accrued foreign taxes, the lender must submit proper documentation under section 905(b) of the Code and section 1.905-2 of the regulations. This documentation requirement is not satisfied by, and is independent of, the inclusion of additional income resulting from the borrowers's [sic] assumption of the lender's foreign tax liability.

"When an income item is properly accrued and subsequently becomes uncollectible, a taxpayer's remedy is by way [of] a deduction rather than through elimination of the accrual. Moreover, this rule is applicable even when the item is accrued and becomes uncollectible during the same taxable year." Rev. Rul. 80-361, 1980-2 C.B. 164, *citing Spring City Foundry Co. v. Commissioner* [4 USTC ¶1276], 292 U.S. 182 (1934), III-1 C.B. 28 (1934) and *Atlantic Coast Line Railroad Co. v. Commissioner* [Dec. 8817], 31 B.T.A. 730, 751 (1934) acq. XIV-2 C.B. [7252] (1935). Although the lender may not reverse a proper accrual of income, it may be entitled to a bad debt deduction under section 166 of the Code. The foreign borrower's contractual obligation to pay the lender's foreign tax liability is a bona fide debt which, if in default, would qualify for the deduction. *See* section 1.166-1(c) of the regulations.

§A.17.3 Examiner's Position

1. The lender must accrue additional income on "net" loans at the time foreign taxes assumed by borrowers would have been accruable by the lender as tax obligations pursuant to section 1.461-1(a) of the regulations and not when the liability is ultimately satisfied by the borrowers;

2. Such additional income may not be adjusted by a reversal of income to reflect the amount of foreign taxes actually paid unless the initial accrual of income was not proper, but may take a deduction under section 166 for the appropriate charge to its bad debt reserve to the extent the

foreign borrower's failure to pay the foreign tax liability meets the bad debt requirements of section 166 and the regulations thereunder.

3. In order to receive a foreign tax credit for the accrued foreign taxes, the lender must submit proper documentation under IRC 905(b) and Section 1.905-2 of the Regulations.

§ A.18 SUPERVISORY GOOD WILL—SETTLEMENT GUIDELINE

§ A.18.1 Issues

1. Whether supervisory goodwill is covered by I.R.C. § 597.
2. Whether taxpayers can establish a tax basis in supervisory goodwill.
3. Whether taxpayers are entitled to losses under I.R.C. § 165 with respect to supervisory goodwill based upon worthlessness, abandonment or confiscation.
4. Whether taxpayers are entitled to depreciation or amortization deductions under I.R.C. § 167 with respect to supervisory goodwill.

§ A.18.2 Compliance Division Position

1. Supervisory goodwill is a creature of regulatory accounting and is not financial assistance provided by the Federal Savings and Loan Insurance Corporation under § 406(f) of the National Housing Act. Therefore, supervisory goodwill does not qualify as "money or other property" under § 597.
2. Taxpayers cannot establish that they have a tax basis in supervisory goodwill because, generally, thrift acquisitions were tax-free transactions and the taxpayers took a carryover basis in the acquired assets. Consequently, no basis was assigned to regulatory intangibles such as supervisory goodwill at the time of the acquisitions. Further, the taxpayers' assertion of tax basis on Forms 1120X is insufficient to establish that tax basis in supervisory goodwill exists.
3. Since taxpayers cannot establish that tax basis in supervisory goodwill exists, they are not entitled to § 165 losses based upon worthlessness, abandonment or confiscation. Moreover, even if a taxpayer were able to establish a tax basis in supervisory goodwill, that taxpayer must affirmatively establish that it met the other requirements of § 165 for the loss as claimed in the tax years for which the amended returns were filed.
4. Taxpayers cannot establish a tax basis in supervisory goodwill and, therefore, they are not entitled to deductions under § 167 for depreciation or amortization with respect to supervisory goodwill. Even if a taxpayer could establish a tax basis in supervisory goodwill, that taxpayer must affirmatively establish that it satisfied Newark Morning Ledger's requirements before it would be entitled to such deductions. However, even if a taxpayer could satisfy all of the requirements with respect to supervisory goodwill, the taxpayer is not entitled to deductions under § 167 with respect to supervisory goodwill that result from the taxpayer's use of an amended return to effectuate an impermissible retroactive change in method of accounting.

§ A.18.3 Taxpayer Position

1. Taxpayers take the position that supervisory goodwill qualifies as other property for purposes of § 597 and is a form of financial assistance

provided by the Federal Savings and Loan Insurance Corporation under § 404(f) of the National Housing Act. As such, the asset was properly excluded from gross income pursuant to § 597(a).

2. Taxpayers take the position that § 597 applies to provide a source from which basis can be said to derive.

3. Taxpayers argue that they are entitled to claim a loss under § 165(a) in the year in which their supervisory goodwill was abandoned, deemed worthless, or confiscated. Further, even though taxpayers may have filed lawsuits against the Federal government for damages relating to the loss of the use of supervisory goodwill, any damages ultimately received do not constitute "compensation" derived for a "claim for reimbursement" within the meaning of Reg. § 1.165-1(d)(2)(i). Furthermore, taxpayers argue there was no reasonable prospect of recovery even though lawsuits may have been filed.

4. As an alternative to their argument under § 165, taxpayers claim entitlement to amortization deductions under § 167. Taxpayers claim that they have an ascertainable tax basis in supervisory goodwill and that this asset has a limited useful life that could be ascertained with reasonable accuracy. The enactment of FIRREA established a useful life for supervisory goodwill that could be reasonably and accurately measured. Taxpayers argue that the enactment of FIRREA and the promulgation of regulations by the Office of Thrift Supervision phasing out the use of supervisory goodwill on a sliding scale basis from 1990 through 1994 altered the indeterminate life of the tax asset.

§ A.18.4 Discussion—Background/Facts

The Savings & Loan Crisis of the 1980s

For a more detailed discussion of the origins of the Savings & Loan crisis and its impact on regulatory accounting issues involving insolvent institutions, see *United States v. Winstar Corporation, et al*, 518 U.S. 839, 844-858 (1996), and the sources cited therein.[1] The following discussion summarizes the salient facts for purposes of framing the tax issue denominated as "supervisory goodwill."

The Federal Home Loan Bank Board ("FHLBB" or "Bank Board") was created in 1932 by the Federal Home Loan Bank Act to channel funds to the savings and loan ("thrift") industry for loans on houses and for preventing foreclosures on them. The FHLBB required that thrifts maintain adequate capital reserves as a cushion against losses. The Federal Savings & Loan Insurance Corporation ("FSLIC") was created in 1934 by the National Housing Act to insure deposits and regulate the thrift industry. The FSLIC, upon appointment, was authorized to act as receiver or conservator for a defaulted insured institution.

---

[1] All subsequent references to *Winstar* are to the Supreme Court's opinion unless otherwise noted.

In the late 1970's and early 1980's, high interest rates created a crisis in the thrift industry. High interest rate payments to depositors on short-term obligations exceeded low interest rate revenue from long-term home mortgages. Hundreds of thrifts found themselves facing insolvency. At the beginning of the crisis, the FSLIC, as insurer, provided financial assistance in the form of cash to failing thrifts and their acquirers. Later in the crisis when the FSLIC's funds began running short, the FSLIC provided a combination of cash and notes in an effort to keep thrifts from failing. Further into the crisis, when the FSLIC itself struggled with the insolvency of the savings and loan insurance fund, an accounting arrangement known as "supervisory goodwill" was developed to minimize the amount of cash outlay by the FSLIC to resolve institutions in receivership.

The FHLBB encouraged healthy thrifts and investors to take over failing thrifts through "supervisory mergers." The principal inducement for these mergers was an understanding that the acquisitions would be subject to a "special accounting treatment" that would help the acquiring institution to meet its capital reserve requirements. The FHLBB allowed these supervisory mergers to be accounted for under the purchase method of accounting where the assets and liabilities were recorded using fair market value. Under the purchase method of accounting, any excess of the purchase price (including liabilities assumed) over the fair market value of the identifiable assets acquired was designated as goodwill. The resulting goodwill in these supervisory mergers was generally referred to as "supervisory goodwill."

When the acquiring thrifts assumed liabilities that exceeded the fair market value of the assets acquired, these supervisory mergers gave rise to a deficit or negative net worth. FSLIC did not have sufficient cash in many cases to make up these deficits. To alleviate the insolvent condition presented in many of these mergers, the acquiring thrifts were allowed to use "special accounting treatments" either in lieu of direct financial assistance or in addition to direct financial assistance. One of the special accounting treatments allowed by the FHLBB permitted the resulting thrifts to count the supervisory goodwill for purposes of meeting their reserve/regulatory capital requirements and to amortize it for regulatory purposes over the applicable period used by the acquirer for book under GAAP (up to 40 years maximum).

The supervisory goodwill was generally recorded as an amortizable asset on the balance sheet of the acquiring institution for financial book purposes, and the institution then amortized the supervisory goodwill for both financial book and regulatory purposes. The supervisory goodwill was taken into account in determining whether the thrifts had sufficient capital reserves to meet regulatory requirements. Capital reserves, expressed as a percentage of total assets, serve as a cushion against losses. By allowing the supervisory goodwill to be accounted for in this manner, thrifts that otherwise would have been impaired or insolvent for regulatory purposes remained in compliance. Thus, as pointed out in the Coordinated Issue Paper ("CIP"), supervisory goodwill represented a form of "regulatory forbearance" that relieved taxpayers of otherwise applicable regulatory capital requirements.[2]

In 1989, Congress noted that this special accounting treatment actually worsened the thrift crisis. In August 1989, Congress enacted the Financial Institutions Reform, Recovery & Enforcement Act, Pub. L.101-73 ("FIRREA") which phased out, over a five-year period, the thrifts' ability to count supervisory goodwill for the purpose of meeting regulatory capital reserve requirements. Beginning in 1989, the thrift capital requirements were generally revised to reflect the elimination of supervisory goodwill by December 31, 1994. In some cases, a thrift may have written off the balance of the supervisory goodwill prior to 1994.

As a result of the change in law, many financial institutions immediately fell out of compliance with regulatory capital requirements, subjecting them to seizure by thrift regulators. Over one hundred financial institutions filed actions against the United States ("U.S.") asserting that the government breached contractual promises to allow thrifts to count supervisory goodwill for the purpose of meeting regulatory requirements. The breach of contract issue reached the Supreme Court in *Winstar*. The Court held that the U.S. was contractually obligated to permit financial institutions to use special accounting treatments with regard to their acquisitions of failing thrifts pursuant to agreements with the federal thrift regulatory agencies. The Court further held that the U.S. breached those contractual obligations when the agencies barred the use of those methods pursuant to FIRREA. The Court remanded the *Winstar* case to the Court of Appeals for the Federal Circuit for further proceedings to determine the appropriate amount of damages. (At the time of the writing of this guideline, there were over one hundred *Winstar*-type damage claim cases (hereafter "damage claim cases") pending in either the Court of Appeals for the Federal Circuit or the Court of Federal Claims.)

Subsequent Tax Claims

At the time of the supervisory mergers, the acquiring thrifts did not assign any tax basis to the supervisory goodwill. The mergers were treated for federal income tax purposes as nontaxable reorganizations pursuant to § 368(a)(1) and the acquiring thrifts took a carryover basis in the acquired assets of the insolvent thrifts pursuant to § 362. The carryover tax basis of these assets generally exceeded the fair market value of the assets.[3] In many cases, shortly after the mergers, the acquiring institutions either sold the assets at a loss for tax purposes, or wrote them off for tax purposes.

On original tax returns, taxpayers did not record any supervisory goodwill as a tax asset attributable to the acquisition.

On amended returns, some taxpayers have claimed that the contractual "right to use" the purchase method of accounting, along with the resultant

---

[2] The CIP suggests that the tax analysis contained therein applies, generally, to other regulatory rights such as the right to operate branches across state lines.

[3] Since the carryover tax basis of the assets acquired presumably exceeded the fair market value of such assets, it would appear that any purchased goodwill was reflected in the higher tax basis.

purchased goodwill, results in a tax asset also denominated as supervisory goodwill. Taxpayers believe that this tax asset of supervisory goodwill qualifies as other property for purposes of § 597. Under § 597, financial assistance received from the FSLIC in a supervisory merger is not includible in income, nor is a reduction in basis of other assets required.

These tax claims are premised on the theory that the supervisory goodwill recorded for book purposes by the acquiring thrift on the acquisition of a failing thrift should have been assigned a tax basis. Taxpayers state that a tax basis for supervisory goodwill has been established through the mechanics of § 597. Taxpayers typically claim an abandonment loss occurred as a result of the enactment of FIRREA which phased out the ability to count supervisory goodwill for purposes of calculating regulatory capital. In most cases, the abandonment loss has been claimed for tax year 1994. In some instances, taxpayers have claimed they are entitled to amortization deductions over the useful life of the asset.

§ A.18.5 Legal Analysis

Issue (1) Whether supervisory goodwill is covered by I.R.C. § 597 and Issue (2) Whether taxpayers can establish a tax basis in supervisory goodwill[4]

The Nature of Supervisory Goodwill

The Supreme Court recognized that regulatory and statutory accounting gimmicks played a principal role in the thrift crisis. See Winstar at 845 and 846 (referring to H.R. Rep. No. 101-54, pt. 1, pp. 297-298). Supervisory goodwill is the product of such accounting gimmicks. But, supervisory goodwill, even though the offspring of such accounting gimmicks, produced real financial accounting and regulatory consequences of benefit for the acquiring thrifts, mainly because they were allowed to use supervisory goodwill to meet regulatory capital requirements. Thus, the right to treat supervisory goodwill as regulatory capital had real value to the acquiring thrifts that booked it for financial and regulatory purposes. At footnote 6 of the Winstar decision, supervisory goodwill is described from a regulatory perspective "as kind of the engine that made this transaction go . . . [b]ecause without it, there wouldn't have been any train pulling out of the station, so to speak."

Following are various excerpts drawn from the *Winstar* opinion that describe the nature of supervisory goodwill and its significance to the thrift industry:

> Because FSLIC had insufficient funds to make up the difference between a failed thrift's liabilities and assets, the Bank Board had to offer a "cash substitute" to induce a healthy thrift to assume a failed thrift's obligations. [Pages 849, 850.]
>
> [T]he treatment of supervisory goodwill as regulatory capital was attractive because it inflated the institution's reserves, thereby allowing the thrift to leverage more loans (and, it hoped, make more profits). [Page 851.]

[4] For discussion purposes, Issues (1) and (2) can be combined. Taxpayers acknowledge that in order to establish tax basis, § 597 must apply to supervisory goodwill.

Indeed, the rationale for recognizing goodwill stands on its head in a supervisory merger: ordinarily, goodwill is recognized as valuable because a rational purchaser would not pay more than assets are worth; here, however, the purchase is rational only because of the accounting treatment for the shortfall. [Citation omitted.] In the end, of course, such reasoning circumvented the whole purpose of the reserve requirements, which was to protect depositors and the deposit insurance fund. As some in Congress later recognized, "[g]oodwill is not cash. It is a concept, and a shadowy one at that. When the Federal Government liquidates a failed thrift, goodwill is simply no good. It is valueless. That means, quite simply, that the taxpayer picks up the tab for the shortfall." [Citation to the Congressional Record omitted.] [S]ee also White 84 (acknowledging that in some instances supervisory goodwill" involved the creation of an asset that did not have real value as protection for the FSLIC"). Pages 854-855.

"[To] a considerable extent, the size of the thrift crisis resulted from the utilization of capital gimmicks that masked the inadequate capitalization of thrifts." [Citation omitted.][Page 857.]

In the present case, the Government chose to regulate capital reserves to protect FSLIC's insurance fund . . . The regulation thus protected the Government in its capacity analogous to a private insurer, the same capacity in which it entered into supervisory merger agreements to convert some of its financial insurance obligations into responsibilities of private entrepreneurs. In this respect, the supervisory mergers bear some analogy to private contracts for reinsurance. [Footnote omitted.] [Page 894.]

Supervisory goodwill was significant to an acquiring institution for two reasons. First, the acquiring institution was permitted by thrift regulators to count supervisory goodwill toward its reserve requirements. This treatment inflated the thrift's reserves, allowing the thrift to leverage more loans. Second, the regulators allowed the goodwill to be amortized over a long period (40 years in some cases). The long write-off period allowed an acquiring thrift to seem more profitable than it in fact was. See *Winstar* at 850-851.

Statutory Framework & Legislative History of § 597

Section 597 was added to the Code by § 244 of the Economic Recovery Tax Act of 1981, P.L. 97-34 (Aug. 13, 1981). Section 597 has been amended a number of times since 1981. Generally, for the tax years in which supervisory goodwill is an issue, § 597(a) provided as follows:

a) Exclusion from Gross Income.—Gross income of a domestic building and loan association does not include any amount of money or other property received from the Federal Savings and Loan Insurance Corporation pursuant to section 406(f) of the National Housing Act (12 U.S.C. sec. 1729(f)[5]), regardless of whether any note or other instrument is issued in exchange therefore.

[5] Section 1729(f) was repealed in 1989 by FIRREA. The repeal coincided with major changes made by FIRREA including the replacement of the FSLIC by the Federal Deposit Insurance Corporation ("FDIC"), and the replacement of the FHLBB by the Office of Thrift Supervision ("OTS").

Section 597(b) provided:

> b) No reduction in Basis of Assets.—No reduction in the basis of assets of a domestic building and loan association shall be made on account of money or other property received under the circumstances referred to in subsection (a).

Section 246(c) of the Act made § 597 of the Code applicable "to any payment made on or after January 1, 1981."

Under § 406(f) of the National Housing Act (as amended by the Garn-St. Germain Depository Institutions Act of 1982, Pub. L. 97-320, 96 Stat. 1469 (Oct. 15, 1982)), the FSLIC was authorized to provide assistance to insured thrift institutions that encountered severe financial conditions. Specifically, in order to prevent the default of such institutions, the FSLIC was authorized "to make loans to, to make deposits in, to purchase the assets or securities of, to assume the liabilities of, or to make contributions to, any insured institution." 12 U.S.C. § 1729(f)(1). The FSLIC, in order to facilitate a merger or consolidation of an insured institution as defined by statute, was further authorized: to purchase any such assets or assume any such liabilities; to make loans or contributions to, or deposits in, or purchase the securities of, such other insured institution; and to guarantee such other institution against loss. See 12 U.S.C. § 1729(f)(2).

Section 1729(f) of 12 U.S.C. does not make any reference to "supervisory goodwill" or "favorable regulatory consideration allowing goodwill to be counted as an asset for regulatory capital purposes". The terms "loans", "deposits", "purchase", and "contributions" reflected in the statute suggest that Congress intended for financial assistance to mean payments of money or money equivalents (such as promissory notes).

The legislative history to § 244 of the Act supports a conclusion that § 597 covers only financial assistance such as payments of money or money equivalents. The Conference Report supporting the enactment of Section 597 states:

> Under present law, contributions to capital by nonshareholder[s] are excluded from the income of a recipient corporation (see 118), but the basis of property is reduced by such contribution (sec. 362(c)).
>
> The bill excludes from income of [an insured thrift] all money or property contributed to the thrift institution by [the FSLIC] under its financial assistance program without reduction in basis of property. The amendment applies to assistance payments whether or not the association issues either a debt or equity instrument in exchange therefore . . .

H.R. Conf. Rep. No. 97-215, 97th Cong., 1st Sess. 284 (1981).

There is nothing in the congressional reports to indicate that the term "money or other property" includes favorable regulatory treatment of supervisory goodwill.

Some Taxpayer Arguments

Notwithstanding that neither the statute nor the congressional reports say anything about § 597 applying to supervisory goodwill, taxpayers' position is that supervisory goodwill does qualify as other property. Taxpayers argue that §

597(a) does not contain exclusions for certain types of property, and that the IRS was not given by statute any regulatory authority to limit or carve out exceptions for certain types of property.

In some instances, the statement has been made by taxpayers that supervisory goodwill was **contributed** to acquiring or acquired institutions to induce and facilitate the acquiring institution's participation in supervisory mergers. This characterization of supervisory goodwill having been **contributed** (thus equating the **contribution** of supervisory goodwill to a **contribution** of, for example, cash or notes) is misleading. The regulatory agencies did not have a storehouse of available goodwill to contribute to an acquiring institution during a supervisory merger. Supervisory goodwill was not something that could have been transferred from an agency to a taxpayer. Supervisory goodwill, in and of itself, did not constitute a contract. Supervisory goodwill by itself was the excess of the fair market value of liabilities over the fair market value of assets acquired as determined under the purchase method of accounting. Without the use of the special accounting treatment (that is, the ability to count the goodwill toward reserve requirements and long term amortization), the goodwill recorded for book purposes would have been of little use to an acquiring thrift.

Taxpayers also argue that the FSLIC and the FHLBB used supervisory goodwill to guarantee acquiring institutions against loss. A guaranty is normally thought of as a pledge by which one person commits to the payment of another's debt or the fulfillment of another's obligation in the event of default. The contractual right to count supervisory goodwill in meeting capital reserve requirements fell far short of a commitment to pay the debts of the acquiring institution. If supervisory goodwill constituted a guaranty as the taxpayer argues, the widespread use of it would likely have aggravated the thrift crisis far sooner. Congress ultimately eliminated the use of supervisory goodwill arrangements with the enactment of FIRREA. It is hard to view supervisory goodwill as a guaranty when it has been characterized by others as a "shadowy concept" and an "accounting gimmick."

Taxpayers also may characterize supervisory goodwill as being similar to net worth certificates because the supervisory goodwill was used in supervisory mergers for the same reasons that net worth certificates were used: to induce healthy institutions' participation in supervisory mergers, to provide assistance to increase the acquired thrift's net worth, and to minimize any losses to the acquiring institution as a result of the acquired thrift's poor financial condition. Net worth certificates represented a promise by the FSLIC to pay money to the acquiring institution at some future date. Supervisory goodwill required no future payment of money by FSLIC. While it is agreed that both were used to induce healthy institutions' participation in supervisory mergers, there is a large difference between money and a note on the one hand and a "special accounting treatment" on the other. The fact that both affected capital reserve requirements is not determinative as to whether supervisory goodwill is property within the meaning of § 597.

Taxpayers also argue that the total or face amount of the supervisory goodwill is automatically the amount of such "property" eligible for exclusion under § 597. Taxpayers' argument does not distinguish the face amount of the supervisory goodwill from the value of the **ability** to use such face amount toward capital reserve requirements. The ability to use the amount of supervisory goodwill toward capital reserve requirements and the ability to amortize the amount was the contractual obligation that the *Winstar* court addressed.

Taxpayers note that contract rights held by a taxpayer ordinarily constitute "property" for income tax purposes. The Service does not necessarily disagree with this statement. The threshold question, however, is whether the contract right to count supervisory goodwill for regulatory capital is "other property" for purposes of § 597. A second question concerns the value of this contract right.

FHLBB vs. FSLIC

Because the FSLIC had insufficient funds to make up the difference between a failed thrift's liabilities and assets, the special accounting treatment was offered as a "cash substitute" to induce a healthy thrift to assume a failed thrift's obligations. The CIP states:

> Supervisory goodwill, however, resulted from grants of regulatory forbearance by the FHLBB, not the FSLIC. [Footnote omitted.]Even though the FSLIC was authorized to enter into assistance agreements in connection with the acquisitions at issue, it was the FHLBB from whom taxpayers sought and received permission to use the purchase method of accounting and to count any resulting goodwill towards their regulatory capital requirements as supervisory goodwill. Thus, supervisory goodwill is also not covered by § 597 because it was not provided by FSLIC.

The CIP says that a comparison of two sections of the Economic Recovery Tax Act of 1981 support treating the FSLIC and the FHLBB as separate entities. Section 241 of the Act states that for purposes of § 368(a)(3)(D) relating to agency receivership proceedings involving financial institutions, the term "Board" means the FHLBB or the FSLIC. On the other hand, section 244 which deals directly with § 597, refers only to the exclusion from gross income of money or other property received from the FSLIC.

Taxpayers refer to language in the *Winstar* decision to rebut Compliance's position. At page 890, the Court states:

> There is no question . . . that the Bank Board [the FHLBB] and FSLIC had ample statutory authority [to promise] to permit respondents to count supervisory goodwill and capital credits toward regulatory capital and to pay respondents' damages if that performance became impossible. The organic statute creating FSLIC as an arm of the Bank Board, 12 U.S.C. § 1725(d) (1988 ed.) (repealed 1989), generally empowered it "[t]o make contracts" [Footnote omitted] and § 1729(f)(2), enacted in 1978, delegated more specific powers in the context of supervisory mergers.

Also at page 890, the Court states:

> Nor is there any reason to suppose that the breadth of this authority was not meant to extend to contracts governing treatment of regulatory capital . . . [And,] there is no serious question that FSLIC (and the Bank Board acting through it) was authorized to make the contracts in issue.

Taxpayers rely on this language in the Winstar opinion in arguing that the FSLIC was authorized to offer cash substitutes, such as the special accounting treatment, to healthy thrifts in the context of the supervisory mergers.

Taxpayers also cite to12 U.S.C. § 1730h(d) as support for the idea that Congress specifically recognized the FSLIC's authority to permit thrifts to count supervisory goodwill toward capital requirements when it modified the National Housing Act in 1987. Section 1730h(d), prior to repeal in 1989, stated:

> No provision of this section shall affect the authority of the [FSLIC] to authorize insured institutions to utilize subordinated debt and goodwill in meeting reserve and other regulatory requirements.

This statutory provision, although enacted in 1987, refers specifically to the FSLIC's authority in authorizing insured institutions to use goodwill in meeting reserve and other regulatory requirements. Whether the FHLBB, the FSLIC, or the two combined were authorized to offer the cash substitute is not entirely clear. At page 850 in Winstar, the Court recognizes that, because the FSLIC lacked sufficient funds, "the Bank Board had to offer a 'cash substitute' to induce a healthy thrift to assume a failed thrift's obligations." In these types of cases, however, the FHLBB ratified the merger and incorporated a resolution into a "Supervisory Action Agreement". The resolution referred to a stipulation that any goodwill arising from the transaction shall be determined and amortized in accordance with FHLBB Memorandum R-31b (the "Memorandum"). The Memorandum permitted the acquiring institution to use the purchase method of accounting and to recognize goodwill as an asset subject to amortization.

The statutory provision at issue, § 597, refers only to the FSLIC. Congress could have easily added the FHLBB to the language in the statute. A logical explanation for the exclusion of the FHLBB from the statute is that, at the time the statute was enacted in August 1981, the FSLIC was authorized to make loans, deposits, contributions, and provide other forms of financial assistance but was not otherwise empowered to provide regulatory relief from the FHLBB's established capital requirements. Alternatively, supervisory goodwill may not have been perceived as a "cash substitute" in August 1981.

Whether supervisory goodwill was authorized by the FSLIC or the FHLBB is not entirely clear. The Supreme Court's language and § 1730h(d) of the National Housing Act noted above appear to support the idea that the FSLIC authorized acquiring institutions to count supervisory goodwill toward capital requirements. See *Winstar* at 891.

Is Supervisory Goodwill "Other Property" for Purposes of § 597?

Whether the FSLIC or the FHLBB authorized the use of supervisory goodwill seems less important than whether the special accounting treatment qualifies as financial assistance pursuant to § 597. Section 597 refers to financial assistance received from the FSLIC, and the applicable provision under title 12 generally refers to "loans, deposits, purchases, and contributions." The failure of either statutory provision (or its relevant legislative history) to include the "special accounting treatment" at issue here as a form of financial assistance places the taxpayer at a disadvantage on the issue of whether supervisory goodwill is covered by § 597.

The amount of supervisory goodwill recorded by an acquiring institution (i.e. liabilities in excess of assets on a fair value basis) was the computational result of the merger being accounted for under the purchase method of accounting. Supervisory goodwill does not resemble a "loan", "deposit", "purchase", "contribution", or "guarantee" as those terms are used in § 597. Neither is the special accounting treatment a loan, deposit, purchase, etc. Whether the special accounting treatment is "other property" within the meaning of § 597 is questionable. Even if it were, it is unlikely that the value of the special accounting treatment equals the amount of supervisory goodwill recorded by the acquiring institution.

Taxpayers observe somewhat incidentally that if supervisory goodwill received by an acquiring institution from the FSLIC had not been excluded from gross income under § 597, such property would have been taxable. We do not necessarily agree with this observation. Although under § 61 gross income means all income from whatever source derived, in a number of cases the creation of property rights under a government regulatory arrangement has not resulted in gross income to the recipient. This is true even though in some cases, the rights are transferable, have an ascertainable value, and are acquired at no cost or for a negligible fee. See, for example, GCM 39606 (Feb. 27, 1987) (opining that the receipt of airport takeoff and landing rights is not an event that results in the realization of gross income). The GCM posits that the value of rights conferred by a governmental body in furtherance of government regulatory policies does not give rise to taxable income. Whether agreements between the FHLBB/ FSLIC and acquiring institutions that furthered the regulators' duty of requiring thrifts to maintain adequate capital reserves could give rise to gross income is highly questionable. In our opinion, § 597 was not intended to create income with respect to an item that otherwise would not have been an item of gross income within the meaning of § 61. We do not agree that supervisory goodwill would have been viewed as an income item in the absence of § 597.

Taxpayers' position is that the face amount of the supervisory goodwill booked by the acquiring institution represented its fair market value. As mentioned earlier, the amount of goodwill resulting from a supervisory merger represented the excess of the fair market value of the liabilities over the fair market value of the assets of the acquired thrift. This figure was a **negative** net worth figure that appeared on the asset side of the balance sheet, but it certainly wasn't an asset in the traditional sense. It wasn't something that could have been independently transferred or sold in the marketplace. It also wasn't something that could have been acquired independently of the merger. The figure represented a plug on the balance sheet and, in our opinion, there is little rationale for saying that the fair market value of such an item was equal to the amount booked.

Taxpayers state that it was widely known in the thrift industry that supervisory goodwill was a valuable intangible that could be obtained in the context of supervisory mergers. It is irrational, say taxpayers, to think that acquiring institutions would have been willing to assume millions of dollars of excess liabilities without receiving something of value in return. Thus, they argue, the government created supervisory goodwill as a "cash substitute" and intended that it take the place of cash, notes, and other financial assistance that the FSLIC was unable to provide.

The valuable asset was not so much the supervisory goodwill, the negative net worth figure, but the right to use the special accounting treatment and the right to count supervisory goodwill toward capital reserve requirements. Yet, taxpayers' position equates the value of these rights to the full amount of supervisory goodwill. If the acquiring institution had a choice of receiving cash or an equal amount of supervisory goodwill, it is irrational to think that the acquirer would have preferred the supervisory goodwill. The right to use the special accounting treatment and the right to count supervisory goodwill toward regulatory capital requirements were of some value to an acquiring institution in the context of a supervisory merger. See *Winstar* at 850.

A review of some of the pending litigation involving *Winstar* damage claim cases is helpful with respect to the issue of whether supervisory goodwill, or more precisely the right to use supervisory goodwill to meet capital reserve requirements, had a value equal to its face amount. Various plaintiffs have filed suit against the U.S. government in connection with the breach of contract issue.[6] The Court of Federal Claims and the Court of Appeals for the Federal Circuit have determined that supervisory goodwill represented a bargained-for promise from the government that had real economic value. For example, in *Glass v. U.S.*, 47 Fed. Cl. 316 (2000), the Court of Federal Claims awarded $2,100,000 in damages to the plaintiff-intervenor FDIC, as successor to the breach of contract claims of the defunct thrift. The Court of Federal Claims concluded that this was the value of the supervisory goodwill capital destroyed by the government's breach. On appeal, the Court of Appeals for the Federal Circuit reversed the lower court's decision and vacated the damage award on the ground that the FDIC lacked standing to intervene in the case. *U.S. v. Glass*, 258 F.3d 1349 (July 24, 2001). Although a final outcome has not yet been reached in this case, the proceedings involving the valuation of supervisory goodwill are informative.

The face amount of supervisory goodwill in *Glass* was about $6,400,000 at the date of the contract, or acquisition date. Plaintiff FDIC's economic expert, Dr. Arnold Heggestad, testified at trial that the cash value of supervisory goodwill is less than 100% of its face because, first, the goodwill becomes less as it is amortized and, second, goodwill is not negotiable or transferable, it cannot be invested, and it has no potential to increase. He determined that the value of the goodwill at the date of contract was about $2,500,000. He determined the value by calculating the amount of direct cash assistance the FSLIC would have had to provide in place of the supervisory goodwill. The benefit of having supervisory

[6] Plaintiffs include acquiring institutions, shareholders of failed institutions and, in some cases, the FDIC, as successor in interest to some of the acquiring institutions that went into receivership as a result of FIRREA.

goodwill on the books is that it provides cash flow. The replacement of cash flow is what Dr. Heggestad's model sought to replicate using the hypothetical of a preferred stock issuance. The government, as defendant in the case, argued that the replacement cost of an asset is not necessarily related to the value of the asset to the company. In the FDIC's *Memorandum in Support of Its Cross-Motion for Summary Judgment on Selected Damage Issues and in Opposition to Defendant's Motion for Summary Judgment*, the FDIC noted that the defendant's expert in another damage claim case (referred to as Glendale), Dr. Ruback (who was dropped before trial), ""first articulated the basic approach to valuing goodwill that the FDIC's expert, Dr. Heggestad, is presenting in this case."

Information from the damage claim cases is somewhat helpful in that the courts have generally concluded, in the context of a breach of contract action, that the true economic value of supervisory goodwill is not equal to the face amount booked by the acquiring institution. Tax claims filed by taxpayers in connection with the alleged worthlessness of supervisory goodwill have been filed for the face amount of goodwill that resulted from the merger transactions. The drafter is unaware of any tax claim where the taxpayer has supported such tax claim with an expert opinion or valuation of the goodwill at the date of contract.

There were other things that acquiring institutions received in supervisory mergers besides the right to use supervisory goodwill to meet capital reserve requirements. Some acquiring institutions received a promise from the FHLBB to refrain from enforcing regulatory capital-ratio requirements for a period of time. This promise has been referred to as forbearance. Some institutions obtained the right to open branches in additional states. It isn't clear whether, at the contract date, these other items could have been separately identified from the concept of supervisory goodwill, or valued independently of supervisory goodwill. In any event, the drafter believes that, generally, such a valuation was not undertaken by taxpayers.

Statement of Financial Accounting Standards # 72

As pointed out by the Supreme Court in *Winstar*, in some merger transactions involving supervisory goodwill the FSLIC also contributed an amount of cash to assist the merger transaction. The regulators permitted the acquiring institution to count the cash contribution as a permanent credit to regulatory capital. By failing to require the thrift to subtract the cash contribution from the amount of supervisory goodwill generated by the merger, "regulators effectively permitted double counting of the cash as both a tangible and an intangible asset. [Citation omitted.] Capital credits thus inflated the acquiring thrift's regulatory capital and permitted leveraging of more and more loans." *Winstar*, at 853.

To eliminate this double counting of cash, in 1983 the Financial Accounting Standards Board promulgated Statement of Financial Accounting Standards No. 72 ("SFAS 72") which applied specifically to the acquisition of a savings and loan association. In addition to allowing supervisory goodwill to be amortized for book purposes, SFAS 72 also required that financial assistance from regulatory authorities be deducted from supervisory goodwill in order to avoid a double counting of the cash as both a tangible and an intangible asset. See *Winstar,* at 855. Thus, in 1983, the Financial Accounting Standards Board recognized the distinction between cash and supervisory goodwill. In the context of a supervisory merger, supervisory goodwill was something that had to be adjusted by the amount of financial assistance (i.e., cash) received.

Can Taxpayer Establish Tax Basis Under § 1012?

As the CIP discusses, pursuant to § 1012, the tax basis of acquired property is generally its cost. Absent certain provisions that provide for the tax-free receipt of property, taxpayers generally must include in income the fair market value of property they receive in order to obtain a tax basis in such property.

Some discussion has taken place suggesting that an acquiring entity incurred a cost in the acquisition of a failing thrift, to the extent that liabilities assumed exceeded the value of the assets acquired. The net cost was the excess of liabilities over assets. Such net cost, representing the amount of supervisory goodwill recorded in the transaction, established a tax basis in supervisory goodwill.

This discussion appears to disregard the fact that the acquiring institution was permitted to record the acquisition as a tax-free reorganization under § 368(a)(1) whereby the acquiring institution took a carryover basis in the acquired assets. In such a tax-free reorganization, there appears to be no room for establishing additional basis, unless § 597 applies to the property in question.

Taxpayers generally appear to have abandoned this position.

Issue (3) Whether taxpayers are entitled to losses under § 165 with respect to supervisory goodwill based upon worthlessness, abandonment or confiscation

Under § 165(a), a taxpayer is allowed a deduction for any loss sustained during the taxable year for which the taxpayer is not compensated by insurance or otherwise. The amount of the deduction is the taxpayer's adjusted basis under § 1011 for determining a loss from the sale or other disposition of property. To be allowable as a deduction under § 165(a), a loss must be evidenced by closed and completed transactions, fixed by identifiable events, and actually sustained during the taxable year. Treas. Reg. § 1.165-1(b).

If an event occurs which may result in a loss, and in the year of the event there exists a claim for reimbursement with respect to which there is a reasonable prospect of recovery, no portion of the loss with respect to which reimbursement may be received is sustained until it can be ascertained with reasonable certainty whether or not such reimbursement will be received. Whether a reasonable prospect of recovery exists is a question of fact to be determined upon examination of all facts and circumstances. Reg. § 1.165-1(d)(2)(i).

The first position in the CIP is that the taxpayer has not established any tax basis in supervisory goodwill. Therefore, taxpayer does not have a deductible tax loss under § 165(a).

Assuming a taxpayer can establish a tax basis in supervisory goodwill, the CIP says the taxpayer is still not entitled to deduct a loss under § 165 because the taxpayer has not affirmatively established that it met the other requirements of § 165 for the loss as claimed in the tax years for which the amended returns were filed. The taxpayer, according to the CIP, cannot establish the amount of any deductible loss based on worthlessness while that taxpayer is pursuing a Winstar-type damage claim.

Scofield Estate v. Commissioner, 266 F.2d 154 (6th Cir. 1959), *aff'g in part and rev'g in part*, 25 T.C. 774 (1956), is a leading case involving the "prospect of recovery". The taxpayer in this case sued the original trustees of a trust to recover money they had embezzled from the trust. The taxpayer filed suit in 1935 and did not recover until 1948, 13 years later. The court held that a loss was properly deducted by the trust in the year in which the litigation terminated. There was a possibility of recovery from a bank depositary of trust funds up to 1948, and a further possibility of recovery from trustees. The court said:

> In the absence of such circumstances [that show]such litigation to be specious, speculative, or wholly without merit and that the taxpayer hence was not reasonable in waiting to claim the loss as a deduction, a taxpayer who feels that chance of recovery is sufficiently probable to warrant bringing a suit and prosecuting it with reasonable diligence to a conclusion is normally reasonable in waiting until the termination thereof to claim a Section 23(e) deduction.

The court in *Scofield* also discussed the substantive merits of the taxpayer's claim, the fact that the taxpayer, an attorney, consulted with senior counsel before instituting the lawsuit, and whether or not the defendants had sufficient assets to pay a judgment.

California Fed. Bank v. United States, 43 Fed. Cl. 445 (1999), *aff'd in part and vacated in part*, 245 F.3d 1342 (Fed. Cir. 2001), is one example of the many damage claim cases that are pending in either the Court of Federal Claims or the Court of Appeals for the Federal Circuit. In 1997, the lower court held on summary judgment in *California Fed Bank* that the government was liable for breach of contract and referred the case for trial on the issue of damages. In 1999, the lower court awarded the plaintiff almost $23,000,000 in damages as the cost of replacing the regulatory capital lost due to the phase-out of goodwill under FIRREA. The government appealed this result and the appeals court ultimately remanded the case back to the lower court to reconsider the damage award.

There are at least 120 of these suits pending against the government for damages relating to the *Winstar* litigation. The magnitude of this litigation and the conclusions reached at both the trial court and the appeals court suggest that there was a reasonable prospect of recovery at the time the tax claims were filed. The suits are being prosecuted "with reasonable diligence." The defendant, the U.S. government, has sufficient assets to pay a judgment.

Taxpayers claim there isn't sufficient nexus between the potential damages that may be received by taxpayers and the losses sustained on the worthlessness of the supervisory goodwill. According to taxpayers, the potential damages under the breach of contract claim would compensate taxpayers for losses incurred in no longer being able to count the supervisory goodwill towards minimum capital requirements. In other words, the compensation would be for the loss of benefits that were derived from the asset and not from for the loss of the asset itself.

Taxpayers cite *Forward Communications Corp. v. U.S.*, 608 F. 2d. 485 (Ct.Cl. 1979), as support for the argument that the *Winstar* claim is collateral to its loss. In that case, the taxpayer, a local television station, claimed a § 165 loss based on termination of its affiliation agreement with the CBS network. Taxpayer was compensated for its loss of the CBS affiliation by increased revenues from affiliation with the ABC network. The Court of Claims held that § 165 does not bar a deduction merely because the taxpayer is able to effect an offsetting gain in a different although contemporaneous transaction.

The facts and circumstances in *Forward Communications* are different from those in the instant situation. Any recovery pursuant to the Winstar claims would compensate the taxpayer precisely for the loss of its right to use supervisory goodwill in meeting regulatory capital requirements. The damage claims and the tax claims originate from precisely the same event—the enactment of FIRREA. The connection between the Winstar-related damage claims and the tax losses claimed by taxpayers is direct and undeniable.

Reasonable Prospect of Recovery at 12/31/94?

The CIP points out that "whether a reasonable prospect for recovery exists is a factual issue, determined upon an objective examination of the facts and circumstances surrounding the loss **as of the close of the taxable year in which the deduction is claimed**." [Emphasis added]

The tax year for which most of the tax claims have been filed is tax year 1994. FIRREA effectively eliminated by December 31, 1994, the ability of the acquiring institutions to count supervisory goodwill for capital reserve requirements. Taxpayers argue that it was not until 1996 that the Supreme Court held in *Winstar* that the government breached its contracts when it enacted FIRREA. Until such time as the Supreme Court decided the Winstar case on July 1, 1996, recovery was merely possible, not probable, according to taxpayers.

The Supreme Court decision, however, was not the first victory for the plaintiffs in the breach of contract litigation. The *Winstar* litigation began almost immediately after FIRREA was enacted. In July 1990, the Claims Court held that summary judgment on the liability question was precluded because a genuine issue of material fact remained. 21 Ct. Cl. 112. In April 1992, the Claims Court denied the government's motion for dismissal or summary judgment, finding that a binding contract existed between the parties which the government breached by enacting FIRREA. 25 Ct. Cl. 541. In July 1992, the Claims Court granted the plaintiffs' motions for summary judgment because the government breached its contracts with them. 26 Cl. Ct. 904. In May 1993, the Court of Appeals for the Federal Circuit reversed and remanded. 994 F. 2d 797. But in August 1995, on rehearing en banc, the Court of Appeals reversed the panel decision and affirmed the Court of Federal Claims. 64 F. 3d 1531. Certiorari was then granted in January 1996.

The *Winstar* plaintiffs were successful throughout, with the exception of a short period of time from May 1993 to August 1995.

Subsequent to the Supreme Court's opinion in Winstar, taxpayers began filing amended returns claiming tax losses with respect to supervisory goodwill. Although the claims are for 1994 and subsequent tax years, the claims were not actually filed until 1996 at the earliest. In other words, at the time claims were filed, the Supreme Court had decided the contract breach issue and had remanded for damages. It would appear that at the time taxpayers filed these claims, there was a reasonable prospect of recovery. At the end of 1994, there may have been somewhat less of a prospect of recovery. But given that plaintiffs were successful almost throughout, except for a short period of time that included December 31, 1994, it would appear that there was a reasonable prospect of recovery even at the end of 1994. It isn't clear whether the filing of the tax claim in a year subsequent to 1994 would tend to mitigate the principle that "reasonable prospect for recovery" should be determined upon the facts and circumstances as of the close of the taxable year in which the deduction is claimed.

Did Worthlessness Occur in 1994?

Even if taxpayers are capable of establishing a tax basis for supervisory goodwill under § 597, some fact patterns raise an additional question of whether taxpayers have claimed losses in the proper tax year, notwithstanding that there may have been a reasonable prospect of recovery.

When FIRREA was enacted in 1989, the amount of supervisory goodwill that could be used to meet regulatory capital requirements was greatly reduced. FIRREA required thrifts to satisfy three new minimum capital standards: "tangible" capital, "core" capital, and "risk-based" capital. 12 U.S.C. § 1464(t). As a result of FIRREA, supervisory goodwill could no longer be included in satisfying minimum "tangible" capital. The amount of supervisory goodwill that could be included in satisfying "core" capital decreased each year and was entirely phased out on December 31, 1994. Supervisory goodwill could be used to maintain "risk-based" capital, but for this purpose FIRREA limited its amortization to a period of no more than 20 years.

As a result of FIRREA, many thrifts **immediately** fell out of compliance with capital requirements and became subject to seizure. The three plaintiffs in the *Winstar* case fell out of compliance well before December 31, 1994. See *Winstar v. U.S.*, 64 F.3d 1531 (1995). Winstar fell out of compliance as soon as the FIRREA capital requirements became effective, and was placed in receivership by the Office of Thrift Supervision in May 1990. Statesman likewise fell out of compliance immediately and was placed in receivership in July 1990. Glendale fell out of compliance with the risk-based capital standard in March 1992. 64 F.3d at 1539.

Assuming a taxpayer can establish that it has a tax basis in supervisory goodwill, that a § 165 loss is allowable, and that there was no reasonable prospect of recovery when the taxpayer fell out of regulatory compliance, the ensuing tax loss may have been in a tax year prior to 1994.

Abandonment

The CIP addresses the taxpayer's claim that it is entitled to an abandonment loss under § 165, following FIRREA. The CIP concludes that the taxpayer is not entitled to an abandonment loss because the taxpayer does not have any tax basis in supervisory goodwill. However, even if the taxpayer can establish a tax basis, there must be an affirmative act of abandonment; the mere diminution in the value of property is not enough to establish an abandonment loss. Neither FIRREA's statutory provisions nor the government's subsequent regulatory curtailment of the ability to use supervisory goodwill to meet the taxpayer's capital requirements constitutes an affirmative act of abandonment by a taxpayer.

Taxpayers contend that the enactment of FIRREA did not merely reduce the value of supervisory goodwill. FIRREA rendered the asset completely and irrevocably worthless.

Once again, a distinction must be made between the face amount of supervisory goodwill booked, and the proper value of the right to use the face amount to meet capital reserve requirements. It would appear that FIRREA effectively eliminated by December 31, 1994 the ability of the acquiring institutions to count supervisory goodwill for capital reserve requirements.

Confiscation

The CIP also addresses the taxpayer's claim that it is entitled to a § 165 loss because the government allegedly confiscated its property as a result of the FIRREA changes. The CIP concludes that taxpayers pursuing *Winstar*-type contract claims have a reasonable prospect of recovery for contract damages. No further position was stated in the CIP regarding the confiscation nature of the loss.

Whether the alleged loss is characterized as a worthlessness, abandonment or confiscation loss seems immaterial. The crucial factor is whether there was a reasonable prospect of recovery.

Issue (4) Whether taxpayers are entitled to depreciation or amortization deductions under I.R.C. § 167 with respect to supervisory goodwill

This issue appears to have been raised by taxpayers as an alternative to the position that a loss is allowable under § 165. Taxpayers believe that supervisory goodwill has an ascertainable basis as a result of the application of § 597 and further argue that, as a result of the enactment of FIRREA, the asset has a limited useful life.

The CIP first concludes that taxpayers are not entitled to depreciation or amortization because taxpayers lack a tax basis in supervisory goodwill. However, even if taxpayers can establish a tax basis, the CIP concludes, based on the regulations under § 167, that taxpayers are not entitled to depreciation or amortization because no such deduction is allowable for residual goodwill. Moreover, a mere diminution in value, even over an identifiable period (such as the 5 year phase out of the right to count supervisory goodwill towards certain regulatory capital requirements) does not suffice to establish a limited useful life for a residual intangible such as the regulatory accounting asset of supervisory goodwill.

Treasury Regulation § 1.167(a)-3 reads, in part, as follows:

> If an intangible asset is known from experience or other factors to be of use in the business or in the production of income for only a limited period, the length of which can be estimated with reasonable accuracy, such an intangible asset may be the subject of a depreciation allowance. Examples are patents and copyrights. An intangible asset, the useful life of which is not limited, is not subject to the allowance for depreciation. No allowance will be permitted merely because, in the unsupported opinion of the taxpayer, the intangible asset has a limited useful life. No deduction for depreciation is allowable with respect to goodwill.

The threshold question is whether supervisory goodwill was goodwill in the traditional sense, or whether it was an identifiable intangible asset that could have been valued separate from that traditional goodwill and amortized over a determinable useful life. We discuss above that taxpayers have not established the real economic value of the right to use supervisory goodwill to meet regulatory requirements that might be embedded in the face amount of supervisory goodwill.

§A.18.6 Settlement Guidelines

In our opinion, a Settlement Guideline must take into account three significant issues:

- Whether the true economic value of supervisory goodwill for tax purposes was the face amount claimed by the taxpayer, or some lower amount,
- Whether the right to use supervisory goodwill to meet regulatory capital requirements represents "other property" within the context of § 597,
- Where a damage claim was filed, whether there was a reasonable prospect of recovery as of the close of the taxable year in which the loss deduction was claimed.

Valuation

The first significant issue concerns the valuation question surrounding the concept of supervisory goodwill. It is important to draw a distinction between what has been referred to as the "face amount of supervisory goodwill" and the value of the "right to use supervisory goodwill" to meet capital reserve requirements. The face amount of supervisory goodwill represented the excess of the value of the liabilities over the value of the assets of a failing thrift. It represented the negative net worth of a failing thrift and, as such, it did not represent an asset in the traditional sense. It was a bookkeeping entry used to implement the purchase method of accounting in the context of a supervisory merger. The face amount of supervisory goodwill, when viewed in and of itself, offered no real asset value to an acquiring thrift.

The "special accounting treatments" associated with supervisory goodwill were, on the other hand, contract rights or bargained-for-promises from the government that had a measure of economic value. The special accounting treatments included: (1) the right to use the face amount of the goodwill to meet capital reserve requirements, and (2) the right to amortize, for regulatory accounting purposes, the face amount over a longer period of time thus allowing the acquired thrift to seem more profitable than it really was.

As the damage claim cases demonstrate, the value of the right to use the special accounting treatment was necessarily less than 100% of the face amount of supervisory goodwill. Various economic experts have testified in the damage claim cases that, because supervisory goodwill was not an asset in the traditional sense, its value to the acquiring thrift was not equal to its face amount. Supervisory goodwill was not a negotiable or transferable asset, nor could it have been invested. It was not the equivalent of cash. It provided the ability to leverage more loans, but ultimately the accounting concept of supervisory goodwill worsened the financial crisis in the thrift industry during the 1980s. See *Winstar* at 854-955.

The supervisory goodwill tax refund claims that have been filed by taxpayers reflect claimed losses or deductions for the face amount of supervisory goodwill recorded in the regulatory merger transaction. Assuming that taxpayers can establish a tax basis for supervisory goodwill, the economic value to the acquiring institution at the acquisition date of the right to use supervisory goodwill to meet capital reserve requirements and to amortize the amount for book purposes has not been determined. Assuming taxpayers can establish a tax basis, then within the face amount of supervisory goodwill there may be an intangible asset that might be separable from goodwill much like the newspaper subscriber list was found to be separate from goodwill in *Newark Morning Ledger Co v. U.S.*, 507 U.S. 546 (1993). But taxpayers have not, for income tax purposes, ascertained such an intangible asset's value nor determined its useful life.

Section 597

The second issue to consider is whether the right to use supervisory goodwill represents "other property" within the context of § 597. There are two sub-issues within this overall issue. First, was the right to use supervisory goodwill received from **the FSLIC**? Second, was the right to use supervisory goodwill **other property** within the meaning of § 597?

The Supreme Court stated:

> There is no question, . . . that the [the FHLBB]and FSLIC had ample statutory authority to permit respondents to count supervisory goodwill and capital credits toward regulatory capital and to pay respondent's damages if that performance became impossible. The organic statute creating FSLIC as an arm of the Bank Board, 12 U.S.C. § 1725 (1988 ed.) (repealed1989), generally empowered it "[t]o make contracts" and § 1729(f)(2), enacted in 1978, delegated more specific powers in the context of supervisory mergers.

Winstar, at 890.

The Court refers to both the FHLBB and the FSLIC as having statutory authority to permit acquiring thrifts to count supervisory goodwill toward regulatory capital. The Court also states that the FSLIC was empowered to make contracts in the context of supervisory mergers.

When Congress amended the National Housing Act in 1987, it enacted § 1730h(d) which states:

> No provision of this section shall affect the authority of the Corporation to authorize insured institutions to utilize subordinated debt and goodwill in meeting reserve and other regulatory requirements.

The "Corporation" referred to in this statute is the FSLIC. Taxpayers have argued that when Congress enacted this statute it must have thought that FSLIC possessed the authority to permit acquiring institutions to use goodwill in meeting reserve requirements.

Section 597 refers to "any amount of money or other property received from the FSLIC pursuant to § 406(f) of the National Housing Act." Section 406(f) of the National Housing Act describes FSLIC assistance to include making loans, making contributions, purchasing assets, assuming liabilities, and guaranteeing against loss. Each of these actions involves either an immediate or eventual payment of money. An agreement reached between an acquiring thrift and the FHLBB/FSLIC that permitted the thrift the right to use supervisory goodwill for regulatory requirements did not require a current or future payment of money. When a supervisory merger involving the special accounting treatments occurred, the acquiring institution could not have anticipated that the special accounting treatments would be taken away as they were upon enactment of FIRREA. Consequently, on the regulatory merger date, the parties to the regulatory merger, including the acquiring institution and the FHLBB/FSLIC, could not have anticipated that any money would change hands with respect to the thrifts' use of the special accounting treatments. Although the enactment of FIRREA ultimately resulted in the filing of damage claims, at the time of the acquisitions, the special accounting treatments were not types of property that were backed by the promise of an eventual payment of money by the FSLIC.

The special accounting treatments associated with supervisory goodwill were promises by regulators to protect the viability of the acquiring thrifts. These regulatory promises, referred to by the Supreme Court as a substitute for cash, were not in fact cash equivalents.

If a damage claim case has not been filed, the ISP Coordinator should be contacted for further advice.

Summary

The risk factors outlined above must be converted into a computational proposal. The taxpayer must prevail on all significant issues in order to achieve success on the overall issue of its entitlement to a tax refund.

First, the taxpayer must convince a court of the value of the right to use supervisory goodwill to meet certain regulatory capital requirements.

Second, the taxpayer must convince a court that § 597 applies to the right to use supervisory goodwill to meet regulatory capital requirements.

Third, if the taxpayer has filed a damage claim, the taxpayer must convince a court that there was a tax loss and that there was no reasonable prospect of recovery at the time the loss was claimed.

Where a settlement is reached, and some measure of tax loss is allowed in a specific taxable year, the settlement should be accompanied by a closing agreement that disposes of these issues for all taxable years.

If the facts of a particular case do not follow the scenario above, the ISP Coordinator should be contacted for further advice.

Furthermore, the taxpayer should make available documentary evidence to support the facts. The following documents and substantiation are generally a part of a typical supervisory merger:

- Assistance agreement
- Forbearance agreement
- Merger Agreement
- Substantiation of the recording of supervisory goodwill for book purposes
- Substantiation of the amortization of supervisory goodwill for book purposes
- Schedules showing how supervisory goodwill contributed to meeting capital reserve requirements both before FIRREA and after FIRREA
- Substantiation of book write-off of supervisory goodwill

§ A.19 SUPERVISORY GOODWILL—LMSB COORDINATED ISSUE[1]

§ A.19.1 Issues

1. Whether supervisory goodwill is covered by I.R.C. § 597.[2]
2. Whether taxpayers[3] can establish a tax basis in supervisory goodwill.
3. Whether taxpayers are entitled to losses under I.R.C. § 165 with respect to supervisory goodwill based upon worthlessness, abandonment or confiscation.
4. Whether taxpayers are entitled to depreciation or amortization deductions under I.R.C. § 167 with respect to supervisory goodwill.

§ A.19.2 Facts

Supervisory goodwill is a regulatory intangible created under special accounting rules used by the Federal Home Loan Bank Board ("FHLBB") during the 1980s in connection with acquisitions of insolvent savings and loans and other similarly chartered institutions ("thrifts"), the deposits of which were insured by the Federal Savings and Loan Insurance Corporation ("FSLIC"). As a general matter, the Service does not recognize supervisory goodwill as an asset having tax basis.

Under the FHLBB's rules, taxpayers were permitted to record the acquisitions for financial reporting purposes using the purchase method of accounting. Under this method, taxpayers booked the excess of their cost (including liabilities assumed) over the then fair market value of the assets acquired as purchased goodwill on their balance sheets. Taxpayers were also allowed under the FHLBB's rules to count purchased goodwill (which was termed "supervisory goodwill" for regulatory purposes) towards meeting their regulatory capital requirements. For financial reporting and book purposes, purchased goodwill was amortized over a period not to exceed 40 years. The regulatory amortization period for supervisory goodwill, however, could be shorter.

Without the ability to count supervisory goodwill towards capital, many taxpayers would not have met their regulatory capital requirements after the acquisition. Upon enactment of the Financial Institutions Reform, Recovery, and Enforcement Act of 1989 (FIRREA), the regulatory benefits associated with supervisory goodwill changed, and the taxpayers' ability to count supervisory goodwill towards capital became subject to an accelerated five year phase out.

---

[1] Various regulatory rights are often conveyed to a taxpayer in connection with the acquisition of an insolvent institution. For the years at issue, these rights often included (1) the right to use the purchase method of accounting for financial reporting purposes to record the acquisition, (2) the right to use supervisory goodwill to meet regulatory capital requirements, and (3) the right to operate branches across state lines (so-called "branching rights"). Regardless of the regulatory rights conveyed in connection with these acquisitions, the issues are similar and the tax analysis used herein is generally applicable.

[2] All references to statutory provisions (including § 597) are to applicable provisions of law in effect prior to the 1989 enactment of the Financial Institutions Reform, Recovery, and Enforcement Act of 1989, Pub. L. No. 101-73 ("FIRREA").

[3] As used herein, taxpayer(s) may refer to the original acquirer of the insolvent institution, its successor in interest, its common parent, or a consolidated return group to which it belonged.

A number of taxpayers sued the federal government for damages arguing that FIRREA constituted a breach of contract for which damages were appropriate. They prevailed in the Supreme Court, which found that the federal government had breached these contracts. **See United States v. Winstar Corp.**, 518 U.S. 839 (1996). The cases were remanded for a determination of appropriate damages. A number of these **Winstar** damages-related actions are still pending in the United States Court of Federal Claims.

Prior to FIRREA, taxpayers did not amortize or depreciate supervisory goodwill or claim losses based on the worthlessness, confiscation or abandonment of supervisory goodwill on their tax returns. After FIRREA, taxpayers began asserting that they had a tax asset called supervisory goodwill. Taxpayers claim that they have a tax basis in supervisory goodwill because it is property under § 597 of the Code and assistance under § 406 of the National Housing Act ("NHA").[4] Further, taxpayers now claim to have incurred losses under § 165 of the Code because supervisory goodwill was abandoned, confiscated, or made worthless as a result of FIRREA's enactment.

In addition, some taxpayers are claiming depreciation or amortization deductions under I.R.C. § 167 for supervisory goodwill. Relying on **Newark Morning Ledger Co. v. United States**, 507 U.S. 546 (1993), these taxpayers claim that supervisory goodwill has an ascertainable value and a limited useful life which could be determined with reasonable accuracy after FIRREA's enactment.

For federal income tax purposes, however, taxpayers treated the acquisitions as nontaxable reorganizations in accordance with I.R.C. §§ 368(a)(1)(G) and 368(a)(3)(D). Pursuant to I.R.C. § 362, they took a carryover basis in the acquired assets of the insolvent thrift. Because supervisory goodwill was not an asset of the insolvent thrift, it was not reflected on the taxpayers' original federal income tax returns for the acquisition year.[5]

Although taxpayers are asserting that they have a tax basis in supervisory goodwill, they have not actually established how that tax basis arose. Because of the tax-free reorganization treatment, all of the taxpayers' originally identified sources of tax basis were properly reflected in their carryover tax basis for the acquired assets at the time of the original acquisitions. In addition, supervisory goodwill is not money or other property provided by the FSLIC pursuant to § 406(f) of the NHA. Therefore, § 597 is also not available to provide taxpayers with a nontaxable source of tax basis in supervisory goodwill. As taxpayers have not identified any source for their alleged tax basis in supervisory goodwill, they are not entitled to any tax relief as a result of FIRREA's changes in the regulatory treatment of supervisory goodwill. The appropriate remedy, if any, for these taxpayers for any breach by the federal government with respect to supervisory goodwill is contract damages.

---

[4] Section 406 of the NHA was codified at 12 U.S.C. § 1729.

[5] The regulatory asset of supervisory goodwill corresponds to the book asset of purchased goodwill. However, there is no corresponding tax asset because the excess amount that was booked by taxpayers as purchased goodwill is already reflected in their higher carryover tax basis for the same assets.

§ A.19.3 Discussion of Issues

Issue 1: Whether supervisory goodwill is covered by § 597.

Under § 597(a), a thrift's gross income did not include money or other property received from the FSLIC pursuant to § 406(f) of the NHA. A review of the legislative history of § 597 indicates that Congress intended § 597 to apply only to forms of financial assistance authorized by § 406(f) of the NHA. With respect to the provision ultimately enacted as § 597, the accompanying Conference Report states:

The bill excludes from income of [an insured thrift] all money or property contributed to the thrift institution by [the FSLIC] under its financial assistance program without reduction in basis of property. The amendment applies to assistance payments whether or not the association issues either a debt or equity instrument in exchange therefore....

H.R. Conf. Rep. No. 97-215, 97th Cong., 1st Sess. 284 (1981).

The types of financial assistance commonly available from the FSLIC under § 406(f) of the NHA included cash contributions, cash deposits, asset purchases, assumptions of liability, guarantees, and loans. As a general matter, these types of positive, tangible contributions from the FSLIC to the net worth of a thrift would be available to meet any future demands from depositors. Because of the types of tangible financial assistance expressly authorized under § 406(f) of the NHA, Congress could not intend § 597 to apply to any form of assistance other than transfers of money or similar property (for example, net worth notes) from the FSLIC.

Supervisory goodwill represents a form of regulatory forbearance that relieved taxpayers of otherwise applicable accounting and regulatory capital requirements. Because supervisory goodwill lacks independent value, it is not an asset available to meet the future demands of depositors. As it is not comparable to the types of financial assistance described under § 406(f) of the NHA, supervisory goodwill is not money or other property for purposes of § 597.

In addition, § 597 requires that the FSLIC provide the assistance under § 406(f) of the NHA. Supervisory goodwill, however, resulted from grants of regulatory forbearance by the FHLBB, not the FSLIC.[6] Even though the FSLIC was authorized to enter into assistance agreements in connection with the acquisitions at issue, it was the FHLBB from whom taxpayers sought and received permission to use the purchase method of accounting and to count any resulting goodwill towards their regulatory capital requirements as supervisory goodwill. Thus, supervisory goodwill is also not covered by § 597 because it was not provided by FSLIC.

---

[6] After **Winstar**, taxpayers also argue that the actions of FSLIC and FHLBB are interchangeable for purposes of § 406 of the NHA. The legislative history to § 597 and related contemporaneously enacted tax provisions, however, supports treating FSLIC and FHLBB as separate entities. Compare section 241 of the Economic Recovery Tax Act of 1981, Pub. L. No. 97-34 (Aug. 13, 1981) ("ERTA") (in which Congress spoke to actions taken by either FSLIC or FHLBB) with sections 243 and 244 of ERTA (in which Congress spoke to actions taken solely by FSLIC). Section 597 was added by section 244 of ERTA.

Some taxpayers also now argue that the "right to use" supervisory goodwill towards regulatory capital requirements is the relevant property for purposes of § 597 of the Code. However, neither this right alone, nor in combination with the bundle of other rights comprising the regulatory forbearance conferred by the FHLBB, is covered by § 597. As discussed above, regulatory forbearance is not an asset of the type described in § 406(f) of the NHA, and it is not assistance provided by the FSLIC.

Supervisory goodwill (including those rights comprising the related regulatory forbearance) remains a creature of regulatory accounting. It is not assistance provided by FSLIC pursuant to § 406(f) of the NHA, and it is not "money or other property" within the meaning of § 597.[7] Consequently, supervisory goodwill is not covered by § 597.

Issue 2: Whether taxpayers can establish a tax basis in supervisory goodwill.

Special basis rules apply to property acquired in tax free reorganizations. Under these rules, taxpayers usually step into the shoes of the transferors and, generally, receive a carryover basis. I.R.C. § 362(b). Since supervisory goodwill was not reflected on the books of the insolvent thrift, taxpayers cannot establish a carryover basis for it. *See* I.R.C. § § 362(a)-(b), and 1032(a).

Taxpayers identified and valued all of the assets and liabilities received in connection with these acquisitions at the time of the acquisition. Any additional consideration paid in connection with the acquisition was also allocated contemporaneously to the acquired assets. Taxpayers did not identify supervisory goodwill as a separate asset for tax purposes at the time of the acquisition. Taxpayers cannot now assert that any tax basis exists for it after FIRREA.[8] Rather, taxpayers must affirmatively establish that they have a tax basis in supervisory goodwill. *See* § § 362(b), 357(a)-(c), and 1012(a); Treas. Reg. § 1.61-(2)(d).

Taxpayers have not established that they incurred any additional cost with respect to supervisory goodwill. Pursuant to I.R.C. § 1012, the tax basis of acquired property is usually its cost. According to Treas. Reg. § 1.1012-1(a), cost is the amount paid (in money or other property) for property. Absent certain provisions which provide for the tax free receipt of property, taxpayers generally must include in income the fair market value of property they receive in order to obtain a tax basis in such property.[9] Treas. Reg. § 1.61-2(d). Taxpayers have not established a cost basis in supervisory goodwill.

Since taxpayers cannot point to any cost incurred in obtaining supervisory goodwill, and since they cannot assert a carryover tax basis in it, they may assert that they have a nontaxable source (such as § 597) from which to derive additional tax basis. However, because taxpayers have not established that at the

[7] See also **Washington Mutual, Inc. v. United States**, No. C06-1550-JCC (W.D. Wash. August 12, 2008), in which the United States District Court for the Western District of Washington, in an unpublished Order, granted the Government's motion for partial summary judgment on this issue.

[8] This also holds true for the "right to use" supervisory goodwill which would be construed as "other property" for purposes of § 1012.

[9] As discussed under Issue 1, § 597 does not apply to supervisory goodwill. Therefore, taxpayers cannot rely on § 597 to provide a nontaxable source for their asserted tax basis in supervisory goodwill.

time of the acquisition they had either a taxable or nontaxable source of tax basis for supervisory goodwill, they are not now entitled to claim that, after FIRREA, they have any tax basis in it.

Issue 3: Whether taxpayers are entitled to losses under § 165 with respect to supervisory goodwill based upon worthlessness, abandonment or confiscation.

After FIRREA, taxpayers began claiming tax losses based upon the worthlessness, abandonment or confiscation of supervisory goodwill and their right to use it to meet regulatory capital requirements. As discussed above, however, taxpayers are not entitled to any losses for supervisory goodwill because they lack tax basis in it. Even if a taxpayer could establish tax basis in supervisory goodwill, the deductible amount of any loss and the proper tax year for claiming such loss are not yet fixed.

Under § 165(a), a taxpayer is allowed a deduction for any loss sustained during the taxable year for which the taxpayer is not compensated by insurance or otherwise. Pursuant to § 165(b), the amount of the deduction is determined by reference to the taxpayer's adjusted basis under I.R.C. § 1011 for determining a loss from the sale or other disposition of property. But, before any loss is allowed as a deduction under § 165(a), it must be evidenced by "closed and completed transactions fixed by identifiable events." Treas. Reg. § 1.165-1(b). *See also* Treas. Reg. § 1.165-1(d); **United States v. S.S. White Dental Mfg. Co.**, 274 U.S. 398, 401 (1927).

Worthlessness

As stated above, taxpayers have not established any tax basis in supervisory goodwill. Therefore, they do not have deductible tax losses under § 165(a). Assuming a taxpayer does have a tax basis in supervisory goodwill, that taxpayer can deduct a loss under § 165 for it only in the year the loss is sustained and only to the extent the taxpayer is not compensated for that loss. Treas. Reg. § 1.165-1(a). If an event occurs that may result in a loss by a taxpayer and the taxpayer makes a claim for reimbursement for which a reasonable prospect of recovery exists, the taxpayer's loss is not considered to be sustained until the prospect of recovery can be ascertained with reasonable certainty. *See* Treas. Reg. § 1.165-1(d)(1) and (2)(i).

Whether a reasonable prospect for recovery exists is a factual issue, determined upon an objective examination of the facts and circumstances surrounding the loss as of the close of the taxable year in which the deduction is claimed. *See* **Boehm v. Commissioner**, 326 U.S. 287, 292-93 (1945); **Ramsay Scarlett & Co. v. Commissioner**, 61 T.C. 795, 811 (1974), aff'd, 521 F.2d 786 (4th Cir. 1975); **Brown v. Commissioner**, T.C. Memo. 1996-284. Thus, where a taxpayer is actively pursuing other remedies such as a lawsuit, and there exists a reasonable prospect for recovery by means of such remedies, the requirements of § 165 are not met. In such cases, the appropriate time for claiming a tax loss would be at the conclusion of the lawsuit (i.e., when there is a closed and completed transaction fixed by identifiable events which establish the proper taxable year and the amount of any loss). *See* Treas. Reg. § 1.165-1(d).

As noted above, certain taxpayers are still pursuing their **Winstar**-type contract claims in litigation and, currently, they appear to have a reasonable prospect of success. Taxpayers filed these **Winstar** lawsuits seeking reimbursement for damages that arose out of the same events underlying the tax losses being claimed on their amended federal income tax returns. Because these taxpayers have a reasonable prospect for recovery in their **Winstar** cases, they have not sustained the claimed tax loss for worthlessness with respect to supervisory goodwill. *See* **Ramsay Scarlett & Co**, supra, at 812-13; **Dawn v. Commissioner**, 675 F.2d 1077,1078 (9th Cir. 1982); **Estate of Scofield v. Commissioner**, 266 F.2d 154, 159 (6th Cir. 1959); **Brown, supra**. *See also* **Boehm, supra**, at 292-93; **Jeppsen v. Commissioner**, T.C. Memo. 1995-342, aff'd, 128 F.3d 1410 (10th Cir. 1997), **cert. denied**, 524 U.S. 916 (1998). Therefore, even assuming that a taxpayer establishes a tax basis in supervisory goodwill, the taxpayer cannot establish the amount of any deductible loss based on worthlessness or the proper tax year for claiming such loss while that taxpayer is pursuing **Winstar**-type litigation with respect to supervisory goodwill. The proper time for claiming such a loss would be when there is a closed and completed transaction fixed by identifiable events (such as the conclusion of the litigation).

Abandonment

Section 165 also permits taxpayers to deduct losses based on the abandonment of an asset used in a business or in a transaction entered into for profit. *See, e.g.*, Treas. Reg. § 1.165-2. To find that a taxpayer has suffered an abandonment loss, there must be (1) an intention by the owner to abandon the asset and (2) an affirmative act of abandonment. **A.J. Industries, Inc. v. United States**, 503 F.2d 660, 670 (9th Cir. 1974); **Citron v. Commissioner**, 97 T.C. 200, 209 (1991); **CRST, Inc. v. Commissioner**, 92 T.C. 1249, 1257 (1989), **aff'd**, 909 F.2d 1146 (8th Cir. 1990). Further, and as discussed above, the transaction must be closed and completed within the meaning of Treas. Reg. § 1.165-1(b). *See* **Illinois Cereal Mills, Inc. v. Commissioner**, T.C. Memo. 1983-469, **aff'd**, 789 F. 2d 1234 (7th Cir.), **cert. denied**, 479 U.S. 995 (1986). The taxable year in which such a loss is sustained need not be the taxable year in which the overt act of abandonment occurs. *See* Treas. Reg. § 1.165-2(a).

Intangible assets may be the subject of an abandonment loss. **Parmelee Transportation Co. v. United States**, 351 F.2d 619 (Ct. Cl. 1965). *See also* **Massey-Ferguson, Inc. v. Commissioner**, 59 T.C. 220 (1959), acq., 1973-2 C.B. 2; **Solar Nitrogen Chemicals, Inc. v. Commissioner**, T.C. Memo. 1978-486. Treas. Reg. § 1.165-2(a) provides that an abandonment loss with respect to a nondepreciable asset (including such historically nonamortizable intangible assets as goodwill) is allowable only in the taxable year in which such loss is sustained.

Generally, goodwill may not be abandoned until the business to which it relates ceases to operate. **Thrifticheck Service Corp. v. Commissioner**, 33 T.C. 1038 (1960), **aff'd**, 287 F.2d 1 (2d Cir. 1961); **Illinois Cereal Mills, Inc., supra**. This is because until the related business has ceased to operate, the transaction is not considered to be "closed and completed" within the meaning of Treas. Reg. § 1.165-1(b). *See* **Illinois Cereal Mills, supra**. An exception to the general proscription against an early abandonment of items like goodwill can exist where the taxpayer abandons a portion of its business having a distinct transferable value. *See* **Metropolitan Laundry Co. v. United States**, 100 F.Supp. 803 (N.D. Cal. 1951) (taxpayer permitted to claim an abandonment loss on a portion of a customer list attributable to a particular geographic area).

The court in **Metropolitan Laundry** explained that while goodwill is not severable from the underlying ongoing business, it is possible that an ongoing concern can dispose of a portion of its business in a particular area, along with attendant goodwill, without completely ceasing operations. Thus, as long as the business and the goodwill disposed can be assigned a "distinct transferable value," the transaction can be considered "closed and completed" for tax purposes. **Metropolitan Laundry**, 100 F.Supp. at 806-07. In **Massey-Ferguson**, 59 T.C. at 225, the Tax Court followed Metropolitan Laundry, and held that the abandonment of an identifiable and severable intangible asset entitled the taxpayer to a currently deductible abandonment loss.[10]

Under § 165, an affirmative act of abandonment is required. The taxpayer's intent to abandon property standing alone is generally insufficient to establish an abandonment loss for § 165 purposes. *See* **Brountas v. Commissioner**, 692 F.2d 152 (1st Cir. 1982), **cert. denied**, 462 U.S. 1106 (1983), **Beus v. Commissioner**, 261 F.2d 176, (9th Cir. 1958), **Citro** n, 97 T.C. at 210; **Zurn v. Commissioner**, T.C. Memo. 1996-386. Moreover, abandonment does not automatically result from the mere cessation of use of the asset by the taxpayer. **Beus**, 261 F.2d at 180.

Further, a taxpayer's participation in a government program requiring the taxpayer to cease certain operations will not be construed as an affirmative act of abandonment absent a showing of the requisite taxpayer intent to abandon the business. *See* **Standley v. Commissioner**, 99 T.C. 259 (1992), **aff'd without published opinion**, 24 F.3d 249 (9th Cir. 1994). Additionally, restrictive actions by the government are generally construed to affect only the value of the property where the taxpayer continues to hold onto that property. *See* **CRST v. Commissioner**, 92 T.C. at 1259-61; **Beatty v. Commissioner**, 46 T.C. 835 (1966); and **Consolidated Freight Lines, Inc. v. Commissioner**, 37 B.T.A. 576 (1938), **aff'd**, 101 F.2d 813 (9th Cir.), **cert. denied**, 308 U.S. 562 (1939).

Following FIRREA, some taxpayers claimed abandonment losses under § 165 with respect to supervisory goodwill. As discussed above, because taxpayers have not established that they have a tax basis in supervisory goodwill or that they have otherwise met the requirements for deduction under § 165 with respect to it, they are not entitled to the claimed deductions. However, even if a taxpayer can establish a tax basis in supervisory goodwill and satisfy the other requirements of § 165, there must be an affirmative act of abandonment by the taxpayer. The mere diminution in the value of property is not enough to establish an abandonment loss. *See* **Kraft Inc. v. United States**, 30 Fed. Cl. 739, 785-86 (1994); **Lakewood Associates v. Commissioner**, 109 T.C. 450, 456 (1997), **aff'd**

[10] In **Massey-Ferguson**, the taxpayer argued that it had abandoned the use of the going concern value of a previously acquired business operation even though it continued to manufacture and distribute similar products under its own name after that time.

without published opinion, 173 F.3d 850 (4th Cir. 1998); and **S.S. White Dental Mfg.**, 274 U.S. at 401. Moreover, neither FIRREA's statutory provisions nor the government's subsequent regulatory curtailment of the ability to use supervisory goodwill to meet taxpayers' capital requirements constitutes an affirmative act of abandonment by a taxpayer.[11]

Confiscation

Some taxpayers have also argued that they are entitled to a § 165 loss because the government allegedly confiscated their property as a result of the FIRREA changes and, therefore, the "reasonable prospect of recovery" standard outlined above does not apply. This argument is based on **S.S. White Dental Mfg.**, 274 U.S. at 403, which allowed the taxpayer a deduction equal to its investment in a subsidiary that had been confiscated by the German government in 1918. In allowing the deduction, the Court pointed to the fact that the taxpayer could have no more than a remote hope of recovering its property from the wreck of war. The Court did not, however, discard the reasonable prospect of recovery standard for cases in which taxpayers do have a reasonable hope of recovery.

Unlike the taxpayer in **S.S. White Dental Mfg.**, taxpayers pursuing **Winstar**-type contract claims have a reasonable prospect of recovery for contract damages. The Supreme Court in **Winstar** stated that the petitioners there were entitled to damages. Similarly situated taxpayers would have equally viable prospects. Thus, the prospect of recovery for taxpayers in these supervisory goodwill cases cannot be deemed so remote a hope as that facing the taxpayer in **S.S. White Dental Mfg.** Where the prospect of recovery is reasonably certain, the mere existence of facts supporting a cause of action has been held sufficient to bar a loss deduction. **Premji v. Commissioner**, T.C. Memo. 1996-304, **aff'd without published opinion**, 139 F.3d 912 (10th Cir. 1998).

Thus, even if a taxpayer can establish that it had a tax basis in supervisory goodwill, that taxpayer would generally not be able to establish that it is entitled to a deductible loss under § 165(a) based upon worthlessness, abandonment, or confiscation for the reasons set forth above.

Issue 4: Whether taxpayers are entitled to depreciation or amortization deductions under I.R.C. § 167 with respect to supervisory goodwill.

Taxpayers are not entitled to depreciation or amortization deductions under § 167 with respect to supervisory goodwill (which corresponds to residual goodwill).[12] Section § 167(a) provides a depreciation deduction for a reasonable allowance for the exhaustion, wear and tear (including obsolescence) of property used in a trade or business including intangibles. *See* Treas. Reg. § 1.167(a)-3.

[11] Generally, for purposes of claiming an abandonment loss with respect to supervisory goodwill, taxpayers have argued that the tax asset of supervisory goodwill is akin to the residual value remaining after all other assets acquired in connection with the insolvent thrift's acquisition have been identified, valued and lifed. The result of this argument is that supervisory goodwill resembles the tax asset of goodwill (referred to as "residual goodwill" under Issue 4 below).

[12] See footnote 11 above for further clarification of the use of the phrase "residual goodwill" in this context.

However, Treas. Reg. § 1.167(a)-3 also provides that no depreciation deduction is allowable for such residual goodwill. This regulation further states that intangible assets which do not have a limited useful life are not subject to the depreciation deduction and that no allowance will be permitted "merely because, in the unsupported opinion of the taxpayer, the intangible asset has a limited useful life."

Moreover, a mere diminution in value, even over an identifiable period (such as the 5 year phase out of the right to count supervisory goodwill towards certain regulatory capital requirements) does not suffice to establish a limited useful life for a residual intangible such as the regulatory accounting asset of supervisory goodwill. Thus, taxpayers are not entitled to depreciation or amortization deductions under § 167 with respect to supervisory goodwill. Even if the regulations did not prohibit such a depreciation or amortization deduction, since taxpayers cannot establish a tax basis in supervisory goodwill they are not entitled to § 167 amortization deductions with respect thereto. As explained above in Issue 2, taxpayers have not established a tax basis in supervisory goodwill (including the right to use it). Since taxpayers lack a tax basis in supervisory goodwill, their depreciable basis is zero pursuant to I.R.C. §§ 167(c)(1), 1011, and 1016 and Treas. Reg. § 1.167(g)-1.

Further, even if a taxpayer could establish a tax basis in supervisory goodwill in excess of zero, that taxpayer must still satisfy the requirements of **Newark Morning Ledger Co. v. Unites States**, 507 U.S. 546 (1993). Once an intangible has been identified, **Newark Morning Ledger** requires that the value of that asset be ascertained (for basis) and its useful life be reasonably determined. As shown above, taxpayers cannot meet these tests with respect to the residually determined supervisory goodwill. Moreover, the determinations of value and useful life must be based upon information available to the taxpayer at the time of the transaction. **Banc One Corp. v. Commissioner**, 84 T.C. 476, 499 (1985), **aff'd without published opinion**, 815 F.2d 75 (6th Cir. 1987). A subsequent change from no determinable useful life to a limited remaining useful life is not a mere change in useful life for purposes of § 167. Rather, such a change is a change in the nature of the asset.

Finally, even assuming that a taxpayer establishes a tax basis in excess of zero and otherwise satisfies **Newark Morning Ledger's** requirements, if the taxpayer is changing the treatment of supervisory goodwill from a non-depreciable capital asset to a depreciable capital asset, the taxpayer has two choices to implement this change pursuant to CC-2004-007 (January 28, 2004) and CC-2004-024 (July 12, 2004) because the taxpayer would have placed the supervisory goodwill in service in taxable years ending before December 30, 2003. That is, the taxpayer may either (i) implement the change by filing amended returns for the earliest open year (but in no event earlier than the placed-in-service year of the supervisory goodwill), or (ii) treat the change as a change in method of accounting under § 446(e) by filing a Form 3115 for the current taxable year. If the taxpayer files amended returns to implement the change in treatment of supervisory goodwill, the taxpayer is taking the position that this change is not a change in method of accounting and, consequently, an adjustment under § 481 is neither required nor permitted. If the taxpayer is treating the change in treatment of supervisory goodwill as a change in method of accounting under § 446(e), the taxpayer must file a Form 3115 for the current taxable year to secure the Commissioner's consent to change the treatment of supervisory goodwill prior to making the change. Consequently, the taxpayer is not entitled to make a retroactive method change with respect to supervisory goodwill. *See* Treas. Reg. §§ 1.446-1(e)(2)(i) and 1.446-1(e)(3)(i).

Except in specifically authorized situations, not present in these types of matters, an accounting method cannot be changed by a taxpayer's filing of an amended return as that would constitute a retroactive method change. *See, e.g.*, Rev. Rul. 90-38, 1990-1 C.B. 57. Thus, assuming a taxpayer can prove a basis in supervisory goodwill in excess of zero, if that taxpayer files amended returns to implement the change in treatment of supervisory goodwill, it is not entitled to deductions under § 167 attributable to supervisory goodwill for any closed year. Alternatively, and also assuming a taxpayer can prove a basis in supervisory goodwill in excess of zero, if that taxpayer treats the change in treatment of supervisory goodwill as a change in method of accounting, the taxpayer is entitled to an adjustment under § 481(a) for the taxable year in which the Form 3115 is filed for the prior years' deductions under § 167 attributable to supervisory goodwill.

§ A.19.4 Conclusions

Issue 1: Supervisory goodwill is a creature of regulatory accounting and is not FSLIC financial assistance under § 406(f) of the NHA (as codified at 12 C.F.R. § 1729(f)). Therefore, supervisory goodwill does not qualify as "money or other property" under § 597.

Issue 2: Taxpayers cannot establish that they have a tax basis in supervisory goodwill because, generally, thrift acquisitions were tax free transactions and the taxpayers took a carryover basis in the acquired assets. Consequently, no basis was assigned to regulatory intangibles such as supervisory goodwill at the time of the acquisitions. Further, the taxpayers' assertion of tax basis on Forms 1120X is insufficient to establish that tax basis in supervisory goodwill exists.

Issue 3: Since taxpayers cannot establish that tax basis in supervisory goodwill exists, they are not entitled to § 165 losses based upon worthlessness, abandonment or confiscation. Moreover, even if a taxpayer were able to establish a tax basis in supervisory goodwill, that taxpayer must affirmatively establish that it met the other requirements of § 165 for the loss as claimed in the tax years for which the amended returns were filed.

Issue 4: Taxpayers cannot establish a tax basis in supervisory goodwill and, therefore, they are not entitled to deductions under § 167 for depreciation or amortization with respect to supervisory goodwill. Even if a taxpayer could establish a tax basis in supervisory goodwill, that taxpayer must affirmatively establish that it satisfied **Newark Morning Ledger's** requirements before it would be entitled to such deductions.

§A.20 BAD DEBTS: INDUSTRY DIRECTOR GUIDELINES ON AUDITING BANK BAD DEBT CONFORMITY ELECTION

December 12, 2001

MEMORANDUM FOR INDUSTRY DIRECTORS
DIRECTOR, FIELD SPECIALISTS
DIRECTOR, PREFILING AND TECHNICAL GUIDANCE

FROM: David B. Robison /s/David B. Robison
Industry Director, Financial Services

SUBJECT: Industry Directive on the Conformity Election for Bank Bad Debts

The purpose of this memorandum is to provide a directive to examiners in the audit of the bad debt conformity election for banking institutions, in light of and as a companion to the publication of Rev. Rul. 2001-59 in I.R.B. 2001-51. This Revenue Ruling resulted from the banking industry's and the Service's joint effort to clarify the conformity election as part of the Industry Issue Resolution Pilot Program.

The bad debt conformity election for banks was added to the Treasury Regulations in response to the September, 1991 Treasury White Paper, "Report to The Congress on The Tax Treatment of Bad Debts by Financial Institutions", which addressed industry requests for book/tax conformity in the bad debt area. The conformity election under Treas. Reg. § 1.166-2(d)(3) is an accounting method available to banks to establish a conclusive presumption of worthlessness, either in whole or in part, for its loans. If a bank has properly complied with the terms of the conformity election, the bank is entitled to a bad debt deduction for loans classified as "loss assets", which were charged off for regulatory purposes.

Proper election of the conformity method of accounting substantially reduces the time required for auditing bad debts, thus saving resources for both the bank and the Service. The attached guidelines are intended to assist examiners in determining whether a proper conformity election was made and to provide assistance to examiners on the efficient use of time and resources in the analysis of this issue. The commitment of staffing to examine conformity election bad debts is usually not an effective utilization of resources. Approaches to planning and conducting an examination of the conformity election are explained in the attachment.

This LMSB Directive is not an official pronouncement of the law or the Service's position and cannot be used, cited or relied upon as such.

If you have any questions, please contact me at (212) 298-2130 or either Jeffrey Kammerman, Commercial Banking/Savings & Loan Technical Advisor, at (212) 719-6569 or Jody Botsford, Savings & Loan/Commercial Banking Technical Advisor, at (626) 312-5101.

§ A.21 BAD DEBTS: ATTACHMENT TO INDUSTRY DIRECTOR GUIDELINES ON AUDITING BANK BAD DEBT CONFORMITY ELECTION

In general, a deduction is allowed under IRC § 166 for any debt which becomes worthless within the taxable year. However, no precise test exists for determining whether a debt is worthless. In many situations, no single factor or identifiable event clearly demonstrates whether a debt has become worthless. Instead, a series of factors or events in the aggregate establishes whether the debt is worthless.

For tax years ending on or after December 31, 1991, a bank, within the meaning of IRC § 581,[1] may obtain a conclusive presumption of worthlessness for bad debts that it owns by making a conformity election under Treas. Reg. § 1.166-2(d)(3). Under this election, a debt charged off for regulatory purposes is conclusively presumed to be worthless, in whole or in part, if either (1) the charge-off results from a specific order from a regulatory authority or (2) the charge-off corresponds to the bank's classification of the debt as a "loss asset". Treas. Reg. § 1.166-2(d)(3)(ii)(C) defines the term "loss asset" as a debt that the bank has assigned to a class that corresponds to a loss asset classification under the standards set forth in the "Uniform Agreement on the Classification of Assets and Appraisal of Securities Held by Banks" or similar guidance issued by the bank's supervisory authority.

Rev. Rul. 2001-59, published on December 17, 2001 in I.R.B. 2001-51, provides clarification of the classification of a loan as a "loss asset" in order to meet the bad debt conformity election. Following an analysis of the applicable legal authorities, the Revenue Ruling concludes that a bank's board of directors' resolution authorizing charge-offs of only "loss asset" loans is sufficient to demonstrate classification of the loans as loss assets for purposes of Treas. Reg. § 1.166-2(d)(3). The Revenue Ruling also provides examples of other procedures a bank can use to classify loans (or loan portions) as loss assets.

Furthermore, Rev. Rul. 2001-59 addresses the situation where a bank erroneously charged off loans for regulatory purposes, but the error was not substantial enough for the Commissioner to revoke the bank's conformity election under Treas. Reg. § 1.166-2(d)(3)(iv)(D). In such a situation, the revenue ruling concludes that even the erroneously charged off loans are entitled to the conclusive presumption of worthlessness and an adjustment is not warranted.

§ A.21.1 I. Guidelines for Auditing Conformity Election Requirements

When auditing a bank under the conformity method of accounting, the examiner must confirm that four requirements have been met for the conclusive presumption of worthlessness to apply to loans owned by the bank. Those four requirements are: (1) a valid conformity election; (2) a valid Express Determination Letter; (3) the loan must be charged off for book purposes; and (4) the loan must be classified as a loss asset (unless charge-off was ordered by the bank's

[1] See Treas. Reg. § 1.166-2(d)(4)(i).

regulator). If a bank fails to meet either the conformity election or the Express Determination Letter requirements, the bank will not be entitled to utilize the conformity method.

The two remaining requirements of book charge-off and loss asset classification apply to each loan separately. A bank's failure to meet either of these two remaining requirements for a specific loan will not result in an adjustment, unless this failure or a pattern of failures is substantial enough to result in a determination to revoke the bank's conformity election under Treas. Reg. § 1.166-2(d)(3)(iv)(D).

For example, in the situation where a bank erroneously charged off loans for regulatory purposes, but the error was not substantial enough to revoke the conformity election, Rev. Rul. 2001-59 concludes that even the erroneously charged off loans are entitled to the conclusive presumption of worthlessness and an adjustment is not warranted. However, if a bank had a computer input error that inadvertently resulted in the addition of an extra 0 (e.g. $5,000,000 vs. $500,000), this would be considered the correction of a clerical error and the adjustment should be made. See, for example, IRC § 6213(b)(1) and Treas. Reg. § 1.446-1(e)(2)(ii)(b).

In order to determine whether a bank has met the above four requirements of the conformity election and is entitled to a conclusive presumption of worthlessness for its charged off loans, it is recommended that the examiner initially request the following information:

Form 3115 electing conformity

Express Determination Letter(s)

Reconciliation of book charge-offs to tax deductions Bank's policies and procedures on loan classification Annual reports

Bank's Reports of Condition and Income (Call Reports)/ Savings and Loan's Thrift Financial Reports

Securities and Exchange Commission (SEC) filings, e.g. Forms 10-Q, 10-K, 8-K

A Valid Conformity Election

One of the initial documents an examiner must obtain is the bank's Form 3115 (Application for Change in Accounting Method) electing conformity. A Form 3115 must be filed by an existing bank to elect the conformity method of accounting. This election must be made on a bank by bank basis and could have been made for years as early as 1991. New banks adopt the conformity method by filing a statement with their initial tax return.

Express Determination Letter

In addition, the examiner must also obtain the bank's Express Determination Letter(s) (EDL) covering the years under audit. Pursuant to Treas. Reg. § 1.166-2(d)(3)(iii) (D), every bank under the conformity method must obtain an EDL from its Federal supervisory authority verifying that the bank maintains and applies loan loss classification standards that are consistent with the supervisory authority's regulatory standards. The necessary language for an EDL can be found in Rev. Proc. 92-84, 1992-2 C.B. 489.

At the end of each regulatory examination by its supervisory authority, the bank must request and receive a new EDL. Retroactive EDLs covering earlier regulatory examination periods are not acceptable. Banks are generally examined by their regulator every 18 months.

If a bank fails to obtain the required EDL, the conformity election is automatically revoked as of the beginning of the tax year that includes the date as of which the supervisory authority conducts its examination.

Book Charge-Off Required

It is also recommended that the examiner obtain from the bank a reconciliation of the bank's charge-offs to its bad debt deductions, since a loan must be charged off on the books and records of the bank for the conclusive presumption of worthlessness to apply.[2] Under the conformity election, the bad debt deduction is limited to the year of the book charge-off. Accordingly, the examiner should compare the book charge-offs and bad debt deductions to see if there are any obvious inconsistencies, which should be reconciled.

For book purposes, a savings & loan (S&L) may establish a specific allowance for loans classified as either substandard, doubtful, or loss. Pursuant to Treas. Reg. § 1.166-2(d)(4)(ii), for banks regulated by the Office of Thrift Supervision (OTS), the term "charge-off" includes the establishment of a specific allowance for loan losses in the amount of 100 percent of the portion of a debt classified as a loss. This section was added to clarify that the term "charge-off," as it pertains to S&Ls, includes the establishment of specific allowances for loan losses.

Although the establishment of a specific allowance will satisfy the charge-off requirements of the conformity election, the loans charged to a specific allowance must also meet the standards of a loss asset to qualify for a conclusive presumption of worthlessness. A loan classified as substandard or doubtful and charged to a specific allowance by an S&L will not meet the standards of a loss asset.

Loan Must Be Classified as a Loss Asset

A loan must also be classified as a "loss asset" by the bank for the conclusive presumption of worthlessness to apply, unless the loan was charged off pursuant to a regulator's specific order. Treas. Reg. § 1.166-2(d)(3)(ii)(C) defines the term "loss asset" as a debt that the bank has assigned to a class that corresponds to a loss asset classification under the standards set forth by the bank's supervisory authority. Therefore, it is recommended that the examiner obtain the bank's policies and procedures on loan classification.

Rev. Rul. 2001-59 provides that various procedures can be used by a bank to classify loans, in whole or in part, as loss assets. This evidence could include the

[2] Discussions of books in this context refer to the bank's Regulatory Accounting Principles (RAP) books.

board of directors' resolution referred to in the Revenue Ruling, credit committee reports or notations on loan files.

For example, an officer or employee may record that a loan has been classified as a loss asset on the internal form used by the bank at the time of charge-off. Copies of these internal forms could then be centrally filed by the bank making it easier for the examiner to verify that the classification requirement has been met. Additionally, if under a board of directors' resolution, the officers and employees are authorized to charge off loans only if the loans are "loss asset" loans, then the charge-offs of these loans demonstrates that the loans have been classified as loss assets.

Bank's Reports and Filings

Finally, it is recommended that the examiner obtain the bank's annual reports, call reports to its regulator and SEC filings. The examiner should analyze these filings to determine whether the bank's charge-offs and recovery rates warrant further review. For SEC registrants, the quarterly and annual Management Discussion and Analysis (MD&A) reports should provide information about the bank's loan loss methodologies, policies and procedures.[3]

The examiner should use professional judgement to determine whether the bank's charge-off and recovery rates warrant further review. Some of the factors to be considered include the rate of charge-offs and recoveries in prior years and the change to charge-offs in comparison to prior year(s). The regulatory and SEC filings may help to determine the bank's historical recovery rates for applicable loan categories.

If the bank has met the conformity election requirements and its charge-off and recovery rates appear reasonable, no further audit steps are warranted.

However, if the bank's charge-off and recovery rates do not initially appear reasonable, the examiner should then consider the charge-off and recovery rates experienced by the bank in relation to its peers. Peer groups are often determined with reference to the bank's asset size, lines of business and/or geographic location. Federal studies (such as the Federal Reserve Bank of New York's publication "Current Issues in Economics and Finance") that track current industry charge-off averages may be useful in this analysis.

For example, if the current industry charge-off average is six percent of outstanding loans for a particular loan category and the taxpayer is charging off 12 percent, a material deviation may exist. The bank should be given the opportunity to explain what economic or other circumstances caused the difference.

A bank's experience with recoveries, as compared to its peers, may also reflect a charge-off in excess of reasonable business judgement. For example, if a

[3] See the Securities and Exchange Commission Staff Accounting Bulletin: No. 102 - Selected Loan Loss Allowance Methodology and Documentation Issues (July 6, 2001) and the Board of Governors on the Federal Reserve System, Division of Banking Supervision and Regulation: SR 01-17 (SUP) - Final Interagency Policy Statement on Allowance for Loan and Lease Losses (ALLL) Methodologies and Documentation for Banks and Savings Institutions.

bank were recovering 25 percent or more of the charged-off loans for a particular loan category, while peer data would indicate that 12 percent recover rate was more common, a material deviation may exist. The examiner should then question the bank as to why its recovery rate appears to be out of line with the industry.

If the bank is unable to adequately explain the above deviations, it may be appropriate to sample the loan files to see if the data supports the bank's chargeoffs. A bank's failure to meet the loan loss classification or charge-off requirements for a specific loan, generally will not result in an individual loan adjustment. If the pattern of failures is substantial enough, however, it may result in a determination to revoke the bank's conformity election.

If the review of the loan files leads to the determination that the charge-offs were substantially in excess of reasonable business judgement, revocation of the election may be warranted. It should be noted that revocation of the conformity election is an extraordinary step when the procedural requirements have been met.

§ A.21.2 II. Revocation of Conformity Election

As stated previously, if a bank fails to meet either the conformity election or the Express Determination Letter requirements, the bank will not be entitled to utilize the conformity method. However, a bank's failure to meet either the book charge-off and loss asset classification requirements for a specific loan will not result in an adjustment, unless this failure or a pattern of failures is substantial enough to result in a determination to revoke the bank's conformity election under Treas. Reg. § 1.166-2(d)(3)(iv)(D).

Pursuant to Treas. Reg. § 1.166-2(d)(3)(iv)(D), the Commissioner may revoke a bank's election to use the conformity method, if an electing bank fails to follow the conformity method of accounting to determine when debts become worthless, or if the bank's charge-offs are substantially in excess of those warranted by reasonable business judgement in applying the regulatory standards of the bank's supervisory authority. Accordingly, if an examination of a bank's books and records reveals that there is a pattern of charge-offs in the wrong year or under all the facts and circumstances the charge-offs were substantially in excess of reasonable business judgment in applying the regulatory standards of the bank's supervisory authority, the conformity election may be revoked.

For example, the conformity bad debt deduction should match book charge-offs. The examiner should determine, based upon a review of the reconciliation schedules provided, whether the bank has engaged in a practice of charging off loans in the wrong year, either early or late. A pattern of charge offs in the wrong year could lead to a revocation of the conformity election.

In addition, as stated above, a bank's failure to meet the loan loss classification or charge-off requirements for a specific loan, generally will not result in an individual loan adjustment. If the pattern of failures is substantial enough, however, it may result in a determination to revoke the bank's conformity election.

Finally, in the case of an S&L where the creation of a specific reserve for loan losses results in a tax deduction for 100 percent of the portion of the debt classified as loss assets, electing conformity is not intended to allow a double deduction. Such a double deduction could result from the fluctuation in the specific reserve from one reporting period to the next. The examiner should compare the prior specific reserves per the Thrift Financial Reports to ensure that the same specific reserve for a particular loan does not result in a duplication of the tax deduction. If this duplication becomes a pattern, the examiner should consider revocation.

The examiner should use professional judgement in determining whether to pursue the extraordinary step of revoking a bank's conformity election. Based on the data collected, the Team Manager and Team Coordinator should determine the extent of resources to devote to this issue. Conversations with the taxpayer and the Banking Technical Advisors may assist the examiner in setting the scope and depth for examining this issue and help minimize the audit burden on both the taxpayer and the examination team.

§ A.21.3 III. Examples of Loans Not Subject to Conformity Election[4]

It should also be remembered that not all loans of a bank are entitled to the conclusive presumption of worthlessness under the conformity election. For example, the examiner should confirm the bank owns the worthless loans for both book and tax purposes. Loans not owned for book purposes are not subject to regulatory loan loss classification standards and thus are outside the scope of the conformity election. In addition, the examiner should be aware that the bank's bad debt tax basis might be affected by the mark to market provisions under IRC § 475.

The following are examples of some loans or portions of loans not subject to the conformity election because they are not subject to regulatory loan loss classification standards:

Securitized Loans –Many securitizations are treated as sales for book purposes, but are treated as financing arrangements for tax purposes. In these circumstances, if the bank does not own the loans for book/regulatory purposes, the loans cannot be charged off on the bank's books under the loss classification standards and, therefore, the conformity election cannot apply to the securitized loans. For example, credit card, installment and auto loan securitizations have generally been treated as sales for book purposes, but financing transactions for tax purposes. The determination of sale versus financing is highly fact intensive and requires a case by case analysis of the benefits and burdens of ownership.

Restructured Loans –A loan may be significantly modified for tax purposes. This significant modification requires the tax recognition of gain or loss, which may not exist for book purposes. See Treas. Reg. § 1.1001-3.

---

[4] Bad debt deductions for loans not subject to regulatory loss classification standards are determined under the general rules of IRC § 166.

Interest on Nonperforming Loans –A bank may cease to accrue interest income for book purposes, even though it continues to accrue the interest for tax purposes. Thus, there is no loan on the books for this unpaid interest.

Loans Accounted for on a Cost Recovery Basis – A bank with a loan that is considered delinquent or nonperforming may still receive cash payments from the borrower. The bank may apply these payments first to principal for book purposes. However, for tax purposes, these payments may be recognized as interest income, based upon the terms of the loan document.

Interest Accrual Reversals –For book purposes, a bank may be required to reverse previously accrued interest income, when a loan is impaired or nonperforming. However, interest income cannot be reversed for tax purposes. Thus, there is no loan of this interest for tax purposes.

In-Substance Foreclosures –In-Substance Foreclosures (ISF) represent the physical possession of the collateral property by a bank. An ISF is recorded as Other Real Estate Owned (OREO) for book purposes, even though a technical foreclosure has not taken place. In an ISF circumstance, the loan no longer exits for book purposes, but it still exists for tax purposes.

§ A.21.4 IV. Previously Published Determinations Concerning The Conformity Election

Prior published determinations by the Chief Counsel's office in the conformity election area are being provided for informational purposes only. Please note that pursuant to IRC § 6110(k)(3), Chief Counsel Advice may not be used or cited as precedent. Such advice generally involves specific taxpayers based on specific facts and represents the thinking of Chief Counsel's office at the time of issuance.

The following are examples of some loans or portions of loans not subject to the conformity election because they are not subject to regulatory loan loss classification standards:

FSA 199912005, Released March 26, 1999:

In response to a request for Field Service Advice, Counsel concluded that only loans classified as "loss" assets for regulatory purposes qualify as deductible bad debts under a valid conformity election, while loans classified as "substandard" or "doubtful" do not.

FSA 200018017, Released May 5, 2000:

On the facts presented, Counsel recommended in this Field Service Advice that Exam consider revoking the taxpayer's conformity election in the earliest open year under examination in accordance with Treas. Reg. § 1.166-(d)(3)(iv)(D). Also, any such revocation must be handled as a cut-off method with no attendant adjustment under IRC § 481(a) with respect to loan amounts previously charged off for book purposes.

ITA 200027036, Released July 7, 2000:

In response to a request for Technical Assistance concerning the revocation of the conformity election under Treas. Reg. § 1.166-2(d)(3), Counsel concluded that the Service may audit a bank that has made the conformity election. The audit determines whether the bank complied with the requirements of the accounting method in particular, as well as the requirements for a bad debt deduction in general.

This advice also discusses instances in which the conformity election may be revoked.

The case of **United States v. U.S. Bancorp**, 12 F.Supp. 2d 982 (D.Minn.1998) is cited in a footnote in this advice. In this summons enforcement case, the bank argued that under a valid conformity election, the information sought by the Service was irrelevant, since the election provides a conclusive presumption of worthlessness for bad debts. The court concluded that the conclusive presumption does not make information regarding those debts irrelevant to the legitimate determination of the bank's tax liabilities and the accuracy of the bank's tax return. Accordingly, the bank was required to comply with the summons.

CCA 200045030, Released November 9, 2000:

In response to a request for Technical Assistance concerning the conformity election under Treas. Reg. § 1.166-2(d)(3), Counsel concluded, in part, that:

The conclusive presumption of worthlessness standard set forth in Treas. Reg. § 1.166-2(d)(3)(ii) can apply to consumer loans such as credit card loans and installment loans that are classified as a regulatory loss asset after the applicable period passes, assuming the bank owns the debt instrument or credit account for both regulatory and tax purposes; and

The Service does not have the authority to question a bank's loan loss classification standards when a bank makes a conformity election and has received an Express Determination Letter. However, the Service may revoke the conformity election, if a bank fails to follow the method of accounting required by the conformity election, or the bank's charge-offs were substantially in excess of reasonable business judgement in applying the regulatory standards of the bank's supervisory authority.

FSA 200129003, Released July 20, 2001

In this Field Service Advice dealing with whether a building and loan association's treatment of bad debt losses was an accounting method change, Counsel stated that the conformity election under Treas. Reg. § 1.166-2(d)(3) can apply equally to banks using the reserve method of accounting for bad debts and to banks using the specific charge-off method.[5]

---

[5] See Statement of Financial Accounting Standards (SFAS) 125 and 140.

§A.22 BAD DEBTS: UNIFORM AGREEMENT ON CLASSIFICATION OF SECURITIES[1]

This Joint Statement of the Office of the Comptroller of the Currency, the Federal Deposit Insurance Corporation, the Board of Governors of the Federal Reserve System, the Office of Thrift Supervision (the Agencies) sets forth uniform supervisory standards on the classification of assets and appraisal of securities held by banks and thrifts.

§A.22.1 I. The Classification of Assets in Bank and Thrift Examinations

Classification units are designated as "Substandard," "Doubtful," and "Loss." A Substandard Asset is inadequately protected by the current sound worth and paying capacity of the obligor or of the collateral pledged, if any. Assets so classified must have a well-defined weakness or weaknesses that jeopardize the liquidation of the debt. They are characterized by the distinct possibility that the institution will sustain some loss if the deficiencies are not corrected. An asset classified Doubtful has all the weaknesses inherent in one classified Substandard with the added characteristic that the weaknesses make collection or liquidation in full, on the basis of currently existing facts, conditions, and values, highly questionable and improbable. Assets classified Loss are considered uncollectible and of such little value that their continuance as bankable assets is not warranted. This classification does not mean that the asset has absolutely no recovery or salvage value, but rather it is not practical or desirable to defer writing off this basically worthless asset even though partial recovery may be effected in the future. Amounts classified Loss should be promptly charged off.

§A.22.2 II. The Appraisal of Securities in Bank and Thrift Examinations

In an effort to streamline the examination process and achieve as much consistency as possible, examiners will use the published ratings provided by nationally recognized statistical ratings organizations (NRSROs) as a proxy for the supervisory classification definitions. Examiners may, however, assign a more or less severe classification for an individual security depending upon a review of applicable facts and circumstances.

A. Investment quality debt securities

Investment quality debt securities are marketable obligations in which the investment characteristics are not distinctly or predominantly speculative. This group generally includes investment securities in the four highest rating categories provided by nationally recognized statistical rating organizations (NRSROs) and unrated debt securities of equivalent quality.

---

[1] Revises examination procedures established in 1938 and revised July 15, 1949, and May 7, 1979.

Since investment quality debt securities do not exhibit weaknesses that justify an adverse classification rating, examiners will generally not classify them. However, published credit ratings occasionally lag demonstrated changes in credit quality and examiners may, in limited cases, classify a security notwithstanding an investment grade rating. Examiners may use such discretion, when justified by credit information the examiner believes is not reflected in the rating, to properly reflect the security's credit risk.

B. Sub-investment quality debt securities

Sub-investment quality debt securities are those in which the investment characteristics are distinctly or predominantly speculative. This group generally includes debt securities, including hybrid equity instruments (e.g., trust preferred securities), in grades below the four highest rating categories, unrated debt securities of equivalent quality, and defaulted debt securities.

In order to reflect asset quality properly, an examiner may in limited cases "pass" a debt security that is rated below investment quality. Examiners may use such discretion for example when the institution has an accurate and robust credit risk management framework and has demonstrated, based on recent, materially positive, credit information, that the security is the credit equivalent of investment grade.

C. Rating differences

Some debt securities may have investment quality ratings by one (or more) rating agencies and sub-investment quality ratings by others. Examiners will generally classify such securities, particularly when the most recently assigned rating is not investment quality. However, an examiner has discretion to "pass" a debt security with both investment and sub-investment quality ratings. The examiner may use that discretion if, for example, the institution has demonstrated through its documented credit analysis that the security is the credit equivalent of investment grade.

D. Split/partially-rated securities

Some individual debt securities have ratings for principal, but not interest. The absence of a rating for interest typically reflects uncertainty regarding the source and amount of interest the investor will receive. Because of the speculative nature of the interest component, examiners will generally classify such securities, regardless of the rating for the principal.

E. Non-rated debt securities

The Agencies expect institutions holding individually large non-rated debt security exposures, or having significant aggregate exposures from small individual holdings, to demonstrate that they have made prudent pre-acquisition credit decisions and have effective, risk-based standards for the ongoing assessment of credit risk. Examiners will review the institution's program for monitoring and measuring the credit risk of such holdings and, if the assessment process is considered acceptable, generally will rely upon those assessments during the examination process. If an institution has not established independent risk-based standards and a satisfactory process to assess the quality of such exposures, examiners may classify such securities, including those of a credit quality deemed to be the equivalent of subinvestment grade, as appropriate.

Some non-rated debt securities held in investment portfolios represent small exposures relative to capital, both individually and in aggregate. While institutions generally have the same supervisory requirements (as applicable to large holdings) to show that these holdings are the credit equivalent of investment grade at purchase, comprehensive credit analysis subsequent to purchase may be impractical and not cost effective. For such small individual exposures, institutions should continue to obtain and review available financial information, and assign risk ratings. Examiners may rely upon the bank's internal ratings when evaluating such holdings.

F. Foreign debt securities

The Interagency Country Exposure Review Committee (ICERC) assigns transfer risk ratings for cross border exposures. Examiners should use the guidelines in this Uniform Agreement rather than ICERC transfer risk ratings in assigning security classifications, except when the ICERC ratings result in a more severe classification.

G. Treatment of declines in fair value below amortized cost on debt securities

Under generally accepted accounting principles (GAAP), an institution must assess whether a decline in fair value[2] below the amortized cost of a security is a "temporary" or "other-than-temporary" impairment. When the decline in fair value on an individual security represents "other-than-temporary" impairment, the cost basis of the security must be written down to fair value, thereby establishing a new cost basis for the security, and the amount of the write-down must be reflected in current period earnings. If an institution's process for assessing impairment is considered acceptable, examiners may use those assessments in determining the appropriate classification of declines in fair value below amortized cost on individual debt securities.

Any decline in fair value below amortized cost on defaulted debt securities will be classified as indicated in the table below. Apart from classification, for impairment write-downs or charge-offs on adversely classified debt securities, the existence of a payment default will generally be considered a presumptive indicator of "other-than-temporary" impairment.

H. Classification of Other Types of Securities

Some investments, such as certain equity holdings or securities with equity-like risk and return profiles, have highly speculative performance characteristics. Examiners should generally classify such holdings based upon an assessment of the applicable facts and circumstances.

---

[2] As currently defined under GAAP, the fair value of an asset is the amount at which that asset could be bought or sold in a current transaction between willing parties, that is, other than in a forced or liquidation sale. Quoted market prices are the best evidence of fair value and must be used as the basis for measuring fair value, if available..

§ A.22.3 III. Summary Table of Debt Security Classification Guidelines

The following table outlines the uniform classification approach the agencies will generally use when assessing credit quality in debt securities portfolios:

General Debt Security Classification Guidelines

Type of Security	*Substandard*	*Classification Doubtful*	*Loss*
Investment quality debt securities with "temporary" impairment	—	—	—
Investment quality debt securities with "other-than-temporary" impairment	—	—	Impairment
Sub-investment quality debt securities with "temporary" impairment[3]	Amortized Cost	—	—
Sub-investment quality debt securities with "other-than-temporary" impairment, including defaulted debt securities	Fair Value	—	Impairment

NOTE: Impairment is the amount by which amortized cost exceeds fair value.

The General Debt Security Classification Guidelines do not apply to private debt and equity holdings in a small business investment company or Edge Act Corporation. The Uniform Agreement does not apply to securities held in trading accounts, provided the institution demonstrates through its trading activity a short-term holding period or holds the security as a hedge for a valid customer derivative contract.

§ A.22.4 IV. Credit Risk Management Framework for Securities

When an institution has developed an accurate, robust, and documented credit risk management framework to analyze its securities holdings, examiners may choose to depart from the General Guidelines in favor of individual asset review in determining whether to classify those holdings. A robust credit risk management framework entails appropriate pre-acquisition credit due diligence, by qualified staff that grades a security's credit risk based upon an analysis of the repayment capacity of the issuer and the structure and features of the security. It also involves the on-going monitoring of holdings to ensure that risk ratings are reviewed regularly and updated in a timely fashion when significant new information is received.

The credit analysis of securities should vary based on the structural complexity of the security, the type of collateral, and external ratings. The credit risk management framework should reflect the size, complexity, quality, and risk

[3] For sub-investment quality available-for-sale (AFS) debt securities with "temporary" impairment, amortized cost rather than the lower amount at which these securities are carried on the balance sheet, i.e., fair value, is classified Substandard. This classification is consistent with the regulatory capital treatment of AFS debt securities. Under GAAP, unrealized gains and losses on AFS debt securities are excluded from earnings and reported in a separate component of equity capital. In contrast, these unrealized gains and losses are excluded from regulatory capital. Accordingly, the amount classified Substandard on these AFS debt securities, i.e., amortized cost, also excludes the balance sheet adjustment for unrealized losses..

characteristics of the securities portfolio, the risk appetite and policies of the institution, and the quality of its credit risk management staff, and should reflect changes to these factors over time. Policies and procedures should identify the extent of credit analysis and documentation required to satisfy sound credit risk management standards.

§ A.23 LB&I DIRECTIVE RELATED TO § 166 DEDUCTIONS FOR ELIGIBLE DEBT AND ELIGIBLE SECURITIES

LB&I-04-1004-008

October 24, 2014

MEMORANDUM FOR All LB&I Employees

FROM: Heather C. Maloy /s/ Heather C. Maloy
Commissioner, Large Business & International Division

SUBJECT: LB&I Directive Related to § 166 Deductions for Eligible Debt and Eligible Debt Securities

I. INTRODUCTION

This Directive provides Large Business & International (LB&I) examiners with guidance regarding bad debt deductions claimed under § 166 by a Bank or Bank Subsidiary. In addition, this Directive clarifies that LB&I examiners will not challenge the inclusion of certain estimated selling costs in a Bank or Bank Subsidiary's bad debt deduction.

Independently determining worthlessness amounts under § 166 imposes a significant burden on Banks, Bank Subsidiaries, and LB&I examiners. Moreover, changes in bank regulatory standards and processes have created concerns about how to comply with the conclusive presumption regulations under § 166. Notice 2013-35, 2013-24 IRB 1240, solicits comments on possible changes to the conclusive presumption regulations.

Pending any future guidance modifying or superseding this Directive, this Directive provides an administrative resolution generally based on accepting charge-off amounts reported by Banks and Bank Subsidiaries for GAAP and regulatory purposes as sufficient evidence of worthlessness. This Directive is intended to provide an efficient manner of resolving many bad debt deduction issues for Banks and Bank Subsidiaries and to more efficiently manage LB&I's audit resources until further guidance under § 166 is issued.

This Directive does not apply to small banks that use the reserve method of accounting for loan losses under § 585, but is available to small banks that do not use the reserve method of accounting for loan losses. LB&I may consider issuing a separate directive for determining the amount and timing of charge-offs under § 585.

II. DEFINITIONS

"Applicable Financial Statement" means: (1) a financial statement that is required to be filed by a Bank and/or Bank Subsidiary (see definitions below) with the Securities and Exchange Commission (the 10-K or the Annual Statement to Shareholders); or (2) a financial statement that is required to be provided by a Bank and/or Bank Subsidiary to a Bank Regulator.

"Bank" means a bank within the meaning of Treas. Reg. § 1.166-2(d)(4)(i) (modifying the definition with respect to foreign corporations by substituting the words "Eligible Debt or Eligible Debt Securities" for "loans") and is subject to regulation by a Bank Regulator.

"Bank Regulator" means the Office of the Comptroller of the Currency (OCC), the Federal Reserve Board, the Federal Deposit Insurance Corporation (FDIC), the Office of Thrift Supervision (OTS) prior to its merger with the OCC, the Farm Credit Administration, any successor to any of the foregoing entities, or State authorities maintaining substantially equivalent standards as these Federal regulatory authorities. A "Bank's Regulator" means the Bank Regulator responsible for the supervision of the Bank and its Bank Subsidiaries.

"Bank Subsidiary" means an entity that (a) is not a Bank, but conducts businesses that a Bank may conduct, (b) is a member of the same affiliated group (within the meaning of § 1504(a)(1)), determined without regard to the exception for S corporations contained in § 1504(b)(8)) as a Bank ("Owning Bank") (or would be a member of the same affiliated group as Owning Bank after the application of the following sentence), (c) bears the same relationship to Owning Bank that the members of an affiliated group bear to their common parent under § 1504(a)(1), and (d) is under the supervision of Owning Bank's Regulator. For purposes of this definition (including for purposes of determining whether a partnership would be an "includible corporation" within the meaning of § 1504(b)), any partnership whose interests are wholly and directly owned by Owning Bank, a Bank wholly owned by Owning Bank, and/or one or more Bank Subsidiaries shall be treated as if it were a corporation; provided, however, that a partnership shall not be treated as wholly and directly owned by Owning Bank and/or one or more Bank Subsidiaries if any interests in such partnership are owned by one or more entities in which the partnership, directly or indirectly, owns an interest.

"Charge-off of Eligible Debt" means an accounting entry or set of accounting entries for a taxable year that reduces the basis of the Eligible Debt when the Eligible Debt is recorded in whole or part as a Loss Asset on the Bank or Bank Subsidiary's Applicable Financial Statement for that year.

"Charge-off of Eligible Debt Security" means an accounting entry or set of accounting entries for a taxable year that reduces the Eligible Debt Security's carrying value and results in a realized loss or a charge to the statement of operations (as opposed to recognition of an unrealized loss) that is recorded on a Bank or Bank Subsidiary's Applicable Financial Statement for that year.

"Eligible Debt" means any debt (whether originated or acquired) reported in the Applicable Financial Statement (balance sheet) of a Bank or Bank Subsidiary that is subject to a bad debt deduction under § 166, is not a security as described in § 165(g)(2)(C), is not subject to § 475, and is either within the scope of Accounting Standards Codification (ASC) 450 or ASC 310-40 under U.S. GAAP, or the predecessors or successors of such accounting standards, or would be subject to such accounting standards (or such predecessors or successors) if such debt were accounted for under U.S. GAAP (for example, accounted for under IFRS).

"Eligible Debt Securities" means any debt securities reported in the Applicable Financial Statement (balance sheet) of a Bank or Bank Subsidiary that are subject to a bad debt deduction under § 166, are not debt securities described in § 165(g)(2) (unless these are debt securities described in § 165(g)(2)(C) and held by a Bank), are not subject to § 475, and are either within the scope of ASC 320 under U.S. GAAP, or the predecessors or successors of such accounting standard, or would be subject to such accounting standard (or such predecessors or successors) if such debt were accounted for under U.S. GAAP (for example, accounted for under IFRS).[1]

"Express Determination Letter" means a written determination that satisfies the express determination requirement described by Treas. Reg. § 1.166-2(d)(3)(iii)(D).

"Loss Asset" means an Eligible Debt or Eligible Debt Security that meets the requirements of the loss asset classification under the regulatory standards and established policies of the Bank Regulator.

III. § 166 DEDUCTIONS FOR ELIGIBLE DEBT AND ELIGIBLE DEBT SECURITIES

A. Background

Section 166(a)(1) provides that "[t]here shall be allowed as a deduction any debt which becomes worthless within the taxable year."

Section 166(a)(2) provides that "[w]hen satisfied that a debt is recoverable only in part, the Secretary may allow such debt, in an amount not in excess of the part charged off within the taxable year, as a deduction."

Treas. Reg. § 1.166-2(a) provides that "[i]n determining whether a debt is worthless in whole or in part the district director will consider all pertinent evidence, including the value of the collateral, if any, securing the debt and the financial condition of the debtor."

Banks can determine their bad debt deduction in one of four ways. First, they may apply the general facts and circumstances test under Treas. Reg. § 1.166-2(a) to determine whether a debt is worthless in the same manner as other types of taxpayers. In the alternative, Banks may use one of two special rules provided in Treas. Reg. § 1.166-2(d)(1) and (3). Finally, small banks are entitled to apply the reserve method of accounting for loan losses. See § 585.

Section 1.166-2(d)(1) provides a "conclusive presumption rule" under which worthlessness is generally presumed to occur in the same year that a bank, or other regulated corporation, charges off a debt in whole or in part pursuant to Federal or state bank regulatory rules and established policies, or pursuant to a specific order by a bank regulator.

Section 1.166-2(d)(3) provides a "conformity election" under which worthlessness is conclusively presumed if a Bank's Bank Regulator makes an express determination that the bank maintains and applies loan loss classification standards that are consistent with regulatory standards.

Many Banks have subsidiaries that are not themselves Banks, but are facilitative of the Banks' banking and lending businesses. In general, a Bank's controlled subsidiaries are subject to the same supervision and oversight by Bank Regulators as the Bank, and a Bank Regulator generally applies identical standards to a Bank's controlled subsidiaries as they do to the Bank, where the controlled subsidiaries conduct any business that can be conducted by the Bank.[2]

B. Issue Tracking:

Any cases having this issue should use the following Uniform Issue List number:

UIL 166.07-00 - Bad Debt Deductions for Eligible Debt and Eligible Debt Securities - Banks and Bank Subsidiaries.

C. Examination Guidance:

LB &I examiners should not challenge a Bank or Bank Subsidiary's bad debt deduction for Eligible Debt or Eligible Debt Securities as follows:

1. Bank or Bank Subsidiary using the general facts and circumstances test of Treas. Reg. § 1.166-2(a).

Do not challenge a Bank or Bank Subsidiary's bad debt deduction for Eligible Debt and Eligible Debt Securities if the deduction is the same amount as the amount of the credit-related impairment portion of its Charge-off of Eligible Debt and the amount of the credit-related impairment portion of its Charge-off of Eligible Debt Securities as reported on its Applicable Financial Statement.

In no event, however, may the post-deduction tax basis of Eligible Debt be less than the post-Charge-off book basis of the Eligible Debt as increased by any portion of the Charge-off not related to credit impairment, nor may the post-deduction tax basis of Eligible Debt Securities be less than the post-Charge-off carrying amount of the Eligible Debt Securities as increased by any portion of the Charge-off not related to credit impairment.

In addition, do not challenge the inclusion in the Bank or Bank Subsidiary's bad debt deduction for Eligible Debt of estimated selling costs to the extent such estimated selling costs are included in the Charge-off reported in the Bank or Bank Subsidiary's Applicable Financial Statement.

2. Bank or Bank Subsidiary using the conclusive presumption rule of Treas. Reg. § 1.166-2(d)(1).

Do not challenge a Bank or Bank Subsidiary's bad debt deduction for Eligible Debt and Eligible Debt Securities if the deduction is the sum of: (1) the amount of the credit-related impairment portion of its Charge-off of Eligible Debt and the amount of the credit-related impairment portion of its Charge-off of Eligible Debt Securities as reported on its Applicable Financial Statement; and (2) the portion of the Charge-off of Eligible Debt and Eligible Debt Securities in excess of the credit-related impairment that was taken pursuant to a specific order or written confirmation (as described in Treas. Reg. § 1.166-2(d)(1)) by a Bank Regulator as reported on its Applicable Financial Statement.

Do not challenge regardless of whether or not a Bank or Bank Subsidiary presents a specific order by Bank Regulators or confirmation in writing as described in Treas. Reg. § 1.166-2(d)(1). However, a signed Certification Statement from the Bank or the Bank Subsidiary is required.

In no event, however, may the post-deduction tax basis of Eligible Debt be less than the post-Charge-off book basis of the Eligible Debt as increased by any portion of the Charge-off not related to credit impairment and reduced by any amount of the Charge-off in excess of the credit-related impairment that was taken pursuant to a specific order or written confirmation (as described in Treas. Reg. § 1.166-2(d)(1)) by a Bank Regulator, nor may the post-deduction tax basis of Eligible Debt Securities be less than the post-Charge-off carrying value of the Eligible Debt Securities as increased by any portion of the Charge-off not related to credit impairment and reduced by any amount of the Charge-off in excess of the credit-related impairment that was taken pursuant to a specific order or written confirmation (as described in Treas. Reg. § 1.166-2(d)(1)) by a Bank Regulator.

In addition, do not challenge the inclusion in the Bank or Bank Subsidiary's bad debt deduction for Eligible Debt of estimated selling costs to the extent such estimated selling costs are included in the Charge-off reported in the Bank or Bank Subsidiary's Applicable Financial Statement.

3. Bank using the conformity election under Treas. Reg. § 1.166-2(d)(3).

Do not challenge a Bank's bad debt deduction for Eligible Debt and Eligible Debt Securities if a Bank made a proper conformity election under Treas. Reg. § 1.166-2(d)(3) regardless of whether or not the express determination requirement as described in Treas. Reg. § 1.166-2(d)(3)(iii)(D) is satisfied.

In addition, do not challenge the inclusion in the Bank bad debt deduction for Eligible Debt of estimated selling costs to the extent such estimated selling costs are included in the Charge-off reported in the Bank Applicable Financial Statement.

D. Implementation

1. In General

This Directive applies on an entity-by-entity basis. A Bank or Bank Subsidiary may apply this Directive no earlier than its 2010 taxable year and no later than a taxable year that begins in 2014. Pending any future guidance modifying or superseding this Directive, once a Bank or Bank Subsidiary chooses to apply this Directive, it must apply it consistently going forward from year to year.

If a Bank or Bank Subsidiary chooses to follow the provisions of this Directive, it may implement any applicable changes by filing amended returns or making the changes in its current taxable year. If a Bank or Bank Subsidiary is under examination, LB&I examiners, in consultation with the Taxpayer, may decide whether it is appropriate to change the amount of bad debt deduction for the Eligible Debt and Eligible Debt Securities for the open taxable year(s) under examination to be consistent with this Directive or to allow the Taxpayer to file amended returns.

In addition, do not challenge the inclusion in the Bank or Bank Subsidiary's bad debt deduction for Eligible Debt of estimated selling costs to the extent such estimated selling costs are included in the Charge-off reported in the Bank or Bank Subsidiary's Applicable Financial Statement.

1. First Year Adjustment

If a Bank or Bank Subsidiary described in C.1 or C.2 above chooses to follow the provisions of this Directive, its first taxable year in which changes are made is the "Adjustment Year." For the Adjustment Year, LB&I Examiners should not challenge a Bank or Bank Subsidiary's bad debt deduction if the amount of the deduction is determined as provided in C.1, and, where applicable, in C.2 above, reduced or increased by a positive or negative adjustment, determined on December 31 of the Adjustment Year (or the last day of the Adjustment Year, if different from December 31) as set out below. The overall Adjustment Year bad debt deduction may be negative, and, depending on the size of the adjustment, may be an income item.

A. Bank or Bank Subsidiary described in C.1 for Eligible Debt and Eligible Debt Securities.

- The first step in determining the amount of the First Year Adjustment for Eligible Debt and Eligible Debt Securities of a Bank or Bank Subsidiary described in C.1 above is to determine the amount of the bad debt deduction in the Adjustment Year as provided in C.1.
- The second step in determining the amount of the First Year Adjustment for Eligible Debt and Eligible Debt Securities is to determine the amount that is the difference between (i) the pre-Charge-off tax basis of the Eligible Debt or Eligible Debt Securities over (ii) the post-Charge-off book basis of the same Eligible Debt (reflecting estimated selling costs as part of the Charge-off) or post-Charge-off carrying value of the Eligible Debt Securities; the amount of this difference is increased by any portion of the Charge-off not related to credit impairment and not allowed as deductible under this Directive.
- The third step in determining the amount of the First Year Adjustment for Eligible Debt and Eligible Debt Securities is to determine the amount representing the difference (whether positive or negative) between the amount determined in the first step in this section D.2.A over the amount determined in the second step in this section D.2.A. This is the amount of the First Year Adjustment.
- In no event may the post-deduction tax basis of Eligible Debt or Eligible Debt Securities be less than the post-Charge-off book basis of the Eligible Debt or the post-Charge-off carrying value of the Eligible Debt Securities increased by any portion of the Charge-off not related to credit impairment and not allowed as deductible under this Directive.

B. Bank or Bank Subsidiary described in C.2 for Eligible Debt and Eligible Debt Securities.

- The first step in determining the amount of the First Year Adjustment for Eligible Debt and Eligible Debt Securities of a Bank or Bank Subsidiary described in C.2 above is to determine the amount of the bad debt deduction in the Adjustment Year as provided in C.2.
- The second step in determining the amount of the First Year Adjustment for Eligible Debt and Eligible Debt Securities is to determine the amount that is the difference between (i) the pre-Charge-off tax basis of the Eligible Debt or Eligible Debt Securities over (ii) the post-Charge-off book basis of the same Eligible Debt (reflecting estimated selling costs as part of the Charge-off) or the post-Charge-off carrying value of the Eligible Debt Securities where the Charge-off was taken for credit-related impairment and any amount in excess of credit-related impairment pursuant to a specific order by a Bank Regulator, or pursuant to a written confirmation that a Charge-off was made in accordance with the regulatory standards and established policies of the Bank Regulator; the amount of this difference is increased by any portion of the Charge-off not related to credit impairment and not allowed as deductible under this Directive.
- The third step in determining the amount of the First Year Adjustment for Eligible Debt and Eligible Debt Securities is to determine the amount representing the difference (whether positive or negative) between the amount determined in the first step in this section D.2.B over the amount determined in the second step in this section D.2.B. This is the amount of the First Year Adjustment.
- In no event may the post-deduction tax basis of Eligible Debt or Eligible Debt Securities be less than the post-Charge-off book basis of the Eligible Debt or the post-Charge-off carrying value of the Eligible Debt Securities increased by any portion of the Charge-off not related to credit impairment, and reduced by any amount of the Charge-off in excess of credit-related impairment that was taken pursuant to a specific order or written confirmation (as described in Treas. Reg. § 1.166-2(d)(1)) by a Bank Regulator.

2. Charge-off Conformity in Subsequent Years

For each taxable year beginning after the Adjustment Year, the amount of the bad debt deduction under § 166 for Eligible Debt and Eligible Debt Securities should be determined as provided in C.1 for Banks and Bank Subsidiaries described in section C.1, and as provided in section C.2 for Banks and Bank Subsidiaries described in section C.2.

IV. CERTIFICATION STATEMENT

If the Taxpayer has claimed a bad debt deduction under § 166 in compliance with the provisions of this Directive, then upon examination, the Taxpayer must sign and complete the attached LB&I Directive on § 166 Bad Debt Deduction for Eligible Debt and Eligible Securities ("Certification Statement").

The Taxpayer must complete all sections of the Certification Statement, have the statement signed by an authorized individual, and provide the statement to the LB&I examiner within 30 days of a request for the Certification Statement. A separate Certification Statement may be requested for each taxable year under audit. For a consolidated Federal income tax return, a separate Certification Statement may be requested for each Bank and Bank Subsidiary applying the terms of this Directive. A LB&I examiner will consider any Taxpayer not in compliance with these requirements ineligible for this Directive and subject to regular audit procedures.

The Certification Statement must be signed by an individual who is authorized to execute the Taxpayer's Federal income tax return for the taxable year under audit, and must certify, under penalty of perjury that, for the taxable year under audit, for:

1) Taxpayers described in C.1 and C.2, A) the bad debt deduction claimed on the Taxpayer's Federal income tax return for Eligible Debt and Eligible Debt Securities is the same amount as the amount of the credit-related impairment portion its Charge-off of Eligible Debt and the same amount of the credit-related impairment portion of its Charge-off of Eligible Debt Securities as reported on the Taxpayer's Applicable Financial Statement for the same accounting period, subject to 2) below for Taxpayers described in C.2, and B) the post-deduction tax basis of Eligible Debt or Eligible Debt Securities is not less than the post Charge-off book basis of the same Eligible Debt or the carrying value of the same Eligible Debt Securities, as applicable under C.1 or C.2 above.
2) Taxpayers described in C.2, if the bad debt deduction claimed in the Taxpayer's Federal income tax return is in excess of the credit-related impairment portion of the Charge-offs reported on the Taxpayer's Applicable Financial Statement, then such excess amount was charged-off pursuant to a specific order or written confirmation (as described in Treas. Reg. § 1.166-2(d)(1)) by a Bank Regulator as reported on its Applicable Financial Statement.

In addition, the Taxpayer should retain the underlying accounting documentation that would permit the LB&I examiner to reconcile the Taxpayer's Applicable Financial Statement with the amount of its bad debt deduction for Eligible Debt and Eligible Debt Securities reported on the Taxpayer's Federal income tax return. If a Taxpayer fails to properly and timely submit the requested documentation, then the Industry Director or his/her delegate may determine that this Directive does not apply to the Taxpayer.

Footnotes:

[1] Debt securities classified as trading securities are excluded from the definition of Eligible Debt Securities.

[2] See 12 USC 24a (subsidiaries of national banks); 12 USC 1831a (subsidiaries of FDIC insured State banks); 12 USC 1467a(c)(1), (2), (9) (subsidiaries of federal savings associations and savings and loan holding companies). See also 12 CFR 5.34 (operating subsidiaries of national banks); 12 CFR 362.1 -362.4

(subsidiaries of FDIC insured State banks); 12 CFR 238.53, 238.54 (subsidiaries of thrift holding companies, previously at 12 CFR 584.2); 12 CFR 239.11 (subsidiaries of thrift holding companies in mutual form, previously at 12 CFR 575.14).

LB&I Directive Related to § 166 Deductions for Eligible Debt and Eligible Debt Securities Certification Statement

Taxpayer Name: ______________________

Taxpayer EIN: ______________________

Tax Year: ______________________

Relevant Period of the Applicable Financial Statement: ______________________

Status of Taxpayer (Bank or Bank Subsidiary): ______________________

Taxpayer's Bank Regulator: ______________________

(For a Bank Subsidiary, list the Owning Bank's Regulator)

Specify whether the Taxpayer is described in the Directive under: C.1, C.2, or C.3: ______________________

Please provide the following information for:

Taxpayers described in the Directive under C.1, C.2, and C.3:

A. Amount of the Charge-off reported on the Applicable Financial Statement for:

1) Eligible Debt: ______________________

2) Eligible Debt Securities: ______________________

B. Amount of the § 166 bad debt deduction reported on Federal income return for:

1) Eligible Debt: ______________________

2) Eligible Debt Securities: ______________________

C. Post-Charge-off:

1) Book basis for Eligible Debt: ______________________

2) Carrying value for Eligible Debt Securities: ______________________

D. Post-deduction tax basis for:

1) Eligible Debt: ______________________

2) Eligible Debt Securities: ______________________

Taxpayers described in the Directive under C.1 and C.2:

E. The portion of the Charge-off not related to credit impairment, if any::

1) Eligible Debt: ______________________

2) Eligible Debt Securities: ______________________

F. The First Year Adjustment determined on December 31 of the Adjustment Year (or the last day of the Adjustment Year, if different):

1) Eligible Debt: ________________________________

2) Eligible Debt Securities: ________________________________

Taxpayers described in the Directive under C.2:

G. The portion of the Charge-off charged-off pursuant to a specific order or written confirmation by a Bank Regulator:

1) Eligible Debt: ________________________________

2) Eligible Debt Securities: ________________________________

CERTIFICATION

By signing this certification statement, the taxpayer agrees to readily provide (upon request of the IRS) all relevant data and records to establish to the satisfaction of the IRS that the statements made in this certification statement are true, correct and complete.

I certify, under penalties of perjury, that for the taxable year under audit, for:

1) Taxpayers described in C.1 and C.2, A) the bad debt deduction claimed on the Taxpayer's Federal income tax return for Eligible Debt and Eligible Debt Securities is the same amount as the amount of the credit-related impairment portion its Charge-off of Eligible Debt and the same amount of the credit-related impairment portion of its Charge-off of Eligible Debt Securities as reported on the Taxpayer's Applicable Financial Statement for the same accounting period, subject to 2) below for Taxpayers described in C.2, and B) the post-deduction tax basis of Eligible Debt or Eligible Debt Securities is not less than the post Charge-off book basis of the same Eligible Debt or the carrying value of the same Eligible Debt Securities, as applicable under C.1 or C.2 above.

2) Taxpayers described in C.2, if the bad debt deduction claimed in the Taxpayer's Federal income tax return is in excess of the credit-related impairment portion of the Charge-offs reported on the Taxpayer's Applicable Financial Statement, then such excess amount was charged-off pursuant to a specific order or written confirmation (as described in Treas. Reg. § 1.166-2(d)(1)) by a Bank Regulator as reported on its Applicable Financial Statement.

Signature: ________________________________

Title: ________________________________

Date: ________________________________

For corporations, the certification must be signed by an individual authorized under I.R.C. section 6062.

§ A.24 MARK-TO-MARKET: I.R.C. § 475 FIELD DIRECTIVE ON VALUATION

April 14, 2011

MEMORANDUM FOR INDUSTRY DIRECTORS
DIRECTOR, FIELD SPECIALISTS
DIRECTOR, PREFILING AND TECHNICAL GUIDANCE
DIRECTOR, INTERNATIONAL BUSINESS COMPLIANCE

FROM: Walter L. Harris /s/ Walter L. Harris
Industry Director, Financial Services

SUBJECT: I.R.C. § 475: Field Directive related to Mark-to-Market Valuation

This Industry Director Directive ("IDD") provides that Large Business & International (LB&I) examiners should not challenge mark-to-market values reported on a qualified financial statement for the tax valuation requirement of I.R.C. § 475. This IDD applies to all taxpayers who are required to, or elect to, mark-to-market securities and/or commodities under I.R.C. § 475 and are required to file a financial statement with the U.S. Securities and Exchange Commission ("SEC") under Section 13(a) or Section 15(d) of the Securities Exchange Act of 1934, and/or under Rule 17a-5 or Rule 17a-12 promulgated thereunder.[1]

The financial accounting valuation requirements for marking to market values that are reported on qualified financial statements are substantially similar to the valuation requirements under I.R.C. § 475. In addition, independently valuing securities and commodities subject to I.R.C. § 475 imposes a significant administrative burden on both taxpayers and LB&I.

Therefore, in an effort to balance current resources and workload priorities, LB&I examiners are directed not to challenge mark-to-market values reported on a qualified financial statement for the tax valuation requirement of I.R.C. § 475 if the requirements set forth in this IDD are satisfied. If a taxpayer has a tax valuation requirement under I.R.C. § 475, but does not meet the requirements of this IDD, traditional audit procedures will apply.

This IDD is not an official pronouncement of law, and cannot be used, cited, or relied upon as such.

Background

I.R.C. § 475 requires dealers in securities to mark their securities to market. I.R.C. § 475 allows traders in securities or commodities, as well as dealers in commodities, to elect to mark-to-market their securities or commodities to market annually. Traditionally, gains and losses are deferred until disposition, but the mark-to-market provisions of I.R.C. § 475 require income recognition without realization. Thus, if a security or commodity subject to I.R.C. § 475 is held at the end of the taxable year, it must be treated as if it were sold on the last business

[1] 15 U.S.C.S § § 78m, 78o, 17 C.F.R. § § 240.17a-12, 240.17a-5.

day of the taxable year for its fair market value and the appropriate gain or loss must be recognized.

For many securities and/or commodities that are subject to I.R.C. §475, no readily available public valuation benchmarks, such as public price quotations, exist. Taxpayers value these instruments internally, using highly subjective and complex mathematical models. Generally, valuation audits are extremely burdensome for both taxpayers and LB&I because of the subjectivity of valuation and the need for significant resources to verify the taxpayer's determinations. Valuation audits of complex, non-publicly traded securities and/or commodities are additionally burdensome because of the complexity of valuation. Further, individual taxpayers may have a significant volume of such securities and/or commodities that are required by I.R.C. §475 to be valued annually. For example, a large financial services firm may have thousands of non-publicly traded securities that must be valued annually for purposes of computing I.R.C. §475 mark-to-market losses and gains. Currently, conducting an I.R.C. §475 mark-to-market valuation audit of such taxpayers requires a substantial commitment of limited LB&I audit resources.

For financial accounting purposes, many taxpayers subject to I.R.C. §475 are required to value these same securities and/or commodities and report these values to the SEC. To improve the administrability of the valuation requirements of I.R.C. §475, LB&I should accept mark-to-market values reported on a qualified financial statement if the taxpayer follows the requirements outlined below.

Issue Tracking:

Any cases having this issue should use the following ITAC tracking code:

ITAC 4475: "Industry Directive on I.R.C. §475 Valuation"

Examination Guidance:

For taxpayers who are required or elect to mark-to-market securities and/or commodities under the provisions of I.R.C. §475, LB&I examiners should accept mark-to-market values reported on a qualified financial statement for the tax valuation requirement of I.R.C. §475. Taxpayers must use the mark-to-market values reported on a qualified financial statement for all securities and/or commodities that are subject to the tax valuation requirement of I.R.C. §475.

A taxpayer currently under examination may not have used their mark-to-market values reported on qualified financial statements for the tax valuation requirement of I.R.C. §475, but would like to change to that method under the provisions of this IDD. For such a taxpayer, LB&I examiners, in consultation with the taxpayer, will decide whether the most appropriate way to make the change is to (1) change the taxpayer's method of accounting for the taxable year under examination to one that is consistent with this IDD or (2) allow the taxpayer to request advance consent to change their method to one that is consistent with this IDD for the current taxable year. With respect to an advance consent, LB&I would grant the taxpayer consent under section 6.01(4) of Rev. Proc. 97-27 to request the voluntary change in method of accounting. In addition, for any taxpayer requesting an advance consent, attaching a completed Certification

Statement (described below) to their Form 3115 will generally satisfy the documentation requirements of Lines 19-21 of Form 3115

Upon examination, if a taxpayer has used its mark-to-market values reported on a qualified financial statement for the tax valuation requirement of I.R.C. § 475, the taxpayer must sign and complete the attached "Industry Directive on I.R.C. § 475 Valuation Certification Statement" ("the Certification Statement"). A taxpayer must complete all sections of the Certification Statement, must have the Certification Statement signed by an authorized individual, and must provide the Certification Statement to the LB&I examiner within 30 days of a request for the Certification Statement. A separate Certification Statement may be requested for each tax year under audit. A LB&I examiner will consider any taxpayer not in compliance with these requirements ineligible for this IDD and subject to traditional audit procedures.

The Certification Statement must be signed by an individual who is authorized to execute the taxpayer's federal income tax return for the taxable year under audit, and must certify, under penalty of perjury, that, for the tax year under audit, the taxpayer's mark-to-market values reported on its qualified financial statements are consistent with the I.R.C. § 475 values for the same securities and/or commodities reported on the taxpayer's federal income tax return for the relevant taxable year. Taxpayers should retain the underlying financial accounting valuation documentation that would permit the LB&I examiner to reconcile the taxpayer's financial accounting mark-to-market values with the taxpayer's tax mark-to-market values. If a taxpayer fails to properly and timely submit a Certification Statement or if a taxpayer fails to timely submit requested valuation documentation that would permit the examiner to reconcile the taxpayer's financial accounting values with the taxpayer's tax mark-to-market values, then the Industry Director or his/her delegate may determine that this IDD does not apply to the taxpayer.

Definitions:

Qualified Financial Statements: A qualified financial statement is a financial statement that is required to be filed with the SEC under Section 13(a) or Section 15(d) of the Securities Exchange Act of 1934, and/or under Rule 17a-5 or Rule 17a-12 promulgated thereunder.

Certification Statement: To be eligible for this IDD, a taxpayer must certify that their mark-to-market values reported on a qualified financial statement are the same values being used for the tax valuation requirement of I.R.C. § 475. Upon audit, this certification must be completed on the attached Certification Statement and must be provided to an LB&I examiner within 30 days of a request. For corporations, the certification must be signed by an individual authorized under I.R.C. § 6062. For partnerships, the certification must be signed by an individual authorized under I.R.C. § 6063. All Certification Statements must be signed under penalties of perjury.

Contacts:

If you have any questions, please contact I.R.C. § 475 Technical Advisor Ann Schultz at 703-462-5994 or Securities and Financial Services firms Industry Counsel Nicole Cammarota at 917-421-4637.

Documents:

Industry Directive on I.R.C. § 475 Valuation Certification Statement

INDUSTRY DIRECTIVE ON I.R.C. § 475 VALUATION

CERTIFICATION STATEMENT

Taxpayer Name: ______________________________

Taxpayer EIN: ______________________________

Tax Year: ______________________________

Qualified Financial Statement: ______________________________

Relevant Period of the
Qualified Financial Statement: ______________________________

Certification

By signing this certification statement, the taxpayer agrees to readily provide (upon request of the IRS) all relevant data and records to establish to the satisfaction of the IRS that the statements made in this certification statement are true, correct and complete.

I certify, under penalty of perjury, that for the tax year to which this certification statement applies, the taxpayer's mark-to-market values reported on its qualified financial statements are consistent with the I.R.C. § 475 values for the same securities and/or commodities reported on the taxpayer's federal income tax return for the relevant tax year for all entities included in the consolidated tax return that use the I.R.C. § 475 mark-to-market method of accounting.

I certify, under penalty of perjury, that no tax return Schedule M adjusting entries or other book to tax adjusting entries were made regarding the I.R.C. § 475 mark-to-market values.

I certify, under penalty of perjury, that no deferred tax assets, deferred tax liabilities, or valuation allowances were reported for U.S. GAAP (FAS 109/ASC 740) purposes regarding any I.R.C. § 475 mark-to-market values.

I certify, under penalty of perjury, that I have examined this certification statement, and to the best of my knowledge and belief, it is true, correct, and complete.

Signature: ______________________________

Date: ______________________________

Title: ______________________________

For corporations, the certification must be signed by an individual authorized under I.R.C. § 6062. For partnerships, the certification must be signed by an individual authorized under I.R.C. § 6063. All certifications must be signed under penalties of perjury.

APPENDIX B
Audit Technique Guide for Commercial Banking

July 1997

The taxpayer names and addresses shown in this publication are hypothetical. They were chosen at random from a list of names of American colleges and universities as shown in Webster's Dictionary or from a list of names of counties in the United States as listed in the United States Government Printing Office Style Manual.

This material was designed specifically for training purposes only. Under no circumstances should the contents be used or cited as authority for setting or sustaining a technical position.

Department of the Treasury

Internal Revenue Service

Training 3149-104 (7-97)

TPDS 89400K

Table of Contents

INTRODUCTION

Formation of the Group 905

Utilization of the Commercial Banking Guide 905

CHAPTER 1—GENERAL OVERVIEW OF THE BANKING INDUSTRY

Definition of a Bank 906

Industry Regulation 907

The Office of the Comptroller of the Currency 909

The Federal Reserve Bank 909

The Federal Deposit Insurance Company 909

The Office of Thrift Supervision 909

State Regulatory Agencies 909

CHAPTER 2—STARTING THE EXAMINATION PROCESS

Introduction to the Audit 913

Coordinated Issues 914

Significant Issues 915

Return Identification Process 915

Pre-Audit Planning 916

CHAPTER 3—SPECIALIZATION WITHIN THE IRS

Involving Specialists in an Examination 918

Engineer 918

Computer Audit Specialist 918
Financial Products Specialist 919
International Examiner 920
Employee Plans Specialist 920
Employment Tax Specialist 921
Insurance Specialist 921
Economist 922
District Counsel and Industry Counsel 922
Market Segment Specialization Program 922
Industry Specialization Program 923
Summary 924
CHAPTER 4—INTEREST ON NONPERFORMING LOANS
Introduction 939
Examination Techniques 940
Law 943
Summary 943
CHAPTER 5—CORE DEPOSITS AND COVENANTS NOT TO COMPETE
Core Deposits 944
IRC Section 197 944
Examination Techniques for Cases Under IRC Section 197 945
Core Deposits Prior to IRC Section 197 945
Intangibles Settlement Initiatives—Pre-IRC Section 197 Cases 946
Application of Pre-IRC Section 197 Law to Core Deposit Intangibles 946
Examination Techniques for Cases Before IRC Section 197 948
Covenants Not to Compete 948
The Economic Reality Test 950
The Mutual Intent Test 952
The Strong Proof Doctrine and the Danielson Rule 954
Valuation of a Convenant Not to Compete 955
Effect of IRC Section 197 956
Examination Techniques 957
Summary 958
CHAPTER 6—GAIN/LOSS ON FORECLOSED PROPERTY
Introduction 960
Computing the Basis of the Loan for Tax Purposes 961
Examination Techniques 962
Coordinated Issue Paper 964
CHAPTER 7—GROSS-UP NET LOANS
Introduction 964
Coordinated Issue Paper 964
International Tax Issues 965
Brazilian Foreign Tax Credits 966
Mexican Foreign Tax Credits 966
Articles 966
CHAPTER 8—MORTGAGE SERVICING RIGHTS
Introduction 967
Examination Areas 968
Background Information 968

Sale of Mortgage Loans & Mortgage Backed Securities 969
Excess Servicing Fee 969
Computation of the Excess Servicing Fee 970
Prepayment of Mortgages 970
Law 971
SFAS 65 971
Examination Limits and Restrictions 972
Examination Techniques 972
Analysis of Rulings 974
Articles 975
CHAPTER 9—LOAN ORIGINATION COSTS
Introduction 975
Book Reporting of Loan Origination Costs 975
Tax Reporting of Loan Origination Costs 976
Law 978
Change in Accounting Method 980
Examination Techniques 981
Summary 983
CHAPTER 10—BAD DEBTS
Introduction 984
Definition of a "Large" Bank 984
Reserve Method 985
Specific Charge-Off Method 986
Charge-Off Mandated by Regulations 986
Breakdown of Loan Classifications Used by Banking Regulators 987
Conformity Election for Bad Debt Charge-Offs 988
Bad Debt Recoveries 989
Bad Debt Reserve Recapture 989
Examination Techniques 990
Miscellaneous Items/Terms 992
Summary 993
CHAPTER 11—FSLIC ASSISTANCE
Background 993
Enactment of FIRREA 994
S&L's Acquired Prior to FIRREA 995
Analysis of the Issue 995
Years Ending On or After March 4, 1991 996
Examination Techniques 996
Post FIRREA Federal Assistance Payments 997
CHAPTER 12—FAILED THRIFT INSTITUTIONS OPERATED BY THE RTC
Introduction 998
Who is Covered by the Agreement 998
Failed Thrift Receiverships 999
RTC Certification 1000
Taxes Covered by the Agreement 1001
Case Processing 1001
Examination Considerations 1001
Report Preparation 1001

Joint Committee Considerations 1002
Case Closing 1002
Unagreed Cases 1002
Refunds 1003
Service Center Overview 1003

CHAPTER 13—ACQUISITION COSTS AND OTHER CAPITAL EXPENSES

Introduction 1003
Examination Techniques 1005
Law and Discussion 1006
General Information 1006
Takeover Attempts 1007
Abandoned Mergers 1008
Target vs. Acquiring Company 1008
Other Capital Expenditures 1009
Branch Costs 1009
Credit Card Start-Up Costs 1009
Automatic Teller Machine Fees 1009
Advertising 1010
Summary 1010

CHAPTER 14—LEVERAGED BUYOUT LOANS

Introduction 1010
Investment Bankers 1011
Examination Techniques—Non-Cash Compensation 1011
Examination Techniques—Fees Paid to the Bank 1012
Summary 1013

CHAPTER 15—AMORTIZATION

Introduction 1013
Law Changes 1013
Amortization Items 1014
Law 1014
General Examination Techniques 1014
Purchased Servicing Rights 1016
Examination Techniques 1017
Organizational and Business Start-Up Costs 1017
Examination Techniques 1019
Work Force in Place 1019
Generic Position Papers 1019
Amortization of Assembled Workforce 1020
Covenants Not to Compete 1020
Customer Based Intangibles 1020
Employment Contracts 1020
Amortization of Market Based Intangibles 1020
Amortization of Order Backlog 1020

CHAPTER 16—FEE INCOME

Introduction 1020
Commitment Fees 1020
Service Fees 1021
Points 1021

Examination Techniques 1022
Law 1024
Original Issue Discount 1024
Summary 1027
CHAPTER 17—INCOME RECEIVED IN ADVANCE
Introduction 1028
Law 1028
Accrual Method of Accounting 1029
Issues 1029
Credit Card Fees 1029
Rental/Lease Income 1030
Prepaid Interest 1031
Commitment Fees and Service Fees 1031
Automobile Lease Payments 1031
Examination Techniques 1032
Summary 1033
CHAPTER 18—TAX-EXEMPT OBLIGATIONS
Introduction 1033
Determination of Tax-Exempt Status 1033
Examination Techniques 1034
Interest and Expenses Relating to Tax-Exempt Income 1034
Examination Techniques 1036
Sale of Tax-Exempt Obligations 1036
Examination Techniques 1036
Bond Premiums on Tax-Exempt Obligations 1037
Original Issue Discount on Tax-Exempt Obligations 1037
Summary 1037
CHAPTER 19—DISCHARGE OF INDEBTEDNESS
Introduction 1038
Premature Withdrawal Penalties 1038
Repurchase of Bonds 1039
Examination Techniques 1040
Forgiveness of a Borrower's Indebtedness 1040
Summary 1041
CHAPTER 20—LOAN SWAPS
Introduction 1041
Mortgages Swapped for Mortgage Backed Securities 1042
Mortgage Pools Swapped for Mortgage Pools 1043
Foreign Loans Swapped for Foreign Loans 1044
Repurchase Agreements 1045
Real Estate Mortgage Investment Conduits (REMIC) 1046
Loan Restructurings 1047
Examination Techniques 1049
Summary 1049
CHAPTER 21—MISCELLANEOUS ISSUES
Introduction 1050
Accrual of Original Issue Discount and Market Discount 1050
CAP Interest 1051

Change of Accounting Method 1051
Currency Transaction Reporting (CTR) 1051
Dividend Received Deduction 1052
Entrance and Exit Fees Paid to Convert From an S&L to a Bank 1052
Exemption for Insolvent Banks 1053
Miscellaneous Income 1053
Net Operating Loss Carrybacks 1053
Regulatory Agency Penalties 1053
Stock Dividend and Issuance Costs 1054
Built-In-Loss Limitations on NOLS 1054
S-Corporation Status 1054
APPENDIX
Resource & Reference Materials
Banking Research Manuals 1055
Banking Publications 1055
IRS Materials 1056
Non-Tax Publications 1056
Bank Tax Seminars and Conferences 1056
Synopsis of Law, Decisions, & Rulings
Introduction 1059
Bad Debts 1059
Capital Expenditures 1060
Core Deposits and Other Intangibles 1060
Financial Products 1061
Foreign Banking 1062
Loan Origination Costs 1062
Loan Swaps 1062
Miscellaneous Issues 1062
Mortgage Servicing Rights 1063
Nonperforming Loans 1063
Original Issue Discount 1063
Premature Withdrawal Penalty Income 1064

INTRODUCTION

FORMATION OF THE GROUP

The Detroit District formed a Financial Group in 1986 when it recognized the need to improve the quality of the examinations of both banking and insurance returns. Approximately one half of the agents in the group specialize in the audit of banks and savings and loans. The other agents specialize in the examination of life and casualty insurance companies.

There is no formal specialized training for agents who audit financial returns. The agents learned to examine banks by studying the banking research services, by reviewing the ISP digest, and by working together. They regularly share with each other what they learn. Additionally, close contact is maintained with the National Banking ISP, Savings and Loan ISP, and National Office personnel. The Detroit District provides resources to attend ISP meetings and outservice seminars. They have also funded subscriptions to bank tax research services and several banking trade publications.

Our Financial Group audits banks, savings and loans, and mortgage companies of all sizes, including several which are included in the Coordinated Examination Program (CEP). Industry issues and substantial "general" issues can be found in returns of any size but are more prominent in cases where assets exceed one billion dollars.

Through specialization, the group significantly improved the quality of bank examinations because of:

1. Improved communication

2. Consistency in issue development

3. More efficient use of audit time.

This audit specialization guide was developed from information available in the financial group, from the Banking Industry Specialist, and from Internal Revenue Agents from around the country. Even though commercial banking is specifically addressed in this guide, many of the issues and techniques are appropriate for use during the audit of savings and loans, mortgage companies, and finance companies.

UTILIZATION OF THE COMMERCIAL BANKING GUIDE

The Commercial Banking Guide is intended to be a tool to assist Internal Revenue Agents who are not familiar with auditing bank returns. It is useful as a reference during pre-audit planning to identify potential issues. It will also assist you, the examiner, in knowing the types of records and techniques necessary to identify and develop the issues. Also, familiarity with terminology unique to banking will enable you to communicate more effectively with the taxpayers and representatives throughout the audit process.

This guide should *not* be used as your sole source of technical information, nor should complete reliance be placed on the suggested audit techniques. It is important to understand the merits of an issue so you can assess how much time and documentation is needed to develop the issue. The technical treatment of issues often changes over time due to legislation, court cases, Revenue Rulings, *etc.* You may determine the current position on an industry issue by contacting the Banking Industry Specialist, Appeals ISP

Coordinator, or Industry Counsel. Above all, continue to use your imagination and initiative to identify and develop new issues which can be shared with the rest of us.

We hope you find this guide useful. If you would like clarification of an examination technique listed in the guide or have suggestions for improvements, you may contact the Michigan District Market Segment Specialization Program Coordinator. Technical questions can be directed to your District ISP Coordinator. Questions on significant industry issues should be directed to the Commercial Banking Industry Specialist who is the focal point for all coordinated and other significant industry issues.

CHAPTER 1—GENERAL OVERVIEW OF THE BANKING INDUSTRY

DEFINITION OF A BANK

Generally, the income and deductions of a banking entity are computed in the same way as those of other corporations. They are also subject to the same federal income tax rates that apply to other corporations. The term "bank" in recent years has become increasingly blurred, but is usually applied to any establishment engaged in the various functions associated with a bank. These functions include the receiving, collecting, lending, and servicing of money. IRC sections 581 through 585 provide special rules directly applicable to the taxation of banks.

Section 581 of the Internal Revenue Code provides us with a *technical* definition of a bank.[1]

EXTRACT

IRC section 581

For purposes of IRC sections 582 and 584, the term "bank" means a bank or trust company incorporated and doing business under the laws of the United States (including laws relating to the District of Columbia) or of any State, a substantial part of the business of which consists of receiving deposits and making loans and discounts, or of exercising fiduciary powers similar to those permitted to national banks under authority of the Comptroller of the Currency, and which is subject by law to supervision and examination by State, or Federal authority having supervision over banking institutions. Such term also means a domestic building and loan association.

After reading the above paragraph you realize that the above definition of a bank is superficial. You will recognize a bank when one is assigned to you. The examination of a bank is different in some ways, as you will find out later in this guide. Yet, in many other ways, bank examinations are similar to other examinations that you have already come in contact with.

Essentially, banks are categorized into two very broad groups: Commercial banks and noncommercial bank institutions, such as savings and loan associations, mutual savings banks, and credit unions.

Commercial banks are broken down into three separate classifications

[1] Banks may also engage in a broad range of securities dealing activities that could give rise to issues not discussed in this guide.

based on the authority which chartered the bank:

1. *National Banks*

   These are banks which are chartered by the Comptroller of the Currency and operated under the supervision of the Federal Government. National banks are required to be members of the Federal Reserve system and to carry deposit insurance through the FDIC.

2. *State Member Banks*

   These are banks which are chartered and regulated by their respective state banking departments and have elected to join the Federal Reserve System. All member banks are required to carry deposit insurance and follow the regulations of the FDIC, similar to that of a national bank.

3. *State Nonmember Banks*

   These are banks that are chartered by the state banking departments and have not elected to join the Federal Reserve System. All nonmember banks are subject only to the state banking department regulations. The actual number of State nonmember banks is relatively small.

For tax purposes, banks receive yet another designation. A bank is treated as being a *large bank* if, for any taxable year after December 31, 1986, the total assets of the bank exceed $500 million, or the bank is part of a controlled group and the group's average total assets exceed $500 million. The large bank category will be specifically discussed later in this guide.

This MSSP guide is being written principally to address the issues unique to the commercial banking industry, *not* those dealing with the examination of a Saving and Loan Association (S&L) or a Credit Union. An S&L, while similar to a bank in that it receives deposits and makes loans to its customers, is not the same as a bank. Savings institutions, also known as thrifts, are defined in the IRC section 591(b) (mutual savings banks), IRC section 7701(a)(19) (domestic building and loan associations) and IRC section 7701(a)(32) (cooperative banks). The rules governing an S&L are covered under IRC sections 591 through 597 and deal primarily with rules applicable to mutual saving banks, cooperative banks, or similar associations covered under federal or state law. To qualify as a savings and loan association, at least 60 percent of the total assets of such an entity must consist of qualifying assets, such as loans for residential real property. These entities qualify for benefits not available to a bank. Credit unions do not have capital stock. They are organized and operated for mutual purposes and are exempt from tax under IRC section 501(c)(14). They also are *not* covered under this guide.

See Exhibit 1-1 at the end of this chapter for a copy of a flow chart titled "**How banks make money.**" This chart provides a somewhat simplistic view of the operations of a bank. However, it also provides a basic understanding of the flow of money through the bank and how the bank makes money from its customers' money. This basic information is essential during the examination of a bank.

INDUSTRY REGULATION

The banking industry is highly regulated. There are numerous state and federal laws that govern the industry. The enforcement of these banking laws is the responsibility of various regulatory agencies, such as the Office of the Comptroller of the Currency (OCC), the Board of Governors of the Federal Reserve (FRB), the Federal Deposit Insurance Company (FDIC), the Office of Thrift Supervision (OTS), and each particular state's governing authority.

Regulations of the OCC, the FRB, the FDIC, and the OTS are codified in Title 12 of the Code of Federal Regulations. The various agencies clarify their policies and provide guidance through the issuance of advisory letters, bulletins, manuals, news releases, *etc.* They also issue written guidance to the particular banks during their examinations.

There has been significant legislation enacted relating to financial institutions in the past few years. The Financial Institutions Reform, Recovery, and Enforcement Act of 1989 (FIRREA) increased the powers of the regulators. It also provided for the regulation of additional entities that were related to financial institutions. The Federal Deposit Insurance Corporation Improvement Act (FDICIA) was enacted in 1991. The FDICIA provided for far reaching reforms of regulatory auditing and accounting standards. It also provided for supervisory actions to be taken when an institution's capital level decreases below acceptable levels. Additionally, the FDICIA provided additional capitalization to the FDIC's Bank Insurance Fund.[2] Title III of the Omnibus Budget Reconciliation Act of 1993 created a national deposit preference.

FIRREA and FDICIA deal primarily with the *regulation* of the banking industry, rather than with *tax* law. However, there are some tax provisions included in FIRREA and FDICIA. These will be discussed later in this guide.

Banks are required to file reports of condition (balance sheets) and reports of income (income statements) with the regulatory agencies. Nationally chartered banks file their reports with the Comptroller of the Currency. The Federal Reserve receives reports from state member banks. Insured nonmember banks file with the FDIC.

Banks are examined frequently by one or more regulatory agencies. In the past, the supervisory agencies conducted their examinations independently. This would result in a bank being examined by several different agencies. Recently, the FDIC and the OTS have been performing joint examinations. Additionally, the FDIC and the Conference of State Bank Supervisors have reached agreement on having cooperative examinations.

The bank examiners' reports are considered the property of the respective regulatory agencies. The banks are prohibited from providing copies of the reports to anyone outside the bank without permission. Although most of the agencies are part of the Treasury Department, the IRS has had difficulty securing complete copies of examination reports from them. IRC section 4083 provides the procedures for requesting certain portions of the OCC's and FDIC's examination reports which relate to charged off assets and adverse classification of balance sheet items. There has been some success in making arrangements to review the examination reports of the OTS and certain State banking regulators. However, this is not uniformly the case.

---

[2] **AICPA Audit Risk Alert,** Depository Institutions Industry Developments—1992, pp. 5-12.

A brief description of each of the regulatory agencies is given below.

The Office of the Comptroller of the Currency

The OCC is the primary regulator for national banks. The Code of Federal Regulations, Title 12, section 1.1 states, "The Comptroller of the Currency is charged by the national banking laws with execution of all laws of the United States relating to the organization, operation, regulation, and supervision of national banks and in particular with the execution of 12 U.S.C. 24 which sets forth the corporate powers of national banks. "The OCC also regulates certain activities of banks in the District of Columbia and state banks that are members of the Federal Reserve System.

The Federal Reserve Bank

The Federal Reserve functions as the central bank of the United States. It consists of 12 regional banks. The Federal Reserve is run by a seven member Board of Governors which is appointed by the President. Although the FRB is accountable to the Government, it is actually owned by banks which have purchased its stock. Banks are required to keep a certain percentage of the amount of their customer deposits in accounts at the FRB to lend money. The FRB sets the discount rate, loans money to member banks, regulates the money supply, and serves as the nation's leading check clearing system. Additionally, it is the primary regulator for state member banks.

The Federal Deposit Insurance Company

The FDIC is a government corporation which insures customer deposits up to $100,000. It is responsible for the examination of insured state nonmember banks. Banks that are not members of the FRB can still apply for deposit insurance from the FDIC. There are very few uninsured state banks.

The Office of Thrift Supervision

The OTS is the primary regulator for savings and loan associations. It was established by FIRREA in 1989. The OTS replaced the Federal Home Loan Bank Board. If a bank has a savings and loan subsidiary, it will also be examined by the OTS. Otherwise, the OTS would not become involved in the regulatory examinations of a bank.

State Regulatory Agencies

If a state chartered bank is not a member of the FDIC or the FRB, it is subject only to state laws and state banking department regulations. However, all FDIC or FRB member state chartered banks will be subject to examination by federal agencies and by their state. Further, the state regulator may examine other types of institutions, as well as, state chartered commercial banks. For example the Michigan Financial Institutions Bureau (FIB) is responsible for the chartering, regulation, examination, and supervision of state chartered banks, credit unions, and savings and loan associations. It also licenses and supervises the activities of various other types of companies, such as credit card issuers and mortgage companies. The state banking regulator can furnish information regarding the laws for banks operating in the state. It may also be able to provide you with information on a particular state chartered bank that you are auditing regarding merger activity, directed charge-offs, illegal activities, penalties, *etc.*

IRM 4083 discusses how information can be requested from various government agencies. Portions of that manual section have been provided below in Figure 1-1.

Figure 1-1

IRM 4083 discusses how information can be requested from various government agencies. Portions of that manual section have been provided below:

4083 ***(4-5-79)***

Information Requested From Government Agencies

4083.1 ***(1-11-91)***

National Office Liasion Activities

(1) Many Government agencies located in Washington, D.C., obtain information in the conduct of their activities which may be significantly helpful to the Service in examining tax returns and in determining tax liabilities. Such information may be useful in examining specific taxpayers, or for general consideration in identifying actual or potential areas of taxpayer noncompliance.

(2) To facilitate the securing of useful information in an orderly manner from Government agencies without undue inconvenience to them, the National Office, serves as an agent in securing such information for Examination field personnel.

(3) Examination personnel should avail themselves of this liaison relationship when information from a Government agency is deemed essential to the conduct of effective examinations. Needed information may be requested even thought the requester is not certain which agency has the information.

(4) All requests should be addressed to the Office of Quality and Customer Advocacy (Attention EX:Q:CA:Q). Each request should set forth all the particulars, including the name, address, Social Security Number or Employer Identification Number (if known), and taxable year(s) for each taxpayer involved, the information on hand and the information desired. Also, please give the name and FTS telephone number of the person to contact for further information. The information desired should first be requested from the taxpayer or his/her representative and documentation to this effect should be included in the audit workpapers. The request should contain a statement that this has been done.

(5) The Office of Quality and Customer Advocacy (Attention EX:Q:CA:Q), will control, process, and evaluate the requests, make contacts with the agencies, as appropriate. Contacts with Government agencies, whether in connection with requests by field offices or otherwise through the liaison established, may lead to identification of indicated broad areas of taxpayer noncompliance; and the Office of Quality and Customer Advocacy, in such cases, coordinates the matter with all field offices affected in the interest of improving voluntary compliance by taxpayers.

(6) In contacts with personnel from other Government agencies, consideration must be given to the disclosure requirements as it relates to

investigative disclosures under IRC 6103(k)(6) and regulations issued pursuant thereto. In such situations, Examination personnel may only disclose return information as defined in IRC 6103(b)(2), and only to the extent necessary, in obtaining information from a Government agency. The law contains strict penalties on the unauthorized disclosure of confidential tax return information. See IRM 1272, Disclosure of Official Information Handbook, for additional instructions concerning such matters.

(7) Examination personnel will normally follow the foregoing procedures when requesting information from Government agencies, unless other Manual provisions are applicable; e.g., IRM 4742 and 4744. Exceptions are also permissible in the following situations.

(a) If an effective liaison or contact has already been established with a local office of a Government agency to obtain information on specific cases, such procedure may be continued.

(b) Information of a routine nature may be requested by Examination personnel directly from the agency involved or appropriate district office in accordance with IRM 4083.(13) and 4083.(14). Also, examiners should check with local offices of other agencies to secure public documents prior to any request to the National Office for assistance.

4083.(11) ***(5-13-82)***

Federal Deposit Insurance Corporation (FDIC)

(1) The FDIC is an independent agency of the Government established to promote and preserve public confidence in banks and to protect the money supply through provision of insurance coverage for bank deposits and periodic examinations of insured state-chartered banks which are not members of the Federal Reserve System.

(2) The FDIC will release certain portions of their confidential Report of Examination to the Service. These portions relate to FDIC's adverse classification of balance sheet items, such as assets, reserves, debts, and loans.

(3) When requesting information on a bank from the FDIC, the bank should be under examination and it will be necessary to list the related taxpayers on which the Service wishes information.

(4) Under no circumstances should a summons be served on the bank for the FDIC Report of Examination, since it is the property of FDIC and the summons will be forwarded to them.

4083.(10)1 ***(3-2-84)***

Comptroller of the Currency (OCC)

(1) Field personnel should follow the instructions in IRM 4232.9, Techniques Handbook for Specialized Industries-Financial Institutions.

(2) Requests for information must contain specific details of data needed so that the Comptroller's Office can process the IRS request.

(3) OCC's examination reports that are provided to the banks is the property of OCC, and the disclosure of its contents to non-bank related persons or organizations is not permitted.

(4) OCC does not restrict access to their "Summary of Charged Off

Assets" (Form CC-1424-OX) and Form CC-1427-OX which lists installment loans charged off. If the bank rejects the agents request for these, the agent should refer the bank to their local OCC field office.

(5) The request must be processed in accordance with IRM 4083.1:(4).

4083.(12) ***(5-13-82)***

Federal Reserve System

(1) The Federal Reserve System is charged with administering and making policy for the nation's credit and monetary affairs. The Board of Governors of the Federal Reserve System has jurisdiction over the admission of state banks and trust companies to membership in the Federal Reserve System. It receives copies of condition reports and has the power to examine all member banks.

(2) To secure a copy of the Federal Reserve System examiner's report the following information is needed:

(a) Name of the bank;

(b) Address of the bank;

(c) Tax years under examination; and

(d) Specific information as to what is needed, such as bad debts deduction.

(3) Request should contain the following statement:

"We agree that no public use of this information, other than to the taxpayer and/or the taxpayer's representative, will be made without the prior approval of the Board of Governors."

(4) Under no circumstances should a summons be served on the bank for the Federal Reserve examiner's report, since it is the property of the Federal Reserve System and the summons will be forwarded to them.

Exhibit 1-1
HOW BANKS MAKE MONEY

TAKING MONEY IN

Depositors

Most comes from depositors, who put cash into banks for safekeeping in savings and checking accounts and certificates of deposit. Banks pay interest, but this is a cheap, stable source of funds.

Money Markets

Banks can go into the money markets and pay investors for funds. Bankers refer to this as hot money because the funds are usually lent on short maturities and can become costly if interest rates jump.

Federal Reserve

Banks also borrow funds from 12 Federal Reserve Banks located throughout the United states in what's known as the federal funds market.

Generating Fees

Banks make money by performing services for customers. They charge a service fee for handling savings accounts. They charge you money for bouncing a check or using your ATM card. Banks also receive fees for managing trust accounts, helping businesses manage cash and servicing mortgage portfolios.

GIVING MONEY OUT

Lending Money

After taking money in, bankers turn around and loan it out. They make loans to individuals buying new cars, boats and homes, and to businesses to build plants and buy equipment. They lend to developers to build shopping malls and office buildings. The riskier the loan, the more interest they charge.

By charging customers more to borrow money than they pay depositors on their accounts, banks make money. The difference is called the spread. There's an old banking motto known as the 3-6-3 rule: Pay 3 percent on deposits, charge 6 percent for loans and be on the golf course by 3 p.m.

Accounting for bad loans: Not all loans pay off. Some businesses go bankrupt and some people never finish paying off boats or homes. When loans go bad, and can't be repaid, banks lose the money they can't recover. This comes out of profits.

Making Investments

In a lousy business climate, banks might want to cut back on lending and sin money into investments that will pay them interest. Banks typically invest in very safe securities, such as mortgage-backed securities and U.S. Treasury securities.

Paying Bills

Banks can't pocket all the money they take in from interest earned on loans. They have plenty of bills to pay: employee salaries, rent on branch buildings, utilities and other business expenses, including income tax.

MAKING MONEY, THE BOTTOM LINE

Money left over after all bills are paid and interest payments are made is called profit. If a bank minds its spread, holds costs in check and doesn't make stupid loans, it should make a profit. Public companies such as Comerica pay some profit to shareholders in the form of dividends.

CHAPTER 2—STARTING THE EXAMINATION PROCESS

INTRODUCTION TO THE AUDIT

The purpose of this guide is to provide the revenue agent with a source of reference for issues which are currently common in the commercial banking industry. The guide should be used by the examiner as an *audit tool* to assist in recognizing certain issues and other unique areas in the banking industry where adjustments may exist. In addition, the guide provides various general and technical information useful to the examiner during the preliminary stages of an examination. The guide is not intended to be all inclusive, nor was it meant to be cited as an authority for a case.

The information contained in this guide is based upon data gathered from a limited number of examinations over a period of time. The objective of the MSSP project is to evaluate compliance within the commercial banking industry and to determine common areas of adjustments based on our audit results. We have attempted to develop a guide which will assist other examiners based on this experience. The fact that a particular issue is addressed in this banking guide does *not* imply that the issue must be examined in all cases, or that no other issues exist. There is nothing like the inquisitive and innovative mind of the revenue agent to come up with a new issue.

Before the examiner contacts the taxpayer, some time should be spent to become familiar with the banking industry. A listing of some of the resource and reference materials available to the agent is provided in the Appendix. These books should be used to become familiar with the accounting procedures used by the banking profession and the unique features of a bank tax return. The agent should also review the portion of the guide dealing with the technical issues. This will enable the agent to recognize issues when encountered during the examination. The first meeting with the taxpayer usually establishes the momentum of the examination. Take advantage of this opportunity to learn as much as possible about the methods and procedures used by the bank you are examining.

One thing to keep in mind is that the size of the asset base of a bank does not necessarily correspond to the complexity of the examination. At first, the rather large numbers may seem insurmountable, especially to someone who has no experience with large cases or is used to auditing only manufacturing firms. However, if you take out the amount of interest income and interest expense, the numbers no longer seem so overwhelming.

COORDINATED ISSUES

ISP Coordinated Issue Papers are written to ensure uniform treatment on issues unique to an industry. An issue does not become coordinated until the Assistant Commissioner (Examination) approves the issuance of the coordinated issue paper.

Delegation Order No. 247 (1996-21 IRB 7 (May 20, 1996)) gives case managers in the CEP program the authority to settle coordinated issues with the concurrence of both the Examination and Appeals ISP coordinators. Issues eligible for this authority are those coordinated issues for which Appeals has written approved settlement position.

Issues become *coordinated* after considering the following factors:

1. Whether the issue is *unique* to a particular industry
2. Whether the issue is generally *applicable* to all taxpayers in the industry
3. The *complexity* of the issue
4. Whether a *compliance* problem can potentially exist with respect to the issue.

There are currently *four* coordinated issues in the Commercial Banking area. These issues are discussed later in this guide.

The national coordinators for the Commercial Banking and the Savings & Loan Industry are as follows:

COMMERCIAL BANKING:
MS MARY GRADY
INTERNAL REVENUE SERVICE
6TH FLOOR
110 WEST 44TH STREET
NEW YORK, NY 10036
PHONE # (212) 719-6170
FAX # (212) 719-6005

SAVINGS AND LOAN ASSOCIATIONS:
MS JODY BOTSFORD
INTERNAL REVENUE SERVICE
ROOM 4012

300 N. LOS ANGELES ST.
LOS ANGELES, CA 90012
PHONE # (213) 894-0918
FAX # (213) 894-6432

Whenever your case includes an adjustment involving one of the coordinated issues, the Industry Specialists *must* be contacted in the event the formal position is not followed for any reason. It is recommended you contact the DISP or the ISP to get updates on the coordinated and other significant issues since the IRS position can change.

SIGNIFICANT ISSUES

Significant issues involve areas with considerable examination potential. They are issues which are encountered in the field but are not yet coordinated. The banking ISP has identified *eight* significant issues which should be considered during all examinations.

Listed below are the eight significant issues along with a brief explanation of each item. Some of these issues are discussed in further detail later in this guide.

1. Mortgage Servicing Rights

The recognition of income on the sale of mortgage pools where the seller separates and retains the mortgage servicing rights. The issue involves the allocation of basis to the rights retained.

2. SFAS 91

The current inclusion into income of all fees, and the capitalization of all direct expenses related to the origination of a loan.

3. Other Real Estate Owned (OREO)

This issue involves the recognition of gain or loss on the repossession of OREO property, the discount factor used to determine FMV, the write-down of OREO property after it is repossessed, and the handling of OREO expenses where the property is not being used as rental property.

4. Hedging Gains and Losses

Are taxpayers properly identifying hedging transactions or should IRC section 1256 apply?

5. Foreign Tax Credit

What level of substantiation must the taxpayer provide in order to be allowed a foreign tax credit? Can the taxpayer use "borrower" letters as proof of payment?

6. Brazilian Foreign Tax Credit

Is the Brazilian Foreign Tax Credit a creditable foreign tax for U.S. tax purposes and if the tax is creditable, is the Brazilian Central Bank exempt from tax?

7. Interest Expense (1120F)

Adjustments which are made to conform the taxpayer's balance sheet to U.S. standards.

8. Home Office Allocation (1120F)

What is the proper method for allocating expenses from the parent company to the branch operation?

RETURN IDENTIFICATION PROCESS

If a bank return is assigned to you, it will be obvious from a review of the return that it is a bank. Usually, the name of the entity will include the word "bank." If the concern is a holding company, the names on the subsidiary list will reflect whether they are banks. There are several ways that you can secure bank returns:

1. Banking returns can be identified by their business activity codes. The Principal Industry Activity (PIA) codes for bank holding companies and regular banks are 6060 and 6090, respectively.

2. In Michigan District, for example, the Planning and Special Projects (PSP) unit automatically receives all financial institution returns for activity codes 215 and above. These returns are segregated from the other tax returns and are classified by revenue agents who specialize in examining banks.

3. The *American Banker* newspaper provides an annual list of the largest 100 bank holding companies and the largest 300 commercial banks in the United States. *Crain's Detroit Business,* a weekly publication, ranks Michigan banks by assets each year. Business publications for many other major cities would likely provide similar lists. These can be reviewed to identify bank returns which are located in your examination area.

4. State banking regulatory agencies can be contacted to obtain information on banks under their authority. In Michigan, the Financial Institutions Bureau distributes two publications each year which summarize the activities of Michigan banks. These are titled "19XX Annual Report-Financial Institutions Bureau" and "Annual Report-19XX Data Analysis, 19XX Enforcement Activity." They provide information on loans, assets, merger activity, capital, minority loans, deposits, *etc.* of the various banks.

5. When our group was formed, one of the agents requested to be put on the mailing lists of the publicly held financial institutions in Michigan. Our group receives annual reports, quarterly reports, 10K's, press releases, *etc.*, from these banks. The group's banking agents also clip articles from local newspapers and publications. This information is compiled in planning folders under each entity's name. This way we are able to keep aware of potential issues that might warrant examination of a particular bank. We have also found this information helpful in planning the examination of banks which have been selected for examination.

In summary, usually banking returns will be easily identified when they are received. If you are interested in obtaining additional returns, there are several sources. PSP can use PIA codes to identify bank returns. The *American Banker*, local business publications, and the State banking authorities can be consulted for lists of banks in your area. Local banks may be contacted for information that they provide to the public.

PRE-AUDIT PLANNING

As with any journey, the audit must begin with a first step. A comprehensive *pre-audit analysis* is one of the most important steps in any examination. It sets the stage for the scope of the audit, the issues, and any unusual items to be examined. Since this is a *banking* guide, the normal pre-audit steps encountered in all examinations are not detailed. Rather, only those areas which have an impact on a bank examination will be discussed.

1. When you are assigned a bank to examine, take some time to read this guide and review any other available reference material. You cannot properly classify a return, or determine the audit potential of a case without first knowing what to look for.

2. A thorough review of the tax return must be made to determine which issues exist. It is impor tant to remember that not all banks are worth auditing, so make sure that you have

some potential issues in your case. Normally, banks with an activity code of 215 or above are automatically sent out to the district. Therefore, returns may be sent out to the group which have no significant tax potential. In those cases, it is a waste of valuable time and resources to examine these returns.

3. After you decide to examine a particular return, it is very important to determine up-front all of the *businesses* the bank operates. In many cases, it cannot be easily determined from just looking at the return. It is common practice for a bank to bury a business within the main operating subsidiary of the bank. The answer to each of the questions below will have a big impact on the scope of your examination. Determine at the very onset of the audit the answers to the following questions.

a. Does the bank have a *mortgage servicing* department?
b. Does the bank operate or engage in any type of *leasing* activity?
c. Does the bank operate a *securities* or brokerage department for trading stocks and bonds for individual or corporate customers?
d. Does the bank engage in interest rate or commodity *hedging*?
e. Does the bank own or operate any institution acquired from the FDIC or RTC?
f. Does the bank have any *foreign* operations?
g. Does the bank regularly purchase from or sell securities to customers in the ordinary course of a trade or business?

A positive answer to any of these questions will lead you to potential issues which will be discussed later. Review those areas of the guide to determine whether that particular issue should be examined.

4. Read the company's annual reports and the Securities and Exchange Commission (SEC) filings for answers to the above questions, while at the same time looking for other areas of potential examination. The information included in these documents is extremely helpful in understanding the business operations of the taxpayer. If the bank has stock that is publicly traded, you can call the bank and request copies of these reports from them. This information is readily available to potential investors.

5. Consider going to the public library to do some research on the bank to determine any other activities the bank may be involved in along with any recent articles on the bank which may have tax implications.

6. Banks can become very cyclical if their investments are not diversified. A bank that loans heavily to the automotive industry, for example, may incur significant losses in an auto industry downturn. Always ask the taxpayer to provide you with the current outlook for the bank. If significant loan losses are anticipated in the near future, this may affect the examination potential, and therefore, the scope of the examination. For tax years beginning after December 31, 1986, and before January 1, 1994, banks using the specific charge-off method of accounting for bad debts are entitled to carry back NOL's for *10* years for losses related to bad debt deductions.

7. Contact your District ISP Coordinator for information on banks in your area.

CHAPTER 3—SPECIALIZATION WITHIN THE IRS

INVOLVING SPECIALISTS IN AN EXAMINATION

One of the objectives of a revenue agent is to know how to identify a potential issue and to know when to seek assistance from a trained specialist. During pre-audit planning, determine which of the available specialists will be needed for the bank examination. Usually, it will be evident from a review of the return which referrals should be made. However, sometimes you will not know until after the examination has begun. Once you realize a specialist is needed, a referral should be made as soon as possible. The specialists available for your examination are discussed below.

Engineer

IRM 42(16)2.2 states engineering referrals are mandatory on all corporate returns with assets of at least $10,000,000. Assistance can also be requested whenever there is a significant valuation issue. An engineering referral is made on Form 5202. Informal consultations with engineers are usually available at any time.

We have found engineering assistance to be particularly valuable when a bank has acquired the assets of another institution. If the bank revalued acquired assets, engineers can be used to determine whether the values and lives that were assigned to assets such as servicing rights, buildings, *etc.* were accurate. Usually, the acquiring bank will have paid an amount in excess of the value of the purchased tangible assets. This premium may be allocated among intangible assets such as: Core deposits, covenants not to compete, goodwill, *etc.* Banks will attempt to allocate as much of the premium as possible to depreciable and amortizable assets. Therefore, it is important that an IRS engineer reviews these valuations to determine whether they are acceptable. The core deposit and intangible issues will be discussed thoroughly in a later chapter.

Banks often have expensive buildings for their headquarters. We used an engineer on one of our cases to assist in determining whether the taxpayer properly allocated payments to its contractor for construction of a new headquarters building. The bank brought in engineers from another state to value the assets during the construction process. They took the position that a number of the assets were not structural components of the building and could be depreciated over shorter lives. The IRS engineer reviewed their studies to determine which assets should have been considered part of the building.

Computer Audit Specialist

IRM 42(13)3.3 requires an examiner to request the assistance of a computer audit specialist (CAS): 1) whenever the Examination Return Chargeout states there is a record retention agreement on file or 2) if the tax return has an activity code of 219 or above. Banks have a large asset base relative to their business activity. Therefore, you may not actually need the assistance of a CAS just because a referral is mandatory. At the beginning of the examination, discuss with your bank whether they can easily provide hard copy documents. If so, this should be mentioned on Form RC-C-Gen 4-873, Request for ADP Assistance, so the CAS manager can decide whether or not to accept the referral.

If a CAS is assigned to your bank, there are a number of ways he or she can assist you. The specialist can review, analyze, and understand the taxpayer's flow of documents through the bank's accounting system. If the bank uses a service bureau, the CAS may be familiar with their system from another exam. Once the CAS evaluates the system, he or she may enter into a record retention agreement with the taxpayer to keep the necessary machine-sensible records for use in current and future examinations.

The CAS is also a specialist in statistical sampling. Statistical sampling can be used when examining line items on the return. It may also be used when reviewing loans written off as bad debts or loans where the taxpayer has stopped accruing interest. (These issues will be discussed later in this guide.) To reduce the sampling error, a large sample must be drawn. It can be very time consuming to review the related documentation. Practically speaking, we have found examiner's judgment in selecting loan samples to be superior to the use of statistical sampling because we have found significant adjustments in substantially less time.

There has been a lot of merger and acquisition activity between banks in recent years. Because of these changes in business form, companies may revalue their assets. A CAS can work with an engineer to determine whether software or other assets were properly valued.

Probably the most important functions the CAS can perform are the various computer applications. See Exhibit 3-1, "Computer Specialist Assistance." This exhibit was written by a CAS who is experienced in the examination of financial institutions. You and the CAS who is assigned to your audit should review this exhibit. Much of the exhibit is designed to be used by the CAS when performing the computer applications or securing a record retention agreement. Therefore, you need not be too concerned with those portions of the exhibit.

Financial Products Specialist

Banks often participate in a number of complicated financial transactions. A review of the Glossary may have exposed you to some new terminology such as: Arbitrage, basis points, collateralized mortgage obligations, *etc.* A trained financial products specialist will be familiar with this terminology and with the mechanics, accounting, tax law, and audit issues of the financial products industry.

The annual report, of publicly held banks, usually has an area which discusses the bank's various financial transactions. The annual report should disclose whether the bank is a party to any interest rate futures, caps and floors, or forward contracts. Many banks also enter into interest rate swap agreements to hedge against fluctuations in the interest rates. They may also enter into repurchase agreements and reverse repurchase agreements.

Do not be concerned if you do not understand the nature of these financial instruments. Your goal should be ascertain whether or not your bank is involved in any of these transactions. The tax manager or tax preparer with whom you are working is likely to be as unfamiliar with this area as you are. The financial products specialist will probably need to interview the bank employee responsible for these types of transactions. The specialist should be able to review the bank's financial products to determine the nature of gains and losses, whether transactions should be treated as sales versus financing transactions, whether any items should be marked-to-market, *etc.*

There are financial products groups in each region. Questions concerning financial products can be directed to the Chief, Technical Field Support, Illinois District, or the Chief, Financial Industry Studies, New York. The Office of Financial Products and Transactions is headquartered in Washington, D.C. This office is responsible for providing any assistance relating to financial products issues. The office provides technical support and performs on-site visits to develop financial products aspects of cases.

International Examiner

Most smaller banks do not participate in international operations. Therefore, it is likely that your bank would not have any issues requiring the assistance of an international examiner. However, many banks do have branches in foreign countries, issue securities outside of the United States, make loans to foreign countries, invest in foreign securities, *etc.*

There are several ways to identify international issues. "International Issue" may be stamped on the front of the tax return. The tax return will often include Form 5471, Information Return with Respect to a Foreign Corporation; Form 5472, Information Return of a Foreign Owned Corporation; Form 1118, Computation of Foreign Tax Credit; or other international forms. The annual report may discuss international activity. Lastly, the taxpayer should be asked whether it has any foreign branches, loans to foreign countries, foreign securities, *etc.*

It is often very difficult to obtain documentation for foreign banking transactions. Therefore, it is very important to determine early in the examination whether assistance is needed from an international specialist. If so, a referral should be made on Form 2962. IRM 42(10)0 discusses international examinations and provides the referral criteria and procedures.

The international examiner will analyze the foreign activity of the bank to determine whether there are any tax consequences. Often, the bank will be deducting bad debts prematurely or deferring foreign source income. The specialist will determine the effect of any adjustments on the taxable income of the bank and may need to recompute the foreign tax credit. One of the banking Coordinated Issue Papers discusses foreign withholding taxes.

Employee Plans Specialist

A bank will usually have at least one retirement plan for its employees. Often, employee plans specialists will independently contact the taxpayer to review its plans prior to an examination by a revenue agent. If the bank's plans were not previously examined, Form 4632-A, Employee Plans Referral Checksheet, should be completed. If assistance is needed, Form 4632, Employee Plans Referral should be used. IRM 45(10)0 provides additional information regarding referrals.

If a referral is accepted, the employee plans specialist will evaluate whether the requirements of the employer's plan(s) have been met. Since taxpayers sometimes deduct amounts in excess of what is needed to fund the plan, the specialist may also calculate the allowable deduction.

Employment Tax Specialist

Some districts assign employment tax specialists to review the employment tax issues on the larger companies. The specialist may review information reporting documents, employment tax returns, Forms W-4, *etc.* He or she may also look at issue areas such as: Employee reimbursement policies, medical reimbursement plans, meal reimbursements, *etc.* The procedures for making referrals to the employment tax groups vary between districts.

The package audit requirements are essentially the same for banks as they are for any other taxpayer. An exception is made for the review of Forms 4789 that are filed by federally regulated banks. (This is the form the bank is required to file if a customer deposits at least $10,000 of cash in one or more related transactions.) Per IRM 1229, the banking regulators are given specific authority to verify that banks are complying with the filing requirements for these forms. The IRS generally does not have jurisdiction in this area.

Banks file numerous Forms 1099 because of the interest and dividends that they pay to their customers. In addition, they file Forms 1098 and 1099 to report mortgage transactions. They retain copies of this information on magnetic tape, rather than on hard copy. In lieu of reviewing these Forms 1099, we generally ask the taxpayer to provide a letter explaining its policy on issuance of Forms 1099 for interest and dividends. Forms 1099 for subcontractors, rent, *etc.* should still be inspected by the agent. Also, the taxpayer's use of Form 1099-A for abandoned property should be reviewed for accuracy and timeliness. Forms 1099-C (post-'93) and 1099-G (pre-'94) for cancellation of indebtedness should also be reviewed.

Banks receive a 1099-B Notice each year. This Notice is issued by the IRS to inform taxpayers of errors in the reporting of names and social security numbers on Forms 1099. Rev. Proc. 93-37, 1993-2 C.B. 477 (modifying Rev. Proc. 92-32, 1992-1 C.B. 776) provides guidance on notifying customers that their taxpayer identification numbers are incorrect. It is effective for B Notices sent on or after September 1, 1993. The penalties from this notice may be waived if the taxpayer has used due diligence when obtaining this information from the customer. Generally, the bank will correspond directly with the IRS Service Center regarding the penalties.

Insurance Specialist

Banks may elect to include certain types of insurance companies as part of their consolidated returns. An insurance company must have been a member of the affiliated group for the 5 taxable years preceding the taxable year for which the election was made. Unless the bank makes a valid election, a separate return must be filed for the related insurance company.

The examination of insurance companies is very difficult. As with banks, there are special code sections that relate only to them. Insurance companies file their returns on Form 1120L or Form 1120PC, rather than on Form 1120.

Although most districts do not have a separate group that specializes in the examination of insurance companies, they usually do have particular agents that have experience in this area. If your bank has an insurance company, consider consulting with an insurance specialist to determine whether there is any audit potential. The life insurance industry specialist is located in New York. The casualty insurance industry specialist is located in Boston.

Economist

IRM 42(12)0 discusses the economic assistance program and the various ways that an examiner may use an economist in analyzing and evaluating the economic factors in his or her case. The economist can assist the examiner with the value of intangible assets, industry and trade practices, the value of functions performed, profit ratios, the value of a closely held business, *etc.* There are economists assigned to some of the district offices in the key regions. Form 9276 is used to request economic assistance. Generally, referrals should be limited to issues where the potential deficiency is at least $500,000.

District Counsel and Industry Counsel

Usually, there is ongoing litigation affecting banking issues. District Counsel receives pending issue reports from the Office of the Associate Chief Counsel (Domestic). They should be able to provide information regarding the current status of any court cases that might affect your examination issues.

There are also banking and savings and loan industry counsel who are responsible for overseeing court cases directly related to financial institutions. These attorneys should be contacted when there are unagreed industry issues. They also want to be made aware of cases that may need to be litigated in the future. Sometimes they are looking for litigation vehicles for particular issues.

MARKET SEGMENT SPECIALIZATION PROGRAM

The IRS' Market Segment Specialization Program (MSSP) focuses on developing examiner expertise through the examination of particular market segments. An industry, a profession, an occupation, or an issue may be selected as a market segment. Once the market segment is identified, qualified examiners are selected to accumulate information about all aspects of that industry's business activities. Returns of the industry are examined in an effort to gain knowledge and to identify industry-wide issues. Based on the knowledge and understanding gained through this process, audit procedures and techniques are incorporated into a written guide to be shared with other districts. The techniques guide provides examiners with information on how the industry operates, its accounting/business practices, common procedures within the industry, sources of information, and unique tax issues.

Specialization puts the Service on a level playing field with both the taxpayer and the practitioner community. MSSP increases the educational level of the examiner while increasing job satisfaction and the self-confidence level of the examiner. In this process, the public image of the IRS is also strengthened. MSSP increases the efficiency and effectiveness of the Service through the development of issues of merit while providing a high degree of consistency in the treatment of those issues. MSSP provides a resource for other examiners to consult to avoid the immeasurable duplication of effort when each agent has to "reinvent the wheel." Specialization is a powerful way for the IRS to acknowledge and respond to the unique business practices of an industry. Such an approach maximizes IRS resources, thus increasing the overall productivity of the Service.

Each District has an MSSP Coordinator who has information on all the market segments in the MSSP program. He or she would be one of your first contacts to obtain industry information. The local MSSP Coordinator receives current updates to the audit guides and industry issues. In addition, there is an MSSP bulletin board that can be accessed to receive industry information. To obtain access to this bulletin board, contact your local MSSP Coordinator.

MSSP has both similarities and differences with ISP. While all examinations have audit techniques and specific tax issues as major components, the primary emphasis of MSSP is development of uniform and effective examination *techniques.* The major emphasis of ISP is the uniform identification, development, and resolution of tax *issues* in larger examinations. The MSSP is directed at the general program and examination of all types and sizes of returns. Both programs emphasize knowledge of the industry and its business and accounting practices. They also treat communication with the industry's customers and representatives as an integral part of the process.

The Market Segment Specialization Program IRM Handbook can be referenced for additional information on MSSP.

INDUSTRY SPECIALIZATION PROGRAM

Commercial banking is included in the Industry Specialization Program (ISP). ISP was established to ensure uniform and consistent treatment of issues nationwide. It also helps to provide for better identification and development of issues. Each industry in the program has released Coordinated Issue Papers and a list of potential issues for use by revenue agents. The Industry Specialist for Commercial Banking is located in New York City. The National Industry Specialist is generally only contacted if an issue has significant nationwide impact, if a Request for Technical Advice is submitted on industry issues, for approval of resolution of a coordinated issue on a basis different than that in the Coordinated Issue Paper, or for Coordinated Examination Program cases.

Each district also has an industry coordinator who is an excellent resource for information on all the industries in the ISP. He or she would generally be your first contact to obtain industry information. The district industry coordinator receives current updates to the Coordinated Issue Papers and industry issues. Contact him or her to obtain copies of the current ISP Coordinated Issue Papers.

Internal Revenue Manual (IRM) 42(14)0 describes the Industry Specialization Program. IRM 42(14)5.23 requires that at the beginning of each examination of a taxpayer included in the ISP, a letter be sent to the taxpayer or its representative. Along with this letter, the taxpayer is to receive copies of the IRM section and the ISP Coordinated Issue Papers for the industry. The banking industry specialist recommends that we provide the taxpayer with copies of both the banking and the savings and loan Coordinated Issue Papers. Exhibit 3-2 contains the sample letter.

It may seem unusual that we are required to inform the taxpayers at the onset of the examination at what areas we will be looking. However, you will find that most banks are aware of the issues and it is helpful to begin discussing their treatment of these items very early in the examination. There are currently four coordinated banking issues: Interest on nonperforming loans, core deposits, gain or loss on foreclosed property, and gross-up net loans. These will all be discussed later in this guide.

The four coordinated savings and loan issues are: Accrued interest on nonperforming loans, core deposit intangibles, validity of Treas. Reg. section 1.593-6A(b)(5)(vi), and interest income on the sale of foreclosed property. The first two issues are discussed in this guide. The last two issues would be applicable to a bank only if it has a savings and loan subsidiary. The Industry Specialist for Savings and Loans is located in Los Angeles.

SUMMARY

As soon as you identify a potential issue that requires the assistance of a specialist, a referral should be made. Sometimes the specialists may be able to assist each other. Therefore, it is important that you frequently communicate with them so you can determine how they can help you and each other.

Exhibit 3-1
Computer Specialist Assistance

Purpose and Utilization

Given the volume and complexity of bank accounting records, auditing techniques often should include CAS support to convert the massive quantity of data into analytical reports. The taxpayer's files are more convenient to review by using computerized reports. The large banks are virtually impossible to examine without the assistance of a Computer Audit Specialist (CAS).

Once a Computer Audit Specialist assistance referral is accepted, it is important to quickly identify which taxpayer data files are needed to provide maximum support for the revenue agent's audit plan. These files should be requested via an Information Document Request (IDR). A sample of an IDR follows.

[SAMPLE INFORMATION DOCUMENT REQUEST, Form 4564, Rev. 6/88. Not Reproduced.]

The following are basic applications, with a brief explanation, of how they may be utilized as banking examination audit tools.

APPLICATIONS

Since the bank's files are usually voluminous, strip the consolidated general ledger by company (each legal entity within the consolidated group) prior to any runs.

1. General Ledger Compare (GLC): The GLC lists each GL account with year end totals for two or three years. The differences are reflected in dollars or percent. The revenue agent (RA) can quickly focus in on accounts with significant changes or unusual trends.

2. Stratification: The stratification is used in conjunction with the GLC. The transaction volume by dollar ranges and monthly distribution for the questionable accounts are shown on the stratification.

This report provides the revenue agent with convenient access to general ledger history which can be analyzed on-site or off-site.

The stratification may be modified for specific "Journal Entry Selections." This may best be accomplished by incorporating an internal sort for journal entry numbers (journal entry number— primary and account number—secondary). Select only the journal entry codes relative to accruals and deferrals. (Request journal voucher and source code listings from taxpayer.) This report will show the distribution of each affected account's accrual or deferral transactions only.

There are several commercial banking potential issues based upon improper accruals and deferrals.

3. Account Selection: After analysis of the stratification, a report can be developed showing all the available, relevant detail for each selected account.

To identify fragmented invoices, sort the general ledger transaction file by invoice number sequence. Invoices, in excess of a specified monetary value, can be printed. Invoices from certain vendors, or invoices charged to certain accounts may also be a selection criteria.

4. W-2 Employment Tax: This program identifies employees whose Federal income tax withholding was under a certain percentage of their gross wages. This application can be performed in lieu of a W-4 check.

5. Data Transfer from Hardcopy or Tape to MICRO (PC): The following are two of several methods to accomplish downloading:

a. Taxpayer's files stored on magnetic media in ASCII or EPCIDIC format may be transferred by direct access/transfer and converted via software such as Data Junction into Enable database or spreadsheet.

b. Taxpayer's files stored on hard copy may be scanned to create magnetic files.

Using the Enable database, the CAS or RA can produce reports. As an alternative, the scanned files may be uploaded to a mainframe for CAS applications.

Frequently, commercial banks do not have sufficient Accounts Payable volume for mainframe maintenance. Instead, they are entered on a PC in Lotus 123 and stored on a floppy disk. Since revenue agents do not have Lotus 123 software, the data may need to be transferred or converted to ASCII. CAS support reports or RA reports can then be generated using Enable's spreadsheet or database software.

COMPUTER AUDIT SPECIALIST ASSISTANCE BY ISSUE

1. Core Deposits

a. *Data Transfer from Hardcopy to MICRO (PC)*:

Banks will usually have a hard copy printout of their calculation of the value of the core deposits.

To accomplish the downloading, the bank's printout of deposit base valuation calculations may be scanned into ASCII format, edited to delete unnecessary titles and fields, and imported to enable spreadsheet or database. Then, the engineer will be able to crunch numbers to correct CORE values, analyze taxpayer's computations, and generate reports as needed.

b. *Statistical Sample*:

A sampling plan may be devised to analyze the customer bank accounts used as the basis to compute the value of the CORE deposit intangible. Some examples of items to consider are listed below:

1) Determine whether intercompany accounts were included in the computation.

2) Identify accounts opened between the date of acquisition and date of final merger. (These are accounts of the acquiring bank.)

3) Determine whether accounts used to manage travelers checks were included in the computation.

4) Determine whether the average balance rather than the balance at the date of acquisition was used.

5) Identify whether accounts with small balances are used. (These have no value in determining core deposit intangibles.)

2. Loan Servicing Rights:

To compute the value of the basis which should be allocated to retained servicing rights, there has been a Lotus spreadsheet developed which includes complex formulas. It is necessary for the CAS to make the following adjustments to the spreadsheet for the Revenue Agent's independent use.

a. Column B Line 21 is the first month of the mortgage term. From here down to the last month of the term, a formula to generate the correct date relative to the "Sales Date" must be input as in the following examples:

Month 1

A:B21:(D4) @if(@Month(D8) + 1=2,@date value(D8 + 28),@if (@month(D8) + 1=4*or*@month

(d8) + 1=6#or#@month(D8) + 1=9#or#@month

(D8) + 1=11, @date value (D3 + 30), @ date value (D8 + 31)))

Month 2

A:B22:(D4) @if(@Month(B21) + 1=2,@date value(B21 + 28), @if (@month(B21) + 1=4#or#@month

(B21) + 1=6#or#@month(B21) + 1=9#or#@month

(B21) + 1=11, @date value (B21 + 30),@date value (D8 + 31)))

Month 3

A:B23:(D4) @if(@Month(B22) + 1=2, @ date value (B22 + 28), @if (@month B22) + 1=4#or#@month

(B22) + 1=6#or#@month(B22) + 1=9#or#@month

(B22) + 1=11, @date value (B22 + 30), @ date value (D8 + 31)))

b. Expand columns to accommodate large dollar amounts.
c. Add column to summarize yearly total of the net spread.
d. Add column to summarize yearly total of the OID income.
e. Reduce size in print option, change font, and print using Lotus Sideways.
f. Condense: "PKZIP new filename. ZIP old filename." (PKZIP is Detroit District's standard for data compression software. We have a site license for the program. You can download it from the District Bulletin Board System (BBS).)
g. Save to 3 1/2" high density disk.
h. To reverse compression: "PKZIP new filename. ZIP"

3. Fee Income:

The combination of stratification and account selection applications may assist the revenue agent in determining whether fee income such as VISA fees were booked as income upon receipt or amortized. The revenue agent will usually request detail from selected liability accounts to test both sides (debit and credit) of entries. The Journal Voucher Number normally can show all accounts related to one transaction.

The Stratification is used to identify the liability accounts, the Account Selection gives significant detail which includes journal voucher code or source code, and the Journal Voucher Selection shows all related accounts.

4. SFAS 91:

Generally, SFAS 91 requires lenders to net nonrefundable fees and direct costs associated with generating a loan, and defer and recognize the excess over the life of the related loan as an adjustment to yield. SFAS 91, section 5. The statement provides that similar loans may be aggregated for purposes of recognizing fees, costs, premium, and discount so long as the resulting amount does not differ materially from a loan-by-loan computation. SFAS 91, section 4.

The stratification may be used to help identify possible Balance Sheet accounts which relate to such costs. Once such accounts are identified, the account selections may identify specific entries for further investigation for potential issues such as improper accruals of income.

5. General Expenses:

The following expenses are often selected for an in-depth review. Stratifications and Account Selections are used to show transaction volume and unusual items:

a. Commission expense
b. Bad debts
c. Contingent liabilities expensed in error
d. Building expense
e. OREO or REO expenses (Other Real Estate Owned)—costs related to property the bank has repossessed or foreclosed upon
f. Leasing
g. Merger and acquisition costs.

Record Retention Agreement

In addition to the regular files requested to be retained, (that is, general ledger, accounts payable, vendor master, and W-2 Payroll Master File) retention of the following files should be considered for commercial banks:

Extract from Mortgage Loan Accounts' Records

File Content: This file will contain taxable year end information for Mortgage Loans and Mortgage-backed Securities sold with servicing retained. This file will include the following: Current Principal Balance, Current Escrow Balance, Current Interest Rate, Current Principal Payment, Current Interest Payment, Pre-Calculated Interest, Escrow Payment, Original Amount, Current Year-to-Date Interest, SWAP Lock Principal Amount, Current Pre-Paid Interest, Interest Change Date, First Payment Date, Last Payment Date, Balloon Type, Balloon Terms, Balloon Loan Maturity Date, Secondary Market Code, Percent Sold, Interest Method, Payment Frequency, Loan Instrument, Loan Type, Property Classification, Loan-To-Value Ratio, and Pass Through Rate to Investor.

Extract from Asset Account & Accumulated Account

File Content: This file will contain Real & Personal Property information such as Cost Basis, Description, Asset Code, Placed-In-Service Date, Useful Life, Current Year Depreciation, Prior Year Accumulated Depreciation Method, ITC, and Disposition (that is, Gains, Losses, and ITC Recapture).

Extract from Sale of Mortgage Backed Securities

File Content: This file will contain Owner at Sale Date, Pool Number, Agency or other entity sold to, Mortgage Term, Type of Mortgage (fixed, variable, *etc.*), Weighted Average Mortgage Rate, Weighted Average Coupon Rate, Guarantee Fee, Mortgage Principal at sales date, Sales Date, Mortgage Date, Maturity Date, Mortgage Group Number, Effective Yield or Discount Rate, Sales Price, Gain/Loss on Sale, SFAS 65 Servicing Gain, Book Amortization of the Servicing, Tax Servicing Gain if different from books, Tax Amortization if different from books, and Deferred Fee for sales in month originated.

Extract from Secondary Market Mortgage Backed Securities

File Content: This file will contain Pool Number, Purchase Date, Face Amount, Type, Date, Maturity, Rate, Factors for 4 Months, Outstanding Balance, Original Discount, Cusip Number, Original WAC, Original WAM, Calculated Remaining Term, Purchased Contractual Term, Historical or Estimated Payments.

Extract from Escrow File

File Content: Monthly history for each mortgage loan escrow account, that is, Date & Amount of Monthly Escrow Deposits and Payments.

Extract from Investment Package Reports

File Content: Monthly data of investment portfolio that is, Premiums, Discounts, Amortization, Interest Earned, Names of Securities, Dates Acquired, Dates Sold, Sales Amounts, and Acquisition Costs.

The above file contents are examples of what have been agreed upon in prior record retention agreements by the revenue agent, taxpayer's information systems personnel, and the computer audit specialist.

It has been found that mortgage and investment data files are usually maintained on a separate database with numerous data fields. The revenue agent and CAS should review the fields to determine which of them may be needed for adjustment calculations. Once these data fields are selected, it is requested they be retained in a flat sequential fixed-length format on magnetic tape reel-to-reel, 3.5" diskette, or 5.25" diskette.

Bank mergers may require special consideration. It will be important to ensure data files from newly acquired companies are *accessible and retainable by the acquiring company* as soon as the acquired company becomes a legal affiliated group member. Record Retention Agreements should be updated to include the computer records of the acquired company.

Exhibit 3-2
4200 Income Tax Examinations

42(14)0 ***(10-23-80)***

Industry Specialization Program

42(14)1 ***(6-11-85)***

General

(1) Industry specialization includes the concepts of Industrywide Studies, Industry Specialists, National Industry Coordinator, Designated Industries, Identified Industry Cases, and Coordinated Issues.

(2) Industry specialization has been established to ensure uniform and consistent treatment of issues nationwide and to provide better identification and development of issues.

(3) Additionally, industry specialization provides a vehicle for continued industry coordination. Since all industry taxpayers (CEP and non-CEP) are included in the Program, the continuity provided by industry specialization expands its benefits beyond the districts which have a concentration of large cases in an industry thereby benefiting those districts lacking wide experience in a highly complex industry.

42(14)2 ***(6-11-85)***

Definitions

(1) *Industrywide Study* is a concurrent evaluation of a particular industry and its principal taxpayers under the direction of an interim Industry Specialist. The concept encompasses the identification of unique industry accounting practices and audit techniques, the identification of common issues, and the pursuit of potential coordinated issues. Taxpayers included for direct participation in the study, represent a cross section of the major cases in the industry. The concept anticipates direct communications between the Interim Industry Specialist and case or group managers and other district management including onsite visitations. Industrywide meetings are also anticipated when appropriate. The purpose of the Industrywide Study is the identification of those industries which merit inclusion as Designated Industries under the continuing coordination of an Industry Specialist. The Study includes:

(a) The definition of business activity and the parameters of the industry;

(b) The identification of industry cases;

(c) The creation of a communications network among service personnel involved in the examination of industry cases;

(d) The analysis and identification of business or economic factors peculiar to the industry;

(e) The identification of tax problems, inconsistencies, *etc.*, within the industry.

(2) *Industry Specialist* serves as a nationwide specialist for an industry selected for specialization (Designated Industry). Effective formal and informal communication skills (horizontal and vertical) are critical to the performance of the job. (See IRM 42(14)6 and 42(15)3.3)

(3) *National Industry Coordinator* is a senior program analyst in the National Programs Section within the Office of National and International Programs, Assistant Commissioner (Examination). The Coordinator, a former case or group manager, provides program oversight and assistance to the Industry Specialists. (See IRM 42(14)3.2)

(4) *Designated Industries* are those industries identified as warranting continuing coordination and to which Industry Specialists have been assigned. Additions or deletions of Designated Industries may be made as circumstances warrant. See Exhibit 42(14)0-2 for the Designated Industries and the regions to which they are assigned with the Specialist's name and location.

(5) *Identified Industry Cases* are those cases within an industry that have been identified for regular monitoring by the Industry Specialist.

(6) *Coordinated Issues* are major issues of particular importance to an industry that have been selected for industrywide coordination. (See IRM 42(11)8—Handbook for Field Examination Case Managers, text 952).

42(14)3 ***(10-23-80)***

National Office Organizational Responsibility

42(14)3.1 ***(6-11-85)***

The National Office Examination Function will:

(1) designate a National Industry Coordinator;

(2) maintain a file of preliminary evaluations of industries conducted by regions and act as a clearinghouse to prevent duplication;

(3) select those industries warranting continuing coordination as Designated Industries and designate a region from which the Industry Specialist will be selected. Industry selections will be made from those recommended as a result of Industrywide Studies;

(4) Provide a resource allocation of at least a full staff year for the Industry Specialist in each industry, unless the workload for that industry dictates otherwise;

(5) assist the Industry Specialist by identifying and securing speakers for meetings. Provide for liaison with other government agencies;

(6) assist regions in identifying additional major industries where industrywide studies are feasible. Upon identification of an industry by a region, and a recommendation for an industrywide study (approved by the National Office), provide temporary staffing allocation for an interim Industry Specialist for the study and assist the region in planning and conducting the study.

(7) coordinate special industrywide projects and issues crossing regional lines;

(8) monitor the progress and examination status of cases utilizing quarterly report Forms 4451 (Large Case Status Report), Report Symbol NO-4000-164, submitted by Case Managers (expiration date 12/85) and Forms 6352 (Industry Specialization Report) Report Symbol NO-4000-440, submitted by the Industry Specialists; (expiration date 12/85)

(9) provide overall program direction and assistance to regions.

42(14)3.2 *(6-11-85)*

National Industry Coordinator will:

(1) function as a focal point of communication for all industry managers. Communicate directly with Industry Specialists, district and regional management officials and specialist managers when warranted;

(2) ensure that findings in the Designated Industries and industry studies are disseminated to all regions;

(3) assist the Industry Specialist in planning and arranging industrywide meetings;

(4) ensure that periodic industrywide reports are compiled and distributed to all examiners;

(5) make program visitations as needed;

(6) recommend to the Assistant Commissioner (Examination) additions, deletions or modifications of industries identified for coordination;

(7) develop and maintain effective communications between Technical and Examination to ensure that requests for technical advice involving industrywide issues are expedited;

(8) In conjunction with the Industry Specialist determine the need to revise or update existing IRM 4232, Techniques Handbook for Specialized Industries, or, if one does not exist, determine the need to develop one. Assist the Industry Specialist and appropriate regional personnel in creating a task force (chaired by the Industry Specialist) to revise or develop the Handbook. Develop, in conjunction with the task force, an action plan with specific target dates for completion of the Handbook;

(9) participate in the selection of Coordinated Issues. (See IRM 42(11)8—Handbook for Field Examination Case Managers, Chapter 952).

42(14)4 *(6-11-85)*

Regional Office Organizational Responsibilities

(1) The office of the Assistant Regional Commissioner (Examination) should:

(a) cooperate with districts in the identification of industries which lend themselves to industrywide studies. After clearing with the National Office that it is not duplicative of other regions' efforts, initiate a preliminary evaluation of a specific industry. Recommend industrywide studies when appropriate. With the concurrence of the Assistant Commissioner (Examination), conduct industrywide studies;

(b) recommend to the National Office, industries warranting continuing coordination to be classified as Designated Industries. Usually, this recommendation is made after the results of an industrywide study indicate the need for continuing coordination;

(c) recommend to the National Office appropriate alternatives when the results of an industrywide study do not indicate the need for continuing coordination;

(d) select Industry Specialists. Usually the selection will be made from a district having significant CEP cases within the particular industry. If the Industry Specialist position is to be a full time one and industry or management factors so dictate, the position may, at the discretion of the region, be placed on the staff of the ARC (Examination).

(e) The Regional office should have flexibility in the application of the following criteria (which is not all inclusive) in recommending the placement of the Specialist:

(1) Multiple staff-year allocation for the Specialist Program. (Full-time Specialist in addition to full-time assistants)

(2) Widespread international activity.

(3) Significant involvement in foreign exchange programs.

(4) Coordinated pricing issues.

(5) Need to conduct centralized studies.

(6) Need for economist assistance.

(f) cooperate with the districts to ensure that Industry Specialists are provided with adequate resources;

(g) cooperate with the districts to ensure that Industry Specialists are relieved of all or the appropriate portion of other duties in order to adequately fulfill the responsibilities outlined in IRM 42(14)5.1. Where the Specialist is to continue as a case manager, only one CEP case will usually be assigned;

(h) annually assess staffing needs of each Designated Industry and provide necessary technical and clerical staffing for the ISP activity;

(i) assist the Industry Specialist in planning, arranging and conducting meetings. Provide resources for the processing and distribution of information;

(j) provide liaison between the National Office, the Industry Specialist and other regions; and

(k) provide appropriate international training to Industry Specialists;

(l) monitor the progress and effectiveness of the region's Industry Specialization Program. Monitoring should be sufficiently adequate to ensure the timely responsiveness of all case managers within the region to the requests of all Industry Specialists;

(m) make program visits as needed. Visits should include CEP and General Program areas.

42(14)5 ***(10-23-80)***

District Office Organizational Responsibilities

42(14)5.1 ***(6-11-85)***

General

(1) The District Examination function should:

(a) be alert to identify an industry which is susceptible to industry-wide study techniques and report such findings to the region;

(b) recommend through channels to the National Industry Coordinator, an industry to be classified as a Designated Industry;

(c) nominate to the Regional Office a manager to serve as Industry Specialist. Usually nominees will be case managers but for selected industries a specialist manager (CAS, Engineer, or International) may be equally appropriate;

(d) ensure that Industry Specialists are relieved of a portion of their duties in order to have adequate time to fulfill his/her responsibilities, and, ensure that the Specialist has adequate resources such as subscriptions to trade and professional magazines and other publications, storage and working space, clerical and technical support *etc.*;

(e) provide at least a full staff year allocation to each Designated Industry program. The allocation may be accomplished either by the Specialist or a combination of Specialist and technical assistant time. In unusual situations the current workload for a particular industry may warrant a lesser allocation;

(f) work with the Industry Specialist to determine the district cases to be included in the district's Industry Specialization Program;

(g) comply with requests of Industry Specialists from outside the district;

(h) provide the necessary involvement of district management to assure cooperation of all participants in industrywide studies and within Designated Industries. All followup requests by Specialists will be made through the District CEP Coordinator;

(i) maintain responsibility for the conduct of the program. Branch, group and case reviews should include consideration of ISP objectives;

(j) not withdraw a case from an industrywide study without the concurrence of the Industry Specialist and the National Industry Coordinator. Such withdrawal should be considered only when most unusual circumstances, such as a joint investigation or a grand jury probe, exist;

(k) secure the prior concurrence of the Industry Specialist to any disposition of a coordinated issue in identified industry cases;

(l) not adopt a position contrary to that reflected in a coordinated issue on any cases without the specific concurrence of the Industry Specialist;

(m) not blanketly held cases open. However, before any case involving a coordinated issue is closed the Industry Specialist should approve such closure after considering all the facts and circumstances.

(n) the manager of the Industry Specialist (branch or section chief) should:

  (1) provide overall support and direction of the program;

  (2) be involved to the extent necessary to ensure that the objectives of the industry program, are met. This degree of involvement requires the manager to have knowledge of the action plan and objectives to the extent necessary to achieve program success; and

  (3) evaluate the performance of the Industry Specialist based on a personal knowl-

edge of his/ her performance and from evaluative inputs from the National and Regional Offices.

42(14)5.2 *(6-11-85)*

Case and Group Managers

42(14)5.21 *(6-11-85)*

Case Manager—General

(1) District case managers examining cases within an industry will:

(a) be directly advised by the Industry Specialist when their case has been included as an identified industry case;

(b) be regularly provided with the ISP Digest. Each issue of the Digest will contain a complete listing of coordinated issues for each Designated Industry. A description of the business activity will also be included for each industry;

(c) advise the Industry Specialist of any CEP case which is engaged in the business activity of a particular Designated Industry and is not an identified industry case. This will also apply to cases where the taxpayer is engaged in the business activity only through a division or subsidiary;

(d) consult with the appropriate Industry Specialist for planning input during step one of the plan on all identified industry cases. In multi-industry cases the case manager will consult with all appropriate Industry Specialists;

(e) consult with the appropriate Industry Specialist prior to submitting a Request for Technical Advice on industry issues.

(f) follow the decisions on coordinated issues formulated by the Industry Specialist. Resolution of a coordinated issue on a basis different than that formulated by the Industry Specialist requires the approval of the Industry Specialist and the National Industry Coordinator. In identified industries cases, decisions to avoid pursuit of a coordinated issue area also require the concurrence of the Specialist. This applies also to cases that must be closed due to an imminent statute expiration prior to issuance of the Industry Specialist's final report on the issue(s).

(g) when mutually agreeable, arrange for the participation of the Industry Specialist in the critique process on identified industry cases;

(h) on identified industry cases, provide timely responses to requests from the Industry Specialist for notifications, forms, reports, *etc.*, whether on a one time or continuing basis.

42(14)5.22 *(6-11-85)*

Group Managers—General

(1) Group managers will be regularly provided with the Industry Specialization Program Digest and will maintain these in a library. Group managers who have revenue agents examining cases within an industry will:

(a) ensure that ISP coordinated issues are included in the examination plan;

(b) ensure that examiners review ISP Digests and, when considered appropriate, consult with the Industry Specialists;

(c) consult with the appropriate Industry Specialist prior to submitting a Request for Technical Advice on industry issues;

(d) follow the decisions on coordinated issues formulated by the Industry Specialist. Resolution of a coordinated issue on a basis different than that formulated by the Industry Specialist requires the approval of the Industry Specialist and the National Industry Coordinator.

(e) ensure that the provisions of IRM 42(14)5.23 are complied with.

42(14)5.23 ***(6-11-85)***

Informing the Taxpayer

(1) At the beginning of each examination of a taxpayer included in the Industry Specialization Program the managers will ensure that a letter is sent to the appropriate representative of the taxpayer which contains the following information:

(a) advise the taxpayer that the Service has an Industry Specialization Program to ensure uniform and consistent treatment of issues on an industrywide basis, and one or more of the designated industries includes the taxpayer's corporation. For purposes of informing the taxpayer about the program, advise that a description of the Program and a copy of the Internal Revenue Manual Procedures are being forwarded with the letter. This information should be included in the opening paragraph of the letter;

(b) also advise the taxpayer that a description of the issues currently being coordinated in the industry is being transmitted with the letter. Inform the taxpayer that the Service would appreciate a review of the issues along with comments and recommendations concerning the issues. Also request the taxpayer to advise the Service as to other potential issues which may benefit from consideration on an industrywide basis. This information should be included in the second paragraph of the letter; and

(c) advise the taxpayer in the closing paragraph that the case manager is available to discuss and answer any questions concerning the Industry Specialization Program with the taxpayer's representative or members of the representative's staff. Include case managers telephone and mailing address.

(2) The letter is required to be sent to all taxpayers included in the Industry Specialization Program. An example of such letter is shown in Exhibit 42(14)0-1. The contents of the letter may be modified and other relevant information added except for the contents outlined in (1)(a) and (1)(b) above.

42(14)6 ***(10-23-80)***

Industry Specialist

42(14)6.1 ***(6-11-85)***

General

(1) The Industry Specialist will provide an overview of the industry as a whole with special emphasis on forward planning and monitoring indus-

try trends and direction. It is essential that the specialist gather sufficient information on current industry activities to be able to forecast the effect on future examinations. As the industry focal point he/she will provide case managers and group managers with the additional tools necessary to plan the examination of taxpayers in a designated industry.

(2) In most Designated Industries at least one staff year should be allocated to ISP activities. This allocation will be accomplished by any appropriate combination of full-time Specialists, Specialists with one CEP case assigned, or technical assistants. Occasionally, current industry circumstances may dictate a lesser annual commitment.

(3) The experience which a new specialist brings to the position should depend on the needs of the industry program. In most cases prior experience as a case manager with cases in the industry would be the preferable background. In some situations however, it might be preferable to use a specialty manager such as Engineering, or International, if more appropriate to the needs of the particular industry.

(4) The Industry Specialist should be rotated at least every seven years which includes a one year transitional period. However, normal rotation (policy statement P-4-5) will be adhered to with respect to any case being managed by him/her.

(5) To ensure effectiveness of the program, the industry specialist should have easy accessibility to:

(a) Economists;

(b) Engineers;

(c) International Examiners;

(d) Employment/Excise Examiners;

(e) Computer Audit Specialists;

(f) Pension Trust Specialists;

(g) District Review personnel; and

(h) National Office Technical personnel.

(6) See Chapter 900 of IRM 42(11)8, Handbook for Field Examination Case Managers, for additional duties, responsibilities and techniques.

42(14)6.2 ***(6-11-85)***

Duties

(1) The Industry Specialist will study the industry on a continuing basis to identify new problems, trends, economic developments and potential issues as they arise in an attempt to stay abreast of industry taxpayers in their tax planning. By acting on this type of information as it is obtained rather than waiting until the returns are filed, the Specialist can gain considerable insight into what is needed in future examination plans. This is especially true as we become more current in the Coordinated Examination Program since, in many instances, we are initiating examinations as soon as the tax returns are filed.

(2) The forward planning duties can be accomplished by the following methods in an effort to recognize and identify or define new, novel, and/ or controversial activities or accounting and financial approaches or transactions.

(a) Studying the industry as a whole by analyzing news media, national business oriented publications, trade journals, market reports, corporate prospectus brochures, stockholders' reports, *etc.*

(b) Establish a communications network with case managers, group managers and specialty managers, to facilitate the upward flow of information which could then be used by the Industry Specialist in forward planning.

(c) Attend industry conferences, conventions and meetings.

(d) Meet with other federal, state and local governmental agency personnel which regulate, monitor, evaluate or otherwise affect industry taxpayers.

(e) Establish a liaison with industry trade associations and the Tax Executive Institute.

(3) Obtain feedback from case managers engaged in the examination of taxpayers in the industry and then communicate, formally or informally, with the case managers in that respective industry.

(4) Select identified industry cases, formally notify respective case managers of inclusion on the industry list, and develop controls for the general monitoring of all identified industry cases. At a minimum, the monitoring will include communication on new trends, current economic developments, coordinated issues and reporting on general case progress and developments.

(5) Each year, identify a segment of identified industry cases to receive more in-depth involvement by the Specialist. Such involvement may include participation in planning or critique meetings, review of plans, issue proposals, or case files, or any other activity considered to be of value to the Specialist. The specific cases to receive this in-depth involvement and the extent of such involvement on specific cases are left to the discretion of the Industry Specialist. The region will determine an appropriate number of "identified industry cases" for in depth involvement.

(6) At the inception of a cycle on any identified industry case, provide the case manager with planning input and with the requirements for reporting to the Specialist that will be applicable to the cycle. The case manager should also, at that point, be advised of the anticipated extent of Specialist involvement.

(7) Review proposed coordinated issues in CEP cases to ensure uniformity. Determine if technical advice should be solicited on any particular issue. (Case managers examining cases within an industry should consult with the appropriate specialist prior to submitting a request for technical advice. The specialist may request that a copy of the proposed technical advice request be forwarded to him/her.) Attempt to reconcile inconsistent positions, and if necessary, utilize Regional and National Office assistance to resolve differences.

(8) Review Coordinated Examination Program examination plans to assure that coordinated issues are being considered.

(9) Communicate with case managers on all coordinated issues in identified industry cases under guidelines established in IRM 42(11)— Handbook for Field Examination Case Managers.

(10) Assist in identifying foreign corporate operations which should be subject to industry wide foreign onsite examinations.

(11) In connection with International Programs Section OP:EX:N:I, assist in the conduct of simultaneous examinations and industrywide exchanges with treaty partners. (See IRM 42(10)(10)).

(12) Conduct periodic meetings, as needed, with case and group managers to discuss common issues, audit procedures, problems, means of solution, current trends, and identification of new issues. Such meetings may be local, regional, or industrywide in scope. When appropriate, meetings should be extended beyond CEP cases. For example, in the insurance industry, representatives of districts examining non-CEP taxpayers should be included in industrywide meetings for both their input as well as to provide a tool for the dissemination of information and assistance of agents in those districts. Industrywide meetings may be held annually or as needed. Meetings should be coordinated with the National Industry Coordinator. Industrywide meetings should be planned and implemented under guidelines set in IRM 42(11)8.

(13) Cooperate with the National Industry Coordinator to determine the need to revise or update existing IRM 4232, Techniques Handbook for Specialized Industries, or, if one does not exist, determine the need to develop one and serve as chairperson on a task force created to revise or develop the Handbook.

(14) Prepare a quarterly report using Form 6352, Industry Specialization Report (NO-4000-440) expiration date 12/25. Forward the report to the National Industry Coordinator. The report is due to the Coordinator on the 15th calendar day following the end of the quarter.

(15) Update, as appropriate, the listings of identified industry cases and coordinated issues and the definition of industry business activity.

(16) Provide narrative input to the National Industry Coordinator for publication in the ISP Digest. The Coordinator will prescribe the content, format, and scheduling of such input.

42(14)6.3 *(3-7-88)*

Petroleum Industry Program

(1) The oil industrywide examination program, the crude oil pricing issue program, and the windfall profit tax (WPT) Unit have been merged into one specialized group, the Petroleum Industry Program. This program is part of the Office of the Assistant Regional Commissioner (Examination), Southwest Region.

(2) The Petroleum Industry Program will be responsible for pricing and freight issues, and will also assume the responsibility for coordinating industrywide issues as well as providing coordination and assistance in WPT examinations.

(3) The unit is composed of four units:

(a) Technical and Research

(b) District Support and Coordination

(c) Controlled Issues; and

(d) Windfall Profit Tax.

(4) The responsibilities of the Industry Specialist will be similar to those mentioned in IRM 42(14)6.

(5) IRM 42(15)0 describes this program in detail.

Exhibit 3-3

INTERNAL REVENUE SERVICE	Department of the Treasury
	Person to Contact:
	Telephone Number:
Name and Address	Refer Reply to:
	Date:

As I stated on the telephone, ABC Bank's Federal income tax return for the year ended December 31, 19XX, has been assigned to me for examination. This letter is to confirm our appointment for June XX, 19XX, at 8:00 A.M., at your office. I have attached a list of documents that I will need to start the audit.

I have also enclosed copies of Publications 1 and 556 which explain the examination process and your appeal rights. At our initial appointment, I can answer any questions you may have regarding this.

The banking industry is part of our industry specialization program. The Internal Revenue Service has an industry specialization program to ensure uniform and consistent treatment of issues on an industry-wide basis throughout the Nation. To better acquaint you with this program, I have enclosed a copy of our Internal Revenue Manual procedures. Also, enclosed are descriptions of the issues currently being coordinated in the banking industry. I would appreciate it if you would review these issues and provide me with your comments and recommendations. We would also like additional suggestions as to other potential issues that may benefit from consideration on an industry-wide basis. I am available to discuss and answer questions concerning the Industry Specialization Program with you.

Please call me if you have any questions. Otherwise, I will plan to meet with you at the scheduled appointment mentioned above.

Sincerely,

Internal Revenue Agent

Enclosures:

CHAPTER 4—INTEREST ON NONPERFORMING LOANS

INTRODUCTION

For financial accounting purposes, banks are required to stop accruing interest income when payments on loans become delinquent. For tax purposes, the requirement is much more stringent. The bank cannot stop accruing the interest income on a loan until (1) the bank has been given specific instruction by a regulatory agency that the underlying loan should be charged off as a bad debt or (2) the interest has been shown to be uncollectible on loans that have not been charged off. If interest was properly accrued, but subsequently becomes uncollectible, it is charged off as a bad debt rather than eliminated as an accrual. Banks and the IRS often disagree as to when interest accrual should cease. Since this is a coordinated issue, it needs to be considered during every bank examination.

Historically, banks will stop accruing interest once a loan is 90 days delinquent. Recently, bank regulators have allowed institutions to exercise more judgment in determining when accrual should stop. Interest can continue to be accrued if the collateral for the loan is sufficient, if collection efforts are being made, and if there is a reasonable expectation of collecting the delinquent interest. However, for small accounts, such as unsecured credit card receivables, most institutions still use a cut-off period to stop interest accrual.

For tax purposes, a bank must generally determine on a loan by loan basis the interest on that loan is collectible. The interest on certain loans in nonperforming status are more likely to be accruable for income tax purposes than for regulatory purposes; this is especially true if the interest on the loan is OID. The key distinction between book and tax reporting is that interest must be uncollectible for tax nonaccrual purposes and not merely delinquent as for regulatory nonaccrual purposes. Some examples of loans that would be accruable for tax purposes are listed below:

1. Loans placed in nonperforming status based upon the lapsing of time, such as, 30, 60, or 90 days
2. Loans with partial write-offs
3. Loans with sporadic payments of interest or principal
4. Loans to borrowers who are in default on other loans
5. Highly leveraged transaction loans.

EXAMINATION TECHNIQUES

1. The accrual for tax purposes often continues longer than accrual for book purposes; this is especially true if the interest on the loan is OID. Therefore, review the M-1 schedule to determine whether there is an M-1 adjustment on the tax. If not, you will probably have an issue. If there is an M-1 adjustment, you will still want to analyze the taxpayer's interest accrual method to ensure it is consistent with the IRS position.

2. Review the bank's annual report to see whether it discusses the corporation's policy regarding the accrual of interest on delinquent loans. It will usually list the amount of interest that would have been accrued if the loans were not in default. This amount provides an indication of the potential amount of the adjustment. However, nonaccrual of a portion of this interest will probably be allowable for tax purposes. Therefore, you will need to request specific information from the taxpayer to determine the amount of interest that should be accrued.

3. Ask the taxpayer to explain the bank's policy for nonaccrual of interest and whether the bank stopped the accrual of interest differently for books than for tax reporting. Also, ask what criteria the bank used to determine when accrual should cease.

4. A sample IDR (see Exhibit 4-1) shows the type of information that can be requested to develop this issue. Request the account balances for interest on nonperforming loans. Also, request lists of the specific loans that were in nonaccrual status at year end. Since it is important to know the current status of these loans, request the bank's most current list of loans in nonaccrual status. Each bank maintains its records differently, inquire as to how you can determine whether the loans were eventually written off or brought current.

5. You need to evaluate the taxpayer's policy for determining when the accrual of interest should stop for tax purposes. Some banks will do a loan by loan analysis to determine when the accrual of interest should

stop. There is less audit potential for these taxpayers than for banks which have no book/tax difference. If the bank has analyzed each loan to determine the collectability of its interest, sample the loans to determine whether nonaccrual is proper. Banks which do not have any book/tax differences will often have significant audit potential.

6. Your next step will be to review a sample of the files for loans where interest accrual has stopped. Once payments are delinquent on a loan the bank will establish a file which may contain these items: correspondence with the borrower, property appraisals, the borrower's financial statements, bank internal memoranda regarding collectability, copies of lawsuits, original loan application, statements regarding third-party guarantors, prospectus, bankruptcy records, history of the customer, statements from regulators, memoranda of meetings with the borrower, *etc.* The following are some items to consider when you are reviewing the loan files:

a. The appraisals in the loan file should show whether the value of the loan collateral is greater than the outstanding interest and loan balances. If so, the taxpayer should continue to accrue interest. Sometimes the debt may be collectible, but the accrued interest will not be. Accrual would not be necessary in those cases. Outside appraisals should be given more credibility than in-house valuations. Ensure that the taxpayer is using market value, not distressed value. The latter is the price the property would sell for if the owner had to sell it immediately.

If the loans are small and there is not any collateral, consider whether the bank's policy regarding nonaccrual of interest is reasonable. It is not always productive to do a case by case analysis of these loans.

b. The loan file should contain information on whether the borrower is continuing to make payments. Even though the borrower may have missed some payments, the loan and interest may be collectible in full. Interest accrual should continue as long as it can be collected.

c. The bank may have initiated legal action against the borrower. Often the bank will anticipate being paid in full once the lawsuit is settled. There should be paperwork in the loan file discussing this activity. Accrual should continue if the borrower has assets which can be used to pay off the loan.

d. The loan file should contain documentation for the restructuring or the renegotiation of loans where the borrower is having difficulty making payments. The bank may stop interest accrual even though the borrower will be able to make full payment under the new terms. Interest should be accrued for tax purposes under the terms of the new agreement. Refer to the discussion of IRC section 1001 later in this guide.

7. Information on foreign loans should be requested from the taxpayer. If the loan is guaranteed by a foreign government, payment of the interest should be reported unless an Allocated Transfer Risk Reserve (ATRR) report

has been issued. However, banks often stop accrual of interest on foreign loans when they are delinquent.

8. The taxpayer for tax purposes must continue to accrue interest on loans not charged off until, on a loan by loan basis, the taxpayer substantiates that interest is uncollectible in accordance with Rev. Rul. 80-361, 1980-2 C.B. 164.

9. A taxpayer for book purposes will not accrue interest on a loan that is past due 90 days. In addition, the taxpayer will reverse the unpaid interest that was accrued since the beginning of the quarter or the year. The taxpayer for tax purposes, however, should not reduce interest by the accrued but unpaid amount. Unpaid interest that has been accrued as income and becomes uncollectible must be charged against the bad debt reserve or charged off under IRC section 166. As you will read later, large banks cannot use the reserve method and beginning in 1996 thrifts cannot use the IRC section 593 reserve method. However, this issue may affect banks and thrifts in tax years for which a reserve method was used. Therefore, even if you agree that the nonaccural of interest is proper, you should determine that previously accrued interest was properly charged off.

10. GAAP and RAP generally provide that payments are to be applied first to principal if the loan is in nonperforming status. It is common for banks to also apply the payments on delinquent loans to principal, rather than to interest for tax purposes. However, some banks allocate delinquent payments to interest income for book reporting, but to principal for tax reporting. A bank may prefer to allocate these payments to interest for several reasons. First, it increases the book income that is reported to the shareholders. Second, often the bank charges interest on the principal, but not necessarily on the interest. Lastly, in the event the bank has to obtain a judgment against the borrower, the court is less likely to dismiss principal than interest. Often the tax department is not aware that the payments have been allocated differently for books than for tax.

There should be documents in the loan file indicating how the payments have been applied. If not, obtain a payment history from the taxpayer. If the loan documents indicate that the delinquent payments should be applied first to interest, but the taxpayer has applied them to principal, an adjustment should be made for the unreported interest.

11. It is important to keep in mind that interest on nonperforming loans is a timing issue. The collectibility of the interest is usually resolved in one of three ways within a relatively short period of time:

a. The borrower may become current in payments. If so, any nonaccrued delinquent interest would be reported by the taxpayer in the year of payment. Therefore, if you have made an adjustment in the earlier year, the taxpayer should reverse the interest in the subsequent year.

b. The loan may be charged off. If the loan has become uncollectible, the interest will also be uncollectible. Therefore, any unpaid interest that was accrued by the bank will be deductible in the year of the charge-off.

c. The loan may still be delinquent. The amount of nonaccrued interest for a subsequent year may include the balance from the prior year. Therefore, if you are making this adjustment for 2 years, be sure to include the same interest only once.

12. You can read the following article for further information on this subject: Koslov, "Tax Consequences of Managing a Bank's Nonperforming Assets," Journal of Bank Taxation, 1989.

LAW

The Coordinated Issue Paper for accrued interest on nonperforming loans discusses the law in detail. Revenue Ruling 80-361, 1980-2 C.B. 164, which is discussed therein, provides guidelines as to when interest accrual should stop. Contact your district ISP coordinator for a copy of the Coordinated Issue Paper.

After the Coordinated Issue Paper was issued, another court case was decided in favor of the Government regarding the accrual of interest on delinquent loans. In *European American Bank and Trust Co. v. United States,* Cl. Ct. No. 135-82T, 92-1 U.S.T.C. ¶50,026 (Fed. Cir. 1992), *aff'g* 20 Cl. Ct. 594 (Cl. Ct. 1990) [90-2 USTC ¶50,333], the Federal Circuit decided that whether the principal on a loan was likely to be repaid was irrelevant to whether the bank could avoid tax on interest income. The bank had applied delinquent payments to principal even though the loan documents provided that the payments were to be first applied to interest. The court said that income should be accrued unless there is no reasonable expectation that it will be paid.

SUMMARY

This issue is directly related to the bad debt issue that is discussed later in this guide. Often, the examination of the nonaccrual of interest and the charge-off of a loan is considered at the same time. When a debt is determined to be worthless, the accrued but uncollected interest will also be charged off. The facts must be considered for each loan to determine whether accrual should continue. It is not appropriate to use blanket criteria, such as a set number of days, to determine when accrual should stop on delinquent loans.

This issue should be considered during every bank examination. It is important to put the taxpayer on the proper method for accruing interest since this is a permanent timing adjustment. Judgment should be used when determining which accounts and how much deferred interest will be reviewed.

Exhibit 4-1

[SAMPLE INFORMATION DOCUMENT REQUEST, Form 4564, Rev. 6/88. Not Reproduced.]

CHAPTER 5—CORE DEPOSITS AND COVENANTS NOT TO COMPETE

CORE DEPOSITS

An institution that acquires a bank will typically pay more than the excess of the banks' assets over its liabilities. A portion of this excess amount is attributable to an intangible asset called "core deposits." Core deposits are the deposit base of demand and savings accounts which are generally expected to remain with the bank in the future. Since the depositors have done their banking at the acquired institution for a period of time, it is expected that they will continue to bank there. The bank pays its depositors a lower interest rate than it would pay for borrowed funds. Therefore, this available inexpensive source of funds has value.

IRC SECTION 197

IRC section 197 was enacted on August 10, 1993. It provides that the capitalized costs of specified intangible assets, now referred to as "IRC section 197 intangibles," are ratably amortized over a 15-year period beginning in the month of acquisition. The 15-year amortization period applies regardless of the actual useful life of the IRC section 197 intangible. No other depreciation or amortization deduction may be claimed on an IRC section 197 intangible that is amortizable under this provision. Proposed Treas. Reg. section 1.197-2 was published in the Federal Register on January 16, 1997.

Any acquired bank's core deposit base is now defined under the provisions of IRC section 197, as a "customer-based intangible." A customerbased intangible refers to the composition of a market, a market share, and any other value resulting from the future provision of goods or services resulting from relationships (contractual or otherwise) with customers in the ordinary course of business.

According to the House Committee Report, typical examples of customer-based intangibles include: The portion of an acquired trade or business attributable to the existence of a customer base, circulation base, undeveloped market or market growth, insurance in force, investment management contracts, or other relationships with customers that involve the future provision of goods or services.

The term "customer-based intangible" includes the core deposit base and any similar asset of a financial institution. Such assets include items such as checking accounts, savings accounts, and escrow accounts.

The amortizable basis is the adjusted basis (for the purpose of determining gain) of an amortizable IRC section 197 intangible. Generally, this is its cost. The adjusted basis of an IRC section 197 intangible acquired from another entity is determined under the present-law principles applicable to the acquisition of tangible property. For example, if a portion of the cost of acquiring an amortizable IRC section 197 intangible is contingent, its adjusted basis is generally increased as of the beginning of the month that the contingent amount is paid or incurred. This additional amount is amortized ratably over the remaining months in the 15-year amortization period that applies to the intangible as of the beginning of the month that the contingent amount is paid or incurred.

If a taxpayer acquires a trade or business in a transaction treated under present law as an asset acquisition under either IRC section 338(b)(5) or IRC section 1060, the House Committee Report indicates that the purchase price should be allocated among the amortizable IRC section 197 intangibles using the residual method. It is anticipated that the regulations will be modified to treat all amortizable IRC section 197 intangibles as Class IV assets for this purpose.

The new rules are in effect after August 10, 1993. Transitional rules allow taxpayers to elect to apply the new rules to all property acquired after July 25, 1991. Under this election, the 15-year amortization period applies on a retroactive basis. The election is binding on all taxpayers under common control with the electing taxpayer any time between August 2, 1993, and the date of the election.

Alternatively, taxpayers can elect to apply prior law, rather than the new rules, to property acquired under a binding written contract in effect on August 10, 1993, even if the acquisition date is after August 10, 1993. The law for earlier years is discussed below. See Treas. Reg. section 1.197-1T.

EXAMINATION TECHNIQUES FOR CASES UNDER IRC SECTION 197

1. Review the amortization schedule to verify that customer based intangibles (as well as all amortizable IRC section 197 intangibles) are be ing amortized on a straight line basis over 15 years.

2. An engineer can review the taxpayer's valuation of the acquired bank to ensure that the taxpayer did not overvalue assets with shorter depreciable lives. Proper valuation is also necessary to determine the amount of gain or loss in the event the taxpayer sells a portion of the acquired assets.

CORE DEPOSITS PRIOR TO IRC SECTION 197

The Internal Revenue Service recognizes the existence of intangible assets and allows for their amortization over their economic useful life. To be an amortizable intangible asset, it must be separately identifiable and have a reasonably determinable economic life. If the life is indeterminate, the asset is considered goodwill and no amortization is allowed.

Prior to the enactment of IRC section 197, the Code did not specify whether customer-based intangibles, such as core deposits, were intangible assets subject to amortization per Treas. Reg. section 1.167(a)-3. The crux of the issue is determining whether the customer base (core deposit intangible), existent at the time of the acquisition, is a separable asset from goodwill or going concern value. If it is separable, a further determination must be made as to whether it has a determinable useful life and whether its value has been proven.

In the past, the Government's primary position was that the core deposit intangible was nonamortizable as a matter of law. This was explained in both the banking and savings and loan ISP Coordinated Issue Papers on core deposits. Contact your District ISP coordinator to determine the current status of these papers due to the Supreme

Court's opinion in *Newark Morning Ledger.*

Because of the Court's decision, it is now especially important to determine whether core deposits are properly lifed and valued. Core deposit issues should be referred to engineers or economists for analysis. The engineer will critique the taxpayer's methodology, the reasonableness of the assumptions and conclusions, *etc.* The engineer will revalue the core deposit intangible, or require the taxpayer to recalculate this intangible based on current and historical data. Cases sent to Appeals without an analysis of the taxpayer's study will be returned as premature referrals.

INTANGIBLES SETTLEMENT INITIATIVE—PRE-IRC SECTION 197 CASES

On February 9, 1994, the Service announced the Intangible Settlement Initiative (ISI) which gives taxpayers a one-time opportunity to resolve intangibles disputes in tax years not affected by IRC section 197. Under the settlement initiative, a taxpayer must agree to adjust the basis of its amortized intangibles by the greater of a 50 percent cost recovery adjustment or a 15 percent minimum concession adjustment. The amount of the required concession depends on the position taken on the return. For further information on the Intangibles Settlement Initiative, consult the ISI Handbook, IRS Document 9233(2)94), Catalog Number 20566N, or contact your District's large case program.

APPLICATION OF PRE-IRC SECTION 197 LAW TO CORE DEPOSIT INTANGIBLES

If the taxpayer declines the ISI offer, allowance of amortization turns on whether the taxpayer can establish that it has accurately determined the life and value of the claimed core deposit intangible. See *Newark Morning Ledger Co. v. United States,* 507 U.S.—, 113 S.Ct. 1670, 123 L.Ed 2d 288 (1993) [93-1 USTC ¶50,228]. The *Newark Morning Ledger* opinion states that the taxpayer's burden is substantial. Whether a taxpayer can meet this burden depends on the quality and reasonableness of the taxpayer's lifing and valuation methods, and the extent to which they conform to valuation methods mandated in the decided cases and sound financial analysis.

The following is a list of pre-IRC section 197 cases which address lifing and valuation of core deposit intangibles:

1. *Citizens & Southern Corp. v. Commissioner,* 91 T.C. 463 (1988) [CCH Dec. 45,036], *aff'd without published opinion,* 900 F.2d 266 (11th Cir. 1990), *aff'd per curiam,* 919 F.2d 1492 (1990) [91-1 USTC ¶50,043].

2. *IT&S of Iowa, Inc. v. Commissioner,* 97 T.C. 496 (1991) [CCH Dec. 47,735].

3. *Banc One Corp. v. Commissioner,* 84 T.C. 476 (1985) [CCH Dec. 41,985], *aff'd* 815 F.2d 75 (6th Cir. 1987).

4. *Colorado National Bankshares, Inc. v. Commissioner,* T.C. Memo. 1990-495 [CCH Dec. 49,813(M)], *aff'd,* 984 F.2d 383 (10th Cir. 1993) [93-1 USTC ¶50,077].

5. *Trustmark Corp. v. Commissioner,* T.C. Memo. 1994-184 [CCH Dec. 49,813(M)].
6. *Peoples Bancorporation v. Commissioner,* T.C. Memo. 1992-285 [CCH Dec. 48,226(M)].
7. *First Chicago Corp. v. Commissioner,* T.C. Memo. 1994-300 [CCH Dec. 49,938(M)].

The Tax Court has generally accepted taxpayer attempts to predict the attrition rate for the acquisition date deposit funds using historical de posit account attrition rates. The Tax Court seems generally willing to assume that the acquisition date pool of core deposits will diminish at the same rate at which the acquired bank's accounts closed, provided that the projected life is based on pre-acquisition account closing or attrition data. The following factors should be considered in evaluating the reliability of the claimed life in a particular case:

1. Use of the acquired bank's pre-acquisition attrition data is preferable to industry estimates or other potentially non-comparable data.
2. A pre-acquisition observation period of at least one year.
3. The taxpayer's methodology must identify and eliminate account closings due to transfers of funds to other accounts maintained by the same depositor.
4. Historical attrition in high balance accounts should be studied and projected separately from smaller accounts since 95 percent of a bank's total deposits are typically found in less than 5 percent of the accounts and these high balance accounts are much longer-lived than smaller accounts.

The core deposit valuation methodology approach, accepted by the Tax Court, is to quantify the value of core deposits as a low-cost funding source by comparing the bank's projected cost to maintain the core deposits of the acquired bank which exist on the acquisition date (interest paid on deposits plus expenses less service fees) to the estimated cost of the next cheapest alternative source of funds. The value of the core deposit intangible is the present value of the cost savings generated as the pool of deposits diminishes over time.

1. The Tax Court has rejected the "income" method of valuing core deposit intangible and has required taxpayers to present a valuation using the "cost-savings" method described above.
2. The alternative cost of funds, which must be used under the cost savings method, is the rate offered on CDs by the acquired bank, the taxpayer, or competitor banks on the valuation date.
3. Core deposits generally consist of business and personal checking accounts and regular savings accounts. Generally, certificates of deposits, money market deposit accounts, Super NOW accounts, NOW accounts, or other accounts bearing interest rates which fluctuate in response to market conditions are not considered core deposits unless the taxpayer proves that such accounts are not interest rate sensitive. Such interest rate sensitive accounts must be excluded in valuing the core deposit intangible.

4. The Service is not bound by contract allocations to core deposit intangible at least where the allocation does not reflect an arm's length bargain between parties with adverse tax interests.

5. Although the deposit in question may not meet the court's definition of an amortizable core deposit, the deposit may still be amortizable. Thus, if the taxpayer can meet the Supreme Court test for amortization stated in *Newark Morning Ledger*, show with reasonable accuracy that the deposit in question has an ascertainable value separate and apart from goodwill and going concern value of the acquired bank and has a limited useful life, the taxpayer may amortize that deposit. However, this may be a difficult test to meet if the deposit is sensitive to interest rates.

EXAMINATION TECHNIQUES FOR CASES BEFORE IRC SECTION 197

1. The facts bearing on the life and value of an acquired bank's core deposit intangible should be developed by the agent, by IDRs, summons procedures, or interviews. Internal memoranda, corporate minutes, acquisition studies conducted by outside consultants, all documents relating to the price negotiations, the purchase agreement, and applications for regulatory approval and related documents should be obtained and reviewed for evidence relating to the acquired bank's deposits.

2. To assist the valuation engineer, the following specific items should be requested from the taxpayer:

a. A copy of the taxpayer's valuation report or, if no formal appraisal was prepared, a written explanation of the methodology used to arrive at the claimed value,

b. Copies of the appraiser's work papers and all documents relied on in determining life and value of the intangible,

c. CD rates needed to calculate the cost of alternative funds,

d. Detailed financial statements,

e. Historical account closing data, and

f. List of deposit accounts and balances on the valuation date.

3. Obtain and review the appraisal of all of the tangible and intangible assets (Class III assets) of the acquired bank.

4. Review all M)1 adjustments and related work papers. Taxpayers often use different values, amortization periods, and amortization methods for book purposes than for tax purposes.

5. A diskette is available to assist agents in redefining the core deposit base and recalculating the deduction based on the *IT&S of Iowa* and *Peoples Bancorporation* cases. This diskette is available on the ISP bulletin board file under CD.ssf.

6. A computer audit specialist can assist you in examining the core deposits issue. Refer to Chapter 3 for additional information.

COVENANTS NOT TO COMPETE

A covenant not to compete (also referred to as a noncompetition agreement) is a contract between the buyer and seller of a business, whereby the seller (or officers or key personnel of the seller) agrees to refrain from operating a competing business within a specified territory for a specified length of time. The covenant not to compete may also require that the seller (also called a "covenanter") not hold employment with a competitor. If the terms of the covenant not to compete are reasonable, and if the covenanter is truly being compensated for giving up his or her right to forego business opportunities in a competitive market, then the buyer is entitled to amortize the lump sum payment or installment payments to the seller over the life of the covenant.

Amounts received by the seller for a covenant not to compete are considered to be given as lost earnings and, consequently, are taxable as ordinary income. Conversely, amounts received by the seller constitute capital gains to the extent they are received as consideration for the goodwill or going concern value of the business, or for the sale of stock.

Prior to 1987, the buyer and seller had competing and conflicting tax interests in the allocation of the purchase price of the business to a covenant not to compete. Due to the differential in tax rates between capital gains and ordinary income, the seller benefited with respect to his or her taxes by allocating as little as possible to the covenant not to compete, and allocating as much as possible to the purchase of the business or its goodwill. Similarly, consideration received in payment for stock was preferable to a seller because such payments represent capital gain to the seller to the extent that the consideration exceeds the seller's basis in the stock. The buyer, on the other hand, preferred to allocate as much as possible to the covenant not to compete because that amount is amortizable, *Ullman v. Commissioner*, 264 F.2d 305 (2d Cir. 1959) [59-1 USTC ¶9314], allowing him or her a deduction against ordinary income, *Sonnleitner v. Commissioner*, 598 F.2d 464, 466 (5th Cir. 1979) [79-2 USTC ¶9464], whereas an allocation to goodwill or going concern value represents a nondepreciable capital investment.

The Tax Reform Act of 1986, generally, eliminated the preferential tax rate for capital gains. Thus, for transactions occurring after 1986, the tax interests of the buyer and the seller with respect to a covenant not to compete are not adverse. With the elimination of the preferential rate, the seller of a business no longer suffers any significant tax disadvantage if more of the purchase price is allocated to the covenant not to compete. Consequently, the seller will be more inclined to agree to a covenant not to compete and to a greater allocation of the purchase price to the covenant. The buyer benefits because he or she can amortize a greater portion of the total purchase price of the acquired business.

In tax years in which there is rough parity between marginal ordinary income and capital gains tax rates, the Service is concerned that excessive amounts are being allocated to the covenants not to compete. In the case of a stock purchase, an amount paid for a covenant not to compete may actually be disguised stock purchase price. Consequently, we can expect to encounter overstated amortization deductions by buyers. Additionally, buyers may attempt to allocate a portion of the purchase price of the business to covenants not to compete because such assets are amortizable, even though the formal agreements between the buyers and sellers contain no allocation to the covenant. Thus, covenants not to compete must be closely scrutinized in order to ascertain whether the allocation lacks economic reality.

Effective for tax years beginning after 1992, the Revenue Reconciliation Act of 1993 increased the maximum ordinary income tax rate to 39.6 percent, while the net capital gains rate continued at 28 percent. However, the enactment of IRC section 197 causes this difference in rates to be important only to the seller. Under IRC section 197, it does not generally matter to the buyer whether an amount is allocated to goodwill or to a covenant not to compete because the buyer can amortize that amount over 15 years. In fact, it may be beneficial to the buyer to have the purchase contract not state an amount allocable to a covenant not to compete so that the buyer can attempt to allocate that portion of the purchase price to a tangible asset that has a shorter useful life. For years after 1992, it may also be beneficial to the seller to have the purchase contract not state an allocation to a covenant not to compete so that the seller does not flag the transaction for the Service, which would require the seller to report the amount paid for the covenant not to compete as ordinary income rather than as capital gain from the sale of the business or asset.

The focus generally is upon the *genuineness* and the *value* of the covenant. To the extent that the value of a covenant not to compete is overstated, this amount represents, in substance, what the buyer paid for the seller's goodwill. The courts have developed several tests for determining the validity and value of covenants not to compete.

THE ECONOMIC REALITY TEST

The economic reality test is primarily concerned with whether a covenant not to compete is genuine, that is, whether it has independent business or economic significance. This test was enunciated in *Schulz v. Commissioner,* 294 F.2d 52, 54 (9th Cir. 1961) [61-1 USTC ¶9648], in which the court stated that "the covenant must have some independent basis in fact or some arguable relationship with business reality such that reasonable men, genuinely concerned with their economic future, might bargain for such an agreement." Where the seller is, objectively, likely to pose a threat of competition, courts will probably sustain some allocation to the covenant. Some of the factors that should be considered include:

1. Did the seller have the ability to compete with the buyer?

This question actually embraces a number of considerations:

a. Seller's customer network and experience.

   Compare *Sonnleitner v. Commissioner, supra* (seller had business contacts and demonstrated selling ability) with *General Insurance Agency, Inc. v. Commissioner,* 401 F.2d 324 (4th Cir. 1968) [68-2 USTC ¶9600] (seller, widow of agency owner, was not considered serious competition because of her inability to successfully manage the company) and *Schulz v. Commissioner, supra* (seller did not have the business contacts and background necessary to compete, and economic conditions were such that it was unlikely that he could successfully compete).

b. Seller's financial ability to compete.

Compare *Illinois Cereal Mills, Inc. v. Commissioner*, T.C. Memo. 1983-469 [CCH Dec. 40,342(M)], *aff'd*, 789 F.2d 1234 (7th Cir.) [86-1 USTC ¶9371], *cert. denied*, 479 U.S. 995 (1986) [86-2 USTC ¶9808] (Seller had economic resources to compete with purchaser.) with *Krug v. Commissioner*, *T.C. Memo.* 1981-522 [CCH Dec. 38,260(M)] (Seller was ill and lacked the financial resources to compete.).

c. Seller's physical ability to compete, that is, age and state of health.

See, for example, *Major v. Commissioner*, 76 T.C. 239 (1981) [CCH Dec. 37,679] (Covenant had minimal value where the seller was of advanced age and had health problems).

d. Non-contractual restrictions that would have prohibited the seller from competing in absence of the covenant not to compete, such as limited market entry.

This factor may be important where a covenant is granted in conjunction with the transfer of a franchise, license, or operating authority where market entry is limited. See, for example, *Forward Communications Corp. v. United States*, 608 F.2d 485 (Ct. Cl. 1979) [79-2 USTC ¶9638] (Seller would need an FCC license to compete, which it was unlikely to obtain.); *Major v. Commissioner, supra* (Seller of freight firm would have to acquire interstate operating authorities, which were difficult to obtain from ICC.).

e. Seller's intention to compete, either by acquiring or by starting a new business in the same market, or by seeking employment with an existing competitor.

A covenant not to compete is not meaningful if the grantor of the covenant has stated his intention to retire or to leave the geographic area covered by the covenant, and thus, poses no real threat of competition. If the grantor has the ability to change plans and re-enter the market, the covenant is more likely to meet the economic reality test. See, for example, *Ansan Tool and Manufacturing Co., Inc. v. Commissioner*, T.C. Memo. 1992-121 [CCH Dec. 48,037(M)] (Court agreed that taxpayer's management had reason to be concerned that departing shareholder-manager might accept employment from a rival firm and take clients away, and thus it was of paramount importance that a covenant not to compete be included in the final buy-sell agreement.) *Illinois Cereal Mills, Inc. v. Commissioner*, T.C. Memo. 1983-469 [CCH Dec. 40,342(M)], *aff'd*, 789 F.2d 1243 (7th Cir.) [86-1 USTC ¶9371], *cert. denied*, 479 U.S. 995 (1986) [86-2 USTC ¶9808] (Covenant not to compete negotiated in conjunction with taxpayer's purchase of another corporation's cereal binder operations was of considerable value to the taxpayer because other corporation would continue to sell resincoated sand in the foundry market in competition with cereal binders; Tax Court found that covenant was valid where other corporation possessed the resources to re-enter the cereal binder market.).

2. Was the payment intended as compensation to the seller in lieu of his employment in a competing venture?

This issue goes to whether the amount purportedly paid for the covenant not compete was actually paid as an inducement for the seller to refrain from competition. It embraces such questions as:

a. Does the payment for the covenant realistically compensate the seller for his loss of earnings by not competing?

b. If the payment for the covenant is to be made in installments, are the payments to the seller conditioned on his or her survival, or is the remaining balance of payments payable to the estate?

In *Ackerman v. Commissioner*, T.C. Memo 1983-469 [CCH Dec. 40,342(M)], *aff'd*, 789 F.2d 1243 (7th Cir.) [86-1 USTC ¶9371], *cert. denied*, 479 U.S. 995 (1986) [86-2 USTC ¶9808], one of the factors which influenced the Tax Court to find that a portion of the purchase price was mutually intended as consideration for the taxpayer's covenant not to compete was the fact that the payments due with respect to the covenant during the term of the covenant terminated in the event of the seller's death.

3. Are there any other factors that reflect the economic reality of the covenant?

Numerous additional factors have been considered by courts in reaching a determination concerning the economic reality of a covenant not to compete. They include:

a. Formalities of the covenant

b. Enforceability of the covenant

c. Scope of the covenant

See, for example, *Dixie Finance Co., Inc. v. United States*, 474 F.2d 501 (5th Cir. 1973) [73-1 USTC ¶9204](Court found covenants lacked economic reality where payments to shareholders were based upon percentage of stockholding, including payments to two shareholders who refused to sign the noncompetition agreement, and purchaser did not police the agreement to ensure that sellers abided by its terms.); *Montesi v. Commissioner*, 40 T.C. 511 (1963) [CCH Dec. 26,175], *aff'd*, 340 F.2d 97 (6th Cir. 1965) [65-1 USTC ¶9173] (Court found covenants bona fide where noncompetition agreements were entered into with only some shareholders, and each covenant was for the same amount irrespective of the shareholder's stock ownership.); *Howard Construction, Inc. v. Commissioner*, 43 T.C. 343 (1964), *acq.*, 1965-2 C.B. 5 (Court found that purchaser lacked concern about competition where covenant prohibited sellers from managing a similar business, but did not prohibit them from purchasing a similar business.).

THE MUTUAL INTENT TEST

The mutual intent test looks at whether the parties to the buy-sell agreement mutually agreed that some portion of the total consideration paid for the going concern was intended for the covenant not to compete. This test is applied where the agreement contains a covenant not to compete, but the purchase price is stated as a lump sum for the entire transaction, that is, there is no express allocation of a specific amount to the covenant. While the failure to allocate a portion of the purchase price appears to be good evidence that the parties did not intend one, *Major v. Commissioner, supra,* 76 T.C. at 250, the mere absence of an allocation to the covenant does not give rise to an inference that the parties affirmatively intended to make *no* allocation (or a zero allocation). *Better Beverages, Inc. v. United States,* 619 F.2d 424 (5th Cir. 1980) [80-2 USTC ¶9516]. Therefore, courts have tended to look at actual contract negotiations to determine whether the parties intended the covenant to have any value. *Patterson v. Commissioner,* 810 F.2d 562 (6th Cir. 1987) [87-1 USTC ¶9168]; *Better Beverages, supra.* Mutual intent is usually found where the parties bargained over the inclusion of the covenant not to compete, or where it was understood that the covenant was an essential part of the agreement. The "economic reality test" plays a role in this inquiry: The covenant not to compete must also have some independent basis in fact such that the parties might bargain for it. Mutual intent may also be found where:

1. Other language in the agreement evidences the parties' intent that the consideration includes an unspecified amount for the covenant. See *Illinois Cereal Mills, supra; Peterson Machine Tool, Inc. v. Commissioner,* 79 T.C. 72 (1982) [CCH Dec. 39,178], *aff'd,* 54 A.F.T.R. 2d 84-5407 (10th Cir. 1984) [84-2 USTC ¶9885].

2. There is uncontroverted testimony regarding the parties' intent. See *Kreider v. Commissioner,* 762 F.2d 580 (7th Cir. 1985) [85-1 USTC ¶9427].

Mutual intent will usually be found where the covenant was an essential part of the sales agreement or was separately bargained for. See *Ansan Tool and Manufacturing Co. v. Commissioner, supra; Peterson Machine Tool, Inc. v. Commissioner, supra.* Under such circumstances, the covenant has *some* value, but an ambiguity exists in the buy-sell agreement—the ambiguity being just how much of the lump sum consideration was exchanged for the covenant. The court will then proceed to resolve the ambiguity—that is, it will assess the covenant's independent economic value. *Patterson, supra.* For example, in *Ansan Tool and Manufacturing Co., supra,* the buyer insisted upon a covenant not to compete due to the seller's prominent role in the business. The seller was capable of competing in a new or existing business, and so the economic reality test was met. However, the stock purchase agreement made no allocation of a part of the purchase price to the covenant. The court held that the buyer had met its burden of establishing that the parties required a covenant, and therefore some allocation was called for. Similarly, in *Wilson Athletic Goods Manufacturing Co. v. Commissioner,* 222 F.2d 355 (7th Cir. 1955) [55-1 USTC ¶9442], the parties did not, in their agreement, allocate a portion of the purchase price to a covenant not to compete which clearly possessed some value. In that case, a major sporting goods manufacturer purchased a shoe factory which produced athletic shoes marketed under the "Wilson" name. The Tax Court found that an unapportioned amount of the purchase price was allocable between goodwill and the seller's covenant. The Seventh Circuit reversed, finding that the taxpayer had demonstrated that all of the unapportioned amount was paid only for the covenant, since Wilson would market the shoes through its own channels and, thus, the seller's goodwill was not of value to it. See also *Kinney v. Commissioner,* 58 T.C. 1038 (1972) [CCH Dec. 31,552]. (Both parties had attached considerable value to the covenant not the compete, but were unable to agree upon a precise allocation.)

It may be, however, that while the parties engaged in negotiations over a covenant not to compete, no mutual agreement was ever reached concerning the allocation of price to the covenant. For example, if the parties discussed a price for the covenant, but a specific allocation to the covenant was not included in the final agreement, this may be evidence that the parties could not reach an agreement.

See, for example, *Patterson v. Commissioner, supra,* 810 F.2d at 573; *Annabelle Candy Co. v. Commissioner,* 314 F.2d 1, 4 (9th Cir. 1963) [63-1 USTC ¶9164]. In *Theophelis v. Commissioner,* 751 F.2d 165 (6th Cir. 1984) [85-1 USTC ¶9105], *aff'g* 571 F. Supp. 516 (E.D. Mich. 1983) [83-2 USTC ¶9630], the seller and buyer never discussed a possible allocation to the covenant not to compete until their final meeting, when they agreed in effect *not* to allocate any specific part of the purchase price to the covenant, but rather, they would allow the Internal Revenue Service to determine its value when the first of the parties to the sale was audited. See also *Forward Communications Corp. v. Commissioner, supra* (Covenant not to compete found to have no value or minimal value where parties agreed to pay a sum certain for the assets of the seller and the purchase price was not altered when the covenant was later added.).

In contrast, where the parties never even discussed the covenant, the courts have found mutual intent to allocate nothing to it. The court will not go further to examine the economic reality of the covenant. See, for example, *Lazisky v. Commissioner,* 72 T.C. 495 (1975) [CCH Dec. 36,135]; *Better Beverages, Inc., supra.* If nothing was paid for the covenant, there is nothing for the buyer to deduct. *Theophelis, supra,* 751 F.2d at 167.

THE STRONG PROOF DOCTRINE AND THE DANIELSON RULE

These tests are applied only when one of the parties to the buy-sell agreement seeks to establish a different value for the covenant than the one specifically stated in the contract. Although the Service is not bound by the allocation, the courts are likely to give effect to the agreed allocation where the parties have tax adversity.

Between the parties, the allocation in their written agreement is generally binding. Where the parties clearly and unequivocally allocated a portion of the total consideration to the covenant, some courts have refused to allow one of the parties to subsequently alter the tax consequences of the expressed amount unless he or she can overcome the contract terms by strong proof that the agreement does not reflect the parties' true intentions. This is known as the "strong proof" doctrine. See, for example, *Meredith Corp. v. Commissioner,* 102 T.C. No. 15 (March 14, 1994), as an example of the Tax Court's use of the strong proof doctrine.

The Commissioner prefers the approach of other appellate courts[1] which, relying on *Commissioner v. Danielson,* 378 F.2d 771 (3d Cir.) [67-1 USTC ¶9423], *cert. denied,* 389 U.S. 858 (1967), require an even stronger degree of proof before one party will be permitted to alter the allocation for tax purposes. Under the "*Danielson* rule," a party may contradict an unambiguous contractual term, for tax purposes, only by offering proof which would be admissible in an action between the parties to alter that construction or to show its unenforceability because of mistake, undue influence, fraud, or duress. 378 F.2d at 778)779.

VALUATION OF A COVENANT NOT TO COMPETE

The taxpayer has the burden of proving that he is entitled to a deduction. *Welch v. Helvering,* 290 U.S. 111 (1933) [3 USTC ¶1164]. Because the amount paid for a covenant not to compete represents compensation to the covenanter, the taxpayer bears the burden of proof for establishing the proper amount attributable to the covenant. The value allocated to the covenant must reflect economic reality. This is a second, separate test from the economic reality test described above. It is possible for a covenant not to compete to possess economic reality, while the amount allocated to its value may not reflect economic reality. The same factors as those listed above have been considered for this purpose.

The purchaser's basis derives from the *cost* that he or she was actually required to pay to obtain the covenant. Evidence of value is material only if probative of actual cost or as to what portion, if any, of the lump sum price was required to obtain the covenant. In *Better Beverages, supra,* the court recognized that there is not a sufficient correlation between the value of a covenant to the purchaser and its value to the covenanter, such that the purchaser's evidence of value to him or her is inadequate to prove actual cost. The interest relinquished by the seller is not parallel to that sought or received by the purchaser:

> The value of such a covenant to a purchaser * * * derives from the projected degree of increased profitability and likelihood of survival of its new enterprise attributable to the insulation of that enterprise, afforded by the covenant, from the deleterious competitive force that the seller could present. Value to the seller, on the other hand, is the measure of his foregoing the opportunity to re-enter a particular market for a given period. Consequently, because they are functions of totally independent sets of considerations, the respective values of the covenant to the buyer and seller are simply unrelated.

See *Better Beverages, Inc. v. United States,* 619 F.2d at 430.

One reasonable method to value a covenant is the compensation-based approach. Under this method, the covenanter's (seller's) average compensa-

[1] The Danielson rule has been adopted by the Third, Fifth, Sixth, and Eleventh Circuits. See *Danielson, infra; Spector v. Commissioner,* 641 F.2d 376 (5th Cir. 1981) [81-1 USTC ¶9308]; *Schatten v. United States,* 746 F.2d 319 (6th Cir. 1984) [84-1 USTC ¶9965]; and *Bradley v. United States,* 730 F.2d 718 (11th Cir. 1984) [84-1 USTC ¶9413]. The Eighth Circuit, in a case decided prior to *Danielson*, adopted a similar rule. *Sullivan v. United States,* 363 F.2d 727 (8th Cir. 1966). Although the Tax Court has rejected the *Danielson* rule, preferring the less stringent strong proof rule, under the doctrine of *Golsen v. Commissioner,* 54 T.C. 742 (1970) [CCH Dec. 30,049], the Tax Court will follow a United States Court of Appeals decision which is squarely on point where appeal of Tax Court decision would lie in a particular circuit.

tion (including salary, bonuses, and benefits) is calculated, this amount is projected over the life of the covenant, and a discount rate is applied to adjust the figure to present value. This method measures the loss of earnings anticipated by the seller as a result of his forbearance from competing in the specified market.

In some complex buy-sell agreements, however, a court may find the compensation-based approach too simplistic. Valuation texts, in discussing covenants not to compete, refer to a second method which values what the buyer acquired: Protection of the continued profitability of the business from the seller's hostile use of his or her contacts in the market. This method calculates the present value of the economic loss to the buyer on the assumption that the seller re-entered the market. Such an approach was sanctioned by the Tax Court in *Ansan Tool and Manufacturing Co. v. Commissioner*, T.C. Memo. 1992-121 [CCH Dec. 48,037(M)], where the compensation-based method was determined inadequate for the unique arrangement between the taxpayer and the seller in a stock buy-out.

Courts will also look to the value claimed for the covenant relative to the values of the other assets acquired. See, for example, *Patterson v. Commissioner, supra; Peterson Machine Tool, Inc. v. United States, supra.* For example, in *Dixie Finance Co. v. United States*, 474 F.2d 501 (5th Cir. 1973) [73-1 USTC ¶9204], where the amount that the taxpayer allocated to the stock purchase was less than its fair market value, the court refused to allocate any of the purchase price to a covenant not to compete. In *Wilson Athletic Goods Manufacturing Co. v. Commissioner, supra,* on the other hand, the court found that the excess purchase price paid for the assets of a shoe manufacturer was allocable to a covenant where the buyer was not interested in acquiring the goodwill of the seller.

Finally, there are situations where the same parties execute both a covenant not to compete and an employment contract. Both agreements need to be evaluated carefully because their provisions may overlap, and thus, so may their values. An employment agreement may convey similar benefits and cover the same time period as a covenant not to compete, and arguably its value is not separate and distinct from the value of the covenant.

EFFECT OF IRC SECTION 197

For transactions occurring after the effective date (including the election-back date) of the Omnibus Budget Reconciliation Act of 1993, a covenant not to compete which is entered into in connection with the direct or indirect acquisition of an interest in a trade or business is an IRC section 197 intangible. Amounts paid or incurred for a covenant not to compete are ratably amortized over 15 years, even if the duration of the covenant is less than 15 years.

An arrangement similar to a covenant not to compete is also treated as an IRC section 197 intangible. For example, excessive compensation or rental paid to former owner of a business for continuing to perform services or to provide the use of property is considered an amount paid for a covenant not to compete. Under the legislative history for IRC section 197, whether compensation is excessive is determined by comparing the compensation under the covenant to the services actually rendered.

An amount paid under a covenant not to compete which actually represents additional consideration paid for stock in a corporation is not an IRC section 197 intangible, and must (as under pre) 1993 case law) be added to the basis of the acquired stock. Proposed Treas. Reg. section 1.197-2 was published in the Federal Register on January 16, 1997. *See also,* Treas. Reg. section 1.197-1T.

EXAMINATION TECHNIQUES

1. Agents are advised to review Form 8594 Asset Acquisition Statement Part II for the allocation of the purchase price to the appropriate asset class. If there are any questions regarding the allocation, your inquiries should be directed to the taxpayer for an explanation.

2. In Part III of Form 8594, special attention should be paid to the column headed "Useful Life." If the amortizable intangible asset is an IRC section 197 intangible, the useful life should be 15 years or more. If it is not, an adjustment should be made to the amortization of the acquired asset.

3. Agents are also advised to request all appraisals relating to tangible assets which were transferred in the acquisition. Under the new law, it will be attractive for taxpayers to allocate more of the purchase to tangible assets than to intangible assets due to the fact that shorter depreciable lives are available under MACRS.

4. The examiner may obtain information relative to the conditions of payment, formalities, enforceability, and scope of the agreement by examining the covenant document itself. However, this usually is inadequate to evaluate the covenant for economic reality and mutual intent. Therefore, the examiner is strongly encouraged to interview both the buyer and the seller to gather facts, rather than rely on opinions. Further, after each interview, the examiner should have the interviewee (especially the buyer) sign an affidavit as part of the factual development since this will improve the chances of the issue being sustained by Appeals.

5. See the sample IDRs in Exhibit 5-1. This may need to be modified depending on whether IRC section 197 applies to the covenant.

6. For covenants not to compete executed in years prior to the enactment date of IRC section 197 (or the election back date available for transactions between July 25, 1991, and August 10, 1993), three tests should generally be applied to determine whether the covenant is amortizable.

a. Economic Reality:

1) Is it genuine? Would or could the seller compete if the covenant did not exist?

2) What is the covenanter's ability to compete? Are there restrictions such as age or health, market entry restrictions, financial limitations?

3) Does the covenanter have business contacts in the industry? What is his or her reputation, both in the firm and the industry?

4) What are the covenanter's intentions? Does he or she have plans for present or future endeavors? Has he or she entered into an employment

agreement with the buyer or with another firm? Does he or she contemplate a move away from the area?

5) Are there market factors that affect the covenanter's ability to engage in competition, such as type, size, territory of the market; barriers to market entry; market saturation; or general economic conditions?

b. Mutual Intent:

1) Is the consideration paid for the covenant not to compete separately stated in the acquisition agreement or in the covenant, or is it included in a lump sum purchase price?

2) Did the parties to the agreement bargain over inclusion of the covenant? Did the buyer make the acquisition conditional upon inclusion of a covenant not to compete? Was the covenant a last-minute addition to the acquisition agreement?

3) Is there other language in the agreement that evidences the parties' intent that the consideration includes an unapportioned amount for the covenant?

4) Do both parties agree that the covenant not to compete has value?

c. Value of the Covenant:

1) Does the taxpayer's claimed basis in the covenant match the allocation in the agreement? Does the apportionment of the purchase price claimed by the buyer match the amount reported by the seller?

2) Does the amount allocated to the covenant not to compete reflect economic reality? If the covenant was given in conjunction with the sale of stock, was the consideration paid for the stock reasonable or excessive? If the covenant was given in conjunction with an asset acquisi tion, does it reflect the value of the covenanter's opportunities foregone?

3) If the seller has an agreement to render post-acquisition services to the buyer or rent property to the buyer, is the consideration for such services or rental excessive?

4) Is there also an employment agreement between the buyer and seller? Do its terms overlap with the covenant not to compete?

5) What is the value of the covenant in relation to the other assets acquired?

SUMMARY

A bank may be amortizing a number of intangible assets for tax purposes. Two of the most common are core deposits and covenants not to compete. If a bank you are examining is amortizing these assets, you may need to request the assistance of an engineer to help determine whether the taxpayer has assigned reasonable values and is using the correct amortization period and method.

Exhibit 5-1

SAMPLE INFORMATION DOCUMENT REQUEST

Form 4564 Rev. 6/88	**Department of the Treasury** **Internal Revenue Service** **INFORMATION DOCUMENT REQUEST**	**Request Number**
TO: Name of Taxpayer and Co. Div. or Branch		Subject Amortization of Intangibles SAIN No. Submitted to:
Please return Part 2 with listed documents to requester identified below.		Dates of Previous Requests

Description of Documents Requested

Provide the following documents regarding each acquisition which occurred during this audit cycle:

1. The Quarterly Reports, Annual Financial Statements, SEC filings, *etc.* for each acquired company for the prior two years.
2. A list of the fixed assets received from each acquired company.
3. A copy of the purchase agreements for each acquired company.
4. A copy of the appraisal of each acquired company.
5. A copy of the lifing studies, valuation studies, *etc.* for any acquired core deposits, servicing rights, or other intangible.
6. A copy of the schedule showing the amount amortized for core deposits, servicing rights, and other intangibles. This should include the total amount subject to amortization, the method of amortization being used, the period over which it is being amortized, the current years' amortization amount, *etc.*
7. Is the amount of amortization computed differently for book purposes than for tax purposes? If so, please explain the differences
8. Copies of M-1 adjustments and work papers for core deposits, purchased servicing rights, and all other intangibles that were acquired.

Information Due By ________ At Next Appointment [ ] Mail In [ ]

FROM:	Name and Title of Requester	Date
	Office Location	

Appendix D

SAMPLE INFORMATION DOCUMENT REQUEST

Form 4564 Rev. 6/88	**Department of the Treasury** **Internal Revenue Service** **INFORMATION DOCUMENT REQUEST**	**Request Number**
TO: Name of Taxpayer and Co. Div. or Branch		Subject Covenant Not to Compete SAIN No. Submitted to:

Please return Part 2 with listed documents to requester identified below.

Dates of Previous Requests

Description of Documents Requested

With respect to the acquisition of the covenant not to compete, please provide the following information and documents:

1. A copy of the covenant(s) not to compete entered into by the various individuals or entities involved.
2. Identify who these individuals are and if there are any non-owners among this group.
3. A complete copy of the purchase agreement including all applicable schedules and exhibits.
4. A copy of any appraisals performed as a result of this acquisition including all supporting schedules and exhibits.
5. The current address and phone number of each of the principle sellers of this business.
6. A copy of the financial statements or tax returns for this business for five years before the acquisition.
7. Copies of M-1 adjustments and work papers for covenant not to compete.

Information Due By ________ At Next Appointment [ ] Mail In [ ]

FROM: Name and Title of Requester Date

Office Location

CHAPTER 6—GAIN/LOSS ON FORECLOSED PROPERTY

INTRODUCTION

Banks typically refer to foreclosed property as OREO property. This is an acronym for other real estate owned. OREO property typically is property obtained by the bank due to the inability of the debtor to pay off a loan.[1]

OREO property can be acquired by the bank in either of two ways:

1. Voluntary conveyance of the property in settlement of the obligation to the bank. This process is known as deed in lieu of foreclosure. This is accomplished when the mortgagee and the mortgagor *agree* to convey the property in settlement of the debt to avoid the costs, delays, the unfavorable publicity, and other problems associated with a foreclosure sale.
2. The property can also be acquired through a *formal foreclosure* of the property by the bank. This method is normally handled through the court system.

In both of the above two situations, the bank will literally take title and possession to the prop erty. The tax consequences to the bank are exactly the same in both a voluntary deed in lieu of foreclosure and in the

[1] The tax treatment of foreclosed property acquired by thrifts is governed by IRC section 595 which will not be discussed in this section. IRC section 595 was repealed for property acquired after December 31, 1995, by section 1616(b)(8) of P.L. 104-188, signed August 20, 1996. The discussion which follows concerns *only* the treatment of foreclosed property acquired by commercial banks.

formal foreclosure proceedings where the deed is transferred under a court order.

A *loan renegotiation* should not be confused with a foreclosure. A modification of the original loan terms usually results in a continuation of the debtor-creditor relationship. The examiner should consider the effects, if any, of *Cottage Savings* and the final Treas. Reg. section 1.1001-3 and determine whether the modification of the loan document is significant. For a more complete discussion of the *Cottage Savings* case and the regulations, refer to the chapter titled Loan Swaps.

Essentially, there are four potential areas for the examiner to consider when reviewing OREO property:

1. Computation of the gain/loss upon foreclosure or repossession, involving,
   a. Fair Market Value of the property received, and
   b. Basis of the loan used for determining gain/loss.
2. Capitalization of costs during and after foreclosure or repossession.
3. Character of the gain or loss reported by the bank.
4. Covered sales.

Each of these areas are discussed in this section of the guide.

The receipt of foreclosed property by a bank is considered to be a payment for the outstanding obligation. The bank *must* recognize a gain or loss on transaction for tax purposes. The amount of the gain or loss is the difference between the basis of the loan and the fair market value of the property received. The starting point for determining the gain or loss in both a foreclosure sale and a transfer of the deed in lieu of foreclosure is the debt's adjusted basis.

COMPUTING THE BASIS OF THE LOAN FOR TAX PURPOSES

1. The starting point is the unpaid balance of the loan remaining at the time the collateral is repossessed by the bank. This amount is reduced by any charge-offs taken for tax purposes during the year, or in prior years. For example, if the bank originally provided a loan for $100,000, received $10,000 in principal payments, and subsequently wrote off $20,000 as being uncollectible, the basis of the loan for tax purposes would be $70,000. This amount does not necessarily tie into the book or legal balance of the obligation remaining for financial reporting purposes.

2. The basis of the loan is *increased* by any interest income which was accrued by the bank and previously reported as taxable income. This assumes that the interest remains uncollected by the bank at the time the property is transferred to OREO property.

3. The basis of the loan is further increased by other costs, such as back taxes, insurance, legal expenses, and similar items paid by the bank for protecting the value of the property *prior* to the transfer of ownership to the bank. Legal costs and other similar expenses incurred in connection with the foreclosure proceedings increase the basis of the OREO property.

This chapter on foreclosed property should be read in conjunction with the chapter on bad debt deductions, which is included later in this guide. A *loss* realized upon foreclosure is normally deducted as part of the bank's overall bad debt deduction, while a *gain* is recognized as ordinary income. See Revenue Ruling 74-159, 1974-1 C.B. 232.

EXAMINATION TECHNIQUES

1. One of the most common issues in the foreclosure area involves the *valuation* of the OREO property when ownership is transferred to the bank. The fair market value of the property must be determined to establish and document the amount of the bank's deductible gain or loss. Generally, the burden of proving the fair market value rests with the bank. *Estimates* of the value of the OREO property should *not* be accepted. However, for purposes of determining gain or loss (other than with respect to the bad debt deduction) on the transaction, the FMV of the property is rebuttably presumed to be the amount bid-in by the taxpayer. The burden, of proving that FMV is not the bid-in price, rests with the party rebutting the presumption. See *Community Bank v. Commissioner,* 62 T.C. 50 (1974).

The easiest and most accurate method for determining the fair market value of the OREO property is to request that the bank provide a written appraisal from a professional independent appraiser. This request is not as unreasonable as it may sound. The bank will normally have already secured a complete appraisal for most, if not all, major property acquired through foreclosure. If the bank does not have an appraisal of the property, secondary evidence should be used. This would include property tax valuations, past appraisals, third party purchase offers for the property, and anything else in the loan file which indicates the value of the OREO. Remember, for purposes of computing its bad debt deduction, it is the taxpayer's responsibility to substantiate the fair market value. Failure to properly document the value of the property at the time of foreclosure can result in the disallowance of the bad debt deduction taken for that OREO property.

2. When reviewing the computation of the gain or loss reported for tax purposes, look very closely at the numbers. The full appraisal amount should be used when computing the taxable gain or loss upon foreclosure. It is common practice for the bank to *reduce* the fair market value of the property by the *projected* selling expenses, the estimated costs to hold the property until sold, the estimated costs of any improvements, plus other related expenses. If the taxpayer uses this net realizable value, the result will be an overstatement of the loss, or an understatement of the gain on the transaction. While this reduction for other costs is required for book purposes, it is *not* acceptable for tax purposes.

3. One of the most common issues to consider in this area deals with the expenses which are deducted by the bank during the period of time the repossessed property is held for sale.

In many cases the bank will deduct as current expenses such items as prior year property taxes, selling expenses, substantial repairs and improvements, and the legal expenses of acquiring the property. These expenses are of a capital nature and are *not* currently deductible. These amounts are considered to be part of the cost of the property until sold.

After the bank takes possession of the property, no portion of the expenses is currently deductible if the bank is holding the property for resale or sale to customers. The OREO property is similar to inventory, and therefore, all expenses are considered to be part of the basis of the property. If, however, the bank is holding the property out for rent, normal maintenance expenses, including depreciation, are deductible by the bank when incurred.

Foreclosure expenses can usually be found on the return under classifications such as ORE expenses, (other real estate expenses), legal expenses, or repossession expenses. These accounts should be thoroughly reviewed for these types of deductions. The bank's policy for these type of expenses should also be reviewed to determine how they are being handled for tax purposes.

4. Another issue which can have significant tax consequences involves the sale of OREO property which is financed by the selling bank. Industry regulators refer to these property sales as *covered* sales. This consists of foreclosed property which is sold by the bank but financed with over 90 percent of funds provided by the selling bank, or the financing offered by the bank is on terms more favorable than customarily offered to its customers.

These transactions are not considered sales for regulatory purposes unless the purchaser contributes over 10 percent of the purchase price. No gain is recognized by the bank since the majority of the funds used to finance the transaction were bank funds. For tax purposes, the property is generally considered sold when title passes. Therefore, it is subject to the gain/loss procedures. A significant amount of deferred gains could exist if the bank finances its foreclosure sales, especially for community banks.

If the bank offers this type of financing, request a statement of the bank's policy concerning these transactions along with a complete list of OREO property financed by the bank. This list should be reviewed to determine if the sale was properly reported for tax purposes.

Schedule M-1 should reflect any book/tax difference on the recognition of these covered transactions.

5. Once a bank has converted a loan to OREO property, no additional bad debt write-downs or charge-off's are permitted for tax purposes with respect to the old loan or the OREO property. If the bank also finances a new buyer's acquisition of the OREO property, that loan should be reflected on the bank's books for tax purposes.

Review the expense accounts for any writedowns the bank may have deducted. In some cases, the bank will have an account titled "OREO write-downs," which will allow you to easily identify any deductions claimed.

It should be noted that the above positions in connection with mortgage foreclosures assume that the bank does not actively sell foreclosed property within the ordinary course of the bank's business. A bank that actively and regularly sells foreclosed property may be classified as a dealer in real estate, in which case the tax implications may be different.

All of the above issues are timing adjustments. Before a lot of time is spent in this area, consideration should be given to the period of time it takes the bank to sell or otherwise dispose of the foreclosed property. This is the turnover rate. If it is the bank's policy to dispose of the property almost immediately, any disagreements over an appraisal or costs to be capitalized are of no consequence. The bank would be entitled to these deductions at the time the property is sold.

COORDINATED ISSUE PAPER

The coordinated issue paper dealing with foreclosed property (which involved the *character* of the gain or loss reportable by a bank on the sale of foreclosed property or securities received as part of a debt restructuring) relied on the "*Corn Products*" doctrine which was substantially modified by the Supreme Court in the *Arkansas Best* case. Therefore, the issue paper as originally written is no longer technically correct. If you have this issue, please contact the Industry Specialist for Commercial Banking for an update of the current IRS position.

It is presumed for both regulatory and financial accounting purposes that OREO property is property held for sale to customers. Although this presumption is not controlling for tax purposes, if such property is held for sale to customers in the ordinary course of the bank's trade or business, then under IRC section 1221(1) gains or losses are ordinary deductions.

CHAPTER 7—GROSS-UP NET LOANS

INTRODUCTION

The fourth and final coordinated issue in the commercial banking area deals with banks involved in foreign or international operations. Normally, the smaller community banks, and even most of the mid-size banks, do not have any international operations and seldom get involved in foreign transactions. Accordingly, this coordinated issue will have no effect on those cases. However, most of the larger banks have significant international operations. These cases will have "international issue" stamped on the front of the tax return and will include various international forms within the return. The revenue agent usually will not examine the international issues. Rather, they will rely on the expertise of a trained international agent. Chapter 3 of this guide includes a section on the involvement of specialists. If your case has any potential international issues, refer to that section for information on requesting the assistance of an international agent.

COORDINATED ISSUE PAPER

The coordinated issue involves the gross-up of net loans.[1] Specifically, whether an amount equal to the foreign withholding taxes due to be paid by borrowers pursuant to "net" loan agreements must be included in the gross income of the lender in the taxable year in which the obligation of the borrower to pay such taxes arose.

If the foreign withholding tax is creditable and included in the income of the lender, whether such taxes recognized for purposes of inclusion in the lender's gross income are also considered documented for purposes of the foreign tax credit, in accordance with IRC section 905.

[1] This issue has also been referred to as the "Foreign Withholding Tax" Issue.

This issue is not as important as it was in the late 70's and early 80's. The banking industry has attempted to comply for the most part with the coordinated issue paper. The real issue is that many banks have grossed-up taxable loans only where they obtain tax receipts.

Part of the problem lies with the substantiation of the foreign tax credits. Taxpayers insist that because they do not have a tax receipt, they can use secondary evidence to verify their foreign tax credits. The secondary evidence provision of Treas. Reg. section 1.905-2(b)(1) has *limited* application. This section specifically cites when secondary evidence can be used, and also what type of evidence is acceptable.

As part of the audit process, examiners should strictly enforce the requirements of IRC section 905 and the applicable regulations. The work papers should clearly document the tax receipts along with any secondary evidence that the tax was actually paid. It is important to identify all evidence provided by the taxpayer into separate categories such as tax letters from borrowers, missing or no exchange rates, *etc.* Such detail summarized by categories assists in the settlement of the issue at a later date.

The opinion in *Continental Illinois Corp. v. Commissioner*, 998 F.2d 513 (7th Cir. 1993) held that borrower letters are not deemed secondary evidence within the provisions of Treas. Reg. section 1.905-2(a)(2) and 2(b)(1). This opinion also rejected the concept of a net loan gross-up without a corresponding tax credit.

See Exhibit 7-1 for a sample IDR detailing information to be requested for the *net loan* issue.

INTERNATIONAL TAX ISSUES

Other foreign issues which have potential tax implications are as follows:

1. Computation and verification of all foreign tax credits claimed on the return.
2. Level of substantiation required for a foreign tax credit to be allowed for tax purposes, and can the taxpayer use *borrower* letters as proof of payment to support the tax credit.
3. Is the Brazilian tax credit a creditable foreign tax credit for U.S. tax purposes, and if it is, is the Brazilian Central Bank exempt from tax? (See item on Brazilian tax credits, discussed below.)
4. The existence of subsidies, refunds, or rebates, which signifies that the foreign tax was not paid for foreign tax credit purposes.
5. Tax implications of foreign transactions, such as sales of foreign debt to third parties, debt-for-debt loan swaps, *etc.*
6. Non-accrual of interest income on foreign debt.
7. Foreign loan charge-offs, some of which are guaranteed by the foreign country. This is an area which can easily be abused by the taxpayer.
8. Foreign hedging transactions and other financial product transactions.
9. Proper application of the Allocated Transfer Risk Reserves (ATRR) charge) off's.
10. Proper application of the Source and Withholding rules.

The above list should be used by the international examiner to determine the scope of the examination. The list is not all inclusive, and is simply a starting point. The agent should also contact the Industry Specialist for Commercial Banking for a copy of the Coordinated Issue Paper and any updates on the issue.

BRAZILIAN FOREIGN TAX CREDITS

One of the issues that continues to come up in the larger cases involves the Brazilian Foreign Tax credit. The IRS has taken the position that the Brazilian tax is not a creditable foreign tax. See Rev. Rul. 89-119, 1989-2 C.B. 132, as modified by Announcement 89-152, 1989-48 I.R.B. 21. A complete breakdown of the foreign tax credits should be secured from the taxpayer as soon as possible to determine whether any Brazilian credits were claimed. This information should be included in the international referral to assist the reviewing agent.

In *Continental Illinois,* the Seventh Circuit affirmed the Tax Court and ruled that the Brazilian tax is potentially creditable, but second or third party rebates must be reduced from the total credit claimed. In *Continental Illinois,* the Court held that these rebates constituted indirect subsidies to the taxpayer, and disallowed foreign tax credits to the extent of the subsidy. *See also, Norwest v. Commissioner,* 69 F.3d 1404 (8th Cir. 1995) [95-2 USTC ¶50,618]. This information should be included in the international referral to assist the reviewing agent.

Regarding the Brazilian Central Bank, the Tax Court held that the Central Bank was not required to pay taxes on its net loan interest remittances on restructured debt because the Central Bank had tax immunity. The Tax Court disallowed the lender's foreign tax credits even though the lender had tax receipts. *Riggs National Corporation v. Commissioner,* 107 T.C. No. 18 (Dec, 10, 1996).

MEXICAN FOREIGN TAX CREDITS

The major issue involving Mexican Foreign Tax Credits centers around the *substantiation* of the credit. One of the main problems that we have come across involves the receipts, and other documentation from the Mexican oil company Petroleos Mexicanos, more commonly known as PEMEX. It is the position of the IRS that as PEMEX is a government agency that has never paid any tax, it is, in effect, tax exempt. This would make any credit being claimed by taxpayers with respect to PEMEX loans, highly questionable. The IRS position was adopted by the Tax Court in *Continental Illinois v. Commissioner,* T.C. Memo. 1991-66 [CCH Dec. 47,178(M)]. The same is true for receipts from Commission Federal de Electricidad.

Because PEMEX is the largest single Mexican borrower of U.S. source loans, there is a strong possibility that a large number of taxpayers, (banks in particular), may be using incorrect and inaccurate documents to substantiate the foreign tax credits which arise from loans to PEMEX.

ARTICLES

Fuller & Kornblatt, "Foreign Tax Credit and Net Loans: A Creditable Attack," 5 J. Bank Taxation, No. 1, 5 (1991).

Exhibit 7-1

[SAMPLE INFORMATION DOCUMENT REQUEST, Form 4564, Rev. 6/88. Not Reproduced.]

CHAPTER 8—MORTGAGE SERVICING RIGHTS

INTRODUCTION

The mortgage servicing area has received a lot of attention in the media over the last couple of years. It involves an issue which has significant tax implications for banks, savings and loan associations, and mortgage bankers. Specifically, the issue deals with the coupon stripping rules of IRC section 1286 which require the allocation of a basis to the servicing rights retained by the bank when the corresponding mortgage is sold in the marketplace.

When a bank sells a mortgage, it simultaneously enters into a contract to service the mortgage for a fee which is based on a percentage of the outstanding principal balance of the loan. This contract is called the *servicing right.*

Servicing a mortgage involves collecting the homeowner's monthly payment, remitting the principal and interest to the investor, accumulating an escrow account for payment of insurance and taxes, disbursing the escrow funds as payments come due, maintaining all records relating to the loan, and handling all delinquency problems. The loan servicer is paid amounts from interest for performing these services.

These amounts are the heart of the issue. If the financial institution receives amounts from interest which are in *excess* of reasonable compensation, basis must be allocated to the servicing right in accordance with the coupon stripping rules of IRC section 1286. The allocation of a portion of the basis to the servicing right will reduce the tax basis of the mortgage instrument and effectively increase the gain or reduce the loss reportable for tax purposes in the year the mortgage is sold.

This issue can be compared to the situation in which interest coupons are stripped from a bond. The real value of the coupons is equivalent to the present value of the income stream of the future payments to be received. This valuation is the basis allocated to the coupons and will proportionally reduce the cost basis of the bond. This allocation directly affects the gain or loss reportable for tax purposes.

The additional amount of income that the taxpayer reports due to the basis allocated to the servicing right is approximately equal to the present value of the *excess* servicing income that the taxpayer will receive in future years.

The value of the *excess* portion of the servicing right retained by the taxpayer is based on the facts and circumstances of each case. The taxpayer can elect to use the safe harbor provisions of Revenue Procedure 91-50, 1991-2 C.B. 778. This revenue procedure provides guidelines for determining what constitutes "reasonable compensation" for mortgage servicing contracts. The election available to the taxpayer is discussed in detail later in this section of the guide.

EXAMINATION AREAS

Consider several different examination areas when reviewing mortgage servicing.

1. Determine if the taxpayer is properly following all of the requirements of Rev. Rul. 91-46, 1991-2 C.B. 358, and has made the appropriate election under Rev. Proc. 91-50, 1991-2 C.B. 778.

2. Many variables are used when computing the value of the servicing right, all of which can significantly affect the amount reported for tax purposes. The computation of the value of the *excess* portion of the servicing right must be reviewed and verified.

BACKGROUND INFORMATION

To obtain a better overall understanding of the issue, it is best to provide some basic information on the subject of mortgage servicing.

The general steps in a typical mortgage process are as follows:

1. A consumer will secure a mortgage loan at a commercial bank, mortgage banker, or savings and loan. The financial institution then has a loan in the place of the cash which it used to pay the seller.
2. The lender then packages the mortgage loans into groups with similar interest rates and terms. The lender then sells the loans. This sale by the lender is a taxable event and is often completed within a few months of the time the loan was originated.
3. Instead of selling the mortgage loans, the lender may choose to exchange them for mortgage backed securities (MBS). The bank may retain the MBS in their own investment portfolio. Alternatively, the bank may sell or exchange the MBS in a taxable event.
4. The purchaser of the mortgages will bundle the loans together and use them as the basis for issuing a mortgage backed security. Security firms on Wall Street will then sell the MBS to investors. This investment carries a low risk because it generally is guaranteed by the Government National Mortgage Association (GNMA), the Federal National Mortgage Association (FNMA), and the Federal Home Loan Mortgage Corporation (FHLMC), or some other government guarantor. With the profits from the sale of the mortgage backed security, the purchaser will then buy additional mortgage loans from a lender and continue the cycle.

Servicing rights are extremely valuable assets. They provide the owner with a predictable cash flow. The mortgage department of a bank, savings and loan, or mortgage company, derives its income almost exclusively from servicing fees, origination fees, and interest income earned on money held in escrow accounts. The servicing portion of the mortgage banking business can be extremely profitable when done in volume.

Some financial institutions purchase individual mortgage loans from other lenders to secure the underlying servicing rights. Then the mortgage will usually be sold along with the mortgages the bank originated. The financial institution which decides to sell the servicing right with the mortgage will do so for various reasons. The bank may not specialize in mortgage servicing or it may not service mortgages for a certain area of the country. When mortgage loans are sold, the seller will always receive more for a mortgage with the servicing right included than for a similar mortgage without the servicing right. For accounting purposes, the difference is called a servicing release premium.

The primary reason for the sale of the mortgage is to eliminate the risk of fluctuations in interest rates. Years ago, many institutions retained the mortgages they originated in the banks' own portfolios. However, when interest rates rose significantly in the early 1980's, the banks were holding fixed rate mortgages paying relatively low interest rates, while they were forced to pay higher rates on funds deposited with the banks. To eliminate this risk, banks sell the mortgages to outside investors. Mortgages are also sold to secure additional funds to lend to future customers. Since the bank has a limited amount of money to lend, it sells the loans and turns the money over indefinitely.

SALE OF MORTGAGE LOANS & MORTGAGE BACKED SECURITIES

The majority of the loans originated by the taxpayers we examined were guaranteed by GNMA and FNMA. These entities along with FHLMC also known as Freddie Mac, dominate the secondary mortgage market. They buy loans from lenders and package them into mortgage backed securities for sale to investors. Their basic purpose is to create a secondary home loan market by buying home loans from financial institutions and selling securities backed by the mortgages to investors. GNMA is a federal agency and FNMA and FHLMC are government sponsored, publicly traded companies.

When the mortgage loans are sold, the servicing of the mortgages is normally required to be retained by the seller. All of the governmental agencies which purchase mortgage loans such as FNMA, GNMA, and FHLMC, will not accept the mortgages with the servicing included. A comparison of pass-through mortgage-backed securities can be obtained from Tax Management Inc., a subsidiary of The Bureau of National Affairs, Inc., Washington, D.C.

EXCESS SERVICING FEE

The fee actually earned by the servicer of the loans will vary depending on the sales price of the loan package. For accounting purposes, servicing fees can be subdivided into two types, *normal servicing* and *excess servicing*. Revenue Ruling 91-46 requires a basis allocation for amounts which exceed reasonable compensation for services to be performed. In Rev. Proc. 91-46, basis was required to be allocated to a portion of normal servicing as well as to excess servicing. Revenue procedure 91-50 provides safe harbor rates that the taxpayer can elect to compute reasonable compensation for servicing one to four family mortgages.

If a taxpayer so elects, the amounts considered to be reasonable compensation in Rev. Rul. 91-46 for purposes of the safe harbor provisions of Rev. Proc. 91-50 are as follow:

1. 25 *basis points* for conventional fixed rate mortgages with an

original principal balance greater than $50,000,

2. 44 *basis points* for loans sold to GNMA and mortgages with an original principal balance of $50,000 or less, or

3. 37.5 *basis points* for all other types of residential mortgages, such as adjustable rate mortgages, sold to parties other than GNMA.

Those amounts are in addition to the guarantee fees charged by GNMA, FNMA, or FHLMC. Thus, it is not uncommon for the spread between mortgage rates and the related MBS to be 50 basis points and result in no basis allocation under IRC section 1286.

The servicer of the loan will remit the home-owner's interest and principal payment, less the servicing fee, to the holder of the mortgage. The fee paid to the servicer is a percentage of the principal balance of the loan remaining at the time of the payment. As the principal balance of the loan is reduced, the fee earned by the servicer of the loan is reduced accordingly.

It should be pointed out that these safe harbor rates apply *only* to one to four unit residential mortgages. There is no guidance on commercial or other mortgage type loans.

COMPUTATION OF THE EXCESS SERVICING FEE

The servicing amounts received are determined by multiplying the remaining principal balance of the mortgage by the difference between the rate collected from the homeowner and the rate that is to be sent to the purchaser of the mortgage. Since these amounts are annual percentage rates, the amount computed is divided by 12 to get the monthly amount. The monthly amounts are used since as each payment is made, the remaining principal balance of the mortgage will be reduced. It is this remaining balance that is used to compute the corresponding amount or fee earned by the servicer of the mortgage.

The total servicing amount, both normal and excess, will be reported by the financial institution as it receives the fees. The taxpayer, however, also is entitled to recover basis allocated to stripped coupons under the OID rules.

Currently, there is a computer program created by IRS personnel which takes into consideration all of the requirements of the new Revenue Procedures and the OID rules. This disk will value the various mortgage pools and compute the correct amount of the excess servicing fee that should be reported as taxable income by the taxpayer. It will also compute the annual deductions allowed to the taxpayer based on variables existing in your case.

Many taxpayers also have programs which compute the present value of excess servicing. The accuracy of their computations can be verified by using the IRS program.

PREPAYMENT OF MORTGAGES

If the mortgage is paid off due to a refinancing or a sale of the residence, then the servicing fee being earned by the servicer of the loan will end. The servicer will no longer be collecting any payments and therefore that individual servicing right will be worthless. The rate of prepayment varies depending on interest rates.

Prepayments, payoffs, and refinancing were fully considered in determining the average life of a mortgage. For every mortgage that is paid off early, there are other mortgages that will go beyond the mortgages average life. In fact, some of the mortgages will not be paid off until the entire 30 years has elapsed. The financial institution will continue to collect the servicing fee on these mortgages to maturity. As anyone with a mortgage knows, the principal balance does not go down very much until the last several years. Therefore, even though the servicing fee may be reduced, it does not go down very much until the very end of the mortgage, which is far beyond the average mortgage life.

The life expectancy of a mortgage is very important. The computation of the value of the excess servicing right uses the present value of the future income stream the bank will receive. This future income stream takes into consideration the length of time the taxpayer will be receiving this income. Secondly, the amount reported as excess servicing fee income is allowed as an amortization deduction in later years. The amortization rate is based on the life expectancy of the servicing right. A reasonable prepayment model, such as the PSA model, should be used to determine the value of retained servicing rights.

LAW

IRC section 1286 discusses the tax treatment of stripped bonds and allocates a tax basis to the coupons when they are stripped from the related coupons. Basis is allocated between the portion of the bond sold and the portion retained.

IRC section 1286 treats the purchaser of a stripped bond as having acquired an original issue discount (OID) instrument with the OID equal to any excess of the stated redemption price at maturity over the bond's purchase price. The seller of the stripped bond is treated as having retained a portion of the bond for an amount equal to the allocated basis under the stripping provisions.

The IRS issued Rev. Rul. 91-46, which ruled that the coupon stripping rules in IRC section 1286 apply to the sale of mortgage loans if the seller retains the right to receive amounts from interest other than as reasonable compensation.

Taking into consideration IRC section 1286, some gain or a reduced amount of loss may be recognized for tax purposes at the date of sale. The basis is allocated between the mortgage instrument and the servicing right based on the fair market value of the items at the date of sale.

SFAS 65

The Financial Accounting Standards Board published SFAS 65 which requires the sales price of mortgages to be adjusted whenever there is excess servicing involved. It attempts to correct the inequities in the recording of the sale of mortgages which involve excess servicing. SFAS 65 requires that the amount of the present value of the excess servicing fees to be received versus the normal servicing fee, is to be included into income for financial reporting. The inclusion of the value of the servicing fees has the effect of increasing the selling price and makes the sale comparable to a normal servicing fee sale in a regular market. If the mortgage had been sold without the retention of the right to future mortgage service income, the mortgage would have been sold at a greater selling price. The increase would approximate the value of the servicing rights. The amount includible into income at the time of the sale of the mortgage is the present value of total fees receivable in excess of normal servicing fees.

SFAS 65 was modified by SFAS 122.

EXAMINATION LIMITS AND RESTRICTIONS

Mortgage servicing involves one of the rare instances where the IRS has moved very quickly to formalize a position on a new issue being developed in the field. The National Office released one Revenue Ruling and three Revenue Procedures dealing directly with mortgage servicing rights on August 8, 1991. These rulings are discussed in detail later in this section of the guide.

It is important to note that the opportunity to pursue this issue is somewhat limited for taxable years ending before August 8, 1991. Revenue Procedure 91-51 provides that the examining agent cannot make adjustments for the value of servicing rights to taxable years prior to publication of the ruling if:

1. The taxpayer was *not* under examination at the time the ruling was issued or
2. The taxpayer was under examination and the servicing rights issue was *not* yet raised by the agent.
3. For these exemptions to apply, the taxpayer *must* have timely filed Form 3115 to change their method of accounting for servicing rights in accordance with Revenue Procedure 91-51 and actually implemented the method change. This method change is subject to verification upon examination.

If the taxpayer elects to change its method of accounting, they do not have to report taxable income for the value of the servicing rights until years ending after August 8, 1991. For calendar year taxpayers, the Revenue Ruling would first apply to the 1991 year. The provisions apply to mortgages which are sold on or after the first day of the taxable year of change.

Subject to the rules applicable to changes in accounting methods, the examining agent can adjust all open years for the full value of the servicing rights retained if the issue was raised during the examination before the taxpayer filed Form 3115.

It should be emphasized that even if you are examining a taxable year ending after August 8, 1991, and the taxpayer has changed its accounting method, potential still exists for an adjustment in this area. Adjustments in the taxpayer's computations valuing the servicing rights may be possible in several areas, including the discount rate used in the present value computations and the retirement rate of the loans for projecting future receipts. Each of these variables can have a significant impact on the computation of the gain reportable for tax purposes and can result in considerable adjustments. These variables are discussed later in this section of the guide.

EXAMINATION TECHNIQUES

1. Review the tax return for elections made by the taxpayer involving a change in the method of accounting for servicing rights, an election for the safe harbor provisions per Revenue Proce-

dure 91-50, or changes in the computation of the gain on the sale of the mortgage. These elections will affect how you proceed on this issue.

2. Review the Schedule M-1 for book to tax differences and analyze the computations by the taxpayer. Most taxpayers have excess servicing for financial reporting purposes. This amount will not necessarily be the same for tax purposes. It should be remembered that the Schedule M-1 adjustment is not indicative of the amount of excess servicing in any one year. Most taxpayers will *net* the excess servicing with the amortization deduction allowable from past year's servicing. These computations should be reviewed by the examining agent and understood in order to know *what* the taxpayer did and *why*.

3. Determine the proper amount of gain or loss on the sale of mortgages to be reported for tax purposes. This examination technique is probably the most important suggestion in this chapter. It involves an area where most of the adjustments will exist in future years, assuming the taxpayer has elected the safe harbor rates of Revenue Procedure 91-50.

This computation includes the following areas:

a. If the taxpayer elected the safe harbor provisions of Revenue Procedure 91-50, make sure that the taxpayer used the correct safe harbor rates and applied them properly.

b. The present value of the servicing rights and the OID valuations can vary significantly depending upon the assumptions and other factors used in the computation. These variables can significantly change the amount of gain or loss reportable for tax purposes.

The variables include:

1) Coupon rate of the mortgage
2) Pass-thru rate
3) Normal servicing rate
4) Discount rate
5) Prepayment speed
6) Method of determining the prepayment:
   a) Constant
   b) Accelerated

The age and remaining term of the mortgages can have an effect on all of the above variables.

c. Changes in the above variables can significantly alter the amount of income to be reported by the taxpayer. They should be reviewed thoroughly and verified as to their accuracy. But most importantly, determine whether the assumptions are *reasonable.* Be alert to differences between assumptions made for book purposes and those made for tax. Consider using the computer program discussed under the caption "Excess Servicing Fee" to determine the amount of servicing that should be included into income for tax purposes based on IRS assumptions.

4. If the taxpayer did *not* elect the safe harbor provisions, the fair market value of the stripped coupons is determined based on all the relevant facts and circumstances in your particular case. Due to the technical aspects of the issue, consider requesting the assistance of an engineer or in some districts, a financial products specialist, to

properly value the servicing rights in this situation.

Also, keep in mind that if your taxpayer did *not* elect to change their method of accounting or include the value of the rights in its return, then an adjustment can be made to all years open under the statute of limitations. Proper consideration must be given to the rules governing changes in accounting method.

ANALYSIS OF RULINGS

The National Office has issued guidelines on the servicing rights issue. One Revenue Ruling, plus three Revenue Procedures were issued. A brief summary of these rulings are as follows:

1. *Revenue Ruling 91-46 (1991-2 C.B. 358)*

IRC section 1286 is applied to certain sales of mortgages where the owner simultaneously enters into an agreement with the purchaser to service those mortgages. Revenue Ruling 66)314 was determined to be obsolete.

2. *Revenue Procedure 91-49 (1991-2 C.B. 777)*

Provides simplified OID procedures for certain mortgage loans that are determined to be stripped bonds under IRC section 1286. Provides guidance on de minimis rule contained in the OID provisions.

3. *Revenue Procedure 91-50 (1991-2 C.B. 778)*

Provides a "safe harbor" that taxpayers may elect for purposes of determining what constitutes reasonable compensation in applying IRC section 1286 to certain mortgage servicing contracts.

The elective safe harbor rules of Revenue Procedure 91-50 are applicable to:

a. One to four unit residential mortgages,

b. Where the servicer provides substantially all of the following services:

   1) Collects periodic mortgage payments from the mortgagor and remits those payments to the owner of the mortgage,

   2) Accumulates escrows, if any, for the payment of insurance and taxes and disburses these funds as payments come due,

   3) Maintains records relating to the mortgage,

   4) Handles delinquency problems.

If the safe harbor provisions are elected, reasonable compensation will be computed as follows:

a. Safe harbor rate, not to exceed contract, plus

b. Income, other than servicing fees, received in the normal course of servicing mortgages.

Safe harbor rates are as follows:

a. 25 basis points for conventional fixed rate mortgages with original mortgage balances exceeding $50,000.

b. 44 basis points for mortgages which are less than one year old and insured or guaranteed by the FHA, VA, or FMHA.

c. 37.5 basis points for any other one to four unit residential mortgage with an original mortgage balance exceeding $50,000.

d. 44 basis points for all mortgages with an original principal balance of $50,000 or less.

These rates are in addition to the amounts paid to GNMA, FNMA, or FHLMC as guarantee fees.

The use of the safe harbor provisions in Rev. Proc. 91-50 is revocable by the taxpayer at any time by filing a statement with the tax return.

4. *Revenue Procedure 91-51 (1991-2 C.B. 779)*

This Revenue Procedure provides guidance to the taxpayer by explaining how to obtain a consent to change their method of accounting for certain sales of mortgage loans from a method that does not comply with IRC section 1286.

a. Provides for automatic change procedures for taxpayers not currently under examination.

b. Provides special procedures for taxpayers under examination, in appeals, or currently before a court.

ARTICLES

Conlon, Butch & Mac Donald, "IRS's New Position on Excess Mortgage Servicing Affects Both Lenders and Investors," 76 J. Taxation 38 (1992).

CHAPTER 9—LOAN ORIGINATION COSTS

INTRODUCTION

One of the primary business activities of every bank is the origination of loans. A loan is originated when a bank lends money to a customer. The bank incurs substantial costs which are directly related to making the loan. Some of these costs are: Employee wages, commissions, office supplies, telephone expenses, and postage. Typically, the bank will capitalize some of the expenditures for book purposes, but expense them for tax purposes. Analyze the bank's loan origination costs to determine whether they should be treated as capital expenditures or currently deducted for tax purposes.

BOOK REPORTING OF LOAN ORIGINATION COSTS

It is important to understand how loan origination costs are treated for financial reporting to determine how they should be treated for tax purposes. Most large financial institutions changed their method of reporting loan fee income and expenses in 1988 as a result of the issuance of Statement of Financial Accounting Standards No. 91. SFAS 91 establishes the rules for accounting for nonrefundable fees and costs associated with lending, committing to lend, or purchasing a loan or a group of loans.

SFAS 91 applies to loans that are purchased from a third party and to loans that are originated by the financial institution. It also applies to leasing transactions. The statement generally relates to transactions entered into in fiscal years beginning after December 15, 1987.

SFAS 91 requires lenders to capitalize fee income and costs from loan originations. Fee income and loan costs are netted. The *net* amount is amortized using the interest method, which is explained in Statement 91. The net amount is considered to be an adjustment to the amount of interest paid by the borrower.

Statement 91 states direct loan origination costs of a completed loan shall include only:

1. Incremental direct costs of loan origination incurred in transac-

tions with independent third parties for that loan and

2. Certain costs directly related to specified activities performed by the lender for that loan. Those activities are: Evaluating the prospective borrower's financial condition; evaluating and recording guarantees, collateral, and other security arrangements; negotiating loan terms, preparing and processing loan documents, and closing the transaction. The costs directly related to those activities shall include only that portion of the employees' total compensation and payroll-related fringe benefits directly related to time spent performing those activities for that loan and other costs related to those activities that would not have been incurred but for that loan.

The Statement requires the lender's *indirect* costs to be expensed, rather than capitalized. These expenditures include costs for advertising, solicitation, servicing, administrative overhead, rent, and equipment. Costs related to unsuccessful loan origination attempts are also expensed.

When adopting Statement 91, many financial institutions established new accounts on their books to record the fee income they received for various loans such as FHA or VA mortgages, adjustable rate mortgages, conventional fixed mortgages, *etc.*

The institutions also may have established new expense accounts such as, loan origination compensation expense contra, loan origination office supplies expense contra, loan origination telephone expense contra, *etc.* This reflects amounts that were capitalized for book purposes.

Often, a bank will compute an average cost per loan origination for a given time period, such as a month. That cost figure is multiplied by the number of loans closed during the period to determine the total amount to be allocated to the previously mentioned accounts.

Typically, the loan fees and costs are tracked on a loan-by-loan basis. If the loan is sold or paid-off, the unamortized portion is included in income or expensed at that time. The net fee income or expense for refinanced loans may also be recognized when the new loan is granted.

TAX REPORTING OF LOAN ORIGINATION COSTS

Historically taxpayers have expensed the costs related to the origination of loans for tax reporting. Banks included these costs in the regular expense accounts for wages, office expenses, *etc.* Since the release of SFAS 91, most banks make M-1 adjustments to reverse the amount of expenses that were capitalized for books. This results in all costs associated with loan originations continuing to be expensed for tax purposes.

Most agents examining banks are taking the position that these costs should be capitalized for tax purposes, as well as for book reporting, because they result in the creation of an asset with a life extending beyond the tax year. This issue has been designated a "significant issue" by the IRS Banking Industry Specialist. The Savings and Loan Industry Specialist is also recommending that agents pursue this issue.

The Service issued Announcement 93-60, 1993-16 I.R.B. 9, to suspend all ruling requests for method changes with respect to this issue while it is under study. This announcement is discussed later in this chapter.

Generally, IRC section 263(a) and case laws provide support for the capitalization of loan origination costs. However, there are a number of unresolved issues presented upon a determination that loan origination costs should be properly capitalized, including issues involving the proper treatment of specific types of costs and the proper computation of basis and the applicable amortization period.

This area is under active consideration in the National Office.

Discussed below are some of the approaches which have been taken by revenue agents:

1. Capitalize *all* costs that are directly related to originating all loans. SFAS 91 costs are used as a starting point, but there may be costs that should be treated differently for tax than for book purposes. Some examples of direct loan origination costs are: Credit report costs, filing and recording fees, and attorney fees.
2. Capitalize the same items for tax that were capitalized for books. Under this approach, however, anomalies may result because of the netting approach permitted by SFAS 91 and the immateriality standard available for book purposes.
3. Net specific fee income against the related costs with the excess of the loan origination costs over certain related fee income being capitalized.

   Note, certain amounts received from borrowers that are paid to third parties for specific charges or services have, generally, been excluded from income or netted against the related costs.

Examiners raising this issue will also need to determine what amortization methods and periods are allowable. The burden is on the taxpayer to establish the life of the loans. Theoretically, if a useful life cannot be established, no amortization would be allowable. (The taxpayer would receive a deduction for the costs in the year the loan is terminated.) Practically speaking, there are usually industry standards for the average lives of the various types of loans. For example, historically 30 year mortgages have lasted 12 years and 15 year mortgages have lasted 8 years. However, these averages have been affected in recent years by lower interest rates, refinancings, *etc.* The taxpayer may have studies showing how long other types of loans, such as car loans or commercial loans, last. It should also be noted that some home equity loans have an indefinite life since they are open-ended.

For book purposes, the bank may track the net of the fee income and the loan costs on a loan-by-loan basis. Some banks have set up their computer systems to separate the fee income and the loan costs. They can then determine whether the loans have been paid off prematurely, the amount being amortized for books, *etc.* Book amortization figures may be used as a starting point for tax amortization.

LAW

The law supporting the IRS' position that loan origination costs should be capitalized is found in part in IRC section 263(a), Treas. Reg. section 1.461-1(a), IRC section 446(a), IRS rulings, and several court cases, including *Indopco, Inc. v. Commissioner,* 503 U.S. 79 (1992) [92-1 USTC ¶50,113]. These are discussed below.

IRC section 263(a) states that no deduction shall be allowed for any amount paid out for new buildings or for permanent improvements or betterments made to increase the value of any property or estate and any amount expended in restoring property or in making good the exhaustion thereof for which an allowance is or has been made.

Treas. Reg. section 1.461-1(a) provides the general rule for the taxable year of deduction. Any expenditure, that results in the creation of an asset having a useful life that extends substantially beyond the close of the taxable year, may not be deductible, or may be deductible only in part, for the taxable year in which incurred.

IRC section 446(a) states that taxable income shall be computed under the method of accounting on the basis of which the taxpayer regularly computes his income in keeping his books. Treas. Reg. section 1.446-1 further provides that the term "method of accounting" includes not only the overall method of accounting of the taxpayer but also the accounting treatment of any item. It further states that a method of accounting which reflects the consistent application of generally accepted accounting principles in a particular trade or business in accordance with accepted conditions or practices in that trade or business will ordinarily be regarded as clearly reflecting income, provided all items of gross income and expense are treated consistently from year to year.

Rules and regulations prescribed by state and federal regulatory authorities may require tax payers to record transactions in a manner inconsistent with the Internal Revenue Code specifications. In the event of such a conflict, the Commissioner is not bound by the regulatory authorities' methods and may require the taxpayer to recompute its taxable income under different methods as required by the Code. See *Old Colony Railroad Co. v. Commissioner,* 284 U.S. 552 (1932) [3 USTC ¶880] and Revenue Ruling 68-220, 1968-1 C.B. 194.[1]

In *Commissioner v. Lincoln Savings & Loan Assoc.,* 403 U.S. 345 (1971) [71-1 USTC ¶9476], the court held that an expenditure should be capitalized if it creates or enhances a separate and distinct asset for which a value can be ascertained.

Consider, for example, home equity lines of credit ("HELOCs"). These credit lines often generate fees for credit reports, filing and recording fees, attorney fees, and related closing costs. As with credit cards and revolving credit lines, the bank typically does not pass these costs to the customer (unlike in a purchase money mortgage loan situation). The Service has treated HELOCs as separate assets having use-

[1] The argument for book-tax conformity per IRC section 446 for loan origination costs supports the capitalization theory only if the bank is following SFAS 91. Some banks did not adopt the statement. In those cases other code sections, regulations, rulings, and court cases should be cited as authority.

ful lives beyond the present tax year. As such, the costs incurred to create or acquire them are subject to the capitalization principles discussed above. Further, the question of capitalization does not turn on whether such costs are paid to employees ("in-house" expenses) or third parties ("out-house" expenses). See Rev. Rul. 57-400, 1957-2 C.B. 520; Rev. Rul. 69-331, 1969-1 C.B. 87. Rather, the principle focus should be on whether the incurred cost directly and significantly contributed to the creation or acquisition of the loan.

Rev. Rul. 57-400, 1957-2 C.B. 520, held that "&1;Finders fees&2;(buying commissions) paid by mutual savings banks, building and loan associations, cooperative banks and other classes of banks, to brokers, title companies, and other third parties for their introduction of acceptable applicants for mortgage loans, constitute a part of the acquisition cost of the loans which must be capitalized and amortized over the lives of the mortgage loans made to such applicants."

Rev. Rul. 69-331, 1969-1 C.B. 87, held that where a taxpayer has paid commissions to its own employees, and the commissions played a direct and significant part in the acquisition of capital assets, the commissions must be capitalized.

In *Indopco, Inc. v. Commissioner,* 112 S.Ct. 1039 (1992) [92-1 USTC ¶50,113], *aff'g National Starch and Chemical Corp. v. Commissioner,* 918 F.2d 426 (1990) [90-2 USTC ¶50,571], *aff'g* 93 T.C. 67 (1989) [CCH Dec. 45,851], the Supreme Court discussed the deductibility of expenses incurred during a friendly takeover. It held that the expenses were not deductible because they created benefits that extended beyond the current year. The creation or enhancement of a separate asset was not a necessary condition to require expenses to be capitalized. The court stated, "Deductions are exceptions to the norm of capitalization and are allowed only if there is clear provision for them in the Code and the taxpayer has met the burden of showing a right to the deduction."

Indopco was significant because it held that the creation of a separate asset was not necessary for capitalization of the related expenditures. *Indopco* strengthens the Government's position that loan origination costs must be capitalized, because it clarifies that expenditures are capitalized when future benefits are created. Some of the future benefits created by originating a loan are the right to receive interest, the right to service the loans, the opportunity to solicit the borrowers for additional business, *etc.*

The uniform capitalization rules of IRC section 263A were enacted by the Tax Reform Act of 1986. UNICAP requires the capitalization of certain expenditures incurred (1) for real or tangible personal property produced by a taxpayer and (2) for real or personal property (tangible or intangible) acquired for resale. Treas. Reg. section 1.263A-1(b)(13) states:

Extract

Treas. Reg. section 1.263A)1(b)(13)

*** the origination of loans is not considered the acquisition of intangible property for resale. (But IRC section 263A(b)(2)(A) does include the acquisition by a taxpayer of pre-existing loans from other persons for resale.)

Therefore, per the regulation, IRC section 263A *does not* apply to originated loans, but *does* apply to loans purchased for resale. Thus, IRC section 263A requires capitalization of certain costs allocable to loans purchased for resale. The regulation applies to costs incurred in taxable years beginning after December 31, 1993. IRS Notice 88-86, 1988-2 C.B. 401, was applicable for years beginning before January 1, 1994. The Notice said that the *origination* of a loan is considered the production of intangible property, rather than the acquisition of intangible property for resale. Therefore, IRC section 263A *does not* apply to originated loans. However, IRC section 263A may apply to the purchase of pre-existing loans from other parties for resale. The applicable portion of Notice 88-86 is reprinted below:

> Commentators have inquired as to whether a taxpayer that originates loans (that is, loans money to other persons in return for promissory notes or other documents evidencing a promise to repay) would be treated as acquiring intangible property for resale under IRC section 263A.
>
> In response to these inquiries, forthcoming regulations shall provide that the origination of a loan shall be treated under IRC section 263A as the production of intangible property for resale. Thus, the capitalization rules of IRC section 263A shall not apply to such activity, because IRC section 263A only applies to the production of tangible personal property. IRC section 263A, however, applies to taxpayers purchasing pre-existing loans from other parties for resale. Such taxpayers are treated as acquiring intangible property for resale, and hence are subject to the uniform capitalization rules. The provisions of this paragraph apply only for purposes of IRC section 263A and no inference relating to the treatment of such property for other purposes of the Code is intended (see for example, Rev. Rul. 72-523, 1972-2 C.B. 242).

Therefore, under both the regulations and the Notice, IRC section 263A applies only to loans purchased for resale, not to loans originated by the taxpayer.

IRC section 263A requires the capitalization of indirect costs that would otherwise be deductible. Since IRC section 263A does not apply to originated loans, IRC section 263 should instead be referenced to determine which expenditures are capital in nature. The applicability of IRC section 263 was discussed above. Fewer expenses are capitalizable under IRC section 263 than would be capitalized under IRC section 263A.

IRC section 263A, however, applies only to IRC section 1221(1) property. *See* IRS section 263A(b)(2)(A). For loans subject to IRC section 475, IRC section 263A will generally not apply. *See* IRC section 475(d)(1). Thus, IRC section 263A will rarely have application even with respect to purchased loans in tax years after the effective date of IRC section 475.

CHANGE IN ACCOUNTING METHOD

The taxpayer's method of accounting must be changed when it is determined that loan origination costs should be capitalized. Announcement 93-60, 1993-16 I.R.B. 9, was released in March 1993 to temporarily suspend the filing of accounting method change requests for loan origination costs. Any Forms 3115 that had been filed were returned to the taxpayers, unless they involved a pending issue before examination or appeals. The following excerpt from the ruling is particularly relevant for revenue agents:

> If a taxpayer is currently under examination or subsequently comes

> under examination, the taxpayer may give the examining agent a copy of the returned Form 3115 and cover letter, or request a change in accounting method (with respect to loan origination costs) by filing a Form 3115 with the examining agent during the first 90 days of the examination or during any of the window periods available under Rev. Proc. 92-20. For taxpayers who file their Form 3115 with the examining agent, any change in method of accounting for loan origination costs will be made under terms no less favorable than those available to taxpayers not under examination. Thus, taxpayers will not be adversely affected by this proscription on filing a method change request regarding this matter with National Office.

Therefore, first determine whether your taxpayer has previously filed Form 3115 or is still within one of the window periods provided by Rev. Proc. 92-20, 1992-1 C.B. 685. If so, the year of change would be later than the year you are examining and you would not want to spend time developing the issue. However, if the bank did not file a request for a change and is no longer within one of the window periods, the issue can be raised.

EXAMINATION TECHNIQUES

1. Review the tax return. Taxpayers sometimes attach disclosure statements which discuss their treatment of loan origination costs. Often there will be a line item on the Other Deduction schedule for loan origination costs.

2. Review the Schedule M-1 to determine if there is an adjustment to expense costs that were capitalized for book purposes. (This adjustment is often identical to the amount on the Other Deduction schedule.) Also, see whether there is an item adjusting fee income that was amortized for book purposes. Taxpayers may have two separate M-1 adjustments for these items, one to decrease book income for the expenses and another to increase book income for the fees. However, they may net these two items and have only one M-1 adjustment. Since the fee income is usually larger than the related expenses, the net M-1 often will increase book income. Therefore, you may have an issue even if book income is not being decreased. Look at the M-1 work papers to determine how loan origination costs have been handled.

3. Determine whether the bank has filed a Form 3115 regarding the tax treatment of loan origination costs. As mentioned earlier, refer to Announcement 93-60 if the taxpayer previously filed a Form 3115 or files one within 90 days of the start of the examination. You would not want to pursue this issue if the taxpayer is still within one of the window periods for filing a Form 3115.

4. Interview the tax manager extensively regarding the bank's book and tax treatment of loan origination costs. He or she should be able to explain the method of capitalizing costs, whether M-1 adjustments were made, the types of costs that may have been capitalized, *etc.* If not, interview another bank employee who is knowledgeable in this area.

5. Determine early in the examination the types of loans the bank makes and which of these they retain. If the bank sells a particular type of loan shortly after it is originated, you will need to decide whether the related costs are significant enough to warrant capitalization. For example, if the bank sells all of its mortgages within one month of origination they would get a

deduction for the costs one month after they were capitalized. Your time may be better spent reviewing the expenditures for loans that the bank retains.

6. Some banks prepare a report for their executive boards to provide them with information regarding loan closings and costs. The report generally will list the number of loans closed during the month, the number of loans in the process of being closed (in the "pipeline"), the fees received on the loans, the per loan costs, the types of loans closed, *etc.* Inquire whether the bank you are examining prepares this type of report and request copies of them.

7. Request that the bank provide a listing of sample journal entries used to record SFAS 91 transactions. This should include entries that are made from the time the borrower applies for the loan through the time fee income and loan expenses are amortized. This will help you develop a better understanding of the bank's practices and may assist in developing the issue. See Exhibit 9-1 for a sample IDR.

8. Review the general ledger to see whether particular accounts have been set up to record SFAS 91 expenses. Also, use the account stratification that was prepared by the CAS to identify balance sheet accounts which relate to SFAS 91 costs. Once the accounts are identified, review account selections and identify specific entries for further analysis. The detail will probably consist of a number of journal entries. Request the back up documents for a sample of the entries.

9. Determine whether the bank pays handling fees or commissions to automobile dealerships for processing loans for customers who purchase vehicles. The dealerships' employees prepare the loan documents on behalf of the bank. The bank pays the dealer a fee, usually a percentage of the loan amount, for performing this service. Banks will normally capitalize this cost for books, but expense it for tax purposes. This fee is no different from other loan origination costs and should be capitalized for tax reporting also.

10. Read the applicable portions of the taxpayer's accounting manual which provide explanations for the types of transactions that are recorded in the accounts.

11. The costs that have been included for SFAS 91 purposes may not be the same as those that should be capitalized for tax purposes. Analyze the taxpayer's expenses to determine if additional costs should be capitalized.

12. If the bank did not capitalize any loan origination costs under SFAS 91, you will need to reconstruct the amounts. Determine which bank personnel are directly involved in the origination of loans and allocate a portion of their salaries. Also, take into consideration office supplies, telephone costs, travel expenditures, and other directly related costs. If the bank used SFAS 91 in subsequent years, you may be able to use those cost figures as a guideline. The bank should have records regarding the number of loans closed each year. If you calculate the average costs per loan, this amount can be multiplied by the number of loans that were closed to estimate the amount that should be capitalized.

13. Since this issue involves the change of an accounting method, an IRC section 481 adjustment may need to be computed. This can be very difficult since the taxpayer is unlikely to

have computed its SFAS 91 costs for years prior to 1988. You may want to use costs from the years you are examining and project them backwards, allowing for inflation. The taxpayer may be able to assist you in determining what the prior years' costs would be.

The taxpayer may request that you make adjustments in the current years only and allow the bank to continue to report prior year loans under the old method. The taxpayer has the burden of proof as to the proper IRC section 481(a) adjustment. *Hitachi Sales Corporation of America v. Commissioner,* T.C. Memo. 1994-159 [CCH Dec. 49,783(M)]. The use of the cut-off method has not been approved for loan origination costs.

14. If the useful life of the loans can be determined with reasonable accuracy, calculate the allowable amortization. The amount capitalized is usually amortized on a straight line basis over the life of the related loans. If the bank tracks its loan origination costs on a loan by loan basis, you may consider doing the same for tax purposes.

15. Several articles have been written on this topic. Keep in mind that these articles express the point of view of the banking industry, not the IRS. However, you can review these for further information on this issue:

a. Alexander and Conjura, "IRS haunts banks by applying FAS 91 at tax audits," *ABA Bankers Weekly,* August 18, 1992.

b. Goeller, "Will Accounting Rules Bar Deductibility of Loan Origination Costs?", *Journal of Bank Taxation,* Vol 6/No 2, Winter 1993, p.3.

c. Andaloro and Alexander, "IRS Fails to Consider Loan Origination Costs in Overall Business Context," *Journal of Bank Taxation,* Vol 6/No 2, Winter 1993, p.7.

d. Ruempler and Salfi, "Tax Treatment of Loan Origination Costs and Fees," September 27, 1993, Tax Notes 1745.

SUMMARY

The capitalization of loan origination costs should be reviewed during the examination of every financial institution. This issue has been identified as a significant issue by the banking industry specialist and the National Office is working on the topic. Determine whether a position has been announced and whether the taxpayer has filed Form 3115 prior to spending a lot of time in this area.

You must use a considerable amount of judgment in developing this issue. You need to determine which costs to capitalize, their amounts, which loans to consider, their amortization periods, *etc.* SFAS 91 costs can be used as a starting point, but additional costs may be capitalizable for tax purposes.

Exhibit 9-1

[SAMPLE INFORMATION DOCUMENT REQUEST, Form 4564, Rev. 6/88. Not Reproduced.]

CHAPTER 10—BAD DEBTS

INTRODUCTION

The primary business of a bank is to lend money to its customers. A bank will claim a bad debt deduction for losses resulting from loans that are not fully repaid, therefore, the amount deducted for bad debts can be significant. The bad debt deduction is an area for potential adjustments since the determination of worthlessness requires a facts and circumstances analysis. Therefore, a fair amount of time should be spent ascertaining the allowable tax deduction.

Prior to the Tax Reform Act of 1986, all banks could elect to deduct their bad debts using either of two methods:

1. *Reserve Method*

   Under the reserve method a bank is allowed to take a deduction for debts that are expected to become worthless in the future. This method permits the bank to establish a *reserve* for these future worthless debts. The amount deducted is normally based on a 6 year moving average of prior experience. IRC section 585 is the authority for banks to use the reserve method for deducting loan losses. The reserve method authorized by IRC section 593 is available only to thrifts. Note that the reserve method of IRC section 593 was repealed for tax years beginning after December 31, 1995, by section 1616(a) of P.L. 104-188 signed August 20, 1996.

2. *Specific Charge-Off Method*

   Under this method, a bad debt deduction is allowed *only* in the year a loan is determined to be wholly or partially worthless. IRC section 166 allows the deduction for the portion of the debt that becomes worthless during the year.

The Tax Reform Act of 1986 *repealed* the use of the reserve method for all taxpayers except for commercial banks with $500 million or less in assets and thrift institutions.[1] Large banks are allowed to use *only* the specific charge-off method for computing their bad debt deductions for years beginning after 1986. In addition, these large banks must *recapture* their entire loan loss reserve balance for tax purposes beginning with the 1987 year. The specific requirements of the reserve recapture are discussed later in this chapter.

DEFINITION OF A "LARGE" BANK

A bank is considered to be a *large bank* if for any taxable year beginning after December 31, 1986, the sum of the average adjusted tax basis of all assets of such bank exceeds $500 million. If the bank is a member of a controlled group, the test is met if the sum of the average adjusted basis of all assets of such group, including bank and nonbank members exceeds $500 million. If you are examining a case which has an asset base close to the $500 million amount, refer to Treas. Reg. section 1.585-5(c) which provides additional guidance to assist you in determining whether this threshold has been exceeded. Final regulations were issued December 29, 1993, covering section 1.585-5 through 1.585-8. See 58 Fed. Reg. 68753 as corrected by 59 Fed. Reg. 4583 (Feb. 1, 1994).

---

[1] Insurance reserves are governed by subchapter L of the Code and were not directly affected by the repeal of former IRC section 166(c).

Once a bank is formally classified as a large bank, it will *always* be considered to be a large bank, even if the asset base drops below $500 million in a later year.

RESERVE METHOD

For banks which are still permitted to use the reserve method, the issue is more computational than technical. The reserve method permits a bad debt deduction for the amount which is determined to be a reasonable addition to the reserve. IRC section 585(b)(1) provides that the reasonable addition to the reserve for bad debts of a financial institution is determined by the experience method.

IRC section 585(b)(2) provides that the amount determined under the experience method shall be the amount necessary to increase the balance of the reserve for losses on loans to the greater of:

Extract

IRC section 585(b)(2)(A)

(A) the amount which bears the same ratio to loans outstanding at the close of the taxable year as (i) the total bad debts sustained during the taxable year and the five preceding taxable years * * * adjusted for recoveries of bad debts during such period, bears to (ii) the sum of the loans outstanding at the close of such six or fewer taxable years, or

(B) the lower of—

(i) the balance of the reserve at the close of the base year, or

(ii) if the amount of loans outstanding at the close of the taxable year is less than the amount of loans outstanding at the close of the base year, the amount which bears the same ratio to loans outstanding at the close of the taxable year as the balance of the reserve at the close of the base year bears to the amount of loans outstanding at the close of the base year.

* * *

To put it very simply, the experience method permits a deduction in the amount necessary to increase the reserve for loan losses to the level determined using a 6-year moving average, or the amount required to increase the loan loss reserve to the balance existing in the base year. The base year is the last taxable year before the most recent adoption of the experience method except that for taxable years beginning after 1987, the base year is the last taxable year beginning before 1988. While this may seem confusing, these computations are usually included with the tax return and simply must be reviewed for accuracy by the examining agent.

If the reserve method is being used, verify that the taxpayer includes only *permissible* loans in computing the addition to the reserve for bad debts. Permissible loans refers to those loans acquired (including originated) in the normal course of business. Additional information on the reserve method for bad debts can be found by referring to one of the publications listed in the Resource and Reference Materials chapter in this guide.

SPECIFIC CHARGE-OFF METHOD

Under the specific charge-off method, a bad debt deduction is allowed only in the year in which the loan is determined to be wholly or partially worthless. Treas. Reg. section 1.166-2(a) provides that in determining whether a debt is worthless, all pertinent evidence including the value of the collateral and the financial condition of the debtor will be considered.

An examiner should consider the following factors in determining the deductibility of a bad debt:

1. A true debtor-creditor relationship must exist:

a. There must be a valid and enforceable obligation to pay a fixed and determinable sum of money.

b. If a creditor has a disputed claim for which the amount due cannot be accurately determined, the disputed amount is not allowable as a bad debt deduction since the existence of a bona-fide debt has not been established.

2. Debt's worthlessness must be considered:

a. The determination of whether a particular loan is worthless, either in whole or in part, is primarily a question of fact. The value of the underlying collateral, the financial condition of the debtor, along with any other factors affecting the possibility of collection must be considered. The burden of proof as to the worthlessness of the debt is on the taxpayer, not the IRS.

b. Bankruptcy of a debtor is not in and of itself a valid indication as to the worthlessness of a debt. Take into consideration other factors such as the value of the collateral supporting the debt and the reason the debtor filed for bankruptcy.

c. The taxpayer must exhaust all reasonable means of collection before worthlessness can be established. The taxpayer must retain documentation showing the attempts made to collect the debt. The mere fact that a debt is difficult to collect does not make it worthless for tax purposes. However, a creditor does not have to pursue legal action if in all probability this action will not result in the collection of the debt.

d. Taxpayer must have a charge-off, that is, the taxpayer must take some action to remove the worthless portion of the asset from its books. See *Brandtjen & Kluge, Inc. v. Commissioner*, 34 T.C. 416 (1960) [CCH Dec. 24,213], *acq.*, 1960-2 C.B. 4. This issue is also illustrated in PLR 9338044.

e. The interaction between debt modification under IRC section 1001 and partially worthless debt is addressed by temporary regulation 1.166-3T, T.D. 8676, 1996-30 IRB 4 (July 22, 1996) and F1-59-94 1996-30 IRB 24 (July 22, 1996).

CHARGE-OFF MANDATED BY REGULATORS

Special provisions in Treas. Reg. section 1.166-2(d) apply to a bank which is subject to Federal or State supervision and which charges off a debt in whole or in part. In these cases, the debt is conclusively presumed to be worthless in whole or in part if the charge-off is made:

1. In obedience to the specific orders of such authorities or
2. In accordance with established policies of such authorities, and upon their first audit of the bank after the charge-off, such authorities confirm in writing that the charge-off would have been subject to such specific orders if the audit had been made on the date of the charge-off.

Simply stated, a debt charged off by the bank per written instructions of a regulatory agency is *conclusively presumed* to be worthless. The charge-off must be in the *loss* category described below. Loans designated as substandard or doubtful are not deductible for tax purposes.

Practically speaking, we do not see charge-off letters very often because we are reviewing loan files which were written off by the bank prior to supervisory examination. The regulators take a conservative approach and usually will not review loans already determined to be uncollectible by the bank. The bank examiner is much more concerned with loans remaining on the books. Therefore, no written opinion by the regulators on charged-off loans will exist. As to the second item listed above, it is unusual to have the banking examiners give a charge-off letter to the bank *after* the fact.

For an example in which a bank was not entitled to a presumption of worthlessness on a participation loan which it charged off *prior* to receiving the Shared National Credit Review, refer to PLR 9253003.

BREAKDOWN OF LOAN CLASSIFICATIONS USED BY BANKING REGULATORS

Regulatory examiners categorize a loan (or some portion of a loan) according to the degree of *risk* associated with a particular loan and its potential for future losses. The banks use similar criteria in their internal loan review process.

The various loan loss classifications are as follows:

Loss Loans

Loans classified as *loss* are considered to be uncollectible. This classification does not mean that the loan has no recovery or salvage value. However, the amount of any potential recovery would be small. The amount of the loan classified as "loss" should be completely charged off for both book and tax purposes. This is the only loan classification which permits a deduction for tax purposes.

Doubtful Loans

Doubtful loans have all the weaknesses of substandard loans but are one step closer to being uncollectible. Based on all the facts existing at the time and considering the valuation of the assets involved, the possibility of full collection of the loan is highly unlikely. Even though the probability of a portion of the loan being uncollected is very high, the classification of this loan to the "loss" category is deferred due to a reasonable expectation of a full recovery. Potential factors which may influence the classification are a potential merger, additional collateral, an injection of new capital, or a new financing source.

Substandard Loans

The *substandard* category is applied to those loans which are inadequately protected from future losses. This may be due to a lack of security pledged as collateral for the loan, due to the current financial condition of the obligor, or other reasons. These loans have the potential for a portion of the loan to be uncollectible if additional collateral is not secured or the financial condition of the obligor does not improve.

Special Mention Loans

This category involves potentially weak loans but which are currently fully protected by the value of the collateral pledged, or the paying capacity of the obligor. The loans are mentioned by the banking examiner since they constitute a credit risk due to the deteriorating financial condition of the obligor, but would not justify any further downgrade in the rating of the loan at this time.

Unclassified Loans

Unclassified loans do not have any greater than normal risk. The obligation is expected to be fully repaid and no loss is anticipated.

The following table lists the various classifications of loans used by the regulators and the applicable deduction of the amount of the loan so designated for book and tax purposes. The amount written off for book purposes for both substandard and doubtful loans are based upon each bank's history of loan losses as determined by the regulators. The percentages used below for these classifications are the normal amounts by an average bank.

Loan Classification	*Book Purposes*	*Tax Purposes*
Loss	100% deduction required	100% deduction allowed
Doubtful	50% deduction required	0% deduction allowed
Substandard	30% deduction required	0% deduction allowed
Special Mention	0% deduction required	0% deduction allowed
Unclassified	0% deduction required	0% deduction allowed

CONFORMITY ELECTION FOR BAD DEBT CHARGE-OFFS

New regulations finalized in February 1992 allow banks to *elect* to account for bad debts in a manner corresponding more closely to bank regulatory classifications. These regulations allow a regulated financial institution a conclusive presumption that debts which are properly chargedoff for regulatory purposes are also worthless for tax purposes, if certain conditions are met. This presumption applies to loans classified under regulatory standards as "loss" assets. These provisions provide conformity with the regulatory standards on loan review and loss classification.

Treasury Decision 8492, 1993-2 C.B. 73, states that:

> Treas. Reg. section 1.166-2(d)(3) permits supervised banks to elect a method of accounting under which their debts generally are conclusively presumed to be worthless for Federal income tax purposes when the debts are charged off for regulatory purposes. One of the requirements for this "conformity presumption" is that the bank obtain an express determination letter from its [Federal]supervisory authority in connection with the most recent examination involving the bank's loan review process.

* * *

*** The final regulations in this document amend Treas. Reg. [section] 1.166-2(d)(3) to require that a bank's supervisory authority expressly determine that the bank maintains and applies "loan loss classification standards" * * * that are consistent with regulatory standards. * * * In addition, the transition rules in Treas. Reg. [section] 1.166-2(d)(3) allow a bank to make the conformity election without an express determination letter until its first examination (involving the loan review process) that is after October 1, 1992, * * *

Certain important facts to consider in this area are:

1. The conformity presumption is *limited* to debts that are classified "*loss*".
2. The conformity presumption applies only to tax years ending on or after December 31, 1991.
3. A bank need not obtain an express determination letter until the completion of its first Federal examination that is after October 1, 1992. The key here is the date the examination report was issued, not the period being examined.
4. Under Notice 93-50, 1993-2 C.B. 336, a bank can, under certain circumstances, elect this accounting method via an amended return for tax years ending on or after December 31, 1991.
5. Rev. Proc. 92-84, 1992-2 C.B. 489 (modifying and superseding Rev. Proc. 92-18, 1992-1 C.B. 684), discusses requirements for obtaining an express determination letter and describes the contents of the letter.
6. The Comptroller of the Currency Examining Circular 216 Supplement 1 issued October 2, 1992 discusses the process for National Banks.

BAD DEBT RECOVERIES

The tax treatment for recoveries of debts which were previously deducted for tax purposes depends upon the method used by the bank to deduct its bad debts.

Specific charge-off method:

Recoveries are included in income and fully taxable to the extent a tax benefit was derived by the bank at the time of the deduction.

Reserve Method:

Recovery of a debt which was previously charged against the reserve is credited to the reserve, rather than included in income. This affects the computation of the reserve deduction in future years. No deduction is allowed for the amount of the recovery credited to the reserve.

BAD DEBT RESERVE RECAPTURE

The Tax Reform Act of 1986 required that large banks recapture their entire loan loss reserve balance beginning in 1987. If the bank does not meet the criteria for being a large bank at that time, then the loan loss reserve balance will be recaptured beginning in the first taxable year in which the total assets of the bank exceeds the $500 million limit.

The switch to the specific charge-off method by the bank is considered to be a change in a method of accounting. This change in method of accounting is treated as being made with the Commissioner's consent.

The 1986 Tax Reform Act stipulated that the loan loss reserve balance is to be recaptured by using one of the following elective methods:

1. *Fixed Percentage Recapture*—General Method

This method requires the reserve balance to be recaptured over a 4-year period using the following percentages:

a. 10 percent of the reserve balance starting in the disqualification year, 1987, or the year the bank becomes a large bank, whichever is later

b. 20 percent in the second succeeding year

c. 30 percent in the third year

d. 40 percent in the fourth year.

2. *Variable Percentage Recapture*—Alternative Method

The bank can recapture any amount of the reserve up to 100 percent, in the disqualification year, with a minimum recapture of 10 percent. The balance of the reserve is recaptured in the subsequent 3 years using the following ratios:

—2/9s, 3/9s, and 4/9s.

3. *Cut-Off Method Recapture*

Under this method, all charge-offs and other losses and recoveries on loans in the bank's portfolio as of the end of the taxable year preceding the disqualification year would be accounted for as adjustments to the reserve account, and not as separate items of income and expense.

4. *Troubled Bank Exception*

The loan loss reserve recapture is *not* required during any year in which the bank is formally classified as being "financially troubled." However, a troubled bank may elect to report the recapture amount for the first year of the recapture period. This is usually done by a bank with expiring NOLs or tax credits that might otherwise not be used.

A financially troubled bank is defined in IRC section 585(c)(3)(B) as any bank in which the nonperforming loan percentage exceeds 75 percent. This percentage is computed as follows:

The sum of the outstanding balance of nonperforming loans as of the close of each quarter.

The sum of the equity capital balance of the bank as of the close of each quarter.

See Example 3 in Treas. Reg. section 1.585-6(d)(5).

The amount of nonperforming loans and equity capital are determined by the banking regulators in accordance with federal regulatory guidelines.

Recently, finalized regulations under IRC section 585(c) provide that large banks may not use the reserve method of IRC section 585 for taxable years beginning after December 31, 1986. Treas. Reg. section 1.585-8 provides rules for making and revoking elections regarding the recapture of the reserve and the use of the cut-off method. These rules do not authorize the opening of closed years to make or revoke elections or to file amended returns.

EXAMINATION TECHNIQUES

1. Review the tax return to determine whether the taxpayer has elected the new regulatory/tax conformity presumption of worthlessness accounting method which is effective for taxable years ending on or after December 31, 1991. If so, the following procedures should be followed:

a. The examiner should request a copy of the "Express Determination Letter" which confirms that the taxpayer maintains classification standards in conformity with the regulators. Refer to Rev. Proc. 92-84, 1992-2 C.B. 489.

b. Review the bad debts claimed for book purposes to verify that the bank deducts only amounts actually categorized under the *lossc-lassification*. Whatever is claimed on the books automatically becomes a bad debt deduction for tax purposes, but *only* for the loss classification. The taxpayer must have total book/tax conformity in this classification.

c. This election does not provide relief for taxable years prior to 1991. Make sure that the taxpayer does not attempt to apply these rules retroactively. The burden is on the taxpayer to support all deductions claimed.

2. If the taxpayer is using the reserve method, which is available only for banks with $500 million or less in assets, verify the computation of the deduction claimed for tax purposes. Ask the taxpayer to adequately explain any large or unusual items included in the computation.

3. If the reserve method is being used for tax purposes, make sure that the taxpayer does not deduct loan loss amounts elsewhere on the return. It is possible that bad debt deductions could be buried in Schedule D, Form 4797, or in Other Deductions. All bad debt losses should be run through the reserve account, including charge-off's of previously accrued interest income.

A loan restructure should be deemed a sale or exchange of property within the meaning of IRC section 1001 and the loss, if any, should be deductible under IRC section 165 rather than a bad debt deduction.

4. If the taxpayer is on the specific charge-off method, request a complete listing of all loans deducted for tax purposes. This amount should tie exactly into the amount claimed on the tax return. Any discrepancies in these amounts should be explained by the taxpayer.

Usually, we do not request specific verification for loan charge-offs under a certain dollar amount. This amount would depend on the size of the bank being examined and upon the discretion of the examiner.

5. Request a meeting with someone from the bank who handles loans currently in default.

Discuss with him or her the procedures used by the bank to determine when a loan should be charged off, and the bank's loan classification policies. In most of our cases, the tax department was unaware of these procedures and simply deducted for tax purposes whatever the loan control department instructed them to deduct for book purposes. Book accounting and tax requirements are different. That is why it is important to talk to someone familiar with the bank's policies and procedures in this area.

6. Check for any book to tax differences on schedule M-1 dealing with the bad debt deductions. Is the bank taking a deduction for tax purposes but not for book? Analyze any differences. It should be emphasized that the taxpayer cannot deduct a bad debt for tax purposes *unless* and *until* there is a book charge off. For partially worthless debts, a book deduction should always be taken *before* a tax deduction.

7. From the listing of loans charged-off for tax purposes, selectively request the complete loan files for all large, unusual, or interesting loans. In multiple year examinations, emphasis should be placed on the most

recent charge-offs since subsequent collections on earlier loans will have already been reported as a recovery.

8. When reviewing the loan file, make sure the taxpayer has provided you with the *entire* file. Look for recent notes indicating that the file is up-to-date and complete. An outdated loan file is of no value. In order to make a proper determination, you must have the most current information available for each and every loan file requested.

9. Review the loan files for comments and notes by the loan officer on the possibility of subsequent events that could affect the collectibility or recoveries in future years.

10. Request the current status reports for several of the larger loans. Analyze the bad debt recoveries in subsequent years. A large recovery and consistent future payments on a particular loan may indicate that the loan should not have been written off during the examination year.

An analysis of the loan file can help put the bad debt issue in perspective. However, it should be noted that the taxpayer is not bound by subsequent events, such as recoveries or future events to determine a charge-off. Also, the IRS does not have to accept subsequent events to determine if a debt is bad in the current year.

11. An aggressive position can be taken on the charge-offs. It is the bank's responsibility to establish the worthlessness of the debt. Failure to properly document the reduced value of the debt precludes the taxpayer from taking a deduction.

a. The taxpayer must document the worthlessness of each loan. The documentation for one loan does not permit the deduction for any other loan. Each loan stands on its own merits and substantiation, or lack thereof.

b. Failure by the taxpayer to provide a loan file can give rise to a complete disallowance of any deduction taken for that particular loan. Unusual facts and circumstances should be considered that would affect the availability of the loan file.

c. It should be remembered that a loan officer's determination as to the collection potential for a particular loan is self serving. In fact, in some cases the loan officer is probably arguing that the loan will be collected in as much as the loan officer was responsible for making the loan in the first place. His or her comments should not automatically be accepted without other substantiating evidence supporting their opinion. The facts contained in the loan file should speak for themselves.

d. In our cases, many of the adjustments we made were based on the taxpayer's failure to provide sufficient proof of worthlessness. The taxpayer was also unable to show that sufficient attempts were made to collect the debt at the point in time of the charge-off.

MISCELLANEOUS ITEMS/ TERMS PARTICIPATION LOAN

A loan made by a bank or financial institution to a borrower, if the lender thereafter sells, assigns, or otherwise transfers a portion of the loan to one or more institutions.

SYNDICATION LOAN

A multi-financial institution loan in which all of the lenders are named as parties to the loan and have privity of contract with the borrower.

SHARED NATIONAL CREDIT EXAM

An examination of a large participation loan shared by more than one federally insured bank.

SHARED NATIONAL CREDIT REVIEW

A list of ratings of large participation loans. The list is compiled annually.

SUMMARY

With the elimination of the reserve method for large banks, the timing and substantiation requirements for charge-offs take on even greater significance. Large banks have less flexibility in managing their tax position with respect to their bad debt deduction. Therefore, the examining agent should take the time to closely scrutinize all bad debt deductions claimed by the taxpayer.

CHAPTER 11—FSLIC ASSISTANCE

BACKGROUND

To encourage investors to acquire troubled savings and loan or thrift institutions, the now defunct Federal Savings and Loan Insurance Corporation (FSLIC) often provided various forms of financial assistance or incentives to acquiring institutions. These acquisitions normally included some or all of the following types of assistance:

1. Issuance of a note receivable to the purchaser

The purpose of a note receivable is to compensate the acquiring institution for the insolvency of the thrift. The amount of the note usually equaled the negative net worth of the thrift. In other words, the amount by which the S&L's liabilities exceeded the value of the underlying assets.

2. Yield maintenance subsidies on loans or other assets

This type of assistance involved the guarantee of additional interest, or provided for a minimum amount of interest, to be received by the purchaser on certain specified interest bearing assets.

3. Reimbursement of losses on disposition of certain assets

These payments reimbursed the acquiring institution for all assets specifically covered in the agreement which were sold for amounts less than a specified amount or became worthless.

4. Indemnification against undisclosed liabilities and litigation resulting from the acquisition

5. Various tax attributes

Under the terms of the agreement, the acquiring institution may be entitled to use various tax benefits of the thrift, such as net operating loss or credit carryovers. However, the agreement may stipulate that FSLIC is entitled to share in the utilization of these tax benefits.

The majority of the assistance payments from the Government were made to cover losses incurred from the sale of the assets of the troubled institution. That's because for the most part, the thrifts which were taken over were insolvent. Prior to the revision of IRC section 597, these assistance payments were excluded from income.

The issue which is discussed in this chapter of the guide involves those cases in which a bank has *acquired* an insolvent thrift from the FSLIC and receives assistance payments to reimburse losses from the sale of the thrift's assets or their subsequent worthlessness.

For tax purposes, our concern centers around these non-taxable reimbursements. The taxpayer will claim a deduction for the loss on the sale of the assets acquired from the thrift, even though the amount of the loss is fully reimbursed. Since these reimbursed losses account for the majority of the tax benefits, the emphasis is on those acquisitions structured during the period of time when assistance payments were excluded from income and a corresponding loss deduction was taken for tax purposes.

ENACTMENT OF FIRREA

IRC section 597 was amended by the Financial Institutions Reform, Recovery, and Enforcement Act of 1989 (FIRREA) to rectify the above situation and eliminate this preferential treatment for subsequent acquisitions of troubled thrifts. This act was signed by the President on August 9, 1989, and is part of Public Law No. 101-73.

The purpose of FIRREA was to restore the public's confidence in the savings and loan industry. The Act grew out of the massive financial crisis in the thrift industry caused by a regional economic collapse, fraud, and insider abuse that ultimately cost the taxpayers hundreds of millions of dollars.

The Act abolished the Federal Home Loan Bank Board (FHLBB) and created the Office of Thrift Supervision (OTS) which is part of the Department of the Treasury. OTS assumed the role of thrift regulator, and is responsible for the examination and supervision of all savings institutions. FIRREA also abolished the Federal Savings and Loan Insurance Corporation (FSLIC) and gave the Federal Deposit Insurance Corporation (FDIC) the duty of insuring the deposits of savings associations as well as banks. The insurance funds are kept separate with thrift funds in the Savings Association Insurance Fund (SAIF) and the bank funds in the Bank Insurance Fund (BIF). Both SAIF and BIF are administered by the FDIC.

FIRREA also established the Resolution Trust Corporation (RTC), whose purpose was to resolve failed thrifts. The RTC went out of existence on December 31, 1995. IRC section 501(b)(11)(B)(i) of FIRREA, which added new IRC section 21A to the Federal Home Loan Bank Act (12 U.S.C. section 1421, et seq.), provided that one of the RTC's responsibilities was to:

> Review and analyze all insolvent institution cases resolved by the Federal Savings and Loan Insurance Corporation between January 1, 1988, and the date of enactment of the Financial Institutions Reform, Recovery, and Enforcement Act of 1989, and actively review all means by which it can reduce costs under existing Federal Savings and Loan Insurance Corporation agreements relating to such cases, including restructuring such agreements * * *

Taxpayers who acquired a thrift institution may have renegotiated the original purchase agreements with the RTC or FDIC.

This chapter does not deal directly with those cases in which the Resolution Trust Corporation or the Federal Deposit Insurance Corporation has taken over the institution and continues to *operate* the business under their control. However, these types of cases are discussed in the next chapter to provide a better overall understanding of the issue.

S&L's ACQUIRED PRIOR TO FIRREA

Prior to the *revision* of IRC section 597 by FIRREA, all money or property contributed by the Federal Savings and Loan Insurance Corporation under the FSLIC's financial assistance program was generally *excluded* from the institution's income. In addition, the receipt of this assistance did not require a reduction in the basis of the thrift's assets. Approximately 100 thrift institutions were acquired during the years 1988 and 1989 which involved federal assistance prior to the revisions to IRC section 597.

The Tax Reform Act of 1986 had scheduled for repeal old IRC section 597 along with the special treatment for FSLIC payments for amounts received after December 31, 1988, unless these payments were made pursuant to an acquisition or merger occurring before that date. The Technical and Miscellaneous Revenue Act of 1988, also known as TAMRA, initially extended these provisions through December 31, 1989, with certain modifications and reductions in tax attributes. However, the enactment of FIRREA subsequently changed IRC section 597 for those amounts received or accrued on or after May 10, 1989.

Specifically, the new law provided that financial assistance from federal insurers to troubled financial institutions generally is taxable income to the institutions. The changes to the Code effectively eliminated the generous tax break that initially lured other banks and investors into buying sick thrifts from the Government prior to 1989.

ANALYSIS OF THE ISSUE

The major tax issue involves pre-FIRREA assisted transactions. Specifically, it involves those acquisitions of troubled institutions which were entered into *prior* to the changes in the law. During this period of time, the law permitted the acquiring corporation to *exclude* from income the payments received from the Government to cover losses or expenses on the sale or disposition of covered assets. The problem is that the bank then claims a deduction for the losses or expenses asso ciated with the sale of the assets, even though fully reimbursed.

This practice, commonly called *double dipping,* also gave the bank an incentive to sell the thrift's assets at the lowest price. The lower the price, the larger the tax deduction. Keep in mind that the entire amount of the loss is reimbursed by the Government, so the acquiring entity simply received a larger tax benefit.

For example, if the acquired thrift sells a covered asset for $70 which was originally carried on the books at $100, the Government would reimburse the acquiring institution for the total amount of the loss, or in this case $30. The thrift then deducted that $30 from its taxable income while receiving a tax free reimbursement of the loss from the Government.

The March 1991 Report on Tax Issues Relating to the 1988/89 Federal Savings and Loan Insurance Corporation Assisted Transactions concluded that "assisted institutions should not be allowed to deduct losses and expenses that are reimbursed by the FDIC."

On January 20, 1992, the Office of Chief Counsel issued Notice N(35)000-98 which stated that they will consider litigating the deductibility of covered asset losses in appropriate cases. More recently, as part of the Omnibus Budget Reconciliation Act of 1993, Congress provided that taxpayers could not obtain tax deductions under IRC sections 165, 166, 585, or 593 for losses reimbursed by tax exempt assistance. The provision is effective for tax years ending on or after March 4, 1991. With respect to losses or reimbursements that occurred prior to March 4, 1991, contact the ISP (S&L) Industry Specialist.

YEARS ENDING ON OR AFTER MARCH 4, 1991

IRC section 13224 of the Omnibus Budget Reconciliation Act of 1993 (Pub. L. No. 103-66) provides a legislative solution to the FSLIC double dip issue for tax years ending on or after March 4, 1991. FSLIC Assistance with respect to any loss of principal, capital, or similar amount upon the disposition of any asset shall be taken into account as compensation for such loss for purposes of IRC section 165. See Act section 13224(a)(1).

Any FSLIC Assistance with respect to any debt shall be taken into account for purposes of IRC sections 166, 585, or 593 in determining whether such debt is worthless or the extent to which such debt is worthless and in determining the amount of any addition to a reserve for bad debts arising from the worthlessness or partial worthlessness of such debts. See Act section 13224(a)(2).

As a result of this new legislation, agents should carefully examine any losses or bad debts being claimed in years ending after March 4, 1991, which were the subject of FSLIC assistance.

EXAMINATION TECHNIQUES

1. Prior to devoting any significant audit time to this issue, make sure that the position in this guide is current. At a minimum, contact the S&L Industry Specialist for an update on how the issue should be handled and find out what your options are as an examiner in the field.

2. Transactions involving these types of acquisitions are extremely complex and usually involve agreements of several hundred pages. If your institution is involved in the acquisition of a thrift institution, ask them to provide any letter rulings or other agreements with the IRS concerning the transaction. This will allow you to determine exactly what the primary provisions and stipulations of the acquisition are before you begin to read the multitude of pages in the agreement.

3. There is a considerable emphasis to renegotiate agreements issued by the FSLIC prior to 1989, specifically, those agreements in which the acquiring institution received an overly generous tax break. In the event that your taxpayer was involved in a pre-1989 acquisition, request any renegotiated agreement or closing agreements signed by the taxpayer.

4. Review the schedule M-1 adjustments for any book to tax differences in this area. Normally the taxpayer will handle the acquisition differently for book purposes and a review of the accounts and computations which make up the book numbers may give you a better understanding of the

transaction and lead you to other potential areas.

5. Keep in mind that even though this issue primarily affects earlier year acquisitions, restrictions in the acquisition agreement may limit the use of the losses on the disposition of the assets to future years. Therefore, the issue can also come up when examining a bank with an NOL carryforward.

POST FIRREA FEDERAL ASSISTANCE PAYMENTS

Thrift and bank acquisitions which occur after May 9, 1989, fall under IRC section 597 as amended by FIRREA. In these cases, assistance payments paid to troubled financial institutions generally are taxable income to the institution.

The final regulations under IRC section 597 were published in the Internal Revenue Bulletin (1996-6 IRB 4 (February 5, 1996)) and outline the tax treatment of post-FIRREA Federal assis tance. The following is a summary of the major provisions of the regulations:

1. Federal Financial Assistance (FFA) is ordinary income.
2. The financial institution receiving assistance for its losses must recognize income. The income generally should match the institution's losses less any acquisition premium paid by the acquirer. Provisions permit the institution to defer recognition of FFA income to the extent that the use of current expenses and NOLs have not completely exhausted shareholders' equity.
3. The IRS will not collect tax due to Federal assistance if a government agency would bear the burden of tax.
4. All tax attributes of the failed institution are eliminated.
5. The Agency making the assistance payments can not use IRC section 7507 except in direct pay out situations.
6. The final regulations allow a retroactive election to deconsolidate upon computation of a "toll charge." We don't expect an actual "toll charge" to be paid unless there is a negative capital account for the subsididiary. The potential therefore exists that some audit adjustments could be nullified by this election.

The Service issued Notice 89-102, 1989-2 C.B. 436, on September 7, 1989, which provides preliminary guidance when dealing with taxable acquisitions of troubled financial institutions and which involve the receipt of assistance payments. This notice covers post FIRREA acquisitions prior to the effective date of the proposed IRC section 597. It does not deal with FSLIC assisted "tax-free" reimbursements.

Post FIRREA acquisitions by banking institutions should not involve the covered asset loss issue discussed earlier in this chapter. However, these acquisitions could involve audit issues in other areas, such as claims for refund, tentative allowances, consolidated return restrictions, *etc.*

CHAPTER 12—FAILED THRIFT INSTITUTIONS OPERATED BY THE RTC

INTRODUCTION

Savings and loan institutions which failed between May 10, 1989, and December 31, 1995, were placed under the control of the Resolution Trust Corporation (RTC) until an acquirer could be found or the deposits could be transferred to another institution. The RTC went out of existence on December 31, 1995, and institutions still under RTC control on that date were transferred to a special unit of the Federal Deposit Insurance Corporation (FDIC) in Dallas, Texas.

The examination of a failed savings and loan (thrift) under the control of the RTC provided an unusual dilemma for the IRS in light of the Congressionally funded clean-up effort. Questions arose as to whether to pursue audits or collection of taxes if the amounts would ultimately be paid by the U.S. Treasury.

After more than 2 years of intense study and negotiation, the Internal Revenue Service and Resolution Trust Corporation Inter-Agency Agreement was signed on December 10, 1992. This Agreement was entered into in order to facilitate the disposition of cases involving failed thrifts under the control of the RTC in an orderly and cost efficient manner. Without this Agreement, both Agencies were destined to spend substantial resources challenging and defending tax issues which would only produce a circular flow of cash from one Treasury pocket (RTC through increased Treasury funding) to another Treasury pocket (IRS). A summary of the major provisions of the Agreement and examination processing procedures follows.

For those institutions previously under RTC control, the FDIC has ratified the Inter-Agency Agreement. As a result, the provisions of the agreement continue to apply to those former RTC cases. The Agreement does not, however, apply to institutions which were always under FDIC control. To avoid confusion and make it clear that the special procedures discussed in this chapter apply only to institutions previously under RTC control, these cases will continue to be referred to as RTC cases even though the RTC no longer exists.

WHO IS COVERED BY THE AGREEMENT

Not all failed financial institutions are covered by the Agreement. Covered institutions, (referred to in the Agreement as thrifts), include any federal or state chartered savings institution for which the RTC was appointed conservator or receiver, regardless of whether or not the institution meets the requirements of IRC section 7701(A)(19).

The Agreement does not cover commercial banks or institutions always under the control of the FDIC

This is an important distinction since savings institutions which failed in 1988 or early 1989 (often called '88 deal cases) were placed under the control of the Federal Savings & Loan Insurance Corporation (FSLIC). When FSLIC was abolished by FIRREA in 1989, these institutions were transferred to the control of the FDIC. While it may appear on the surface that these cases also involve Treasury funds, *the situation is not the same and they are not covered by this Agreement* since they are not under the control of the RTC. The Bank Insurance Fund (BIF) which insures commercial banks is funded by the industry, not by Treasury.

In examinations involving a parent corporation not controlled by the RTC, the Inter-Agency Agreement does not apply, and it is business as usual although the RTC-controlled subsidiary may be protected by the noncollection provision of the Inter-Agency Agreement.

Please refer to Exhibit 12-1, a flow chart, to assist you in determining whether the IRS/RTC Inter-Agency Agreement applies to your case.

A video user guide entitled "Failed S&L's" (Document 9073 (3-93)) was mailed to each District and outlines the procedures to be followed by examination personnel in the processing of these cases.

FAILED THRIFT RECEIVERSHIPS

It may be helpful at this point to briefly explain the typical life cycle of a failed thrift. In dealing with an insolvent savings and loan, the RTC typically used two receiverships. When a savings and loan institution was determined to be insolvent (or otherwise in jeopardy due to unsafe and unsound business practices by prior management or liquidity problems encountered by the thrift) the RTC was appointed its receiver. This first receivership is often referred to as a pass-through receivership because substantially all the deposits and assets are transferred to an interim or "bridge" savings and loan under the RTC's control in conservatorship.

The RTC conservatorship continued to operate the historic business of the old savings and loan by accepting deposits and making or purchasing loans. To the public there may have been little indication that the institution was under RTC control. If the institution was originally known as ABC Savings and Loan, it may now be known as ABC Federal Savings and Loan. For tax purposes, we treat the bridge institution and the original institution as the same taxpayer. The tax year should not end and the EIN should remain the same. It is, however, important to use both names when preparing statute extensions, closing agreements, or audit reports. The bridge institution will remain in operation for as long as necessary to find an acquirer or, in rare instances, to fully liquidate the institution. This can span several tax years.

At the time of the second receivership, the RTC generally stops the operation of the bridge institution. In many instances, the second receiver transfers substantially all the deposits and assets to an acquirer. In some cases a substantial amount of assets (usually "bad" assets) may remain in the receivership for ultimate liquidation. The RTC often referred to this receivership as a liquidating receivership or final receivership.

The RTC may contribute federal financial assistance to the original insolvent institution, the bridge institution or the acquirer. The tax consequences of this assistance are governed by IRC section 597, Notice 89-102 (1989-2 C.B. 436) and final regulations under IRC section 597 (T.D. 8641, 1996-6 I.R.B. 4 (February 5, 1996)).

RTC CERTIFICATION

Once you have determined that the RTC controlled your thrift, request the required written certification from the FDIC. Previously, this certification was provided by the RTC. FDIC has delegated signature authority for these certifications to several people. The FDIC names you will see most often are Jonnie Wells, David Jones, Richard Cywinski, Sharon Kelley, and Sharon Shroder. If you see other names, contact your local FDIC office and obtain a copy of the delegation order authorizing that person to sign. This written certification provides information specific to the thrift and will state that:

1. The assets of such thrift are insufficient to satisfy the claims of the thrift's depositors;
2. If the IRS were to collect taxes before all depositors were paid in full, additional Treasury funds would be used to satisfy depositor claims;
3. The Federal Income Tax Liability will not be borne by the thrift on account of a tax sharing agreement.

The FDIC is required to provide the certification for each thrift that meets the certification criteria, they cannot selectively certify. The certification will follow one of two formats:

1. Federal Deposit Insurance Corporation

FDIC AS SUCCESSOR RECEIVER TO RESOLUTION TRUST CORPORATION CERTIFICATION OF TREASURY FUNDS USAGE

This certification, also known as FDIC 4360/88, indicates that the RTC controlled a thrift that was either a stand-alone corporation or was the parent of a consolidated group. These are institutions to which all the provisions of the Agreement apply since these are the situations which would produce a circular flow of cash from one Treasury pocket to another.

2. Federal Deposit Insurance Corporation

FDIC AS SUCCESSOR RECEIVER TO RESOLUTION TRUST CORPORATION NON-COLLECTION STATEMENT

This certification, also known as FDIC 4360/89, indicates that the RTC controlled a thrift which was itself a part of a consolidated group for which the RTC did not control the parent. For these institutions only the special non-collection provisions of the Agreement apply. Those provisions only protect the RTC from collection of the tax liability. Collection of the liability from the non-controlled parent of the group will occur under normal procedures.

If the certification criteria cannot be met, the Agreement does not apply and the case will be processed in the normal manner. Although we know of no case to date for which the certification cannot be made, it is possible that in the future, as the new regulatory capital requirements take effect, marginally solvent institutions will be placed in receivership. In those cases, federal taxes may be assessed and collected without affecting the payment of depositors. If you believe you have such a case, immediately contact either the Industry Specialist for Savings and Loans in Los Angeles, or the Industry Counsel for Savings and Loans in Denver.

TAXES COVERED BY THE AGREEMENT

The Agreement covers federal income tax matters. The essence of the Agreement is that the Service will continue to assess all taxes, interest, and penalties against insolvent institutions in RTC receiverships.

The "assess but not collect" rule does not apply to:

1. Employment or trust fund taxes
2. Refunds pursuant to IRC section 6402(i)
3. Certain separate income tax liabilities of a subsidiary of an insolvent institution
4. Cases in which the certification of the use of Treasury funds is erroneous
5. Liabilities arising from tax-sharing agreements.

CASE PROCESSING

Once you have determined that the Agreement applies in its entirety (that is, the RTC controlled thrift is either a stand alone entity or the parent of a group) to your case, special handling rules apply. To avoid transferring money between Treasury pockets, the IRS has agreed not to *collect* income tax from the RTC on behalf of failed thrifts if Treasury funds are needed to pay depositors. In exchange for our agreement not to collect income taxes, the RTC has agreed not to challenge the amount of tax determined by the IRS. This means the RTC will not be exercising their normal appeal rights.

EXAMINATION CONSIDERATIONS

In determining whether to conduct an examination, or how involved the examination should be, consideration should be given to the spirit of the Inter-Agency Agreement which is to reduce the burden and administrative cost to both the IRS and the RTC while still determining the proper tax. It was decided, nonetheless, that resources should continue to be used for limited audits to ensure that an insolvent institution's tax liabilities are properly determined and assessed. These assessments can reduce potential refunds or eliminate the carry-forward of beneficial tax attributes. Moreover, these assessments will permit an accounting of foregone tax revenue that can be used by the Treasury Department to determine the aggregate cost of federal assistance to insolvent financial institutions. Resource expenditures should be carefully weighed both in light of this Agreement and in light of the emphasis the Service is placing upon collectibility in general.

REPORT PREPARATION

Upon completion of the examination, prepare a Revenue Agent Report (RAR) and a closing agreement. After coordinating the proposed closing agreement with Industry Counsel in Denver, solicit agreement from the RTC. Meritorious issues should be included on the RAR. Include all years examined in the report, particularly where there are adjustments which would offset other adjustments or would eliminate net operating losses or claims already filed. Include both the deficiency years and the overassessment years. If the net result is an overassessment, RTC will waive its right to the refund. If the net result is a deficiency, IRS will not *collect* this amount under the Agreement.

In CEP cases, prepare Forms 4549-A, 870, and a closing agreement. For non-CEP cases, prepare Form 4549 and a closing agreement. Closing agreement examples for both consolidated and non-consolidated returns are available. Authority to sign these closing agreements is covered by Delegation Order 245.

JOINT COMMITTEE CONSIDERATIONS

The normal Joint Committee jurisdictional rules (IRC section 6405) apply to tax returns for insolvent thrifts under RTC control. Therefore, if refunds or tentative allowances have already been paid in excess of the $1 million threshold, a report to the Joint Committee on Taxation must be prepared. The closing agreement should not be countersigned on behalf of the IRS until Joint Committee approval has been received. Since under the agreement the IRS will no longer be paying refunds and the RTC will no longer be filing claims for refunds or tentative allowances for cases governed by the Agreement, it is anticipated that Joint Committee volume will decrease significantly.

CASE CLOSING

Attach a copy of Form 3198 "Special Handling Notice" to the case file. Check the "other" box and insert the following instructions:

> This taxpayer is covered by the Internal Revenue service and Resolution Trust Corporation Inter-Agency Agreement. Please assess the tax, additions to tax, penalties, and interest. In processing the assessment input TC 530, closing code 15.

This closing code will alert other Service personnel that Collection efforts beyond the initial notice and filing of the proofs of claim are not warranted. In addition, this code causes notices to be frozen and separates these cases in the Accounts Receivable Dollar Inventory (ARDI). It provides information on the tax costs of the savings and loan bailout.

UNAGREED CASES

The Agreement curtails litigation activity (with some limited exceptions concerning appellate litigation) and provides that all tax disputes be resolved administratively between the IRS and the RTC at whatever stage the case may be when the S&L comes under RTC control. This means that the RTC will agree to IRS assessments without litigation or challenge. Cases in Examination will be settled at the Examination level and cases docketed in Tax Court will be settled without trial by District Counsel. The expeditious resolution of issues at the lowest possible level conserves resources and promotes consistency of position and result.

For those situations in which the RTC does not agree with the revenue agent's determination of tax, interest, penalties, and additions to tax, normal appeal procedures will not apply. Do not issue either a 30-day letter or a statutory notice of deficiency. Contact the S&L ISP Industry Specialist or Industry Counsel to review your adjustments. If an agreement cannot be reached, the RTC National Office representative will be afforded an opportunity to either instruct their field personnel to agree with the proposed adjustments or present the unagreed issues to the IRS National Office for a final determination. This procedure will function primarily to resolve questions of tax policy and to ensure consistent treatment of tax issues. The National Office should sustain the agent's reasonable adjustments.

REFUNDS

For those cases to which the entire Agreement applies, the IRS will no longer make any payments to an insolvent thrift or to the RTC as a result of income tax claims for refund, tentative allowances, or refund suits. This prohibition on payment of refunds includes income tax returns filed which show an overpayment of estimated taxes and cases already approved by the Joint Committee where the refund has not yet been issued. Before any payment is authorized to such an insolvent thrift or the RTC, please contact the S&L ISP Industry Specialist, or Industry Counsel. For any claims which have not yet been paid by IRS, RTC will agree in writing to withdraw the claim. The RTC will not file or pursue any further income tax related refund claims for thrifts under its jurisdiction except as specifically provided in the separate IRS/RTC 6402(i) agreement dated September 27, 1991.

SERVICE CENTER OVERVIEW

Special return screening procedures are in place to identify returns to which the Agreement may apply. A classification specialist in each Service Center reviews these returns to determine whether the Agreement applies and whether additional information is necessary to process the return. If you have questions on how these returns are processed at the Service Center, contact the Program Analyst, Coordinated Examination Program, in the National Office.

CHAPTER 13—ACQUISITION COSTS AND OTHER CAPITAL EXPENSES

INTRODUCTION

If you are examining a bank that merged with another bank, acquired a bank, or was acquired by another entity, consider the appropriate tax treatment of the expenses which were incurred. Generally, merger and acquisition expenditures should be capitalized, rather than deducted currently. They usually are not amortizable. The applicable law for this treatment is discussed later in this chapter.

In recent years there have been numerous mergers and acquisitions of large national banks as well as smaller local banks. Banks may decide to merge to reduce operating expenses through elimination of extra personnel and branches, to expand geographically, cheaply, and quickly, or to discourage an acquisition by an undesirable bank.

Acquisitions of banks are also common. A bank may seek a buyer, such as when the owners of a closely held bank wish to retire and receive cash for their investments. Bank acquisitions are "unfriendly" or "hostile" when they are opposed by the target bank. Publicly held banks, whose stocks are undervalued in relationship the value of their assets, are potential takeover targets. Also, troubled institutions may be taken over by the Federal Deposit Insurance Corporation or the Resolution Trust Corporation. These organizations may then sell the assets to healthy financial institutions.

There are various types of expenses that a bank can incur when it undergoes a change in structure. A number of these expenses are discussed below:

1. *Legal Expenses*—A substantial amount is paid to attorneys for drafting agreements, negotiating prices, resolving Community Reinvestment Act protests, fighting lawsuits, *etc.* Normally the bank will hire a particular law firm which specializes in mergers and acquisitions. Ask the taxpayer which firm they used and review those specific invoices. Allocation of the bank's in-house attorneys' salaries should also be considered.

2. *Investment Banker Expenses*—Investment bankers perform several services in relation to merger and acquisition activities. They often render a fairness opinion as to whether the consideration offered is reasonable. They also may market a company that is interested in being purchased.

3. *Appraisal Costs*—Accountants and engineers may be hired to value certain tangible and intangible assets. As discussed in an earlier chapter, a bank may pay a premium for an existing deposit base. There are companies that specialize in the valuation of these core deposits. In a tax free stock merger, appraisers may still be hired to value assets for book purposes.

4. *Regulatory Fees*—Banks are required to receive regulatory approval before a merger or acquisition can be finalized. The regulatory agencies may charge a fee for the work that they do in processing and approving the merger or acquisition. For example, the fee charged by the Financial Institutions Bureau in Michigan as of June 1992 was $10,000. Fees are also paid to the Security and Exchange Commission.

5. *Accounting Fees*—Accountants may be hired to perform various functions. They may provide tax advice to the different parties. An analysis of the banks' different computer and accounting systems may be made in order to efficiently combine them. Also, they may do studies to determine the value of assets. The banks may also incur in-house costs for this type of work, which may be subject to capitalization.

6. *Payment for Due Diligence Study*—The Board of Directors will often hire an accounting or investment firm to study all aspects of the proposed transaction. They will render an opinion as to whether the merger or acquisition is in the best interests of the company. This protects the directors from shareholders who may not be pleased with the change.

7. *Shareholder Costs*—The bank is required to receive shareholder approval for any changes in business structure. The bank will incur costs for notices in newspapers, printing of prospec-

tuses, mailings to shareholders, *etc.*

8. *Salaries and Wages*—As mentioned above, bank employees, such as attorneys and accountants may spend considerable time working on the merger or acquisition. The key officers of the bank will also be involved in negotiations, decision making, traveling, *etc.* A portion of their salaries should also be considered for capitalization.

There are a number of issues related to merger and acquisition activity. Some of them, such as core deposits, recapture of bad debt reserves, and FSLIC assistance payments are discussed elsewhere in this guide. Other merger and acquisition issues such as the type of reorganization, the gain/loss that should be recognized, recapture provisions, *etc.* are complex and are beyond the scope of this guide. In this chapter, we will limit our discussion to the examination techniques and tax treatment for acquisition and merger expenses. Several other types of capital expenditures by financial institutions will also be discussed.

EXAMINATION TECHNIQUES

1. First review the tax return. Since many of these expenses are capitalized for book purposes, the taxpayer may have made an M-1 adjustment to expense them for tax purposes. Sometimes the taxpayer will attach a disclosure statement to the tax return to disclose that merger or acquisition costs were expensed. Also, the detail schedule for "other deductions" may include these expenses as a separate line item.

2. Read the portion of the bank's annual report that discusses past, present, and pending business combinations. It will provide general information as to your bank's merger and acquisition activity.

3. The corporate minute book should be reviewed to obtain more detailed information. It may disclose activity that was considered, but never consummated. The minute book may also discuss some of the costs associated with mergers and acquisitions.

4. Once you have determined that a bank incurred expenses related to merger or acquisition activity, an IDR should be issued requesting specific cost information. A sample IDR is included (See Exhibit 13-1.) which shows the type of information that can be requested. Most banks keep detailed records of their costs because they need to report this information to their regulatory authorities. Also, they use the information for internal planning purposes. However, the tax department often is not aware that merger and acquisition cost information is readily available. They may need to check with the legal department to find out what records were maintained.

5. Request a copy of the Notification and Report Form for Certain Mergers and Acquisitions that the bank files under the Hart-Scott-Rodino Antitrust Improvement Act of 1976. This form is provided to the Federal Trade Commission and the Antitrust Division of the Department of Justice to allow them to consider the anti-competitive effects of the proposed merger or acquisition.

6. If the bank has not kept detailed records, you may need to review the

specific transactions which were recorded in accounts titled "Legal Expenses," "Accounting Fees," "Consulting Fees," *etc.* A computer audit specialist can perform stratifications and account selections to assist you in selecting a sample.

7. Interview employees that were involved with the mergers or acquisitions to determine what types of expenses were incurred, especially if inhouse legal or other work was performed. An allocation can be made for the salaries of bank employees who assisted in the merger or acquisition.

LAW AND DISCUSSION

The tax treatment of merger and acquisition expenses may vary depending on whether the expenses are paid to defend against a takeover attempt, whether the proposed merger or acquisition is abandoned, or whether the institution you are examining is the acquiring or the target bank. Each of these items is discussed below.

General Information

The most important court opinion in this area is *Indopco, Inc. v. Commissioner*, 503 U.S. 79 (1992), *aff'g National Starch and Chemical Corp. v. Commissioner*, 918 F.2d 426 (3d Cir. 1990) [CCH Dec. 45,851], *aff'g* 93 T.C. 67 (1989) [90-2 USTC ¶50,571]. The Supreme Court held that the investment banking fees and expenses incurred during a friendly takeover were not deductible under IRC section 162. The Court stated in *Indopco* at p. 1040:

> Petitioner's expenses do not qualify for deduction under IRC section 162(a). Deductions are exceptions to the norm of capitalization and are allowed only if there is clear provision for them in the Code and the taxpayer has met the burden of showing a right to the deduction. *Commissioner v. Lincoln Savings & Loan Assn.*, 403 U.S. 345, 354, holds simply that the creation of a separate and distinct asset may be a sufficient condition for classification as a capital expenditure, not that it is a prerequisite to such classification. Nor does *Lincoln Savings* prohibit reliance on future benefit as means of distinguishing an ordinary business expense from a capital expenditure. Although the presence of an incidental future benefit may not warrant capitalization, a taxpayer's realization of benefits beyond the year in which the expenditure is incurred is important in determining whether the appropriate tax treatment is immediate deduction or capitalization. The record in the instant case amply supports the lower courts' findings that the transaction produced significant benefits to petitioner extending beyond the tax year in question.

This case was significant because the Supreme Court said that the creation or enhancement of a separate asset was not a necessary condition for capitalization. Instead, the creation of a long term benefit was sufficient to require the expenses to be capitalized. Some of the benefits that resulted from this merger were (1) additional technological resources, (2) synergy, (3) a reduction in shareholder expenses, and (4) administrative advantages from the reduction in shares. The court determined that the taxpayer, National Starch, believed that the shift in ownership was in its best interest and would benefit the company for many future years.

IRC section 197 was added by the Revenue Reconciliation Act of 1993. The new law provides for the amortization of certain purchased intangible assets. However, there are a number of intangible assets which are specifically excluded from the application of IRC section 197. IRC section 197(e)(8) provides that any fees for professional services or other transaction costs with respect to transactions in which gain or loss is not recognized under IRC sections 351-368 cannot be amortized under IRC section 197. Therefore, most merger and acquisition costs are specifically excluded.

The Conference Committee's report indicates that it was not Congress' intent to overturn *Indopco* by enacting IRC section 197. Since these transaction costs are specifically excluded from IRC section 197, they should be treated as they were prior to the section's enactment. Therefore, continue to look to *Indopco* to determine the nature of these expenditures. If merger or acquisition costs create a long term benefit, they should be capitalized and not amortized.

Revenue Ruling 73-580, 1973-2 C.B. 86, states "compensation paid for services performed by employees relating to the acquisition of other corporations is not distinguishable from fees paid for similar services performed by outsiders." Thus, a corporation must capitalize the portion of the compensation paid to its employees that is reasonably attributable to services performed in connection with corporate mergers and acquisitions.

Takeover Attempts

Whether a proposed corporate takeover is friendly or hostile is not determinative of the proper tax treatment with respect to professional fees. *A.E. Staley Mfg. Co. v. Commissioner,* 105 T.C. 166 (1995) [CCH Dec. 50,882]. *Butsee United States v. Federated Department Stores,* 171 Bankr. 603 (S.D. Ohio 1994), *appeal pending* (6th Cir. No. 94-4676). The focus should be on whether the target corporation obtained a long-term benefit as a result of making the expenditures. The taxpayer must demonstrate that it did not obtain a long-term benefit. Expenditures for professional fees incurred in a takeover attempt, labeled hostile or friendly, may be classified as either currently deductible under IRC section 162 or capitalizable under IRC section 263, depending on the specific facts and circumstances of each case.

Costs incurred by the target company in repurchasing its stock from the corporate raider should also be considered. Assume that a target company makes a lump sum payment to the corporate raider for reimbursement of the raider's fees and for expenses which were incurred as a result of the unsuccessful takeover attempt. Both of these expenses are treated as nondeductible capital expenditures since they relate to the repurchase of stock where the repurchase was not essential to the corporation's continued existence.

In summary, some of the expenses incurred in defending a takeover may be deductible. The primary factor in determining deductibility is whether the expenditure resulted in a long term benefit. If so, the expense should be capitalized. If not, the cost can be expensed. For a more detailed discussion of loan fees in connection with a redemption of stock, see the Mergers & Acquisitions ISP Coordinated Position Paper on this issue. [The "Loan Commitment Fee In a Stock Redemption" paper was originally issued as a LBO Industry Coordinated Issue Paper; however, the LBO ISP has been redesignated as the Mergers & Acquisitions ISP.]

Abandoned Mergers

Merger and acquisition costs, otherwise capitalizable, are generally deductible losses under IRC section 165 when the transaction is abandoned. See Rev. Rul. 73-580, 1973-2 C.B. 86. However, if an expense is incurred for an item used subsequently, the costs would generally not be deductible. Each cost should be analyzed to determine whether it created a long term benefit. For example, a target company may reject several takeover bids prior to accepting a final offer. If the taxpayer can establish through careful documentation that particular expenses relate only to the abandoned proposals, those expenses may be deductible. However, any expenses that relate to both the abandoned and the adopted merger should be capitalized. For example, valuations of stock or appraisals of property could be used to evaluate more than one offer.

There have been several court cases and revenue rulings which discuss the deductibility of expenses related to abandoned projects. In *Sibley, Lindsay & Curr Co. v. Commissioner*, 15 T.C. 106 (1950) [CCH Dec. 17,788], the court held that the taxpayer was entitled to deduct as ordinary and necessary expenses the costs attributable to an abandoned merger. The merger was one of three proposals that were *not* alternatives and the taxpayer could have accepted any or all of them. It cited *Doernbecher Manufacturing Co. v. Commissioner*, 30 BTA 973 (1934) [CCH Dec. 8606], which determined that the amount paid by the taxpayer as its share of expenses of investigating the possibilities of forming a merger were deductible in the year in which the plan to form the merger was abandoned. *Doernbecher* was also mentioned in Rev. Rul. 67-125, 1967-1 C.B. 31. This revenue ruling discusses the treatment of legal expenses for securing advice on the tax consequences prior to the consummation of a merger, stock split, and partial redemption. The ruling states that these expenditures are capital in nature, but could be deducted in the year of abandonment if the proposed redemption of stock is subsequently abandoned.

Rev. Rul. 73-580, which was discussed above, held that amounts paid to employees with respect to abandoned plans for mergers or acquisitions are deductible as losses under IRC section 165(a) in the year of the abandonment.

However, if the proposed transactions are alternatives, only one of which can be accepted, no abandonment loss is proper unless the entire transaction is abandoned. *See Staley*, 105 T.C. at 200.

Target vs. Acquiring Company

The general rule that merger and acquisition expenses are nondeductible and capital may be clearer for the acquiring company than for the target company. It is readily apparent that the acquiring company would not incur these expenses unless it anticipated that they would benefit the company for a period of time. However, a target company may incur expenses in defending a hostile takeover or in evaluating friendly take-over proposals which were later abandoned. The general theory from *Indopco* should be applied, namely that costs should be capitalized if they create a future benefit.

OTHER CAPITAL EXPENDITURES

There are a number of other situations in which a bank incurs expenses that may be subject to capitalization. The general philosophy as to whether a separate asset or a future benefit is present should be considered to determine whether an expenditure should be capitalized or expensed. Some of the areas where potential issues exist are discussed below:

Branch Costs

When a bank opens new branch offices, it incurs numerous expenses such as attorney fees, studies of various site locations, application fees to obtain regulatory approval, *etc.* The bank may form a new corporate subsidiary for the new branches. Regulatory approval generally must be obtained prior to opening a new branch. This creates an intangible right the bank did not previously have. The general position of the Service has been that branch expansion costs are capitalized since a separate and distinct asset is created. The *Indopco* case discussed above provides additional support for the Government's position since the opening of a branch office would create a future benefit. However, the banking industry takes the position that these costs should be currently deductible under IRC section 162. The banks feel that they are merely extending their current business activity by opening new branches. The Fourth Circuit has allowed banks to deduct their expansion costs, while the Fifth Circuit and Eleventh Circuits have denied the deduction.[1] Some taxpayers have elected to amortize these costs over 60 months per IRC section 195 for Start-Up Expenditures.

Each cost should be independently analyzed to determine whether it creates a future benefit. If so, that expenditure should be capitalized, even though other business expansion costs may be currently deductible. See *Indopco, Inc. v. Commissioner,* 503 U.S. 79 (1992).

Credit Card Start-Up Costs

The theory behind whether or not a bank can deduct the costs it incurs for credit card start-up costs is very similar to whether or not new branch costs can be expensed. The taxpayers maintain that these costs are an extension of their current business.

However, the IRS can argue that some of the expenditures result in the creation of a future benefit or a separate asset. In general the courts have held that when payment was made to allow a bank to join a particular credit card system, it was capital in nature since it had value to the bank for its duration. However, expenses for credit reports, advertising, *etc.* were allowed as current deductions.[2]

Automatic Teller Machine Fees

Banks pay one time fees to join some of the automatic teller machine (ATM) systems. However, some ATM systems do not require any initial fee

---

[1] *North Carolina National Bank v. United States,* 78-2 U.S.T.C. ¶9661 (D. N.C. 1978) [684 F3d 285], *rev'd,* 651 F.2d 942 (4th Cir. 1981) [81-2 USTC ¶9501], *aff'd upon reh. en banc,* 684 F.2d 285 (4th Cir. 1982); *Central Texas S&L Association v. United States,* 84-1 U.S.T.C. ¶9471 (5th Cir. 1984) [731 F2d 1181]; *Ellis Banking Corp. v. Commissioner,* 688 F.2d 1376 (11th Cir. 1982) [82-2 USTC ¶9630], *cert denied,* 103 S. Ct. 3537.

[2] See the discussion of this issue in Charles W. Wheeler, JD and Jack B. Wilson, Jr., CPA, *The Bank Income Tax Return Manual-1992,* p. 5-89 to 5-90.

to be paid. NYCE, CIRRUS, and MAC are a few of the systems which do charge upfront fees. The bank acquires the future right to use the ATM system indefinitely. Therefore, this cost would be a capital expenditure.

Advertising

There was considerable discussion after the opinion in *Indopco* on whether advertising expenses created a future benefit that should be capitalized. The IRS issued Revenue Ruling 92-80, 1992-2 C.B. 57, to clarify its position. The ruling provides that the *Indopco* decision does not affect the treatment of advertising costs under IRC section 162(a). These costs are generally deductible under that section even though advertising may have some future effect on business activities, as in the case of institutional or goodwill advertising.* * * Only in the unusual circumstance where advertising is directed towards obtaining future benefits significantly beyond those traditionally associated with ordinary product advertising or with institutional or goodwill advertising, must the costs of that advertising be capitalized.

SUMMARY

Because of the proliferation of mergers and acquisitions in the last decade, it is very likely that the bank that you are examining may have been considered as a takeover target or may have considered acquiring another institution. If so, the bank would have incurred considerable expenses that should be capitalized.

Prior to the *Indopco* opinion, many taxpayers were expensing merger and acquisition related costs. Some continue to do so. Determine early in the examination whether the bank has any of these types of expenses. If so, each expenditure should be analyzed carefully to determine whether it should be capitalized.

Even if the bank did not have any merger or acquisition related expenses, you may need to evaluate whether other types of costs were improperly expensed. Consideration should be given to whether these expenditures contributed to the creation of a separate asset or a future benefit. If so, they should be capitalized.

Exhibit 13-1

[SAMPLE INFORMATION DOCUMENT REQUEST, Form 4564, Rev. 6/88. Not Reproduced.]

CHAPTER 14—LEVERAGED BUYOUT LOANS

INTRODUCTION

A leveraged buyout (LBO) involves the purchase of a company in which a substantial portion of the purchase price is paid by borrowed funds which are secured by the assets of the company. The debt is repaid from the future earnings of the company, sale of company assets, issuance of public stock, additional capital contributions, or any combination of the above.

Since the early 1980's, the stock market has seen an explosion of leveraged buyouts. Mergers and acquisitions became common in almost every industry. The banking industry participated in the leveraged buyout boom in that a significant portion of the financing for these transactions was provided by the banks. A change in the Federal Reserve regulations allowed investment bankers to arrange financing for the acquisition of stock in public companies.

As discovered within the last couple of years, a lot of the leveraged buy out loans made by financial institutions did *not* come without substantial risk. The collapse of several institutions can be directly related to the financing or participation in highly leveraged LBO loans along with so called "junk bonds." However, if successful, these LBO loans could be very lucrative to the banks in the form of higher interest rates, substantial fees paid up-front for participating in the loan, and possibly even a financial interest in the company itself.

INVESTMENT BANKERS

Investment bankers, in most cases, are the primary people involved in the leveraged buyout field. They are often referred to as LBO "specialists." Investment bankers find companies for sale, structure the deal, and negotiate with both the selling and buying groups. They also arrange debt financing and equity investments. After a buyout, the investment banker will continue to monitor the company in the event additional assistance is needed, such as a public offering of the stock. The vast majority of the LBO activity is conducted by big investment firms and companies specializing in this area.

EXAMINATION TECHNIQUES—NONCASH COMPENSATION

If your case involves a bank that was only a participant in the financing of an LBO loan, as opposed to being the investment banker, the issue is fairly simple. The Securities and Exchange Commission (SEC) requires that a bank disclose the extent of their LBO activity in their annual reports.

1. Review this report to determine the extent the bank is involved in this type of investment. If no formal annual report is prepared by the bank, this information can usually be found in the regulatory or SEC filings.
2. If you determine that the financial institution participated in LBO transactions, secure a complete list of the individual LBO loans from the taxpayer. These loans should tie into the amounts reflected in the annual report.
3. Specifically, inquire as to whether there were any "perks" given to the bank as an incentive to participate in the leveraged buyout.

   These perks, also known as "sweeteners," consist of stock warrants or other noncash consideration which allows the bank to earn *additional* profits based on the success of the company. Stock warrants are simply a *right* to purchase the stock of the company for a specified price for a certain period of time. The bank does not pay any money or give up any other consideration that may be due in exchange for these warrants. The warrants are an additional payment to the bank for providing the funding necessary for the LBO.
4. Also request a signed statement from someone with personal knowledge of these transactions to explain the extent of the

bank's involvement in these types of transactions. This is the easiest way to determine if any issues exist and whether the bank received any compensation in return for its participation.

5. A random check should also be made of selected loan files to verify the taxpayer's statement.

In most of our examinations, we have found that it was the bank's policy *not* to request this additional consideration. However, if warrants or other incentives were given to the bank and accepted without any restrictions or further requirements of the bank, these rights are considered to be *additional compensation*. The fair market value of the warrants is fully taxable to the bank as ordinary income at the point in time the warrants are issued as part of an investment unit under IRC section 1273.

The fair market value of the warrants which was previously included in income will become the basis for the warrants. If the warrants are exercised instead of sold, the basis in the warrants becomes part of the bank's basis in the stock.

The primary reason these warrants are offered to the lender is to give the bank a reason for wanting the company to be successful. If times became tough, the bank would be reluctant to foreclose on the property because the value of the company would be diminished. By receiving these warrants, the bank has received a partial ownership in the success of the company.

The most difficult part of this issue involves the *valuation* of the rights.

Treasury Reg. section 1.83-7(b)(3) provides the following insight in determining the value of an option:

Extract

Treas. Reg. section 1.83)7(b)(3)

* * * the fair market value of an option to buy includes the value of the right to benefit from any future increase in the value of the property subject to the option (relative to the option exercise price), without risking any capital. Therefore, the fair market value of an option is not merely the difference that may exist at a particular time between the option's exercise price and the value of the property subject to the option, but also includes the value of the option privilege for the remainder of the exercise period. * * *

This last sentence is very important because it allows a value to be placed on the *future* prospects of a company, *not* just the value of the company at the point in time the option was granted. The value of a warrant or other similar option cannot easily be determined and must be based on the facts and circumstances of your case. If an issue is found in this area, a specialist may be required to determine the fair market value and the amount of the adjustment.

EXAMINATION TECHNIQUES—FEES PAID TO THE BANK

Another issue in the leverage buyout area involves the *fees* paid to the bank, other than fees paid for the loan, to participate in the LBO transaction, or for other services rendered. These fees are all taxable when the cash is received by the bank. These amounts cannot be deferred for tax purposes, such as over the life of the loan, or any other method of deferral.

1. A sample LBO loan file should be reviewed to determine the amount of fees received by the bank. Verify that these amounts are properly reported on the tax return. Most banks will have a separate account for these types of fees, and therefore tracing the fees to the tax return should not be that difficult.
2. Request also that the bank provide its current *policy* as to how these amounts are reported for tax purposes.
3. Review the schedule M-1 adjustments for any differences in the timing of income or deduction for financial and tax purposes relating to LBO fees or expenses. All of these areas can lead to potential adjustments.

SUMMARY

Currently, there is an LBO specialist in the Industry Specialization Program. Several Coordinated Issue Papers have been proposed in the leveraged buyout area. The majority of the issues involve the tax implications to the LBO target entity. However, there are also issues involving investment banking activities. The ISP has a data base on LBO transactions. This data base can help to identify potential leads on your case.

If you are examining a large entity which is involved in investment banking services, the LBO coordinated issues should be reviewed. Since these issues involve only a limited number of banks, they are beyond the scope of this guide.

CHAPTER 15—AMORTIZATION

INTRODUCTION

Amortization is the method of allocating the cost of an intangible asset over its useful life. When a deduction for amortization is claimed, Part VI of Form 4562, Depreciation and Amortization, should be completed by the taxpayer. The amount deducted for amortization should be included as part of line 26 of the tax return, *other deductions.*

Amortization issues are usually seen in cases where an entire business or a group of assets is purchased. In these cases, a portion of the purchase price is normally allocated to an intangible asset. In the past, it was common for the taxpayer to allocate as much of the purchase price as possible to intangible assets which are amortizable for tax purposes. This reduced the remaining value allocated to goodwill or going concern value. The larger the allocation of the purchase price to an amortizable intangible, the bigger the deduction for tax purposes. Treas. Reg. section 1.167(a)-3 provides: "no deduction for depreciation is allowable with respect to goodwill." The historical position of the IRS has been that an amortization deduction was not allowed for amounts allocable to intangible assets such as work force in place and going concern value. However, recent changes in the law have significantly affected this issue.

LAW CHANGES

Congress passed the Revenue Reconciliation Act of 1993 which provides that the capitalized cost of specified intangible assets referred to as "IRC section 197 intangibles" are to be ratably amortized over a 15-year period. This provision of the law provides that the 15-year amortization period is applicable regardless of the actual useful life of the intangible property. The new law was intended to eliminate controversies between the Service and taxpayers over allocations of purchase price between amortizable intangibles and nonamortizable goodwill. It carries some loss deferral rules but taxes gains on early dispositions of IRC section 197 intangibles.

The enactment of this law will significantly affect how we examine the amortization and intangible areas for tax purposes. See discussion of the Intangibles Settlement Initiative in Chapter 5. Proposed Treas. Reg. section 1.197-2 was published in the Federal Register on January 16, 1997. *See also* Treas. Reg. section 1.197-1T.

AMORTIZATION ITEMS

Amortization is normally applicable to intangible assets. Some of the most common banking assets which are subject to the amortization provisions are as follows:

* 1. Core deposit intangibles

* 2. Covenant not to compete

* 3. Merger and acquisition costs

* 4. Loan origination costs—SFAS 91

* 5. *Originated* servicing rights

* 6. Credit card start-up costs

* 7. Entrance and exit fees for bank insurance funds

8. *Purchased* servicing rights

9. Organizational and business start-up costs

10. Work force in place.

* Items 1-7 are discussed in detail elsewhere in this guide. The remaining items are discussed below. Suggested examination techniques and potential issues are provided.

LAW

Internal Revenue Code section 167(a) states:

Extract

IRC section 167(a)

* * * There shall be allowed as a depreciation deduction a reasonable allowance for the exhaustion, wear and tear (including a reasonable allowance for obsolescence)—

(1) of property used in the trade or business, or

(2) of property held for the production of income.

Federal income tax Treas. Reg. section 1.167(a)-3 states in part:

Extract

Treas. Reg. section 1.167(a)-3

* * * If an intangible asset is known from experience or other factors to be of use in the business or in the production of income for only a limited period, the length of which can be estimated with reasonable accuracy, such an intangible asset may be the subject of a depreciation allowance. Examples are patents and copyrights. An intangible asset, the useful life of which is not limited, is not subject to * * * depreciation. * * *

GENERAL EXAMINATION TECHNIQUES

1. It is important to keep in mind that just because the taxpayer does not include an amortization amount on Form 4562, does *not* mean that an amortization deduction was not claimed by the taxpayer. It has been our experience that it is common for the taxpayer to include the amortization expense elsewhere on the return, even if it is not specifically listed on Form 4562. Since the amount deducted for amortization is included as part of line 26, other deductions, the amount can easily be combined with another account, netted against income, misla-

beled, or just included as part of miscellaneous expenses.

Therefore, the taxpayer should be specifically asked whether any amortization deductions were claimed on the return. If any exist, then request a complete list of the assets being amortized along with the worksheets computing the amount of the deduction taken on the return. All of these items should be reconciled and tied into the amount on the return. On one of our cases, the taxpayer acquired another bank with a core deposit. The amortization deduction was buried in a subsidiary bank which was not being examined. Obtaining a detailed listing of the assets being amortized for all entities in the consolidated return group from the taxpayer is helpful for identifying these issues.

2. The taxpayer is not required to include on its tax return a detailed listing of the items being amortized from prior years. For example, if the taxpayer were to acquire and amortize a Core Deposit in a year preceding the examination year, this fact would not be apparent from reviewing the tax return. The taxpayer is required to provide only the *amount* of the amortization deduction being claimed for assets acquired in prior years. A description of the property, the cost of the property, and the method of amortization is only required for intangible assets acquired during the current year. Therefore, always review prior year amortization deductions and request adequate documentation.

3. Review the annual report or SEC filings for any indication as to whether or not assets are being amortized. Usually, there is a section in the annual report dealing with income taxes and accounting policies which may mention intangible assets and give you clues as to potential areas to examine. This latter section may also discuss the method of amortization being utilized for financial reporting purposes.

4. Review Schedule M-1 for any book to tax differences in the amount of amortization being claimed by the taxpayer. There should always be an M-1 adjustment if the taxpayer is amortizing goodwill or similar assets for book purposes since these deductions are not allowed for tax purposes. Amortization deductions in excess of the amount taken for book purposes should be closely scrutinized.

5. The *life* of the asset and the *method* of computing the amortization are also areas which should be thoroughly reviewed. A shorter useful life, or the use of an accelerated method will produce a larger deduction for the taxpayer. These computations should always be reviewed to determine if they are technically correct and reasonable.

6. Normally, the straight-line method of amortization is used for tax purposes. Any accelerated method claimed on the return should be closely scrutinized. However, under certain circumstances, taxpayers are permitted to take additional amortization if they can show that it properly reflects the actual decline in value of the asset.

For example, if all or a portion of the mortgage servicing rights were sold or unanticipated prepayments were made (such as might occur if interest rates declined), the value of the remaining asset may decrease more rapidly than provided for by the original straight-line amortization. Based on the facts and circumstances, the taxpayer may be able to support an additional amortization deduction to match the anticipated servicing income stream on the remaining principle balances of the associated mortgages.

7. One of the biggest problems encountered with an amortization issue deals with the *valuation* of the intangible assets. This is especially true where the purchase price is not allocated to the individual assets in the purchase contact. These valuations are dependent on the facts and circumstances of each particular case and normally require the assistance of an engineer. Even if the taxpayer has secured a sophisticated appraisal or paid for an expert valuation report, the reasonableness of the conclusions must be evaluated by an IRS engineer.

PURCHASED SERVICING RIGHTS

Mortgage servicing can be very profitable to a bank if done in volume. A bank that decides to operate a mortgage servicing department will occasionally purchase servicing rights from other banking entities. The bank may also purchase servicing rights from another servicer in bulk. The primary reason for purchasing these additional servicing rights is that the bank cannot originate enough servicing rights fast enough to become profitable.

While *purchased* servicing rights are similar to originatedservicing rights, the issue should not be confused. The purchased servicing rights issue deals solely with the computation of the amortization deduction claimed by the taxpayer on servicing rights which it has purchased. Originated servicing rights are obtained when a bank lends money for a mortgage and retains the right to service the loan after it is sold.

As discussed in detail under the originated servicing issue, the servicing rights have significant underlying value. A bank will pay a premium for these rights. It is this premium which is being amortized by the purchasing bank.

As also discussed in detail under the originated servicing issues, rights to receive mortgage servicing fees are stripped coupons within the meaning of IRC section 1286(e)(3) to the extent, if any, that they exceed reasonable compensation for the services to be performed under the servicing contract. This is true not only for originated servicing rights, but also for purchased servicing rights. Rev. Proc. 91-50, 1991-2 C.B. 778, provides guidance on determining the extent to which mortgage servicing fees constitute reasonable compensation.

IRC section 1286(a) provides that stripped coupons are treated as having original issue discount (OID). Therefore, the basis attributable to any portion of mortgage servicing fees that exceeds reasonable compensation is recovered in accordance with the OID rules. In contrast, any basis attributable to the portion of purchased servicing that constitutes reasonable compensation is subject to IRC section 197. The legislative history of this section makes it clear that IRC section 197 does not apply to amounts that exceed reasonable compensation.

Under IRC section 197, purchased mortgage servicing rights will be amortizable over 9 years provided they relate to indebtedness secured by residential real property and they were not acquired as part of the acquisition of a trade or business. Other purchased mortgage servicing rights will be amortizable over 15 years. The new provisions are effective for property acquired after August 10, 1993. The taxpayer may elect, subject to some stringent rules, to apply the new rules to all property acquired after July 25, 1991. Questions remain about the possible interplay between IRC sections 197 and 475 for purchased mortgage servicing rights.

EXAMINATION TECHNIQUES

1. As mentioned earlier in this guide, one of the first questions to ask the taxpayer is whether the bank operates a mortgage servicing department. If they do, request the taxpayer to provide the purchase contract and verify the amortization deductions for all servicing rights acquired from outside parties, along with any related work papers.

2. Review the taxpayer's computations to determine whether the amount of the deduction is accurate. This issue normally does not involve a valuation problem. Rather, the issue involves the *method* and *life* over which the rights are amortized by the purchasing bank. The amount of premium paid for the servicing rights is usually evidenced by a purchase agreement. However, when servicing rights are purchased along with other assets, such as in a acquisition, an allocation of the cost must be made. The amount allocated to the rights should be amortized over its useful life as discussed below.

3. The correct method or life for amortization purposes must be determined based on the facts of your particular case. Usually, a 12-year life for a 30-year fixed rate mortgage is the norm, with an 8-year life for a 15-year mortgage. The determination of the life is complicated if the mortgages are aged, if there is a combination of 15-year and 30-year mortgages, or if there are both conventional and adjustable rate mortgages. Salomon Brothers publishes a table showing the estimated useful lives of mortgages depending on the age of the mortgage and also takes into consideration the interest rate of the mortgage. This book, or a similar type book is usually available from the mortgage department of the bank.

4. The straight line method of amortization is required unless the taxpayer can substantiate otherwise. Because of the large number of mortgages that were refinanced in the early 90's, the taxpayer may argue that the useful lives of earlier mortgages are shorter than the 8 and 12 years mentioned normally allowed for amortization. Normally, we will allow the taxpayer to deduct the actual run-off of the mortgage repayments if the amounts can be adequately substantiated. However, in those cases the life of the mortgage servicing may extend beyond 12 years. Theoreti cally, lower interest rate mortgages have longer lives, especially if interest rates have increased, because there would be fewer people refinancing.

ORGANIZATIONAL AND BUSINESS START-UP COSTS

Organizational expenditures are those costs directly related to the creation of a corporation. All costs associated with starting up the business are not allowed as a current deduction and must be capitalized. However, an election to amortize the expenses can be made.

IRC section 195 deals with start-up expenditures. It provides in part that:

Extract

IRC section 195

(a) CAPITALIZATION OF EXPENDITURES.—Except as otherwise provided in this section, no deduction shall be allowed for start-up expenditures.

(b) ELECTION TO AMORTIZE.—

(1) IN GENERAL.—Start-up expenditures may, at the election of the taxpayer, be treated as deferred expenses. Such deferred expenses shall be allowed as a deduction prorated equally over such period of not less than 60 months as may be selected by the taxpayer * * *

* * *

(c) DEFINITIONS.—For purposes of this section—

(1) START-UP EXPENDITURES.—The term "start-up expenditures" means any amount—

(A) paid or incurred in connection with -

(i) investigating the creation or acquisition of an active trade or business, or

(ii) creating an active trade or business, or

(iii) any activity engaged in for profit and for the production of income before the day on which the active trade or business begins, in anticipation of such activity becoming an active trade or business, * * *

* * *

IRC section 195 provides that start-up expenses be deferred and amortized at the election of the taxpayer over a period of not less than 60 months. The election to amortize organizational expenditures must be made in a statement attached to the return for the taxable year in which the business begins.

Both IRC section 195 and IRC section 248 allow these costs to be capitalized and then amortized over 60 months. It thus might not seem important to distinguish between the two types of costs; after all, both receive the same treatment. This might well be the case for the regular income tax.

But it is important for the Alternative Minimum Tax. IRC section 56(g)(4)(D)(ii) requires an Adjusted Current Earnings (ACE) adjustment for IRC section 248 organizational costs. There is, however, no corresponding adjustment for IRC section 195 start-up costs. Thus, the distinction between IRC section 248 organizational costs and IRC section 195 start-up costs is important for the AMT.

Taxpayers might want to take IRC section 248 organizational costs and recharacterize them as IRC section 195 start-up costs to reduce their alternative minimum taxable income (AMTI).

EXAMINATION TECHNIQUES

1. Review Form 851, Affiliations Schedule, which is attached to the return to determine if the taxpayer started any new businesses or subsidiaries during the examination years. The issue is most common in those entities which are expanding their asset bases through new businesses.

2. Analyze all of the cost areas associated with the creation of the new company, such as legal expenses, salaries, and fees paid. It has been our experience that the taxpayer will actually capitalize many of the direct costs clearly associated with a new business. However, many of the indirect costs such as officers' salaries and in-house legal costs are overlooked by the taxpayer and should be capitalized.

Some examples of the costs which must be capitalized are as follows:

a. Legal services related to the creation of the corporation such as drafting the corporate charter, bylaws, minutes of organizational meetings, and similar expenditures,

b. Accounting services,

c. Expenses of organizational meetings of the board of directors or shareholders, and

d. Fees paid to the state of incorporation.

The chapter on acquisition costs provides additional examples of the type of expenses you may encounter.

3. Review the minute book and annual report for clues as to any plans the corporation may have to expand into new areas. Research the bank in a local library, and secure any other public informa tion concerning your bank to assist in this examination area.

If the corporation fails to make the proper election to amortize the organizational expenses, they must be capitalized and will remain on the books until the year of dissolution or liquidation. At that time they will be deductible as a loss from the sale or exchange of a capital asset.

WORK FORCE IN PLACE

When a bank acquires another institution, it may allocate a portion of the purchase price to an intangible asset which they call "work force in place." This is the name given to the employees of the acquired company which are retained by the new entity. Historically, the IRS position has been that an amortization deduction for this type of intangible asset is *not* allowable. However, this issue may be affected by the Supreme Court's decision in *Newark Morning Ledger* and by the enactment of IRC section 197. *See Ithaca Industries, Inc. v. Commissioner*, 97 T.C. 253 (1991) [CCH Dec. 47,536], *aff'd*, 17 F.3d 684 (4th Cir. 1994) [94-1 USTC ¶50,100]. A complete discussion of this issue is beyond the scope of this guide. This issue usually involves a rather large deduction and we recommend the assistance of an engineer be requested.

GENERIC POSITION PAPERS

The following Coordinated Issue Papers deal with various amortization issues. They were issued in *generic form* which means that they can apply to industries across the board as opposed to any specialized industry. Copies of the complete Issue Papers are available from your ISP/MSSP District coordinator. However, in view of the enactment of IRC section 197, a revision of the Issue Papers may be required. Contact your District ISP Coordinator for an update.

Amortization of Assembled Workforce

Whether in the context of an acquisition of a business, the benefit inherent in acquiring a trained staff of employees already in place is an amortizable asset.

Covenants Not to Compete

Whether covenants not to compete entered into during acquisition negotiations are amortizable.

Customer Based Intangibles

In the acquisition of a going business, whether customer based intangible assets, in which a cost basis has been allocated, are amortizable under IRC section 167. In other words, whether the particular customer based intangible is an asset separate and distinct from the goodwill of the acquired business.

Employment Contracts

Whether employment contracts entered into by a target company during acquisition negotiations are an asset of the target company where there is no substantial business purpose for the target company independent of the proposed sale of the company.

Amortization of Market Based Intangibles

Whether a benefit derived from a competitive market position is an amortizable asset under IRC section 167(a).

Amortization of Order Backlog

Whether a benefit derived from acquiring unfilled customer orders at the acquisition date is an amortizable asset under IRC section 167(a).

CHAPTER 16—FEE INCOME

INTRODUCTION

Although interest income is the primary source of a bank's revenue, fee income can also be a significant income source. There are many types of fee income; however, labels are not determinative of their treatment. This chapter will discuss commitment fees, service fees, and points (also called loan origination fees).

COMMITMENT FEES

A commitment fee is generally a nonrefundable charge for making funds available for a specific period of time at a fixed rate of interest. This fee is not considered interest income since the fee is not paid for the use or forbearance of money. For example, someone building a home may pay a commitment fee to the bank to guarantee that it will lend $100,000 within 90 days at 8 percent.

For cash basis banks, the commitment fee is income in the year it is received. For accrual basis banks, the fee is included in income in the year it becomes due or when received, whichever is earlier.[1]

Keep in mind that many banks are required to use the accrual method of accounting after 1986. Banks with gross receipts of more than $5 million are prohibited from using the cash

[1] Rev. Rul. 70-540, 1970-2 C.B. 102.

method of accounting, except for certain specified transactions.

SERVICE FEES

Banks charge fees for services rendered in connection with loaning money such as: escrow fees, recording fees, credit inspection fees, appraisal fees, *etc.* The tax treatment of these fees depends on whether the taxpayer reports its income on the cash or accrual method and when payment for the fees was received.

Taxpayers using the accrual method report their fee income when it is earned or received, whichever is earlier. Therefore, accrual basis taxpayers will report service fees in the year the loan is made regardless of whether cash was received or whether the fees were added to the loan balance.

Cash basis taxpayers report service fees as income when received. Therefore, if the service fees are paid at closing they are reportable at that time. However, if the amount of the fees is added to the loan balance instead of paid at closing, a cash basis taxpayer includes the fee in taxable income ratably, as payments are made on the loan.[2]

POINTS

Revenue Ruling 70-540, 1970-2 C.B. 101, defines points as a charge made by the lender to the borrower, which is in addition to the stated annual interest rate, and is paid by the borrower to the lender as an adjustment of the stated interest to reflect the actual cost of borrowing money. The number of points charged by the lender is determined based on the factors that dictate an acceptable rate of interest. Points are paid for the use or forbearance of money and are considered to be interest.

For example, if the market rate of interest for a zero point mortgage is 8 percent, a borrower might pay one point to lower the interest rate to 7.75 percent. One point is 1 percent of the loan balance, for example, $1500 for a $150,000 loan.

Rev. Rul. 70-540, amplified by Rev. Rul. 74-607, 1974-2 C.B. 149, provided guidance concerning when points charged by a lender were to be included in the lender's income. In general, Rev. Rul. 70-540 held that points were includable in a lender's income upon receipt. The final original issue discount (OID) regulations, however, change the lender's treatment of points.[3]

Treas. Reg. section 1.1173-1 defines OID as the excess of a loan's stated redemption price at maturity over its issue price. Under Treas. Reg. section 1.1173-2(g), points paid when a loan is originated reduce the issue price of the loan, thereby creating or increasing the amount of discount on the loan.[4] If the points are financed by the lender, the loan's stated redemption price at maturity is increased by the amount of the points. Thus, all points charged on a

[2] *Ibid.*

[3] Rev. Rul. 70-540 (to the extent of any holdings concerning the lender's treatment of points) and Rev. Rul. 74-607 were made obsolete by Rev. Proc. 94-29, 1994-1 C.B. 616.

[4] For example, if a borrower pays at closing $2,000 in points on a loan with a stated principal amount of $100,000, the loan's issue price is $98,000, the loan's stated redemption price at maturity is $100,000, and, therefore, the loan has discount of $2,000.

loan create or increase the amount of discount on the loan.[5]

If the amount of the discount on a loan is more than a de minimis amount (as determined under Treas. Reg. section 1.1173-1(d), the lender includes the discount (OID) in income over the term of the loan. See Treas. Reg. section 1.1172-1. If the amount of the discount on the loan is a de minimis amount, the lender includes the discount (de minimis OID) in income as stated principal payments are made on the loan. See Treas. Reg. section 1.1173-1(d)(5).

On April 4, 1994, the Service released three revenue procedures dealing with accounting method changes for OID and de minimis OID (including discount attributable to points): (1) Rev. Proc. 94-28, 1994-1 C.B. 614, (2) Rev. Proc. 94-29, 1994-1 C.B. 616 and (3) Rev. Proc. 94-30, 1994-1 C.B. 621. The revenue procedures are discussed in more detail later in this chapter.

A distinction should be made between points that are paid for the use or forbearance of money and points that are paid as reimbursement for closing costs. Points that are charged for specific services by the lender are not interest and can not be deferred. Examples of fees for services not considered to be interest are the appraisal fee, preparation costs, settlement fees, and notary fees. The final OID regulations do not change the treatment of service fees.[6]

Both cash and accrual banks must report service fees as income when the loan closes if they are paid at closing. Accrual basis banks must report financed service fees as income when earned at closing.

EXAMINATION TECHNIQUES

1. The taxpayer should be questioned extensively regarding all the types of fee income the bank earns. Fee income may be properly reported for one type of loan, but improperly deferred for another type of loan. For example the bank may report cash fees for adjustable rate mortgages, but amortize the cash fees for 30 year conventional mortgages.

2. Review the general ledger for deferred income accounts. There are likely to be different accounts for each type of loan, such as: 30-year fixed conventional, 15-year adjustable rate mortgages, 30-year FHA, *etc.* The accounts in the general ledger should be compared to the M-1 work papers to determine which accounts have not been adjusted for tax purposes.

3. Review the M-1 schedule to ensure that the bank's fee income was reported differently for tax than for books. For book purposes, banks are required to report most of their fee income as an adjustment to yield over the life of the related loans, regardless of whether the borrower paid or financed the fees. Therefore, many fees are required to be reported earlier for tax than for book, especially if they were not financed by the borrower. The M-1 adjustment for this item is often titled "Deferred Fee Income."

The M-1 adjustment may either increase or decrease book income de-

[5] The rule in Treas. Reg. section 1.1273-2(g) does not apply to the borrower's treatment of the points if the points are deductible under section 461(g)(2) of the Code.

[6] Under Treas. Reg. section 1.1273-2(g), a payment by the borrower for services provided by the lender in a lending transaction, such as commitment fees or loan processing costs, does not reduce the issue price of the loan.

pending primarily on whether lending activity has increased or decreased during the year. Analyze the taxpayer's M-1 work papers to obtain a complete understanding of what adjustments are being made. The following computation is a very simple example of what the work papers might show:

Fee income reported for books	$400,000
Deferred fee income balance 1/1	(300,000)
Deferred fee income balance 12/31	500,000
Taxable fee income	$600,000

The M-1 adjustment is $200,000. This represents the change in deferred fees for the year. The deferred fee account is increased by any cash fees that were not reported as income on the books and is decreased as the fees are subsequently recognized for books.

4. Determine whether the taxpayer filed a Form 3115 to change its method of accounting for fee income. Even if the IRS has approved the change, you still need to verify that the facts are the same as they were represented in the ruling.

5. If the taxpayer is deferring fee income (other than points) for tax purposes, a complete analysis of the loan documents must be made. Consider the following items:

a. Did the borrower bring cash to closing? If so, deferral of fees (other than points) may not be allowable. This may be true even if the taxpayer contends these funds were for reimbursement of the bank's costs, such as for filing fees.

b. Evaluate the loan documents to determine the terms of the agreement between the bank and the customer. Unless there is a clear understanding between the lender and the borrower that the fees are being financed and this is confirmed by the loan documents, the fees (other than points) should not be deferred.

6. If the bank earns fees which can be deferred, you will need to determine whether they are being amortized into income properly. Some of the amortization methods that you may encounter are discussed below:

a. Sum of the month's digits and straight line have been allowed as amortization methods for both cash and accrual basis taxpayers.

b. The composite straight line method has been allowed for use by accrual basis taxpayers for tax years prior to the OID regulations. Under this method fees are recognized ratably over the life of the loans. See Rev. Rul. 54-367, 1954-2 C.B. 109.

c. For years prior to the application of the OID regulations, the liquidation method has been approved for use by cash basis taxpayers. Under this method, the percentage of the fees recognized each month is equal to the percentage of principal liquidated during the month. See Rev. Rul. 64-178, 1964-2 C.B. 120.

d. A constant interest rate method is to be used whenever fee income is in the nature of original issue discount (OID). Some loan fees, such as points, may meet the definition of OID. This will be discussed in more detail later in this chapter.

Revenue Rulings 54-367 and 64-178, *infra,* which permitted amortization under the composite and liquidation methods, were issued before the original issue discount (OID) rules were changed by DRA 1984 and TRA 1986. You are very likely to encounter taxpayers using those methods who should instead be including income on a constant interest rate method.

e. Rev. Rul. 54-367, 1954-2 C.B. 109, and Rev. Rul. 64-278, 1964-2 C.B. 120, were made obsolete by Rev. Proc. 94-29. Thus, a taxpayer may no longer rely on these rulings for any loan required to be accounted for in accordance with the final OID regulations.

A discussion of the mechanics of each of these methods is beyond the scope of this guide. If a taxpayer that you are examining is amortizing fees into income you will need to (1) determine which method is being used, (2) do research to determine whether it is an appropriate method, and (3) analyze the taxpayer's workpapers to evaluate whether the method is being utilized properly.

7. Determine whether the bank you are auditing sells its loans, such as mortgages, shortly after they are originated. When the loans are sold any unamortized fee income would be recognized immediately. If you determine the bank was improperly deferring loan fees and required them to include the fees in income when the loans were originated, your adjustment would be reversed as soon as the loans were sold. Although this would result in a permanent timing difference, it may not be significant enough to warrant spending the time needed to examine this area.

LAW

Section 451 of the Internal Revenue Code states "the amount of any item of gross income shall be included in the gross income for the taxable year in which received by the taxpayer, unless, under the method of accounting used in computing taxable income, such amount is to be properly accounted for as of a different period." Treas. Reg. section 1.451-1 provides that under the cash method of accounting items of income are includible in gross income when actually or constructively received. Under the accrual method of accounting, income is includible in gross income when all the events have occurred which fix the right to receive such income and the amount thereof can be determined with reasonable accuracy.

Rev. Rul. 70-540 discusses the taxable year in which lending institutions are to include in income commitment fees and service fees charged by them in connection with real estate mortgage loans. The conclusions reached in this ruling were explained previously. Rev. Proc. 94-29, 1994-1 C.B. 616, made obsolete the discussion in Rev. Rul. 70-540 concerning the treatment of points by a lender.

ORIGINAL ISSUE DISCOUNT

Original issue discount or OID is the excess (if any) of the stated redemption price at maturity over the issue price of a debt instrument (for example, a loan). See IRC section

1173(a)(1). OID consists of all "interest" that is payable on a debt instrument other than interest that is payable at a fixed rate at least annually over the entire term of the instrument.

Example 1

A debt instrument is issued on January 1, 1995, for $750. The debt instrument provides for a payment of $1,000 on January 1, 1998. The debt instrument has $250 of OID. (The debt instrument is a "Zero-coupon bond.")

Example 2

A debt instrument is issued on January 1, 1995, for $500. The debt instrument provides for a payment of $500 on January 1, 1999, and for interest payments of $125 on January 1, 1997, and January 1, 1999. The debt instrument has $250 of OID. (The debt instrument is an "Installment obligation.")

Example 3

A debt instrument is issued on January 1, 1995, for $500. The debt instrument providesfor a payment of $500 on January 1, 1999, and for interest payments of $40 on January 1 of each year, beginning on January 1, 1996, and ending on January 1, 1999. Because all interest is payable annually at a fixed rate over the entire term of the instrument, the debt instrument has no OID.

In Example 1, it would make no difference if the $250 payable at maturity in excess of the $750 amount loaned was designated either as interest or principal by the parties—the $250 would be taxed as interest under the OID provisions.

The Tax Reform Act of 1984 revised the rules for original issue discount, including the extension of the OID rules to loans issued by individuals, such as mortgage loans. Proposed regulations relating to OID were issued on December 22, 1992, which substantially revised the proposed regulations issued on April 6, 1986.

On February 2, 1994, the Service published final rules for the treatment of OID, de minimis OID, stated interest, and unstated interest. See generally sections 1.163-7, 1.446-2, 1.483-1 through 1.483-3, 1.1001-1(g), 1.1012-1(g), and 1.1171-0 through 1.1175-5 of the Income Tax Regulations (the final OID regulations). In general, the final OID regulations are effective for debt instruments issued on or after April 4, 1994. A taxpayer, however, may rely on the final OID regulations for debt instruments issued on or after December 22, 1992, and before April 4, 1994.

On April 4, 1994, the Service released three revenue procedures dealing with accounting method changes for OID and de minimis OID, including any discount attributable to points: (1) Rev. Proc. 94-28, (2) Rev. Proc. 94-29, and (3) Rev. Proc. 94-30.

Rev. Proc. 94-28 provides taxpayers with procedures to obtain automatic consent to change their methods of accounting to conform to the final OID regulations. This revenue procedure applies only to changes in methods of accounting for taxable years that end on or after December 22, 1992, or begin on or before April 4, 1994. If a taxpayer is making a change under this revenue procedure. the taxpayer generally must choose one of the following cut-off dates to make the change: (1) December 22, 1992, (2) the first day of any taxable year beginning after December 22, 1992, and before April 4, 1994, or (3) April 4, 1994. Because the changes made under this revenue procedure are made only for debt instruments (loans) originated on or after the cut-off date, no section 481(a) adjustment is necessary, and taxpayers do not obtain audit protection for loans originated before the cut-off date.

Rev. Proc. 94-28 also provides special rules for any change in method of accounting for de minimis OID, including de minimis OID attributable to points. For example, if a taxpayer is making a change under this revenue procedure for de minimis OID, the taxpayer also may choose the first day of the taxpayer's first taxable year beginning after April 4, 1994, as the cut-off date for the change.

Rev. Proc. 94-29 allows a taxpayer to use the principal reduction method of accounting, an aggregate method of accounting for de minimis OID, including de minimis OID attributable to points, on certain loans originated by the taxpayer. The principal reduction method of accounting, which is based on the principles of Treas. Reg. section 1.1173-1(d)(5), allows a taxpayer to take aggregate de minimis OID into account as principal on the underlying debt instruments is liquidated, in the proportion that the liquidated principal bears to the total outstanding principal. The revenue procedure specifies certain categories into which loans and related de minimis OID must be classified to perform the calculations, and requires that the calculations of liquidated principal be performed monthly. In addition, the revenue procedure requires that detailed books and records be kept to support a taxpayer's calculations. Because this method gives taxpayers an immediate increase in basis for the de minimis OID amount even though the income recognition is spread over the period principal is received, a potential problem exists if the related loan is then "marked to market" at yearend under IRC section 475. The Service published Notice 96-23, 1996-16, I.R.B. 23 (April 15, 1996) to solicit comments on the interaction of the two provisions and to put the taxpayers on notice that they cannot take an inconsistent position until the conflict is resolved.

Rev. Proc. 94-29 also prescribes exclusive procedures for taxpayers to use in changing to the principal reduction method of accounting. Taxpayers that follow the procedures receive automatic consent to make the change. In general, taxpayers may change to this method for loans originated on or after the "cut-off date" chosen by the taxpayer. For purposes of this revenue procedure, the cut-off date is the first day of any taxable year ending on or after December 22, 1992. Special rules are provided, however, to determine the cut-off date if the year of change includes either December 22, 1992, or April 4, 1994. Because the change made under this revenue procedure is made only for loans originated on or after the cut-off date, no IRC section 481(a) adjustment is necessary, and taxpayers do not receive audit protection for loans originated prior to the cut-off date.

Finally, Rev. Proc. 94-29 obsoletes several earlier revenue rulings that provided taxpayers additional methods of accounting for points, including the composite method and the loan liquidation method. See section 10 of this revenue procedure for the list of obsolete revenue rulings.

If a taxpayer is changing its method of accounting for de minimis OID, including de minimis OID attributable to points, under either Rev. Proc. 94-28 or Rev. Proc. 94-29, the change only applies to loans originated on or after the applicable cut-off date. Rev. Proc. 94-30 provides the exclusive procedures for a taxpayer to obtain the Commissioner's consent to change its method of accounting for points on loans acquired before the cut-off date, and prescribes the only methods of accounting for points to which a taxpayer may change for these loans. Under Rev. Proc. 94-30, the year of change may be no later than the first taxable year beginning after April 4, 1994.

For points previously accounted for under the current inclusion method (that is, included in income on origination of a loan), the taxpayer may change to a deferred recognition method known as "the revised loan liquidation method." This method is modeled on the principal reduction method described in Rev. Proc. 94-29, with certain modifications. Taxpayers also may change to a loan by loan basis of accounting for points originally subject to the current inclusion method of accounting, taking points into account as stated principal payments on each loan are made. The change in method of accounting for points previously recognized under the current inclusion method is made for all loans held by the taxpayer as of the cut-off date. Accordingly, a negative IRC section 481(a) adjustment is necessary for this change.

For points previously accounted for under some type of deferred recognition method (that is, a method other than the current inclusion method), taxpayers may change only to "the revised loan liquidation method" of accounting. This change is effected on a cut-off basis, and no IRC section 481(a) adjustment is allowed. Special rules apply if the taxpayer, at the time of the filing of the Form 3115 to make the change is under examination, before an appeals office, or before any federal court.

SUMMARY

When examining a bank consider the proper tax treatment of the fee income it receives. As discussed earlier, the fees may be reportable in the initial year or deferred over time depending on whether they represent interest and whether they were paid when the loan was originated.

Review the loan documents carefully to determine when the fees are reportable for tax purposes, since this often differs from book reporting. Unless the loan documents clearly show that there is a clear understanding between the bank and the borrower that the fees are being financed and the loan documents confirm this agreement, the fees (other than points) should not be deferred. If the taxpayer is allowed to defer fee income, the amortization method being used should be evaluated.

CHAPTER 17—INCOME RECEIVED IN ADVANCE

INTRODUCTION

Under the accrual method of accounting, the *right to receive* income generally determines when to report that amount for tax purposes. However, *prepaid* income received without restriction must be included in taxable income when *received*. This is true even if these amounts have *not* yet been earned by the bank.

Prepaid amounts must be included in taxable income even if the bank may be required to repay the amount at some future time. A deduction may be taken by an accrual basis bank in the year in which the bank satisfies the "all events" test for liability to repay the income. The all events test will not be met earlier than when economic performance with respect to such liability occurs.

The general rule involving prepaid income assumes the bank is using the accrual method of accounting which is defined later in this chapter. Example applications of these provisions are also provided below.

LAW

Treas. Reg. section 1.451-5(b)(1) defines the taxable year of inclusion. This provision provides in general that:

Advance payments must be included in income either—

(1) In the taxable year of receipt; or

(2) In the tax year in which properly accruable under the method used for tax purposes unless the method used for financial purposes results in an earlier accrual.

In addition, in *Schlude v. Commissioner*, 372 U.S. 128 (1963) [63-1 USTC ¶ 9284], the Supreme Court required the taxpayer to report not only advance cash payments but other payments falling due, but not paid, that were for future services. However, although this is the gerneral rule, it may not apply to certain types of financial transactions. For example, the regulations under IRC section 446 that apply to swap transactions and the OID regulations discussed elsewhere provide different rules.

Rev. Rul. 66-347, 1966-2 C.B. 196, discusses the year income must be recognized when it is received without restriction as to its disposition, use, or enjoyment. It also discusses income which has been received subject to a contingent liability requiring a portion of the income to be returned. This ruling holds that the income must be reported in the year of receipt and a deduction is taken only in the year that a refund is made.

The theory behind this position can be applied to any type of an advanced payment of income issue. Although the tax treatment of prepaid interest has been affected by the final OID regulations, the analysis in *Continental Illinois*, T.C. Memo. 1989-636 [CCH Dec. 46,180(M)], *aff'd* 998 F.2d 513 (7th Cir. 1993) [93-2 USTC ¶ 50,400], can be cited as the authority for an adjustment in some other situations. The following is a summary of the Tax Court opinion.

1. The burden of proof was on the accrual basis taxpayer to show that the income should *not* be taxed when received.

2. The Commissioner has broad discretion in determining the proper method of accounting that a taxpayer may use. Also, the Commissioner did not exceed his discretionary powers in this case.

3. The court determined that since *Continental Illinois* met the two prong claim of right doctrine test, income should be included upon receipt.

ACCRUAL METHOD OF ACCOUNTING

One of the most important requirements of a method of accounting is that it must clearly reflect income. The Tax Reform Act of 1986 substantially limited a bank's flexibility in selecting a method of accounting. For taxable years after 1986, banks with gross receipts of more than 5 million dollars are *required* to use the accrual method. Under this method, it is the *right to receive the* income, as opposed to the actual *receipt* of the money, that determines when to include the amount in gross income. The advantage of the accrual method over any other method of accounting is that it more accurately reflects income on a periodic basis.

Treas. Reg. section 1.451-1(a) provides that under the accrual method of accounting, income is included in gross income in the taxable year in which:

1. All events have occurred which fix the right to receive the income and

2. The amount of such income can be determined with reasonable accuracy.

ISSUES

When a bank *earns* a fee for services or *receives* cash payments in advance, determining the point in time that it must report these amounts as income can sometimes be confusing. Simply put, is the bank required to report income when received or when earned? The general rule is that advance payments are income when received, even to an accrual basis taxpayer, unless an exception applies. To better understand this area, several potential issues are discussed below. In each situation, the bank receives an advance payment and could attempt to defer a portion of this income until future years.

CREDIT CARD FEES

Most commercial banks that offer customers credit card services will charge the user an annual fee for the use of the card. The fee is charged to the customer at the inception of the account and on each anniversary date of the issuance of the card. The fee is approximately $25 per card holder, and covers the use of the card for the subsequent 12 months. The fee is usually nonrefundable.

The issue is whether the entire annual fee for the use of the credit card should be included in income in the taxable year in which the payment is made, or should the fee be included in income on a ratable basis over the time period covered by the use of the card.

The IRS views these credit card fees as amounts received for the right to utilize the credit card rather than as income for services rendered. The annual credit card fee does *not* represent a charge for the use of money and also, does *not* represent a fee for future services. Therefore, the credit card fees should be reported in income when received by the bank. The amounts should *not* be deferred and subsequently reported as income evenly over a 12-month period.

Many commercial banks have taken the position that credit card fees are amounts received for services to be performed ratably over a 1-year period. The banks therefore claim to be entitled to use the 1-year deferral of income provisions of Rev. Proc. 71-21, 1971-1 C.B. 549. There is frequently a factual question whether the annual fees are actually intended to compensate for services. Two cases, issued the same day by the United States Tax Court, highlight this dispute. In *Barnett Banks of Florida, Inc. v. Comissioner,* 106 T.C. 163 (1996), the court after receiving testimony of bank officers, concluded that the fees were for services and allowed the fees to be included ratably over the 12 month period. However, in *Signet Banking Corporation v. Commissioner,* 106 T.C. 117 (1996) [CCH Dec. 51,192], based upon the language of the written agreement between the bank and credit card customers and the nonrefundable nature of the fees, the court found that the fees were not for future services and denied the deferral of income.

The National Office is considering whether, even if the fees are for credit card processing or other potential services, banks may utilize Rev. Proc. 71-21 for their credit card businesses. Contact the National Office if this issue arises. However, the examining agent should always request the credit card agreement to ascertain whether the credit card fees are provided for future services.

RENTAL/LEASE INCOME

Banks frequently own buildings and other commercial property which are leased out to tenants. This includes property obtained by the bank through foreclosure proceedings.[1] The rental or lease income of the bank is treated in the same manner as rental income received by any other taxpayer. The amount is includible in the gross income of the bank when received regardless of the period covered or the method of accounting employed by the taxpayer. See Treas. Reg. section 1.61-8(b).

Rents received in *advance* are includible in gross income, regardless of the bank's accounting method. However, gross income usually does *not* include amounts received as security deposits or the value of property attributable to improvements made by the tenant, unless such improvements were made in lieu of rent.

On occasion, you may come across a lease agreement which provides for uneven rental payments over the term of the lease, with no reasonable basis for this type of payment arrangement. These uneven payments may constitute an attempt to defer a portion of the rental income. In these cases, the lease agreement should be reviewed to determine potential tax implications. *See* IRC section 467.

---

[1] The tax treatment of foreclosure property by thrifts under IRC section 595 is beyond the scope of this document. IRC section 595 was repealed for property acquired after December 31, 1995, and by section 1616(b)(8) of P.L. 104-188 (August 20, 1996). Contact the Savings and Loan Industry Specialist in Los Angeles if you are examining a thrift.

PREPAID INTEREST

The treatment of prepaid interest has been changed by the final OID regulations. Under the regulations, a payment generally is treated first as a payment of interest (or OID) to the extent of accrued but unpaid interest (or OID), and then as a payment of principal. Thus, no portion of any payment is treated as prepaid interest. See Treas. Reg. sections 1.446-2(e) and 1.1275-2(a). Because there is no accrued but unpaid interest (or OID) at the time of a "prepayment," the payment is treated as a principal payment, which is not includable in income. In effect, the payment reduces the issue price (or adjusted issue price) of the loan.

COMMITMENT FEES AND SERVICE FEES

These types of fees normally comprise the major portion of the fee income earned by a bank. A complete discussion of the tax implications of these items is included in the "Fee Income" chapter and will not be repeated at this time.

AUTOMOBILE LEASE PAYMENTS

One issue we came across during our examination involved whether lessee down payments made to an automobile dealership at the inception of an automobile lease should be treated as an advance payment to the bank to which the vehicle and related lease are sold. For tax purposes, the auto lease is reflected on the books of the bank as a purchase and subsequent lease of the vehicle. The bank depreciates the vehicle and reports the lease payments in income as they are earned. However, for financial reporting, the bank considers the lease a financing arrangement which bears little resemblance to the tax accounting entries.

The advance payment rules pertain only to the question of *when* an item is to be taken into income; they do *not* pertain to whether an item is income. Accordingly, the threshold question in analyzing an auto lease transaction is not whether the down payment is an advance payment to the bank, but rather whether it is includible in the bank's income at all.[2] In the commonly used leasesale transaction described below, the advance payment rules do *not* apply to the bank because the lessee down payment—made to and retained by an auto dealership—is not includible in the bank's income.

A typical auto lease-sale transaction involves three unrelated parties and two steps. L, an individual lessee, begins the transaction by entering into a lease with D, an auto dealer. L and D negotiate the amount of L's down payment and agree to the amount of rent that L will pay over a specified lease term. The down payment and rental payments will vary inversely: the

---

[2] *See generally Commissioner v. Indianapolis Power & Light Co.*, 493 U.S. 203 (1990) (customer deposits were not income to public utility because utility did not have unfettered dominion over deposits at time payments were made). In determining whether the deposits should be treated as taxable advance payments or instead as of non-taxable security deposits, the supreme Court of the United States began by expressly distinguishing between "when" and "whether" questions:

This Court has held that an accrual-basis taxpayer is required to treat advance payments as income in the year of receipt. [Citations omitted.] These cases concerned payments—nonrefundable fees for services—that indisputably constituted income; the issue was *when* that income was taxable. Here, in contrast, the issue is whether these deposits, as such, are income at all. (493 U.S. at 208; emphasis in original.)

higher the down payment, the less the monthly rental payments.

Second, D sells the vehicle to a bank or finance company (B), subject to the lease and net of the down payment.[3] B becomes the owner of the car and assignee of the lease, L's obligation to pay rent runs to B, rather than to D, and B begins depreciating the vehicle, using as its IRC section 1012 cost basis the amount that B paid D for the vehicle.

For example, suppose that a vehicle is worth $20,000, that L makes a $2,000 down payment to D, and that D sells the car, subject to the lease, to B for $18,000 in the type of transaction just described. In this circumstance, the advance payment rules do not apply to B because the down payment is never income to B in the first place. B cannot properly be required to include in income a down payment which it never actually (or constructively) receives, from which B derives no economic benefit, and over which B exercises no dominion or control. Under IRC section 1012, B has a cost basis in the vehicle of $18,000, the amount that represents the fair market value of the vehicle less the down payment.

There may be other common forms of the lease transactions in which the results may be different because the facts do not fit the prototype just described.

The National Office plans to develop guidance concerning various types of lease transactions and is available for consultation should the transactions you examine differ materially from the prototype discussed herein.

EXAMINATION TECHNIQUES

1. Banks normally follow a somewhat conservative approach to accounting and reporting their income. Therefore, it is important to identify any reserve accounts existing in the trial balance or chart of accounts. The liability section of the balance sheet should disclose the existence of any deferred income accounts.

2. Banks usually have manuals which provide explanations or descriptions of all accounts available to the bank. These manuals are used by employees for reference purposes and can provide the agent with valuable information as to the purpose of each of these accounts. These manuals should be requested from the bank since they will assist in determining the purpose of any deferred income accounts and whether any portion of this income should be reported currently.

3. Review the "significant accounting policy" section of the bank's annual report along with the SEC filings for clues as to the existence of any deferred income accounts. Determine how these accounts were handled for tax purposes.

[3] The calculation of the sale price may be made on a standardized purchase order worksheet that B provides to D. One worksheet we have seen provides that the sales price of the vehicle to B is the "vehicle purchase price." That price equals the stated selling price (including preparation, options, and accessories), plus the federal luxury tax and state sales tax, less the value of any trade-in or the amount of any cash down payment made by L. Stated differently, the worksheet takes the selling price of the vehicle, plus any additional up-front costs, to arrive at the capitalized cost. Any cash down payment or trade-in value on another vehicle is subtracted from the capitalized cost. The amount remaining—described as the "balance subject to lease charge" —is thus the amount that B is willing to pay D for the vehicle and the lease, net of any down payment or trade in.

4. Request all internal policy statements from the bank which stipulate how they handle advance payments for tax purposes.

5. Review the schedule M-1 for book and tax differences in the reporting of income items. Also, ask the tax manager to explain any deferred income accounts and how the bank handles them for tax purposes.

6. Review any leasing or rental activity in the consolidated banking return and look for deferred income accounts. Verify that all amounts were properly reported for tax purposes.

7. Review the consolidated return for other entities which may be involved with advance payments or deferred income items.

8. Included in this guide is a chapter titled "Specialization Within the IRS". That chapter, which discusses the use of a CAS to assist the examining agent in determining the amount of fee income reported by the taxpayer and other potential issues, should be referred to for additional information.

SUMMARY

It is important that all deferred income accounts be analyzed to determine whether amounts were properly reported for tax purposes. Many of the issues will be straight forward but others may be difficult to find. It is very important that an agent understand the numerous business operations of the bank to locate potential deferred income items.

CHAPTER 18—TAX-EXEMPT OBLIGATIONS

INTRODUCTION

The money deposited by a customer can be invested by the bank in many ways. Municipal obligations are one of the most common investments of a bank. The major advantage for purchasing this type of investment is the tax benefit. IRC section 103 provides that interest received on obligations of a state, territory, a possession of the United States, or any political subdivision thereof, is specifically *exempt* from federal income tax. Potential examination issues in this area follow.

DETERMINATION OF TAX-EXEMPT STATUS

Not all municipal bonds are tax-exempt. There are many rules and restrictions which limit the tax-exempt status of a particular obligation. During our examinations, very few adjustments were found in this area. Since the IRS is examining the bank and not the municipality, it is difficult to accurately determine the taxable status of a bond by simply looking at the prospectus or other information on the bond offering.

It has been our experience that the bank will adequately review the obligation to verify that it qualifies for tax-exempt status. Often, the taxpayer will have a file containing background information such as the purpose for the bond, authorization for the bond, a legal opinion with respect to taxability, copies of forms registering the bonds as tax-exempt, and any IRS rulings which may have been secured.

In many cases, it was found that the banks have inserted a provision in the purchase agreement for the municipal bonds that guarantee that the investments would qualify for tax-exempt status. If for any reason a bond's tax-exempt status was disqualified, the bank would be adequately reimbursed by the issuing party.

EXAMINATION TECHNIQUES

1. Interest income received on tax-exempt obligations is not included in taxable income. However, these amounts are reported for financial purposes. A schedule M-1 adjustment will indicate the total amount of tax free interest income received by the bank. A complete breakdown of this amount should be requested from the taxpayer and tied directly into the M-1 adjustment. These amounts should be scanned for any large or unusual items, or items which do not appear to be municipal obligations.

2. If the tax-exempt status of any portion of the bank's portfolio is in question, contact Exempt Organizations. The listing provided by the taxpayer in item 1 above, can be used to select several items to be reviewed.

3. The taxpayer should always be asked to provide all available information it maintains on the tax-exempt obligations which may be helpful. If the taxpayer does not have any information, contact Exempt Organizations for assistance.

4. A bank may exclude the interest from taxexempt obligations from gross income *only* if it actually owns the bonds. If the bonds are being held as collateral for a loan the interest is *not* taxexempt to the bank because it holds the securities as collateral, and not as the owner. While reviewing the bond file, this should be considered as a potential adjustment area.

5. In addition, interest will *not* be tax-exempt if it is paid with respect to an obligation in which the principal or interest is guaranteed by the Federal Government. This item should also be kept in mind while reviewing the files.

6. Smaller bond issues where a single bank has purchased the entire bond issue should receive the closest scrutiny. That's because there usually is no other regulatory supervision with respect to this issue and, therefore, may be subject to an oversight on the part of the taxpayer.

The Cumulative Bulletin Digest index will identify recent rulings that have questioned the taxability of various types of bond issues and may provide information that is similar to an issue in your case.

INTEREST AND EXPENSES RELATING TO TAX-EXEMPT INCOME

As a general rule, a nonbank taxpayer could *not* deduct expenses incurred in connection with acquiring or carrying assets that produce tax-exempt interest. Historically, banks were not subject to these rules. Thus, a bank could deduct interest and other expenses on indebtedness incurred in the ordinary course of business where the expenses were *not* directly related to the purchase of tax-exempt bonds.

Effective for tax years beginning after December 31, 1982, the scaleback provisions of IRC section 291(a)(3) were enacted. This section became a major disadvantage for banks that invested heavily in tax-exempt obligations. Even though a financial institution could deduct interest incurred in the ordinary course of its business, IRC section 291(a)(3) provided that the amount of interest a bank incurred to purchase and carry tax-exempt obligations was considered to be a tax preference item. Accordingly, the law provided that the amount of interest expense deducted for debts incurred to carry tax-exempt securities acquired after 1982, was subject to a 15-percent reduction. The Tax Reform Act of 1984 increased the disallowance of the interest expense from 15 percent to 20 percent for securities purchased after December 31, 1982.

Specifically, IRC section 291(e)(1)(B)(i) provides that a financial institution preference item includes the following.

Extract

IRC section 291(e)(1)(B)(i)

> * * * In the case of a financial institution which is a bank * * * the amount of interest on indebtedness incurred or continued to purchase or carry obligations acquired after December 31, 1982, and before August 8, 1986 the interest on which is exempt from taxes for the taxable year, to the extent that a deduction would * * * be allowable with respect to such interest for such taxable year.

To summarize, IRC section 291 disallows a portion of the interest expense deduction claimed by the bank attributable to its investment in taxexempt securities.

The Tax Reform Act of 1986 significantly changed the rules governing the tax exemption of interest for obligations issued after August 7, 1986.

IRC section 265(b)(1) was added to the Code and was effective for tax years beginning after December 31, 1986. This section provides in part that "no deduction shall be allowed for that portion of the taxpayer's interest expense which is allocable to tax-exempt interest." In other words, 100 percent of a financial institution's interest expense allocable to tax-exempt income on obligations acquired after August 7, 1986, is not allowed as a deduction. The 20 percent disallowance rule under IRC section 291, continues to apply to obligations acquired before August 8, 1986.

IRC section 291 and IRC section 265 both provide that, unless the taxpayer can establish otherwise, the portion of the taxpayer's interest expense which is allocable to tax-exempt obligations is an amount which bears the same ratio to such interest expense as:

1. The taxpayer's average adjusted basis of tax-exempt obligations bears to
2. Such average adjusted basis for all assets of the taxpayer.

The average adjusted basis of tax-exempt obligations is generally computed by determining the adjusted basis of such obligations at the end of each month and averaging them over the taxable year.

The average adjusted basis for all assets is generally determined by averaging the basis of all assets at the beginning of the year, with the basis in all assets existing at the end of the year. There usually is no need to use monthly figures since a bank's total asset base does not fluctuate significantly during the year.

As with most sections of the Code, there is an exception to the general rule. IRC section 265(b)(3) provides that the 100 percent disallowance rule does *not* apply to *qualified* tax-exempt obligations. Under IRC section 265(b)(3)(B)(i), a tax-exempt obligation must meet *three* criteria in order to qualify for this exception.

1. First, the obligation must be issued by a qualified small issuer which reasonably anticipates that

it will not issue more than $10 million of tax-exempt obligations during a calendar year.

2. Second, it cannot be a private activity bond.
3. Finally, the issuer must specifically designate the bond as a qualified tax-exempt obligation.

In the event that the bank meets the three requirements listed above, the amounts are still subject to the 20 percent disallowance per IRC section 291, instead of the 100 percent disallowance.

EXAMINATION TECHNIQUES

1. The amount of interest *expense* treated as being disallowed by the bank under IRC section 291 and IRC section 265 will normally be reflected as a schedule M-1 adjustment on the tax return. These amounts should be reconciled to the general ledger and the tax workpapers. They should also be tied to the taxpayer's computations of the disallowed interest.

2. During the examination of a bank, it is important to properly determine the date the tax-exempt securities were issued and subsequently acquired by the bank. The reissuing of tax-exempt securities after August 7, 1986, trigger the provisions of IRC sections 291 or 265.

3. During our examinations, adjustments were found in two separate areas. These issues were discovered by reviewing the computations the bank had already compiled for the tax return. Both of the adjustments we came across were apparent after reviewing the taxpayer's work papers and related computations.

a. In the first issue, the taxpayer incorrectly applied the percentage of interest to be disallowed for tax purposes. (20 percent of the interest rather than 100 percent.) Specifically, the *date* the municipal bond was acquired by the bank, did not correspond to the proper percentage of interest expense to be disallowed.

b. In the second issue, errors were found in the mathematical computation of the interest expense allocable to the tax-exempt obligations. The adjustment was based on the equation discussed above. We simply recomputed the amounts used in the equation to determine the correct amount of interest expense to be disallowed.

SALE OF TAX-EXEMPT OBLIGATIONS

It is important to remember that the gain on the sale of a state, municipal, or governmental security is fully *taxable,* even though the interest earned on the obligation is tax-exempt. The gain or loss on the sale of these securities gives rise to ordinary income/loss and is not subject to the capital gain/loss provisions.

EXAMINATION TECHNIQUES

1. Our examinations did not result in any adjustments in this area. However, fluctuating interest rates may result in adjustments if the municipal bonds are currently trading at a pre mium. The bank may want to take advantage of this opportunity to sell some of their bonds in the open market. The sale of these bonds will not be reflected anywhere on the tax return if they consider the gain to be tax-exempt.

Therefore, a complete review should be made of the municipal bonds in the bank's portfolio at year end to look for any changes from one year to the next.

2. A review of the annual report may indicate sales of tax-exempt obligations. Obligations of states and other municipal obligations will usually be separately stated on the balance sheet. You may also find information on the sale of tax-exempt obligations in the executive committee minute book.

3. Finally, a request should be made for the bank to document all municipal bond sales which occurred during the year to determine if they were properly handled for tax purposes.

BOND PREMIUMS ON TAX-EXEMPT OBLIGATIONS

Generally, if a bond is purchased for an amount in *excess* of the face value of the bond, the difference in price is considered to be a bond *premium.* A bond premium is considered a reduction of the interest income received by the purchaser. This premium is amortized over the life of the bond for taxable securities. However, since the interest from tax-exempt obligations is not taxable, the reduction in interest attributable to the premium is *not* deductible.

While the premiums paid for the purchase of municipal bonds are nondeductible, any premium *received* by the bank due to the early redemption of the bond is considered an amount received from the sale of the bond and, therefore, is taxable.

This latter issue may be significant when there are declines in interest rates. A premium may be paid by the issuer when a bond is called prior to maturity. This additional payment is fully taxable to the bank.

The audit techniques for this issue are similar to those discussed under the sale of tax-exempt obligations, discussed above.

ORIGINAL ISSUE DISCOUNT ON TAX-EXEMPT OBLIGATIONS

If the original bond is issued at a *discount* from its face value, the difference between the issue price and the redemption price is the original issue discount (OID). The OID on obligations issued by a governmental unit is considered tax-exempt interest income. This income is apportioned ratably over the term of the obligation. See IRC section 1288.

Only the discount, when the bond is first issued, qualifies as tax-exempt interest. A discount arising from a subsequent repurchase of a bond, does not qualify for the tax exemption. Thus, if a dealer purchases exempt obligations at par or above, and subsequently resells them at a discount, this discount does *not* qualify as tax-exempt interest income in the hands of the subsequent holders. That's because it is not part of the *original* issue discount.

If the obligation originally issued at a discount is sold prior to the redemption date or the maturity date of the obligation, the original issue discount is apportioned between the original holder and subsequent purchaser of the obligation.

SUMMARY

IRC section 103 generally allows interest on obligations of a state or political subdivision to be exempt from federal tax. However, recent changes in the law have limited the benefit of tax-exempt obligations. The agent should reconcile the amount of tax-exempt income and the portion of interest expense disallowed under IRC sections 291 and 265 shown on schedule M-1. The examiner should also identify the source, and verify all computations made by the taxpayer in determining the amount of interest expense to be disallowed. In most cases, the taxpayer will maintain adequate records enabling the agent to verify the computations without too much trouble.

CHAPTER 19—DISCHARGE OF INDEBTEDNESS

INTRODUCTION

Gross income includes income from the discharge of indebtedness, except as otherwise provided in the Code. The most common situation in which a bank may have had discharge of indebtedness income is when an institution purchased its own bonds on the open market at less than their face amount.

IRC section 108 provides the criteria under which income from discharge of indebtedness can be excluded from gross income. If the taxpayer is entitled to exclude income under IRC section 108, an election must be made to adjust the bases of assets by the amount of income excluded, in accordance with IRC section 1017.

IRC sections 108 and 1017 were enacted to provide relief for bankrupt and insolvent entities. By allowing taxpayers to recognize the discharge of indebtedness income over time through the reduction of depreciation expense, borrowers would not be discouraged from renegotiating or repurchasing their debt for fear of an immediate increase in their tax liability.

Prior to 1987, taxpayers could exclude discharges which occurred (1) in a title 11 case, (2) when the taxpayer was insolvent, or (3) if the discharged debt was qualified business indebtedness. The 1986 Tax Reform Act repealed the third provision which allowed the exclusion of discharged qualified business indebtedness.

The Omnibus Budget Reconciliation Act of 1993 added another category for exclusion if the indebtedness which is discharged is qualified real property business indebtedness per IRC section 108(a)(1)(D). This exclusion is not available to a C-Corporation. Thus, it could apply to a borrower, but would not be available for the bank. Refer to Temporary Treas. Reg. section 1.108(c)-1T which was published December 27, 1993, in TD 8509.

The procedures used when a taxpayer elects to defer income per IRC sections 108 and 1017 will not be reviewed here since they are not any different for banks than for other entities. Instead, issues that are related to the discharge of a bank's indebtedness will be discussed.

PREMATURE WITHDRAWAL PENALTIES

During the early 1980's, when interest rates were rising, many bank customers were cashing in their certificates of deposit (CD's) prior to maturity. The interest or principal that the depositors forfeited were more than offset by the higher interest rates being offered on new CD's. Banks were receiving significant income from these prepayment penalties. Some banks elected to defer this income as income from discharge of indebtedness.

In Revenue Ruling 83-60, 1983-1 C.B. 39, the Service concluded that premature withdrawal penalties were not income from discharge of indebtedness and, therefore, could not be excluded from income under IRC section 108. The penalties were the consideration the bank received because it lost the right to use the funds through the maturity dates of the certificates.

The Supreme Court in *United States v. Centennial Savings Bank, FSB*, 499 U.S. 573, 91-1 U.S.T.C. ¶50188 (1991) stated with respect to this issue:

> Penalties collected by a savings and loan institution when its customers prematurely withdrew their certificates of deposit could not be treated as discharge of indebtedness income and excluded from the savings and loan's taxable income. No discharge of indebtedness occurred, because the customers did not forgive or release any repayment obligation of the financial institution when they accepted an amount equal to the principal and accrued interest minus the penalty. Such amount was exactly what the bank was obligated to pay under the terms of the certificate of deposit agreements.

Therefore, taxpayers should be including all premature withdrawal penalties in income in the year the CD's are cashed in. Banks should not be deferring this as discharge of indebtedness income. You should not see this issue on any returns after 1986, since the provision for excluding discharged qualified business indebtedness was repealed. However, you may encounter this item if your taxpayer has carry backs to years prior to 1987 or if the bases of assets being depreciated or sold in the year you are examining have been adjusted per IRC section 1017.

REPURCHASE OF BONDS

It is not uncommon for banks to repurchase bonds that they previously issued. Treas. Reg. section 1.61-12(c)(3) states, "If bonds are issued by a corporation and are subsequently repurchased by the corporation at a price which is exceeded by the issue price plus any amount of discount already deducted. * * * minus any amount of premium already returned as income, the amount of such excess is income for the taxable year." In other words, this is considered a discharge of a portion of the amount that the company owed to the bondholders and it is therefore, taxable. A debenture, note, or other evidence of indebtedness, issued by a corporation and bearing interest is given the same treatment as a bond. Proposed regulations under IRC section 61 were issued in 1996. Therefore, Treas. Reg. section 1.61-12(c)(3) may not be effective when you face this issue.

The reportable income is increased by any premium that was not previously included in income and decreased by any discount that was not previously taken as a deduction.

The amount of income is also decreased by any unamortized bond issuance expense remaining when the bonds are repurchased. The issuance expense is treated the same as unamortized discount and cannot be deducted in the year of the discharge if the taxpayer elected to exclude income under IRC sections 108 and 1017. See Rev. Rul. 68-288, 1968-1 C.B. 53.

Example 1

ABC Bank issued 5 percent interest bearing bonds with a total face value of $100,000 for $90,000. (Since market interest rates were greater than 5 percent, the bonds were issued at a discount so that the effective interest rate was greater than 5 percent.) The bank incurred issuance expenses of $5,000.

When market interest rates rose higher, the value of these fixed rate bonds declined. ABC Bank repurchased all of the bonds on the open market for $60,000. At the time of the repurchase there was unamortized discount of $6,000 and unamortized issuance expenses of $3,000. The taxpayer's gain is computed as follows:

Face value of bonds	$94,000
Repurchase price	60,000
Gain before adjustments	34,000
Less: Unamortized expenses	(3,000)
Net gain	$31,000

For years prior to 1987, taxpayers could elect the provisions of IRC sections 108 and 1017 to exclude this discharge from income. However, beginning in 1987 taxpayers should be reporting the discharge of debt from the repurchase of bonds as income in the year they are repurchased. Therefore, it is unlikely you would examine a taxpayer who made this election in current years. However, you may want to determine whether the bank you are examining repurchased any bonds to ensure that any discharge income was reported.

EXAMINATION TECHNIQUES

1. Review the tax return to see whether the taxpayer filed Form 982 to adjust the bases of its depreciable assets. If so, information should be requested from the taxpayer to determine the nature of the deferred income.

2. If the deferral is allowable, the taxpayer's depreciation schedule should be reviewed to verify that the bases of the assets were reduced. The taxpayer should have work papers showing these computations. The current year's depreciation schedule can be compared with the prior year's schedule to ensure the reduction was made.

3. Review the bank's annual report and minute book to see whether they discuss any repurchased bonds, renegotiated loans, *etc.* If so, ensure that any discharge of indebtedness was properly reported.

4. If you have a carryback loss to a year where the taxpayer improperly made an election to exclude income, such as from premature withdrawal penalties, you may want to consider adjusting that item. Consider the amount of deferred income, the amount of the carryback, and whether the taxpayer has since recognized most of this income through reduced depreciation deductions.

FORGIVENESS OF A BORROWER'S INDEBTEDNESS

Banks sometimes renegotiate borrower's loans for less than the original loan amount. This is common in markets where the value of real estate has declined significantly. If the value of the collateral has decreased below the loan amount, the borrower may choose to walk away from the property, rather than continue to make the loan payments. Even if the borrower is solvent, he or she may stop making payments if not personally liable for the loan.

If the value of collateralized property has decreased significantly, the banks may have a lot of nonperforming loans. In most situations, it is better for a bank to refinance the loan than to repossess the property. If the FDIC/ RTC has taken over an institution, it may also prefer to renegotiate the loan, rather than to sell the asset. See IRC section 108(e)(10) to determine the amount of forgiveness of indebtedness income in a refinancing.

When the principal balance of the loan is decreased, the borrower is likely to have forgiveness of indebtedness income. Consider a review of the borrower's return if the decrease in the loan balance is significant.

Financial institutions described in IRC sections 581 or 591(a) which discharge (in whole or in part) the indebtedness of any person must file information returns under IRC section 6050P provided (1) the discharge is at least $600.00 and (2) the discharge occurs after December 31, 1993.

Temporary Treas. Reg. sections 1.6050P-0T through 1.6050P-1T (TD 8506) were published December 27, 1993. In addition to discussing the general reporting requirements on Form 1099-C, these regulations provide guidance on when an indebtedness is considered discharged and the determination of the amount discharged.

These information reporting requirements also apply to the FDIC and the RTC for discharges occurring after August 10, 1993. See Notice 93-52, 1993-2 C.B. 337, which provides for interim governmental entity reporting via Form 1099-G (with modifications) for 1993.

Since this text was written, the Service has issued final regulations under IRC section 6050P which become effective December 22, 1996 (T.D. 8654, 1996-11, I.R.B. 14) and final regulations on backup witholding (T.D. 8664, 1996-20 I.R.B. 7).

SUMMARY

Prior to the changes made by the 1986 Tax Reform Act, banks frequently elected to reduce their depreciable assets, rather than report in come from discharge of indebtedness. Since this election can now be made only by insolvent or bankrupt taxpayers, it will not be applicable for most banks. Instead they should be reporting discharge of indebtedness income in full in the year of the forgiveness. For tax years after December 31, 1993, banks may be required to file Forms 1099-C with respect to incidents of forgiveness of borrowers' indebtedness.

CHAPTER 20—LOAN SWAPS

INTRODUCTION

A loan swap is when a bank exchanges or "swaps" loans for other loans, rather than cash. Often, they will do this for valid business purposes. However, sometimes loans are swapped primarily to obtain tax benefits. The following types of exchanges will be discussed:

1. Mortgages swapped for mortgage backed securities
2. Mortgage pools swapped for other mortgage pools
3. Foreign loans swapped for other foreign loans
4. Repurchase agreements
5. Real estate mortgage investment conduits (REMICs)
6. Loan restructuring.

MORTGAGES SWAPPED FOR MORTGAGE BACKED SECURITIES

The Federal Home Loan Mortgage Corporation (FHLMC), the Federal National Mortgage Association (FNMA), and the Government National Mortgage Association (GNMA) have mortgage swap programs. Under these programs, banks can exchange pools of mortgages for mortgage backed securities issued by the agencies. Ownership of a mortgage backed security represents ownership in the *exact* same mortgages that were exchanged.

One reason financial institutions swap mortgages for mortgage backed securities is that the agency guarantees that the bank will be paid the interest and principal, even if the homeowners become delinquent on the mortgages. The interest rate for these participation certificates is less than the interest rate on the mortgages that were transferred. For swaps with Freddie Mac and Fannie Mae, a portion of the difference between the interest rate on the mortgages and the rate on the mortgage backed security is retained by the agency to cover the cost of the guarantee. The balance of the difference between the mortgage rate and the pass through rate is the servicing fee that is kept by the bank.

Payment on Ginnie Mae mortgage backed certificates are guaranteed by the Federal Government since they are represented by FHA and VA mortgages. Therefore, no guarantee fee is paid to Ginnie Mae. The difference between the mortgage rate and the pass through rate is the servicing fee retained by the bank.

Another reason financial institutions securitize their mortgages is to make them easier to sell. Mortgage backed securities are actively traded. They are purchased by other banks, pension plans, insurance companies, *etc.* Therefore, if a bank needs an influx of cash, it can quickly sell a certificate in the open market. It would be much more difficult to sell a group of unsecuritized mortgage loans.

The Service has treated the transfer of mortgages to the FHLMC in exchange for participation certificates as a nonrecognition event under IRC section 1001. This is illustrated in PLR 8327008. Banks are also not required to report a gain or loss on these swaps for book purposes. Therefore, you will not see any indication on the income statement or M-1 Schedule that this transaction has occurred. Mortgage loans will be recategorized on the balance sheet as mortgage backed securities or participation certificates, but the dollar amount of the assets will not change.

Since it is not a taxable event, you would not have any examination issues in this area at the time the mortgages are swapped for the mortgage backed securities. However, if the bank later sells the mortgage backed securities, you should consider the servicing rights issue which is explained in detail in the chapter on mortgage servicing rights. That chapter also has information on mortgage backed securities, the agencies involved, related terminology, *etc.*

MORTGAGE POOLS SWAPPED FOR MORTGAGE POOLS

When interest rates increased significantly in the late 1970's, many financial institutions continued to hold numerous old mortgages with low interest rates. These banks were receiving interest at a low rate while simultaneously paying their depositors at a high rate. One way to become more liquid would have been to sell the old loans. Since newly originated mortgages were paying higher interest, the old mortgages would have been sold at large losses. These losses could then be used to generate tax refunds.

However, selling the mortgages at losses would have decreased the institutions' net worth and possibly put them in danger of closure by the regulatory agencies. The Office of Examination and Supervision of the Federal Home Loan Bank Board responded to this situation by issuing Memorandum R-49 in June 1980. R-49 provided that savings and loans did not need to report losses from the exchange of mortgages for substantially identical mortgages held by another institution. The memorandum provided 10 criteria for evaluating whether mortgages were substantially identical, such as: Type of mortgages, same interest rates, same terms to maturity, *etc.* The FHLBB acknowledged that it issued R-49 to facilitate transactions that would generate tax losses, but that would not substantially affect the economic position of the institutions. In essence, the sole purpose of the mortgage swaps was to generate tax refunds.

The Internal Revenue Service responded by issuing Revenue Ruling 81-204, 1981-2 C.B. 157. It held that the losses upon the exchange of mortgage loans that were similar in type, term, and rates were *not* deductible. The ruling states:

> The taxpayers have not met the requirements of Treas. Reg. section 1.1001-1(a) since they have exchanged mortgage pools that do not differ materially either in kind or in extent and, therefore, pursuant to IRC section 1001 and the regulations thereunder, no loss may be recognized on the exchange. Furthermore, deduction is also precluded because the exchange had no purpose or utility apart from the anticipated tax consequences.

Later Revenue Ruling 85-125, 1985-2 C.B. 180, was issued which similarly disallowed losses from interdependent sales and purchases of mortgage pools. It ruled that these transactions were in essence mortgage swaps which resulted in the institutions acquiring assets that were not materially different from the assets they transferred.

The Supreme Court addressed this issue in *Cottage Savings Association v. Commissioner*, 499 U.S. 554 (1991), 91-1 U.S.T.C. ¶50,187. The Court held that Cottage Savings Association realized deductible losses when it exchanged participation interests in its residential mortgages for participation interests in residential mortgages held by other savings and loans. The exchange was a realization event, because the interests that were exchanged were materially different. The underlying mortgages were made to different obligors and were secured by different homes, therefore, the participation interests embodied legally distinct entitlements.

Additionally, the losses were treated as bona fide, because no contention had been made that the transaction was not at arm's length or that the taxpayer retained ownership of the participation interests that were traded.

The Court concluded that Treas. Reg. section 1.1001-1, which requires that an exchange of property can be treated as a disposition only if the properties exchanged are materially different, is a reasonable interpretation of IRC section 1001(a). However, it disagreed with the IRS that these exchanges were not for materially different assets. The court stated that "mortgages can be substantially identical for Memorandum R-49 purposes and still exhibit 'differences' that are 'material' for purposes of the Internal Revenue Code." The loans were considered to be materially different since the mortgages were made to different obligors and secured by different homes, resulting in legally distinct entitlements.

If the swap of mortgage pools results in an exchange of property under IRC section 1001, the financial institution has an amount realized on the disposition of the mortgage pool. In this case, the general rule of IRC section 1001(b) applies and the amount realized is the fair market value of property received in the exchange.

Note, that in the swap of mortgage pools, two holders are *exchanging* instruments that have already been issued. The borrower now owes its debt to a new party. Since there has not been an issuance of a new debt in exchange for property, the amount realized is not determined under Treas. Reg. section 1.1001-1(g) or, for transactions prior to enactment of the OID provisions, Revenue Ruling 79-292, 1979-2 C.B. 287. [Revenue Ruling 79-292, which required accrual basis taxpayers to realize the face amount (and not the fair market value) of debt instruments that were received *in exchange for property sold to the issuer* does not apply to an exchange of debt instruments by two holders.]

When mortgage interest rates are low, it is unlikely that you will encounter transactions where an institution is exchanging loans to generate a tax loss. However, if you examine a taxpayer who is deducting losses which were not reported for books, review the transactions to determine whether loans were swapped. If so, you will need to evaluate whether the swapped loans are materially different assets. The *Cottage Savings* case can be used as a guide. However, the particular facts for each transaction will need to be reviewed.

FOREIGN LOANS SWAPPED FOR FOREIGN LOANS

Many banks have made loans to lesser developed) countries (LDC). Shareholders, regulators, depositors, and creditors of these banks have been concerned about whether the banks' balance sheets overstated the value of these loans since payment of the principal and interest was doubt ful. The banks have written off many of these loans for book purposes. However, it is the IRS' position that the loans cannot be presumed worthless for tax purposes unless the regulators have issued assigned transfer risk reserves (ATRR) designations to them. In the absence of an ATRR, the taxpayer must establish worthlessness on a loan-by-loan basis from all of the facts and circumstances.

Some banks have swapped this foreign debt for the foreign debt of other banks. The banks may swap identical debt, such as Mexican loans for Mexican loans. However, they usually swap debt that is different, such as Mexican loans for Brazilian loans. One party to the transaction may also pay cash if the value of the loans received is treater than the value of the loans given up.

Regardless of the type of debt that has been exchanged, the banks often take a loss for the difference between their basis in the loans and the fair market value" of the loans. Frequently, the banks have purchased similar loans from third parties prior to the exchange to establish their fair market value. They may also use a broker familiar with dealing in foreign debt to value the loans.

If a bank has swapped its foreign loans with another bank for different foreign loans, that is, Mexican for Brazilian, the swap results in an exchange under IRC section 1001. This assumes, however, that the wash sale rules of IRC section 1091 do not apply to prevent the recognition of loss on the sale and repurchase of substantially identical securities (that is, loans issued by the same country with identical interest rates and maturity dates).

If there is an exchange, the general rule of IRC section 1001(b) applies and the amount realized by the bank is the fair market value of property received (the foreign loan) in the exchange.

Note, that in the swap of foreign loans, two holders are *exchanging* instruments that have already been issued. The borrower now owes its debt to a new party. Since there has not been debt issued in exchange for property, the amount realized is *not* determined under Treas. Reg. section 1001-1(g) or, for transactions prior to the enactment of the OID provisions, Revenue Ruling 79-292.

Note, that if a bank agrees with a foreign country to modify the terms of a debt instrument, the transaction is a "loan restructuring" which is discussed below.

REPURCHASE AGREEMENTS

Repurchase agreements (repos) are simultaneous contracts to sell and repurchase identical securities within a specified time at a specified price.[1,2] The agreements may cover securities such as, Treasury bonds, bills, notes, mortgage backed securities, or commercial paper. Since the agreements are entered into simultaneously, the transactions are considered to be equivalent to borrowing and lending funds equal to the sales price of the related securities. This is recorded as a financing transaction, not as a sale. The difference between the sale and purchase prices represents interest for use of the funds.

For example, Bank A may sell a particular Treasury bond to Bank B for $1,000,000. At the same time, they agree that Bank A will repurchase the same security 180 days later for $950,000. The difference of $50,000 rep-

[1] Please note that the terminology used in this chapter may vary between tax, accounting, and regulatory sources. For example, the AICPA Audit and Accounting Guides for banks and savings and loans use different terminology when discussing repurchase agreements.

[2] The other side of the transaction, a contract to purchase and resell at a later date, is known as a reverse repurchase agreement.

resents the interest on the "borrowed" funds. The interest earned on the security and the pay down of the principal balance will also affect the transaction.

Although the transactions are similar, dollar rolls are different from repurchase agreements. Dollar rolls are contracts to sell and repurchase *similar but not identical* securities, generally mortgage backed securities. Dollar rolls are recorded as financing transactions for books only if the securities that are sold and repurchased are similar enough to consider the transaction borrowing and lending of funds. Otherwise, the transaction is considered a sale and purchase of securities.

Banks enter into these agreements to obtain funds by leveraging their investment portfolios. The terms of the agreements are generally for 1 to 6 months, but can range from only a day to in excess of a year. Sometimes the agreements are extended beyond the original terms.

Generally, repurchase agreements have been treated as financing transactions for tax, as well as, for books. However, the facts for the transaction were considered to determine whether the taxpayer had substantially relinquished its ownership and whether there was a shifting of the economic risk of loss. See Rev. Rul. 79-195, 1979-1 C.B. 177; Rev. Rul. 74-27, 1974-1 C.B. 24; Rev. Rul. 77-59, 1977-1 C.B. 196; *American National Bank of Austin v. United States,* 421 F.2d 442 (5th Cir. 1970) [70-1 USTC ¶9184], *cert. denied,* 400 U.S. 819 (1970); *Citizens National Bank of Waco v. United States,* 551 F.2d 832, 843 (Ct.Cl. 1977) [77-1 USTC ¶9298].

The proposed regulations, for IRC section 1001, clarify when a modification of a debt instrument will be deemed to be an exchange of properties that differ materially either in kind or extent. The theory behind the regulations is to avoid recognition of gains or losses unless the exchanges are material. Although the proposed regulations do not apply to dollar rolls, they do give some guidance on what differences in the terms of debt instruments are considered to be material. Consideration should be given to the regulations when determining whether recognition is required for dollar rolls.

Practically speaking, most repurchase agreements and dollar rolls are resolved in a very short time, sometimes a few days. Therefore, it may not make any difference whether the transaction is treated as a sale and subsequent repurchase or a financing transaction. Hopefully, additional guidance will be issued on this issue in the near future.

REAL ESTATE MORTGAGE INVESTMENT CONDUITS (REMIC)

REMIC's were created by the 1986 Tax Reform Act as a vehicle for the securitization of mortgages. The tax law relating to REMIC's is extremely complex and, therefore, will not be discussed in this guide. However, some general background information will be provided.

A REMIC may be formed as a partnership, trust, corporation, or other agreed upon entity. A REMIC may also be formed as a segregated pool of assets rather than as a separate entity. An organization, such as a bank, transfers real estate loans to the REMIC in exchange for interests in it.

Interests are then sold to third party investors and gain or loss is recognized on the sale. There are both "regular interests" and "residual interests."

REMIC's are generally not subject to taxation. Instead, the income of the REMIC is taxable to holders of interests in the REMIC. The regular interests are treated as debt obligations. The residual interest holders are taxed on the net income of the REMIC. A portion of the income allocable to a residual interest, referred to as an "excess inclusion," is, with an exception for thrift institutions, subject to Federal income taxation in all events. Residual interest holders other than thrift institutions may not offset excess inclusions with otherwise allowable deductions.

You may audit a bank that holds either a regular interest, a residual interest, or both. If you decide to examine this area you will need to do considerable research. The law relating to REMIC's is found in IRC sections 860A through 860G. Also, Tax Management has a portfolio that discusses REMIC's.

LOAN RESTRUCTURINGS

Final regulations under IRC section 1001 were published as T.D. 8675 (1996-29, I.R.B. 5 (July 15, 1996)). The discussion which follows was written before these regulations were finalized so any resulting changes have not been incorporated in this text. For questions concerning application of the final regulations, contact the Industry Specialist.

Banks, often, will renegotiate the terms of a debt instrument with a borrower. If the changes are material, there is a deemed exchange for tax purposes of the original debt instrument for a new debt instrument with the modified terms. Sometimes, this type of exchange is referred to as a swap, though it differs from the transactions discussed above that involve an exchange between holders of instruments of different obligors.

If the modification of the debt rises to the level of a deemed exchange, the bank will have gain or loss on the disposition of the original instrument. In addition, the bank will hold a new instrument that may be subject to the rules for original issue discount under IRC sections 1272 through 1275 or the unstated interest rules of IRC section 483.

Treas. Reg. section 1.1001-1(a) provides that gain or loss is realized on the sale of property or on *the exchange of property for other property differing materially either in kind or in extent.* This rule applies not only to actual exchanges of properties between owners, but also to deemed exchanges arising from the modification of the terms of debt instruments. However, *see* Treas. Reg. section 1.1001-1(g) for special rules for using issue price to determine the amount realized for OID instruments. After the opinion in *Cottage Savings,* there was considerable discussion as to how the Court's interpretation of the definition of a material difference should be applied to debt modifications.

The IRS responded by proposing changes to the Regulations for IRC section 1001. Proposed Treas. Reg. section 1.1001-3 provides the rules for determining when a modification of a debt instrument will be deemed to be an exchange of properties that differ materially either in kind or in extent. Gain or loss recognition is not required if the modification of the debt instrument is not significant.

A brief outline of the proposed regulations is provided below.

1. A significant modification of a debt instrument is treated as an exchange of the original instrument for a modified instrument that differs materially either in kind or extent. If the modification is not significant, it is not an exchange.
2. An alteration of a legal right or obligation of the holder or the issuer is a modification unless the alteration was provided for in the original terms of the instrument and does not require consent or consideration from the other party. However, a temporary waiver of a default or similar right by the holder after the issuer fails to perform an obligation is not a modification.
3. Rules are provided which determine whether changes in (a) yield, (b) timing or amounts of payments, (c) obligor or security, or (d) the nature of the instrument are considered significant.
4. If multiple, simultaneous changes are made to the debt instrument which are not significant, they do not collectively constitute a significant modification.
5. Multiple changes to a debt instrument over any period of time constitute a significant modification if, had they been done as a single change, the change would have resulted in a significant modification.

If the taxpayer you are examining has renegotiated debt with its customers, you will need to consider whether it resulted in a taxable event. Usually when debt restructuring occurs, it is because the borrower is having financial trouble. Therefore, the restructured loan will have more favorable terms for the borrower and therefore, be worth less. Since this would result in a loss, the taxpayer may want to treat changes that are not material as being significant modifications. Although the proposed regulations have not yet been finalized, you may want to review them to get a better understanding of the issue.

The proposed regulations, for the most part, follow the existing authorities as to when a debt modification would rise to the level of an exchange under IRC section 1001. The proposed regulations, however, are prospective only. For transactions occurring before the proposed regulations take effect, rely on existing authorities.

The main issue on the deemed disposition of the original note is the amount realized. Banks may try to claim that the amount realized is the fair market value of the new debt instrument.

Under Treas. Reg. section 1.1001-1(g), if a debt instrument is given in exchange for property, the amount realized on the disposition of the property is the issue price of the debt instrument received as determined under the OID rules. The regulation is effective as of April 4, 1994, but has been proposed in substantially the same form since 1986. Amendments were made to this section in 1996. (This regulation was part of the

OID package and is separate from Proposed Treas. Reg. section 1.1001-3.)

Under rules in IRC sections 1273, 1274, and the regulations, the issue price of the new debt that provides for interest at or above the applicable Federal rate (AFR) will generally be the debt instrument's face amount. If either the old or new debt instrument in the exchange is publicly traded (listed on an exchange or regularly quoted by dealers in the over-the-counter market), however, the issue price of the new debt instrument will be fair market value, as measured by the traded debt. Narrow bid/ask spreads for bonds (based on evidence of contemporaneous quotes) are a strong indication that the bonds are regularly quoted.

For exchanges occurring prior to the enactment of the OID rules in 1984, Revenue Ruling 79-292 requires accrual basis taxpayers to realize the face amount, not the fair market value, of the debt obligations that are received upon the disposition of property. Since the taxpayer has an unconditional right to receive the face amount of the note, the fair market value is not relevant.

EXAMINATION TECHNIQUES

1. The taxpayer should be questioned extensively to determine whether they have exchanged any loans during the years under examination. Ask specifically about mortgage loan swaps, foreign loan swaps, repurchase agreements, *etc.*

2. Keep in mind that some of these swaps might not require book recognition. If the principal amount has not changed during the swap, there usually would not be any book entries. Therefore, the tax department may not be aware that any swaps took place. A person from the bank that is knowledgeable in this area should be interviewed.

3. Review the M-1 schedule and related work papers to see if there are any book/tax differences in the reporting of loan losses. Large and unusual items should be analyzed further.

4. If the taxpayer has exchanged loans, you will need to do research to determine whether the exchange resulted in a taxable event. Since there have been new interpretations of the law in this area, you may want to discuss the issue with the industry specialist or a financial product specialist.

5. If the taxpayer has restructured loans, obtain copies of both the new and old loan documents to determine whether there are substantial modifications.

6. Once you determine that the taxpayer had a taxable exchange, do research to determine whether face value or fair market value should be used for the amount realized. The taxable gain or loss can then be computed.

7. Additional examination techniques were discussed in each of the above sections. Those should be reviewed when you encounter that particular type of swap.

SUMMARY

As discussed above, there are several types of loan swaps that banks may enter into. Each type of exchange must be evaluated to determine whether the taxpayer properly reported the gain or loss from the transaction. The Supreme Court's opinion in *Cottage Savings* should be considered when determining the proper tax treatment of the swaps.

CHAPTER 21—MISCELLANEOUS ISSUES

INTRODUCTION

During the examination of a bank, you may encounter issues which are not explained elsewhere in this guide. This miscellaneous issues section is included to provide a *brief* explanation of these topics. This portion of the guide was not meant to consider all of the potential aspects of an issue. The explanations are simply a starting point to be used when developing a new issue.

ACCRUAL OF ORIGINAL ISSUE DISCOUNT AND MARKET DISCOUNT

Original issue discount (OID) is simply the excess of a debt instrument's stated redemption price at maturity over its issue price.

IRC section 1272(a)(1) provides that:

Extract

> IRC section 1272(a)(1)
>
> *** For purposes of this title, there shall be included in the gross income of the holder of any debt instrument having original issue discount issued after July 1, 1982, an amount equal to the sum of the daily portions of the original issue discount for each day during the taxable year on which such holder held such debt instrument.

In other words, the holder of any debt instrument having original issue discount must include in income a ratable portion of the discount computed on a daily basis.

In February 1994, the Service published final rules for the treatment of OID, de minimis OID, stated interest, and unstated interest. See, generally, Treas. Reg. sections 1.163-7, 1.446-2, 1.483-1 through 1.483-3, 1.1012-1(g), and 1.1271-0 through 1.1275-5.

Original issue discount should *not* be confused with market discount. A market discount involves the purchase of a security at a discount after its original issuance. This discount is generally not taxed until maturity or disposition. However, the Tax Reform Act of 1986 provides that some of the market discount would be currently taxable if a portion of the principal is included with the interest payment. If a financial institution is *not* required to report all of the accrued market discount, IRC section 1277(a) may require the deferral of a portion of the bank's interest expense deduction that is allocable to obligations purchased at a discount.

Banks normally invest a significant amount of funds in mortgage backed securities issued by the Governmental National Mortgage Association (GNMA), Federal National Mortgage Association (FNMA), and the Federal Home Loan Mortgage Association (FHLMC). These obligations can be purchased at a *discount* from the face value of the note. Payments on these obligations include the interest due, *plus* a portion of the principal of the original obligation. Therefore, each payment contains a portion of the *discount*. The amount of the discount is taxable income when received or accrued by the bank.

CAP INTEREST

The tax treatment of prepaid interest was, generally, changed by the final original issue discount (OID) regulations. A debt instrument with an overall instrument rate cap is subject to the OID rules, either under the rules for variable rate debt instruments or for contingent payment debt instruments.

Prior to December 1992, CAP interest was one of the five coordinated issues in the commercial banking area. The CAP interest issue was formally *decontrolled* in December 1992, thus it is no longer a coordinated issue. In the event you come across an issue in this area, contact the Industry Specialist for Commercial Banking for an update.

CHANGE OF ACCOUNTING METHOD

Rev. Proc. 92-20, 1992-1 C.B. 685, was issued in March 1992 to provide new procedures for changes in accounting methods. It modified and superseded Rev. Proc. 84-74, 1984-1 C.B. 118. In general, the revenue procedure provides incentives for taxpayers to file requests to change from improper accounting methods *before* they are contacted by the IRS for an examination. The terms and conditions for accounting method changes are dependent on when the method change is requested and upon the impropriety of the method that had been used.

The revenue procedure states that if the practice does not permanently affect the taxpayer's lifetime taxable income, but does or could change the taxable year in which taxable income is reported, it involves timing and is therefore considered a method of accounting.

In other words, *timing adjustments* fall under the rules for changing accounting methods.

These procedures apply to all taxpayers, not just banks. It is being mentioned in this guide so that it is properly considered during the course of your examination. A complete analysis of this revenue procedure is available in most research libraries.

It is important that you inform the taxpayer whenever you change the bank's accounting method so that there is no question which method they should use in subsequent years.

CURRENCY TRANSACTION REPORTING (CTR)

In an attempt to track the flow of cash by individuals and businesses, the Federal Government has imposed strict reporting requirements in recent years. One of the most common requirements for banks involves currency transaction reporting. Forms must be filed with the Internal Revenue Service by financial institutions for each deposit, withdrawal, exchange of currency, or other payment or transfer, by, through, or to such financial institution which involves a transaction in currency in excess of $10,000.

Treasury Form 4789 is used to report cash transactions over $10,000 which are deposited with the financial institution in one or more related transactions. It is the obligation of the bank to properly file these forms when appropriate. The form identifies the individual making the transaction, the person or organization for whom the transaction was conducted, the institution reporting the transaction, and the amount of cash deposited. As explained in Chapter 5, the IRS does not have jurisdiction to examine this area for federally regulated banks.

Treasury Form 8300 is required for cash payments over $10,000 which are received by the bank other than from depositors. It identifies the customer and provides a description of the transaction and method of payment.

Forms filed by taxpayers are available to the revenue agent through the Currency and Banking Retrieval System.

DIVIDEND RECEIVED DEDUCTION

The dividend received deduction is disallowed on any stock which was not held for the required holding period. In addition, no dividend received deduction is allowed to the extent the taxpayer is under an obligation to make related payments with respect to positions in substantially similar or related property. See Revenue Ruling 94-28, 1994-1 C.B. 86, which discusses the availability of the dividends received deduction for some new financial products.

ENTRANCE AND EXIT FEES PAID TO CONVERT FROM AN S&L TO A BANK

A number of savings and loans have converted to banks in recent years. There are several reasons why they might choose to do this. First, the public image of a bank is better than that of a thrift. Second, a savings and loan is required to invest primarily in mortgage loans. If the institution determines that they would be more profitable being diversified, it may be willing to give up the tax advantages afforded to savings and loans. Third, at one point, the insurance premiums paid to the Bank Insurance Fund ("BIF") were lower than those paid to the Savings Association Insurance Fund ("SAIF"). Last, banks which acquire savings and loans may want them to be similar types of institutions.

When a savings and loan converts to a bank, it is required to pay a fee to exit SAIF and another fee to join BIF. Consideration needs to be given to whether either or both of these fees are capital in nature. Many people in the industry concur that the entrance fee should not be expensed. It is the cost of changing the institution's form of doing business and will create a future benefit. It may be argued that the exit fee should also be capitalized since it is part of the overall conversion which results in a future benefit. Some banks argue that the exit fee is a cost of ceasing to do business in the old form and therefore, should be expensed.

The Service is treating the SAIF exit fee and the BIF entrance fee as part of an integrated transaction. Both fees are required to be paid in any conversion transaction and confer significant benefits which extend beyond the taxable year. As a result, both the exit fee and the entrance fee are capital expenditures under IRC section 263. Since the benefits of these fees continue indefinitely as long as membership in the insurance fund is re tained (as opposed to continuing only for the life of the specific deposits transferred), the exit fee and entrance fee are not subject to an allowance for depreciation under IRC section 167(a).

The potential effect of new IRC section 197 has not yet been addressed as it did not apply to the years under consideration. It is not known whether entrance and exit fees paid after the effective date of IRC section 197 will be amortizable. If you encounter this situation, contact the Commercial Banking or Savings & Loan Industry Specialist for the IRS' current position.

EXEMPTION FOR INSOLVENT BANKS

Under certain very restrictive circumstances, insolvent banks are *exempted* from federal income taxes under IRC section 7507. This section provides for payment of depositors' claims ahead of other creditors, including the U.S. Government. The fact that a bank is taken over by the FDIC does *not* automatically mean that it is insolvent. It is the Service position that IRC section 7507 applies only in very *rare* circumstances. The FDIC has attempted to discourage IRS examinations of banks it is operating by claiming that they are insolvent and, therefore, exempt from federal income taxes. If you have this issue, please contact the Industry Specialist.

MISCELLANEOUS INCOME

Banks, generally, report many miscellaneous items of income in a manner consistent with their overall method of accounting. Service charges such as safe deposit fees, traveler checks fees, overdraft charges, and other miscellaneous fees are generally included in income as earned or received, whichever is earlier.

NET OPERATING LOSS CARRYBACKS

IRC section 172(b)(1)(D)

Pursuant to IRC section 172(b)(1)(D) for taxable years beginning after December 31, 1986 and before January 1, 1994, banks using the specific charge-off method for bad debt loss deductions, are allowed a 10-year carry-back and a 5-year carryforward for NOL's attributable specifically to bad debt losses. This differs from a regular corporation which is allowed only a 3-year carry back for net operating losses. This carryback period was changed by the Tax Reform Act of 1986. Previously, the law had allowed a 10-year carryback for *all* losses incurred by a bank.

Because of the extended carryback provisions, banks may file claims for a number of years if they have bad debts which create a net operating loss. If allowable claims exceed $1,000,000, Joint Committee case procedures must be followed.

First Alex Bancshares Inc. v. United States, 93-2 U.S.T.C. ¶50,542 (W.D. Okla. 1993) [830 FSupp 581], held that the 10-year NOL carryback applies only to bad debt deductions claimed under IRC section 166. Banks using the reserve method under IRC section 585 cannot claim a 10-year carryback. See Rev. Rul. 93-69, 1993-2 C.B. 75.

IRC section 172(f)

If you have any cases involving the 10-year carryback provisions of IRC section 172(f), please contact the ISP Specialist for Savings and Loans.

REGULATORY AGENCY PENALTIES

The Federal Reserve and other regulatory agencies have the authority to charge a bank various penalties for failing to comply with banking regulations. IRC section 162(f) provides that no deduction shall be allowed for any fine or similar penalty paid to the government for the violation of any act. Penalties by the regulators which are punitive in nature may constitute a nondeductible civil penalty within the meaning of Treas. Reg. section 1.162-21(b)(1)(ii). However, the mere designation as a penalty is not determinative.

The easiest way to obtain penalty information is through the use of Lexis. Search the Lexis libraries for any regulatory agencies that examine your bank. Your search request should include the name of the bank and the word *fine* or *penalty*. If you come across this issue, please contact either the Industry Specialist or Industry Counsel for Commercial Banking (or Savings and Loan if you are examining a thrift).

STOCK DIVIDEND AND ISSUANCE COSTS

Costs directly associated with the issuance of additional capital stock or stock dividends are not tax deductible expenses. A review of the annual report or the corporate minute book will usually indicate if any new stock or stock dividends were issued. Some examples of the type of expenses that cannot be deducted are legal fees, printing costs, mailing costs, and other distribution expenses.

BUILT-IN-LOSS LIMITATIONS ON NOLS

In *Idaho First National Bank, Moore Financial Group, Inc. v. Commissioner*, 997 F.2d 1285 (9th Cir. 1993) [93-2 USTC ¶50,373], the court ruled that losses resulting from the financial failures of the acquired corporation prior to acquisition were "built-in deductions" rather than rehabilitating deductions and thus were limited under Treas. Reg. section 1.1502-15(a).

S-CORPORATION STATUS

As a result of the August 20, 1996, enactment of P.L. 104-188, the Small Business Job Protection Act of 1996, banks and thrifts not using a reserve method of accounting for bad debts are now eligible to convert to S-Corporations in tax years beginning after December 31, 1996. Prior to Act section 1315, IRC section 1361(b)(2) prohibited financial institutions to which IRC sections 585 and 593 applied from electing S-Corporation status. In a related measure, Act section 1301 increased the number of shareholders permitted in an S-Corporation from 35 to 75. Conversion from a reserve method of bad debts to the specific charge off method will trigger the recapture of some or all of the bad debt reserve.

APPENDIX RESOURCE & REFERENCE MATERIALS

There are many resource and reference materials available which can assist you during the examination of a financial institution. The majority of these materials are published commercially for use by banks and accountants. There are also various seminars held periodically. Information regarding these items and a list of IRS personnel who are involved with the tax treatment of financial institutions is provided below. Please keep in mind that this information may have changed since the publication date of this guide.

BANKING RESEARCH MANUALS

TAXATION OF FINANCIAL INSTITUTIONS

This is a three volume set authored by partners at KPMG Peat Marwick and published by Matthew Bender. The first two volumes provide detailed, but easy-to-read explanations of bank and thrift tax issues. Sample returns are also included. Volume three includes code sections, regulations, revenue rulings, applicable federal rates, revenue procedures, and letter rulings applicable to financial institutions.

Most of the larger banks subscribe to this research service so you may be able to use the bank's copy. Ordering information is provided below:

Address: Matthew Bender & Company, Inc.
Customer Services Department-Special Accounts
1275 Broadway, Albany, N.Y. 12204
Phone: (800) 833-9844
Cost: $525 for the first year, $389 for each subsequent year

THE BANK INCOME TAX RETURN MANUAL

This manual is published each year by Warren Gorham Lamont and is written by Charles W. Wheeler, JD, and Jack B. Wilson, Jr., CPA. The manual is comprised of text, practice aids, checklists, tables, and sample tax returns. Although this is not as large as the *Taxation of Financial Institutions,* it provides very good explanations of bank tax law. It does not include information applicable to thrift institutions. Ordering information is provided below:

Address: Warren Gorham Lamont
Ted Ward, Federal Government Representative
210 South Street, Boston, MA 02111
Phone: (800) 950-1229 X8277
Cost: $117.76 (Government rate)

FEDERAL INCOME TAXATION OF BANKS & FINANCIAL INSTITUTIONS

This manual is also published by Warren Gorham Lamont and is authored by Lance W. Rook. It provides detailed information on the federal income taxation of banks and other financial institutions. The manual also includes worksheets and a table of code sections, regulations, and rulings. Ordering information is provided below:

Address: Warren Gorham Lamont
Ted Ward, Federal Government Representative
210 South Street, Boston, MA 02111
Phone: (800) 950-1229 X8277
Cost: $505.58 per year, including 4 updates
(Government rate) $215 for initial yearly fill with no updates

BANKING PUBLICATIONS

THE JOURNAL OF BANK TAXATION

The Journal of Bank Taxation is published quarterly by Warren Gorham Lamont. The periodical includes articles by various bank tax professionals on current topics. It also may contain information on upcoming conferences, bank tax planning, state bank developments, international banking, *etc.* Ordering information is provided below:

Address: Warren Gorham Lamont
Ted Ward, Federal Government Representative
210 South Street, Boston, MA 02111
Phone: (800) 950-1229 X8277
Cost: $128.70 per year (Government rate)

AMERICAN BANKER

The *American Banker* is a newspaper which is published Monday through Friday. It provides current information on all banking activities, such as mergers, earnings, legislation, *etc.*, not just bank taxation. Magazines are also published each year which include consumer surveys and rankings of banks. Ordering information is provided below:

Address: American Banker
One State Street Plaza, New York, N.Y. 10004
Phone: (800) 221-1809
Cost: $750 per year (lower group rates may be available)

IRS MATERIALS

INTERNAL REVENUE MANUAL 4232.9

This handbook was prepared to assist agents in the examination of financial institutions. Chapter 200 provides general information on records, accounting methods, issues, *etc.* which are applicable to bank and trust companies. This section of the manual also discusses savings and loans, mutual savings banks, cooperative banks, commercial credit agencies, regulated investment companies, small business investment companies, and bank holding companies.

NON-TAX PUBLICATIONS

COMPTROLLER'S MANUAL FOR NATIONAL BANKS

This manual contains selected statutes, regulations, and rulings related to the operations of banks. It is updated every few years to include subsequent changes to the law. It can be secured from the Comptroller of the Currency by written request. There generally is not a charge to the IRS if you request a complimentary copy. Ordering information is provided below:

Address: Ellen Stockdale, Director of Communication
250 E Street SW
Washington D.C. 20219
Phone: (202) 622-2000
Cost: $0 (Government rate)

AUDITS OF BANKS

The AICPA publishes an audit and accounting guide which describes the accounting and financial reporting practices for the banking industry. It also discusses the audits of banks' financial statements. The guide is updated annually. It can be ordered as follows:

Address: American Institute of Certified Public Accountants
P.O. Box 9264
Church Street Station
New York, NY 10256-9264
Phone: (800) 862-4272
Cost: $29.75 ($27 for AICPA members)

BANK TAX SEMINARS AND CONFERENCES

ANNUAL BANK TAX INSTITUTE

Executive Enterprises sponsors the Bank Tax Institute which is held each December. Approximately 20 general sessions and workshops are held on various topics such as, bad debts, financial products, mortgage banking, IRS developments, international banking, mergers, *etc.* The sessions are intended for individuals who are familiar with the banking industry and the specific bank tax issues. Speakers include the IRS banking and savings and loan industry specialists, accountants, and bank tax managers. Although the sessions are geared towards educating accountants and bank personnel they can also be very informative for IRS agents. There are several hundred people who attend this conference. For registration information contact the following:

Address: Executive Enterprises, Inc.
22 West 21st Street
New York, NY 10010-6990
Phone: (800) 831-8333
Cost: $995

THE HOTTEST ISSUES IN BANK TAXATION

This small group training session is also sponsored by Executive Enterprises. The course leader is Ronald Blasi, a professor at the College of Law at Georgia State University. This conference covers fewer topics than the Bank Tax Institute, but explores them in more depth. The instructor encourages the class to interact and welcomes IRS agents' comments. There are usually several sessions offered each year. Registration information follows:

Address: Executive Enterprises, Inc.
22 West 21st Street
New York, NY 10010-6990
Phone: (800) 831-8333
Cost: $995

IRS RESOURCE PEOPLE

The following list is provided to assist IRS personnel in contacting specific members of the banking and savings and load ISP teams. They are not part of the MSSP program.

Banking ISP Team

Name	*Title*	*Phone/FAX #*
Mary Grady	Industry Specialist	(212) 719-6270
	- Manhattan	(212) 719-6005
John Sweeney	Foreign Banking Specialist	(212) 719-6271
	- Manhattan	(212) 719-6005
Victor Bellino	Asst. Industry Specialist	(212) 719-6295
	- Manhattan	(212) 719-6005
John Conley	Appeals Coordinator	(212) 264-3734
	- Manhattan	(212) 264-9758
Roland Barral	Industry Counsel	(212) 264-7940
	- Manhattan	(212) 264-4089
Peter La Belle	Industry Counsel	(212) 264-7829
	- Manhattan	(212) 264-4089
Dante Lucas	Industry Counsel	(212) 264-7872
	- Manhattan	(212) 264-4089
Diane Thaler	Industry Counsel	(212) 264-7920
	- Manhattan	(212) 264-4089
Steve Glickstein	Counsel to the Asst.	(202) 622-4439
	Chief Counsel (FI&P)	(202) 622-4425
Arnold Golub	ISP Coordinator	(202) 622-3950
	Counsel - FI&P	(202) 622-4425
Peter Cinquergrani	ISP Coordinator	(202) 622-3920
	Counsel - FI&P	(202) 622-4425
Craig Wojay	ISP Coordinator	(202) 622-3920
	Counsel - FI&P	(202) 622-4425
Tina Jannotta	ISP Coordinator	(202) 622-7870
	Counsel - FS:FI&P	(202) 622-6889
Grace Matueszeski	ISP Coordinator	(202) 622-7900
	Counsel - FS:IT&A	(202) 622-6889
Richard Hoge	ISP Coordinator	(202) 622-3870
	Counsel - International	(202) 622-4484
Lewis Brickates	ISP Coordinator	(202) 622-7770
	Counsel - Corporate	(202) 622-6834
Kelly Alton	ISP Coordinator	(202) 622-4950
	Counsel - IT&A	(202) 622-6316

Savings and Loan ISP Team

Name	*Title*	*Phone/FAX #*
Jody Botsford	Industry Specialist	(213) 894-0918
	- Los Angeles	(213) 894-6432
Rubs Reynolds	Appeals Coordinator	(213) 894-4680
	- Los Angeles	(213) 894-6282
Bill Boulet	Industry Counsel	(303) 844-3258

	- Denver	(303) 844-3294
Mark Petersen	Industry Counsel	(414) 297-4248
	- Milwaukee	(414) 297-4285
Steve Glickstein	Counsel to the Asst.	(202) 622-4439
	Chief Counsel (FI&P)	(202) 622-4425
Mark Smith	ISP Coordinator	(202) 622-3930
	Counsel - FI&P	(202) 622-4425
Arnold Golub	ISP Coordinator	(202) 622-3950
	Counsel - FI&P	(202) 622-4425
Peter Cinquergrani	ISP Coordinator	(202) 622-3920
	Counsel - FI&P	(202) 622-4425
Craig Wojay	ISP Coordinator	(202) 622-3920
	Counsel - FI&P	(202) 622-4425
Tina Jannotta	ISP Coordinator	(202) 622-7870
	Counsel -FS:FI&P	(202) 622-6889
Roy Hirschhorn	ISP Coordinator	(202) 622-3610
	Counsel - GL	(202) 622-6834
Walt Ryan	ISP Coordinator	(202) 622-3610
	Counsel - GL	(202) 622-3766

SYNOPSIS OF LAW, DECISIONS, & RULINGS

INTRODUCTION

There are a number of recent regulations, court cases, revenue rulings, revenue procedures, *etc.* which affect the taxation of financial institutions. The most significant decisions have been summarized below to assist you in your research. Information on other useful reading materials is provided. Also refer to the banking coordinated issue papers for discussions of older court cases which affect the coordinated issues.

Information relating to the following issues are discussed in this chapter:

1. Bad Debts
2. Capital Expenditures
3. Core Deposits and Other Intangibles
4. Financial Products
5. Foreign Banking
6. Loan Origination Costs
7. Loan Swaps
8. Miscellaneous Issues
9. Mortgage Servicing Rights
10. Nonperforming Loans
11. Original Issue Discount
12. Premature Withdrawal Penalty Income

BAD DEBTS

T.D. 8676, 1996-30, I.R.B. 4. These temporary regulations (1.166-3T) under IRC section 166 were issued in July 1996 and discuss the interaction between debt modifications under IRC section 1001 and partially worthless debt.

T.D. 8513, 1994-1 C.B. 169. These final regulations under IRC section 585 were issued on December 29, 1993.

T.D. 8492, 1993-2 C.B. 73. This Treasury decision amends Treas. Reg. section 1.166-2(d)(3) regarding the conclusive presumption of worthlessness for bad debt charge-offs.

T.D. 8396, 1992-1 C.B. 95. This Treasury decision contains final regulations under IRC section 166 relating to a bank's determination of worthlessness of a debt. The regulations provide for a conclusive presumption of worthlessness of debts based on the application of a single set of standards for both regulatory and tax accounting purposes.

Rev. Rul. 92-14, 1992-1 C.B. 93. The portion of an international loan that is subject to an allocated transfer risk reserve (ATRR) is treated as a debt charge-off in obedience to a specific order of the bank's supervisory authority for purposes of the conclusive presumption regulations.

Rev. Proc. 92-18, 1992-1 C.B. 684. The procedures are provided for obtaining an express determination letter from the bank's supervisory authority. A sample uniform express determination letter is provided.

Rev. Proc. 92-84, 1992-2 C.B. 489. Discusses requirements for obtaining an express determination letter and describes the contents of the letter.

Notice 93-50, 1993-2 C.B. 336. A bank can, under certain circumstances, elect the conformity method via an amended return for tax years ending on or after December 31, 1991.

CAPITAL EXPENDITURES

Indopco, Inc. v. Commissioner, 503 U.S. 79 (1992) [92-1 USTC ¶50,113], *aff'g National Starch and Chemical Corp. v. Commissioner,* 918 F.2d 426 (3d Cir. 1990) [90-2 USTC ¶50,571], *aff'g* 93 T.C. 67 (1989) [CCH Dec. 45,851]. Expenses incurred during a friendly takeover were not deductible because benefits were created that extended beyond the current year. The creation or enhancement of a separate asset was not a necessary condition to require expenses to be capitalized.

Rev. Rul. 92-80, 1992-2 C.B. 57. This ruling held that advertising costs are generally deductible under IRC section 162.

CORE DEPOSITS AND OTHER INTANGIBLES

Citizens & Southern Corp. v. Commissioner, 91 T.C. 463 (1988), *aff'd without published opinion,* 900 F.2d 266 (11th Cir. 1990), *aff'd per curiam,* 919 F.2d 1492. The deposit base which was acquired by a bank had an ascertainable cost basis distinct from goodwill and had a limited useful life. The bank was allowed to depreciate the deposit base.

Colorado National Bankshares, Inc. v. Commissioner, T.C. Memo. 1990-495, *aff'd* 984 F.2d 383 (10th Cir. 1993). The core deposit intangible was held to have an ascertainable value separate and distinct from the goodwill and going-concern value of the acquired banks. The core had a limited useful life. Therefore, the taxpayer was entitled to a depreciation deduction.

IT&S of Iowa, Inc. v. Commissioner, 97 T.C. 496 (1991). The core deposit intangible asset is separate and distinct from goodwill and has a limited useful life. It may be depreciated on an accelerated basis. However, the bank erroneously calculated the value of the core deposit by including interest sensitive deposits, by failing to reduce the core for reserve requirements and float on deposits, by using an inappropriate alternative funding source, and by using an incorrect discount rate.

Newark Morning Ledger Co. v. United States, 507 U.S.—, 113 S. Ct. 1670, 123 L.Ed.2d. 288 (1993), *rev'g* 945 F.2d 555 (3d Cir. 1992), *rev'g* 736 F. Supp. 176 (D.N.J. 1990). If the taxpayer can successfully meet its burden of proving that an asset has value and a limited useful life, it is depreciable even if its value is related to the expectancy of continued patronage.

Peoples Bancorporation v. Commissioner, T.C. Memo. 1992-285. The core deposits were determined to be separate from goodwill and amortizable. They had limited useful lives of 18 and 20 years. The values were determined using a modified cost-savings method.

Trustmark Corp. v. Commissioner, T.C. Memo. 1994-184. The court allowed the use of subsequent studies of account closings to corroborate the reasonable accuracy of the taxpayer's projections.

IRC section 197. The capitalized costs of specified intangible assets are ratably amortized over a 15 year period. A bank's core deposit base is now defined under the provisions of IRC section 197.

T.D. 8528, 1994-1 C.B. 81, and PS-55-93, 1994-1 C.B. 830. The temporary and proposed regulations under IRC sections 167 and 168 relate to certain elections for intangible property.

Other Useful Reading:

Intangibles Settlement Initiative, IRS Document 9233 (2-94), Catalog No. 20566N. The settlement initiative gives taxpayers a one-time opportunity to resolve intangibles disputes in tax years not affected by the Omnibus Budget Reconciliation Act of 1993.

FINANCIAL PRODUCTS

Arkansas Best Corporation v. Commissioner, 485 U.S. 212 (1988), 88-1 U.S.T.C. ¶9210. The Supreme Court determined that an ordinary loss is allowable upon the sale of an asset only if the property is specifically excluded from capital asset treatment per IRC section 1221. The case discussed the treatment of hedging transactions.

Federal National Mortgage Association v. Commissioner, 100 T.C. No. 36 (1993), 65 T.C.M. (CCH) 4178 (1993). Certain hedging transactions were allowed ordinary loss treatment. The hedges were surrogates for mort gages and were excepted from the definition of a capital asset. Foreign currency swap transactions were also discussed.

Circle K Corp. v. United States, 23 Cl. Ct. 665, 91-2 U.S.T.C. ¶50383 (1991), vacating and reissuing, 23 Cl. Ct. 161, 91-1 U.S.T.C. ¶50260 (1991). The court allowed a gasoline retailer to deduct a loss on the sale of stock it purchased in an oil company as an ordinary loss. The purchase was characterized as an integral part of the company's inventory-purchase system and was excluded from the definition of a capital asset. The decision seems to be in direct conflict with the Arkansas Best decision.

IRC section 475. Beginning in 1994, dealers in securities are required to report unrealized gains and losses at year end if the securities are not held for investment.

T.D. 8493, 1993-2 C.B. 255. These new regulations, under IRC section 1221, define what transactions will qualify as hedging transactions. Ordinary gain or loss treatment is allowed for business hedges.

T.D. 8491, 1993-2 C.B. 215. These new regulations, under IRC section 446, govern the tax treatment of notional principal contracts. They deal with the year and amounts that should be reported for tax purposes.

FI-54-93, 1993-2 C.B. 615. These proposed regulations, under IRC section 446, would require that a taxpayer's method of accounting for hedging transactions clearly reflect income.

Notice 93-45, 1993-2 C.B. 334. Dealers must identify securities for mark to market.

Rev. Rul. 93-76, I.R.B. 93-35. This ruling elaborates on who will be considered a "dealer in securities." It amplifies and supersedes Notice 93-45.

Rev. Rul. 94-7, 1994-1 C.B. 151. This ruling corrects Rev. Rul. 93-76.

Proposed regulations under IRC section 475, FI-42-94, were published in the Federal Register on January 4, 1995.

T.D. 8653, 1996-12 I.R.B. 4, covers the final hedging regulations.

Rev. Proc 96-21, 1996-4 I.R.B. 96, deals with hedging.

Notice 96-12, 1996-10 I.R.B. 29, discusses mark to market accounting.

T.D. 8676, 1996-30 I.R.B. 4, provides temporary regulations on certain assignments of notional principal contracts.

FOREIGN BANKING

Continental Illinois Corp. v. Commissioner, T.C. Memo. 1991-66 [CCH Dec. 47,178(M)], *aff'd in part and rev'd in part, remanded,* 93 T.N.T. 148-11 (7th Cir. 1993), 93-2 U.S.T.C. ¶50400. The taxpayer was legally liable for Brazilian tax. However, the bank was entitled to foreign tax credits only when it substantiated that the withholding tax was paid.

Rev. Proc. 91-22, 1991-1 C.B. 526, superseded by Rev. Proc. 96-53, 1996-49 I.R.B. 22. This revenue procedure explains how to secure an advance pricing agreement covering the prospective determination and application of transfer pricing methodologies for international of foreign or domestic taxpayers. The revenue procedure has been corrected by and cited in several subsequent rulings.

LOAN ORIGINATION COSTS

Announcement 93-60, 1993-16 IRB 9. This announcement temporarily suspending the filing of accounting method change requests for loan origination costs.

Indopco, Inc. v. Commissioner, 503 U.S. 79 (1992), *aff'g National Starch and Chemical Corp. v. Commissioner,* 918 F.2d 426 (3d Cir. 1990), *aff'g* 93T.C. 67 (1989). Expenses incurred during a friendly takeover were not deductible because benefits were created that extended beyond the current year. The creation or enhancement of a separate asset was not a necessary condition to require expenses to be capitalized. Notice 96-7, 1996-6, I.R.B. 22 (February 5, 1996).

LOAN SWAPS

T.D. 8675, 1996-29 I.R.B. 5 (July 15, 1996). Final regulations under IRC section 1001 deal with debt modification.

Cottage Savings Association v. Commissioner, 499 U.S. 554 (1991), 91-1 U.S.T.C. ¶50187, remanded, 934 F.2d 739 (6th Cir. 1992), 92-1 U.S.T.C. ¶50221. The taxpayer realized deductible losses when it exchanged participation interests in mortgages for mortgages that were materially different. The losses were treated as bona fide because no contention had been made that the transaction was not at arm's length or that the taxpayer retained ownership of the participation interests that were traded.

FI-31-92, 1992-2 C.B. 683. The proposed regulations under IRC section 1001 provide the rules for determining when a modification of a debt instrument will be deemed to be an exchange of properties that differ materially either in kind or in extent.

MISCELLANEOUS ISSUES

First Alex Bancshares Inc. v. United States, 93-2 U.S.T.C. ¶50,542 (W.D. Okla. 1993) [830 F Supp 581]. The court held that the 10 year NOL carryback applies only to bad debt deductions claimed under IRC section 166.

Rev. Rul. 93-69, 1993-2 C.B. 75. A commercial bank may not use the special 10 year net operating loss carryback provision of IRC section 172(b)(1)(D) for the portion of its net operating loss that is attributable to a deduction for an addition to its bad debt reserve.

Idaho First National Bank, Moore Financial Group, Inc. v. Commissioner, 997 F.2d 1285 (9th Cir. 1993) [93-2 USTC ¶50,373]. The court ruled that losses resulting from the financial failures of the acquired corporation prior to acquisition were "built-in deductions" rather than rehabilitating deductions and thus were limited under Treas. Reg. section 1.1502-15(a).

Security Bank of Minnesota v. Commissioner, 994 F.2d 432 (8th Cir. 1993) [93-1 USTC ¶50,301], *aff'g* 98 T.C. 33 (1992) [CCH Dec. 49,941]. The court ruled that a *cash* basis bank was not required to accrue interest income on short term loans under IRC section 1281(a)(2). The Service's nonacquiescence to this decision was announced at 1995-2 C.B. 2 and in Notice 95-57, 1995-2, C.B. 337 and in an Action on Decision, 1995-52 I.R.B. 4. The Service will not follow this decision or allow changes of accounting method which reflect this decision outside the 8th Circuit.

Rev. Proc. 92-20, 1992-1 C.B. 685. This revenue procedure explains the new procedures for taxpayers to change their accounting methods. Taxpayers are given more favorable treatment the earlier they file for method changes.

Rev. Rul. 94-28, 1994-1 C.B. 86. The revenue ruling discusses the availability of the dividends received

MORTGAGE SERVICING RIGHTS

Rev. Rul. 91-46, 1991-2 C.B. 358. IRC section 1286 is applied to sales of mortgages when the seller enters into a contract to service the mortgages. If the taxpayer is entitled to receive amounts that exceed reasonable compensation for the services to be performed, the mortgages are stripped bonds. The excess servicing rights are stripped coupons.

Rev. Proc. 91-49, 1991-2 C.B. 777. The procedure provides simplified tax treatment for original issue discount for certain mortgages that are stripped bonds under IRC section 1286.

Rev. Proc. 91-50, 1991-2 C.B. 778. Taxpayers may elect to use safe harbor rates in computing the amount of excess servicing. The safe harbor rates represent the amount of reasonable compensation that the taxpayer is entitled to receive under a mortgage servicing contract.

Rev. Proc. 91-51, 1991-2 C.B. 779. Taxpayers can elect to automatically change their accounting method for servicing rights on a cutoff basis.

NONPERFORMING LOANS

European American Bank and Trust Co. v. United States, Cl. Ct. No. 135-82T, 92-1 U.S.T.C. ¶50,026 (Fed. Cir. 1992), *aff'g* 20 Cl. Ct. 594 (Cl. Ct. 1990). Interest income should be accrued unless there is no reasonable expectation that it will be paid. The accrual of interest income was not dependent on whether the principal on a loan was likely to be repaid. If a lender expects to receive payment for interest, but not necessarily payment for the principal, interest should still be accrued.

ORIGINAL ISSUE DISCOUNT

T.D. 8517, 1994-1 C.B. 38. [Treas. Reg. sections 1.163-7, 1.446-2, 1.483-1 through 1.483-3, 1.1001-1(g), 1.1012-1(g), and 1.1271-0 through 1.1275-5.] These regulations contain the final rules for the treatment of OID, de minimis OID, stated interest, and unstated interest.

Rev. Proc. 94-28, 1994-1 C.B. 614. This contains the procedures for taxpayers to obtain automatic consent to change their methods of accounting to conform to the final OID regulations.

Rev. Proc. 94-29, 1994-1 C.B. 616. This procedure includes special rules for any change in method of accounting for de minimis OID, including de minimis OID attributable to points.

Rev. Proc. 94-30, 1994-1 C.B. 621. This procedure allows a taxpayer to use the principal reduction method of accounting on certain loans originated by the taxpayer.

T.D. 8674, 1996-28, I.R.B. 7 (July 8, 1996), contains final regulations on contingent debt.

Rev. Rul. 95-70, 1995-2, C.B. 124, provides the definition of qualified stated interest, however, amendments contained in T.D. 8674 have affected these rulings.

Notice 96-23, 1996-16, IRB 23 (April 15, 1996), discusses the interaction between the Rev. Proc. 94-29 method and mark to market.

PREMATURE WITHDRAWAL PENALTY INCOME

United States v. Centennial Savings Bank, FSB, 499 U.S. 573 (1991), 91-1 U.S.T.C. ¶50188. The court held that premature withdrawal penalties could not be treated as discharge of indebtedness and excluded from taxable income. The penalty income was includible in taxable income in the current year.

Table of Cases

Numbers refer to section (§) numbers.

A

A.E. Staley Mfg. Co. v. Commissioner 8.5
A.J. Industries v. United States 8.21
A.N. McQuown v. Commissioner . . 11.3
Advertisers Exch., Inc. v. Commissioner 2.2
Affiliated Capital Corp. v. Commissioner 8.6
Alice Phelan Sullivan Corp. v. United States 10.6
Allen v. Trust Co. of Georgia 10.6
Allstate Savings & Loan Association v. Commissioner 7.6
American Central Utilities Co. v. Commissioner 5.3
American Finance & Mortgage CO. v. Commissioner 10.3
American Fork & Hoe Co. v. Commissioner 5.3
American National Bank of Austin v. United States. 2.9, 10.7
AmSouth Bancorporation v. United States 11.3
Andrews v. Commissioner 4.4
Annapolis Federal Savings & Loan Association v. Commissioner . . . 10.7
Anschutz v. Commissioner 14.6
Appalachian Trail Co. v. Commissioner 10.3
Appeal of Bank of Hartsville . . . 2.2, 2.6.1
Appeal of C.F. Hovey Co. 11.3
Appeal of Chatham & Pheonix National Bank 2.2, 2.6.1
Appeal of First National Bank of Kulm 2.2
Appeal of Franklin Brown and Otto Thomen 4.4
Appeal of Madison & Kedzie State Bank 2.2, 2.6.1
Appeal of National Bank of New Jersey 2.2
Appeal of Somers Lumber Co. 5.3
Arctic Ice Machine v. Commissioner 11.5
Arkansas Best Corp. v. United States 4.4, 7.6
Associated Milk Producers v. Commissioner 8.10
Atl. Coast Line Railroad Co. v. Commissioner 5.3
Atl. Coast Realty Co. v. Commissioner 7.5.1
Austin State Bank v. Commissioner . 1.4, 1.5.4
Austin v. Helvering 10.2

B

B.L. Battelstein v. Internal Revenue Service 6.3
Baird v. Meyer et al 9.2
Banc One Corporation v. Commissioner 11.3
Bank of Kirksville v. United States . . 2.2, 5.3, 7.3, 10.3
Bank of Wyoming v. Commissioner . 10.2
Barber v. Commissioner 2.8
Barnett Banks v. Commissioner 2.8
Barnett Banks, Inc. & Subsidiaries v. Commissioner 1.5, 1.7
Barnett Banks of Florida, Inc. v. Commissioner 2.2, 2.7
Barretville Bank & Trust Company v. Commissioner 2.2
Bazley v. Commissioner 11.5
Bell Federal Savings & Loan v. Commissioner 3.3.2, 10.9
Bellefontaine Federal Savings and Loan Association v. Commissioner 5.3

Numbers refer to section (§) numbers.

Beneficial Corporation and Subsidiaries v. United States 10.7, 10.8
Bentsen v. Phimey 11.5
Bercy Industries Inc. v. Commissioner 11.5
Bettendorf Co. v. Commissioner 5.3
Beus. v. Commissioner 8.3
Biedenharn Realty Co. v. United States 7.5.1, 7.6,
Bielfeldt v. Commissioner 4.3, 4.4
Bixby v. Commissioner 11.3
Black Industries, Inc. v. Commissioner 11.3
Black Motor Co. v. Commissioner . . 10.8
Blair v. Commissioner 10.3
Blair v. First Trust & Savings Bank of Miami, Fla. 2.8
Blitzer v. United States 2.7
Boe v. Commissioner 11.3
Boehm v. Commissioner 8.21
Boise Cascade Corp. v. United States 2.7
Bonded Mortgage Co. of Baltimore v. Commissioner 2.8
Borge v. Commissioner 9.4.3
Bradstreet Co. of Maine v. Commissioner 2.2
Bramblett. v. Commissioner . . . 7.5.1, 7.6
Brandtjen & Kluge, Inc. v. Commissioner 10.3
Briarcliff Candy Corp. v. United States 8.10
Brimberry v. Commissioner 10.3
Broderick v. Anderson 5.3
Brountas v. Commissioner 8.12
Brown v. Helvering 2.7
Brown v. United States 3.6, 4.4, 8.21
Buff v. Commissioner 8.2.2
Bull v. Smith 4.4
Bullock v. Commissioner 10.3
Buono v. Commissioner 7.5.1, 7.6
Burbank Liquidating Corp. v. Commissioner 4.3, 4.4, 8.18
Burnet v. Logan 5.3

C

C.E. Wilson v. Commissioner 4.4
C.F. Lukens Steel Co. v. Commissioner 8.2
C.T. Investment Co. v. Commissioner 11.5
Caldwell v. Commissioner 2.2
Calloway v. Commissioner 4.6
Captial Fed. Sav. & Loan Association & Sub. v. Commissioner 2.2
Captial National Bank of Sacramento v. Commissioner 10.3
Captial One Financial Corporation and Subsidiaries 2.1, 2.2, 2.3
Captial Savings & Loan Association v. United States 11.5
Casey v. Commissioner 2.2
Cassatt v. Commissioner 8.10
Catholic News Publishing Co. v. Commissioner 8.10
Centennial Savings Bank, FSB v. United States 6.2
Central Cuba Sugar Co. v. Commissioner 2.7
Central National Bank of Lincoln, Nebraska v. Commissioner 11.5
Central National Bank of Richmond v. Commissioner 10.4.1
Central Pennsylvania Savings Association v. Commissioner . . . 10.9
Central Texas Savings & Loan Association v. United States . 8.3, 8.10
Centralia Fed. Savings & Loan Association v. Commissioner . . . 10.7
Charles Kay Bishop v. Commissioner 8.2.2
Cheltenham Federal Savings and Loan Association v. Commissioner . . . 10.9
Chemung Canal Trust Company v. Commissioner 2.2
Chesapeake Financial Corp. v. Commissioner 2.8
Chicago & North Western Ry. v. Commissioner 5.3

Numbers refer to section (§) numbers.

Citizens and Southern Corp. & Subsidiaries v. Commissioner . . . 8.12, 11.3
Citizens National Bank of Orange v. Commissioner 10.4.1
Citizens National Bank & Trust v. Commissioner 10.6
Citizens National Bank of Waco v. United States 2.9
City Bank Farmers Trust Co. v. Hoey 6.2
Clemens v. Commissioner 10.3
Cleveland Allerton Hotel v. Commissioner 8.10
Cleveland Electric Illuminating Co. v. United States 8.10
Clifton Mfg. Co. v. Commissioner . . . 5.3
Cohan v. Commissioner 11.3
Cole v. Commissioner 10.3
Colonial Fabrics, Inc. v. Commissioner 4.4
Colonial Savings Association v. Commissioner 2.12
Colorado County Federal Savings & Loan Association v. Commissioner . . . 10.7
Colorado National Bankshares, Inc. v. Commissioner 11.3
Colorado Springs National Bank v. United States 8.8, 8.10
Columbia State Savings Bank v. Commissioner 2.8
Commercial Savings and Loan Association v. Commissioner . . . 10.7
Commissioner v. Brown 2.9
Commissioner v. Capento Securities Corp. 11.5
Commissioner v. Danielson 11.3
Commissioner v. First National Bank of Altoona 11.5
Commissioner v. Idaho Power Co. . . . 2.2, 8.3, 8.10
Commissioner v. Killian 11.3
Commissioner v. MacDonald Engineering 10.3
Commissioner v. New Hampshire Fire Insurance Company 5.3
Commissioner v. Seaboard Finance 11.3
Commissioner v. Standard Life & Accident Ins. Co. 2.2
Commissioner v. Tellier . . . 8.3, 8.6, 8.10
Commissioner v. Tufts 4.4.8
Commissioner v. Valley Morris Plan . 1.4
Commissioner v. Williams 7.5.1, 7.6
Community Bank v. Commissioner . . 7.3
Community Trust Bancorp, Inc. v. United States 4.4
Computing & Software, Inc. v. Commissioner 11.3
Concord Control Inc. v. Commissioner 11.3
Connelly v. Commissioner 4.4
Continental Illinois Corp. v. Commissioner 3.3.3, 9.3
Continental Illinois Corp. v. Commissioner 9.3
Continental Illinois National Bank & Trust Co. of Chicago v. Commissioner 7.6, 10.6
Cooley v. Commissioner 4.4
Copperhead Coal Co., Inc. v. Commissioner 11.3
Corliss v. Bowers 3.3.3
Corn Exchange Bank v. United States 5.3
Corn Products Refining Co. v. Commissioner 4.3, 7.6
Cortland Specialty Co. v. Commissioner 11.5
Cottage Savings Association v. Commissioner . 4.3, 5.3, 6.1, 6.2.1, 6.3
Crane v. Commissioner 4.4.8, 11.3
CRST, Inc. v. Commissioner 8.21
Cuba Railroad Company v. Commissioner 5.3
Cullen F. Thomas v. Commissioner 11.5

D

D.L. Wilkerson v. Commissioner . . . 3.4.3
D.P. Harris Hardware & Mfg. C o. v. Commissioner 10.2

Numbers refer to section (§) numbers.

Dallmeyer . v. Commissioner 10.3
Danco Products Inc. v. Commissioner 8.21
David Ullman v. Commissioner ... 11.3
Denman v. Slayton 9.5
Denver and Rio Grande Western R.R. Co. v. Commissioner 10.5
Department of Banking and Commerce v. Clark 10.8
Deputy v. DuPont 8.3, 8.5
Dominion National Bank v. Commissioner 8.12
Donrey, Inc. v. Commissioner 11.3
Doris Havemeyer v. Commissioner . 10.2
Dudley T. Humphrey v. Commissioner 6.3
Drybrough v. Commissioner 9.4.3
Duecaster v. Commissioner 8.9
Dunlap v. Oldham Lumber Co. 7.5.1
Dunn and McCarthy, Inc. v. Commissioner 11.3
Dustin v. Commissioner 10.3

E

E.A. Phillips v. Frank 5.3
E.P. Wright, Executors v. Commissioner 2.3
Earl Drown Corp. v. Commissioner . 9.5
Eckert v. Burnet 10.2
Ehrman v. Commissioner 7.5.1
Eisner v. Macomber 4.4
Eline Realty Co. v. Commissioner .. 7.5.1
Elko Realty Company v. Commissioner 9.4.3
Ellis Banking Corp. v. Commissioner 8.5, 8.9
Ellis, Holyoke & Company v. Commissioner 4.4
Emery v. Commissioner 6.2
Empire Case Goods Company v. Commissioner 10.7
Encyclopedia Britannica v. Commissioner 8.3, 8.9, 8.10
Enoch v. Commissioner 9.6
Enterprises International, Inc. v. Commissioner 9.5
Erforth v. Commissioner 4.4
Estate of Bennet v. Commissioner ... 4.4
Estate of Bright v. United States 4.4
Estate of Gilford v. Commissioner ... 4.4
Estate of Mixon v. Commissioner ... 9.2
Estate of Schieffelin v. Commissioner 7.3
Estate of William H. Block v. Commissioner 10.6
Etheridge and Vanneman, Inc. v. Commissioner 2.7
European American Bank and Trust Co. v. United States 2.3, 2.6, 5.3
Eustace v. Commissioner 12.1
Everett v. United States 11.5
Ewald & Co. v. Commissioner 10.3

F

FDIC v. Godshall 8.12
FMNA v. Commissioner 4.3
FMR Corp. v. Commissioner 8.10
Factor v. Commissioner 4.4
Fahey v. O. Melveny & Meyers 2.14
Fairbanks, Morse & Co. v. Harrison 10.6, 10.8
Fairless v. Commissioner 10.3.2
Fall River Electric Light Company v. Commissioner 9.2
Farmers & Merchants National Bamk of Nocona, Tex. v. Commissioner .. 10.2
Federal National Mortgage Association v. Commissioner 7.6
FedEx Corp. v. United States 12.1.1, 12.1.3, 12.1.4
Fidelity Associates, Inc. v. Commissioner 8.10
Findley v. Commissioner 10.3, 11.6
First Charter Financial Corp. v. United States 7.3, 7.4, 7.5, 7.6
First Federal Savings & Loan Ass'n. v. United States 11.5
First Federal Savings & Loan Association of Bristol v. United States 7.5, 7.6

First Federal Savings Bank of Washington v. United States 10.9
First National Bank v. Commissioner 10.6
First National Bank in Houston v. Scofield 10.6
First National Bank in Little Rock v. Commissioner 10.8
First National Bank in Plant City, Fla. v. Dickinson 1.4
First National Bank of Charlotte v. National Exchange Bank of Baltimore 4.3
First National Bank of Chicago v. Commissioner 10.8
First National Bank of South Carolina v. United States 8.8, 8.10
First Northwest Industries of America v. Commissioner 11.3
First Pennsylvania Banking and Trust Corp. v. Commissioner 2.7, 11.3
First Savings and Loan Association v. Commissioner 6.3, 10.9
First Wisconsin Bankshares Corp. v. United States 10.6, 10.8
Fourth Financial Corp. v. Commissioner 9.3
FPL Group, Inc & Subs. v. Commissioner 2.2
Francis v. Commissioner 2.8
Francis Ward Paine v. Commissioner 6.2, 6.3
Frank Lyon Co. v. United States 12.2
Fraser v. Commissioner 10.3
Fredricksburg Federal Savings and Loan Association v. Commissioner 10.9
Frontier Savings Ass'n v. Commissioner 2.14.2

G

Gamble v. Commissioner 7.5.1, 7.6
Garcia v. Commissioner 4.4.11
Gatlin v. Commissioner 4.4
General Utilities & Operating Co. v. Helvering 11.3
George L. Castner, Co., Inc. v. Commissioner 6.3
George R. Kemon v. Commissioner 4.4
Georgia Federal Bank v. Commissioner 10.9
Georgia School-Book Depository, Inc. v. Commissioner 2.7
Gibraltar Financial Corp. of Calif. v. United States 7.3, 7.4, 7.6
Girard Trust Co. v. United States 6.2, 6.3
Girard Trust Corn Exchanges Bank v. Commissioner 7.5.1
Girardi Trust v. Commissioner 7.6
Goldberg v. Commissioner 4.4.2
Goodwin v. Commissioner 3.4.3, 2.7
Gottesman & Co. v. Commissioner 9.5
Great Northern Ry. Co. v. Commissioner 5.3
Great W. Bank v. Office of Thrift Supervision 8.12
Gregory v. Helvering 11.5
Guarantee Title & Trust Co. v. Commissioner 2.7
Guaranty Employees Association, Inc. v. United States 1.5
Guardian Industries Corp. 4.4

H

H. Enterprises International, Inc. v. Commissioner 9.4.3
H. Liebes & Co. v. Commissioner 5.3
H. B. Quinn v. Commissioner 8.2.2
Hadley Falls Trust Co. v. United States 7.4
Hall Paving Co. v. United States 9.4.3
Hammitt v. Commissioner 2.2
Hancock v. Commissioner 7.5.1, 7.6
Hancock County Federal Savings & Loan Association of Chester v. Commissioner 9.3
Harman v. Commissioner 8.12
Harmont Plaza, Inc. v. Commissioner 5.3
Harris v. Commissioner 7.5.1, 7.6

Numbers refer to section (§) numbers.

Harris Trust & Savings Bank v. Commissioner 5.3
Harriman National Bank v. Commissioner 2.2, 4.4
Helvering v. Enright's Estate 2.2
Helvering v. Fried 4.4
Helvering v. Lazarus & Co. 2.4
Helvering v. Midland Mutual Life Insurance Co. 7.4
Helvering v. Minnesota Tea Co. . . . 11.5
Helvering v. Safe Deposit Co. 4.4
Helvering v. Southwest Consolidated Corp. 11.5
Helvering v. Winmill 4.3
Henry B. Miller v. Commissioner . . 8.10
Herndon v. Commissioner 11.3
Highland Farms, Inc. v. Commissioner 2.9
Holden Fuel Oil Co. v. Commissioner 11.3
Home Savings v. Commissioner . . . 10.7
Home Savings & Loan Ass'n v. United States 11.5
Homes by Ayres v. Commissioner . . 7.5.1
Houston Chronicle Publishing Co. v. United States 11.3
Howell v. Commissioner 7.5.1
Hubble v. Commissioner 10.3
Hudson City Savings Bank v. Commissioner 9.2, 9.3
Huntington-Redondo Company v. Commissioner 2.3
Hustead v. Commissioner 7.5.1

I

Idaho First Nat. Bank and its Subsidiaries v. Commissioner . . 10.4.1
Illinois Cereal Mills Inc. v. Commissioner 8.21
INDOPCO, Inc. v. Commissioner . . . 8.3, 8.4, 8.8, 8.12, 11.3
In Re Landbank Equity Corp. 10.3
Independent Bankers Ass'n of America v. Heimann 11.2
Indiana Broadcasting Corp. v. Commissioner 11.3
Intergraph Corporation v. Commissioner 10.2
Investment Company Institute v. FDIC 11.2
Iowa Trust & Savings v. Commissioner 11.3
Iowa-Des Moines National Bank v. Commissioner 8.3, 8.8, 8.10
Ithaca Industries Inc. v. Commissioner 8.10, 8.12

J

J. Leonard Schmitz v. Commissioner 11.3
J.B.N. Telephone Co., Inc. v. United States 5.3
J.E. Davant v. Commissioner 11.5
J.P. Morgan & Chase Co. v. Commissioner 4.4
J.T. Bennett v. Commissioner 2.2
Jack Daniel Distillery v. United States 11.3
Jackson v. Commissioner 7.5.1
James v. United States 3.3.3
Joe W. Scales v. Commissioner . . 6.2, 6.3
John A. Nelson Co. v. Helvering . . . 11.5, 11.5.1
Jones Lumber Co., Inc. v. Commissioner 5.3, 6.3

K

KFOX, Inc. v. United States 11.3
K.F. Knetsch v. United States 12.2
K.L. Mulholland v. United States . . 2.6.1
Kaiser Steel Corp. v. United States . . 8.2
Kanawha Valley Bank v. Commissioner 7.6
Keller v. Commissioner 10.5
Keman v. Commissioner 7.5.1
Kishi v. Humble Oil & Refining Co. . 9.2
Kistler Co. v. Commissioner 2.8
Knetsch v. Commissioner 12.1
Koehring Company v. United States . 5.3

Numbers refer to section (§) numbers.

L

L. Heller & Son, Inc. v. Commissioner 8.10
La Caisse Popularire Ste. Marie (St. Mary's Bank) v. United States . . . 1.4
LaStaiti v. Commissioner 10.3
Leach Corp. v. Blacklidge 4.4
Leader Federal Savings and Loan Association v. Commissioner . . . 10.9
Lebron v. National R.R. Passenger Corp. 8.12
Leslie v. Commissioner 9.5
Leslie S. Ray Ins. Agency Inc. v. United States 11.3
LeTulle v. Scofield 11.5
Levelland Savings & Loan Association v. United States 10.7
Lincoln Savings & Loan Association v. Commissioner . 8.3, 8.4, 8.9, 8.10, 8.12
Lio v. Commissioner 4.4
Lippmann v. Commissioner 4.4
Lloyd-Smith v. Commissioner 4.4
Lomas & Nettlecon Financial Corp. v. United States 5.3
Longview Hilton Hotel Co. v. Commissioner 9.6
Lord v. United States 2.2
Los Angeles Gas & Electric Corp. v. Railroad Comm'n 11.3
Lovejoy v. Commissioner 9.6
Lowell v. Commissioner 4.4
Lukens Steel Corp. v. United States . . 8.2
Lyon v. Commissioner 12.1
Lykes Energy, Inc. v. Commissioner 8.10

M

M.L. Grinsten v. Commissioner 5.3
M. Liftin v. Commissioner 5.3
Makoff v. Commissioner 4.4
Malat v. Riddell 4.4
Malden Trust Co. v. Commissioner . 10.3, 10.5
Mann, Estate of v. U.S. 10.3
Mapco, Inc. v. United States 2.4
Marjorie K. Campbell v. Commissioner 6.2
Marr v. United States 6.2
Marrin v. Commissioner 4.4
Massey-Ferguson, Inc.v. Commissioner 8.21
Mathews v. Commissioner 7.5.1, 7.6
Matz v. Commissioner 7.5.1, 7.6
Mauldin v. Commissioner 7.5.1
Maurice Mittleman v. Commissioner 11.3
McCain v. Commissioner 10.3
McDonald's Restaurants of Ill., Inc. v. Commissioner 11.5
Mellinger v. United States 6.2, 6.3
Merchants National Bank v. Commissioner 2.2, 4.3
Messing v. Commissioner 4.4
Metrobank v. Commissioner 8.12
Metropolitan Laundry Co. v. United States 8.21
Metropolitan Mortgage Fund, Inc. v. Commissioner 2.4, 2.7
Metropolitan National Bank of New York v. St. Louis Post Dispatch 11.3
Metropolitan Properties Corp. v. Commissioner 9.6
Midlantic National Bank v. Commissioner 11.3
Miller v. Commissioner 8.10
Millinary Center Building Corp. v. Commissioner 8.10
Minneapolis St. Paul & S. Ste. M. R.R.. v. U.S. 10.3
Mitchell. v. Commissioner 10.3
Moline Properties, Inc. v. Commissioner 9.4.3
Moneygram International, Inc. v. Commissioner 1.5.4, 1.5.8
MoneyGram International and Subsidiaries v. Commissioner . . . 1.5.4
Montgomery Co. v. Commissioner . . 11.3
Moock Electric Supply Co. 10.3
Morgan Guaranty Trust Co. of N.Y. v. United States 2.2, 3.3.3

Numbers refer to section (§) numbers.

Morris Plan Bank of New Haven v. Smith 1.4

Motel Corp. v. Commissioner 2.3

Motor Products Corp. v. Commissioner 6.2

Motor Securities Co., Inc. v. Commissioner 2.8

Murchison National Bank . . 10.3, 10.4.1

Mutual Savings and Loan Co., Inc. of Norfolk v. Commissioner 1.4

N

NCNB Corp. v. Commissioner . . 8.3, 8.5

NCNB Corp. v. United States . . . 2.2, 8.3, 8.10

N.W. Menz v. Commissioner 6.3

National Bank of Commerce in Memphis v. United States 11.5

National Bank of Commerce of Norfolk v. United States 11.5

National Bank of Commerce of Seattle v. Commissioner 10.6

National Bank of Fort Benning v. United States 2.2

National Bank of South Carolina v. Lucas 2.2

NationsBank of North Carolina v. Variable Annuity Life Insurance Co. 4.3

Neal T. Baker Enters. v. Commissioner 7.5.1

Nebraska Department of Revenue v. Loewnstein 2.9

Nestle Holdings, Inc. v. Commissioner 6.3

New Colonial Ice Company v. Helvering 8.3

Neuman, Est. of v. Commissioner . . 9.4.3

Newport Federal Savings & Loan Association v. United States 10.7

Newark Corp. v. Commissioner . . . 12.1

Newark Morning Ledger Co. v. United States 8.12, 11.3

New Mexico Bancorporation and Subsidiaries v. Commissioner 9.5

Nichols v. Commissioner 7.4

Noteman v. Welch 2.7

North American Oil Consolidated v. Burnet 3.3.3, 5.3

Northeast Bancorp, Inc. v. The Board of Governors of the Fed 11.2

Northeastern Surety Co. v. Commissioner 4.3

Norwest Corp. and Subsidiairies v. Commissioner 8.5, 12.1

O

O. Liquidating Corp. 2.2

Old Colony Railroad Co. v. Commissioner 5.3

Old Virgina Brick Co. Inc. 1.6

Oregon State University Alumni Assoc. v. Commissioner 2.8

Orth v. Commissioner 4.4

O'Sullivan Rubber Co. v. Commissioner 5.3

P

PNC Bancorp, Inc. v. Commissioner . 8.3, 8.4, 8.10

Pacific First Federal Savings & Loan Association v. Commissioner 2.7, 10.9

Pacific Nat'l Co.v. Welch 2.2

Pacific Securities v. Commissioner . . 4.4

Palm Beach Trust Co. v. Commissioner 1.4

Pan-American Bank & Trust Co. v. Commissioner 4.4

Parmelee Transportation Co. v. United States 8.21

Particelli v. Commissioner 11.3

Pate v. Commissioner 10.3

Paulsen v. Commissioner 11.5

Peerless Weighing and Vending Machine Corp. v. Commissioner 8.4, 8.10

Peoples Bancorporation & Subsidiaries v. Commissioner 11.3

Peoples Bank and Trust Company v. Commissioner 9.3

Numbers refer to section (§) numbers.

Peoples Federal Savings & Loan Association v. United States 10.7

Peoples Federal Savings & Loan Association of Sydeny v. Commissioner 10.9

Permanent Savings & Loan Association v. United States 1.6, 10.7

Perry v. Commissioner 10.3

Phellis v. United States, ... 6.2

Philadelphia National Bank v. United States 2.5.1

Philadelphia Steel & Iron Corp. v. Commissioner 11.3

Phil Gluckstern's, Inc. v. Commissioner 8.10

Pig & Whistle Co. v. Commissioner . 8.10

Pinellas Ice & Cold Storage Co. v. Commissioner 4.4, 11.5

Pittman v. Commissioner 8.3

Plainfield-Union Water Company v. Commissioner 8.3

Poncin Corp. v. Commissioner 11.3

Porter v. Commissioner 10.2

Prazen v. Commissioner 2.2

Production Steel, Inc. v. Commissioner 10.3

Propstra v. United States 4.4

Putnam v. Commissioner 10.2

R

RCA Corp. V. United States 2.2

R.E. Purvis v. Commissioner 4.4

R.G. Goodwin v. Commissioner . 2.4, 2.6

R.M. Smith, Inc. v. Commissioner . 11.3

R.O. Holton v. Commissioner 4.4

Rafferty v. Commissioner 11.5

Ramsey Scarlett & Company v. Commissioner 8.21

Redwood Empire Savings & Loan Association v. Commissioner 7.6

Reef Corp. v. Commissioner 11.5

Reese v. Commissioner 7.5.1, 7.6

Richmond Hill Savings Bank v. Commissioner 10.9

Richmond Television Corp. v. United States 8.9

Rio Grande Building & Loan Association v. Commissioner 10.7, 10.7.10

Ripple v. Mortgage & Acceptance Corporation 9.2

Riss v. Commissioner 10.3

Robert J. Dial v. Commissioner .. 6.2, 6.3

Rocky Mountain Federal Savings & Loan Ass'n v. United States 11.5

Rodeway Inns of America, v. Commissioner 8.10

Rollingwood Corp. v. Commissioner 7.5.1

Roth Steel Tube Co. v. Commissioner 10.3

Roy Moody Bell v. Commissioner ... 2.2

S

S & L Bldg. Corp. v. Commissioner .. 9.6

Samueli v. Commissioner 4.6

San Antonio Savings Association v. Commissioner 6.2

San Francisco Stevedoring Co. v. Commissioner 2.2

Savings Assurance Agency, Inc. v. Commissioner 1.3

Schafer v. Helvering 4.4

Schieffelin v. Commissioner 7.3

Schlude v. Commissioner 2.7

Schram v. United States 2.2

Schuster v. Helvering 2.8

Seaboard loan & Sav. Association v. Commissioner 11.2

Securities Industry Ass'n v. Comptroller 11.2

Securities-Intermountain, Inc. v. United States 2.7

Securities Mortgage Co. v. Commissioner 7.3

Security Bank Minnesota v. Commissioner ... 3.3.5, 3.4.8, 3.2, 9.3

Security Fed. Sav. & Loan Association of St. Augustine v. United States .. 10.7

Security State Bank v. Commissioner 3.3.5, 3.4.8

Numbers refer to section (§) numbers.

Sherman v. Commissioner 9.3
Sierra Club, Inc. v. Commissioner . . 2.8
Signet Banking Corp. v. Commissioner 2.2, 2.7
Silverman v. Commissioner 4.4
Silverton Loan and Building Company v. United States 10.7
Simon v. Commissioner 10.3, 10.7
Smothers v. United States 11.5
Snow v. Commissioner 8.10
Society For Savings v. Bowers 11.5
Solar Nitrogen Chemicals Inc. v. Commissioner 8.21
Sollitt Construction Co. v. United States 8.21
Southern Bancorporation v. United States 11.3
Southern Pacific Transportation Co. v. Commissioner 11.3
Spreckles v. Helvering 4.3
Spring City Foundry Co. v. Commissioner 2.2, 5.3, 6.3, 10.2
State Bank of Bloomington v. Commissioner 11.5
Staunton Industrial Loan Corporation v. Commissioner 1.4
Stern Bros. v. Commissioner 4.4
Stevens Bros. Foundations, Inc. v. Commissioner 9.3
Stevenson v. Commissioner 5.3
Stokes v. Rothensies 2.2, 4.4
Stratton v. Commissioner 4.4
Streckfus Steamers, Inc. v. Commissioner 10.6
Sun Microsystems, Inc. v. Commissioner 8.3, 8.8, 8.10, 8.22
Summit v. Commissioner 4.4.11
Super Food Services, Inc. v. United States 11.3

T

T.J. Enterprises Inc. v. Commissioner 8.10
The 12701 Shaker Boulevard Company v. Commissioner 8.18
The Austin Co., Inc. v. Commissioner 10.3
The Charles Schwab Corp. v. Commissioner 2.7
The Home Group, Inc. v. Commissioner 10.7
The Limited, Inc. v. Commissioner . . 1.3, 1.5
The Seagrove Corp. v. Commissioner 2.5.2
Theodore R. Plunckett v. Commissioner 2.3
Thomas Emery v. Commissioner . 6.2, 6.3
Thomas Watson v. Commissioner . . . 6.2
Thompson Lumber Company v. Commissioner 7.5.1, 7.6
Thor Power Tool Company v. Commissioner 2.2, 8.3, 10.2
Thorndson v. Commissioner 11.3
Thriftcheck Service Corp. v. Commissioner 8.21
Title Insurance Co. of Hampden County v. United States 2.8
Toledo Home Federal Savings and Loan Assoc. v. United States 10.7
Tower Bldg. Corp. v. Commissioner 11.5
Trustmark Corporation & Subsidiaries v. Commissioner 11.3

U

Ullman v. Commissioner 11.3
Union Pacific R.R. Co. v. Commissioner 5.3
Union Planters National Bank of Memphis v. United States 2.9
Union Trust Co. of Indianapolis v. United States 4.4, 10.2
United States v. Basye 9.4.3
United States v. Cartwright 4.4, 7.3
United States v. Centennial Savings Bank 2.12
United States v. Chinook Inv. Co. . . . 4.4
United States v. Davis 2.14
United States v. E. L. Bruce Co. . . . 8.10

Numbers refer to section (§) numbers.

United States v. General Dynamics Corp. 8.12

United States v. Hughes Properties, Inc. 8.12

United States v. Merrill 8.2.2

United States v. Midland Ross Corporation 3.1

United States v. Nordberg 7.5.1

United States v. S.S. White Dental Mfg. Co. 10.3

United States v. Seattle First International Corp. 1.4

United States v. Winstar Corp. 8.12, 8.21

United States v. Wood 4.4

U.S. Freightways Corp. v. Commissioner 8.4

United States Freight Co. v. U.S. 4.4.7

United Stationers, Inc. v. United States 12.1

Urquahart. v. Commissioner 8.4

V

Vainisi v. Commissioner 1.6.5, 9.6

Van Iderstine Co. v. Commissioner . 8.10

Van Suetendael v. Commissioner . . . 4.4

Vancoh Realty Company v. Commissioner 2.4, 2.8, 5.3, 6.3

Vaughan v. Commissioner 4.4

VGS Corp. v. Commissioner 11.3

Victor Meat Co., Inc. v. Commissioner 11.3

Victory Markets v. Commissioner . . . 8.9

W

W.A. Drake v. Commissioner 4.4.7

W.B. Dozier v. Commissioner 3.4.3

W.C. & A.N. Miller Dev. Co. v. Commissioner 7.5.1

W.Credit Co. v. Commissioner 2.7

W.E. Underhill v. Commissioner 5.3

Warner Co. v. Commissioner 2.3

Washington Mutual, Inc. v. United States 11.3.3

Weis v. Commissioner 5.3

Welch v. Helvering 8.3, 8.9

Wells Fargo Bank & Union Trust Co., Trustee v. Commissioner 8.5, 8.9

West v. Commissioner 2.7

Western Credit Co. v. Commissioner . 2.7

Western Federal Saving & Loan Ass'n v. Commissioner 2.14.2

Western Mortgage Corp. v. United States 2.7

Westside Federal Savings & Loan Ass'n of Fairview Park v. United States . . 11.5

White v. Commissioner 4.4

William Justin Petit, et. al. v. Commissioner 2.3

Williams v. Commissioner 5.3

Winn-Dixie Montgomery, Inc. v. United States 11.3

Winter & Hirsch v. United States . . 10.7

Wisconsin Bankshares Corp. v. United States 10.6

Wisconsin Cheeseman, Inc. v. United States 9.5

Woodward v. Commissioner 4.3, 8.3

Wright v. Commissioner 4.4.11

Wright v. United States 11.5

Wright Contracting Co.v. United States 2.2

Z

Zurn v. Commissioner 8.21

Table of I.R.C. Sections

Sections	§Number
1	1.6.6; 6.2.3; 9.5.8; 12.2.3
1(c)	1.4.2
1(c)(4)	12.2.11
1(f)(3)	12.2.10
1(f)(4)	12.2.10
1(h)	1.6.5
11	1.4.1; 1.6.5
38	12.2; 12.3.1
38(c)	12.2
39	10.7.11; 12.2
41	8.11; 12.1; 12.1.1; 12.1.2; 12.1.4; 12.1.5;
41(a)	12.1.4
41(b)(1)	12.1.4
41(b)(2)	12.1.4
41(b)(3)	12.1.4
42	12.2; 12.2.11; 12.2.12; 12.2.2; 12.3.2
45D	12.3
45D(f)	12.3.2
49(a)(1)	12.2.2
49(a)(2)	12.2.2
52	12.1
55	1.6.5; 10.12.1
55(b)	10.12.1
55(d)	1.6.2
56	1.5.7
56(b)	12.1.6
56(b)(2)(A)(ii)	12.1.6
56(b)(2)(D)	12.1.6
56(c)	12.1.6
56(d)	8.20
56(g)(4)(F)	8.3.4
57	10.12.1; 12.1.6
57(a)(4)	1.5.7; 10.9; 10.12.1
59(e)	12.1.6
59(i)	9.5.4
61	1.5.4, 11.3.1
61(a)(12)	6.3.2; 6.3.3
63	10.9.3; 10.12.1
71	11.4.17
72	4.4.4
75	3.7; 4.4.1
75(a)	3.7.2
75(b)(1)	3.7
83	2.2.1; 11.5.7
103	1.7.7; 2.3; 2.5; 2.9.1; 7.5.2; 9.5.8; 10.8.6; 12.2.1; 12.2.2
103(b)	2.5; 10.8.6
103(b)(1)	2.5.1
103(c)	2.5
103(j)	9.7
104(a)	1.5.3
105B	4.6
108	2.13; 11.5.6
108(a)(1)	6.3.2; 6.3.3
108(a)(1)(B)	6.3.3
108(a)(1)(C)	11.5.6
108(b)(5)	11.5.6
108(c)(1)	2.13
108(e)(7)	4.4.9; 7.6.2
108(e)(10)	6.3.2; 11.5.6
108(e)(10)(A)	6.3.3
108(e)(10)(B)	6.3.3; 11.5.6
108(e)(10)(C)	11.5.6
111	8.17; 10.6; 10.7.9
111(a)	1.6.8; 10.6
118	9.5.7; 11.6
133	2.5.3

Sections	§Number
141	9.5.5
141	2.5.1
142	12.2.3; 12.2.4
145	9.5.5
146	12.2.1; 12.2.1; 12.2.2; 12.2.9
146(j)	12.2.11
148	2.5; 9.5.3
149	2.5; 9.7
161	8.3.1; 8.3.4; 9.5.8
162	1.2; 1.6.5; 8.3.1; 8.3.2; 8.3.3; 8.3.4; 8.4.4; 8.5.1; 8.5.2; 8.5; 8.8.2; 8.8.3; 8.9.1; 8.9.2; 8.10.2; 8.10.3; 8.10.6; 8.10.7; 8.10.8; 8.10.9; 8.11; 8.15; 8.16; 8.17; 9.2; 11.3.3; 12.1.1
162(a)	8.3.4; 8.5.2; 8.8.2; 8.9.2; 8.10.4.2; 8.10.5; 8.10.7; 8.10.9; 11.3.4
162(k)	8.5.1
163	1.5.7; 2.3; 8.6; 8.9.2; 9.2; 9.5.8
163(a)	9.2; 9.4.3
163(d)	12.2
163(e)	9.3.4
163(f)	9.7
163(j)	9.7
164	7.5.1; 8.9.2
165	1.2; 2.8.1; 4.3.3; 4.4.7; 4.4.9; 6.2.1; 6.3.2; 7.3.1; 8.5.2; 8.10.9; 8.18; 8.19; 8.21.2; 8.21; 10.2.3
165(a)	6.2.1; 8.21
165(b)	4.3
165(g)	4.4.7
165(g)(1)	4.3.3
165(g)(2)	4.4.7; 11.4.20; 11.4
165(g)(2)(C)	4.3; 4.4.7; 4.4.9; 10.2.3; 10.8.6; 10.9.2
165(h)	10.2.3
165(j)	9.7
165(l)(3)(A)	1.5.5
166	1.6.4; 3.3.2; 4.3.3; 4.3.3; 4.4.9; 5.1; 5.3.2; 5.3.7; 5.3.8; 5.3.14; 5.3.15; 6.3.2; 6.3.3; 7.5.2; 7.6.2; 10.2.1; 10.2.3; 10.3; 10.3.1; 10.3.2; 10.4.4; 10.4.5; 10.7.1; 10.7.4; 10.7.5; 10.7.6; 10.7.10; 10.7.11; 10.8.6; 10.9; 11.4.; 11.4.11; 11.6.9
166(a)	5.3.15; 8.20.2; 10.2.3; 10.3; 10.4.4; 10.4.5; 10.7.4
166(a)(1)	10.3.2
166(a)(2)	6.3.3; 10.2.2; 10.2.3; 10.3.2; 10.3; 10.7.5; 11.6.9
166(b)	10.2.2
166(c)	4.3.3; 10.2.3; 10.4.4; 10.7.1; 10.7.3; 10.7.4; 10.7.5; 10.9.3
166(d)	10.2.3
166(e)	10.2.3
167	2.7.4; 7.5.1; 8.3.1; 8.4.5; 8.19; 11.3.2; 11.3.4; 11.3.5
167(a)	2.7.4; 8.13; 11.3.2; 11.3.5
167(a)(1)	2.7.4
167(a)(2)	2.7.4
167(f)	2.7.4; 11.3.3
167(f)(1)	11.3.2; 11.3.5

Sections	*§Number*
167(f)(1)(A)	8.7
167(f)(3)	2.7.4; 11.3.2; 11.3.5
167(g)	11.3.5
167(k)	12.2.2
168	2.7.4; 11.3.2
168(a)	11.3.2
168(b)	11.3.2
168(c)	11.3.2
168(d)	11.3.2
168(e)(3)(B)	11.3.2
168(e)(3)(C)	11.3.2
168(k)	12.1.7
168(k)(1)	11.3.2
168(k)(2)	12.1.7
168(k)(4)	12.1.7
168(k)(4)	12.1.7
170	1.6.5
170(c)	1.6.2
171	1.2; 2.10.2; 2.10.3; 3.7.4; 3.7.5; 3.7; 8.7; 11.3.5
171(a)	3.7.2
171(b)(1)(A)	3.7.5
171(b)(1)(B)(ii)	3.7.5
171(b)(3)	3.7.4
171(b)(3)(A)	3.7.4
171(c)	2.10.3; 3.7
171(c)(2)	3.7.1
171(d)	3.7.3
171(e)	3.7; 9.2
171(f)	3.7
171(i)	3.7.5
172	8.20.2; 8.20.3; 10.7.1; 10.9.3
172(a)	8.20
172(b)	8.20
172(b)(1)(A)	8.20.2
172(b)(1)(D)	8.20.2; 10.2.3
172(b)(1)(F)	8.20.1; 8.20.2
172(b)(1)(H)	8.20.4
172(b)(1)(L)	8.20.2
172(b)(1)(L)[K]	8.20.2
172(b)(1)(L)[K]and	8.20.2
172(b)(1)(M)	8.20.2
172(b)(3)	8.20.3; 8.20.4
172(g)	8.20.2
174	8.4.3; 8.9.2; 8.11; 12.1.1; 12.1.2; 12.1.4; 12.1.5
174(a)	12.1.1
174]	12.1.1
178	8.7
178(a)	11.3.5
179(d)(2)	12.2.2
179(d)(7)	12.2.2
183	12.2
195	1.2; 1.2.1; 7.6.4; 8.1; 8.3.1; 8.3.4; 8.4.4; 8.5.1; 8.5.2; 8.6.2; 8.9.1; 8.9.2; 8.9.4; 8.9.5; 8.10.2; 8.10.6
195(b)(1)	8.9.2
195(b)(2)	8.10.2
195(c)	11.3.4
195(c)(1)	8.9.2
195(c)(1)(A)(i)	8.6.2; 8.9.2
195(c)(1)(A)(ii)	8.9.2
195(c)(1)(A)(iii)	8.9.2)
195(c)(1)(B)	8.9.2
195(c)(2)	8.9.2
195(d)	8.9.2
195(d)(1)	8.9.5
196	8.3.1
197	1.2; 2.7.4; 8.3.1; 8.5.1; 8.7; 8.9.2; 8.13; 8.21.1; 10.12.2; 11.3.3; 11.3.4; 11.3.5; 11.3.6; 11.3.7; 11.3.8
197(a)	2.7.4; 11.3.3
197(c)	8.21.1
197(c)(1)	11.3.3

Sections	*§Number*
197(c)(2)(A)	11.3.4
197(d)	11.3.3
197(e)	11.3.5
197(e)(5)(B)	11.3.5
197(e)(7)	2.7.4; 11.3.5
197(f)(1)	8.21.1
197(f)	11.3.6
197(f)(7)	2.7.4
199(c)(2)	11.3.3
212	11.3.3
243	1.6.6; 2.14.3; 10.9.3; 10.9
244	10.9
245	10.9
246(a)(2)	2.14.3
246A(c)(3)(B)(i)	1.5.5
247	10.9.3
248	7.6.4; 8.9.1; 8.9.2; 8.9.3; 8.9.4; 8.9.5
248(a)	8.9.3
248(b)	8.9.3; 8.9.5
248(b)(2)	8.9.3
261	8.3.1
263	1.2; 2.2.1; 8.3.1; 8.3.2; 8.3.3; 8.3.4; 8.4.4; 8.5; 8.6.2; 8.8.2; 8.9.1; 8.9.2; 8.10.2; 8.10.6; 8.10.8; 8.10.9; 8.10; 9.5.4
263(A)	4.4.8
263(a)	8.1; 8.3.1; 8.3.3; 8.3.4; 8.4.1; 8.4.4; 8.5.1; 8.6.2; 8.9.2; 8.10; 8.10.2; 8.10.4.2; 8.10.6; 8.10.8; 8.10.9
263(a)(1)	8.3.1
263(g)	4.4.2; 4.4.8; 4.4.11
263(g)(3)	7.6.1(a)
263A	2.2.1; 4.4.1; 4.4.2; 4.4.11; 7.1; 7.5.1; 8.3.1; 9.1; 9.4.3

Sections	*§Number*
263A(b)	9.4.3
263A(b)(1)	9.4.3
263A(f)	9.4.3
263A(f)(1)(A)	9.4.3
263A(f)(1)(B)	9.4.3
263A(g)(1)	9.4.3
265	1.5.5; 9.5.1; 9.5.4; 9.5.8; 10.10.1
265(2)	9.4.2; 9.5.1; 9.5.2; 9.5.3; 9.5.8
265(a)	9.4.2; 9.5.1; 9.5.2; 9.5.4; 9.5.6; 9.5.8
265(a)(2)	9.4.3; 9.5.1; 9.5.8
265(a)(5)	3.6.3
265(b)	1.2.5; 1.5.5; 1.6.3; 9.4.2; 9.5.1; 9.5.2; 9.5.4; 9.5.5; 9.5.6; 9.5.7; 9.5.8; 9.5.9; 9.6
265(b)(3)(G)	9.5.5
265(b)(3)(G)(iii)	9.5.5
265(b)(2)	9.5.4
265(b)(2)(A)	9.5.8
265(b)(3)	9.5.5; 9.6
265(b)(3)(A)	9.6
265(b)(3)(B)	9.5.5
265(b)(3)(C)	9.5.5
265(b)(3)(D)	9.5.5
265(b)(3)(E)	9.5.5
265(b)(3)(F)	9.5.5
265(b)(4)	9.5.4
265(b)(4)(B)	9.5.4
265(b)(5)	4.4.4; 10.4.1; 10.10.4
265(b)(6)	9.5.2
265(b)(7)	9.5.2
265(e)	9.5.4
266	9.5.4
267	4.4.4; 11.3.4
267(a)	10.10.1
267(b)	8.5.1; 10.10.1; 12.2.2(a)

Sections	§Number
267(b)(2)	4.4.4
267(b)(3)	4.4.4
267(b)(10)	4.4.4
267(b)(11)	4.4.4
267(b)(12)	4.4.4
267(c)	4.4.4
269	9.4.3; 11.5.1
271(a)	1.5.5; 10.2.3
279	9.5.1
279(c)(5)(A)	1.5.5
280C(c)(1)	12.1.5
280C(c)(3)(A)	12.1.5
280C(c)(3)(B)	12.1.5
280H	8.3.1
291	1.5.5; 1.6.3; 1.6.5; 9.4.2; 9.5.3; 9.6; 10.10.1; 10.12.2; 11.3.4
291(a)(3)	1.5.5; 9.5.3; 9.5.4
291(e)	9.5.4; 9.5.5; 9.5.6; 9.5.8; 9.6
291(e)(1)(A)	10.12.2
291(e)(1)(B)	9.5.3; 9.5.3; 9.5.4; 9.5.8
291(e)(1)(B)(4)	9.5.4
291(e)(1)(B)(i)	9.5.3
291(e)(1)(B)(ii)	3.6.3; 9.4.2
291(e)(1)(I)	9.5.8
301	2.14.2; 2.14.3; 2.14.4
302	2.14.3; 11.5.2
305	9.2.1; 11.5.7
305(a)	2.14.2; 2.14.4
305(b)	2.14.2
305(e)(5)(B)	9.2.1
307	2.14.4
311(a)	11.3.1
312	10.9.3; 10.9.5
312(m)	9.7
316	11.5.7
318	11.4.17
332	1.6.3; 6.2.3; 10.10.2; 11.3.1; 11.4.22; 11.4.2
336	11.3.1
337	11.3.1
338	1.6.1; 6.2.3; 9.5.7; 10.10.1; 11.3.1; 11.3.2; 11.3.3; 11.3.8; 11.4.9; 11.4.11; 11.6.6
338(a)	11.3.2
338(b)(5)	11.3.2
338(d)(3)	11.3.8
338(h)(2)	9.5.7
338(h)(10)	11.3.4; 11.5.5
338(h)(10)(A)	11.5.5
351	2.10.4; 4.4.5; 4.4.7; 8.5.1; 9.5.7; 10.7.11; 11.3.5; 11.5.2; 11.5.3; 11.5.7
351(a)	2.10.4
351(b)	11.5.3
351(e)	2.10.4
351(e)(1)	2.10.4
351(g)	4.3.4
351(g)(3)(A)	9.2.1
354	4.4.7; 8.5.1; 11.5.1; 11.5.2; 11.5.4; 11.5.7
354(a)	11.5.8
354(a)(2)(G)(ii)	11.5.5
354(b)(1)	11.5.8
354(b)(1)(A)	11.5.8
354(b)(1)(B)	11.5.5; 11.5.8
355	11.4.24; 11.5.1; 11.5.4
355(a)(1)	11.5.4
356	6.3.2; 11.5.1
356(a)	6.3.2; 11.5.2
356(d)	6.3.2
357	11.5.3

Sections	*§Number*
357(a)	11.5.2; 11.5.3; 11.5.4
358	11.5.1; 11.5.2
358(a)(1)	11.5.2; 11.5.3; 11.5.4
358(d)(1)	11.5.3
360E(e)	2.10.3
361	4.4.7; 6.2.3; 11.5.1; 11.5.2
361(a)	11.5.2; 11.5.3; 11.5.4; 11.5.5
361(c)	11.5.4
361(c)(4)	11.3.1
362	11.5.1; 11.5.3
362(a)	11.5.3
362(b)	11.5.2; 11.5.3; 11.5.4; 11.5.7
362(c)	11.6
368	4.4.7; 8.5.1; 9.5.7; 11.1; 11.4.22; 11.5.1; 11.5.8
368(a)	11.5.1
368(a)(1)	10.11; 11.5.8
368(a)(1)(A)	8.5.1; 11.5.2
368(a)(1)(B)	1.6.3; 9.4.1; 11.5.3
368(a)(1)(C)	11.5.2; 11.5.3; 11.5.5
368(a)(1)(D)	1.2.3; 8.5.1; 11.5.4; 11.5.5
368(a)(1)(F)	11.5.7
368(a)(1)(G)	11.5.8
368(a)(2)(A)	11.5.4
368(a)(3)	11.5.8
368(b)	11.5.2
368(c)	11.5.3
368(e)	11.5.3
371	11.5.8
372	11.5.8
381	10.10.2; 11.5.1; 11.5.2; 11.5.7; 11.5.8
381(a)	6.2.3; 9.4.1; 10.10.1; 10.10.2 11.4.22; 11.5.2
381(a)(2)	11.5.8
381(b)(3)	11.5.7
381(c)	11.5.2
381(c)(1)	11.5.2
381(c)(2)	11.5.2
381(c)(4)	10.7.8; 10.11; 11.5.2; 11.5.8
381(c)(12)	10.6
381(c)(19)	11.5.2
381(c)(26)	11.5.2
382	4.4.10; 10.12.2; 11.1; 11.4.11; 11.4.17; 11.4.1; 11.4.23; 11.4.25; 11.4.5; 11.4.6; 11.4.8; 11.4; 11.5.1; 11.5.2; 11.5.7; 11.5.8
382(a)	11.4; 11.5.7
382(a)(1)(C)	11.5.7
382(a)(2)	11.5.7
382(b)	11.5.7
382(b)(1)	11.4.1; 11.4.5
382(b)(3)	11.5.7
382(b)(6)	11.5.2
382(b)(7)	11.5.8
382(c)	11.5.7
382(g)(4)(D)	11.4.20
382(h)	11.4.11; 11.4.9; 11.4
382(h)(1)	11.4.6
382(h)(2)	11.4.11
382(h)(2)(A)	11.4.11; 11.4.9
382(h)(2)(B)	11.4.11
382(h)(3)	11.4.7; 11.4.11
382(h)(4)	11.4.9
382(h)(6)(A)	11.4.11
382(h)(8)	11.4.9
382(k)(1)	11.4.2
382(l)(1)	11.4.24; 11.4

Sections	§Number
382(l)(3)(A)	11.4.17
382(l)(8)	11.4.2
382(m)	11.4.23
383	11.4; 11.5.2
384	11.3.5; 11.5.2
385	6.2.3; 10.2.3; 10.8.6
401(a)	1.6.1; 1.6.2
404	8.10.9
404(a)	8.10.9
418(a)	10.10.2
443	11.4.5
446	2.2.1; 2.2.3; 2.6; 2.12.3; 2.12.4; 2.12.7; 4.4.8; 5.3.1; 10.2.3; 10.7.1; 10.7.2
446(a)	2.2.1; 2.2.2; 8.3.4
446(b)	2.2.1; 9.5.8
446(c)	1.6.5; 2.2.1
446(d)	2.2.4
446(e)	2.2.1; 2.2.3; 3.4.4; 10.7.1; 10.10.2
448	2.2.1; 2.2.1
448(a)	1.6.5
448(c)	1.6.5; 2.12; 8.20.4
448(c)(1)	2.2.1
448(c)(3)(C)	2.2.1
448(d)(7)	2.2.1
451	5.1; 5.3.14; 5.3.15; 5.3.18; 5.3.1; 5.3.2; 5.3.7; 10.7.2
453	6.2.2; 7.6.1; 11.4.11; 11.5.2(c)
453B(a)	6.2.2
454	3.3.4
455	2.7.2; 11.4.9
456	2.7.2
460	2.2.1
461	8.14; 9.3.1
461(3)	9.4.1
461(e)	9.4.1
461(g)(2)	3.4.3
461(h)	2.2.1; 8.2; 9.3.1
461(h)(2)(A)(iii)	8.2.1
461(h)(2)(B)	8.2.1
461(h)(2)(C)	8.2.1; 11.4.11
461(h)(3)	2.2.1; 8.2.1
461(h)(5)	2.2.1
461(i)	8.2.1
465	1.1; 12.2
465(c)(7)(D)(iv)	1.5.5
467	2.7.2
469	1.6.5; 1.6.7; 12.2
469(g)	1.1
469(h)	12.1.6; 12.2.11
469(i)	12.2
471	2.2.1; 4.4.2; 4.4.5
475	1.2; 1.6.3; 2.2.1; 2.2.4; 2.12; 3.6; 3.7.2; 3.7.5; 3.7; 4.1; 4.3.3; 4.4.1; 4.4.2; 4.4.3; 4.4.4; 4.4.5; 4.4.6; 4.4.7; 4.4.8; 4.4.9; 4.4.11; 4.4.12; 5.3.7; 5.3.9; 6.1; 6.3.1; 6.3; 8.7; 9.5.2; 9.5.8; 10.2.2; 10.2.3; 10.3.2; 10.8.5; 10.8.6; 11.5.1; 11.6.9; 12.3.8
475(a)	4.4.8; 10.2.2; 10.8.5
475(a)(1)	4.4.8; 6.3.1; 11.6.9
475(a)(2)	4.4.8; 11.6.9
475(a)(3)	6.3.1
475(b)	4.4.3; 4.4.4; 4.4.6; 4.4.7; 6.3.1
475(b)(1)	4.4.4; 4.4.5
475(b)(1)(A)	4.4.3; 4.4.4; 4.4.9; 11.6.9
475(b)(1)(B)	4.4.3
475(b)(1)(C)	4.4.3
475(b)(2)	4.4.4; 4.4.5

Sections	§Number
475(b)(4)	4.4.4; 4.4.6
475(c)(1)	4.4.5; 4.4.11
475(c)(1)(A)	4.4.5
475(c)(1)(B)	4.4.5
475(c)(1)(F)	4.4.11
475(c)(2)	4.4.8; 4.6; 5.3.9
475(c)(2)(D)	4.4.4
475(c)(2)(E)	4.4.4
475(c)(2)(F)	4.4.4; 4.4.7
475(c)(3)	4.4.7
475(d)(1)	4.4.11
475(d)(2)	4.4.4
475(d)(3)	4.4.5; 4.4.6; 4.4.9
475(d)(3)(A)(i)	4.4.5
475(d)(3)(B)	4.4.6; 4.4.9
475(d)(3)(B)(ii)	4.4.5
475(d)(3)(ii)	4.4.9
475(e)	4.4.8
475(e)(2)	4.4.8
475(f)	4.4.6
475(f)(1)	4.4.6
475(f)(1)(B)(i)	4.4.6
475(f)(1)(B)(ii)	4.4.6
475(f)(2)	4.4.6
475(f)(3)	4.4.6
481	2.2.1; 2.2.3; 4.4.12; 10.4.4; 10.7.1; 10.10.2; 10.11
481(a)	1.6.4; 2.2.1; 2.2.3; 4.4.6; 5.3.18; 8.4.6; 9.7; 10.4.4; 10.7.1; 10.10.2; 10.10.4; 10.11.1; 10.11.2; 10.11
481(b)(1)	10.10.2
482	1.6.3; 4.4.8; 9.4.3; 9.5.8
483	3.2.4; 6.3.3
501(a)	1.6.1; 1.6.2; 12.2.11

Sections	§Number
501(c)(3)	1.6.2; 1.6.2; 2.5.1; 9.5.5; 12.2.11; 12.2.2; 12.2.4
501(c)(4)	12.2.2
501(c)(14)	1.3; 10.9.4
511	2.10.3
512(a)(5)	4.6
531	1.4.2; 1.6.5
532	1.4.2
532(a)	1.4.2
542(c)(2)	1.4.1; 1.5.5; 1.5.7; 1.6.5
542(c)(6)	1.5.7; 1.6.7
581	1.2; 1.3; 1.4.1; 1.5.3; 1.5.4; 1.5.5; 1.5.6; 1.5.7; 1.5.10; 1.6.1; 1.6.6; 1.6.7; 1.7.4; 1.7.5; 2.7.4; 5.3.6; 5.3.7; 5.3.8; 8.20; 10.1; 10.2.3; 10.4.2; 10.4.4; 10.7.6; 10.8.4; 10.11.3; 11.3.4
581	1.5.6
582	1.1; 1.5.4; 1.5.5; 1.6.3; 2.7.4; 3.7.2; 4.3.1; 4.3.3; 4.4.9; 7.3.1; 7.6.1; 10.2.3; 10.7.4; 11.3.4
582(a)	4.4.7; 4.4.9; 10.2.3; 10.2.3; 11.4
582(b)	4.3.3
582(c)	3.6.1; 3.6.3; 4.3.3; 4.3.5; 10.2.3; 10.4.1
582(c)(1)	2.7.4; 2.10.3; 4.3.3
582(c)(2)	4.3.4; 11.3.4
582(c)(2)(A)	11.3.4
582(c)(2)(A)(i)	2.7.4
582(c)(2)(A)(ii)	2.7.4
582(c)(2)(C)	4.3.3
582(c)(5)	1.5.5
584	1.5.4, 1.5.5

Sections	§Number
585	1.3; 1.5.5; 1.6.1; 2.2.1; 3.3.2; 4.4.7; 5.3.7; 5.3.8; 7.3.1; 7.5.2; 9.5.9; 9.7; 10.2.1; 10.2.3; 10.4.4; 10.6; 10.7.1; 10.7.2; 10.7.3; 10.7.4; 10.7.5; 10.7.6; 10.7.7; 10.7.8; 10.7.9; 10.7.10; 10.7.11; 10.8.4; 10.8.5; 10.8.6; 10.9.1; 10.9; 10.10.1; 10.10.2; 10.11.2; 10.11; 11.6.9
585(a)	10.4.1; 10.7.1; 10.7.4
585(a)(2)	1.5.5; 10.7.4
585(a)(2)(A)	1.5.5
585(a)(2)(B)	1.5.5; 10.7.6
585(b)	10.7.7; 10.8.4; 10.9.3
585(b)(2)	2.10.2; 7.3.1; 10.7.3; 10.8.2; 10.8; 10.10.2
585(b)(2)(A)	10.7.3; 10.8.1; 10.8.2; 10.8; 10.11.2; 11.5.3
585(b)(2)(B)	10.8.2; 10.8; 11.5.3
585(b)(2)(B)(ii)	10.8.3; 10.11.1
585(b)(3)	2.10.2; 10.8.6; 10.9.5; 10.9.6
585(b)(3)(A)	10.12.1
585(b)(4)	10.8.6
585(b)(4)(A)(B)	10.8.6
585(b)(4)(C)	10.8.6
585(b)(4)(D)	10.8.6
585(b)(4)(E)	10.8.6
585(b)(4)(F)	10.8.6
585(c)	1.2; 1.5.5; 1.6.8; 2.10.2; 9.5.9; 10.2.1; 10.7.6; 10.10.1; 10.10.2; 11.6.9
585(c)(2)	10.11.1; 10.11.2
585(c)(2)(A)	10.10.1
585(c)(3)	10.10.2; 10.10.2; 10.11.2
585(c)(3)(A)	10.10.4
585(c)(3)(A)(iii)	10.10.2
585(c)(3)(B)	10.10.2; 10.10.4
585(c)(3)(B)(ii)	10.10.4
585(c)(3)(B)(iii)	10.10.4
585(c)(3)(B)(iv)	10.10.4
585(c)(3)(C)	10.10.4
585(c)(3)(I)	10.10.4
585(c)(4)	4.4.9; 10.10.2; 10.11.1
585(c)(5)	10.10.1
585(c)(5)(A)	10.10.1
585(c)(5)(B)	10.10.1
585(i)	10.10.1
591	1.5.5; 1.5.7; 1.5.10; 1.7.1; 1.7.7; 2.7.4; 2.13; 9.2; 9.3; 9.3.2; 9.3.4; 9.4.1; 9.5.6; 10.9.5
591(a)	9.2; 9.3.2
591(b)	1.3; 1.4.1; 1.7.1; 7.3.2; 9.3.2

Sections	§Number
593	1.3; 1.5.5; 1.5.10; 1.6.6; 1.6.8; 1.7.2; 1.7.5; 1.7.7; 1.7.9; 2.2.1; 7.5.2; 9.7; 10.2.1; 10.2.3; 10.4.4; 10.7.1; 10.7.3; 10.7.4; 10.7.5; 10.7.6; 10.7.7; 10.7.8; 10.7.9; 10.7.10; 10.7.11; 10.8; 10.8.6; 10.9; 10.9.1; 10.9.3; 10.9.5; 10.11; 10.12.1; 10.12.2; 11.5.3; 11.5.8
593(a)	1.6.6; 10.9; 11.5.3
593(a)(1)	10.7.6
593(a)(2)	1.7.7; 10.9
593(b)	10.7.4
593(b)(1)	10.9.3
593(b)(1)(A)	10.9.6
593(b)(1)(B)	10.7.7
593(b)(1)(B)(i)	10.9.5
593(b)(1)(ii)	10.9.5
593(b)(2)	10.9
593(b)(2)(A)	10.9.3; 10.9.4
593(b)(2)(B)	10.9.6
593(b)(2)(C)	10.9.5; 10.9.6
593(b)(2)(D)(i)	10.9.3
593(b)(2)(D)(ii)	10.9.3
593(b)(2)(D)(iii)	10.9.3
593(b)(2)(D)(v)	10.9.3
593(b)(2)(E)(iv)	10.9.3
593(b)(3)	10.7.3
593(c)	10.7.10; 10.7.9
593(d)	10.8.6
593(d)(1)	7.3.2; 10.9.1
593(d)(1)(A)-(D)	10.9.2
593(d)(1)(B)(ii)	1.5.5
593(d)(2)	10.9.2
593(d)(3)	10.8.6
593(d)(4)	10.8.6; 10.9.1
593(e)	1.6.6; 10.9.3; 10.11.1; 10.11.3; 11.5.2; 11.5.7
593(g)	1.6.8; 10.11
593(g)(1)(B)	10.11
593(g)(1)(C)	10.11
593(g)(1)(C)(i)	10.11
593(g)(2)	1.6.6
593(g)(2)(A)	10.11.1
593(g)(2)(B)	10.11.2
593(g)(2)(B)(i)	10.11.2
593(g)(2)(B)(ii)	10.11.2
593(g)(3)	10.11
593(g)(5)(A)	10.11.2
593(g)(5)(B)	10.11.1
593(g)(6)	10.11.3
593(g)(8)	10.11.3
595	1.3; 1.5.5; 1.5.10; 1.7.6; 3.3.2; 7.1; 7.3.2; 7.5.1; 7.5.2; 7.6.1; 7.6.3; 10.4.5; 10.8.6;
595(a)	7.3.2; 7.4; 10.9.1
595(b)	7.3.2; 7.5.2; 10.4.5
595(c)	7.3.2
596	1.5.5; 1.5.10; 10.9.3; 10.9
597	8.19; 11.6; 11.6.1; 11.6.2; 11.6.8; 11.6
597(a)	8.19; 8.21.2
597(b)	8.21.2
597(c)	11.6.1
597(d)	11.6.1
650(a)	10.7.8
678	1.6.2
701	9.4.3
703(a)	9.4.3
704(c)	2.10.4
707	4.4.4
707(b)	10.10.1; 12.2.2
707(b)(3)	4.4.4
709	8.9.2

Sections	*§Number*
709(b)	8.9.3
709(b)(1)-(3)	8.9.3
721(a)	2.10.4
721(b)	2.10.4
722	2.10.4
817	4.4.4
848	8.3.4
856	2.10
857	2.10
860(a)(2)	2.10.3
860(a)(3)	2.10.3
860A-860G	2.10.3
860B(a)	2.10.3
860B(c)	2.10.3
860C(a)(1)	2.10.3
860C(a)(2)	2.10.3
860C(c)	2.10.3
860C(d)	2.10.3
860D	2.10
860E(e)(5)	2.10.3
860F(b)(1)(A)	2.10.3; 4.4.5
860F(b)(1)(B)	2.10.3
860F(b)(1)(C)	2.10.3
860F(b)(1)(D)(ii)	2.10.3
860G(a)(2)	2.10.3
860G(a)(3)	2.10.3
860G(a)(7)(C)	2.10.3
860H(a)	2.11.1
860H(b)(1)	2.11.1
860H(b)(2)	2.11.1
860H(b)(4)	2.11.1
860H(c)(1)	2.11.1
860I	2.11.1
860I(a)(2)	2.11.1
860I(b)	2.11.1
860I(d)(1)(A)	2.11.1
860I(d)(1)(A)(ii)	2.11.1
860I(d)(1)(B)	2.11.1
860I(e)(1)	2.11.1
860I(e)(2)	2.11.1
860J(a)	2.11.1
860J(b)	2.11.1
860L(a)(1)	2.11.1
860L(a)(2)	2.11.1
860L(b)(1)	2.11.1
860L(c)	2.11.1
860L(e)(1)	2.11.1
860L(e)(2)	2.11.1
860L(e)(3)	2.11.1
861(c)(1)	1.5.8
863	4.4.5
864	1.5.7
864(c)	1.5.5; 10.4.4
904	2.12.7
936(j)	1.6.1
956	1.3; 10.2.3; 1.5.7
956(b)(2)(A)	1.5.7
988	2.12; 2.12.3; 2.12.7; 4.4.11
988(a)(1)	2.12.7
988(a)(1)(A)	4.4.11
988(a)(3)	2.12.7
988(a)(3)(C)	2.12.7
988(c)(1)	2.12.7
988(c)(1)(E)(iv)	2.12.7
988(d)	2.12; 2.12.7; 4.4.2; 4.4.11
1001	2.9.1; 4.3; 6.1; 6.2.1; 6.2.2; 6.3; 6.3.1; 6.3.3; 7.6.3; 7.6; 8.3.1; 8.5.1; 9.5.7; 11.3.1; 11.3.8; 11.6.4
1001(a)	4.3; 6.2.1; 6.3.1; 7.1; 7.6
1001(b)	4.3; 6.3.1; 6.3.2; 11.3.2; 11.6.6
1001(c)	4.3.1; 4.3; 4.4.1; 4.4.5
1001-3(g)	3.3.2
1011	4.3; 6.3.1; 10.2.2
1011(a)	11.6.9
1012	2.9.1; 7.1; 7.6.1; 11.3.2; 11.3.8; 11.5.7; 12.3.2

Sections	*§Number*
1012(a)	11.6.9
1016	6.3.1; 9.5.9
1016(a)(1)	6.3.1
1016(a)(5)	3.7.2
1016(a)(6)	3.7.2
1017	2.13
1032	4.4.7; 11.5.1; 11.5.3
1032(a)	11.5.2; 11.5.3; 11.5.4; 11.5.7
1036	4.6
1037	6.2.2; 6.3.2
1042	1.6.5
1044(c)(3)	12.3.3
1055	10.11.4
1055(c)	10.9.1
1058	2.9.1; 4.6
1058(a)	4.6
1058(b)	4.6
1060	2.7.4; 11.3.2; 11.3.4; 11.3.5; 11.3.8
1060(a)	11.3.2
1060(a)(1)	11.3.2
1060(c)	11.3.2
1061	11.3.2
1091	2.9.1; 4.3.1; 4.4.2; 4.3.3; 4.4.1; 4.4.5; 4.4.11
1091(a)	4.3.1
1092	2.12.7; 4.4.2; 4.4.11
1092(c)	2.12.7
1092(d)(1)	4.4.6
1092(e)	7.6.1
1202	1.1
1211	4.3.5
1211(a)	2.14.3
1212	2.14.3; 7.5.1; 10.9.3
1221	1.1; 2.7.4; 2.12; 4.3.3; 4.3.5; 4.4.3; 4.4.5; 4.4.9; 7.1; 7.6.1; 10.2.3; 11.3.4
1221(a)(1)	2.7.4; 4.4.9; 7.6.1
1221(a)(2)	2.7.4; 7.6.1
1221(4)	4.3.5
1221(a)(1)	4.3.3; 4.4.4; 7.6.1
1221(a)(1)-(8)	4.3.3
1221(a)(4)	2.7.4; 4.3.3
1221(a)(7)	2.12
1221(b)(2)(A)(iii)	2.12
1221(i)	2.12
1223	9.5.4; 9.5.7
1223(1)	11.5.1; 11.5.2; 11.5.3; 11.5.4
1223(2)	11.5.1; 11.5.2; 11.5.3; 11.5.4; 11.5.7
1223(6)	11.5.7
1231	2.7.4 7.6.1; 8.9.2; 10.9.3; 11.3.2; 11.5.3
1233(g)	7.6.1
1236	4.3.3; 4.4.4; 4.4.7; 4.4.9
1236(a)	4.3.3
1236(a)(1)	4.4.4
1236(b)	4.3.3
1236(c)	4.3.3; 4.4.7; 4.6
1236(d)	4.3.3
1239	9.5.8
1245	7.6.1; 7.6.2
1245(b)	3.6.1
1250	7.6.1
1253(b)(1)	11.3.4
1253(d)(1)	11.3.4
1253(d)(1)(B)	11.3.4
1256	1.2; 2.12.7; 4.4.2; 4.4.11; 4.4.5; 4.4.7
1256(a)	4.4.7
1256(a)(3)	4.4.11
1256(b)	4.4.7

Sections	§Number
1256(b)(2)(B)	2.12.2; 4.4.11
1256(d)	2.12.7
1256(e)	7.6.1
1256(e)(1)	4.4.11
1256(g)	2.12.7
1271	1.2; 3.1; 4.4.1; 6.2.2; 10.3
1271(a)	4.3
1271(a)(1)	10.3
1271(a)(2)(B)	10.3
1271(a)(3)(C)	3.2.1
1271(b)	3.3.1; 10.3
1271(c)	3.6
1272	2.2.1; 2.6; 2.6.2; 2.10.2; 3.3.4; 3.4.6; 3.4.7; 3.5.5; 6.1; 8.6; 9.4.2
1272(a)	3.3.4
1272(a)(1)	3.3.7; 3.4.6; 3.4.7; 3.5.5
1272(a)(3)	3.2.4; 3.3.1; 3.4.6
1272(a)(4)	3.2.4; 3.4.6
1272(a)(5)	3.2.4
1272(a)(6)	3.4.7; 3.5.5; 10.3
1272(a)(6)(C)(i)	3.5.5
1272(a)(6)(C)(iii)	3.4.7; 3.5.5
1272(d)(2)	3.3.7; 3.4.4
1273	3.4.4; 3.4.5; 6.3.3
1273(a)	3.2.1; 8.6; 11.3.5
1273(a)(1)	3.2.4; 3.4.4; 3.4.5; 3.5.5
1273(a)(2)	3.2.4; 3.4.5
1273(a)(3)	3.3.4; 3.4.1
1273(a)(12)	3.2.4
1273(b)	6.3.3
1273(b)(1)	3.2.4; 3.4.5
1273(b)(2)	3.2.4; 3.5.5
1273(b)(3)	3.2.4
1273(b)(4)	3.2.4
1273(b)(4)(B)	3.2.4
1273(b)(5)	3.2.4
1273(c)	3.2.4
1274	3.2.4; 3.4.5; 6.2.3; 6.3.2; 6.3.3
1274(a)	6.3.3
1274(a)(1)	3.2.4
1274(a)(2)	3.2.4; 6.3.3
1274(b)	3.2.4; 6.3.3
1274(b)(2)	6.3.3
1274(b)(3)	3.2.4
1274(c)(1)	3.2.4
1274(c)(2)	6.3.3
1274(c)(4)	3.2.4; 6.2.3
1274(d)(1)	12.2.1
1274(d)(1)(A)	6.3.3
1275	2.3; 3.1
1275(a)	9.3.4
1275(a)(1)(A)	3.3.4; 3.4.5
1275(a)(4)	6.3.1
1275(c)	3.3.8
1275(c)(1)	3.3.8
1275(c)(2)	2.10.3
1276	3.6.1; 3.6.3; 9.4.2
1276(a)(1)	3.6.1
1276(a)(3)	3.6.1
1276(a)(4)	3.6.1
1276(b)	3.6.1
1276(b)(1)	3.6.2
1276(b)(2)	3.6.1; 3.6.2
1276(d)	3.6.1
1277	3.6.3; 5.3.13; 9.4.2
1277(a)	3.6.3; 9.4.2
1277(b)	9.4.2
1277(b)(1)	3.6.3; 9.4.2
1277(b)(1)(C)	3.6.3
1277(b)(2)	3.6.3; 9.4.2
1277(b)(2)(B)	3.6.3; 9.4.2
1277(c)	1.5.5; 3.6.3; 9.4.2; 9.5.4
1278(a)	9.4.2
1278(a)(2)	3.2.1; 3.6
1278(a)(3)	9.4.2
1278	2.10.3; 3.6.3; 3.6.4; 3.6

Sections	*§Number*
1278(b)(2)	3.6
1278(b)(3)	3.6
1281	1.6.3; 2.2.1; 3.3.4; 3.3.5; 3.6.2
1281(a)	3.6
1281(a)(1)	3.3.5; 3.6.2
1281(a)(2)	3.3.5
1281(b)	3.3.4
1281(b)(1)(C)	1.5.5; 3.3.1
1282(b)(1)	3.2.4
1282(b)(2)	3.2.4
1283	3.3.4
1283(a)	3.2.1; 3.6.2
1283(a)(1)	3.3.4; 9.3.4(a)
1283(a)(1)(A)	3.6.2
1283(a)(2)	3.6
1283(b)	3.6.2
1283(b)(1)	3.3.1
1283(b)(2)	3.3.1
1286	2.7.4; 4.3.2; 11.3.5
1286(b)	2.7.4
1286(b)(3)	4.3.2
1286(e)(1)	2.7.4
1286(e)(2)	2.7.4
1286(e)(5)	2.7.4
1361	1.4.1; 9.6
1361(b)(2)	10.2.1
1361(b)(2)(A)	10.4.1
1361(b)	1.6.1; 1.6.6; 9.5.2
1361(b)(1)	1.6.1; 9.6
1361(b)(1)(A)	1.6.1
1361(b)(1)(B)	1.6.2
1361(b)(1)(C)	1.6.1
1361(b)(1)(D)	1.6.1
1361(b)(2)	1.6; 1.6.1; 1.6.3; 1.6.6;
1361(b)(2)(A)	1.6.1; 1.6.6
1361(b)(3)	1.6.3; 9.6
1361(b)(3)(A)	9.6
1361(b)(3)(A)(i)	1.6.3
1361(b)(3)(A)(ii)	1.6.3
1361(c)(1)	1.6.1
1361(c)(1)(B)	1.6.2
1361(c)(2)	1.6.1; 1.6.2
1361(c)(2)(A)(i)	1.6.2
1361(c)(2)(A)(ii)	1.6.2
1361(c)(2)(A)(iii)	1.6.2
1361(c)(2)(A)(iv)	1.6.2
1361(c)(2)(A)(v)	1.6.2
1361(c)(2)(A)(vi)	1.6.2
1361(c)(2)(B)(i)	1.6.2
1361(c)(2)(B)(iv)	1.6.2
1361(c)(6)	1.6.1; 1.6.2
1361(d)	1.6.2
1361(d)(1)	1.6.2
1361(d)(2)	1.6.2
1361(d)(3)	1.6.2
1361(e)(2)	1.6.2
1361(g)	1.6.4
1362(a)	1.6.5
1362(b)(5)	1.6.4
1362(d)	1.6.7
1362(d)(1)	1.6.1
1362(d)(3)	1.6.7
1362(d)(3)(C)(v)	1.6.7
1362(d)(3)(F)	1.6.7
1362(f)	1.6.4
1363(b)	9.6
1363(b)(3)	9.6
1363(b)(4)	1.6.3; 1.6.5; 9.6
1366	7.5.1
1366(b)	1.6.5
1366(f)(2)	1.6.8
1366(f)(3)	1.6.7
1366(f)(3)(A)	1.6.7
1366(f)(3)(B)	1.6.7
1367	1.6.5
1368	1.6.6
1371	1.6; 9.6
1371(b)	1.6.6
1371(d)(2)	1.6.9
1372	1.6.6
1374	1.6.6; 1.6.8; 11.4.11

Sections	§Number
1374(a)	1.6.9
1374(b)(2)	1.6.6
1374(d)(1)	1.6.8
1374(d)(3)	1.6.8; 1.6.8
1374(d)(4)	1.6.8
1374(d)(7)	1.6.8
1374(d)(7)(B)	1.6.8(a)
1374(d)(7)(C)	1.6.8(a)
1375	1.6.6; 1.6.7
1375(a)	1.6.7; 1.6.9
1375(b)(3)	1.6.7
1375(b)(4)	1.6.7
1375(d)	1.6.7
1378	1.6.6
1381(a)(2)(c)	2.10.3
1397(C)(e)	12.3.6
1397C(e)	12.3.6
1400(c)(1)(A)	12.2
1400(c)(1)(B)	12.2
1400N(c)(1)	12.2.12
1400N(c)(1)(C)	12.2.12
1400N(c)(2)	12.2.12
1400N(c)(3)	12.2; 12.2.2(a)
1400N(c)(4)	12.2.4(a)
1400N(m)	12.3.1; 12.3.4
1501	9.4.3
1502	9.5.7
1504	10.9.2
1504(a)	4.4.5; 8.20; 9.4.3; 10.9.2
1504(a)(1)	10.4.1
1504(a)(1)(A)	9.4.3
1504(a)(2)	1.6.7
1504(a)(4)	11.4.23; 11.4.25; 11.5.7
1504(b)	10.9.2
1504(b)(1)	9.4.3
1504(b)(2)	1.2; 9.4.3
1504(b)(3)	9.4.3
1504(b)(8)	9.4.3; 10.4.1
1504(c)(1)	1.2
1504(c)(2)	1.2
1563(a)(1)	10.10.1; 10.10.4; 10.11.4
1563(a)(1)(A)	10.10.1
1563(a)(2000)	10.10.1
1563(b)(2)	10.10.1
1958(b)	4.6
1986	9.5.4(c)
1999	12.1.5
2032A(e)(5)(A)	12.3.6
2679f(2)	10.3.1
3081(b)	12.1.7
3401(c)	8.4.4
4975	1.6.1; 1.6.2
6032	1.5.5
6049(c)	3.3.8
6049(d)(6)	3.3.8
6050J	7.2
6411(a)	8.20.4
6501	10.4.4
6511(a)	10.7.8
6511(d)(1)	10.3.1
6511(d)(2)	10.7.8
6621	12.2.14
6621(a)(2)	12.2.14
6655(d)(1)(B)(ii)	1.6.9
6655(d)(2)(B)	1.6.9
6655(e)	1.6.9
6655(e)(2)(A)	10.10.4
6655(g)(4)	1.6.9
6655(g)(4)(E)	1.6.9
6662(d)(2)(B)	5.1
6695(f)	1.5.5
7507	1.4.1; 1.7.3; 11.6.7
7512(b)	1.5.5
7701	9.5.8
7701(a)(1)	9.4.3; 9.7
7701(a)(1)(C)	10.9.6
7701(a)(3)	11.6.5
7701(a)(5)	9.7
7701(a)(14)	9.4.3

Sections	*§Number*
7701(a)(19)	1.3; 1.5.4; 1.5.5; 1.5.10; 1.7.1; 1.7.4; 1.7.5; 1.7.7; 1.7.9; 7.3.2; 10.7.6; 10.9.5; 10.9.6; 11.3.4
7701(a)(19)(A)-(B)	11.6.1
7701(a)(19)(A)-(C)	1.7.4
7701(a)(19)(B)	1.7.6
7701(a)(19)(C)	1.7.7; 1.7.8; 10.7.11; 10.9; 10.9.1; 10.9.6
7701(a)(19)(C)(v)	1.7.7; 10.11.4
7701(a)(19)(c)	10.9
7701(a)(19)(iii)-(xi)	10.9.3
7701(a)(23)	1.4.2
7701(a)(30)	2.12.7; 9.7
7701(a)(32)	1.3; 1.5.10; 7.3.2
7701(f)	9.4.3; 9.5.2; 9.5.6; 9.5.8
7701(f)(1)	9.4.3
7701(g)	4.4.8
7701(i)(1)	2.10.2
7701(i)(2)	2.10.2
7702	4.4.4
7805(a)	8.4.4; 10.8.6
7805(b)	3.4.4; 9.5.8
7871(d)	10.8.6
7872(f)	9.5.8

Table of Other Statutory Provisions and Statements of Financial Accounting Standards

Statutes	*§Number*
12 U.S.C. § 1	1.4
12 U.S.C. § 24	1.4, 8.10, 11.2
12 U.S.C. § 24(7)	1.4, 4.3, 11.2
12 U.S.C. § 27	1.4
12 U.S.C. § 29	7.2
12 U.S.C. § 36	11.2
12 U.S.C. § 36(c)	8.10, 11.2
12 U.S.C. § 72	1.6
12 U.S.C. § 81	11.2
12 U.S.C. § 92a(a)	1.4
12 U.S.C. § 215	11.5
12 U.S.C. § 321	11.2
12 U.S.C. § 372	10.8
12 U.S.C. § 377	11.2
12 U.S.C. § 378	11.2
12 U.S.C. § 482	8.5
12 U.S.C. § 611	10.4.3, 11.2
12 U.S.C. § 1426(a)	2.14
12 U.S.C. § 1426(b)	2.14
12 U.S.C. § 1426(c)	2.14
12 U.S.C. § 1430	1.6
12 U.S.C. § 1430(b)	1.6
12 U.S.C. § 1430(e)(1)	2.14
12 U.S.C. § 1431(e)	1.6
12 U.S.C. § 1462(d)	1.6
12 U.S.C. § 1464	1.6
12 U.S.C. § 1464(c)(4)(B)	11.2
12 U.S.C. § 1467(a)	1.6
12 U.S.C. § 1467(m)	1.6, 2.14
12 U.S.C. § 1724(a)	1.6
12 U.S.C. § 1725(e)	1.3, 1.6
12 U.S.C. § 1729(f)	8.19, 11.5
12 U.S.C. § 1730(a)	11.2
12 U.S.C. § 1811	8.7
12 U.S.C. § 1813	1.4
12 U.S.C. § 1813(b)	1.6
12 U.S.C. § 1813(b)(2)	1.6
12 U.S.C. § 1813(c)(1)	1.4
12 U.S.C. § 1813(f)	1.6
12 U.S.C. § 1813(l)	1.5
12 U.S.C. § 1813(w)(1)	4.3
12 U.S.C. § 1815(d)(2)(A)(ii)	8.13
12 U.S.C. § 1815(d)(2)(C)	8.13
12 U.S.C. § 1815(d)(2)(D)	11.3
12 U.S.C. § 1815(d)(2)(E)	8.13
12 U.S.C. § 1815(d)(2)(F)	8.13
12 U.S.C. § 1815(d)(2)(G)	8.13
12 U.S.C. § 1815(d)(3)	8.13
12 U.S.C. § 1815(d)(3)(A)	8.13
12 U.S.C. § 1815(d)(3)(B)	8.13
12 U.S.C. § 1815(d)(3)(C)	8.13
12 U.S.C. § 1815(d)(3)(G)	8.13
12 U.S.C. § 1817	8.13
12 U.S.C. § 1817(i)(1-2)	1.5

Statutes	*§Number*
12 U.S.C. § 1817(i)(3)	1.5
12 U.S.C. § 1817(j)	11.2
12 U.S.C. § 1821(a)	1.6
12 U.S.C. § 1821(a)(1)(C)	1.5
12 U.S.C. § 1821(a)(1)(E)	1.5
12 U.S.C. § 1821(a)(4)(A)	1.5
12 U.S.C. § 1828	11.2
12 U.S.C. § 1828(d)(1)	11.2
12 U.S.C. § 1831(n)	5.2
12 U.S.C. § 1832(a)(5)	1.5
12 U.S.C. § 1832(a)(5)(B)(i)	1.5
12 U.S.C. § 1841	11.2
12 U.S.C. § 1841(a)	1.6
12 U.S.C. § 1841(a)(1)	11.2
12 U.S.C. § 1841(a)(2)	11.2
12 U.S.C. § 1841(b)	11.2
12 U.S.C. § 1841(c)	1.4, 11.2
12 U.S.C. § 1841(c)(2)(F)	1.5
12 U.S.C. § 1842	11.2
12 U.S.C. § 1842(d)(1)	11.2
12 U.S.C. § 1843	11.2
12 U.S.C. § 1843(c)(1)(C)	11.2
12 U.S.C. § 1843(c)(6)	11.2
12 U.S.C. § 1843(c)(8)	4.3, 11.2
12 U.S.C. § 1844	11.2
12 U.S.C. § 1845	11.2
12 U.S.C. § 1846	11.2
12 U.S.C. § 1847	11.2
12 U.S.C. § 1848	11.2
12 U.S.C. § 1849	11.2
12 U.S.C. § 1850	11.2
12 U.S.C. § 1861	11.2
12 U.S.C. § 1863	11.2
12 U.S.C. § 1864	11.2
12 U.S.C. § 1964(d)(6)	11.5
12 U.S.C. § 2001	1.5, 1.7
12 U.S.C. § 2002(a)	1.5
12 U.S.C. § 2011(a)	1.5
12 U.S.C. § 2071(a)	1.5
12 U.S.C. § 2071(b)(7)	1.5
12 U.S.C. § 2091	1.4
12 U.S.C. § 2091(a)	1.5
12 U.S.C. § 2091(b)(4)	1.5
12 U.S.C. § 2093	1.4
12 U.S.C. § 2121	1.5
12 U.S.C. § 2141	1.5
12 U.S.C. § 2802(2)(A)	1.6
12 U.S.C. § 3502	2.12, 9.3
12 U.S.C. § 482	8.14
12 U.S.C. § 5201	9.2.1
12 U.S.C. § 5213(1)	9.2.1
12 U.S.C. § 5261(d)-(e)	4.3.4
15 U.S.C. § 78(a)-78(kk)	4.3
15 U.S.C. § 1127	11.3
26 U.S.C. § 401(d)	1.5
29 U.S.C. § 1002	1.5

Public Law	*§Number*
63-16	1.3, 1.6
65-50	9.5
74-740	1.3
82-183	1.3, 1.6
85-866	4.3
87-834	1.3, 1.6, 7.1
89-485	1.4
90-255	11.2
90-321	2.6
91-172	1.3, 1.6
91-607	1.4

Public Law	*§Number*
94-455	8.20, 11.5
95-630	11.2
96-211	9.3
96-221	2.10, 7.2, 9.3
96-589	11.5
96-605	8.6, 11.3
97-34	1.3, 1.6, 4.3, 11.5, 11.6, 12.1
97-248	3.2, 9.5, 11.5
97-320	1.2, 11.2
97-760	9.5
98-181	10.4.4
98-369	3.4.8, 3.6, 4.3, 8.2, 8.9, 9.3, 9.4, 9.5, 11.5
99-514	1.3, 1.6, 2.2, 2.10, 3.6, 4.3, 4.4, 7.5, 8.3, 8.8, 8.20, 9.4, 9.5, 10.7 10.9, 10.11, 11.3, 11.6, 12.1, 12.2
99-597	11.5
100-86	1.4, 8.10, 11.2
100-233	8.16
100-647	2.2, 4.3, 8.5, 8.22, 9.5,10.10, 11.6
101-73	1.6, 2.14, 8.13, 8.21, 10.7, 11.3, 11.6
101-239	4.3, 12.1
101-508	4.3, 10.7, 10.8, 10.12, 12.1
101-227	12.1
102-242	5.2
103-66	4.4, 11.3
103-328	11.2
104-188	1.2, 1.5, 1.6, 2.5, 2.11, 2.12, 7.1, 9.6, 10.2, 10.7, 10.9
105-34	1.3, 1.5, 2.10, 3.4.2, 3.5.1, 4.3, 4.4, 9.6
106-102	1.2, 4.3, 11.1, 11.2
106-170	7.6. 12.1.5
108-359	2.10
108-375	1.1, 1.6, 8.6
109-135	12.3
109-171	1.5
109-432	12.1.4, 12.1.5
110-28	1.6.3
110-289	12.1.7, 12.2
110-343	4.3, 8.20, 9.2.1, 11.4, 11.6, 12.1-12.3
111-5	8.20, 9.5, 11.4, 12.2, 12.3
111-92	8.20
111-203	1.5, 2.12.1
511	1.4
591	8.4

Statements of Financial Accounting Standards	*§Number*
2	8.9
5	5.2
12	4.3, 4.4
15	5.2
65	4.3, 4.4
71	8.9
72	11.3
91	2.2, 2.8, 4.3, 8.3
112	2.7
114	5.1, 5.2, 6.1, 6.2
115	4.3, 4.4
118	5.1, 5.2
125	2.7
140	2.7

Table of Treasury Regulations

Proposed Regulations	*§Number*
1.41-4	12.1.1; 12.1.3; 12.1.4
1.41-4(a)(8)	12.1.1
1.41-4(c)(6)	12.1.3
1.41-4(c)(6)(iv)(A)	12.1.3
1.41-4(c)(6)(vi)(A)-(C)	12.1.3
1.45D-1(d)	12.3.4; 12.3.6
1.197-2(11)	11.3.5
1.197-2(c)(4)	11.3.5
1.263(a)-4	8.9.2
1.263(a)-4(d)(7)	8.10.9
1.263(a)-4(o)	8.3.4
1.355-2(b)	11.5.1
1.368-2(j)	11.5.2; 11.5.3
1.446	2.12.4
1.475(a)	10.5
1.475(a)-1(f)	4.4.9; 10.2.3; 10.3.2
1.475(a)-1(g)(1)	10.8.5
1.475(a)-1(g)(2)	10.9.3
1.475(b)-3(b)	4.4.7
1.475(f)-2(a)(3)	4.4.6
1.475(f)-2(a)(4)	4.4.6
1.1001-1(a)	4.6
1.1001-3	9.5.7
1.1296	1.5.7

Temporary Regulations	*§Number*
1.41-8T(b)(5)	12.1.5
1.45D-1T(h)	12.3.1
1.163-5T	9.7
1.197-1T	11.3.3
1.338(b)-2T	11.3.2
1.382-2T(a)(1)	11.4.12
1.382-2T(a)(2)(i)	11.4.12
1.382-2T(a)(2)(i)(B)	11.4.12
1.382-2T(c)	11.4.13
1.382-2T(e)(1)	11.4.13
1.382-2T(f)(9)	11.4.12; 11.4.13
1.382-2T(g)(1)	11.4.13
1.382-2T(h)(4)	11.4.19
1.382-2T(j)	11.4.13
1.382-2T(j)(2)	11.4.13
1.382-2T(j)(2)(iii)(A)	11.4.21
1.382-2T(d)	11.4.16
1.382-2T(f)(18)	11.4.18
1.382-2T(f)(18)(i)	11.4.12; 11.4.18
1.382-2T(h)(2)(i)(A)	11.4.17
1.382-2T(h)(2)(i)(B)	11.4.17
1.382-2T(h)(3)	11.4.17
1.382-2T(h)(4)	11.4.17
1.382-2T(k)(3)	11.4.17
1.444-2T	1.6.2(c)
1.956-2T	10.2.3
1.1060-1T(a)(1)	11.3.2
1.1060-1T(b)(2)	2.7.4
1.1060-1T(d)	11.3.2
1.1060-1T(d)(1)	11.3.2
1.1060-1T(d)(2)	11.3.2
1.1060-1T(d)(2)(iii)	11.3.2
1.1060-1T(e)	11.3.2
1.1221-2T(a)(1)	7.6.1
1.1221-2T(a)(2)	7.6.1
1.1286-1T	2.7.4

Temporary Regulations	*§Number*
1.6050J-1T	7.2
7.0	8.20.3

Treasury Regulations	*§Number*
1.41-1(a)	12.1.5
1.41-2	12.1.1
1.41-4	12.1; 12.1.1
1.41-4(a)(3)	12.1.1
1.41-4(c)(6)(iv)(A)	12.1.3
1.42(d)(4)	12.2.2
1.42-2(c)(3)	12.2.2
1.42-2(d)(1)	12.2.2
1.42-2(d)(3)	12.2.2
1.42-3	12.2.1
1.42-4(a)	12.2
1.42-4(b)	12.2
1.42-6(a)(2)(ii)	12.2.11
1.42-8(a)(2)	12.2.1
1.42-8(a)(4)(i)	12.2.1
1.42-8(a)(4)(ii)	12.2.1
1.42-8(a)(5)	12.2.1
1.42-8(a)(6)	12.2.1
1.42-8(a)(6)(i)	12.2.1
1.42-8(a)(6)(ii)	12.2.1
1.42-8(b)(2)	12.2.1
1.42-8(b)(3)	12.2.1
1.42-8(b)(4)(i)	12.2.1
1.42-8(b)(4)(ii)	12.2.1
1.42-9	12.2.3
1.42-10(b)(1)	12.2.3
1.42-10(b)(2)	12.2.3
1.42-10(b)(3)	12.2.3
1.42-10(b)(4)(i)	12.2.3
1.42-10(b)(4)(ii)	12.2.3
1.42-10(c)	12.2.3
1.42-10(c)(1)	12.2.3
1.42-10(c)(2)	12.2.3
1.42-11	12.2.3
1.42-12	12.2.1
1.42-12(a)(3)	12.2.1
1.42-12(a)(4)	12.2.3

Treasury Regulations	*§Number*
1.42-13(b)	12.2.12
1.42-13(b)(3)(iv)	12.2.12
1.42-13(d)	12.2.12
1.42-14(a)(1)	12.2.11
1.42-14(b)	12.2.11
1.42-14(c)	12.2.11
1.42-14(d)(1)	12.2.11
1.42-14(d)(2)(iv)(A)	12.2.11
1.42-14(h)	12.2.11
1.42-15(c)	12.2.3
1.42-15(d)	12.2.3
1.42-15(e)	12.2.3
1.42-15(f)	12.2.3
1.42-16(a)	12.2.2
1.42-16(b)	12.2.2
1.42-16(c)	12.2.2
1.45(d)(1)(ii)(B)	12.3.5
1.45D-1	12.3.1
1.45D-1(b)(4)	12.3.2
1.45D-1(c)	12.3.2
1.45D-1(c)(3)(i)	12.3.2
1.45D-1(c)(3)(ii)	12.3.2
1.45D-1(c)(3)(ii)(A)	12.3.2
1.45D-1(c)(3)(ii)(B)	12.3.2
1.45D-1(c)(3)(iv)	12.3.2
1.45D-1(c)(4)	12.3.2
1.45D-1(c)(5)	12.3.2
1.45D-1(c)(5)(iii)	12.3.2
1.45D-1(c)(5)(iv)	12.3.2
1.45D-1(c)(7)	12.3.2
1.45D-1(c)(3)(ii)	12.3.2
1.45D-1(d)(1)	12.3.5
1.45D-1(d)(1)(iv)	12.3.5
1.45D-1(d)(4)	12.3.6
1.45D-1(d)(4)(i)	12.3.6
1.45D-1(d)(4)(i)(E)(1)(i)	12.3.6
1.45D-1(d)(4)(i)(E)(1)(ii)	12.3.6
1.45D-1(d)(4)(i)(E)(2)	12.3.6
1.45D-1(d)(4)(ii)	12.3.6
1.45D-1(d)(4)(iii)	12.3.6
1.45D-1(d)(4)(iv)(A)	12.3.6

Treasury Regulations	§Number
1.45D-1(d)(5)	12.3.6
1.45D-1(d)(6)(i)	12.3.6
1.45D-1(d)(6)(ii)(A)	12.3.6
1.45D-1(d)(6)(ii)(B)	12.3.6
1.45D-1(d)(6)(ii)(C)	12.3.2; 12.3.6
1.45D-1(d)(6)(ii)(C)(3)(ii)	12.3.2
1.45D-1(d)(7)	12.3.5
1.45D-1(e)	12.3.8
1.45D-1(e)(6)	12.3.8
1.45D-1(g)(1)	12.3.8
1.45D-1(g)(2)(i)(B)	12.3.8
1.45D-1(g)(4)	12.3.1
1.45D-1(h)	12.3.1
1.45D-1(h)(2)	12.3.6
1.45D-D(c)(3)(i)	12.3.2
1.57-1(g)(4)	10.12.1
1.57-1(g)(4)(i)	10.12.1
1.61-6(a)	11.3.2(d)
1.61-7(c)	2.4; 3.2.1; 3.4.4
1.61-8(b)	2.7.2
1.61-12(c)(2)(ii)	6.3.3
1.103-1(b)	2.5.1
1.103-16	2.5.2
1.111-1	10.6
1.111-1(a)(1)	10.7.9
1.162-1(a)	8.8.3
1.162-10	8.10.9
1.162-11(a)	11.3.5
1.162-20(a)(2)	8.10.2
1.163-1(c)	9.2
1.163-3(d)	9.3.4
1.163-4	9.2; 9.3.4
1.163-5	9.7
1.163-5(c)	9.7
1.163-7(b)(2)	8.6
1.163-13(a)	8.6
1.163-13(c)	8.6
1.165-1(b)	4.4.1; 6.2.1; 8.18; 8.21
1.165-1(c)(1)	8.21
1.165-1(c)(4)	8.21
1.165-1(d)(2)(i)	8.21
1.165-2(a)	8.21
1.165-5	10.2.3
1.165-8(d)	10.2.3
1.165-12	9.7
1.166-1(b)	10.7.1
1.166-1(b)(1)	10.7.5
1.166-1(b)(3)	10.7.1
1.166-1(c)	10.2.2; 10.2.3; 10.8.6
1.166-1(d)	10.2.2
1.166-1(d)(1)	10.2.2
1.166-1(f)	10.6; 10.7.9
1.166-1(g)(2)	10.2.3
1.166-1(g)(1)	10.2.3
1.166-1(g)(2)	10.2.3
1.166-2(a)	10.3.1; 10.4.1
1.166-2(c)	10.3.1
1.166-2(d)	5.3.16; 5.3.17; 10.5
1.166-2(d)(1)	10.4.1; 10.4.3; 11.6.9
1.166-2(d)(2)	10.3; 10.4.1.; 10.5
1.166-2(d)(2)(I)	10.5
1.166-2(d)(2)(ii)	10.5
1.166-2(d)(3)	5.3.16; 5.3.3; 6.3.3; 10.2.3; 10.4.1; 10.4.4; 10.8.6; 11.6.9
1.166-2(d)(3)(ii)(C)	10.3.2
1.166-2(d)(3)(iii)(B)	10.4.4
1.166-2(d)(3)(iii)(B)(3)	4.4.9; 6.3.3; 10.4.4; 10.8.6
1.166-2(d)(3)(iv)(C)	10.4.4
1.166-2(d)(3)(iv)(C)(2)	10.4.4
1.166-2(d)(3)(iv)(C)(3)	10.4.4
1.166-2(d)(3)(iv)(C)(4)	10.4.4
1.166-2(d)(3)(iii)(D)	10.4.1
1.166-2(d)(3)(iv)(D)	10.4.4
1.166-2(d)(3)(iv)(E)	10.4.4
1.166-2(d)(4)(I)	10.4.4

Treasury Regulations	§Number
1.166-2(d)(4)(ii)	10.3.2; 10.4.4
1.166-2(d)(4)(ii)(C)	10.4.4
1.166-3	6.3.3; 10.2.3; 10.3
1.166-3(a)(2)	10.3; 10.5
1.166-3(a)(2)(ii)	10.3.1
1.166-3(a)(3)(iii)	6.3.3; 10.3.2
1.166-3(d)(iv)(D)	10.4.4
1.166-6	7.3.1
1.166-6(a)	7.3.1
1.166-6(a)(1)	7.3.1
1.166-6(a)(2)	7.3.1
1.166-6(b)	7.3.1
1.166-6(b)(2)	7.3.1
1.166-6(d)	7.3.2
1.166-9	10.2.3
1.166-9(a)	10.2.3
1.166-9(c)	10.2.3
1.166-9(e)	10.2.3
1.167(a)-1(a)	2.7.4
1.167(a)-1(b)	2.7.4; 11.3.2; 11.3.3
1.167(a)-3	11.3.2; 11.3.3
1.167(a)-3(b)(ii)	8.7
1.167(a)-3(b)(iii)	8.7
1.167(a)-3(b)(iv)	8.7
1.167(a)-5	11.3.2
1.167(a)-8	2.7.4
1.167(b)-1	2.7.4
1.171-1	3.7
1.171-1(a)(2)	3.7
1.171-2(a)(1)	3.7.5
1.171-2(d)	3.7.5
1.171-2(f)	3.7.4
1.171-3(a)	3.7.1
1.171-4(a)	3.7.3
1.174-2(a)(1)	12.1.1
1.195-1	8.9.2
1.195-1(a)	8.9.5
1.195-1(c)	8.9.2
1.197-2	8.4.3
1.197-2(b)(1)	8.4.2
1.197-2(b)(3)	8.4.2
1.197-2(b)(6)	8.4.2
1.197-2(b)(7)	8.4.2
1.197-2(b)(10);	8.4.2
1.197-2(c)(11)	2.7.4
1.197-2(e)(1)	2.7.4
1.197-2(g)(1)(i)(B)	8.21.1
1.197-14(d)	2.7.4
1.197-14(d)(2)(i)	2.7.4
1.197-14(d)(2)(ii)	2.7.4
1.248(b)(3)	8.9.4
1.248-1(a)(2)	8.9.5
1.248-1(a)(3)	8.9.2
1.248-1(b)(2)	8.9.4
1.248-1(b)(3)	8.9.4
1.248-1(c)	8.9.5
1.263	8.4.3; 8.4.4
1.263(a)	8.9.2
1.263(a)-1	8.3.1
1.263(a)-1(f)(1)(ii)(D)	8.4.4
1.263(a)-2	8.3.1(a)
1.263(a)-4	8.3.1; 8.3.2; 8.3.4; 8.4.1; 8.4.3; 8.4.4; 8.4.5; 8.4.6; 8.5.1; 8.7; 8.10.4
1.263(a)-4(a)	8.4.1
1.263(a)-4(b)(1)	8.3.3; 8.4.1
1.263(a)-4(b)(1)(i)	8.4.1
1.263(a)-4(b)(1)(ii)	8.4.1
1.263(a)-4(b)(1)(iii)	8.4.1
1.263(a)-4(b)(1)(iv)	8.4.1
1.263(a)-4(b)(1)(v)	8.4.1; 8.4.4
1.263(a)-4(b)(2)	8.3.3; 8.4.1
1.263(a)-4(b)(3)	8.4.1
1.263(a)-4(b)(3)(i)	8.4.1
1.263(a)-4(b)(3)(ii)	8.4.1
1.263(a)-4(b)(3)(iii)	8.4.1
1.263(a)-4(b)(3)(iv)	8.4.1

Treasury Regulations	*§Number*
1.263(a)-4(b)(3)(v)	8.4.1
1.263(a)-4(b)(4)(i)	8.3.3; 8.4.1
1.263(a)-4(b)(i)(ii)	8.4.4
1.263(a)-4(c)	8.7
1.263(a)-4(c)(1)	8.4.2
1.263(a)-4(c)(1)(i)-(iv)	8.4.3
1.263(a)-4(c)(1)(i)-(xv)	8.4.2
1.263(a)-4(c)(1)(vi)	8.4.1
1.263(a)-4(d)	8.3.3; 8.4.1; 8.4.3; 8.13
1.263(a)-4(d)(1)	8.4.3
1.263(a)-4(d)(2)	8.4.4; 8.7
1.263(a)-4(d)(2)(i)	8.4.3
1.263(a)-4(d)(2)(i)(A)	8.4.3
1.263(a)-4(d)(2)(i)(A)-(F)	8.4.3
1.263(a)-4(d)(2)(i)(B)	8.4.4
1.263(a)-4(d)(2)(i)(C)(1)-(5)	8.4.3
1.263(a)-4(d)(2)(i)(D)	8.4.3
1.263(a)-4(d)(2)(i)(E)	8.4.3
1.263(a)-4(d)(2)(i)(F)	8.4.3
1.263(a)-4(d)(2)(ii)	8.4.3
1.263(a)-4(d)(2)(vi)	8.4.3
1.263(a)-4(d)(3)	8.4.3; 8.12
1.263(a)-4(d)(3)(ii)	8.12
1.263(a)-4(d)(4)	8.4.3
1.263(a)-4(d)(5)(i)	8.4.3
1.263(a)-4(d)(5)(ii)	8.4.3
1.263(a)-4(d)(5)(v)	8.4.5; 8.5.1
1.263(a)-4(d)(6)	8.4.4
1.263(a)-4(d)(6)(i)	8.4.3
1.263(a)-4(d)(6)(i)(A)	8.4.3
1.263(a)-4(d)(6)(i)(B)	8.4.3
1.263(a)-4(d)(6)(i)(C)	8.4.3
1.263(a)-4(d)(6)(i)(E)	8.4.3
1.263(a)-4(d)(6)(ii)	8.4.3
1.263(a)-4(d)(6)(iii)	8.4.3
1.263(a)-4(d)(6)(iv)	8.4.3
1.263(a)-4(d)(6)(v)	8.4.3; 8.4.4
1.263(a)-4(d)(7)	8.4.3
1.263(a)-4(d)(7)(i)	8.4.4
1.263(a)-4(d)(7)(i)(A)	8.4.3; 8.10.9
1.263(a)-4(d)(7)(i)(B)	8.4.3
1.263(a)-4(d)(7)(i)(C)	8.4.3
1.263(a)-4(d)(8)(i)	8.4.3
1.263(a)-4(d)(8)(ii)	8.4.3
1.263(a)-4(d)(9)	8.4.3
1.263(a)-4(e)	8.4.2
1.263(a)-4(e)(1)(i)	8.4.4; 8.6.2
1.263(a)-4(e)(1)(ii)	8.4.4
1.263(a)-4(e)(1)(iii)	8.4.4
1.263(a)-4(e)(1)(iv)	8.4.4
1.263(a)-4(e)(1)(v)	8.4.4
1.263(a)-4(e)(3)	8.4.4
1.263(a)-4(e)(4)	8.4.1; 8.4.4
1.263(a)-4(e)(4)(A)(iii)	8.4.4
1.263(a)-4(e)(4)(ii)(A)	8.4.4
1.263(a)-4(e)(4)(ii)(B)	8.4.4
1.263(a)-4(e)(4)(iii)	8.4.3; 8.4.4
1.263(a)-4(e)(4)(iii)(A)	8.4.4; 8.4.5; 8.10.8
1.263(a)-4(e)(4)(iii)(B)	8.4.4
1.263(a)-4(e)(4)(iv)	8.4.4; 8.4.6
1.263(a)-4(e)(5)	8.4.4
1.263(a)-4(e)(4)(i)	8.4.4
1.263(a)-4(e)(4)(ii)	8.4.4
1.263(a)-4(f)	8.4.1; 8.4.3; 8.4.4; 8.12
1.263(a)-4(f)(1)	8.4.4
1.263(a)-4(f)(1)(i)	8.4.4
1.263(a)-4(f)(3)	8.4.4
1.263(a)-4(f)(4)	8.4.4
1.263(a)-4(f)(5)	8.4.4; 8.12
1.263(a)-4(f)(5)(iii)	8.4.4
1.263(a)-4(f)(7)	8.4.4; 8.4.6
1.263(a)-4(f)(8)	8.4.4
1.263(a)-4(g)(1)	8.4.4; 8.5.1
1.263(a)-4(h)	8.4.3; 8.4.4; 8.4.5
1.263(a)-4(h)(2)	8.4.5
1.263(a)-4(h)(4)	8.4.5

Treasury Regulations	§Number
1.263(a)-4(h)(5)	8.4.5
1.263(a)-4(h)(6)	8.4.5
1.263(a)-4(l)	8.4.4
1.263(a)-4(p)	8.5.1
1.263(a)-4)(e)(1)(i)	8.6.2
1.263(a)-5	7.6.4; 8.4.1; 8.4.3; 8.4.4; 8.4.6; 8.5.1; 8.5.2
1.263(a)-5(a)(1)	8.5.1
1.263(a)-5(a)(1)-(10)	8.5.1
1.263(a)-5(a)(2)	8.5.1
1.263(a)-5(a)(3)	8.5.1
1.263(a)-5(a)(4)	8.5.1
1.263(a)-5(a)(5)	8.5.1
1.263(a)-5(a)(6)	8.5.1
1.263(a)-5(a)(7)	8.5.1
1.263(a)-5(a)(8)	8.5.1
1.263(a)-5(a)(9)	8.5.1; 8.6
1.263(a)-5(a)(10)	8.5.1
1.263(a)-5(b)(1)	8.5.1
1.263(a)-5(b)(2)	8.5.1
1.263(a)-5(c)(1)	8.5.1
1.263(a)-5(c)(1)-(8)	8.5.1
1.263(a)-5(c)(2)	8.5.1
1.263(a)-5(c)(3)	8.5.1
1.263(a)-5(c)(4)	8.5.1
1.263(a)-5(c)(5)	8.5.1
1.263(a)-5(c)(6)	8.5.1
1.263(a)-5(c)(7)	8.5.1
1.263(a)-5(c)(8)	8.5.1
1.263(a)-5(d)(1)	8.5.1
1.263(a)-5(d)(2)(ii)	8.5.1
1.263(a)-5(d)(3)	8.4.3
1.263(a)-5(e)(1)	8.5.1
1.263(a)-5(e)(1)(i)	8.5.1; 8.6.2; 8.9.2
1.263(a)-5(e)(2)	8.5.1; 8.6.2
1.263(a)-5(e)(2)(i)	8.5.1
1.263(a)-5(e)(2)(ii)	8.5.1
1.263(a)-5(e)(2)(iii)	8.5.1
1.263(a)-5(e)(2)(iv)	8.5.1; 8.9.2
1.263(a)-5(e)(2)(v)	8.5.1
1.263(a)-5(e)(2)(vi)	8.5.1
1.263(a)-5(e)(3)(i)	8.5.1
1.263(a)-5(e)(3)(ii)	8.5.1
1.263(a)-5(e)(3)(iii)	8.5.1
1.263(a)-5(f)	8.5.1
1.263(a)-5(g)	8.5.1
1.263(a)-5(g)(2)(i)	8.5.1
1.263(a)-5(g)(2)(ii)	8.5.1
1.263(a)-5(l)	8.5.1
1.263(a)-5(n)	8.5.1
1.263(a)-5(n)(3)	8.4.6
1.263-1	8.3.1
1.263A-1	7.5.1
1.263A-1(b)(13)	8.3.1
1.263A-3	4.4.1; 7.5.1
1.263A-8(b)(4)	9.4.3
1.263A-9(a)(1)	9.4.3
1.263A-9(a)(2)(i)	9.4.3
1.263A-9(a)(4)	9.4.3
1.263A-9(b)(1)	9.4.3
1.263A-9(b)(2)	9.4.3
1.263A-9(b)(3)	9.4.3
1.263A-9(g)(5)(i)	9.4.3
1.263A-9(g)(5)(ii)	9.4.3
1.263A-9(g)(5)(iii)	9.4.3
1.263A-10	9.4.3
1.265-1(a)	4.4.1
1.1273-2(f)	2.4; 6.3.3
1.274-2(c)(1)	11.6.9
1.307-1	2.14.4
1.312-11	11.5.3
1.312-11(b)	11.5.7
1.312-11(c)	11.5.7
1.338(b)-1(a)	11.3.2
1.338-2(b)(2)(ii)	11.3.8
1.351-1(c)(1)	2.10.4
1.358-1(a)	11.5.4
1.368-1(b)	11.5.2
1.368-1(c)	11.5.1

Treasury Regulations	*§Number*
1.368-1(d)	11.5.1
1.368-1(d)(3)(ii)	11.5.1
1.368-2(b)(1)	11.5.2
1.368-2(b)(2)	11.5.2; 11.5.3
1.368-2(g)	11.5.1
1.381(b)-(1)(a)(2)	11.5.7
1.381(b)-1(b)	11.5.2
1.381(c)(2)-1	11.5.2
1.381(c)(4)-1(a)(1)	11.5.2
1.381(c)(4)-1(b)(3)	10.10.1
1.381(c)(4)-1(c)(2)	10.10.1
1.382-2(a)(1)	11.4.2
1.382-2(a)(1)(iii)	11.4.22
1.382-2(a)(1)(iv)(ii)	11.4.22
1.382-3(a)(1)	11.4.13; 11.4.4
1.382-3(k)	11.4.21
1.382-4	11.4.19
1.382-4(d)(3)	11.4.19
1.382-4(d)(4)	11.4.19
1.382-4(d)(5)	11.4.19
1.382-4(d)(6)	11.4.19
1.382-4(d)(7)	11.4.19
1.382-5(c)	11.4.5
1.382-5(d)	11.4.5
1.382-8(b)(2)	11.4.8
1.382-10	11.4.17
1.382-11(a)	11.4.12
1.446-1(a)	2.2.1; 2.2.2; 2.6
1.446-1(a)(2)	2.2.2; 2.2.4
1.446-1(a)(4)	2.2.2
1.446-1(c)(1)(I)	2.2.1
1.446-1(c)(1)(ii)	2.2.1; 5.3.1
1.446-1(c)(1)(ii)(A)	2.2.1
1.446-1(c)(1)(ii)IC)	8.2
1.446-1(c)(1)(iv)	2.2.1
1.446-1(c)(1)(iv)(b)(2)	2.2.1
1.446-1(c)(2)(ii)	5.3.14
1.446-1(d)(1)	2.2.4; 2.7.3
1.446-1(d)(2)	2.2.4
1.446-1(d)(3)	2.2.4
1.446-1(e)	2.2.3; 10.10.2(d)
1.446-1(e)(2)(ii)(a)	3.4.9
1.446-1(e)(2)(ii)(b)	2.2.3
1.446-2	2.2.1; 2.6; 5.3.6; 9.2
1.446-2(a)(2)	2.2.1
1.446-2(e)	2.3; 3.3.3
1.446-3	2.2.1
1.446-3(c)(1)(i)	2.12.2
1.446-3(c)(1)(iv)	2.12.3
1.446-3(c)(3)	2.12.2
1.446-3(c)(4)(ii)	6.2.3
1.446-3(d)	2.12.4
1.446-3(e)(1)	2.12.4
1.446-3(e)(2)	2.12.4
1.446-3(f)(1)	2.12.4
1.446-3(f)(2)(i)	2.12.4
1.446-3(f)(2)(ii)	2.12.5
1.446-3(f)(2)(iii)(A)	2.12.5
1.446-3(f)(2)(iii)(B)	2.12.5
1.446-3(f)(2)(iv)	2.12.6
1.446-3(f)(2)(v)	2.12.6
1.446-3(f)(2)(v)(A)	2.12.6
1.446-3(f)(2)(v)(C)	2.12.6
1.446-3(g)(1)	2.12.3
1.446-3(h)(1)	2.12.4
1.446-3(h)(2)	2.12.4
1.446-3(h)(3)	2.12.4
1.446-3(h)(4)(i)	2.12.4
1.446-3(h)(4)(ii)	2.12.4
1.446-3(i)	2.12.3
1.446-4(a)	2.12
1.446-4(a)(1)	2.12
1.446-4(a)(2)(i)	2.12
1.446-4(a)(2)(iii)	2.12
1.446-4(g)	2.12
1.446-5	8.5.1
1.446-5(a)	8.6
1.446-5(b)(3)	8.6
1.448-1(g).	2.2.1

Treasury Regulations	§Number
1.448-1(h)(4)	2.2.3
1.451-1	2.6.1
1.451-1(a)	2.2.1; 5.3.14; 5.3.1
1.451-5	11.4.9
1.453-6(a)	6.3.2
1.461(g)(1)(iv)	8.2.1
1.461-1(a)	8.9.2
1.461-1(a)(1)	8.3.3; 9.3.1
1.461-1(a)(2)	8.2; 8.3.3; 9.3.1
1.461-1(d)	8.2.1
1.461-1(d)(3)(i)	8.2.1
1.461-1(d)(3)(ii)	8.2.1
1.461-1(e)(1)(ii)	9.4.1
1.461-1(e)(3)(i)	9.4.1
1.461-1(e)(3)(ii)	9.4.1
1.461-1(e)(3)(iii)	9.4.1
1.461-1(e)(1)	9.4.1
1.461-1(e)(2)	9.4.1
1.461-4(d)(4)	8.2.1
1.461-4(d)(6)(ii)	8.2.1
1.461-4(e)	9.3.1
1.461-4(g)	11.4.11
1.461-4(g)(1)(i)	8.2.1
1.461-4(g)(1)(ii)(C)	8.2.1
1.461-4(g)(8)	8.16
1.461-4(g)(1)(ii)	8.2.1
1.461-4(g)(2)	8.2.1
1.461-4(g)(6)	8.2.1
1.461-5	2.2.1
1.461-5(b)(3)	8.2.1
1.466-1(e)(2)(iii)	10.2.2
1.471-5	4.4.1; 4.4.5; 4.4.6; 7.5.1
1.475	4.4.4; 4.4.5
1.475(a)-3(a)(1)	4.4.10
1.475(a)-3(a)(2)	4.4.10
1.475(a)-3(b)(1)	4.4.10
1.475(a)-4	4.4.8
1.475(a)-4(c)(1)	4.4.8
1.475(a)-4(d)(2)	4.4.8
1.475(a)-4(d)(3)	4.4.8
1.475(a)-4(e)	4.4.8
1.475(a)-4(g)	4.4.8
1.475(a)-4(h)	4.4.8
1.475(b)-1	4.4.3; 4.4.4
1.475(b)-1(a)	4.4.3
1.475(b)-1(b)(1)	4.4.4
1.475(b)-1(b)(2)	4.4.4
1.475(b)-1(b)(3)	4.4.4
1.475(b)-1(b)(i)	4.4.4
1.475(b)-1(b)(ii)	4.4.4
1.475(b)-1(c)	4.4.4
1.475(b)-1(d)	4.4.4
1.475(b)-2(a)	4.4.3; 4.4.4
1.475(b)-2(a)(1)	4.4.4
1.475(b)-2(b)	4.4.4
1.475(b)-2(c)(2)	4.4.4
1.475(b)-2(c)(3)	4.4.4
1.475(b)-3	4.4.7
1.475(b)-3(a)	4.4.3
1.475(b)-4(a)	4.4.4
1.475(c)-1	4.4.5
1.475(c)-2	4.4.7
1.475(c)-2(a)(1)	4.4.7
1.475(c)-2(a)(2)	4.4.7; 11.6.9
1.475(c)-2(a)(3)	4.4.7
1.475(d)-1	4.4.9
1.475(d)-1(b)	4.4.4
1.475(e)-1(e)(2)	4.4.4
1.475(e)-1(e)(3)	4.4.4
1.481-1(c)(1)	2.2.3; 5.3.18
1.483-1(a)(1)	6.3.3
1.537-1(a)-2(b)	1.4.2
1.537-1(b)	1.4.2
1.543-1(b)(5)(ii)	4.4.5
1.581-1	1.4.1
1.582-1(a)	10.2.3
1.582-1(d)	4.3.3
1.585-1(a)	10.7.10 10.7.8
1.585-1(b)	10.7.6
1.585-1(c)(1)	10.10.1

Treasury Regulations	*§Number*
1.585-2	10.7.2; 10.8.6
1.585-2(a)(2)	10.7.7
1.585-2(c)(1)(ii)	10.8.4; 10.10.2
1.585-2(c)(2)	10.8.4
1.585-2(c)(2)(ii)	10.8.4
1.585-2(c)(2)(ii)(A)(2)	10.8.4
1.585-2(d)	10.7.1
1.585-2(d)(2)	10.7.1
1.585-2(d)(3)	10.7.1
1.585-2(e)(2)	4.4.7; 10.8.6; 11.4
1.585-2(e)(2)(i)(A)	10.8.6
1.585-2(e)(2)(i)(B)	10.8.6
1.585-2(e)(2)(i)(C)	10.8.6
1.585-2(e)(2)(ii)(A)	10.8.6
1.585-2(e)(2)(ii)(C)	10.8.6; 10.9.2
1.585-2(e)(2)(ii)(D)	10.8.6
1.585-2(e)(2)(ii)(E)	10.8.6
1.585-2(e)(2)(ii)(F)	10.8.6
1.585-2(e)(3)	10.8.6
1.585-2(e)(3)(iii)(A)	10.8.6
1.585-2(e)(3)(iii)(B)	10.8.6
1.585-2(e)(3)(iii)(C)	10.8.6
1.585-2(e)(5)	10.8.4
1.585-2(e)(6)	10.8.4
1.585-2(e)(7)	10.8.4
1.585-3	10.8.5
1.585-3(a)	10.7.9
1.585-3(b)	10.7.1; 10.7.10; 10.7.11
1.585-3(ii)(A)	10.8.6
1.585-3(ii)(B)	10.8.6
1.585-3(ii)(C)	10.8.6
1.585-3(ii)(D)	10.8.6
1.585-3(ii)(E)	10.8.6
1.585-4	5.3.6
1.585-5(b)	9.5.9; 10.10.1
1.585-5(b)(2)	10.10.1
1.585-5(b)(2)(ii)	10.10.1
1.585-5(b)(2)(iii)	10.10.1
1.585-5(b)(2)(iv)	10.10.1
1.585-5(b)(3)	10.10.1
1.585-5(b)(d)(iv)	10.10.1
1.585-5(b)(iii)	10.10.1
1.585-5(c)	9.5.9
1.585-5(c)(2)	9.5.9; 10.10.1
1.585-5(c)(2)(i)	9.5.9; 10.10.1
1.585-5(c)(2)(ii)	10.10.1
1.585-5(c)(2)(iii)	10.10.1; 10.10.1
1.585-5(c)(3)	9.5.9; 10.10.1
1.585-5(c)(3)(i)	10.10.1
1.585-5(c)(4)	10.10.1
1.585-5(c)(4)(i)	10.10.1
1.585-5(d)	10.10.1
1.585-5(d)(2)	10.10.1
1.585-5(d)(3)	10.10.1
1.585-6	10.10.4
1.585-6(a)	10.10.1
1.585-6(b)	10.10.2
1.585-6(c)	10.10.2
1.585-6(d)	10.10.4
1.585-7	4.4.9
1.585-7(a)	10.10.2
1.585-7(a)(1)	10.10.2
1.585-7(b)(2)	10.10.2
1.585-7(b)(3)	10.10.2
1.585-7(d)(2)	10.10.2
1.585-7(d)(2)(i)	10.10.2
1.585-7(d)(2)(ii)	10.10.2
1.585-8	10.10.1; 10.10.2
1.585-8(a)	10.10.4
1.585-8(b)	10.10.4
1.585-8(d)	10.10.2
1.591-1(a)(2)	9.3.2
1.591-1(b)	9.2; 9.3.4
1.593-1	10.7.7
1.593-1(a)	10.7.1; 10.7.5
1.593-1(b)	10.7.1
1.593-1(d)(2)(iii)	10.9.5
1.593-1(d)(3)	10.9.5

Treasury Regulations	*§Number*
1.593-1(d)(2)	10.9.5
1.593-1(d)(2)(ii)	10.9.5
1.593-4	10.7.6
1.593-5(b)	10.7.11
1.593-5(b)(2)	10.7.11
1.593-6	10.9.3
1.593-6(a)	10.7.7; 10.7.8
1.593-6(a)(3)	10.7.7
1.593-6(a)(1)(ii)	10.7.8
1.593-6(e)	10.9.5
1.593-6(f)(2)	10.9.5
1.593-6(f)(3)	10.9.5
1.593-6(f)(1)	10.9.5
1.593-6(f)(2)	10.9.5
1.593-6A	10.9.3
1.593-6A(a)(1)	10.7.3; 10.7.7
1.593-6A(b)(2)(i)	10.7.11; 10.9.6
1.593-6A(b)(5)(vi)	10.9.3; 12.3.8
1.593-6A(b)(5)(vii)	10.9.3
1.593-6A(e)	10.9.5
1.593-7	10.7.10
1.593-7(a)(2)	10.7.11; 10.7.10
1.593-7(b)	10.7.10
1.593-7(c)(3)(ii)	10.7.9
1.593-7(c)(3)(iii)	10.7.9
1.593-7(c)(2)	10.8.6
1.593-11	10.7.7; 10.9.2
1.593-11(b)	10.9.1
1.593-11(b)(2)	10.9.1
1.593-11(b)(5)(i)	10.9.2
1.593-11(b)(5)(ii)	10.9.2
1.593-11(b)(5)(iii)	10.9.2
1.593-14	10.11
1.595(e)(1)	7.3.2
1.595-1(a)	7.3.2; 7.4; 7.6.1
1.595-1(b)	7.3.2
1.595-1(b)(2)	7.3.2
1.595-1(d)	7.3.2
1.595-1(e)(1)	7.5.1
1.595-1(e)(3)	7.5.1; 7.6.1
1.595-1(e)(6)	7.5.2; 7.6.3
1.595-1(e)(6)(i)	7.5.2; 7.6.1
1.595-1(e)(6)(ii)	7.5.2
1.595-1(e)(7)	7.5.1
1.595-1(e)(8)	7.5.1
1.596-1(c)	10.9
1.597(4)(g)(4)(v)	11.6.5
1.597-1	11.6.1; 11.6.3
1.597-1(b)	11.6.1; 11.6.2; 11.6.4; 11.6.5; 11.6.6
1.597-2	11.6.2; 11.6.3
1.597-3(a)	11.6.2
1.597-3(b)	11.6.8
1.597-3(c)	11.6.8
1.597-4(b)	11.6.5
1.597-4(d)	11.6.5
1.597-4(d)(2)	11.6.5
1.597-4(e)	11.6.5
1.597-4(f)	11.6.5
1.597-4(g)(2)(v)	11.6.5
1.597-4(g)(3)	11.6.5
1.597-4(g)(4)	11.6.5
1.597-4(g)(5)(i)	11.6.5
1.597-4(g)(5)(i)(B)	11.6.5
1.597-4(g)(6)	11.6.5
1.597-5(a)(1)	11.6.6
1.597-5(b)	11.6.6
1.597-5(b)(2)	11.6.6
1.597-5(c)(1)	11.6.6
1.597-5(c)(2)	11.6.6
1.597-5(c)(3)	11.6.6
1.597-5(c)(3)(ii)	11.6.6
1.597-5(d)(1)	11.6.6
1.597-5(d)(2)	11.6.6
1.597-5(f)	11.6.6
1.597-6	11.6.7
1.597-6(a)	11.6.2
1.597-6(e)(1)	11.6.7
1.597-6(e)(2)	11.6.7
1.597-6(f)	11.6.7

Treasury Regulations	*§Number*
1.597-7	11.6.1
1.597-7(d)(2)	11.6.1
1.597-8	11.6.1
1.856-2	2.10.4
1.860F-2(b)(2)	2.10.3
1.860F-2(b)(4)	2.10.3
1.860F-2(b)(4)(i)-(iv)	2.10.3
1.860G-1(a)(3)	2.10.3
1.863-7(a)(1)	4.4.5
1.988-1(a)(11)	2.12.7
1.988-2(e)(3)(iv)	2.12.7
1.988-2(e)(7)	2.12.7
1.988-2(f)	2.12.7
1.988-3(a)	4.4.7
1.1001-1	8.21
1.1001-1(a)	6.2.1; 6.2.3
1.1001-1(g)	4.4.4; 6.1; 11.6.9
1.1001-3	4.3; 6.1; 6.2.1; 6.2.3; 10.2.3
1.1001-3(b)	11.6.9
1.1001-3(c)	6.2.3
1.1001-3(c)(1)(ii)	6.2.3
1.1001-3(c)(2)(i)	6.2.3
1.1001-3(c)(2)(ii)	6.2.3
1.1001-3(c)(2)(iii)	6.2.3
1.1001-3(c)(3)	6.2.3
1.1001-3(c)(3)(i)	6.2.3
1.1001-3(c)(3)(ii)	6.2.3
1.1001-3(c)(3)(iii)	6.2.3
1.1001-3(c)(4)(i)	6.2.3
1.1001-3(c)(4)(ii)	6.2.3
1.1001-3(c)(5)	6.2.3
1.1001-3(c)(ii)	6.2.3
1.1001-3(d)	6.2.3
1.1001-3(e)	6.2.3
1.1001-3(e)(1)	6.2.3; 6.3.2
1.1001-3(e)(2)	6.2.3
1.1001-3(e)(2)-(5)	6.2.3
1.1001-3(e)(3)	6.2.3
1.1001-3(e)(3)(ii)	6.2.3

Treasury Regulations	*§Number*
1.1001-3(e)(4)	6.2.3
1.1001-3(e)(4)(B)	6.2.3
1.1001-3(e)(4)(i)(B)	6.2.3
1.1001-3(e)(4)(i)(E)	6.2.3
1.1001-3(e)(4)(i)(F)	6.2.3
1.1001-3(e)(4)(iii)	6.2.3
1.1001-3(e)(4)(iv)(B)	6.2.3
1.1001-3(e)(4)(v)	6.2.3
1.1001-3(e)(5)(i)	6.2.3
1.1001-3(e)(5)(ii)(A)	6.2.3
1.1001-3(e)(5)(ii)(B)(2)	6.2.3
1.1001-3(e)(6)	6.2.3
1.1001-3(e)(1)	6.2.3
1.1001-3(e)(2)	6.2.3
1.1001-3(e)(4)	6.2.3
1.1001-3(e)(4)(i)	6.2.3
1.1001-3(e)(4)(ii)	6.2.3
1.1001-3(g)	6.2.3
1.1001-6(g)	6.2.3
1.1016-5(b)	3.7.2
1.1016-9(a)	3.7.2
1.1016-9(b)	3.7.2
1.1016-9(c)	3.7.3
1.1052-42	10.9.5
1.1058-1	4.6
1.1091-1(a)	4.3.1
1.1091-2	4.3.1
1.1221-2	4.4.9
1.1221-2(c)(3)	2.12
1.1221-2(d)(ii)(B)	4.4.2
1.1221-2(d)(1)	4.4.5
1.1221-2(f)(2)(ii)	2:12; 4.4.4
1.1236-1(d)(1)	4.4.4
1.171-1(a)(2)	10.3
1.1272-1	3.3.2; 3.5.1
1.1272-1(a)	2.2.1
1.1272-1(a)(1)	3.3.4
1.1272-1(b)	3.3.2; 3.4.6; 3.5.1
1.1272-1(b)(1)	3.3.7; 3.4.4; 3.4.6

Treasury Regulations	§Number
1.1272-1(b)(1)(ii)	3.2.4
1.1272-1(b)(1)(iv)	3.2.4; 3.3.1; 3.4.6
1.1272-1(g)	3.3.7
1.1272-1	3.5.1
1.1272-2(b)(6)	3.3.7
1.1272-3	3.3.2
1.1272-3(a)	3.3.2
1.1272-3(c)(2)	3.3.7
1.1272-3(d)	3.4.2
1.1273-1(a)	3.2.1
1.1273-1(b)	3.2.4; 3.4.5; 3.5.5; 6.2.3
1.1273-1(c)(1)	3.2.4
1.1273-1(c)(i)(i)	3.2.4
1.1273-1(c)(ii)	3.2.4
1.1273-1(c)(iii)	3.2.4
1.1273-1(d)	3.3.4
1.1273-1(d)(1)	3.3.2; 3.4.1; 3.4.2
1.1273-1(d)(2)	3.4.1
1.1273-1(d)(3)	3.3.2; 3.4.1
1.1273-1(d)(5)	3.4.2
1.1273-1(d)(5)(i)	3.3.2
1.1273-1(e)(1)	3.4.1
1.1273-1(e)(2)	3.4.1
1.1273-1(e)(3)	3.4.1
1.1273-2	2.6.2
1.1273-2(a)	3.2.4
1.1273-2(a)(1)	3.2.4; 3.4.5; 3.5.5; 6.3.3
1.1273-2(a)(2)	3.2.4
1.1273-2(b)	3.2.4
1.1273-2(c)	3.2.4; 3.4.5
1.1273-2(c)(1)	3.2.4; 6.3.3
1.1273-2(d)	3.2.4
1.1273-2(d)(1)	3.2.4
1.1273-2(g)	3.3.3; 3.4.3; 3.4.5
1.1273-2(g)(2)	3.4.5
1.1273-2(g)(4)	3.4.8
1.1273-2(g)(5)	3.4.5
1.1273-3(a)	3.3.2
1.1274-1(a)	6.3.3
1.1274-2(b)(1)	3.4.5; 11.6.9
1.1274-2(b)(2)	11.6.9
1.1274-5(c)	6.3.3
1.1275-1(b)(1)	3.4.6
1.1275-2(a)	2.3; 3.3.3; 5.3.1
1.1275-2(a)(1)	5.3.5
1.1275-2(f)	3.3.7
1.1275-2(f)(1)	3.6.1
1.1275-2(f)(2)	3.3.7; 3.6.1
1.1275-3	3.3.8
1.1275-3(b)	3.3.8
1.1275-4(a)(3)	5.3.12
1.1275-4(b)	2.12.4
1.1361-1(g)(1)(i)	1.6.1
1.1361-1(h)(1)(v)	1.6.2
1.1361-1(j)(1)	1.6.2
1.1361-1(j)(1)(iii)	1.6.2
1.1361-1(j)(2)(i)	1.6.2
1.1361-1(j)(2)(ii)	1.6.2
1.1361-1(j)(2)(ii)(B)	1.6.2
1.1361-1(j)(6)	1.6.2
1.1361-1(j)(6)(iii)	1.6.2
1.1361-1(j)(6)(iii)(A)	1.6.2
1.1361-1(j)(6)(iii)(B)	1.6.2
1.1361-1(j)(9)	1.6.2
1.1361-1(j)(10)	1.6.2
1.1361-1(j)(11)	1.6.2
1.1361-1(m)	1.6.2
1.1361-4(a)(3)	1.6.3; 9.5.2
1.1361-5(b)	1.6.3
1.1361-5(b)(3)	1.6.3
1.1362-2(c)(5)(iii)(B)(2)	1.6.7
1.1362-2(c)(1)(i)	1.6.7
1.1362-2(c)(6)	1.6.7
1.1362-8(a)	1.6.7
1.1362-8(b)(1)	1.6.7
1.1362-8(b)(2)	1.6.7
1.1362-8(b)(3)	1.6.7

Treasury Regulations	§Number
1.1362-8(b)(4)	1.6.7
1.1362-8(b)(5)	1.6.7
1.1374-4(b)(1)	11.4.11
1.1374-4(b)(2)	11.4.11
1.1374-4(f)	1.6.8; 11.4.11
1.1374-4(h)	11.4.11
1.1375-1(d)	1.6.7
1.1502-1(h)	4.4.5
1.1502-11(a)(1)	9.4.3
1.1502-11(a)(3)	1.1
1.1502-13	4.4.10; 4.4.5; 4.4.9; 9.5.7; 10.8.6; 11.4.6
1.1502-13(a)(2)	4.4.5
1.1502-13(c)(4)(ii)	4.4.5
1.1502-13(c)(7)	7.6
1.1502-13(c)(7)(ii)	1.6.3
1.1502-13(g)(3)	10.8.6
1.1502-13(g)(5)	9.5.6
1.1502-13(g)(6)	10.8.6
1.1502-13(k)(2)	9.4.3
1.1502-26(a)(3)	10.9
1.1502-26(a)(4)	10.9
1.1502-42(e)	10.9.3
1.1502-42(e)(1)	10.9.3
1.1502-42(e)(3)	10.9.3
1.1502-42(f)	10.9.3
1.1502-42(f)(1)(i)	10.9.3
1.1502-42(f)(4)(iv)	10.9.3
1.1502-42(f)(4)(iv)(B)	10.9.3
1.1502-42(g)	10.9.3
1.1502-42(g)(1)(i)	10.9.3
1.1502-42(g)(1)(ii)	10.9.3
1.1502-42(g)(2)	10.9.3
1.1502-47	1.2
1.1502-77(a)	8.20.3
20.2031(b)	4.4.8
20.2031(c)	4.4.8
20.2031-1(b)	4.4.8; 7.3.1; 11.3.2; 11.3.2
20.2031-2(b)	4.4.8

Treasury Regulations	§Number
20.2031-2(e)	4.4.8
20.2031-2(f)	4.4.8
20.2031-2(h)	4.4.8
20.2031-4	4.4.8
20.2031-8(b)	4.4.8
25.2512-1	4.4.8
204.2(c)(1)(i)	2.13
301.7701(4)(c)	2.10.2
301.7701-1	6.2.3
301.7701(i)-1(a)	2.10.2
301.7701-2	1.4.3; 2.10.2
301.7701-2(b)	1.4.1; 1.5.7
301.7701-2(b)(5)	1.4.3
301.7701-2(c)(2)(ii)	9.5.2
301.7701-4(c)	2.10.2
301.7701-13	10.9
301.7701-13(a)	1.7.6
301.7701-13(b)	1.7.6
301.7701-13(d)	1.7.6
301.7701-13(e)	1.7.6
301.7701-13(e)(1)	1.7.6
301.7701-13(e)(5)	1.7.7
301.7701-13(e)(6)	1.7.7
301.7701-13(e)(7)	1.7.7
301.7701-13(e)(8)	1.7.7
301.7701-13(e)(10)	1.7.7
301.7701-13(e)(11)	1.7.6
301.7701-13A	1.7.5; 1.7.6; 1.7.8; 10.9
301.7701-13A(b)	1.7.5
301.7701-13A(b)-(d)	1.7.4
301.7701-13A(c)	1.7.6
301.7701-13A(c)(2)	1.7.6; 10.9.5
301.7701-13A(c)(3)	1.7.6
301.7701-13A(d)	1.7.7
301.7701-13A(e)	1.7.7
301.7701-14	1.5.10
301.9100-1(b)	3.4.2
301.9100-1(c)	3.4.2
301.9100-3	2.7.4

Table of Revenue Rulings and Procedures

Revenue Rulings	*§Number*	*Revenue Rulings*	*§Number*
53-216	2.6, 3.4	66-23	11.5
53-258	3.4, 3.6	66-26	10.7, 10.8
54-367	2.6	66-49	2.5
54-501	6.3	66-290	11.3, 11.5
55-79	11.3	66-321	10.2
55-391	10.9	66-335	10.4
55-435	10.9	66-347	2.5
56-136	2.8	66-365	11.5
56-359	8.10	67-260	9.5
56-404	10.7	67-352	9.3
56-572	11.5	68-3	10.8
57-167	4.4	68-83	2.2
57-276	11.5	68-220	2.2
57-278	11.5	68-285	11.5
57-518	11.5	68-475	10.7
57-535	6.3	68-524	10.8
58-238	8.10	68-608	11.3
58-605	1.4	68-609	11.3
59-83	10.7	68-630	10.8
59-227	11.5	69-3	11.5
59-259	11.5	69-6	11.5
59-260	9.3	69-129	11.5
60-25	6.3	69-147	9.3
60-85	2.6	69-188	2.6
60-195	6.2	69-263	6.3
60-346	4.4	69-330	8.5, 8.6
61-175	2.10	69-491	8.16
63-57	2.2, 2.3	69-511	8.10
64-73	11.5	69-539	11.3
64-160	4.4	69-617	11.5
64-278	1.6, 2.6, 3.4	69-646	11.5
65-92	10.7, 10.8	69-648	11.5
65-95	4.4	70-5	10.7
65-122	11.3	70-121	9.2

Revenue Rulings	*§Number*
70-142	2.7, 2.8
70-224	11.5
70-271	11.5
70-360	9.6
70-385	1.4
70-540	2.7, 2.8, 3.4
70-544	2.10
70-545	2.10, 10.8
70-598	4.3, 11.5
70-647	2.3, 2.6
71-63	9.3
71-133	10.7
71-163	9.5
71-191	2.8
71-233	11.5
71-299	2.5
71-365	2.7
71-381	10.2
71-399	2.10, 10.8, 10.9
71-568	4.3
72-100	2.6, 5.3
72-238	7.3
72-315	2.8
72-376	2.10, 10.9
72-523	4.4, 9.5
73-16	11.5
73-116	7.6
73-160	6.2
73-221	9.3
73-403	4.3
73-427	11.3
74-27	2.9
74-34	10.7
74-159	7.5.1, 7.6
74-169	2.10, 10.8
74-218	4.3
74-221	10.9
74-270	2.2
74-280	2.2
74-300	2.10, 10.9
74-372	2.7
74-383	2.2
74-395	2.2, 2.5, 2.8
74-409	10.7, 10.8
74-546	11.5
74-548	10.9
74-584	10.8
74-604	10.7
74-607	2.8, 3.4, 5.3
75-46	8.17
75-83	11.5
75-95	11.5
75-172	2.8, 9.6
75-455	10.7
75-541	2.8
75-560	10.7
76-245	10.7
76-308	9.3
76-430	10.8
76-489	4.4
76-528	11.5
77-128	10.7
77-135	2.2
77-164	10.8
77-165	10.8
77-215	10.2
77-216	10.8
77-232	2.5
77-265	10.9
77-307	11.5
77-333	10.7
77-349	2.6, 2.10, 10.8, 10.9
77-417	2.7
77-426	2.14
78-37	9.3
78-40	2.7
78-88	2.9
78-94	7.6
78-226	10.7
78-250	11.3
78-280	11.5

Revenue Rulings	*§Number*
78-286	11.5
78-365	2.7
78-397	11.5
78-407	10.9
79-123	10.7
79-198	10.7
79-214	10.4
79-228	2.6
79-283	8.10
79-292	6.3
79-378	2.2
79-434	11.5
80-56	4.3, 7.3
80-57	4.3
80-96	2.10, 10.9
80-105	11.5
80-180	10.4
80-230	2.2, 8.8, 8.14
80-270	10.7
80-361	3.4, 5.3
81-18	5.3, 10.4
81-25	11.5
81-37	1.4
81-142	9.3
81-160	2.5, 2.8
81-161	9.6
81-169	6.2
81-172	1.4, 10.7, 10.12
81-200	9.5
81-203	2.10, 10.9
81-204	4.3
82-10	3.6
82-26	10.8
83-60	2.12, 9.3
83-68	2.14
83-84	2.2, 2.6
83-176	1.4
84-10	2.10, 10.8, 10.9
84-94	10.4, 10.7
84-95	10.4
84-104	11.5

Revenue Rulings	*§Number*
85-125	4.3
85-171	10.7, 10.11
85-198	11.5
86-35	2.2
86.67	9.6
87-19	6.2, 9.5
87-76	11.5
88-18	1.3, 1.4, 1.6
89-23	8.3, 8.10
89-59	10.9
89-62	2.7
89-78	8.13
89-122	6.2, 6.3
90-7	10.9
90-38	2.2, 2.7
90-44	9.4, 9.5, 10.10
90-60	12.2
90-98	2.14
91-46	2.7, 11.3
92-14	10.3, 10.4, 10.7, 10.8
92-80	8.5, 8.10
93-12	4.4
93-76	4.4
93-79	1.6
94-7	4.4
94-12	8.8
94-70	8.5
94-77	8.8, 8.10
95-32	8.3, 8.4, 8.8, 8.9, 8.10
95-70	3.4
96-62	8.3, 8.4, 8.8, 8.10
97-27	4.4
97-32	4.3
97-39	4.4, 5.3
98-60	2.7
99-23	8.5, 8.9
2001-59	5.3, 10.3,10.4
2004-47	9.5

Revenue Rulings	*§Number*
2007-1	2.7
2007-32	5.1, 5.3, 9.5, 10.3, 10.6

Revenue Procedures	*§Number*
65-332	1.6
69-21	8.3, 8.7, 8.8, 8.10, 12.1
70-20	9.5
71-21	2.7
72-18	9.5
77-37	11.5
78-34	9.5
80-55	9.5
81-16	9.5
82-13	11.5
83-40	2.5
83-91	9.5
84-27	2.5
84-28	2.5
84-29	2.5
84-30	2.5
84-74	2.7
85-8	10.7
85-22	11.5
85-34	11.5
89-50	11.5
91-49	2.7
91-50	2.7, 2.7.4
92-18	10.4
92-20	2.2, 3.4, 5.3, 8.3
92-84	10.4
93-3	8.3
94-27	2.6
94-28	1.6, 2.6
94-29	1.6, 2.6, 3.2, 4.4
94-30	1.6, 2.6
95-28	12.2

Revenue Procedures	*§Number*
97-27	1.6, 2.2, 2.5, 2.7, 3.4, 4.4, 5.3, 8.3, 10.10
97-38	2.7
97-43	4.4
97-50	8.5, 8.10, 12.1
98-60	1.5, 2.2, 2.5, 3.4
99-11	12.2
99-17	4.4
99-49	1.5, 2.2, 4.4, 2.5, 3.4
99-514	8.3
2001-10	2.2
2001-25	3.4
2001-52	2.2
2002-9	1.6, 2.2, 2.2.3, 2.6, 2.7, 4.4, 5.3, 8.4, 10.10
2002-18	2.2
2002-19	2.2
2002-54	5.3
2003-23	1.6.1
2003-82	12.2
2004-14	1.6.1
2004-23	2.7, 8.4
2004-33	3.4, 2.7
2004-34	2.7, 11.4
2004-57	8.4
2004-82	12.2
2005-9	8.4
2005-37	12.2
2006-53	12.2
2005-47	2.7, 3.4
2007-32	5.3
2007-33	5.1, 5.3, 10.4
2007-41	4.4
2007-72	6.2
2008-47	2.10, 6.2
2008-18	1.6
2008-28	2.10
2008-47	2.10

Revenue Procedures	*§Number*
2008-52	2.1, 2.2, 4.4
2008-63	4.6
2008-64	4.3.4
2008-65	12.1
2008-72	2.10
2009-19	8.20
2009-39	2.1
2009-45	2.10
2010-17	12.3
2011-14	2.1, 2.2, 2.2.3, 2.6.1, 3.4.7; 3.5.1
2011-18	2.7.6
2013-26	3.5.1
2013-29	2.7.6
2016-29	2.2.3

Table of IRS Private Letter Rulings and Other Releases

General Counsel Memorandum	*§Number*
14839	2.5
21497	7.6
22056	6.2
25605	10.8
33640	10.7
33820	10.7
34436	10.7
35681	8.8
36301	10.7
37002	6.3
37884	6.3
38292	10.7
38838	4.3
39149	4.4
39225	6.2
39276	10.7
39434	2.7
39469	10.7
39551	4.3
39667	9.5
39668	5.3
39701	10.9
39760	10.7, 10.9

Private Letter Rulings	*§Number*
7829021	9.3
7831003	8.2
7921016	10.2, 10.8
7943021	10.7
7945011	10.7
8001006	1.4, 10.12
8009003	10.7
8025163	9.3
8113004	1.4
8142072	11.5
8243150	11.5
8243159	11.5
8243166	11.5
8327016	9.5
8329020	9.5
8425036	10.9
8425059	10.8
8427025	10.8
8427072	11.5
8428091	10.9
8430112	10.9
8434039	10.9
8438003	9.5
8447001	8.18
8451012	6.3
8504049	6.2
8509083	11.5
8511017	11.5
8512012	8.20
8519011	2.6
8524062	11.5
8526062	11.5
8527004	8.20
8533025	11.5
8533072	11.5
8533073	11.5
8533075	11.5
8534027	11.5
8534049	11.5
8534054	11.5
8534063	11.5
8534073	11.5

Private Letter Rulings	*§Number*
8534082	11.5
8535005	11.5
8535008	11.5
8535024	11.5
8535040	11.5
8535051	11.5
8535054	11.5
8537048	11.5
8539045	11.5
8539078	11.5
8539084	11.5
8541105	11.5
8542018	11.5
8544038	11.5
8544044	11.5
8544070	8.20
8544071	11.5
8549026	11.5
8551064	11.5
8552068	11.5
8571043	10.9
8601040	10.8
8612063	11.5
8620019	10.9
8625004	10.9
8649046	6.2
8650035	2.3, 5.3
8652014	10.7
8701040	10.7
8701041	1.6
8714034	6.2
8715011	1.5
8724035	10.9
8735006	11.5
8737033	9.5
8738030	9.5
8740001	9.5
8742032	6.2
8745024	2.11
8807046	10.7
8814053	1.4
8821002	1.3
8822001	10.8, 10.9
8822048	10.9
8824036	11.5
8825039	10.9
8830065	10.9
8901001	3.3.2
8903001	10.8
8903016	1.4
8918026	10.9
8919035	10.8
8928002	10.8
8929061	10.8
8932067	6.2
9020015	11.5
9031009	11.5
9044046	1.4
9113032	11.4
9205013	9.5
9207028	11.5
9312017	1.6
9330027	11.4
9333005	8.15
9338044	10.3
9348003	8.13
9402002	8.8
9409033	11.5
9423002	10.8
9434022	11.5
9436057	11.3
9451031	7.6
9508009	11.3
9528013	11.5
9535011	8.8
9551032	1.4
9607016	8.10
9615007	3.2
9615028	8.10
9725039	11.4
9729004	3.6
97434038	11.5

Private Letter Rulings	*§Number*
9744003	2.10
9743013	4.4
9751022	5.3
9801015	1.5
9801056	1.5
9805032	9.5
9824026	9.5
9836030	1.5, 1.6, 10.7
9838026	8.3
9839001	2.5, 2.9
9844021	6.2
9847004	10.6
199909043	9.5
199918022	8.10
199935017	4.4
199937032	10.11
199938035	1.5
200027021	1.5
200217048	1.6
200243002	11.3
200247004	8.10
200447004	5.5
200645006	5.5
201701017	2.7.4
201720004	3.4.2

Technical Advice Memorandum	*§Number*
7905009	10.8
7905011	11.5
7921016	10.8
8001006	1.4, 10.7
8009003	10.7
8009007	11.3
8023017	10.7
8031062	10.7
8052023	6.2
8113004	1.4
8134013	2.5
8137004	5.3
8141033	8.5, 8.10

Technical Advice Memorandum	*§Number*
8141035	4.4
8145027	8.20
8147004	10.8
8214016	10.8
8232010	10.2
8242001	10.9
8243009	11.5
8251001	5.3
8435015	10.7
8437007	10.7, 10.9
8442002	10.7, 10.9
8442003	10.7, 10.9
8451012	6.2
8453002	10.7, 10.9
8516003	3.3.2
8516006	3.3.2
8516009	3.3.2
8527004	8.20
8537002	2.7
8543004	2.8
8547001	6.2
8602006	4.3
8641004	4.3
8706001	3.3.2
8706002	2.5
8706003	2.5
8706004	2.5
8707001	2.5
8710001	3.3.2
8712001	3.3.2
8723005	3.3.2
8723006	3.3.2
8724004	3.3.2
8740001	9.4.3
8741006	5.3, 10.2
8806005	10.9
8809002	10.9
8822001	10.8
8838004	9.5
8901001	3.3.2

Technical Advice Memorandum	*§Number*
8928002	2.10
9024003	8.8
9253003	10.2, 10.4
9402006	8.15
9439002	2.7
9522005	2.7
9538007	2.5, 5.3
9544001	8.8
9641004	8.8
9645002	8.8, 8.10
9822009	1.3
9825005	8.9
9901004	8.9
9924060	8.13
2000309004	9.4.3
200434021	9.5
200434029	9.5
200439041	10.8
200533023	2.5, 2.7
200839033	4.3

I.R.S. Announcements	*§Number*
81-43	8.9
91-112	12.2
93-60	8.3
2004-9	12.1
2008-41	4.3, 4.4

I.R.S. Notices	*§Number*
87-79	11.4
88-86	8.3
89-21	2.5
89-102	8.7
90-27	11.4
93-45	4.4
93-50	10.4
96-12	4.4
96-23	4.4
97-4	1.5

I.R.S. Notices	*§Number*
97-5	1.5, 9.6
97-12	1.5
97-20	1.5
97-49	1.5
97-66	2.9
97-67	1.5
2001-19	12.1
2001-76	1.6, 2.2
2002-14	2.2
2002-17	1.6
2002-79	2.7
2003-65	11.4
2004-100	5.1
2005-69	12.2
2006-11	12.2
2006-60	12.3
2008-41	9.5
2008-71	4.4
2008-76	11.4
2008-78	11.4
2008-83	11.4
2008-84	11.4
2008-88	9.5
2008-100	11.4
2008-101	11.6
2009-38	11.4
2010-2	11.4
2011-99	3.4.7
2013-35	10.4.1; 10.4.2

Field Service Advisories	*§Number*
199909007	4.4, 11.6.9
199910012	8.3
199912005	10.4
199918013	8.5
199938018	8.7
199941009	2.7
199944014	10.11
200028001	8.21
200013006	8.21

Field Service Advisories	*§Number*
200018017	5.3
200024004	10.5
2000470012	4.4
200129003	7.3, 7.5, 10.3, 10.4, 10.7
200129009	9.5
200130009	2.10
200136010	9.6

Chief Counsel Advisories	*§Number*
200019041	2.6
200045030	10.3, 10.4
200145013	2.7, 3.3.2
200210053	8.19
20040302F	8.9, 8.10
200731029	4.4
200817035	4.4
201136022	2.8
201450011	10.2.3

Index

References are to section (§) numbers.

A

Abandonment losses
. for customer lists . . . 8.21.1
. deduction . . . 8.2
. supervisory goodwill . . . 8.21.2

Accounting methods . . . 2.6.2
. accrual method of accounting . . . 2.2.1
. . "all-events test . . . 2.2.1, 2.8.1, 3.3.3, 8.2
. . economic performance . . . 2.2.1
. . enrolled merchant fees . . . 3.5.7
. . interest income . . . 2.6
. . securities dealers . . . 2.2.4, 2.7.3
. . semiannual assessment . . . 2.2.1
. accrual of interest . . . 2.2.2
. additional depreciation . . . 2.2.2
. bank's securities inventory . . . 2.2.1
. cash method of accounting . . . 2.2.1, 2.2.4
. . enrolled merchant fees . . . 3.5.7
. . gross receipts less than $5,000,000 . . . 2.2.1
. . qualifying small business taxpayer . . . 2.2.1
. . service fee income . . . 3.5.8
. . short term obligation . . . 2.2.1
. change in accounting method . . . 2.2.2-2.2.3, 3.4.7, 10.7.1
. . automatic change procedure . . . 2.2.3
. . change in facts . . . 2.2.3
. . change in material item . . . 2.2.3
. . change in overall plan . . . 2.2.3
. . consent requirement . . . 2.2.3
. . credit card cardholder agreement . . . 2.2.3
. . installment loan . . . 2.2.3
. . involuntary change procedures . . . 2.2.3
. . retroactive change . . . 2.2.3
. . section 481(a) adjustments . . . 2.2.3
. . voluntary change procedures . . . 2.2.3

Accounting methods—continued
. changes . . . 8.4.6
. clear reflection of income . . . 2.2.1-2.2.2
. composite method
. . purchase discount . . . 2.6.2
. conformity with book accounting rules . . . 2.2.2
. conformity with regulatory rules . . . 2.2.2
. constant yield method . . . 2.2.1, 2.6
. credit card service fees . . . 2.2.2
. dealer securities activities . . . 2.2.4
. debt charged off . . . 2.2.2
. deference to regulatory agency . . . 2.2.2
. economic accrual method
. . interest income . . . 2.6
. for bad debt . . . 10.11
. for loan origination costs . . . 8.3.4
. hybrid method . . . 2.2.1
. late fees . . . 2.2.1
. loan liquidation method
. . interest income . . . 2.6.2
. . mechanical operation . . . 1.7.6
. loan origination fee income . . . 2.2.2
. multiple businesses of single taxpayer . . . 2.2.4
. overall method . . . 2.2.1
. proportional method . . . 3.5.1
. qualified subchapter S subsidiary . . . 2.2.1
. recovery of bad debt . . . 2.2.1
. reflecting income . . . 2.7.3
. reserve method . . . 2.2.1
. . bad debt recovery . . . 2.2.1
. . bad debt deductions . . . 10.7.1
. S corporations
. . bad-debt . . . 1.6.4
. . cash method . . . 1.6.5
. separate book . . . 2.2.4
. thrift changing . . . 10.11
. trust business . . . 2.2.4

References are to section (§) numbers.

Accounting methods—continued
. writedown of fixed assets . . . 2.2.2

Accrual method of accounting
. deduction of liabilities . . . 8.2
. interest expense deduction . . . 9.3.1

Accumulated earnings tax
. accumulatd taxable income . . . 1.4.2
. banks subject to . . . 1.4.2
. S corporation status to avoid . . . 1.6.5

Acquisitions costs
. abandonment losses
. . customer lists . . . 8.21.1
. . goodwill . . . 8.21.2
. amortization
. . safe harbor . . . 8.7
. . salvage value . . . 8.7
. business expansion and new products . . . 8.10
. . advertising . . . 8.10.5
. . bailout . . . 8.10.8
. . branch pre-opening . . . 8.10.1
. . credit cards . . . 8.10.7
. . geographic expansion . . . 8.10.2
. . lease termination payments . . . 8.10.9
. . mutual fund . . . 8.10.6
. . program implementation . . . 8.10.9
. . promotions . . . 8.10.4
. . severance pay . . . 8.10.9
. . training . . . 8.10.3
. capitalization regulations . . . 8.5.1
. . asset sale costs . . . 8.5.1
. . bankruptcy reorganization costs . . . 8.5.1
. . borrowing costs . . . 8.5.1
. . hostile acquisitions . . . 8.5.1
. . integration costs . . . 8.5.1
. . ordering rules . . . 8.5.1
. . registrar and transfer agent costs . . . 8.5.1
. . scope . . . 8.5.1
. . simplifying conventions . . . 8.5.1
. . stock distribution costs . . . 8.5.1
. . stock issuance costs . . . 8.5.1
. . success-based fees . . . 8.5.1
. . termination costs . . . 8.5.1
. . treatment of capitalized cost . . . 8.5.1
. code section 195
. . activities test . . . 8.9.2

Acquisitions costs—continued
. code section 195—continued
. . book accounting . . . 8.9.2
. . carrying on a trade or business . . . 8.9.2
. . deductibility test . . . 8.9.2
. . electing . . . 8.9.2
. . generally . . . 8.9.2
. . investigatory expense . . . 8.9.2
. . judicial precedent . . . 8.9.2
. . legislative history . . . 8.9.2
. code section 248
. . electing . . . 8.9.5
. comparison of 195 and 248
. . neither section 195 nor 248 expenditures . . . 8.9.4
. . section 195 expenditures . . . 8.9.4
. . section 248 expenditures . . . 8.9.4
. de minimus O.I.D. . . . 8.6
. debt issuance . . . 8.6
. deposit insurance assessment . . . 8.12
. . exit and entrance fees . . . 8.13
. directors' and officers' insurance . . . 8.16
. discount for early mortgage pay-off . . . 8.18
. facilitation costs
. . bright-line date rule . . . 8.5.1
. . covered transactions . . . 8.5.1
. . generally . . . 8.5.1
. farm credit assessment . . . 8.15
. net operating loss
. . 1987-1993 . . . 8.20.2
. . alternative minimum tax . . . 8.20
. . present-law carryback . . . 8.20.4
. organizational expenditures
. . legislative history . . . 8.9.3
. . operation of section 248 . . . 8.9.3
. pre-regulation IRS pronouncements . . . 8.8
. . advertising and other expenditures . . . 8.8.3
. . home equity lines of credit . . . 8.8.1
. . origination of mortgage loans . . . 8.8.2
. premiums on debtors' life insurance . . . 8.17
. Regulation section 1.263(a)-5
. . legal expenses . . . 8.5.1
. regulatory examination assessment . . . 8.14
. supervisory goodwill . . . 8.19

References are to section (§) numbers.

Acquisitions costs—continued
. year 2000 costs . . . 8.11

Acquisitions . . . 11.1-11.5.8
. accounting method by transferor . . . 10.11
. allocation of purchase price . . . 11.3.2
. bankruptcy reorganizations costs . . . 8.8.5
. borrowing costs . . . 8.8.5
. bright line date rule . . . 8.5.1
. capitalization of costs . . . 8.5.1-8.5.2
. conversion transactions between insurers . . . 8.13
. covered transaction . . . 8.5.1
. friendly . . . 8.3.3
. general rules . . . 8.5.1
. hostile . . . 8.5.1
. indirect . . . 11.3.2
. inherently facilitative amounts . . . 8.5.1
. intangibles, capitalization of costs . . . 8.4-8.4.5, 8.5.1
. investigatory costs . . . 8.5.2, 8.9.2
. low-income housing buildings . . . 12.2.13
. mandatory stock distributions . . . 8.5.5
. maximizing purchase price . . . 11.1
. mortgage loans . . . 8.8.1
. qualified stock purchase . . . 10.10.1
. simplifying conventions for costs . . . 8.5.1
. start-up expenses . . . 8.5-8.5.2
. success-based fees . . . 8.5.1
. tax planning . . . 11.1
. whether-and-which test . . . 8.9.2

Adjusted issue price
. computing . . . 3.3.6

Advance payment
. deferral . . . 2.7.2

Advertising costs
. deductibility . . . 8.5.2, 8.10.5
. goodwill . . . 8.10.5
. start-up businesses . . . 8.10.5

Affinity card . . . 2.7.5

Allocated Transfer Risk Reserve (ATRR)
. bad-debt deductions . . . 10.4.3
. transfer of debt . . . 10.3.2, 10.4.3

Allocation of receipts
. defaulted bond . . . 2.3

Allocation of receipts—continued
. installment loan payment . . . 2.3
. partial repayment . . . 2.3

Alternative minimum tax
. avoiding . . . 1.6.5
. exemption for Electing Small Business Trust (ESBT) . . . 1.6.2
. items of tax preference . . . 10.12.1
. net operating losses
. . acquisition costs . . . 8.20

American Jobs Creation Act of 2004, The . . . 1.1, 1.6.1, 1.6.2, 1.6.6, 1.6.7, 2.10.3, 2.11.1, 12.3.1, 12.3.6.1

American Recovery and Reinvestment Act of 2009, The . . . 8.20.3, 9.5.2, 9.5.4, 9.5.5, 11.4, 12.2.10, 12.3.1
. acquisition costs
. . net operating losses . . . 8.20.3

Amortization
. bond premium . . . 3.4.8
. business expenses . . . 8.6.2
. cap premium . . . 2.12.6
. debt costs . . . 8.4.1, 8.6, 8.7
. mortgage servicing fees . . . 2.7.4
. nonperiodic swap payments . . . 2.12.5–2.12.6

Applicable excess reserves
. large bank . . . 10.11.1
. recapturing . . . 10.11
. small bank . . . 10.11.2

Applicable federal rate (AFR) as discount rate
. present value determination . . . 6.3.3

Arbitage bond . . . 2.5

Asset backed securities
. FASITs . . . 2.11.1
. hedging transaction . . . 2.12

Asset sales
. costs to facilitate . . . 8.5.5

Asset test for thrifts
. quick reference table for . . . 1.7.9

ATM Fees . . . 2.7.2

References are to section (§) numbers.

Audit
. adjustment to accounting method . . . 2.1
. revenue procedure . . . 5.3.18
. statistical sampling of non performing loans . . . 5.1, 5.3.18

Authorization years
. bad-debt deductions
. . experience method . . . 10.8.4

Average adjusted tax basis
. computing . . . 9.5.9

B

Bad-debt deductions . . . 1.6.8, 10.1–10.12.2
. ATRR loans . . . 10.8.6
. ''charge off'' test . . . 5.3.5, 5.3.15
. "uncollectible" test . . . 5.3.5, 5.3.15
. alternative minimum tax . . . 10.12
. amount
. . accrued interest receivable . . . 10.2.2
. . change in method of accounting . . . 10.2.2
. applicable excess reserve
. . large bank . . . 10.11.1
. . small bank . . . 10.11.2
. available methods . . . 10.2.1
. bookkeeping . . . 10.7.11
. building and loan associations
. . reserve method . . . 1.7.5
. change in accounting method for . . . 10.11
. charge-off . . . 10.3.2
. commercial bank reserve recapture
. . large bank . . . 10.10
. commissioner's discretion revoked . . . 10.7.5
. computing . . . 10.6
. conformity election . . . 10.1, 10.4.4
. . background . . . 10.4.4
. . charge-off . . . 10.4.4
. . conclusive presumption . . . 10.4.4
. . eligible taxpayers . . . 10.4.4
. . express determination letter . . . 10.4.4
. . Form 3115 . . . 10.4.4
. . historical presumption contrasted . . . 10.4.4
. . loss assets . . . 10.4.4

Bad-debt deductions—continued
. conformity election—continued
. . rebutting conclusive presumption . . . 10.4.4
. . revocation . . . 10.4.4
. . revocation consequences . . . 10.4.4
. corporate preference item . . . 10.12.2
. deferral of . . . 10.5
. defined . . . 10.2.2
. direct charge-off method . . . 10.3–10.3.2
. eligible taxpayers
. . foreign corporation . . . 10.7.6
. eliminated from taxpayer's book . . . 10.3.2
. establishing and maintaining reserves
. . negative reserve balance . . . 10.7.10
. experience method
. . base-year reserve . . . 10.8.2
. . change in risk of loss . . . 10.8.4
. . comparable bank . . . 10.8.4
. . decline in economic conditions . . . 10.8.4
. . decline in loan balance . . . 10.8.3
. . loans defined . . . 10.8.5
. . moving-average formula . . . 10.8.1
. . new banks . . . 10.8.4
. . reserve restoration . . . 10.8.2
. . shorter experience period . . . 10.8.4
. extraordinary loan losses . . . 10.8.6
. . eligible loans . . . 10.8.6
. . insured loans . . . 10.8.6
. . loans secured by deposits . . . 10.8.6
. . loans to banks . . . 10.8.6
. . loans to governments . . . 10.8.6
. . mortgage loans . . . 10.8.6
. . REMICs . . . 10.8.6
. foreclosures . . . 7.3.1
. involuntary charge-off . . . 10.5
. issuer default . . . 10.2.3
. large bank
. . adjusted tax basis . . . 10.10.1
. . average adjusted basis . . . 10.10.1
. . controlled group . . . 10.10.1
. . disqualification year . . . 10.10.1
. . Federal Financial Institutions Examination Council (FFIEC) . . . 10.10.4
. . financially troubled . . . 10.10.4
. . nonperforming loans . . . 10.10.4

References are to section (§) numbers.

Bad-debt deductions—continued
. large bank—continued
. . report date . . . 10.10.1
. . resulting from transfer . . . 10.10.1
. . tax basis . . . 10.10.1
. . tax/book ratio . . . 10.10.1
. limitations on reserve additions
. . deposits and withdrawable accounts . . . 10.9.5
. . pre-1987 reduction . . . 10.9.6
. . surplus, undivided profits and reserves . . . 10.9.5
. mortgage backed securities . . . 2.10.2
. net operating loss . . . 8.20.3
. non-bank . . . 10.2.3
. non-loans
. . commercial paper . . . 10.8.6
. . distortion loans . . . 10.8.6
. . illegal loans . . . 10.8.6
. . loans to affiliates . . . 10.8.6
. . noncustomer loans . . . 10.8.6
. . pending loans . . . 10.8.6
. . securities . . . 10.8.6
. . security property . . . 10.8.6
. . unrecognized discount . . . 10.8.6
. percentage of taxable income method
. . applicable percentages . . . 10.9.4
. . consolidated losses . . . 10.9.3
. . dividends received . . . 10.9.3
. . limitations on addition . . . 10.9.5
. . net gains . . . 10.9.3
. . net operating losses deductions . . . 10.9.3
. . nondeductible distributions . . . 10.9.3
. . nonqualifying loans . . . 10.9.2
. . qualifying real property loans . . . 10.9
. . reserve additions . . . 10.9.3
. pre-1987 rules . . . 10.7.3
. presumption of worthlessness . . . 10.1, 10.4-10.4.5
. property acquired in . . . 7.1, 7.5.2
. property acquired in foreclosure . . . 7.1, 7.5.2
. Qsubs . . . 1.6.8
. qualified bad-debt
. . capital contribution . . . 10.2.3
. . guarantor payments . . . 10.2.3
. . impairment loss . . . 10.2.3

Bad-debt deductions—continued
. qualified bad-debt—continued
. . loan v. joint venture . . . 10.2.3
. . nonbank . . . 10.2.3
. . other-than-temporary impairments . . . 10.2.3
. . renegotiated debt . . . 10.2.3
. . securities losses . . . 10.2.3
. . theft and other losses . . . 10.2.3
. recapture for thrifts . . . 10.11-10.11.4
. recapture methods
. . accelerated method . . . 10.10.2-10.10.3
. . advantages/disadvantages . . . 10.10.3
. . cut-off method . . . 10.10.2-10.10.3
. . deferral method . . . 10.10.2-10.10.3
. . financially troubles . . . 10.10.4
. recoveries . . . 10.6, 10.7.9
. reserve methods . . . 10.7.1-10.7.11
. . binding effect of election . . . 10.7.1
. . bookkeeping . . . 10.7.11
. . eligible loans . . . 10.7.3
. . Form 3115 . . . 10.7.1
. . legislative history . . . 10.7.2
. . minimum reserve addition . . . 10.7.7
. . net operating losses . . . 10.7.2
. . post-1986 rules . . . 10.7.3
. . pre-1987 rules . . . 10.7.3
. . record keeping requirements . . . 10.7.11
. . recoveries . . . 10.7.9
. . retroactive increase . . . 10.7.7
. . Small Business and Job Protection Act of 1996 . . . 10.7
. . special procedure for election . . . 10.7.1
. . Tax Reform Act of 1986 . . . 10.7
. S corporations
. . applicable excess reserves . . . 1.6.8
. . reserve recapture . . . 1.6.8
. . tax benefit rule . . . 1.6.8
. section 481(a) adjustments
. . accelerated method . . . 10.10.2
. . cut-off method . . . 10.10.2
. . deferral method . . . 10.10.2
. . disposing of loans . . . 10.10.2
. separate and distinct asset test . . . 8.31.-8.3.2
. statute of limitations . . . 10.3.1
. subsequent disallowance . . . 10.3.1

References are to section (§) numbers.

Bad-debt deductions—continued
. tax planning . . . 10.13.1
. Tax Reform Act repeal of deduction . . . 10.2.3
. thrift bad-debt reserve recapture . . . 10.11
. . acquisition and dispositions . . . 10.11.3
. . residential loan requirement . . . 10.11.4
. thrifts . . . 1.3, 1.7.2
. worthlessness . . . 10.3.1
. . confirmation letters . . . 10.4.3
. . historical presumption . . . 10.4.3
. . shared national credit review . . . 10.4.3

Bank
. accepting deposits . . . 9.6
. as LLCs . . . 1.4.3
. charitable contributions limit for . . . 1.6.5
. chartering requirement . . . 1.5.6
. classification of entities . . . 1.1
. commercial
. . definition . . . 1.1
. . use of term . . . 1.3
. cooperative
. . treatment as domestic building and loan association . . . 1.3, 1.5.10
. CRA ratings of . . . 1.2.2
. defined . . . 1.5-1.5.9
. deposit requirement . . . 1.5
. expansion of branches of, amortizable costs of . . . 8.1
. financial subsidiaries . . . 1.2.3
. insolvency . . . 1.7.3
. large . . . 10.7.2-10.7.6, 10.10.1-10.10.4, 10.11.1
. loans . . . 10.8.6
. national service fee . . . 2.4
. partnership election . . . 1.4.3
. S corporations . . . 1.1, 1.6
. savings, qualification as thrift . . . 1.7.4
. supervisory requirement . . . 1.5.8
. "well-capitalized" . . . 1.4.2

Bank Holding company (BHC)
. acquisitions . . . 11.1
. as FHC . . . 1.2.1-1.2.2
. directors' shares . . . 1.6.1
. interstate activities . . . 11.2.1-11.2.2

Bank Holding company (BHC)—continued
. merger of newly formed subsidiary . . . 11.5.2
. parent of Qsub bank . . . 1.6.1
. sale of stock . . . 1.6
. sale of stock of thrift . . . 11.5.7
. Type D reorganization as method to enter another state . . . 11.5.4

Bank Holding Company Act of 1956 (BHCA) . . . 1.2, 1.2.1, 1.6.7
. banks defined . . . 1.5.3
. continuing to operate . . . 1.2.2
. FHC requirements in amendments to . . . 1.2.1
. Financial Modernization Act as amending . . . 1.2
. locations permitted . . . 11.2.2
. nonbank subsidiary activities permissible . . . 1.2.2
. passive investment income . . . 1.6.7
. permissible activities defined . . . 11.2.2

Bank Insurance Fund (BIF)
. assessments . . . 8.10.2
. commercial bank funds insured by . . . 1.7.5
. conversion from SAIF participation to . . . 8.10.3

Bank Regulatory Rules . . . 1.4.2
. CAMEL rating system . . . 1.4.2
. capital ratios
. . adequately capitalized . . . 1.4.2
. . leverage ratio . . . 1.4.2
. . tier 1 risk-based capital . . . 1.4.2

Bankcard association costs, tax treatment of . . . 8.7

Banking Act of 1933
. Financial Modernization Act as amending . . . 1.2, 1.2.5
. parity of branching rights of state and national banks under . . . 11.2.1

Bankruptcy
. bad-debt deduction . . . 10.3.1

Bankruptcy Tax Act of 1980, Type G reorganizations created by . . . 11.5.8

References are to section (§) numbers.

Basis
. allocation
. . mortgage sales . . . 2.8.3
. bonds reduced by amortizable bond premium . . . 3.4.8
. costs capitalized in taxable acquisitive transactions . . . 8.5.1
. Federal Home Loan Bank . . . 2.14.3
. low-income housing credit
. . eligibility . . . 12.2.2
. unadjusted debt obligations . . . 3.3.7

Bond premium
. amortization . . . 3.7, 3.7.5
. debt issuance costs . . . 8.9
. defined . . . 3.7.3
. election to amortize . . . 3.7.4

Bonds
. defined . . . 3.7.3
. premium . . . 3.7.5
. tax-exempt
. . premium . . . 3.7
. taxable
. . premium . . . 3.7.5

Boot in mergers . . . 11.1

Branch Banking Act of 1994
. permissible interstate activities . . . 11.2.1

Building and loan associations
. acquiring savings . . . 1.7.6
. asset test . . . 1.7.7
. business operations test . . . 1.7.6
. conformity test . . . 1.7.6
. deferred fee income . . . 1.7.6
. defined . . . 1.7
. eligible entities . . . 1.7.4
. gross income test . . . 1.7.6
. investment in loans . . . 1.7.6
. QTL test . . . 1.7.8
. real property held for investment or sale . . . 1.7.6
. real property rented . . . 1.7.6
. savings of the public . . . 1.7.6
. special bank tax rules . . . 1.7.3
. supervisory test . . . 1.7.5

Built-in gains tax
. core deposit intangible . . . 1.6.8
. net recognized built-in gains . . . 1.6.8
. rate of tax . . . 1.6.8
. S corporations
. . former C corporations . . . 1.6.8
. . net operating loss . . . 1.6.6
. valuation of assets . . . 1.6.8
. branch expansions . . . 8.10.2

Business expenses . . . 8.1-8.22
. branch expansions . . . 8.10.2
. costs of reducing or eliminating future expenses . . . 8.1
. economic performance requirement . . . 8.2.1
. expansion and new product development . . . 8.9.2, 8.10
. future benefits test . . . 8.1
. I.R.S. pronouncements related to capitalizing . . . 8.8.1–8.8.2
. investigatory costs . . . 8.9.2, 8.10
. loan origination expenditures as . . . 8.3.1, 8.8.2
. nondeductible (capital) . . . 8.3.1
. ordinary and necessary . . . 8.3.1, 8.3.4, 8.9.1–8.9.2, 8.10
. organizational . . . 8.9.3
. promotional and selling expenses . . . 8.10.4
. regulatory examination assessment . . . 8.10.4
. tax planning . . . 8.1
. taxable year of deduction . . . 8.2–8.2.1
. training costs . . . 8.9.5, 8.10.3
. year 2000 conversions . . . 8.11

Business-purpose test of tax-free reorganizations . . . 11.5.1

C

C corporations
. accumulated earnings and profits . . . 1.6.7
. distributions by subsidiaries . . . 1.6.7
. taxation of banks as . . . 1.4.1, 1.6.8

CAMEL rating system . . . 1.4.2
. loan charge-offs . . . 5.3.14

References are to section (§) numbers.

CAP loan
. inclusion in income . . . 3.3.3

Capital asset
. separate and distinct test . . . 8.3.2–8.3.3, 8.10

Capitalization of costs to acquire
. assembled workforce . . . 8.4.2
. copyrights . . . 8.4.2
. customer list . . . 8.4.2
. derivatives . . . 8.4.2
. foreign currency contract . . . 8.4.2
. forward contract . . . 8.4.2
. futures contract . . . 8.4.2
. Goodwill or going concern value . . . 8.4.2
. lease . . . 8.4.1, 8.4.2
. notional principal contracts . . . 8.4.2
. options . . . 8.4.2, 8.5.1
. patents . . . 8.4.2
. servicing rights . . . 8.4.2
. trademarks or trade names . . . 8.4.2

Capitalization of expenditures . . . 8.3-8.3.4
. Announcement 93-60 . . . 8.3.4
. book treatment . . . 8.3.4
. create goodwill . . . 8.1
. deductibility versus . . . 8.3.1-8.3.3
. future benefits test . . . 8.3.1, 8.3.3, 8.10
. . twelve-month rule . . . 8.3.3
. loan origination costs . . . 8.3.4
. priority ordering rule . . . 8.5.1
. section 263(a) . . . 8.3.1
. . burden of proof . . . 8.3.1
. . incidental future benefit . . . 8.3.1
. . separate and distinct asset . . . 8.3.1
. . supremacy . . . 8.3.1
. separate and distinct asset test . . . 8.3.2
. start-up companies . . . 8.9.1
. twelve-month rule . . . 8.4.4
. UNICAP rule . . . 8.3.1

Capitalization of intangibles
. regulations
. . goodwill . . . 8.4.1
. . intangibles required to be capitalized . . . 8.4.1
. . separate and distinct intangible asset . . . 8.4.1

Capitalization of intangibles—continued
. regulations—continued
. . simplifying conventions . . . 8.4.1
. . substantial future benefit . . . 8.4.1

Capitalized borrowing costs . . . 9.6

Capitalized transaction costs
. date rule . . . 8.4.4
. de minimis costs . . . 8.4.4
. . commissions . . . 8.4.4
. . pooling . . . 8.4.4
. election to capitalize . . . 8.4.4
. employee compensation . . . 8.4.4
. general rule . . . 8.4.4
. simplifying conventions . . . 8.4.4
. twelve-month rule
. . contract terminations . . . 8.4.4
. . election to capitalize . . . 8.4.4
. . indefinite duration . . . 8.4.4
. . measuring the period . . . 8.4.4
. . pooling method . . . 8.4.4
. . renewal periods . . . 8.4.4

Caps and floors . . . 2.12.6

Cash method of accounting
. interest expense . . . 9.3.1

Central Bank for Cooperatives . . . 1.5.3

Certificates of deposit . . . 1.5.7
. early withdrawal from . . . 9.3.4
. interest expense . . . 9.3.4

Character of gains or losses
. certain preferred stock
. . applicable financial institutions . . . 4.3.4
. . partnerships . . . 4.3.4
. . pass-through certificates . . . 4.3.4
. debt securities
. . deductible . . . 4.3.3
. . subsidiary bank . . . 4.3.3
. . wash sale . . . 4.3.3
. foreclosed property . . . 7.6.1
. mutual fund investments
. . capital losses . . . 4.3.5
. . judicial exception . . . 4.3.5

Charge-off
. allowance for loan losses . . . 10.4.4
. defined . . . 10.3.2

References are to section (§) numbers.

Charge-off—continued
. involuntary . . . 10.5

Charge-off of accrued interest
. experience formula . . . 5.3.7
. mark-to-market rules . . . 5.3.7

Charitable contributions . . . 1.6.5

Charter stripping
. Type C and D Reorganizations . . . 11.5.5

Chartering requirement . . . 1.5.6

Classification of entities . . . 1.1

Code Sec. 382, Loss Carryovers . . . 11.4. 11.4.1
. capital contributions . . . 11.4.24
. entity . . . 11.4.4
. limitation on built-in losses from loans . . . 11.4.4
. loss corporations . . . 11.4.2
. net operating loss: built-in loss . . . 11.4.6
. net unrealized built-in gain (NUBIG) . . . 11.4.7
. . calculating . . . 11.4.11
. . recognized built-in gain (RBIG) . . . 11.4.9
. . threshold requirement . . . 11.4.10
. net unrealized built-in loss (NUBIL) . . . 11.4.7
. . calculating . . . 11.4.11
. . recognized built-in loss (RBIL) . . . 11.4.9
. . taxable year . . . 11.4.8
. . threshold requirement . . . 11.4.10
. pre-change loss and post-change year . . . 11.4.3
. recapitalized financial institutions . . . 11.4.25
. seized financial corporations . . . 11.4.23
. . Fannie Mae and Freddie Mac . . . 11.4.23
. short tax year . . . 11.4.5

Code Section 481(a) adjustments . . . 1.6.4

Code Section 581 . . . 1.5.5
. foreign banks . . . 1.5.5
. thrifts . . . 1.5.5

Collar . . . 2.12.2, 2.12.6

Collateralized mortgage obligations (CMOs)
. advantages . . . 2.10.1
. tax treatment . . . 2.10.2

Commission
. loan origination . . . 2.8.2
. refundable loan . . . 2.8.2
. securities . . . 2.8.3, 8.3.1

Commitment fees
. intangible property rights . . . 2.8.1
. standby fees . . . 2.8.1

Commodity swaps . . . 2.12.2

Community Development Institutions Fund
. certification as CDE . . . 12.3.2

Community Reinvestment Act (CRA) . . . 1.2.2
. banking services requirements . . . 1.2.2
. national bank ratings . . . 1.2.3

Community Renewal Relief Act of 2000, New Markets Tax Credit under . . . 12.3.1

Comparable bank
. bad-debt deductions
. . experience method . . . 10.8.4

Competitive Equality Banking Act of 1987 (CEBA), moratorium on conversion transactions in . . . 8.13

Composite method of accounting . . . 2.5.6

Computer software
. acquisition . . . 8.4.1, 8.4.2
. amortization . . . 11.3.5
. conversion or replacement costs . . . 8.8.2
. held for sale, lease, or license . . . 12.1.1
. internal use . . . 12.1.3–12.1.4
. not section 197 intangible . . . 11.3.5
. R&D credit . . . 12.1, 12.1.1

Consolidated dissallowance . . . 9.5.8

Consolidated group
. advantages . . . 1.1
. bank net operating loss . . . 8.20
. common parent as agent . . . 8.20.5
. corporate structure . . . 1.6.3
. disallowance of interest expense . . . 9.5.2
. election to capitalize . . . 8.4.4

References are to section (§) numbers.

Consolidated group—continued
. election to forego NOL carryback . . . 8.20.5
. exclude entities . . . 1.2
. of bank and nonbank members . . . 8.20
. thrift joining in . . . 10.9.3

Consolidate returns
. S corporations . . . 1.6.3

Constant yield method of accounting . . . 2.2.1, 2.5.4
. acquisition discount . . . 3.5.8
. amortizable bond premium . . . 3.7.4
. bond premium amortization . . . 3.7.4
. calculation of discount . . . 3.3.1, 3.3.7

Constant-interest rate method
. market discount deferrals . . . 3.5.2

Contingent liabilities
. accrual accounting method . . . 8.2

Continuity-of-business-enterprise test . . . 11.5.1

Continuity-of-proprietary-interest test . . . 11.5.1

Contract termination payments, capitalization rules for . . . 8.1

Controlled group
. large bank
. . bad-debt deductions . . . 10.10.1
. S corporations . . . 1.6.3

Cost recovery
. applicable asset acquisition . . . 11.3.2
. Section 197 intangibles
. . Omnibus Budget Reconciliation Act of 1993 . . . 11.3.3
. open and speculative transactions . . . 5.3.13

Cost recovery table using different recovery periods . . . 11.3.2

Coupon stripping bond rules for sale of mortgages . . . 2.7.4

Covenants-not-to-compete as section 197 intangibles . . . 11.3.4

Covered asset losses . . . 8.22

CRA Ratings . . . 1.2.6

Credit Card Costs . . . 8.10.7

Credit card defaults, IRS examination of treatment of . . . 5.1

Credit card fees
. annual, ratable inclusion method . . . 2.7.3
. cash advance . . . 2.7.3
. late charge . . . 2.7.3
. over-the-limit . . . 2.7.3
. treatment as interest . . . 2.7.3

Credit card receivables, securitizing . . . 9.6

Credit card system entry fees . . . 8.1

Credit evaluation costs, current deductibility of . . . 8.3.1

Credit union . . . 1.3

Currency gain or loss . . . 2.12.7

Currency swaps . . . 2.12.2
. exchange gain or loss for . . . 2.12.7
. notional principal contract . . . 2.12.7

Customer list
. abandonment loss . . . 8.21.1

D

De Minimis Rule . . . 3.3.1

Dealers
. code section 475
. . bank securities transactions . . . 4.4.5
. . consolidated group . . . 4.4.5
. . intragroup-customer elections . . . 4.4.5
. . loan participants . . . 4.4.5
. . nonstatutory exceptions . . . 4.4.5
. . notional principal contract . . . 4.4.5
. . originating loans . . . 4.4.5
. . REMICs . . . 4.4.5
. . safe harbor rules . . . 4.4.5
. . separate branches . . . 4.4.5
. intercompany transactions
. . consolidated returns . . . 4.4.5
. . deferred intercompany gain . . . 4.4.5
. negligible sales election
. . 5 percent of total basis . . . 4.4.5
. . 60 debt instruments . . . 4.4.5
. . intragroup-customer election . . . 4.4.5

References are to section (§) numbers.

Dealers—continued
. negligible sales election—continued
. . nondealer affiliate . . . 4.4.5
. . recurring business activity . . . 4.4.5
. nonfinancial goods and services
. . customer paper . . . 4.4.5
. . non-cash transactions . . . 4.4.5
. . REMICs . . . 4.4.5
. securitiazation transactions
. . pooling loans . . . 4.4.5
. traders and speculators
. . commodity . . . 4.4.5
. . Taxpayer Relief Act of 1997 . . . 4.4.5

Debt
. bona fide . . . 10.2.3

Debt exchange
. amount realized . . . 6.3.3
. deemed charge-off . . . 6.3.3
. deemed exchange . . . 6.1
. I.R.S. position . . . 6.3.2
. in foreclosures . . . 7.3.1
. measuring gain or loss on . . . 6.3–6.3.3

Debt instruments
. alteration of contract for . . . 6.2.3
. capitalization of issuance costs for . . . 8.4.1, 8.6–8.7
. change between recourse and nonrecourse . . . 6.2.3
. change in obligor . . . 6.2.3
. change in payment expectations . . . 6.2.3
. change in yield . . . 6.2.3
. change of fair market value . . . 6.2.2
. change to non debt instruments . . . 6.2.3
. containing both stated interest and O.I.D . . . 5.3.12
. defined . . . 3.3.4
. determining issue price . . . 3.3.6
. fair market value (FMV) . . . 6.3.2
. options; unilateral versus bilateral . . . 6.2.3
. renegotiated . . . 6.1–6.3.3
. substitution of new for old . . . 6.2

Debt-equity swap . . . 11.5.6

Deduction of refunded interest . . . 8.2.2

Deed-in-lieu-of-foreclosure . . . 7.2, 7.3.2, 7.6

Deemed charge-off for debt exchanges . . . 6.3.3

Deemed sale of assets, gain on, offset by consolidated NOL . . . 11.3.8

Deep rent skewed projects
. special low-income housing . . . 12.2.14
. special low-income housing rule . . . 12.2.14

Defaulted bond, distribution considered return of principal for . . . 2.3

Deferral
. advance payments . . . 2.7.6
. bad-debt deductions . . . 10.5
. commitment fees . . . 2.8.1
. interest expense deduction . . . 3.6.2–3.6.3, 9.4.1–9.4.3
. loan origination fees . . . 8.3.4
. market discount . . . 3.6
. payments for debt obligation . . . 6.2.3
. prepaid income . . . 3.3.3, 3.7.1
. service fee income . . . 2.7.2

Deferred interest expense
. market discount bonds
. . allocable interest expense . . . 9.4.2
. . deductions . . . 9.4.2
. . defined . . . 9.4.2
. . general rule . . . 9.4.2
. . legislative history . . . 9.4.2
. . net direct interest expense . . . 9.4.2
. prepaid interest by a thrift
. . deferral rule . . . 9.4.1
. . exceptions to deferral rule . . . 9.4.1
. UNICAP rule . . . 9.4.3

Deficiency judgment
. unpaid principal . . . 7.2

Deficit Reduction Act of 1984
. deferred interest expense
. . market discount bonds . . . 9.4.2
. market discount bond rule . . . 9.4.2
. recharacterization of gain under . . . 3.6, 3.6.1

Definition
. bank
. . Bank Holding Company Act of 1956 (BHCA) . . . 1.5.3

References are to section (§) numbers.

Definition—continued
. bank—continued
. . classical definition . . . 1.5.1
. . code definition . . . 1.5.4
. . Competitive Equality Banking Act of 1987 (CEBA) . . . 1.5.3
. . Farm Credit Act of 1933 . . . 1.5.3
. . Federal Deposit Insurance Act . . . 1.5.3
. . Judicial definition . . . 1.5.2
. . National Bank Act of 1864 . . . 1.5.3
. building and loan associations . . . 1.7, 1.7.8
. commercial bank . . . 1.1
. grace period . . . 3.4.7
. interest . . . 2.4
. large bank . . . 10.10
. loan
. . bad-debt deductions . . . 10.8.5
. mortgage backed securities (MBSs) . . . 2.10
. mutual savings bank . . . 1.7.1
. notional principal contract . . . 2.12.2
. original issue discount (O.I.D.) . . . 3.4.7
. points . . . 3.4.3
. qualified bond . . . 2.5.1
. real estate investment trust (REIT) . . . 2.10.4
. Small Business Corporation . . . 1.6.1
. state or local bond . . . 2.5.1
. thrift . . . 1.3
. total payments . . . 5.3.6

Delinquent interest
. all events test . . . 5.3.1
. reasonable expectancy standard . . . 5.3.3
. . delay in payment . . . 5.3.3
. . receivership . . . 5.3.3

Deposit requirement . . . 1.5.7

Depository Institutions Deregulation Act of 1980 (DIDC), premature withdrawal penalty prescribed by . . . 2.13

Depository Institutions Deregulation and Monetary Control Act . . . 7.2

Depreciation
. foreclosed property . . . 7.1, 7.5.1, 7.6.2
. stock acquired in foreclosure
. . recapture . . . 7.6.2

Depreciation deduction, calculating annual . . . 11.3.2

Determining gains or losses
. stripped bonds
. . Tax Reform Act of 1984 . . . 4.3.2
. wash sale rule
. . commodity futures . . . 4.3.1
. . holding period . . . 4.3.1
. . mark-to-market rules . . . 4.3.1
. . mortgage loans . . . 4.3.1
. . mortgage swaps . . . 4.3.1

Directors' and officers' liability insurance, deductibility of . . . 8.16

Discount income, accrual of
. debt obligations . . . 3.3.2
. taxable corporate and governmental bonds . . . 3.3.1

Discount income on early mortgage pay-off . . . 8.10.8

Disregarded entity . . . 1.6.3

Dividends received deduction
. FHLB dividends . . . 2.14.2
. S corporations not allowed . . . 1.6.6

Dodd-Frank Wall Street Reform and Consumer Protection Act . . . 2.12.1

E

Economic accrual method of accounting . . . 2.5.4

Economic Recovery Tax Act of 1981 (ERTA)
. federal financial assistance . . . 11.6
. FIRREA repeal of certain tax rules . . . 8.22
. mutual savings bank redefined . . . 1.7.1
. rules for financially troubled thrift institutions in . . . 11.5.8
. Type G reorganization
. . general rules . . . 11.5.8

Economic significance rule for modification of debt instruments . . . 6.2.3

Edge Act Corporations
. permissible interstate activities . . . 11.2.1

References are to section (§) numbers.

Effective interest method for amortization of bond premium . . . 3.7.5

Elderly and handicapped projects . . . 12.2.3

Electing small business trust (ESBT) . . . 1.6.2
. alternative minimum tax exemption . . . 1.6.2
. as shareholder of S corporation . . . 1.6.2
. distributable net income . . . 1.6.2
. election . . . 1.6.2, 1.6.4
. grace period to dispose of stock . . . 1.6.2,
. taxation of . . . 1.6.2
. nonresident alien . . . 1.6.2
. potential current beneficiary . . . 1.6.2
. separate trust . . . 1.6.2
. taxation . . . 1.6.2

Emergency Economic Stabilization Act of 2008 . . . 11.4, 12.1.4
. character of gain or losses on certain preferred stock . . . 4.3.4
. deducting dividend payments on TARP-preferred stock . . . 9.2.1
. recapitalized financial institutions . . . 11.4.25

Emergency Low Income Housing Preservation Act of 1987
. waiver for prepayment . . . 12.2.2

Emergency medical services . . . 2.5.2

Employee stock ownership plan (ESOP)
. as shareholder of S corporation . . . 1.6.5
. loan . . . 2.5.3
. purchasing S corporation stock . . . 1.6.1

Equity and equity index swaps . . . 2.12.2

Equity structure shift . . . 11.4.14

ESOP loan
. refinancing . . . 2.5.3
. Small Business Job Protection Act of 1996 . . . 2.5.3

Excess purchase price as indication of goodwill and going concern value . . . 11.3.4

Exchange treatment
. change in maturity date . . . 6.2.2

Exchange treatment—continued
. change in security . . . 6.2.2
. change in yield . . . 6.2.2
. cottage savings association . . . 6.2.1
. mortgage pool . . . 6.2.1

Experience method for computing reserve balance . . . 10.8–10.8.6
. authorization years . . . 10.8.4
. comparable bank . . . 10.8.4
. experience period . . . 10.8.4
. items not considered to be loans . . . 10.8.6
. moving-average formula for additions . . . 10.8–10.8.1
. not available for large banks . . . 10.8
. reserve balances determined by reference to base year . . . 10.8, 10.8.2
. reserve restoration upon decline in loan balance . . . 10.8.3

Extended low-income housing commitment, 15-year . . . 12.2.9

F

Fair Housing Act, low-income housing credit . . . 12.2.14

Fair market value (FMV)
. debt obligations . . . 6.3.2
. foreclosed property . . . 7.3.1–7.3.2, 7.4
. low-income housing credit . . . 12.2.10

Fair market value allocation method . . . 11.3.2

Fannie Mae pass-throughs, character of gains or losses, certain preferred stock . . . 4.3.4

Farm Credit Act of 1933, banks defined for . . . 1.5.3, 1.5.7

Farm Credit System, creation of . . . 1.5.3

Farm Credit System Financial Assistance Corporation (FAC), assessment of . . . 8.10.5

Farmers' Home Administration (FMHA) assistance . . . 12.2.3

FAS No. 114, impairment of loan . . . 5.2.2

References are to section (§) numbers.

Federal Deposit Insurance Act, character of gains or losses, certain preferred stock . . . 4.3.4

Federal Deposit Insurance Corporation (FDIC)
. branches approved . . . 11.2.1
. deposit insurance assessment . . . 8.12
. federal financial assistance . . . 11.6.1
. insurance of thrifts . . . 1.7.5
. insured institutions . . . 1.7.5
. phantom income from loan modifications . . . 1.7.5
. regulations . . . 1.4.3
. Savings Association Insurance Fund (SAIF) . . . 1.7.5
. state-chartered bank classified as corporation by . . . 1.4.3

Federal Deposit Insurance Corporation Act . . . 1.2.6, 1.4.3, 1.7.5
. approval of new branches by FDIC required by . . . 11.2.1
. Financial Modernization Act as amending . . . 1.2, 1.2.6
. insured banks defined . . . 11.2.2
. uniformity of GAAP and RAP . . . 5.2.2

Federal Financial Institutions Examination Council (FFIEC)
. bad-debt deductions
. . large bank . . . 10.10.4
. loan standards . . . 10.10.4

Federal Financial Insurance (FFA) . . . 11.6
. bridge banks and residual entitles . . . 11.6.5
. defined . . . 11.6.1
. Econcomic Recovery Tax Act of 1981 (ERTA) . . . 11.6
. Emergency Economic Stabilization Act of 2008 . . . 11.6.1
. Financial Institutions Reform, Recovery, and Enforcement Act of 1989 (FIRREA) . . . 11.6
. income inclusion . . . 11.6.3
. limitation on collection of income tax . . . 11.6.7
. miscellaneous rules . . . 11.6.8

Federal Financial Insurance (FFA)—continued
. principles used in prescribing regulations . . . 11.6.2
. taxable transfers . . . 11.6.6
. transfer of property by institution . . . 11.6.4

Federal Home Loan Bank Board (FHLBB)
. conformity test . . . 1.7.6
. distributions from systems
. . basis . . . 2.14.3
. . stock . . . 2.14.1
. federal control of banks under . . . 2.14.4
. FIRREA abolishment . . . 1.7.6
. interest charge-off . . . 5.3.16
. savings and loan associations . . . 6.2.1
. stock . . . 1.7.8
. . basis . . . 2.14.3
. . redemption . . . 2.14.2
. supervisory goodwill . . . 11.6.1
. system . . . 2.14.4
. waiver of continuity-of-interest rule . . . 11.5.8

Federal Home Loan Bank Board (FHLBB) rules
. conformity test under . . . 1.7.6
. FIRREA abolishment of . . . 1.7.6
. for waiver of continuity-of-interest rule . . . 11.5.8

Federal Home Loan Mortgage Corporation (FHLMC, Freddie Mac)
. federally guaranteed mortgage certificates . . . 10.8.6

Federal Housing Authority (FHA)
. amortizing loan premiums for mortgages insured by . . . 3.4.8
. insurance of Ginnie Mae pass-throughs . . . 2.10.1

Federal Modernization Act
. amendments to Federal Deposit Insurance Act . . . 1.2.6

Federal National Mortgage Association (FNMA) (Fannie Mae)
. federally guaranteed mortgage certificates . . . 10.8.6
. income . . . 1.5.8

References are to section (§) numbers.

Federal National Mortgage Association (FNMA) (Fannie Mae)—continued
. mortgage pass-through securities . . . 2.10.1

Federal rental assistance payments . . . 12.2.2

Federal Reserve; section 20 subsidiaries . . . 1.2.5

Federal Reserve Act . . . 1.2
. activities between bank and its financial subsidiary . . . 1.2.3
. branching limitations identical for state and national banks . . . 11.2.1
. Financial Modernization Act as amending . . . 1.2

Federal Reserve Board (FRB) approval of branches . . . 11.2.1
. value of BHC structure affected by . . . 11.2.2

Federal Savings and Loan Insurance Corporation (FSLIC)
. abolition . . . 1.7.5
. acquisition costs
. . abandonment losses . . . 8.21.2
. assistance to financially troubled thrifts . . . 11.5.8
. federal financial assistance . . . 11.6
. payments to acquiring institution by . . . 8.22
. supervisory goodwill . . . 11.6.1

Federally guaranteed mortgage certificates . . . 10.8.6

Federally subsidized building for low-income housing credit . . . 12.2.1

Fee for services
. in cash basis accounting . . . 8.2.2

Fiduciary institutions, categorization as . . . 1.5.9

Fiduciary powers . . . 1.5.9

Financial Accounting Standards Board (FASB), credit card fees . . . 2.7.3

Financial asset securitization trust (FASIT)
. credit card fees . . . 2.7.3
. credit card receivables . . . 2.11.1

Financial asset securitization trust (FASIT)—continued
. defined . . . 2.11.1
. eligible corporation . . . 2.11.1
. ownership interest . . . 2.11.1
. permitted asset . . . 2.11.1
. prohibited transaction . . . 2.11.1
. regular interest . . . 2.11.1

Financial holding companies (FHCs) . . . 1.2, 1.2.1
. conversion to FHC . . . 1.2.1
. dividends received deduction . . . 1.2.4
. electing status . . . 1.2.2
. financial activities . . . 1.2.1, 1.2.3
. insurance activities . . . 1.2.2–1.2.4
. intercompany elimination . . . 1.2.4
. life insurance business . . . 1.2.4
. permitted under Financial Modernization Act . . . 1.2
. registered broker-dealer affiliates . . . 1.2.5
. registration exemptions . . . 1.2.5
. requirements under amendments to Bank Holding Company Act . . . 1.2.1
. Section 20 subsidiaries . . . 1.2.5
. securities activities . . . 1.2.2, 1.2.5
. state tax implications . . . 1.2.4
. title insurance activities . . . 1.2.4

Financial Institution Reform, Recovery, and Enforcement Act of 1989 (FIRREA) . . . 1.7.5
. abandonment loss . . . 8.21.2
. control measures to prevent exodus from SAIF . . . 8.13
. federal financial assistance . . . 11.6
. repeal of certain tax rules . . . 8.22

Financial Institution's Reform, Recovery, and Enforcement Act of 1989
. acquisition costs
. . abandonment losses . . . 8.21.2
. . covered losses . . . 8.21.3

Financial interests not considered section 197 intangibles . . . 11.3.5

Financial Modernization Act . . . 1.2
. Federal Deposit Insurance Act amended for state bank activities . . . 1.2.6

References are to section (§) numbers.

Financial Modernization Act—continued
. insurance activities permitted to FHCs . . . 1.2.3–1.2.4
. National Bank Act amended to expand national banks' financial activities . . . 1.2.3
. permitted financial holding companies . . . 1.2
. restriction on affiliation between banks and securities dealers repealed by . . . 1.2.5

Financial subsidiaries . . . 1.2.3
. activities allowed for . . . 1.2.3
. firewall restrictions . . . 1.2.3
. National Bank Act amendments . . . 1.2.3

Fire Department loans . . . 2.5.2

Foreclosure property
. capital asset treatment . . . 7.6.1
. used for lender's own business . . . 7.6, 7.6.1

Foreclosures . . . 1.3, 7.1–7.6.4
. acquisition costs . . . 7.3.2
. acquisition of property . . . 7.1, 7.2
. as troubled debt restructuring . . . 5.2.2, 10.10.4
. bid price adjustments by banks . . . 7.3.1
. by thrifts . . . 7.3.2
. capital assets . . . 7.6.1
. code section 263A UNICAP rule . . . 7.1
. debt collection . . . 7.3.1
. deed-in-lie-of-foreclosure . . . 7.2
. deficiency judgment . . . 7.2
. determining fair market value
. . clear and convincing proof . . . 7.3.1
. disposal of property
. . gains and losses . . . 7.1, 7.6-7.6.4
. expenses to carry . . . 7.1
. foreclosure sale . . . 7.2
. intercompany transactions . . . 7.6.1
. interest income . . . 7.4, 7.6.3
. legal aspects . . . 7.2
. other real estate owned (OREO) . . . 7.2, 7.5.1, 7.6.1
. partially-worthless bad debt . . . 7.3.2
. post-acquisition income . . . 7.5.2
. power of sale . . . 7.2
. sale costs . . . 7.3.1

Foreclosures—continued
. separate entity to avoid tort liability . . . 7.6.4
. stages . . . 7.1
. stock acquired . . . 7.6.2
. strict foreclosure . . . 7.2
. tax planning . . . 7.1
. tax treatment of gain or loss . . . 7.3.1–7.3.2
. writ of entry . . . 7.2
. as troubled debt restructurings, not loans . . . 5.2.2, 10.10.4

Foreign banks, treatment as banks of . . . 1.5.5

Forms
. Form 2553, Election by a Small Business Corporation, from parent corporation . . . 1.6.4
. Form 3115 . . . 2.7.2, 5.3.18
. . conformity election for bad debts . . . 10.4.4
. . loan origination costs . . . 8.3.4
. Form 8281
. . issuer of O.I.D. obligation as filing . . . 3.3.8
. Form 8609
. . election not to treat partnership as a taxpayer for low-income housing credit . . . 12.2.14
. . election to come under 20-50 or 40-60 test . . . 12.2.4
. . election to reduce eligible basis of subsidized building . . . 12.2.1
. . filed to obtain housing credit allocation . . . 12.2.4
. Form 8693
. . low-income housing disposition bond . . . 12.2.14
. Form 8869, Qualified Subchapter S Subsidiary Election

Forward and Future contracts . . . 2.12.7

Franchises as section 197 intangibles . . . 11.3.4

Freddie Mac
. character of gains or losses
. . certain preferred stock . . . 4.3.4

References are to section (§) numbers.

Freddie Mac—continued
. mortgage pass-through securities . . . 2.10.1

G

Garn-St. Germain Depository Institutions Act of 1982
. differences between commercial banks and thrifts' activities reduced by . . . 1.3
. formation of bank service corporations permitted by . . . 11.2.1
. permissible interstate activities . . . 11.2.1

General business credit components . . . 12.2

General ledger accounts monitored for inadvertent changes . . . 2.1

General Utilities doctrine, repeal of . . . 11.3.1

Generally accepted accounting principles (GAAP)
. conformity with RAP under FDIC Act . . . 5.2.2
. requirement to adopt SFAS No. 114 of . . . 5.1

Gift Cards . . . 2.7.6

Ginnie Mae pass-throughs . . . 2.8.1

Glass-Steagall Act . . . 1.2, 1.2.5

Goodwill
. capitalization . . . 8.4.1

Goodwill or going concern value
. cost recovery of . . . 11.3.3
. defined . . . 11.3.4
. in purchase price . . . 11.3.7

Government National Mortgage Association (GNMA, Ginnie Mae)
. federally guaranteed mortgage certificates . . . 10.8.6

Governmental obligations
. accrued discount . . . 3.3.1
. loans collateralized . . . 10.8.6

Grace period defined . . . 3.4.7

Grace period interest
. actual experience . . . 3.4.7
. credit card receivables . . . 3.4.7
. included in income . . . 2.1
. reasonable assumption . . . 3.4.7
. Taxpayer Relief Act of 1997 . . . 3.4.7

Grantor trust holding mortgages . . . 2.10.2

Gross income
. amount of discount includible . . . 3.3.1
. interest on state or local bond . . . 2.3.1

Gross income test
. real estate investment trust (REIT) . . . 2.10.4

Gross rent for low-income housing credit . . . 12.2.4

Gulf Opportunity Zone Act of 2005 . . . 12.3.1, 12.3.4, 12.3.6.2

H

Hedging transaction
. caps and floors . . . 2.12.6
. currency exchange hedging . . . 2.12
. currency gain or loss
. . forward and future contracts . . . 2.12.7
. . functional currency . . . 2.12.7
. . loss deferral rule . . . 2.12.7
. . nonfunctional currency . . . 2.12.7
. . section 988 transaction . . . 2.12.7
. . sourcing rules . . . 2.12.7
. . straddles . . . 2.12.7
. dealer . . . 2.12
. nonperiodic payments . . . 2.12.4
. notional principal contract . . . 2.12.2
. . accounting . . . 2.12.3
. . collar . . . 2.12.2
. . commodity swap . . . 2.12.2
. . interest rate swap . . . 2.12.2
. periodic payments . . . 2.12.4
. swaps . . . 2.12.5
. termination payments . . . 2.12.4
. tax treatment . . . 7.6.1

Home equity lines of credit, capitalization of costs to establish . . . 8.8.1

References are to section (§) numbers.

HOME Investment Partnerships Act, assistance under . . . 12.2.1

Home Owners Loan Act (HOLA), reference to federal savings and loan association under . . . 1.7.4

Housing Act of 1937, voucher or certificate of eligibility under . . . 12.2.10
. qualified rental assistance program under . . . 12.2.2

Housing Act of 1949, waiver for prepayment under . . . 12.2.2

Housing and Community Development Act of 1974, below-market HUD block grants under . . . 12.2.1

Housing and Urban Development (HUD), Department of
. nondiscrimination housing policy . . . 12.2.3
. pass-through mortgage securities . . . 2.10.1

Housing Assistance Tax Act of 2008 . . . 12.1.7, 12.2

Hybrid method of accounting . . . 2.2.1

I

Identification of securities
. approved methods
. . common depository account . . . 4.4.4
. . identification statement . . . 4.4.4
. . limitation on loss . . . 4.4.4
. . parent corporation's . . . 4.4.4
. . software system . . . 4.4.4
. books and records . . . 4.4.4
. dealers
. . "primarily" for sale . . . 4.4.4
. . customers . . . 4.4.4
. . entity-by-entity basis . . . 4.4.4
. . floor specialist . . . 4.4.4
. . mortgage corporation . . . 4.4.4
. . options market maker . . . 4.4.4
. deemed identification
. . constructive stock ownership . . . 4.4.4
. endowment . . . 4.4.4
. hedging transactions . . . 4.4.4

Identification of securities—continued
. inadvertent error . . . 4.4.4
. life insurance contract . . . 4.4.4
. negative identification . . . 4.4.4
. partnership of trust . . . 4.4.4
. protective identification . . . 4.4.4
. timing
. . 30-day rule . . . 4.4.4
. . mortgage loans . . . 4.4.4
. . one-day rule . . . 4.4.4
. . synthetic debt . . . 4.4.4

Imputed principal amount . . . 3.3.6

Income forecast depreciation of mortgage servicing rights . . . 2.7.4

Individual retirement accounts (IRAs) . . . 1.6.1

Industry loan company . . . 1.5.6-1.5.8

Industry Issue Resolution Program "IIR Program" . . . 5.1

Insolvency . . . 1.7.3

Installment obligations; pool . . . 2.6.2

Insurance activities permitted for FHCs . . . 1.2.3–1.2.4

Insurance company . . . 1.5.9

Intangible assets
. abandonment loss . . . 8.21.1
. amortizable section 197 . . . 8.4.2, 8.21.1, 11.3.4
. amortization period for . . . 8.6.1, 11.3.4
. benefits arising from real property . . . 8.4.3
. capitalization of acquisition or creation of . . . 8.4.1–8.4.5
. capitalization of expenses . . . 8.3.3, 8.3.4
. capitalization of transaction costs . . . 8.4.4
. contract rights . . . 8.4.3
. contract terminations . . . 8.4.3
. core deposit . . . 11.3.4
. cost recovery . . . 11.3.3
. created, capitalized costs of . . . 8.4.3, 8.10
. customer-based . . . 8.4.2, 11.3.4, 11.3.7
. *de minimis* rule . . . 8.4.4
. defense of perfection of title . . . 8.4.3
. estimated useful life of . . . 8.6.1

References are to section (§) numbers.

Intangible assets—continued
. excess purchase price . . . 11.3.4
. financial interests . . . 8.4.3
. general rule . . . 8.4.2
. ISO 9000 certification . . . 8.4.3
. membership and privileges . . . 8.4.3
. pooling method . . . 8.4.4–8.4.5
. pre-paid expenses . . . 8.4.3
. rights obtained from governmental agency . . . 8.4.3
. safe harbor amortization rules . . . 8.6.1
. section 197 . . . 11.3.3-11.3.5
. separate and distinct . . . 8.4.1
. simplifying conventions . . . 8.4.4
. supplier-based . . . 11.3.4

Integration costs for business operations in acquisitions . . . 8.5.1

Interchange fees . . . 3.5.7

Intercompany distributions of foreclosed property . . . 7.6

Interest
. defined . . . 9.2
. deductible vs. nondeductible . . . 9.2

Interest expense . . . 9.1–9.6
. acquisition date . . . 9.5.7
. allocation to tax-exempt obligations . . . 9.1
. automatic disallowance rules for . . . 9.1, 9.5.1
. avoided cost method . . . 9.4.3
. capitalization under UNICAP . . . 9.4.3
. consolidated disallowance . . . 9.5.8
. . bank rules . . . 9.5.8
. . consolidated exclusion . . . 9.5.8
. . judicial analysis . . . 9.5.8
. . statutory rule . . . 9.5.8
. crediting . . . 9.3.3
. deductibility . . . 9.2–9.3.4
. deferral of deduction for . . . 3.6.1, 9.4.1–9.4.3
. defined . . . 9.5.6
. disallowed . . . 9.5.1–9.5.10
. . administrative difficulties . . . 9.5.2
. . application to banks . . . 9.5.2
. . de minimis exception . . . 9.5.2
. . generally . . . 9.5.1

Interest expense—continued
. disallowed—continued
. . repurchase agreements . . . 9.5.2
. . short-term financial obligations . . . 9.5.2
. federal funds . . . 9.5.6
. qualified tax-exempt obligations
. . Tax Reform Act of 1986 . . . 9.5.5
. S Corporation banks . . . 9.6
. . mortgage pool . . . 9.7
. . registration-required obligations . . . 9.7
. savings certificates and O.I.D.
. . amount . . . 9.3.4
. . early withdrawal . . . 9.3.4
. . Regulation Q . . . 9.3.4
. . timing . . . 9.3.4
. tax basis of assets and tax-exempts; average adjusted basis . . . 9.5.9
. tax planning . . . 9.1
. Tax Reform Act of 1986
. . legislative history . . . 9.5.4
. . scope of disallowance . . . 9.5.4
. TEFRA disallowance . . . 1.6.3
. . legislative history . . . 9.5.3
. . scope . . . 9.5.3
. thrifts . . . 9.3.2
. timing . . . 9.2.1
. . cash method . . . 9.2.1
. . economic performance . . . 9.2.1

Interest holiday; issued upon debt obligation . . . 3.3.6

Interest income . . . 2.4
. accrual
. . discontinuance . . . 5.3.1–5.3.16, 5.3.11
. charge-off of accrued . . . 5.3.7
. clear reflection of income . . . 2.7.3
. compared to service fee income . . . 2.7.1
. credit card fees . . . 2.7.3
. defined . . . 2.4
. delinquent . . . 5.1–5.3.11, 5.2.1-5.3.18
. economic accrual method . . . 2.6
. foreclosures . . . 7.4, 7.6.3
. income
. . creditor recognition under FASB No. 18 . . . 5.2.2
. installment loan . . . 2.6.1
. loan origination fee income . . . 2.4

References are to section (§) numbers.

Interest income—continued
. National Banking Act . . . 2.4
. refunded, lender deduction of . . . 2.5.8
. repurchase agreement . . . 2.9–2.9.2
. resumption of accrual . . . 5.3.10
. service fee . . . 2.4
. tax-exempt . . . 2.5.1

Interest rate cap agreement . . . 2.12.2

Interest rate swap agreement . . . 2.12.2, 2.12.4

Interests in land not considered section 197 intangibles . . . 11.3.5

Interests under debt instruments or leases not considered section 197 intangibles . . . 11.3.5

Internal Revenue Service (I.R.S.) "Audit Technique Guide for Commercial Banking" (Market Segment Specialization Program) . . . 5.3.14

Internal Revenue Service (I.R.S.) Commissioner
. authority to determine use of reserve method . . . 10.7.5
. exceptions to seeking permission to change accounting method from . . . 8.9
. revocation of conformity election by . . . 10.4.4

International banking subsidiaries ("Edge Act" corporations) . . . 11.2.1-11.2.2

J

Joint ventures, funding not characterized as loans but . . . 10.2.3

Judicial sale pursuant to court order for sale of foreclosed property . . . 7.2

L

LB&I Directive Related to §166 Deductions for Eligible Debt/Securities
. charge-off and financial statement requirement . . . 10.4.1
. defined . . . 10.4.1

LB&I Directive Related to §166 Deductions for Eligible Debt/Securities—continued
. qualifying banks and subsidiaries . . . 10.4.1
. taxpayers applied to . . . 10.4.1
. "worthlessness" regulations . . . 10.4.1

Large bank . . . 10.10

Lease termination or cancellation payments . . . 8.1

License or permit as section 197 intangible . . . 11.3.4

Life insurance on borrower, deduction of premiums paid by bank for . . . 8.17

Limited liability companies (LLCs), banks as . . . 1.4.3, 1.6.3

Loan liquidation method of accounting
. interest income apportioned using . . . 2.5.6
. mechanical operation of . . . 1.7.6

Loan modifications
. phantom income . . . 11.6.9
. . eliminating . . . 11.6.9
. . production . . . 11.6.9
. treatment . . . 11.6.9

Loan origination
. commission . . . 2.8.2
. fee income
. . deferral . . . 2.2.2, 2.8.1
. . disaggregation . . . 3.1
. . interest income . . . 2.4, 2.6.2
. production of intangible property for resale . . . 8.8

Loan origination costs
. current deductions versus capitalization of . . . 8.3.1, 8.3.4
. employee compensation and overhead related to . . . 8.3.4, 8.4.4

Loan premium
. for mortgages insured by FHA . . . 3.4.8
. not considered section 197 intangible . . . 11.3.5

Loans
. ATTR . . . 10.8.6
. below-market federal . . . 12.2.1
. book balance . . . 10.1

References are to section (§) numbers.

Loans—continued
. by community development entity . . . 12.3.5
. classified as loss assets . . . 10.4.4
. collateral dependent . . . 5.2.2
. defined
. . bad-debt deductions . . . 10.8.5
. disposal . . . 10.10.2
. experience method calculation . . . 10.8.6
. for improvement of residential real property . . . 10.11.4
. illegal . . . 10.8.6
. impaired . . . 5.2.2
. installment . . . 2.6.1
. international . . . 10.4.3
. issue price . . . 3.3.6
. joint ventures . . . 10.2.3
. lacking economic substance . . . 9.2
. noncustomer . . . 10.8.6
. nonperforming . . . 5.1–5.3.11, 10.10.4
. payment ordering rule for . . . 2.3
. pending . . . 10.8.6
. purchased . . . 8.6.1, 12.3.5
. recharacterizing agreements for . . . 10.2.3
. reconciling tax and book basis of . . . 5.3.7
. refinance to ESOP loan . . . 2.5.1
. S corporations, charge-off method to determine deductions for . . . 1.6.6
. safe harbor rates . . . 2.8.3
. secured by deposits . . . 10.8.6
. secured by real property . . . 10.9.1, 10.11.4
. Shared National Credit Review of . . . 10.4.3
. thrifts' investment in . . . 1.7.6
. to affiliates . . . 10.8.6, 10.9.2
. to banks . . . 10.8.6, 10.9.2
. to government . . . 10.8.6, 10.9.2
. types of . . . 1.7.7, 4.4.2

Loan of Securities . . . 4.6

Loss assets
. classifying loans as . . . 10.4.4
. defined . . . 10.4.4

Loss deferral rule . . . 2.12.7

Low-income community defined . . . 12.3.4

Low-income credit housing building . . . 12.2.10

Low-income housing credit . . . 12.2–12.2.14
. "adjusted investor equity" . . . 12.2.10
. 15-year compliance period for low-income use . . . 12.2.10, 12.2.14
. acquisition of existing buildings . . . 12.2.13
. additional credit . . . 12.2.6
. agency authorization . . . 12.2.9
. allocated between seller and purchaser upon disposition . . . 12.2.7
. allocation authority . . . 12.2.12
. applicable percentage . . . 12.2.1
. applicable percentage of qualified basis . . . 12.2.1
. apportioned between estate or trust and beneficiaries . . . 12.2.8
. as component of general business credit . . . 12.2
. authority from state or local agency . . . 12.2.9
. credit period . . . 12.2.5, 12.2.12
. disposition of building . . . 12.2.7
. election to determine percentage applicable to building in advance . . . 12.2.1
. elections of appropriate percentage month . . . 12.2.1
. . agency authorization . . . 12.2.1
. . binding commitment . . . 12.2.1
. . tax-exempt bonds . . . 12.2.1
. for homeless occupants . . . 12.2.3
. for single parent and children . . . 12.2.3
. for students . . . 12.2.3
. Form 8609 . . . 12.2.9
. Gulf Opportunity Zone property . . . 12.2.2, 12.2.3, 12.2.12
. housing use agreement . . . 12.2.10
. increases in tenant income . . . 12.2.3, 12.2.14
. maximum allocable . . . 12.2.11
. qualified basis . . . 12.2.2, 12.2.6
. . at-risk rules . . . 12.2.2
. . eligible basis . . . 12.2.2
. . federally assisted building . . . 12.2.2
. . low-income building . . . 12.2.2
. . qualified census tract . . . 12.2.2
. recapture bond . . . 12.2.14
. recapture of credit
. . recapture amount . . . 12.2.14

References are to section (§) numbers.

Low-income housing credit—continued
. recapture of credit—continued
. . recapture bond . . . 12.2.14
. . recapture events . . . 12.2.14
. . recapture-early disposition . . . 12.2.14
. . recapture-increases in tenant income . . . 12.2.14
. reduced first-year . . . 12.2.5
. state or local agency approval for . . . 12.2.2
. subsidized buildings . . . 12.2.1
. substantial rehabilitation . . . 12.2.2
. tax-exempt bond financed buildings . . . 12.2.1
. tenant's right to acquire building receiving . . . 12.2.8
. tenant's right to acquisition . . . 12.2.8
. utility allowances . . . 12.2.3
. waiver of 10-year holding period . . . 12.2.2

Low-income housing project
. defined . . . 12.2.4
. minimum set-aside . . . 12.2.4
. rent restrictions . . . 12.2.4

Low-income unit
. available unit rule for . . . 12.2.3
. defined . . . 12.2.3
. qualification rules
. . residential rental units . . . 12.2.3
. rent restriction . . . 12.2.4

M

Mandatory allocation rule for purchase price . . . 11.3.2

Mark-to-market
. bad debt deductions . . . 4.4.8
. . worthless debts . . . 4.4.8
. . treatment of gain or loss . . . 4.4.8
. change in accounting method . . . 4.4.12
. character of gains or losses
. . bad debt deductions . . . 4.4.9
. . equity instrument . . . 4.4.9
. . mortgage company . . . 4.4.9
. . Section 20 subsidiary . . . 4.4.9
. charge-off of accrued interest . . . 5.3.7
. Code section 1256 contrasts . . . 4.4.11
. for purchased loans . . . 8.6.1

Mark-to-market—continued
. foreign currency transaction . . . 4.4.11
. gains or losses from debt exchanges . . . 6.1
. measuring gain or loss . . . 6.3.1
. . fair market value . . . 4.4.8
. . illiquid securities . . . 4.4.8
. . inter-branch transactions . . . 4.4.8
. . interest rate swaps . . . 4.4.8
. . pools . . . 4.4.8
. . restrictions on marketability . . . 4.4.8
. . safe harbor rule . . . 4.4.8
. tax basis of loan . . . 10.8.5
. tax-free acquisitions . . . 4.4.10
. unrealized gain or loss . . . 3.6

Market discount
. creation . . . 3.6, 9.4.2
. deferral of interest expense deduction . . . 3.6.3–3.6.4
. included in gross income . . . 3.6.4
. purchase of assets or loans . . . 3.6

Market discount bond
. defined . . . 9.4.2
. net direct interest expense . . . 9.4.2

Maturity date of obligation, change in, taxable exchange not triggered by . . . 6.2.2

McFadden Act of 1927
. permissible interstate activities . . . 11.2.1

McFadden Act of 1927, branch banking under . . . 11.2.1

Measuring gain or loss
. amount realized . . . 6.3.2
. IRS position . . . 6.3.2
. mark-to-market rules . . . 6.3.1
. O.I.D. rules
. . deemed charge-off . . . 6.3.3
. . introduction . . . 6.3.2

Merchant fees
. deduction from credit sales remittances . . . 3.4.6

Method of accounting
. bad-debt deductions
. . conformity election . . . 10.4.4

Minimum additions to reserves . . . 10.7.7

References are to section (§) numbers.

Modified debt . . . 6.1–6.3.3
. charge-off preceding . . . 6.3.3
. economic significance rule . . . 6.2.3
. exchange treatment . . . 6.1
. tax planning . . . 6.1

Mortgage backed securities (MBSs) . . . 2.10.1
. certificate holder treatment
. . late payment charges . . . 2.10.2
. . original issue discount (O.I.D.) . . . 2.10.2
. . servicing fees . . . 2.10.2
. collateralized mortgage obligations (CMOs) . . . 2.10.2
. credit risk . . . 2.10.1
. defined . . . 2.10
. mortgage backed . . . 2.10.1
. mortgage participation certificate . . . 2.10.1
. mortgage pass-through securities . . . 2.10.1
. pass-through investor . . . 2.10.1
. pool of loans . . . 2.10
. reserve loss . . . 2.10.2
. securitization vehicles . . . 2.10
. stripped . . . 2.10.1
. tranches . . . 2.10.1
. transfer of mortgages into trust . . . 2.10.2
. trust characterization
. . grantor trust . . . 2.10.2
. . REMICs . . . 2.10.2
. . Tax Reform Act of 1986 . . . 2.10.2
. types of . . . 2.10.1

Mortgage bank Association (MBA) . . . 5.2.2

Mortgage buy-downs, creation of O.I.D. by . . . 3.5.1

Mortgage participation certificates . . . 2.10.1

Mortgage pass-through securities
. transfer of mortgages . . . 2.10.2

Mortgage pool . . . 2.10.2
. exchange treatment . . . 6.2.1
. interest expense deduction
. . S Corporation banks . . . 9.7

Mortgage servicing fees
. accounting rules . . . 2.7.4
. amortization period . . . 2.7.4
. basis . . . 2.7.4

Mortgage servicing fees—continued
. cost recovery for purchased rights to . . . 2.8.3, 11.3.5
. coupon stripping bond rules . . . 2.7.4
. income forecast method . . . 2.7.4
. mortgage servicing-character of gain or loss, sale of . . . 2.7.4
. multiple accounts . . . 2.7.4
. pool of mortgages . . . 2.7.4
. safe harbor . . . 2.7.4, 2.8.3
. servicing rights-cost recovery, purchase of . . . 2.7.4
. single asset . . . 2.7.4
. straight-line method . . . 2.7.4

Mortgages
. acquiring . . . 8.3.1
. assumed by purchasers . . . 6.2.3
. early pay-off of, discount for . . . 8.18
. market discount for purchases of . . . 3.4.8
. mortgage backed securities backed by pool of . . . 2.8
. prepayment . . . 12.2.2
. sale . . . 2.8.3, 4.4.2, 6.2, 8.5.1
. transferred to trust . . . 2.10.2
. valuing . . . 2.10.1

Mutual funds
. bailout costs for . . . 8.7.6, 8.10.8
. capital losses . . . 4.3.5

Mutual holding company formation . . . 11.5.3

Mutual savings bank
. adoption of stock corporation structure . . . 11.5.2
. conversion into stock bank of . . . 11.5.6
. defined . . . 1.4.1, 1.7.1

N

National Bank Act
. banks defined . . . 1.5.3
. Financial Modernization Act as amending . . . 1.2
. interest income . . . 2.4
. loan production offices . . . 11.2.1
. permissible securities activities . . . 4.2

References are to section (§) numbers.

National Housing Act, insured institutions within . . . 1.7.5

national recognized statistical ratings organizations (NRSROs) . . . 10.4.4

Native American Housing Assistance and Self-Determination Act of 1996 . . . 12.2.1

Net operating loss (NOL)
. 2008 NOL elective carryback period . . . 8.20.3
. acquisition costs . . . 8.20
. bad-debt deductions
. . percentage of taxable income method . . . 10.9.3
. bifurcation under Tax Reform Act of 1986 . . . 8.20.2
. of C corporation, 2-year carryback and 20-year carryforward for . . . 8.20.4
. carryback for 10 years before 1987 . . . 8.11.1, 10.7.2
. carryback rules for Type F reorganization . . . 11.5.7
. carryforward rules for Type G reorganization . . . 11.5.8
. consolidated . . . 11.3.8
. election to forego carryback . . . 8.20.5
. of commercial bank . . . 8.20.2
. of thrift . . . 8.20.2, 10.7.8
. S corporations . . . 1.6.6
. special bank rule . . . 8.20, 8.20.2, 10.7.2
. special rule during 1982–1985 . . . 8.20.4
. taxable income effect under PTI method . . . 10.9.3

New Markets Tax Credit (NMTC) . . . 12.3.1–12.3.8
. allocation . . . 12.3.2
. allowance dates . . . 12.3.7
. CDE receiving allocation . . . 12.3.2
. component of general business credit . . . 12.3.1
. credit allowance date . . . 12.3.1
. generally . . . 12.3.1
. low-income community . . . 12.3.4
. low-income community investment . . . 12.3.5
. . GO zone targets populations . . . 12.3.6.2

New Markets Tax Credit (NMTC)— continued
. low-income community investment—continued
. . targeted populations . . . 12.3.6.1
. qualified active low-income community business . . . 12.3.6
. qualified equity investment . . . 12.3.2
. qualified low-income community investment . . . 12.3.2
. recapture . . . 12.3.8

Nominee corporations to hold acquired security property . . . 7.6.4

Non-sufficient fund fee . . . 3.5.5

Nonperforming loans . . . 5.1–5.3.11
. all events test . . . 5.3.2
. Appeals Settlement Guideline . . . 5.3.16
. automatic change of accounting method . . . 5.1, 5.3.18
. bad-debt deductions
. . large bank . . . 10.10.4
. book treatment of delinquent interest . . . 5.1–5.2.1
. coordinated issue price . . . 5.1, A.8
. historical treatment . . . 5.2.1
. open . . . 5.3.13
. practice of I.R.S. . . . 5.3.17
. reasonable expectancy standard . . . 5.1, 5.3.3
. regulatory rules . . . 5.2.1
. safe harbor method . . . 5.3.6
. SFAS No. 114 guidance . . . 5.1, 5.2.2
. speculative . . . 5.3.13
. tax planning . . . 5.1
. tax treatment . . . 5.1-5.2.2

Nonperiodic payments . . . 2.12.4

Notional principal contracts
. accounting for . . . 2.12.3
. defined . . . 2.12.2
. exchange gain or loss on . . . 2.12.7
. mark-to-market method for . . . 2.12.4
. non-periodic payments under . . . 2.12.4
. periodic payments generated by . . . 2.12.4
. termination payments of . . . 2.12.4

References are to section (§) numbers.

O

Oakar transaction, adjusted attributable deposit amounts in . . . 8.13

Odd days interest . . . 3.4.9

Office of Thrift Supervision (OTS)
. core deposits defined . . . 11.3.4
. creation of . . . 1.7.6
. gross income test under . . . 1.7.6
. as primary federal regulator of thrifts . . . 1.7.5

Omnibus Budget Reconciliation Act of 1989 . . . 12.2

Omnibus Budget Reconciliation Act of 1990
. bad-debt deductions
. . corporate preference items . . . 10.12.2

Omnibus Budget Reconciliation Act of 1993, recovery of purchase price under . . . 11.3.3

Organizational expenditures, non-start-up . . . 8.9.3

Original issue discount (O.I.D.)
. accrual . . . 3.3.1, 3.3.2, 3.3.6, 5.3.12, 6.1
. . contingent obligations . . . 5.3.12
. amortization of debt issuance costs . . . 8.6
. amount realized in debt exchange . . . 6.3.2-6.3.3
. applied to any debt instrument . . . 3.3.4
. constant-yield method to calculate . . . 3.3.7
. *de minimis* . . . 8.6
. deductible . . . 9.3.4
. deferral of prepaid interest . . . 3.1, 3.3.3
. defined . . . 3.4.7
. financed . . . 3.4.4
. interest portion of mortgage . . . 2.7.4
. mortgage buy-downs creating . . . 3.5.1
. points . . . 3.4.4-3.4.6
. recordkeeping . . . 3.3.8
. short-term obligations . . . 3.3.6
. stated redemption price . . . 3.3.6, 3.4.7, 3.5.7
. statutory framework . . . 5.3.12

Ownership Changes . . . 11.4.12
. disregarded stock . . . 11.4.18
. equity structure shift . . . 11.4.14

Ownership Changes—continued
. multiple transactions . . . 11.4.15
. mutual funds . . . 11.4.21
. options . . . 11.4.19
. shift involving five-percent shareholders . . . 11.4.13
. short testing periods . . . 11.4.16
. stock ownership rules . . . 11.4.17
. worthless stock . . . 11.4.20

P

Parent-subsidiary controlled group . . . 10.10.1

Partnership
. character of gains of losses
. . certain preferred stock . . . 4.3.4
. interest expense . . . 2.6.1
. tax treatment
. . election of business entities . . . 1.4.3

Pass-through trusts
. character of gains or losses
. . certain preferred stock . . . 4.3.4

Passive investment income . . . 1.6.7
. banking assets . . . 1.6.7

Percentage of eligible loans method for computing reserve additions . . . 10.7.3

Percentage of taxable income (PTI) method for thrifts
. allowable reserve addition . . . 10.9.3, 10.9.6
. tests . . . 10.9

Periodic payments . . . 2.12.4

Personal holding company tax, avoiding . . . 1.6.5

Personal property, costs of lease termination for . . . 8.1

Phantom gain by acquiring property in foreclosure . . . 7.1

Points
. adjusted issue price . . . 3.4.6
. CAP loan . . . 3.3.3
. claim of right . . . 3.3.3
. construction loan . . . 3.4.6

References are to section (§) numbers.

Points—continued
. daily portions . . . 3.4.6
. *de minimis* . . . 3.4.1–3.4.2
. defined . . . 3.4.3
. financed . . . 3.4.4
. fresh funds . . . 3.4.4
. HUD settlement statement . . . 3.4.4
. income inclusion . . . 3.4.6
. issue price . . . 3.3.3
. material distortion . . . 3.3.3
. net disbursement . . . 3.4.3
. pre-regulation treatment . . . 3.4.4
. ratable portions . . . 3.4.6
. refundable payments . . . 3.3.3
. risk of forfeiture . . . 3.3.3
. treatment before 1994 O.I.D. regulations . . . 3.4.4
. treatment under O.I.D. regulations . . . 3.4.5
. yield to maturity . . . 3.4.6

Pooling costs . . . 8.4.4

Pooling methods
. accounting method . . . 8.4.5
. composition . . . 8.4.5
. consistency rule . . . 8.4.5
. de minimis transaction costs . . . 8.4.5
. distortion . . . 8.4.5
. IRS authority . . . 8.4.5

Power of sale for acquiring property in foreclosure . . . 7.2

Pre-opening and -operational costs for banks . . . 8.1

Premature withdrawal penalties
. cancellation of indebtness . . . 2.13
. Depository Institutions Deregulation Act of 1980 . . . 2.13
. forfeited interest . . . 2.13
. Tax Reform Act of 1986 . . . 2.13

Prepaid interest . . . 3.3.3

Prepayment
. defined . . . 3.3.7
. proportional method of accounting . . . 3.5.1

Principal reduction method
. determining income inclusion . . . 3.3.7

Private (non-agency) pass-throughs . . . 2.10.1

Private activity bonds
. loan to university . . . 2.5.1
. private business use test . . . 2.5.1
. qualified bond . . . 2.5.1
. QTEO . . . 2.5.1, 9.5.5

Privately placed debt
. issue price . . . 3.3.6

Program implementation costs for reducing future costs . . . 8.1

Property
. adapted to new or different use . . . 8.3.1

Proportional Method of Accounting . . . 3.1.5

Public Housing Authority (PHA) utility allowances . . . 12.2.3

Publicly offered debt
. issue price . . . 3.3.6

Purchase method of accounting, supervisory goodwill . . . 8.19

Q

QSubs
. consolidated returns for . . . 1.6.3
. deemed liquidation . . . 1.6.3
. deemed reincorporation . . . 1.6.3
. election . . . 1.6.4, 1.6.7-1.6.8
. ineligible corporation . . . 1.6.3
. qualifying as . . . 1.6.3
. reversed deemed liquidation . . . 1.6.3

Qualified active low-income community business . . . 12.3.6
. GO Zone targeted populations . . . 12.3.6.2
. targeted populations generally . . . 12.3.6.1

Qualified bond defined . . . 2.5.1

Qualified census tract designated by HUD . . . 12.2.2

Qualified community development entity (CDE)
. defined . . . 12.3.3
. loans . . . 12.3.5, 12.3.6

References are to section (§) numbers.

Qualified community development entity (CDE)—continued
. NMTC . . . 12.3.1
. qualified equity investments . . . 12.3.2
. redemption of investment . . . 12.3.8
. services . . . 12.3.5

Qualified equity investment defined . . . 12.3.2

Qualified low-income community investment
. four types of investments . . . 12.3.5
. made by CDE . . . 12.3.2

Qualified low-income housing project
. minimum set-aside and rent restriction tests for . . . 12.2.4
. qualified low-income building required to be part of . . . 12.2.3
. for state allocation of credits . . . 12.2.11

Qualified nonprofit organization defined . . . 12.2.11

Qualified real property loan for foreclosed property . . . 7.3.2

Qualified stated interest (QSI) . . . 3.4.7
. defined . . . 3.3.6
. not included in stated redemption price at maturity . . . 3.3.6

Qualified stock purchase qualifying as Type A reorganization . . . 11.3.8

Qualified subchapter S trust (QSST) . . . 1.6.2
. consent to revoke election . . . 1.6.2
. election . . . 1.6.2
. husband and wife . . . 1.6.2
. obligation to support . . . 1.6.2
. reform trust provisions . . . 1.6.2
. revocation of election . . . 1.6.2

Qualified tax-exempt obligations (QTEOs) . . . 9.5.5

Qualified thrift investments in QTL test . . . 1.7.1, 1.7.8, 1.7.9

Qualifying real property loan for PTI method . . . 10.9.1, 10.9.5

Qualifying small business taxpayer, cash accounting method for . . . 2.2.1

R

Real estate investment trusts (REIT)
. capital gains . . . 2.10.4
. defined . . . 2.10.4
. gross income test . . . 2.10.4
. income and asset tests . . . 2.10.4
. investment company . . . 2.10.4
. prohibited transaction . . . 2.10.4
. qualifying as . . . 2.10.4
. tax treatment of . . . 2.11.1
. umbrella partnership real estate investment trust . . . 2.10.4

Real estate mortgage investment conduit (REMIC)
. daily portion . . . 2.10.3
. defined . . . 2.10.3
. election . . . 2.10.3
. issue price . . . 2.10.3
. market discount bonds . . . 2.10.3
. ordinary income . . . 2.10.3
. permitted investments . . . 2.10.3
. purpose . . . 2.10.3
. qualified mortgage . . . 2.10.3
. regular interests . . . 2.10.3
. residual interests . . . 2.10.3
. sponsor's gains or losses, character of . . . 2.10.3
. tax treatment . . . 2.10.3, 2.11.1

Recurring liabilities, economic performance . . . 8.2.1

Redemptions, Federal Home Loan Bank . . . 2.14.2

Refunded interest . . . 8.2.2

Refundable loan commissions . . . 2.8.2

Registrar and transfer agent fees . . . 8.5.5

Registration-required obligations, disallowance . . . 9.5.9

Regulatory accounting principles (RAP) rule
. conformity with GAAP under FDIC Act of . . . 5.2.2

References are to section (§) numbers.

Regulatory accounting principles (RAP) rule—continued
. discontinuing interest accrual for loans in default . . . 5.1

Regulatory rules, delinquent interest . . . 5.2.1

Renegotiated debt
. alteration of operation of original terms . . . 6.2.3
. automatic alteration . . . 6.2.3
. change in nature of instrument . . . 6.2.3
. change in obligor . . . 6.2.3
. change in payment expectations . . . 6.2.3
. change in security, credit enhancement, priority, or payment expectations . . . 6.2.3
. change in timing of payments . . . 6.2.3
. economic significance rule . . . 6.2.3
. failure to perform . . . 6.2.3
. four specific situations . . . 6.2.3
. general rules . . . 6.2.3
. real estate mortgage investment conduits (REMICs) . . . 6.2.3
. Treasury regulations . . . 6.1, 6.2.1
. unilateral alteration . . . 6.2.3

Repurchase agreements
. defined . . . 2.9
. reporting interest income from . . . 2.9
. sale v. loan . . . 2.9.1
. tax treatment . . . 2.9, 2.9.1–2.9.2
. typical . . . 2.9.1

Research and development (R&D) credit . . . 12.1–12.1.7
. accelerated . . . 12.1.7
. bank expenditures affected . . . 8.1
. calculating . . . 12.1.5
. computer software . . . 12.1
. deductions reduced . . . 12.1.5
. election to claim accelerated research credit in lieu of bonus depreciation . . . 12.1.7
. expenditures eligible for credit . . . 12.1.1
. expenditures ineligible for credit . . . 12.1.2
. ineligibility
. . market research . . . 12.1.2
. . quality control . . . 12.1.2

Research and development (R&D) credit—continued
. ineligible expenditures . . . 8.11, 12.1.2
. internal use software . . . 12.1.3
. *Nortwest Corp.* . . . 12.1.4
. qualified research expenses . . . 12.1-12.1.1
. strategic banking system . . . 12.1.4
. tests applied by Tax Court . . . 12.1.4
. treatment of research and experimental expenditures as tax preference items . . . 12.1.6

Research or experimental expenditures
. defined . . . 12.1.1

Reserve method of accounting
. bad debt deduction . . . 10.2.2, 10.7–10.7.11
. electing . . . 10.7.1–10.7.8
. for loan losses of banks . . . 7.3.1, 10.7
. net operating losses . . . 8.20.4, 10.7.2
. partial worthlessness of debt . . . 10.2
. record requirements . . . 10.7.10
. securities losses by bank . . . 10.8.6

Reserve recapture
. S corporations . . . 1.6.6

Residential loan requirement . . . 10.11.4

Residual allocation method, classes of assets in . . . 11.3.2

Residual interest . . . 2.10.3

Retroactive Reserve Adjustments . . . 10.7.10

Revenue Act of 1936, taxation of banks under . . . 1.4.1

Revenue Act of 1951, thrift exemption repealed by . . . 1.7.2

Revenue Act of 1962
. building and loan associations defined in . . . 1.7.1, 1.7.2
. practical tax exemption for thrifts eliminated by . . . 1.7.2

Revenue Reconciliation Act of 1990
. bad-debt deductions . . . 10.12.1

Revised Loan Liquidation Method (RLLM)
. permitted use . . . 3.4.2

References are to section (§) numbers.

Rigle-Neil Interstate Banking and Branching Efficiency Act of 1994 (Branch Banking Act of 1994) . . . 11.2.1

Risk-based capital ratio of banks . . . 1.4.2

Rule of 78s method . . . 2.2.1, 2.6.1

Rural Housing Service (RHS), Ginnie Mae pass-throughs insured by . . . 2.10.1

S

S corporations
. accounting method
. . accrual method . . . 2.2.1
. . cash method . . . 1.6.5
. accumulated adjustments account (AAA) . . . 1.6.6
. advantages of status . . . 1.6.5
. affiliated group . . . 1.6.3
. bad-debt deductions
. . applicable excess reserves . . . 1.6.6, 1.6.8
. . reserve recapture . . . 1.6.6, 1.6.8
. . tax benefit rule . . . 1.6.8
. banks . . . 1.6, 9.5.9
. built-in gains tax . . . 1.6.3, 1.6.6, 1.6.8
. C corporation holding company . . . 1.6.3
. consolidated returns . . . 1.6.3
. defective elections . . . 1.6.2
. deferred income tax accounts . . . 1.6.6
. directors shares . . . 1.6.1
. disadvantages of status . . . 1.6.6
. distributions of income . . . 1.6.6
. dividends received deduction . . . 1.6.6
. election . . . 1.6.3-1.6.4
. Employee stock ownership plan (ESOP) . . . 1.6.5
. entities permitted to be shareholders . . . 1.6.5
. estimated tax payments . . . 1.6.9
. family members . . . 1.6.1
. inadvertently terminated . . . 1.6.1
. individual tax rates . . . 1.6.6
. ineligible corporation . . . 1.6.1
. IRA or Roth IRA as shareholder . . . 1.6.6
. maximum number of shareholders . . . 1.6.6
. net operating losses (NOL) . . . 1.6.6
. parent of bank . . . 1.1

S corporations—continued
. passive investment income . . . 1.6.7
. predecessor C corporations for . . . 1.6.6
. QSSTs holding stock . . . 1.6.2
. Qsub bank . . . 1.6.1
. qualification for treatment . . . 1.6.1
. reserve method . . . 1.6.6
. restrictions on shareholders of . . . 1.6.2
. retirement plans as shareholders . . . 1.6.1-1.6.2
. sale of stock . . . 1.6.3
. second class of stock . . . 1.6.1
. specially taxed items . . . 1.6.5
. specific taxed items . . . 1.6.5
. voting trust . . . 1.6.2

Safe harbor method
. acquisition or disposition . . . 5.3.6
. mortgage servicing fees . . . 2.7.4
. recovery percentage . . . 5.3.6
. shorter experience period . . . 5.3.6
. total payments . . . 5.3.6

Savings and loan (S&L) association
. adoption of stock corporation structure . . . 11.5.2
. as conduit for mortgage lender . . . 1.7.6
. decline during 1970s in value of mortgages held by . . . 6.2.1
. qualification as bank of federally chartered . . . 1.7.4
. regulation . . . 6.2.1

Savings Association Insurance Fund (SAIF), assessments for . . . 8.12

Savings Association Insurance Fund (SAIF), conversion to BIF of participants in, fees for . . . 8.13

Schedule M
. market discount . . . 3.6
. start-up and organizational expenditures . . . 8.9.2

Second-tier allocation method for purchase price . . . 11.3.2

Section 197 intangibles . . . 11.3.4

Section 20 subsidiaries allowed by Federal Reserve . . . 1.2.5

References are to section (§) numbers.

Section 988 transaction . . . 2.12.7

Securities
. acquired at discount . . . 3.2.1
. acquired in foreclosure . . . 7.6.2
. real estate mortgage investment conduit (REMIC) . . . 2.10.3
. repurchase agreements for . . . 2.9, 4.6

Securities and Exchange Commission (SEC), registration as broker-dealer with . . . 1.2.5

Securities dealers
. accrual method of accounting . . . 2.2.4
. code section 475
. . exceptions to mark-to-market rules . . . 4.4.7
. . identification of securities . . . 4.4.7
. . mortgage loans . . . 4.4.7
. . primarily for sale to customer . . . 4.4.7
. . REMICs . . . 4.4.7
. commission . . . 2.8.3
. deemed taxable exchanges . . . 6.3.1
. defined . . . 4.3.3
. Financial Modernization Act as repealing prohibition against affiliations between banks and . . . 1.2.5
. permissible securities activities . . . 4.2
. tax planning . . . 4.1
. valuation rules
. . cost method . . . 4.4.1
. . lower of the cost or market . . . 4.4.1
. . market method . . . 4.4.1

Securities Exchange Act of 1934, Financial Modernization Act as amending . . . 1.2, 1.2.5

Securities exchange system
. execution of transactions . . . 2.7.3

Securities inventory rules
. measuring gain or loss . . . 6.3.1

Securities losses by bank on reserve method . . . 10.8

Security
. accrued interest . . . 5.3.7

Security investment transactions
. FAS No. 115 . . . 4.5.1

Security property
. capital asset treatment
. . judicial exception . . . 7.6.1
. disposing
. . deficiency judgments . . . 7.6
. . intercompany distribution . . . 7.6
. holding
. . property taxes . . . 7.5.1

Self-Amortizing Method (SAM)
. computing *de minimis* amount . . . 3.4.1

Separate and distinct test, capital assets . . . 8.3.2, 8.10

Service fee income
. advance payments . . . 2.7.2
. annual fees . . . 2.7.3
. ATM fees . . . 3.5.6
. cash advance . . . 3.5
. cash method of accounting . . . 2.7.4
. commitment fee . . . 3.5.1
. compared to interest income . . . 2.7.1
. contingent services . . . 3.5.1
. credit card fee
. . cash advance . . . 3.5.4
. . interchange fees . . . 3.5.5
. . late charge . . . 3.5.3
. . merchant fees . . . 3.5.7
. . non-sufficient funds fees . . . 3.5.8
. . over the limit fees . . . 3.5.2
. fixed and definite . . . 2.7.2
. inclusion . . . 2.7.2
. revolving line of credit . . . 2.7.3
. unearned payments . . . 2.7.2
. mortgage servicing fees . . . 2.7.4

Severance payments, deductibility . . . 8.4.4, 8.10

Shared National Credit Review of large participation loans . . . 10.4.3

Short-term loan
. accrual of interest not required for . . . 3.3.5
. automatic changes . . . 3.3.5
. discount . . . 3.3.5
. Rule of 78s method . . . 2.6.1
. state interest . . . 3.3.5
. treasury bill . . . 3.3.5

References are to section (§) numbers.

Short-term obligation
. defined . . . 3.6
. interest expense . . . 9.5.3
. loans made by a bank . . . 3.3.4

Simplifying conventions
. costs to acquire trade or business . . . 8.5.6
. intangibles . . . 8.4.4

Small Business and Work Opportunity Act of 2007 . . . 1.6.3, 12.2

Small Business Job Protection Act of 1996 . . . 1.3, 1.5.5, 1.6, 1.7.2. 2.11.1
. bad-debt deduction . . . 10.2.1
. . reserve methods . . . 10.7
. exclusion of interest income from ESOP loan . . . 2.5.1
. repeal of bad debt reserve method . . . 1.7.2, 10.2.1, 10.7
. S corporation election for banks . . . 1.6, 9.6

Software development qualifying and not qualifying for R&D credit . . . 12.1, 12.1.1

Sourcing rules . . . 2.12.7

Specially computed taxable income under PTI method . . . 10.9.3

Specific charge-off method
. at foreclosures . . . 7.3.1
. bad-debt deductions of large banks . . . 10.7.4
. worthless debts . . . 10.2.1–10.2.2, 10.3, 10.7–10.7.1

Speculative obligation . . . 5.3.13

Start-up expenditures . . . 1.2.1, 8.1, 8.6.2, 8.9.1–8.9.5
. acquisition expenditures . . . 8.9.2
. activities and deductibility tests to qualify . . . 8.9.2
. amortization deductions . . . 8.9.3–8.9.4, 8.10
. amortization period in . . . 8.9.1
. capitalization in . . . 8.9.2
. case law . . . 8.1
. costs not subject to FASB SOP . . . 8.9.2
. expansion of existing business treated separately from . . . 8.1

Start-up expenditures—continued
. judicial precedent . . . 8.9.2
. legislative history . . . 8.9.2
. ordinary and necessary . . . 8.9.1–8.9.2
. organizational expenditures . . . 8.9.1, 8.9.3

State bank provisions . . . 1.2.6

State chartered trust company, qualification as bank of . . . 1.5.9

State housing credit agencies, allocation authority of . . . 12.2.12

State insurance regulators, unchanged current law for . . . 1.2.6

State law for acquiring security property . . . 7.2

State or local bond
. defined . . . 2.5.1
. exclusion from gross income . . . 2.5.1

State principal amount . . . 3.3.6

Stated redemption price at maturity (SRPM . . . 2.5.15
. defined . . . 3.3.6
. excess of points over issue price . . . 3.4.5, 3.4.7
. market discount . . . 3.6

Stepped interest rate . . . 3.3.6

Stock acquisition costs as amortizable asset acquisitions cost . . . 8.6.2

Stock bank, conversion of mutual savings bank to . . . 11.5.6

Stock dividends, FHLB . . . 2.14.2

Stock issuance costs of open-end regulated investment companies . . . 8.5.5

Straddles . . . 2.12.7

Straight line depreciation
. accelerated amortization versus . . . 3.7.5
. mortgage servicing rights . . . 2.7.4
. on bond premium . . . 3.7.4

Strict foreclosure for acquiring property in foreclosure . . . 7.2

Supervisory goodwill . . . 11.6.1

References are to section (§) numbers.

Supervisory goodwill—continued
. abandonment loss . . . 8.21.2
. financial assistance as . . . 8.19

Supervisory requirement . . . 1.5.8

Swaps
. nonperiodic payments under general rule for . . . 2.10.4
. notional principal amount of . . . 9.5.8

T

Tax Deficit Reduction Act of 1984, interest expense for consolidated returns under . . . 9.5.2

Tax Equity and Fiscal Responsibility Act of 1982 (TEFRA)
. disallowance interest expense . . . 9.5.1
. interest expense
. . disallowance . . . 9.5.3
. issue price . . . 3.3.6
. privately placed debt . . . 3.3.6

Tax planning
. acquisitions . . . 11.1
. bad-debt deductions . . . 10.1
. business expenses . . . 8.1
. for accounting for interest, fee and other income . . . 2.1
. for classification of entities subject to bank tax rules . . . 1.1
. for foreclosures . . . 7.1
. for non performing loans . . . 5.1
. for taxation of discounts, points, and premiums . . . 3.1
. interest expense . . . 9.1
. modified debt . . . 6.1

Tax preference item
. AMT increased by tax preference items . . . 10.12.1
. corporate preference items for reserve additions . . . 10.12.2
. research and experimental expenditures . . . 12.1.6

Tax Reform Act of 1969
. building and loan associations definition modified in . . . 1.7.1

Tax Reform Act of 1984
. discharges of indebtedness . . . 11.5.6
. taxable year of deduction . . . 8.2.1
. wash sale rule . . . 4.3.1

Tax Reform Act of 1986
. acquisition costs
. . covered asset losses . . . 8.21.3
. allocating purchase price among assets . . . 11.3.2
. asset and income tests liberalized by . . . 1.7.1
. averaging rules . . . 9.5.8
. bad debt deduction reduced by . . . 1.7.2, 10.2.3
. bad-debt deductions . . . 10.2.3
. . reserve methods . . . 10.7.4
. cancellation of indebtedness exclusion by . . . 2.13
. capitalization of expenditures . . . 8.3.1
. cash method of accounting . . . 2.2.1
. deduction for reasonable reserve addition repealed . . . 10.7.4
. deferred interest expense
. . market discount bonds . . . 9.4.2
. expanded financial activities under . . . 1.3
. FIRREA repeal of certain tax rules extended by . . . 8.22
. General Utilities Doctrine . . . 11.3.1
. interest expense disallowance rule . . . 9.5.1, 9.5.2, 9.5.4, 9.5.5
. large commercial banks prohibited from using reserve method . . . 10.7
. NOL treatment for banks changed by . . . 8.20.2
. recognition of gain on corporate liquidation required by . . . 11.3.1
. REMICs . . . 1.7.1, 2.10.2, 2.10.3
. reserve method . . . 10.7–10.7.1, 10.7.5
. taxable income allowable as deduction reduced . . . 10.9.6
. Type G reorganization
. . general rules . . . 11.5.8
. UNICAP rule added to Code by . . . 8.3.1

Tax Relief and Health Care Act of 2006 (TRHCA) . . . 12.1, 12.1.4, 12.1.5

Tax Relief Extension Act of 1999 . . . 12.1.5

References are to section (§) numbers.

Tax-exempt bonds marketability
. interest expense temporary de minimis safe harbor . . . 9.5.4

Tax-exempt interest . . . 2.5.

Tax-exempt obligations
. accrual of discount income . . . 3.3.1
. acquisition date . . . 9.5.7
. disallowance rule for interest expense . . . 9.5.1–9.5.2
. nexus . . . 9.5.2
. tax basis . . . 9.5.9

Tax-free reorganizations
. boot received . . . 11.5.1
. judicial tests . . . 11.5.1, 11.5.8
. tax treatment . . . 11.5.1–11.5.8
. taxable purchases by bank or BHC . . . 11.1
. types . . . 11.5.1

Taxable governmental obligations
. maturity date of one year or less . . . 3.3.1

Taxable purchase acquisitions . . . 11.1, 11.3.1–11.3.8
. cost recovery rules . . . 11.3.2
. determining and allocating purchase price . . . 11.3.2
. taxation of selling corporations . . . 11.3.1
. treatment of liabilities . . . 11.3.1

Taxable year of deduction . . . 8.2.1
. economic performance
. . tort liabilities, and other liabilities . . . 8.2.1
. . use of property . . . 8.2.1

Taxpayer Relief Act of 1997
. exception to the QSub deemed liquidation rule under . . . 9.6
. grace period interest . . . 3.4.7
. traders and speculators . . . 4.4.6

Technical and Miscellaneous Revenue Act of 1988 (TAMRA)
. acquisition costs
. . covered asset losses . . . 8.21.3
. FIRREA repeal of tax rules . . . 8.22, 11.6

Termination payments . . . 2.12.4

Termination payments—continued
. business acquisition agreement . . . 8.4.3, 8.5.5

The Bank Holding Company Act of 1956
. permissible interstate activities
. . BHC Activities . . . 11.2.2
. Douglas Amendment . . . 11.2.2

The Banking Act of 1933
. permissible interstate activities . . . 11.2.1

The Revenue Act of 1921
. deduction of partially worthless debts . . . 10.3

Theft loss, bad debt deductions . . . 10.2.3

Thrift
. acquisition of assets . . . 10.11.3
. applicable excess reserves for . . . 10.11.1–10.11.2
. bad-debt recapture by . . . 10.11–10.11.4
. bad-debt reserve methods . . . 10.1, 10.3.2, 10.7, 10.7.11, 10.9.4-10.9.5
. business operations test . . . 1.7.5-1.7.6
. conformity election for bad debts . . . 10.4.4
. conversion of mutually organized into stock . . . 11.5.7
. deduction for dividends (interest expense) on deposits by . . . 9.2, 9.3, 9.3.2
. elimination of practical exemption . . . 1.7.2
. foreclosures . . . 7.3.2, 7.5.1
. gross income test . . . 1.7.6
. income in Code Section 581 definition . . . 1.5.5
. insurance for . . . 1.7.5
. net operating losses . . . 8.20.2, 10.7.8
. overlapping activities with commercial bank . . . 1.3
. percentage of taxable income method . . . 10.9.6
. prepaid interest . . . 9.4.1
. qualifying assets
. . bad debt computation . . . 1.6.10
. regulatory versus tax definition . . . 1.1, 1.7.8
. repeal of exemption . . . 1.7.2
. reserve addition for qualifying loans of . . . 10.9.6

References are to section (§) numbers.

Thrift—continued
. surplus, undivided profits, and reserves of . . . 10.9.5
. suspended reserve of . . . 10.11.3
. tax treatment . . . 1.3, 1.7.2
. terminating depositor or shareholder . . . 9.4.1
. use of term . . . 1.3

Time deposits, premature withdrawal penalties on . . . 2.13

Tort liabilities, economic performance for . . . 8.2.1

Trade or business, determining whether assets constitute . . . 11.35

Trader, Investors and Speculators . . . 4.4.6
. Code section 475(f) election . . . 4.4.6
. mark-to-market method . . . 4.4.6

Trademark or trade name
. as section 197 intangible . . . 11.3.4

Triangular mergers
. in Type A reorganizations, forward and reverse . . . 11.5.2
. in Type G reorganizations . . . 11.5.8

Troubled Asset Relief Program (TARP)
. deducting dividend payments . . . 9.2.1

Trust powers . . . 1.5.9

Trusts
. as S corporation shareholder . . . 1.6.2

Truth-in-Lending Act, accounting methods . . . 2.6.2

Type A reorganization
. continuity-of-interest . . . 11.1
. general rules . . . 11.5.2
. merger of mutual associations . . . 11.5.2
. overlap with Types B and C of triangular . . . 11.5.3
. qualified stock purchase . . . 11.3.8

Type B reorganization, solely voting stock in . . . 11.5.3

Type C reorganization
. charter stripping . . . 11.5.5
. solely voting stock in . . . 11.5.3

Type D reorganization
. charter stripping . . . 11.5.5
. divisive and nondivisive . . . 11.5.4
. Type G reorganization compared with . . . 11.5.8

Type E reorganization to recapitalize structure of existing corporation . . . 11.5.6

Type F reorganization, NOL carryback rules for . . . 11.5.7

Type G reorganization to help rehabilitate troubled businesses . . . 11.5.8

U

Umbrella partnership real estate investment trust (UPREIT) . . . 2.10.4

Uniform Agreement on the Classification of Assets and Appraisal of Securities Held by Banks . . . 10.4.4

Uniform capitalization (UNICAP) rules
. capitalization of interest expense . . . 9.1, 9.4.3
. general rule . . . 8.8

United States Housing Act of 1937, low-income family formula of . . . 12.2.4
. assistance under . . . 12.2.3

University loan . . . 2.5.1

Unused state housing credit ceiling . . . 12.2.11

V

Veterans Affairs (VA), Department of, Ginnie Mae pass-throughs insured by . . . 2.10.1

Volcker Rule . . . 2.12.1
. defintion . . . 2.12.1
. effect of hedging . . . 2.12.1
. purpose . . . 2.12.1

Voluntary conveyance (deed-in-lieu-of-foreclosure) . . . 7.2, 7.3.2, 7.6

References are to section (§) numbers.

W

Weighted Average Method (WAM)
. computing de minimus amount . . . 3.4.1

Worker, Homeownership, and Business Assistance Act of 2009 (WHBAA) . . . 8.20.4

Workers' compensation, economic performance . . . 8.2.1

Worthlessness of debts
. establishing . . . 10.3.1
. presumption . . . 10.1, 10.4–10.4.5

Write-down of bonds . . . 10.2.3